The Founders' Constitution

The Founders' Constitution

Edited by
Philip B. Kurland
and
Ralph Lerner

VOLUME TWO

Preamble through Article 1,

Section 8, Clause 4

Liberty Fund

This book is published by Liberty Fund, Inc., a foundation established to encourage study of the ideal of a society of free and responsible individuals.

The cuneiform inscription that serves as our logo and as a design element for Liberty Fund books is the earliest-known written appearance of the word "freedom" (*amagi*), or "liberty." It is taken from a clay document written about 2300 B.C. in the Sumerian city-state of Lagash.

Philip B. Kurland was the William R. Kenan, Jr., Distinguished Service Professor in the College and professor in the Law School, University of Chicago.

Ralph Lerner is the Benjamin Franklin Professor in the College and professor in the Committee on Social Thought, University of Chicago.

Printed in the United States of America

23 24 25 26 27 P 10 9 8 7 6

Library of Congress Cataloging-in-Publication Data

The Founders' Constitution / edited by Philip B. Kurland and Ralph Lerner.
    p.   cm.
    Originally published: Chicago: University of Chicago Press, 1987.
    Includes bibliographical references and index.
    Contents: v. 1. Major themes—v. 2. Preamble through Article 1, Section 8, Clause 4—v. 3. Article 1, Section 8, Clause 5, through Article 2, Section 1—v. 4. Article 2, Section 2, through Article 7—v. 5. Amendments I–XII.
    ISBN 0-86597-279-6 (set: pbk.: alk. paper)—ISBN 0-86597-302-4 (v. 1: pbk.: alk. paper)—ISBN 0-86597-303-2 (v. 2: pbk.: alk. paper)
    1. Constitutional history—United States—Sources. I. Kurland, Philip B. II. Lerner, Ralph.

KF4502 .F68 2000
342.73′029—dc21   99-052811

ISBN 0-86597-304-0 (v. 3 pbk.: alk. paper)
ISBN 0-86597-305-9 (v. 4 pbk.: alk. paper)
ISBN 0-86597-306-7 (v. 5 pbk.: alk. paper)

Liberty Fund, Inc.
11301 North Meridian Street
Carmel, Indiana 46032
libertyfund.org

Cover design by Erin Kirk New, Watkinsville, Georgia

Printed and bound by Sheridan Books, Chelsea, Michigan

To Mary Jane

Contents

VOLUME TWO: PREAMBLE THROUGH ARTICLE 1, SECTION 8, CLAUSE 4
(For detailed contents, see box at opening of each item or group of items listed below)

Note on References

References to documents follow a consistent pattern both in the cross-references (in the detailed tables of contents) and in the indexes. Where a document in volume 1 is being cited, reference is to chapter and document number; thus, for example, ch. 15, no. 23. Where the document is to be found in one of the subsequent volumes, which are organized by Constitutional article, section, and clause, or by amendment, reference is in this mode: 1.8.8, no. 12; or, Amend. I (religion), no. 66. Each document heading consists of its serial number in that particular chapter; an author and title (or letter writer and addressee, or speaker and forum); date of publication, writing, or speaking; and, where not given in the first part of the heading, an identification of the source of the text being reprinted. These sources are presented in short-title form, the author of the source volume being presumed (unless otherwise noted) to be the first proper name mentioned in the document heading. Thus, for example, in the case of a letter from Alexander Hamilton to Governor George Clinton, "Papers 1:425–28" would be understood to refer to the edition fully described under "Hamilton, Papers" in the list of short titles found at the back of each volume.

A somewhat different form has been followed in the case of the proceedings of the Constitutional Convention that met in Philadelphia from late May to mid-September of 1787. As might be expected, we have included many extracts from the various records kept by the participants while they were deliberating over the shape and character of a new charter of government. For any particular chapter or unit, those extracts have been grouped as a single document, titled "Records of the Federal Convention," and placed undated in that chapter's proper time slot. The bracketed note that precedes each segment within that selection of the "Records" lists the volume and opening page numbers in the printed source (Max Farrand's edition), the name of the participant whose notes are here being reproduced (overwhelmingly Madison, but also Mason, Yates, others, and the Convention's official Journal), and the month and day of 1787 when the reported transaction took place.

Preamble

We the People of the United States, in Order to form a more perfect Union, establish Justice, insure domestic Tranquillity, provide for the common defence, promote the general Welfare, and secure the Blessings of Liberty to ourselves and our Posterity, do ordain and establish this Constitution for the United States of America.

1

JOHN LOCKE, SECOND TREATISE, § 131
1689

131. But though Men when they enter into Society, give up the Equality, Liberty, and Executive Power they had in the State of Nature, into the hands of the Society, to be so far disposed of by the Legislative, as the good of the Society shall require; yet it being only with an intention in every one the better to preserve himself his Liberty and Property; (For no rational Creature can be supposed to change his condition with an intention to be worse) the power of the Society, or *Legislative* constituted by them, *can never be suppos'd to extend farther than the common good;* but is obliged to secure every ones Property by providing against those three defects above-mentioned, that made the State of Nature so unsafe and uneasie. And so whoever has the Legislative or Supream Power of any Common-wealth, is bound to govern by establish'd *standing Laws,* promulgated and known to the People, and not by Extemporary Decrees; by *indifferent* and upright *Judges,* who are to decide Controversies by those Laws; And to imploy the force of the Community at home, *only in the Execution of such Laws,* or abroad to prevent or redress Foreign Injuries, and secure the Community from Inroads and Invasion. And all this to be directed to no other *end,* but the *Peace, Safety,* and *publick good* of the People.

2

WILLIAM BLACKSTONE, COMMENTARIES 1:157
1765

(See vol. 1, ch. 3, no. 3)

3

VIRGINIA DECLARATION OF RIGHTS, SECS. 2–3
12 June 1776

Mason Papers 1:287

(See vol. 1, ch. 1, no. 3)

4

DECLARATION OF INDEPENDENCE
4 July 1776

Tansill 22

(See vol. 1, ch. 1, no. 5)

5

VERMONT CONSTITUTION OF 1777, PREAMBLE
Thorpe 6:3737

Whereas, all government ought to be instituted and supported, for the security and protection of the community, as such, and to enable the individuals who compose it, to enjoy their natural rights, and the other blessings which the Author of existence has bestowed upon man; and whenever those great ends of government are not obtained, the people have a right, by common consent, to change it, and take such measures as to them may appear necessary to promote their safety and happiness.

6

VERMONT CONSTITUTION OF 1786, PREAMBLE
Thorpe 6:3751

Therefore it is absolutely necessary, for the welfare and safety of the inhabitants of this State, that it should be henceforth a free and independent State, and that a just, permanent, and proper form of government should exist

in it, derived from and founded on the authority of the people only, agreeable to the direction of the honourable American Congress.

We the Representatives of the freemen of Vermont, in General Convention met, for the express purpose of forming such a government—confessing the goodness of the great Governor of the universe (who alone knows to what degree of earthly happiness mankind may attain by perfecting the arts of government) in permitting the people of this State, by common consent, and without violence, deliberately to form for themselves such just rules as they shall think best, for governing their future society; and being fully convinced, that it is our indispensable duty to establish such original principles of government as will best promote the general happiness of the people of this State, and their posterity, and provide for future improvements, without partiality for, or prejudice against, any particular class, sect, or denomination of men whatever; do, by virtue of authority vested in us by our constituents, ordain, declare and establish the following Declaration of Rights, and Frame of Government, to be the Constitution of this Commonwealth, and to remain in force therein forever unaltered, except in such articles as shall hereafter on experience be found to require improvement, and which shall, by the same authority of the people, fairly delegated, as this Frame of Government directs, be amended or improved, for the more effectual obtaining and securing the great end and design of all government, herein before mentioned.

7

RECORDS OF THE FEDERAL CONVENTION

[1:20; Madison, 29 May]

Resolutions proposed by Mr Randolph in Convention.

1. Resolved that the articles of Confederation ought to be so corrected & enlarged as to accomplish the objects proposed by their institution; namely. "common defence, security of liberty and general welfare."

[1:30; Journal, 30 May]

It was then moved by Mr Randolph and seconded by Mr. G Morris to substitute the following resolution in the place of the first resolution

Resolved that an union of the States, merely foederal, will not accomplish the objects proposed by the articles of confederation, namely "common defence, security of liberty, and general welfare.

It was moved by Mr Butler seconded by Mr Randolph to postpone the consideration of the said resolution in order to take up the following resolution submitted by Mr Randolph namely

Resolved that a national government ought to be established consisting of a supreme legislative, judiciary and executive.

[1:242; Madison, 15 June]

The propositions from N. Jersey moved by Mr. Patterson were in the words following.

1. Resd. that the articles of Confederation ought to be so revised, corrected & enlarged, as to render the federal Constitution adequate to the exigences of Government, & the preservation of the Union.

[4:37; Committee of Detail, IV]

In the draught of a fundamental constitution, two things deserve attention:

    1. To insert essential principles only; lest the operations of government should be clogged by rendering those provisions permanent and unalterable, which ought to be accomodated to times and events: and

    2. To use simple and precise language, and general propositions, according to the example of the constitutions of the several states.

1. A preamble seems proper. Not for the purpose of designating the ends of government and human polities—This display of theory, howsoever proper in the first formation of state governments, is unfit here; since we are not working on the natural rights of men not yet gathered into society, but upon those rights, modified by society, and interwoven with what we call the rights of states—Nor yet is it proper for the purpose of mutually pledging the faith of the parties for the observance of the articles—This may be done more solemnly at the close of the draught, as in the confederation—But the object of our preamble ought to be briefly to declare, that the present foederal government is insufficient to the general happiness; that the conviction of this fact gave birth to this convention; and that the only effectual mode which they can devise, for curing this insufficiency, is the establishment of a supreme legislative executive and judiciary—Let it be next declared, that the following are the constitution and fundamentals of government for the United States—

[2:565; Committee of Style, 10 Sept.]

We the People of the States of New-Hampshire, Massachusetts, Rhode-Island and Providence Plantations, Connecticut, New-York, New-Jersey, Pennsylvania, Delaware, Maryland, Virginia, North-Carolina, South-Carolina, and Georgia, do ordain, declare and establish the following Constitution for the Government of Ourselves and our Posterity.

Article I.

The stile of this Government shall be, "The United States of America."

II.

The Government shall consist of supreme legislative, executive and judicial powers.

[2:590; Committee of Style, 12 Sept.]

We, the People of the United States, in order to form a more perfect union, to establish justice, insure domestic tranquillity, provide for the common defence, promote the general welfare, and secure the blessings of liberty to ourselves and our posterity, do ordain and establish this Constitution for the United States of America.

8

JAMES WILSON, PENNSYLVANIA RATIFYING CONVENTION
11 Dec. 1787
McMaster 384–85

This, Mr. President, is not a government founded upon compact; it is founded upon the power of the people. They express in their name and their authority, *"We the People do ordain and establish,"* &c., from their ratification, and their ratification alone it is to take its constitutional authenticity; without that it is no more than *tabula rasa.*

I know very well all the common-place rant of State sovereignties, and that government is founded in original compact. If that position was examined, it will be found not to accede very well with the true principle of free government. It does not suit the language or genius of the system before us. I think it does not accord with experience, so far as I have been able to obtain information from history.

The greatest part of governments have been founded on conquest; perhaps a few early ones may have had their origin in paternal authority. Sometimes a family united, and that family afterwards extended itself into a community. But the greatest governments which have appeared on the face of the globe have been founded in conquest. The great empires of Assyria, Persia, Macedonia and Rome, were all of this kind. I know well that in Great Britain, since the revolution, it has become a principle that the constitution is founded in contract; but the form and time of that contract no writer has yet attempted to discover. It was, however, recognized at the time of the revolution, therefore is politically true. But we should act very imprudently to consider our liberties as placed on such foundation.

If we go a little further on this subject, I think we see that the doctrine of original compact cannot be supported consistently with the best principles of government. If we admit it, we exclude the idea of amendment; because a contract once entered into between the governor and governed becomes obligatory, and cannot be altered but by the mutual consent of both parties. The citizens of United America, I presume, do not wish to stand on that footing, with those to whom, from convenience, they please to delegate the exercise of the general powers necessary for sustaining and preserving the Union. They wish a principle established, by the operation of which the legislatures may feel the direct authority of the people. The people possessing that authority, will continue to exercise it by amending and improving their own work. This constitution may be found to have defects in it; amendments hence may become necessary; but the idea of a government founded on contract, destroys the means of improvement. We hear it every time the gentlemen are up, "Shall we violate the confederation, which directs every alteration that is thought necessary to be established by the State legislatures only?" Sir, those gentlemen must ascend to a higher source; the people fetter themselves by no contract. If your State legislatures have cramped themselves by compact, it was done without the authority of the people, who alone possess the supreme power.

I have already shown, that this system is not a compact or contract; the system itself tells you what it is; it is an ordinance and establishment of the people. I think that the force of the introduction to the work, must by this time have been felt. It is not an unmeaning flourish. The expressions declare, in a practical manner, the principle of this constitution. It is ordained and established by the people themselves; and we, who give our votes for it, are merely the proxies of our constituents. We sign it as their attorneys, and as to ourselves, we agree to it as individuals.

9

LUTHER MARTIN, GENUINE INFORMATION
1788

(See vol. 1, ch. 8, no. 32)

10

JAMES MADISON, FEDERALIST, NO. 37,
233–39
11 Jan. 1788

. . . many allowances ought to be made for the difficulties inherent in the very nature of the undertaking referred to the Convention.

The novelty of the undertaking immediately strikes us. It has been shewn in the course of these papers, that the existing Confederation is founded on principles which are fallacious; that we must consequently change this first foundation, and with it, the superstructure resting upon it. It has been shewn, that the other confederacies which could be consulted as precedents, have been viciated by the same erroneous principles, and can therefore furnish no other light than that of beacons, which give warning of the course to be shunned, without pointing out that which ought to be pursued. The most that the Convention could do in such a situation, was to avoid the errors suggested by the past experience of other countries, as well as of our own; and to provide a convenient mode of rectifying their own errors, as future experience may unfold them.

Among the difficulties encountered by the Convention, a very important one must have lain, in combining the requisite stability and energy in Government, with the inviolable attention due to liberty, and to the Republican form. Without substantially accomplishing this part of their undertaking, they would have very imperfectly fulfilled the object of their appointment, or the expectation of the public: Yet, that it could not be easily accomplished, will be denied by no one, who is unwilling to betray his ignorance of the subject. Energy in Government is essential to that security against external and internal danger, and to that prompt and salutary execution of the laws, which enter into the very definition of good Government. Stability in Government, is essential to national character, and to the advantages annexed to it, as well as to that repose and confidence in the minds of the people, which are among the chief blessings of civil society. An irregular and mutable legislation, is not more an evil in itself, than it is odious to the people; and it may be pronounced with assurance, that the people of this country, enlightened as they are, with regard to the nature, and interested, as the great body of them are, in the effects of good Government, will never be satisfied, till some remedy be applied to the vicissitudes and uncertainties, which characterize the State administrations. On comparing, however, these valuable ingredients with the vital principles of liberty, we must perceive at once, the difficulty of mingling them together in their due proportions. The genius of Republican liberty, seems to demand on one side, not only that all power should be derived from the people; but, that those entrusted with it should be kept in dependence on the people, by a short duration of their appointments; and, that, even during this short period, the trust should be placed not in a few, but in a number of hands. Stability, on the contrary, requires, that the hands, in which power is lodged, should continue for a length of time, the same. A frequent change of men will result from a frequent return of electors, and a frequent change of measures, from a frequent change of men: whilst energy in Government requires not only a certain duration of power, but the execution of it by a single hand. How far the Convention may have succeeded in this part of their work, will better appear on a more accurate view of it. From the cursory view, here taken, it must clearly appear to have been an arduous part.

Not less arduous must have been the task of marking the proper line of partition, between the authority of the general, and that of the State Governments. Every man will be sensible of this difficulty, in proportion, as he has been accustomed to contemplate and discriminate objects, extensive and complicated in their nature. The faculties of the mind itself have never yet been distinguished and defined, with satisfactory precision, by all the efforts of the most acute and metaphysical Philosophers. Sense, perception, judgment, desire, volition, memory, imagination, are found to be separated by such delicate shades, and minute gradations, that their boundaries have eluded the most subtle investigations, and remain a pregnant source of ingenious disquisition and controversy. The boundaries between the great kingdoms of nature, and still more, between the various provinces, and lesser portions, into which they are subdivided, afford another illustration of the same important truth. The most sagacious and laborious naturalists have never yet succeeded, in tracing with certainty, the line which separates the district of vegetable life from the neighboring region of unorganized matter, or which marks the termination of the former and the commencement of the animal empire. A still greater obscurity lies in the distinctive characters, by which the objects in each of these great departments of nature, have been arranged and assorted. When we pass from the works of nature, in which all the delineations are perfectly accurate, and appear to be otherwise only from the imperfection of the eye which surveys them, to the institutions of man, in which the obscurity arises as well from the object itself, as from the organ by which it is contemplated; we must perceive the necessity of moderating still farther our expectations and hopes from the efforts of human sagacity. Experience has instructed us that no skill in the science of Government has yet been able to discriminate and define, with sufficient certainty, its three great provinces, the Legislative, Executive and Judiciary; or even the privileges and powers of the different Legislative branches. Questions daily occur in the course of practice, which prove the obscurity which reigns in these subjects, and which puzzle the greatest adepts in political science. The experience of ages, with the continued and combined labors of the most enlightened Legislators and jurists, have been equally unsuccessful in delineating the several objects and limits of different codes of laws and different tribunals of justice. The precise extent of the common law, the statute law, the maritime law, the ecclesiastical law, the law of corporations and other local laws and customs, remain still to be clearly and finally established in Great-Britain, where accuracy in such subjects has been more industriously pursued than in any other part of the world. The jurisdiction of her several courts, general and local, of law, of equity, of admiralty, &c. is not less a source of frequent and intricate discussions, sufficiently denoting the indeterminate limits by which they are respectively circumscribed. All new laws, though penned with the greatest technical skill, and passed on the fullest and most mature deliberation, are considered as more or less obscure and equivocal, until their meaning be liquidated and ascertained by a series of particular discussions and adjudications. Besides the obscurity arising from the complexity of objects, and the imperfection of the human faculties, the medium through which the conceptions of men are conveyed to each other, adds a fresh embarrassment. The use of words is to express ideas. Perspicuity therefore requires not only that the ideas should be distinctly formed, but that they should be expressed by words distinctly and exclusively appropriated to them. But no language is so copious as to supply words and phrases for every complex idea, or so correct as not to include many equivocally denoting different ideas. Hence, it must happen, that however accurately objects may be discriminated in themselves, and however accurately the discrimination may be considered, the definition of them may be rendered inaccurate by the inaccuracy of the terms in which it is delivered. And this un-

avoidable inaccuracy must be greater or less, according to the complexity and novelty of the objects defined. When the Almighty himself condescends to address mankind in their own language, his meaning, luminous as it must be, is rendered dim and doubtful, by the cloudy medium through which it is communicated. Here then are three sources of vague and incorrect definitions; indistinctness of the object, imperfection of the organ of conception, inadequateness of the vehicle of ideas. Any one of these must produce a certain degree of obscurity. The Convention, in delineating the boundary between the Federal and State jurisdictions, must have experienced the full effect of them all.

To the difficulties already mentioned, may be added the interfering pretensions of the larger and smaller States. We cannot err in supposing that the former would contend for a participation in the Government, fully proportioned to their superior wealth and importance; and that the latter would not be less tenacious of the equality at present enjoyed by them. We may well suppose that neither side would entirely yield to the other, and consequently that the struggle could be terminated only by compromise. It is extremely probable also, that after the ratio of representation had been adjusted, this very compromise must have produced a fresh struggle between the same parties, to give such a turn to the organization of the Government, and to the distribution of its powers, as would encrease the importance of the branches, in forming which they had respectively obtained the greatest share of influence. There are features in the Constitution which warrant each of these suppositions; and as far as either of them is well founded, it shews that the Convention must have been compelled to sacrifice theoretical propriety to the force of extraneous considerations.

Nor could it have been the large and small States only which would marshal themselves in opposition to each other on various points. Other combinations, resulting from a difference of local position and policy, must have created additional difficulties. As every State may be divided into different districts, and its citizens into different classes, which give birth to contending interests and local jealousies; so the different parts of the United States are distinguished from each other, by a variety of circumstances, which produce a like effect on a larger scale. And although this variety of interests, for reasons sufficiently explained in a former paper, may have a salutary influence on the administration of the Government when formed; yet every one must be sensible of the contrary influence which must have been experienced in the task of forming it.

Would it be wonderful if under the pressure of all these difficulties, the Convention should have been forced into some deviations from that artificial structure and regular symmetry, which an abstract view of the subject might lead an ingenious theorist to bestow on a Constitution planned in his closet or in his imagination? The real wonder is, that so many difficulties should have been surmounted; and surmounted with a unanimity almost as unprecedented as it must have been unexpected. It is impossible for any man of candor to reflect on this circumstance, without partaking of the astonishment. It is impossible for the man of pious reflection not to perceive in it, a finger of that Almighty hand which has been so frequently and signally extended to our relief in the critical stages of the revolution. We had occasion in a former paper, to take notice of the repeated trials which have been unsuccessfully made in the United Netherlands, for reforming the baneful and notorious vices of their Constitution. The history of almost all the great councils and consultations, held among mankind for reconciling their discordant opinions, assuaging their mutual jealousies, and adjusting their respective interests, is a history of factions, contentions, and disappointments; and may be classed among the most dark and degrading pictures which display the infirmities and depravities of the human character. If, in a few scattered instances, a brighter aspect is presented, they serve only as exceptions to admonish us of the general truth; and by their lustre to darken the gloom of the adverse prospect to which they are contrasted. In revolving the causes from which these exceptions result, and applying them to the particular instance before us, we are necessarily led to two important conclusions. The first is, that the Convention must have enjoyed in a very singular degree, an exemption from the pestilential influence of party animosities; the diseases most incident to deliberative bodies, and most apt to contaminate their proceedings. The second conclusion is, that all the deputations composing the Convention, were either satisfactorily accommodated by the final act; or were induced to accede to it, by a deep conviction of the necessity of sacrificing private opinions and partial interests to the public good, and by a despair of seeing this necessity diminished by delays or by new experiments.

11

CHARLES PINCKNEY, SOUTH CAROLINA HOUSE
OF REPRESENTATIVES
16 Jan. 1788
Elliot 4:253–63

Hon. CHARLES PINCKNEY (one of the delegates of the Federal Convention) rose in his place, and said that, although the principles and expediency of the measures proposed by the late Convention will come more properly into discussion before another body, yet, as their appointment originated with them, and the legislatures must be the instrument of submitting the plan to the opinion of the people, it became a duty in their delegates to state with conciseness the motives which induced it.

It must be recollected that, upon the conclusion of the definitive treaty, great inconveniences were experienced, as resulting from the inefficacy of the Confederation. The one first and most sensibly felt was the destruction of our commerce, occasioned by the restrictions of other nations, whose policy it was not in the power of the general government to counteract. The loss of credit, the inability in

our citizens to pay taxes, and languor of government, were, as they ever must be, the certain consequences of the decay of commerce. Frequent and unsuccessful attempts were made by Congress to obtain the necessary powers. The states, too, individually attempted, by navigation acts and other commercial provisions, to remedy the evil. These, instead of correcting, served but to increase it; their regulations interfered not only with each other, but, in almost every instance, with treaties existing under the authority of the Union. Hence arose the necessity of some general and permanent system, which should at once embrace all interests, and, by placing the states upon firm and united ground, enable them effectually to assert their commercial rights. Sensible that nothing but a concert of measures could effect this, Virginia proposed a meeting of commissioners at Annapolis, from the legislature of each state, who should be empowered to take into consideration the commerce of the Union; to consider how far a uniform system in their commercial regulations might be necessary to their common interest; and to report to the states such an act as, when unanimously ratified by them, would enable Congress effectually to provide for the same. In consequence of this, ten states appointed delegates. By accident, or otherwise, they did not attend, only five states being represented. The gentlemen present, not being a majority of the Union, did not conceive it advisable to proceed; but in an address to their constituents, which was also transmitted to the other legislatures, acquainted them with the circumstances of their meeting; that there appeared to them to be other and more material defects in the federal system than merely those of commercial powers. That these, upon examination, might be found greater than even the acts of their appointments implied, was at least so far probable, from the embarrassments which mark the present state of national affairs, foreign and domestic, as to merit, in their opinions, a deliberate and candid discussion in some mode which would unite the sentiments and councils of all the states. They therefore suggested the appointment of another convention, under more extensive powers, for the purpose of devising such further provisions as should appear to them necessary to render the federal government adequate to the exigencies of the Union.

Under this recommendation the late Convention assembled; for most of the appointments had been made before the recommendation of Congress was formed or known. He thought proper concisely to mention the manner of the Convention's assembling, merely to obviate an objection which all the opposers of the federal system had used, viz., that, at the time the Convention met, no opinion was entertained of their departing from the Confederation— that merely the grant of commercial powers, and the establishment of a federal revenue, were in agitation; whereas nothing can be more true, than that its promoters had for their object a firm national government. Those who had seriously contemplated the subject were fully convinced that a total change of system was necessary— that, however the repair of the Confederation might for a time avert the inconveniences of a dissolution, it was impossible a government of that sort could long unite this growing and extensive country. They also thought that the public mind was fully prepared for the change, and that no time could be more proper for introducing it than the present—that the total want of government, the destruction of commerce, of public credit, private confidence, and national character, were surely sufficiently alarming to awaken their constituents to a true sense of their situation.

Under these momentous impressions the Convention met, when the first question that naturally presented itself to the view of almost every member, although it was never formally brought forward, was the formation of a new, or the amendment of the existing system. Whatever might have been the opinions of a few speculative men, who either did, or pretended to, confide more in the virtue of the people than prudence warranted, Mr. Pinckney said he would venture to assert that the states were unanimous in preferring a change. They wisely considered that, though the Confederation might possess the great outlines of a general government, yet that it was, in fact, nothing more than a federal union; or, strictly speaking, a league founded in paternal and persuasive principles, with nothing permanent and coercive in its construction, where the members might, or might not, comply with their federal engagements, as they thought proper—that no power existed of raising supplies but by the requisitions or quotas on the states—that this defect had been almost fatally evinced by the experience of the states for the last six or eight years, in which not one of them had completely complied; but a few had even paid up their specie proportions; others very partially; and some, he had every reason to believe, had not to this day contributed a shilling to the common treasury since the Union was formed. He should not go into a detail of the conduct of the states, or the unfortunate and embarrassing situation to which their inattention has reduced the Union; these have been so often and so strongly represented by Congress, that he was sure there could not be a member on the floor unacquainted with them. It was sufficient to remark that the Convention saw and felt the necessity of establishing a government upon different principles, which, instead of requiring the intervention of thirteen different legislatures between the demand and the compliance, should operate upon the people in the first instance.

He repeated, that the necessity of having a government which should at once operate upon the people, and not upon the states, was conceived to be indispensable by every delegation present; that, however they may have differed with respect to the quantum of power, no objection was made to the system itself. They considered it, however, highly necessary that, in the establishment of a constitution possessing extensive national authorities, a proper distribution of its powers should be attended to. Sensible of the danger of a single body, and that to such a council the states ought not to intrust important rights, they considered it their duty to divide the legislature into two branches, and, by a limited revisionary power, to mingle, in some degree, the executive in their proceedings—a provision that he was pleased to find meets with universal approbation. The degree of weight which each state was to have in the federal council became a question of much ag-

itation. The larger states contended that no government could long exist whose principles were founded in injustice; that one of the most serious and unanswerable objections to the present system was the injustice of its tendency in allowing each state an equal vote, notwithstanding their striking disparity. The small ones replied, and perhaps with reason, that, as the states were the pillars upon which the general government must ever rest, their state governments must remain; that, however they may vary in point of territory or population, as political associations they were equal; that upon these terms they formally confederated, and that no inducement whatsoever should tempt them to unite upon others; that, if they did, it would amount to nothing less than throwing the whole government of the Union into the hands of three or four of the largest states.

After much anxious discussion,—for, had the Convention separated without determining upon a plan, it would have been on this point,—a compromise was effected, by which it was determined that the first branch be so chosen as to represent in due proportion to the people of the Union; that the Senate should be the representatives of the states, where each should have an equal weight. Though he was at first opposed to this compromise, yet he was far from thinking it an injudicious one. The different branches of the legislature being intended as checks upon each other, it appeared to him they would more effectually restrain their mutual intemperances under this mode of representation than they would have done if both houses had been so formed upon proportionable principles; for, let us theorize as much as we will, it will be impossible so far to divest the majority of the federal representatives of their state views and policy, as to induce them always to act upon truly national principles. Men do not easily wean themselves of those preferences and attachments which country and connections invariably create; and it must frequently have happened, had the larger states acquired that decided majority which a proportionable representation would have given them in both houses, that state views and policy would have influenced their deliberations. The ease with which they would, upon all occasions, have secured a majority in the legislature, might, in times less virtuous than the present, have operated as temptations to designing and ambitious men to sacrifice the public good to private views. This cannot be the case at present; the different mode of representation for the Senate will, as has already been observed, most effectually prevent it. The purpose of establishing different houses of legislation was to introduce the influence of different interests and principles; and he thought that we should derive, from this mode of separating the legislature into two branches, those benefits which a proper complication of principles is capable of producing, and which must, in his judgment, be greater than any evils that may arise from their temporary dissensions.

The judicial he conceived to be at once the most important and intricate part of the system. That a supreme federal jurisdiction was indispensable, cannot be denied. It is equally true that, in order to insure the administration of justice, it was necessary to give it all the powers, original as well as appellate, the Constitution has enumerated; without it we could not expect a due observance of treaties—that the state judiciary would confine themselves within their proper sphere, or that general sense of justice pervade the Union which this part of the Constitution is intended to introduce and protect—that much, however, would depend upon the wisdom of the legislatures who are to organize it—that, from the extensiveness of its powers, it may be easily seen that, under a wise management, this department might be made the keystone of the arch, the means of connecting and binding the whole together, of preserving uniformity in all the judicial proceedings of the Union—that, in republics, much more (in time of peace) would always depend upon the energy and integrity of the judicial than on any other part of the government—that, to insure these, extensive authorities were necessary; particularly so were they in a tribunal constituted as this is, whose duty it would be not only to decide all national questions which should arise within the Union, but to control and keep the state judicials within their proper limits whenever they shall attempt to interfere with its power.

And the executive, he said, though not constructed upon those firm and permanent principles which he confessed would have been pleasing to him, is still as much so as the present temper and genius of the people will admit. Though many objections had been made to this part of the system, he was always at a loss to account for them. That there can be nothing dangerous in its powers, even if he was disposed to take undue advantages, must be easily discerned from reviewing them. He is commander-in-chief of the land and naval forces of the Union, but he can neither raise nor support forces by his own authority. He has a revisionary power in the making of laws; but if two thirds of both houses afterwards agree notwithstanding his negative, the law passes. He cannot appoint to an office without the Senate concurs; nor can he enter into treaties, or, in short, take a single step in his government, without their advice. He is, also, to remain in office but four years. He might ask, then, From whence are the dangers of the executive to proceed? It may be said, From a combination of the executive and the Senate, they might form a baneful aristocracy.

He had been opposed to connecting the executive and the Senate in the discharge of those duties, because their union, in his opinion, destroyed that responsibility which the Constitution should, in this respect, have been careful to establish; but he had no apprehensions of an aristocracy. For his part, he confessed that he ever treated all fears of aristocracies or despotisms, in the federal head, as the most childish chimeras that could be conceived. In a Union extensive as this is, composed of so many state governments, and inhabited by a people characterized, as our citizens are, by an impatience under any act which even looks like an infringement of their rights, an invasion of them by the federal head appeared to him the most remote of all our public dangers. So far from supposing a change of this sort at all probable, he confessed his apprehensions were of a different kind: he rather feared that it was impossible, while the state systems continue—and continue they must—to construct any government upon republican principles sufficiently energetic to extend its influence through all its parts. Near the federal seat, its influence may have complete effect; but he much doubted its efficacy in the more remote districts. The state governments will too naturally slide into an opposition against the general one, and be easily induced to consider themselves as rivals. They will, after a time, resist the collection of a revenue; and if the general government is obliged to concede, in the smallest degree, on this point, they will of course neglect their duties, and despise its authority: a great degree of weight and energy is necessary to enforce it; nor is any thing to be apprehended from them. All power being immediately derived from the people, and the state governments being the basis of the general one, it will easily be in their power to interfere, and to prevent its injuring or invading their rights. Though at first he considered some declaration on the subject of trial by jury in civil causes, and the freedom of the press, necessary, and still thinks it would have been as well to have had it inserted, yet he fully acquiesced in the reasoning which was used to show that the insertion of them was not essential. The distinction which has been taken between the nature of a federal and state government appeared to be conclusive—that in the former, no powers could be executed, or assumed, but such as were expressly delegated; that in the latter, the indefinite power was given to the government, except on points that were by express compact reserved to the people.

On the subject of juries, in civil cases, the Convention were anxious to make some declaration; but when they reflected that all courts of admiralty and appeals, being governed in their propriety by the civil law and the laws of nations, never had, or ought to have, juries, they found it impossible to make any precise declaration upon the subject; they therefore left it as it was, trusting that the good sense of their constituents would never induce them to suppose that it could be the interest or intention of the general government to abuse one of the most invaluable privileges a free country can boast; in the loss of which, themselves, their fortunes and connections, must be so materially involved, and to the deprivation of which, except in the cases alluded to, the people of this country would never submit. When we reflect that the exigencies of the government require that a general government upon other principles than the present should be established,—when we contemplate the difference between a federal union and a government operating upon the people, and not upon the states,—we must at once see the necessity of giving to it the power of direct taxation. Without this, it must be impossible for them to raise such supplies as are necessary to discharge the debts, or support the expenses, of the Union—to provide against the common dangers, or afford that protection to its members which they have a right to expect from the federal head. But here he begged leave to observe that, so far from apprehending danger from the exercise of this power, few or no inconveniences are to be expected. He had not a doubt that, except in time of war, or pressing necessity, a sufficient sum would always be raised, by impost, to defray the general expenses. As to the power of raising troops, it was unnecessary to remark upon it further than merely to say, that this is a power the government at present possesses and exercises; a power so essential, that he should very much doubt the good sense or information of the man that should conceive it improper. It is guarded by a declaration that no grants for this purpose shall be longer than two years at a time. For his own part, notwithstanding all that had been said upon this popular topic, he could not conceive that either the dignity of a government could be maintained, its safety insured, or its laws administered, without a body of regular forces to aid the magistrate in the execution of his duty. All government is a kind of restraint. We may be told, a free government imposes no restraint upon the private wills of individuals which does not conduce in a greater degree to the public happiness; but all government is restraint, and founded in force. We are the first nation who have ever held a contrary opinion, or even attempted to maintain one without it. The experiment has been made, and he trusted there would hereafter be few men weak enough to suppose that some regular force ought not to be kept up, or that the militia ever can be depended upon as the support or protection of the Union.

Upon the whole, he could not but join those in opinion who have asserted that this is the best government that has ever yet been offered to the world, and that, instead of being alarmed at its consequences, we should be astonishingly pleased that one so perfect could have been formed from such discordant and unpromising materials. In a system founded upon republican principles, where the powers of government are properly distributed, and each confined to a separate body of magistracy, a greater degree of force and energy will always be found necessary than even in a monarchy. This arises from the national spirit of union being stronger in monarchies than in republics: it is said to be naturally strong in monarchies, because, in the absence both of manners and principles, the compelling power of the sovereign collects and draws every thing to a point; and thereby, in all common situations, effectually supplies their place. But in free countries it is naturally weak, unless supported by public spirit; for as, in most cases, a full spirit of national union will require that the separate and partial views of private interest be on every occasion sacrificed to the general welfare, so, when this principle prevails not, (and it will only prevail in moments of enthusiasm,) the national union must ever be destroyed by selfish views and private interest. He said that, with respect to the Union, this can only be remedied by a strong government, which, while it collects its powers to a point, will prevent that spirit of disunion from which the most serious consequences are to be apprehended. He begged leave, for a moment, to examine what effect this spirit of disunion must have upon us, as we may be affected by a foreign enemy. It weakens the consistency of all public measures, so that no extensive scheme of thought can be carried into action, if its accomplishment demand any long continuance of time. It weakens not only the consistency, but the vigor and expedition, of all public measures; so that, while a divided people are contending about the

means of security or defence, a united enemy may surprise and invade them. These are the apparent consequences of disunion. Mr. Pinckney confessed, however, that, after all that had been said upon the subject, our Constitution was in some measure but an experiment; nor was it possible yet to form a just conclusion as to its practicability.

It had been an opinion long established, that a republican form of government suited only the affairs of a small state; which opinion is founded in the consideration, that unless the people in every district of the empire be admitted to a share in the national representation, the government is not to them as a republic; that in a democratic constitution, the mechanism is too complicated, the motions too slow, for the operations of a great empire, whose defence and government require execution and despatch in proportion to the magnitude, extent, and variety of its concerns. There was, no doubt, weight in these reasons; but much of the objection, he thought, would be done away by the continuance of a federal republic, which, distributing the country into districts, or states, of a commodious extent, and leaving to each state its internal legislation, reserves unto a superintending government the adjustment of their general claims, the complete direction of the common force and treasure of the empire. To what limits such a republic might extend, or how far it is capable of uniting the liberty of a small commonwealth with the safety of a peaceful empire; or whether, among coördinate powers, dissensions and jealousies would not arise, which, for want of a common superior, might proceed to fatal extremities,—are questions upon which he did not recollect the example of any nation to authorize us to decide, because the experiment has never been yet fairly made. We are now about to make it upon an extensive scale, and under circumstances so promising, that he considered it the fairest experiment that had been ever made in favor of human nature. He concluded with expressing a thorough conviction that the firm establishment of the present system is better calculated to answer the great ends of public happiness than any that has yet been devised.

12

BRUTUS, NO. 12
7 Feb. 1788
Storing 2.9.150–51

To discover the spirit of the constitution, it is of the first importance to attend to the principal ends and designs it has in view. These are expressed in the preamble, in the following words, viz. "We, the people of the United States, in order to form a more perfect union, establish justice, insure domestic tranquility, provide for the common defence, promote the general welfare, and secure the blessings of liberty to ourselves and our posterity, do ordain and establish this constitution," &c. If the end of the government is to be learned from these words, which are clearly designed to declare it, it is obvious it has in view every object which is embraced by any government. The preservation of internal peace—the due administration of justice—and to provide for the defence of the community, seems to include all the objects of government; but if they do not, they are certainly comprehended in the words, "to provide for the general welfare." If it be further considered, that this constitution, if it is ratified, will not be a compact entered into by states, in their corporate capacities, but an agreement of the people of the United States, as one great body politic, no doubt can remain, but that the great end of the constitution, if it is to be collected from the preamble, in which its end is declared, is to constitute a government which is to extend to every case for which any government is instituted, whether external or internal. The courts, therefore, will establish this as a principle in expounding the constitution, and will give every part of it such an explanation, as will give latitude to every department under it, to take cognizance of every matter, not only that affects the general and national concerns of the union, but also of such as relate to the administration of private justice, and to regulating the internal and local affairs of the different parts.

Such a rule of exposition is not only consistent with the general spirit of the preamble, but it will stand confirmed by considering more minutely the different clauses of it.

13

ALEXANDER HAMILTON, FEDERALIST, NO. 84,
578–79
28 May 1788

Here, in strictness, the people surrender nothing, and as they retain every thing, they have no need of particular reservations. "WE THE PEOPLE of the United States, to secure the blessings of liberty to ourselves and our posterity, do *ordain* and *establish* this constitution for the United States of America." Here is a better recognition of popular rights than volumes of those aphorisms which make the principal figure in several of our state bills of rights, and which would sound much better in a treatise of ethics than in a constitution of government.

14

PATRICK HENRY, VIRGINIA RATIFYING
CONVENTION
4 June 1788
Elliot 3:22–23

And here I would make this inquiry of those worthy characters who composed a part of the late federal Conven-

tion. I am sure they were fully impressed with the necessity of forming a great consolidated government, instead of a confederation. That this is a consolidated government is demonstrably clear; and the danger of such a government is, to my mind, very striking. I have the highest veneration for those gentlemen; but, sir, give me leave to demand, What right had they to say, *We, the people?* My political curiosity, exclusive of my anxious solicitude for the public welfare, leads me to ask, Who authorized them to speak the language of, *We, the people,* instead of, *We, the states?* States are the characteristics and the soul of a confederation. If the states be not the agents of this compact, it must be one great, consolidated, national government, of the people of all the states. I have the highest respect for those gentlemen who formed the Convention, and, were some of them not here, I would express some testimonial of esteem for them. America had, on a former occasion, put the utmost confidence in them—a confidence which was well placed; and I am sure, sir, I would give up any thing to them; I would cheerfully confide in them as my representatives. But, sir, on this great occasion, I would demand the cause of their conduct. Even from that illustrious man who saved us by his valor, I would have a reason for his conduct: that liberty which he has given us by his valor, tells me to ask this reason; and sure I am, were he here, he would give us that reason. But there are other gentlemen here, who can give us this information. The people gave them no power to use their name. That they exceeded their power is perfectly clear. It is not mere curiosity that actuates me: I wish to hear the real, actual, existing danger, which should lead us to take those steps, so dangerous in my conception. Disorders have arisen in other parts of America; but here, sir, no dangers, no insurrection or tumult have happened; every thing has been calm and tranquil. But, notwithstanding this, we are wandering on the great ocean of human affairs. I see no landmark to guide us. We are running we know not whither. Difference of opinion has gone to a degree of inflammatory resentment in different parts of the country, which has been occasioned by this perilous innovation. The federal Convention ought to have amended the old system; for this purpose they were solely delegated; the object of their mission extended to no other consideration. You must therefore, forgive the solicitation of one unworthy member to know what danger could have arisen under the present Confederation, and what are the causes of this proposal to change our government.

15

DEBATE IN NORTH CAROLINA RATIFYING
CONVENTION
24 July 1788
Elliot 4:15–26

Mr. CALDWELL. Mr. Chairman, if they mean, *We, the people,*—the people at large,—I conceive the expression is improper. Were not they who framed this Constitution the representatives of the legislatures of the different states? In my opinion, they had no power, from the people at large, to use their name, or to act for them. They were not delegated for that purpose.

Mr. MACLAINE. The reverend gentleman has told us, that the expression, *We, the people*, is wrong, because the gentlemen who framed it were not the representatives of the people. I readily grant that they were delegated by states. But they did not think that they were the people, but intended it for the people, at a future day. The sanction of the state legislatures was in some degree necessary. It was to be submitted by the legislatures to the people; so that, when it is adopted, it is the act of the people. When it is the act of the people, their name is certainly proper. This is very obvious and plain to any capacity.

Mr. DAVIE. Mr. Chairman, the observation of the reverend gentleman is grounded, I suppose, on a supposition that the Federal Convention exceeded their powers. This objection has been industriously circulated; but I believe, on a candid examination, the prejudice on which this error is founded will be done away. As I had the honor, sir, to be a member of the Convention, it may be expected I would answer an objection personal in its nature, and which contains rather a reflection on our conduct, than an objection to the merits of the Constitution. After repeated and decisive proofs of the total inefficiency of our general government, the states deputed the members of the Convention to revise and strengthen it. And permit me to call to your consideration that, whatever form of confederate government they might devise, or whatever powers they might propose to give this new government, no part of it was binding until the whole Constitution had received the solemn assent of the people. What was the object of our mission? "To decide upon the most effectual means of removing the defects of our federal union." This is a general, discretional authority to propose any alteration they thought proper or necessary. Were not the state legislatures afterwards to review our proceedings? Is it not immediately through their recommendation that the plan of the Convention is submitted to the people? And this plan must still remain a dead letter, or receive its operation from the fiat of this Convention. Although the Federal Convention might recommend the concession of the most extensive powers, yet they could not put one of them into execution. What have the Convention done that can merit this species of censure? They have only recommended a plan of government containing some additional powers to those enjoyed under the present feeble system; amendments not only necessary, but which were the express object of the deputation. When we investigate this system candidly and accurately, and compare all its parts with one another, we shall find it absolutely necessary to confirm these powers, in order to secure the tranquillity of the states and the liberty of the people. Perhaps it would be necessary, to form a true judgment of this important question, to state some events, and develop some of those defects, which gave birth to the late Convention, and which have produced this revolution in our federal government. With the indulgence of the committee, I will attempt this detail with as much precision as I am capable of. The general objects of the union are, 1st, to protect us against foreign invasion; 2d, to defend us against internal commotions and insurrections; 3d, to promote the commerce, agriculture, and manufacturers, of America. These objects are requisite to make us a safe and happy people, and they cannot be attained without a firm and efficient system of union.

As to the first, we cannot obtain any effectual protection from the present Confederation. It is indeed universally acknowledged, that its inadequacy in this case is one of its greatest defects. Examine its ability to repel invasion. In the late glorious war, its weakness was unequivocally experienced. It is well known that Congress had a *discretionary right* to raise men and money; but they had no power to do either. In order to preclude the necessity of examining the whole progress of its imbecility, permit me to call to your recollection one single instance. When the last great stroke was made which humbled the pride of Britain, and put us in possession of peace and independence, so low were the finances and credit of the United States, that our army could not move from Philadelphia, until the minister of his most Christian majesty was prevailed upon to draw bills to defray the expense of the expedition. These were not obtained on the credit or interest of Congress, but by the personal influence of the commander-in-chief.

Had this great project miscarried, what fatal events might have ensued! It is a very moderate presumption, that what has once happened may happen again. The next important consideration, which is involved in the external powers of the Union, are *treaties*. Without a power in the federal government to compel the performance of our engagements with foreign nations, we shall be perpetually involved in destructive wars. The Confederation is extremely defective in this point also. I shall only mention the British treaty as a satisfactory proof of this melancholy fact. It is well known that, although this treaty was ratified in 1784, it required the sanction of a law of North Carolina in 1787; and that our enemies, presuming on the weakness of our federal government, have refused to deliver up several important posts within the territories of the United States, and still hold them, to our shame and disgrace. It is unnecessary to reason on facts, the perilous consequences of which must in a moment strike every mind capable of reflection.

The next head under which the general government may be considered, is the regulation of commerce. The United States should be empowered to compel foreign nations into commercial regulations that were either founded on the principles of justice or reciprocal advantages. Has the present Confederation effected any of these things? Is not our commerce equally unprotected abroad by arms and negotiation? Nations have refused to enter into treaties with us. What was the language of the British court on a proposition of this kind? Such as would insult the pride of any man of feeling and independence.—"You can make engagements, but you cannot compel your citizens to comply with them. We derive greater profits from the present situation of your commerce than we could expect under a treaty; and you have no kind of power that can compel us to surrender any advantage to you." This was the language of our enemies; and while our government remains as feeble as it has been, no nation will form any connection with us that will involve the relinquishment of the least advantage. What has been the consequence? A general decay of trade, the rise of imported merchandise, the fall of produce, and an uncommon decrease of the value of lands. Foreigners have been reaping the benefits and emoluments which our citizens ought to enjoy. An unjustifiable perversion of justice has pervaded almost all the states, and every thing presented to our view a spectacle of public poverty and private wretchedness!

While this is a true representation of our situation, can our general government recur to the ordinary expedient of *loans?* During the late war, large sums were advanced to us by foreign states and individuals. Congress have not been enabled to pay even the interest of these debts, with honor and punctuality. The requisitions made on the states have been every where unproductive, and some of them have not paid a stiver. These debts are a part of the price of our liberty and independence—debts which ought to be regarded with gratitude and discharged with honor. Yet many of the individuals who lent us money in the hour of our distress, are now reduced to indigence in consequence of our delinquency. So low and hopeless are the finances of the United States, that, the year before last Congress were obliged to borrow money even to pay the interest of the principal which we had borrowed before. This wretched resource of turning interest into principal, is the most humiliating and disgraceful measure that a nation could take, and approximates with rapidity to absolute ruin. Yet it is the inevitable and certain consequence of such a system as the existing Confederation.

There are several other instances of imbecility in that system. It cannot secure to us the enjoyment of our own territories, or even the navigation of our own rivers. The want of power to establish a uniform rule for naturalization through the United States is also no small defect, as it must unavoidably be productive of disagreeable controversies with foreign nations. The general government ought in this, as in every other instance, to possess the means of preserving the peace and tranquillity of the Union. A striking proof of the necessity of this power recently happened in Rhode Island: A man who had run off with a vessel and cargo, the property of some merchants in Holland, took sanctuary in that place: application was made for him as a citizen of the United Netherlands by the minister, but, as he had taken the oath of allegiance, the state refused to deliver him up, and protected him in his villany. Had it not been for the peculiar situation of the states at that time, fatal consequences might have resulted from such a conduct, and the contemptible state of Rhode Island might have involved the whole Union in a war.

The encroachments of some states on the rights of others, and of all on those of the Confederacy, are incontestable proofs of the weakness and imperfection of that system. Maryland lately passed a law granting exclusive privileges to her own vessels, contrary to the Articles of the Confederation. Congress had neither power nor influence

to alter it; all they could do was to send a contrary recommendation. It is provided, by the 6th Article of the Confederation, that no compact shall be made between two or more states without the consent of Congress; yet this has been recently violated by Virginia and Maryland, and also by Pennsylvania and New Jersey. North Carolina and Massachusetts have had a considerable body of forces on foot, and those in this state raised for two years, notwithstanding the express provision in the Confederation that no force should be kept up by any state in time of peace.

As to internal tranquillity,—without dwelling on the unhappy commotions in our own back counties, —I will only add that, if the rebellion in Massachusetts had been planned and executed with any kind of ability, that state must have been ruined; for Congress were not in a situation to render them any assistance.

Another object of the federal union is, to promote the agriculture and manufactures of the states—objects in which we are so nearly concerned. Commerce, sir, is the nurse of both. The merchant furnishes the planter with such articles as he cannot manufacture himself, and finds him a market for his produce. Agriculture cannot flourish if commerce languishes; they are mutually dependent on each other. Our commerce, as I have before observed, is unprotected abroad, and without regulation at home, and in this and many of the states ruined by partial and iniquitous laws—laws which, instead of having a tendency to protect property and encourage industry, led to the depreciation of the one, and destroyed every incitement to the other—laws which basely warranted and legalized the payment of just debts by *paper,* which represents nothing, or property of very trivial value.

These are some of the leading causes which brought forward this new Constitution. It was evidently necessary to infuse a greater portion of strength into the national government. But Congress were but a single body, with whom it was dangerous to lodge additional powers. Hence arose the necessity of a different organization. In order to form some balance, the departments of government were separated, and as a necessary check, the legislative body was composed of *two branches.* Steadiness and wisdom are better insured when there is a second branch, to balance and check the first. The stability of the laws will be greater when the popular branch, which might be influenced by local views, or the violence of party, is checked by another, whose longer continuance in office will render them more experienced, more temperate, and more competent to decide rightly.

The Confederation derived its sole support from the state legislatures. This rendered it weak and ineffectual. It was therefore necessary that the foundations of this government should be laid on the broad basis of the people. Yet the state governments are the pillars upon which this government is extended over such an immense territory, and are essential to its existence. The House of Representatives are immediately elected by the people. The senators represent the sovereignty of the states; they are directly chosen by the state legislatures, and no legislative act can be done without their concurrence. The election of the executive is in some measure under the control of the legislatures of the states, the electors being appointed under their direction.

The difference, in point of magnitude and importance, in the members of the confederacy, was an additional reason for the division of the legislature into two branches, and for establishing an equality of suffrage in the Senate. The protection of the small states against the ambition and influence of the larger members, could only be effected by arming them with an equal power in one branch of the legislature. On a contemplation of this matter, we shall find that the jealousies of the states could not be reconciled any other way. The lesser states would never have concurred unless this check had been given them, as a security for their political existence, against the power and encroachments of the great states. It may be also proper to observe, that the executive is separated in its functions from the legislature, as well as the nature of the case would admit, and the judiciary from both.

Another radical vice in the old system, which was necessary to be corrected, and which will be understood without a long deduction of reasoning, was, that it legislated on states, instead of individuals; and that its powers could not be executed but by fire or by the sword—by military force, and not by the intervention of the civil magistrate. Every one who is acquainted with the relative situation of the states, and the genius of our citizens, must acknowledge that, if the government was to be carried into effect by military force, the most dreadful consequences would ensure. It would render the citizens of America the most implacable enemies to one another. If it could be carried into effect against the small states, yet it could not be put in force against the larger and more powerful states. It was therefore absolutely necessary that the influence of the magistrate should be introduced, and that the laws should be carried home to individuals themselves.

In the formation of this system, many difficulties presented themselves to the Convention.

Every member saw that the existing system would ever be ineffectual, unless its laws operated on individuals, as military coercion was neither eligible nor practicable. Their own experience was fortified by their knowledge of the inherent weakness of all confederate governments. They knew that all governments merely federal had been short-lived, or had existed from principles extraneous from their constitutions, or from external causes which had no dependence on the nature of their governments. These considerations determined the Convention to depart from that solecism in politics—the principle of legislation for states in their political capacities.

The great extent of country appeared to some a formidable difficulty; but a confederate government appears, at least in theory, capable of embracing the various interests of the most extensive territory. Founded on the state governments solely, as I have said before, it would be tottering and inefficient. It became, therefore, necessary to bottom it on the people themselves, by giving them an immediate interest and agency in the government. There was, however, some real difficulty in conciliating a number of jarring interests, arising from the incidental but unalterable difference in the states in point of territory, situation, climate, and rivalship in commerce. Some of the states are very extensive, others very limited: some are manufacturing states, others merely agricultural: some of these are exporting states, while the carrying and navigation business are in the possession of others. It was not easy to reconcile such a multiplicity of discordant and clashing interests. Mutual concessions were necessary to come to any concurrence. A plan that would promote the exclusive interests of a few states would be injurious to others. Had each state obstinately insisted on the security of its particular local advantages, we should never have come to a conclusion. Each, therefore, amicably and wisely relinquished its particular views. The Federal Convention have told you, that the Constitution which they formed "was the result of a spirit of amity, and of that mutual deference and concession which the peculiarity of their political situation rendered indispensable." I hope the same laudable spirit will govern this Convention in their decision on this important question.

The business of the Convention was to amend the Confederation by giving it additional powers. The present form of Congress being a single body, it was thought unsafe to augment its powers, without altering its organization. The act of the Convention is but a mere proposal, similar to the production of a private pen. I think it a government which, if adopted, will cherish and protect the happiness and liberty of America; but I hold my mind open to conviction. I am ready to recede from my opinion if it be proved to be ill-founded. I trust that every man here is equally ready to change an opinion he may have improperly formed. The weakness and inefficiency of the old Confederation produced the necessity of calling the Federal Convention. Their plan is now before you; and I hope, on a deliberate consideration, every man will see the necessity of such a system. It has been the subject of much jealousy and censure out of doors. I hope gentlemen will now come forward with their objections, and that they will be thrown out and answered with candor and moderation.

Mr. CALDWELL wished to know why the gentlemen who were delegated by the states, styled themselves *We, the people.* He said that he only wished for information.

Mr. IREDELL answered, that it would be easy to satisfy the gentleman; that the style, *We, the people,* was not to be applied to the members themselves, but was to be the style of the Constitution, when it should be ratified in their respective states.

Mr. JOSEPH TAYLOR. Mr. Chairman, the very wording of this Constitution seems to carry with it an assumed power. *We, the people,* is surely an assumed power. Have they said, We, the delegates of the people? It seems to me that, when they met in Convention, they assumed more power than was given them. Did the people give them the power of using their name? This power was in the people. They did not give it up to the members of the Convention. If, therefore, they had not this power, they assumed it. It is the interest of every man, who is a friend to liberty, to oppose the assumption of power as soon as possible. I see no reason why they assumed this power. Matters may be carried still farther. This is a consolidation of all the states.

Had it said, *We, the states,* there would have been a federal intention in it. But, sir, it is clear that a consolidation is intended. Will any gentleman say that a consolidated government will answer this country? It is too large. The man who has a large estate cannot manage it with convenience. I conceive that, in the present case, a consolidated government can by no means suit the genius of the people. The gentleman from Halifax (Mr. Davie) mentioned reasons for such a government. They have their weight, no doubt; but at a more convenient time we can show their futility. We see plainly that men who come from New England are different from us. They are ignorant of our situation; they do not know the state of our country. They cannot with safety legislate for us. I am astonished that the servants of the legislature of North Carolina should go to Philadelphia, and, instead of speaking of the *state* of North Carolina, should speak of the *people.* I wish to stop power as soon as possible; for they may carry their assumption of power to a more dangerous length. I wish to know where they found the power of saying *We, the people,* and of consolidating the states.

Mr. MACLAINE. Mr. Chairman, I confess myself astonished to hear objections to the preamble. They say that the delegates to the Federal Convention assumed powers which were not granted them; that they ought not to have used the words *We, the people.* That they were not the delegates of the people, is universally acknowledged. The Constitution is only a mere proposal. Had it been binding on us, there might be a reason for objecting. After they had finished the plan, they proposed that it should be recommended to the people by the several state legislatures. If the people approve of it, it becomes their act. Is not this merely a dispute about words, without any meaning whatever? Suppose any gentleman of this Convention had drawn up this government, and we thought it a good one; we might respect his intelligence and integrity, but it would not be binding upon us. We might adopt it if we thought it a proper system, and then it would be our act. Suppose it had been made by our enemies, or had dropped from the clouds; we might adopt it if we found it proper for our adoption. By whatever means we found it, it would be our act as soon as we adopted it. It is no more than a blank till it be adopted by the people. When that is done here, is it not the people of the state of North Carolina that do it, joined with the people of the other states who have adopted it? The expression is, then, right. But the gentleman has gone farther, and says that the people of New England are different from us. This goes against the Union altogether. They are not to legislate for us; we are to be represented as well as they. Such a futile objection strikes at all union. We know that without union we should not have been debating now. I hope to hear no more objections of this trifling nature, but that we shall enter into the spirit of the subject at once.

Mr. CALDWELL observed, that he only wished to know why they had assumed the name of the people.

Mr. JAMES GALLOWAY. Mr. Chairman, I trust we shall not take up more time on this point. I shall just make a few remarks on what has been said by the gentleman from Halifax. He has gone through our distresses, and those of the other states. As to the weakness of the Confederation, we all know it. A sense of this induced the different states to send delegates to Philadelphia. They had given them certain powers; we have seen them, they are now upon the table. The result of their deliberations is now upon the table also. As they have gone out of the line which the states pointed out to them, we, the people, are to take it up and consider it. The gentlemen who framed it have exceeded their powers, and very far. They will be able, perhaps, to give reasons for so doing. If they can show us any reasons, we will, no doubt, take notice of them. But, on the other hand, if our civil and religious liberties are not secured, and proper checks provided, we have the power in our own hands to do with it as we think proper. I hope gentlemen will permit us to proceed.

16

A NATIVE OF VIRGINIA, OBSERVATIONS UPON THE PROPOSED PLAN OF FEDERAL GOVERNMENT
1788
Monroe Writings 1:356

The introduction, like a preamble to a law, is the Key of the Constitution. Whenever federal power is exercised, contrary to the spirit breathed by this introduction, it will be unconstitutionally exercised, and ought to be resisted by the people.

17

HOUSE OF REPRESENTATIVES, AMENDMENTS TO THE CONSTITUTION
14 Aug. 1789
Annals 1:717–19

Mr. SMITH wished to transpose the words of the first amendment, as they did not satisfy his mind in the manner they stood.

Mr. GERRY said, they were not well expressed; we have it here "government being intended for the benefit of the people;" this holds up an idea that all the Governments of the earth are intended for the benefit of the people. Now, I am so far from being of this opinion, that I do not believe that one out of fifty is intended for any such purpose. I believe the establishment of most Governments is to gratify the ambition of an individual, who, by fraud, force, or accident, had made himself master of the people. If we contemplate the history of nations, ancient or modern, we shall find they originated either in fraud or force, or both. If this is demonstrable, how can we pretend to say that Governments are intended for the benefit of those who are most oppressed by them. This maxim does not appear to me to be strictly true in fact, therefore I think we ought not to insert it in the constitution. I shall therefore propose to amend the clause, by inserting "of right," then it will stand as it ought. I do not object to the principle, sir; it is a good one, but it does not generally hold in practice.

The question on inserting the words "of right" was put, and determined in the negative.

Mr. TUCKER.—I presume these propositions are brought forward under the idea of being amendments to the constitution; but can this be esteemed an amendment of the constitution? If I understand what is meant by the introductory paragraph, it is the preamble to the constitution; but a preamble is no part of the constitution. It is, to say the best, a useless amendment. For my part, I should as soon think of amending the concluding part, consisting of General Washington's letter to the President of Congress, as the preamble; but if the principle is of importance, it may be introduced into a bill of rights.

Mr. SMITH read the amendments on this head, proposed by the conventions of New York, Virginia, and North Carolina, from which it appeared that these States had expressed a desire to have an amendment of this kind.

Mr. TUCKER replied, that the words "We the people do ordain and establish this constitution for the United States of America," were a declaration of their action; this being performed, Congress have nothing to do with it. But if it was necessary to retain the principle, it might come in at some other place.

Mr. SUMTER thought this was not a proper place to introduce any general principle; perhaps, in going through with the amendments, something might be proposed subversive of what was there declared; wherefore he wished the committee would pass over the preamble until they had gone through all the amendments, and then, if alterations were necessary, they could be accommodated to what had taken place in the body of the constitution.

Mr. LIVERMORE was not concerned about the preamble; he did not care what kind it was agreed to form in the committee; because, when it got before the House, it would be undone if one member more than one-third of the whole opposed it.

Mr. PAGE thought the preamble no part of the constitution; but if it was, it stood in no need of amendment; the words "We the people," had the neatness and simplicity, while its expression was the most forcible of any he had ever seen prefixed to any constitution. He did not doubt the truth of the proposition brought forward by the committee, but he doubted its necessity in this place.

Mr. MADISON.—If it be a truth, and so self-evident that it cannot be denied; if it be recognised, as is the fact in many of the State constitutions; and if it be desired by three important States, to be added to this, I think they must collectively offer a strong inducement to the mind desirous of promoting harmony, to acquiesce with the report; at least, some strong arguments should be brought forward to show the reason why it is improper.

My worthy colleague says, the original expression is neat and simple; that loading it with more words may destroy the beauty of the sentence; and others say it is unnecessary, as the paragraph is complete without it. Be it so, in

their opinion; yet, still it appears important in the estimation of three States, that this solemn truth should be inserted in the constitution. For my part, sir, I do not think the association of ideas anywise unnatural; it reads very well in this place; so much so, that I think gentlemen, who admit it should come in somewhere, will be puzzled to find a better place.

Mr. SHERMAN thought they ought not to come in in this place. The people of the United States have given their reasons for doing a certain act. Here we propose to come in and give them a right to do what they did on motives which appeared to them sufficient to warrant their determination; to let them know that they had a right to exercise a natural and inherent privilege, which they have asserted in a solemn ordination and establishment of the constitution. Now, if this right is indefeasible, and the people have recognised it in practice, the truth is better asserted than it can be by any words whatever. The words "We the people" in the original constitution, are as copious and expressive as possible; any addition will only drag out the sentence without illuminating it; for these reasons, it may be hoped the committee will reject the proposed amendment.

18

MARTIN V. HUNTER'S LESSEE
1 Wheat. 304 (1816)

(See 3.2.1, no. 65)

19

McCULLOCH V. MARYLAND
4 Wheat. 316 (1819)

[MARSHALL, C. J.] In discussing this question, the counsel for the State of Maryland have deemed it of some importance, in the construction of the constitution, to consider that instrument not as emanating from the people, but as the act of sovereign and independent States. The powers of the general government, it has been said, are delegated by the States, who alone are truly sovereign; and must be exercised in subordination to the States, who alone possess supreme dominion.

It would be difficult to sustain this proposition. The Convention which framed the constitution was indeed elected by the State legislatures. But the instrument, when it came from their hands, was a mere proposal, without obligation, or pretensions to it. It was reported to the then existing Congress of the United States, with a request that it might "be submitted to a Convention of Delegates, chosen in each State by the people thereof, under the recommendation of its Legislature, for their assent and ratification." This mode of proceeding was adopted; and by the

Convention, by Congress, and by the State Legislatures, the instrument was submitted to the people. They acted upon it in the only manner in which they can act safely, effectively, and wisely, on such a subject, by assembling in Convention. It is true, they assembled in their several States—and where else should they have assembled? No political dreamer was ever wild enough to think of breaking down the lines which separate the States, and of compounding the American people into one common mass. Of consequence, when they act, they act in their States. But the measures they adopt do not, on that account, cease to be the measures of the people themselves, or become the measures of the State governments.

From these Conventions the constitution derives its whole authority. The government proceeds directly from the people; is "ordained and established" in the name of the people; and is declared to be ordained, "in order to form a more perfect union, establish justice, ensure domestic tranquillity, and secure the blessings of liberty to themselves and to their posterity." The assent of the States, in their sovereign capacity, is implied in calling a Convention, and thus submitting that instrument to the people. But the people were at perfect liberty to accept or reject it; and their act was final. It required not the affirmance, and could not be negatived, by the State governments. The constitution, when thus adopted, was of complete obligation, and bound the State sovereignties.

It has been said, that the people had already surrendered all their powers to the State sovereignties, and had nothing more to give. But, surely, the question whether they may resume and modify the powers granted to government does not remain to be settled in this country. Much more might the legitimacy of the general government be doubted, had it been created by the States. The powers delegated to the State sovereignties were to be exercised by themselves, not by a distinct and independent sovereignty, created by themselves. To the formation of a league, such as was the confederation, the State sovereignties were certainly competent. But when, "in order to form a more perfect union," it was deemed necessary to change this alliance into an effective government, possessing great and sovereign powers, and acting directly on the people, the necessity of referring it to the people, and of deriving its powers directly from them, was felt and acknowledged by all.

The government of the Union, then, (whatever may be the influence of this fact on the case,) is, emphatically, and truly, a government of the people. In form and in substance it emanates from them. Its powers are granted by them, and are to be exercised directly on them, and for their benefit.

This government is acknowledged by all to be one of enumerated powers. The principle, that it can exercise only the powers granted to it, would seem too apparent to have required to be enforced by all those arguments which its enlightened friends, while it was depending before the people, found it necessary to urge. That principle is now universally admitted. But the question respecting the extent of the powers actually granted, is perpetually arising, and will probably continue to arise, as long as our system shall exist.

20

JAMES MONROE, VIEWS OF THE PRESIDENT OF THE UNITED STATES ON THE SUBJECT OF INTERNAL IMPROVEMENTS
4 May 1822
Richardson 2:147–49

The Constitution of the United States was formed by a convention of delegates from the several States, who met in Philadelphia, duly authorized for the purpose, and it was ratified by a convention in each State which was especially called to consider and decide on the same. In this progress the State governments were never suspended in their functions. On the contrary, they took the lead in it. Conscious of their incompetency to secure to the Union the blessings of the Revolution, they promoted the diminution of their own powers and the enlargement of those of the General Government in the way in which they might be most adequate and efficient. It is believed that no other example can be found of a Government exerting its influence to lessen its own powers, of a policy so enlightened, of a patriotism so pure and disinterested. The credit, however, is more especially due to the people of each State, in obedience to whose will and under whose control the State governments acted.

The Constitution of the United States, being ratified by the people of the several States, became of necessity to the extent of its powers the paramount authority of the Union. On sound principles it can be viewed in no other light. The people, the highest authority known to our system, from whom all our institutions spring and on whom they depend, formed it. Had the people of the several States thought proper to incorporate themselves into one community, under one government, they might have done it. They had the power, and there was nothing then nor is there anything now, should they be so disposed, to prevent it. They wisely stopped, however, at a certain point, extending the incorporation to that point, making the National Government thus far a consolidated Government, and preserving the State governments without that limit perfectly sovereign and independent of the National Government. Had the people of the several States incorporated themselves into one community, they must have remained such, their Constitution becoming then, like the constitution of the several States, incapable of change until altered by the will of the majority. In the institution of a State government by the citizens of a State a compact is formed to which all and every citizen are equal parties. They are also the sole parties and may amend it at pleasure. In the institution of the Government of the United States by the citizens of every State a compact was formed between the whole American people which has the same force and partakes of all the qualities to the extent of its powers as a compact between the citizens of a State in the formation of their own constitution. It can not be altered except by those who formed it or in the mode prescribed by the parties to the compact itself.

This Constitution was adopted for the purpose of remedying all defects of the Confederation, and in this it has succeeded beyond any calculation that could have been formed of any human institution. By binding the States together the Constitution performs the great office of the Confederation; but it is in that sense only that it has any of the properties of that compact, and in that it is more effectual to the purpose, as it holds them together by a much stronger bond; and in all other respects in which the Confederation failed the Constitution has been blessed with complete success. The Confederation was a compact between separate and independent States, the execution of whose articles in the powers which operated internally depended on the State governments. But the great office of the Constitution, by incorporating the people of the several States to the extent of its powers into one community and enabling it to act directly on the people, was to annul the powers of the State governments to that extent, except in cases where they were concurrent, and to preclude their agency in giving effect to those of the General Government. The Government of the United States relies on its own means for the execution of its powers, as the State governments do for the execution of theirs, both governments having a common origin or sovereign, the people—the State governments the people of each State, the National Government the people of every State—and being amenable to the power which created it. It is by executing its functions as a Government thus originating and thus acting that the Constitution of the United States holds the States together and performs the office of a league. It is owing to the nature of its powers and the high source from whence they are derived—the people—that it performs that office better than the Confederation or any league which ever existed, being a compact which the State governments did not form, to which they are not parties, and which executes its own powers independently of them.

There were two separate and independent governments established over our Union, one for local purposes over each State by the people of the State, the other for national purposes over all the States by the people of the United States. The whole power of the people, on the representative principle, is divided between them. The State governments are independent of each other, and to the extent of their powers are complete sovereignties. The National Government begins where the State governments terminate, except in some instances where there is a concurrent jurisdiction between them. This Government is also, according to the extent of its powers, a complete sovereignty. I speak here, as repeatedly mentioned before, altogether of representative sovereignties, for the real sovereignty is in the people alone.

The history of the world affords no such example of two separate and independent governments established over

the same people, nor can it exist except in governments founded on the sovereignty of the people. In monarchies and other governments not representative there can be no such division of power. The government is inherent in the possessor; it is his, and can not be taken from him without a revolution. In such governments alliances and leagues alone are practicable. But with us individuals count for nothing in the offices which they hold; that is, they have no right to them. They hold them as representatives, by appointment from the people, in whom the sovereignty is exclusively vested. It is impossible to speak too highly of this system taken in its twofold character and in all its great principles of two governments, completely distinct from and independent of each other, each constitutional, founded by and acting directly on the people, each competent to all its purposes, administering all the blessings for which it was instituted, without even the most remote danger of exercising any of its powers in a way to oppress the people. A system capable of expansion over a vast territory not only without weakening either government, but enjoying the peculiar advantage of adding thereby new strength and vigor to the faculties of both; possessing also this additional advantage, that while the several States enjoy all the rights reserved to them of separate and independent governments, and each is secured by the nature of the Federal Government, which acts directly on the people, against the failure of the others to bear their equal share of the public burdens, and thereby enjoys in a more perfect degree all the advantages of a league, it holds them together by a bond altogether different and much stronger than the late Confederation or any league that was ever known before—a bond beyond their control, and which can not even be amended except in the mode prescribed by it. So great an effort in favor of human happiness was never made before; but it became those who made it. Established in the new hemisphere, descended from the same ancestors, speaking the same language, having the same religion and universal toleration, born equal and educated in the same principles of free government, made independent by a common struggle and menaced by the same dangers, ties existed between them which never applied before to separate communities. They had every motive to bind them together which could operate on the interests and affections of a generous, enlightened, and virtuous people, and it affords inexpressible consolation to find that these motives had their merited influence.

In thus tracing our institutions to their origin and pursuing them in their progress and modifications down to the adoption of this Constitution two important facts have been disclosed, on which it may not be improper in this stage to make a few observations. The first is that in wresting the power, or what is called the sovereignty, from the Crown it passed directly to the people. The second, that it passed directly to the people of each colony and not to the people of all the colonies in the aggregate; to thirteen distinct communities and not to one. To these two facts, each contributing its equal proportion, I am inclined to think that we are in an eminent degree indebted for the success of our Revolution. By passing to the people it vested in a community every individual of which had equal rights and a common interest. There was no family dethroned among us, no banished pretender in a foreign country looking back to his connections and adherents here in the hope of a recall; no order of nobility whose hereditary rights in the Government had been violated; no hierarchy which had been degraded and oppressed. There was but one order, that of the people, by whom everything was gained by the change. I mention it also as a circumstance of peculiar felicity that the great body of the people had been born and educated under these equal and original institutions. Their habits, their principles, and their prejudices were therefore all on the side of the Revolution and of free republican government.

Had distinct orders existed, our fortune might and probably would have been different. It would scarcely have been possible to have united so completely the whole force of the country against a common enemy. A contest would probably have arisen in the outset between the orders for the control. Had the aristocracy prevailed, the people would have been heartless. Had the people prevailed, the nobility would probably have left the country, or, remaining behind, internal divisions would have taken place in every State and a civil war broken out more destructive even than the foreign, which might have defeated the whole movement. Ancient and modern history is replete with examples proceeding from conflicts between distinct orders, of revolutions attempted which proved abortive, of republics which have terminated in despotism. It is owing to the simplicity of the elements of which our system is composed that the attraction of all the parts has been to a common center, that every change has tended to cement the union, and, in short, that we have been blessed with such glorious and happy success.

21

JOSEPH STORY, COMMENTARIES ON THE
CONSTITUTION, 1:§§ 459, 462–63, 469–70,
471–76, 482–86, 489, 493–97, 500–501, 506
1833

---

§ 459. The importance of examining the preamble, for the purpose of expounding the language of a statute, has been long felt, and universally conceded in all juridical discussions. It is an admitted maxim in the ordinary course of the administration of justice, that the preamble of a statute is a key to open the mind of the makers, as to the mischiefs, which are to be remedied, and the objects, which are to be accomplished by the provisions of the statute.

. . . . .

§ 462. And, here, we must guard ourselves against an error, which is too often allowed to creep into the discussions upon this subject. The preamble never can be resorted to, to enlarge the powers confided to the general government, or any of its departments. It cannot confer any power *per se;* it can never amount, by implication, to an enlargement of any power expressly given. It can never be the legitimate source of any implied power, when otherwise withdrawn from the constitution. Its true office is to expound the nature, and extent, and application of the powers actually conferred by the constitution, and not substantively to create them. . . .

§ 463. We have already had occasion, in considering the nature of the constitution, to dwell upon the terms, in which the preamble is conceived, and the proper conclusion deducible from it. It is an act of the people, and not of the states in their political capacities. It is an ordinance or establishment of government and not a compact, though originating in consent; and it binds as a fundamental law promulgated by the sovereign authority, and not as a compact or treaty entered into and *in fieri,* between each and all the citizens of the United States, as distinct parties. The language is, "We, the *people* of the United States," not, We, the *states,* "do *ordain* and *establish;*" not, do *contract* and enter into a *treaty* with each other; "this *constitution* for the United States of America," not this *treaty* between the several states. And it is, therefore, an unwarrantable assumption, not to call it a most extravagant stretch of interpretation, wholly at variance with the language, to substitute other words and other senses for the words and senses incorporated, in this solemn manner, into the substance of the instrument itself. We have the strongest assurances, that this preamble was not adopted as a mere formulary; but as a solemn promulgation of a fundamental fact, vital to the character and operations of the government. The obvious object was to substitute a government of the people, for a confederacy of states; a constitution for a compact.

. . . . .

§ 469. The constitution, then, was adopted first "to form a more perfect union." Why this was desirable has been in some measure anticipated in considering the defects of the confederation. When the constitution, however, was before the people for ratification, suggestions were frequently made by those, who were opposed to it, that the country was too extensive for a single national government, and ought to be broken up into several distinct confederacies, or sovereignties; and some even went so far, as to doubt, whether it were not, on the whole, best, that each state should retain a separate, independent, and sovereign political existence. Those, who contemplated several confederacies, speculated upon a dismemberment into three great confederacies, one of the northern, another of the middle, and a third of the southern states. The greater probability, certainly, then was of a separation into two confederacies; the one composed of the northern and middle states, and the other of the southern. The reasoning of the Federalist on this subject seems absolutely irresistible. The progress of the population in the western territory, since that period, has materially changed the basis of all that reasoning. There could scarcely now, upon any dismemberment, exist, with a view to local interests, political associations, or public safety, less than three confederacies, and most probably four. And it is more than probable, that the line of division would be traced out by geographical boundaries, which would separate the slave-holding from the non-slave-holding states. Such a distinction in government is so fraught with causes of irritation and alarm, that no honest patriot could contemplate it without many painful and distressing fears.

§ 470. But the material consideration, which should be kept steadily in view, is, that under such circumstances a national government, clothed with powers at least equally extensive with those given by the constitution, would be indispensable for the preservation of each separate confederacy. Nay, it cannot be doubted, that much larger powers, and much heavier expenditures would be necessary. No nation could long maintain its public liberties, surrounded by powerful and vigilant neighbours, unless it possessed a government clothed with powers of great efficiency, prompt to act, and able to repel every invasion of its rights. Nor would it afford the slightest security, that all the confederacies were composed of a people descended from the same ancestors, speaking the same language, professing the same religion, attached to the same principles of government, and possessing similar manners, habits, and customs. If it be true, that these circumstances would not be sufficient to hold them in a bond of peace and union, when forming one government, acting for the interests, and as the representatives of the rights of the whole; how could a better fate be expected, when the interests and the representation were separate; and ambition, and local interests, and feelings, and peculiarities of climate, and products, and institutions, and imaginary or real aggressions and grievances, and the rivalries of commerce, and the jealousies of dominion, should spread themselves over the distinct councils, which would regulate their concerns by independent legislation? The experience of the whole world is against any reliance for security and peace between neighbouring nations, under such circumstances. . . .

§ 471. The same reasoning would apply with augmented force to the case of a dismemberment, when each state should by itself constitute a nation. The very inequalities in the size, the revenues, the population, the products, the interests, and even in the institutions and laws of each, would occasion a perpetual petty warfare of legislation, of border aggressions and violations, and of political and personal animosities, which, first or last, would terminate in the subjugation of the weaker to the arms of the stronger. In our further observations on this subject, it is not proposed to distinguish the case of several confederacies from that of a complete separation of all the states; as in a general sense the remarks apply with irresistible, if not with uniform, force to each.

§ 472. Does, then, the extent of our territory form any solid objection against forming "this more perfect union?" This question, so far as respects the original territory included within the boundaries of the United States by treaty of peace of 1783, seems almost settled by the experience of the last forty years. It is no longer a matter of conjecture, how far the government is capable (all other things being equal) of being practically applied to the whole of that territory. The distance between the utmost limits of our present population, and the diversity of interests among the whole, seem to have presented no obstacles under the beneficent administration of the general government, to the most perfect harmony and general advancement of all. Perhaps it has been demonstrated, (so far as our limited experience goes,) that the increased facilities of intercourse, the uniformity of regulations and laws, the common protection, the mutual sacrifices of local interests, when incompatible with that of all, and the pride and confidence in a government, in which all are represented, and all are equal in rights and privileges; perhaps, we say, it has been demonstrated, that these effects of the Union have promoted, in a higher degree, the prosperity of every state, than could have been attained by any single state, standing alone, in the freest exercise of all its intelligence, its resources, and its institutions, without any check or obstruction during the same period. The great change, which has been made in our internal condition, as well as in our territorial power, by the acquisition of Louisiana and Florida, have, indeed, given rise to many serious reflections, whether such an expansion of our empire may not hereafter endanger the original system. But time alone can solve this question; and to time it is the part of wisdom and patriotism to leave it.

§ 473. When, however, the constitution was before the people for adoption, objections, as has been already suggested, were strenuously urged against a general government, founded upon the then extent of our territory. And the authority of Montesquieu was relied on in support of the objections. It is not a little surprising, that Montesquieu should have been relied on for this purpose. He obviously had in view, when he recommends a moderate extent of territory, as best suited to a republic, small states, whose dimensions were far less than the limits of one half of those in the Union; so that upon strictly following out his suggestions, the latter ought to have been divided. But he suggests the appropriate remedy of a confederate republic, (the very form adopted in the constitution,) as the proper means of at once securing safety and liberty with extensive territory. The truth is, that what size is safe for a nation, with a view to the protection of its rights and liberties, is a question, which admits of no universal solution. Much depends upon its local position, its neighbours, its resources, the facilities of invasion, and of repelling invasion, the general state of the world, the means and weapons of warfare, the interests of other nations in preserving or destroying it, and other circumstances, which scarcely admit of enumeration. How far a republican government can, in a confederated form, be extended, and be at once efficient abroad and at home, can ensure general happiness to its own citizens, and perpetuate the principles of liberty, and preserve the substance of justice, is a great problem in the theory of government, which America is now endeavouring to unfold, and which, by the blessing of God, we must all earnestly hope, that she may successfully demonstrate.

§ 474. In the mean time, the following considerations may serve to cheer our hopes, and dispel our fears. First, (1.) that extent of territory is not incompatible with a just spirit of patriotism; (2.) nor with a general representation of all the interests and population within it; (3.) nor with a due regard to the peculiar local advantages or disadvantages of any part; (4.) nor with a rapid and convenient circulation of information useful to all, whether they are rulers or people. On the other hand, it has some advantages of a very important nature. (1.) It can afford greater protection against foreign enemies. (2.) It can give a wider range to enterprize and commerce. (3.) It can secure more thoroughly national independence to all the great interests of society, agriculture, commerce, manufactures, literature, learning, religion. (4.) It can more readily disarm and tranquillize domestic factions in a single state. (5.) It can administer justice more completely and perfectly. (6.) It can command larger revenues for public objects without oppression or heavy taxation. (7.) It can economise more in all its internal arrangements, whenever necessary. In short, as has been said, with equal truth and force: "One government can collect and avail itself of the talents and experience of the ablest men, in whatever part of the Union they may be found. It can move on uniform principles of policy. It can harmonize, assimilate, and protect the several parts and members, and extend the benefit of its foresight and precautions to each. In the formation of treaties, it will regard the interests of the whole, and the particular interests of the parts, as connected with that of the whole. It can apply the revenues of the whole to the defence of any particular part, and that more easily and expediciously, than state governments or separate confederacies can possibly do, for want of concert, and unity of system." Upon some of these topics, we may enlarge hereafter.

§ 475. The union of these states, "the more perfect union" is, then, and must for ever be invaluable to all, in respect both to foreign and domestic concerns. It will prevent some of the causes of war, that scourge of the human race, by enabling the general government, not only to negotiate suitable treaties for the protection of the rights and interests of all, but by compelling a general obedience to them, and a general respect for the obligations of the law of nations. It is notorious, that even under the confederation, the obligations of treaty stipulations, were openly violated, or silently disregarded; and the peace of the whole confederacy was at the mercy of the majority of any single state. If the states were separated, they would, or might, form separate and independent treaties with different nations, according to their peculiar interests. These treaties would, or might, involve jealousies and rivalries at home, as well as abroad, and introduce conflicts between nations struggling for a monopoly of the trade with each state. Retaliatory or evasive stipulations would be made, to counteract the injurious system of a neighbouring or distant state, and thus the scene be again acted over with renewed violence, which succeeded the peace of 1783, when the common interests were forgotten in the general struggle for superiority. It would manifestly be the interest of foreign nations to promote these animosities and jealousies, that, in the general weakness, the states might seek their protection by an undue sacrifice of their interests, or fall an easy prey to their arms.

§ 476. The dangers, too, to all the states, in case of division, from foreign wars and invasion, must be imminent, independent of those from the neighbourhood of the colonies and dependencies of other governments on this continent. Their very weakness would invite aggression. The ambition of the European governments, to obtain a mastery of power in colonies and distant possessions, would be perpetually involving them in embarrassing negotiations or conflicts, however peaceable might be their own conduct, and however inoffensive their own pursuits, and objects. America, as of old, would become the theatre of warlike operations, in which she had no interests; and with a view to their own security, the states would be compelled to fall back into a general colonial submission, or sink into dependencies of such of the great European powers, as might be most favourable to their interests, or most commanding over their resources.

· · · · ·

§ 482. But not to dwell farther on these important inducements "to form a more perfect union," let us pass to the next object, which is to "establish justice." This must for ever be one of the great ends of every wise government; and even in arbitrary governments it must, to a great extent, be practised, at least in respect to private persons, as the only security against rebellion, private vengeance, and popular cruelty. But in a free government it lies at the very basis of all its institutions. Without justice being freely, fully, and impartially administered, neither our persons, nor our rights, nor our property, can be protected. And if these, or either of them, are regulated by no certain laws, and are subject to no certain principles, and are held by no certain tenure, and are redressed, when violated, by no certain remedies, society fails of all its value; and men may as well return to a state of savage and barbarous independence. No one can doubt, therefore, that the establishment of justice must be one main object of all our state governments. Why, then, may it be asked, should it form so prominent a motive in the establishment of the national government?

§ 483. This is now proposed to be shown in a concise manner. In the administration of justice, foreign nations, and foreign individuals, as well as citizens, have a deep stake; but the former have not always as complete means of redress as the latter; for it may be presumed, that the state laws will always provide adequate tribunals to redress the grievances and sustain the rights of their own citizens. But this would be a very imperfect view of the subject. Citizens of contiguous states have a very deep interest in the administration of justice in each state; and even those, which are most distant, but belonging to the same confederacy, cannot but be affected by every inequality in the provisions, or the actual operations of the laws of each other. While every state remains at full liberty to legislate upon the subject of rights, preferences, contracts, and remedies, as it may please, it is scarcely to be expected, that they will all concur in the same general system of policy. The natural tendency of every government is to favour its own citizens; and unjust preferences, not only in the administration of justice, but in the very structure of the laws, may reasonably be expected to arise. Popular prejudices, or passions, supposed or real injuries, the predominance of home pursuits and feelings over the comprehensive views of a liberal jurisprudence, will readily achieve the most mischievous projects for this purpose. And these, again, by a natural reaction, will introduce correspondent regulations, and retaliatory measures in other states.

§ 483 [sic]. Now, exactly what this course of reasoning has led us to presume as probable, has been demonstrated by experience to be true in respect to our own confederacy during the short period of its existence, and under circumstances well calculated to induce each state to sacrifice many of its own objects for the general good. Nay, even when we were colonies, dependent upon the authority of the mother country, these inequalities were observable in the local legislation of several of the states, and produced heart-burnings and discontents, which were not easily appeased.

§ 484. First, in respect to foreign nations. After the confederacy was formed, and we had assumed the general rights of war as a sovereign belligerent nation, authority to make captures, and to bring in ships and cargoes for adjudication naturally flowed from the proper exercise of these rights by the law of nations. The states respectively retained the power of appointing prize tribunals, to take cognizance of these matters in the first instance; and thus thirteen distinct jurisdictions were established, which acted entirely independent of each other. It is true, that the articles of confederation had delegated to the general government the authority of establishing courts for receiving and determining, finally, appeals in all cases of captures. Congress accordingly instituted proper appellate tribunals, to which the state courts were subordinate, and, upon constitutional principles, were bound to yield obedience. But it is notorious, that the decisions of the appellate tribunals were disregarded, and treated as mere nullities, for no power to enforce them was lodged in congress. They operated, therefore, merely by moral influence and requisition, and, as such, soon sunk into insignificance. Neutral individuals, as well as neutral nations, were left wholly without any adequate redress for the most inexcusable injustice, and the confederacy subjected to imminent hazards. And until the constitution of the United States was established, no remedy was ever effectually administered. Treaties, too, were formed by congress with various nations; and above all, the treaty of peace of 1783, which gave complete stability to our independence against Great Britain. These treaties were, by the theory of the confederation, absolutely obligatory upon all the states. Yet their provisions were notoriously violated both by state legislation and state judicial tribunals. The non-fulfilment of the stipulations of the British treaty on our part more than once threatened to involve the whole country again in war. And the provision in that treaty for the payment of British debts was practically disregarded in many, if not in all, the state courts. These debts never were enforced, until the constitution gave them a direct and adequate sanction, independently of state legislation and state courts.

§ 485. Besides the debts due to foreigners, and the obligations to pay the same, the public debt of the United States was left utterly unprovided for; and the officers and soldiers of the revolution, who had achieved our independence, were, as we have had occasion to notice, suffered to languish in want, and their just demands evaded, or passed by with indifference. No efficient system to pay the public creditors was ever carried into operation, until the constitution was adopted; and, notwithstanding the increase of the public debt, occasioned by intermediate wars, it is now on the very eve of a total extinguishment.

§ 486. These evils, whatever might be their magnitude, did not create so universal a distress, or so much private discontent, as others of a more domestic nature, which were subversive of the first principles of justice. Independent of the unjustifiable preferences, which were fostered in favour of citizens of the state over those belonging to other states, which were not few nor slight, there were certain calamities inflicted by the common course of legislation in most of the states, which went to the prostration of all public faith and all private credit. Laws were constantly made by the state legislatures violating, with more or less degrees of aggravation, the sacredness of private contracts. Laws compelling the receipt of a depreciated and depreciating paper currency in payment of debts were generally, if not universally, prevalent. Laws authorizing the payment of debts by instalments, at periods differing entirely from the original terms of the contract; laws suspending, for a limited or uncertain period, the remedies to recover debts in the ordinary course of legal proceedings; laws authorizing the delivery of any sort of property, however unproductive or undesirable, in payment of debts upon an arbitrary or friendly appraisement; laws shutting up the courts for certain periods and under certain circumstances, were not infrequent upon the statute books of many of the states now composing the Union. In the rear of all these came the systems of general insolvent laws, some of which were of a permanent nature, and others again were adopted upon the spur of the occasion, like a sort of gaol delivery under the Lords' acts in England, which had so few guards against frauds of every kind by the debtor, that in practice they amounted to an absolute discharge from any debt, without any thing more than a nominal dividend; and sometimes even this vain mockery was dispensed with. In short, by the operations of paper currency, tender laws, installment laws, suspension laws, appraisement laws, and insolvent laws, contrived with all the dexterous ingenuity of men oppressed by debt, and popular by the very extent of private embarrassments, the states were almost universally plunged into a ruinous poverty, distrust, debility, and indifference to justice. The local tribunals were bound to obey the legislative will; and in the few instances, in which it was resisted, the independence of the judges was sacrificed to the temper of the times. It is well known, that Shays's rebellion in Massachusetts took its origin from this source. The object was to prostrate the regular administration of justice by a system of terror, which should prevent the recovery of debts and taxes.

. . . . .

§ 489. The next clause in the preamble is "to ensure domestic tranquillity." The illustrations appropriate to this head have been in a great measure anticipated in our previous observations. The security of the states against foreign influence, domestic dissensions, commercial rivalries, legislative retaliations, territorial disputes, and the petty irritations of a border warfare for privileges, exemptions, and smuggling, have been already noticed. The very habits of intercourse, to which the states were accustomed with each other during their colonial state, would, as has been justly remarked, give a keener edge to every discontent excited by any inequalities, preferences, or exclusions, growing out of the public policy of any of them. These, however, are not the only evils. In small communities domestic factions may well be expected to arise, which, when honest, may lead to the most pernicious public measures; and when corrupt, to domestic insurrections, and even to an overthrow of the government. The dangers to a republican government from this source have been dwelt upon by the advocates of arbitrary government with much exultation; and it must be confessed, that the history of free governments has furnished but too many examples to apologize for, though not to justify their arguments, drawn not only against the forms of republican government, but against the principles of civil liberty.

. . . . .

§ 493. One of the ordinary results of disunion among neighbouring states is the necessity of creating and keeping up standing armies, and other institutions unfavourable to liberty. The immediate dangers from sudden inroads and invasions, and the perpetual jealousies and discords incident to their local position, compel them to resort to the establishment of armed forces, either disproportionate to their means, or inadequate for their defence. Either alternative is fraught with public mischiefs. If they do not possess an adequate military force to repel invasion, they have no security against aggression and insult. If they possess an adequate military force, there is much reason to dread, that it may, in the hands of aspiring or corrupt men, become the means of their subjugation. There is no other refuge in such cases, but to seek an alliance always unequal, and to be obtained only by important concessions to some powerful nation, or to form a confederacy with other states, and thus to secure the co-operation and the terror of numbers. Nothing has so strong a tendency to suppress hostile enterprises, as the consciousness, that they will not be easily successful. Nothing is so sure to produce moderation, as the consciousness, that resistance will steadily maintain the dictates of justice. Summary, nay, even arbitrary authority, must be granted, where the safety of a state cannot await the slow measures of ordinary legislation to protect it. That government is, therefore, most safe in its liberties, as well as in its domestic peace, whose numbers constitute a preventive guard against all internal, as well as external attacks.

§ 494. We now proceed to the next clause in the preamble, to "provide for the common defence." And many of the considerations already stated apply with still greater force under this head. One of the surest means of preserving peace is said to be, by being always prepared for war. But a still more sure means is the power to repel, with effect, every aggression. That power can scarcely be attained without a wide extent of population, and at least a moderate extent of territory. A country, which is large in its limits, even if thinly peopled, is not easily subdued. Its variety of soil and climate, its natural and artificial defences, nay, its very poverty and scantiness of supplies, make it difficult to gain, or to secure a permanent conquest. It is far easier to overrun, than to subdue it. Armies must be divided, distant posts must be maintained, and channels of supplies kept constantly open. But where the territory is not only large, but populous, permanent conquest can rarely occur, unless (which is not our case) there are very powerful neighbours on every side, having a common interest to assist each other, and to subjugate their enemy. It is far otherwise, where there are many rival and independent states, having no common union of government or interests. They are half subdued by their own dissensions, jealousies, and resentments before the conflict is begun. They are easily made to act a part in the destruction of each other, or easily fall a prey for want of proper concert and energy of operations.

§ 495. Besides;—The resources of a confederacy must be far greater than those of any single state belonging to it, both for peace and war. It can command a wider range of revenue, of military power, of naval armaments, and of productive industry. It is more independent in its employments, in its capacities, and in its influences. In the present state of the world, a few great powers possess the command of commerce, both on land and at sea. In war, they trample upon the rights of neutrals who are feeble; for their weakness furnishes an excuse both for servility and disdain. In peace, they control the pursuits of the rest of the world, and force their trade into every channel by the activity of their enterprise, their extensive navigation, and their flourishing manufactures. They little regard the complaints of those, who are sub[di]vided into petty states with varying interests; and use them only as instruments to annoy or check the enterprise of each other. Such states are not formidable in peace or in war. To secure their rights and maintain their independence they must become a confederated nation, and speak with the force of numbers, as well as the eloquence of truth. The navy or army, which could be maintained by any single state in the Union, would be scarcely formidable to any second rate power in Europe. It would be a grievous public burthen, and exhaust the whole resources of the state. But a navy or army for all the purposes of home defence, or protection upon the ocean, is within the compass of the resources of the general government, without any severe exaction. And with the growing strength of the Union must be at once more safe for us, and more formidable to foreign nations. The means, therefore, to provide for the common defence are ample; and they can only be rendered inert and inadequate by a division among the states, and a want of unity of operations.

§ 496. We pass, in the next place, to the clause to "promote the general welfare." And it may be asked, as the state governments are formed for the same purpose by the people, why should this be set forth, as a peculiar or prominent object of the constitution of the United States? To such an inquiry two general answers may be given. The states, separately, would not possess the means. If they did possess the means, they would not possess the power to carry the appropriate measures into operation.

§ 497. First, in respect to means. It is obvious, that from the local position and size of several of the states, they must for ever possess but a moderate revenue, not more than what is indispensable for their own wants, and, in the strictest sense, for domestic improvements. In relation to others more favourably situated for commerce and navigation, the revenues from taxation may be larger; but the main reliance must be placed upon the taxation by way of imposts upon importations. Now, it is obvious, from the remarks already made, that no permanent revenue can be raised from this source, when the states are separated. The evasions of the laws, which will constantly take place from the rivalries, and various interests of the neighbouring states; the facilities afforded by the numerous harbours, rivers, and bays, which indent and intersect our coasts; the strong interest of foreigners to promote smuggling; the want of uniformity in the duties laid by the different states; the means of intercourse along the internal territorial boundaries of the commercial states; these, and many other causes, would inevitably lead to a very feeble administration of any local revenue system, and would make its returns moderate and unsatisfactory. What could New-York do with a single sea-port, surrounded on each side by jealous maritime neighbours with numerous ports? What could Massachusetts, or Connecticut do with the intermediate territory of Rhode-Island, running into the heart of the states by water communications admirably adapted for the security of illicit trade? What could Maryland or Virginia do with the broad Chesapeake between them with its thousand landing places? What could Pennsylvania oppose to the keen resentments, or the facile policy of her weaker neighbour, Delaware? What could any single state on the Mississippi do to force a steady trade for itself with adequate protecting duties? In short, turn to whichever part of the continent we may, the difficulties of maintaining an adequate system of revenue would be insurmountable, and the expenses of collecting it enormous. After some few struggles for uniformity, and co-operation for mutual support, each state would sink back into listless indifference or gloomy despondency; and rely, principally, upon direct taxation for its ordinary supplies. The experience of the few years succeeding the peace of 1783 fully justifies the worst apprehensions on this head.

. . . . .

§ 500. But if the means were completely within the power of the several states, it is obvious, that the jurisdiction would be wanting to carry into effect any great or comprehensive plan for the welfare of the whole. The idea of a permanent and zealous co-operation of thirteen (and now of twenty-four) distinct governments in any scheme for the common welfare, is of itself a visionary notion. In the first place, laying aside all local jealousies and accidental jars, there is no plan for the benefit of the whole, which would not bear unequally upon some particular parts. Is it a regulation of commerce or mutual intercourse, which is proposed? Who does not see, that the agricultural, the

manufacturing, and the navigating states, may have a real or supposed difference of interest in its adoption. If a system of regulations, on the other hand, is prepared by a general government, the inequalities of one part may, and ordinarily will, under the guidance of wise councils, correct and meliorate those of another. The necessity of a sacrifice of one for the benefit of all may not, and probably will not, be felt at the moment by the state called upon to make it. But in a general government, representing the interests of all, the sacrifice, though first opposed, will, in the end, be found adequately recompensed by other substantial good. Agriculture, commerce, manufactures, may, each in turn, be compelled to yield something of their peculiar benefits, and yet, on the whole, be still each a gainer by the general system. The very power of thus redressing the evils, felt by each in its intercourse with foreign nations, by prohibitory regulations, or countervailing duties, may secure permanent privileges of an incalculable value. And the fact has been, as theoretical reasoning would lead us to suppose. The navigation and commerce, the agriculture and manufactures of all the states, have received an advancement in every direction by the union, which has far exceeded the most sanguine expectation of its warmest friends.

§ 501. But the fact alone of an unlimited intercourse, without duty or restriction, between all the states, is of itself a blessing of almost inconceivable value. It makes it an object with each permanently to look to the interests of all, and to withdraw its operations from the narrow sphere of its own exclusive territory. Without entering here into the inquiry, how far the general government possesses the power to make, or aid the making of roads, canals, and other general improvements, which will properly arise in our future discussions, it is clear, that if there were no general government, the interest of each state to undertake, or to promote in its own legislation any such project, would be far less strong, than it now is; since there would be no certainty, as to the value or duration of such improvements, looking beyond the boundaries of the state. The consciousness, that the union of the states is permanent, and will not be broken up by rivalries, or conflicts of policy, that caprice, or resentment, will not divert any state from its proper duties, as a member of the Union, will give a solid character to all improvements. Independent of the exercise of any authority by the general government for this purpose, it was justly foreseen, that roads would be every where shortened and kept in better order; accommodations for travellers would be multiplied and meliorated; an interior navigation on our eastern side would be opened throughout the whole extent of our coast; and, by canals and improvements in river navigation, a boundless field opened to enterprise and emigration, to commerce and products, through the interior states, to the farthest limits of our western territories.

. . . . .

§ 506. The last clause in the preamble is to "secure the blessings of liberty to ourselves and our posterity." And surely no object could be more worthy of the wisdom and ambition of the best men in any age.

Article 1, Section 1

All legislative Powers herein granted shall be vested in a Congress of the United States, which shall consist of a Senate and House of Representatives.

1

JOHN LOCKE, SECOND TREATISE, §§ 134–42
1689

(See vol. 1, ch. 17, no. 5)

2

WILLIAM BLACKSTONE, COMMENTARIES
1:149–51, 156–57
1765

II. The constituent parts of a parliament are the next objects of our enquiry. And these are, the king's majesty, sitting there in his royal political capacity, and the three estates of the realm; the lords spiritual, the lords temporal, (who sit, together with the king, in one house) and the commons, who sit by themselves in another. And the king and these three estates, together, form the great corporation or body politic of the kingdom, of which the king is said to be *caput, principium, et finis.* For upon their coming together the king meets them, either in person or by representation; without which there can be no beginning of a parliament; and he also has alone the power of dissolving them.

It is highly necessary for preserving the ballance of the constitution, that the executive power should be a branch, though not the whole, of the legislature. The total union of them, we have seen, would be productive of tyranny; the total disjunction of them for the present, would in the end produce the same effects, by causing that union, against which it seems to provide. The legislature would soon become tyrannical, by making continual encroachments, and gradually assuming to itself the rights of the executive power. Thus the long parliament of Charles the first, while it acted in a constitutional manner, with the royal concurrence, redressed many heavy grievances and established many salutary laws. But when the two houses assumed the power of legislation, in exclusion of the royal authority, they soon after assumed likewise the reins of administration; and, in consequence of these united powers, overturned both church and state, and established a worse oppression than any they pretended to remedy. To hinder therefore any such encroachments, the king is himself a part of the parliament: and, as this is the reason of his being so, very properly therefore the share of legislation, which the constitution has placed in the crown, consists in the power of *rejecting,* rather than *resolving;* this being sufficient to answer the end proposed. For we may apply to the royal negative, in this instance, what Cicero observes of the negative of the Roman tribunes, that the crown has not any power of *doing* wrong, but merely of *preventing* wrong from being done. The crown cannot begin of itself any alterations in the present established law; but it may approve or disapprove of the alterations suggested and consented to by the two houses. The legislative therefore cannot abridge the executive power of any rights which it now has by law, without it's own consent; since the law must perpetually stand as it now does, unless all the powers will agree to alter it. And herein indeed consists the true excellence of the English government, that all the parts of it form a mutual check upon each other. In the legislature, the people are a check upon the nobility, and the nobility a check upon the people; by the mutual privilege of rejecting what the other has resolved: while the king is a check upon both, which preserves the executive power from encroachments. And this very executive power is again checked, and kept within due bounds by the two houses, through the privilege they have of enquiring into, impeaching, and punishing the conduct (not indeed of the king, which would destroy his constitutional independence; but, which is more beneficial to the public) of his evil and pernicious counsellors. Thus every branch of our civil polity supports and is supported, regulates and is regulated, by the rest; for the two houses naturally drawing in two directions of opposite interest, and the prerogative in another still different from them both, they mutually keep each other from exceeding their proper limits; while the whole is prevented from separation, and artificially connected together by the mixed nature of the crown, which is a part of the legislative, and the sole executive magistrate. Like three distinct powers in mechanics, they jointly impel the machine of government in a direction different from what either, acting by themselves, would have done; but at the same time in a direction partaking of each, and formed out of all; a direction which constitutes the true line of the liberty and happiness of the community.

. . . . .

The power and jurisdiction of parliament, says Sir Edward Coke, is so transcendent and absolute, that it cannot be confined, either for causes or persons, within any bounds. And of this high court he adds, it may be truly said *"si antiquitatem spectes, est vetustissima; si dignitatem, est honoratissima; si juridictionem, est capacissima."* It hath sovereign and uncontrolable authority in making, confirming, enlarging, restraining, abrogating, repealing, reviving, and expounding of laws, concerning matters of all possible denominations, ecclesiastical, or temporal, civil, military, maritime, or criminal: this being the place where that absolute despotic power, which must in all governments reside somewhere, is entrusted by the constitution of these kingdoms. All mischiefs and grievances, operations and remedies, that transcend the ordinary course of the laws, are within the reach of this extraordinary tribunal. It can regulate or new model the succession to the crown; as was done in the reign of Henry VIII and William III. It can alter the established religion of the land; as was done in a variety of instances, in the reigns of king Henry VIII and his three children. It can change and create afresh even the constitution of the kingdom and of parliaments themselves; as was done by the act of union, and the several statutes for triennial and septennial elections. It can, in short, do every thing that is not naturally impossible; and therefore some have not scrupled to call it's power, by a figure rather too bold, the omnipotence of parliament.

True it is, that what they do, no authority upon earth can undo. So that it is a matter most essential to the liberties of this kingdom, that such members be delegated to this important trust, as are most eminent for their probity, their fortitude, and their knowlege; for it was a known apothegm of the great lord treasurer Burleigh, "that "England could never be ruined but by a parliament:" and, as sir Matthew Hale observes, this being the highest and greatest court, over which none other can have jurisdiction in the kingdom, if by any means a misgovernment should any way fall upon it, the subjects of this kingdom are left without all manner of remedy. To the same purpose the president Montesquieu, though I trust too hastily, presages; that as Rome, Sparta, and Carthage have lost their liberty and perished, so the constitution of England will in time lose it's liberty, will perish: it will perish, whenever the legislative power shall become more corrupt than the executive.

3

JOHN ADAMS, THOUGHTS ON GOVERNMENT
Apr. 1776

(See vol. 1, ch. 4, no. 5)

4

RECORDS OF THE FEDERAL CONVENTION

[1:21; Madison, 29 May]

6. Resolved that each branch ought to possess the right of originating Acts; that the National Legislature ought to be impowered to enjoy the Legislative Rights vested in Congress by the Confederation & moreover to legislate in all cases to which the separate States are incompetent, or in which the harmony of the United States may be interrupted by the exercise of individual Legislation; to negative all laws passed by the several States, contravening in the opinion of the National Legislature the articles of Union; and to call forth the force of the Union agst. any member of the Union failing to fulfill its duty under the articles thereof.

[1:47; Journal, 31 May]

"That the national legislature ought to be empowered"

"to enjoy the legislative rights vested in Congress by the confederation; and moreover

To legislate in all cases, to which the separate States are incompetent: [Ayes—9; noes—0; divided—1.] or

in which the harmony of the united States may be interrupted by the exercise of individual legislation

To negative all laws, passed by the several States, contravening, in the opinion of the national legislature, the articles of union: (the following words were added to this clause on motion of Mr Franklin, "or any Treaties subsisting under the authority of the union

Questions being taken separately on the foregoing clauses of the sixth resolution they were agreed to.

[1:53; Madison, 31 May]

On the proposition for giving "Legislative power in all cases to which the State Legislatures were individually incompetent".

Mr. Pinkney, & Mr. Rutledge objected to the vagueness of the term *incompetent,* and said they could not well decide how to vote until they should see an exact enumeration of the powers comprehended by this definition.

Mr. Butler repeated his fears that we were running into an extreme in taking away the powers of the States, and called on Mr. Randolp for the extent of his meaning.

Mr. Randolph disclaimed any intention to give indefinite powers to the national Legislature, declaring that he was entirely opposed to such an inroad on the State jurisdictions, and that he did not think any considerations whatever could ever change his determination. His opinion was fixed on this point.

Mr. Madison said that he had brought with him into the Convention a strong bias in favor of an enumeration and definition of the powers necessary to be exercised by the national Legislature; but had also brought doubts concerning its practicability. His wishes remained unaltered; but his doubts had become stronger. What his opinion might ultimately be he could not yet tell. But he should shrink from nothing which should be found essential to such a form of Govt. as would provide for the safety, liberty and happiness of the Community. This being the end of all our deliberations, all the necessary means for attaining it must, however reluctantly, be submitted to.

On the question for giving powers, in cases to which the States are not competent,

Massts. ay. Cont. divd. (Sharman no Elseworth ay) N.Y. ay. N.J. ay. Pa. ay. Del. ay. Va. ay. N.C. ay, S. Carolina ay. Georga. ay. [Ayes—9; noes—0; divided—1.]

The other clauses giving powers necessary to preserve harmony among the States (to negative all State laws contravening in the opinion of the Nat Leg the articles of Union down to the last clause, (the words "or any treaties subsisting under the authority of the Union", being added after the words "contravening &c. the articles of the Union"; on motion of Dr. Franklin) were agreed to witht. debate or dissent.

[1:225, 229; Journal, 13 June]

Resolved that the national Legislature ought to be empowered.

to enjoy the legislative rights vested in Congress by the confederation; and moreover.

to legislate in all cases to which the separate States are incompetent: or in which the harmony of the United States may be interrupted by the exercise of individual legislation.

to negative all laws passed by the several States contravening, in the opinion of the national legislature,

the articles of union; or any treaties subsisting under the authority of the Union

. . . . .

6. Resolved. that the national Legislature ought to be empowered

to enjoy the legislative rights vested in Congress by the confederation—and moreover

to legislate in all cases to which the separate States are incompetent: or in which the harmony of the United States may be interrupted by the exercise of individual legislation.

to negative all laws passed by the several States contravening, in the opinion of the national legislature, the articles of union, or any treaties subsisting under the authority of the union.

[1:243; Madison, 15 June]

2. Resd. that in addition to the powers vested in the U. States in Congress, by the present existing articles of Confederation, they be authorized to pass acts for raising a revenue, by levying a duty or duties on all goods or merchandizes of foreign growth or manufacture, imported into any part of the U. States, by Stamps on paper, vellum or parchment, and by a postage on all letters or packages passing through the general post-Office, to be applied to such federal purposes as they shall deem proper & expedient; to make rules & regulations for the collection thereof; and the same from time to time, to alter & amend in such manner as they shall think proper: to pass Acts for the regulation of trade & commerce as well with foreign nations as with each other: provided that all punishments, fines, forfeitures & penalties to be incurred for contravening such acts rules and regulations shall be adjudged by the Common law Judiciarys of the State in which any offence contrary to the true intent & meaning of such Acts rules & regulations shall have been committed or perpetrated, with liberty of commencing in the first instance all suits & prosecutions for that purpose in the superior Common law Judiciary in such State, subject nevertheless, for the correction of all errors, both in law & fact in rendering judgment, to an appeal to the Judiciary of the U. States

[1:291; Madison, 18 June]

I "The Supreme Legislative power of the United States of America to be vested in two different bodies of men; the one to be called the Assembly, the other the Senate who together shall form the Legislature of the United States with power to pass all laws whatsoever subject to the Negative hereafter mentioned.

[1:336; Madison, 20 June]

The 2d. Resoln. "that the national Legislature ought to consist of two branches". taken up. the word "national" struck out as of course.

Mr. Lansing, observed that the true queston here was, whether the Convention would adhere to or depart from the foundation of the present Confederacy; and moved instead of the 2d Resolution "that the powers of Legislation be vested in the U. States in Congress". . He had already assigned two reasons agst. such an innovation as was proposed. 1. the want of competent powers in the Convention—2. the state of the public mind. It had been observed by (Mr. Madison) in discussing the first point, that in two States the Delegates to Congs. were chosen by the people. Notwithstanding the first appearance of this remark, it had in fact no weight, as the Delegates however chosen, did not represent the people merely as so many individuals; but as forming a sovereign State. (Mr. Randolph) put it, he said, on its true footing namely that the public safety superseded the scruple arising from the review of our powers. But in order to feel the force of this consideration, the same impression must be had of the public danger. He had not himself the same impression, and could not therefore dismiss his scruple. (Mr Wilson) contended that as the Convention were only to recommend, they might recommend what they pleased. He differed much from him. any act whatever of so respectable a body must have a great effect, and if it does not succeed, will be a source of great dissentions. He admitted that there was no certain criterion of the public mind on the subject. He therefore recurred to the evidence of it given by the opposition in the States to the scheme of an Impost. It could not be expected that those possessing Sovereignty could ever voluntarily part with it. It was not to be expected from any one State, much less from thirteen. He proceeded to make some observations on the plan itself and the argumts. urged in support of it. The point of Representation could receive no elucidation from the case of England. The corruption of the boroughs did not proceed from their comparative smallness: but from the actual fewness of the inhabitants, some of them not having more than one or two. a great inequality existed in the Counties of England. Yet the like complaint of peculiar corruption in the small ones had not been made. It had been said that Congress represent the State Prejudices: will not any other body whether chosen by the Legislatures or people of the States, also represent their prejudices? It had been asserted by his Colleague (Col. Hamilton) that there was no coincidence of interests among the large States that ought to excite fears of oppression in the smaller. If it were true that such a uniformity of interests existed among the States, there was equal safety for all of them, whether the representation remained as heretofore, or were proportioned as now proposed. It is proposed that the genl. Legislature shall have a negative on the laws of the States. Is it conceivable that there will be leisure for such a task? there will on the most moderate calculation, be as many Acts sent up from the States as there are days in the year. Will the members of the general Legislature be competent Judges? Will a gentleman from Georgia be a Judge of the expediency of a law which is to operate in N. Hamshire. Such a Negative would be more injurious than that of Great Britain heretofore was. It is said that the National Govt. must have the influence arising from the grant of offices and honors. In order to render such a Government effectual he believed such an influence to be necessary. But if the States will not agree to it, it is in vain, worse than in vain to make the proposition. If this influence is to be attained, the States must be entirely abolished. Will any one say this would ever be agreed to? He doubted whether any Genl Govern-

ment equally beneficial to all can be attained. That now under consideration he is sure, must be utterly unattainable. He had another objection. The system was too novel & complex. No man could foresee what its operation will be either with respect to the Genl. Govt. or the State Govts. One or other it has been surmised must absorb the whole.

Col. Mason. did not expect this point would have been reagitated. The essential differences between the two plans, had been clearly stated. The principal objections agst. that of Mr. R. were the *want of power* & the *want of practicability*. There can be no weight in the first as the fiat is not to be *here*, but in the people. He thought with his colleague Mr. R. that there were besides certain crisises, in which all the ordinary cautions yielded to public necessity. He gave as an example, the eventual Treaty with G. B. in forming which the Commsrs of the U.S. had boldly disregarded the improvident shackles of Congs. had given to their Country an honorable & happy peace, and instead of being censured for the transgression of their powers, had raised to themselves a monument more durable than brass. The *impracticability* of gaining the public concurrence he thought was still more groundless. (Mr. Lansing) had cited the attempts of Congress to gain an enlargment of their powers, and had inferred from the miscarrige of these attempts, the hopelessness of the plan which he (Mr. L) opposed. He thought a very different inference ought to have been drawn; viz. that the plan which (Mr. L.) espoused, and which proposed to augument the powers of Congress, never could be expected to succeed. He meant not to throw any reflections on Congs. as a body, much less on any particular members of it. He meant however to speak his sentiments without reserve on this subject; it was a privilege of Age, and perhaps the only compensation which nature had given for, the privation of so many other enjoyments; and he should not scruple to exercise it freely. Is it to be thought that the people of America, so watchful over their interests; so jealous of their liberties, will give up their all, will surrender both the sword and the purse, to the same body, and that too not chosen immediately by themselves? They never will. They never ought. Will they trust such a body, with the regulation of their trade, with the regulation of their taxes; with all the other great powers, which are in contemplation? Will they give unbounded confidence to a secret Journal—to the intrigues—to the factions which in the nature of things appertain to such an Assembly? If any man doubts the existence of these characters of Congress, let him consult their Journals for the years, 78, 79, & 80—It will be said, that if the people are averse to parting with power, why is it hoped that they will part with it to a National Legislature. The proper answer is that in this case they do not part with power: they only transfer it from one sett of immediate Representatives to another sett. Much has been said of the unsettled state of the mind of the people. he believed the mind of the people of America, as elsewhere, was unsettled as to some points; but settled as to others. In two points he was sure it was well settled. 1. in an attachment to Republican Government. 2. in an attachment to more than one branch in the Legislature. Their constitutions accord so generally in both these circumstances, that they seem almost to have been preconcerted. This must either have been a miracle, or have resulted from the genius of the people. The only exceptions to the establishmt. of two branches in the Legislatures are the State of Pa. & Congs. and the latter the only single one not chosen by the people themselves. What has been the consequence? The people have been constantly averse to giving that Body further powers—It was acknowledged by (Mr. Patterson) that his plan could not be enforced without military coertion. Does he consider the force of this concession. The most jarring elements of nature; fire & water themselves are not more incompatible that such a mixture of civil liberty and military execution. Will the militia march from one State to another, in order to collect the arrears of taxes from the delinquent members of the Republic? Will they maintain an army for this purpose? Will not the citizens of the invaded State assist one another till they rise as one Man, and shake off the Union altogether. Rebellion is the only case in which the military force of the State can be properly exerted agst. its Citizens. In one point of view he was struck with horror at the prospect of recurring to this expedient. To punish the non-payment of taxes with death, was a severity not yet adopted by depotism itself: yet this unexampled cruelty would be mercy compared to a military collection of revenue, in which the bayonet could make no discrimination between the innocent and the guilty. He took this occasion to repeat. that notwithstanding his solicitude to establish a national Government, he never would agree to abolish the State Govts. or render them absolutely insignificant. They were as necessary as the Genl. Govt. and he would be equally careful to preserve them. He was aware of the difficulty of drawing the line between them, but hoped it was not insurmountable. The Convention, tho' comprising so many distinguished characters, could not be expected to make a faultless Govt. And he would prefer trusting to posterity the amendment of its defects, rather than push the experiment too far.

Mr. Luther Martin agreed with (Col Mason) as to the importance of the State Govts. he would support them at the expense of the Genl. Govt. which was instituted for the purpose of that support. He saw no necessity for two branches, and if it existed Congress might be organized into two. He considered Congs as representing the people, being chosen by the Legislatures who were chosen by the people. At any rate, Congress represented the Legislatures; and it was the Legislatures not the people who refused to enlarge their powers. Nor could the rule of voting have been the ground of objection, otherwise ten of the States must always have been ready, to place further confidence in Congs. The causes of repugnance must therefore be looked for elsewhere.—At the separation from the British Empire, the people of America preferred the Establishment of themselves into thirteen separate sovereignties instead of incorporating themselves into one: to these they look up for the security of their lives, liberties & properties: to these they must look up—The federal Govt. they formed, to defend the whole agst. foreign nations, in case of war, and to defend the lesser States agst. the ambition of the larger: they are afraid of granting powers

unnecessarily, lest they should defeat the original end of the Union; lest the powers should prove dangerous to the sovereignties of the particular States which the Union was meant to support; and expose the lesser to being swallowed up by the larger. He conceived also that the people of the States having already vested their powers in their respective Legislatures, could not resume them without a dissolution of their Governments. He was agst. Conventions in the States: was not agst. assisting States agst. rebellious subjects; thought the *federal* plan of Mr. Patterson did not require coercion more than the *national one*, as the latter must depend for the deficiency of its revenues on requisitions & quotas, and that a national Judiciary extended into the States would be ineffectual, and would be viewed with a jealousy inconsistent with its usefulness.

Mr. Sherman 2ded & supported Mr. Lansing's motion. He admitted two branches to be necessary in the State Legislatures, but saw no necessity for them in a Confederacy of States. The Examples were all, of a single Council. Congs. carried us thro' the war, and perhaps as well as any Govt. could have done. The complaints at present are not that the views of Congs. are unwise or unfaithful, but that that their powers are insufficient for the execution of their views. The national debt & the want of power somewhere to draw forth the National resources, are the great matters that press. All the States were sensible of the defect of power in Congs. He thought much might be said in apology for the failure of the State Legislatures to comply with the confederation. They were afraid of bearing too hard on the people, by accumulating taxes; no *constitutional* rule had been or could be observed in the quotas,—the accounts also were unsettled & every State supposed itself in advance, rather than in arrears. For want of a general system taxes to a due amount had not been drawn from trade which was the most convenient resource. As almost all the States had agreed to the recommendation of Congs. on the subject of an impost, it appeared clearly that they were willing to trust Congs. with power to draw a revenue from Trade. There is no weight therefore in the argument drawn from a distrust of Congs. for money matters being the most important of all, if the people will trust them with power as to them, they will trust them with any other necessary powers. Congs. indeed by the confederation have in fact the right of saying how much the people shall pay, and to what purpose it shall be applied: and this right was granted to them in the expectation that it would in all cases have its effect. If another branch were to be added to Congs. to be chosen by the people, it would serve to embarrass. The people would not much interest themselves in the elections, a few designing men in the large districts would carry their points, and the people would have no more confidence in their new representatives than in Congs. He saw no reason why the State Legislatures should be unfriendly as had been suggested, to Congs. If they appoint Congs. and approve of their measures, they would be rather favorable and partial to them. The disparity of the States in point of size he perceived was the main difficulty. But the large States had not yet suffered from the equality of votes enjoyed by the small ones. In all great and general points, the interests of all the States were the same. The State of Virga. notwithstanding the equality of votes, ratified the Confederation without, or even proposing, any alteration. Massts. also ratified without any material difficulty &c. In none of the ratifications is the want of two branches noticed or complained of. To consolidate the States as some had proposed would dissolve our Treaties with foreign nations, which had been formed with us, as *Confederated* States. He did not however suppose that the creation of two branches in the Legislature would have such an effect. If the difficulty on the subject of representation can not be otherwise got over, he would agree to have two branches, and a proportional representation in one of them, provided each State had an equal voice in the other. This was necessary to secure the rights of the lesser States; otherwise three or four of the large States would rule the others as they please. Each State like each individual had its peculiar habits usages and manners, which constituted its happiness. It would not therefore give to others a power over this happiness, any more than an individual would do, when he could avoid it.

Mr. Wilson, urged the necessity of two branches; observed that if a proper model was not to be found in other Confederacies it was not to be wondered at. The number of them was small & the duration of some at least short. The Amphyctionic & Achaean were formed in the infancy of political Science; and appear by their History & fate, to have contained radical defects, The Swiss & Belgic Confederacies were held together not by any vital principle of energy but by the incumbent pressure of formidable neighbouring nations: The German owed its continuance to the influence of the H. of Austria. He appealed to our own experience for the defects of our Confederacy. He had been 6 years in the 12 since the commencement of the Revolution, a member of Congress and had felt all its weaknesses. He appealed to the recollection of others whether on many important occasions, the public interest had not been obstructed by the small members of the Union. The success of the Revolution was owing to other causes, than the Constitution of Congress. In many instances it went on even agst. the difficulties arising from Congs. themselves— He admitted that the large States did accede as had been stated, to the Confederation in its present form. But it was the effect of necessity not of choice. There are other instances of their yielding from the same motive to the unreasonable measures of the small States. The situation of things is now a little altered. He insisted that a jealousy would exist between the State Legislatures & the General Legislature: observing that the members of the former would have views & feelings very distinct in this respect from their constituents. A private citizen of a State is indifferent whether power be exercised by the Genl. or State Legislatures, provided it be exercised most for his happiness. His representative has an interest in its being exercised by the body to which he belongs. He will therefore view the National Legisl: with the eye of a jealous rival. He observed that the addresses of Congs. to the people at large, had always been better received & pro-

duced greater effect, than those made to the Legislatures.

On the question for postponing in order to take up Mr. Lansings proposition "to vest the powers of Legislation in Congs."

Masst. no. Cont. ay. N. Y. ay. N. J. ay. Pa. no. Del. ay Md. divd. Va. no. N. C. no. S. C. no. Geo. no [Ayes—4; noes—6; divided—1.]

On motion of the Deputies from Delaware, the question on the 2d. Resolution in the Report from the Committee of the whole was postponed till tomorrow.

adjd.

[1:344; Yates, 20 June]

Met pursuant to adjournment. Present 11 states.

Judge Elsworth. I propose, and therefore move, to expunge the word *national,* in the first resolve, and to place in the room of it, *government of the United States*—which was agreed to, *nem. con.*

Mr. Lansing then moved, that the first resolve be postponed, in order to take into consideration the following: *That the powers of legislation ought to be vested in the United States in congress.*

I am clearly of opinion that I am not authorized to accede to a system which will annihilate the state governments, and the Virginia plan is declarative of such extinction. It has been asserted that the public mind is not known. To some points it may be true, but we may collect from the fate of the requisition of the impost, what it may be on the principles of a national government.—When many of the states were so tenacious of their rights on this point, can we expect that *thirteen* states will surrender their governments up to a national plan? Rhode-Island pointedly refused granting it. Certainly she had a federal right so to do; and I hold it as an undoubted truth, as long as state distinctions remain, let the national government be modified as you please, both branches of your legislature will be impressed with local and state attachments. The Virginia plan proposes a negative on the state laws where *in the opinion* of the national legislature, they contravene the national government: and no state laws can pass unless approved by them.—They will have more than a law in a day to revise; and are they competent to judge of the wants and necessities of remote states?

This national government will, from their power, have great influence in the state governments; and the existence of the latter are only saved in appearance. And has it not been asserted that they expect their extinction? If this be the object, let us say so, and extinguish them at once. But remember, if we devise a system of government which will not meet the approbation of our constituents, we are dissolving the union—but if we act within the limits of our power, it will be approved of; and should it upon experiment prove defective, the people will entrust a future convention again to amend it. Fond as many are of a general government, do any of you believe it can pervade the whole continent so effectually as to secure the peace, harmony and happiness of the whole? The excellence of the British model of government has been much insisted on; but we are endeavoring to complicate it with state governments, on principles which will gradually destroy the one or the other. You are sowing the seeds of rivalship, which must at last end in ruin.

Mr. Mason. The material difference between the two plans has already been clearly pointed out. The objection to that of Virginia arises from the want of power to institute it, and the want of practicability to carry it into effect. Will the first objection apply to a power merely recommendatory? In certain seasons of public danger it is commendable to exceed power. The treaty of peace, under which we now enjoy the blessings of freedom, was made by persons who exceeded their powers. It met the approbation of the public, and thus deserved the praises of those who sent them. The impracticability of the plan is still less groundless. These measures are supported by one who, at his time of life, has little to hope or expect from any government. Let me ask, will the people entrust their dearest rights and liberties to the determination of one body of men, and those not chosen by them, and who are invested both with the *sword* and *purse*? They never will—they never can—to a conclave, transacting their business secret from the eye of the public. Do we not discover by their public journals of the years 1778–9, and 1780, that factions and party spirit had guided many of their acts? The people of America, like all other people, are unsettled in their minds, and their principles fixed to no object, except that a republican government is the best, and that the legislature ought to consist of two branches. The constitutions of the respective states, made and approved of by them, evince this principle. Congress, however, from other causes, received a different organization. What, would you use military force to compel the observance of a social compact? It is destructive to the rights of the people. Do you expect the militia will do it, or do you mean a standing army? The first will never, on such an occasion, exert any power; and the latter may turn its arms against the government which employs them. I never will consent to destroy state governments, and will ever be careful to preserve the one as the other. If we should, in the formation of the latter, have omitted some necessary regulation, I will trust my posterity to amend it. That the one government will be productive of disputes and jealousies against the other, I believe; but it will produce mutual safety. I shall close with observing, that though some gentlemen have expressed much warmth on this and former occasions, I can excuse it, as the result of sudden passion; and hope that although we may differ in some particular points, if we mean the good of the whole, that our good sense upon reflection, will prevent us from spreading our discontent further.

Mr. Martin. I know that government must be supported; and if the one was incompatible with the other, I would support the state government at the expense of the union—for I consider the present system as a system of slavery. Impressed with this idea, I made use, on a former occasion, of expressions perhaps rather harsh. If gentlemen conceive that the legislative branch is dangerous, divide them into two. They are as much the representatives of the states, as the state assemblies are the representatives of the people. Are not the powers which we here exercise

given by the legislatures? (After giving a detail of the revolution and of state governments, Mr. M. continued). I confess when the confederation was made, congress ought to have been invested with more extensive powers; but when the states saw that congress indirectly aimed at sovereignty, they were jealous, and therefore refused any farther concessions. The time is now come that we can constitutionally grant them not only new powers, but to modify their government, so that the state governments are not endangered. But whatever we have now in our power to grant, the grant is a state grant, and therefore it must be so organized that the state governments are interested in supporting the union. Thus systematized, there can be no danger if a small force is maintained.

Mr. Sherman. We have found during the war that though congress consisted of but one branch, it was that body which carried us through the whole war, and we were crowned with success. We closed the war, performing all the functions of a good government, by making a beneficial peace. But the great difficulty now is, how we shall pay the public debt incurred during that war. The unwillingness of the states to comply with the requisitions of congress, has embarrassed us greatly.—But to amend these defects in government I am not fond of speculation. I would rather proceed on experimental ground. We can so modify the powers of congress, that we will all be mutual supporters of one another. The disparity of the states can be no difficulty. We know this by experience—Virginia and Massachusetts were the first who unanimously ratified the old confederation. They then had no claim to more votes in congress than one. Foreign states have made treaties with us as confederated states, not as a national government. Suppose we put an end to that government under which those treaties were made, will not these treaties be void?

Mr. Wilson. The question before us may admit of the three following considerations:

1. Whether the legislature shall consist of one or two branches.

2. Whether they are to be elected by the state governments or by the people.

3. Whether in proportion to state importance, or states individually.

Confederations are usually of a short date. The amphyctionic council was instituted in the infancy of the Grecian republics—as those grew in strength, the council lost its weight and power. The Achaean league met the same fate—Switzerland and Holland are supported in their confederation, not by its intrinsic merit, but the incumbent pressure of surrounding bodies. Germany is kept together by the house of Austria. True, congress carried us through the war even against its own weakness. That powers were wanting, you Mr. President, must have felt. To other causes, not to congress, must the success be ascribed. That the great states acceded to the confederation, and that they in the hour of danger, made a sacrifice of their interest to the lesser states is true. Like the wisdom of Solomon in adjudging the child to its true mother, from tenderness to it, the greater states well knew that the loss of a limb was fatal to the confederation—they too, through tenderness sacrificed their dearest rights to preserve the whole. But the time is come, when justice will be done to their claims—Situations are altered.

Congress have frequently made their appeal to the people. I wish they had always done it—the national government would have been sooner extricated.

Question then put on Mr. Lansing's motion and lost.—6 states against 4—one divided. New-York in the minority.

Adjourned till to-morrow morning.

[1:350; Hamilton, 20 June]

Mr. Lansing—Resolved that the powers of legislation ought to be vested in the United States in Congress—

—If our plan be not adopted it will produce those mischiefs which we are sent to obviate—

Principles of System—

—Equality of Representation—

Dependence of members of Congress on States—

So long as state distinctions exist state prejudices will operate whether election be by *states* or *people*—

—If no interest to *oppress* no need of *apportionment*—

—Virginia 16—Delaware 1—

—Will General Government have liesure to examine state laws—?

—Will G Government have the necessary information?

—Will states agree to surrender?

—Let us meet public opinion & hope the progress of sentiment will make future arrangements—

—Would like my system if it could be established—

System without example—

Mr. Mason—Objection to granting power to Congress arose from their constitution.

Sword and *purse* in one body—

Two principles in which *America* are unanimous

1 attachment to Republican government

2 ———to two branches of legislature—

—Military *force & liberty* incompatible—

—Will people maintain a standing army?

—Will endeavour to preserve state governments & draw lines—trusting to posterity to amend—

Mr. Martin—General Government originally formed for the preservation of state governments—

Objection to giving power to Congress has originated with the legislatures—

10 of the states interested in an equal voice—

Real motive was an opinion that there ought to be distinct governments & not a general government—

If we should form a general government twould break to pieces—

—For common safety instituted a General government—

Jealousy of power the motive—

People have delegated all their authority to state government—

Coertion necessary to both systems—

Requisitions necessary upon one system as upon another—

In their *system* made requisitions necessary in the first instance but left Congress in the second instance—to assess themselves—

Judicial tribunals in the different states would become odious—

If we always to make a change shall be always in a state of infancy—

☞ States will not be disposed hereafter to strengthen the general government.

Mr. Sherman—Confederacy carried us through the war—

Non compliances of States owing to various embarrassment

Why should state legislatures be unfriendly?

State governments will always have the confidence & government of the people: if they cannot be conciliated no efficacious government can be established.

Sense of all states that one *branch is sufficient.*

If consolidated all treaties will be void.

State governments more fit for local legislation customs habits etc

[1:354; Madison, 21 June]

Mr. Jonathan Dayton from N. Jersey took his seat.

Doctr. Johnson. On a comparison of the two plans which had been proposed from Virginia & N. Jersey, it appeared that the peculiarity which characterized the latter was its being calculated to preserve the individuality of the States. The plan from Va. did not profess to destroy this individuality altogether, but was charged with such a tendency. One Gentleman alone (Col. Hamilton) in his animadversions on the plan of N. Jersey, boldly and decisively contended for an abolition of the State Govts. Mr. Wilson & the gentleman from Virga. who also were adversaries of the plan of N. Jersey held a different language. They wished to leave the States in possession of a considerable, tho' a subordinate jurisdiction. They had not yet however shewn how this cd. consist with, or be secured agst. the general sovereignty & jurisdiction, which they proposed to give to the national Government. If this could be shewn in such a manner as to satisfy the patrons of the N. Jersey propositions, that the individuality of the States would not be endangered, many of their objections would no doubt be removed. If this could not be shewn their objections

31

would have their full force. He wished it therefore to be well considered whether in case the States, as was proposed, shd. retain some portion of sovereignty at least, this portion could be preserved, without allowing them to participate effectually in the Genl. Govt., without giving them each a distinct and equal vote for the purpose of defending themselves in the general Councils.

Mr. Wilson's respect for Dr. Johnson, added to the importance of the subject led him to attempt, unprepared as he was, to solve the difficulty which had been started. It was asked how the genl. Govt. and individuality of the particular States could be reconciled to each other; and how the latter could be secured agst. the former? Might it not, on the other side be asked how the former was to be secured agst. the latter? It was generally admitted that a jealousy & rivalship would be felt between the Genl. & particular Govts. As the plan now stood, tho' indeed contrary to his opinion, one branch of the Genl.—Govt. (the Senate or second branch) was to be appointed by the State Legislatures. The State Legislatures, therefore, by this participation in the Genl. Govt. would have an opportunity of defending their rights. Ought not a reciprocal opportunity to be given to the Genl. Govt. of defending itself by having an appointment of some one constituent branch of the State Govts. If a security be necessary on one side, it wd. seem reasonable to demand it on the other. But taking the matter in a more general view, he saw no danger to the states from the Genl. Govt. In case a combination should be made by the large ones it wd produce a general alarm among the rest; and the project wd. be frustrated. But there was no temptation to such a project. The States having in general a similar interest, in case of any proposition in the National Legislature to encroach on the State Legislatures, he conceived a general alarm wd. take place in the National Legislature itself, that it would communicate itself to the State Legislatures, and wd. finally spread among the people at large. The Genl. Govt. will be as ready to preserve the rights of the States as the latter are to preserve the rights of individuals; all the members of the former, having a common interest, as representatives of all the people of the latter, to leave the State Govts. in possession of what the people wish them to retain. He could not discover, therefore any danger whatever on the side from which it had been apprehended. On the contrary, he conceived that in spite of every precaution the General Govt. would be in perpetual danger of encroachments from the State Govts.

Mr. Madison was of opinion that there was 1. less danger of encroachment from the Genl. Govt. than from the State Govts. 2. that the mischief from encroachments would be less fatal if made by the former, than if made by the latter. 1. All the examples of other confederacies prove the greater tendency in such systems to anarchy than to tyranny; to a disobedience of the members than to usurpations of the federal head. Our own experience had fully illustrated this tendency.—But it will be said that the proposed change in the principles & form of the Union will vary the tendency, that the Genl. Govt. will have real & greater powers, and will be derived in one branch at least from the people not from the Govts. of the States. To give

full force to this objection, let it be supposed for a moment that indefinite power should be given to the Gen'l Legislature, and the States reduced to corporations dependent on the Genl. Legislature; why shd. it follow that the Gen'l Govt. wd. take from the States any branch of their power as far as its operation was beneficial, and its continuance desirable to the people? In some of the States, particularly in Connecticut, all the Townships are incorporated, and have a certain limited jurisdiction. Have the Representatives of the people of the Townships in the Legislature of the State ever endeavored to despoil the Townships of any part of their local authority? As far as this local authority is convenient to the people they are attached to it; and their representatives chosen by & amenable to them naturally respect their attachment to this, as much as their attachment to any other right or interest: The relation of a Genl. Govt. to State Govts. is parallel. 2. Guards were more necessary agst. encroachments of the State Govts.—on the Genl. Govt. than of the latter on the former. The great objection made agst. an abolition of the State Govts. was that the Genl. Govt. could not extend its care to all the minute objects which fall under the cognizance of the local jurisdictions. The objection as stated lay not agst. the probable abuse of the general power, but agst. the imperfect use that could be made of it throughout so great an extent of country, and over so great a variety of objects. As far as its operation would be practicable it could not in this view be improper; as far as it would be impracticable, the conveniency of the Genl. Govt. itself would concur with that of the people in the maintenance of subordinate Governments. Were it practicable for the Genl. Govt. to extend its care to every requisite object without the cooperation of the State Govts. the people would not be less free as members of one great Republic than as members of thirteen small ones. A citizen of Delaware was not more free than a citizen of Virginia: nor would either be more free than a citizen of America. Supposing therefore a tendency in the Genl. Government to absorb the State Govts. no fatal consequence could result. Taking the reverse of the supposition, that a tendency should be left in the State Govts. towards an independence on the General Govt. and the gloomy consequences need not be pointed out. The imagination of them, must have suggested to the States the experiment we are now making to prevent the calamity, and must have formed the chief motive with those present to undertake the arduous task.

On the question for resolving "that the Legislature ought to consist of two Branches"

Mass ay. Cont. ay. N. Y. no. N. Jersey no Pa. ay. Del. no. Md. divd. Va. ay. N. C. ay. S. C. ay. Geo. ay [Ayes—7; noes—3; divided—1.]

[1:362; Yates, 21 June]

Met pursuant to adjournment. Present 11 states.

Dr Johnson—It appears to me that the Jersey plan has for its principal object, the preservation of the state governments. So far it is a departure from the plan of Virginia, which although it concentres in a distinct national government, it is not totally independent of that of the states. A gentleman from New-York, with boldness and decision, proposed a system totally different from both; and though he has been praised by every body, he has been supported by none. How can the state governments be secured on the Virginia plan? I could have wished, that the supporters of the Jersey system could have satisfied themselves with the principles of the Virginia plan and that the individuality of the states could be supported. It is agreed on all hands that a portion of government is to be left to the states. How can this be done? It can be done by joining the states in their legislative capacity with the right of appointing the second branch of the national legislature, to represent the states individually.

Mr. Wilson. If security is necessary to preserve the one, it is equally so to preserve the other. How can the national government be secured against the states? Some regulation is necessary. Suppose the national government had a component number in the state legislature? But where the one government clashed with the other, the state government ought to yield, as the preservation of the general interest must be preferred to a particular. But let us try to designate the powers of each, and then no danger can be apprehended nor can the general government be possessed of any ambitious view to encroach on the state rights.

Mr. Madison. I could have wished that the gentleman from Connecticut had more accurately marked his objections to the Virginia plan. I apprehended the greatest danger is from the encroachment of the states on the national government—This apprehension is justly founded on the experience of ancient confederacies, and our own is a proof of it.

The right of negativing in certain instances the state laws, affords one security to the national government. But is the danger well founded? Have any state governments ever encroached on the corporate rights of cities? And if it was the case that the national government usurped the state government, if such usurpation was for the good of the whole, no mischief could arise.—To draw the line between the two, is a difficult task. I believe it cannot be done, and therefore I am inclined for a general government.

If we cannot form a general government, and the states become totally independent of each other, it would afford a melancholy prospect.

The 2d resolve was then put and carried—7 states for—3 against—one divided. New-York in the minority.

[1:366; King, 21 June]

Johnson—The Gentleman from NYk is praised by every gentleman, but supported by no gentleman—He goes directly to ye abolition of the State Governts. and the erection of a Genl. Govt.—All other Gentlemen agree that the national or Genl. Govt. shd. be more powerful—& the State Govts. less so. Provision is made in the Virgina Project to secure the Genl. Govt: but no provision is made for the security of the State Government—The plan from N Jersey provides for the security of the State & Genl. Govt.—If the advocates for the Genl. Govt. agreeably to the Virgin. Plan can show that the State Govts. will be secure from the Genl. Govt. we may all agree—

Wilson—We have provided that the States or yr. Legislatures shall appt. a Brh. of the national Govt. let the Natl. Govt. have a reciprocal power to elect or appoint one Br. of each State Govt—I dont see how the State Govts will be endangered—what power will the states possess, which the Genl. Govt. will wish to possess? their powers if added wd. not be of any considerable consequence—the attempt. however to acquire these powers wd. alarm the Citizens, who gave them to the States individually, and never intended them for the Genl. Govt.—The people wd. not suffer it—

Madison—The history of antient Confedys. proves that there never has existed a danger of the destruction of the State Govts. by encroachments of the Genl. Govts the converse of the proposition is true—I have therefore been assiduous to guard the Genl. from the power of the State Governments—the State Govts. regulate the conduct of their Citizens, they punish offenders—they cause Justice to be administered and do those arts wh endear the Govt. to its Citizens. The Citizens will not therefore suffer the Genl. Govt. to injure the State Govts—

The Convention agree yt the Legislature shd. consist of two Brs—

[2:14; Journal, 16 July]

It was moved and seconded to agree to the first clause of the sixth resolution reported from the Committee of the whole House namely

"That the national Legislature ought to possess the legislative rights vested in Congress by the confederation"

which passed unanimously in the affirmative

[2:16; Madison, 16 July]

The 6th Resol: in the Report from the Come. of the whole House, which had been postponed in order to consider the 7 & 8th. Resol'ns; was now resumed. see the Resoln:

The 1s. member "That the Natl. Legislature ought to possess the Legislative Rights vested in Congs. by the Confederation." was Agreed to nem. Con.

The next "And moreover to legislate in all cases to which the separate States are incompetent; or in which the harmony of the U.S. may be interrupted by the exercise of individual legislation," being read for a question

Mr. Butler calls for some explanation of the extent of this power; particularly of the word *incompetent*. The vagueness of the terms rendered it impossible for any precise judgment to be formed.

Mr. Ghorum. The vagueness of the terms constitutes the propriety of them. We are now establishing general principles, to be extended hereafter into details which will be precise & explicit.

Mr. Rutlidge, urged the objection started by Mr. Butler and moved that the clause should be committed to the end that a specification of the powers comprised in the general terms, might be reported.

On the question for a commitment, the States were equally divided

Mas. no. Cont. ay. N.J. no. Pa. no. Del. no. Md. ay. Va. ay. N.C. no. S.C. ay. Geo. ay: So it was lost. [Ayes—5; noes—5.]

[2:21; Journal, 17 July]

It was moved and seconded to postpone the considn of the second clause of the Sixth resolution reported from the Committee of the whole House in order to take up the following

"To make laws binding on the People of the United States in all cases which may concern the common interests of the Union: but not to interfere with the government of the individual States in any matters of internal police which respect the government of such States only, and wherein the general welfare of the United States is not concerned."

which passed in the negative [Ayes—2; noes—8.]
It was moved and seconded to alter the second clause of the 6th resolution so as to read as follows, namely

"and moreover to legislate in all cases for the general interests of the Union, and also in those to which the States are separately incompetent, or in which the harmony of the United States may be interrupted by the exercise of individual legislation

which passed in the affirmative [Ayes—6; noes—4.]

[To agree to the second clause of the 6. resolution as amended. Ayes—8; noes—2.]
On the question to agree to the following clause of the sixth resolution reported from the Committee of the whole House, namely,

"to negative all laws passed by the several States contravening in the opinion of the national legislature, the articles of union, or any treaties subsisting under the authority of the Union"

it passed in the negative [Ayes—3; noes—7.].

[2:25; Madison, 17 July]

Mr. Governr. Morris moved to reconsider the whole Resolution agreed to yesterday concerning the constitution of the 2 branches of the Legislature. His object was to bring the House to a consideration in the abstract of the powers necessary to be vested in the general Government. It had been said, Let us know how the Govt. is to be modelled, and then we can determine what powers can be properly given to it. He thought the most eligible course was, first to determine on the necessary powers, and then so to modify the Governt. as that it might be justly & properly enabled to administer them. He feared if we proceded to a consideration of the powers, whilst the vote of yesterday including an equality of the States in the 2d. branch, remained in force, a reference to it, either mental or expressed, would mix itself with the merits of every question concerning the powers.—this motion was not seconded. (It was probably approved by several members, who either despaired of success, or were apprehensive that the attempt would inflame the jealousies of the smaller States.)

The 6th. Resoln. in the Report of the Come. of the whole relating to the powers, which had been postponed in order to consider the 7 & 8th. relating to the Constitution of the, Natl. Legislature, was now resumed—

Mr. Sherman observed that it would be difficult to draw the line between the powers of the Genl. Legislatures, and those to be left with the States; that he did not like the definition contained in the Resolution, and proposed in place of the words "of individual legislation" line 4 inclusive, to insert "to make laws binding on the people of the United States in all cases which may concern the common interests of the Union; but not to interfere with the Government of the individual States in any matters of internal police which respect the Govt. of such States only, and wherein the General welfare of the U. States is not concerned."

Mr. Wilson 2ded. the amendment as better expressing the general principle.

Mr Govr Morris opposed it. The internal police, as it would be called & understood by the States ought to be infringed in many cases, as in the case of paper money & other tricks by which Citizens of other States may be affected.

Mr. Sherman, in explanation of his ideas read an enumeration of powers, including the power of levying taxes on trade, but not the power of *direct taxation.*

Mr. Govr. Morris remarked the omission, and inferred that for the deficiencies of taxes on consumption, it must have been the meaning of Mr. Sherman, that the Genl. Govt. should recur to quotas & requisitions, which are subversive of the idea of Govt.

Mr. Sherman acknowledged that his enumeration did not include direct taxation. Some provision he supposed must be made for supplying the deficiency of other taxation, but he had not formed any.

On Question on Mr. Sherman's motion, it passed in the negative

Mas. no. Cont. ay. N. J. no. Pa. no. Del. no. Md. ay. Va. no. N. C. no. S. C. no. Geo. no. [Ayes—2; noes—8.]

Mr. Bedford moved that the 2d. member of Resolution 6. be so altered as to read "and moreover to legislate in all cases for the general interests of the Union, and also in those to which the States are separately incompetent," or in which the harmony of the U. States may be interrupted by the exercise of individual Legislation".

Mr. Govr. Morris 2ds. the motion.

Mr. Randolph. This is a formidable idea indeed. It involves the power of violating all the laws and constitutions of the States, and of intermeddling with their police. The last member of the sentence is also superfluous, being included in the first.

Mr. Bedford. It is not more extensive or formidable than the clause as it stands: no *State* being *separately* competent to legislate for the *general interest* of the Union.

On question for agreeing to Mr. Bedford's motion. it passed in the affirmative.

Mas. ay. Cont. no. N. J. ay. Pa. ay. Del. ay. Md. ay. Va. no. N. C. ay. S. C. no. Geo. no.[Ayes—6; noes—4.]

On the sentence as amended, it passed in the affirmative.

Mas. ay. Cont. ay. N. J. ay. Pa. ay. Del. ay. Md. ay. Va. ay. N. C. ay. S. C. no. Geo. no.[Ayes—8; noes—2.]

The next.— "To negative all laws passed by the several States contravening in the opinion of the Nat: Legislature the articles of Union, or any treaties subsisting under the authority of ye Union"

Mr. Govr. Morris opposed this power as likely to be terrible to the States, and not necessary, if sufficient Legislative authority should be given to the Genl. Government.

Mr. Sherman thought it unnecessary, as the Courts of the States would not consider as valid any law contravening the Authority of the Union, and which the legislature would wish to be negatived.

Mr. L. Martin considered the power as improper & inadmissable. Shall all the laws of the States be sent up to the Genl. Legislature before they shall be permitted to operate?

Mr. Madison, considered the negative on the laws of the States as essential to the efficacy & security of the Genl. Govt. The necessity of a general Govt. proceeds from the propensity of the States to pursue their particular interests in opposition to the general interest. This propensity will continue to disturb the system, unless effectually controuled. Nothing short of a negative on their laws will controul it. They can pass laws which will accomplish their injurious objects before they can be repealed by the Genl Legislre. or be set aside by the National Tribunals. Confidence can not be put in the State Tribunals as guardians of the National authority and interests. In all the States these are more or less dependt. on the Legislatures. In Georgia they are appointed annually by the Legislature. In R. Island the Judges who refused to execute an unconstitutional law were displaced, and others substituted, by the Legislature who would be willing instruments of the wicked & arbitrary plans of their masters. A power of negativing the improper laws of the States is at once the most mild & certain means of preserving the harmony of the system. Its utility is sufficiently displayed in the British System. Nothing could maintain the harmony & subordination of the various parts of the empire, but the prerogative by which the Crown, stifles in the birth every Act of every part tending to discord or encroachment. It is true the prerogative is sometimes misapplied thro' ignorance or a partiality to one particular part of ye. empire: but we have not the same reason to fear such misapplications in our System. As to the sending all laws up to the Natl. Legisl: that might be rendered unnecessary by some emanation of the power into the States, so far at least, as to give a temporary effect to laws of immediate necessity.

Mr. Govr. Morris was more & more opposed to the negative. The proposal of it would disgust all the States. A law that ought to be negatived will be set aside in the Judiciary departmt. and if that security should fail; may be repealed by a Nationl. law.

Mr. Sherman. Such a power involves a wrong principle, to wit, that a law of a State contrary to the articles of the Union, would if not negatived, be valid & operative.

Mr. Pinkney urged the necessity of the Negative.

On the question for agreeing to the power of negativing laws of States &c." it passed in the negative.

Mas. ay. Ct. no. N. J. no. Pa. no. Del. no. Md. no. Va. ay. N. C. ay. S. C. no. Geo. no. [Ayes—3; noes—7.]

[2:131, 151; *Committee of Detail, I, V*]

Resolved That the Legislature of the United States ought to possess the legislative Rights vested in Congress by the Confederation; and moreover to legislate in all Cases for the general Interests of the Union, and also in those Cases to which the States are separately incompetent, or in which the Harmony of the United States may be interrupted by the Exercise of individual Legislation.

. . . . .

The Continuation of the Scheme

1. To treat of the Powers of the legislative
2. To except from those Powers certain specified Cases
3. To render in certain Cases a greater Number than a Majority necessary
4. To assign to H. Repr—any Powers peculiarly belonging to it
5. To assign, in same Manner, Powers which may, with Propriety be vested in it.

[2:321; *Journal, 18 Aug.*]

The following additional powers proposed to be vested in the Legislature of the United States having been submitted to the consideration of the Convention—It was moved and seconded to refer them to the Committee to whom the proceedings of the Convention were referred
which passed in the affirmative
The propositions are as follows

To dispose of the unappropriated lands of the United States

To institute temporary governments for new States arising thereon

To regulate affairs with the Indians as well within as without the limits of the United States

To exercise exclusively Legislative authority at the seat of the general Government, and over a district around the same, not exceeding   square miles: the consent of the Legislature of the State or States comprising such district being first obtained

To grant charters of incorporation in cases where the public good may require them, and the authority of a single State may be incompetent

To secure to literary authors their copy rights for a limited time

To establish an University

To encourage, by proper premiums and provisions, the advancement of useful knowledge and discoveries

To authorise the Executive to procure and hold for the use of the United States landed property for the erection of forts, magazines, and other necessary buildings

To fix and permanently establish the seat of Government of the United-States in which they shall possess the exclusive right of soil and jurisdiction

To establish seminaries for the promotion of literature and the arts and sciences

To grant charters of incorporation

To grant patents for useful inventions

To secure to authors exclusive rights for a certain time

To establish public institutions, rewards and immunities for the promotion of agriculture, commerce, trades, and manufactures.

That Funds which shall be appropriated for payment of public Creditors shall not during the time of such appropriation be diverted or applied to any other purpose—and to prepare a clause or clauses for restraining the Legislature of the United States from establishing a perpetual revenue

To secure the payment of the public debt.

To secure all Creditors, under the new Constitution, from a violation of the public faith. when pledged by the authority of the Legislature

To grant letters of marque and reprisal

To regulate Stages on the post-roads.

It was moved and seconded That a Committee to consist of a Member from each State be appointed to consider the necessity and expediency of the debts of the several States being assumed by the United States

        which passed in the affirmative [Ayes—6; noes—4; divided—1.]

critical situation, to have deserted their country? No. Every man who hears me, every wise man in the United States, would have condemned them. The Convention were obliged to appoint a committee for accommodation. In this committee, the arrangement was formed as it now stands, and their report was accepted. It was a delicate point, and it was necessary that all parties should be indulged. Gentlemen will see that, if there had not been a unanimity, nothing could have been done; for the Convention had no power to establish, but only to recommend, a government. Any other system would have been impracticable. Let a convention be called to-morrow; let them meet twenty times,—nay, twenty thousand times; they will have the same difficulties to encounter, the same clashing interests to reconcile.

5

ALEXANDER HAMILTON, NEW YORK
RATIFYING CONVENTION
20 June 1788
Elliot 2:235–36

6

WILLIAM R. DAVIE, NORTH CAROLINA
RATIFYING CONVENTION
24 July 1788
Elliot 4:20–21

In order that the committee may understand clearly the principles on which the general Convention acted, I think it necessary to explain some preliminary circumstances. Sir, the natural situation of this country seems to divide its interests into different classes. There are navigating and non-navigating states. The Northern are properly navigating states: the Southern appear to possess neither the mean nor the spirit of navigation. This difference of situation naturally produces a dissimilarity of interests and views respecting foreign commerce. It was the interest of the Northern States that there should be no restraints on their navigation, and they should have full power, by a majority in Congress, to make commercial regulations in favor of their own, and in restraint of the navigation of foreigners. The Southern States wish to impose a restraint on the Northern, by requiring that two thirds in Congress should be requisite to pass an act in regulation of commerce. They were apprehensive that the restraints of a navigation law would discourage foreigners, and, by obliging them to employ the shipping of the Northern States, would probably enhance their freight. This being the case, they insisted strenuously on having this provision ingrafted in the Constitution; and the Northern States were as anxious in opposing it. On the other hand, the small states, seeing themselves embraced by the Confederation upon equal terms, wished to retain the advantages which they already possessed. The large states, on the contrary, thought it improper that Rhode Island and Delaware should enjoy an equal suffrage with themselves. From these sources a delicate and difficult contest arose. It became necessary, therefore, to compromise, or the Convention must have dissolved without effecting any thing. Would it have been wise and prudent in that body, in this

These are some of the leading causes which brought forward this new Constitution. It was evidently necessary to infuse a greater portion of strength into the national government. But Congress were but a single body, with whom it was dangerous to lodge additional powers. Hence arose the necessity of a different organization. In order to form some balance, the departments of government were separated, and as a necessary check, the legislative body was composed of *two branches*. Steadiness and wisdom are better insured when there is a second branch, to balance and check the first The stability of the laws will be greater when the popular branch, which might be influenced by local views, or the violence of party, is checked by another, whose longer continuance in office will render them more experienced, more temperate, and more competent to decide rightly.

The Confederation derived its sole support from the state legislatures. This rendered it weak and ineffectual. It was therefore necessary that the foundations of this government should be laid on the broad basis of the people. Yet the state governments are the pillars upon which this government is extended over such an immense territory, and are essential to its existence. The House of Representatives are immediately elected by the people. The senators represent the sovereignty of the states; they are directly chosen by the state legislatures, and no legislative act can be done without their concurrence. The election of the executive is in some measure under the control of the legislatures of the states, the electors being appointed under their direction.

The difference, in point of magnitude and importance, in the members of the confederacy, was an additional reason for the division of the legislature into two branches, and for establishing an equality of suffrage in the Senate. The protection of the small states against the ambition and influence of the larger members, could only be effected by arming them with an equal power in one branch of the legislature. On a contemplation of this matter, we shall find that the jealousies of the states could not be reconciled any other way. The lesser states would never have concurred unless this check had been given them, as a security for their political existence, against the power and encroachments of the great states. It may be also proper to observe, that the executive is separated in its functions from the legislature, as well as the nature of the case would admit, and the judiciary from both.

7

JAMES IREDELL, NORTH CAROLINA RATIFYING CONVENTION
25 July 1788
Elliot 4:38–39

I believe sir, it was the general sense of all America, with the exception only of one state, in forming their own state constitutions, that the legislative body should be divided into two branches, in order that the people might have a double security. It will often happen that, in a single body, a bare majority will carry exceptionable and pernicious measures. The violent faction of a party may often form such a majority in a single body, and by that means the particular views or interests of a part of the community may be consulted, and those of the rest neglected or injured. Is there a single gentleman in this Convention, who has been a member of the legislature, who has not found the minority in the most important questions to be often right? Is there a man here, who has been in either house, who has not at some times found the most solid advantages from the coöperation or opposition of the other? If a measure be right, which has been approved of by one branch, the other will probably confirm it; if it be wrong, it is fortunate that there is another branch to oppose or amend it. These principles probably formed one reason for the institution of a Senate, in the form of government before us. Another arose from the peculiar nature of that government, as connected with the government of the particular states.

The general government will have the protection and management of the general interests of the United States. The local and particular interests of the different states are left to their respective legislatures. All affairs which concern this state only are to be determined by our representatives coming from all parts of the state; all affairs which concern the Union at large are to be determined by representatives coming from all parts of the Union. Thus, then, the general government is to be taken care of, and the state governments to be preserved. The former is done by a numerous representation of the people of each state, in proportion to its importance. The latter is effected by giving each state an equal representation in the Senate. The people will be represented in one house, the state legislatures in the other.

Many are of the opinion that the power of the Senate is too great; but I cannot think so, considering the great weight which the House of Representatives will have. Several reasons may be assigned for this. The House of Representatives will be more numerous than the Senate. They will represent the immediate interests of the people. They will originate all money bills, which is one of the greatest securities in any republican government. The respectability of their constituents, who are the free citizens of America, will add great weight to the representatives; for a power derived from the people is the source of all real honor, and a demonstration of confidence which a man of any feeling would be more ambitious to possess, than any other honor or any emolument whatever. There is, therefore, always a danger of such a house becoming too powerful, and it is necessary to counteract its influence by giving great weight and authority to the other. I am warranted by well-known facts in my opinion that the representatives of the people at large will have more weight than we should be induced to believe from a slight consideration.

8

WAYMAN v. SOUTHARD
10 Wheat. 1 (1825)

The counsel for the defendants contend, that this clause, if extended beyond the mere regulation of practice in the court, would be a delegation of legislative authority which congress can never be supposed to intend, and has not the power to make. But congress has expressly enabled the courts to regulate their practice, by other laws. The 17th section of the judiciary act of 1789, c. 20, enacts, "that all the said courts shall have power,"—"to make and establish all necessary rules for the orderly conducting business in the said courts, provided such rules are not repugnant to the laws of the United States;" and the 7th section of the act, "in addition to the act, entitled, an act to establish the judicial courts of the United States" (Act of 1793, ch. 22, § 7), details more at large the powers conferred by the 17th section of the judiciary act. These sections give the court full power over all matters of practice; and it is not reasonable to suppose, that the process act was intended solely for the same object. The language is different; and the two sections last mentioned have no reference to state laws.

It will not be contended, that congress can delegate to the courts, or to any other tribunals, powers which are strictly and exclusively legislative. But congress may certainly delegate to others, powers which the legislature may rightfully exercise itself. Without going further for examples, we will take that, the legality of which the counsel for the defendants admit. The 17th section of the judiciary act, and the 7th section of the additional act, empower the courts respectively to regulate their practice. It certainly will not be contended, that this might not be done by congress. The courts, for example, may make rules, directing the returning of writs and processes, the filing of declarations and other pleadings, and other things of the same description. It will not be contended, that these things might not be done by the legislature, without the intervention of the courts; yet it is not alleged, that the power may not be conferred on the judicial department.

The line has not been exactly drawn which separates those important subjects, which must be entirely regulated by the legislature itself, from those of less interest, in which a general provision may be made, and power given to those who are to act under such general provisions, to fill up the details. To determine the character of the power given to the courts by the process act, we must inquire into its extent. It is expressly extended to those forms and modes of proceeding in suits at common law, which were used in the state courts in September 1789, and were adopted by that act.

9

BANK OF THE UNITED STATES V. HALSTEAD

10 Wheat. 51 (1825)

It is said, however, that this is the true exercise of legislative power, which could not be delegated by congress to the courts of justice. But this objection cannot be sustained. There is no doubt, that congress might have legislated more specifically on the subject, and declared what property should be subject to executions from the courts of the United States. But it does not follow, that because congress might have done this, they necessarily must do it, and cannot commit the power to the courts of justice. Congress might regulate the whole practice of the courts, if it was deemed expedient so to do: but this power is vested in the courts; and it never has occurred to any one, that it was a delegation of legislative power. The power given to the courts over their process is no more than authorizing them to regulate and direct the conduct of the marshal, in the execution of the process. It relates, therefore, to the ministerial duty of the officer; and partakes no more of legislative power, than that discretionary authority intrusted to every department of the government in a variety of cases. And, as is forcibly observed by the court, in the case of *Wayman* v. *Southard,* the same objection arises to delegating this power to the state authorities, as there does to intrusting it to the courts of the United States; it is as much a delegation of legislative power in the one case as in the other. It has been already decided, in the case referred to, that the 34th section of the judiciary act has no application to the practice of the courts of the United States, so as in any manner to govern the form of the process of execution. And all the reasoning of the court,

which denies the application of this section to the form, applies with equal force to the effect or extent and operation of the process. If, therefore, congress has legislated at all upon the effect of executions, they have either adopted and limited it to that which would have been given to the like process from the supreme courts of the respective states, in the year 1789, or have provided for changes, by authorizing the courts of the United States to make such alterations and additions in the process itself, as to give it a different effect.

To limit the operation of an execution *now,* to that which it would have had in the year 1789, would open a door to many and great inconveniences, which congress seems to have foreseen, and to have guarded against, by giving ample powers to the courts, so to mould their process, as to meet whatever changes might take place. And if any doubt existed, whether the act of 1792 vests such power in the courts, or with respect to its constitutionality, the practical construction heretofore given to it, ought to have great weight in determining both questions. It is understood, that it has been the general, if not the universal practice of the courts of the United States, so to alter their executions, as to authorize a levy upon whatever property is made subject to the like process from the state courts; and under such alterations, many sales of land have no doubt been made, which might be disturbed, if a contrary construction should be adopted. That such alteration, both in the form and effect of executions, has been made by the circuit court for the district of Kentucky, is certain, from the case now before us, as, in 1789, land in Kentucky could not be sold on execution.

If the court, then, had the power so to frame and mould the execution in this case, as to extend to lands, the only remaining inquiry is, whether the proceedings on the execution could be arrested and controlled by the state law. And this question would seem to be put at rest by the decision in the case of *Wayman* v. *Southard.* The law of Kentucky, as has been already observed, does not in terms profess to exercise any such authority; and if it did, it must be unavailing. An officer of the United States cannot, in the discharge of his duty, be governed and controlled by state laws, any further than such laws have been adopted and sanctioned by the legislative authority of the United States. And he does not, in such case, act under the authority of the state law, but under that of the United States, which adopts such law. An execution is the fruit and end of the suit, and is very aptly called the life of the law. The suit does not terminate with the judgment; and all proceedings on the execution, are proceedings in the suit, and which are expressly, by the act of congress, put under the regulation and control of the court out of which it issues. It is a power incident to every court from which process issues, when delivered to the proper officer, to enforce upon such officer a compliance with his duty, and a due execution of the process, according to its command. But we are not left to rest upon any implied power of the court, for such authority over the officer. By the 7th section of the act of the 2d of March 1793 (1 U.S. Stat. 335), it is delcared, that "it shall be lawful for the several courts of the United States, from time to time, as occasion may require, to make rules and orders for their respective courts, directing the returning of writs and processes, &c., and to regulate the practice of the said courts respectively, in such manner as shall be fit and necessary for the advancement of justice, and especially to the end to prevent delays in proceedings." To permit the marshal, in this case, to be governed and controlled by the state law, is not only delaying, but may be entirely defeating the effect and operation of the execution, and would be inconsistent with the advancement of justice.

Upon the whole, therefore, the opinion of this court is, that the circuit court had authority to alter the form of the process of execution, so as to extend to real as well as personal property, when, by the laws of Kentucky, lands were made subject to the like process from the state courts; and that the act of the general assembly of Kentucky does not operate upon, and bind, and direct the mode in which the *venditioni exponas* should be enforced by the marshal, so as to forbid a sale of the land levied upon, unless it commanded three-fourths of its value, according to the provisions of the said act; and that, of course, the return of the marshal is insufficient, and ought to be quashed. This renders it unnecessary to inquire into the constitutionality of the law of Kentucky.

10

JAMES KENT, COMMENTARIES 1:207–10
1826

The power of making laws is the supreme power in a state, and the department in which it resides will naturally have such a preponderance in the political system, and act with such mighty force upon the public mind, that the line of separation between that and the other branches of the government ought to be marked very distinctly, and with the most careful precision.

The constitution of the United States has effected this purpose with great felicity of execution, and in a way well calculated to preserve the equal balance of the government, and the harmony of its operations. It has not only made a general delegation of the legislative power to one branch of the government, of the executive to another, and of the judicial to the third, but it has specially defined the general powers and duties of each of those departments. This was essential to peace and safety in a government clothed only with specific powers for national purposes, and erected in the midst of numerous state governments retaining the exclusive control of their local concerns. It will be the object of this lecture to review the legislative department, and I shall consider this great title in our national polity under the following heads: (1.) The constituent parts of congress, and the mode of their appointment; (2.) Their joint and separate powers and privileges; (3.) Their method of enacting laws, with the qualified negative of the President.

(1.) By the constitution, all the legislative powers therein granted, are vested in a congress, consisting of a senate and house of representatives.

The division of the legislature into two separate and independent branches, is founded in such obvious principles of good policy, and is so strongly recommended by the unequivocal language of experience, that it has obtained the general approbation of the people of this country. The great object of this separation of the legislature into two houses, acting separately, and with co-ordinate powers, is to destroy the evil effects of sudden and strong excitement, and of precipitate measures springing from passion, caprice, prejudice, personal influence, and party intrigue, and which have been found, by sad experience, to exercise a potent and dangerous sway in single assemblies. A hasty decision is not so likely to arrive to the solemnities of a law, when it is to be arrested in its course, and made to undergo the deliberation, and probably the jealous and critical revision, of another and a rival body of men, sitting in a different place, and under better advantages to avoid the prepossessions and correct the errors of the other branch. The legislatures of Pennsylania and Georgia consisted originally of a single house. The instability and passion which marked their proceedings were very visible at the time, and the subject of much public animadversion; and in the subsequent reform of their constitutions, the people were so sensible of this defect, and of the inconvenience they had suffered from it, that in both states a senate was introduced. No portion of the political history of mankind is more full of instructive lessons on this subject, or contains more striking proof of the faction, instability, and misery of states, under the dominion of a single unchecked assembly, than that of the Italian republics of the middle ages; and which arose in great numbers, and with dazzling but transient splendour, in the interval between the fall of the Western and the Eastern empire of the Romans. They were all alike ill constituted, with a single unbalanced assembly. They were all alike miserable, and all ended in similar disgrace.

Many speculative writers and theoretical politicians, about the time of the commencement of the French revolution, were struck with the simplicity of a legislature with a single assembly, and concluded that more than one house was useless and expensive. This led the elder President Adams to write and publish his great work, entitled, "A Defence of the Constitutions of Government of the United States," in which he vindicates, with much learning and ability, the value and necessity of the division of the legislature into two branches, and of the distribution of the different powers of the government into distinct departments. He reviewed the history, and examined the construction of all mixed and free governments which had ever existed, from the earliest records of time, in order to deduce with more certainty and force his great practical truth, that single assemblies, without check or balance, or a government with all authority collected into one centre, according to the notion of M. Turgot, were visionary, violent, intriguing, corrupt and tyrannical dominations of majorities over minorities, and uniformly and rapidly terminating their career in a profligate despotism.

This visionary notion of a single house of the legislature was carried into the constitution which the French national assembly adopted in 1791. The very nature of things, said the intemperate and crude politicians of that assembly, was adverse to every division of the legislative body; and that, as the nation which was represented was one, so the representative body ought to be one also. The will of the nation was indivisible, and so ought to be the voice which pronounced it. If there were two chambers, with a *veto* upon the acts of each other, in some cases they would be reduced to perfect inaction. By such reasoning, the national assembly of France, consisting of upwards of one thousand members, after a short and tumultuous debate, almost unanimously voted to reject the proposition of an upper house. The same false and vicious principle continued for some time longer to prevail with the theorists of that country; and a single house was likewise established in the plan of government published by the French convention in 1793. The instability and violent measures of that convention, which continued for some years to fill all Europe with astonishment and horror, tended to display in a most forcible and affecting light, the miseries of a single unchecked body of men, clothed with all the legislative powers of the state. It is very possible that the French nation might have been hurried into the excesses of a revolution even under a better organization of their government; but if the proposition of M. Lally Tolendal to constitute a senate, or upper house, to be composed of members chosen for life, had prevailed, the constitution would have had much more stability, and afforded infinitely greater probability of preserving the nation in order and tranquillity. Their own sufferings taught the French people to listen to that oracle of wisdom, the experience of other countries and ages, and which for some years they had utterly disregarded, amidst the hurry and the violence of those passions by which they were inflamed. No people, said M. Boissy d'Angles in 1795, can testify to the world with more truth and sincerity than Frenchmen can do, the dangers inherent in a single legislative assembly, and the point to which factions may mislead an assembly without reins or counterpoise. We accordingly find that in the next constitution, which arose in 1797, there was a division of the legislature, and a council of ancients was introduced to give stability and moderation to the government; and this idea of two houses was never afterwards abandoned.

SEE ALSO:

Records of the Federal Convention, Farrand 1:20, 27, 45–46, 48, 54, 55, 57, 60, 61, 225, 235, 291, 334, 349–50

George Mason to George Mason, Jr., 20 May 1787, Farrand 3:23

George Read to John Dickinson, 21 May 1787, Farrand 3:25

William Grayson to James Madison, 24 May 1787, Farrand 3:26

Charles Pinckney, Observations on the Plan of Government, 1787, Farrand 3:110

Charles Pinckney, South Carolina Ratifying Convention, 16 Jan. 1788, Elliot 4:256–57

Benjamin Franklin to M. LeVeillard, 22 April 1788, Farrand 3:297

Robert Lansing, New York Ratifying Convention, 24 June 1788, Elliot 2:294

Debates in New York Ratifying Convention, 26 June–1 July 1788, Elliot 2:330–78

James Monroe, Virginia Ratifying Convention, June 1788, Elliot 3:214–16

A Native of Virginia, Observations upon the Proposed Plan of Federal Government, 1788, Monroe Writings 1:356

Debate in House of Representatives, 8 Mar. 1792, Annals 3:437–52

House of Representatives, The President's Speech, 20 Nov. 1792, Annals 3:703–8

St. George Tucker, Blackstone's Commentaries 1:App. 3–6 (1803)

Senate Instructions of State Legislatures to Their Senators, 14, 19 Feb. 1811, Annals 22:193–201, 308–9

The Aurora v. *United States*, 7 Cranch 382 (1813)

Lewis v. *Webb*, 3 Maine 326 (1825)

Joseph Story, Commentaries on the Constitution 2:§§ 547–51, 554–57 (1833)

United States v. *Bailey*, 9 Pet. 238 (1835)

Article 1, Section 2, Clause 1

The House of Representatives shall be composed of Members chosen every second Year by the People of the several States, and the Electors in each State shall have the Qualifications requisite for Electors of the most numerous Branch of the State Legislature.

1

DELAWARE CHARTER OF 1701
Thorpe 1:559

II.

FOR the well governing of this Province and Territories, there shall be an Assembly yearly chosen, by the Freemen thereof, . . .

2

ADDRESS OF GENERAL ASSEMBLY OF NEW YORK TO LT. GOVERNOR GEORGE CLARKE
7 Sept. 1737
J. Gen. Assembly Colony of New York 1:706–7 (1764)

Persons that are fairly and freely chosen, have only right to represent the People, and are most likely to do the most effectual, as well as the most acceptable Service to the Publick: Whereas those who have recourse to Frauds and unbecoming Arts, to procure themselves to be raised to those Stations, must be under the Government of narrow and selfish Views, unworthy any Representation of a free People, and will no doubt basely submit to the same detestable Measures, to continue themselves (by any Means) in the Exercise of a Trust unjustly acquired. It is by such as these, that the Liberties of the most free People have been in various Ages of the World, undermined and subverted: And it is to prevent this, as much as we may, that we gave Leave to bring in the Bill, for regulating of Elections.

The Mischief that is by it endeavoured to be prevented, has been but too generally practised, and the many Laws of that Kind, both in *England* and the Plantations, that have had the Royal Assent in different Reigns, proves that our Kings did not at any Time think, that Bills of that Nature, were Attempts upon their royal and just Prerogatives, but just and necessary to secure the Liberties of their Subjects; which it always was and ever will be their Honour, as well as their true Interest, to preserve and maintain.

As it is absolutely necessary in the Nature of Things, that Elections of Representatives should be free, otherwise they cannot with any Propriety of Speech be called Elections, so it seems equally necessary for the Safety of the People, that they should be frequent, for which Reason, we gave Leave to bring in a Bill for that Purpose.

No Government can be safe without proper Checks upon those intrusted with Power, and the wisest Governments where the Chief Magistrates were Elective, took especial Care, that it should not continue long, in the same Hands, Experience having taught them, that Men, how much so ever esteemed, had really not Virtue enough for so great a Trust, and generally used it ill when they had it.

The Experience of *England* has shewn, that long Parliaments have been dangerous to their Choosers, as well as to their Kings, and whatever Advantages may be hoped from any Set of Men properly disposed to come into particular Measures, the Success has seldom (if ever) answered the Expectation; for Men being Men, and as such changeable, according to the different Appearances of Things by which they have been affected; it has not seldom been found, that those very Men on whom was the greatest Dependence, have acted a quite contrary Part from what has been expected from them; and therefore in our Mother Country, frequent Parliaments, were antiently judged necessary to preserve that just Ballance of Power, without which, the State and Constitution it self could not long be preserved. This the Legislature of *England* saw, when they enacted trianeal Parliaments, and though for evident and good Reasons, that Term has been there since that Time prolonged, yet that they should be often elected, seems to be a Point agreed upon as a Thing in itself necessary. If it may be lawful to compare small Things with great, this Country has not been without its Uneasiness, at the long Continuance of an Assmbly; which your Honour found it necessary, for his Majesty's Honour and the Interest and Prosperity of the Province to dissolve; for doing of which, we in the Name of our Constituents return you our Thanks, and doubt not that above nineteen Twentieths of the People of this Colony, heartily join with us in doing so. By that Dissolution, you gave the Country an Opportunity of a new Choice, which they and the Assembly themselves, had long and earnestly desired, and often in vain attempted to procure. . . .

Though none can have more warm and hearty Affections for the Interest of our Country than we have, or would do more for its Service according to our Knowledge and Abilities; yet from what we have observed in others, we have some Reason to distrust ourselves, and fear a long Continuance in Assembly, will render us, as unfit to answer the Ends of our Choice, as it has done others before us. We doubt not from your late Conduct, that you have seen and observed the Inconvenience of long Assemblies, and are fully persuaded of the Necessity and Use of frequent Elections, as the most likely Way of inducing them to act as becomes them to do. Frequent Elections is what all our neighbouring Charter Governments enjoy, and the Benefits conceived to accrue by such a Constitution, has been the great, if not the only Cause of the superior Numbers of Inhabitants in those Colonies; and we believe the want of it, no small Inducement to Numbers of our own to remove; it has been a Constitution indulged to most of the King's Plantations in *America,* and (as we conceive) not found to be prejudicial to his Majesty's Service, or destruc-

tive of his just Prerogatives; and therefore, we hope your Honour's Assent to this Bill, will be readily given when it comes before you.

3

WILLIAM BLACKSTONE, COMMENTARIES 1:165–66
1765

---

1. As to the qualifications of the electors. The true reason of requiring any qualification, with regard to property, in voters, is to exclude such persons as are in so mean a situation that they are esteemed to have no will of their own. If these persons had votes, they would be tempted to dispose of them under some undue influence or other. This would give a great, an artful, or a wealthy man, a larger share in elections than is consistent with general liberty. If it were probable that every man would give his vote freely, and without influence of any kind, then, upon the true theory and genuine principles of liberty, every member of the community, however poor, should have a vote in electing those delegates, to whose charge is committed the disposal of his property, his liberty, and his life. But, since that can hardly be expected in persons of indigent fortunes, or such as are under the immediate dominion of others, all popular states have been obliged to establish certain qualifications; whereby some, who are suspected to have no will of their own, are excluded from voting, in order to set other individuals, whose wills may be supposed independent, more thoroughly upon a level with each other.

And this constitution of suffrages is framed upon a wiser principle than either of the methods of voting, by centuries, or by tribes, among the Romans. In the method by centuries, instituted by Servius Tullius, it was principally property, and not numbers that turned the scale: in the method by tribes, gradually introduced by the tribunes of the people, numbers only were regarded and property entirely overlooked. Hence the laws passed by the former method had usually too great a tendency to aggrandize the patricians or rich nobles; and those by the latter had too much of a levelling principle. Our constitution steers between the two extremes. Only such as are entirely excluded, as can have no will of their own: there is hardly a free agent to be found, but what is entitled to a vote in some place or other in the kingdom. Nor is comparative wealth, or property, entirely disregarded in elections; for though the richest man has only one vote at one place, yet if his property be at all diffused, he has probably a right to vote at more places than one, and therefore has many representatives. This is the spirit of our constitution: not that I assert it is in fact quite so perfect as I have here endeavoured to describe it; for, if any alteration might be wished or suggested in the present frame of parliaments, it should be in favour of a more complete representation of the people.

4

VIRGINIA DECLARATION OF RIGHTS, SEC. 6
12 June 1776

(See vol. 1, ch. 1, no. 3)

5

NORTH CAROLINA CONSTITUTION
OF 1776, ARTS. 7–9
Thorpe 5:2790

VII. That all freemen, of the age of twenty-one years, who have been inhabitants of any one county within the State twelve months immediately preceding the day of any election, and possessed of a freehold within the same county of fifty acres of land, for six months next before, and at the day of election, shall be entitled to vote for a member of the Senate.

VIII. That all freemen of the age of twenty-one years, who have been inhabitants of any one county within this State twelve months immediately preceding the day of any election, and shall have paid public taxes, shall be entitled to vote for members of the House of Commons for the county in which he resides.

IX. That all persons possessed of a freehold in any town in this State, having a right of representation, and also all freemen, who have been inhabitants of any such town twelve months next before, and at the day of election, and shall have paid public taxes, shall be entitled to vote for a member to represent such town in the House of Commons:—Provided always, That this section shall not entitle any inhabitant of such town to vote for members of the House of Commons, for the county in which he may reside, nor any freeholder in such county, who resides without or beyond the limits of such town, to vote for a member for said town.

6

GEORGIA CONSTITUTION OF 1777, ART. 9
Thorpe 1:779

ART. IX. All male white inhabitants, of the age of twenty-one years, and possessed in his own right of ten pounds value, and liable to pay tax in this State, or being of any mechanic trade, and shall have been resident six months in this State, shall have a right to vote at all elections for representatives, or any other officers, herein agreed to be chosen by the people at large; and every person having a right to vote at any election shall vote by ballot personally.

7

NEW YORK CONSTITUTION OF 1777, ART. 7
Thorpe 5:2630–31

VII. That every male inhabitant of full age, who shall have personally resided within one of the counties of this State for six months immediately preceding the day of election, shall, at such election, be entitled to vote for representatives of the said county in assembly; if, during the time aforesaid, he shall have been a freeholder, possessing a freehold of the value of twenty pounds, within the said county, or have rented a tenement therein of the yearly value of forty shillings, and been rated and actually paid taxes to this State: *Provided always*, That every person who now is a freeman of the city of Albany, or who was made a freeman of the city of New York on or before the fourteenth day of October, in the year of our Lord one thousand seven hundred and seventy-five, and shall be actually and usually resident in the said cities, respectively, shall be entitled to vote for representatives in assembly within his said place of residence.

8

VERMONT CONSTITUTION OF 1786, CH. 2, ART. 18
Thorpe 6:3757

XVIII. Every man, of the full age of twenty-one years, having resided in this State, for the space of one whole year, next before the election of representatives, and is of a quiet and peaceable behaviour, and will take the following oath, (or affirmation) shall be entitled to all the privileges of a freeman of this State.

You solemnly swear, (or affirm) that whenever you give your vote or suffrage, touching any matter that concerns the State of Vermont, you will do it so as in your conscience you shall judge will most conduce to the best good of the same, as established by the Constitution, without fear or favour of any man.

9

RECORDS OF THE FEDERAL CONVENTION

[1:48; Madison, 31 May]

Resol: 4. first clause "that the members of the first branch of the National Legislature ought to be elected by the people of the several States" being taken up,

Mr. Sherman opposed the election by the people, insisting that it ought to be by the State Legislatures. The people he said, immediately should have as little to do as may be about the Government. They want information and are constantly liable to be misled.

Mr. Gerry. The evils we experience flow from the excess of democracy. The people do not want virtue; but are the dupes of pretended patriots. In Massts. it has been fully confirmed by experience that they are daily misled into the most baneful measures and opinions by the false reports circulated by designing men, and which no one on the spot can refute. One principal evil arises from the want of due provision for those employed in the administration of Governnt. It would seem to be a maxim of democracy to starve the public servants. He mentioned the popular clamour in Massts. for the reduction of salaries and the attack made on that of the Govr. though secured by the spirit of the Constitution itself. He had he said been too republican heretofore: he was still however republican, but had been taught by experience the danger of the levilling spirit.

Mr. Mason. argued strongly for an election of the larger branch by the people. It was to be the grand depository of the democratic principle of the Govt. It was, so to speak, to be our House of Commons—It ought to know & sympathise with every part of the community; and ought therefore to be taken not only from different parts of the whole republic, but also from different districts of the larger members of it, which had in several instances particularly in Virga., different interests and views arising from difference of produce, of habits &c &c. He admitted that we had been too democratic but was afraid we sd. incautiously run into the opposite extreme. We ought to attend to the rights of every class of the people. He had often wondered at the indifference of the superior classes of society to this dictate of humanity & policy, considering that however affluent their circumstances, or elevated their situations, might be, the course of a few years, not only might but certainly would, distribute their posterity thoughout the lowest classes of Society. Every selfish motive therefore, every family attachment, ought to recommend such a system of policy as would provide no less carefully for the rights—and happiness of the lowest than of the highest orders of Citizens.

Mr. Wilson contended strenuously for drawing the most numerous branch of the Legislature immediately from the people. He was for raising the federal pyramid to a considerable altitude, and for that reason wished to give it as broad a basis as possible. No government could long subsist without the confidence of the people. In a republican Government this confidence was peculiarly essential. He also thought it wrong to increase the weight of the State Legislatures by making them the electors of the national Legislature. All interference between the general and local Governmts. should be obviated as much as possible. On examination it would be found that the opposition of States to federal measures had proceded much more from the Officers of the States, than from the people at large.

Mr. Madison considered the popular election of one branch of the national Legislature as essential to every plan of free Government. He observed that in some of the States one branch of the Legislature was composed of men already removed from the people by an intervening body of electors. That if the first branch of the general legislature should be elected by the State Legislatures, the second branch elected by the first—the Executive by the second together with the first; and other appointments again made for subordinate purposes by the Executive, the people would be lost sight of altogether; and the necessary sympathy between them and their rulers and officers, too little felt. He was an advocate for the policy of refining the popular appointments by successive filtrations, but thought it might be pushed too far. He wished the expedient to be resorted to only in the appointment of the second branch of the Legislature, and in the Executive & judiciary branches of the Government. He thought too that the great fabric to be raised would be more stable and durable if it should rest on the solid foundation of the people themselves, than if it should stand merely on the pillars of the Legislatures.

Mr. Gerry did not like the election by the people. The maxims taken from the British constitution were often fallacious when applied to our situation which was extremely different. Experience he said had shewn that the State Legislatures drawn immediately from the people did not always possess their confidence. He had no objection however to an election by the people if it were so qualified that men of honor & character might not be unwilling to be joined in the appointments. He seemed to think the people might nominate a certain number out of which the State legislatures should be bound to choose.

Mr. Butler thought an election by the people an impracticable mode.

On the question for an election of the first branch of the national Legislature, by the people, Massts. ay. Connect. divd. N. York ay. N. Jersey no. Pena. ay. Delawe. divd. Va. ay. N. C. ay. S. C. no. Georga. ay. [Ayes—6; noes—2; divided—2.]

[1:132; Madison, 6 June]

Mr. Pinkney according to previous notice & rule obtained, moved "that the first branch of the national Legislature be elected by the State Legislatures, and not by the people". contending that the people were less fit Judges in such a case, and that the Legislatures would be less likely to promote the adoption of the new Government, if they were to be excluded from all share in it.

Mr. Rutlidge 2ded. the motion.

Mr. Gerry. Much depends on the mode of election. In England, the people will probably lose their liberty from the smallness of the proportion having a right to suffrage. Our danger arises from the opposite extreme: hence in Massts. the worst men get into the Legislature. Several members of that Body had lately been convicted of infamous crimes. Men of indigence, ignorance & baseness, spare no pains however dirty to carry their point agst. men who are superior to the artifices practiced. He was not disposed to run into extremes. He was as much principled as ever agst. aristocracy and monarchy. It was necessary on the one hand that the people should appoint one branch of the Govt. in order to inspire them with the necessary confidence. But he wished the election on the other to be so modified as to secure more effectually a just preference of merit. His idea was that the people should nominate certain persons in certain districts, out of whom the State Legislatures shd. make the appointment.

Mr. Wilson. He wished for vigor in the Govt. but he wished that vigorous authority to flow immediately from the legitimate source of all authority. The Govt. ought to possess not only 1st. the *force* but 2ndly. the *mind or sense* of the people at large. The Legislature ought to be the most exact transcript of the whole Society. Representation is made necessary only because it is impossible for the people to act collectively. The opposition was to be expected he said from the *Governments,* not from the Citizens of the States. The latter had parted as was observed (by Mr. King) with all the necessary powers; and it was immaterial to them, by whom they were exercised, if well exercised. The State officers were to be losers of power. The people he supposed would be rather more attached to the national Govt. than to the State Govts. as being more important in itself, and more flattering to their pride. There is no danger of improper elections if made by *large* districts. Bad elections proceed from the smallness of the districts which give an opportunity to bad men to intrigue themselves into office.

Mr. Sherman. If it were in view to abolish the State Govts. the elections ought to be by the people. If the State Govts. are to be continued, it is necessary in order to preserve harmony between the national & State Govts. that the elections to the former shd. be made by the latter. The right of participating in the National Govt. would be sufficiently secured to the people by their election of the State Legislatures. The objects of the Union, he thought were few. 1. defence agst. foreign danger. 2. agst. internal disputes & a resort to force. 3. Treaties with foreign nations 4. regulating foreign commerce, & drawing revenue from it. These & perhaps a few lesser objects alone rendered a Confederation of the States necessary. All other matters civil & criminal would be much better in the hands of the States. The people are more happy in small than large States. States may indeed be too small as Rhode Island, & thereby be too subject to faction. Some others were perhaps too large, the powers of Govt not being able to pervade them. He was for giving the General Govt. power to legislate and execute within a defined province.

Col. Mason. Under the existing Confederacy, Congs. represent the *States* not the *people* of the States: their acts operate on the *States* not on the individuals. The case will be changed in the new plan of Govt. The people will be represented; they ought therefore to choose the Representatives. The requisites in actual representation are that the Reps. should sympathize with their constituents; shd. think as they think, & feel as they feel; and that for these purposes shd. even be residents among them. Much he sd. had been alledged agst. democratic elections. He admitted that much might be said; but it was to be considered that

no Govt. was free from imperfections & evils; and that improper elections in many instances, were inseparable from Republican Govts. But compare these with the advantage of this Form in favor of the rights of the people, in favor of human nature. He was persuaded there was a better chance for proper elections by the people, if divided into large districts, than by the State Legislatures. Paper money had been issued by the latter when the former were against it. Was it to be supposed that the State Legislatures then wd. not send to the Natl. legislature patrons of such projects. if the choice depended on them.

Mr. Madison considered an election of one branch at least of the Legislature by the people immediately, as a clear principle of free Govt. and that this mode under proper regulations had the additional advantage of securing better representatives, as well as of avoiding too great an agency of the State Governments in the General one.— He differed from the member from Connecticut (Mr. Sherman) in thinking the objects mentioned to be all the principal ones that required a National Govt. Those were certainly important and necessary objects; but he combined with them the necessity, of providing more effectually for the security of private rights, and the steady dispensation of Justice. Interferences with these were evils which had more perhaps than any thing else, produced this convention. Was it to be supposed that republican liberty could long exist under the abuses of it practiced in some of the States. The gentleman (Mr. Sherman) had admitted that in a very small State, faction & oppression wd. prevail. It was to be inferred then that wherever these prevailed the State was too small. Had they not prevailed in the largest as well as the smallest tho' less than in the smallest; and were we not thence admonished to enlarge the sphere as far as the nature of the Govt. would admit. This was the only defence agst. the inconveniences of democracy consistent with the democratic form of Govt. All civilized Societies would be divided into different Sects, Factions, & interests, as they happened to consist of rich & poor, debtors & creditors, the landed the manufacturing, the commercial interests, the inhabitants of this district, or that district, the followers of this political leader or that political leader, the disciples of this religious sect or that religious sect. In all cases where a majority are united by a common interest or passion, the rights of the minority are in danger. What motives are to restrain them? A prudent regard to the maxim that honesty is the best policy is found by experience to be as little regarded by bodies of men as by individuals. Respect for character is always diminished in proportion to the number among whom the blame or praise is to be divided. Conscience, the only remaining tie is known to be inadequate in individuals: In large numbers, little is to be expected from it. Besides, Religion itself may become a motive to persecution & oppression.—These observations are verified by the Histories of every Country antient & modern. In Greece & Rome the rich & poor, the creditors & debtors, as well as the patricians & plebeians alternately oppressed each other with equal unmercifulness. What a source of oppression was the relation between the parent Cities of Rome, Athens &

Carthage, & their respective provinces: the former possessing the power & the latter being sufficiently distinguished to be separate objects of it? Why was America so justly apprehensive of Parliamentary injustice? Because G. Britain had a separate interest real or supposed, & if her authority had been admitted, could have pursued that interest at our expense. We have seen the mere distinction of colour made in the most enlightened period of time, a ground of the most oppressive dominion ever exercised by man over man. What has been the source of those unjust laws complained of among ourselves? Has it not been the real or supposed interest of the major number? Debtors have defrauded their creditors. The landed interest has borne hard on the mercantile interest. The Holders of one species of property have thrown a disproportion of taxes on the holders of another species. The lesson we are to draw from the whole is that where a majority are united by a common sentiment and have an opportunity, the rights of the minor party become insecure. In a Republican Govt. the Majority if united have always an opportunity. The only remedy is to enlarge the sphere, & thereby divide the community into so great a number of interests & parties, that in the 1st. place a majority will not be likely at the same moment to have a common interest separate from that of the whole or of the minority; and in the 2d. place, that in case they shd. have such an interest, they may not be apt to unite in the pursuit of it. It was incumbent on us then to try this remedy, and with that view to frame a republican system on such a scale & in such a form as will countroul all the evils wch. have been experienced.

Mr. Dickinson considered it as essential that one branch of the Legislature shd. be drawn immediately from the people; and as expedient that the other shd. be chosen by the Legislatures of the States. This combination of the State Govts. with the National Govt. was as politic as it was unavoidable. In the formation of the Senate we ought to carry it through such a refining process as will assimilate it as near as may be to the House of Lords in England. He repeated his warm eulogiums on the British Constitution. He was for a strong National Govt. but for leaving the States a considerable agency in the System. The objection agst. making the former dependent on the latter might be obviated by giving to the Senate an authority permanent & irrevocable for three, five or seven years. Being thus independent they will speak & decide with becoming freedom.

Mr. Read. Too much attachment is betrayed to the State Govermts. We must look beyond their continuance. A national Govt. must soon of necessity swallow all of them up. They will soon be reduced to the mere office of electing the national Senate. He was agst. patching up the old federal System: he hoped the idea wd. be dismissed. It would be like putting new cloth on an old garment. The confederation was founded on temporary principles. It cannot last: it cannot be amended. If we do not establish a good Govt. on new principles, we must either go to ruin, or have the work to do over again. The people at large are wrongly suspected of being averse to a Genl. Govt. The

aversion lies among interested men who possess their confidence.

Mr. Pierce was for an election by the people as to the 1st. branch & by the States as to the 2d. branch; by which means the Citizens of the States wd. be represented both *individually* & *collectively*.

General Pinkney wished to have a good national Govt. & at the same time to leave a considerable share of power in the States. An election of either branch by the people scattered as they are in many States, particularly in S. Carolina was totally impracticable. He differed from gentlemen who thought that a choice by the people wd. be a better guard agst. bad measures, than by the Legislatures. A majority of the people in S. Carolina were notoriously for paper money as a legal tender; the Legislature had refused to make it a legal tender. The reason was that the latter had some sense of character and were restrained by that consideration. The State Legislatures also he said would be more jealous, & more ready to thwart the National Govt. if excluded from a participation in it. The Idea of abolishing these Legislatures wd. never go down.

Mr. Wilson, would not have spoken again, but for what had fallen from Mr. Read; namely, that the idea of preserving the State Govts. ought to be abandoned. He saw no incompatability between the national & State Govts. provided the latter were restrained to certain local purposes; nor any probability of their being devoured by the former. In all confederated systems antient & modern the reverse had happened; the Generality being destroyed gradually by the usurpations of the parts composing it.

On the question for electing the 1st. branch by the State Legislatures as moved by Mr. Pinkney; it was negatived:

Mass. no. Ct. ay. N. Y. no. N. J. ay. Pa. no. Del. no. Md. no. Va. no. N. C. no. S. C. ay. Geo. no. [Ayes—3; noes—8.]

[1:214; Madison, 12 June]

Mr. Sharman & Mr. Elseworth moved to fill the blank left in the 4th Resolution for the periods of electing the members of the first branch with the words "every year." Mr. Sharman observing that he did it in order to bring on some question.

Mr. Rutlidge proposed "every two years."

Mr. Jennifer propd. "every three years." observing that the too great frequency of elections rendered the people indifferent to them, and made the best men unwilling to engage in so precarious a service.

Mr. Madison seconded the motion for three years. Instability is one of the great vices of our republics, to be remedied. Three years will be necessary, in a Government so extensive, for members to form any knowledge of the various interests of the States to which they do not belong, and of which they can know but little from the situation and affairs of their own. One year will be almost consumed in preparing for and traveling to & from the seat of national business.

Mr. Gerry. The people of New England will never give up the point of annual elections. they know of the transition made in England from triennial to Septennial elections, and will consider such an innovation here as the prelude to a like usurpation. He considered annual Elections as the only defence of the people agst. tyranny. He was as much agst. a triennial House as agst. a hereditary Executive.

Mr. Madison. observed that if the opinions of the people were to be our guide, it wd. be difficult to say what course we ought to take. No member of the Convention could say what the opinions of his Constituents were at this time; much less could he say what they would think if possessed of the information & lights possessed by the members here; & still less what would be their way of thinking 6 or 12 months hence. We ought to consider what was right & necessary in itself for the attainment of a proper Governmt. A plan adjusted to this idea will recommend itself—The respectability of this convention will give weight to their recommendation of it. Experience will be constantly urging the adoption of it. and all the most enlightened & respectable citizens will be its advocates. Should we fall short of the necessary & proper point, this influential class of citizens will be turned against the plan, and little support in opposition to them can be gained to it from the unreflecting multitude.

Mr. Gerry repeated his opinion that it was necessary to consider what the people would approve. This had been the policy of all Legislators. If the reasoning of Mr. Madison were just, and we supposed a limited Monarchy the best form in itself, we ought to recommend it, tho' the genius of the people was decidedly adverse to it, and having no hereditary distinctions among us, we were destitute of the essential materials for such an innovation.

On the question for triennial election of the 1st branch Mass. no. (Mr King ay.) Mr. Ghorum wavering. Cont. no. N. Y. ay. N. J. ay. Pa. ay. Del. ay. Md. ay. Va. ay. N. C. no. S. C. no. Geo. ay. [Ayes—7; noes—4.]

[1:235; Madison, 13 June]

3. Resd. that the members of the first branch of the National Legislature ought to be elected by the people of the several States for the term of three years, to receive fixed Stipends by which they may be compensated for the devotion of their time to public service, to be paid out of the National Treasury: to be ineligible to any office established by a particular State, or under the authority of the U. States, (except those peculiarly belonging to the functions of the first branch), during the term of service, and under the national Government for the space of one year after its expiration.

[1:358; Madison, 21 June]

Genl. Pinkney moved "that the 1st. branch, instead of being elected by the people, shd. be elected in such manner as the Legislature of each State should direct." He urged 1. that this liberty would give more satisfaction, as the Legislature could then accomodate the mode to the conveniency & opinions of the people. 2. that it would avoid the undue influence of large Counties which would prevail if the elections were to be made in districts as must be the mode intended by the Report of the Committee. 3. that otherwise disputed elections must be referred to the General Legislature which would be attended with intolerable expence and trouble to the distant parts of the republic.

Mr. L. Martin seconded the Motion.

Col. Hamilton considered the motion as intended manifestly to transfer the election from the people to the State Legislatures, which would essentially vitiate the plan. It would increase that State influence which could not be too watchfully guarded agst. All too must admit the possibility, in case the Genl. Govt. shd. maintain itself, that the State Govts. might gradually dwindle into nothing. The system therefore shd. not be engrafted on what might possibly fail.

Mr. Mason urged the necessity of retaining the election by the people. Whatever inconveniency may attend the democratic principle, it must actuate one part of the Govt. It is the only security for the rights of the people.

Mr. Sherman, would like an election by the Legislatures, best, but is content with plan as it stands.

Mr. Rutlidge could not admit the solidity of the distinction between a mediate & immediate election by the people. It was the same thing to act by oneself, and to act by another. An election by the Legislature would be more refined than an election immediately by the people: and would be more likely to correspond with the sense of the whole community. If this Convention had been chosen by the people in districts it is not to be supposed that such proper characters would have been preferred. The Delegates to Congs. he thought had also been fitter men than would have been appointed by the people at large.

Mr. Wilson considered the election of the 1st. branch by the people not only as the corner Stone, but as the foundation of the fabric: and that the difference between a mediate and immediate election was immense. The difference was particularly worthy of notice in this respect: that the Legislatures are actuated not merely by the sentiment of the people, but have an official sentiment opposed to that of the Genl: Govt. and perhaps to that of the people themselves.

Mr. King enlarged on the same distinction. He supposed the Legislatures wd. constantly choose men subservient to their own views as contrasted to the general interest; and that they might even devise modes of election that wd. be subversive of the end in view. He remarked several instances in which the views of a State might be at variance with those of the Gen'l. Govt. and mentioned particularly a competition between the National & State debts, for the most certain & productive funds.

Genl. Pinkney was for making the State Govts. a part of the General System. If they were to be abolished, or lose their agency, S. Carolina & other States would have but a small share of the benefits of Govt.

On the question for Genl. Pinkney motion to substitute election of 1st branch in such mode as the Legislatures should appoint, in stead of its being elected by the people Masst. no. Cont. ay. N. Y. no. N. J. ay. Pa. no. Del. ay. Md. divd. Va. no. N. C. no. S. C. ay. Geo. no. [Ayes—4; noes—6; divided—1.]

Genl. Pinkney then moved that the 1st. branch be

elected *by the people* in such mode as the Legislatures should direct; but waved it on its being hinted that such a provision might be more properly tried in the detail of the plan.

On the question for ye election of the 1st branch by the *people*"

Massts. ay. Cont. ay. N. Y. ay. N. J. no. Pa. ay. Del. ay. Md. divd. Va. ay. N. C. ay. S. C. ay Geo. ay. [Ayes—9; noes—1; divided—1.]

Election of the 1st. branch "for the term of three years," considered

Mr. Randolph moved to strike out, "three years" and insert "two years"—he was sensible that annual elections were a source of great mischiefs in the States, yet it was the want of such checks agst. the popular intemperance as were now proposed, that rendered them so mischievous. He would have preferred annual to biennial, but for the extent of the U. S. and the inconveniency which would result from them to the representatives of the extreme parts of the Empire. The people were attached to frequency of elections. All the Constitutions of the States except that of S. Carolina, had established annual elections.

Mr. Dickenson. The idea of annual elections was borrowed from the antient usage of England, a country much less extensive than ours. He supposed biennial would be inconvenient. He preferred triennial: and in order to prevent the inconveniency of an entire change of the whole number at the same moment, suggested a rotation, by an annual election of one third.

Mr. Elseworth was opposed to three years. supposing that even one year was preferable to two years. The people were fond of frequent elections and might be safely indulged in one branch of the Legislature. He moved for 1 year.

Mr. Strong seconded & supported the motion.

Mr. Wilson being for making the 1st. branch an effectual representation of the people at large, preferred an annual election of it. This frequency was most familiar & pleasing to the people. It would be not more inconvenient to them, than triennial elections, as the people in all the States have annual meetings with which the election of the National representatives might be made to coin——cide. He did not conceive that it would be necessary for the Natl. Legisl: to sit constantly; perhaps not half—perhaps not one fourth of the year.

Mr. Madison was persuaded that annual elections would be extremely inconvenient and apprehensive that biennial would be too much so: he did not mean inconvenient to the electors; but to the representatives. They would have to travel seven or eight hundred miles from the distant parts of the Union; and would probably not be allowed even a reimbursement of their expences. Besides, none of those who wished to be re-elected would remain at the seat of Governmt. confiding that their absence would not affect them. The members of Congs. had done this with few instances of disappointment. But as the choice was here to be made by the people themselves who would be much less complaisant to individuals, and much more susceptible of impressions from the presence of a Rival candidate, it must be supposed that the members from the most distant States would travel backwards & forwards at least as often as the elections should be repeated. Much was to be said also on the time requisite for new members who would always form a large proportion, to acquire that knowledge of the affairs of the States in general without which their trust could not be usefully discharged.

Mr. Sherman preferred annual elections, but would be content with biennial. He thought the representatives ought to return home and mix with the people. By remaining at the seat of Govt. they would acquire the habits of the place which might differ from those of their Constituents.

Col. Mason observed that the States being differently situated such a rule ought to be formed as would put them as nearly as possible on a level. If elections were annual the middle States would have a great advantage over the extreme ones. He wished them to be biennial; and the rather as in that case they would coincide with the periodical elections of S. Carolina as well as of the other States.

Coll. Hamilton urged the necessity of 3 years. there ought to be neither too much nor too little dependence, on the popular sentiments. The checks in the other branches of Governt. would be but feeble, and would need every auxiliary principle that could be interwoven. The British House of Commons were elected septennially, yet the democratic spirit of ye Constitution had not ceased. Frequency of elections tended to make the people listless to them; and to facilitate the success of little cabals. This evil was complained of in all the States. In Virga. it had been lately found necessary to force the attendance & voting of the people by severe regulations.

On the question for striking out "three years"

Massts. ay. Cont. ay. N. Y. no. N J. divd. Pa. ay. Del. no. Md. no. Va. ay. N. C. ay. S. C. ay. Geo. ay. [Ayes—7; noes—3; divided—1.]

The motion for "two years." was then inserted nem. con.

[2:201; Madison, 7 Aug.]

Mr. Govr. Morris moved to strike out the last member of the section beginning with the words "qualifications" of Electors." in order that some other provision might be substituted which wd. restrain the right of suffrage to freeholders.

Mr. Fitzsimmons 2ded. the motion

Mr. Williamson was opposed to it.

Mr. Wilson. This part of the Report was well considered by the Committee, and he did not think it could be changed for the better. It was difficult to form any uniform rule of qualifications for all the States. Unnecessary innovations he thought too should be avoided. It would be very hard & disagreeable for the same persons, at the same time, to vote for representatives in the State Legislature and to be excluded from a vote for those in the Natl. Legislature.

Mr. Govr. Morris. Such a hardship would be neither great nor novel. The people are accustomed to it and not dissatisfied with it, in several of the States. In some the qualifications are different for the choice of the Govr. & Representatives; In others for different Houses of the Legislature. Another objection agst. the clause as it stands is that it makes the qualifications of the Natl. Legislature depend on the will of the States, which he thought not proper.

Mr. Elseworth. thought the qualifications of the electors stood on the most proper footing. The right of suffrage was a tender point, and strongly guarded by most of the State Constitutions. The people will not readily subscribe to the Natl. Constitution, if it should subject them to be disfranchised. The States are the best Judges of the circumstances and temper of their own people.

Col. Mason. The force of habit is certainly not attended to by those gentlemen who wish for innovations on this point. Eight or nine States have extended the right of suffrage beyond the freeholders. What will the people there say, if they should be disfranchised. A power to alter the qualifications would be a dangerous power in the hands of the Legislature.

Mr. Butler. There is no right of which the people are more jealous than that of suffrage Abridgments of it tend to the same revolution as in Holland, where they have at length thrown all power into the hands of the Senates, who fill up vacancies themselves, and form a rank aristocracy.

Mr. Dickenson. had a very different idea of the tendency of vesting the right of suffrage in the freeholders of the Country. He considered them as the best guardians of liberty; And the restriction of the right to them as a necessary defence agst. the dangerous influence of those multitudes without property & without principle, with which our Country like all others, will in time abound. As to the unpopularity of the innovation it was in his opinion chemirical. The great mass of our Citizens is composed at this time of freeholders, and will be pleased with it.

Mr Elseworth. How shall the freehold be defined? Ought not every man who pays a tax to vote for the representative who is to levy & dispose of his money? Shall the wealthy merchants and manufacturers, who will bear a full share of the public burdens be not allowed a voice in the imposition of them—taxation and representation ought to go together.

Mr. Govr. Morris. He had long learned not to be the dupe of words. The sound of Aristocracy therefore, had no effect on him. It was the thing, not the name, to which he was opposed, and one of his principal objections to the Constitution as it is now before us, is that it threatens this Country with an Aristocracy. The aristocracy will grow out of the House of Representatives. Give the votes to people who have no property, and they will sell them to the rich who will be able to buy them. We should not confine our attention to the present moment. The time is not distant when this Country will abound with mechanics & manufacturers who will receive their bread from their employers. Will such men be the secure & faithful Guardians of liberty? Will they be the impregnable barrier agst. aristocracy?—He was as little duped by the association of the words, "taxation & Representation"—The man who does not give his vote freely is not represented. It is the man who dictates the vote. Children do not vote. Why? because they want prudence. because they have no will of their own. The ignorant & the dependent can be as little trusted

with the public interest. He did not conceive the difficulty of defining "freeholders" to be insuperable. Still less that the restriction could be unpopular. 9/10 of the people are at present freeholders and these will certainly be pleased with it. As to Merchts. &c. if they have wealth & value the right they can acquire it. If not they don't deserve it.

Col. Mason. We all feel too strongly the remains of antient prejudices, and view things too much through a British Medium. A Freehold is the qualification in England, & hence it is imagined to be the only proper one. The true idea in his opinion was that every man having evidence of attachment to & permanent common interest with the Society ought to share in all its rights & privileges. Was this qualification restrained to freeholders? Does no other kind of property but land evidence a common interest in the proprietor? does nothing besides property mark a permanent attachment. Ought the merchant, the monied man, the parent of a number of children whose fortunes are to be pursued in their own Country, to be viewed as suspicious characters, and unworthy to be trusted with the common rights of their fellow Citizens

Mr. Madison. the right of suffrage is certainly one of the fundamental articles of republican Government, and ought not to be left to be regulated by the Legislature. A gradual abridgment of this right has been the mode in which Aristocracies have been built on the ruins of popular forms. Whether the Constitutional qualification ought to be a freehold, would with him depend much on the probable reception such a change would meet with in States where the right was now exercised by every description of people. In several of the States a freehold was now the qualification. Viewing the subject in its merits alone, the freeholders of the Country would be the safest depositories of Republican liberty. In future times a great majority of the people will not only be without landed, but any other sort of, property. These will either combine under the influence of their common situation; in which case, the rights of property & the public liberty, will not be secure in their hands: or which is more probable, they will become the tools of opulence & ambition, in which case there will be equal danger on another side. The example of England has been misconceived (by Col Mason). A very small proportion of the Representatives are there chosen by freeholders. The greatest part are chosen by the Cities & boroughs, in many of which the qualification of suffrage is as low as it is in any one of the U. S. and it was in the boroughs & Cities rather than the Counties, that bribery most prevailed, & the influence of the Crown on elections was most dangerously exerted.

Docr. Franklin. It is of great consequence that we shd. not depress the virtue & public spirit of our common people; of which they displayed a great deal during the war, and which contributed principally to the favorable issue of it. He related the honorable refusal of the American seamen who were carried in great numbers into the British Prisons during the war, to redeem themselves from misery or to seek their fortunes, by entering on board the Ships of the Enemies to their Country; contrasting their patriotism with a contemporary instance in which the British seamen made prisoners by the Americans, readily entered on the ships of the latter on being promised a share of the prizes that might be made out of their own Country. This proceeded he said, from the different manner in which the common people were treated in America & G. Britain. He did not think that the elected had any right in any case to narrow the privileges of the electors. He quoted as arbitrary the British Statute setting forth the danger of tumultuous meetings, and under that pretext, narrowing the right of suffrage to persons having freeholds of a certain value; observing that this Statute was soon followed by another under the succeeding Parliamt. subjecting the people who had no votes to peculiar labors & hardships. He was persuaded also that such a restriction as was proposed would give great uneasiness in the populous States. The sons of a substantial farmer, not being themselves freeholders, would not be pleased at being disfranchised, and there are a great many persons of that description.

Mr. Mercer. The Constitution is objectionable in many points, but in none more than the present. He objected to the footing on which the qualification was put, but particularly to the *mode of election* by the people. The people can not know & judge of the characters of Candidates. The worse possible choice will be made. He quoted the case of the Senate in Virga. as an example in point- The people in Towns can unite their votes in favor of one favorite; & by that means always prevail over the people of the Country, who being dispersed will scatter their votes among a variety of candidates.

Mr. Rutledge thought the idea of restraining the right of suffrage to the freeholders a very unadvised one. It would create division among the people & make enemies of all those who should be excluded.

On the question for striking out as moved by Mr. Govr. Morris, from the word "qualifications" to the end of the III article

N. H. no. Mas. no. Ct. no. Pa. no. Del. ay. Md. divd. Va. no. N. C. no. S. C. no. Geo. not prest. [Ayes—1; noes—7; divided—1; absent—1.]

[2:215; Madison, 8 Aug.]

Art: IV. Sect. 1.—Mr. Mercer expressed his dislike of the whole plan, and his opinion that it never could succeed.

Mr. Ghorum. He had never seen any inconveniency from allowing such as were not freeholders to vote, though it had long been tried. The elections in Phila. N. York & Boston where the Merchants, & Mechanics vote are at least as good as those made by freeholders only. The case in England was not accurately stated yesterday (by Mr. Madison) The Cities & large towns are not the seat of Crown influence & corruption. These prevail in the Boroughs, and not on account of the right which those who are not freeholders have to vote, but of the smallness of the number who vote. The people have been long accustomed to this right in various parts of America, and will never allow it to be abridged. We must consult their rooted prejudices if we expect their concurrence in our propositions.

Mr. Mercer did not object so much to an election by the people at large including such as were not freeholders, as to their being left to make their choice without any guidance. He hinted that Candidates ought to be nominated by the State Legislatures.

On question for agreeing to Art: IV–Sect. 1 it passd. nem. con.

10

CATO, NO. 5
Fall 1787
Storing 2.6.36–37

But with respect to the first objection, it may be remarked that a well digested democracy has this advantage over all others, to wit, that it affords to many the opportunity to be advanced to the supreme command, and the honors they thereby enjoy fill them with a desire of rendering themselves worthy of them: hence this desire becomes part of their education, is matured in manhood, and produces an ardent affection for their country, and it is the opinion of the great Sidney, and Montesquieu that this is in a great measure produced by annual election of magistrates.

If annual elections were to exist in this government, and learning and information to become more prevalent, you never will want men to execute whatever you could design—Sidney observes *that a well governed state is as fruitful to all good purposes as the seven headed serpent is said to have been in evil; when one head is cut off, many rise up in the place of it.* He remarks further, that *it was also thought, that free cities by frequent elections of magistrates became nurseries of great and able men, every man endeavoring to excel others, that he might be advanced to the honor he had no other title to, than what might arise from his merit, or reputation,* but the framers of this *perfect government,* as it is called, have departed from this democratical principle, and established bi-ennial elections for the house of representatives, who are to be chosen by the people, and sextennial for the senate, who are to be chosen by the legislatures of the different states, and have given to the executive the unprecedented power of making temporary senators, in case of vacancies, by resignation or otherwise, and so far forth establishing a precedent for virtual representation (though in fact, their original appointment is virtual) thereby influencing the choice of the legislatures, or if they should not be so complaisant as to conform to his appointment—offence will be given to the executive and the temporary members will appear ridiculous by rejection; this temporary member, during his time of appointment, will of course act by a power derived from the executive, and for, and under his immediate influence.

11

"JOHN DEWITT," NO. 3
Fall 1787

Storing 4.3.14

These considerations, added to their share above mentioned in the Executive department must give them a decided superiority over the House of Representatives.—But that superiority is greatly enhanced, when we consider the difference of time for which they are chosen. They will have become adepts in the mystery of administration, while the House of Representatives may be composed perhaps two thirds of members, just entering into office, little used to the course of business, and totally unacquainted with the means made use of to accomplish it.—Very possible also in a country where they are total strangers.—But, my fellow-citizens, the important question here arises, who are this House of Representatives? "A representative Assembly, says the celebrated Mr. Adams, is the sense of the people, and the perfection of the portrait, consists in the likeness."—Can this Assembly be said to contain the sense of the people?—Do they resemble the people in any one single feature?—Do you represent your wants, your grievances, your wishes, in person? If that is impracticable, have you a right to send one of your townsmen for that purpose?—Have you a right to send one from your county? Have you a right to send more than one for every thirty thousand of you? Can he be presumed knowing to your different, peculiar situations—your abilities to pay publick taxes, when they ought to be abated, and when encreased? Or is there any possibility of giving him information? All these questions must be answered in the negative. But how are these men to be chosen? Is there any other way than by dividing the State into districts? May not you as well at once invest your annual Assemblies with the power of choosing them—where is the essential difference? The nature of the thing will admit of none. Nay, you give them the power to prescribe the mode. They may invest it in themselves.—If you choose them yourselves, you must take them upon credit, and elect those persons you know only by common fame. Even this privilege is denied you annually, through fear that you might withhold the shadow of controul over them. In this view of the System, let me sincerely ask you, where is the people in this House of Representatives?—Where is the boasted popular part of this much admired System?—Are they not couzin germans in every sense to the Senate? May they not with propriety be termed an Assistant Aristocratical Branch, who will be infinitely more inclined to co-operate and compromise with each other, than to be the careful guardians of the rights of their constituents? Who is there among you would not start at being told, that instead of your present House of Representatives, consisting of members chosen from every town, your future Houses were to consist of but ten in number, and these to be chosen by districts?—

What man among you would betray his country and approve of it? And yet how infinitely preferable to the plan proposed?—In the one case the elections would be annual, the persons elected would reside in the center of you, their interests would be yours, they would be subject to your immediate controul, and nobody to consult in their deliberations—But in the other, they are chosen for double the time, during which, however well disposed, they become strangers to the very people choosing them, they reside at a distance from you, you have no controul over them, you cannot observe their conduct, and they have to consult and finally be guided by twelve other States, whose interests are, in all material points, directly opposed to yours. Let me again ask you, What citizen is there in the Commonwealth of Massachusetts, that would deliberately consent laying aside the mode proposed, that the several Senates of the several States, should be the popular Branch, and together, form one National House of Representatives?—And yet one moment's attention will evince to you, that this blessed proposed Representation of the People, this apparent faithful Mirror, this striking Likeness, is to be still further refined, and more Aristocratical four times told.—Where now is the exact balance which has been so diligently attended to?

12

JAMES WILSON, PENNSYLVANIA RATIFYING
CONVENTION
4 Dec. 1787

Elliot 2:473–75

We are told, in the next place, by the honorable gentleman from Fayette, (Mr. Smilie,) that, in the different orders of mankind, there is that of a natural aristocracy. On some occasions there is a kind of magical expression, used to conjure up ideas that may create uneasiness and apprehension. I hope the meaning of the words is understood by the gentleman who used them. I have asked repeatedly of gentlemen to explain, but have not been able to obtain the explanations of what they meant by a consolidated government. They keep round and round about the thing, but never define. I ask now what is meant by a natural aristocracy. I am not at a loss for the etymological definition of the term; for, when we trace it to the language from which it is derived, an aristocracy means nothing more or less than a government of the best men in the community, or those who are recommended by the words of the Constitution of Pennsylvania, where it is directed that the representatives should consist of those most noted for wisdom and virtue. Is there any danger in such representation? I shall never find fault that such characters are employed. How happy for us, when such characters can be obtained! If this is meant by a natural aristocracy,—and I know no other,—can it be objectionable that men should be employed that are most noted for their virtue and talents? And are attempts made to mark out these as the most improper persons for the public confidence?

I had the honor of giving a definition—and I believe it was a just one—of what is called an *aristocratic government*. It is a government where the supreme power is not retained by the people, but resides in a select body of men, who either fill up the vacancies that happen, by their own choice and election, or succeed on the principle of descent, or by virtue of territorial possessions, or some other qualifications that are not the result of personal properties. When I speak of personal properties, I mean the qualities of the head and the disposition of the heart.

We are told that the representatives will not be known to the people, nor the people to the representatives, because they will be taken from large districts, where they cannot be particularly acquainted. There has been some experience, in several of the states, upon this subject; and I believe the experience of all who had experience, demonstrates that the larger the district of election, the better the representation. It is only in remote corners of a government that little demagogues arise. Nothing but real weight of character can give a man real influence over a large district. This is remarkably shown in the commonwealth of Massachusetts. The members of the House of Representatives are chosen in very small districts; and such has been the influence of party cabal, and little intrigue in them, that a great majority seem inclined to show very little disapprobation of the conduct of the insurgents in that state.

The governor is chosen by the people at large, and that state is much larger than any district need be under the proposed Constitution. In their choice of their governor, they have had warm disputes; but, however warm the disputes, their choice only vibrated between the most eminent characters. Four of their candidates are well known—Mr. Hancock, Mr. Bowdoin, General Lincoln, and Mr. Goreham, the late president of Congress.

I apprehend it is of more consequence to be able to know the true interest of the people than their faces, and of more consequence still to have virtue enough to pursue the means of carrying that knowledge usefully into effect. And surely, when it has been thought, hitherto, that a representation, in Congress, of from five to two members, was sufficient to represent the interest of this state, is it not more than sufficient to have ten members in that body—and those in a greater comparative proportion than heretofore? The citizens of Pennsylvania will be represented by eight, and the state by two. This, certainly, though not gaining enough, is gaining a good deal; the members will be more distributed through the state, being the immediate choice of the people who hitherto have not been represented in that body.

13

DEBATE IN MASSACHUSETTS RATIFYING CONVENTION
14–15 Jan. 1788
Elliot 2:4–17, 19–20

[*14 Jan.*]

It had been mentioned by some gentlemen, that the introduction of tyranny into several nations had been by lengthening the duration of their parliaments or legislative bodies; and the fate of those nations was urged as a caution against lengthening the period for which Congress is to be chosen. Mr. SEDGWICK wished to know what were the nations which had been thus deprived of their liberties; he believed they were few in number; in fact, he did not recollect any. After showing, by several examples, how nations had been deprived of their liberties, he continued,—Is it not necessary, Mr. President, that the federal representatives should be chosen for two years? Annual elections, in a single state, may be the best for a variety of reasons; but when the great affairs of thirteen states—where their commerce may be extended, and where it is necessary to be restricted—what measures may be most expedient, and best adapted to promote the general prosperity thereof, are to be the objects of deliberation, is not such a period too short? Can a man, called into public life, divest himself of local concerns, and instantly initiate himself into a general knowlege of such extensive and weighty matters? . . .

Mr. G. DENCH wished to know how the representation was secured; as, by the 4th section, Congress were empowered to make or alter the regulation of the times, places, and manner of holding elections. Mr. D. was continuing, but was called to order by Mr. Parsons, who said the subject in debate was the *expediency of biennial elections,* and that an answer to the gentleman from Hopkinton would more properly be given when the 4th section was under consideration.

Dr. TAYLOR. Mr. President, I am opposed to *biennial,* and am in favor of *annual* elections. Annual elections have been the practice of this state ever since its settlement, and no objection to such a mode of electing has ever been made. It has, indeed, sir, been considered as the safeguard of the liberties of the people; and the annihilation of it, the avenue through which tyranny will enter. By the Articles of Confederation, annual elections are provided for, though we have additional securities in a right to recall any or all of our members from Congress, and a provision for rotation. In the proposed Constitution, there is no provision for rotation; we have no right by it to recall our delegates. In answer to the observations, that, by frequency of elections, good men will be excluded, I answer, if they behave well, it is probable they will be continued; but if they behave ill, how shall we remedy the evil? It is possible that rulers may be appointed who may wish to root out the liberties of the people. Is it not, Mr. President, better, if such a case should occur, that at a short period they should politically die, than that they should be proceeded against by impeachment? These considerations, and others, said the doctor, make me in favor of annual elections; and the further we deviate therefrom, the greater is the evil.

The Hon. Mr. SPRAGUE was in favor of the section as it stood. He thought the same principles ought not to guide us when considering the election of a body whose jurisdiction was coëxtensive with a great continent, as when regulating that of one whose concerns are only those of a single state.

Mr. T. DAWES, after a short exordium, said he had not heard it mentioned by any gentleman who had spoken in the debate, that the right of electing representatives in the Congress, as provided for in the proposed Constitution, will be the acquisition of a new privilege by the people, as it really will be. The people will then be immediately represented in the federal government; at present they are not; therefore it will be in favor of the people, if they are chosen for forty instead of two years;—and he adduced many reasons to show that it would not conduce to the interests of the United States, or the security of the people, to have them for a shorter period than two years.

The Hon. Mr. WHITE said he was opposed to the section; he thought the security of the people lay in frequent elections; for his part, he would rather they should be for six months than for two years;—and concluded by saying he was in favor of annual elections.

[15 Jan.]

The Hon. Mr. STRONG rose to reply to the inquiry of the Hon. Mr. Adams, why the alteration of *elections* from annual to biennial was made; and to correct an inaccuracy of the Hon. Mr. Gorham, who, the day before, had said that *that* alteration was made to gratify South Carolina. He said he should then have arisen to put his worthy colleague right, but his memory was not sufficiently retentive to enable him immediately to collect every circumstance. He had since recurred to the original plan. When the subject was at first discussed in Convention, some gentlemen were for having the term extended for a considerable length of time; others were opposed to it, as it was contrary to the ideas and customs of the Eastern States; but a majority was in favor of three years, and it was, he said, urged by the Southern States, which are not so populous as the Eastern, that the expense of more frequent elections would be great;—and concluded by saying that a general concession produced the term as it stood in the section, although it was agreeable to the practice of South Carolina.

Mr. AMES . . . I am sensible, sir, that the doctrine of frequent elections has been sanctioned by antiquity, and is still more endeared to us by our recent experience and uniform habits of thinking. Gentlemen have expressed their zealous partiality for it. They consider this as a leading question in the debate, and that the merits of many other parts of the Constitution are involved in the decision. I confess, sir, and I declare that my zeal for frequent elections is not inferior to their own. I consider it as one of the first securities for popular liberty, in which its very essence may be supposed to reside. But how shall we make the best use of this pledge and instrument of our safety?

A right principle, carried to an extreme, becomes useless. It is apparent that a declaration for a very short term, as for a single day, would defeat the design of representation. The election, in that case, would not seem to the people to be of any importance, and the person elected would think as lightly of his appointment. The other extreme is equally to be avoided. An election for a very long term of years, or for life, would remove the member too far from the control of the people, would be dangerous to liberty, and in fact repugnant to the purposes of the delegation. The truth, as usual, is placed somewhere between the extremes, and I believe is included in this proposition: The term of election must be so long, that the representative may understand the interest of the people, and yet so limited, that his fidelity may be secured by a dependence upon their approbation.

Before I proceed to the application of this rule, I cannot forbear to premise some remarks upon two opinions, which have been suggested.

Much has been said about the people divesting themselves of power, when they delegate it to representatives; and that all representation is to their disadvantage, because it is but an image, a copy, fainter and more imperfect than the original, the people, in whom the light of power is primary and unborrowed, which is only reflected by their delegates. I cannot agree to either of these opinions. The representation of the people is something more than the people. I know, sir, but one purpose which the people can effect without delegation, and that is to destroy a government. That they cannot erect a government, is evinced by our being thus assembled on their behalf. The people must govern by a majority, with whom all power resides. But how is the sense of this majority to be obtained? It has been said that a pure democracy is the best government for a small people who assemble in person. It is of small consequence to discuss it, as it would be inapplicable to the great country we inhabit. It may be of some use in this argument, however, to consider, that it would be very burdensome, subject to faction and violence; decisions would often be made by surprise, in the precipitancy of passion, by men who either understand nothing or care nothing about the subject; or by interested men, or those who vote for their own indemnity. It would be a government not by laws, but by men.

Such were the paltry democracies of Greece and Asia Minor, so much extolled, and so often proposed as a model for our imitation. I desire to be thankful that our people (said Mr. Ames) are not under any temptation to adopt the advice. I think it will not be denied that the people are gainers by the election of representatives. They may destroy, but they cannot exercise, the powers of government in person, but by their servants *they* govern: they do not renounce their power; they do not sacrifice their rights; they become the true sovereigns of the country when they delegate that power, which they cannot use themselves to their trustees.

I know, sir, that the people talk about the liberty of nature, and assert that we divest ourselves of a portion of it when we enter into society. This is declamation against matter of fact. We cannot live without society; and as to liberty, how can I be said to enjoy that which another may take from me when he pleases? The liberty of one depends not so much on the removal of all restraint from him, as on the due restraint upon the liberties of others. Without such restraint, there can be no liberty. Liberty is so far from being endangered or destroyed by this, that it is extended and secured. For I said that we do not enjoy that which another may take from us. But civil liberty cannot be taken from us, when any one may please to invade it; for we have the strength of the society on our side.

I hope, sir, that these reflections will have some tendency to remove the ill impressions which are made by proposing to divest the people of their power.

That they may never be divested of it, I repeat that I am in favor of frequent elections. They who commend annual elections are desired to consider, that the question is, whether biennial elections are a defect in the Constitution; for it does not follow, because annual elections are safe, that biennial are dangerous; for both may be good. Nor is there any foundation for the fears of those, who say that if we, who have been accustomed to choose for one year only, now extend it to two, the next stride will be to five or seven years, and the next for term of life; for this article, with all its supposed defects, is in favor of liberty. Being inserted in the Constitution, it is not subject to be repealed by law. We are sure that it is the worst of the case. It is a fence against ambitious encroachments, too high and too strong to be passed. In this respect, we have greatly the advantage of the people of England, and of all the world. The law which limits their Parliaments is liable to be repealed.

I will not defend this article by saying that it was a matter of compromise in the federal Convention. It has my entire approbation as it stands. I think that we ought to prefer, in this article, biennial elections to annual; and my reasons for this opinion are drawn from these sources:—

From the extent of the country to be governed;

The objects of their legislation;

And the more perfect security of our liberty.

It seems obvious that men who are to collect in Congress from this great territory, perhaps from the Bay of Fundy, or from the banks of the Ohio, and the shore of Lake Superior, ought to have a longer term in office, than the delegates of a single state, in their own legislature. It is not by riding post to and from Congress that a man can acquire a just knowledge of the true interests of the Union. This term of election is inapplicable to the state of a country as large as Germany, or as the Roman empire in the zenith of its power.

If we consider the objects of their delegation, little doubt will remain. It is admitted that annual elections may be highly fit for the state legislature. Every citizen grows up with a knowledge of the local circumstances of the state. But the business of the federal government will be very different. The objects of their power are few and national. At least two years in office will be necessary to enable a man to judge of the trade and interests of the state which

he never saw. The time, I hope, will come, when this excellent country will furnish food, and freedom, (which is better than food, which is the food of the soul,) for fifty millions of happy people. Will any man say that the national business can be understood in one year?

Biennial elections appear to me, sir, an essential security to liberty. These are my reasons:—

Faction and enthusiasm are the instruments by which popular governments are destroyed. We need not talk of the power of an aristocracy. The people, when they lose their liberties, are cheated out of them. They nourish factions in their bosoms, which will subsist so long as abusing their honest credulity shall be the means of acquiring power. A democracy is a volcano, which conceals the fiery materials of its own destruction. These will produce an eruption, and carry desolation in their way. The people always mean right; and, if time is allowed for reflection and information, they will do right. I would not have the first wish, the momentary impulse of the public mind, become law; for it is not always the sense of the people, with whom I admit that all power resides. On great questions, we first hear the loud clamors of passion, artifice, and faction. I consider biennial elections as a security that the sober, second thought of the people shall be law. There is a calm review of public transactions, which is made by the citizens who have families and children, the pledges of their fidelity. To provide for popular liberty, we must take care that measures shall not be adopted without due deliberation. The member chosen for two years will feel some independence in his seat. The factions of the day will expire before the end of his term.

The people will be proportionably attentive to the merits of a candidate. Two years will afford opportunity to the member to deserve well of them, and they will require evidence that he has done it.

But, sir, the representatives are the grand inquisition of the Union. They are, by impeachment, to bring great offenders to justice. One year will not suffice to detect guilt, and to pursue it to conviction; therefore they will escape, and the balance of the two branches will be destroyed, and the people oppressed with impunity. The senators will represent the sovereignty of the states. The representatives are to represent the people. The offices ought to bear some proportion in point of importance. This will be impossible if they are chosen for one year only.

Will the people, then, blind the eyes of their own watchmen? Will they bind the hands which are to hold the sword for their defence? Will they impair their own power by an unreasonable jealousy of themselves?

For these reasons, I am clearly of opinion that the article is entitled to our approbation as it stands; and as it has been demanded, why annual elections were not preferred to biennial, permit me to retort the question, and to inquire, in my turn, what reason can be given, why, if annual elections are good, biennial elections are not better?

. . . . .

The Hon. Mr. BOWDOIN remarked on the idea suggested by the honorable gentleman from Scituate, [Mr. Turner,] who had said that nature pointed out the propriety of *annual* elections, by the *annual* renewal, and observed, that if the revolution of the heavenly bodies is to be the principle to regulate elections, it was not fixed to any period, as in some of the systems it would be very short; and in the last-discovered planet it would be eighty of our years. Gentlemen, he said, who had gone before him in debate, had clearly pointed out the alteration of the election of our federal representatives, from annual to biennial, to be justifiable. Annual elections may be necessary in this state, but in the choice of representatives from the continent, it ought to be longer; nor did he see any danger in its being so. Who, he asked, are the men to be elected? Are they not to be from among us? If they were to be a distinct body, then the doctrine of precaution, which gentlemen use, would be necessary; but, sir, they can make no laws, nor levy any taxes, but those to which they themselves must be subservient; they themselves must bear a part; therefore our security is guarantied by their being thus subject to the laws, if by nothing else.

Gen. HEATH. Mr. President, I consider myself not as an inhabitant of Massachusetts, but as a citizen of the United States. My ideas and views are commensurate with the continent; they extend in length from the St. Croix to the St. Maria, and in breadth from the Atlantic to the Lake of the Woods; for over all this extensive territory is the federal government to be extended.

I should not have risen on this paragraph, had it not been for some arguments which gentlemen have advanced respecting elections, and which, I think, tend to make dangerous impressions on the minds of the rising generation. It has been the general opinion that the liberties of the people are principally secured by the frequency of elections, and power returning again into their own hands. The first Parliament ever called in Europe was called by Constantine the Third, and to continue for one year. The worthy gentleman from Boston [Mr. Dawes] has mentioned a writer as a good authority, and who, he says, was twenty years compiling his works. I will produce one observation from this celebrated writer, Baron Montesquieu; it is as follows: "The greatness of power must be compensated by the brevity of the duration; most legislators have fixed it to a year; a longer space would be dangerous." Here, sir, we have not only the opinion of this celebrated writer, but he has also mentioned that most legislators were of the like opinion; but I shall come to our own country, where we shall find in what respect annual elections have always been held. This was the wisdom of our ancestors; it has been confirmed by time; therefore, sir, before we change it, we should carefully examine whether it be for the better. Local circumstances may render it expedient; but we should take care not to hold up to the rising generation, that it is a matter of indifference whether elections be annual or not; and this is what induced me to rise.

It is a novel idea, that representatives should be chosen for a considerable time, in order that they may learn their duty. The representative is one who appears in behalf of, and acts for, others; he ought, therefore, to be fully acquainted with the feelings, circumstances, and interests of the persons whom he represents; and this is learnt among them, not at a distant court. How frequently, on momentary occasions, do the members of the British Parliament wish to go home and consult their constituents, before they come to decision! This shows from what quarter they wish to obtain their information. With respect to the obtaining a knowledge of the circumstances and abilities of the other states, in order to an equal taxation, this must be acquired from the returns of the number of inhabitants, &c., which are to be found on the files of Congress; for I know not how length of time could furnish other information, unless the members should go from state to state, in order to find out the circumstances of the different states. I think representatives ought always to have a general knowledge of the interests of their constituents, as this alone can enable them properly to represent them.

But, sir, if there be charms in the paragraph now under consideration, they are these: Congress, at present, are continually sitting; but under the new Constitution, it is intended that Congress shall sit but once annually, for such time as may be necessary, and then adjourn. In this view, every gentleman acquainted with the business of legislation knows that there is much business, in every session, which is taken up and partly considered, but not finished; an adjournment keeps all this business alive; and at the next session it is taken up and completed, to the benefit of the people, in a great saving of expense, which would otherwise be lost; for a new legislature would not see through the eyes of those who went before them; consequently all business partly finished would be time lost, to the injury of the public. Therefore, as it seems to be intended that Congress shall have but two sessions in the two years for which the representatives are to be chosen, this consideration has reconciled me to the paragraph, and I am in favor of biennial elections.

Mr. TURNER, in reply to the Hon. Mr. Bowdoin, said he thought it an important consideration whether the elections were to be for one or for two years. He was, he said, greatly in favor of annual elections, and he thought, in the present instance, it would be establishing a dangerous precedent to adopt a change; for, says he, the principle may so operate, as, in time, our elections will be as *seldom* as the revolution of the star the honorable gentleman talks of.

Mr. DAWES, in answer to Gen. Heath, said, that the passage quoted from Montesquieu applied to *single* governments, and not to *confederate* ones.

Gen. BROOKS, (of Medford,) in reply to Gen. Heath, said, he recollected the passage of Montesquieu, but he also recollected that that writer had spoken highly of the British government. He then adverted to the objection to this section of Gen. Thompson and others, that biennial elections were a novelty, and said, we were not to consider whether a measure was new, but whether it was proper. Gentlemen had said that it had been the established custom of this country to elect annually; but, he asked, have we not gone from a colonial to an independent situation? We were then provinces; we are now an independent empire; our measures, therefore, says he, must change with our situation. Under our old government, the objects of legislation were few and divided; under our present, there are many, and must be united; and it appears necessary that, according to the magnitude and multiplicity of the business, the duration should be extended, he did not, he said, undertake to say how far. He then went into a view of the history of Parliaments: the modern northern nations, he said, had Parliaments; but they were called by their kings; and the time, business, &c., of them, depended wholly on their wills.

We can, therefore, says he, establish nothing from these. One general remark was, that, in the reigns of weak princes, the power and importance of Parliaments increased; in the reigns of strong and arbitrary kings, they always declined; and, says he, they have been *triennial,* and they have been *septennial.* The general combated the idea *that the liberties of the people depended on the duration of Parliament,* with much ability. Do we hear, asked he, that the people of England are deprived of their liberties? or that they are not as free now as when they had short Parliaments? On the contrary, do not writers agree, that life, liberty, and property, are nowhere better secured than in Great Britain, and that this security arises from their Parliaments being chosen for seven years? As such is the situation of the people of England, and as no instance can be given wherein biennial elections have been destructive to the liberties of the people, he concluded by asking, whether so much danger is to be apprehended from such elections as gentlemen imagined.

Gen. THOMPSON. Sir, Gentlemen have said a great deal about the history of old times. I confess I am not acquainted with such history; but I am, sir, acquainted with the history of my own country. I had the honor to be in the General Court last year, and am in it this year. I think, sir, that had the last administration continued one year longer, our liberties would have been lost, and the country involved in blood. Not so much, sir, from their bad conduct, but from the suspicions of the people of them. But, sir, a change took place; from this change pardons have been granted to the people, and peace is restored. This, sir, I say, is in favor of frequent elections.

. . . . .

He thought a change of election was for the best, even if the administration pleased the people. Do the members of Congress, says he, displease us, we call them home, and they obey. Now, where is the difference of their having been elected for one or two years? It is said that the members cannot learn sufficiently in that time. Sir, I hope we shall never send men who are *not learned.* Let these members know their dependence upon the people, and I say it will be a check on them, even if they were not good men. Here the general broke out in the following pathetic apostrophe: "O my country, never give up your annual elections! young men, never give up your jewel!" He apologized for his zeal. He then drew a comparison between the judges, &c., of this country before the revolution, who were dependent on Great Britain for their salaries, and those representatives dependent on the Continent. He concluded by hoping that the representatives would be annually elected, and thereby feel a greater dependence on the people.

Mr. GORE. It has been observed, that, in considering this great and momentous question, we ought to consult the sentiments of wise men, who have written on the subject of government, and thereby regulate our decision on this business. A passage is adduced from Montesquieu, stating that, where the people delegate great power, it ought to be compensated for by the shortness of the duration. Though strictly agreeing with the author, I do not see that it applies to the subject under consideration. This might be perfectly applicable to the ancient governments, where they had no idea of representation, or different checks in the legislature or administration of government; but, in the proposed Constitution, the powers of the whole government are limited to certain national objects, and are accurately defined. The House of Representatives is but one branch of the system, and can do nothing of itself. Montesquieu, in the sentiment alluded to, must have had in his mind the Epistates of Athens, or the Dictators of Rome; but certainly observations drawn from such sources can have no weight in considering things so efficiently different. Again, sir, gentlemen have said that annual elections were necessary to the preservation of liberty, and that, in proportion as the people of different nations have lengthened, beyond the term of a year, the duration of their representatives, they have lost their liberties, and that all writers have agreed in this. I may mistake; but I know no such thing as a representation of the people in any of the ancient republics. In England, from whence we receive many of our ideas on this subject, King John covenanted with his people to summon certain classes of men to Parliament. By the constitution of that country, the king alone can convoke, and he alone, previous to the revolution, could dissolve, the Parliament; but in the reign of William the Third, the patriots obtained an act limiting the duration of Parliament to three years. Soon after, a Parliament then sitting, and near expiring, a rebellion broke out, and the tories and Jacobites were gaining strength to support the Pretender's claim to the crown. Had they dissolved themselves, and a new Parliament been convoked, probably many of the very opponents to the government might have been elected. In that case they might have effected by law what they in vain attempted by arms.

. . . . .

[The Hon. Mr. KING] If, then, history can afford little or no instruction on this subject, the Convention must determine the question upon its own principles. It seems proper that the representative should be in office time enough to acquire that information which is necessary to form a right judgment; but that the time should not be so long as to remove from his mind the powerful check upon his conduct, that arises from the frequency of elections, whereby the people are enabled to remove an unfaithful representative, or to continue a faithful one. If the question is examined by this standard, perhaps it will appear that an election for two years is short enough for a representative in Congress. If one year is necessary for a representative to be useful in the state legislature, where the objects of his deliberations are local, and within his constant observation, two years do not appear too long, where the objects of deliberation are not confined to one state, but extend to thirteen states; where the complicated interests of united America are mingled with those of foreign nations; and where the great duties of national sovereignty will require his constant attention. When the representatives of the colony of Massachusetts were first chosen, the country was not settled more than twenty miles from Boston; they then held their offices for one year. The emigrants from Massachusetts, who settled on Connecticut River, appointed the representatives to meet in the General Court of that colony for only six months. Massachusetts, although her settlements have extended over almost her whole territory, has continued to depute representatives for only one year, and Connecticut for only six months; but as, in each of these colonies, when under the British government, the duties of the representatives were merely local, the great duties of sovereignty being vested in their king, so, since the revolution, their duties have continued local, many of the authorities of sovereignty being vested in Congress. It is now proposed to increase the powers of Congress; this will increase the duties of the representatives, and they must have a reasonable time to obtain the information necessary to a right discharge of their office.

It has been said that our ancestors never relinquished the idea of annual elections: this is an error. In 1643, the colonies of Plymouth, Massachusetts, Connecticut, and New Haven, united in a confederacy, which continued about forty years; each colony sent two commissioners as their representatives, and by the articles they were to be annually elected. About the year 1650, the General Court of Massachusetts instructed their commissioners to propose that the elections, instead of being annual, should be only once in three years. The alteration did not take place, but the anecdote proves that our ancestors have not had a uniform predilection for annual elections.

14

James Madison, Federalist, no. 52, 354–59
8 Feb. 1788

The qualifications of the elected being less carefully and properly defined by the State Constitutions, and being at the same time more susceptible of uniformity, have been very properly considered and regulated by the Convention. A representative of the United States must be of the age of twenty-five years; must have been seven years a citizen of the United States, must at the time of his election, be an inhabitant of the State he is to represent, and during the time of his service must be in no office under the United States. Under these reasonable limitations, the door of this part of the Foederal Government, is open to merit of every description, whether native or adoptive, whether young or old, and without regard to poverty or wealth, or to any particular profession of religious faith.

The term for which the Representatives are to be elected, falls under a second view which may be taken of this branch. In order to decide on the propriety of this article, two questions must be considered; first, whether

biennial elections will, in this case, be safe; secondly, whether they be necessary or useful.

First. As it is essential to liberty that the government in general, should have a common interest with the people; so it is particularly essential that the branch of it under consideration, should have an immediate dependence on, & an intimate sympathy with the people. Frequent elections are unquestionably the only policy by which this dependence and sympathy can be effectually secured. But what particular degree of frequency may be absolutely necessary for the purpose, does not appear to be susceptible of any precise calculation; and must depend on a variety of circumstances with which it may be connected. Let us consult experience, the guide that ought always to be followed, whenever it can be found.

The scheme of representation, as a substitute for a meeting of the citizens in person, being at most but very imperfectly known to ancient polity; it is in more modern times only, that we are to expect instructive examples. And even here, in order to avoid a research too vague and diffusive, it will be proper to confine ourselves to the few examples which are best known, and which bear the greatest analogy to our particular case. The first to which this character ought to be applied, is the House of Commons in Great Britain. The history of this branch of the English Constitution, anterior to the date of Magna Charta, is too obscure to yield instruction. The very existence of it has been made a question among political antiquaries. The earliest records of subsequent date prove, that Parliaments were to *sit* only, every year; not that they were to be *elected* every year. And even these annual sessions were left so much at the discretion of the monarch, that under various pretexts, very long and dangerous intermissions, were often contrived by royal ambition. To remedy this grievance, it was provided by a statute in the reign of Charles the second, that the intermissions should not be protracted beyond a period of three years. On the accession of Wil. III. when a revolution took place in the government, the subject was still more seriously resumed, and it was declared to be among the fundamental rights of the people, that Parliaments ought to be held *frequently*. By another statute which passed a few years later in the same reign, the term 'frequently' which had alluded to the triennial period settled in the time of Charles II. is reduced to a precise meaning, it being expressly enacted that a new parliament shall be called within three years after the determination of the former. The last change from three to seven years is well known to have been introduced pretty early in the present century, under an alarm for the Hanoverian succession. From these facts it appears, that the greatest frequency of elections which has been deemed necessary in that kingdom, for binding the representatives to their constituents, does not exceed a triennial return of them. And if we may argue from the degree of liberty retained even under septennial elections, and all the other vicious ingredients in the parliamentary constitution, we cannot doubt that a reduction of the period from seven to three years, with the other necessary reforms, would so far extend the influence of the people over their representatives, as to satisfy us, that biennial elections under the foederal system, cannot possibly be dangerous to the requisite dependence of the house of representatives on their constituents.

Elections in Ireland till of late were regulated entirely by the discretion of the crown, and were seldom repeated except on the accession of a new Prince, or some other contingent event. The parliament which commenced with George II. was continued throughout his whole reign, a period of about thirty-five years. The only dependence of the representatives on the people consisted, in the right of the latter to supply occasional vacancies, by the election of new members, and in the chance of some event which might produce a general new election. The ability also of the Irish parliament, to maintain the rights of their constituents, so far as the disposition might exist, was extremely shackled by the controul of the crown over the subjects of their deliberation. Of late these shackles, if I mistake not, have been broken; and octennial parliaments have besides been established. What effect may be produced by this partial reform, must be left to further experience. The example of Ireland, from this view of it, can throw but little light on the subject. As far as we can draw any conclusion from it, it must be, that if the people of that country have been able, under all these disadvantages, to retain any liberty whatever, the advantage of biennial elections would secure to them every degree of liberty which might depend on a due connection between their representatives and themselves.

Let us bring our enquiries nearer home. The example of these States when British colonies claims particular attention; at the same time that it is so well known, as to require little to be said on it. The principle of representation, in one branch of the Legislature at least, was established in all of them. But the periods of election were different. They varied from one to seven years. Have we any reason to infer from the spirit and conduct of the representatives of the people, prior to the revolution, that biennial elections would have been dangerous to the public liberties? The spirit which every where displayed itself at the commencement of the struggle; and which vanquished the obstacles to independence, is the best of proofs that a sufficient portion of liberty had been every where enjoyed to inspire both a sense of its worth, and a zeal for its proper enlargement. This remark holds good as well with regard to the then colonies, whose elections were least frequent, as to those whose elections were most frequent. Virginia was the colony which stood first in resisting the parliamentary usurpations of Great-Britain: it was the first also in espousing by public act, the resolution of independence. In Virginia nevertheless, if I have not been misinformed, elections under the former government were septennial. This particular example is brought into view, not as a proof of any peculiar merit, for the priority in those instances, was probably accidental; and still less of any advantage in *septennial* elections, for when compared with a greater frequency they are inadmissible: but merely as a proof, and I conceive it to be a very substantial proof, that the liberties of the people can be in no danger from *biennial* elections.

The conclusion resulting from these examples will be not a little strengthened by recollecting three circumstances. The first is that the Foederal Legislature will possess a part only of that supreme legislative authority which is vested completely in the British parliament, and which with a few exceptions was exercised by the colonial Assemblies and the Irish Legislature. It is a received and well founded maxim, that, where no other circumstances affect the case, the greater the power is, the shorter ought to be its duration; and, conversely, the smaller the power, the more safely may its duration be protracted. In the second place, it has, on another occasion, been shewn that the Foederal Legislature will not only be restrained by its dependence on the people as other legislative bodies are, but that it will be moreover watched and controuled by the several collateral Legislatures, which other legislative bodies are not. And in the third place, no comparison can be made between the means that will be possessed by the more permanent branches of the Foederal Government for seducing, if they should be disposed to seduce, the House of Representatives from their duty to the people; and the means of influence over the popular branch, possessed by the other branches of the governments above cited. With less power therefore to abuse, the Foederal Representatives, can be less tempted on one side, and will be doubly watched on the other.

15

JAMES MADISON, FEDERALIST, NO. 53, 359–66
9 Feb. 1788

I shall here perhaps be reminded of a current observation, "that where annual elections end, tyranny begins." If it be true as has often been remarked, that sayings which become proverbial, are generally founded in reason, it is not less true that when once established, they are often applied to cases to which the reason of them does not extend. I need not look for a proof beyond the case before us. What is the reason on which this proverbial observation is founded? No man will subject himself to the ridicule of pretending that any natural connection subsists between the sun or the seasons, and the period within which human virtue can bear the temptations of power. Happily for mankind, liberty is not in this respect confined to any single point of time; but lies within extremes, which afford sufficient latitude for all the variations which may be required by the various situations and circumstances of civil society. The election of magistrates might be, if it were found expedient, as in some instances it actually has been, daily, weekly, or monthly, as well as annual; and if circumstances may require a deviation from the rule on one side, why not also on the other side? Turning our attention to the periods established among ourselves, for the election of the most numerous branches of the state legislatures, we find them by no means coinciding any more in this instance, than in the elections of other civil magistrates. In Connecticut and Rhode-Island, the periods are half-yearly. In the other states, South-Carolina excepted, they are annual. In South-Carolina, they are biennial; as is proposed in the federal government. Here is a difference, as four to one, between the longest and shortest periods; and yet it would be not easy to shew that Connecticut or Rhode-Island is better governed, or enjoys a greater share of rational liberty than South-Carolina; or that either the one or the other of these states are distinguished in these respects, and by these causes, from the states whose elections are different from both.

In searching for the grounds of this doctrine, I can discover but one, and that is wholly inapplicable to our case. The important distinction so well understood in America between a constitution established by the people, and unalterable by the government; and a law established by the government, and alterable by the government, seems to have been little understood and less observed in any other country. Wherever the supreme power of legislation has resided, has been supposed to reside also, a full power to change the form of the government. Even in Great-Britain, where the principles of political and civil liberty have been most discussed; and where we hear most of the rights of the constitution, it is maintained that the authority of the parliament is transcendent and uncontroulable, as well with regard to the constitution, as the ordinary objects of legislative provision. They have accordingly, in several instances, actually changed, by legislative acts, some of the most fundamental articles of the government. They have in particular, on several occasions, changed the periods of election; and on the last occasion, not only introduced septennial, in place of triennial, elections; but by the same act continued themselves in place four years beyond the term for which they were elected by the people. An attention to these dangerous practices has produced a very natural alarm in the votaries of free government, of which frequency of elections is the corner stone; and has led them to seek for some security to liberty against the danger to which it is exposed. Where no constitution paramount to the government, either existed or could be obtained, no constitutional security similar to that established in the United States, was to be attempted. Some other security therefore was to be sought for; and what better security would the case admit, than that of selecting and appealing to some simple and familiar portion of time, as a standard for measuring the danger of innovations, for fixing the national sentiment, and for uniting the patriotic exertions. The most simple and familiar portion of time, applicable to the subject, was that of a year; and hence the doctrine has been inculcated by a laudable zeal to erect some barrier against the gradual innovations of an unlimited government, that the advance towards tyranny was to be calculated by the distance of departure from the fixed point of annual elections. But what necessity can there be of applying this expedient to a government, limited as the federal government will be, by the authority of a paramount constitution? Or who will pretend that the liberties of the people of America will not be more secure under biennial

elections, unalterably fixed by such a constitution, than those of any other nation would be, where elections were annual or even more frequent, but subject to alterations by the ordinary power of the government?

The second question stated is, whether biennial elections be necessary or useful? The propriety of answering this question in the affirmative will appear from several very obvious considerations.

No man can be a competent legislator who does not add to an upright intention and a sound judgment, a certain degree of knowledge of the subjects on which he is to legislate. A part of this knowledge may be acquired by means of information which lie within the compass of men in private as well as public stations. Another part can only be attained, or at least thoroughly attained, by actual experience in the station which requires the use of it. The period of service ought therefore in all such cases to bear some proportion to the extent of practical knowledge, requisite to the due performance of the service. The period of legislative service established in most of the states for the more numerous branch is, as we have seen, one year. The question then may be put into this simple form; does the period of two years bear no greater proportion to the knowledge requisite for federal legislation, than one year does to the knowledge requisite for state legislation? The very statement of the question in this form, suggests the answer that ought to be given to it.

In a single state the requisite knowledge, relates to the existing laws which are uniform throughout the state, and with which all the citizens are more or less conversant; and to the general affairs of the state, which lie within a small compass, are not very diversified, and occupy much of the attention and conversation of every class of people. The great theatre of the United States presents a very different scene. The laws are so far from being uniform, that they vary in every state; whilst the public affairs of the union are spread throughout a very extensive region, and are extremely diversified by the local affairs connected with them, and can with difficulty be correctly learnt in any other place, than in the central councils, to which a knowledge of them will be brought by the representatives of every part of the empire. Yet some knowledge of the affairs, and even of the laws of all the states, ought to be possessed by the members from each of the states. How can foreign trade be properly regulated by uniform laws, without some acquaintance with the commerce, the ports, the usages, and the regulations, of the different states? How can the trade between the different states be duly regulated without some knowledge of their relative situations in these and other points? How can taxes be judiciously imposed, and effectually collected, if they be not accommodated to the different laws and local circumstances relating to these objects in the different states? How can uniform regulations for the militia be duly provided without a similar knowledge of many internal circumstances by which the states are distinguished from each other? These are the principal objects of federal legislation, and suggest most forceably, the extensive information which the representatives ought to acquire. The other inferior objects will require a proportional degree of information with regard to them.

It is true that all these difficulties will by degrees be very much diminished. The most laborious task will be the proper inauguration of the government, and the primeval formation of a federal code. Improvements on the first draught will every year become both easier and fewer. Past transactions of the government will be a ready and accurate source of information to new members. The affairs of the union will become more and more objects of curiosity and conversation among the citizens at large. And the increased intercourse among those of different states will contribute not a little to diffuse a mutual knowledge of their affairs, as this again will contribute to a general assimilation of their manners and laws. But with all these abatements the business of federal legislation must continue so far to exceed both in novelty and difficulty, the legislative business of a single state as to justify the longer period of service assigned to those who are to transact it.

A branch of knowledge which belongs to the acquirements of a federal representative, and which has not been mentioned, is that of foreign affairs. In regulating our own commerce he ought to be not only acquainted with the treaties between the United States and other nations, but also with the commercial policy and laws of other nations. He ought not to be altogether ignorant of the law of nations, for that as far as it is a proper object of municipal legislation is submitted to the federal government. And although the house of representatives is not immediately to participate in foreign negotiations and arrangements, yet from the necessary connection between the several branches of public affairs, those particular branches will frequently deserve attention in the ordinary course of legislation, and will sometimes demand particular legislative sanction and cooperation. Some portion of this knowledge may no doubt be acquired in a man's closet; but some of it also can only be derived from the public sources of information; and all of it will be acquired to best effect by a practical attention to the subject during the period of actual service in the legislature.

There are other considerations of less importance perhaps, but which are not unworthy of notice. The distance which many of the representatives will be obliged to travel, and the arrangements rendered necessary by that circumstance, might be much more serious objections with fit men to this service if limited to a single year than if extended to two years. No argument can be drawn on this subject from the case of the delegates to the existing Congress. They are elected annually it is true; but their re-election is considered by the legislative assemblies almost as a matter of course. The election of the representatives by the people would not be governed by the same principle.

A few of the members, as happens in all such assemblies, will possess superior talents, will by frequent re-elections, become members of long standing; will be thoroughly masters of the public business, and perhaps not unwilling to avail themselves of those advantages. The greater the proportion of new members, and the less the information of the bulk of the members, the more apt will they be to

fall into the snares that may be laid for them. This remark is no less applicable to the relation which will subsist between the house of representatives and the senate.

It is an inconveniency mingled with the advantages of our frequent elections, even in single states where they are large and hold but one legislative session in the year, that spurious elections cannot be investigated and annulled in time for the decision to have its due effect. If a return can be obtained, no matter by what unlawful means, the irregular member, who takes his seat of course, is sure of holding it a sufficient time, to answer his purposes. Hence a very pernicious encouragement is given to the use of unlawful means for obtaining irregular returns. Were elections for the federal legislature to be annual, this practice might become a very serious abuse, particularly in the more distant states. Each house is, as it necessarily must be, the judge of the elections, qualifications and returns of its members, and whatever improvements may be suggested by experience for simplifying and accelerating the process in disputed cases. So great a portion of a year would unavoidably elapse, before an illegitimate member could be dispossessed of his seat, that the prospect of such an event, would be little check to unfair and illicit means of obtaining a seat.

All these considerations taken together warrant us in affirming that biennial elections will be as useful to the affairs of the public, as we have seen that they will be safe to the liberties of the people.

16

A NATIVE OF VIRGINIA, OBSERVATIONS UPON THE PROPOSED PLAN OF FEDERAL GOVERNMENT 1788
Monroe Writings 1:356–57

It will be asked by some,—Why should the Representatives to Congress be elected for two years, when in Virginia and the other States, the State Delegates are annually chosen? In answer to this question a variety of reasons occur; such as that they will have a great distance to go: That the purposes of their Legislation being purely federal, it will take them some time to become acquainted with the situation and interests of the respective States, as well as the relative situation and interest of the whole Union. That it would be difficult to get men of abilities to serve in an office, the re-election to which would be so frequent. If the election had been once in three years, it would perhaps have been an improvement. The unstable councils, the feeble laws, the relaxation of government which afflict this, and almost every State in the Union, may justly be attributed to the frequent changes which take place among the rulers in all the American governments.

17

James Madison to Thomas Jefferson
8 Oct. 1788
Papers 11:276

A law has also passed in that State [Pennsylvania] providing for the election of members for the House of Representatives and electors of the President. The act proposes that every Citizen throughout the State shall vote for the whole number of members allotted to the State. This mode of election will confine the choice to characters of general notoriety, and so far be favorable to merit. It is however liable to some popular objections urged against the tendency of the new system. In Virginia, I am inclined to think the State will be divided into as many districts, as there are to be members. In other States, as in Connecticut the Pena. example will probably be followed. And in others again a middle course be taken. It is perhaps to be desired that various modes should be tried, as by that means only the best mode can be ascertained.

18

James Wilson, The Legislative Department, Lectures on Law
1791
Works 1:407–11

By the constitution of the United States, the members of the house of representatives shall be chosen by the people of the several states. The electors, in each state, shall have the qualifications requisite for electors of the most numerous branch of the state legislature.

This regulation is generous and wise. It is generous; for it intrusts to the constitutions or to the legislatures of the several states, the very important power of ascertaining and directing the qualifications of those, who shall be entitled to elect the most numerous branch of the national legislature. This unsuspicious confidence evinces, in the national constitution, the most friendly disposition towards the governments of the several states. For how can such a proper disposition be evinced more strongly, than by providing that its legislature, so far as respects the most numerous branch of it, should stand upon the same foundation with theirs; and by providing farther, that this foundation should be continued or altered by the states themselves?

This regulation is wise as well as generous. An attention to its genuine principle and tendency must have a strong effect, in preventing or destroying the seeds of jealousy, which might otherwise spring up, with regard to the genius and views of the national government. It has embarked itself on the same bottom with the governments of the different states: can a stronger proof be given of its determination to sink or swim with them? Can proof be given of a stronger desire to live in mutual harmony and affection? This is an object of the last importance; for, to adopt an expression used by my Lord Bacon, "the uniting of the hearts and affections of the people is the life and true end of this work."

The remarks which I have made on this subject place, in a clear and striking point of view, the propriety, and indeed the political necessity, of a regulation made in another part of this constitution. In the fourth section of the fourth article it is provided, that, "the United States shall guaranty to every state in this Union a republican form of government." Its own existence, as a government of this description, depends on theirs.

As the doctrine concerning elections and the qualifications of electors is, in every free country, a doctrine of the first magnitude; and as the national constitution has, with regard to this doctrine, rested itself on the governments of the several states; it will be highly proper to take a survey of those provisions, which, on a subject so interesting, have been made by the different state constitutions: for every state has justly deemed the subject to be of constitutional importance.

In the constitution of Pennsylvania, the great principle, which animates and governs this subject, is secured by an explicit declaration, that "elections shall be free and equal." This is enumerated among the great points, which are "excepted out of the general powers of government, and shall for ever remain inviolate." The practical operation of this great and inviolable principle is thus specified and directed: "In elections by the citizens, every freeman of the age of twenty one years, having resided in the state two years next before the election, and within that time paid a state or county tax, which shall have been assessed at least six months before the election, shall enjoy the rights of an elector."

It well deserves, in this place, to be remarked, how congenial, upon this great subject, the principles of the constitution of Pennsylvania are to those adopted by the government of the Saxons. The Saxon freemen, as we have already seen, had votes in making their general laws. The freemen of Pennsylvania, as we now see, enjoy the rights of electors. This right, it has been shown, is equivalent, and, in a state of any considerable extent, must, on every principle of order and convenience, be substituted to the other. This is far from being the only instance, in which we shall have the pleasure of finding the old Saxon maxims of government renewed in the American constitutions. Particular attention will be paid to them, as they present themselves.

By the constitution of New Hampshire, "every male inhabitant, with town privileges, of twenty one years of age, paying for himself a poll tax, has a right to vote, in the town or parish wherein he dwells, in the election of representatives."

In Massachussetts, this right is, under the constitution, enjoyed by "every male person, being twenty one years of age, and resident in any particular town in the commonwealth for the space of one year next preceding, having a freehold estate within the same town, of the annual income of three pounds, or any estate of the value of sixty pounds." Every one so qualified may "vote in the choice of a representative for the said town."

The right to choose representatives in Rhode Island is vested in "the freemen of the respective towns or places." This regulation is specified in the charter of Charles the second. The state of Rhode Island and Providence Plantations has not assumed a form of government different from that, which is contained in the abovementioned charter.

The qualifications requisite, in the state of Connecticut, to entitle a person to vote at elections, are, maturity in years, quiet and peaceable behaviour, a civil conversation, and forty shillings freehold, or forty pounds personal estate; if the selectmen of this town certify a person qualified in those respects, he is admitted a freeman on his taking an oath of fidelity to the state.

It ought to be observed, by the way, that this power to admit persons to be freemen, or to exclude them from being freemen, according to the sentiments which others entertain concerning their conversation and behaviour, is a power of a very extraordinary nature; and is certainly capable of being exercised for very extraordinary purposes.

The constitution of New York ordains, "that every male inhabitant of full age, who shall have personally resided within one of the counties of the state, for six months immediately preceding the day of election, shall, at such election, be entitled to vote for representatives of the said county in assembly; if during the time aforesaid he shall have been a freeholder, possessing a freehold of the value of twenty pounds, within the said county, or have rented a tenement therein of the yearly value of forty shillings; and been rated and actually paid taxes to the state."

"All inhabitants of New Jersey, of full age, who are worth fifty pounds, proclamation money, clear estate within that government, and have resided within the county, in which they shall claim a vote, for twelve months immediately preceding the election, shall be entitled to vote for representatives in assembly."

The right of suffrage is not specified in the constitution of Delaware; but it is provided, that, in the election of members of the legislature, it "shall remain as exercised by law at present."

In Maryland, "all freemen above twenty one years of age, having a freehold of fifty acres of land in the county, in which they offer to vote, and residing therein; and all freemen having property in the state above the value of thirty pounds current money, and having resided in the county, in which they offer to vote, one whole year next preceding the election, shall have a right of suffrage in the election of delegates for such county."

We find, in the constitution of Virginia, no specification of the right of suffrage: it is declared, however, that this right shall remain as it was exercised at the time when that constitution was made.

It is provided by the constitution of North Carolina, "that all freemen of the age of twenty one years, who have been inhabitants of any county within the state twelve months immediately preceding the day of any election, and shall have paid publick taxes, shall be entitled to vote for members of the house of commons, for the county in which they reside."

According to the constitution of South Carolina, "every free white man, of the age of twenty one years, being a citizen of the state, and having resided in it two years previous to the day of election, and who has a freehold of fifty acres of land, or a town lot, of which he hath been legally seized and possessed at least six months before such election, or, not having such freehold or lot, has resided within the election district, in which he offers to give his vote, six months before the election, and has, the preceding year, paid a tax of three shillings sterling towards the support of government, shall have a right to vote for members of the house of representatives for the election district, in which he holds such property, or is so resident."

I am not possessed of the present constitution of Georgia. By its late constitution, it was provided, that "all male white inhabitants, of the age of twenty one years, and possessed, in their own right, of ten pounds value, and liable to pay tax in the state, or being of any mechanick trade, and shall have been a resident six months in the state, shall have a right to vote at all elections for representatives."

From the foregoing enumeration—its length and its minuteness will be justified by its importance—from the foregoing enumeration of the provisions, which have been made, in the several states, concerning the right of suffrage, we are well warranted, I think, in drawing this broad and general inference—that, in the United States, this right is extended to every freeman, who, by his residence, has given evidence of his attachment to the country, who, by having property, or by being in a situation to acquire property, possesses a common interest with his fellow citizens; and who is not in such uncomfortable circumstances, as to render him necessarily dependent, for his subsistence, on the will of others.

By the same enumeration, we are enabled, with conscious pleasure, to view and to display the close approximation, which, on this great subject, the constitutions of the American States have made, to what we have already seen to be the true principles and the correct theory of freedom.

Again; the same enumeration places in the strongest and most striking light, the wisdom and the generous confidence, which rested one of the principal pillars of the national government upon the foundation prepared for it by the governments of the several states.

19

ST. GEORGE TUCKER,
BLACKSTONE'S COMMENTARIES 1:APP. 208–15
1803

I. The constituent parts of the British parliament, are, the house of commons, the house of lords, and the king, sitting there in his royal political capacity, in the union of which three estates the body politic of the kingdom consists. Analogous to which, though very differently constituted, we have seen the house of representatives and senate of the United States, and *sub modo* the president of the United States forming the general congress, or the supreme political legislature of the federal government. Thus far the great outlines of both governments appear to run parallel: they will however upon a nearer scrutiny be found frequently to diverge. We shall begin with the house of commons, which forms the democractical part of the British constitution.

"In a free state" says the author of the commentaries "every man who is supposed a free agent, ought to be in some measure his own governor, and therefore a branch at least of the legislative power should reside in the whole body of the people. In so large a state as Britain, therefore, it is very wisely contrived that the people should do that by their representatives, which it is impracticable to perform in person; representatives, chosen by a number of minute and separate districts, wherein all the voters are, or easily may be, distinguished. He adds, elsewhere, "In a democracy there can be no exercise of sovereignty, but by suffrage, which is the declaration of the people's will. In all democracies, therefore, it is of the utmost importance to regulate by whom and in what manner the suffrages are to be collected. In England where the people do not debate in a collective body, but by representation, the exercise of their sovereignty consists in the choice of representatives"

Such are the principles laid down by this distinguished writer, from whence one would be led to conclude that the elections for members of the house of commons were regulated in a manner as conformable thereto as possible. That where there was an equality of right, an equality of representation would also be found; and that the right of suffrage would be regulated by some uniform standard, so that the same class of men should not possess privileges in one place, which they are denied in another.

1. By equality of representation, it will be understood, that I mean the right which any given number of citizens possessing equal qualifications in respect to the right of suffrage, have, to an equal share in the councils of the nation by their representatives, as an equal number of their fellow citizens in any other part of the state enjoy.

In England and in Wales there are fifty-two counties, represented by knights, elected by the proprietors of lands; the cities and boroughs are represented by citizens and burgesses, chosen by the mercantile part, or supposed trading part of the nation. . . . The whole number of English representatives, is 513 and of Scots, 45. The members of boroughs now bear above a quadruple proportion to those for counties; from whence one would, at first, be apt to conclude, that the population or at least the number of electors in the counties were equal; and, that the boroughs were at least four times as populous as the counties, collectively. The former of these suppositions would be perfectly unfounded in truth; the latter perhaps may approach nearer to it. In truth, were the latter supposition well founded, the equality of representation would not be much advanced by it. . . . In London which is supposed to contain near a seventh part of the number of the inhabitants of all England, they are entitled to four members only in parliament. The inconsiderable borough of Melcomb Regis in Dorsetshire sends as many. Manchester and Birmingham, two large populous, flourishing, manufacturing towns have no representative, whilst the depopulated borough of Old Sarum, without a house or an inhabitant, is the vehicle through which two members obtain their seats in parliament; a representation equal to that of the most populous county.

Many other corresponding instances might be adduced to prove the inequality of representation; but they are unnecessary. . . . In America the representation is in exact proportion to the inhabitants. Every part of the states is therefore equally represented, and consequently has an equal share in the government. Here the principle that the whole body of the people should have a share in the legislature, and every individual entitled to vote, possess an equal voice, is practically enforced. . . . In England it is a mere illusion.

It is but justice to acknowledge that attempts have repeatedly been made, to effect a reform in this part of the British constitution: the voice of the nation has more than once loudly demanded it . . . but their rulers, like the God Baal, have been otherwise employed; or deaf, or peradventure asleep, and could not be awaked.

2. As to the right of suffrage in the individual, nearly the same principle seems to prevail in respect to the qualification in lands, in both countries; and the different manner of ascertaining it, is not sufficient to require any remark. I shall only observe that copy-holders, whose interest, in almost every other respect in their lands, seem to be equal to that of a free-holder, (at least, such as have inheritances in them) are not admitted to the right of suffrage. The proportion of copy-holders for life, or of inheritance, to the freehold tenants of the counties, I have never heard estimated: it is, however, very considerable.

"The right of voting in boroughs is various," says Blackstone, "depending entirely on the several charters, customs, and constitutions of the respective places, which has occasioned infinite disputes." It may vary no less perhaps in the different states of America, but there is this advantage, that however various, there can be little room for doubts, or disputes on the subject. In Virginia the qualification to vote in boroughs, is as fixed and invariable as in the counties. One principle however must not be lost sight of, which perhaps should have come under the last head. No borough can ever be entitled to a representative, whenever the number of inhabitants shall, for the space of seven years together, be less than half the number of the inhabitants of any county in Virginia. In England the boroughs retain the right of representation, as we have seen, even after they have lost their inhabitants. Another circumstance respecting them is no less notorious; though the right of suffrage is in the burgher, the power of sending the member to parliament is in the lord of the soil; a number of the boroughs being private property, and the burghers, who are tenants, bound to vote as their lord shall direct: the shadow of the right of suffrage is all these burghers possess . . . to the exercise of that right they are as much strangers, as to the pyramids of Egypt, or the ruins of Palmyra. It is scarcely possible that the electors of America should ever be degraded to a similar state of political mechanism.

3. The qualification of the members is the next object of our comparison. In England a knight of the shire must possess an estate in lands of the value of 600*l.* sterling, per annum, and a member for a borough of one half that value, except the eldest sons of peers; and of persons qualified to be knights of shires, and members of the two universities.

This at first view appears to be a proper and necessary precaution, as far as it extends, to secure the independence of the members of that branch of the legislature. But this argument is neither conclusive in fact, nor even in theory. Neither of these sums is an adequate support for a man moving in the rank of a member of the British parliament. Luxury has taken too deep root in the nation to authorize the supposition generally; and if it fails in general, it is of little avail that a few instances may be found of persons in that sphere, whose expences do not exceed the requisite qualification in point of fortune. But if the principle be admitted that an independent fortune be necessary to secure the independence of the member in his legislative conduct, it would seem that the measure ought to be the same to all the members, since, according to the doctrine laid down by our author, a member though chosen by a particular district, when elected, serves the whole realm, the end of his election not being particular, but general. An equality of qualification should then have taken place; and if 600*l.* is necessary to secure the independence of the member, those who possess but half as much ought to be excluded; on the other hand, if 300*l.* be a competent sum for that purpose, how injurious must that law be to the rights of the citizen, which requires the qualification which is acknowledged to be sufficient for every good purpose, to be doubled. But a qualification in respect to estate is neither equally nor uniformly required; if the member elected should happen to be the eldest son of a peer, or of a person qualified to be knight of the shire; in either of these cases it is altogether dispensed with. The effect of this, as it respects the former of these classes of men, we shall speak of hereafter. As to the latter, it is sufficient to say, that presumption is allowed to supply the place of evidence; and both the exceptions prove the deviation from the general principle to have originated in the influence of the aristocratical interest of the nation.

In America no qualification in point of estate is required in the representative in congress by the constitution; and perhaps we may with some propriety insist that any such qualification would be not only unnecessary, but contrary to the true interests of their constituents. In England the interests of the crown, of the nobles, and of the people, are confessedly distinct and often diametrically opposite. In America all are citizens possessing equal rights in their civil capacities and relations; there are no distinct orders among us, except while in the actual exercise of their several political functions. When the member quits his seat, or the magistrate descends from the bench, he is instantly one of the people. The pageantry of office reaches not beyond the threshold of the place where it is exercised; and civil distinctions privileges or emoluments independent of the office are interdicted by the principles of our government. To secure the independence of the members conduct, perhaps no previous qualification, in point of estate may be requisite; though such a qualification might for another reason have been not improper: that by sharing in the burthens of government, he might be restrained from an undue imposition of them upon his constituents. The law of the state indeed requires that the representative should be a freeholder, as well as a resident in the district; but both these provisions, as they require qualifications which the constitution does not, may possibly be found to be nugatory, should any man possess a sufficient influence in a district in which he neither resides nor is a freeholder, to obtain a majority of the suffrages in his favor. But how strong soever the reasons in favour of a qualification in point of estate might have been, on the grounds last spoken of, they were overbalanced probably by two considerations.

First, that in a representative government, the people have an undoubted right to judge for themselves of the qualification of their delegate, and if their opinion of the integrity of their representative will supply the want of estate, there can be no reason for the government to interfere, by saying, that the latter must and shall overbalance the former.

Secondly; by requiring a qualification in estate it may often happen, that men the best qualified in other respects might be incapacitated from serving their country. To which we may add, that the compensation which the members receive for their services, is probably such an equivalent, as must secure them from undue influence, or concessions from motives of interest.

A second qualification required by the British constitution is, that the person elected shall be of the age of twenty-one years at the time of his election: ours with more caution and perhaps with better reason, requires that he shall have attained to the age of twenty-five years.

These are all the positive qualifications, in which there appears to be any very material difference worth remarking. Of negative ones, those which relate to the incapacity of certain descriptions of placemen and pensioners in England, are limited to a very small part of the host of the former who depend upon the crown for support; and in respect to the latter only such pensioners as hold during the pleasure of the crown, are excluded. A list of placemen and pensioners in either the present or last parliament of England was published some years ago. . . . I do not recollect their exact number, but I can be positive that it exceeded two hundred. A number sufficient to secure the most unlimited influence in the crown: to these let us add the eldest sons of peers, and ask whether in a question between the commons and the nobility, it would be probable, that they would give an independent vote, against the order in which they soon hoped to obtain a permanent rank and station.

Lastly, let me ask, if the conduct of those borough members who hold their seats by the appointment of members of the other house, or perhaps of their own, may reasonably be expected to be uninfluenced by the nod of their patrons? Can a house thus constituted be said to represent the people, the democratic part of the government? Can they be said to form a check upon the proceedings of the nobility, or the measures of the crown? The question only requires to be understood, to be answered decidedly in the negative.

We have seen that no person holding any office under the United States, shall be a member of either house during his continuance in office; and that no member of congress shall during the time for which he was elected, be appointed to any civil office under the authority of the United States, which shall have been created, or the emoluments thereof increased during such time. These provisions appear to be more effectual to secure the independence of the members, than any qualification in respect to estate: but, they seem not to have been carried quite far enough.

20

JOSEPH STORY, COMMENTARIES ON THE CONSTITUTION 2:§§ 572–80
1833

§ 572. First; the principle of representation. The American people had long been in the enjoyment of the privilege of electing, at least, one branch of the legislature; and, in some of the colonies, of electing all the branches composing the legislature. A house of representatives, under various denominations, such as a house of delegates, a house of commons, or, simply, a house of representatives, emanating directly from, and responsible to, the people, and possessing a distinct and independent legislative authority, was familiar to all the colonies, and was held by them in the highest reverence and respect. They justly thought, that as the government in general should always have a common interest with the people, and be administered for their good; so it was essential to their rights and liberties, that the most numerous branch should have an immediate dependence upon, and sympathy with, the people. There was no novelty in this view. It was not the mere result of a state of colonial dependence, in which their jealousy was awake to all the natural encroachments of power in a foreign realm. They had drawn their opinions and principles from the practice of the parent country. They knew the inestimable value of the house of commons, as a component branch of the British parliament; and they believed, that it had at all times furnished the best security against the oppressions of the crown, and the

aristocracy. While the power of taxation, of revenue, and of supplies, remained in the hands of a popular branch, it was difficult for usurpation to exist for any length of time without check; and prerogative must yield to that necessity, which controlled at once the sword and the purse. No reasoning, therefore, was necessary to satisfy the American people of the advantages of a house of representatives, which should emanate directly from themselves; which should guard their interests, support their rights, express their opinions, make known their wants, redress their grievances, and introduce a pervading popular influence throughout all the operations of the government. Experience, as well as theory, had settled it in their minds, as a fundamental principle of a free government, and especially of a republican government, that no laws ought to be passed without the co-operation and consent of the representatives of the people; and that these representatives should be chosen by themselves without the intervention of any other functionaries to intercept, or vary their responsibility.

§ 573. The principle, however, had been hitherto applied to the political organization of the state legislatures only; and its application to that of the federal government was not without some diversity of opinion. This diversity had not its origin in any doubt of the correctness of the principle itself, when applied to simple republics; but, the propriety of applying it to cases of confederated republics was affected by other independent considerations. Those, who might wish to retain a very large portion of state sovereignty, in its representative character, in the councils of the Union, would naturally desire to have the house of representatives elected by the state in its political character, as under the old confederation. Those, on the other hand, who wished to impart to the government a national character, would as naturally desire an independent election by the people themselves in their primary meetings. Probably these circumstances had some operation upon the votes given on the question in the convention itself. For it appears, that upon the original proposition in the convention, "That the members of the first branch of the national legislature ought to be elected by the *people* of the several states, six states voted for it, two against it, and two were divided. And upon a subsequent motion to strike out the word "people," and insert in its place the word "legislatures," three states voted in the affirmative and eight in the negative. At a subsequent period a motion, that the representatives should be appointed in such manner as the legislature of each state should direct, was negatived, six states voting in the affirmative, three in the negative, and one being divided; and the final vote in favour of an election by the people was decided by the vote of nine states in the affirmative, one voting in the negative, and one being divided. The result was not therefore obtained without much discussion and argument; though at last an entire unanimity prevailed. It is satisfactory to know, that a fundamental principle of public liberty has been thus secured to ourselves and our posterity, which will for ever indissolubly connect the interests of the people with the interests of the Union. Under the confederation, though the delegates to congress might have been elected by the people, they were, in fact, in all the states except two, elected by the state legislature.

§ 574. We accordingly find, that in the section under consideration, the house of representatives is required to be composed of representatives chosen by the people of the several states. The choice, too, is to be made immediately by them; so that the power is direct; the influence direct; and the responsibility direct. If any intermediate agency had been adopted, such as a choice through an electoral college, or by official personages, or by select and specially qualified functionaries *pro hac vice*, it is obvious, that the dependence of the representative upon the people, and the responsibility to them, would have been far less felt, and far more obstructed. Influence would have naturally grown up with patronage; and here, as in many other cases, the legal maxim would have applied, *causa proxima, non remota, spectatur*. The select body would have been at once the patrons and the guides of the representative; and the people themselves have become the instruments of subverting their own rights and power.

§ 575. The *indirect* advantages from this immediate agency of the people in the choice of their representatives are of incalculable benefit, and deserve a brief mention in this place, because they furnish us with matter for most serious reflection, in regard to the actual operations and influences of republican governments. In the first place, the right confers an additional sense of personal dignity and duty upon the mass of the people. It gives a strong direction to the education, studies, and pursuits of the whole community. It enlarges the sphere of action, and contributes, in a high degree, to the formation of the public manners, and national character. It procures to the common people courtesy and sympathy from their superiors, and diffuses a common confidence, as well as a common interest, through all the ranks of society. It awakens a desire to examine, and sift, and debate all public proceedings, and thus nourishes a lively curiosity to acquire knowledge, and, at the same time, furnishes the means of gratifying it. The proceedings and debates of the legislature; the conduct of public officers from the highest to the lowest; the character and conduct of the executive and his ministers; the struggles, intrigues, and conduct of different parties; and the discussion of the great public measures and questions, which agitate and divide the community, are not only freely canvassed, and thus improve and elevate conversation; but they gradually furnish the mind with safe and solid materials for judgment upon all public affairs; and check that impetuosity and rashness, to which sudden impulses might otherwise lead the people, when they are artfully misguided by selfish demagogues, and plausible schemes of change.

§ 576. But this fundamental principle of an immediate choice by the people, however important, would alone be insufficient for the public security, if the right of choice had not many auxiliary guards and accompaniments. It was indispensable, secondly, to provide for the qualifications of the electors. It is obvious, that even when the principle is established, that the popular branch of the legislature shall emanate directly from the people, there still remains a very serious question, by whom and in what manner the choice shall be made. It is a question vital to the system, and in a practical sense decisive, as to the durability and efficiency of the powers of government. Here, there is much room for doubt, and ingenious speculation, and theoretical inquiry; upon which different minds may arrive, and indeed have arrived, at very different results. To whom ought the right of suffrage, in a free government, to be confided? Or, in other words, who ought to be permitted to vote in the choice of the representatives of the people? Ought the right of suffrage to be absolutely universal? Ought it to be qualified and restrained? Ought it to belong to many, or few? If there ought to be restraints and qualifications, what are the true boundaries and limits of such restraints and qualifications?

§ 577. These questions are sufficiently perplexing and disquieting in theory; and in the practice of different states, and even of free states, ancient as well as modern, they have assumed almost infinite varieties of form and illustration. Perhaps they do not admit of any general, much less of any universal answer, so as to furnish an unexceptionable and certain rule for all ages and all nations. The manners, habits, institutions, characters, and pursuits of different nations; the local position of the territory, in regard to other nations; the actual organizations and classes of society; the influences of peculiar religious, civil, or political institutions; the dangers, as well as the difficulties, of the times; the degrees of knowledge or ignorance pervading the mass of society; the national temperament, and even the climate and products of the soil; the cold and thoughtful gravity of the north; and the warm and mercurial excitability of tropical or southern regions; all these may, and probably will, introduce modifications of principle, as well as of opinion, in regard to the right of suffrage, which it is not easy either to justify or to overthrow.

§ 578. The most strenuous advocate for universal suffrage has never yet contended, that the right should be absolutely universal. No one has ever been sufficiently visionary to hold, that all persons, of every age, degree, and character, should be entitled to vote in all elections of all public officers. Idiots, infants, minors, and persons insane or utterly imbecile, have been, without scruple, denied the right, as not having the sound judgment and discretion fit for its exercise. In many countries, persons guilty of crimes have also been denied the right, as a personal punishment, or as a security to society. In most countries, females, whether married or single, have been purposely excluded from voting, as interfering with sound policy, and the harmony of social life. In the few cases, in which they have been permitted to vote, experience has not justified the conclusion, that it has been attended with any correspondent advantages, either to the public, or to themselves. And yet it would be extremely difficult, upon any mere theoretical reasoning, to establish any satisfactory principle, upon which the one half of every society has thus been systematically excluded by the other half from all right of participating in government, which would not, at the same time, apply to and justify many other exclusions. If it be said, that all men have a natural, equal, and unalienable right to vote, because they are all born free, and equal; that they all have common rights and interests entitled to protection, and therefore have an equal right to decide, either personally or by their chosen representatives, upon the laws and regulations, which shall control, measure, and sustain those rights and interests; that they cannot be compelled to surrender, except by their free consent, what, by the bounty and order of Providence, belongs to them in common with all their race;—what is there in these considerations, which is not equally applicable to females, as free, intelligent, moral, responsible beings, entitled to equal rights, and interests, and protection, and having a vital stake in all the regulations and laws of society? And if an exception, from the nature of the case, could be felt in regard to persons, who are idiots, infants, and insane; how can this apply to persons, who are of more mature growth, and are yet deemed minors by the municipal law? Who has an original right to fix the time and period of pupilage, or minority? Whence was derived the right of the ancient Greeks and Romans to declare, that women should be deemed never to be of age, but should be subject to perpetual guardianship? Upon what principle of natural law did the Romans, in after times, fix the majority of females, as well as of males, at twenty-five years? Who has a right to say, that in England it shall, for some purposes, be at fourteen, for others, at seventeen, and for all, at twenty-one years; while, in France, a person arrives, for all purposes, at majority, only at thirty years, in Naples at eighteen, and in Holland at twenty-five? Who shall say, that one man is not as well qualified, as a voter, at eighteen years of age, as another is at twenty-five, or a third at forty; and far better, than most men are at eighty? And if any society is invested with authority to settle the matter of the age and sex of voters, according to its own view of its policy, or convenience, or justice, who shall say, that it has not equal authority, for like reasons, to settle any other matter regarding the rights, qualifications, and duties of voters?

§ 579. The truth seems to be, that the right of voting, like many other rights, is one, which, whether it has a fixed foundation in natural law or not, has always been treated in the practice of nations, as a strictly civil right, derived from, and regulated by each society, according to its own circumstances and interests. It is difficult, even in the abstract, to conceive how it could have otherwise been treated. The terms and conditions, upon which any society is formed and organized, must essentially depend upon the will of those, who are associated; or at least of those, who constitute a majority, actually controlling the rest. Originally, no man could have any right but to act for himself; and the power to choose a chief magistrate or other officer to exercise dominion or authority over others, as well as himself, could arise only upon a joint consent of the others to such appointment; and their consent might be qualified exactly according to their own interests, or power, or policy. The choice of representatives to act in a legislative capacity is not only a refinement of much later stages of actual association and civilization, but could scarcely occur, until the society had assumed to itself the right to introduce such institutions, and to confer such privileges, as it deemed conducive to the public good, and to prohibit the existence of any other. In point of fact, it is well known, that representative legislative bodies, at least in the form now used, are the peculiar invention of modern times, and were unknown to antiquity. If, then, every well organized society has the right to consult for the common good of the whole, and if, upon the principles of natural law, this right is conceded by the very union of society, it seems difficult to assign any limit to this right, which is compatible with the due attainment of the end proposed. If, therefore, any society shall deem the common good and interests of the whole society best promoted under the particular circumstances, in which it is placed, by a restriction of the right of suffrage, it is not easy to state any solid ground of objection to its exercise of such an authority. At least, if any society has a clear right to deprive females, constituting one half of the whole population, from the right of suffrage, (which, with scarcely an exception, has been uniformly maintained,) it will require some astuteness to find upon what ground this exclusion can be vindicated, which does justify, or at least excuse, many other exclusions. Government (to use the pithy language of Mr. Burke) has been deemed a practical thing, made for the happiness of mankind, and not to furnish out a spectacle of uniformity to gratify the schemes of visionary politicians.

§ 580. Without laying any stress upon this theoretical reasoning, which is brought before the reader, not so much because it solves all doubts and objections, as because it presents a view of the serious difficulties attendant upon the assumption of an original and unalienable right of suffrage, as originating in natural law, and independent of civil law, it may be proper to state, that every civilized society has uniformly fixed, modified, and regulated the right of suffrage for itself, according to its own free will and pleasure. Every constitution of government in these United States has assumed, as a fundamental principle, the right of the people of the state to alter, abolish, and modify the form of its own government, according to the sovereign pleasure of the people. In fact, the people of each state have gone much farther, and settled a far more critical question, by deciding, who shall be the voters, entitled to approve and reject the constitution framed by a delegated body under their direction. In the adoption of no state constitution has the assent been asked of any but the qualified voters; and women, and minors, and other persons, not recognised as voters by existing laws, have been studiously excluded. And yet the constitution has been deemed entirely obligatory upon them, as well as upon the minority, who voted against it. From this it will be seen, how little, even in the most free of republican governments, any abstract right of suffrage, or any original and indefeasible privilege, has been recognised in practice. If this consideration does not satisfy our minds, it at least will prepare us to presume, that there may be an almost infinite diversity in the established right of voting, without any state being able to assert, that its own mode is exclusively founded in natural justice, or is most conformable to sound policy, or is best adapted to the public security. It will teach us, that the question is necessarily complex and intricate in its own nature, and is scarcely susceptible of any simple solution, which shall rigidly apply to the circumstances and conditions, the interests and the feelings, the institutions and the manners of all nations. What may best promote the public weal, and secure the public liberty, and advance the public prosperity in one age or nation, may totally fail of similar results under local, physical, or moral predicaments essentially different.

SEE ALSO:

Ashby v. *White*, 92 Eng. Rep. 126 (Q.B. 1783)
Records of the Federal Convention, Farrand 1:20, 27–28, 46, 56, 130, 140–41, 142–44, 353–54, 364–66, 367–68; 2:151, 153, 163–64, 178, 206–8, 209–10
Elbridge Gerry to Senate President and House Speaker in Massachusetts, 18 Oct. 1787, Farrand 3:128

James McHenry, Maryland House of Delegates, 29 Nov. 1787, Farrand 3:146–47
Thomas McKean, Pennsylvania Ratifying Convention, 11 Dec. 1787, Elliot 2:532–33
George Nicholas, Virginia Ratifying Convention, 3 June 1788, Elliot 3:8–9
James Maclaine, North Carolina Ratifying Convention, 24 July 1788, Elliot 4:28–29
Georgia Constitution of 1789, art. 4, Thorpe 2:789
Charles Pinckney to Rufus King, 26 Jan. 1789, Farrand 3:355
Charles Pinckney to James Madison, 28 Mar. 1789, Farrand 3:355
Alabama Constitution of 1819, art. 3, sec. 5, Thorpe 1:99
New York Constitution of 1821, art. 2, secs. 1–4, Thorpe 5:2642–43
James Kent, Commentaries 1:215–16 (1826)
William Rawle, A View of the Constitution of the United States 41–42 (2d ed. 1829)
Joseph Story, Commentaries on the Constitution 2:§§ 582–609 (1833)

Article 1, Section 2, Clause 2

No Person shall be a Representative who shall not have attained to the age of twenty five Years, and been seven Years a Citizen of the United States, and who shall not, when elected, be an Inhabitant of that State in which he shall be chosen.

1. William Blackstone, Commentaries (1765)
2. Records of the Federal Convention
3. Debate in Massachusetts Ratifying Convention, 17 Jan. 1788
4. A Republican Federalist, no. 6, 2 Feb. 1788
5. Wilson Nicholas, Virginia Ratifying Convention, 4 June 1788
6. James Madison, House of Representatives, 22 May 1789
7. James Wilson, The Legislative Department, Lectures on Law, 1791
8. House of Representatives, Maryland Contested Election, 12, 16 Nov. 1807
9. Thomas Jefferson to Joseph C. Cabell, 31 Jan. 1814
10. Joseph Story, Commentaries on the Constitution (1833)

1

WILLIAM BLACKSTONE, COMMENTARIES 1:169–70
1765

2. Our second point is the qualification of persons to be elected members of the house of commons. This depends upon the law and custom of parliaments, and the statutes referred to in the margin.[1] And from these it appears, 1.

[1] 1 Hen. V. c. 1.   23 Hen. VI. c. 15.   1 W. & M. st. 2. c. 2.   5 & 6 W. & M. c. 7.   11 & 12 W. III. c. 2.   12 & 13 W. III. c. 10.   6 Ann. c. 7.   9 Ann. c. 5.   1 Geo. I. c. 56.   15 Geo. II. c. 22.   33 Geo. II. c. 20.

That they must not be aliens born, or minors. 2. That they must not be any of the twelve judges, because they sit in the lords' house; nor of the clergy, for they sit in the convocation; nor persons attainted of treason or felony, for they are unfit to sit anywhere. 3. That sheriffs of counties, and mayors and bailiffs of boroughs, are not eligible in their respective jurisdictions, as being returning officers; but that sheriffs of one county are eligible to be knights of another. 4. That, in strictness, all members ought to be inhabitants of the places for which they are chosen: but this is intirely disregarded. 5. That no persons concerned in the management of any duties or taxes created since 1692, except the commissioners of the treasury, nor any of the officers following, (viz. commissioners of prizes, transports, sick and wounded, wine licences, navy, and victualling; secretaries or receivers of prizes; comptrollers of the army accounts; agents for regiments; governors of plantations and their deputies; officers of Minorca or Gibraltar; officers of the excise and customs; clerks or deputies in the several offices of the treasury, exchequer, navy, victualling, admiralty, pay of the army or navy, secretaries of state, salt, stamps, appeals, wine licences, hackney coaches, hawkers and pedlars) nor any persons that hold any new office under the crown created since 1705, are capable of being elected members. 6. That no person having a pension under the crown during pleasure, or for any term of years, is capable of being elected. 7. That if any member accepts an office under the crown, except an officer in the army or navy accepting a new commission, his seat is void; but such member is capable of being re-elected. 8. That all knights of the shire shall be actual knights, or such notable esquires and gentlemen, as have estates sufficient to be knights, and by no means of the degree of yeomen. This is reduced to a still greater certainty, by ordaining, 9. That every knight of a shire shall have a clear estate of freehold or copyhold to the value of six hundred pounds *per annum*, and every citizen and burgess to the value of three hundred pounds; except the eldest sons of peers, and of persons qualified to be knights of shires, and except the members for the two universities: which somewhat ballances the ascendant which the boroughs have gained over the counties, by obliging the trading interest to make choice of landed men: and of this qualification the member must make oath, and give in the particulars in writing, at the time of his taking his seat. But, subject to these restrictions and disqualifications, every subject of the realm is eligible of common right. It was therefore an unconstitutional prohibition, which was inserted in the king's writs, for the parliament holden at Coventry, 6 Hen. IV, that no apprentice or other man of the law should be elected a knight of the shire therein: in return for which, our law books and historians have branded this parliament with the name of *parliamentum indoctum,* or the lack-learning parliament; and sir Edward Coke observes with some spleen, that there was never a good law made thereat.

2

RECORDS OF THE FEDERAL CONVENTION

[1:375; Madison, 22 June]

Col. Mason moved to insert "twenty five years of age as a qualification for the members of the 1st. branch". He thought it absurd that a man to day should not be permitted by the law to make a bargain for himself, and tomorrow should be authorized to manage the affairs of a great nation. It was the more extraordinary as every man carried with him in his own experience a scale for measuring the deficiency of young politicians; since he would if interrogated be obliged to declare that his political opinions at the age of 21. were too crude & erroneous to merit an

influence on public measures. It had been said that Congs. had proved a good school for our young men. It might be so for any thing he knew but if it were, he chose that they should bear the expence of their own education.

Mr. Wilson was agst. abridging the rights of election in any shape. It was the same thing whether this were done by disqualifying the objects of choice, or the persons chusing. The motion tended to damp the efforts of genius, and of laudable ambition. There was no more reason for incapacitating *youth* than *age*, when the requisite qualifications were found. Many instances might be mentioned of signal services rendered in high stations to the public before the age of 25: The present Mr. Pitt and Lord Bolingbroke were striking instances.

On the question for inserting "25 years of age"
Massts. no. Cont. ay. N. Y. divd. N. J. ay. Pa. no. Del. ay. Md. ay. Va. ay. N. C. ay. S. C. ay. Geo. no. [Ayes—7; noes—3; divided—1.]

[2:121; Madison, 26 July]

Mr Mason moved "that the Committee of detail be instructed to receive a clause requiring certain qualifications of landed property & citizenship of the U. States in members of the Legislature, and disqualifying persons having unsettled Accts. with or being indebted to the U. S. from being members of the Natl. Legislature"—He observed that persons of the latter descriptions had frequently got into the State Legislatures, in order to promote laws that might shelter their delinquencies; and that this evil had crept into Congs. if Report was to be regarded.

Mr Pinckney seconded the motion

Mr Govr. Morris. If qualifications are proper, he wd. prefer them in the electors rather than the elected. As to debtors of the U. S. they are but few. As to persons having unsettled accounts he believed them to be pretty many. He thought however that such a discrimination would be both odious & useless. and in many instances unjust & cruel. The delay of settlemt. had been more the fault of the public than of the individuals. What will be done with those patriotic Citizens who have lent money, or services or property to their Country, without having been yet able to obtain a liquidation of their claims? Are they to be excluded?

Mr. Ghorum was for leaving to the Legislature, the providing agst such abuses as had been mentioned.

Col. Mason mentioned the parliamentary qualifications adopted in the Reign of Queen Anne, which he said had met with universal approbation

Mr. Madison had witnessed the zeal of men having accts. with the public, to get into the Legislatures for sinister purposes. He thought however that if any precaution were to be taken for excluding them, the one proposed by Col. Mason ought to be new modelled. It might be well to limit the exclusion to persons who had recd money from the public, and had not accounted for it.

Mr Govr. Morris—It was a precept of great antiquity as well as of high authority that we should not be righteous overmuch. He thought we ought to be equally on our guard agst. being wise over much. The proposed regulation would enable the Govent. to exclude particular persons from office as long as they pleased He mentioned the case of the Commander in chief's presenting his account for secret services, which he said was so moderate that every one was astonished at it; and so simple that no doubt could arise on it. Yet had the Auditor been disposed to delay the settlement, how easily might he have affected it, and how cruel wd. it be in such a case to keep a distinguished & meritorious Citizen under a temporary disability & disfranchisement. He mentioned this case merely to illustrate the objectionable nature of the proposition. He was opposed to such minutious regulations in a Constitution. The parliamentary qualifications quoted by Col. Mason, had been disregarded in practice; and was but a scheme of the landed agst the monied interest.

Mr Pinckney & Genl. Pinckney moved to insert by way of amendmt. the words Judiciary & Executive so as to extend the qualifications to those departments which was agreed to nem con

Mr. Gerry thought the inconveniency of excluding a few worthy individuals who might be public debtors or have unsettled accts ought not to be put in the Scale agst the public advantages of the regulation, and that the motion did not go far enough.

Mr. King observed that there might be great danger in requiring landed property as a qualification since it would exclude the monied interest, whose aids may be essential in particular emergencies to the public safety.

Mr. Dickenson. was agst. any recital of qualifications in the Constitution. It was impossible to make a compleat one, and a partial one would by implication tie up the hands of the Legislature from supplying the omissions, The best defence lay in the freeholders who were to elect the Legislature. Whilst this Source should remain pure, the public interest would be safe. If it ever should be corrupt, no little expedients would repel the danger. He doubted the policy of interweaving into a Republican constitution a veneration for wealth. He had always understood that a veneration for poverty & virtue, were the objects of republican encouragement. It seemed improper that any man of merit should be subjected to disabilities in a Republic where merit was understood to form the great title to public trust, honors & rewards.

Mr Gerry if property be one object of Government, provisions for securing it can not be improper.

Mr. Madison moved to strike out the word *landed*, before the word, "qualifications". If the proposition sd. be agreed to he wished the Committee to be at liberty to report the best criterion they could devise. Landed possessions were no certain evidence of real wealth. Many enjoyed them to a great extent who were more in debt than they were worth. The unjust laws of the States had proceeded more from this class of men, than any others. It had often happened that men who had acquired landed property on credit, got into the Legislatures with a view of promoting an unjust protection agst. their Creditors. In the next place, if a small quantity of land should be made the standard. it would be no security.—if a large one, it would exclude the proper representatives of these classes of Citizens who were not landholders. It was politic as well as just that the interests & rights of every class should be

duly represented & understood in the public Councils. It was a provision every where established that the Country should be divided into districts & representatives taken from each, in order that the Legislative Assembly might equally understand & sympathise, with the rights of the people in every part of the Community. It was not less proper that every class of Citizens should have an opportunity of making their rights be felt & understood in the public Councils. The three principle classes into which our citizens were divisible, were the landed the commercial, & the manufacturing. The 2d. & 3rd. class, bear as yet a small proportion to the first. The proportion however will daily increase. We see in the populous Countries in Europe now, what we shall be hereafter. These classes understand much less of each others interests & affairs, than men of the same class inhabiting different districts. It is particularly requisite therefore that the interests of one or two of them should not be left entirely to the care, or the impartiality of the third. This must be the case if landed qualifications should be required; few of the mercantile, and scarcely any of the manufacturing class, chusing whilst they continue in business to turn any part of their Stock into landed property. For these reasons he wished if it were possible that some other criterion than the mere possession of land should be devised. He concurred with Mr. Govr. Morris in thinking that qualifications in the Electors would be much more effectual than in the elected. The former would discriminate between real & ostensible property in the latter; But he was aware of the difficulty of forming any uniform standard that would suit the different circumstances & opinions prevailing in the different States.

Mr. Govr Morris 2ded. the motion.

On the Question for striking out "landed"

N. H. ay. Mas. ay. Ct. ay N. J. ay. Pa. ay. Del. ay. Md. no Va. ay. N. C. ay. S. C. ay. Geo. ay. [Ayes—10; noes—1.]

On Question on 1st. part of Col. Masons proposition as to qualification of property & citizenship" as so amended N. H. ay. Masts. ay. Ct. no. N. J. ay. Pa. no. Del. no. Md. ay. Va. ay. N. C. ay. S. C. ay. Geo. ay. [Ayes—8; noes—3.]

"The 2d. part, for disqualifying debtors, and persons having unsettled accounts", being under consideration

Mr. Carrol moved to strike out "having unsettled accounts"

Mr. Ghorum seconded the motion; observing that it would put the commercial & manufacturing part of the people on a worse footing than others as they would be most likely to have dealings with the public.

Mr. L– Martin. if these words should be struck out, and the remaining words concerning debtors retained, it will be the interest of the latter class to keep their accounts unsettled as long as possible.

Mr. Wilson was for striking them out. They put too much power in the hands of the Auditors, who might combine with rivals in delaying settlements in order to prolong the disqualifications of particular men. We should consider that we are providing a Constitution for future generations, and not merely for the peculiar circumstances of the moment. The time has been, and will again be when the public safety may depend on the voluntary aids of individuals which will necessarily open accts. with the public, and when such accts. will be a characteristic of patriotism. Besides a partial enumeration of cases will disable the Legislature from disqualifying odious & dangerous characters.

Mr. Langdon was for striking out the whole clause for the reasons given by Mr Wilson. So many Exclusions he thought too would render the system unacceptable to the people.

Mr. Gerry. If the argumts. used to day were to prevail, we might have a Legislature composed of public debtors, pensioners, placemen & contractors. He thought the proposed qualifications would be pleasing to the people. They will be considered as a security agst unnecessary or undue burdens being imposed on them He moved to add "pensioners" to the disqualified characters which was negatived.

N. H. no Mas. ay. Con. no. N. J. no Pa. no. Del no Maryd. ay. Va. no. N. C. divided. S. C. no. Geo. ay. [Ayes—3; noes—7; divided—1.]

Mr. Govr. Morris The last clause, relating to public debtors will exclude every importing merchant. Revenue will be drawn it is foreseen as much as possible, from trade. Duties of course will be bonded. and the Merchts. will remain debtors to the public. He repeated that it had not been so much the fault of individuals as of the public that transactions between them had not been more generally liquidated & adjusted. At all events to draw from our short & scanty experience rules that are to operate through succeeding ages, does not savour much of real wisdom.

On question for striking out "persons having unsettled accounts with the U. States."

N. H. ay. Mas. ay. Ct. ay. N. J. no. Pa. ay. Del. ay. Md. ay. Va. ay. N. C. ay. S. C. ay. Geo. no. [Ayes—9; noes—2.]

Mr. Elseworth was for disagreeing to the remainder of the clause disqualifying public debtors; and for leaving to the wisdom of the Legislature and the virtue of the Citizens, the task of providing agst. such evils. Is the smallest as well largest debtor to be excluded? Then every arrear of taxes will disqualify. Besides how is it to be known to the people when they elect who are or are not public debtors. The exclusion of pensioners & placemen in Engd is founded on a consideration not existing here. As persons of that sort are dependent on the Crown, they tend to increase its influence.

Mr. Pinkney sd. he was at first a friend to the proposition, for the sake of the clause relating to qualifications of property; but he disliked the exclusion of public debtors; it went too far. It wd. exclude persons who had purchased confiscated property or should purchase Western territory of the public, and might be some obstacle to the sale of the latter.

On the question for agreeing to the clause disqualifying public debtors

N. H. no. Mas– no. Ct. no. N. J. no. Pa. no. Del. no. Md. no. Va. no. N. C. ay. S. C. no. Geo. ay. [Ayes—2; noes—9.]

[2:216; Madison, 8 Aug.]

Art. IV. Sect. 2. taken up.

Col. Mason was for opening a wide door for emigrants; but did not chuse to let foreigners and adventurers make laws for us & govern us. Citizenship for three years was not enough for ensuring that local knowledge which ought to be possessed by the Representative. This was the principal ground of his objection to so short a term. It might also happen that a rich foreign Nation, for example Great Britain, might send over her tools who might bribe their way into the Legislature for insidious purposes. He moved that "seven" years instead of "three," be inserted.

Mr. Govr. Morris 2ded. the motion, & on the question, All the States agreed to it except Connecticut.

Mr. Sherman moved to strike out the word "resident" and insert "inhabitant," as less liable to misconstruction.

Mr. Madison 2ded. the motion. both were vague, but the latter least so in common acceptation, and would not exclude persons absent occasionally for a considerable time on public or private business. Great disputes had been raised in Virga. concerning the meaning of residence as a qualification of Representatives which were determined more according to the affection or dislike to the man in question, than to any fixt interpretation of the word.

Mr. Wilson preferred "inhabitant."

Mr. Govr. Morris was opposed to both and for requiring nothing more than a freehold. He quoted great disputes in N. York occasioned by these terms, which were decided by the arbitrary will of the majority. Such a regulation is not necessary. People rarely chuse a nonresident—It is improper as in the 1st. branch, *the people at large,* not the *States* are represented.

Mr. Rutlidge urged & moved that a residence of 7 years shd. be required in the State Wherein the Member shd. be elected. An emigrant from N. England to S. C. or Georgia would know little of its affairs and could not be supposed to acquire a thorough knowledge in less time.

Mr. Read reminded him that we were now forming a *Natil* Govt and such a regulation would correspond little with the idea that we were one people.

Mr. Wilson—enforced the same consideration.

Mr. Madison suggested the case of new States in the West, which could have perhaps no representation on that plan.

Mr. Mercer. Such a regulation would present a greater alienship among the States than existed under the old federal system. It would interweave local prejudices & State distinctions in the very Constitution which is meant to cure them. He mentioned instances of violent disputes raised in Maryland concerning the term "residence"

Mr Elseworth thought seven years of residence was by far too long a term: but that some fixt term of previous residence would be proper. He thought one year would be sufficient, but seemed to have no objection to three years.

Mr. Dickenson proposed that it should read "inhabitant actually resident for ——— year." This would render the meaning less indeterminate.

Mr. Wilson. If a short term should be inserted in the blank, so strict an expression might be construed to exclude the members of the Legislature, who could not be said to be actual residents in their States whilst at the Seat of the Genl. Government.

Mr. Mercer. It would certainly exclude men, who had once been inhabitants, and returning from residence elswhere to resettle in their original State; although a want of the necessary knowledge could not in such case be presumed.

Mr. Mason thought 7 years too long, but would never agree to part with the principle. It is a valuable principle. He thought it a defect in the plan that the Representatives would be too few to bring with them all the local knowledge necessary. If residence be not required, Rich men of neighbouring States, may employ with success the means of corruption in some particular district and thereby get into the public Councils after having failed in their own State. This is the practice in the boroughs of England.

On the question for postponing in order to consider Mr Dickinsons motion

N. H. no. Mas. no. Ct. no. N. J. no. Pa. no. Del. no. Md. ay. Va. no. N. C. no. S. C. ay. Geo. ay. [Ayes—3; noes—8.]

On the question for inserting "inhabitant" in place of "resident"—Agd. to nem. con.

Mr. Elseworth & Col. Mason move to insert "one year" for previous inhabitancy

Mr. Williamson liked the Report as it stood. He thought "resident" a good eno' term. He was agst requiring any period of previous residence. New residents if elected will be most zealous to Conform to the will of their constituents, as their conduct will be watched with a more jealous eye.

Mr. Butler & Mr. Rutlidge moved "three years" instead of "one year" for previous inhabitancy

On the question for 3 years.

N. H. no. Mas. no. Ct. no. N. J. no. Pa. no. Del. no. Md. no. Va. no. N. C. no. S. C. ay. Geo. ay [Ayes—2; noes—9.]

On the question for "1 year"

N. H. no—Mas—no. Ct. no. N. J. ay. Pa. no. Del. no. Md. divd. Va. no— N– C. ay– S. C. ay. Geo—ay [Ayes—4; noes—6; divided—1.]

Art. IV– Sect. 2. As amended in manner preceding, was agreed to nem. con.

[2:268; Madison, 13 Aug.]

Mr. Wilson & Mr. Randolph moved to strike out "7 years" and insert "4 years," as the requisite terms of Citizenship to qualify for the House of Reps. Mr. Wilson said it was very proper the electors should govern themselves by this consideration; but unnecessary & improper that the Constitution should chain them down to it.

Mr. Gerry wished that in future the eligibility might be confined to Natives. Foreign powers will intermeddle in our affairs, and spare no expence to influence them. Persons having foreign attachments will be sent among us & insinuated into our councils, in order to be made instruments for their purposes. Every one knows the vast sums laid out in Europe for secret services—He was not singular in these ideas. A great many of the most influential men in Massts. reasoned in the same manner.

Mr. Williamson moved to insert 9 years instead of seven. He wished this Country to acquire as fast as possible national habits. Wealthy emigrants do more harm by their luxurious examples, than good, by the money, they bring with them.

Col. Hamilton was in general agst. embarrassing the Govt. with minute restrictions. There was on one side the possible danger that had been suggested—on the other side, the advantage of encouraging foreigners was obvious & admitted. Persons in Europe of moderate fortunes will be fond of coming here where they will be on a level with the first Citizens. He moved that the section be so altered as to require merely Citizenship & inhabitancy. The right of determining the rule of naturalization will then leave a discretion to the Legislature on this subject which will answer every purpose.

Mr Madison seconded the motion. He wished to maintain the character of liberality which had been professed in all the Constitutions & publications of America. He wished to invite foreigners of merit & republican principles among us. America was indebted to emigration for her settlement & Prosperity. That part of America which had encouraged them most had advanced most rapidly in population, agriculture & the arts. There was a possible danger he admitted that men with foreign predilections might obtain appointments but it was by no means probable that it would happen in any dangerous degree. For the same reason that they would be attached to their native Country, our own people wd. prefer natives of this Country to them. Experience proved this to be the case. Instances were rare of a foreigner being elected by the people within any short space after his coming among us—If bribery was to be practised by foreign powers, it would not be attempted among the electors, but among the elected; and among natives having full Confidence of the people not among strangers who would be regarded with a jealous eye.

Mr. Wilson. Cited Pennsylva. as a proof of the advantage of encouraging emigrations. It was perhaps the youngest (except Georgia) settlemt. on the Atlantic; yet it was at least among the foremost in population & prosperity. He remarked that almost all the Genl. officers of the Pena. line of the late army were foreigners. And no complaint had ever been made against their fidelity or merit. Three of her deputies to the Convention (Mr. R. Morris, Mr. Fitzsimmons & himself) were also not natives. He had no objection to Col. Hamiltons motion & would withdraw the one made by himself.

Mr. Butler was strenuous agst. admitting foreigners into our public Councils.

Question on Col. Hamilton's Motion

N. H. no. Mas. no. Ct. ay. N. J. no. Pa. ay. Del. no Md. ay. Va. ay. N. C. no. S. C. no. Geo. no. [Ayes—4; noes —7.]

Question on Mr. Williamson's moution, to insert 9 years instead of seven.

N. H. ay. Masts. no. Ct. no. N. J. no. Pa. no. Del. no. Md. no. Va no. N– C. no. S. C. ay. Geo. ay. [Ayes—3; noes—8.]

Mr. Wilson's renewed the motion for 4 years instead of 7. & on question

N. H. no Mas. no. Ct. ay. N. J. no. Pa. no. Del. no. Md.

ay. Va. ay. N. C. no. S. C. no Geo. no. [Ayes—3; noes—8.]

Mr. Govr. Morris moved to add to the end of the section (art IV. s. 2) a proviso that the limitation of seven years should not affect the rights of any person now a Citizen.

Mr. Mercer 2ded. the motion. It was necessary he said to prevent a disfranchisement of persons who had become Citizens under the faith & according to—the laws & Constitution from being on a level in all respects with natives.

Mr. Rutledge. It might as well be said that all qualifications are disfranchisemts. and that to require the age of 25 years was a disfranchisement. The policy of the precaution was as great with regard to foreigners now Citizens; as to those who are to be naturalized in future.

Mr. Sherman. The U. States have not invited foreigners nor pledged their faith that they should enjoy equal privileges with native Citizens. The Individual States alone have done this. The former therefore are at liberty to make any discriminations they may judge requisite.

Mr. Ghorum. When foreigners are naturalized it wd. seem as if they stand on an equal footing with natives. He doubted then the propriety of giving a retrospective force to the restriction.

Mr. Madison animadverted on the peculiarity of the doctrine of Mr. Sharman. It was a subtilty by which every national engagement might be evaded. By parity of reason, Whenever our public debts, or foreign treaties become inconvenient nothing more would be necessary to relieve us from them, than to new model the Constitution. It was said that the *U.S.* as such have not pledged their faith to the naturalized foreigners, & therefore are not bound. Be it so, & that the States alone are bound. Who are to form the New Constitution by which the condition of that class of citizens is to be made worse than the other class? Are not the States ye agents? will they not be the members of it? Did they not appoint this Convention? Are not they to ratify its proceedings? Will not the new Constitution be their Act? If the new Constitution then violates the faith pledged to any description of people will not the makers of it, will not the States, be the violators. To justify the doctrine it must be said that the States can get rid of their obligation by revising the Constitution, though they could not do it by repealing the law under which foreigners held their privileges. He considered this a matter of real importance. It woud expose us to the reproaches of all those who should be affected by it, reproaches which wd. soon be echoed from the other side of the Atlantic; and would unnecessarily enlist among the Adversaries of the reform a very considerable body of Citizens: We should moreover reduce every State to the dilemma of rejecting it or of violating the faith pledged to a part of its citizens.

Mr. Govr. Morris considered the case of persons under 25 years, as very different from that of foreigners. No faith could be pleaded by the former in bar of the regulation. No assurance had ever been given that persons under that age should be in all cases on a level with those above it. But with regard to foreigners among us, the faith had been pledged that they should enjoy the privileges of Citizens. If the restriction as to age had been confined to natives, & had left foreigners under 25 years, eligible in this case, the discrimination wd. have been an equal injustice on the other side.

Mr. Pinkney remarked that the laws of the States had varied much the terms of naturalization in different parts of America; and contended that the U.S. could not be bound to respect them on such an occasion as the present. It was a sort of recurrence to first principles.

Col- Mason was struck not like (Mr. Madison), with the *peculiarity*, but the *propriety* of the doctrine of Mr. Sharman. The States have formed different qualifications themselves, for enjoying different rights of citizenship. Greater caution wd. be necessary in the outset of the Govt. than afterwards. All the great objects wd. be then provided for. Every thing would be then set in Motion. If persons among us attached to G- B. should work themselves into our Councils, a turn might be given to our affairs & particularly to our Commercial regulations which might have pernicious consequences. The great Houses of British Merchants would spare no pains to insinuate the instruments of their views into the Govt—

Mr. Wilson read the clause in the Constitution of Pena. giving to foreigners after two years residence all the rights whatsoever of Citizens, combined it with the Article of Confederation making the Citizens of one State Citizens of all, inferred the obligation Pena. was under to maintain the faith thus pledged to her citizens of foreign birth, and the just complaints which her failure would authorize: He observed likewise that the Princes & States of Europe would avail themselves of such breach of faith to deter their subjects from emigrating to the U.S.

Mr. Mercer enforced the same idea of a breach of faith.

Mr. Baldwin could not enter into the force of the arguments agst. extending the disqualification to foreigners now Citizens. The discrimination of the place of birth, was not more objectionable than that of age which all had concurred in the propriety of.

Question on the proviso of Mr Govr. Morris in favor of foreigners now Citizens

N. H. no. Mas. no. Ct. ay. N. J. ay. Pa. ay. Del. no. Maryd. ay. Va. ay. N- C. no. S. C. no. Geo. no. [Ayes—5; noes–6.]

Mr. Carrol moved to insert "5 years" instead "of seven," in section 2d. Art: IV

N- H. no. Mas. no. Ct. ay. N. J. no. Pa. divd. Del. no. Md. ay. Va. ay. N. C. no. S. C. no. Geo. no. [Ayes—3; noes—7; divided—1.]

The Section (Art IV. Sec. 2) as formerly amended was then agreed to nem. con.

3

DEBATE IN MASSACHUSETTS RATIFYING CONVENTION
17 Jan. 1788
Elliot 2:35–36

Gen. THOMPSON thought that there should have been some *qualification of property* in a representative; for, said he when men have *nothing to lose*, they have *nothing to fear*.

Hon. Mr. SEDGWICK said, that this *objection* was founded on an anti-democratical principle, and was surprised that gentlemen who appeared so strenuously to advocate the rights of the people, should wish to exclude from the federal government a *good* man, because he was not a *rich* one.

Mr. KING said, that gentlemen had made it a question, why a qualification of property in a representative is omitted, and that they thought the provision of such a qualification necessary. He thought otherwise; he never knew that *property* was an index to abilities. We often see men, who, though destitute of property, are superior in knowledge and rectitude. The men who have most injured the country have most commonly been rich men. Such a qualification was proposed in Convention; but by the delegates of Massachusetts it was contested that it should not obtain. He observed, that no such qualification is required by the Confederation. In reply to Gen. Thompson's question, why disqualification of age was not added, the honorable gentleman said, that it would not extend to all parts of the continent alike. Life, says he, in a great measure, depends on climate. What in the Southern States would be accounted *long life*, would be but the *meridian* in the Northern; what here is the time of *ripened judgment* is *old age* there. Therefore the want of such a disqualification cannot be made an objection to the Constitution.

4

A REPUBLICAN FEDERALIST, NO. 6
2 Feb. 1788
Storing 4.13.26

I am sensible it will be said the Constitution provides "that the electors in each State shall have the qualification requisite for electors of the most numerous branch of the State legislatures." But the new Constitution was evidently intended to, and must in its operation inevitably produce an abolition of the State governments, and when this is accomplished, the rule of apportionment of representatives according to property, must and will apply to electors, and have the effect mentioned. There would nevertheless be some consolation, if these were the only objections relative to representation in the new system, but

in the second sect. of the first art. there is a provision that "no person shall be a representative who shall not have attained to the age of twenty-five years, and been seven years a citizen of the United States," &c. had this provision extended to the foreigners who under the government of the United States, had contended for the establishment of our independence, it would have met with no objection; but as it now stands, any foreigner having attained the age of twenty five years, having been seven years a citizen of the United States, and being an inhabitant of any State, may be elected a representative—and the right of being elected senators, is confirmed to foreigners who shall have attained "the age of thirty years," and "who shall have been nine years a citizen of the United States, &c." Thus are we to have a supreme legislature over us, to consist as well of foreigners, as of freemen of the United States.— CITIZENS OF AMERICA! What have you for a number of years been contending for? To what purpose have you expended so freely the blood and treasures of this country? To have a government with unlimited powers administered by foreigners? Will there not be immediately planted in the several States, men of abilities, who, having the appearance of privates, will nevertheless be in the pay of foreign powers? Will not such men ingratiate themselves into your favour, or, which will be much better for them, into the favour of the new government? And after seven years residence, will they not be in your federal house of representatives, or after nine years residence in your senate? Will not the most important secrets of your executive, respecting treaties and other matters, be by these means always open to European powers? Will you not be engaged in their trials? Will not your interest be sacrificed to their politicks? And will you not be the puppets of foreign Courts? Perhaps you will be told that this provision will encourage emigrants, who will bring their money to America; but will you for such precarious and futile prospects consent to part with the right of governing yourselves? How carefully is this point guarded by Great-Britain. Judge Blackstone, book first, chap. tenth, says, "naturalization cannot be performed but by act of parliament, for by this an alien is put in exactly the same state as if he had been born in the king's legiance, *except* only that he is *incapable* as well as a denizen of being *a member of the privy council, or of parliament*, no bill for naturalization can be received in either house of parliament without such disqualifying clause in it." Other European powers are equally careful to exclude foreigners from their councils, whilst we, *too wise* to be benefited by the experience of governments which have existed for ages, and have attained the zenith of power, are adopting new principles, and exposing ourselves to evils which must inevitably lead us to destruction.

5

WILSON NICHOLAS, VIRGINIA RATIFYING
CONVENTION
4 June 1788
Elliot 3:8–9

Secondly, as it respects the qualifications of the elected. It has ever been considered a great security to liberty, that very few should be excluded from the right of being chosen to the legislature. This Constitution has amply attended to this idea. We find no qualifications required except those of age and residence, which create a certainty of their judgment being matured, and of being attached to their state. It has been objected, that they ought to be possessed of landed estates; but, sir, when we reflect that most of the electors are landed men, we must suppose they will fix on those who are in a similar situation with themselves. We find there is a decided majority attached to the landed interest; consequently, the landed interest must prevail in the choice. Should the state be divided into districts, in no one can the mercantile interest by any means have an equal weight in the elections; therefore, the former will be more fully represented in the Congress; and men of eminent abilities are not excluded for the want of landed property.

6

JAMES MADISON, HOUSE OF REPRESENTATIVES
22 May 1789
Papers 12:179–82

I think the merit of the question is now to be decided, whether the gentleman is eligible to a seat in this house or not, but it will depend on the decision of a previous question, whether he has been seven years a citizen of the United-States or not.

From an attention to the facts which have been adduced, and from a consideration of the principles established by the revolution, the conclusion I have drawn is, that Mr. Smith, was on the declaration of independence a citizen of the United-States, and unless it appears that he has forfeited his right, by some neglect or overt act, he had continued a citizen until the day of his election to a seat in this house. I take it to be a clear point, that we are to be guided in our decision, by the laws and constitution of South-Carolina, so far as they can guide us, and where the laws do not expressly guide us, we must be guided by principles of a general nature so far as they are applicable to the present case.

It were to be wished, that we had some law adduced more precisely defining the qualities of a citizen or an alien; particular laws of this kind, have obtained in some of the states; if such a law existed in South-Carolina, it might have prevented this question from ever coming before us; but since this has not been the case, let us settle some general principles before we proceed to the presumptive proof arising from public measures under the law, which tend to give support to the inference drawn from such principles.

It is an established maxim that birth is a criterion of allegiance. Birth however derives its force sometimes from place and sometimes from parentage, but in general place is the most certain criterion; it is what applies in the United States; it will therefore be unnecessary to investigate any other. Mr. Smith founds his claim upon his birthright; his ancestors were among the first settlers of that colony.

It is well known to many gentlemen on this floor, as well as to the public, that the petitioner is a man of talents, one who would not lightly hazard his reputation in support of visionary principles: yet I cannot but think he has erred in one of the principles upon which he grounds his charge. He supposes, when this country separated from Great Britain, the tie of allegiance subsisted between the inhabitants of America and the king of that nation, unless by some adventitious circumstance the allegiance was transferred to one of the United States. I think there is a distinction which will invalidate his doctrine in this particular, a distinction between that primary allegiance which we owe to that particular society of which we are members, and the secondary allegiance we owe to the sovereign established by that society. This distinction will be illustrated by the doctrine established by the laws of Great Britain, which were the laws of this country before the revolution. The sovereign cannot make a citizen by any act of his own; he can confer denizenship, but this does not make a man either a citizen or subject. In order to make a citizen or subject, it is established, that allegiance shall first be due to the whole nation; it is necessary that a national act should pass to admit an individual member. In order to become a member of the British empire, where birth has now endowed the person with that privilege, he must be naturalized by an act of parliament.

What was the situation of the people of America when the dissolution of their allegiance took place by the declaration of independence? I conceive that every person who owed this primary allegiance to the particular community in which he was born retained his right of birth, as the member of a new community; that he was consequently absolved from the secondary allegiance he had owed to the British sovereign: If he was not a minor, he became bound by his own act as a member of the society who separated with him from a submission to a foreign country. If he was a minor, his consent was involved in the decision of that society to which he belonged by the ties of nature. What was the allegiance as a citizen of South-Carolina, he owed to the King of Great Britain? He owed his allegiance to him as a King of that society to which, as a society he owed his primary allegiance. When that society separated from Great Britain, he was bound by that act and his allegiance transferred to that society, or the sovereign which that society should set up, because it was through his membership of the society of South-Carolina, that he owed allegiance to Great Britain.

This reasoning will hold good, unless it is supposed that the separation which took place between these states and Great Britain, not only dissolved the union between those countries, but dissolved the union among the citizens themselves: that the original compact, which made them altogether one society, being dissolved, they could not fall into pieces, each part making an independent society, but must individually revert into a state of nature; but I do not conceive that this was of necessity to be the case; I believe such a revolution did not absolutely take place. But in supposing that this was the case lies the error of the memorialist. I conceive the colonies remained as a political society, detached from their former connection with another society, without dissolving into a state of nature; but capable of substituting a new form of government in the place of the old one, which they had for special considerations abolished. Suppose the state of South Carolina should think proper to revise her constitution, abolish that which now exists, and establish another form of government: Surely this would not dissolve the social compact. It would not throw them back into a state of nature. It would not dissolve the union between the individual members of that society. It would leave them in perfect society, changing only the mode of action, which they are always at liberty to arrange. Mr. Smith being then, at the declaration of independence, a minor, but being a member of that particular society, he became, in my opinion, bound by the decision of the society with respect to the question of independence and change of government; and if afterward he had taken part with the enemies of his country, he would have been guilty of treason against that government to which he owed allegiance, and would have been liable to be prosecuted as a traitor.

If it is said, that very inconvenient circumstances would result from this principle, that it would constitute all those persons who are natives of America, but who took part against the revolution, citizens of the United States, I would beg leave to observe, that we are deciding a question of right, unmixed with the question of expediency, and must therefore pay a proper attention to this principle. But I think it can hardly be expected by gentlemen that the principle will operate dangerously. Those who left their country to take part with Britain were of two descriptions, minors, or persons of mature age. With respect to the latter nothing can be inferred with respect to them from the decision on the present case; because they had the power of making an option between the contending parties: whether this was a matter of right or not is a question which need not be agitated in order to settle the case before us. Then, with respect to those natives who were minors at the revolution, and whose case is analogous to Mr. Smith's, if we are bound by the precedent of such a decision as we are about to make, and it is declared, that they owe a primary allegiance to this country, I still think we are not likely to be inundated with such characters; so far as any of them took part against us they violated their allegiance and opposed our laws; so then there can be only

a few characters, such as were minors at the revolution, and who have never violated their allegiance by a foreign connection, who can be affected by the decision of the present question. The number I admit is large who might be acknowledged citizens on my principles; but there will very few be found daring enough to face the laws of the country they have violated, and against which they have committed high treason.

So far as we can judge by the laws of Carolina, and the practice and decision of that state, the principles I have adduced are supported; and I must own that I feel myself at liberty to decide, that Mr. Smith was a citizen at the declaration of independence, a citizen at the time of his election, and consequently entitled to a seat in this legislature.

7

JAMES WILSON, THE LEGISLATIVE DEPARTMENT,
LECTURES ON LAW
1791
Works 1:413

2. Before one can be a representative, he must have been seven years a citizen of the United States.

Two reasons may be assigned for this provision. 1. That the constituents might have a full and mature opportunity of knowing the character and merit of their representative. 2. That the representative might have a full and mature opportunity of knowing the dispositions and interests of his constituents.

3. The representative must, when elected, be an inhabitant of that state, in which he is chosen.

The qualification of residence we have found to be universally insisted on with regard to those who elect: here the same qualification is insisted on with regard to those who are elected. The same reasons, which operated in favour of the former qualification, operate with equal, indeed, with greater force, in favour of this. A provision, almost literally the same with the present one, was made in England three centuries and a half ago. By a statute made in the first year of Henry the fifth, it was enacted, that "the knights of the shires, which from henceforth shall be chosen in every shire, be not chosen, unless they be resident within the shire where they shall be chosen, the day of the date of the writ of the summons of the parliament"—"And moreover it is ordained and established, that the citizens and burgesses of the cities and boroughs be chosen men, citizens and burgesses, resiant, dwelling, and free in the same cities and boroughs, and no other in any wise." to this moment, this statute continues unrepealed— a melancholy proof, how far degenerate and corrupted manners will overpower the wisest and most wholesome laws. From Sir Bulstrode Whitlocke we learn, that, above a century ago, noncompliance with this statute was "connived at." The statute itself has been long and openly disregarded. The consequences of this disregard may be seen in the present state of the representation in England.

8

HOUSE OF REPRESENTATIVES, MARYLAND CONTESTED ELECTION
12, 16 Nov. 1807
Annals 17:882–86, 911–15

[*12 Nov.*]

[Mr. RANDOLPH. The] House had never been called upon to make a more important decision than the one now proposed. He wished he was prepared for the discussion. He had scarcely run over the report of the Committee of Elections; but it was one of those questions upon which his mind had been so long unalterably fixed, that he could not refrain from the endeavor to warn the Committee of the dangerous ground which they were invited to tread. In undertaking to decide upon the validity of the law of the State, they touched upon a subject which should never be approached but under the most imperious necessity, and where no shadow of doubt could hang upon their decision. It might be said that with the *reasoning* of the report they had nothing to do; it was the committee's reasoning, not theirs; that they acted on the naked resolution only. But it was obvious to the meanest capacity, that when the committee thought the fact of Mr. McCreery's residence in Baltimore so unimportant that no question was taken upon it, and grounded their resolution solely upon the unconstitutionality of the law requiring it, that House could not affirm the resolution without affirming, at the same time, the only point upon which the committee had decided in favor of the sitting member. What were they required to do? To declare the law of Maryland, long reverenced and obeyed, under which successive elections had been held, and never before questioned—to pronounce this law to be a dead letter, entitled to no respect, even from her own citizens, and to absolve them from all obedience to it! Was it matter of surprise that the members of the House were startled at an innovation so daring and so dangerous? He had laid it down as a principle not to be questioned, that Congress should never undertake to pronounce upon State regulations, but in cases too clear to admit a contest, and where the decision could not be evaded without manifest detriment to the public good. If he were called upon to establish a criterion, an infallible touchstone of the soundness of political principles, it should be made to consist of nothing so much as a sacred regard for the rights of the States. An enlarged and liberal construction of State rights was, with him, an indispensable requisite, and he could never give his confidence to a politician indisposed to such a construction. He viewed the proposed measure but as the commencement of a series, as the entering wedge. If they began with declaring one law of one State unconstitutional, where were they to stop? They might, they would go on (it was the natural tendency

of power never to be satiated as long as there was anything left to devour) until the State Governments, stripped of all authority, rendered contemptible in the eyes of the people for their imbecility, and odious for their expense, mere skeletons of Governments, the shadows of their former greatness, should be forever abolished, and a great consolidated empire established upon their ruins. Mr. R. looked forward to such an event as the death warrant of the existing Constitution, and the people's liberties. If they wished to preserve the Constitution, they must learn to respect the rights of the States, and not bring the whole artillery of the Federal Government to bear upon them. In such a contest, the States must fall, and when they did fall, there was an end of all republican government in the country.

The second paragraph of the second section of the first article of the Constitution had, to his extreme surprise, been construed by the Committee of Elections as restricting the States from annexing qualifications to a seat in the House of Representatives. He could not view it in that light. Mark the distinctions between the first and second paragraphs. The first is affirmative and positive. "They shall have the qualifications necessary to the electors of the most numerous branch of the State Legislature." The second merely negative. "No person shall be a Representative who shall not have attained the age of twenty-five years," &c. No man could be a member without these requisites; but it did not follow that he who had them was entitled to set at naught such other requisites as the several States might think proper to demand. If the Constitution had meant (as was contended) to have settled the qualification of members, its words would have naturally ran thus: "*Every person* who has attained the age of twenty-five years, and been seven years a citizen of the United States, and who shall, when elected, be an inhabitant of the State from which he shall be chosen, shall be eligible to a seat in the House of Representatives." But so far from fixing the qualifications of members of that House, the Constitution merely enumerated a few *disqualifications* within which the States were left to act. It said to the States, you have been in the habit of electing young men barely of age; you shall send us none but such as are five and twenty: some of you have elected persons just naturalized; you shall not elect any to this House who have not been seven years citizens of the United States. Sometimes mere sojourners and transient persons have been clothed with legislative authority; you shall elect none whom your laws do not consider as inhabitants. Thus guarding against too great laxity in the State regulations, by general and negative provisions, leaving them, however, within the limits of those restrictions, to act for themselves; to consult the genius, habits, and if you will, the prejudices of their people.

The first paragraph which he had read was positive and affirmative. By it, *every* person having the qualification requisite to an elector of the most numerous branch of his State Legislature, was entitled to vote for members of the House of Representatives. Yet, nevertheless, the qualification rested with the State. They might make it a part of the qualification of an elector, that he should reside within his district, county, or borough. Would it not be absurd to say that a man might take his seat in that House, who, at the same time, was not qualified to vote for a member of it? It had always been supposed that the elected should possess higher qualifications than the elector; yet here it would be entirely reversed. And why should it be supposed that whilst the Constitution had vested in the State the greater power, that which was most capable of abuse, the unlimited right of prescribing the qualifications of the voter, it had denied to them, by a forced implication, the right of prescribing the qualification of the person voted for, having respect, however, to the disqualifications enumerated in it? The construction of the Constitution, for which he had contended, was so obvious and natural, that it had been adopted by the States, and acted upon from the commencement of the Government, without any man dreaming of, or starting an objection to it. And the uniform practice of near twenty years, and the laws of the States in which the practice originated, were to be overturned at once, with as little ceremony as they would change one of their rules. If the doctrine of the Committee of Elections be sanctioned, Mr. R. said he did not know by what authority he himself could claim his seat. The law of Virginia, under which he held it, was equally unconstitutional with the law of Maryland. Indeed, it might be demonstrated, perhaps, that we had been living for years under an unconstitutional Government. Laws could not be valid which were passed by persons unconstitutionally elected. We should rip up the Government to its very foundations. The State of Virginia appointed her electors by a general ticket, (to keep out the heathen,) but each elector was to come from a particular *district*, notwithstanding twenty-four separate districts sent twenty-four electors by general ticket. If the State had no right to prescribe that the elector should be a resident of his district, the President had been unconstitutionally elected, in the first instance, by the electors, and in the second by members of that House voting by States, which members themselves had no right to their seats, the law under which they were appointed being null, void, and of no effect. Were gentlemen prepared for such conclusions as these?

Mr. R. said a gentleman from Maryland had obliged him by calling his attention to that article of the Constitution which enjoins that "the citizens of each State shall be entitled to all the privileges and immunities of citizens in the several States." Now, if it were laid down as a principle that the State had no right to require the residence of a member of that House within his district, the whole representation of Maryland might be taken (as they would be taken) from the town of Baltimore. Transient persons from other States, happening to arrive at Baltimore on the day before the election, who, if elected, would declare their determination to become permanent residents, might be returned as members of that House, and must maintain their seats under this decision. The House of Representatives would become a mere shadow, a mockery of representation; not such as the people were attached to, in support of their claim to which they had bled, but such a representation as an English lawyer allowed us to possess in the British House of Commons, when he discovered that the different grants in America, being held as part

and parcel of the manor of East Greenwich, all the Colonies were represented by the knights of the shire for Kent. He believed they would possess just as much knowledge of the interest of their constituents in the one case, as has been exhibited in the other, and would demonstrate the same sort of care of their persons and purses. Mr. R. said he held residence within the body of the county or district, to be of the very essence of representation. To be a good Representative, a man must not only reside among the people, he must be one of them, bound to them by every tie of habit, interest, and affection; not a stranger, having no common feeling with them, known to them only by report, and imposed upon them by cabal, intrigue, and corruption.

He believed there were no gentlemen of that House who had maintained a more uninterrupted harmony with each other, than that which subsisted between himself and the two gentlemen from Baltimore, (Messrs. Moore and McCreery.) Their whole intercourse had consisted of an interchange of civilities and courtesies. But this could not affect his opinion upon the present question. But whilst he thought Mr. McCreery certainly, and Mr. Moore *possibly*, not entitled to a seat, he could not agree with a gentleman from North Carolina, that Mr. Barney was duly elected. He would never consent to a man's sitting in that House upon the votes of a minority of the qualified electors of his district. He respected the rights of the people not less than the rights of the States. If a majority of the electors had voted for an unqualified person, believing him to be qualified, he believed the election should be set aside, and it should be put into the power of the people to send the man of their choice, who should be duly qualified. Mr. R. said that the votes not being given in exact conformity to law, perhaps the whole election should be set aside; but he inclined to the opinion that Mr. Moore was duly elected as the county member; that the votes given to Mr. McCreery were under the idea that he still continued a resident of the city; that being unqualified, his seat should be vacated, and a new writ issued to fill the vacancy.

If the report of the Committee of Elections should be affirmed, it would be an era in the history of this Government. For the first time, and when the nation was supposed to be under the guidance of men supposed to be friendly to the interests of the States and people, the law of a State was to be declared unconstitutional. Before the Committee undertook to pronounce this sentence, to set this awful precedent, it behooved them to pause and consider well. This decision, said Mr. R., will not be final. It will be but the forerunner of a long series of acts, abrogating the laws and usages of the States, endeared to the people by habit, and sanctified by reason. Before you enter upon this fatal act, be you well assured that the right is indisputably your own, and that you are called upon to exercise it by considerations which it would be criminal to resist. Beware lest, whilst you proudly assert your power, you do not meet the reprobation of the great body of the American people.

[*16 Nov.*]

Mr. KEY: The Convention who formed the Constitution

of the United States, represented not the States, but the people of the United States. They met to form not a State government, but a National Government for the people of the United States. The sovereignty of each State was solemnly guarantied by the Constitution, and as each State, whether great or small, was equally sovereign and independent, each State is equally represented in the Senate of the United States; each State sends two members; and this is the federative feature in our Constitution; but the House of Representatives was intended as the immediate representation of the people of the United States. The Constitution begins: "We, the people of the United States;" and the Constitution having defined the qualifications of the electors, it proceeds to define those of the Representative, or elected. It was surely competent to the Convention, who represented the people of the United States, to say what qualifications their agent, Representative, or law-maker, should possess, and they accordingly fix three: 1st, That he shall be above the age of twenty-five. 2d. Seven years a citizen of the United States. And, 3d, An inhabitant, when elected, of the State in which he shall be chosen. Uniformity could not, I have shown, be obtained as to the qualification of the electors; but it was most desirable in the elected, and, as it could be easily obtained, is accordingly specified in the Constitution; and the expression of these qualifications in the Constitution, is the exclusion of all others; so, to define the qualifications of the elected, was within the power of the Convention, was their duty, and is set forth in the Constitution itself.

But it is objected that the expressions used in the Constitution are negative ones, and do not prevent the States from superadding other qualifications. To this I answer, first, that if the words are changed into positive instead of negative terms, it makes no difference in the meaning; for instance, each Representative shall be above the age of twenty-five, &c., creates no difference in the construction or meaning of the article. You may make a new article to remove the difficulty, but the present one cannot be altered in signification, whether the terms remain negative, or are changed to affirmative ones. I will hereafter consider the effect of these words, when used to describe the qualifications of President.

Secondly. As to the power of the States to superinduce other qualifications to the three enumerated in the Constitution of the United States, I say, and I lay it down as a political truth, that the States, in their sovereign capacities, have no power, right or authority to interfere with the elections of Representatives to Congress, except so far as the Constitution of the United States gives them special powers so to do. By what authority do the several States interfere in elections of Representatives to Congress? Let each man honestly put this question to himself. Is it under the principles of State sovereignty? No. By what authority, then? I answer, by the express authority of the Constitution of the United States, in these words; first paragraph of fourth section of article first: "The times, places, and manner of holding elections for Senators and Representatives shall be prescribed in each State by the Legislature thereof; but Congress may, at any time, by law, make or alter such regulations, except as to the places of choosing

Senators." Every man acquainted with our political institutions must say that the State Legislatures derive their authority from the above article, to interfere with the United States elections. It was impracticable for the Convention to introduce an election law into the Constitution; they, therefore, left certain powers with the States. What are those powers? To regulate the time, place, and manner of holding elections. It is a special, limited power, for particular designated objects. The first branch of the power gives authority to the State Legislatures to regulate the time of holding the election; surely the time of holding the election has no relation to the previous residence or qualification of the candidate. Secondly. The State Legislatures may regulate the place of holding elections; manifestly this power has no reference to the qualification of the candidate. And thirdly: The State Legislatures may regulate the manner of holding elections. Now the manner of holding an election has no connexion with the previous residence or qualification of a candidate; but it implies that the election may be *viva voce*, by ballot, by districts for the convenience of the voters, or by the States in a general ticket. When the Constitution designates three qualifications, and no more, and when that same Constitution gives to the States the limited power to prescribe the time, place, and manner of holding elections, can any reasonable man believe that the States have power to add qualifications of age, property, or residence? If the States have power to add one qualification, they have power to create all. If they can make one year's previous residence in a district necessary, they have equal power to make forty necessary; and if they can limit the residence (as in this case of McCreery) to a particular part of the district, they may to a particular house in the district, and so localize a man as to take all power of election from the people; totally destroy the elective franchise. They may say, with equal power, that no man under £1,000 a year shall be a Representative. Mr. Chairman, the people of every State in the Union have a direct interest in every member of the House of Representatives; these members do not represent, in this House, the people of any particular State, but the people of the United States generally, and are competent to raise taxes from the whole people of the United States, though all the Representatives of any one State should oppose the law, and to bind all the people in every State by their votes and acts: hence the people in each State are interested in the qualifications of the Representatives of every State, and no one State can destroy the right. It was from this great principle that every Representative, from whatever State he comes, may, by his acts and votes, bind the citizens of other States, declare war, or lay taxes, that the Constitution defined the qualifications of the elected; limited the power of the States simply to the time, place, and manner of holding the elections; and declared, in terms too plain to be perverted, "We the people" of the United States have declared who may elect, and who be elected, and we leave to the States (until Congress shall otherwise direct) the power to prescribe the time, place, and manner of letting such qualified electors choose such qualified Representatives.

It has been said, but faintly relied on, that if the States

have power to fix election districts for the electors, they may equally locate the Representative. But this is a great mistake. The Constitution, in permitting the States to determine the manner of holding elections, permits them, if it suits their convenience, to hold them in districts; but the attempt to curtail and rob the people of their elective franchise, by making the eligibility of the candidate depend on the locality of his residence, is out of their power, and not given to them by the Constitution. As to the propriety and policy of such power being placed in a State, it is not now a question. We are not framing a constitution. We are examining where it is placed by our Constitution. If it is not well placed, there is a Constitutional mode of altering it.

But gentlemen say that the States, for twenty years past, have added qualifications of residence to Representatives. To this I answer, that if the Representative is a resident of the district, he must, *ex necessitate,* be of the State and of course have the Constitutional qualification. But I perceive great danger in this doctrine. Violations of the Constitution, by some of the States, are now cited as precedents from which destructive conclusions are drawn, although the cases cited have never been acted on. Thus the assumption of power by the Legislatures of some States, is made to justify itself. If these innovations, thus practised, and never brought judicially into view of this House, are permitted to go on, they will, in time, like water dropping on a stone, wear away the very substance of the Constitution.

Now is the time to act on the subject. It is fairly before us on the report of the committee; and in what capacity do we act? In our judicial capacity, as judges, under these words in the first article of the fifth section: "Each House shall be the judge of the elections, returns, and qualifications of its own members." We have no discretion as a legislative body. We cannot look into the policy or propriety of the qualifications. We are sworn to support the Constitution. We sit as judges under it, and it is our bounden duty to declare if the State of Maryland has violated the United States Constitution, by imposing on a Representative other qualifications than that instrument requires.

It is a sound rule, in construing instruments, to examine the different parts of them, and if the same words are used on a similar subject, they must have the same interpretation. I pass by the Senatorial qualifications, where the same negative expressions are used. I will proceed to the qualifications of the President of the United States, article 2, section 1, paragraph 5: "No person, except a natural born citizen, or a citizen of the United States at the adoption of this Constitution, shall be eligible to the office of President; neither shall any person be eligible to that office who shall not have attained to the age of thirty-five years, and been fourteen years a resident within the United States." The expressions used in this article are in negative terms, in the same manner as those used with respect to qualifications of the Representatives; and does any reasonable man, and does any friend of the Constitution, say that the States can superinduce or add any other qualification to the President than those designated by the Constitution? If negative expressions apply to one case, so they do to the other. If the doctrine of reserved powers applies to

one case, so it does to the other. What would be the absurd consequence of investing the State sovereignties with power to add other qualifications to the President? The nine small States might add qualifications of age, residence, or property, and the eight large States, from their numbers, might elect a President without any of the qualifications limited by the majority of the States. What a singular phenomenon this would produce! A President elected by a large majority of the electors without the qualifications prescribed by a majority of the States? An argument producing such absurdities need not be pressed further. It is impossible to let the States interfere with the qualifications of the Representatives, and yet restrain them from interfering with the qualifications of the President. Very nearly the same expressions are used in each case in the same instrument, defining the qualifications.

A distinction is attempted which cannot be maintained, viz: "that the President is elected for the United States, and that no State can alter the qualifications in which all have an interest." I admit it; and this argument is most strongly in my favor, for all the citizens of the United States have an interest in each Representative, and therefore no State can alter the qualifications of a Representative; each Representative may, by his single voice, declare war or lay taxes. He who can command the sword and the purse of the people must represent them; and consequently each member must represent the people of the United States, not the people of his State; for to say that a person can, by his voice, lay taxes on persons whom he does not represent, or make them go to war, is a principle hostile to republicanism, and tears up the foundation of our Government.

It is said the States ought to have power to add qualifications of residence, or the people may choose transient persons; but this argument proves too much, because, when pushed far, it proves the people not competent to self-government.

I derive some consolation from the circumstance that I am a young member, of little or no political influence; hence, my arguments have nothing to recommend them but their intrinsic weight, and, in a Constitutional question, this is most desirable. We should be on our guard against the high character and influence of the gentleman from Virginia, whose opinions, from his talents and standing in society, may be received as correct, without accurately investigating them. But, is my doctrine new, Mr. Chairman? No, sir; it is a doctrine coeval with the Constitution, and supported by our ablest men. In a work of high celebrity, *The Federalist,* composed by JAY, HAMILTON, and MADISON, men eminently distinguished for their patriotism and their talents, and who, with dignified reputation, have filled the highest offices in our country, this doctrine is explicitly stated and ably maintained. The same doctrine is supported in the debates in the Virginia Convention, where some illustrious characters exhibited their acknowledged talents. There, sir, an objection was taken, that there was no freehold qualification in the Representative, the darling object of Virginia. Those who made this objection, never supposed the qualifications were not fixed by the Constitution; for, men of such talents and reputation would never have urged that as an objection to the Constitution if, for a moment, they had supposed the Legislatures of the States competent to make such alteration.

9

THOMAS JEFFERSON TO JOSEPH C. CABELL
31 Jan. 1814
Works 11:379–81

You ask my opinion on the question, whether the States can add any qualifications to those which the constitution has prescribed for their members of Congress? It is a question I had never before reflected on; yet had taken up an off-hand opinion, agreeing with your first, that they could not; that to add new qualifications to those of the constitution, would be as much an alteration as to detract from them. And so I think the House of Representatives of Congress decided in some case; I believe that of a member from Baltimore. But your letter having induced me to look into the constitution, and to consider the question a little, I am again in your predicament, of doubting the correctness of my first opinion. Had the constitution been silent, nobody can doubt but that the right to prescribe all the qualifications and disqualifications of those they would send to represent them, would have belonged to the State. So also the constitution might have prescribed the whole, and excluded all others. It seems to have preferred the middle way. It has exercised the power in part, by declaring some disqualifications, to wit, those of not being twenty-five years of age, of not having been a citizen seven years, and of not being an inhabitant of the State at the time of election. But it does not declare, itself, that the member shall not be a lunatic, a pauper, a convict of treason, of murder, of felony, or other infamous crime, or a non-resident of his district; nor does it prohibit to the State the power of declaring these, or any other disqualifications which its particular circumstances may call for; and these may be different in different States. Of course, then, by the tenth amendment, the power is reserved to the State. If, wherever the constitution assumes a single power out of many which belong to the same subject, we should consider it as assuming the whole, it would vest the General Government with a mass of powers never contemplated. On the contrary, the assumption of particular powers seems an exclusion of all not assumed. This reasoning appears to me to be sound; but, on so recent a change of view, caution requires us not to be too confident, and that we admit this to be one of the doubtful questions on which honest men may differ with the purest motives; and the more readily, as we find we have differed from ourselves on it.

I have always thought where the line of demarcation between the powers of the General and the State governments was doubtfully or indistinctly drawn, it would be prudent and praiseworthy in both parties, never to approach it but under the most urgent necessity. Is the necessity now urgent, to declare that no non-resident of his district shall be eligible as a member of Congress? It seems to me that, in practice, the partialities of the people are a sufficient security against such an election; and that if, in any instance, they should ever choose a non-resident, it must be one of such eminent merit and qualifications, as would make it a good, rather than an evil; and that, in any event, the examples will be so rare, as never to amount to a serious evil. If the case then be neither clear nor urgent, would it not be better to let it lie undisturbed? Perhaps its decision may never be called for.

10

JOSEPH STORY, COMMENTARIES ON THE
CONSTITUTION 2:§§ 612–28
1833

---

§ 612. It is obvious, that the inquiry, as to the due qualifications of representatives, like that, as to the due qualifications of electors in a government, is susceptible, in its own nature, of very different answers, according to the habits, institutions, interests, and local peculiarities of different nations. It is a point, upon which we can arrive at no universal rule, which will accommodate itself to the welfare and wants of every people, with the same proportionate advantages. The great objects are, or ought to be, to secure, on the part of the representatives, fidelity, sound judgment, competent information, and incorruptible independence. The best modes, by which these objects can be attained, are matters of discussion and reasoning, and essentially dependent upon a large and enlightened survey of the human character and passions, as developed in the different stages of civilized society. There is great room, therefore, for diversities of judgment and opinion upon a subject so comprehensive and variable in its elements. It would be matter of surprise, if doctrines essentially different, nay, even opposite to each other, should not, under such circumstances, be maintained by political writers, equally eminent and able. Upon questions of civil policy, and the fundamental structure of governments, there has hitherto been too little harmony of opinion among the greatest men to encourage any hope, that the future will be less fruitful in dissonances, than the past. In the practice of governments, a very great diversity of qualifications has been insisted on, as prerequisites of office; and this alone would demonstrate, that there was not admitted to exist any common standard of superior excellence, adapted to all ages, and all nations.

§ 613. In Great-Britain, besides those negative qualifications, which are founded in usage, or positive law, such as the exclusion of persons holding certain offices and pensions, it is required, that every member for a country, or knight of a shire, (as he is technically called,) shall have a clear estate of freehold, or copyhold, to the value of £600 sterling per annum; and every member for a city or borough, to the value of £300, except the eldest sons of peers, and of persons qualified to be knights of shires, and except the members of the two universities.

§ 614. Among the American colonies antecedent to the revolution, a great diversity of qualifications existed; and the state constitutions, subsequently formed, by no means lessen that diversity. Some insist upon a freehold, or other property, of a certain value; others require a certain period of residence, and citizenship only; others require a freehold only; others a payment of taxes, or an equivalent; others, again, mix up all the various qualifications of property, residence, citizenship, and taxation, or substitute some of these, as equivalents for others.

§ 615. The existing qualifications in the states being then so various, it may be thought, that the best course would have been, to adopt the rules of the states respectively, in regard to the most numerous branch of their own legislatures. And this course might not have been open to serious objections. But, as the qualifications of members were thought to be less carefully defined in the state constitutions, and more susceptible of uniformity, than those of the electors, the subject was thought proper for regulation by the convention. And it is observable, that the positive qualifications are few and simple. They respect only age, citizenship, and inhabitancy.

§ 616. First, in regard to age. The representative must have attained twenty-five years. And certainly to this no reasonable objection can be made. If experience, or wisdom, or knowledge be of value in the national councils, it can scarcely be pretended, that an earlier age could afford a certain guaranty for either. That some qualification of age is proper, no one will dispute. No one will contend, that persons, who are minors, ought to be eligible; or, that those, who have not attained manhood, so as to be entitled by the common law to dispose of their persons, or estates, at their own will, would be fit depositaries of the authority to dispose of the rights, persons, and property of others. Would the mere attainment of twenty-one years of age be a more proper qualification? All just reasoning would be against it. The characters and passions of young men can scarcely be understood at the moment of their majority. They are then new to the rights of self-government; warm in their passions; ardent in their expectations; and, just escaping from pupilage, are strongly tempted to discard the lessons of caution, which riper years inculcate. What they will become, remains to be seen; and four years beyond that period is but a very short space, in which to try their virtues, develop their talents, enlarge their resources, and give them a practical insight into the business of life adequate to their own immediate wants and duties. Can the interests of others be safely confided to those, who have yet to learn how to take care of their own? The British constitution has, indeed, provided only for the members of the house of commons not being minors; and illustrious instances have occurred to show, that great statesmen may be formed even during their minority. But such instances are rare, they are to be looked at as prodigies, rather than as examples; as the extraordinary growth of a peculiar education and character, and a hot-bed precocity in a monarchy, rather than as the sound and thrifty

growth of the open air, and the bracing hardihood of a republic. In the convention this qualification, as to age, did not pass without a struggle. It was originally carried by a vote of seven states against three, one being divided; though it was ultimately adopted without a division. In the state conventions it does not seem to have formed any important topic of debate.

§ 617. Secondly, in regard to citizenship. It is required, that the representative shall have been a citizen of the United States seven years. Upon the propriety of excluding aliens from eligibility, there could scarcely be any room for debate; for there could be no security for a due administration of any government by persons, whose interests and connexions were foreign, and who owed no permanent allegiance to it, and had no permanent stake in its measures or operations. Foreign influence, of the most corrupt and mischievous nature, could not fail to make its way into the public councils, if there was no guard against the introduction of alien representatives. It has accordingly been a fundamental policy of most, if not of all free states, to exclude all foreigners from holding offices in the state. The only practical question would seem to be, whether foreigners, even after naturalization, should be eligible as representatives; and if so, what was a suitable period of citizenship for the allowance of the privilege. In England, all aliens born, unless naturalized, were originally excluded from a seat in parliament; and now, by positive legislation, no alien, though naturalized, is capable of being a member of either house of parliament. A different course, naturally arising from the circumstances of the country, was adopted in the American colonies antecedent to the revolution, with a view to invite emigrations, and settlements, and thus to facilitate the cultivation of their wild and waste lands. A similar policy had since pervaded the state governments, and had been attended with so many advantages, that it would have been impracticable to enforce any total exclusion of naturalized citizens from office. In the convention it was originally proposed, that three years' citizenship should constitute a qualification; but that was exchanged for seven years by a vote of ten states to one. No objection seems even to have been suggested against this qualification; and hitherto it has obtained a general acquiescence or approbation. It certainly subserves two important purposes. 1. That the constituents have a full opportunity of knowing the character and merits of their representative. 2. That the representative has a like opportunity of learning the character, and wants, and opinions of his constituents.

§ 618. Thirdly, in regard to inhabitancy. It is required, that the representative shall, when elected, be an inhabitant of the state, in which he shall be chosen. The object of this clause, doubtless, was to secure an attachment to, and a just representation of, the interests of the state in the national councils. It was supposed, that an inhabitant would feel a deeper concern, and possess a more enlightened view of the various interests of his constituents, than a mere stranger. And, at all events, he would generally possess more entirely their sympathy and confidence. It is observable, that the inhabitancy required is within the state, and not within any particular district of the state, in which the member is chosen. In England, in former times, it was required, that all the members of the house of commons should be inhabitants of the places, for which they were chosen. But this was for a long time wholly disregarded in practice, and was at length repealed by statute of 14 Geo. 3, ch. 58. The circumstance is not a little remarkable in parliamentary history; and it establishes, in a very striking manner, how little mere theory can be regarded in matters of government. It was found by experience, that boroughs and cities were often better represented by men of eminence, and known patriotism, who were strangers to them, than by those chosen from their own vicinage. And to this very hour some of the proudest names in English history, as patriots and statesmen, have been the representatives of obscure, and, if one may so say, of ignoble boroughs.

§ 619. An attempt was made in the convention to introduce a qualification of one year's residence before the election; but it failed, four states voting in favour of it, six against it, and one being divided. The omission to provide, that a subsequent non-residence shall be a vacation of the seat, may in some measure defeat the policy of the original limitation. For it has happened, in more than one instance, that a member, after his election, has removed to another state, and thus ceased to have that intimate intercourse with, and dependence upon his constituents, upon which so much value has been placed in all his discussions on this subject.

§ 620. It is observable, that no qualification, in point of estate, has been required on the part of members of the house of representatives. Yet such a qualification is insisted on, by a considerable number of the states, as a qualification for the popular branch of the state legislature. The probability is, that it was not incorporated into the constitution of the Union from the difficulty of framing a provision, that would be generally acceptable. Two reasons have, however, been assigned by a learned commentator for the omission, which deserve notice. First, that in a representative government the people have an undoubted right to judge for themselves of the qualification of their representative, and of their opinion if his integrity and ability will supply the want of estate, there is better reason for contending, that it ought not prevail. Secondly, that by requiring a property qualification, it may happen, that men, the best qualified in other respects, might be incapacitated from serving their country. There is, doubtless, weight in each of these considerations. The first, however, is equally applicable to all sorts of qualifications whatsoever; and proceeds upon an inadmissible foundation; and that is, that the society has no just right to regulate for the common good, what a portion of the community may deem for their special good. The other reason has a better foundation in theory; though, generally speaking, it will rarely occur in practice. But it goes very far towards overturning another fundamental guard, which is deemed essential to public liberty; and that is, that the representative should have a common interest in measures with his constituents. Now, the power of taxation, one of the most delicate and important in human society, will rarely be exerted oppressively by those, who are to share the common

burthens. The possession of property has in this respect a great value among the proper qualifications of a representative; since it will have a tendency to check any undue impositions, or sacrifices, which may equally injure his own, as well as theirs.

§ 621. In like manner there is a total absence of any qualification founded on religious opinions. However desirable it may be, that every government should be administered by those, who have a fixed religious belief, and feel a deep responsibility to an infinitely wise and eternal Being; and however strong may be our persuasion of the everlasting value of a belief in Christianity for our present, as well as our immortal welfare; the history of the world has shown the extreme dangers, as well as difficulties, of connecting the civil power with religious opinions. Half the calamities, with which the human race have been scourged, have arisen from the union of church and state; and the people of America, above all others, have too largely partaken of the terrors and the sufferings of persecution for conscience' sake, not to feel an excessive repugnance to the introduction of religious tests. Experience has demonstrated the folly, as well as the injustice, of exclusions from office, founded upon religious opinions. They have aggravated all other evils in the political organization of societies. They carry in their train discord, oppression, and bloodshed. They perpetuate a savage ferocity, and insensibility to human rights and sufferings. Wherever they have been abolished, they have introduced peace and moderation, and enlightened legislation. Wherever they have been perpetuated, they have always checked, and in many cases have overturned all the securities of public liberty. The right to burn heretics survived in England almost to the close of the reign of Charles the Second; and it has been asserted, (but I have not been able to ascertain the fact by examination of the printed journals,) that on that occasion the whole bench of bishops voted against the repeal. We all know how slowly the Roman Catholics have recovered their just rights in England and Ireland. The triumph has been but just achieved, after a most painful contest for a half century. In the catholic countries, to this very hour, protestants are, for the most part, treated with a cold and reluctant jealousy, tolerated perhaps, but never cherished. In the actual situation of the United States a union of the states would have been impracticable from the known diversity of religious sects, if any thing more, than a simple belief in Christianity in the most general form of expression, had been required. And even to this some of the states would have objected, as inconsistent with the fundamental policy of their own charters, constitutions, and laws. Whatever, indeed, may have been the desire of many persons, of a deep religious feeling, to have embodied some provision on this subject in the constitution, it may be safely affirmed, that hitherto the absence has not been felt, as an evil; and that while Christianity continues to be the belief of the enlightened, and wise, and pure, among the electors, it is impossible, that infidelity can find an easy home in the house of representatives.

§ 622. It has been justly observed, that under the reasonable qualifications established by the constitution, the door of this part of the federal government is open to merit of every description, whether native or adoptive, whether young or old, and without regard to poverty or wealth, or any particular profession of religious faith.

§ 623. A question, however, has been suggested upon this subject, which ought not to be passed over without notice. And that is, whether the states can superadd any qualifications to those prescribed by the constitution of the United States. The laws of some of the states have already required, that the representative should be a freeholder, and be resident within the district, for which he is chosen. If a state legislature has authority to pass laws to this effect, they may impose any other qualifications beyond those provided by the constitution, however inconvenient, restrictive, or even mischievous they may be to the interests of the Union. The legislature of one state may require, that none but a Deist, a Catholic, a Protestant, a Calvinist, or a Universalist, shall be a representative. The legislature of another state may require, that none shall be a representative but a planter, a farmer, a mechanic, or a manufacturer. It may exclude merchants, and divines, and physicians, and lawyers. Another legislature may require a high monied qualification, a freehold of great value, or personal estate of great amount. Another legislature may require, that the party shall have been born, and always lived in the state, or district; or that he shall be an inhabitant of a particular town or city, free of a corporation, or eldest son. In short, there is no end to the varieties of qualifications, which, without insisting upon extravagant cases, may be imagined. A state may, with the sole object of dissolving the Union, create qualifications so high, and so singular, that it shall become impracticable to elect any representative.

§ 624. It would seem but fair reasoning upon the plainest principles of interpretation, that when the constitution established certain qualifications, as necessary for office, it meant to exclude all others, as prerequisites. From the very nature of such a provision, the affirmation of these qualifications would seem to imply a negative of all others. And a doubt of this sort seems to have pervaded the mind of a learned commentator. A power to add new qualifications is certainly equivalent to a power to vary them. It adds to the aggregate, what changes the nature of the former requisites. The house of representatives seems to have acted upon this interpretation, and to have held, that the state legislatures have no power to prescribe new qualifications, unknown to the constitution of the United States. A celebrated American statesman [Jefferson], however, with his avowed devotion to state power, has intimated a contrary doctrine. "If," says he, "whenever the constitution assumes a single power out of many, which belong to the same subject, we should consider it as assuming the whole, it would vest the general government with a mass of powers never contemplated. On the contrary, the assumption of particular powers seems an exclusion of all not assumed. This reasoning appears to me to be sound, but on so recent a change of view, caution requires us not to be over confident." He intimates, however, that unless the case be either clear or urgent, it would be better to let it lie undisturbed.

§ 625. It does not seem to have occurred to this celebrated statesman, that the whole of this reasoning, which is avowedly founded upon that amendment to the constitution, which provides, that "the powers not delegated nor prohibited to the states, are reserved to the states respectively, or to the people," proceeds upon a basis, which is inapplicable to the case. In the first place, no powers could be reserved to the states, except those, which existed in the states before the constitution was adopted. The amendment does not profess, and indeed, did not intend to confer on the states any new powers; but merely to reserve to them, what were not conceded to the government of the Union. Now, it may properly be asked, where did the states get the power to appoint representatives in the national government? Was it a power, that existed at all before the constitution was adopted? If derived from the constitution, must it not be derived exactly under the qualifications established by the constitution, and none others? If the constitution has delegated no power to the states to add new qualifications, how can they claim any such power by the mere adoption of that instrument, which they did not before possess?

§ 626. The truth is, that the states can exercise no powers whatsoever, which exclusively spring out of the existence of the national government, which the constitution does not delegate to them. They have just as much right, and no more, to prescribe new qualifications for a representative, as they have for a president. Each is an officer of the Union, deriving his powers and qualifications from the constitution, and neither created by, dependent upon, nor controllable by, the states. It is no original prerogative of state power to appoint a representative, a senator, or president for the Union. Those officers owe their existence and functions to the united voice of the whole, not of a portion, of the people. Before a state can assert the right, it must show, that the constitution has delegated and recognised it. No state can say, that it has reserved, what it never possessed.

§ 627. Besides; independent of this, there is another fundamental objection to the reasoning. The whole scope of the argument is, to show, that the legislature of the state has a right to prescribe new qualifications. Now, if the state in its political capacity had it, it would not follow, that the legislature possessed it. That must depend upon the powers confided to the state legislature by its own constitution. A state, and the legislature of a state, are quite different political beings. Now it would be very desirable to know, in which part of any state constitution this authority, exclusively of a national character, is found delegated to any state legislature. But this is not all. The amendment does not reserve the powers to the states exclusively, as political bodies; for the language of the amendment is, that the powers not delegated, &c. are reserved to the states, or to the *people*. To justify, then, the exercise of the power by a state, it is indispensable to show, that it has not been reserved to the people of the state. The people of the state, by adopting the constitution, have declared what their will is, as to the qualifications for office. And here the maxim, if ever, must apply, *Expressio unius est exclusio alterius*. It might further be urged, that the constitution, being the act of the whole people of the United States, formed and fashioned according to their own views, it is not to be assumed, as the basis of any reasoning, that they have given any control over the functionaries created by it, to any state, beyond what is found in the text of the instrument. When such a control is asserted, it is matter of proof, not of assumption; it is matter to be established, as of right, and not to be exercised by usurpation, until it is displaced. The burthen of proof is on the state, and not on the government of the Union. The affirmative is to be established; the negative is not to be denied, and the denial taken for a concession.

§ 628. In regard to the power of a state to prescribe the qualification of inhabitancy or residence in a district, as an additional qualification, there is this forcible reason for denying it, that it is undertaking to act upon the very qualification prescribed by the constitution, as to inhabitancy in the state, and abridging its operation. It is precisely the same exercise of power on the part of the states, as if they should prescribe, that a representative should be forty years of age, and a citizen for ten years. In each case, the very qualification fixed by the constitution is completely evaded, and indirectly abolished.

SEE ALSO:

Records of the Federal Convention, Farrand 1:20, 116–17, 210, 370; 2:129, 134, 139, 153, 164, 213, 225, 226, 245, 251, 265–66, 281, 565, 590

James McHenry, Maryland House of Delegates, 29 Nov. 1787, Farrand 3:147

David Ramsay to James Madison, 4 Apr. 1789, Papers 12:44–45

Article 1, Section 2, Clause 3

Representatives and direct Taxes shall be apportioned among the several States which may be included within this Union, according to their respective Numbers, which shall be determined by adding to the whole Number of free Persons, including those bound to Service for a Term of Years, and excluding Indians not taxed, three fifths of all other Persons. The actual Enumeration shall be made within three Years after the first Meeting of the Congress of the United States, and within every subsequent Term of ten Years, in such Manner as they shall by Law direct. The Number of Representatives shall not exceed one for every thirty Thousand, but each State shall have at Least one Representative; and until such enumeration shall be made, the State of New Hampshire shall be entitled to chuse three, Massachusetts eight, Rhode-Island and Providence Plantations one, Connecticut five, New-York six, New Jersey four, Pennsylvania eight, Delaware one, Maryland six, Virginia ten, North Carolina five, South Carolina five, and Georgia three.

1

CONTINENTAL CONGRESS, TAXATION AND REPRESENTATION
12 July 1776
Jefferson Autobiography, 1821, Works 1:43–57

On Friday July 12. [1776] the Committee [of the Continental Congress] appointed to draw the articles of confederation reported them, and on the 22d. the house resolved themselves into a committee to take them into consideration. On the 30th. & 31st. of that month & 1st. of the ensuing, those articles were debated which determined the proportion or quota of money which each state should furnish to the common treasury, and the manner of voting in Congress. The first of these articles were expressed in the original draught in these words. "Art. XI. All charges of war & all other expenses that shall be incurred for the common defence, or general welfare, and allowed by the United States assembled, shall be defrayed out of a common treasury, which shall be supplied by the several colonies in proportion to the number of inhabitants of every age, sex & quality, except Indians not paying taxes, in each colony, a true account of which, distinguishing the white inhabitants, shall be triennially taken & transmitted to the Assembly of the United States."

Mr. [Samuel] Chase moved that the quotas should be fixed, not by the number of inhabitants of every condition, but by that of the "white inhabitants." He admitted that taxation should be alwais in proportion to property, that this was in theory the true rule, but that from a variety of difficulties, it was a rule which could never be adopted in practice. The value of the property in every State could never be estimated justly & equally. Some other measure for the wealth of the State must therefore be devised, some standard referred to which would be more simple. He considered the number of inhabitants as a tolerably good criterion of property, and that this might alwais be obtained. He therefore thought it the best mode which we could adopt, with one exception only. He observed that negroes are property, and as such cannot be distinguished from the lands or personalities held in those States where there are few slaves, that the surplus of profit which a Northern farmer is able to lay by, he invests in cattle, horses, &c. whereas a Southern farmer lays out that same surplus in slaves. There is no more reason therefore for taxing the Southern states on the farmer's head, & on his slave's head, than the Northern ones on their farmer's heads & the heads of their cattle, that the method proposed would therefore tax the Southern states according to their numbers & their wealth conjunctly, while the Northern would be taxed on numbers only: that negroes in fact should not be considered as members of the state more than cattle & that they have no more interest in it.

Mr. John Adams observed that the numbers of people were taken by this article as an index of the wealth of the state, & not as subjects of taxation, that as to this matter it was of no consequence by what name you called your people, whether by that of freemen or of slaves. That in some countries the labouring poor were called freemen, in others they were called slaves; but that the difference as to the state was imaginary only. What matters it whether a landlord employing ten labourers in his farm, gives them annually as much money as will buy them the necessaries of life, or gives them those necessaries at short hand. The ten labourers add as much wealth annually to the state increase it's exports as much in the one case as the other. Certainly 500 freemen produce no more profits, no greater surplus for the paiment of taxes than 500 slaves. Therefore the state in which are the labourers called freemen should be taxed no more than that in which are those called slaves. Suppose by any extraordinary operation of nature or of law one half the labourers of a state could in the course of one night be transformed into slaves: would the state be made the poorer or the less able to pay taxes? That the condition of the laboring poor in most countries, that of the fishermen particularly of the Northern states, is as abject as that of slaves. It is the number of labourers which produce the surplus for taxation, and numbers therefore indiscriminately, are the fair index of wealth. That it is the use of the word "property" here, & it's application to some of the people of the state, which produces the fallacy. How does the Southern farmer procure slaves? Either by importation or by purchase from his neighbor. If he imports a slave, he adds one to the number of labourers in his country, and proportionably to it's profits & abilities to pay taxes. If he buys from his neighbor it is only a transfer of a labourer from one farm to another, which does not change the annual produce of the state, & therefore should not change it's tax. That if a Northern farmer works ten labourers on his farm, he can, it is true, invest the surplus of ten men's labour in cattle: but so may the Southern farmer working ten slaves. That a state of one hundred thousand freemen can maintain no more cattle than one of one hundred thousand slaves. Therefore they have no more of that kind of property. That a slave may indeed from the custom of speech be more properly called the wealth of his master, than the free labourer might be called the wealth of his employer: but as to the state, both were equally it's wealth, and should therefore equally add to the quota of it's tax.

Mr. [Benjamin] Harrison proposed as a compromise, that two slaves should be counted as one freeman. He affirmed that slaves did not do so much work as freemen; and doubted if two effected more than one. That this was proved by the price of labor. The hire of a labourer in the Southern colonies being from 8 to £12. while in the Northern it was generally £24.

Mr. [James] Wilson said that if this amendment should take place the Southern colonies would have all the benefit of slaves, whilst the Northern ones would bear the burthen. That slaves increase the profits of a state, which the Southern states mean to take to themselves; that they also increase the burthen of defence, which would of course fall so much the heavier on the Northern. That slaves occupy the places of freemen and eat their food. Dismiss your slaves & freemen will take their places. It is our duty to lay every discouragement on the importation of slaves; but this amendment would give the jus trium liberorum to him who would import slaves. That other kinds of property were pretty equally distributed thro' all the colonies: there were as many cattle, horses, & sheep, in the North as the South, & South as the North; but not so as to slaves. That experience has shown that those colonies have been alwais able to pay most which have the most inhabitants, whether they be black or white, and the practice of the Southern colonies has alwais been to make every farmer pay poll taxes upon all his labourers whether they be black or white. He acknowledges indeed that freemen work the most; but they consume the most also. They do not produce a greater surplus for taxation. The slave is neither fed nor clothed so expensively as a freeman. Again white women are exempted from labor generally, but negro women are not. In this then the Southern states have an advantage as the article now stands. It has sometimes been said that slavery is necessary because the commodities they raise would be too dear for market if cultivated by freemen; but now it is said that the labor of the slave is the dearest.

Mr. Payne [Robert Treat Paine] urged the original resolution of Congress, to proportion the quotas of the states to the number of souls.

Dr. [John] Witherspoon was of opinion that the value of lands & houses was the best estimate of the wealth of a nation, and that it was practicable to obtain such a valuation. This is the true barometer of wealth. The one now proposed is imperfect in itself, and unequal between the States. It has been objected that negroes eat the food of freemen & therefore should be taxed. Horses also eat the food of freemen; therefore they also should be taxed. It has been said too that in carrying slaves into the estimate of the taxes the state is to pay, we do no more than those states themselves do, who alwais take slaves into the estimate of the taxes the individual is to pay. But the cases are not parallel. In the Southern colonies slaves pervade the whole colony; but they do not pervade the whole continent. That as to the original resolution of Congress to proportion the quotas according to the souls, it was temporary only, & related to the monies heretofore emitted: whereas we are now entering into a new compact, and therefore stand on original ground.

Aug. 1. The question being put the amendment proposed was rejected by the votes of N. Hampshire, Massachusetts, Rhode island, Connecticut, N. York, N. Jersey, & Pennsylvania, against those of Delaware, Maryland, Virginia, North & South Carolina. Georgia was divided.

The other article was in these words. "Art. XVII. In determining questions each colony shall have one vote."

July 30. 31. Aug. 1. Present 41. members. Mr. Chase observed that this article was the most likely to divide us of any one proposed in the draught then under consideration. That the larger colonies had threatened they would not confederate at all if their weight in congress should not be equal to the numbers of people they added to the confederacy; while the smaller ones declared against a

union if they did not retain an equal vote for the protection of their rights. That it was of the utmost consequence to bring the parties together, as should we sever from each other, either no foreign power will ally with us at all, or the different states will form different alliances, and thus increase the horrors of those scenes of civil war and bloodshed which in such a state of separation & independence would render us a miserable people. That our importance, our interests, our peace required that we should confederate, and that mutual sacrifices should be made to effect a compromise of this difficult question. He was of opinion the smaller colonies would lose their rights, if they were not in some instances allowed an equal vote; and therefore that a discrimination should take place among the questions which would come before Congress. That the smaller states should be secured in all questions concerning life or liberty & the greater ones in all respecting property. He therefore proposed that in votes relating to money, the voice of each colony should be proportioned to the number of its inhabitants.

Dr. Franklin thought that the votes should be so proportioned in all cases. He took notice that the Delaware counties had bound up their Delegates to disagree to this article. He thought it a very extraordinary language to be held by any state, that they would not confederate with us unless we would let them dispose of our money. Certainly if we vote equally we ought to pay equally; but the smaller states will hardly purchase the privilege at this price. That had he lived in a state where the representation, originally equal, had become unequal by time & accident he might have submitted rather than disturb government; but that we should be very wrong to set out in this practice when it is in our power to establish what is right. That at the time of the Union between England and Scotland the latter had made the objection which the smaller states now do. But experience had proved that no unfairness had ever been shown them. That their advocates had prognosticated that it would again happen as in times of old, that the whale would swallow Jonas, but he thought the prediction reversed in event and that Jonas had swallowed the whale, for the Scotch had in fact got possession of the government and gave laws to the English. He reprobated the original agreement of Congress to vote by colonies and therefore was for their voting in all cases according to the number of taxables.

Dr. Witherspoon opposed every alteration of the article. All men admit that a confederacy is necessary. Should the idea get abroad that there is likely to be no union among us, it will damp the minds of the people, diminish the glory of our struggle, & lessen it's importance; because it will open to our view future prospects of war & dissension among ourselves. If an equal vote be refused, the smaller states will become vassals to the larger; & all experience has shown that the vassals & subjects of free states are the most enslaved. He instanced the Helots of Sparta & the provinces of Rome. He observed that foreign powers discovering this blemish would make it a handle for disengaging the smaller states from so unequal a confederacy. That the colonies should in fact be considered as individuals; and that as such, in all disputes they should have an equal vote; that they are now collected as individuals making a bargain with each other, & of course had a right to vote as individuals. That in the East India company they voted by persons, & not by their proportion of stock. That the Belgic confederacy voted by provinces. That in questions of war the smaller states were as much interested as the larger, & therefore should vote equally; and indeed that the larger states were more likely to bring war on the confederacy in proportion as their frontier was more extensive. He admitted that equality of representation was an excellent principle, but then it must be of things which are co-ordinate; that is, of things similar & of the same nature: that nothing relating to individuals could ever come before Congress; nothing but what would respect colonies. He distinguished between an incorporating & a federal union. The union of England was an incorporating one; yet Scotland had suffered by that union: for that it's inhabitants were drawn from it by the hopes of places & employments. Nor was it an instance of equality of representation; because while Scotland was allowed nearly a thirteenth of representation they were to pay only one fortieth of the land tax. He expressed his hopes that in the present enlightened state of men's minds we might expect a lasting confederacy, if it was founded on fair principles.

John Adams advocated the voting in proportion to numbers. He said that we stand here as the representatives of the people. That in some states the people are many, in others they are few; that therefore their vote here should be proportioned to the numbers from whom it comes. Reason, justice, & equity never had weight enough on the face of the earth to govern the councils of men. It is interest alone which does it, and it is interest alone which can be trusted. That therefore the interests within doors should be the mathematical representatives of the interests without doors. That the individuality of the colonies is a mere sound. Does the individuality of a colony increase it's wealth or numbers. If it does, pay equally. If it does not add weight in the scale of the confederacy, it cannot add to their rights, nor weigh in argument. A. has £50. B. £500. C. £1000. in partnership. Is it just they should equally dispose of the monies of the partnership? It has been said we are independent individuals making a bargain together. The question is not what we are now, but what we ought to be when our bargain shall be made. The confederacy is to make us one individual only; it is to form us, like separate parcels of metal, into one common mass. We shall no longer retain our separate individuality, but become a single individual as to all questions submitted to the confederacy. Therefore all those reasons which prove the justice & expediency of equal representation in other assemblies, hold good here. It has been objected that a proportional vote will endanger the smaller states. We answer that an equal vote will endanger the larger. Virginia, Pennsylvania, & Massachusetts are the three greater colonies. Consider their distance, their difference of produce, of interests & of manners, & it is apparent they can never have an interest or inclination to combine for the oppression of the smaller. That the smaller will naturally divide on all questions with the larger. Rhode isld, from it's relation, similarity & intercourse will generally pursue the same objects with Massachusetts; Jersey, Delaware & Maryland, with Pennsylvania.

Dr. [Benjamin] Rush took notice that the decay of the liberties of the Dutch republic proceeded from three causes. 1. The perfect unanimity requisite on all occasions. 2. Their obligation to consult their constituents. 3. Their voting by provinces. This last destroyed the equality of representation, and the liberties of great Britain also are sinking from the same defect. That a part of our rights is deposited in the hands of our legislatures. There it was admitted there should be an equality of representation. Another part of our rights is deposited in the hands of Congress: why is it not equally necessary there should be an equal representation there? Were it possible to collect the whole body of the people together, they would determine the questions submitted to them by their majority. Why should not the same majority decide when voting here by their representatives? The larger colonies are so providentially divided in situation as to render every fear of their combining visionary. Their interests are different, & their circumstances dissimilar. It is more probable they will become rivals & leave it in the power of the smaller states to give preponderance to any scale they please. The voting by the number of free inhabitants will have one excellent effect, that of inducing the colonies to discourage slavery & to encourage the increase of their free inhabitants.

Mr. [Stephen] Hopkins observed there were 4 larger, 4 smaller, & 4 middle-sized colonies. That the 4 largest would contain more than half the inhabitants of the confederated states, & therefore would govern the others as they should please. That history affords no instance of such a thing as equal representation. The Germanic body votes by states. The Helvetic body does the same; & so does the Belgic confederacy. That too little is known of the ancient confederations to say what was their practice.

Mr. Wilson thought that taxation should be in proportion to wealth, but that representation should accord with the number of freemen. That government is a collection or result of the wills of all. That if any government could speak the will of all, it would be perfect; and that so far as it departs from this it becomes imperfect. It has been said that Congress is a representation of states; not of individuals. I say that the objects of its care are all the individuals of the states. It is strange that annexing the name of "State" to ten thousand men, should give them an equal right with forty thousand. This must be the effect of magic, not of reason. As to those matters which are referred to Congress, we are not so many states, we are one large state. We lay aside our individuality, whenever we come here. The Germanic body is a burlesque on government; and their practice on any point is a sufficient authority & proof that it is wrong. The greatest imperfection in the constitution of the Belgic confederacy is their voting by provinces. The interest of the whole is constantly sacrificed to that of the small states. The history of the war in the Reign of Q. Anne sufficiently proves this. It is asked shall nine colonies put it into the power of four to govern them as they please? I invert the question, and ask shall two millions of people put it in the power of one million to govern them as they please? It is pretended too that the smaller colonies will be in danger from the greater. Speak in honest language & say the minority will be in danger from the majority. And is there an assembly on earth where this danger may not be equally pretended? The truth is that our proceedings will then be consentaneous with the interests of the majority, and so they ought to be. The probability is much greater than the larger states will disagree than that they will combine. I defy the wit of man to invent a possible case or to suggest any one thing on earth which shall be for the interests of Virginia, Pennsylvania & Massachusetts, and which will not also be for the interest of the other states.

These articles reported July 12. 76 were debated from day to day, & time to time for two years, were ratified July 9, '78, by 10 states, by N. Jersey on the 26th. of Nov. of the same year, and by Delaware on the 23d. of Feb. following. Maryland alone held off 2 years more, acceding to them Mar. 1, 81. and thus closing the obligation.

2

RECORDS OF THE FEDERAL CONVENTION

[1:35; Madison, 30 May]

The following Resolution being the 2d. of those proposed by Mr. Randolph was taken up. viz—"that the rights of suffrage in the National Legislature ought to be proportioned to the quotas of contribution, or to the number of free inhabitants, as the one or the other rule may seem best in different cases."

Mr. Madison observing that the words "or to the number of free inhabitants." might occasion debates which would divert the Committee from the general question whether the principle of representation should be changed, moved that they might be struck out.

Mr. King observed that the quotas of contribution which would alone remain as the measure of representation, would not answer; because waving every other view of the matter, the revenue might hereafter be so collected by the general Govt. that the sums respectively drawn from the States would not appear; and would besides be continually varying.

Mr. Madison admitted the propriety of the observation, and that some better rule ought to be found.

Col. Hamilton moved to alter the resolution so as to read "that the rights of suffrage in the national Legislature ought to be proportioned to the number of free inhabitants. Mr. Spaight 2ded. the motion.

It was then moved that the Resolution be postponed, which was agreed to.

Mr. Randolph and Mr. Madison then moved the following resolution—"that the rights of suffrage in the national Legislature ought to be proportioned"

It was moved and 2ded. to amend it by adding "and not according to the present system"—which was agreed to.

It was then moved and 2ded. to alter the resolution so as to read "that the rights of suffrage in the national Legislature ought not to be according to the present system."

It was then moved & 2ded. to postpone the Resolution moved by Mr. Randolph & Mr. Madison, which being agreed to;

Mr. Madison, moved, in order to get over the difficulties, the following resolution—"that the equality of suffrage established by the articles of Confederation ought not to prevail in the national Legislature, and that an equitable ratio of representation ought to be substituted" This was 2ded. by Mr. Govr. Morris, and being generally relished, would have been agreed to; when,

Mr. Reed moved that the whole clause relating to the point of Representation be postponed; reminding the Come. that the deputies from Delaware were restrained by their commission from assenting to any change of the rule of suffrage, and in case such a change should be fixed on, it might become their duty to retire from the Convention.

Mr. Govr. Morris observed that the valuable assistance of those members could not be lost without real concern, and that so early a proof of discord in the convention as a secession of a State, would add much to the regret; that the change proposed was however so fundamental an article in a national Govt. that it could not be dispensed with.

Mr. Madison observed that whatever reason might have existed for the equality of suffrage when the Union was a federal one among sovereign States, it must cease when a national Governt. should be put into the place. In the former case, the acts of Congs. depended so much for their efficacy on the cooperation of the States, that these had a weight both within & without Congress, nearly in proportion to their extent and importance. In the latter case, as the acts of the Genl. Govt. would take effect without the intervention of the State legislatures, a vote from a small State wd. have the same efficacy & importance as a vote from a large one, and there was the same reason for different numbers of representatives from different States, as from Counties of different extents within particular States. He suggested as an expedient for at once taking the sense of the members on this point and saving the Delaware deputies from embarrassment, that the question should be taken in Committee, and the clause on report to the House be postponed without a question there. This however did not appear to satisfy Mr. Read.

By several it was observed that no just construction of the Act of Delaware, could require or justify a secession of her deputies, even if the resolution were to be carried thro' the House as well as the Committee. It was finally agreed however that the clause should be postponed: it being understood that in the event the proposed change of representation would certainly be agreed to, no objection or difficulty being started from any other quarter than from Delaware.

[1:176; Madison, 9 June]

Mr. Patterson moves that the Committee resume the clause relating to the rule of suffrage in the Natl. Legislature.

Mr. Brearly seconds him. He was sorry he said that any question on this point was brought into view. It had been much agitated in Congs. at the time of forming the Confederation and was then rightly settled by allowing to each sovereign State an equal vote. Otherwise the smaller States must have been destroyed instead of being saved. The substitution of a ratio, he admitted carried fairness on the face of it; but on a deeper examination was unfair and unjust. Judging of the disparity of the States by the quota of Congs. Virga. would have 16 votes, and Georgia but one. A like proportion to the others will make the whole number ninity. There will be 3. large states and 10 small ones. The large States by which he meant Massts. Pena. & Virga. will carry every thing before them. It had been admitted, and was known to him from facts within N. Jersey that where large and small counties were united into a district for electing representatives for the district, the large counties always carried their point, and Consequently that the large States would do so. Virga. with her sixteen votes will be a solid column indeed, a formidable phalanx. While Georgie with her Solitary vote, and the other little States will be obliged to throw themselves constantly into the scale of some large one, in order to have any weight at all. He had come to the convention with a view of being as useful as he could in giving energy and stability to the Federal Government. When the proposition for destroying the equality of votes came forward, he was astonished, he was alarmed. Is it fair then it will be asked that Georgia should have an equal vote with Virga.? He would not say it was. What remedy then? One only, that a map of the U. S. be spread out, that all the existing boundaries be erased, and that a new partition of the whole be made into 13 equal parts

Mr. Patterson considered the proposition for a proportional representation as striking at the existence of the lesser States. He wd. premise however to an investigation of this question some remarks on the nature structure and powers of the Convention. The Convention he said was formed in pursuance of an Act of Congs. that this act was recited in several of the Commissions, particularly that of Massts. which he required to be read: That the amendment of the confederacy was the object of all the laws and commissions on the subject; that the articles of the confederation were therefore the proper basis of all the proceedings of the Convention. We ought to keep within its limits, or we should be charged by our constituents with usurpation. that the people of America were sharpsighted and not to be deceived. But the Commissions under which we acted were not only the measure of our power. they denoted also the sentiments of the States on the subject of our deliberation. The idea of a national Govt. as contradistinguished from a federal one, never entered into the mind of any of them, and to the public mind we must accommodate ourselves. We have no power to go beyond the federal scheme, and if we had the people are not ripe for any other. We must follow the people; the people will not follow us. *The proposition* could not be maintained whether considered in reference to us as a nation, or as a confederacy. A confederacy supposes sovereignty in the members composing it & sovereignty supposes equality. If we are to be considered as a nation, all State distinctions must be abolished, the whole must be thrown into hotchpot, and when an equal division is made, then there may be fairly an equality of representation. He held up Virga. Massts. & Pa. as the three large States, and the other ten as small ones; repeating the calculations of Mr. Brearly as to the disparity of votes which wd. take place, and affirming that the small States would never agree to it. He said there was no more reason that a great individual State contributing much, should have more votes than a small one contributing little, than that a rich individual citizen should have more votes than an indigent one. If the rateable property of A was to that of B as 40 to 1. ought A for that reason to have 40 times as many votes as B. Such a principle would never be admitted, and if it were admitted would put B entirely at the mercy of A. As A. has more to be protected than B so he ought to contribute more for the common protection. The same may be said of a large State wch. has more to be protected than a small one. Give the large States an influence in proportion to their magnitude, and what will be the consequence? Their ambition will be proportionally increased, and the small States will have every thing to fear. It was once proposed by Galloway & some others that America should be represented in the British Parlt. and then be bound by its laws. America could not have been entitled to more than ⅓ of the no. of Representatives which would fall to the share of G. B. Would American rights & interests have been safe under an authority thus constituted? It has been said that if a Natl. Govt. is to be formed so as to operate on the people and not on the States, the representatives ought to be drawn from the people. But why so? May not a Legislature filled by the State Legislatures operate on the people who chuse the State Legislatures? or may not a practicable coercion be found. He admitted that there was none such in the existing System. He was attached strongly to the plan of the existing confederacy, in which the people chuse their Legislative representatives; and the Legislatures their federal representatives. No other amendments were wanting than to mark the orbits of the States with due precision, and provide for the use of coercion, which was the great point. He alluded to the hint thrown out heretofore by Mr. Wilson of the necessity to which the large States might be reduced of confederating among themselves, by a refusal of the others to concur. Let them unite if they please, but let them remember that they have no authority to compel the others to unite. N. Jersey will never confederate on the plan before the Committee. She would be swallowed up. He had rather submit to a monarch, to a despot, than to such a fate. He would not only oppose the plan here but on his return home do everything in his power to defeat it there

Mr. Wilson. hoped if the Confederacy should be dissolved, that a *majority*, that a *minority* of the States would unite for their safety. He entered elaborately into the defence of a proportional representation, stating for his first position that as all authority was derived from the people, equal numbers of people ought to have an equal no. of representatives, and different numbers of people different numbers of representatives. This principle had been improperly violated in the Confederation, owing to the urgent circumstances of the time. As to the case of A. & B, stated by Mr. Patterson, he observed that in districts as large as the States, the number of people was the best measure of their comparative wealth. Whether therefore wealth or numbers were to form the ratio it would be the same. Mr. P. admitted persons, not property to be the measure of suffrage. Are not the citizens of Pena. equal to those of N. Jersey? does it require 150 of the former to balance 50 of the latter? Representatives of different districts ought clearly to hold the same proportion to each other, as their respective constituents hold to each other. If the small States will not confederate on this plan, Pena. & he presumed some other States, would not confederate on any other. We have been told that each State being sovereign, all are equal. So each man is naturally a sovereign over himself, and all men are therefore naturally equal. Can he retain this equality when he becomes a member of civil Government? He can not. As little can a Sovereign State, when it becomes a member of a federal Governt. If N. J. will not part with her Sovereignty it is in vain to talk of Govt. A new partition of the States is desireable, but evidently & totally impracticable.

Mr. Williamson, illustrated the cases by a comparison of the different States, to Counties of different sizes within the same State; observing that proportional representation was admitted to be just in the latter case, and could not therefore be fairly contested in the former.

The question being about to be put Mr. Patterson hoped that as so much depended on it, it might be thought best to postpone the decision till tomorrow, which was done nem. con—

[1:196; Madison, 11 June]

The clause concerning the rule of suffrage in the natl. Legislature postponed on Saturday, was resumed.

Mr. Sharman proposed that the proportion of suffrage in the 1st branch should be according to the respective numbers of free inhabitants; and that in the second branch or Senate, each State should have one vote and no more. He said as the States would remain possessed of certain individual rights, each State ought to be able to protect itself: otherwise a few large States will rule the rest. The House of Lords in England he observed had certain particular rights under the Constitution, and hence they have an equal vote with the House of Commons that they may be able to defend their rights.

Mr. Rutlidge proposed that the proportion of suffrage in the 1st branch should be according to the quotas of contribution. The justice of this rule he said could not be contested. Mr. Butler urged the same idea: adding that money was power; and that the States ought to have weight in the Govt.—in proportion to their wealth.

Mr. King & Mr. Wilson in order to bring the question to a point moved "that the right of suffrage in the first branch of the national Legislature ought not to be according the rule established in the articles of Confederation, but according to some equitable ratio of representation". The clause so far as it related to suffrage in the first branch was postponed in order to consider this motion:

Mr. Dickenson contended for the *actual* contributions of the States as the rule of their representation & suffrage in the first branch. By thus connecting the interest of the States with their duty, the latter would be sure to be performed.

Mr. King remarked that it was uncertain what mode might be used in levying a national revenue; but that it was probable, imports would be one source of it. If the *actual* contributions were to be the rule the non-importing States, as Cont. & N. Jersey, wd. be in a bad situation indeed. It might so happen that they wd. have no representation. This situation of particular States had been always one powerful argument in favor of the 5 Per Ct. impost.

The question being abt. to be put Docr. Franklin sd. he had thrown his ideas of the matter on a paper wch. Mr. Wilson read to the Committee in the words following—

Mr Chairman

It has given me a great pleasure to observe that till this point, the proportion of representation, came before us, our debates were carried on with great coolness & temper. If any thing of a contrary kind, has on this occasion appeared. I hope it will not be repeated; for we are sent here to *consult* not to *contend*, with each other; and declarations of a fixed opinion, and of determined resolution, never to change it, neither enlighten nor convince us. Positiveness and warmth on one side, naturally beget their like on the other; and tend to create and augment discord & division in a great concern, wherein harmony & Union are extremely necessary to give weight to our Councils, and render them effectual in promoting & securing the common good.

I must own that I was originally of opinion it would be better if every member of Congress, or our national Council, were to consider himself rather as a representative of the whole, than as an Agent for the interests of a particular State; in which case the proportion of members for each State would be of less consequence, & it would not be very material whether they voted by States or individually. But as I find this is not to be expected, I now think the number of Representatives should bear some proportion to the number of the Represented; and that the decisions shd. be by the majority of members, not by the majority of States. This is objected to from an apprehension that the greater States would then swallow up the smaller. I do not at present clearly see what advantage the greater States could propose to themselves by swallowing the smaller, and therefore do not apprehend they would attempt it. I recollect that in the beginning of this Century, when the Union was proposed of the two Kingdoms, England & Scotland, the Scotch Patriots were full of fears, that unless they had an equal number of Representatives in Parliament, they should be ruined by the superiority of the English. They finally agreed however that the different proportions of importance in the Union, of the two Nations should be attended to, whereby they were to have only forty members in the House of Commons, and only sixteen in the House of Lords; A very great inferiority of numbers! And yet to this day I do not recollect that any thing has been done in the Parliament of Great Britain to the prejudice of Scotland; and whoever looks over the lists of public officers, Civil & military of that nation will find I believe that the North Britons enjoy at least their full proportion of emolument.

But, Sir, in the present mode of voting by States, it is equally in the power of the lesser States to swallow up the greater; and this is mathematically demonstrable. Suppose for example, that 7 smaller States had each 3 members in the House, and the 6 larger to have one with another 6 members; and that upon a question, two members of each smaller State should be in affirmative and one in the Negative, they will make

Affirmatives 14   .... Negatives   7
And that all the larger States should
    be unanimously
in the negative, they would
        make .... Negatives   36
                                    In all ...   43

It is then apparent that the 14 carry the question against the 43. and the minority overpowers the majority, contrary to the common practice of Assemblies in all Countries and Ages.

The greater States Sir are naturally as unwilling to have their property left in the disposition of the smaller, as the smaller are to have theirs in the disposition of the greater. An honorable gentleman has, to avoid this difficulty, hinted a proposition of equalizing the States. It appears to me an equitable one, and I should, for my own part, not be against such a measure, if it might be found practicable. Formerly, indeed, when almost every province had a different Constitution, some with greater others with fewer privileges, it was of importance to the borderers when their boundaries were contested, whether by running the division lines, they were placed on one side or the other. At present when such differences are done away, it is less material. The Interest of a State is made up of the interests of its individual members. If they are not injured, the State is not injured. Small States are more easily well & happily governed than large ones. If therefore in such an equal division, it should be found necessary to diminish Pennsylvania, I should not be averse to the giving a part of it to N. Jersey, and another to Delaware. But as there would probably be considerable difficulties in adjusting such a division; and however equally made at first, it would be continually varying by the augmentation of inhabitants in some States, and their [more] fixed proportion in others; and thence frequent occasion for new divisions, I beg leave to propose for the consideration of the Committee another mode which appears to me to be as equitable, more easily carried into practice, and more permanent in its nature.

Let the weakest State say what proportion of money or force it is able and willing to furnish for the general purposes of the Union.

Let all the others oblige themselves to furnish each an equal proportion.

The whole of these joint supplies to be absolutely in the disposition of Congress.

The Congress in this case to be composed of an equal number of Delegates from each State:

And their decisions to be by the majority of individual members voting.

If these joint and equal supplies should on particular occasions not be sufficient, Let Congress make requisitions on the richer and more powerful States for farther aids, to be voluntarily afforded, leaving to each State the right of considering the necessity and utility of the aid desired, and of giving more or less as it should be found proper.

This mode is not new, it was formerly practiced with success by the British Government with respect to Ireland and the Colonies. We sometimes gave even more than they expected, or thought just to accept; and in the last war carried on while we were united, they gave us back in five years a million Sterling. We should probably have continued such voluntary contributions, whenever the occasions appeared to require them for the common good of the Empire. It was not till they chose to force us, and to deprive us of the merit and pleasure of voluntary contributions that we refused & resisted. Those contributions however were to be disposed of at the pleasure of a Government in which we had no representative. I am therefore persuaded, that they will not be refused to one in which the Representation shall be equal

My learned colleague (Mr. Wilson) has already mentioned that the present method of voting by States, was submitted to originally by Congress, under a conviction of its impropriety, inequality, and injustice. This appears in the words of their Resolution. It is of Sepr. 6. 1774. The words are

"Resolved that in determining questions in this Congs. each colony or province shall have one vote: the Congs. not being possessed of or at present able to procure materials for ascertaining the importance of each Colony."

On the question for agreeing to Mr. Kings and Mr. Wilsons motion. it passed in the affirmative Massts. ay. Ct. ay. N. Y no. N. J. no. Pa. ay. Del. no. Md. divd. Va. ay. N. C. ay. S. C. ay. Geo. ay. [Ayes—7; noes—3; divided—1.]

It was then moved by Mr. Rutlidge 2ded. by Mr. Butler to add to the words "equitable ratio of representation" at the end of the motion just agreed to, the words "according to the quotas of Contribution." On motion of

Mr. Wilson seconded by Mr. C. *Pinckney,* this was postponed; in order to add, after, after the words "equitable ratio of representation" the words following "in proportion to the whole number of white & other free Citizens & inhabitants of every age sex & condition including those bound to servitude for a term of years and three fifths of all other persons not comprehended in the foregoing description, except Indians not paying taxes, in each State." this being the rule in the Act of Congress agreed to by eleven States, for apportioning quotas of revenue on the States. and requiring a census only every 5—7, or 10 years.

Mr. Gerry thought property not the rule of representation. Why then shd. the blacks, who were property in the South, be in the rule of representation more than the cattle & horses of the North.

On the question.

Mass: Con: N. Y. Pen: Maryd. Virga. N. C. S. C. and

Geo: were in the affirmative: N. J. & Del: in the negative. [Ayes—9; noes—2.]

[1:436; Madison, 27 June]

Mr. Rutledge moved to postpone the 6th. Resolution, defining the powers of Congs.: in order to take up the 7 & 8 which involved the most fundamental points; the rules of suffrage in the 2 branches which was agreed to nem. con.

A question being proposed on Resol: 7 declaring that the suffrage in the first branch sd. be according to an equitable ratio

Mr L. Martin contended at great length and with great eagerness that the General Govt. was meant merely to preserve the State Governts: not to govern individuals: that its powers ought to be kept within narrow limits; that if too little power was given to it, more might be added; but that if too much, it could never be resumed: that individuals as such have little to do but with their own States; that the Genl. Govt. has no more to apprehend from the States composing the Union while it pursues proper measures, that a Govt. over individuals has to apprehend from its subjects: that to resort to the Citizens at large for their sanction to a new Governt. will be throwing them back into a State of Nature: that the dissolution of the State Govts. is involved in the nature of the process: that the people have no right to do this without the consent of those to whom they have delegated their power for State purposes; through their tongue only they can speak, through their ears, only, can hear: that the States have shewn a good disposition to comply with the Acts, of Congs. weak, contemptibly weak as that body has been; and have failed through inability alone to comply: that the heaviness of the private debts, and the waste of property during the war, were the chief causes of this inability; that he did not conceive the instances mentioned by Mr. Madison of conpacts between Va. & Md. between Pa. & N. J. or of troops raised by Massts. for defence against the Rebels, to be violations of the articles of confederation—that an equal vote in each State was essential to the federal idea, and was founded in justice & freedom, not merely in policy: that tho' the States may give up this right of sovereignty, yet they had not, and ought not: that the States like individuals were in a State of nature equally sovereign & free. In order to prove that individuals in a State of nature are equally free & independent he read passages from Locke, Vattel, Lord Summers—Priestly. To prove that the case is the same with States till they surrender their equal sovereignty, he read other passages in Locke & Vattel, and also Rutherford: that the States being equal cannot treat or confederate so as to give up an equality of votes without giving up their liberty: that the propositions on the table were a system of slavery for 10 States: that as Va. Masts. & Pa. have 42/90 of the votes they can do as they please without a miraculous Union of the other ten: that they will have nothing to do, but to gain over one of the ten to make them compleat masters of the rest, that they can then appoint an Execute: & Judiciary & legislate for them as they please: that there was & would continue a natural predilection & partiality in men for their own States; that the

States, particularly the smaller, would never allow a negative to be exercised over their laws: that no State in ratifying the Confederation had objected to the equality of votes; that the complaints at present run not agst. this equality but the want of power; that 16 members from Va. would be more likely to act in concert than a like number formed of members from different States; that instead of a junction of the small States as a remedy, he thought a division of the large States would be more eligible.—This was the substance of a speech which was continued more than three hours. He was too much exhausted he said to finish his remarks, and reminded the House that he should tomorrow, resume them.

[1:444; Madison, 28 June]

Mr. L. Martin resumed his discourse, contending that the Genl. Govt. ought to be formed for the States, not for individuals: that if the States were to have votes in proportion to their numbers of people, it would be the same thing whether their representatives were chosen by the Legislatures or the people; the smaller States would be equally enslaved; that if the large States have the same interest with the smaller as was urged, there could be no danger in giving them an equal vote; they would not injure themselves, and they could not injure the large ones on that supposition without injuring themselves and if the interests were not the same the inequality of suffrage wd— be dangerous to the smaller States: that it will be in vain to propose any plan offensive to the rulers of the States, whose influence over the people will certainly prevent their adopting it: that the large States were weak at present in proportion to their extent: & could only be made formidable to the small ones, by the weight of their votes; that in case a dissolution of the Union should take place, the small States would have nothing to fear from their power; that if in such a case the three great States should league themselves together, the other ten could do so too: & that he had rather see partial Confederacies take place, than the plan on the table. This was the substance of the residue of his discourse which was delivered with much diffuseness & considerable vehemence.

Mr. Lansing & Mr. Dayton moved to strike out "not." so that the 7 art: might read that the rights of suffrage in the 1st branch ought to be according to the rule established by the Confederation"

Mr. Dayton expressed great anxiety that the question might not be put till tomorrow; Governr. Livingston being kept away by indisposition, and the representation of N. Jersey thereby suspended.

Mr. Williamson. thought that if any political truth could be grounded on mathematical demonstration, it was that if the states were equally sovereign now, and parted with equal proportions of sovereignty, that they would remain equally sovereign. He could not comprehend how the smaller States would be injured in the case, and wished some gentleman would vouchsafe a solution of it. He observed that the small States, if they had a plurality of votes would have an interest in throwing the burdens off their own shoulders on those of the large ones. He begged that the expected addition of new States from the Westward might be kept in view. They would be small States, they would be poor States, they would be unable to pay in proportion to their numbers; their distance from market rendering the produce of their labour less valuable; they would consequently be tempted to combine for the purpose of laying burdens on commerce & consumption which would fall with greatest weight on the old States.

Mr. Madison sd. he was much disposed to concur in any expedient not inconsistent with fundamental principles, that could remove the difficulty concerning the rule of representation. But he could neither be convinced that the rule contended for was just, nor necessary for the safety of the small States agst. the large States. That it was not just, had been conceded by Mr. Breerly & Mr. Patterson themselves. The expedient proposed by them was a new partition of the territory of the U. States. The fallacy of the reasoning drawn from the equality of Sovereign States in the formation of compacts, lay in confounding mere Treaties, in which were specified certain duties to which the parties were to be bound, and certain rules by which their subjects were to be reciprocally governed in their intercourse, with a compact by which an authority was created paramount to the parties, & making laws for the government of them. If France, England & Spain were to enter into a Treaty for the regulation of commerce &c. with the Prince of Monacho & 4 or 5 other of the smallest sovereigns of Europe, they would not hesitate to treat as equals, and to make the regulations perfectly reciprocal. Wd. the case be the same if a Council were to be formed of deputies from each with authority and discretion, to raise money, levy troops, determine the value of coin &c? Would 30 or 40. million of people submit their fortunes into the hands, of a few thousands? If they did it would only prove that they expected more from the terror of their superior force, than they feared from the selfishness of their feeble associates Why are Counties of the same States represented in proportion to their numbers? Is it because the representatives are chosen by the people themselves? so will be the representatives in the Nationl. Legislature. Is it because, the larger have more at stake than the smaller? The case will be the same with the larger & smaller States. Is it because the laws are to operate immediately on their persons & properties? The same is the case in some degree as the articles of confederation stand; the same will be the case in a far greater degree under the plan proposed to be substituted. In the cases of captures, of piracies, and of offenses in a federal army, the property & persons of individuals depend on the laws of Congs. By the plan proposed a compleat power of taxation, the highest prerogative of supremacy is proposed to be vested in the National Govt. Many other powers are added which assimilate it to the Govt. of individual States. The negative on the State laws proposed, will make it an essential branch of the State Legislatures & of course will require that it should be exercised by a body established on like principles with the other branches of those Legislatures.— That it is not necessary to secure the small States agst. the large ones he conceived to be equally obvious: Was a combination of the large ones dreaded? this must arise either from some interest common to Va. Masts. & Pa. & distin-

guishing them from the other States or from the mere circumstance of similarity of size. Did any such common interest exist? In point of situation they could not have been more effectually separated from each other by the most jealous citizen of the most jealous State. In point of manners, Religion and the other circumstances, which sometimes beget affection between different communities, they were not more assimilated than the other States.—In point of the staple productions they were as dissimilar as any three other States in the Union.

The Staple of Masts. was *fish,* of Pa. *flower,* of Va. *Tobo.* Was a Combination to be apprehended from the mere circumstance of equality of size? Experience suggested no such danger. The journals of Congs. did not present any peculiar association of these States in the votes recorded. It had never been seen that different Counties in the same State, conformable in extent, but disagreeing in other circumstances, betrayed a propensity to such combinations. Experience rather taught a contrary lesson. Among individuals of superior eminence & weight in society, rivalships were much more frequent than coalitions. Among independent nations preeminent over their neighbours, the same remark was verified. Carthage & Rome tore one another to pieces instead of uniting their forces to devour the weaker nations of the Earth. The Houses of Austria & France were hostile as long as they remained the greatest powers of Europe. England & France have succeeded to the pre-eminence & to the enmity. To this principle we owe perhaps our liberty. A coalition between those powers would have been fatal to us. Among the principal members of antient & modern confederacies, we find the same effect from the same cause. The contentions, not the coalitions of Sparta, Athens & Thebes, proved fatal to the smaller members of the Amphyctionic Confederacy. The contentions, not the combinations of Prussia & Austria, have distracted & oppressed the Germanic empire. Were the large States formidable *singly* to their smaller neighbours? On this supposition the latter ought to wish for such a general Govt. as will operate with equal energy on the former as on themselves. The more lax the band, the more liberty the larger will have to avail themselves of their superior force. Here again Experience was an instructive monitor. What is ye situation of the weak compared with the strong in those stages of civilization in which the violence of individuals is least controuled by an efficient Government? The Heroic period of Antient Greece the feudal licentiousness of the middle ages of Europe, the existing condition of the American Savages, answer this question. What is the situation of the minor sovereigns in the great society of independent nations, in which the more powerful are under no controul but the nominal authority of the law of Nations? Is not the danger to the former exactly in proportion to their weakness. But there are cases still more in point. What was the condition of the weaker members of the Amphyctionic Confederacy. Plutarch (life of Themistocles) will inform us that it happened but too often that the strongest cities corrupted & awed the weaker, and that Judgment went in favor of the more powerful party. What is the condition of the lesser States in the German Confederacy? We all know that they are exceedingly trampled upon and that they owe their safety as far as they enjoy it, partly to their enlisting themselves, under the rival banners of the preeminent members, partly to alliances with neighbouring Princes which the Constitution of the Empire does not prohibit. What is the state of things in the lax system of the Dutch Confederacy? Holland contains about ½ the people, supplies about ½ of the money, and by her influence, silently & indirectly governs the whole Republic. In a word; the two extremes before us are a perfect separation & a perfect incorporation, of the 13 States. In the first case they would be independent nations subject to no law, but the law of nations. In the last, they would be mere counties of one entire republic, subject to one common law. In the first case the smaller states would have every thing to fear from the larger. In the last they would have nothing to fear. The true policy of the small States therefore lies in promoting those principles & that form of Govt. which will most approximate the States to the condition of Counties. Another consideration may be added. If the Genl. Govt. be feeble, the large States distrusting its continuance, and foreseeing that their importance & security may depend on their own size & strength, will never submit to a partition. Give to the Genl. Govt. sufficient energy & permanency, & you remove the objection. Gradual partitions of the large, & junctions of the small States will be facilitated, and time may effect that equalization, which is wished for by the small States, now, but can never be accomplished at once.

Mr. Wilson. The leading argument of those who contend for equality of votes among the States is that the States as such being equal, and being represented not as districts of individuals, but in their political & corporate capacities, are entitled to an equality of suffrage. According to this mode of reasoning the representation of the burroughs in Engld which has been allowed on all hands to be the rotten part of the Constitution, is perfectly right & proper. They are like the States represented in their corporate capacity like the States therefore they are entitled to equal voices, old Sarum to as many as London. And instead of the injury supposed hitherto to be done to London, the true ground of complaint lies with old Sarum; for London instead of two which is her proper share, sends four representatives to Parliament.

Mr. Sherman. The question is not what rights naturally belong to men; but how they may be most equally & effectually guarded in Society. And if some give up more than others in order to attain this end, there can be no room for complaint. To do otherwise, to require an equal concession from all, if it would create danger to the rights of some, would be sacrificing the end to the means. The rich man who enters into Society along with the poor man, gives up more than the poor man. yet with an equal vote he is equally safe. Were he to have more votes than the poor man in proportion to his superior stake, the rights of the poor man would immediately cease to be secure. This consideration prevailed when the articles of confederation were formed.

The determination of the question from striking out the word "not" was put off till to morrow at the request of the Deputies of N. York.

[1:461; Madison, 29 June]

Doctr. Johnson. The controversy must be endless whilst Gentlemen differ in the grounds of their arguments; Those on one side considering the States as districts of people composing one political Society; those on the other considering them as so many political societies. The fact is that the States do exist as political Societies, and a Govt. is to be formed for them in their political capacity, as well as for the individuals composing them. Does it not seem to follow, that if the States as such are to exist they must be armed with some power of self-defence. This is the idea of (Col. Mason) who appears to have looked to the bottom of this matter. Besides the Aristocratic and other interests, which ought to have the means of defending themselves, the States have their interests as such, and are equally entitled to likes means. On the whole he thought that as in some respects the States are to be considered in their political capacity, and in others as districts of individual citizens, the two ideas embraced on different sides, instead of being opposed to each other, ought to be combined; that in *one* branch the *people*, ought to be represented; in the *other*, the *States*.

Mr. Ghorum. The States as now confederated have no doubt a right to refuse to be consolidated, or to be formed into any new system. But he wished the small States which seemed most ready to object, to consider which are to give up most, they or the larger ones. He conceived that a rupture of the Union wd. be an event unhappy for all, but surely the large States would be least unable to take care of themselves, and to make connections with one another. The weak therefore were most interested in establishing some general system for maintaining order. If among individuals, composed partly of weak, and partly of strong, the former most need the protection of law & Government, the case is exactly the same with weak & powerful States. What would be the situation of Delaware (for these things he found must be spoken out, & it might as well be done first as last) what wd. be the situation of Delaware in case of a separation of the States? Would she not lie at the mercy of Pennsylvania? would not her true interest lie in being consolidated with her, and ought she not now to wish for such a union with Pa. under one Govt. as will put it out of the power of Pena. to oppress her? Nothing can. be more ideal than the danger apprehended by the States, from their being formed into one nation. Massts. was originally three colonies, viz old Massts.—Plymouth—& the province of Mayne. These apprehensions existed then. An incorporation took place; all parties were safe & satisfied; and every distinction is now forgotten. The case was similar with Connecticut & Newhaven. The dread of Union was reciprocal; the consequence of it equally salutary and satisfactory. In like manner N. Jersey has been made one society out of two parts. Should a separation of the States take place, the fate of N. Jersey wd. be worst of all. She has no foreign commerce & can have but little. Pa. & N. York will continue to levy taxes on her consumption. If she consults her interest she wd. beg of all things to be annihilated. The apprehensions of the small States ought to be appeased by another reflection. Massts. will be divided. The province of Maine is already considered as approaching the term of its annexation to it; and Pa. will probably not increase, considering the present state of her population, & other events that may happen. On the whole he considered a Union of the States as necessary to their happiness, & a firm Genl. Govt. as necessary to their Union. He shd. consider it as his duty if his colleagues viewed the matter in the same light he did to stay here as long as any other State would remain with them, in order to agree on some plan that could with propriety be recommended to the people.

Mr. Elseworth, did not despair. He still trusted that some good plan of Govt. wd. be divised & adopted.

Mr. Read. He shd. have no objection to the system if it were truly national, but it has too much of a federal mixture in it. The little States he thought had not much to fear. He suspected that the large States felt their want of energy, & wished for a genl. Govt. to supply the defect. Massts. was evidently labouring under her weakness and he believed Delaware wd. not be in much danger if in her neighbourhood. Delaware had enjoyed tranquillity & he flattered himself wd. continue to do so. He was not however so selfish as not to wish for a good Genl. Govt. In order to obtain one the whole States must be incorporated. If the States remain, the representatives of the large ones will stick together, and carry every thing before them. The Executive also will be chosen under the influence of this partiality, and will betray it in his administration. These jealousies are inseparable from the scheme of leaving the States in Existence. They must be done away. The ungranted lands also which have been assumed by particular States must also be given up. He repeated his approbation of the plan of Mr. Hamilton, & wished it to be substituted in place of that on the table.

Mr. Madison agreed with Docr. Johnson, that the mixed nature of the Govt. ought to be kept in view; but thought too much stress was laid on the rank of the States as political societies. There was a gradation, he observed from the smallest corporation, with the most limited powers, to the largest empire with the most perfect sovereignty. He pointed out the limitations on the sovereignty of the States. as now confederated; their laws in relation to the paramount law of the Confederacy were analogous to that of bye laws to the supreme law, within a State. Under the proposed Govt. the powers of the States will be much farther reduced. According to the views of every member, the Genl. Govt. will have powers far beyond those exercised by the British Parliament when the States were part of the British Empire. It will in particular have the power, without the consent of the State Legislatures, to levy money directly on the people themselves; and therefore not to divest such *unequal* portions of the people as composed the several States, of an *equal* voice, would subject the system to the reproaches & evils which have resulted from the vicious representation in G. B.

He entreated the gentlemen representing the small States to renounce a principle wch. was confessedly unjust, which cd. never be admitted, & if admitted must infuse mortality into a Constitution which we wished to last forever. He prayed them to ponder well the consequences of suffering the Confederacy to go to pieces. It had been sd. that the want of energy in the large states wd. be a security to the small. It was forgotten that this want of energy proceded from the supposed security of the States agst. all external danger. Let each State depend on itself for its security, & let apprehensions arise of danger from distant powers or from neighbouring States, & the languishing condition of all the States, large as well as small, wd. soon be transformed into vigorous & high toned Govts. His great fear was that their Govts. wd. then have too much energy, that these might not only be formidable in the large to the small States, but fatal to the internal liberty of all. The same causes which have rendered the old world the Theatre of incesssant wars, & have banished liberty from the face of it, wd. soon produce the same effects here. The weakness & jealousy of the small States wd. quickly introduce some regular military force agst. sudden danger from their powerful neighbours. The example wd. be followed by others, and wd. soon become universal. In time of actual war, great discretionary powers are constantly given to the Executive Magistrate. Constant apprehension of War, has the same tendency to render the head too large for the body. A standing military force, with an overgrown Executive will not long be safe companions to liberty. The means of defence agst. foreign danger, have been always the instruments of tyranny at home. Among the Romans it was a standing maxim to excite a war, whenever a revolt was apprehended. Throughout all Europe, the armies kept up under the pretext of defending, have enslaved the people. It is perhaps questionable, whether the best concerted system of absolute power in Europe cd. maintain itself, in a situation, where no alarms of external danger cd. tame the people to the domestic yoke. The insular situation of G. Britain was the principal cause of her being an exception to the general fate of Europe. It has rendered less defence necessary, and admitted a kind of defence wch. cd. not be used for the purpose of oppression.—These consequences he conceived ought to be apprehended whether the States should run into a total separation from each other, or shd. enter into partial confederacies. Either event wd. be truly deplorable; & those who might be accessary to either, could never be forgiven by their Country, nor by themselves.

Mr. Hamilton observed that individuals forming political Societies modify their rights differently, with regard to suffrage. Examples of it are found in all the States. In all of them some individuals are deprived of the right altogether, not having the requisite qualification of property. In some of the States the right of suffrage is allowed in some cases and refused in others. To vote for a member in one branch, a certain quantum of property, to vote for a member in another branch of the Legislature, a higher quantum of property is required. In like manner States may modify their right of suffrage differently, the larger exercising a larger, the smaller a smaller share of it. But as States are a collection of individual men which ought we to respect most, the rights of the people composing them, or of the artificial beings resulting from the composition. Nothing could be more preposterous or absurd than to sacrifice the former to the latter. It has been sd. that if the smaller States renounce their *equality,* they renounce at the same time their *liberty.* The truth is it is a contest for power, not for liberty. Will the men composing the small States be less free than those composing the larger. The State of Delaware having 40,000 souls will *lose power,* if she has ⅒ only of the votes allowed to Pa. having 400,000: but will the people of Del: *be less free,* if each citizen has an equal vote with each citizen of Pa. He admitted that common residence within the same State would produce a certain degree of attachment; and that this principle might have a certain influence in public affairs. He thought however that this might by some precautions be in a great measure excluded: and that no material inconvenience could result from it, as there could not be any ground for combination among the States whose influence was most dreaded. The only considerable distinction of interests, lay between the carrying & non-carrying States, which divide instead of uniting the largest States. No considerable inconvenience had been found from the division of the State of N. York into different districts, of different sizes.

Some of the consequences of a dissolution of the Union, and the establishment of partial confederacies, had been pointed out. He would add another of a most serious nature. Alliances will immediately be formed with different rival & hostile nations of Europes, who will foment disturbances among ourselves, and make us parties to all their own quarrels. Foreign nations having American dominions are & must be jealous of us. Their representatives betray the utmost anxiety for our fate, & for the result of this meeting, which must have an essential influence on it.—It had been said that respectability in the eyes of foreign Nations was not the object at which we aimed; that the proper object of republican Government was domestic tranquillity & happiness. This was an ideal distinction. No Governmt. could give us tranquillity & happiness at home, which did not possess sufficient stability and strength to make us respectable abroad. This was the critical moment for forming such a government. We should run every risk in trusting to future amendments. As yet we retain the habits of union. We are weak & sensible of our weakness. Henceforward the motives will become feebler, and the difficulties greater. It is a miracle that we were now here exercising our tranquil & free deliberations on the subject. It would be madness to trust to future miracles. A thousand causes must obstruct a reproduction of them.

Mr. Peirce considered the equality of votes under the Confederation as the great source of the public difficulties. The members of Congs. were advocates for local advantages. State distinctions must be sacrificed as far as the general good required: but without destroying the States. Tho' from a small State he felt himself a Citizen of the U. S.

Mr. Gerry, urged that we never were independent States, were not such now, & never could be even on the principles of the Confederation. The States & the advocates for them were intoxicated with the idea of their *sovereignty.* He was a member of Congress at the time the federal articles were formed. The injustice of allowing each State an equal vote was long insisted on. He voted for it, but it was agst. his Judgment, and under the pressure of public danger, and the obstinacy of the lesser States. The present confederation he considered as dissolving. The fate of the Union will be decided by the Convention. If they do not agree on something, few delegates will probably be appointed to Congs. If they do Congs. will probably be kept up till the new System should be adopted—He lamented that instead of coming here like a band of brothers, belonging to the same family, we seemed to have brought with us the spirit of political negociators.

Mr. L. Martin. remarked that the language of the States being *Sovereign & independent,* was once familiar & understood; though it seemed now so strange & obscure. He read those passages in the articles of Confederation, which describe them in that language.

On the question as moved by Mr. Lansing. Shall the word "not" be struck out.

Massts. no. Cont. ay. N. Y. ay. N. J. ay. Pa. no. Del. ay. Md. divd. Va. no. N. C. no. S. C. no. Geo. no [Ayes—4; noes—6; divided—1.]

On the motion to agree to the clause as reported. "that the rule of suffrage in the 1st. branch ought not to be according to that established by the Articles of Confederation. Mass. ay. Cont. no N. Y. no. N. J. no. Pa. ay. Del. no. Md. divd. Va. ay. N. C. ay. S. C. ay. Geo. ay. [Ayes—6; noes—4; divided—1.]

[1:486; Madison, 30 June]

[Madison] . . . It was urged, he said, continually that an equality of votes in the 2d. branch was not only necessary to secure the small, but would be perfectly safe to the large ones whose majority in the 1st. branch was an effectual bulwark. But notwithstanding this apparent defence, the Majority of States might still injure the majority of people. 1. they could *obstruct* the wishes and interests of the majority. 2. they could *extort* measures, repugnant to the wishes & interest of the majority. 3. They could *impose* measures adverse thereto; as the 2d branch will probly exercise some great powers, in which the 1st will not participate. He admitted that every peculiar interest whether in any class of citizens, or any description of States, ought to be secured as far as possible. Wherever there is danger of attack there ought be given a constitutional power of defence. But he contended that the States were divided into different interests not by their difference of size, but by other circumstances; the most material of which resulted partly from climate, but principally from the effects of their having or not having slaves. These two causes concurred in forming the great division of interests in the U. States. It did not lie between the large & small States: it lay between the Northern & Southern. and if any defensive power were necessary, it ought to be mutually given to these two interests. He was so strongly impressed with this important truth that he had been casting about in his mind for some expedient that would answer the purpose. The one which had occurred was that instead of proportioning the votes of the States in both branches, to their respective numbers of inhabitants computing the slaves in the ratio of 5 to 3. they should be represented in one branch according to the number of free inhabitants only; and in the other according to the whole no. counting the slaves as if free. By this arrangement the Southern Scale would have the advantage in one House, and the Northern in the other. He had been restrained from proposing this expedient by two considerations; one was his unwillingness to urge any diversity of interests on an occasion when it is but too apt to arise of itself—the other was the inequality of powers that must be vested in the two branches, and which wd. destroy the equilibrium of interests.

[1:540; Madison, 6 July]

Mr. Govr. Morris moved to commit so much of the Report as relates to "1 member for every 40,000 inhabitants" His view was that they might absolutely fix the number for each State in the first instance; leaving the Legislature at liberty to provide for changes in the relative importance of the States, and for the case of new States.

Mr. Wilson 2ded. the motion; but with a view of leaving the Committee under no implied shackles.

Mr. Ghorum apprehended great inconveniency from fixing directly the number of Representatives to be allowed to each State. He thought the number of Inhabitants the true guide; tho' perhaps some departure might be expedient from the full proportion. The States also would vary in their relative extent, by separations of parts of the largest States. A part of Virga. is now on the point of a separation. In the province of Mayne a Convention is at this time deliberating on a separation from Masts. In such events, the number of representatives ought certainly to be reduced. He hoped to see all the States made small by proper divisions, instead of their becoming formidable as was apprehended, to the Small States. He conceived that let the Genl. Government be modified as it might, there would be a constant tendency in the State Governmts. to encroach upon it: it was of importance therefore that the extent of the States shd. be reduced as much & as fast as possible. The stronger the Govt. shall be made in the first instance the more easily will these divisions be effected; as it will be of less consequence in the opinion of the States whether they be of great or small extent.

Mr. Gerry did not think with his Colleague that the large States ought to be cut up. This policy has been inculcated by the middling and smaller States, ungenerously & contrary to the spirit of the Confederation. Ambitious men will be apt to solicit needless divisions, till the States be reduced to the size of Counties. If this policy should still actuate the small States, the large ones cou'd not confederate safely with them; but would be obliged to consult their safety by confederating only with one another. He favored the Commitment and thought that Representation ought to be in the Combined ratio of numbers of Inhabitants and of wealth, and not of either singly.

Mr. King wished the clause to be committed chiefly in order to detach it from the Report with which it had no connection. He thought also that the Ratio of Representation proposed could not be safely fixed, since in a century

& a half our computed increase of population would carry the number of representatives to an enormous excess; that ye. number of inhabitants was not the proper index of ability & wealth; that property was the primary object of Society; and that in fixing a ratio this ought not to be excluded from the estimate. With regard to New States, he observed that there was something peculiar in the business which had not been noticed. The U. S. were now admitted to be proprietors of the Country, N. West of the Ohio. Congs. by one of their ordinances have impoliticly laid it out into ten States, and have made it a fundamental article of compact with those who may become settlers, that as soon as the number in any one State shall equal that of the smallest of the 13 original States, it may claim admission into the Union. Delaware does not contain it is computed more than 35,000 souls, and for obvious reasons will not increase much for a considerable time. It is possible then that if this plan be persisted in by Congs. 10 new votes may be added, without a greater addition of inhabitants than are represented by the single vote of Pena. The plan as it respects one of the new States is already irrevocable, the sale of the lands having commenced, and the purchasers & settlers will immediately become entitled to all the privileges of the compact.

Mr. Butler agreed to the Commitment if the Committee were to be left at liberty. He was persuaded that the more the subject was examined, the less it would appear that the number of inhabitants would be a proper rule of proportion. If there were no other objection the changeableness of the standard would be sufficient. He concurred with those who thought some balance was necessary between the old & New States. He contended strenuously that property was the only just measure of representation. This was the great object of Governt: the great cause of war, the great means of carrying it on.

Mr. Pinkney saw no good reason for committing. The value of land had been found on full investigation to be an impracticable rule. The contributions of revenue including imports & exports, must be too changeable in their amount; too difficult to be adjusted; and too injurious to the non-commercial States. The number of inhabitants appeared to. him the only just & practicable rule. He thought the blacks ought to stand on an equality with whites: But wd.—agree to the ratio settled by Congs. He contended that Congs. had no right under the articles of Confederation to authorize the admission of new States; no such case having been provided for.

Mr. Davy, was for committing the clause in order to get at the merits of the question arising on the Report. He seemed to think that wealth or property ought to be represented in the 2d. branch; and numbers in the 1st. branch.

On the motion for committing as made by Mr. Govr. Morris.

Masts. ay—Cont. ay. N. Y. no. N. J. no. Pa ay. Del. no. Md. divd. Va. ay. N. C. ay. S. C. ay. Geo. ay. [Ayes—7; noes—3; divided—1.]

The members appd. by Ballot were Mr. Govr. Morris, Mr. Gorham. Mr. Randolph. Mr. Rutledge. Mr. King.

Mr. Wilson signified that his view in agreeing to the

Commitmt. was that the Come might consider the propriety of adopting a scale similar to that established by the Constitution of Masts. which wd give an advantage to ye. small States without substantially departing from a rule of proportion.

[1:559; Madison, 9 July]

Mr. Govr. Morris delivered a report from the Come. of 5 members to whom was committed the clause in the Report of the Come. consisting of a member from each State, stating the proper ratio of Representatives in the 1st. branch, to be as 1 to every 40,000 inhabitants, as follows viz

"The Committee to whom was referred the 1st. clause of the 1st. proposition reported from the grand Committee, beg leave to report I.¶ that in the 1st. meeting of the Legislature the 1st. branch thereof consist of 56. members of which Number N. Hamshire shall have 2. Massts. 7. R.Id.1. Cont. 4. N. Y. 5. N. J. 3. Pa. 8. Del. 1. Md. 4. Va. 9. N. C. 5, S. C. 5. Geo. 2. II¶—. But as the present situation of the States may probably alter as well in point of wealth as in the number of their inhabitants, that the Legislature be authorized from time to time to augment ye. number of Representatives. And in case any of the States shall hereafter be divided, or any two or more States united, or any new States created within the limits of the United States, the Legislature shall possess authority to regulate the number of Representatives in any of the foregoing cases, upon the principles of their wealth and number of inhabitants."

Mr. Sherman wished to know on what principles or calculations the Report was founded. It did not appear to correspond with any rule of numbers, or of any requisition hitherto adopted by Congs.

Mr. Gorham. Some provision of this sort was necessary in the outset. The number of blacks & whites with some regard to supposed wealth was the general guide Fractions could not be observed. The Legislre. is to make alterations from time to time as justice & propriety may require, Two objections prevailed agst. the rate of 1 member for every 40,000. inhts. The 1st. was that the Representation would soon be too numerous: the 2d. that the Westn. States who may have a different interest, might if admitted on that principal by degrees, out-vote the Atlantic. Both these objections are removed. The number will be small in the first instance and may be continued so, and the Atlantic States having ye. Govt. in their own hands, may take care of their own interest, by dealing out the right of Representation in safe proportions to the Western States. These were the views of the Committee.

Mr. L Martin wished to know whether the Come. were guided in the ratio, by the wealth or number of inhabitants of the States, or by both; noting its variations from former apportionments by Congs.

Mr. Govr. Morris & Mr. Rutlidge moved to postpone the 1st. paragraph relating to the number of members to be allowed each State in the first instance, and to take up the 2d. paragraph authorizing the Legislre to alter the number from time to time according to wealth & inhabitants. The motion was agreed to nem. con.

On Question on the 2d. paragh. taken without any debate

Masts. ay. Cont. ay. N. Y. no. N. J. no. Pa. ay. Del. ay. Md. ay. Va. ay. N. C. ay. S. C. ay. Geo. ay. [Ayes—9; noes—2.]

Mr. Sherman moved to refer the 1st. part apportioning the Representatives to a Comme. of a member from each State.

Mr. Govr. Morris seconded the motion; observing that this was the only case in which such Committees were useful.

Mr. Williamson. thought it would be necessary to return to the rule of numbers. but that the Western States stood on different footing. If their property shall be rated as high as that of the Atlantic States, then their representation ought to hold a like proportion. Otherwise if their property was not to be equally rated.

Mr Govr. Morris. The Report is little more than a guess. Wealth was not altogether disregarded by the Come. Where it was apparently in favor of one State whose nos. were superior to the number of another, by a fraction only, a member extraordinary was allowed to the former: and so vice versa. The Committee meant little more than to bring the matter to a point for the consideration of the House.

Mr. Reed asked why Georgia was allowed 2 members, when her number of inhabitants had stood below that of Delaware.

Mr. Govr. Morris. Such is the rapidity of the population of that State, that before the plan takes effect, it will probably be entitled to 2 Representatives

Mr. Randolph disliked the report of the Come. but had been unwilling to object to it. He was apprehensive that as the number was not to be changed till the Natl. Legislature should please, a pretext would never be wanting to postpone alterations, and keep the power in the hands of those possessed of it. He was in favor of the commitmt. to a member from each State

Mr. Patterson considered the proposed estimate for the future according to the Combined rule of numbers and wealth, as too vague. For this reason N. Jersey was agst. it. He could regard negroes slaves in no light but as property. They are no free agents, have no personal liberty, no faculty of acquiring property, but on the contrary are themselves property, & like other property entirely at the will of the Master. Has a man in Virga. a number of votes in proportion to the number of his slaves? and if Negroes are not represented in the States to which they belong, why should they be represented in the Genl. Govt. What is the true principle of Representation? It is an expedient by which an assembly of certain individls. chosen by the people is substituted in place of the inconvenient meeting of the people themselves. If such a meeting of the people was actually to take place, would the slaves vote? they would not. Why then shd. they be represented. He was also agst. such an indirect encouragemt. of the slave trade; observing that Congs. in their act relating to the change of the 8 art: of Confedn. had been ashamed to use the term "Slaves" & had substituted a description.

Mr. Madison, reminded Mr. Patterson that his doctrine

of Representation which was in its principle the genuine one, must for ever silence the pretensions of the small States to an equality of votes with the large ones. They ought to vote in the same proportion in which their citizens would do, if the people of all the States were collectively met. He suggested as a proper ground of compromise, that in the first branch the States should be represented according to their number of free inhabitants; And in the 2d. which had for one of its primary objects the guardianship of property, according to the whole number, including slaves.

Mr. Butler urged warmly the justice & necessity of regarding wealth in the apportionment of Representation.

Mr. King had always expected that as the Southern States are the richest, they would not league themselves with the Northn. unless some respect were paid to their superior wealth. If the latter expect those preferential distinctions in Commerce & other advantages which they will derive from the connection they must not expect to receive them without allowing some advantages in return. Eleven out of 13 of the States had agreed to consider Slaves in the apportionment of taxation; and taxation and Representation ought to go together.

On the question for committing the first paragraph of the Report to a member from each State.
Masts. ay. Cont. ay. N.Y. no. N.J. ay. Pa. ay. Del. ay. Md ay. Va. ay. N.C. ay. S.C. no. Geo. ay. [Ayes—9; noes—2.]

The Come. appointed were. Mr King. Mr. Sherman, Mr. Yates, Mr. Brearly, Mr. Govr. Morris, Mr. Reed, Mr. Carrol, Mr. Madison, Mr. Williamson, Mr. Rutlidge, Mr. Houston.

[1:566; Madison, 10 July]

Mr. King reported from the Come. yesterday appointed that the States at the 1st. meeting of the General Legislature, should be represented by 65 members in the following proportions, to wit. N. Hamshire by 3, Masts. 8. R. Isd. 1. Cont. 5. N.Y. 6. N.J. 4. Pa. 8. Del. 1. Md. 6. Va. 10. N:C. 5. S.C. 5, Georgia 3.

Mr. Rutledge moved that N. Hampshire be reduced from 3 to 2. members. Her numbers did not entitle her to 3 and it was a poor State.

Genl. Pinkney seconds the motion.

Mr. King. N. Hamshire has probably more than 120,000 Inhabts. and has an extensive country of tolerable fertility. Its inhabts therefore may be expected to increase fast. He remarked that the four Eastern States having 800,000 souls, have ⅓ fewer representatives than the four Southern States, having not more than 700,000 souls rating the blacks, as 5 for 3. The Eastern people will advert to these circumstances, and be dissatisfied. He believed them to be very desirous of uniting with their Southern brethren but did not think it prudent to rely so far on that disposition as to subject them to any gross inequality. He was fully convinced that the question concerning a difference of interests did not lie where it had hitherto been discussed, between the great & small States; but between the Southern & Eastern. For this reason he had been ready to yield something in the proportion of representatives for the security of the Southern. No principle would justify the giv-

ing them a majority. They were brought as near an equality as was possible. He was not averse to giving them a still greater security, but did not see how it could be done.

Genl. Pinkney. The Report before it was committed was more favorable to the S. States than as it now stands. If they are to form so considerable a minority, and the regulation of trade is to be given to the Genl. Government, they will be nothing more than overseers for the Northern States. He did not expect the S. States to be raised to a majority of representatives, but wished them to have something like an equality. At present by the alterations of the Come. in favor of the N. States they are removed farther from it than they were before. One member had indeed been added to Virga. which he was glad of as he considered her as a Southern State. He was glad also that the members of Georgia were increased.

Mr. Williamson was not for reducing N. Hamshire from 3 to 2. but for reducing some others. The Southn. Interest must be extremely endangered by the present arrangement. The Northn. States are to have a majority in the first instance and the means of perpetuating it.

Mr. Dayton observed that the line between the Northn. & Southern interest had been improperly drawn: that Pa. was the dividing State, there being six on each side of her.

Genl. Pinkney urged the reduction, dwelt on the superior wealth of the Southern States, and insisted on its having its due weight in the Government.

Mr. Govr. Morris regretted the turn of the debate. The States he found had many Representatives on the floor. Few he fears were to be deemed the Representatives of America. He thought the Southern States have by the report more than their share of representation. Property ought to have its weight; but but not all the weight. If the Southn. States are to supply money. The Northn. States are to spill their blood. Besides, the probable Revenue to be expected from the S. States has been greatly overated. He was agst. reducing N. Hamshire.

Mr. Randolph was opposed to a reduction of N. Hamshire, not because she had a full title to three members: but because it was in his contemplation 1. to make it the duty instead of leaving it in the discretion of the Legislature to regulate the representation by a periodical census. 2. to require more than a bare majority of votes in the Legislature in certain cases & particularly in commercial cases.

On the question for reducing N. Hamshire from 3 to 2 Represents. it passed in the negative
Masts. no. Cont. no. N. J. no. Pa. no. Del. no. Md. no. Va. no. N. C. ay. S. C. ay. Geo. no. [Ayes—2; noes—8.]

Genl. Pinkney & Mr. Alexr. Martin moved that 6 Reps. instead of 5 be allowed to N. Carolina

On the question, it passed in the negative
Masts. no. Cont. no. N. J. no. Pa. no. Del. no. Md. no. Va. no. N. C. ay. S. C. ay Geo. ay. [Ayes—3; noes—7.]

Genl. Pinkney & Mr. Butler made the same motion in favor of S. Carolina

On the Question it passed in the negative
Masts. no. Cont. no. N. Y. no. N.J. no. Pa. no. Del. ay. Md. no. Va. no. N. C. ay. S. C. ay. Geo. ay [Ayes—4; noes—7.]

Genl. Pinkney & Mr. Houston moved that Georgia be allowed 4 instead of 3 Reps. urging the unexampled celerity of its population. On the Question, it passed in the Negative

Masts. no. Cont. no. N. Y. no N. J. no. Pa. no. Del. no. Md. no. Va. ay. N: C. ay. S. C. ay. Geo. ay. [Ayes—4; noes—7.]

Mr. Madison moved that the number allowed to each State be doubled. A *majority* of a *Quorum of 65* members, was too small a number to represent the whole inhabitants of the U. States; They would not possess enough of the confidence of the people, and wd. be too sparsely taken from the people, to bring with them all the local information which would be frequently wanted. Double the number will not be too great even with the future additions from New States. The additional expence was too inconsiderable to be regarded in so important a case. And as far as the augmentation might be unpopular on that score, the objection was overbalanced by its effect on the hopes of a greater number of the popular Candidates.

Mr. Elseworth urged the objection of expence, & that the greater the number, the more slowly would the business proceed; and the less probably be decided as it ought, at last—He thought the number of Representatives too great in most of the State Legislatures: and that a large number was less necessary in the Genl. Legislature than in those of the States, as its business would relate to a few great, national Objects only.

Mr. Sherman would have preferred 50 to 65. The great distance they will have to travel will render their attendance precarious and will make it difficult to prevail on a sufficient number of fit men to undertake the service. He observed that the expected increase from New States also deserved consideration.

Mr. Gerry was for increasing the number beyond 65. The larger the number the less the danger of their being corrupted. The people are accustomed to & fond of a numerous representation, and will consider their rights as better secured by it. The danger of excess in the number may be guarded agst. by fixing a point within which the number shall always be kept.

Col. Mason admitted that the objection drawn from the consideration of expence, had weight both in itself, and as the people might be affected by it. But he thought it outweighed by the objections agst. the smallness of the number. 38, will he supposes, as being a majority of 65, form a quorum. 20 will be a majority of 38. This was certainly too small a number to make laws for America. They would neither bring with them all the necessary information relative to various local interests nor possess the necessary confidence of the people. After doubling the number, the laws might still be made by so few as almost to be objectionable on that account.

Mr. Read was in favor of the motion. Two of the States (Del. & R. I.) would have but a single member if the aggregate number should remain at 65. and in case of accident to either of these one State wd. have no representative present to give explanations or informations of its interests or wishes. The people would not place their con-

fidence in so small a number. He hoped the objects of the Genl. Govt. would be much more numerous than seemed to be expected by some gentlemen, and that they would become more & more so. As to New States the highest number of Reps. for the whole might be limited, and all danger of excess thereby prevented.

Mr. Rutlidge opposed the motion. The Representatives were too numerous in all the States. The full number allotted to the States may be expected to attend & the lowest possible quorum shd. not therefore be considered—. The interests of their Constituents will urge their attendance too strongly for it to be omitted: and he supposed the Genl. Legislature would not sit more than 6 or 8 weeks in the year.

On the question for doubling the number, it passed in the negative.

Masts. no. Cont. no. N. Y. no. N. J. no. Pa. no. Del ay. Md. no. Va. ay. N. C. no. S. C. no. Geo. no. [Ayes—2; noes—9.]

On the question for agreeing to the apportionment of Reps. as amended by the last committee it passed in the affirmative,

Mas. ay. Cont. ay. N. Y. ay. N. J. ay. Pa. ay. Del ay. Md. ay. Va. ay. N. C. ay. S. C. no. Geo. no. [Ayes—9; noes—2.]

Mr. Broom gave notice to the House that he had concurred with a reserve to himself of an intention to claim for his State an equal voice in the 2d. branch: which he thought could not be denied after this concession of the small States as to the first branch.

Mr. Randolph moved as an amendment to the report of the Comme. of five "that in order to ascertain the alterations in the population & wealth of the several States the Legislature should be required to cause a census, and estimate to be taken within one year after its first meeting; and every   years thereafter—and that the Legislre. arrange the Representation accordingly."

Mr Govr. Morris opposed it as fettering the Legislature too much. Advantage may be taken of it in time of war or the apprehension of it, by new States to extort particular favors. If the mode was to be fixed for taking a census, it might certainly be extremely inconvenient; if unfixt the Legislature may use such a mode as will defeat the object: and perpetuate the inequality. He was always agst. such Shackles on the Legislre. They had been found very pernicious in most of the State Constitutions. He dwelt much on the danger of throwing such a preponderancy into the Western Scale, suggesting that in time the Western people wd. outnumber the Atlantic States. He wished therefore to put it in the power of the latter to keep a majority of votes in their own hands. It was objected he said that if the Legislre. are left at liberty, they will never readjust the Representation. He admitted that this was possible, but he did not think it probable unless the reasons agst. a revision of it were very urgent & in this case, it ought not to be done.

[1:578; Madison, 11 July]

Mr. Randolph's motion requiring the Legislre. to take a periodical census for the purpose of redressing inequalities in the Representation was resumed.

Mr. Sherman was agst. Shackling the Legislature too much. We ought to choose wise & good men, and then confide in them.

Mr. Mason. The greater the difficulty we find in fixing a proper rule of Representation, the more unwilling ought we to be, to throw the task from ourselves, on the Genl. Legislre. He did not object to the conjectural ratio which was to prevail in the outset; but considered a Revision from time to time according to some permanent & precise standard as essential to ye. fair representation required in the 1st. branch. According to the present population of America, the Northn. part of it had a right to preponderate, and he could not deny it. But he wished it not to preponderate hereafter when the reason no longer continued. From the nature of man we may be sure, that those who have power in their hands will not give it up while they can retain it. On the Contrary we know they will always when they can rather increase it. If the S. States therefore should have ¾ of the people of America within their limits, the Northern will hold fast the majority of Representatives. ¼ will govern the ¾. The S. States will complain: but they may complain from generation to generation without redress. Unless some principle therefore which will do justice to them hereafter shall be inserted in the Constitution, disagreable as the declaration was to him, he must declare he could neither vote for the system here nor support it, in his State. Strong objections had been drawn from the danger to the Atlantic interests from new Western States. Ought we to sacrifice what we know to be right in itself, lest it should prove favorable to States which are not yet in existence. If the Western States are to be admitted into the Union as they arise, they must, he wd. repeat, be treated as equals, and subjected to no degrading discriminations. They will have the same pride & other passions which we have, and will either not unite with or will speedily revolt from the Union, if they are not in all respects placed on an equal footing with their brethren. It has been said they will be poor, and unable to make equal contributions to the general Treasury. He did not know but that in time they would be both more numerous & more wealthy than their Atlantic brethren. The extent & fertility of their soil, made this probable; and though Spain might for a time deprive them of the natural outlet for their productions, yet she will, because she must, finally yield to their demands. He urged that numbers of inhabitants; though not always a precise standard of wealth was sufficiently so for every substantial purpose.

Mr. Williamson was for making it the duty of the Legislature to do what was right & not leaving it at liberty to do or not do it. He moved that Mr. Randolph's proposition be postpond. in order to consider the following "that in order to ascertain the alterations that may happen in the population & wealth of the several States, a census shall be taken of the free white inhabitants and ⅗ths of those of other descriptions on the 1st year after this Government shall have been adopted and every   year thereafter; and that the Representation be regulated accordingly."

Mr. Randolph agreed that Mr. Williamson's propositon

should stand in the place of his. He observed that the ratio fixt for the 1st. meeting was a mere conjecture, that it placed the power in the hands of that part of America, which could not always be entitled to it, that this power would not be voluntarily renounced; and that it was consequently the duty of the Convention to secure its renunciation when justice might so require; by some constitutional provisions. If equality between great & small States be inadmissible, because in that case unequal numbers of Constituents wd. be represented by equal number of votes; was it not equally inadmissible that a larger & more populous district of America should hereafter have less representation, than a smaller & less populous district. If a fair representation of the people be not secured, the injustice of the Govt. will shake it to its foundations. What relates to suffrage is justly stated by the celebrated Montesquieu, as a fundamental article in Republican Govts. If the danger suggested by Mr. Govr. Morris be real, of advantage being taken of the Legislature in pressing moments, it was an additional reason, for tying their hands in such a manner that they could not sacrifice their trust to momentary considerations. Congs. have pledged the public faith to New States, that they shall be admitted on equal terms. They never would nor ought to accede on any other. The census must be taken under the direction of the General Legislature. The States will be too much interested to take an impartial one for themselves.

Mr. Butler & Genl. Pinkney insisted that blacks be included in the rule of Representation, *equally* with the Whites: and for that purpose moved that the words "three fifths" be struck out.

Mr. Gerry thought that ⅗ of them was to say the least the full proportion that could be admitted.

Mr. Ghorum. This ratio was fixed by Congs. as a rule of taxation. Then it was urged by the Delegates representing the States having slaves that the blacks were still more inferior to freemen. At present when the ratio of representation is to be established, we are assured that they are equal to freemen. The arguments on ye. former occasion had convinced him that ⅗ was pretty near the just proportion and he should vote according to the same opinion now.

Mr. Butler insisted that the labour of a slave in S. Carola. was as productive & valuable as that of a freeman in Massts., that as wealth was the great means of defence and utility to the Nation they were equally valuable to it with freemen; and that consequently an equal representation ought to be allowed for them in a Government which was instituted principally for the protection of property, and was itself to be supported by property.

Mr. Mason. could not agree to the motion, notwithstanding it was favorable to Virga. because he thought it unjust. It was certain that the slaves were valuable, as they raised the value of land, increased the exports & imports, and of course the revenue, would supply the means of feeding & supporting an army, and might in cases of emergency become themselves soldiers. As in these important respects they were useful to the community at large, they ought not to be excluded from the estimate of Representation. He could not however regard them as equal to freemen and could not vote for them as such. He added as worthy of remark, that the Southern States have this peculiar species of property, over & above the other species of property common to all the States.

Mr. Williamson reminded Mr. Ghorum that if the Southn. States contended for the inferiority of blacks to whites when taxation was in view, the Eastern States on the same occasion contended for their equality. He did not however either then or now, concur in either extreme, but approved of the ratio of ⅗.

On Mr. Butlers motion for considering blacks as equal to Whites in the apportionmt. of Representation

Massts. no. Cont. no. (N. Y. not on floor.) N. J. no. Pa. no. Del. ay. Md. no. Va no N. C. no. S. C. ay. Geo. ay. [Ayes—3; noes—7.]

Mr. Govr. Morris said he had several objections to the proposition of Mr. Williamson. 1. It fettered the Legislature too much. 2. it would exclude some States altogether who would not have a sufficient number to entitle them to a single Representative. 3. it will not consist with the Resolution passed on Saturday last authorizing the Legislature to adjust the Representation from time to time on the principles of population & wealth or with the principles of equity. If slaves were to be considered as inhabitants, not as wealth, then the sd. Resolution would not be pursued: If as wealth, then why is no other wealth but slaves included? These objections may perhaps be removed by amendments. His great objection was that the number of inhabitants was not a proper standard of wealth. The amazing difference between the comparative numbers & wealth of different Countries, rendered all reasoning superfluous on the subject. Numbers might with greater propriety be deemed a measure of stregth, than of wealth, yet the late defence made by G. Britain agst. her numerous enemies proved in the clearest manner, that it is entirely fallacious even in this respect.

Mr. King thought there was great force in the objections of Mr. Govr. Morris: he would however accede to the proposition for the sake of doing something.

Mr. Rutlidge contended for the admission of wealth in the estimate by which Representation should be regulated. The Western States will not be able to contribute in proportion to their numbers, they shd. not therefore be represented in that proportion. The Atlantic States will not concur in such a plan. He moved that "at the end of   years after the 1st. meeting of the Legislature, and of every   years thereafter, the Legislature shall proportion the Representation according to the principles of wealth & population"

Mr. Sherman thought the number of people alone the best rule for measuring wealth as well as representation; and that if the Legislature were to be governed by wealth, they would be obliged to estimate it by numbers. He was at first for leaving the matter wholly to the discretion of the Legislature; but he had been convinced by the observations of (Mr. Randolph & Mr. Mason) that the *periods* & the *rule* of revising the Representation ought to be fixt by the Constitution

Mr. Reid thought the Legislature ought not to be too much shackled. It would make the Constitution like Religious Creeds, embarrassing to those bound to conform to them & more likely to produce dissatisfaction and Scism, than harmony and union.

Mr. Mason objected to Mr. Rutlidge motion, as requiring of the Legislature something too indefinite & impracticable, and leaving them a pretext for doing nothing.

Mr. Wilson had himself no objection to leaving the Legislature entirely at liberty. But considered wealth as an impracticable rule.

Mr. Ghorum. If the Convention who are comparatively so little biassed by local views are so much perplexed, How can it be expected that the Legislature hereafter under the full biass of those views, will be able to settle a standard. He was convinced by the arguments of others & his own reflections, that the Convention ought to fix some standard or other.

Mr. Govr. Morris. The argts. of others & his own reflections had led him to a very different conclusion. If we can't agree on a rule that will be just at this time, how can we expect to find one that will be just in all times to come. Surely those who come after us will judge better of things present, than we can of things future. He could not persuade himself that numbers would be a just rule at any time. The remarks of (Mr Mason) relative to the Western Country had not changed his opinion on that head. Among other objections it must be apparent they would not be able to furnish men equally enlightened, to share in the administration of our common interests. The Busy haunts of men not the remote wilderness, was the proper School of political Talents. If the Western people get the power into their hands they will ruin the Atlantic interests. The Back members are always most averse to the best measures He mentioned the case of Pena. formerly. The lower part of the State had ye. power in the first instance. They kept it in yr. own hands. & the country was ye. better for it. Another objection with him agst admitting the blacks into the census, was that the people of Pena. would revolt at the idea of being put on a footing with slaves. They would reject any plan that was to have such an effect. Two objections had been raised agst. leaving the adjustment of the Representation from time to time, to the discretion of the Legislature. The 1. was they would be unwilling to revise it at all. The 2 that by referring to *wealth* they would be bound by a rule which if willing, they would be unable to execute. The 1st. objn. distrusts their fidelity. But if their duty, their honor & their oaths will not bind them, let us not put into their hands our liberty, and all our other great interests. let us have no Govt. at all. 2. If these ties will bind them. we need not distrust the practicability of the rule. It was followed in part by the Come. in the apportionment of Representatives yesterday reported to the House. The best course that could be taken would be to leave the interests of the people to the Representatives of the people.

Mr. *Madison* was not a little surprised to hear this implicit confidence urged by a member who on all occasions, had inculcated So strongly, the political depravity of men, and the necessity of checking one vice and interest by opposing to them another vice & interest. If the Representatives of the people would be bound by the ties he had mentioned, what need was there of a Senate? What of a Revisionary power? But his reasoning was not only inconsistent with his former reasoning, but with itself. at the same time that he recommended this implicit confidence to the Southern States in the Northern Majority, he was still more zealous in exhorting all to a jealousy of a Western majority. To reconcile the gentln. with himself it must be imagined that he determined the human character by the points of the compass. The truth was that all men having power ought to be distrusted to a certain degree. The case of Pena. had been mentioned where it was admitted that those who were possessed of the power in the original settlement, never admitted the new settlmts. to a due share of it. England was a still more striking example. The power there had long been in the hands of the boroughs, of the minority; who had opposed & defeated every reform which had been attempted. Virga. was in a lesser degree another example. With regard to the Western States, he was clear & firm in opinion that no unfavorable distinctions were admissible either in point of justice or policy. He thought also that the hope of contributions to the Treasy. from them had been much underrated. Future contributions it seemed to be understood on all hands would be principally levied on imports and exports. The extent & fertility of the Western Soil would for a long time give to agriculture a preference over manufactures. Trials would be repeated till some articles could be raised from it that would bear a transportation to places where they could be exchanged for imported manufactures. Whenever the Mississpi should be opened to them, which would of necessity be ye. case as soon as their their population would subject them to any considerable share of the public burdin, imposts on their trade could be collected with less expense & greater certainty, than on that of the Atlantic States. In the meantime, as their supplies must pass thro' the *Atlantic States* their contributions would be levied in the same manner with those of the Atlantic States.—He could not agree that any substantial objection lay agst. fixig numbers for the perpetual standard of Representation. It was said that Representation & taxation were to go together; that taxation & wealth ought to go together, that population and wealth were not measures of each other. He admitted that in different climates, under different forms of Govt. and in different stages of civilization the inference was perfectly just. He would admit that in no situation numbers of inhabitants were an accurate measure of wealth. He contended however that in the U. States it was sufficiently so for the object in contemplation. Altho' their climate varied considerably, yet as the Govts. the laws, and the manners of all were nearly the same, and the intercourse between different parts perfectly free, population, industry, arts, and the value of labour, would constantly tend to equalize themselves. The value of labour, might be considered as the principal criterion of wealth and ability to support taxes; and this would find its level in different places where the intercourse should be easy & free, with

as much certainty as the value of money or any other thing. Wherever labour would yield most, people would resort, till the competition should destroy the inequality. Hence it is that the people are constantly swarming from the more to the less populous places—from Europe to Ama from the Northn. & middle parts of the U. S. to the Southern & Western. They go where land is cheaper, because there labour is dearer. If it be true that the same quantity of produce raised on the banks of the Ohio is of less value than on the Delaware, it is also true that the same labor will raise twice or thrice, the quantity in the former, that it will raise in the latter situation.

Col. Mason, Agreed with Mr. Govr. Morris that we ought to leave the interests of the people to the Representatives of the people: but the objection was that the Legislature would cease to be the Representatives of the people. It would continue so no longer than the States now containing a majority of the people should retain that majority. As soon as the Southern & Western population should predominate, which must happen in a few years, the power wd be in the hands of the minority, and would never be yielded to the majority, unless provided for by the Constitution

On the question for postponing Mr. Williamson's motion, in order to consider that of Mr. Rutlidge it passed in the negative. Massts. ay. Cont. no. N. J. no. Pa. ay. Del. ay. Md. no. Va. no. N. C. no. S. C. ay. Geo—ay. [Ayes—5; noes—5.]

On the question on the first clause of Mr. Williamson's motion as to taking a census of the *free* inhabitants. it passed in the affirmative Masts. ay. Cont. ay. N. J. ay. Pa. ay. Del. no. Md. no. Va. ay. N. C. ay. S. C. no. Geo. no. [Ayes—6; noes—4.]

the next clause as to ⅗ of the negroes considered

Mr. King. being much opposed to fixing numbers as the rule of representation, was particularly so on account of the blacks. He thought the admission of them along with Whites at all, would excite great discontents among the States having no slaves. He had never said as to any particular point that he would in no event acquiesce in & support it; but he wd. say that if in any case such a declaration was to be made by him, it would be in this. He remarked that in the temporary allotment of Representatives made by the Committee, the Southern States had received more than the number of their white & three fifths of their black inhabitants entitled them to.

Mr. Sherman. S. Carola. had not more beyond her proportion than N. York & N. Hampshire, nor either of them more than was necessary in order to avoid fractions or reducing them below their proportion. Georgia had more; but the rapid growth of that State seemed to justify it. In general the allotment might not be just, but considering all circumstances, he was satisfied with it.

Mr. Ghorum. supported the propriety of establishing numbers as the rule. He said that in Massts. estimates had been taken in the different towns, and that persons had been curious enough to compare these estimates with the respective numbers of people; and it had been found even including Boston, that the most exact proportion prevailed between numbers & property. He was aware that there might be some weight in what had fallen from his colleague, as to the umbrage which might be taken by the people of the Eastern States. But he recollected that when the proposition of Congs for changing the 8th. art: of Confedn. was before the Legislature of Massts. the only difficulty then was to satisfy them that the negroes ought not to have been counted equally with whites instead of being counted in the ratio of three fifths only.

Mr. Wilson did not well see on what principle the admission of blacks in the proportion of three fifths could be explained. Are they admitted as Citizens? Then why are they not admitted on an equality with White Citizens? Are they admitted as property? then why is not other property admitted into the computation? These were difficulties however which he thought must be overruled by the necessity of compromise. He had some apprehensions also from the tendency of the blending of the blacks with the whites, to give disgust to the people of Pena. as had been intimated by his colleague (Mr. Govr. Morris). But he differed from him in thinking numbers of inhabts. so incorrect a measure of wealth. He had seen the Western settlemts. of Pa. and on a comparison of them with the City of Philada. could discover little other difference, than that property was more unequally divided among individuals here than there. Taking the same number in the aggregate in the two situations he believed there would be little difference in their wealth and ability to contribute to the public wants.

Mr. Govr. Morris was compelled to declare himself reduced to the dilemma of doing injustice to the Southern States or to human nature, and he must therefore do it to the former. For he could never agree to give such encouragement to the slave trade as would be given by allowing them a representation for their negroes, and he did not believe those States would ever confederate on terms that would deprive them of that trade.

On Question for agreeing to include ⅗ of the blacks
Masts. no. Cont. ay N. J. no. Pa. no. Del. no. Mard. no. Va. ay. N. C. ay. S. C. no. Geo. ay [Ayes—4; noes—6.]

On the question as to taking census "the first year after meeting of the Legislature"
Masts. ay. Cont. no. N. J. ay. Pa. ay. Del. ay. Md. no. Va. ay. N. C. ay. S. ay. Geo. no. [Ayes—7; noes—3.]

On filling the blank for the periodical census with 15 years". agreed to nem. con.

Mr. Madison moved to add after "15 years," the words "at least" that the Legislature might anticipate when circumstances were likely to render a particular year inconvenient.

On this motion for adding "at least", it passed in the negative the States being equally divided.
Mas..ay. Cont. no. N. J. no. Pa. no. Del. no. Md. no. Va. ay. N. C. ay. S. C. ay. Geo. ay. [Ayes—5; noes—5.]

A change of the phraseology of the other clause so as to read; "and the Legislature shall alter or augment the representation accordingly" was agreed to nem. con.

On the question on the whole resolution of Mr. Williamson as amended.

Mas. no. Cont. no. N. J. no. Del. no. Md. no. Va. no. N. C. no. S. C. no—Geo—no [Ayes—0; noes—9.]

[1:591; Madison, 12 July]

Mr. Govr. Morris moved to add to the clause empowering the Legislature to vary the Representation according to the principles of wealth & number of inhabts. a "proviso that taxation shall be in proportion to Representation".

Mr Butler contended again that Representation sd. be according to the full number of inhabts. including all the blacks; admitting the justice of Mr. Govr. Morris's motion.

Mr. Mason also admitted the justice of the principle, but was afraid embarrassments might be occasioned to the Legislature by it. It might drive the Legislature to the plan of Requisitions.

Mr. Govr. Morris, admitted that some objections lay agst. his motion, but supposed they would be removed by restraining the rule to *direct* taxation. With regard to indirect taxes on *exports* & imports & on consumption, the rule would be inapplicable. Notwithstanding what had been said to the contrary he was persuaded that the imports & consumption were pretty nearly equal throughout the Union.

General Pinkney liked the idea. He thought it so just that it could not be objected to. But foresaw that if the revision of the census was left to the discretion of the Legislature, it would never be carried into execution. The rule must be fixed, and the execution of it enforced by the Constitution. He was alarmed at what was said yesterday, concerning the Negroes. He was now again alarmed at what had been thrown out concerning the taxing of exports. S. Carola. has in one year exported to the amount of £600,000 Sterling all which was the fruit of the labor of her blacks. Will she be represented in proportion to this amount? She will not. Neither ought she then to be subject to a tax on it. He hoped a clause would be inserted in the system restraining the Legislature from a taxing Exports.

Mr. Wilson approved the principle, but could not see how it could be carried into execution; unless restrained to direct taxation.

Mr. Govr. Morris having so varied his motion by inserting the word "direct". It passd. nem. con. as follows— "provided always that direct taxation ought to be proportioned to representation".

Mr. Davie, said it was high time now to speak out. He saw that it was meant by some gentlemen to deprive the Southern States of any share of Representation for their blacks. He was sure that N. Carola. would never confederate on any terms that did not rate them at least as ⅗. If the Eastern States meant therefore to exclude them altogether the business was at an end.

Dr. Johnson, thought that wealth and population were the true, equitable rule of representation; but he conceived that these two principles resolved themselves into one; population being the best measure of wealth. He concluded therefore that ye. number of people ought to be established as the rule, and that all descriptions including blacks *equally* with the whites, ought to fall within the computation. As various opinions had been expressed on the subject, he would move that a Committee might be appointed to take them into consideration and report thereon.

Mr. Govr. Morris. It has been said that it is high time to speak out. As one member, he would candidly do so. He came here to form a compact for the good of America. He was ready to do so with all the States: He hoped & believed that all would enter into such a Compact. If they would not he was ready to join with any States that would. But as the Compact was to be voluntary, it is in vain for the Eastern States to insist on what the Southn States will never agree to. It is equally vain for the latter to require what the other States can never admit; and he verily belived the people of Pena. will never agree to a representation of Negroes. What can be desired by these States more than has been already proposed; that the Legislature shall from time to time regulate Representation according to population & wealth.

Gen. Pinkney desired that the rule of wealth should be ascertained and not left to the pleasure of the Legislature; and that property in slaves should not be exposed to danger under a Govt. instituted for the protection of property.

The first clause in the Report of the first Grand Committee was postponed

Mr. Elseworth. In order to carry into effect the principle established, moved to add to the last clause adopted by the House the words following "and that the rule of contribution by direct taxation for the support of the Government of the U. States shall be the number of white inhabitants, and three fifths of every other description in the several States, until some other rule that shall more accurately ascertain the wealth of the several States can be devised and adopted by the Legislature"

Mr. Butler seconded the motion in order that it might be committed.

Mr. Randolph was not satisfied with the motion. The danger will be revived that the ingenuity of the Legislature may evade or pervert the rule so as to perpetuate the power where it shall be lodged in the first instance. He proposed in lieu of Mr. Elseworth's motion, "that in order to ascertain the alterations in Representation that may be required from time to time by changes in the relative circumstances of the States, a census shall be taken within two years from the 1st. meeting of the Genl. Legislature of the U. S., and once within the term of every   year afterwards, of all the inhabitants in the manner & according to the ratio recommended by Congress in their resolution of the 18th day of Apl. 1783; (rating the blacks at ⅗ of their number) and that the Legislature of the U. S. shall arrange the Representation accordingly."—He urged strenuously that express security ought to be provided for including slaves in the ratio of Representation. He lamented that such a species of property existed. But as it did exist the holders of it would require this security. It was perceived that the design was entertained by some of excluding slaves altogether; the Legislature therefore ought not to be left at liberty.

Mr. Elseworth withdraws his motion & seconds that of Mr. Randolph.

Mr. Wilson observed that less umbrage would perhaps be taken agst. an admission of the slaves into the Rule of representation, if it should be so expressed as to make them indirectly only an ingredient in the rule, by saying that they should enter into the rule of taxation: and as representation was to be according to taxation, the end would be equally attained. He accordingly moved & was 2ded so to alter the last clause adopted by the House, that together with the amendment proposed the whole should read as follows—provided always that the representation ought to be proportioned according to direct taxation, and in order to ascertain the alterations in the direct taxation which may be required from time to time by the changes in the relative circumstances of the States. Resolved that a census be taken within two years from the first meeting of the Legislature of the U. States, and once within the term of every   years afterwards of all the inhabitants of the U. S. in the manner and according to the ratio recommended by Congress in their Resolution of April 18 1783; and that the Legislature of the U. S. shall proportion the direct taxation accordingly"

Mr. King. Altho' this amendment varies the aspect somewhat, he had still two powerful objections agst. tying down the Legislature to the rule of numbers. 1. they were at this time an uncertain index of the relative wealth of the States. 2. if they were a just index at this time it can not be supposed always to continue so. He was far from wishing to retain any unjust advantage whatever in one part of the Republic. If justice was not the basis of the connection it could not be of long duration. He must be short sighted indeed who does not foresee that whenever the Southern States shall be more numerous than the Northern, they can & will hold a language that will awe them into justice. If they threaten to separate now in case injury shall be done them, will their threats be less urgent or effectual, when force shall back their demands. Even in the intervening period there will no point of time at which they will not be able to say, do us justice or we will separate. He urged the necessity of placing confidence to a certain degree in every Govt. and did not conceive that the proposed confidence as to a periodical readjustment of the representation exceeded that degree.

Mr. Pinkney moved to amend Mr. Randolph's motion so as to make "blacks equal to the whites in the ratio of representation". This he urged was nothing more than justice. The blacks are the labourers, the peasants of the Southern States: they are as productive of pecuniary resources as those of the Northern States. They add equally to the wealth, and considering money as to the sinew of war, to the strength of the nation. It will also be politic with regard to the Northern States as taxation is to keep pace with Representation.

Genl. Pinkney moves to insert 6 years instead of two, as the period computing from 1st meeting of ye Legis— within which the first census should be taken. On this question for inserting six instead of two" in the proposition of Mr. Wilson, it passed in the affirmative

Masts. no. Ct. ay. N. J. ay. Pa. ay. Del. divd. Mayd. ay. Va. no. N. C. no. S. C. ay. Geo. no. [Ayes—5; noes—4; divided—1.]

On a question for filling the blank for ye. periodical census with 20 years, it passed in the negative

Masts. no. Ct. ay. N. J. ay. P. ay. Del. no. Md. no. Va. no. N. C. no. S. C. no. Geo. no. [Ayes—3; noes—7.]

On a question for 10 years, it passed in the affirmative.

Mas. ay. Cont. no. N. J. no. P. ay. Del. ay. Md. ay. Va. ay. N. C. ay. S. C. ay. Geo. ay. [Ayes—8; noes—2.]

On Mr. Pinkney's motion for rating blacks as equal to whites instead of as ⅗.

Mas. no. Cont. no. (Dr Johnson ay) N. J. no. Pa. no. (3 agst. 2) Del. no. Md. no. Va. no. N. C. no. S. C. ay. Geo—ay. [Ayes—2; noes—8.]

Mr. Randolph's proposition as varied by Mr. Wilson being read for question on the whole.

Mr. Gerry, urged that the principle of it could not be carried into execution as the States were not to be taxed as States. With regard to taxes in imports, he conceived they would be more productive—Where there were no slaves than where there were; the consumption being greater—

Mr. Elseworth. In case of a poll tax there wd. be no difficulty. But there wd. probably be none. The sum allotted to a State may be levied without difficulty according to the plan used by the State in raising its own supplies. On the question on ye. whole proposition; as proportioning representation to direct taxation & both to the white & ⅗ of black inhabitants, & requiring a census within six years—& within every ten years afterwards.

Mas. divd. Cont. ay. N. J. no. Pa. ay. Del. no. Md. ay. Va. ay. N. C. ay. S. C. divd. Geo. ay. [Ayes—6; noes—2; divided—2.]

[1:600; Madison, 13 July]

Mr. Gerry, moved to add as an amendment to the last clause agreed to by the House "That from the first meeting of the Legislature of the U. S. till a census shall be taken all monies to be raised for supplying the public Treasury by direct taxation, shall be assessed on the inhabitants of the several States, according to the number of their Representatives respectively in the 1st branch." He said this would be as just before as after the Census: according to the general principle that taxation & Representation ought to go together.

Mr. Williamson feared that N. Hamshire will have reason to complain. 3 members were allotted to her as a liberal allowance for this reason among others, that she might not suppose any advantage to have been taken of her absence. As she was still absent, and had no opportunity of deciding whether she would chuse to retain the number on the condition, of her being taxed in proportion to it, he thought the number ought to be reduced from three to two, before the question on Mr. G's motion

Mr. Read could not approve of the proposition. He had observed he said in the Committee a backwardness in some of the members from the large States, to take their full proportion of Representatives. He did not then see the motive. He now suspects it was to avoid their due share of taxation. He had no objection to a just & accurate adjustment of Representation & taxation to each other.

Mr. Govr. Morris & Mr. Madison answered that the charge itself involved an acquittal, since notwithstanding the augmentation of the number of members allotted to Masts. & Va. the motion for proportioning the burdens thereto was made by a member from the former State & was approved by Mr. M from the latter who was on the Come. Mr. Govr. Morris said that he thought Pa. had her due share in 8 members; and he could not in candor ask for more. Mr. M. said that having always conceived that the difference of interest in the U. States lay not between the large & small, but the N. & Southn. States, and finding that the number of members allotted to the N. States was greatly superior, he should have preferred, an addition of two members to the S. States, to wit one to N & 1 to S. Carla. rather than of one member to Virga. He liked the present motion, because it tended to moderate the views both of the opponents & advocates for rating very high, the negroes.

Mr. Elseworth hoped the proposition would be withdrawn. It entered too much into detail. The general principle was already sufficiently settled. As fractions can not be regarded in apportioning the *no. of representatives*, the rule will be unjust until an actual census shall be made. after that taxation may be precisely proportioned according to the principle established, to the *number of inhabitants*.

Mr. Wilson hoped the motion would not be withdrawn. If it shd. it will be made from another quarter. The rule will be as reasonable & just before, as after a Census. As to fractional numbers, the Census will not destroy, but ascertain them. And they will have the same effect after as before the Census: for as he understands the rule, it is to be adjusted not to the number of *inhabitants*, but of *Representatives*.

Mr. Sherman opposed the motion. He thought the Legislature ought to be left at liberty: in which case they would probably conform to the principles observed by Congs.

Mr. Mason did not know that Virga. would be a loser by the proposed regulation, but had some scruple as to the justice of it. He doubted much whether the conjectural rule which was to precede the census, would be as just, as it would be rendered by an actual census.

Mr. Elseworth & Mr. Sherman moved to postpone the motion of Mr. Gerry, on ye. question, it passed in the negative

Mas. no. Cont. ay. N. J. ay. Pa. no. Del. ay. Md. ay. Va. no. N. C. no. S. C. no. Geo. no. [Ayes—4; noes—6.]

Question on Mr. Gerry's motion, it passed in the negative, the States being equally divided.

Mas. ay. Cont. no. N. J. no. *Pa. ay.* Del. no. Md. no. *Va. no.* N. C. ay. S. C. ay. Geo. ay. [Ayes—5; noes—5.]

Mr. Gerry finding that the loss of the question had proceeded from an objection with some, to the proposed assessment of direct taxes on the *inhabitants* of the States, which might restrain the legislature to a poll tax, moved his proposition again, but so varied as to authorize the assessment on the States, which wd. leave the mode to the Legislature viz "that from the 1st meeting of the Legislature of the U. S. untill a census shall be taken, all monies for supplying the public Treasury by direct taxation shall be raised from the several States according to the number of their representatives respectively in the 1st branch"

On this varied question it passed in the affirmative

Mas. ay. Cont. no. N. J. no. *Pa. divd.* Del. no. Md. no. *Va. ay.* N. C. ay. S. C. ay. Geo. ay. [Ayes—5; noes—4; divided—1.]

On the motion of Mr. Randolph, the vote of saturday last authorizing the Legislre. to adjust from time to time, the representation upon the principles of *wealth* & numbers of inhabitants was reconsidered by common consent in order to strike out "Wealth" and adjust the resolution to that requiring periodical revisions according to the number of whites & three fifths of the blacks: the motion was in the words following—"But as the present situation of the States may probably alter in the number of their inhabitants, that the Legislature of the U. S. be authorized from time to time to apportion the number of representatives: and in case any of the States shall hereafter be divided or any two or more States united or new States created within the limits of the U. S. the Legislature of U. S. shall possess authority to regulate the number of Representatives in any of the foregoing cases, upon the principle of their number of inhabitants; according to the provisions hereafter mentioned."

Mr. Govr. Morris opposed the alteration as leaving still an incoherence. If Negroes were to be viewed as inhabitants, and the revision was to proceed on the principle of numbers of inhabts. they ought to be added in their entire number, and not in the proportion of ⅗. If as property, the word wealth was right, and striking it out would. produce the very inconsistency which it was meant to get rid of.—The train of business & the late turn which it had taken, had led him he said, into deep meditation on it, and He wd. candidly state the result. A distinction had been set up & urged, between the Nn. & Southn. States. He had hitherto considered this doctrine as heretical. He still thought the distinction groundless. He sees however that it is persisted in; and that the Southn. Gentleman will not be satisfied unless they see the way open to their gaining a majority in the public Councils. The consequence of such a transfer of power from the maritime to the interior & landed interest will he foresees be such an oppression of commerce, that he shall be obliged to vote for ye. vicious principle of equality in the 2d. branch in order to provide some defence for the N. States agst. it. But to come now more to the point, either this distinction is fictitious or real: if fictitious let it be dismissed & let us proceed with due confidence. If it be real, instead of attempting to blend incompatible things, let us at once take a friendly leave of each other. There can be no end of demands for security if every particular interest is to be entitled to it. The Eastern States may claim it for their fishery, and for other objects, as the Southn. States claim it for their peculiar objects. In this struggle between the two ends of the Union, what part ought the Middle States in point of policy to take: to join their Eastern brethren according to his ideas. If the Southn. States get the power into their hands, and be joined as they will be with the interior Country they will inevitably bring on a war with Spain for the Mississippi. This language is already held. The interior Country having no property nor interest exposed on the sea, will be little affected by such a war. He wished to know what security the Northn. & middle States will have agst. this danger. It has been said that N. C. S. C. and Georgia only will in a little time have a majority of the people of America. They must in that case include the great interior Country, and every thing was to be apprehended from their getting the power into their hands.

Mr. Butler. The security the Southn. States want is that their negroes may not be taken from them which some gentlemen within or without doors, have a very good mind to do. It was not supposed that N. C. S. C & Geo. would have more people than all the other States, but many more relatively to the other States than they now have. The people & strength of America are evidently bearing Southwardly & S. westwdly.

Mr. Wilson. If a general declaration would satisfy any gentleman he had no indisposition to declare his sentiments. Conceiving that all men wherever placed have equal rights and are equally entitled to confidence, he viewed without apprehension the period when a few States should contain the superior number of people. The majority of people wherever found ought in all questions to govern the minority. If the interior Country should acquire this majority they will not only have the right, but will avail themselves of it whether we will or no. This jealousy misled the policy of G. Britain with regard to America. The fatal maxims espoused by her were that the Colonies were growing too fast, and that their growth must be stinted in time. What were the consequences? first. enmity on our part, then actual separation. Like consequences will result on the part of the interior settlements, if like jealousy & policy be pursued on ours. Further. if numbers be not a proper rule, why is not some better rule pointed out. No one has yet ventured to attempt it. Congs. have never been able to discover a better. No State as far as he had heard, has suggested any other. In 1783, after elaborate discussion of a measure of wealth all were satisfied then as they are now that the rule of numbers, does not differ much from the combined rule of numbers & wealth. Again he could not agree that property was the sole or the primary object of Governt. & Society. The cultivation & improvement of the human mind was the most noble object. With respect to this object, as well as to other *personal* rights, numbers were surely the natural & precise measure of Representation. And with respect to property, they could not vary much from the precise measure. In no point of view however could the establishmt. of numbers as the rule of representation in the 1st. branch vary his opinion as to the impropriety of letting a vicious principle into the 2d. branch.—On the question to strike out *wealth* & to make the change as moved by Mr. Randolph, it passed in the affirmative—

Mas. ay. Cont. ay. N. J. ay. Pa. ay. Del. divd. Md. ay. Va. ay. N. C. ay. S. C. ay. Geo. ay. [Ayes—9; noes—0; divided—1.]

Mr. Reed moved to insert after the word—"divided," "or enlarged by addition of territory" which was agreed to nem. con. (his object probably was to provide for such cases as an enlargmt. of Delaware by annexing to it the Peninsula on the East Side of Chesapeak)

[2:2; Madison, 14 July]

Mr. Gerry. wished before the question should be put, that the attention of the House might be turned to the dangers apprehended from Western States. He was for admitting them on liberal terms, but not for putting ourselves into their hands. They will if they acquire power like all men, abuse it. They will oppress commerce, and drain our wealth into the Western Country. To guard agst. these consequences, he thought it necessary to limit the number of new States to be admitted into the Union, in such a manner, that they should never be able to outnumber the Atlantic States. He accordingly moved "that in order to secure the liberties of the States already confederated, the number of Representatives in the 1st. branch of the States which shall hereafter be established shall never exceed in number, the Representatives from such of the States as shall accede to this confederation.

Mr. King. seconded the motion.

Mr. Sherman, thought there was no probability that the number of future States would exceed that of the Existing States. If the event should ever happen, it was too remote to be taken into consideration at this time. Besides We are providing for our posterity, for our children & our grand Children, who would be as likely to be citizens of new Western States, as of the old States. On this consideration alone, we ought to make no such discrimination as was proposed by the motion.

Mr. Gerry. If some of our children should remove, others will stay behind, and he thought it incumbent on us to provide for their interests. There was a rage for emigration from the Eastern States to the Western Country and he did not wish those remaining behind to be at the mercy of the Emigrants. Besides foreigners are resorting to that Country, and it is uncertain what turn things may take there.—On the question for agreeing to the Motion of Mr. Gerry, it passed in the negative.

Mas. ay. Cont. ay. N. J. no Pa. divd. Del: ay. Md. ay. Va. no. N. C. no. S. C. no Geo. no. [Ayes—4; noes—5; divided—1.]

[2:106; Madison, 24 July]

Mr. Carrol took occasion to observe that he considered the clause declaring that direct taxation on the States should be in proportion to representation, previous to the obtaining an actual census, as very objectionable, and that he reserved to himself the right of opposing it, if the Report of the Committee of detail should leave it in the plan.

Mr. Govr. Morris hoped the Committee would strike out the whole of the clause proportioning direct taxation to representation. He had only meant it as a bridge to assist us over a certain gulph; having passed the gulph the bridge may be removed. He thought the principle laid down with so much strictness, liable to strong objections

[2:178, 182; Committee of Detail, Madison, 6 Aug.]

IV

Sect. 3. The House of Representatives shall, at its first formation, and until the number of citizens and inhabitants shall be taken in the manner herein after described,

consist of sixty five Members, of whom three shall be chosen in New Hampshire, eight in Massachusetts, one in Rhode-Island and Providence Plantations, five in Connecticut, six in New-York, four in New-Jersey, eight in Pennsylvania, one in Delaware, six in Maryland, ten in Virginia, five in North-Carolina, five in South-Carolina, and three in Georgia.

Sect. 4. As the proportions of numbers in [the] different States will alter from time to time; as some of the States may hereafter be divided; as others may be enlarged by addition of territory; as two or more States may be united; as new States will be erected within the limits of the United States, the Legislature shall, in each of these cases, regulate the number of representatives by the number of inhabitants, according to the provisions herein after made, at the rate of one for every forty thousand.

· · · · ·

VII

Sect. 3. The proportions of direct taxation shall be regulated by the whole number of white and other free citizens and inhabitants, of every age, sex and condition, including those bound to servitude for a term of years, and three fifths of all other persons not comprehended in the foregoing description, (except Indians not paying taxes) which number shall, within six years after the first meeting of the Legislature, and within the term of every ten years afterwards, be taken in such manner as the said Legislature shall direct.

[2:219; Madison, 8 Aug.]

The 3. Sect. of Art: IV was then agreed to.

Art: IV. Sect. 4. taken up.

Mr. Williamson moved to strike out "according to the provisions hereinafter made" and to insert the words "according to the rule hereafter to be provided for direct taxation"—See Art VII. sect. 3.

On the question for agreeing to Mr. Williamson's amendment

N. H– ay. Mas. ay. Ct. ay. N. J. no Pa. ay. Del. no. Md. ay. Va ay. N. C. Ay. S. C. ay. Geo. ay. [Ayes—9; noes—2.]

Mr. King wished to know what influence the vote just passed was meant have on the succeeding part of the Report, concerning the admission of slaves into the rule of Representation. He could not reconcile his mind to the article if it was to prevent objections to the latter part. The admission of slaves was a most grating circumstance to his mind, & he believed would be so to a great part of the people of America. He had not made a strenuous opposition to it heretofore because he had hoped that this concession would have produced a readiness which had not been manifested, to strengthen the Genl. Govt. and to mark a full confidence in it. The Report under consideration had by the tenor of it, put an end to all these hopes. In two great points the hands of the Legislature were absolutely tied. The importation of slaves could not be prohibited—exports could not be taxed. Is this reasonable? What are the great objects of the Genl. System? 1. difence agst. foreign invasion. 2. agst. internal sedition. Shall all the States then be bound to defend each; & shall each be at liberty to introduce a weakness which will render defence more difficult? Shall one part of the U. S. be bound to defend another part, and that other part be at liberty not only to increase its own danger, but to withhold the compensation for the burden? If slaves are to be imported shall not the exports produced by their labor, supply a revenue the better to enable the Genl. Govt. to defend their Masters?—There was so much inequality & unreasonableness in all this, that the people of the Northern States could never be reconciled to it. No candid man could undertake to justify it to them. He had hoped that some accommodation wd. have taken place on this subject; that at least a time wd. have been limited for the importation of slaves. He never could agree to let them be imported without limitation & then be represented in the Natl. Legislature. Indeed he could so little persuade himself of the rectitude of such a practice, that he was not sure he could assent to it under any circumstances. At all events, either slaves should not be represented, or exports should be taxable.

Mr. Sherman regarded the slave-trade as iniquitous; but the point of representation having been Settled after much difficulty & deliberation, he did not think himself bound to make opposition; especially as the present article as amended did not preclude any arrangement whatever on that point in another place of the Report.

Mr. Madison objected to 1 for every 40,000 inhabitants as a perpetual rule. The future increase of population if the Union shd. be permanent, will render the number of Representatives excessive.

Mr. Ghorum. It is not to be supposed that the Govt will last so long as to produce this effect. Can it be supposed that this vast Country including the Western territory will 150 years hence remain one nation?

Mr. Elseworth. If the Govt. should continue so long, alterations may be made in the Constitution in the manner proposed in a subsequent article.

Mr. Sherman & Mr. Madison moved to insert the words "not exceeding" before the words "1 for every 40,000, which was agreed to nem. con.

Mr. Govr. Morris moved to insert "free" before the word "inhabitants." Much he said would depend on this point. He never would concur in upholding domestic slavery. It was a nefarious institution—It was the curse of heaven on the States where it prevailed. Compare the free regions of the Middle States, where a rich & noble cultivation marks the prosperity & happiness of the people, with the misery & poverty which overspread the barren wastes of Va. Maryd. & the other States having slaves. Travel thro' ye whole Continent & you behold the prospect continually varying with the appearance & disappearance of slavery. The moment you leave ye E. Sts. & enter N. York, the effects of the institution become visible; Passing thro' the Jerseys and entering Pa—every criterion of superior improvement witnesses the change. Proceed Southwdly, & every step you take thro' ye great regions of slaves, presents a desert increasing with ye increasing proportion of these wretched beings.

Upon what principle is it that the slaves shall be computed in the representation? Are they men? Then make them Citizens & let them vote? Are they property? Why then is no other property included? The Houses in this City (Philada.) are worth more than all the wretched slaves which cover the rice swamps of South Carolina. The admission of slaves into the Representation when fairly explained comes to this: that the inhabitant of Georgia and S. C. who goes to the Coast of Africa, and in defiance of the most sacred laws of humanity tears away his fellow creatures from their dearest connections & damns them to the most cruel bondages, shall have more votes in a Govt. instituted for protection of the rights of mankind, than the Citizen of Pa or N. Jersey who views with a laudable horror, so nefarious a practice. He would add that Domestic slavery is the most prominent feature in the aristocratic countenance of the proposed Constitution. The vassalage of the poor has ever been the favorite offspring of Aristocracy. And What is the proposed compensation to the Northern States for a sacrifice of every principle of right, of every impulse of humanity. They are to bind themselves to march their militia for the defence of the S. States; for their defence agst those very slaves of whom they complain. They must supply vessels & seamen, in case of foreign Attack. The Legislature will have indefinite power to tax them by excises, and duties on imports: both of which will fall heavier on them than on the Southern inhabitants; for the bohea tea used by a Northern freeman, will pay more tax than the whole consumption of the miserable slave, which consists of nothing more than his physical subsistence and the rag that covers his nakedness. On the other side the Southern States are not to be restrained from importing fresh supplies of wretched Africans, at once to increase the danger of attack, and the difficulty of defence; nay they are to be encouraged to it by an assurance of having their votes in the Natl Govt increased in proportion. and are at the same time to have their exports & their slaves exempt from all contributions for the public service. Let it not be said that direct taxation is to be proportioned to representation. It is idle to suppose that the Genl Govt. can stretch its hand directly into the pockets of the people scattered over so vast a Country. They can only do it through the medium of exports imports & excises. For what then are all these sacrifices to be made? He would sooner submit himself to a tax for paying for all the Negroes in the U. States. than saddle posterity with such a Constitution.

Mr. Dayton 2ded. the motion. He did it he said that his sentiments on the subject might appear whatever might be the fate of the amendment.

Mr. Sherman. did not regard the admission of the Negroes into the ratio of representation, as liable to such insuperable objections. It was the freemen of the Southn. States who were in fact to be represented according to the taxes paid by them, and the Negroes are only included in the Estimate of the taxes. This was his idea of the matter.

Mr. Pinkney, considered the fisheries & the Western frontier as more burdensome to the U.S. than the slaves— He thought this could be demonstrated if the occasion were a proper one.

Mr Wilson. thought the motion premature—An agreement to the clause would be no bar to the object of it.

Question On Motion to insert "free" before "inhabitants."

N. H– no. Mas. no. Ct. no. N. J. ay. Pa. no. Del. no. Md. no. Va. no. N C. no. S. C. no. Geo. no. [Ayes—1; noes—10.]

On the suggestion of Mr. Dickenson the words, "provided that each State shall have one representative at least."—were added nem. con.

Art. IV. sect. 4. as amended was Agreed to nem. con.

[2:350; Madison, 20 Aug.]

Sect—3—taken up. "white & other" struck out nem con. as superfluous.

Mr. Elseworth moved to required the first census to be taken within "three" instead of "six" years from the first meeting of the Legislature—and on question

N—H—ay. Mas—ay Ct ay—N J—ay—Pa ay—Del. ay. Md ay Va ay—N—C—ay—S—C. no—Geo—no. [Ayes—9; noes—2.]

Mr. King asked what was the precise meaning of *direct* taxation? No one answd.

Mr. Gerry moved to add to the 3d. Sect. art. VII, the following clause. "That from the first meeting of the Legislature of the U. S. until a Census shall be taken all monies for supplying the public Treasury by direct taxation shall be raised from the several States according to the number of their Representatives respectively in the first branch"

Mr. Langdon. This would bear unreasonably hard on N. H. and he must be agst it.

Mr. Carrol. opposed it. The number of Reps. did not admit of a proportion exact enough for a rule of taxation—

[2:356; Madison, 21 Aug.]

Art: VII. sect. 3. resumed.—Mr. Dickenson moved to postpone this in order to reconsider Art: IV. sect. 4. and to *limit* the number of representatives to be allowed to the large States. Unless this were done the small States would be reduced to entire insignificancy, and encouragement given to the importation of slaves.

Mr. Sherman would agree to such a reconsideration, but did not see the necessity of postponing the section before the House.—Mr. Dickenson withdrew his motion.

Art: VII. sect. 3. then agreed to 10 ays. Delaware alone being no.

Mr. Sherman moved to add to sect 3, the following clause "and all accounts of supplies furnished, services performed, and monies advanced by the several States to the U—States, or by the U. S. to the several States shall be adjusted by the same rule."

Mr. Governr. Morris 2ds. the motion.

Mr. Ghorum, thought it wrong to insert this in the Constitution. The Legislature will no doubt do what is right. The present Congress have such a power and are now exercising it.

Mr Sherman unless some rule be expressly given none will exist under the new system.

Mr. Elseworth. Though The contracts of Congress will be binding, there will be no rule for executing them on the States;—and one ought to be provided.

Mr Sherman withdrew his motion to make way for one of Mr Williamson to add to sect– 3. "By this rule the several quotas of the States shall be determined in Settling the expences of the late war"–

Mr. Carrol brought into view the difficulty that might arise on this subject from the establishment of the Constitution as intended without the *Unanimous* consent of the States

Mr Williamson's motion was postponed nem. con.

Art: VI sect. 12. which had been postponed Aug: 15. was now called for by Col. Mason. who wished to know how the proposed amendment as to money bills would be decided, before he agreed to any further points.

Mr. Gerry's motion of yesterday that previous to a census, direct taxation be proportioned on the States according to the number of Representatives, was taken up– He observed that the principal acts of Government would probably take place within that period, and it was but reasonable that the States should pay in proportion to their share in them.

Mr. Elseworth thought such a rule unjust– there was a great difference between the number of Represents. and the number of inhabitants as a rule in this case. Even if the former were proportioned as nearly as possible to the latter, it would be a very inaccurate rule– A State might have one Representative only, that had inhabitants enough for 1½ or more, if fractions could be applied—&c—. He proposed to amend the motion by adding the words "subject to a final liquidation by the foregoing rule when a census shall have been taken."

Mr. Madison. The last appointment of Congs., on which the number of Representatives was founded, was conjectural and meant only as a temporary rule till a Census should be established.

Mr. Read. The requisitions of Congs. had been accommodated to the impoverishments produced by the war; and to other local and temporary circumstances—

Mr. Williamson opposed Mr Gerry's motion

Mr Langdon was not here when N. H. was allowed three members. If it was more than her share; he did not wish for them.

Mr. Butler contended warmly for Mr Gerry's motion as founded in reason and equity.

Mr. Elseworth's proviso to Mr. Gerry's motion was agreed to nem con.

Mr. King thought the power of taxation given to the Legislature rendered the motion of Mr Gerry altogether unnecessary.

On Mr Gerry's motion as amended

N– H– no Mas– ay. Ct no N– J– no. Pa. no– Del. no– Md no– Va no– N– Ci– divd. S– C. ay. Geo. no– [Ayes—2; noes—8; divided—1.]

[2:511; Madison, 5 Sept.]

Mr. Williamson gave like notice as to the Article fixing the number of Representatives, which he thought too small. He wished also to allow Rho: Island more than one, as due to her probable number of people, and as proper to stifle any pretext arising from her absence on the occasion.

[2:553; Madison, 8 Sept.]

Mr. Williamson moved that previous to this work of the Committee the clause relating to the number of the House of Representatives shd. be reconsidered for the purpose of increasing the number.

Mr Madison 2ded. the Motion

Mr. Sherman opposed it—he thought the provision on that subject amply sufficient.

Col: Hamilton expressed himself with great earnestness and anxiety in favor of the motion. He avowed himself a friend to a vigorous Government, but would declare at the same time, that he held it essential that the popular branch of it should be on a broad foundation. He was seriously of opinion that the House of Representatives was on so narrow a scale as to be really dangerous, and to warrant a jealousy in the people for their liberties. He remarked that the connection between the President & Senate would tend to perpetuate him, by corrupt influence. It was the more necessary on this account that a numerous representation in the other branch of the Legislature should be established.

On the motion of Mr. Williamson to reconsider, it was negatived,

N—H—no. Mas. no. Ct. no. N. J. no. Pa. ay. Del. ay. Md. ay. Va ay—N. C. ay. S. C. no. Geo. no. [Ayes—5; noes—6.]

[2:607; Madison, 13 Sept.]

Art: 1—sect. 2—On motion of Mr. Randolph the word "servitude" was struck out, and "service" unanimously inserted, the former being thought to express the condition of slaves, & the latter the obligations of free persons.

Mr Dickenson & Mr. Wilson moved to strike out "and direct taxes," from sect. 2 art. 1. as improperly placed in a clause relating merely to the Constitution of the House of Representatives.

Mr. Govr. Morris. The insertion here was in consequence of what had passed on this point; in order to exclude the appearance of counting the Negroes in *the Representation*—The including of them may now be referred to the object of direct taxes, and incidentally only to that of Representation—

On the motion to strike out "and direct taxes" from this place

N—H—no—Mas—no—Ct. no. N—J— ay. Pa. no. Del. ay. Md ay. Va. no—N. C. no. S. C. no. Geo. no. [Ayes—3; noes—8.]

[2:612; Madison, 14 Sept.]

Mr. Williamson moved to reconsider in order to increase the number of Representatives fixed for the first Legislature. His purpose was to make an addition of one half generally to the number allotted to the respective States; and to allow two to the smallest States.

On this motion

N. H. no—Mas. no. Ct no. N. J—no. Pa ay—Del. ay. Md ay. Va. ay. N C. ay. S—C. no. Geo no [Ayes—5; noes—6.]

[2:623; Madison, 15 Sept.]

Mr. Langdon. Some gentlemen have been very uneasy that no increase of the number of Representatives has been admitted. It has in particular been thought that one more ought to be allowed to N. Carolina. He was of opinion that an additional one was due both to that State & to Rho: Island. & moved to reconsider for that purpose.

Mr. Sherman. When the Committee of eleven reported the apportionment—five Representatives were thought the proper share of N—Carolina. Subsequent information however seemed to entitle that State to another—

On the motion to reconsider

N—H—ay—Mas—no. Ct ay—N—J. no—Pen. divd. Del. ay. Md. ay. Va. ay—N. C. ay. S—C. ay. Geo. ay. [Ayes—8; noes—2; divided—1.]

Mr. Langdon moved to add 1 member to each of the Representations of N—Carolina & Rho: Island.

Mr. King was agst. any change whatever as opening the door for delays. There had been no official proof that the numbers of N—C are greater than before estimated. And he never could sign the Constitution if Rho: Island is to be allowed two members that is, one fourth of the number allowed to Massts, which will be known to be unjust.

Mr. Pinkney urged the propriety of increasing the number of Reps allotted to N. Carolina.

Mr. Bedford contended for an increase in favor of Rho: Island, and of Delaware also

On the question for allowing two Reps. to Rho: Island it passed in the negative

N. H—ay. Mas. no. Ct. no. N. J. no. Pa. no. Del. ay. Md. ay. Va. no. N. C—ay. S. C. no.—Geo—ay. [Ayes—5; noes—6.]

On the question for allowing six to N. Carolina, it passed in the negative

N.H. no. Mas. no. Ct. no—N.J. no. Pa. no. Del—no—Md. ay. Va. ay. N—C. ay. S—C. ay. Geo. ay. [Ayes—5; noes—6.]

[2:638; Mason, 15 Sept.]

In the House of Representatives there is not the substance but the shadow only of representation; which can never produce proper information in the legislature, or inspire confidence in the people; the laws will therefore be generally made by men little concerned in, and unacquainted with their effects and consequences. This objection has been in some degree lessened by an amendment, often before refused and at last made by an erasure, after the engrossment upon parchment of the word *forty* and inserting *thirty*, in the third clause of the second section of the first article.

[2:643; Madison, 17 Sept.]

Mr. Gorham said if it was not too late he could wish, for the purpose of lessening objections to the Constitution, that the clause declaring "the number of Representatives shall not exceed one for every forty thousand—" which had produced so much discussion, might be yet reconsidered, in order to strike out 40,000 & insert "thirty thousand" This would not he remarked establish that as an absolute rule, but only give Congress a greater latitude which could not be thought unreasonable.

Mr. King & Mr Carrol seconded & supported the ideas of Mr Gorham.

When the President rose, for the purpose of putting the question, he said that although his situation had hitherto restrained him from offering his sentiments on questions depending in the House, and it might be thought, ought now to impose silence on him, yet he could not forbear expressing his wish that the alteration proposed might take place. It was much to be desired that the objections to the plan recommended might be made as few as possible— The smallness of the proportion of Representatives had been considered by many members of the Convention, an insufficient security for the rights & interests of the people. He acknowledged that it had always appeared to himself among the exceptionable parts of the plan; and late as the present moment was for admitting amendments, he thought this of so much consequence that it would give much satisfaction to see it adopted.

No opposition was made to the proposition of Mr. Gorham and it was agreed to unanimously

---

3

LETTER FROM A GENTLEMAN FROM
MASSACHUSETTS
17 Oct. 1787
Storing 4.2.3

My *particular objections* are first to the third paragraph in Sect. 2, Art. 1, which is in the following words—"Representatives and *direct taxes,* shall be apportioned among the several states, which *may be included in this union,* according to their respective numbers, which shall be determined, by adding to the whole number of *free persons,* including those bound to service for a term of years, and excluding *Indians* not taxed, *three fifths of all other persons.*" Was not this form of words thus uncouthly used to avoid using the word *Negroes?* It certainly looks as though the word *Negroes* was omitted from some *design,* it cannot be from any fear of offending that nation of *Africans.* Why must that man that has 500 slaves in our southern states, where slaves are looked upon only as *personal property,* have 300 of them exempted from *capitation,* while an inhabitant of the northern states, possessed of the same number of horned cattle, horses and hogs, be obliged to pay for the whole number? They are all considered as *chattles.* But to proceed, "The number of representatives shall not exceed *one* for every thirty thousand, but each state shall have at least *one representative:* and until such enumeration shall be made, the state of New-Hampshire shall be permitted to chuse *three,* Massachusetts *eight,* Rhode-Island and Providence Plantations *one,* Connecticut *five,* New-York *six,* New-Jersey *four,* Pennsylvania *eight,* Delaware *one,* Maryland *six,* Virginia *ten,* North-Carolina *five,* South-Carolina *five,* and Georgia *three.*" My objections to this part of the paragraph, are, that the representation is by far too small, to transact the business of so large an empire, our state

assemblies may be annihilated, having nothing to do of importance; the power of taxation being vested in Congress, all other business may be transacted in our town meetings.—A large representation has ever been esteemed by the best whigs in Great-Britain, the best barrier against *bribery* and *corruption,* and yet we find a *British king,* having the disposition of all places, civil and military, & an immense *revenue,* SQUEEZED out of the very mouths of his wretched subjects, is able to corrupt the parliament, to vote him any supplies he demands, to support armies, to defend the prerogatives of his crown, and carry fire & sword by his fleets and armies; to desolate whole provinces in the *eastern world,* to aggrandize himself, and satisfy the avarice of his tyrannical subjects.

4

A FEDERAL REPUBLICAN, REVIEW OF
THE CONSTITUTION PROPOSED
BY THE LATE CONVENTION
28 Oct. 1787
Storing 3.6.43–45

The next thing that we come to speak of, is the mode of laying taxes. All direct taxes are to be apportioned among the several states according to their respective numbers.

This is a great and a fundamental error. Direct taxes should always be apportioned according to extent of territory. In framing the present confederation in 1778, this was held to be an essential point. Article 8th says, "all charges of war and other expences which shall be incurred for the common defence and general welfare, and allowed for by the United States in Congress assembled, shall be defrayed out of the common treasury, which shall be supplied by the several states in proportion to the value of land in each state, etc." The value of land in a country increases with its riches, and therefore forms a just criterion. There are many reasons which might be offered to show that the number of inhabitants in any state is an improper measure of apportioning taxes. The inhabitants of some states may be numerous and poor, and those of another, few and wealthy.

The truth is, the ratios both of inhabitants and wealth, conspire to shew that the extent of territory is the only proper measure in apportioning taxes among the several states. Commerce creates wealth, but at the same time luxury and high life, and these again a decrease of inhabitants.

The luxury that is derived from commercial wealth always tends to stop population. From this it clearly appears that the apportioning of taxes according to numbers is not just. On the contrary, the state of agriculture is more favourable to population, but not to wealth. Indeed land must, in the nature of things, afford a just measure. It is true that the value of land is dependent on circumstances.

But the richer the country grows, the more valuable the land. The extent of land in Massachusetts is small in proportion to its inhabitants, but yet it is more valuable—in Virginia it is very great in proportion to the inhabitants, but yet it is not so valuable.

Let direct taxes be apportioned according to the value of land in each state, and it must be just for this reason, that the value of land always increases in an exact proportion to the riches of the country.

5

BRUTUS, NO. 3
15 Nov. 1787
Storing 2.9.38–39

The words are "representatives and direct taxes, shall be apportioned among the several states, which may be included in this union, according to their respective numbers, which shall be determined by adding to the whole number of free persons, including those bound to service for a term of years, and excluding Indians not taxed, three fifths of all other persons."—What a strange and unnecessary accumulation of words are here used to conceal from the public eye, what might have been expressed in the following concise manner. Representatives are to be proportioned among the states respectively, according to the number of freemen and slaves inhabiting them, counting five slaves for three free men.

"In a free state," says the celebrated Montesquieu, "every man, who is supposed to be a free agent, ought to be concerned in his own government. therefore the legislature should reside in the whole body of the people, or their representatives." But it has never been alledged that those who are not free agents, can, upon any rational principle, have any thing to do in government, either by themselves or others. If they have no share in government, why is the number of members in the assembly, to be increased on their account? Is it because in some of the states, a considerable part of the property of the inhabitants consists in a number of their fellow men, who are held in bondage, in defiance of every idea of benevolence, justice, and religion, and contrary to all the principles of liberty, which have been publickly avowed in the late glorious revolution? If this be a just ground for representation, the horses in some of the states, and the oxen in others, ought to be represented—for a great share of property in some of them, consists in these animals; and they have as much controul over their own actions, as these poor unhappy creatures, who are intended to be described in the above recited clause, by the words, "all other persons." By this mode of apportionment, the representatives of the different parts of the union, will be extremely unequal; in some of the southern states, the slaves are nearly equal in number to the free men; and for all these slaves, they will be entitled to a proportionate share in the legislature—this will give them an unreasonable weight in the government, which can derive no additional strength, protection, nor defence from the slaves, but the contrary. Why then should they be represented? What adds to the evil is, that these states are to be permitted to continue the inhuman traffic of importing slaves, until the year 1808—and for every cargo of these unhappy people, which unfeeling, unprincipled, barbarous, and avaricious wretches, may tear from their country, friends and tender connections, and bring into those states, they are to be rewarded by having an increase of members in the general assembly.

6

CATO, NO. 5
Fall 1787
Storing 2.6.38

It is a very important objection to this government, that the representation consists of so few; too few to resist the influence of corruption, and the temptation to treachery, against which all governments ought to take precautions—how guarded you have been on this head, in your own state constitution, and yet the number of senators and representatives proposed for this vast continent, does not equal those of your own state; how great the disparity, if you compare them with the aggregate numbers in the United States. The history of representation in England, from which we have taken our model of legislation, is briefly this[:] before the institution of legislating by deputies, the whole free part of the community usually met for that purpose; when this became impossible, by the increase of numbers the community was divided into districts, from each of which was sent such a number of deputies as was a complete representation of the various numbers and orders of citizens within them; but can it be asserted with truth, that six men can be a complete and full representation of the numbers and various orders of the people in this state? Another thing [that] may be suggested against the small number of representatives is, that but few of you will have the chance of sharing even in this branch of the legislature; and that the choice will be confined to a very few; the more complete it is, the better will your interests be preserved, and the greater the opportunity you will have to participate in government, one of the principal securities of a free people; but this subject has been so ably and fully treated by a writer under the signature of Brutus, that I shall content myself with referring you to him thereon, reserving further observations on the other objections I have mentioned, for my future numbers.

7

JAMES WILSON, PENNSYLVANIA RATIFYING
CONVENTION
30 Nov., 4 Dec. 1787
Elliot 2:442–43, 482–83

[*30 Nov.*]

It is objected that the number of members in the House of Representatives is too small. This is a subject somewhat embarrassing, and the Convention who framed the article felt the embarrassment. Take either side of the question, and you are necessarily led into difficulties. A large representation, sir, draws along with it a great expense. We all know that expense is offered as an objection to this system of government; and certainly, had the representation been greater, the clamor would have been on that side, and perhaps with some degree of justice. But the expense is not the sole objection; it is the opinion of some writers, that a deliberative body ought not to consist of more than one hundred members. I think, however, that there might be safety and propriety in going beyond that number; but certainly there is some number so large that it would be improper to increase them beyond it. The British House of Commons consists of upwards of five hundred. The senate of Rome consisted, it is said, at some times, of one thousand members. This last number is certainly too great.

The Convention endeavored to steer a middle course; and, when we consider the scale on which they formed their calculation, there are strong reasons why the representation should not have been larger. On the ratio that they have fixed, of one for every thirty thousand, and according to the generally received opinion of the increase of population throughout the United States, the present number of their inhabitants will be doubled in twenty-five years, and according to that progressive proportion, and the ratio of one member for thirty thousand inhabitants, the House of Representatives will, within a single century, consist of more than six hundred members. Permit me to add a further observation on the numbers—that a large number is not so necessary in this case as in the cases of state legislatures. In them there ought to be a representation sufficient to declare the situation of every county, town, and district; and if of every individual, so much the better, because their legislative powers extend to the particular interest and convenience of each. But in the general government, its objects are enumerated, and are not confined, in their causes or operations, to a county, or even to a single state. No one power is of such a nature as to require the minute knowledge of situations and circumstances necessary in state governments possessed of general legislative authority. These were the reasons, sir, that, I believe, had influence on the Convention, to agree to the number of thirty thousand; and when the inconveniences and conveniences, on both sides, are compared, it would be difficult to say what would be a number more unexceptionable.

[*4 Dec.*]

In this system, it is declared that the electors in each state shall have the qualifications requisite for electors of the most numerous branch of the state legislature. This being made the criterion of the right of suffrage, it is consequently secured, because the same Constitution guaranties to every state in the Union a republican form of government. The right of suffrage is fundamental to republics.

Sir, there is another principle that I beg leave to mention. *Representation and direct taxation,* under this Constitution, are to be according to numbers. As this is a subject which I believe has not been gone into in this house, it will be worth while to show the sentiments of some respectable writers thereon. *Montesquieu,* in considering the requisites in a confederate republic, book 9th, chap. 3d, speaking of Holland, observes, "It is difficult for the united states to be all of equal power and extent. The Lycian (*Strabo,* lib. 14) republic was an association of twenty-three towns; the large ones had three votes in the common council, the middling ones two, and the small towns one. The Dutch republic consists of seven provinces, of different extent of territory, which have each one voice.

"The cities of Lycia (*Strabo,* lib. 14) contributed to the expenses of the state, according to the proportion of suffrages. The provinces of the United Netherlands cannot follow this proportion; they must be directed by that of their power.

"In *Lycia,* (*Strabo,* lib. 14,) the judges and town magistrates were elected by the common council, and according to the proportion already mentioned. In the republic of Holland, they are not chosen by the common council, but each town names its magistrates. Were I to give a model of an excellent confederate republic, I should pitch upon that of *Lycia.*"

I have endeavored, in all the books that I have access to, to acquire some information relative to the *Lycian republic;* but its history is not to be found; the few facts that relate to it are mentioned only by Strabo; and however excellent the model it might present, we were reduced to the necessity of working without it. Give me leave to quote the sentiments of another author, whose peculiar situation and extensive worth throw a lustre on all he says. I mean Mr. *Necker,* whose ideas are very exalted, both in theory and practical knowledge, on this subject. He approaches the nearest to the truth in his calculations from experience, and it is very remarkable that he makes use of that expression. His words are, (*Necker on Finance,* vol. i. p. 308),—

"Population can therefore be only looked on as an exact measure of comparison when the provinces have resources nearly equal; but even this imperfect rule of proportion ought not to be neglected; and of all the objects which may be subjected to a determined and positive calculation, that of the taxes, to the population, approaches nearest to the truth."

8

THE ADDRESS AND REASONS OF DISSENT OF THE MINORITY OF THE CONVENTION OF PENNSYLVANIA TO THEIR CONSTITUENTS
18 Dec. 1787
Storing 3.11.34–37

The president is to have the controul over the enacting of laws, so far as to make the concurrence of *two* thirds of the representatives and senators present necessary, if he should object to the laws.

Thus it appears that the liberties, happiness, interests, and great concerns of the whole United States, may be dependent upon the integrity, virtue, wisdom, and knowledge of 25 or 26 men—How [i]nadequate and unsafe a representation! Inadequate, because the sense and views of 3 or 4 millions of people diffused over so extensive a territory comprising such various climates, products, habits, interests, and opinions, cannot be collected in so small a body; and besides, it is not a fair and equal representation of the people even in proportion to its number, for the smallest state has as much weight in the senate as the largest, and from the smallness of the number to be chosen for both branches of the legislature; and from the mode of election and appointment, which is under the controul of Congress; and from the nature of the thing, men of the most elevated rank in life, will alone be chosen. The other orders in the society, such as farmers, traders, and mechanics, who all ought to have a competent number of their best informed men in the legislature, will be totally unrepresented.

The representation is unsafe, because in the exercise of such great powers and trusts, it is so exposed to corruption and undue influence, by the gift of the numerous places of honor and emoluments at the disposal of the executive; by the arts and address of the great and designing; and by direct bribery.

The representation is moreover inadequate and unsafe, because of the long terms for which it is appointed, and the mode of its appointment, by which Congress may not only controul the choice of the people, but may so manage as to divest the people of this fundamental right, and become self-elected.

The number of members in the house of representatives *may* be encreased to one for every 30,000 inhabitants. But when we consider, that this cannot be done without the consent of the senate, who from their share in the legislative, in the executive, and judicial departments, and permanency of appointment, will be the great efficient body in this government, and whose weight and predominancy would be abridged by an increase of the representatives, we are persuaded that this is a circumstance that cannot be expected. On the contrary, the number of representatives will probably be continued at 65, although the population of the country may swell to treble what it now is; unless a revolution should effect a change.

9

LUTHER MARTIN, GENUINE INFORMATION
1788
Storing 2.4.14–15, 16, 28–34, 45

You have heard, Sir, the resolutions which were brought forward by the honourable member from Virginia; let me call the attention of this House to the conduct of Virginia, when our confederation was entered into—that State then proposed, and obstinately contended, *contrary to the sense of, and unsupported by the other States, for an inequality of suffrage* founded on *numbers, or some such scale,* which should give *her,* and certain other States, *influence in the Union over the rest;* pursuant to that spirit which then characterized her, and uniform in her conduct, the very second resolve, is calculated expressly for that purpose *to give her a representation proportioned to her numbers,* as if the *want of that* was *the principle defect* in our original system, and this alteration the great means of remedying the evils we had experienced under our present government.

The object of *Virginia,* and *other large States, to encrease their power and influence over the others,* did not escape observation: the subject, however, was discussed with great coolness in the committee of the whole House (for the convention had resolved itself into a committee of the whole to deliberate upon the propositions delivered in by the honourable member from Virginia). Hopes were formed, that the farther we proceeded in the examination of the resolutions, the better the House might be satisfied of the impropriety of adopting them, and that they would finally be rejected by a majority of the committee; if on the contrary, a majority should report in their favour, it was considered, that it would not preclude the members from bringing forward and submitting any other system to the consideration of the convention; and accordingly, while those resolves were the subject of discussion in the committee of the whole House, a number of the members who disapproved them, were preparing *another system,* such as *they thought more conducive to the happiness and welfare of the States*—The propositions originally submitted to the convention having been debated, and undergone a variety of alterations in the course of our proceedings, the committee of the whole House by a *small majority* agreed to a *report,* which I am happy, Sir, to have in my power to lay before you; it was as follows:

. . . . .

7. That the *right of suffrage* in the *first* branch of the national legislature, *ought not to be according to the rule established in the articles of confederation,* but according to some equitable rate of representation, namely, *in proportion to the whole number of white, and other free citizens and inhabitants of every age, sex and condition, including those bound to servitude for a term of years, and three-fifths of all other persons,* not comprehended in the foregoing description, except Indians not paying taxes in each State.

. . . . .

The Jersey propositions being thus rejected, the convention took up those reported by the committee, and proceeded to debate them by paragraphs; it was now that they who disapproved the report found it necessary to make a *warm* and *decided opposition*, which took place upon the discussion of the seventh resolution, which related to the *inequality* of representation in the *first* branch. Those who advocated this inequality, urged, that when the articles of confederation were formed, it was *only* from *necessity* and *expediency* that the States were admitted *each* to have an *equal vote;* but that our situation was *now altered*, and therefore those States who considered it contrary to their interest, would *not longer abide* by it. They said no State ought to wish to have influence in government, except in proportion to what it contributes to it; that if it contributes but little, it ought to have but a small vote; that taxation and representation ought always to go together; that if one State had *sixteen times as many inhabitants* as another, or was *sixteen times as wealthy*, it ought to have *sixteen times as many votes;* that an inhabitant of Pennsylvania ought to have as much weight and consequence as an inhabitant of Jersey or Delaware; that it was contrary to the feelings of the human mind; what the *large States* would *never* submit to; that the *large States* would have *great objects* in view, in which they would never permit the *smaller States* to thwart them; that *equality of suffrage* was the rotten part of the constitution, and that this was a happy time to get clear of it. In fine, that it was the poison which contaminated our whole system, and the source of all the evils we experienced.

This, Sir, is the substance of the arguments, if arguments they may be called, which were used in favour of *inequality of suffrage*.—Those who advocated the *equality of suffrage*, took the matter up on the original principles of government; they urged, that all men considered in a state of nature, before any government formed, are equally free and independent, no one having any right or authority to exercise power over another, and this *without any regard to difference in personal strength, understanding, or wealth*—That when such individuals enter into government, they have *each a right* to an *equal voice* in its first formation, and afterwards have *each* a right to an *equal vote* in every matter which relates to their government—That if it could be done conveniently, they have a right to exercise it in person—Where it cannot be done in person but for convenience, representatives are appointed to act for them, *every person* has a *right* to an *equal vote*, in choosing that representative who is entrusted to do for the whole, that which the whole, if they could assemble, might do in person, and in the transacting of which each would have an equal voice—That if we were to admit, because a man was *more wise, more strong*, or *more wealthy*, he should be entitled to *more votes* than another, it would be *inconsistent with the freedom and liberty of that other*, and would reduce him to *slavery*—Suppose, for instance, ten individuals in a state of nature, about to enter into government, *nine* of whom are *equally wise, equally strong, and equally wealthy*, the *tenth* is *ten times as wise, ten times as strong*, or *ten times as rich;* if for this reason he is to have *ten votes* for *each vote of either of the others*, the *nine* might as well *have no vote at all*, since though the *whole nine* might assent to a measure, yet the *vote* of the *tenth* would *countervail*, and *set aside all their votes*—If this *tenth* approved of what *they* wished to adopt, it would be well, but if he disapproved, he could prevent it, and in the same manner he could carry into execution *any measure he wished, contrary to the opinion of all the others, he* having *ten votes*, and the *other* altogether but *nine*—It is evident that on these principles, *the nine* would have *no will nor discretion of their own*, but must be *totally dependent* on the *will* and *discretion* of the *tenth*, to him *they* would be as *absolutely slaves* as *any negro* is to his *master*—If *he* did not attempt to carry into execution any measures injurious to the *other nine*, it could only be said that they had a *good master*, they would not be the *less slaves*, because *they* would be *totally dependent* on the *will of another*, and not on *their own will*—They might not *feel their chains*, but they would notwithstanding *wear them*, and whenever their *master* pleased he might draw them so tight as to gall them to the bone. Hence it was urged the *inequality of representation*, or giving to one man more votes than another on account of his wealth, etc. was *altogether inconsistent with the principles of liberty*, and in the *same proportion as it should be adopted*, in favour of *one* or *more*, in *that proportion are the others inslaved*—It was urged, that though every individual should have an an equal voice in the government, yet, even the superior wealth, strength, or understanding, would give great and undue advantages to those who possessed them. That wealth attracts respect and attention; superior strength would cause the weaker and more feeble to be cautious how they offended, and to put up with small injuries rather than to engage in an unequal contest—In like manner superior understanding would give its possessor many opportunities of profiting at the expence of the more ignorant. Having thus established these principles with respect to the *rights* of *individuals* in a *state of nature*, and what is due to *each* on entering into government, principles established by every writer on liberty, they proceeded to shew that *States*, when *once formed*, are considered *with respect* to *each other* as *individuals* in a state of nature; that, like individuals, each *State* is considered *equally free* and *equally independent*, the *one* having no right to exercise authority over the *other*, though *more strong, more wealthy*, or *abounding with more inhabitants*—That when a number of *States* unite themselves under a *federal government*, the *same principles apply to them* as when a *number* of *individual men* unite themselves under a *State government*—That every argument which shews *one man* ought not to have *more votes* than *another*, because he is *wiser, stronger* or *wealthier*, proves that *one State* ought not to have *more votes* than *another*, because it is *stronger, richer*, or *more populous*—And that by *giving one State*, or one or two *States more votes* than the *others*, the *others* thereby are *enslaved to such State or States*, having the *greater number of votes*, in the *same manner* as in the case before put of *individuals* where *one* has *more votes than the others*—That the reason why each individual man in forming a State government should have an equal vote is, because each individual before he enters into government is *equally free* and *independent*—So *each State*, when *States enter* into a *federal government*, are entitled to an *equal vote*, because before they entered into such federal government, *each State* was *equally free* and *equally independent*—That *adequate* representation of *men formed into a State government*, consists in *each man* having an *equal voice*, either personally, or if by representatives, that he should have an equal voice in choosing the representative—So adequate representation of *States* in a *federal government*, consists in *each State* having an *equal voice* either in person or by its representative in every thing which relates to the federal government—That this *adequacy of representation* is *more important* in a *federal*, than in a *State* government, because the members of a State government, the *district* of which is *not very large*, have generally such a *common interest*, that laws can scarcely be made by *one* part *oppressive* to the *others*, without *their suffering in common;* but the *different States* composing an *extensive federal empire*, widely distant *one* from the *other*, may have *interests so totally distinct*, that the *one* part might be be greatly *benefited* by what would be *destructive* to the *other*.

They were not satisfied by resting it on principles; they also appealed to history—They shewed that in the Amphyctionic confederation of the Grecian cities, *each city* however *different* in *wealth*, *strength*, and other *circumstances*, sent the same *number* of deputies, and had *each* an *equal voice* in every thing that related to the common concerns of Greece. It was shewn that in the seven Provinces of the United Netherlands, and the confederated Cantons of Switzerland, *each Canton* and *each province* have an *equal vote*, although there are as great distinctions of wealth, strength, population, and extent of territory among *those provinces* and *those Cantons*, as among *these States*. It was said, that the maxim that taxation and representation ought to go together, was true so far, that no person ought to be *taxed* who is not *represented*, but not in the extent insisted upon, to wit, that the *quantum of taxation* and *representation* ought to be *same;* on the contrary, the *quantum of representation* depends upon the quantum of *freedom*, and therefore *all*, whether *individual States*, or individual *men*, who are *equally free*, have a right to *equal representation*—That to those who insist that he who pays the greatest share of taxes, ought to have the greatest number of votes; is a sufficient answer to say, that *this rule* would be *destructive* of the *liberty* of the *others*, and would render *them slaves* to the *more rich* and *wealthy*—That if one man pays *more taxes* than another, it is because he has *more wealth* to be protected by government, and he receives greater benefits from the government—So if one State pays more to the federal government, it is because as a State, she enjoys greater blessings from it; she has more wealth protected by it, or a greater number of inhabitants, whose rights are secured, and who share its advantages.

It was urged, that upon these principles the Pennsylvanian, or inhabitant of a large State, was of as much consequence as the inhabitant of Jersey, Delaware, Maryland, or any other State—That *his consequence* was to be decided by *his situation* in his *own State;* that if he was *there* as *free*, if he had as great share in the forming of his own government, and in the making and executing its laws, as the inhabitants of those other States, then was he equally important and of equal consequence—Suppose a confederation of States had never been adopted, but every State had remained absolutely in its independent situation, no per-

son could with propriety, say that the citizen of the large State was not as important as the citizen of the smaller, the confederation of the States cannot alter the case. It was said, that in all transactions *between State and State*, the freedom, independence, importance and consequence, even the individuality of each citizen of the different States, might with propriety be said to be swallowed up, or concentrated in the independence, the freedom and the individuality *of the State* of which they are citizens—That the *Thirteen States* are *thirteen distinct political individual existences* as to each other; that the *federal* government is or *ought to be* a government *over these thirteen political individual existences*, which form the members of that government; and that as the *largest State* is only a *single individual* of this government, it ought to have only *one vote;* the *smallest State* also being *one individual member* of this government, ought also to have *one vote*—To those who urged that the States have equal suffrage, was contrary to the feelings of the human heart, it was answered, that it was admitted to be contrary to the feelings of *pride* and *ambition;* but those were feelings which ought not to be gratified at the expence of *freedom*.

It was urged, that the position that great States would have great objects in view, in which they would not suffer the less states to thwart them, was one of the strongest reasons why inequality of representation ought not to be admitted. If those great objects were not *inconsistent* with the interest of the *less States*, they would readily concur in them, but if they were *inconsistent* with the *interest* of a *majority of the States* composing the government, in that case *two* or *three States* ought not to have it in their power to *aggrandize themselves* at the *expence of all the rest*—To those who alledged that equality of suffrage in our federal government, was the poisonous source from which all our misfortunes flowed, it was answered, that the allegation was not founded in fact—That *equality of suffrage* had *never been complained of by the States* as a *defect* in our federal system—That among the eminent writers, foreigners and others, who had treated of the defects of our confederation, and proposed alterations, *none had proposed an alteration in this part of the system:* And members of the convention both in and out of Congress, who advocated the equality of suffrage, called upon their opponents both in and out of Congress, and challenged them to produce *one single instance* where a *bad measure* had been adopted, or a *good measure* had failed of adoption in consequence of the States having an *equal vote;* on the contrary, they urged, that all our evils flowed from the *want of power* in the federal head, and that let the *right of suffrage* in the States be *altered in any manner whatever*, if no *greater powers were given* to the government, the *same inconveniences would continue*.

It was denied that the *equality of suffrage* was *originally* agreed to on principles of *necessity* or *expediency*, on the contrary, that it was adopted on the principles of the *rights of men* and the *rights of States* which were *then* well known, and which then influenced our conduct although *now* they seem to be *forgotten*—For this the journals of Congress were appealed to; it was from them shewn, that when the Committee of Congress reported to that body the articles of confederation, the very first article which became the subject of discussion, was that respecting equality of suffrage—That Virginia proposed divers modes of suffrage, all on the principle of inequality, which were *almost unanimously* rejected; that on the question for adopting the article, it passed, Virginia being the *only* State which voted in the *negative*—That after the articles of confederation were submitted to the States by them to be ratified, almost every State proposed certain amendment, which they instructed their delegates to endeavour to obtain before ratification, and that among all the amendments proposed, *not one State*, not even Virginia, proposed an amendment of that *article, securing the equality of suffrage*—the most convincing proof it was agreed to and adopted, not from *necessity*, but *upon a full conviction*, that according to the principles of free government, the States had a *right to that equality of suffrage.*

But, Sir, it was to no purpose that the futility of their objections were shewn—when driven from the *pretence* that the *equality of suffrage* had been originally agreed to on principles of *expediency* and *necessity*, the representatives of the *large States* persisting in a declaration, that they would never agree to admit the *smaller States* to an *equality* of suffrage—In answer to this, they were informed, and informed in terms the *most strong* and *energetic* that could *possibly be used*, that *we never would agree* to a system giving them the *undue influence* and *superiority* they proposed—That we would risque every possible consequence—That from anarchy and confusion *order might arise*—That *slavery* was the *worst* that could ensue, and we considered the *system* proposed to be the *most complete, most abject* system of *slavery* that the wit of man ever devised, under the *pretence* of forming a government for free States—That we never would submit tamely and servilely to a *present certain evil* in dread of a *future,* which might be *imaginary;* that we were sensible the eyes of our country and the world were upon us—That we would not labour under the *imputation* of being *unwilling* to *form a strong* and *energetic federal government;* but we would publish the system which we *approved,* and also that which we *opposed,* and leave it to our country and the world at large to judge between us, who *best understood* the rights of *free men* and *free States,* and who *best advocated them;* and to the same tribunal we would submit, who ought to be answerable for all the consequences which might arise to the union from the convention breaking up, without proposing any system to their constituents.—During this debate we were *threatened,* that if we did not agree to the system proposed, we *never should* have an *opportunity* of *meeting in convention* to deliberate on *another,* and this was frequently urged—In answer, we called upon them to shew *what was to prevent it,* and from what quarter was our danger to proceed; was it from a *foreign enemy?* Our *distance* from Europe, and the *political situation* of that country, left us but little to fear: Was there any *ambitious State* or *States, who in violation of every sacred obligation* was preparing to *enslave* the *other* States, and raise *itself* to *consequence* on the *ruin of the others?* Or was there any such *ambitious individual?* We did not apprehend it to be the case: but suppose it to be true, it rendered it the *more necessary* that *we* should *sacredly guard against a system* which might enable *all those ambitious views to be carried into effect,*

even under the sanction of the constitution and government: In fine, Sir, *all these threats* were treated with *contempt,* and they were told that we apprehended but *one reason* to prevent the States meeting again in convention; that when they discovered the part *this* convention had acted, and how much its members were *abusing the trust* reposed in them, the States would never trust *another* convention. At length, Sir, after every argument had been exhausted by the advocates of equality of representation, the question was called, when a majority decided in favour of the inequality—Massachusetts, Pennsylvania, Virginia, North-Carolina, South-Carolina and Georgia voting for it—Connecticut, New-York, New-Jersey, and Delaware against it; Maryland divided. It may be thought surprising, Sir, that Georgia, a State *now small* and comparatively *trifling* in the union, should advocate this system of *unequal representation,* giving up her *present* equality in the federal government, and sinking herself almost to total insignificance in the scale; but, Sir, it must be considered that Georgia has the *most extensive* territory in the union, being *larger* than the *whole island of Great-Britain,* and *thirty* times as large as *Connecticut.* This system being designed to *preserve to the States their whole territory unbroken,* and to prevent the erection of new States within the territory of any of them: Georgia looked forward *when her population,* being increased in some measure *proportioned to her territory,* she should *rise* in the scale and *give law* to the other States, and hence we found the delegation of Georgia warmly advocating the proposition of giving the States unequal representation.

. . . . .

With respect to *that part* of the *second* section of the *first* article, which relates to the *apportionment of representation* and *direct taxation,* there were considerable objections made to it, besides the great objection of inequality—It was urged, that no principle could justify taking *slaves* into computation in *apportioning* the number of *representatives* a State should have in the government—That it involved the absurdity of *increasing* the power of a State in making laws for *free men* in *proportion* as that State *violated* the *rights of freedom*—That it might be proper to take slaves into consideration, when *taxes* were to be apportioned, because it had a tendency to *discourage slavery;* but to take them into account in *giving representation* tended to *encourage* the *slave trade,* and to make it the *interest* of the States to *continue* that *infamous traffic*—That slaves could not be taken into account as *men,* or *citizens,* because they were not admitted to the *rights of citizens,* in the States which adopted or continued slavery—If they were to be taken into account as *property,* it was asked, what peculiar circumstance should render this property (of *all others* the most *odious* in its nature) entitled to the *high privilege* of conferring *consequence* and *power* in the *government* to its possessors, rather than *any other* property: and why *slaves* should, as property be taken into account rather than *horses, cattle, mules,* or any *other species;* and it was observed by an honourable member from Massachusetts, that he considered it as dishonourable and humiliating to enter into compact with the *slaves of the southern States,* as it would with the *horses* and *mules of the eastern.* It was also objected, that the *numbers* of representatives appointed by this section to be sent by the particular States to compose the *first* legislature, were not precisely *agreeable* to the *rule* of representation adopted by this system, and that the numbers in this section are *artfully lessened* for the *large* States, while the *smaller* States have their *full proportion* in order to prevent the *undue influence* which the *large* States will have in the government from being *too apparent;* and I think, Mr. Speaker, that this objection is *well founded.* I have taken some pains to obtain information of the number of free men and slaves in the different States, and I have reason to believe, that if the estimate was *now* taken, which is directed, and one delegate to be sent for every thirty thousand inhabitants, that Virginia would have at least *twelve* delegates, Massachusetts *eleven,* and Pennsylvania *ten,* instead of the number stated in *this section;* where the *other* States, I believe, would not have more than the number there allowed them, nor would Georgia, most probably at present, send more than *two*—If I am right, Mr. Speaker, upon the enumeration being made, and the representation being apportioned according to the rule prescribed, the *whole number* of delegates would be *seventy-one,* thirty-six of which would be a *quorum* to do business; the delegates of Virginia, Massachusetts, and Pennsylvania, would amount to *thirty-three* of that quorum—Those three States will, therefore, have *much more* than *equal* power and influence in *making* the laws and regulations, which are to affect this continent, and will have a *moral certainty* of *preventing* any laws or regulations which *they disapprove,* although they might be thought ever so *necessary* by a *great majority* of the States— It was further objected, that even if the States who had most inhabitants ought to have a greater number of delegates, yet the *number of delegates* ought not to be in *exact proportion* to the *number of inhabitants,* because the influence and power of those States whose delegates are numerous, will be *greater* when compared to the influence and power of the other States, than the *proportion* which the numbers of their delegates bear to each other; as for instance, though Delaware has *one* delegate, and Virginia but *ten,* yet Virginia has *more* than *ten times* as much *power* and *influence* in the government as Delaware; to prove this, it was observed, that *Virginia* would have a *much greater* chance to carry any measure than *any number of States,* whose delegates were altogether ten (suppose the States of Delaware, Connecticut, Rhode-Island, and New-Hampshire) since the *ten* delegates from Virginia in every thing that related to the interest of that State would *act in union,* and *move one solid and compact body,* whereas the *delegates of these four States,* though collectively *equal* in number to those from Virginia, coming from *different* States, having different *interests,* will be less likely to harmonize and move in concert. As a further proof it was said, that Virginia, as the system is now reported, by uniting with her the delegates of *four* other States, can carry a question *against* the sense and interest of *eight* States by *sixty-four* different combinations; the *four* States voting with Virginia, being every time *so far different* as not to be composed of the *same four;* whereas the State of Delaware can only, by uniting four other States with her, carry a measure against the sense of eight States by *two* different combinations—a

mathematical proof that the State of *Virginia* has *thirty-two* times greater chance of carrying a measure against the sense of eight States than *Delaware,* although Virginia has only *ten times* as many delegates: It was also shewn, that the idea was totally fallacious which was attempted to be maintained, that if a State had *one thirteenth* part of the *numbers composing the delegation in this system,* such State would have *as much influence* as under the articles of confederation; to prove the fallacy of this idea it was shewn, that under the articles of confederation the State of Maryland had but *one* vote in *thirteen,* yet no measure could be carried against her interests without *seven States,* a majority of the whole concurring in it; whereas in this system, though Maryland has *six* votes, which is *more* than the *proportion* of *one in thirteen,* yet *five* States may, in a *variety of combinations,* carry a question *against* her interest, tho' *seven* other States concur with her, and *six* States by a *much greater* number of combinations, may carry a measure against *Maryland,* united with *six other States.* I shall here, Sir, just observe, that as the committee of detail reported the system, the delegates from the different States were to be *one* for every *forty thousand* inhabitants; it was afterwards altered to one for every *thirty* thousand; this alteration was made after I left the convention, at the instance of whom I know not, but it is evident, that the alteration is in favour of the *States* which have large and extensive territory, to increase their power and influence in the government, and to the injury of the *smaller States*—Since it is the States of *extensive* territory, who will *most speedily* increase the number of their *inhabitants* as before has been observed, and will therefore, most speedily procure an increase to the number of their *delegates*—By this alteration Virginia, North-Carolina, or Georgia, by obtaining one hundred and twenty thousand additional inhabitants, will be entitled to *four* additional delegates, whereas such State would only have been entitled to *three,* if *forty thousand* had remained the number by which to apportion the delegation. As to that part of this section that relates to direct taxation, there was also an objection for the following reasons, it was said that a *large sum* of money was to be brought into the national treasury by the *duties* on commerce, which would be almost *wholly* paid by the *commercial States,* it would be *unequal* and *unjust* that the sum which was necessary to be raised by *direct taxation* should be apportioned *equally* upon all the States, obliging the commercial States to pay as large a share of the revenue arising therefrom, as the States from whom no revenue had been drawn by imposts; since the wealth and industry of the inhabitants of the commercial States will in the first place be severely taxed through their commerce, and afterwards be *equally taxed* with the industry and wealth of the inhabitants of the other States, *who have paid no part* of that *revenue,* so that by this provision, the inhabitants of the commercial States are in this system obliged to bear an unreasonable and disproportionate share in the expences of the union, and the payment of that foreign and domestic debt, which was incurred not more for the benefit of the commercial than of the other States.

10

ALEXANDER HAMILTON, FEDERALIST, NO. 36, 226, 229–30
8 Jan. 1788

Let it be recollected, that the proportion of these taxes is not to be left to the discretion of the national Legislature: but is to be determined by the numbers of each State as described in the second section of the first article. An actual census or enumeration of the people must furnish the rule; a circumstance which effectually shuts the door to partiality or oppression. The abuse of this power of taxation seems to have been provided against with guarded circumspection. In addition to the precaution just mentioned, there is a provision that 'all duties, imposts and excises shall be UNIFORM throughout the United States.'

. . . . .

As to poll taxes, I, without scruple, confess my disapprobation of them; and though they have prevailed from an early period in those States which have uniformly been the most tenacious of their rights, I should lament to see them introduced into practice under the national government. But does it follow because there is a power to lay them, that they will actually be laid? Every State in the Union has power to impose taxes of this kind; and yet in several of them they are unknown in practice. Are the State governments to be stigmatised as tyrannies because they possess this power? If they are not, with what propriety can the like power justify such a charge against the national government, or even be urged as an obstacle to its adoption? As little friendly as I am to the species of imposition, I still feel a thorough conviction, that the power of having recourse to it ought to exist in the Foederal Government. There are certain emergencies of nations, in which expedients that in the ordinary state of things ought to be foreborn, become essential to the public weal. And the government from the possibility of such emergencies ought ever to have the option of making use of them. The real scarcity of objects in this country, which may be considered as productive sources of revenue, is a reason peculiar to itself, for not abridging the discretion of the national councils in this respect. There may exist certain critical and tempestuous conjunctures of the State, in which a poll tax may become an inestimable resource. And as I know nothing to exempt this portion of the globe from the common calamities that have befallen other parts of it, I acknowledge my aversion to every project that is calculated to disarm the government of a single weapon, which in any possible contingency might be usefully employed for the general defence and security.

11

DEBATE IN MASSACHUSETTS RATIFYING CONVENTION
17–19 Jan. 1788
Elliot 2:36–45

Mr. KING rose to explain it. There has, says he, been much misconception of this section. It is a principle of this Constitution, that representation and taxation should go hand in hand. This paragraph states that the number of free persons, including those bound to service for a term of years, and excluding Indians not taxed, three fifths of all other persons. These persons are the *slaves*. By this rule are representation and taxation to be apportioned. And it was adopted, because it was the language of all America. According to the Confederation, ratified in 1781, the sums for the general welfare and defence should be apportioned according to the surveyed lands, and improvements thereon, in the several states; but that it hath never been in the power of Congress to follow that rule, the returns from the several states being so very imperfect.

Dr. TAYLOR thought that the number of members to be chosen for the House of Representatives was too small. The whole Union was entitled to send but 65; whereas, by the old Confederation, they send 91—a reduction of 30 per cent. He had heard it objected, that, if a larger number was sent, the house would be unwieldy. He thought our House of Representatives, which sometimes consists of 150, was not unwieldy; and if the number of the federal representatives was enlarged to twice 65, he thought it would not be too large. He then proceeded to answer another objection, "that an increase of numbers would be an increase of expense," and by calculation demonstrated that the salaries of the full number he wished, would, in a year, amount only to £2,980, about one penny on a poll; and by this increase, he thought every part of the commonwealth would be represented. The distresses of the people would thereby be more fully known and relieved.

Mr. WIDGERY asked, if a boy of six years of age was to be considered as a free person.

Mr. KING, in answer, said, all persons born free were to be considered as freemen; and, to make the idea of *taxation by numbers* more intelligible, said that *five negro children of South Carolina are to pay as much tax as the three governors* of New Hampshire, Massachusetts, and Connecticut.

Mr. GORHAM thought the proposed section much in favor of Massachusetts; and if it operated against any state, it was Pennsylvania, because they have more *white persons bound* than any other. Mr. G. corrected an observation of Dr. Taylor's that the states now send 91 delegates to Congress; which was not the case. The states do not, he said, send near the number, and instanced Massachusetts, which sends but four. He concluded by saying that the Constitution provides for an increase of members as numbers increase, and that in fifty years there will be 360; in one hundred years, 14 or 1500, if the Constitution last so long.

Judge DANA, remarking on the assertions of Dr. Taylor, that the *number of representatives* was too small; that the whole Union was now entitled to send but 65, whereas by the Confederation they might send 91,—a reduction of 30 per cent.,—said, if the Constitution under consideration was in fact what its opposers had often called it, a consolidation of the states, he should readily agree with that gentleman that the representation of the people was much too small; but this was a charge brought against it without any foundation in truth. So far from it, that it must be apparent to every one, that the federal government springs out of, and can alone be brought into existence by, the state governments. Demolish the latter, and there is an end of the former. Had the Continental Convention, then, doubled the representation, agreeably to that gentleman's ideas, would not the people of this Commonwealth have been the first to complain of it as an unnecessary burden laid upon them—that, in addition to their own domestic government, they have been charged with the support of so numerous a national government? Would they not have contended for the demolition of the one or the other, as being unable to support both? Would they have been satisfied by being told that doubling the representation would yearly amount only "to about one penny upon a poll"? Does not the gentleman know that the expense of our own numerous representation has excited much ill-will against the government? Has he never heard it said among the people that our public affairs would be as well conducted by half the number of representatives? If he has not, I have, sir, and believe it to be true. But the gentleman says that there is a reduction of 30 per cent. in the federal representation, as the whole Union can send but 65, when under the Confederation they may send 91. The gentleman has not made a fair calculation. For, if to the 65 representatives under the proposed Constitution we add 2 senators from each state, amounting to 26 in all, we shall have the same number, 91; so that in this respect there is no difference. Besides, this representation will increase with the population of the states, and soon become sufficiently large to meet that gentleman's ideas. I would just observe, that by the Confederation this state has a right to send seven members to Congress; yet, although the legislature hath sometimes chosen the whole number, I believe at no time have they had, or wished to have, more than four of them actually in Congress. Have any ill consequences arisen from this small representation in the national council? Have our liberties been endangered by it? No one will say they have. The honorable gentleman drew a parallel between the Eastern and Southern States, and showed the injustice done the former by the present mode of apportioning taxes, according to surveyed land and improvements, and the consequent advantage therefrom to the latter, their property not lying in improvements, in buildings, &c.

In reply to the remark of some gentlemen, that the Southern States were favored in this mode of apportionment, by having five of their *negroes* set against *three persons* in the Eastern, the honorable judge observed, that the *negroes* of the Southern States work no longer than when the eye of the driver is on them. Can, asked he, that land flourish like this, which is cultivated by the hands of freemen? and are not *three* of these independent freemen of more real advantage to a state than *five* of those poor slaves? As a friend to equal taxation, he rejoiced that an opportunity was presented, in this Constitution, to change this unjust mode of apportionment. Indeed, concluded he, from a survey of every part of the Constitution, I think it the best that the wisdom of men could suggest.

Mr. NASSON remarked on the statement of the Hon. Mr. King, by saying that the honorable gentleman should have gone further, and shown us the other side of the question. It is a good rule that works both ways; and the gentleman should also have told us, that *three of our infants in the cradle* are to be rated as *five of the working negroes* of Virginia. Mr. N. adverted to a statement of Mr. King, who had said that five negro children of South Carolina were equally ratable as three governors of New England, and wished, he said, the honorable gentleman had considered this question upon the other side, as it would then appear that this state will pay as great a tax for three children in the cradle, as any of the Southern States will for five hearty, working negro men. He hoped, he said, while we were making a new government, we should make it better than the old one; for, if we had made a bad bargain before, as had been hinted, it was a reason why we should make a better one now.

Mr. RANDALL begged leave to answer a remark of the Hon. Mr. Dana, which, he thought, reflected on the barrenness of the Southern States. He spoke from his own personal knowledge, he said, and he could say, that the land in general, in those states, was preferable to any he ever saw.

Judge DANA rose to set the gentleman right; he said it was not the *quality* of the land he alluded to, but the *manner* of tilling it that he alluded to.

FRIDAY, *January* 18.—The third paragraph of the 2d section of article one still under consideration.

Hon. Mr. DALTON opened the conversation with some remarks on Mr. Randall's positive assertions of the fertility of the Southern States; who said, from his own observation, and from accounts he had seen, which were better, he could say, that the gentleman's remark was not perfectly accurate. The honorable gentleman showed why it was not so, by stating the inconsiderable product of the land, which, though it might in part be owing to the faithlessness and ignorance of the slaves who cultivate it, he said, was in a greater measure owing to the want of heart in the soil.

Mr. RANDALL. Mr. President, I rise to make an observation on the suggestion of the honorable gentleman from Newbury. I have, sir, travelled into the Southern States, and should be glad to compare our knowledge on the subject together. In Carolina, Mr. President, if they don't get more than twenty or thirty bushels of corn from an acre, they think it a small crop. On the low lands they sometimes get forty. I hope, sir, these great men of eloquence and learning will not try to *make* arguments to make this Constitution go down, right or wrong. An old saying, sir, is, that "a good thing don't need praising;" but, sir, it takes the best men in the state to gloss this Constitution, which they say is the best that human wisdom can invent. In praise of it we hear the reverend clergy, the judges of the Supreme Court, and the ablest lawyers, exerting their utmost abilities. Now, sir, suppose all this artillery turned the other way, and these great men would speak half as much against it, we might complete our business and go home in forty-eight hours. Let us consider, sir, we are acting for the people, and for ages unborn; let us deal fairly and above board. Every one comes here to discharge his duty to his constituents, and I hope none will be biased by the best orators; because we are not acting for ourselves. I think Congress ought to have power, such as is for the good of the nation; but what it is, let a more able man than I tell us.

Mr. DAWES said, he was very sorry to hear so many objections raised against the paragraph under consideration. He thought them wholly unfounded; that the *black inhabitants* of the Southern States must be considered either as slaves, and as so much *property*, or in the character of so many freemen; if the former, why should they not be wholly represented? Our own state laws and constitution would lead us to consider these blacks as freemen, and so indeed would our own ideas of natural justice. If, then, they are freemen, they might form an equal basis for representation as though they were all white inhabitants. In either view, therefore, he could not see that the Northern States would suffer, but directly to the contrary. He thought, however, that gentlemen would do well to connect the passage in dispute with another article in the Constitution, that permits Congress, in the year 1808, wholly to prohibit the importation of slaves, and in the mean time to impose a duty of ten dollars a head on such blacks as should be imported before that period. Besides, by the new Constitution, every particular state is left to its own option totally to prohibit the introduction of slaves into its own territories. What could the Convention do more? The members of the Southern States, like ourselves, have *their* prejudices. It would not do to abolish slavery, by an act of Congress, in a moment, and so destroy what our southern brethren consider as property. But we may say, that, although slavery is not smitten by an apoplexy, yet it has received a mortal wound, and will die of a consumption.

Mr. D. said, the paragraph in debate related only to the *rule* of apportioning internal taxes; but the gentleman had gone into a consideration of the question, whether Congress should have the power of laying and collecting such *taxes;* which, he thought, would be more properly discussed under the section relative to the *powers* of Congress; but as objections had been suggested, the answers might be hinted as we went along. By the old articles, said he, Congress have a right to ascertain what are necessary for the Union, and to appropriate the same, but have no authority to draw such moneys from the states. The states are under an *honorary* obligation to raise the moneys; but Congress cannot compel a compliance with the obligation.

So long as we withhold that authority from Congress, so long we may be said to give it to other nations. Let us contemplate the loan we have made with the Dutch. Our ambassador has bound us all, jointly and severally, to pay the money borrowed. When pay-day shall come, how is the money to be raised? Congress cannot collect it. If any one state shall disobey a requisition, the Dutch are left, in such a case, to put their own demand in force for themselves. They must raise by arms what we are afraid Congress shall collect by the law of peace. There is a prejudice, said Mr. Dawes, against direct taxation, which arises from the manner in which it has been abused by the errors of the old Confederation. Congress had it not in their power to draw a revenue from commerce, and therefore multiplied their requisitions on the states. Massachusetts, willing to pay her part, made her own trade law, on which the trade departed to such of our neighbors as made no such impositions on commerce; thus we lost what little revenue we had, and our only course was, to a direct taxation. In addition to this, foreign nations, knowing this inability of Congress, have on that account been backward in their negotiations, and have lent us money at a premium which bore some proportion to the risk they had of getting payment; and this extraordinary expense has fallen at last on the land.

Some gentlemen have said, that Congress may draw their revenue wholly by direct taxes; but they cannot be induced so to do; it is easier for them to have resort to the impost and excise; but as it will not do to overburden the impost, (because that would promote smuggling, and be dangerous to the revenue,) therefore Congress should have the power of applying, in extraordinary cases, to direct taxation. War may take place, in which case it would not be proper to alter those appropriations of impost which may be made for peace establishments. It is inexpedient to divert the public funds; the power of direct taxation would, in such circumstances, be a very necessary power. As to the rule of apportioning such taxes, it must be by the quantity of lands, or else in the manner laid down in the paragraph under debate. But the quantity of lands is an uncertain rule of wealth. Compare the lands of different nations of Europe, some of them have great comparative wealth and less quantities of lands, whilst others have more land and less wealth. Compare Holland with Germany. The rule laid down in the paragraph is the best that can be obtained for the apportionment of the little direct taxes which Congress will want.

Afternoon.—Messrs. King, Gore, Parsons, and Jones, of Boston, spoke of the advantage to the *Northern States* the rule of apportionment in the third paragraph (still under debate) gave to them; as also the Hon. Judge DANA, the sketch of whose speech is as follows:—

The learned judge began with answering some objections to this paragraph, and urging the necessity of Congress being vested with power to levy *direct taxes* on the states, and it was not to be supposed that they would levy such, unless the impost and excise should be found insufficient in case of a war. If, says he, a part of the Union is attacked by a foreign enemy, and we are disunited, how is it to defend itself? Can it by its own internal force? In the late war, this state singly was attacked, and obliged to make the first defence. What has happened may happen again. The state oppressed must exert its whole power, and bear the whole charge of the defence; but common danger points out for common exertion; and this Constitution is excellently designed to make the danger equal. Why should one state expend its blood and treasure for the whole? Ought not a controlling authority to exist, to call forth, if necessary, the whole force and wealth of all the states? If disunited, the time may come when we may be attacked by our natural enemies. Nova Scotia and New Brunswick, filled with tories and refugees, stand ready to attack and devour these states, one by one. This will be the case, if we have no power to draw forth the wealth and strength of the whole, for a defence of a part. Then shall we, continued the honorable gentleman, see, but too late, the necessity of a power being vested somewhere, that could command that wealth and strength when wanted. I speak with earnestness, said he, but it is for the good of my native country. By God and nature made equal, it is with remorse I have heard it suggested by some, that those gentlemen who have had the superior advantages of education, were enemies to the rights of their country. Are there any among this honorable body, who are possessed of minds capable of such narrow prejudices? If there are, it is in vain to reason with them; we had better come to a decision, and go home.

After dilating on this matter a short time, the learned judge begged gentlemen to look around them, and see who were the men that composed the assembly. Are they not, he asked, men who have been foremost in the cause of their country, both in the cabinet and in the field? and who, with halters about their necks, boldly and intrepidly advocated the rights of America, and of humanity, at home and in foreign countries? And are they not to be trusted? Direct *taxation* is a tremendous idea; but may not necessity dictate it to be unavoidable? We all wish to invest Congress with more power. We disagree only in the quantum, and manner, in which Congress shall levy taxes on the states. A capitation tax is abhorrent to the feelings of human nature, and, I venture to trust, will never be adopted by Congress. The learned judge pointed out, on various grounds, the utility of the power to be vested in the Congress, and concluded by observing, that the proposed Constitution was the best that could be framed; that, if adopted, we shall be a great and happy nation; if rejected, a weak and despised one; we shall fall as the nations of ancient times have fallen; that this was his firm belief; and, said he, I would rather be annihilated than give my voice for, or sign my name to, a constitution which in the least should betray the liberties or interests of my country.

Mr. WIDGERY. I hope, sir, the honorable gentleman will not think hard of it, if we ignorant men cannot see as clear as he can. The strong must bear with the infirmities of the weak; and it must be a weak mind indeed that could throw such illiberal reflections against gentlemen of education, as the honorable gentleman complains of. To return to the paragraph. If Congress, continued Mr W., have this power of taxing directly, it will be in their power to enact a poll

tax. Can gentlemen tell why they will not attempt it, and by this method make the poor pay as much as the rich?

Mr. DENCH was at a loss to know how Congress could levy the tax, in which he thought the difficulty of money consisted; yet had no doubt but that Congress would direct that these states should pay it *in their own way*.

The Hon. Mr. FULLER begged to ask Mr. Gerry, "why, in the last requisition of Congress, the portion required of this state was thirteen times as much as of Georgia; and yet we have but eight representatives in the general government, and Georgia has three." Until this question was answered, he was at a loss to know how taxation and representation went hand in hand.

[It was then voted that this question be asked Mr. Gerry. A long and desultory debate ensued on the manner in which the answer should be given: it was at last voted that Mr. G. reduce his answer to writing.]

SATURDAY, *January* 19, 1788, A. M.—The Hon. Mr. SINGLETARY thought we were giving up all our privileges, as there was no provision that men in power should have any *religion;* and though he hoped to see Christians, yet, by the Constitution, a Papist, or an Infidel, was as eligible as they. It had been said that men had not degenerated; he did not think men were better now than when men after God's own heart did wickedly. He thought, in this instance, we were giving great power to we know not whom.

Gen. BROOKS, (of Medford.)—If good men are appointed, government will be administered well. But what will prevent bad men from mischief, is the question. If there should be such in the Senate, we ought to be cautious of giving power; but when that power is given, with proper checks, the danger is at an end. When men are answerable, and within the reach of responsibility, they cannot forget that their political existence depends upon their good behavior. The Senate can frame no law but by consent of the Representatives, and is answerable to that house for its conduct. If that conduct excites suspicion, they are to be impeached, punished, (or prevented from holding any office, which is great punishment.) If these checks are not sufficient, it is impossible to devise such as will be so.

[Mr. Gerry's answer to Mr. Fuller's question was read. The purport is, that Georgia had increased in its numbers by emigration; and if it had not then, would soon be entitled to the proportion assigned her.]

Hon. Mr. KING. It so happened that I was both of the Convention and Congress at the same time; and if I recollect right, the answer of Mr. G. does not materially vary. In 1778, Congress required the states to make a return of the houses and lands surveyed; but one state only complied therewith—New Hampshire. Massachusetts did not. Congress consulted no rule: it was resolved that the several states should be taxed according to their ability, and if it appeared any state had paid more than her just quota, it should be passed to the credit of that state, with lawful interest.

Mr. DALTON said we had obtained a great deal by the new Constitution. By the Confederation each state had an equal vote. Georgia is now content with three eighths of the voice of Massachusetts.

12

A REPUBLICAN FEDERALIST, NO. 5
19 Jan. 1788
Storing 4.13.22

Let is now proceed to the provision in the system for a representation of the people, which is the *corner stone* of a free government. The Constitution provides, art. 1st, sect. 2, "that representatives and direct taxes shall be apportioned among the several States, which may be included within this union, according to their respective numbers, which shall be determined by adding to the whole number of free persons, including those bound to service for a term of years, and excluding Indians not taxed, three fifths of all other persons." Representatives then are to be "apportioned among the several States, according to their respective numbers," and *five* slaves, in computing those numbers, are to be classed with *three* freemen—By which rule, fifty thousand slaves, having neither *liberty* or *property*, will have a representative in that branch of the legislature—to which more especially will be committed, the *protection of the liberties*, and *disposal of all the property* of the freemen of the Union—for thus stands the new Constitution. Should it be said, that not *the slaves* but their *masters* are to send a representative, the answer is plain—If the *slaves* have a *right* to be represented, they are *on a footing* with *freemen, three* of *whom* can then have no more than an equal right of representation with *three slaves,* and these when qualified by property, may elect or be elected representatives, *which is not the case:* But if they have not a right to be represented, their masters can have no right derived from their *slaves,* for *these* cannot transfer to others what they have not themselves. Mr. Locke, in treating of political or civil societies, chap. 7, sect. 85, says, that men "being in the state of slavery, not capable of any property, cannot, in that state, be considered as any part of civil society, the chief end whereof, is the preservation of property." If slaves, then, are no part of civil society, there can be no more reason in admitting them, than there would be in admitting the *beasts* of the field, or *trees* of the forest, to be classed with *free electors.* What covenant are the freemen of Massachusetts about to ratify? A covenant that will degrade them to the *level of slaves,* and give to the States who have as many blacks as whites, *eight* representatives, *for the same number of freemen* as will enable this State to elect *five*—Is this an *equal,* a *safe,* or a *righteous* plan of government? Indeed it is not. But if to encrease these objections, it should be urged, "that representation being regulated by the same rule as taxation, and taxation being regulated by a rule intended to ascertain the relative prop-

erty of the States, representation will then be regulated by the principle of property." This *answer* would be the only one that could be made, for representation, according to the new Constitution is to be regulated, either by *numbers* or *property.*

13

JAMES MADISON, FEDERALIST, NO. 54,
366–72
12 Feb. 1788

The next view which I shall take of the House of Representatives, relates to the apportionment of its members to the several States, which is to be determined by the same rule with that of direct taxes.

It is not contended that the number of people in each State ought not to be the standard for regulating the proportion of those who are to represent the people of each State. The establishment of the same rule for the apportionment of taxes, will probably be as little contested; though the rule itself in this case, is by no means founded on the same principle. In the former case, the rule is understood to refer to the personal rights of the people, with which it has a natural and universal connection. In the latter, it has reference to the proportion of wealth, of which it is in no case a precise measure, and in ordinary cases a very unfit one. But notwithstanding the imperfection of the rule as applied to the relative wealth and contributions of the States, it is evidently the least exceptionable among the practicable rules; and had too recently obtained the general sanction of America, not to have found a ready preference with the Convention.

All this is admitted, it will perhaps be said: But does it follow from an admission of numbers for the measure of representation, or of slaves combined with free citizens, as a ratio of taxation, that slaves ought to be included in the numerical rule of representation? Slaves are considered as property, not as persons. They ought therefore to be comprehended in estimates of taxation which are founded on property, and to be excluded from representation which is regulated by a census of persons. This is the objection, as I understand it, stated in its full force. I shall be equally candid in stating the reasoning which may be offered on the opposite side.

We subscribe to the doctrine, might one of our southern brethren observe, that representation relates more immediately to persons, and taxation more immediately to property, and we join in the application of this distinction to the case of our slaves. But we must deny the fact that slaves are considered merely as property, and in no respect whatever as persons. The true state of the case is, that they partake of both these qualities; being considered by our laws, in some respects, as persons, and in other respects, as property. In being compelled to labor not for himself, but for a master; in being vendible by one master to another master; and in being subject at all times to be restrained in his liberty, and chastised in his body, by the capricious will of another, the slave may appear to be degraded from the human rank, and classed with those irrational animals, which fall under the legal denomination of property. In being protected on the other hand in his life & in his limbs, against the violence of all others, even the master of his labor and his liberty; and in being punishable himself for all violence committed against others; the slave is no less evidently regarded by the law as a member of the society; not as a part of the irrational creation; as a moral person, not as a mere article of property. The Foederal Constitution therefore, decides with great propriety on the case of our slaves, when it views them in the mixt character of persons and of property. This is in fact their true character. It is the character bestowed on them by the laws under which they live; and it will not be denied that these are the proper criterion; because it is only under the pretext that the laws have transformed the negroes into subjects of property, that a place is disputed them in the computation of numbers; and it is admitted that if the laws were to restore the rights which have been taken away, the negroes could no longer be refused an equal share of representation with the other inhabitants.

This question may be placed in another light. It is agreed on all sides, that numbers are the best scale of wealth and taxation, as they are the only proper scale of representation. Would the Convention have been impartial or consistent, if they had rejected the slaves from the list of inhabitants when the shares of representation were to be calculated; and inserted them on the lists when the tariff of contributions was to be adjusted? Could it be reasonably expected that the southern States would concur in a system which considered their slaves in some degree as men, when burdens were to be imposed, but refused to consider them in the same light when advantages were to be conferred? Might not some surprize also be expressed that those who reproach the southern States with the barbarous policy of considering as property a part of their human brethren, should themselves contend that the government to which all the States are to be parties, ought to consider this unfortunate race more compleatly in the unnatural light of property, than the very laws of which they complain!

It may be replied perhaps that slaves are not included in the estimate of representatives in any of the States possessing them. They neither vote themselves, nor increase the votes of their masters. Upon what principle then ought they to be taken into the foederal estimate of representation? In rejecting them altogether, the Constitution would in this respect have followed the very laws which have been appealed to, as the proper guide.

This objection is repelled by a single observation. It is a fundamental principle of the proposed Constitution, that as the aggregate number of representatives allotted to the several States, is to be determined by a foederal rule founded on the aggregate number of inhabitants, so the right of choosing this allotted number in each State is to be exercised by such part of the inhabitants, as the State itself may designate. The qualifications on which the right of suffrage depend, are not perhaps the same in any two States. In some of the States the difference is very material. In every State, a certain proportion of inhabitants are deprived of this right by the Constitution of the State, who will be included in the census by which the Foederal Constitution apportions the representatives. In this point of view, the southern States might retort the complaint, by insisting, that the principle laid down by the Convention required that no regard should be had to the policy of particular States towards their own inhabitants; and consequently, that the slaves as inhabitants should have been admitted into the census according to their full number, in like manner with other inhabitants, who by the policy of other States, are not admitted to all the rights of citizens. A rigorous adherence however to this principle is waved by those who would be gainers by it. All that they ask is, that equal moderation be shewn on the other side. Let the case of the slaves be considered as it is in truth a peculiar one. Let the compromising expedient of the Constitution be mutually adopted, which regards them as inhabitants, but as debased by servitude below the equal level of free inhabitants, which regards the *slave* as divested of two fifth of the *man*.

After all may not another ground be taken on which this article of the Constitution, will admit of a still more ready defence? We have hitherto proceeded on the idea that representation related to persons only, and not at all to property. But is it a just idea? Government is instituted no less for protection of the property, than of the persons of individuals. The one as well as the other, therefore may be considered as represented by those who are charged with the government. Upon this principle it is, that in several of the States, and particularly in the State of New-York, one branch of the government is intended more especially to be the guardian of property, and is accordingly elected by that part of the society which is most interested in this object of government. In the Foederal Constitution, this policy does not prevail. The rights of property are committed into the same hands with the personal rights. Some attention ought therefore to be paid to property in the choice of those hands.

For another reason the votes allowed in the Foederal Legislature to the people of each State, ought to bear some proportion to the comparative wealth of the States. States have not like individuals, an influence over each other arising from superior advantages of fortune. If the law allows an opulent citizen but a single vote in the choice of his representative, the respect and consequence which he derives from his fortunate situation, very frequently guide the votes of others to the objects of his choice; and through this imperceptible channel the rights of property are conveyed into the public representation. A State possesses no such influence over other States. It is not probable that the richest State in the confederacy will ever influence the choice of a single representative in any other State. Nor will the representatives of the larger and richer States possess any other advantage in the Foederal Legislature over the representatives of other States, than what may result from their superior number alone; as far therefore as their superior wealth and weight may justly entitle them to any advantage, it ought to be secured to them by a superior share of representation. The new Constitution is in this respect materially different from the existing confederation, as well as from that of the United Netherlands, and other similar confederacies. In each of the latter the efficacy of the foederal resolutions depends on the subsequent and voluntary resolutions of the States composing the Union. Hence the States, though possessing an equal vote in the public councils, have an unequal influence, corresponding with the unequal importance of these subsequent and voluntary resolutions. Under the proposed Constitution, the foederal acts will take effect without the necessary intervention of the individual States. They will depend merely on the majority of votes in the Foederal Legislature, and consequently each vote whether proceeding from a larger or a smaller State, or a State more or less wealthy or powerful, will have an equal weight and efficacy; in the same manner as the votes individually given in a State Legislature, by the representatives of unequal counties or other districts, have each a precise equality of value and effect; or if there be any difference in the case, it proceeds from the difference in the personal character of the individual representative, rather than from any regard to the extent of the district from which he comes.

Such is the reasoning which an advocate for the southern interests might employ on this subject: And although it may appear to be a little strained in some points, yet on the whole, I must confess, that it fully reconciles me to the scale of representation, which the Convention have established.

In one respect the establishment of a common measure for representation and taxation will have a very salutary effect. As the accuracy of the census to be obtained by the Congress, will necessarily depend in a considerable degree on the disposition, if not the cooperation of the States, it is of great importance that the States should feel as little bias as possible to swell or to reduce the amount of their numbers. Were their share of representation alone to be governed by this rule they would have an interest in exaggerating their inhabitants. Were the rule to decide their share of taxation alone, a contrary temptation would prevail. By extending the rule to both objects, the States will have opposite interests, which will controul and ballance each other; and produce the requisite impartiality.

14

JAMES MADISON, FEDERALIST, NO. 55,
372–78
13 Feb. 1788

The number of which the House of Representatives is to consist, forms another, and a very interesting point of view under which this branch of the federal legislature may be contemplated. Scarce any article indeed in the whole con-

stitution seems to be rendered more worthy of attention, by the weight of character and the apparent force of argument, with which it has been assailed. The charges exhibited against it are, first, that so small a number of representatives will be an unsafe depository of the public interests; secondly, that they will not possess a proper knowledge of the local circumstances of their numerous constituents; thirdly, that they will be taken from that class of citizens which will sympathize least with the feelings of the mass of the people, and be most likely to aim at a permanent elevation of the few on the depression of the many; fourthly, that defective as the number will be in the first instance, it will be more and more disproportionate, by the increase of the people, and the obstacles which will prevent a correspondent increase of the representatives.

In general it may be remarked on this subject, that no political problem is less susceptible of a precise solution, than that which relates to the number most convenient for a representative legislature: Nor is there any point on which the policy of the several states is more at variance; whether we compare their legislative assemblies directly with each other, or consider the proportions which they respectively bear to the number of their constituents. Passing over the difference between the smallest and largest states, as Delaware, whose most numerous branch consists of twenty-one representatives, and Massachusetts, where it amounts to between three and four hundred; a very considerable difference is observable among states nearly equal in population. The number of representatives in Pennsylvania is not more than one-fifth of that in the state last mentioned. New-York, whose population is to that of South-Carolina as six to five, has little more than one third of the number of representatives. As great a disparity prevails between the states of Georgia and Delaware, or Rhode-Island. In Pennsylvania the representatives do not bear a greater proportion to their constituents than of one for every four or five thousand. In Rhode-Island, they bear a proportion of at least one for every thousand. And according to the constitution of Georgia, the proportion may be carried to one for every ten electors; and must unavoidably far exceed the proportion in any of the other States.

Another general remark to be made is, that the ratio between the representatives and the people, ought not to be the same where the latter are very numerous, as where they are very few. Were the representatives in Virginia to be regulated by the standard in Rhode-Island, they would at this time amount to between four and five hundred; and twenty or thirty years hence, to a thousand. On the other hand, the ratio of Pennsylvania, if applied to the state of Delaware, would reduce the Representative assembly of the latter to seven or eight members. Nothing can be more fallacious than to found our political calculations on arithmetical principles. Sixty or seventy men, may be more properly trusted with a given degree of power than six or seven. But it does not follow, that six or seven hundred would be proportionally a better depositary. And if we carry on the supposition to six or seven thousand, the whole reasoning ought to be reversed. The truth is, that in all cases a certain number at least seems to be necessary to secure the benefits of free consultation and discussion, and to guard against too easy a combination for improper purposes: As on the other hand, the number ought at most to be kept within a certain limit, in order to avoid the confusion and intemperance of a multitude. In all very numerous assemblies, of whatever characters composed, passion never fails to wrest the sceptre from reason. Had every Athenian citizen been a Socrates; every Athenian assembly would still have been a mob.

It is necessary also to recollect here the observations which were applied to the case of biennial elections. For the same reason that the limited powers of the Congress and the controul of the state legislatures, justify less frequent elections than the public safety might otherwise require; the members of the Congress need be less numerous than if they possessed the whole power of legislation, and were under no other than the ordinary restraints of other legislative bodies.

With these general ideas in our minds, let us weigh the objections which have been stated against the number of members proposed for the House of Representatives. It is said in the first place, that so small a number cannot be safely trusted with so much power.

The number of which this branch of the legislature is to consist at the outset of the government, will be sixty five. Within three years a census is to be taken, when the number may be augmented to one for every thirty thousand inhabitants; and within every successive period of ten years, the census is to be renewed, and augmentations may continue to be made under the above limitation. It will not be thought an extravagant conjecture, that the first census, will, at the rate of one for every thirty thousand raise the number of representatives to at least one hundred. Estimating the negroes in the proportion of three fifths, it can scarcely be doubted that the population of the United States will by that time, if it does not already, amount to three millions. At the expiration of twenty five years, according to the computed rate of increase, the number of representatives will amount to two hundred; and of fifty years to four hundred. This is a number which I presume will put an end to all fears arising from the smallness of the body. I take for granted here what I shall in answering the fourth objection hereafter shew, that the number of representatives will be augmented from time to time in the manner provided by the constitution. On a contrary supposition, I should admit the objection to have very great weight indeed.

The true question to be decided then is whether the smallness of the number, as a temporary regulation, be dangerous to the public liberty: Whether sixty five members for a few years, and a hundred or two hundred for a few more, be a safe depositary for a limited and well guarded power of legislating for the United States? I must own that I could not give a negative answer to this question, without first obliterating every impression which I have received with regard to the present genius of the people of America, the spirit, which actuates the state legislatures, and the principles which are incorporated with the political character of every class of citizens. I am unable to conceive that the people of America in their pres-

ent temper, or under any circumstances which can speedily happen, will chuse, and every second year repeat the choice of sixty-five or an hundred men, who would be disposed to form and pursue a scheme of tyranny or treachery. I am unable to conceive that the state legislatures which must feel so many motives to watch, and which possess so many means of counteracting the federal legislature, would fail either to detect or to defeat a conspiracy of the latter against the liberties of their common constituents. I am equally unable to conceive that there are at this time, or can be in any short time, in the United States any sixty-five or an hundred men capable of recommending themselves to the choice of the people at large, who would either desire or dare within the short space of two years, to betray the solemn trust committed to them. What change of circumstances time and a fuller population of our country may produce, requires a prophetic spirit to declare, which makes no part of my pretensions. But judging from the circumstances now before us, and from the probable state of them within a moderate period of time, I must pronounce that the liberties of America can not be unsafe in the number of hands proposed by the federal constitution.

From what quarter can the danger proceed? Are we afraid of foreign gold? If foreign gold could so easily corrupt our federal rulers, and enable them to ensnare and betray their constituents, how has it happened that we are at this time a free and independent nation? The Congress which conducted us through the revolution were a less numerous body than their successors will be; they were not chosen by nor responsible to their fellow citizens at large; though appointed from year to year, and recallable at pleasure, they were generally continued for three years; and prior to the ratification of the federal articles, for a still longer term; they held their consultations always under the veil of secrecy; they had the sole transaction of our affairs with foreign nations; through the whole course of the war, they had the fate of their country more in their hands, than it is to be hoped will ever be the case with our future representatives; and from the greatness of the prize at stake and the eagerness of the party which lost it, it may well be supposed, that the use of other means than force would not have been scrupled; yet we know by happy experience that the public trust was not betrayed; nor has the purity of our public councils in this particular ever suffered even from the whispers of calumny.

Is the danger apprehended from the other branches of the federal government? But where are the means to be found by the President or the Senate, or both? Their emoluments of office it is to be presumed will not, and without a previous corruption of the house of representatives cannot, more than suffice for very different purposes: Their private fortunes, as they must all be American citizens, cannot possibly be sources of danger. The only means then which they can possess, will be in the dispensation of appointments. Is it here that suspicion rests her charge? Sometimes we are told that this fund of corruption is to be exhausted by the President in subduing the virtue of the Senate. Now the fidelity of the other house is to be the victim. The improbability of such a mercenary and perfidious combination of the several members of government standing on as different foundations as republican principles will well admit, and at the same time accountable to the society over which they are placed, ought alone to quiet this apprehension. But fortunately the constitution has provided a still further safeguard. The members of the Congress are rendered ineligible to any civil offices that may be created or of which the emoluments may be increased, during the term of their election. No offices therefore can be dealt out to the existing members, but such as may become vacant by ordinary casualties; and to suppose that these would be sufficient to purchase the guardians of the people, selected by the people themselves, is to renounce every rule by which events ought to be calculated, and to substitute an indiscriminate and unbounded jealousy, with which all reasoning must be vain. The sincere friends of liberty who give themselves up to the extravagancies of this passion are not aware of the injury they do their own cause. As there is a degree of depravity in mankind which requires a certain degree of circumspection and distrust: So there are other qualities in human nature, which justify a certain portion of esteem and confidence. Republican government presupposes the existence of these qualities in a higher degree than any other form. Were the pictures which have been drawn by the political jealousy of some among us, faithful likenesses of the human character, the inference would be that there is not sufficient virtue among men for self-government; and that nothing less than the chains of despotism can restrain them from destroying and devouring one another.

15

JAMES MADISON, FEDERALIST, NO. 56,
378–83
16 Feb. 1788

The *second* charge against the House of Representatives is, that it will be too small to possess a due knowledge of the interests of its constituents.

As this objection evidently proceeds from a comparison of the proposed number of representatives, with the great extent of the United States, the number of their inhabitants, and the diversity of their interests, without taking into view at the same time the circumstances which will distinguish the Congress from other legislative bodies, the best answer that can be given to it, will be a brief explanation of these peculiarities.

It is a sound and important principle that the representative ought to be acquainted with the interests and circumstances of his constituents. But this principle can extend no farther than to those circumstances and interests, to which the authority and care of the representative relate. An ignorance of a variety of minute and particular objects, which do not lie within the compass of legislation, is consistent with every attribute necessary to a due performance of the legislative trust. In determining the extent of

information required in the exercise of a particular authority, recourse then must be had to the objects within the purview of that authority.

What are to be the objects of federal legislation? Those which are of most importance, and which seem most to require local knowledge, are commerce, taxation, and the militia.

A proper regulation of commerce requires much information, as has been elsewhere remarked; but as far as this information relates to the laws and local situation of each individual state, a very few representatives would be very sufficient vehicles of it to the federal councils.

Taxation will consist, in great measure, of duties which will be involved in the regulation of commerce. So far the preceding remark is applicable to this object. As far as it may consist of internal collections, a more diffusive knowledge of the circumstances of the state may be necessary. But will not this also be possessed in sufficient degree by a very few intelligent men diffusively elected within the state. Divide the largest state into ten or twelve districts, and it will be found that there will be no peculiar local interest in either, which will not be within the knowledge of the representative of the district. Besides this source of information, the laws of the state framed by representatives from every part of it, will be almost of themselves a sufficient guide. In every state there have been made, and must continue to be made, regulations on this subject, which will in many cases leave little more to be done by the federal legislature, than to review the different laws, and reduce them into one general act. A skilful individual in his closet, with all the local codes before him, might compile a law on some subjects of taxation for the whole union, without any aid from oral information; and it may be expected, that whenever internal taxes may be necessary, and particularly in cases requiring uniformity throughout the states, the more simple objects will be preferred. To be fully sensible of the facility which will be given to this branch of federal legislation, by the assistance of the state codes, we need only suppose for a moment, that this or any other state were divided into a number of parts, each having and exercising within itself a power of local legislation. Is it not evident that a degree of local information and preparatory labour would be found in the several volumes of their proceedings, which would very much shorten the labours of the general legislature, and render a much smaller number of members sufficient for it? The federal councils will derive great advantage from another circumstance. The representatives of each state will not only bring with them a considerable knowledge of its laws, and a local knowledge of their respective districts; but will probably in all cases have been members, and may even at the very time be members of the state legislature, where all the local information and interests of the state are assembled, and from whence they may easily be conveyed by a very few hands into the legislature of the United States.

The observations made on the subject of taxation apply with greater force to the case of the militia. For however different the rules of discipline may be in different states; They are the same throughout each particular state; and depend on circumstances which can differ but little in different parts of the same state.

The attentive reader will discern that the reasoning here used to prove the sufficiency of a moderate number of representatives, does not in any respect contradict what was urged on another occasion with regard to the extensive information which the representatives ought to possess, and the time that might be necessary for acquiring it. This information, so far as it may relate to local objects, is rendered necessary and difficult, not by a difference of laws and local circumstances within a single state; but of those among different states. Taking each state by itself, its laws are the same, and its interests but little diversified. A few men therefore will possess all the knowledge requisite for a proper representation of them. Were the interests and affairs of each individual state, perfectly simple and uniform, a knowledge of them in one part would involve a knowledge of them in every other, and the whole state might be competently represented, by a single member taken from any part of it. On a comparison of the different states together, we find a great dissimilarity in their laws, and in many other circumstances connected with the objects of federal legislation, with all of which the federal representatives ought to have some acquaintance. Whilst a few representatives therefore from each state may bring with them a due knowledge of their own state, every representative will have much information to acquire concerning all the other states. The changes of time, as was formerly remarked, on the comparative situation of the different states, will have an assimilating effect. The effect of time on the internal affairs of the states taken singly, will be just the contrary. At present some of the states are little more than a society of husbandmen. Few of them have made much progress in those branches of industry, which give a variety and complexity to the affairs of a nation. These however will in all of them be the fruits of a more advanced population; and will require on the part of each state a fuller representation. The foresight of the Convention has accordingly taken care that the progress of population may be accompanied with a proper increase of the representative branch of the government.

The experience of Great Britain which presents to mankind so many political lessons, both of the monitory and exemplary kind, and which has been frequently consulted in the course of these enquiries, corroborates the result of the reflections which we have just made. The number of inhabitants in the two kingdoms of England and Scotland, cannot be stated at less than eight millions. The representatives of these eight millions in the House of Commons, amount to five hundred fifty-eight. Of this number one ninth are elected by three hundred and sixty four persons, and one half by five thousand seven hundred and twenty three persons. It cannot be supposed that the half thus elected, and who do not even reside among the people at large, can add any thing either to the security of the people against the government; or to the knowledge of their circumstances and interests, in the legislative councils. On the contrary it is notorious that they are more frequently the representatives and instruments of the executive magistrate, than the guardians and advocates of the popular

rights. They might therefore with great propriety be considered as something more than a mere deduction from the real representatives of the nation. We will however consider them, in this light alone, and will not extend the deduction, to a considerable number of others, who do not reside among their constituents, are very faintly connected with them, and have very little particular knowledge of their affairs. With all these concessions two hundred and seventy nine persons only will be the depository of the safety, interest and happiness of eight millions; that is to say: There will be one representative only to maintain the rights and explain the situation of *twenty eight thousand six hundred and seventy* constituents, in an assembly exposed to the whole force of executive influence, and extending its authority to every object of legislation within a nation whose affairs are in the highest degree diversified and complicated. Yet it is very certain not only that a valuable portion of freedom has been preserved under all these circumstances, but that the defects in the British code are chargeable in a very small proportion, on the ignorance of the legislature concerning the circumstances of the people. Allowing to this case the weight which is due to it: And comparing it with that of the House of Representatives as above explained, it seems to give the fullest assurance that a representative for every *thirty thousand inhabitants* will render the latter both a safe and competent guardian of the interests which will be confided to it.

16

JAMES MADISON, FEDERALIST, NO. 57,
384–90
19 Feb. 1788

The *third* charge against the House of Representatives is, that it will be taken from that class of citizens which will have least sympathy with the mass of the people, and be most likely to aim at an ambitious sacrifice of the many to the aggrandizement of the few.

Of all the objections which have been framed against the Foederal Constitution, this is perhaps the most extraordinary. Whilst the objection itself is levelled against a pretended oligarchy, the principle of it strikes at the very root of republican government.

The aim of every political Constitution is or ought to be first to obtain for rulers, men who possess most wisdom to discern, and most virtue to pursue the common good of the society; and in the next place, to take the most effectual precautions for keeping them virtuous, whilst they continue to hold their public trust. The elective mode of obtaining rulers is the characteristic policy of republican government. The means relied on in this form of government for preventing their degeneracy are numerous and various. The most effectual one is such a limitation of the term of appointments, as will maintain a proper responsibility to the people.

Let me now ask what circumstance there is in the Constitution of the House of Representatives, that violates the principles of republican government; or favors the elevation of the few on the ruins of the many? Let me ask whether every circumstance is not, on the contrary, strictly conformable to these principles; and scrupulously impartial to the rights and pretensions of every class and description of citizens?

Who are to be the electors of the Foederal Representatives? Not the rich more than the poor; not the learned more than the ignorant; not the haughty heirs of distinguished names, more than the humble sons of obscure and unpropitious fortune. The electors are to be the great body of the people of the United States. They are to be the same who exercise the right in every State of electing the correspondent branch of the Legislature of the State.

Who are to be the objects of popular choice? Every citizen whose merit may recommend him to the esteem and confidence of his country. No qualification of wealth, of birth, of religious faith, or of civil profession, is permitted to fetter the judgment or disappoint the inclination of the people.

If we consider the situation of the men on whom the free suffrages of their fellow citizens may confer the representative trust, we shall find it involving every security which can be devised or desired for their fidelity to their constituents.

In the first place, as they will have been distinguished by the preference of their fellow citizens, we are to presume, that in general, they will be somewhat distinguished also, by those qualities which entitle them to it, and which promise a sincere and scrupulous regard to the nature of their engagements.

In the second place, they will enter into the public service under circumstances which cannot fail to produce a temporary affection at least to their constituents. There is in every breast a sensibility to marks of honor, of favor, of esteem, and of confidence, which, apart from all considerations of interest, is some pledge for grateful and benevolent returns. Ingratitude is a common topic of declamation against human nature; and it must be confessed, that instances of it are but too frequent and flagrant both in public and in private life. But the universal and extreme indignation which it inspires, is itself a proof of the energy and prevalence of the contrary sentiment.

In the third place, these ties which bind the representative to his constituents are strengthened by motives of a more selfish nature. His pride and vanity attach him to a form of government which favors his pretensions, and gives him a share in its honors and distinctions. Whatever hopes or projects might be entertained by a few aspiring characters, it must generally happen that a great proportion of the men deriving their advancement from their influence with the people, would have more to hope from a preservation of the favor, than from innovations in the government subversive of the authority of the people.

All these securities however would be found very insufficient without the restraint of frequent elections. Hence, in the fourth place, the House of Representatives is so constituted as to support in the members an habitual recollection of their dependence on the people. Before the sentiments impressed on their minds by the mode of their elevation, can be effaced by the exercise of power, they will be compelled to anticipate the moment when their power is to cease, when their exercise of it is to be reviewed, and when they must descend to the level from which they were raised; there for ever to remain, unless a faithful discharge of their trust shall have established their title to a renewal of it.

I will add as a fifth circumstance in the situation of the House of Representatives, restraining them from oppressive measures, that they can make no law which will not have its full operation on themselves and their friends, as well as on the great mass of the society. This has always been deemed one of the strongest bonds by which human policy can connect the rulers and the people together. It creates between them that communion of interests and sympathy of sentiments of which few governments have furnished examples; but without which every government degenerates into tyranny. If it be asked what is to restrain the House of Representatives from making legal discriminations in favor of themselves and a particular class of the society? I answer, the genius of the whole system, the nature of just and constitutional laws, and above all the vigilant and manly spirit which actuates the people of America, a spirit which nourishes freedom, and in return is nourished by it.

If this spirit shall ever be so far debased as to tolerate a law not obligatory on the Legislature as well as on the people, the people will be prepared to tolerate anything but liberty.

Such will be the relation between the House of Representatives and their constituents. Duty, gratitude, interest, ambition itself, are the chords by which they will be bound to fidelity and sympathy with the great mass of the people. It is possible that these may all be insufficient to controul the caprice and wickedness of man. But are they not all that government will admit, and that human prudence can devise? Are they not the genuine and the characteristic means by which Republican Government provides for the liberty and happiness of the people? Are they not the identical means on which every State Government in the Union, relies for the attainment of these important ends? What then are we to understand by the objection which this paper has combated? What are we to say to the men who profess the most flaming zeal for Republican Government, yet boldly impeach the fundamental principle of it; who pretend to be champions for the right and the capacity of the people to chuse their own rulers, yet maintain that they will prefer those only who will immediately and infallibly betray the trust committed to them?

Were the objection to be read by one who had not seen the mode prescribed by the Constitution for the choice of representatives, he could suppose nothing less than that some unreasonable qualification of property was annexed to the right of suffrage; or that the right of eligibility was limited to persons of particular families or fortunes; or at least that the mode prescribed by the State Constitutions was in some respect or other very grossly departed from. We have seen how far such a supposition would err as to the two first points. Nor would it in fact be less erroneous as to the last. The only difference discoverable between the two cases, is, that each representative of the United States will be elected by five or six thousand citizens; whilst in the individual States the election of a representative is left to about as many hundred. Will it be pretended that this difference is sufficient to justify an attachment to the State Governments and an abhorrence to the Foederal Government? If this be the point on which the objection turns, it deserves to be examined.

Is it supported by *reason?* This cannot be said, without maintaining that five or six thousand citizens are less capable of chusing a fit representative, or more liable to be corrupted by an unfit one, than five or six hundred. Reason, on the contrary assures us, that as in so great a number, a fit representative would be most likely to be found, so the choice would be less likely to be diverted from him, by the intrigues of the ambitious, or the bribes of the rich.

Is the *consequence* from this doctrine admissible? If we say that five or six hundred citizens are as many as can jointly exercise their right of suffrage, must we not deprive the people of the immediate choice of their public servants in every instance where the administration of the government does not require as many of them as will amount to one for that number of citizens?

Is the doctrine warranted by *facts?* It was shewn in the last paper, that the real representation in the British House of Commons very little exceeds the proportion of one for every thirty thousand inhabitants. Besides a variety of powerful causes, not existing here, and which favor in that country, the pretensions of rank and wealth, no person is eligible as a representative of a county, unless he possess real estate of the clear value of six hundred pounds sterling per year; nor of a city or borough, unless he possess a like estate of half that annual value. To this qualification on the part of the county representatives, is added another on the part of the county electors, which restrains the right of suffrage to persons having a freehold estate of the annual value of more than twenty pounds sterling according to the present rate of money. Notwithstanding these unfavorable circumstances, and notwithstanding some very unequal laws in the British code, it cannot be said that the representatives of the nation have elevated the few on the ruins of the many.

But we need not resort to foreign experience on this subject. Our own is explicit and decisive. The districts in New-Hampshire in which the Senators are chosen immediately by the people are nearly as large as will be necessary for her representatives in the Congress. Those of Massachusetts are larger, than will be necessary for that purpose. And those of New-York still more so. In the last State the members of Assembly, for the cities and counties of New-York and Albany, are elected by very nearly as many voters, as will be entitled to a representative in the Congress, calculating on the number of sixty-five representatives only. It makes no difference that in these senatorial districts and counties, a number of representatives are voted for by each elector at the same time. If the same electors, at the same time are capable of choosing four or five representatives, they cannot be incapable of choosing

one. Pennsylvania is an additional example. Some of her counties which elect her State representatives, are almost as large as her districts will be by which her Foederal Representatives will be elected. The city of Philadelphia is supposed to contain between fifty and sixty thousand souls. It will therefore form nearly two districts for the choice of Foederal Representatives. It forms however but one county, in which every elector votes for each of its representatives in the State Legislature. And what may appear to be still more directly to our purpose, the whole city actually elects a *single member* for the executive council. This is the case in all the other counties of the State.

Are not these facts the most satisfactory proofs of the fallacy which has been employed against the branch of the Foederal Government under consideration? Has it appeared on trial that the Senators of New-Hampshire, Massachusetts, and New-York; or the Executive Council of Pennsylvania; or the members of the Assembly in the two last States, have betrayed any peculiar disposition to sacrifice the many to the few; or are in any respect less worthy of their places than the representatives and magistrates appointed in other States, by very small divisions of the people?

But there are cases of a stronger complexion than any which I have yet quoted. One branch of the Legislature of Connecticut is so constituted that each member of it is elected by the whole State. So is the Governor of that State, of Massachusetts, and of this State, and the President of New-Hampshire. I leave every man to decide whether the result of any one of these experiments can be said to countenance a suspicion that a diffusive mode of chusing representatives of the people tends to elevate traitors, and to undermine the public liberty.

17

JAMES MADISON, FEDERALIST, NO. 58,
391–97
20 Feb. 1788

The remaining charge against the House of Representatives which I am to examine, is grounded on a supposition that the number of members will not be augmented from time to time, as the progress of population may demand.

It has been admitted that this objection, if well supported, would have great weight. The following observations will shew that like most other objections against the constitution, it can only proceed from a partial view of the subject; or from a jealousy which discolours and disfigures every object which is beheld.

1. Those who urge the objection seem not to have recollected that the federal constitution will not suffer by a comparison with the state constitutions, in the security provided for a gradual augmentation of the number of representatives. The number which is to prevail in the first instance is declared to be temporary. Its duration is limited to the short term of three years.

Within every successive term of ten years, a census of inhabitants is to be repeated. The unequivocal objects of these regulations are, first, to readjust from time to time the apportionment of representatives to the number of inhabitants; under the single exception that each state shall have one representative at least; Secondly, to augment the number of representatives at the same periods; under the sole limitation, that the whole number shall not exceed one for every thirty thousand inhabitants. If we review the constitutions of the several states, we shall find that some of them contain no determinate regulations on this subject; that others correspond pretty much on this point with the federal constitution; and that the most effectual security in any of them is resolvable into a mere directory provision.

2. As far as experience has taken place on this subject, a gradual increase of representatives under the state constitutions, has at least kept pace with that of the constituents; and it appears that the former have been as ready to concur in such measures, as the latter have been to call for them.

3. There is a peculiarity in the federal constitution which ensures a watchful attention in a majority both of the people and of their representatives, to a constitutional augmentation of the latter. The peculiarity lies in this, that one branch of the legislature is a representation of citizens; the other of the states: in the former consequently the larger states will have most weight; in the latter, the advantage will be in favour of the smaller states. From this circumstance it may with certainty be inferred, that the larger states will be strenuous advocates for increasing the number and weight of that part of the legislature in which their influence predominates. And it so happens that four only of the largest, will have a majority of the whole votes in the house of representatives. Should the representatives or people therefore of the smaller states oppose at any time a reasonable addition of members, a coalition of a very few states will be sufficient to overrule the opposition; a coalition, which notwithstanding the rivalship and local prejudices which might prevent it on ordinary occasions, would not fail to take place, when not merely prompted by common interest, but justified by equity and the principles of the constitution.

It may be alledged, perhaps, that the senate would be prompted by like motives to an adverse coalition; and as their concurrence would be indispensable, the just and constitutional views of the other branch might be defeated. This is the difficulty which has probably created the most serious apprehensions in the zealous friends of a numerous representation. Fortunately it is among the difficulties which, existing only in appearance, vanish on a close and accurate inspection. The following reflections will, if I mistake not, be admitted to be conclusive and satisfactory on this point.

Notwithstanding the equal authority which will subsist between the two houses on all legislative subjects, except the originating of money bills, it cannot be doubted that the house composed of the greater number of members, when supported by the more powerful states, and speaking the known and determined sense of a majority of the people, will have no small advantage in a question depending on the comparative firmness of the two houses.

This advantage must be increased by the consciousness felt by the same side, of being supported in its demands, by right, by reason, and by the constitution; and the consciousness on the opposite side, of contending against the force of all these solemn considerations.

It is farther to be considered that in the gradation between the smallest and largest states, there are several which, though most likely in general to arrange themselves among the former, are too little removed in extent and population from the latter, to second an opposition to their just and legitimate pretensions. Hence it is by no means certain that a majority of votes, even in the senate, would be unfriendly to proper augmentations in the number of representatives.

It will not be looking too far to add, that the senators from all the new states may be gained over to the just views of the house of representatives, by an expedient too obvious to be overlooked. As these states will for a great length of time advance in population with peculiar rapidity, they will be interested in frequent reapportionments of the representatives to the number of inhabitants. The large states therefore, who will prevail in the house of representatives, will have nothing to do, but to make reapportionments and augmentations mutually conditions of each other; and the senators from all the most growing states will be bound to contend for the latter, by the interest which their states will feel in the former.

These considerations seem to afford ample security on this subject; and ought alone to satisfy all the doubts and fears which have been indulged with regard to it. Admitting however that, they should all be insufficient to subdue the unjust policy of the smaller states, or their predominant influence in the councils of the senate; a constitutional and infallible resource, still remains with the larger states, by which they will be able at all times to accomplish their just purposes. The house of representatives can not only refuse, but they alone can propose the supplies requisite for the support of government. They in a word hold the purse; that powerful instrument by which we behold in the history of the British constitution, an infant and humble representation of the people, gradually enlarging the sphere of its activity and importance, and finally reducing, as far as it seems to have wished, all the overgrown prerogatives of the other branches of the government. This power over the purse, may in fact be regarded as the most compleat and effectual weapon with which any constitution can arm the immediate representatives of the people, for obtaining a redress of every grievance, and for carrying into effect every just and salutary measure.

But will not the house of representatives be as much interested as the senate in maintaining the government in its proper functions, and will they not therefore be unwilling to stake its existence of its reputation on the pliancy of the senate? Or if such a trial of firmness between the two branches were hazarded, would not the one be as likely first to yield as the other? These questions will create no difficulty with those who reflect, that in all cases the smaller the number and the more permanent and conspicuous the station of men in power, the stronger must be the interest which they will individually feel in whatever concerns the government. Those who represent the dignity of their country in the eyes of other nations, will be particularly sensible to every prospect of public danger, or of a dishonorable stagnation in public affairs. To those causes we are to ascribe the continual triumph of the British house of commons over the other branches of the government, whenever the engine of a money bill has been employed. An absolute inflexibility on the side of the latter, although it could not have failed to involve every department of the state in the general confusion, has neither been apprehended nor experienced. The utmost degree of firmness that can be displayed by the federal senate or president will not be more than equal to a resistance in which they will be supported by constitutional and patriotic principles.

In this review of the constitution of the house of representatives, I have passed over the circumstance of economy which in the present state of affairs might have had some effect in lessening the temporary number of representatives; and a disregard of which would probably have been as rich a theme of declamation against the constitution as has been furnished by the smallness of the number proposed. I omit also any remarks on the difficulty which might be found, under present circumstances, in engaging in the federal service, a large number of such characters as the people will probably elect. One observation however I must be permitted, to add, on this subject, as claiming in my judgment a very serious attention. It is, that in all legislative assemblies, the greater the number composing them may be, the fewer will be the men who will in fact direct their proceedings. In the first place, the more numerous any assembly may be, of whatever characters composed, the greater is known to be the ascendancy of passion over reason. In the next place, the larger the number, the greater will be the proportion of members of limited information and of weak capacities. Now it is precisely on characters of this description that the eloquence and address of the few are known to act with all their force. In the antient republics, where the whole body of the people assembled in person, a single orator, or an artful statesman, was generally seen to rule with as compleat a sway, as if a sceptre had been placed in his single hands. On the same principle the more multitudinous a representative assembly may be rendered, the more it will partake of the infirmities incident to collective meetings of the people. Ignorance will be the dupe of cunning; and passion the slave of sophistry and declamation. The people can never err more than in supposing that by multiplying their representatives, beyond a certain limit, they strengthen the barrier against the government of a few. Experience will forever admonish them that on the contrary, *after securing a sufficient number for the purposes of safety, of local information, and of diffusive sympathy with the whole society,* they will counteract their own views by every addition to their representatives. The countenance of the government may become

more democratic; but the soul that animates it will be more oligarchic. The machine will be enlarged, but the fewer and often, the more secret will be the springs by which its motions are directed.

As connected with the objection against the number of representatives, may properly be here noticed, that which has been suggested against the number made competent for legislative business. It has been said that more than a majority ought to have been required for a quorum, and in particular cases, if not in all, more than a majority of a quorum for a decision. That some advantages might have resulted from such a precaution, cannot be denied. It might have been an additional shield to some particular interests, and another obstacle generally to hasty and partial measures. But these considerations are outweighed by the inconveniencies in the opposite scale. In all cases where justice or the general good might require new laws to be passed, or active measures to be pursued, the fundamental principle of free government would be reversed. It would be no longer the majority that would rule; the power would be transferred to the minority. Were the defensive privilege limited to particular cases, an interested minority might take advantage of it to screen themselves from equitable sacrifices to the general weal, or in particular emergencies to extort unreasonable indulgences. Lastly, it would facilitate and foster the baneful practice of secessions; a practice which has shewn itself even in states where a majority only is required; a practice subversive of all the principles of order and regular government; a practice which leads more directly to public convulsions, and the ruin of popular governments, than any other which has yet been displayed among us.

18

DEBATE IN VIRGINIA RATIFYING CONVENTION
4–5 June 1788
Elliot 3:11–14, 29–35, 64

[*4 June*]

[WILSON NICHOLAS.] I come now, sir, to consider that part of the Constitution which fixes the number of representatives. It is first necessary for us to establish what the number of representatives is to be. At present it only consists of sixty-five; but let us consider that it is only to continue at that number till the actual enumeration shall be made, which is to be within three years after the first meeting of Congress; and that the number of representatives will be ascertained, and the proportion of taxes fixed, within every subsequent term of ten years. Till this enumeration be made, Congress will have no power to lay direct taxes: as there is no provision for this purpose, Congress cannot impose it; as direct taxation and representation are to be regulated by the enumeration there directed, therefore they have no power of laying direct taxes till the enumeration be actually made. I conceive no apportionment can be made before this enumeration, there being no certain data to go on. When the enumeration shall be made, what will be the consequence? I conceive there will be always one for every thirty thousand. Many reasons concur to lead me to this conclusion. By the Constitution, the allotment now made will only continue till the enumeration be made; and as a new enumeration will take place every ten years, I take it for granted that the number of representatives will be increased, according to the progressive increase of population, at every respective enumeration; and one for every thirty thousand will amount to one hundred representatives, if we compute the number of inhabitants to be only three millions in the United States, which is a very moderate calculation. The first intention was only to have one for every forty thousand, which was afterwards estimated to be too few, and, according to this proportion, the present temporary number is fixed; but as it now stands, we readily see that the proportion of representatives is sufficiently numerous to answer every purpose of federal legislation, and even soon to gratify those who wish for the greatest number. I take it that the number of representatives will be proportioned to the highest number we are entitled to; and that it never will be less than one for every thirty thousand. I formed this conclusion from the situation of those who will be our representatives. They are all chosen for two years; at the end of which term they are to depend on the people for their reëlection. This dependence will lead them to a due and faithful discharge of their duty to their constituents: the augmentation of their number will conciliate the affections of the people at large; for the more the representatives increase in number, the greater the influence of the people in the government, and the greater the chance of reëlection to the representatives.

But it has been said, that the Senate will not agree to any augmentation of the number of representatives. The Constitution will entitle the House of Representatives to demand it. Would the Senate venture to stand out against them? I think they would not, sir. Were they ready to recede from the evident sense of the Constitution, and grasp at power not thereby given them, they would be compelled to desist. But, that I may not be charged with urging suppositions, let us see what ground this stands upon, and whether there be any real danger to be apprehended. The first objection that I shall consider is, that, by paucity of numbers, they will be more liable to depart from their duty, and more subject to influence. I apprehend that the fewer the number of representatives, the freer the choice, and the greater the number of electors, the less liable to the unworthy acts of the candidates will they be; and thus their suffrage, being free, will probably fall on men of the . most merit. The practice of that country, which is situated more like America than any other country in the world, will justify this supposition. The British House of Commons consists, I believe, of five hundred and fifty-eight members; yet the greater number of these are supposed to be under the undue influence of the crown. A single fact from the British history illustrates these observations,—viz., that there is scarcely an instance, for a century

past, of the crown's exercising its undoubted prerogative of rejecting a bill sent up to it by the two houses of Parliament: it is no answer to say, that the king's influence is sufficient to prevent any obnoxious bills passing the two houses; there are many instances, in that period, not only of bills passing the two houses, but even receiving the royal assent, contrary to the private wish and inclination of the prince.

It is objected, however, as a defect in the Constitution, that it does not prohibit the House of Representatives from giving their powers, particularly that respecting the support &c., of armies, out of their hands for a longer term than two years. Here, I think, the enemies to the plan reason unfairly; they first suppose that Congress, from a love of power natural to all, will, in general, abuse that with which they are invested; and then they would make us apprehend that the House of Representatives, notwithstanding their love of power, (and it must be supposed as great in a branch of Congress as in the whole,) will give out of their hands the only check which can insure to them the continuance of the participation of the powers lodged in Congress in general. In England, there is no restraint of this kind on the Parliament; and yet there is no instance of a money bill being passed for a longer term than one year; the proposed plan, therefore, when it declares that no appropriation for the support of an army shall be made for a longer term than two years, introduces a check unknown to the English constitution, and one which will be found very powerful when we reflect that, if the House of Representatives could be prevailed on to make an appropriation for an army for two years, at the end of that time there will be a new choice of representatives. Thus I insist that security does not depend on the number of representatives: the experience of that country also shows that many of their counties and cities contain a greater number of souls than will be entitled to a representation in America; and yet the representatives chosen in those places have been the most strenuous advocates of liberty, and have exerted themselves in the defence of it, even in opposition to those chosen by much smaller numbers. Many of the senatorial districts in Virginia also contain a greater number of souls; and yet I suppose no gentleman within these walls will pay the senators chosen by them so poor a compliment as to attribute less wisdom and virtue to them than to the delegates chosen from single counties; and as there is greater probability that the electors in a large district will be more independent, so I think the representatives chosen in such districts will be more so too; for those who have sold themselves to their representatives will have no right to complain, if they, in their turn, barter away their rights and liberties; but those who have not themselves been bought, will never consent to be sold. Another objection made to the small number of representatives, is, that, admitting they were sufficient to secure their integrity, yet they cannot be acquainted with the local situation and circumstances of their constituents. When we attend to the object of their jurisdiction, we find this objection insupportable. Congress will superintend the great national interests of the Union. Local concerns are left to the state legislatures. When the members compare and communicate to one another their knowledge of their respective districts and states, their collective intelligence will sufficiently enable them to perform the objects of their cognizance. They cannot extend their influence or agency to any objects but those of a general nature; the representatives will, therefore, be sufficiently acquainted with the interests of their states, although chosen by large districts. As long as the people remain virtuous and uncorrupted, so long, we may fairly conclude, will their representatives, even at their present number, guard their interests, and discharge their duty with fidelity and zeal: when they become otherwise, no government can possibly secure their freedom.

. . . . .

Mr. GEORGE MASON. Mr. Chairman, whether the Constitution be good or bad, the present clause clearly discovers that it is a national government, and no longer a Confederation. I mean that clause which gives the first hint of the general government laying direct taxes. The assumption of this power of laying direct taxes does, of itself, entirely change the confederation of the states into one consolidated government. This power, being at discretion, unconfined, and without any kind of control, must carry every thing before it. The very idea of converting what was formerly a confederation to a consolidated government, is totally subversive of every principle which has hitherto governed us. This power is calculated to annihilate totally the state governments. Will the people of this great community submit to be individually taxed by two different and distinct powers? Will they suffer themselves to be doubly harassed? These two concurrent powers cannot exist long together; the one will destroy the other: the general government being paramount to, and in every respect more powerful than the state governments, the latter must give way to the former. Is it to be supposed that one national government will suit so extensive a country, embracing so many climates, and containing inhabitants so very different in manners, habits, and customs? It is ascertained, by history, that there never was a government over a very extensive country without destroying the liberties of the people: history also, supported by the opinions of the best writers, shows us that monarchy may suit a large territory, and despotic governments ever so extensive a country, but that popular governments can only exist in small territories. Is there a single example, on the face of the earth, to support a contrary opinion? Where is there one exception to this general rule? Was there ever an instance of a general national government extending over so extensive a country, abounding in such a variety of climates, &c., where the people retained their liberty? I solemnly declare that no man is a greater friend to a firm union of the American states than I am; but, sir, if this great end can be obtained without hazarding the rights of the people, why should we recur to such dangerous principles? Requisitions have been often refused, sometimes from an impossibility of complying with them; often from that great variety of circumstances which retards the collection of moneys; and perhaps sometimes from a wilful design of procrastinating. But why shall we give up to the national government this power, so dangerous in its nature, and for which its members will not have sufficient information? Is it not well known that what would be a proper tax in one state would be grievous in another? The gentleman who hath favored us with a eulogium in favor of this system, must, after all the encomiums he has been pleased to bestow upon it, acknowledge that our federal representatives must be unacquainted with the situation of their constituents. Sixty-five members cannot possibly know the situation and circumstances of all the inhabitants of this immense continent. When a certain sum comes to be taxed, and the mode of levying to be fixed, they will lay the tax on that article which will be most productive and easiest in the collection, without consulting the real circumstances or convenience of a country, with which, in fact, they cannot be sufficiently acquainted.

The mode of levying taxes is of the utmost consequence; and yet here it is to be determined by those who have neither knowledge of our situation, nor a common interest with us, nor a fellow-feeling for us. The subject of taxation differs in three fourths, nay, I might say with truth, in four fifths of the states. If we trust the national government with an effectual way of raising the necessary sums, it is sufficient: every thing we do further is trusting the happiness and rights of the people. Why, then, should we give up this dangerous power of individual taxation? Why leave the manner of laying taxes to those who, in the nature of things, cannot be acquainted with the situation of those on whom they are to impose them, when it can be done by those who are well acquainted with it? If, instead of giving this oppressive power, we give them such an effectual alternative as will answer the purpose, without encountering the evil and danger that might arise from it, then I would cheerfully acquiesce; and would it not be far more eligible? I candidly acknowledge the inefficacy of the Confederation; but requisitions have been made which were impossible to be complied with—requisitions for more gold and silver than were in the United States. If we give the general government the power of demanding their quotas of the states, with an alternative of laying direct taxes in case of non-compliance, then the mischief would be avoided; and the certainty of this conditional power would, in all human probability, prevent the application, and the sum necessary for the Union would be then laid by the states, by those who know how it can best be raised, by those who have a fellow-feeling for us. Give me leave to say, that the sum raised one way with convenience and ease, would be very oppressive another way. Why, then, not leave this power to be exercised by those who know the mode most convenient for the inhabitants, and not by those who must necessarily apportion it in such manner as shall be oppressive? With respect to the representation so much applauded, I cannot think it such a full and free one as it is represented; but I must candidly acknowledge that this defect results from the very nature of the government. It would be impossible to have a full and adequate representation in the general government; it would be too expensive and too unwieldy. We are, then, under the necessity of having this a very inadequate representation. Is this general representation to be compared with the real, actual, substantial representation of the state legislatures? It cannot bear a comparison. To make representation real and actual, the number of representatives ought to be adequate; they ought to mix with the people, think as they think, feel as they feel,—ought to be perfectly amenable to them, and thoroughly acquainted with their interest and condition. Now, these great ingredients are either not at all, or in a small degree, to be found in our federal representatives; so that we have no real, actual, substantial representation: but I acknowledge it results from the nature of the government. The necessity of this inconvenience may appear a sufficient reason not to argue against it; but, sir, it clearly shows that we ought to give power with a sparing hand to a government thus imperfectly constructed. To a government which, in the nature of things, cannot but be defective, no powers ought to be given but such as are absolutely necessary. There is one thing in it which I conceive to be extremely dangerous. Gentlemen may talk of public virtue and confidence; we shall be told that the House of Representatives will consist of the most virtuous men on the continent, and that in their hands we may trust our dearest rights. This, like all other assemblies, will be composed of some bad and some good men; and, considering the natural lust of power so inherent in man, I fear the thirst of power will prevail to oppress the people. What I conceive to be so dangerous, is the provision with respect to the number of representatives: it does not expressly provide that we shall have one for every thirty thousand, but that the number shall not exceed that proportion. The utmost that we can expect (and perhaps that is too much) is, that the present number shall be continued to us;—"the number of representatives shall not exceed one for every thirty thousand." Now, will not this be complied with, although the present number should never be increased—nay, although it should be decreased? Suppose Congress should say that we should have one for every forty thousand; will not the Constitution be complied with?—for one for every forty thousand does not exceed one for every thirty thousand. There is a want of proportion that ought to be strictly guarded against. The worthy gentleman tells us that we have no reason to fear; but I always fear for the rights of the people. I do not pretend to inspiration; but I think it is apparent as the day, that the members will attend to local, partial interests, to prevent an augmentation of their number. I know not how they will be chosen, but, whatever be the mode of choosing, our present number will be ten; and suppose our state is laid off in ten districts,—those gentlemen who shall be sent from those districts will lessen their own power and influence in their respective districts if they increase their number; for the greater the number of men among whom any given quantum of power is divided, the less the power of each individual. Thus they will have a local interest to prevent the increase of, and perhaps they will lessen their own number. This is evident on the face of the Constitution: so loose an expression ought to be guarded against, for Congress will be clearly within the requisition of the Constitution, although the number of representatives should always continue what it is now, and the population of the country should increase to an immense number. Nay, they may reduce the number from sixty-five to one from each state, without violating the Constitution; and thus the number, which is not too small, would then be infinitely too much so. But my principal objection is, that the Confederation is converted to one general consolidated government, which, from my best judgment of it, (and which perhaps will be shown, in the course of this discussion, to be really well founded,) is one of the worst curses that can possibly befall a nation. Does any man suppose that one general national government can exist in so extensive a country as this? I hope that a government may be framed which may suit us, by drawing a line between the general and state governments, and prevent that dangerous clashing of interest and power, which must, as it now stands, terminate in the destruction of one or the other. When we come to the judiciary, we shall be more convinced that this government will terminate in the annihilation of the state governments: the question then will be, whether a consolidated government can preserve the freedom and secure the rights of the people.

If such amendments be introduced as shall exclude danger, I shall most gladly put my hand to it. When such amendments as shall, from the best information, secure the great essential rights of the people, shall be agreed to by gentlemen, I shall most heartily make the greatest concessions, and concur in any reasonable measure to obtain the desirable end of conciliation and unanimity. An indispensable amendment in this case is, that Congress shall not exercise the power of raising direct taxes till the states shall have refused to comply with the requisitions of Congress. On this condition it may be granted; but I see no reason to grant it unconditionally, as the states can raise the taxes with more ease, and lay them on the inhabitants with more propriety, than it is possible for the general government to do. If Congress hath this power without control, the taxes will be laid by those who have no fellow-feeling or acquaintance with the people. This is my objection to the article now under consideration. It is a very great and important one. I therefore beg gentlemen to consider it. Should this power be restrained, I shall withdraw my objections to this part of the Constitution; but as it stands, it is an objection so strong in my mind, that its amendment is with me a *sine qua non* of its adoption. I wish for such amendments, and such only, as are necessary to secure the dearest rights of the people.

Mr. MADISON. Mr. Chairman, it would give me great pleasure to concur with my honorable colleague in any conciliatory plan. The clause to which the worthy member alludes is only explanatory of the proportion which representation and taxation shall respectively bear to one another. The power of laying direct taxes will be more properly discussed, when we come to that part of the Constitution which vests that power in Congress. At present, I must endeavor to reconcile our proceedings to the resolution we have taken, by postponing the examination of this power till we come properly to it. With respect to converting the confederation to a complete consolidation, I think no such consequence will follow from the Constitution, and that, with more attention, we shall see that he is mistaken; and with respect to the number of representatives, I reconcile it to my mind, when I consider that it may be increased to the proportion fixed, and that, as it may be so increased, *it shall,* because it is the interest of those who alone can prevent it, who are representatives, and who depend on their good behavior for their reëlection. Let me observe, also, that, as far as the number of representatives may seem to be adequate to discharge their duty, they will have sufficient information from the laws of particular states, from the state legislatures, from their own experience, and from a great number of individuals; and as to our security against them, I conceive, sir, that the general limitation of their powers, and the general watchfulness of the states, will be a sufficient guard. As it is now late, I shall defer any further investigation till a more convenient time.

[*5 June*]

[PATRICK HENRY.] Remember, sir, that the number of our representatives is but ten, whereof six is a majority. Will those men be possessed of sufficient information? A particular knowledge of particular districts will not suffice. They must be well acquainted with agriculture, commerce, and a great variety of other matters throughout the continent; they must know not only the actual state of nations in Europe and America, the situations of their farmers, cottagers, and mechanics, but also the relative situations and intercourse of those nations. Virginia is as large as England. Our proportion of representatives is but ten men. In England they have five hundred and fifty-eight. The House of Commons, in England, numerous as they are, we are told, are bribed, and have bartered away the rights of their constituents: what, then, shall become of us? Will these few protect our rights? Will they be incorruptible? You say they will be better men than the English commoners. I say they will be infinitely worse men, because they are to be chosen blindfolded: their election (the term, as applied to their appointment, is inaccurate) will be an involuntary nomination, and not a choice.

19

JAMES MADISON, CENSUS BILL, HOUSE OF
REPRESENTATIVES
25–26 Jan., 2 Feb. 1790
Papers 13:8–9, 15–16

Mr. Madison Observed that they had now an opportunity of obtaining the most useful information for those who should hereafter be called upon to legislate for their country if this bill was extended so as to embrace some other objects besides the bare enumeration of the inhabitants; it would enable them to adapt the public measures to the particular circumstances of the community. In order to know the various interests of the United States, it was necessary that the description of the several classes into which the community was divided, should be accurately known; on this knowledge the legislature might proceed to make a proper provision for the agricultural, commercial and manufacturing interests, but without it they could never make their provisions in due proportion.

This kind of information, he observed, all legislatures had wished for; but this kind of information had never been obtained in any country. He wished, therefore, to avail himself of the present opportunity of accomplishing so valuable a purpose. If the plan was pursued in taking every future census, it would give them an opportunity of marking the progress of the society, and distinguishing the growth of every interest. This would furnish ground for many useful calculations, and at the same time answer the purpose of a check on the officers who were employed to make the enumeration, forasmuch as the aggregate number was divided into parts, any imposition might be discovered with proportionable ease. If these ideas met the approbation of the house, he hoped they would pass over the schedule in the second clause of the bill, and he would endeavor to prepare something to accomplish this object.

. . . . .

Mr. Madison presented a schedule, which he moved should be inserted in lieu of that annexed to the bill, viz.

Free white males, under 16; free white males, above 16; white females, free blacks, and slaves, the heads of families, &c.

And he likewise proposed that a particular schedule should be included in the bill, specifying the number of persons employed in different professions and arts, carried on within the United States; such as merchants, mechanics, manufacturers, &c. &c.

. . . . .

Mr. Madison. If the object to be attained by this particular enumeration be as important in the judgment of this house, as it appears to my mind, they will not suffer a small defect in the plan, to defeat the whole. And I am very sensible, Mr. Speaker, that there will be more difficulty attendant on the taking the census, in the way required by the constitution, and which we are obliged to perform, than there will be in the additional trouble of making all the distinctions contemplated in the bill. The classes of people most troublesome to enumerate, in this schedule, are happily those resident in large towns, the greatest number of artisans live in populous cities, and compact settlements, where distinctions are made with great ease.

I take it, sir, that in order to accommodate our laws to the real situation of our constituents, we ought to be acquainted with that situation. It may be impossible to ascertain it as far as I wish, but we may ascertain it so far as to be extremely useful, when we come to pass laws, affecting any particular description of people. If gentlemen have any doubts with respect to its utility, I cannot satisfy them in a better manner, than by referring them to the debates which took place upon the bills, intend[ed], collaterally, to benefit the agricultural, commercial, and manufacturing parts of the community. Did they not wish then to know the relative proportion of each, and the exact number of every division, in order that they might rest their arguments on facts, instead of assertions and conjectures? Will any gentleman pretend to doubt, but our regulations would have been better accommodated to the real state of the society than they are? If our decisions had been influenced by actual returns, would they not have been varied, according as the one side or the other was more or less numerous? We should have given less encouragement in some instances, and more in others; but in every instance, we should have proceeded with more light and satisfaction.

The gentleman from Massachusetts (Mr. Sedgwick) has asked, why the learned professions were not included: I have no objection to giving a column to the general body. I think the work would be rendered more complete by the addition, and if the decision of such a motion turned upon my voice, they shall be added. But it may nevertheless be observed, that in such a character, they can never be objects of legislative attention or cognizance. As to those employed in teaching and inculcating the duties of religion, there may be some indelicacy in singling them out, as the general government is proscribed from interfering, in any manner whatever, in matters respecting religion; and it may be thought to do this, in ascertaining who, and who are not, ministers of the gospel. Conceiving the extension of the plan to be useful, and not difficult, I hope it may meet the ready concurrence of this house.

20

HYLTON V. UNITED STATES
3 Dall. 171 (1796)

(See 1.9.4, no. 13)

21

ST. GEORGE TUCKER,
BLACKSTONE'S COMMENTARIES
1:APP. 189
1803

This mode of ascertaining the number of representatives, and the inseparable connection thereby established between the benefits and burthens of the state, seems to be more consonant with the true principles of representation than any other which has hitherto been suggested. For every man, in his individual capacity, has an equal right to vote in matters which concern the whole community: no just reason therefore can be assigned why ten men in one part of the community should have greater weight in it's councils, than one hundred in a different place, as is the case in England, where a borough composed of half a dozen freeholders, sends perhaps as many representatives to parliament, as a county which contains as many thousands; this unreasonable disparity appears to be happily guarded against by our constitution. It may be doubted indeed how far the apportionment of the numbers, as it

respects slaves, is founded upon the principles of perfect equality; and if it be not, it may be a further question whether the advantage preponderates on the side of the states that have the most, or the fewest slaves amongst them; for, if on the one hand it be urged, that slaves are not in the rank of persons, being no more than goods or chattels, according to the opinion of the Roman jurists, and consequently not entitled to representation, it may be answered that the ratio of representation and taxation being the same, this additional weight in council is purchased at an expence which secures the opposite party from the abuse of it in the imposition of burthens on the government. On the other hand, it must be remembered, that the two fifths of this class of people who are not represented, are by that means exempted from taxation. An exemption which probably took its rise from the unprofitable condition of that proportion of the number of slaves.

22

JOSEPH STORY, COMMENTARIES ON THE
CONSTITUTION 2:§§ 630–35, 641–47, 673–80
1833

§ 630. . . . It is obvious, that the question, how the apportionment should be made, was one, upon which a considerable diversity of judgment might, and probably would, exist. Three leading principles of apportionment would, at once, present themselves. One was to adopt the rule already existing, under the confederation; that is, an equality of representation and vote by each state, thus giving each state a right to send not less than two, nor more than seven representatives, and in the determination of questions, each state to have one vote. This would naturally receive encouragement from all those, who were attached to the confederation, and preferred a mere league of states, to a government in any degree national. And accordingly it formed, as it should seem, the basis of what was called the New-Jersey Plan. This rule of apportionment met, however, with a decided opposition, and was negatived in the convention at an early period, seven states voting against it, three being in its favour, and one being divided.

§ 631. Another principle might be, to apportion the representation of the states according to the relative property of each, thus making property the basis of representation. This might commend itself to some persons, because it would introduce a salutary check into the legislature in regard to taxation, by securing, in some measure, an equalization of the public burthens, by the voice of those, who were called to give most towards the common contributions. That taxation ought to go hand in hand with representation, had been a favourite theory of the American people. Under the confederation, all the common expenses were required to be borne by the states in proportion to the value of the land within each state. But it has been already seen, that this mode of contribution was extremely difficult and embarrassing, and unsatisfactory in practice, under the confederation. There do not, indeed, seem to be any traces in the proceedings of the convention, that this scheme had an exclusive influence with any persons in that body. It mixed itself up with other considerations, without acquiring any decisive preponderance. In the first place, it was easy to provide a remedial check upon undue direct taxation, the only species, of which there could be the slightest danger of unequal and oppressive levies. And it will be seen, that this was sufficiently provided for, by declaring, that representatives and direct taxes should be apportioned by the same ratio.

§ 632. In the next place, although property may not be directly aimed at, as a basis in the representation, provided for by the constitution, it cannot, on the other hand, be deemed to be totally excluded, as will presently be seen. In the next place, it is not admitted, that property alone can, in a free government, safely be relied on, as the sole basis of representation. It may be true, and probably is, that in the ordinary course of affairs, it is not the interest, or policy of those, who possess property, to oppress those, who want it. But, in every well-ordered commonwealth, persons, as well as property, should possess a just share of influence. The liberties of the people are too dear, and too sacred to be entrusted to any persons, who may not, at all times, have a common sympathy and common interest with the people in the preservation of their public rights, privileges, and liberties. Checks and balances, if not indispensable to, are at least a great conservative in, the operations of all free governments. And, perhaps, upon mere abstract theory, it cannot be justly affirmed, that either persons or property, numbers or wealth, can safely be trusted, as the final repositaries of the delegated powers of government. By apportioning influence among each, vigilance, caution, and mutual checks are naturally introduced, and perpetuated.

§ 633. The third and remaining principle was, to apportion the representatives among the states according to their relative numbers. This had the recommendation of great simplicity and uniformity in its operation, of being generally acceptable to the people, and of being less liable to fraud and evasion, than any other, which could be devised. Besides; although wealth and property cannot be affirmed to be in different states, exactly in proportion to the numbers; they are not so widely separated from it, as, at a hasty glance, might be imagined. There is, if not a natural, at least a very common connexion between them; and, perhaps, an apportionment of taxes according to numbers is as equitable a rule for contributions according to relative wealth, as any, which can be practically obtained.

§634. The scheme, therefore, under all the circumstances, of making numbers the basis of the representation of the Union, seems to have obtained more general favour, than any other in the convention, because it had a natural and universal connexion with the rights and liberties of the whole people.

§ 635. But here a difficulty of a very serious nature arose. There were other persons in several of the states, than those, who were free. There were some persons, who were bound to service for a term of years; though these were so few, that they would scarcely vary the result of the general rule, in any important degree. There were Indians, also, in several, and probably in most, of the states at that period, who were not treated as citizens, and yet, who did not form a part of independent communities or tribes, exercising general sovereignty and powers of government within the boundaries of the states. It was necessary, therefore, to provide for these cases, though they were attended with no practical difficulty. There seems not to have been any objection in including, in the ratio of representation, persons bound to service for a term of years, and in excluding Indians not taxed. The real (and it was a very exciting) controversy was in regard to slaves, whether they should be included in the enumeration, or not. On the one hand, it was contended, that slaves were treated in the states, which tolerated slavery, as property, and not as persons. They were bought and sold, devised and transferred, like any other property. They had no civil rights, or political privileges. They had no will of their own; but were bound to absolute obedience to their masters. There was, then, no more reason for including them in the census of persons, than there would be for including any brute animals whatsoever. If they were to be represented as property, the rule should be extended, so as to embrace all other property. It would be a gross inequality to allow representation for slaves to the southern states; for that, in effect, would be, to allow to their masters a predominant right, founded on mere property. Thus, five thousand free persons, in a slave-state, might possess the same power to choose a representative, as thirty thousand free persons in a non-slave-holding state.

. . . . .

§ 641. The truth is, that the arrangement adopted by the constitution was a matter of compromise and concession, confessedly unequal in its operation, but a necessary sacrifice to that spirit of conciliation, which was indispensable to the union of states having a great diversity of interests, and physical condition, and political institutions. It was agreed, that slaves should be represented, under the mild appellation of "other persons," not as free persons, but only in the proportion of three fifths. The clause was in substance borrowed from the resolve, passed by the continental congress on the 18th of April, 1783, recommending the states to amend the articles of confederation in such manner, that the national expenses should be defrayed out of a common treasury, "which shall be supplied by the several states, in proportion to the whole number of white, or other free inhabitants, of every age, sex, and condition, including those bound to servitude for a term of years, and three fifths of all other persons, not comprehended in the foregoing description, except Indians, not paying taxes, in each state." In order to reconcile the non-slave-holding states to this provision, another clause was inserted, that direct taxes should be apportioned in the same manner as representatives. So, that, theoretically, representation and taxation might go *pari passu*. This provision, however, is more specious than solid; for while, in the levy of direct taxes, it apportions them on three fifths of persons not free, it, on the other hand, really exempts the other two fifths from being taxed at all, as property. Whereas, if direct taxes had been apportioned, as upon principle they ought to be, according to the real value of property within the state, the whole of the slaves would have been taxable, as property. But a far more striking inequality has been disclosed by the practical operations of the government. The principle of representation is constant, and uniform; the levy of direct taxes is occasional, and rare. In the course of forty years, no more than three direct taxes have been levied; and those only under very extraordinary and pressing circumstances. The ordinary expenditures of the government are, and always have been, derived from other sources. Imposts upon foreign importations have supplied, and will generally supply, all the common wants; and if these should not furnish an adequate revenue, excises are next resorted to, as the surest and most convenient mode of taxation. Direct taxes constitute the last resort; and (as might have been foreseen) would never be laid, until other resources had failed.

§ 642. Viewed in its proper light, as a real compromise, in a case of conflicting interests, for the common good, the provision is entitled to great praise for its moderation, its aim at practical utility, and its tendency to satisfy the people, that the Union, framed by all, ought to be dear to all, by the privileges it confers, as well as the blessings it secures. It had a material influence in reconciling the southern states to other provisions in the constitution, and especially to the power of making commercial regulations by a mere majority, which was thought peculiarly to favour the northern states. It has sometimes been complained of, as a grievance; but he, who wishes well to his country, will adhere steadily to it, as a fundamental policy, which extinguishes some of the most mischievous sources of all political divisions,—those founded on geographical positions, and domestic institutions. It did not, however, pass the convention without objection. Upon its first introduction, it was supported by the votes of nine states against two. In subsequent stages of the discussion, it met with some opposition; and in some of the state conventions it was strenuously resisted. The wish of every patriot ought now to be, *requiescat in pace.*

§ 643. Another part of the clause regards the periods, at which the enumeration or census of the inhabitants of the United States shall be taken, in order to provide for new apportionments of representatives, according to the relative increase of the population of the states. Various propositions for this purpose were laid, at different times, before the convention. It was proposed to have the census taken once in fifteen years, and in twenty years; but the vote finally prevailed in favour of ten. The importance of this provision for a decennial census can scarcely be overvalued. It is the only effectual means, by which the relative power of the several states could be justly represented. If the system first established had been unalterable, very gross inequalities would soon have taken place among the states, from the very unequal increase of their population. The representation would soon have exhibited a system very analogous to that of the house of commons in Great-Britain, where old and decayed boroughs send representatives, not only wholly disproportionate to their impor-

tance; but in some cases, with scarcely a single inhabitant, they match the representatives of the most populous counties.

§ 644. In regard to the United States, the slightest examination of the apportionment made under the first three censuses will demonstrate this conclusion in a very striking manner. The representation of Delaware remains, as it was at the first apportionment; those of New-Hampshire, Rhode-Island, Connecticut, New-Jersey, and Maryland have had but a small comparative increase; whilst that of Massachusetts (including Maine) has swelled from eight to twenty; that of New-York, from six to thirty-four; and that of Pennsylvania, from eight to twenty-six. In the mean time, the new states have sprung into being; and Ohio, which in 1803 was only entitled to one, now counts fourteen representatives. The census of 1831 exhibits still more striking results. In 1790, the whole population of the United States was about three millions nine hundred and twenty-nine thousand; and in 1830, it was about twelve millions eight hundred and fifty-six thousand. Ohio, at this very moment, contains at least one million, and New-York two millions of inhabitants. These facts show the wisdom of the provision for a decennial apportionment; and, indeed, it would otherwise have happened, that the system, however sound at the beginning, would by this time have been productive of gross abuses, and probably have engendered feuds and discontents, of themselves sufficient to have occasioned a dissolution of the Union. We probably owe this provision to those in the convention, who were in favour of a national government, in preference to a mere confederation of states.

§ 645. The next part of the clause relates to the total number of the house of representatives. It declares, that "the number of representatives shall not exceed one for every thirty thousand." This was a subject of great interest; and it has been asserted, that scarcely any article of the whole constitution seems to be rendered more worthy of attention by the weight of character, and the apparent force of argument, with which it was originally assailed. The number fixed by the constitution to constitute the body, in the first instance, and until a census was taken, was sixty-five.

§ 646. Several objections were urged against the provision. First, that so small a number of representatives would be an unsafe depositary of the public interests. Secondly, that they would not possess a proper knowledge of the local circumstances of their numerous constituents. Thirdly, that they would be taken from that class of citizens, which would sympathize least with the feelings of the people, and be most likely to aim at a permanent elevation of the few, on the depression of the many. Fourthly, that defective, as the number in the first instance would be, it would be more and more disproportionate by the increase of the population, and the obstacles, which would prevent a correspondent increase of the representatives.

§ 647. Time and experience have demonstrated the fallacy of some, and greatly impaired, if they have not utterly destroyed, the force of all of these objections. The fears, which were at that period so studiously cherished; the alarms, which were so forcibly spread; the dangers to liberty, which were so strangely exaggerated; and the predominance of aristocratical and exclusive power, which were so confidently predicted, have all vanished into air, into thin air. Truth has silently dissolved the phantoms raised by imaginations, heated by prejudice or controversy; and at the distance of forty years we look back with astonishment at the laborious reasoning, which was employed to tranquillize the doubts, and assuage the jealousies of the people.

. . . . .

§ 673. As a fit conclusion of this part of the subject it may be remarked, that congress, at its first session in 1789, in pursuance of a desire expressed by several of the state conventions, in favour of further declaratory and restrictive amendments to the constitution, proposed twelve additional articles. The first was on the very subject now under consideration, and was expressed in the following terms: "After the first enumeration required by the first article of the constitution, there shall be one representative for every thirty thousand, until the number shall amount to one hundred; after which the proportion shall be so regulated by congress, that there shall not be less than one hundred representatives, nor less than one for every forty thousand persons, until the number of representatives shall amount to two hundred; after which, the proportion shall be so regulated by congress, that there shall not be less than two hundred representatives, nor more than one representative for every fifty thousand." This amendment was never ratified by a competent number of the states to be incorporated into the constitution. It was probably thought, that the whole subject was safe, where it was already lodged; and that congress ought to be left free to exercise a sound discretion, according to the future exigencies of the nation, either to increase, or diminish the number of representatives.

§ 674. There yet remain two practical questions of no inconsiderable importance, connected with the clause of the constitution now under consideration. One is, what are to be deemed direct taxes within the meaning of the clause. The other is, in what manner the apportionment of representatives is to be made. The first will naturally come under review in examining the powers of congress, and the constitutional limitations upon those powers; and may, therefore, for the present, be passed over. The other was a subject of much discussion at the time, when the first apportionment was before congress after the first census was taken; and has been recently revived with new and increased interest and ability. It deserves, therefore, a very deliberate examination.

§ 675. The language of the constitution is, that "representatives and direct taxes shall be apportioned among the several states, &c. according to their respective numbers;" and at the first view it would not seem to involve the slightest difficulty. A moment's reflection will dissipate the illusion, and teach us, that there is a difficulty intrinsic in the very nature of the subject. In regard to direct taxes, the natural course would be to assume a particular sum to be raised, as three millions of dollars; and to apportion it among the states according to their relative numbers. But even here, there will always be a very small fractional

amount incapable of exact distribution, since the numbers in each state will never exactly coincide with any common divisor, or give an exact aliquot part for each state without any remainder. But, as the amount may be carried through a long series of descending money fractions, it may be ultimately reduced to the smallest fraction of any existing, or even imaginary coin.

§ 676. But the difficulty is far otherwise in regard to representatives. Here, there can be no subdivision of the unit; each state must be entitled to an entire representative, and a fraction of a representative is incapable of apportionment. Yet it will be perceived at once, that it is scarcely possible, and certainly is wholly improbable, that the relative numbers in each state should bear such an exact proportion to the aggregate, that there should exist a common divisor for all, which should leave no fraction in any state. Such a case never yet has existed; and in all human probability it never will. Every common divisor, hitherto applied, has left a fraction greater, or smaller, in every state; and what has been in the past must continue to be for the future. Assume the whole population to be three, or six, or nine, or twelve millions, or any other number; if you follow the injunctions of the constitution, and attempt to apportion the representatives according to the numbers in each state, it will be found to be absolutely impossible. The theory, however true, becomes practically false in its application. Each state may have assigned a relative proportion of representatives up to a given number, the whole being divisible by some common divisor; but the fraction of population belonging to each beyond the point is left unprovided for. So that the apportionment is, at best, only an approximation to the rule laid down by the constitution, and not a strict compliance with the rule. The fraction in one state may be ten times as great, as that in another; and so may differ in each state in any assignable mathematical proportion. What then is to be done? Is the constitution to be wholly disregarded on this point? Or is it to be followed out in its true spirit, though unavoidably differing from the letter, by the nearest approximation to it? If an additional representative can be assigned to one state beyond its relative proportion to the whole population, it is equally true, that it can be assigned to all, that are in a similar predicament. If a fraction admits of representation in any case, what prohibits the application of the rule to all fractions? The only constitutional limitation seems to be, that no state shall have more than one representative for every thirty thousand persons. Subject to this, the truest rule seems to be, that the apportionment ought to be the nearest practical approximation to the terms of the constitution; and the rule ought to be such, that it shall always work the same way in regard to all the states, and be as little open to cavil, or controversy, or abuse, as possible.

§ 677. But it may be asked, what are the first steps to be taken in order to arrive at a constitutional apportionment? Plainly, by taking the aggregate of population in all the states, (according to the constitutional rule,) and then ascertain the relative proportion of the population of each state to the population of the whole. This is necessarily so in regard to direct taxes; and there is no reason to say, that it can, or ought to be otherwise in regard to representatives; for that would be to contravene the very injunctions of the constitution, which require the like rule of apportionment in each case. In the one, the apportionment may be run down below unity; in the other, it cannot. But this does not change the nature of the rule, but only the extent of its application.

§ 678. In 1790, a bill was introduced into the house of representatives, giving one representative for every thirty thousand, and leaving the fractions unrepresented; thus producing an inequality, which was greatly complained of. It passed the house; and was amended in the senate by allowing an additional representative to the states having the largest fractions. The house finally concurred in the amendment, after a warm debate. The history of these proceedings is summarily stated by the biographer of Washington, as follows:—"Construing," says he, "the constitution to authorize a process, by which the whole number of representatives should be ascertained on the whole population of the United States, and afterwards apportioned among the several states according to their respective numbers, the senate applied the number thirty thousand, as a divisor, to the total population, and taking the quotient, which was one hundred and twenty, as the number of representatives given by the ratio, which had been adopted in the house, where the bill originated, they apportioned that number among the several states by that ratio, until as many representatives, as it would give, were allotted to each. The residuary members were then distributed among the states having the highest fractions. Without professing the principle, on which this apportionment was made, the amendment of the senate merely allotted to the states respectively the number of members, which the process just mentioned would give. The result was a more equitable apportionment of representatives to population, and a still more exact accordance, than was found in the original bill, with the prevailing sentiment, which, both within doors and without, seemed to require, that the popular branch of the legislature should consist of as many members, as the fundamental laws of the government would admit. If the rule of construing that instrument was correct, the amendment removed objections, which were certainly well founded, and was not easily assailable by the advocates of a numerous representative body. But the rule was novel, and overturned opinions, which had been generally assumed, and were supposed to be settled. In one branch of the legislature, it had been already rejected; and in the other, the majority in its favour was only one."

§ 679. The debate in the two houses, however, was purely political, and the division of the votes purely geographical; the southern states voting against it, and the northern in its favour. The president returned the bill with two objections. "1. That the constitution has prescribed, that representatives shall be apportioned among the several states according to their respective numbers; and there is no proportion or divisor, which, applied to the respective numbers of the states, will yield the number and allotment of representatives proposed by the bill. 2. The constitution has also provided, that the number of representatives shall not exceed one for thirty thousand, which restriction is by the context, and by fair and obvious

construction, to be applied to the several and respective numbers of the states, and the bill has allotted to eight of the states more than one for thirty thousand." The bill was accordingly lost, two thirds of the house not being in its favour. It is understood, that the president's cabinet was greatly divided on the question.

§ 680. The second reason assigned by the president against the bill was well founded in fact, and entirely conclusive. The other, to say the least of it, is as open to question, as any one, which can well be imagined in a case of real difficulty of construction. It assumes, as its basis, that a common ratio, or divisor, is to be taken, and applied to each state, let the fractions and inequalities left be whatever they may. Now, this is a plain departure from the terms of the constitution. It is not there said, that any such ratio shall be taken. The language is, that the representatives shall be apportioned among the several states according to their respective numbers, that is, according to the proportion of the whole population of each state to the aggregate of all the states. To apportion according to a ratio, short of the whole number in a state, is not an apportionment according to the respective numbers of the state. If it is said, that it is impracticable to follow the meaning of the terms literally, that may be admitted; but it does not follow, that they are to be wholly disregarded, or language substituted essentially different in its import and effect. If we must depart, we must depart as little as practicable. We are to act on the doctrine of cy pres, or come as nearly as possible to the rule of the constitution. If we are at liberty to adopt a rule varying from the terms of the constitution, arguing ab inconvenienti, then it is clearly just as open to others to reason on the other side from opposing inconvenience and injustice.

SEE ALSO:

Records of the Federal Convention, Farrand 1:31–32, 181–83, 184–85, 185–86, 192–93, 204–6, 207–8, 227, 229, 436–38, 438–41, 442–43, 444, 453–57, 458–59, 460, 470–74, 476–77, 479, 523, 524, 526, 535, 536, 537, 538, 557–58, 575–76, 589–91, 598–99; 2:12, 13–14, 130–31, 135, 138–39, 153–54, 164, 168, 571, 590–91

North Carolina Delegates to Governor Caswell, 18 Sept. 1787, Farrand 3:83

Roger Sherman and Oliver Ellsworth to Governor of Connecticut, 26 Sept. 1787, Farrand 3:99–100

Oliver Ellsworth, The Landholder no. 4, 26 Nov. 1787, Farrand 3:143

James McHenry, Maryland House of Delegates, 29 Nov. 1787, Farrand 3:147

Luther Martin, Maryland House of Delegates, 29 Nov. 1787, Farrand 3:152–54

Thomas McKean, Pennsylvania Ratifying Convention, 11 Dec. 1787, Elliot 2:533–34

Charles Pinckney, South Carolina Legislature, 16 Jan. 1788, Farrand 3:249

Charles Cotesworth Pinckney, South Carolina Legislature, 17 Jan. 1788, Elliot 4:282–85

Debate in Massachusetts Ratifying Convention, 17 Jan. 1788, Elliot 2:37–39

Rufus King, Massachusetts Ratifying Convention, 17 Jan. 1788, Farrand 3:255

Article 1, Section 2, Clause 4

When vacancies happen in the Representation from any State, the Executive Authority thereof shall issue Writs of Election to fill such Vacancies.

1

RECORDS OF THE FEDERAL CONVENTION

[2:140, 154, 164; Committee of Detail, IV, VI, IX]

17. Vacancies by death disability or resignation shall be supplied by a writ from the governor of the state, wherein they shall happen.

. . . . .

The House of Representatives shall be the grand Inquest of this Nation; and all Impeachments shall be made by them. Vacancies in the House of Representatives shall be supplied by Writs of Election from the Executive Authority of the State in the Representation from which they shall happen.

. . . . .

Vacancies in the House of Representatives shall be supplied by Writs of Election from the Executive Authority of the State, in the representation from which they shall happen.

[2:179; Madison, 6 Aug.]

Sect. 7. Vacancies in the House of Representatives shall be supplied by writs of election from the executive authority of the State, in the representation from which it shall happen.

[2:227; Journal, 9 Aug.]

It was moved and seconded to alter the 3rd. clause in the 1st section of the 5. article so as to read as follows, namely

"vacancies happening by refusals to accept resignations or otherwise may be supplied by the Legislature of the State in the representation of which such vacancies shall happen or by the executive thereof until the next meeting of the Legislature"

Which passed in the affirmative

[2:566, 591; Committee of Style]

Sect. 7. Vacancies in the House of Representatives shall be supplied by writs of election from the executive authority of the State, in the representation from which they shall happen.

. . . . .

When vacancies happen in the representation from any state, the Executive authority thereof shall issue writs of election to fill such vacancies.

2

HOUSE OF REPRESENTATIVES, REPRESENTATIVE FROM MARYLAND
22–23 Nov. 1791
Annals 3:205–7, 209

[*22 Nov.*]

The House resolved itself into a Committee of the Whole House on the report of the standing Committee of Elections, to whom was referred the Letter from the Executive of the State of Maryland, containing the resignation of WILLIAM PINKNEY, a member returned to serve in this House for the said State; and also a certificate of the election of JOHN FRANCIS MERCER, in the room of the said WILLIAM PINKNEY.

The law of the State of Maryland regulating elections being called for, was produced and read; by which it appeared that the Governor and Council of that State were authorized to fill up vacancies in the representation of that State in Congress.

Some objections having been offered against accepting the report,

Mr. SENEY observed, that the case appeared to him to be so plain that he was surprised to find gentlemen objecting to an acceptation of the report of the committee. He then stated the whole process of the business, in the resignation of Mr. PINKNEY and the election of Mr. MERCER, in which the law of the State had been strictly adhered to. He concluded by saying, that two cases in point had already occurred in the State of Connecticut, and no difficulty respecting them had taken place in the House.

Mr. GILES said, that he was a member of the select committee which had made the report; and, from an accurate attention to all the circumstances of the case, he was led to think the report a very improper one. From recurring to the Constitution, he was of opinion that a resignation did not constitute a vacancy. The Constitution speaks only of vacancies in general, and does not contemplate one as resulting from a resignation. Adverting to the British House of Commons, he observed that in that body there could be no resignation. This is an established principle. The people having once chosen their representatives, their power ceases, and consequently the body to which the resignation ought to be made no longer exists. From the experience of the British Government in this respect, he argued against a deviation from this rule. He showed from the Constitution, that the Executives of the States who are empowered to fill vacancies, are not at all authorized to declare the existence of such vacancies; for, if they are to judge in the case, the whole power is invested in them of determining the whole business of vacancies—an idea that materially and essentially affects the privileges of the members of the House. He remarked that, even by the law of Maryland, the requisite steps had not been pursued by the Executive of that State. He concluded by saying, that, if the principles he had advanced were just, he hoped the report would not be accepted.

Mr. SMITH (S. C.) had had his doubts on the report; but, on more mature consideration, he was convinced that on account of the inconvenience which would result from rejecting it, and from other considerations, it was proper to adopt it, but not without a full discussion. He then stated some particulars to show that the vacancy which had occurred on this occasion could not properly be called a resignation. Mr. PINKNEY had never taken his seat, nor the requisite oath. He said that there was no analogy between the Parliament of Great Britain and this House; the mode of issuing the writs originally, and of filling up vacancies, is essentially different. No parts of the Constitution prohibits a member from resigning, and for convenience it ought to be concluded that he may resign. The public interest may suffer extremely in cases of sickness or embarrassments, which may prevent a member from attending. This argument from the body's not existing to whom the resignation ought to be made, will apply to the President of the United States, whose resignation is expressly mentioned in the Constitution. The objection urged from the Executives of the States judging of vacancies, he conceived had no great force, for Congress would finally judge in every case of election. It is uncertain how the practice of the British Parliament originated. *Blackstone* says nothing of resignations. When a member wants to resign in that Legislature, he gets appointed to some fictitious office which disqualifies him from sitting in the House. He thought it best to establish some precedent, rather than oblige members who may wish to resign to have recourse to some familiar method, by accepting of some appointment in the State which is incompatible with a seat.

Mr. MURRAY said he was in favor of accepting the report, both on account of propriety and conveniency. Vacancies may happen from various causes—by resignation, by death, or by expulsion—the Executive of the State is the proper judge in the first case. He stated certain differences between a resignation after a person has taken his seat, and a resignation before that event. In the former case, Congress will of course give notice to the Executive of the State; in the latter, the Executive alone can take cognizance of the resignation. He stated the extreme inconveniency which would result from the ideas of the gentleman from Virginia, as it would respect the State of Georgia. He then stated several particulars to show that Mr. PINKNEY was not a member of the House agreeably to the Constitution, and therefore the House cannot proceed with him as one. He said that we ought to be willing to derive information from the experience of every country; but he conceived that no precedents could be drawn that would apply in the present case from a country which had none, to one which had a Constitution that so clearly defined and guarded the rights of the citizens. The custom which had been mentioned as obtaining in that country, arose from a wish to prevent a frequency of elections. From what had been offered by the gentleman from South Carolina, and the ideas he had suggested, he hoped the committee would be induced to accept the report.

Mr. WILLIAMSON said, that it appeared to him that the Constitution contemplates that a member may resign. He read the clause, which says that no member of the Legislature shall accept of an office made *during the time* for which he was chosen—from hence he inferred that resignations were clearly contemplated.

Mr. GERRY said, that he had heard nothing to show that Mr. PINKNEY had ever accepted of his appointment, and therefore it ought to have been expressed that he had declined; but, granting he had resigned after accepting his appointment, he asserted that nothing had been offered to prove that resignations might not take place in one House as well as in the other; and the Constitution plainly expresses that a Senator may resign. The House of Commons originated with the Kings, who formed that body to control the Lords; and hence arose the prohibition against resignations, as they would weaken the body, and the expense of a new election would fall on the King. With respect to the Executive declaring improper vacancies, he observed that Congress was invested with full power to control the Executives of the States in respect to such declarations.

Mr. SENEY observed, upon a distinction made by Mr. GILES between a resignation on the part of a Senator and a Member of the House, he supposed a resignation in either would equally vacate a seat, and that no difference did really exist.

Mr. SEDGWICK observed that, if a power of adjudication was vested in the Executives of the States to determine on a vacancy in cases of resignation, it would involve this consequence, that a power of judging of vacancies in all possible cases would be the necessary result. He thought the proposition involved the most serious effects with respect to the privileges and independency of this House.

This subject was further discussed the next day, and ended in an acceptation of the report of the committee, which was in favor of Mr. MERCER's election.

[*23 Nov.*]

The House again resolved itself into a Committee of the Whole House on the report of the Standing Committee of Elections, to whom was referred the letter from the Executive of Maryland, containing the resignation of WILLIAM PINKNEY, a member returned to serve in this House for the said State; and also a certificate of the election of JOHN FRANCIS MERCER, in the room of the said William Pinkney; and, after some time spent therein, the Chairman reported that the committee had again had the said report under consideration, and made an amendment thereto; which said report and amendment were twice read and agreed to by the House, as follows:

"It appears that, at an election held for the State of Maryland, on the first day of October, one thousand seven hundred and ninety, William Pinkney was duly elected a Representative for that State, to serve in the House of Representatives of the United States; that the certificate of his election has been duly transmitted by the Executive thereof, and heretofore so reported by your committee; that, by letter, dated the twenty-sixth of September, one thousand seven hundred and ninety-one, directed to the Governor and Council of that State, William Pinkney resigned that appointment; and that, in consequence of such resignation, the Executive issued a writ for an election, to supply the vacancy thereby occasioned, and have certified that John Francis Mercer was duly elected, by virtue of that writ, in pursuance of the law of the State of Maryland in that case provided.

"*Resolved,* That it is the opinion of this committee that John Francis Mercer is entitled to take a seat in this House as one of the Representatives for the State of Maryland, in the stead of William Pinkney."

3

JOSEPH STORY, COMMENTARIES ON THE
CONSTITUTION 2:§ 683
1833

---

§ 683. The propriety of adopting this clause does not seem to have furnished any matter of discussion, either in, or out of the convention. It was obvious, that the power ought to reside somewhere; and must be exercised either by the state or national government, or by some department thereof. The friends of state powers would naturally rest satisfied with leaving it with the state executive; and the friends of the national government would acquiesce in that arrangement, if other constitutional provisions existed sufficient to preserve its due execution. The provision, as it stands has the strong recommendation of public convenience, and facile adaptation to the particular local circumstances of each state. Any general regulation would have worked with some inequality.

Impeachment Clauses:

Article 1, Section 2, Clause 5

The House of Representatives shall chuse their Speaker and other Officers; and shall have the sole Power of Impeachment.

Article 1, Section 3, Clauses 6 and 7

The Senate shall have the sole Power to try all Impeachments. When sitting for that Purpose, they shall be on Oath or Affirmation. When the President of the United States is tried the Chief Justice shall preside: And no Person shall be convicted without the Concurrence of two thirds of the Members present.

Judgement in Cases of Impeachment shall not extend further than to removal from Office, and disqualification to hold and enjoy any Office of honor, Trust or Profit under the United States: but the Party convicted shall nevertheless be liable and subject to Indictment, Trial, Judgment and Punishment, according to Law.

Article 2, Section 4

The President, Vice President and all Civil Officers of the United States, shall be removed from Office on Impeachment for, and Conviction of, Treason, Bribery, or other high Crimes and Misdemeanors.

Article 3, Section 1

. . . The Judges, both of the supreme and inferior Courts, shall hold their Offices during good Behaviour. . . .

1. Jefferson's Manual of Parliamentary Practice and Rules of the House of Representatives, sec. 53
2. North Carolina Constitution of 1776, art. 23
3. Delaware Constitution of 1776, art. 23
4. Virginia Constitution of 1776
5. New York Constitution of 1777, arts. 32–34
6. Vermont Constitution of 1777, ch. 2, sec. 20
7. Records of the Federal Convention
8. Luther Martin, Genuine Information, 1788
9. Alexander Hamilton, Federalist, no. 65, 7 Mar. 1788
10. Alexander Hamilton, Federalist, no. 66, 8 Mar. 1788
11. Brutus, no. 15, 20 Mar. 1788
12. A Native of Virginia, Observations upon the Proposed Plan of Federal Government, 1788
13. Debate in North Carolina Ratifying Convention, 24–25, 28 July 1788
14. James Madison, Observations on Jefferson's Draft of a Constitution for Virginia, 15 Oct. 1788, in vol. 1, ch. 17, no. 25
15. James Wilson, Legislative Department, Lectures on Law, 1791
16. Luther Martin, Impeachment Trial of Justice Samuel Chase, Senate, 23 Feb. 1804
17. William Rawle, A View of the Constitution of the United States (2d ed. 1829)
18. Joseph Story, Commentaries on the Constitution (1833)

1

JEFFERSON'S MANUAL OF PARLIAMENTARY
PRACTICE AND RULES OF THE HOUSE OF
REPRESENTATIVES, SEC. 53

House Doc. no. 7, 93d Cong., 1st Sess. (1973)

§ 601. Jurisdiction of Lords and Commons as to impeachments.

These are the provisions of the Constitution of the United States on the subject of impeachments. The following is a sketch of some of the principles and practices of England on the same subject:

Jurisdiction. The Lords can not impeach any to themselves, nor join in the accusation, because they are the judges. *Seld. Judic. in Parl.*, 12, 63. Nor can they proceed against a commoner but on complaint of the Commons. *Ib.*, 84. The Lords may not, by the law, try a commoner for a capital offense, on the information of the King or a private person, because the accused is entitled to a trial by his peers generally; but on accusation by the House of Commons, they may proceed against the delinquent, of whatsoever degree, and whatsoever be the nature of the offense; for there they do not assume to themselves trial at common law. The Commons are then instead of a jury, and the judgment is given on their demand, which is instead of a verdict. So the Lords do only judge, but not try the delinquent. *Ib.*, 6, 7. But Wooddeson denies that a commoner can now be charged capitally before the Lords, even by the Commons; and cites Fitzharris's case, 1681, impeached of high treason, where the Lords remitted the prosecution to the inferior court. *8 Grey's Deb.*, 325–7; *2 Wooddeson*, 576, 601; *3 Seld.*, 1604, 1610, 1618, 1619, 1641; *4 Blackst.*, 25; *9 Seld.*, 1656; *73 Seld.*, 1604–18.

§ 602. Parliamentary law as to accusation in impeachment.

Accusation. The Commons, as the grand inquest of the nation, becomes suitors for penal justice. *2 Wood.*, 597; *6 Grey*, 356. The general course is to pass a resolution containing a criminal charge against the supposed delinquent, and then to direct some member to impeach him by oral accusation, at the bar of the House of Lords, in the name of the Commons. The persons signifies that the articles will be exhibited, and desires that the delinquent may be sequestered from his seat, or be committed, or that the peers will take order for his appearance. *Sachev. Trial*, 325; *2 Wood.*, 602, 605; *Lords' Journ.*, 3 June, 1701; *1 Wms.*, 616; *6 Grey*, 324.

. . . . .

§ 608. The writ of summons for appearance of respondent.

Process. If the party do not appear, proclamations are to be issued, giving him a day to appear. On their return they are strictly examined. If any error be found in them,

a new proclamation issues, giving a short day. If he appear not, his goods may be arrested, and they may proceed. *Seld. Jud.*, 98, 99.

. . . . .

§ 609. Exhibition and form of articles.

Articles. The accusation (articles) of the Commons is substituted in place of an indictment. Thus, by the usage of Parliament, in impeachment for writing or speaking, the particular words need not be specified. *Sach. Tr.*, 325; *2 Wood.*, 602, 605; *Lords' Journ.*, 3 June, 1701; *1 Wms.*, 616.

. . . . .

§ 610. Parliamentary law as to appearance of respondent.

Appearance. If he appear and the case be capital, he answers in custody; though not if the accusation be general. He is not to be committed but on special accusations. If it be for a misdemeanor only, he answers, a lord in his place, a commoner at the bar, and not in custody, unless, on the answer, the Lords find cause to commit him, till he finds sureties to attend, and lest he should fly. *Seld. Jud.*, 98, 99. A copy of the articles is given him, and a day fixed for his answer. *T. Ray.; 1 Rushw.*, 268; *Fost.*, 232; *1 Clar. Hist. of the Reb.*, 379. On a misdemeanor, his appearance may be in person, or he may answer in writing, or by attorney. *Seld. Jud.*, 100. The general rule on accusation for a misdemeanor is, that in such a state of liberty or restraint as the party is when the Commons complain of him, in such he is to answer. *Ib.*, 101. If previously committed by the commons, he answers as a prisoner. But this may be called in some sort judicium parium suorum. *Ib.* In misdemeanors the party has a right to counsel by the common law, but not in capital cases. *Seld. Jud.*, 102, 105.

. . . . .

§ 612. Answer of respondent.

Answer. The answer need not observe great strictness of form. He may plead guilty as to part, and defend as to the residue; or, saving all exceptions, deny the whole or give a particular answer to each article separately. *1 Rush.*, 274; *2 Rush.*, 1374; *12 Parl. Hist.*, 442; *3 Lords' Journ.*, 13 Nov., 1643; *2 Wood.*, 607. But he cannot plead a pardon in bar to the impeachment. *2 Wood.*, 615; *2 St. Tr.*, 735.

. . . . .

§ 613. Other pleadings.

Replication, rejoinder, &c. There may be a replication, rejoinder, &c. *Sel. Jud.*, 114; *8 Grey's Deb.*, 233; *Sach. Tr.*, 15; *Journ. H. of Commons*, 6 March, 1640–1.

. . . . .

§ 614. Examination of witnesses.

Witnesses. The practice is to swear the witnesses in open House, and then examine them there; or a committee may be named, who shall examine them in committee, either on interrogatories agreed on in the House, or such as the committee in their discretion shall demand. *Seld. Jud.*, 120, 123.

. . . . .

§ 615. *Relation of jury trial to impeachment.*

Jury. In the case of Alice Pierce, *1 R., 2,* a jury was impaneled for her trial before a committee. *Seld. Jud., 123.* But this was on a complaint, not on impeachment by the Commons. *Seld. Jud., 163.* It must also have been for a misdemeanor only, as the Lords spiritual sat in the case, which they do on misdemeanors, but not in capital cases. *Id., 148.* The judgment was a forfeiture of all her lands and goods. *Id., 188.* This, Selden says, is the only jury he finds recorded in Parliament for misdemeanors; but he makes no doubt, if the delinquent doth put himself on the trial of his country, a jury ought to be impaneled, and he adds that it is not so on impeachment by the Commons, for they are in loco proprio, and there no jury ought to be impaneled. *Id., 124.* The Ld. Berkeley, *6 E., 3,* was arraigned for the murder of L. 2, on an information on the part of the King, and not on impeachment of the Commons; for then they had been patria sua. He waived his peerage, and was tried by a jury of Gloucestershire and Warwickshire. *Id., 126.* In *1 H., 7,* the Commons protest that they are not to be considered as parties to any judgment given, or hereafter to be given in Parliament. *Id., 133.* They have been generally and more justly considered, as is before stated, as the grand jury; for the conceit of Selden is certainly not accurate, that they are the patria sua of the accused, and that the Lords do only judge, but not try. It is undeniable that they do try; for they examine witnesses as to the facts, and acquit or condemn, according to their own belief of them. And Lord Hale says, "the peers are judges of law as well as of fact;" *2 Hale, P. C., 275;* consequently of fact as well as of law.

．．．．．

§ 616. *Attendance of the Commons.*

Presence of Commons. The Commons are to be present at the examination of witnesses. *Seld. Jud., 124.* Indeed, they are to attend throughout, either as a committee of the whole House, or otherwise, at discretion, appoint managers to conduct the proofs. *Rushw. of Straff., 37; Com. Journ., 4 Feb., 1709–10; 2 Wood., 614.* And judgment is not given till they demand it. *Seld. Jud., 124.* But they are not to be present on impeachment when the Lords consider of the answer or proofs and determine of their judgment. Their presence, however, is necessary at the answer and judgment in case capital *Id., 58, 158,* as well as not capital; *162.*

．．．．．

§ 618. *Voting on the articles in an impeachment trial.*

* * * The Lords debate the judgment among themselves. Then the vote is first taken on the question of guilty or not guilty; and if they convict, the question, or particular sentence, is out of that which seemeth to be most generally agreed on. *Seld. Jud., 167; 2 Wood., 612.*

．．．．．

§ 619. *Judgment in impeachments.*

Judgement. Judgments in Parliament, for death, have been strictly guided per legem terrae, which they can not alter; and not at all according to their discretion. They can neither omit any part of the legal judgment nor add to it. Their sentence must be secundum non ultra legem. *Seld. Jud., 168, 171.* This trial, though it varies in external ceremony, yet differs not in essentials from criminal prosecutions before inferior courts. The same rules of evidence, the same legal notions of crimes and punishments, prevailed; for impeachments are not framed to alter the law, but to carry it into more effectual execution against too powerful delinquents. The judgment, therefore, is to be such as is warranted by legal principles or precedents. *6 Sta. Tr., 14; 2 Wood., 611.* The Chancellor gives judgments in misdemeanors; the Lord High Steward formerly in cases of life and death. *Seld. Jud., 180.* But now the Steward is deemed not necessary. *Fost., 144; 2 Wood., 613.* In misdemeanors the greatest corporal punishment hath been imprisonment. *Seld. Jud., 184.* The King's assent is necessary to capital judgments (but *2 Wood., 614,* contra), but not in misdemeanors. *Seld. Jud., 136.*

．．．．．

§ 620. *Impeachment not interrupted by adjournments.*

Continuance. An impeachment is not discontinued by the dissolution of Parliament, but may be resumed by the new Parliament. *T. Ray 383; 4 Com. Journ., 23 Dec., 1790; Lord's Jour., May 15, 1791; 2 Wood., 618.*

2

NORTH CAROLINA CONSTITUTION OF 1776, ART. 23

Thorpe 5:2792

That the Governor, and other officers, offending against the State, by violating any part of this Constitution, maladministration, or corruption, may be prosecuted, on the impeachment of the General Assembly, or presentment of the Grand Jury of any court of supreme jurisdiction in this State.

3

DELAWARE CONSTITUTION OF 1776, ART. 23

Thorpe 1:566

The president, when he is out of office, and within eighteen months after, and all others offending against the State, either by maladministration, corruption, or other means, by which the safety of the Commonwealth may be endangered, within eighteen months after the offence committed, shall be impeachable by the house of assembly before the legislative council; such impeachment to be prosecuted by the attorney-general, or such other person or persons as the house of assembly may appoint, according to the laws of the land. If found guilty, he or they shall be either forever disabled to hold any office under government, or removed from office *pro tempore*, or subjected to such pains and penalties as the laws shall direct. And all officers shall be removed on conviction of misbehavior at common law, or on impeachment, or upon the address of the general assembly.

4

VIRGINIA CONSTITUTION OF 1776
Thorpe 7:3818

The Governor, when he is out of office, and others, offending against the State, either by mal-administration, corruption, or other means, by which the safety of the State may be endangered, shall be impeachable by the House of Delegates. Such impeachment to be prosecuted by the Attorney-General, or such other person or persons, as the House may appoint in the General Court, according to the laws of the land. If found guilty, he or they shall be either forever disabled to hold any office under government, or be removed from such office *pro tempore*, or subjected to such pains or penalties as the laws shall direct.

If all or any of the Judges of the General Court should on good grounds (to be judged of by the House of Delegates) be accused of any of the crimes or offences above mentioned, such House of Delegates may, in like manner, impeach the Judge or Judges so accused, to be prosecuted in the Court of Appeals; and he or they, if found guilty, shall be punished in the same manner as is prescribed in the preceding clause.

5

NEW YORK CONSTITUTION OF 1777,
ARTS. 32–34
Thorpe 5:2635

ART. XXXII. And this convention doth further, in the name and by the authority of the good people of this State, ordain, determine, and declare, that a court shall be instituted for the trial of impeachments, and the correction of errors, under the regulations which shall be established by the legislature; and to consist of the president of the senate, for the time being, and the senators, chancellor, and judges of the supreme court, or the major part of them; except that when an impeachment shall be prosecuted against the chancellor, or either of the judges of the supreme court, the person so impeached shall be suspended from exercising his office until his acquittal; and,

in like manner, when an appeal from a decree in equity shall be heard, the chancellor shall inform the court of the reasons of his decree, but shall not have a voice in the final sentence. And if the cause to be determined shall be brought up by writ of error, on a question of law, on a judgment in the supreme court, the judges of that court shall assign the reasons of such their judgment, but shall not have a voice for its affirmance or reversal.

ART. XXXIII. That the power of impeaching all officers of the State, for mal and corrupt conduct in their respective offices, be vested in the representatives of the people in assembly; but that it shall always be necessary that two third parts of the members present shall consent to and agree in such impeachment. That previous to the trial of every impeachment, the members of the said court shall respectively be sworn truly and impartially to try and determine the charge in question, according to evidence; and that no judgment of the said court shall be valid unless it be assented to by two third parts of the members then present; nor shall it extend farther than to removal from office, and disqualification to hold or enjoy any place of honor, trust, or profit under this State. But the party so convicted shall be, nevertheless, liable and subject to indictment, trial judgment, and punishment, according to the laws of the land.

ART. XXXIV. *And it is further ordained,* That in every trial on impeachment, or indictment for crimes or misdemeanors, the party impeached or indicted shall be allowed counsel, as in civil actions.

6

VERMONT CONSTITUTION OF 1777, CH. 2, SEC. 20
Thorpe 6:3745

Every officer of State, whether judicial or executive, shall be liable to be impeached by the General Assembly, either when in office, or after his resignation, or removal for mal-administration. All impeachments shall be before the Governor or Lieutenant Governor and Council, who shall hear and determine the same.

7

RECORDS OF THE FEDERAL CONVENTION

[1:85; Madison, 2 June]

Mr. Dickenson moved "that the Executive be made removeable by the National Legislature on the request of a majority of the Legislatures of individual States". It was necessary he said to place the power of removing somewhere. He did not like the plan of impeaching the Great Officers of State. He did not know how provision could be made for removal of them in a better mode than that which he had proposed. He had no idea of abolishing the State Governments as some gentlemen seemed inclined to do. The happiness of this Country in his opinion required considerable powers to be left in the hands of the States.

Mr. Bedford seconded the motion.

Mr. Sherman contended that the National Legislature should have power to remove the Executive at pleasure.

Mr. Mason. Some mode of displacing an unfit magistrate is rendered indispensable by the fallibility of those who choose, as well as by the corruptibility of the man chosen. He opposed decidedly the making the Executive the mere creature of the Legislature as a violation of the fundamental principle of good Government.

Mr. Madison & Mr. Wilson observed that it would leave an equality of agency in the small with the great States; that it would enable a minority of the people to prevent ye removal of an officer who had rendered himself justly criminal in the eyes of a majority; that it would open a door for intrigues agst. him in States where his administration tho' just might be unpopular, and might tempt him to pay court to particular States whose leading partizans he might fear, or wish to engage as his partizens. They both thought it bad policy to introduce such a mixture of the State authorities, when their agency could be otherwise supplied.

Mr. Dickenson considered the business as so important that no man ought to be silent or reserved. He went into a discourse of some length, the sum of which was, that the Legislative, Executive, & Judiciary departments ought to be made as independt. as possible; but that such an Executive as some seemed to have in contemplation was not consistant with a republic; that a firm Executive could only exist in a limited monarchy. In the British Govt. itself the weight of the Executive arises from the attachments which the Crown draws to itself, & not merely from the force of its prerogatives. In place of these attachments we must look out for something else. One source of stability is the double branch of the Legislature. The division of the Country into distinct States formed the other principal source of stability. This division ought therefore to be maintained, and considerable powers to be left with the States. This was the ground of his consolation for the future fate of his Country. Without this, and in case of a consolidation of the States into one great Republic we might read its fate in the history of smaller ones. A limited Monarchy he considered as *one* of the best Governments in the world. It was not *certain* that the same blessings were derivable from any other form. It was certain that equal blessings had never yet been derived from any of the republican form. A limited monarchy however was out of the question. The spirit of the times—the state of our affairs, forbade the experiment, if it were desireable. Was it possible moreover in the nature of things to introduce it even if these obstacles were less insuperable. A House of Nobles was essential to such a Govt. Could these be created by a breath, or by a stroke of the pen? No. They were the growth of ages, and could only arise under a complication of circumstances none of which existed in this Country. But though a form the most perfect *perhaps* in itself be

unattainable. we must not despair. If antient republics have been found to flourish for a moment only & then vanish forever, it only proves that they were badly constituted; and that we ought to seek for every remedy for their diseases. One of these remedies he conceived to be the accidental lucky division of this country into distinct States; a division which some seemed desirous to abolish altogether.

As to the point of representation in the national legislature as it might affect States of different sizes, he said it must probably end in mutual concession. He hoped that each State would retain an equal voice at least in one branch of the National Legislature, and supposed the sums paid within each state would form a better ratio for the other branch than either the number of inhabitants or the quantum of property.

A motion, being made to strike out "on request by a majority of the Legislatures of the individual States" and rejected, Connecticut. S. Carol: & Geo. being ay. the rest no: the question was taken—

On Mr. Dickenson's motion for making Executive removable by Natl. Legislature at request of majority of State Legislatures was also rejected all the States being in the negative except Delaware which gave an affirmative vote.

[1:292; Madison, 18 June]

IX. The Governour Senators and all officers of the United States to be liable to impeachment for mal—and corrupt conduct; and upon conviction to be removed from office, & disqualified for holding any place of trust or profit—all impeachments to be tried by a Court to consist of the Chief   or Judge of the Superior Court of Law of each State, provided such Judge shall hold his place during good behavior and have a permanent salary.

[2:53; Madison, 19 July]

[G. Morris] The Executive is also to be impeachable. This is a dangerous part of the plan. It will hold him in such dependence that he will be no check on the Legislature, will not be a firm guardian of the people and of the public interest. He will be the tool of a faction, of some leading demagogue in the Legislature. These then are the faults of the Executive establishment as now proposed. Can no better establishmt. be devised? If he is to be the Guardian of the people let him be appointed by the people? If he is to be a check on the Legislature let him not be impeachable. Let him be of short duration, that he may with propriety be re-eligible.—It has been said that the candidates for this office will not be known to the people. If they be known to the Legislature, they must have such a notoriety and eminence of Character, that they cannot possibly be unknown to the people at large. It cannot be possible that a man shall have sufficiently distinguished himself to merit this high trust without having his character proclaimed by fame throughout the Empire. As to the danger from an unimpeachable magistrate he could not regard it as formidable. There must be certain great officers of State; a minister of finance, of war, of foreign affairs &c. These he presumes will exercise their functions in subordination to the Executive, and will be amenable by impeachment to the public Justice. Without these ministers the Executive can do nothing of consequence.

[2:64; *Madison, 20 July*]

"to be removeable on impeachment and conviction for malpractice or neglect of duty". See Resol: 9:

Mr. Pinkney & Mr Govr. Morris moved to strike out this part of the Resolution. Mr P. observd. he ought not to be impeachable whilst in office

Mr. Davie. If he be not impeachable whilst in office, he will spare no efforts or means whatever to get himself re-elected. He considered this as an essential security for the good behaviour of the Executive.

Mr. Wilson concurred in the necessity of making the Executive impeachable whilst in office.

Mr. Govr. Morris. He can do no criminal act without Coadjutors who may be punished. In case he should be re-elected, that will be sufficient proof of his innocence. Besides who is to impeach? Is the impeachment to suspend his functions. If it is not the mischief will go on. If it is the impeachment will be nearly equivalent to a displacement, and will render the Executive dependent on those who are to impeach

Col. Mason. No point is of more importance than that the right of impeachment should be continued. Shall any man be above Justice? Above all shall that man be above it, who can commit the most extensive injustice? When great crimes were committed he was for punishing the principal as well as the Coadjutors. There had been much debate & difficulty as to the mode of chusing the Executive. He approved of that which had been adopted at first, namely of referring the appointment to the Natl. Legislature. One objection agst. Electors was the danger of their being corrupted by the Candidates: & this furnished a peculiar reason in favor of impeachments whilst in office. Shall the man who has practised corruption & by that means procured his appointment in the first instance, be suffered to escape punishment, by repeating his guilt?

Docr. Franklin was for retaining the clause as favorable to the executive. History furnishes one example only of a first Magistrate being formally brought to public Justice. Every body cried out agst this as unconstitutional. What was the practice before this in cases where the chief Magistrate rendered himself obnoxious? Why recourse was had to assassination in wch. he was not only deprived of his life but of the opportunity of vindicating his character. It wd. be the best way therefore to provide in the Constitution for the regular punishment of the Executive when his misconduct should deserve it, and for his honorable acquittal when he should be unjustly accused.

Mr. Govr Morris admits corruption & some few other offences to be such as ought to be impeachable; but thought the cases ought to be enumerated & defined:

Mr. Madison—thought it indispensable that some provision should be made for defending the Community agst the incapacity, negligence or perfidy of the chief Magistrate. The limitation of the period of his service, was not a sufficient security. He might lose his capacity after his appointment. He might pervert his administration into a scheme of peculation or oppression. He might betray his trust to foreign powers. The case of the Executive Magistracy was very distinguishable, from that of the Legislative or of any other public body, holding offices of limited duration. It could not be presumed that all or even a majority of the members of an Assembly would either lose their capacity for discharging, or be bribed to betray, their trust. Besides the restraints of their personal integrity & honor, the difficulty of acting in concert for purposes of corruption was a security to the public. And if one or a few members only should be seduced, the soundness of the remaining members, would maintain the integrity and fidelity of the body. In the case of the Executive Magistracy which was to be administered by a single man, loss of capacity or corruption was more within the compass of probable events, and either of them might be fatal to the Republic.

Mr. Pinkney did not see the necessity of impeachments. He was sure they ought not to issue from the Legislature who would in that case hold them as a rod over the Executive and by that means effectually destroy his independence. His revisionary power in particular would be rendered altogether insignificant.

Mr. Gerry urged the necessity of impeachments. A good magistrate will not fear them. A bad one ought to be kept in fear of them. He hoped the maxim would never be adopted here that the chief Magistrate could do no wrong.

Mr. King expressed his apprehensions that an extreme caution in favor of liberty might enervate the Government we were forming. He wished the House to recur to the primitive axiom that the three great departments of Govts. should be separate & independent: that the Executive & Judiciary should be so as well as the Legislative: that the Executive should be so equally with the Judiciary. Would this be the case if the Executive should be impeachable? It had been said that the Judiciary would be impeachable. But it should have been remembered at the same time that the Judiciary hold their places not for a limited time, but during good behaviour. It is necessary therefore that a forum should be established for trying misbehaviour. Was the Executive to hold his place during good behaviour?— The Executive was to hold his place for a limited term like the members of the Legislature; Like them particularly the Senate whose members would continue in appointmt the same term of 6 years. he would periodically be tried for his behaviour by his electors, who would continue or discontinue him in trust according to the manner in which he had discharged it. Like them therefore, he ought to be subject to no intermediate trial, by impeachment. He ought not to be impeachable unless he hold his office during good behavior, a tenure which would be most agreeable to him; provided an independent and effectual forum could be devised; But under no circumstances ought he to be impeachable by the Legislature. This would be destructive of his independence and of the principles of the Constitution. He relied on the vigor of the Executive as a great security for the public liberties.

Mr. Randolph. The propriety of impeachments was a favorite principle with him; Guilt wherever found ought to be punished. The Executive will have great opportunitys of abusing his power; particularly in time of war when the military force, and in some respects the public money will be in his hands. Should no regular punishment be provided, it will be irregularly inflicted by tumults & insurrections. He is aware of the necessity of proceeding with a cautious hand, and of excluding as much as possible the influence of the Legislature from the business. He suggested for consideration an idea which had fallen (from Col Hamilton) of composing a forum out of the Judges belonging to the States: and even of requiring some preliminary inquest whether just grounds of impeachment existed.

Doctr. Franklin mentioned the case of the Prince of Orange during the late war. An agreement was made between France & Holland; by which their two fleets were to unite at a certain time & place. The Dutch fleet did not appear. Every body began to wonder at it. At length it was suspected that the Statholder was at the bottom of the matter. This suspicion prevailed more & more. Yet as he could not be impeached and no regular examination took place, he remained in his office, and strengtheing his own party, as the party opposed to him became formidable, he gave birth to the most violent animosities & contentions. Had he been impeachable, a regular & peaceable inquiry would have taken place and he would if guilty have been duly punished, if innocent restored to the confidence of the public.

Mr. King remarked that the case of the Statholder was not applicable. He held his place for life, and was not periodically elected. In the former case impeachments are proper to secure good behaviour. In the latter they are unnecessary; the periodical responsibility to the electors being an equivalent security.

Mr. Wilson observed that if the idea were to be pursued, the Senators who are to hold their places during the same term with the Executive. ought to be subject to impeachment & removal.

Mr. Pinkney apprehended that some gentlemen reasoned on a supposition that the Executive was to have powers which would not be committed to him: He presumed that his powers would be so circumscribed as to render impeachments unnecessary.

Mr. Govr. Morris,'s opinion had been changed by the arguments used in the discussion. He was now sensible of the necessity of impeachments, if the Executive was to continue for any time in office. Our Executive was not like a Magistrate having a life interest, much less like one having an hereditary interest in his office. He may be bribed by a greater interest to betray his trust; and no one would say that we ought to expose ourselves to the danger of seeing the first Magistrate in foreign pay without being able to guard agst it by displacing him. One would think the King of England well secured agst bribery. He has as it were a fee simple in the whole Kingdom. Yet Charles II was bribed by Louis XIV. The Executive ought therefore to be impeachable for treachery; Corrupting his electors, and incapacity were other causes of impeachment. For the latter he should be punished not as a man, but as an officer, and punished only by degradation from his office. This Magistrate is not the King but the prime-Minister. The people are the King. When we make him amenable to Justice however we should take care to provide some mode that will not make him dependent on the Legislature.

It was moved & 2ded. to postpone the question of impeachments which was negatived. Mas. & S. Carolina only being ay.

On ye. Question, Shall the Executive be removeable on impeachments?

Mas. no. Ct. ay. N. J. ay. Pa. ay. Del. ay. Md. ay. Va. ay. N. C. ay. S. C. no. Geo-ay- [Ayes—8; noes—2.]

[2:427; Madison, 27 Aug.]

The clause for removing the President on impeachment by the House of Reps and conviction in the supreme Court, of Treason, Bribery or corruption, was postponed nem: con: at the instance of Mr. Govr. Morris, who thought the Tribunal an improper one, particularly, if the first judge was to be of the privy Council.

Mr. Govr. Morris objected also to the President of the Senate being provisional successor to the President, and suggested a designation of the Chief Justice.

Mr. Madison added as a ground of objection that the Senate might retard the appointment of a President in order to carry points whilst the revisionary power was in the President of their own body, but suggested that the Executive powers during a vacancy, be administered by the persons composing the Council to the President.

Mr. Williamson suggested that the Legislature ought to have power to provide for occasional successors. & moved that the last clause (of 2 sect. X art:) relating to a provisional successor to the President be postponed.

Mr. Dickinson 2ded. the postponement. remarking that it was too vague. What is the extent of the term "disability" & who is to be the judge of it?

[2:499; Madison, 4 Sept.]

The latter part of Sect. 2. Art: 10. to read as follows.

(9) "He shall be removed from his office on impeachment by the House of Representatives, and conviction by the Senate, for Treason, or bribery, and in case of his removal as aforesaid, death, absence, resignation or inability to discharge the powers or duties of his office, the vice-president shall exercise those powers and duties until another President be chosen, or until the inability of the President be removed."

[2:550; Madison, 8 Sept.]

The clause referring to the Senate, the trial of impeachments agst. the President, for Treason & bribery, was taken up.

Col. Mason. Why is the provision restrained to Treason & bribery only? Treason as defined in the Constitution will not reach many great and dangerous offences. Hastings is not guilty of Treason. Attempts to subvert the Constitution may not be Treason as above defined—As bills of attainder which have saved the British Constitution are forbidden, it is the more necessary to extend: the power of impeachments. He movd. to add after "bribery" "or maladministration". Mr. Gerry seconded him—

Mr Madison So vague a term will be equivalent to a tenure during pleasure of the Senate.

Mr Govr Morris, it will not be put in force & can do no harm— An election of every four years will prevent maladministration.

Col. Mason withdrew "maladministration" & substitutes "other high crimes & misdemeanors" agst. the State"

On the question thus altered

N. H— ay. Mas. ay— Ct. ay. N. J. no Pa no. Del. no. Md ay. Va. ay. N. C. ay. S. C. ay. Geo. ay. [Ayes—8; noes—3.]

Mr. Madison, objected to a trial of the President by the Senate, especially as he was to be impeached by the other branch of the Legislature, and for any act which might be called a misdemesnor. The President under these circumstances was made improperly dependent. He would prefer the supreme Court for the trial of impeachments, or rather a tribunal of which that should form a part.

Mr Govr Morris thought no other tribunal than the Senate could be trusted. The Supreme Court were too few in number and might be warped or corrupted. He was agst. a dependence of the Executive on the Legislature, considering the Legislative tyranny the great danger to be apprehended; but there could be no danger that the Senate would say untruly on their oaths that the President was guilty of crimes or facts, especially as in four years he can be turned out.—

Mr. Pinkney disapproved of making the Senate the Court of Impeachments, as rendering the President too dependent on the Legislature. If he opposes a favorite law, the two Houses will combine agst him, and under the influence of heat and faction throw him out of office.

Mr. Williamson thought there was more danger of too much lenity than of too much rigour towards the President, considering the number of cases in which the Senate was associated with the President—

Mr Sherman regarded the Supreme Court as improper to try the President, because the Judges would be appointed by him.

On motion by Mr. Madison to strike out the words—"by the Senate" after the word "Conviction"

N—H. no. Mas—no. Ct. no. N. J. no—Pa. ay—Del—no. Md. no. Va. ay—N. C. no. S—C—no. Geo. no. [Ayes—2; noes—9.]

In the amendment of Col: Mason just agreed to, the word "State" after the words misdemeanors against" was struck out, and the words "United States" inserted, unanimously in order to remove ambiguity—

On the question to agree to clause as amended,

N. H. ay. Mas. ay. Cont ay N. J. ay. Pa. no. Del. ay Md. ay— Va. ay. N— C. ay. S. C. ay. Geo. ay [Ayes—10; noes—1.]

On motion "The vice-President and other Civil officers of the U. S. shall be removed from office on impeachment and conviction as aforesaid" was added to the clause on the subject of impeachments.

. . . . .

Mr. Govr Morris moved to add to clause (3) of the report made on Sept. 4. the words "and every member shall be on oath" which being agreed to, and a question taken on the clause so amended viz—"The Senate of the U. S. shall have power to try all impeachments: but no person shall be convicted without the concurrence of two thirds of the members present: and every member shall be on oath"

N. H. ay— Mas. ay. Ct. ay. N. J— ay. Pa. no— Del— ay—Md ay. Va. no. N. C. ay. S. C. ay. Geo. ay. [Ayes—9; noes—2.]

[2:563; Madison, 10 Sept.]

Mr. Randolph took this opportunity to state his objections to the System. They turned on the Senate's being made the Court of Impeachment for trying the Executive—

[2:612; Madison, 14 Sept.]

Mr Rutlidge and Mr. Govr. Morris moved "that persons impeached be suspended from their office until they be tried and acquitted"

Mr. Madison— The President is made too dependent already on the Legislature, by the power of one branch to try him in consequence of an impeachment by the other. This intermediate suspension, will put him in the power of one branch only—They can at any moment, in order to make way for the functions of another who will be more favorable to their views, vote a temporary removal of the existing magistrate—

Mr. King concurred in the opposition to the amendment

On the question to agree to it

N—H. no. Mas. no—Ct. ay—N—J. no. Pa. no. Del—no. Md no. Va. no. N—C. no. S. C. ay, Geo. ay, [Ayes—3; noes—8.]

8

LUTHER MARTIN, GENUINE INFORMATION
1788

Storing 2.4.87–88

It was further observed, that the only appearance of responsibility in the President, which the system holds up to our view, is the provision for impeachment; but that when we reflect that he cannot be impeached but by the house of delegates, and that the members of this house are rendered dependant upon, and unduly under the influence of the President, by being appointable to offices of which he has the sole nomination, so that without his favour and approbation, they cannot obtain them, there is little reason to believe, that a majority will ever concur in impeaching the President, let his conduct be ever so reprehensible, especially too, as the final event of that impeachment will depend upon a different body, and the members of the house of delegates will be certain, should the decision be ultimately in favour of the President, to become thereby the objects of his displeasure, and to bar to themselves every avenue to the emoluments of government.

Should he, contrary to probability, be impeached, he is afterwards to be tried and adjudged by the senate, and without the concurrence of two-thirds of the members who shall be present, he cannot be convicted—This senate being constituted a privy council to the President, it is probable many of its leading and influential members may have advised or concurred in the very measures for which he may be impeached; the members of the Senate also are by the system, placed as unduly under the influence of, and dependant upon the President, as the members of the other branch, since they also are appointable to offices, and cannot obtain them but through the favour of the President—There will be great, important and valuable offices under this government, should it take place, more than sufficient to enable him to hold out the expectation of one of them to *each* of the senators—Under these circumstances, will any person conceive it to be difficult for the President always to secure to himself more than one-third of that body? Or, can it reasonably be believed, that a criminal will be convicted, who is constitutionally empowered to bribe his judges, at the head of whom is to preside on those occasions the chief Justice. Which officer in his original appointment, must be *nominated* by the President, and will therefore, probably, be appointed [not] so much for his eminence in legal knowledge and for his integrity, as from favouritism and influence, since the President knowing that in case of impeachment the chief Justice is to preside at his trial, will naturally wish to fill that office with a person of whose voice and influence he shall consider himself secure. These are reasons to induce a belief, that there will be but little probability of the President ever being either impeached or convicted; but it was also urged, that vested with the powers which the system gives him, and with the influence attendant upon those powers, to him it would be of little consequence whether he was impeached or convicted, since he will be able to set both at defiance. These considerations occasioned a part of the convention to give a negative to this part of the system establishing the executive as it is now offered for our acceptance.

9

ALEXANDER HAMILTON, FEDERALIST, NO. 65,
439–45
7 March 1788

A well constituted court for the trial of impeachments, is an object not more to be desired than difficult to be obtained in a government wholly elective. The subjects of its jurisdiction are those offenses which proceed from the misconduct of public men, or in other words from the abuse or violation of some public trust. They are of a nature which may with peculiar propriety be denominated POLITICAL, as they relate chiefly to injuries done immediately to the society itself. The prosecution of them, for this reason, will seldom fail to agitate the passions of the whole community, and to divide it into parties, more or less friendly or inimical, to the accused. In many cases, it will connect itself with the pre-existing factions, and will inlist all their animosities, partialities, influence and interest on one side, or on the other; and in such cases there will always be the greatest danger, that the decision will be regulated more by the comparitive strength of parties than by the real demonstrations of innocence or guilt.

The delicacy and magnitude of a trust, which so deeply concerns the political reputation and existence of every man engaged in the administration of public affairs, speak for themselves. The difficulty of placing it rightly in a government resting entirely on the basis of periodical elections will as readily be perceived, when it is considered that the most conspicuous characters in it will, from that circumstance, be too often the leaders, or the tools of the most cunning or the most numerous faction; and on this account can hardly be expected to possess the requisite neutrality towards those, whose conduct may be the subject of scrutiny.

The Convention, it appears, thought the Senate the most fit depositary of this important trust. Those who can best discern the intrinsic difficulty of the thing will be least hasty in condemning that opinion; and will be most inclined to allow due weight to the arguments which may be supposed to have produced it.

What it may be asked is the true spirit of the institution itself? Is it not designed as a method of NATIONAL INQUEST into the conduct of public men? If this be the design of it, who can so properly be the inquisitors for the nation, as the representatives of the nation themselves? It is not disputed that the power of originating the inquiry, or in other words of preferring the impeachment ought to be lodged in the hands of one branch of the legislative body; will not the reasons which indicate the propriety of this arrangement, strongly plead for an admission of the other branch of that body to a share in the inquiry? The model, from which the idea of this institution has been borrowed, pointed out that course to the Convention: In Great Britain, it is the province of the house of commons to prefer the impeachment; and of the house of lords to decide upon it. Several of the State constitutions have followed the example. As well the latter as the former seem to have regarded the practice of impeachments, as a bridle in the hands of the legislative body upon the executive servants of the government. Is not this the true light in which it ought to be regarded?

Where else, than in the Senate could have been found a tribunal sufficiently dignified, or sufficiently independent? What other body would be likely to feel *confidence enough in its own situation,* to preserve unawed and uninfluenced the necessary impartiality between an *individual* accused, and the *representatives of the people, his accusers?*

Could the Supreme Court have been relied upon as answering this description? It is much to be doubted whether the members of that tribunal would, at all times, be endowed with so eminent a portion of fortitude, as would be called for in the execution of so difficult a task; & it is still more to be doubted, whether they would possess the degree of credit and authority, which might, on certain occasions, be indispensable, towards reconciling the people to a decision, that should happen to clash with an accusation brought by their immediate representatives. A deficiency in the first would be fatal to the accused; in the last, dangerous to the public tranquillity. The hazard in both these respects could only be avoided, if at all, by rendering that tribunal more numerous than would consist with a reasonable attention to oeconomy. The necessity of a numerous court for the trial of impeachments is equally dictated by the nature of the proceeding. This can never be tied down by such strict rules, either in the delineation of the offence by the prosecutors, or in the construction of it by the Judges, as in common cases serve to limit the discretion of courts in favor of personal security. There will be no jury to stand between the Judges, who are to pronounce the sentence of the law and the party who is to receive or suffer it. The awful discretion, which a court of impeachments must necessarily have, to doom to honor or to infamy the most confidential and the most distinguished characters of the community, forbids the commitment of the trust to a small number of persons.

These considerations seem alone sufficient to authorise a conclusion, that the Supreme Court would have been an improper substitute for the Senate, as a court of impeachments. There remains a further consideration which will not a little strengthen this conclusion. It is this. The punishment, which may be the consequence of conviction upon impeachment, is not to terminate the chastisement of the offender. After having been sentenced to a perpetual ostracism from the esteem and confidence, and honors and emoluments of his country; he will still be liable to prosecution and punishment in the ordinary course of law. Would it be proper that the persons, who had disposed of his fame and his most valuable rights as a citizen in one trial, should in another trial, for the same offence, be also the disposers of his life and his fortune? Would there not be the greatest reason to apprehend, that error in the first sentence would be the parent of error in the second sentence? That the strong bias of one decision would be apt to overrule the influence of any new lights, which might be brought to vary the complexion of another decision? Those, who know any thing of human nature, will not hesitate to answer these questions in the affirmative; and will be at no loss to perceive, that by making the same persons Judges in both cases, those who might happen to be the objects of prosecution would in a great measure be deprived of the double security, intended them by a double trial. The loss of life and estate would often be virtually included in a sentence, which, in its terms, imported nothing more than dismission from a present, and disqualification for a future office. It may be said, that the intervention of a jury, in the second instance, would obviate the danger. But juries are frequently influenced by the opinions of Judges. They are sometimes induced to find special verdicts which refer the main question to the decision of the court. Who would be willing to stake his life and his estate upon the verdict of a jury, acting under the auspices of Judges, who had predetermined his guilt?

Would it have been an improvement of the plan, to have united the Supreme Court with the Senate, in the formation of the court of impeachments? This Union would certainly have been attended with several advantages; but would they not have been overballanced by the signal disadvantage, already stated, arising from the agency of the same Judges in the double prosecution to which the offender would be liable? To a certain extent, the benefits of that Union will be obtained from making the Chief Justice of the Supreme Court the President of the court of impeachments, as is proposed to be done in the plan of the Convention; while the inconveniences of an intire incorporation of the former into the latter will be substantially avoided. This was perhaps the prudent mean. I forbear to remark upon the additional pretext for clamour, against the Judiciary, which so considerable an augmentation of its authority would have afforded.

Would it have been desirable to have composed the court for the trial of impeachments of persons wholly distinct from the other departments of the government? There are weighty arguments, as well against, as in favor of such a plan. To some minds, it will not appear a trivial objection, that it would tend to increase the complexity of the political machine; and to add a new spring to the government, the utility of which would at best be questionable. But an objection, which will not be thought by any unworthy of attention, is this—A court formed upon such a plan would either be attended with heavy expence, or might in practice be subject to a variety of casualties and inconveniencies. It must either consist of permanent officers stationary at the seat of government, and of course entitled to fixed and regular stipends, or of certain officers of the State governments, to be called upon whenever an impeachment was actually depending. It will not be easy to imagine any third mode materially different, which could rationally be proposed. As the court, for reasons already given, ought to be numerous; the first scheme will be reprobated by every man, who can compare the extent of the public wants, with the means of supplying them; the second will be espoused with caution by those, who will seriously consider the difficulty of collecting men dispersed over the whole union; the injury to the innocent, from the procrastinated determination of the charges which might be brought against them; the advantage to the guilty, from the opportunities which delay would afford to intrigue and corruption; and in some cases the detriment to the State, from the prolonged inaction of men, whose firm and faithful execution of their duty might have exposed them to the persecution of an intemperate or designing majority in the House of Representatives. Though this latter supposition may seem harsh, and might not be likely often to be verified; yet it ought not to be forgotten, that the demon of faction will at certain seasons extend his sceptre over all numerous bodies of men.

But though one or the other of the substitutes which have been examined, or some other that might be devised, should be thought preferable to the plan, in this respect, reported by the Convention, it will not follow, that the Constitution ought for this reason to be rejected. If mankind were to resolve to agree in no institution of government, until every part of it had been adjusted to the most exact standard of perfection, society would soon become a general scene of anarchy, and the world a desert. Where is the standard of perfection to be found? Who will undertake to unite the discordant opinions of a whole community, in the same judgment of it; and to prevail upon one conceited projector to renounce his *infallible* criterion, for the *fallible* criterion of his more *conceited neighbor?* To answer the purpose of the adversaries of the Constitution, they ought to prove, not merely, that particular provisions in it are not the best, which might have been imagined; but that the plan upon the whole is bad and pernicious.

10

ALEXANDER HAMILTON, FEDERALIST, NO. 66,
445–51
8 March 1788

A review of the principal objections that have appeared against the proposed court for the trial of impeachments, will not improbably eradicate the remains of any unfavourable impressions, which may still exist, in regard to this matter.

The *first* of these objections is, that the provision in question confounds legislative and judiciary authorities in the same body; in violation of that important and well established maxim, which requires a separation between the different departments of power. The true meaning of this maxim has been discussed and ascertained in another place, and has been shewn to be entirely compatible with a partial intermixture of those departments for special purposes, preserving them in the main distinct and unconnected. This partial intermixture is even in some cases not only proper, but necessary to the mutual defence of the several members of the government, against each other. An absolute or qualified negative in the executive, upon the acts of the legislative body, is admitted by the ablest adepts in political science, to be an indefensible barrier against the encroachments of the latter upon the former. And it may perhaps with not less reason be contended that the powers relating to impeachments are as before intimated, an essential check in the hands of that body upon the encroachments of the executive. The division of them between the two branches of the legislature; assigning to one the right of accusing, to the other the right of judging; avoids the inconvenience of making the same persons both accusers and judges; and guards against the danger of persecution from the prevalency of a factious spirit in either of those branches. As the concurrence of two-thirds of the senate will be requisite to a condemnation, the security to innocence, from this additional circumstance, will be as complete as itself can desire.

It is curious to observe with what vehemence this part of the plan is assailed, on the principle here taken notice of, by men who profess to admire without exception the constitution of this state; while that constitution makes the senate, together with the chancellor and judges of the supreme court, not only a court of impeachments, but the highest judiciary in the state in all causes, civil and criminal. The proportion, in point of numbers, of the chancel-

lor and judges to the senators, is so inconsiderable, that the judiciary authority of New-York in the last resort may, with truth, be said to reside in its senate. If the plan of the convention be in this respect chargeable with a departure from the celebrated maxim which has been so often mentioned, and seems to be so little understood, how much more culpable must be the constitution of New-York?

A *second* objection to the senate, as a court of impeachments, is, that it contributes to an undue accumulation of power in that body, tending to give to the government a countenance too aristocratic. The senate, it is observed, is to have concurrent authority with the executive in the formation of treaties, and in the appointment to offices: If, say the objectors, to these prerogatives is added that of deciding in all cases of impeachment, it will give a decided predominancy to senatorial influence. To an objection so little precise in itself, it is not easy to find a very precise answer. Where is the measure or criterion to which we can appeal, for determining what will give the senate too much, too little, or barely the proper degree of influence? Will it not be more safe, as well as more simple, to dismiss such vague and uncertain calculations, to examine each power by itself, and to decide on general principles where it may be deposited with most advantage and least inconvenience?

If we take this course it will lead to a more intelligible, if not to a more certain result. The disposition of the power of making treaties, which has obtained in the plan of the convention, will then, if I mistake not, appear to be fully justified by the considerations stated in a former number, and by others which will occur under the next head of our enquiries. The expediency of the junction of the senate with the executive will, I trust, be placed in a light not less satisfactory, in the disquisitions under the same head. And I flatter myself the observations in my last paper must have gone no inconsiderable way towards proving that it was not easy, if practicable, to find a more fit receptable for the power of determining impeachments, than that which has been chosen. If this be truly the case, the hypothetical danger of the too great weight of the senate ought to be discarded from our reasonings.

But this hypothesis, such as it is has already been refuted in the remarks applied to the duration in office prescribed for the senators. It was by them shewn, as well on the credit of historical examples, as from the reason of the thing, that the most *popular* branch of every government, partaking of the republican genius, by being generally the favorite of the people, will be as generally a full match, if not an overmatch, for every other member of the government.

But independent of this most active and operative principle; to secure the equilibrium of the national house of representatives, the plan of the convention has provided in its favor, several important counterpoises to the additional authorities, to be conferred upon the senate. The exclusive privilege of originating money bills will belong to the house of representatives. The same house will possess the sole right of instituting impeachments: Is not this a complete counterballance to that of determining them? The same house will be the umpire in all elections of the president, which do not unite the suffrages of a majority of the whole number of electors; a case which it cannot be doubted will sometimes, if not frequently, happen. The constant possibility of the thing must be a fruitful source of influence to that body. The more it is contemplated, the more important will appear this ultimate, though contingent power of deciding the competitions of the most illustrious citizens of the union, for the first office in it. It would not perhaps be rash to predict, that as a mean of influence it will be found to outweigh all the peculiar attributes of the senate.

A third objection to the senate as a court of impeachments is drawn from the agency they are to have in the appointments to office. It is imagined that they would be too indulgent judges of the conduct of men, in whose official creation they had participated. The principle of this objection would condemn a practice, which is to be seen in all the state governments, if not in all the governments, with which we are acquainted: I mean that of rendering those, who hold office during pleasure, dependent on the pleasure of those, who appoint them. With equal plausibility might it be alledged in this case that the favoritism of the latter would always be an asylum for the misbehavior of the former. But that practice, in contradiction to this principle, proceeds upon the presumption, that the responsibility of those who appoint, for the fitness and competency of the persons, on whom they bestow their choice, and the interest they will have in the respectable and prosperous administration of affairs, will inspire a sufficient disposition, to dismiss from a share in it, all such, who, by their conduct, shall have proved themselves unworthy of the confidence reposed in them. Though facts may not always correspond with this presumption, yet if it be in the main just, it must destroy the supposition, that the senate, who will merely sanction the choice of the executive, should feel a byass towards the objects of that choice, strong enough to blind them to the evidences of guilt so extraordinary as to have induced the representatives of the nation to become its accusers.

If any further argument were necessary to evince the improbability of such a byass, it might be found in the nature of the agency of the senate, in the business of appointments. It will be the office of the president to *nominate,* and with the advice and consent of the senate to *appoint.* There will of course be no exertion of *choice* on the part of the senate. They may defeat one choice of the executive, and oblige him to make another; but they cannot themselves *choose*—they can only ratify or reject the choice, of the president. They might even entertain a preference to some other person, at the very moment they were assenting to the one proposed; because there might be no positive ground of opposition to him; and they could not be sure, if they withheld their assent, that the subsequent nomination would fall upon their own favorite, or upon any other person in their estimation more meritorious than the one rejected. Thus it could hardly happen that the majority of the senate would feel any other complacency towards the object of an appointment, than such, as the appearances of merit, might inspire, and the proofs of the want of it, destroy.

A fourth objection to the senate, in the capacity of a court of impeachments, is derived from their union with the executive in the power of making treaties. This, it has been said, would constitute the senators their own judges, in every case of a corrupt or perfidious execution of that trust. After having combined with the executive in betraying the interests of the nation in a ruinous treaty, what prospect, it is asked, would there be of their being made to suffer the punishment, they would deserve, when they were themselves to decide upon the accusation brought against them for the treachery of which they had been guilty?

This objection has been circulated with more earnestness and with greater show of reason, than any other which has appeared against this part of the plan; and yet I am deceived if it does not rest upon an erroneous foundation.

The security essentially intended by the constitution against corruption and treachery in the formation of treaties, is to be sought for in the numbers and characters of those who are to make them. The JOINT AGENCY of the chief magistrate of the union, and of two-thirds of the members of a body selected by the collective wisdom of the legislatures of the several states, is designed to be the pledge for the fidelity of the national councils in this particular. The convention might with propriety have meditated the punishment of the executive, for a deviation from the instructions of the senate, or a want of integrity in the conduct of the negociations committed to him: They might also have had in view the punishment of a few leading individuals in the senate, who should have prostituted their influence in that body, as the mercenary instruments of foreign corruption: But they could not with more or with equal propriety have contemplated the impeachment and punishment of two-thirds of the senate, consenting to an improper treaty, than of a majority of that or of the other branch of the national legislature, consenting to a pernicious or unconstitutional law: a principle which I believe has never been admitted into any government. How in fact could a majority of the house of representatives impeach themselves? Not better, it is evident, than two-thirds of the senate might try themselves. And yet what reason is there, that a majority of the house of representatives, sacrificing the interests of the society, by an unjust and tyrannical act of legislation, should escape with impunity more than two-thirds of the senate, sacrificing the same interests in an injurious treaty with a foreign power? The truth is, that in all such cases it is essential to the freedom and to the necessary independence of the deliberations of the body, that the members of it should be exempt from punishment for acts done in a collective capacity; and the security to the society must depend on the care which is taken to confide the trust to proper hands, to make it their interest to execute it with fidelity, and to make it as difficult as possible for them to combine in any interest opposite to that of the public good.

So far as might concern the misbehaviour of the executive in perverting the instructions, or contravening the views of the senate, we need not be apprehensive of the want of a disposition in that body to punish the abuse of their confidence, or to vindicate their own authority. We may thus far count upon their pride, if not upon their virtue. And so far even as might concern the corruption of leading members, by whose arts and influence the majority may have been inveigled into measures odious to the community; if the proofs of that corruption should be satisfactory, the usual propensity of human nature will warrant us in concluding, that there would be commonly no defect of inclination in the body, to divert the public resentment from themselves, by a ready sacrifice of the authors of their mismanagement and disgrace.

11

BRUTUS, NO. 15
20 Mar. 1788

Storing 2.9.192

The only clause in the constitution which provides for the removal of the judges from office, is that which declares, that "the president, vice-president, and all civil officers of the United States, shall be removed from office, on impeachment for, and conviction of treason, bribery, or other high crimes and misdemeanors." By this paragraph, civil officers, in which the judges are included, are removable only for crimes. Treason and bribery are named, and the rest are included under the general terms of high crimes and misdemeanors.—Errors in judgment, or want of capacity to discharge the duties of the office, can never be supposed to be included in these words, *high crimes and misdemeanors*. A man may mistake a case in giving judgment, or manifest that he is incompetent to the discharge of the duties of a judge, and yet give no evidence of corruption or want of integrity. To support the charge, it will be necessary to give in evidence some facts that will shew, that the judges commited the error from wicked and corrupt motives.

12

A NATIVE OF VIRGINIA, OBSERVATIONS UPON THE PROPOSED PLAN OF FEDERAL GOVERNMENT
1788

Monroe Writings 1:361–62

I conceive that the Senators are not impeachable, and therefore Governor Randolph's objection falls to the ground. I am surprised that a man of that gentleman's abilities should have fallen into this mistake. The Senators having a power over their own members, have the right of expulsion. Why then should they be impeachable? For upon impeachments, the punishment is only removal

from, and incapacity to hold offices. Expulsion amounts to the same thing. Besides, the Senators are elected by the people, though mediately, as well as the House of Representatives, and therefore have not the same degree of responsibility annexed to their characters, as the officers of the government: and for this obvious reason,—the former are appointed by the people themselves to stand in their places, and they are the best judges of those who are most fit to serve them: but the latter are appointed by the servants of the people. It is a generally received maxim among writers on government, that the Judiciary and Legislative departments should be kept distinct. The position is true to a certain extent; but this like most other general rules, is liable to exceptions. In the English government, which is certainly the freest in Europe, the House of Lords not only try impeachments, but is the highest civil court in the kingdom. In that Constitution the House of Commons are the impeachers, the House of Lords the triers: But no members either of the House of Commons or House of Lords, was ever impeached as such: But whenever members of either House have been impeached, it was as great officers of State. Under the federal government this is impossible, because the members of neither House can hold any office of State.

If this reasoning be not conclusive, the fourth section of the second article puts it out of doubt, viz. "The President, Vice-President, and all civil officers of the United States, shall be removed from office on impeachment, &c." The Senators are representatives of the people; and by no construction can be considered as civil officers of the State. If this be the case, in whose hands can this power be lodged with greater propriety, or with greater safety, than in those of the Senate? Or how can a better court be appointed? To impeach either the members of Senate or House of Representatives, would be to impeach the representatives of the people, that is the people, themselves which is an absurdity.

13

DEBATE IN NORTH CAROLINA RATIFYING CONVENTION
24–25, 28 July 1788

Elliot 4:32–37, 43–50, 126–28

[*24 July*]

Mr. JOSEPH TAYLOR objected to the provision made for impeaching. He urged that there could be no security from it, as the persons accused were triable by the Senate, who were a part of the legislature themselves; that, while men were fallible, the senators were liable to errors, especially in a case where they were concerned themselves.

Mr. IREDELL. Mr. Chairman, I was going to observe that this clause, vesting the power of impeachment in the House of Representatives, is one of the greatest securities for a due execution of all public offices. Every government requires it. Every man ought to be amenable for his conduct, and there are no persons so proper to complain of the public officers as the representatives of the people at large. The representatives of the people know the feelings of the people at large, and will be ready enough to make complaints. If this power were not provided, the consequences might be fatal. It will be not only the means of punishing misconduct, but it will prevent misconduct. A man in public office who knows that there is no tribunal to punish him, may be ready to deviate from his duty; but if he knows there is a tribunal for that purpose, although he may be a man of no principle, the very terror of punishment will perhaps deter him. I beg leave to mention that every man has a right to express his opinion, and point out any part of the Constitution which he either thinks defective, or has heard represented to be so. What will be the consequence if they who have objections do not think proper to communicate them, and they are not to be mentioned by others? Many gentlemen have read many objections, which perhaps have made impressions on their minds, though they are not communicated to us. I therefore apprehend that the member was perfectly regular in mentioning the objections made out of doors. Such objections may operate upon the minds of gentlemen, who, not being used to convey their ideas in public, conceal them out of diffidence.

Mr. BLOODWORTH wished to be informed, whether this sole power of impeachment, given to the House of Representatives, deprived the state of the power of impeaching any of its members.

Mr. SPAIGHT answered, that this impeachment extended only to the officers of the United States—that it would be improper if the same body that impeached had the power of trying—that, therefore, the Constitution had wisely given the power of impeachment to the House of Representatives, and that of trying impeachments to the Senate.

Mr. JOSEPH TAYLOR. Mr. Chairman, the objection is very strong. If there be but one body to try, where are we? If any tyranny or oppression should arise, how are those who perpetrated such oppression to be tried and punished? By a tribunal consisting of the very men who assist in such tyranny. Can any tribunal be found, in any community, who will give judgment against their own actions? Is it the nature of man to decide against himself? I am obliged to the worthy member from New Hanover for assisting me with objections. None can impeach but the representatives; and the impeachments are to be determined by the senators, who are one of the branches of power which we dread under this Constitution.

His excellency, Gov. JOHNSTON. Mr. Chairman, the worthy member from Granville surprises me by his objection. It has been explained by another member, that only officers of the United States were impeachable. I never knew any instance of a man being impeached for a legislative act; nay, I never heard it suggested before. No member of the House of Commons, in England, has ever been impeached before the Lords, nor any lord, for a legislative misdemeanor. A representative is answerable to no power but his constituents. He is accountable to no being under heaven but the people who appointed him.

Mr. TAYLOR replied, that it now appeared to him in a still worse light than before.

Mr. BLOODWORTH observed, that as this was a Constitution for the United States, he should not have made the observation he did, had the subject not been particularly mentioned—that the words "sole power of impeachment" were so general, and might admit of such a latitude of construction, as to extend to every legislative member upon the continent, so as to preclude the representatives of the different states from impeaching.

Mr. MACLAINE. Mr. Chairman, if I understand the gentleman rightly, he means that Congress may impeach all the people or officers of the United States. If the gentleman will attend, he will see that this is a government for confederated states; that, consequently, it can never intermeddle where no power is given. I confess I can see no more reason to fear in this case than from our own General Assembly. A power is given to our own state Senate to try impeachments. Is it not necessary to point out some tribunal to try great offences? Should there not be some mode of punishment for the offences of the officers of the general government? Is it not necessary that such officers should be kept within proper bounds? The officers of the United States are excluded from offices of honor, trust, or profit, under the United States, on impeachment for, and conviction of, high crimes and misdemeanors. This is certainly necessary. This exclusion from office is harmless in comparison with the regulation made, in similar cases, in our own government. Here it is expressly provided how far the punishment shall extend, and that it shall extend no farther. On the contrary, the limits are not marked in our own Constitution, and the punishment may be extended too far. I believe it is a certain and known fact, that members of the legislative body are never, as such, liable to impeachment, but are punishable by law for crimes and misdemeanors in their personal capacity. For instance; the members of Assembly are not liable to impeachment, but, like other people, are amenable to the law for crimes and misdemeanors committed as individuals. But in Congress, a member of either house can be no officer.

Gov. JOHNSTON. Mr. Chairman, I find that making objections is useful. I never thought of the objection made by the member from New Hanover. I never thought that impeachments extended to any but officers of the United States. When you look at the judgment to be given on impeachments, you will see that the punishment goes no farther than to remove and disqualify civil officers of the United States, who shall, on impeachment, be convicted of high misdemeanors. Removal from office is the punishment—to which is added future disqualification. How could a man be removed from office who had no office? An officer of this state is not liable to the United States. Congress could not disqualify an officer of this state. No body can disqualify, but that body which creates. We have nothing to apprehend from that article. We are perfectly secure as to this point. I should laugh at any judgment they should give against any officer of our own.

Mr. BLOODWORTH. From the complexion of the paragraph it appeared to me to be applicable only to officers of the United States; but the gentleman's own reasoning convinces me that he is wrong. He says he would laugh at them. Will the gentleman laugh when the extension of their powers takes place? It is only by our adoption they can have any power.

Mr. IREDELL. Mr. Chairman, the argument of the gentleman last up is founded upon misapprehension. Every article refers to its particular object. We must judge of expressions from the subject matter concerning which they are used. The sole power of impeachment extends only to objects of the Constitution. The Senate shall only try impeachments arising under the Constitution. In order to confirm and illustrate that position, the gentleman who spoke before explained it in a manner perfectly satisfactory to my apprehension—"under this Constitution." What is the meaning of these words? They signify those arising under the government of the United States. When this government is adopted, there will be two governments to which we shall owe obedience. To the government of the Union, in certain defined cases—to our own state government in every other case. If the general government were to disqualify me from any office which I held in North Carolina under its laws, I would refer to the Constitution, and say that they violated it, as it only extended to officers of the United States.

Mr. BLOODWORTH. The penalty is only removal from office. It does not mention from what office. I do not see any thing in the expression that convinces me that I was mistaken. I still consider it in the same light.

Mr. PORTER wished to be informed, if every officer, who was a creature of that Constitution, was to be tried by the Senate—whether such officers, and those who had complaints against them, were to go from the extreme parts of the continent to the seat of government, to adjust disputes.

Mr. DAVIE answered, that impeachments were confined to cases under the Constitution, but did not descend to petty offices; that if the gentleman meant that it would be troublesome and inconvenient to recur to the federal courts in case of oppressions by officers, and to carry witnesses such great distances, he would satisfy the gentleman, that Congress would remove such inconveniences, as they had the power of appointing inferior tribunals, where such disputes would be tried.

Mr. J. TAYLOR. Mr. Chairman, I conceive that, if this Constitution be adopted, we shall have a large number of officers in North Carolina under the appointment of Congress. We shall undoubtedly, for instance, have a great number of tax-gatherers. If any of these officers shall do wrong, when we come to fundamental principles, we find that we have no way to punish them but by going to Congress, at an immense distance, whither we must carry our witnesses. Every gentleman must see, in these cases, that oppressions will arise. I conceive that they cannot be tried elsewhere. I consider that the Constitution will be explained by the word "sole." If they did not mean to retain a general power of impeaching, there was no occasion for saying the "sole power." I consider therefore that oppressions will arise. If I am oppressed, I must go the House of Representatives to complain. I consider that, when mankind are about to part with rights, they ought only to part with those rights which they can with convenience relinquish, and not such as must involve them in distresses.

In answer to Mr. Taylor, Mr. SPAIGHT observed that, though the power of impeachment was given, yet it did not say that there was no other manner of giving redress—that it was very certain and clear that, if any man was injured by an officer of the United States, he could get redress by a suit at law.

Mr. MACLAINE. Mr. Chairman, I confess I never heard before that a tax-gatherer was worthy of impeachment. It is one of the meanest and least offices. Impeachments are only for high crimes and misdemeanors. If any one is injured in his person or property, he can get redress by a suit at law. Why does the gentleman talk in this manner? It shows what wretched shifts gentlemen are driven to. I never heard, in my life, of such a silly objection. A poor, insignificant, petty officer amenable to impeachment!

Mr. IREDELL. Mr. Chairman, the objection would be right if there was no other mode of punishing. But it is evident that an officer may be tried by a court of common law. He may be tried in such a court for common-law offences, whether impeached or not. As it is to be presumed that inferior tribunals will be constituted, there will be no occasion for going always to the Supreme Court, even in cases where the federal courts have exclusive jurisdiction. Where this exclusive cognizance is not given them, redress may be had in the common-law courts in the state; and I have no doubt such regulations will be made as will put it out of the power of officers to distress the people with impunity.

Gov. JOHNSTON observed, that men who were in very high offices could not be come at by the ordinary course of justice; but when called before this high tribunal and convicted, they would be stripped of their dignity, and reduced to the rank of their fellow-citizens, and then the courts of common law might proceed against them.

[25 July]

Mr. JOHN BLOUNT said, that the sole power of impeachment had been objected to yesterday, and that it was urged, officers were to be carried from the farthest parts of the states to the seat of government. He wished to know if gentlemen were satisfied.

Mr. MACLAINE. Mr. Chairman, I have no inclination to get up a second time, but some gentlemen think this subject ought to be taken notice of. I recollect it was mentioned by one gentleman, that petty officers might be impeached. It appears to me, sir, to be the most horrid ignorance to suppose that every officer, however trifling his office, is to be impeached for every petty offence; and that every man, who should be injured by such petty officers, could get no redress but by this mode of impeachment, at the seat of government, at the distance of several hundred miles, whither he would be obliged to summon a great number of witnesses. I hope every gentleman in this committee must see plainly that impeachments cannot extend to inferior officers of the United States. Such a construction cannot be supported without a departure from the usual and well-known practice both in England and

America. But this clause empowers the House of Representatives, which is the grand inquest of the Union at large, to bring great offenders to justice. It will be a kind of state trial for high crimes and misdemeanors. I remember it was objected yesterday, that the House of Representatives had the sole power of impeachment. The word "sole" was supposed to be so extensive as to include impeachable offences against particular states. Now, for my part, I can see no impropriety in the expression. The word relates to the general objects of the Union. It can only refer to offences against the United States; nor can it be tortured so as to have any other meaning, without a perversion of the usual meaning of language. The House of Representatives is to have the sole power of impeachment, and the Senate the sole power of trying. And here is a valuable provision, not to be found in other governments.

In England, the Lords, who try impeachments, declare solemnly, upon honor, whether the persons impeached be guilty or not. But here the senators are on oath. This is a very happy security. It is further provided, that, when the President is tried, (for he is also liable to be impeached,) the chief justice shall preside in the Senate; because it might be supposed that the Vice-President might be connected, together with the President, in the same crime, and would therefore be an improper person to judge him. It would be improper for another reason. On the removal of the President from office, it devolves on the Vice-President. This being the case, if the Vice-President should be judge, might he not look at the office of President, and endeavor to influence the Senate against him? This is a most excellent caution. It has been objected by some, that the President is in no danger from a trial by the Senate, because he does nothing without its concurrence. It is true, he is expressly restricted not to make treaties without the concurrence of two thirds of the senators present, nor appoint officers without the concurrence of the Senate, (not requiring two thirds.) The concurrence of all the senators, however, is not required in either of those cases. They may be all present when he is impeached, and other senators in the mean time introduced. The chief justice, we ought to presume, would not countenance a collusion. One dissenting person might divulge their misbehavior. Besides, he is impeachable for his own misdemeanors, and as to their concurrence with him, it might be effected by misrepresentations of his own, in which case they would be innocent, though he be guilty. I think, therefore, the Senate a very proper body to try him. Notwithstanding the mode pointed out for impeaching and trying, there is not a single officer but may be tried and indicted at common law; for it is provided, that a judgment, in cases of impeachment, shall not extend farther than to removal from office, and disqualification to hold and enjoy any office of honor, trust, or profit, under the United States; but the party convicted shall, nevertheless, be liable and subject to indictment, trial, judgment, and punishment, according to law. Thus you find that no offender can escape the danger of punishment. Officers, however, cannot be oppressed by an unjust decision of a bare majority; for it further provides, that no person shall be convicted without the con-

currence of two thirds of the members present; so that those gentlemen who formed this government have been particularly careful to distribute every part of it as equally as possible. As the government is solely instituted for the United States, so the power of impeachment only extends to officers of the United States. The gentleman who is so much afraid of impeachment by the federal legislature, is totally mistaken in his principles.

Mr. J. TAYLOR. Mr. Chairman, my apprehension is, that this clause is connected with the other, which gives the sole power of impeachment, and is very dangerous. When I was offering an objection to this part, I observed that it was supposed by some, that no impeachments could be preferred but by the House of Representatives. I concluded that perhaps the collectors of the United States, or gatherers of taxes, might impose on individuals in this country, and that these individuals might think it too great a distance to go to the seat of federal government to get redress, and would therefore be injured with impunity. I observed that there were some gentlemen, whose abilities are great, who construe it in a different manner. They ought to be kind enough to carry their construction not to the mere letter, but to the meaning. I observe that, when these great men are met in Congress, in consequence of this power, they will have the power of appointing all the officers of the United States. My experience in life shows me that the friends of the members of the legislature will get the offices. These senators and members of the House of Representatives will appoint their friends to all offices. These officers will be great men, and they will have numerous deputies under them. The receiver-general of the taxes of North Carolina must be one of the greatest men in the country. Will he come to me for his taxes? No. He will send his deputy, who will have special instructions to oppress me. How am I to be redressed? I shall be told that I must go to Congress, to get him impeached. This being the case, whom am I to impeach? A friend of the representatives of North Carolina. For, unhappily for us, these men will have too much weight for us; they will have friends in the government who will be inclined against us, and thus we may be oppressed with impunity.

I was sorry yesterday to hear personal observations drop from a gentleman in this house. If we are not of equal ability with the gentleman, he ought to possess charity towards us, and not lavish such severe reflections upon us in such a declamatory manner.

These are considerations I offer to the house. These oppressions may be committed by these officers. I can see no mode of redress. If there be any, let it be pointed out. As to personal aspersions, with respect to me, I despise them. Let him convince me by reasoning, but not fall on detraction or declamation.

Mr. MACLAINE. Mr. Chairman, if I made use of any asperity to that gentleman yesterday, I confess I am sorry for it. It was because such an observation came from a gentleman of his profession. Had it come from any other gentleman in this Convention, who is not of his profession, I should not be surprised. But I was surprised that it should come from a gentleman of the law, who must know the contrary perfectly well. If his memory had failed him, he might have known by consulting his library. His books would have told him that no petty officer was ever impeachable. When such trivial, ill-founded objections were advanced, by persons who ought to know better, was it not sufficient to irritate those who were determined to decide the question by a regular and candid discussion?

Whether or not there will be a receiver-general in North Carolina, if we adopt the Constitution, I cannot take upon myself to say. I cannot say how Congress will collect their money. It will depend upon laws hereafter to be made. These laws will extend to other states as well as to us. Should there be a receiver-general in North Carolina, he certainly will not be authorized to oppress the people. His deputies can have no power that he could not have himself. As all collectors and other officers will be bound to act according to law, and will, in all probability, be obliged to give security for their conduct, we may expect they will not dare to oppress. The gentleman has thought proper to lay it down as a principle, that these receivers-general will give special orders to their deputies to oppress the people. The President is the superior officer, who is to see the laws put in execution. He is amenable for any maladministration in his office. Were it possible to suppose that the President should give wrong instructions to his deputies, whereby the citizens would be distressed, they would have redress in the ordinary courts of common law. But, says he, parties injured must go to the seat of government of the United States, and get redress there. I do not think it will be necessary to go to the seat of the general government for that purpose. No persons will be obliged to attend there, but on extraordinary occasions; for Congress will form regulations so as to render it unnecessary for the inhabitants to go thither, but on such occasions.

My reasons for this conclusion are these: I look upon it as the interest of all the people of America, except those in the vicinity of the seat of government, to make laws as easy as possible for the people, with respect to local attendance. They will not agree to drag their citizens unnecessarily six or seven hundred miles from their homes. This would be equally inconvenient to all except those in the vicinity of the seat of government, and therefore will be prevented. But, says the gentleman from Granville, what redress have we when we go to that place? These great officers will be the friends of the representatives of North Carolina. It is possible they may, or they may not. They have the power to appoint officers for each state from what place they please. It is probable they will appoint them out of the state in which they are to act. I will, however, admit, for the sake of argument, that those federal officers who will be guilty of misdemeanors in this state will be near relations of the representatives and senators of North Carolina. What then? Are they to be tried by them only? Will they be the near friends of the senators and representatives of the other states? If not, his objection goes for nothing. I do not understand what he says about detraction and declamation. My character is well known. I am no declaimer; but when I see a gentleman, ever so respectable, betraying his trust to the public, I will publish it loudly; and I say this is not detraction or declamation.

Gov. JOHNSTON. Mr. Chairman, impeachment is very different in its nature from what the learned gentleman from Granville supposes it to be. If an officer commits an offence against an individual, he is amenable to the courts of law. If he commits crimes against the state, he may be indicted and punished. Impeachment only extends to high crimes and misdemeanors in a *public office*. It is a mode of trial pointed out for great misdemeanors against the public. But I think neither that gentleman nor any other person need be afraid that officers who commit oppressions will pass with impunity. It is not to be apprehended that such officers will be tried by their cousins and friends. Such cannot be on the jury at the trial of the cause; it being a principle of law that no person interested in a cause, or who is a relation of the party, can be a juror in it. This is the light in which it strikes me. Therefore the objection of the gentleman from Granville must necessarily fall to the ground on that principle.

Mr. MACLAINE. Mr. Chairman, I must obviate some objections which have been made. It was said, by way of argument, that they could impeach and remove any officer, whether of the United States or any particular state. This was suggested by the gentleman from New Hanover. Nothing appears to me more unnatural than such a construction. The Constitution says, in one place, that the House of Representatives shall have the sole power of impeachment. In the clauses under debate, it provides that the Senate shall have the sole power to try all impeachments, and then subjoins, that judgment, in cases of impeachment, shall not extend further than to removal from office, and disqualification to hold and enjoy any office of honor, trust, or profit, under the United States. And in the 4th section of the 2d article, it says that the President, Vice-President, and all civil officers of the United States, shall be removed from office on impeachment for, and conviction of, treason, bribery, or other high crimes and misdemeanors.

Now, sir, what can be more clear and obvious than this? The several clauses relate to the same subject, and ought to be considered together. If considered separately and unconnectedly, the meaning is still clear. They relate to the government of the Union altogether. Judgment on impeachment only extends to removal from office, and future disqualification to hold offices *under the United States.* Can those be removed from offices, and disqualified to hold offices under the United States, who actually held no office under the United States? The 4th section of the 2d article provides expressly for the removal of the President, Vice-President, and all civil officers of the United States, on impeachment and conviction. Does not this clearly prove that none but officers of the United States are impeachable? Had any other been impeachable, why was not provision made for the case of their conviction? Why not point out the punishment in one case as well as in others? I beg leave to observe, that this is a Constitution which is not made with any reference to the government of any particular state, or to officers of particular states, but to the government of the United States at large.

We must suppose that every officer here spoken of must be an officer of the United States. The words discover the meaning as plainly as possible. The sentence which provides that "judgment, in cases of impeachment, shall not extend further than to removal from office," is joined by a conjunction copulative to the other sentence,—"and disqualification to hold and enjoy any office of honor, trust, or profit, under the United States,"—which incontrovertibly proves that officers of the United States only are referred to. No other grammatical construction can be put upon it. But there is no necessity to refer to grammatical constructions, since the whole plainly refers to the government of the United States at large. The general government cannot intermeddle with the internal affairs of the state governments. They are in no danger from it. It has been urged that it has a tendency to a consolidation. On the contrary, it appears that the state legislatures must exist in full force, otherwise the general government cannot exist itself. A consolidated government would never secure the happiness of the people of this country. It would be the interest of the people of the United States to keep the general and individual governments as separate and distinct as possible.

Mr. BLOODWORTH. Mr. Chairman, I confess I am obliged to the honorable gentleman for his construction. Were he to go to Congress, he might put that construction on the Constitution. But no one can say what construction Congress will put upon it. I do not distrust him, but I distrust them. I wish to leave no dangerous latitude of construction.

[28 July]

[JAMES IREDELL] God forbid that a man, in any country in the world, should be liable to be punished for want of judgment. This is not the case here. As to errors of the heart, there is sufficient responsibility. Should these be committed, there is a ready way to bring him to punishment. This is a responsibility which answers every purpose that could be desired by a people jealous of their liberty. I presume that, if the President, with the advice of the Senate, should make a treaty with a foreign power, and that treaty should be deemed unwise, or against the interest of the country, yet if nothing could be objected against it but the difference of opinion between them and their constituents, they could not justly be obnoxious to punishment. If they were punishable for exercising their own judgment, and not that of their constituents, no man who regarded his reputation would accept the office either of a senator or President. Whatever mistake a man may make, he ought not to be punished for it, nor his posterity rendered infamous. But if a man be a villain, and wilfully abuse his trust, he is to be held up as a public offender, and ignominiously punished. A public officer ought not to act from a principle of fear. Were he punishable for want of judgment, he would be continually in dread; but when he knows that nothing but real guilt can disgrace him, he may do his duty firmly, if he be an honest man; and if he be not, a just fear of disgrace may, perhaps, as to the public, have nearly the effect of an intrinsic principle of virtue. According to these principles, I suppose the only instances, in which the President would be liable to impeachment, would be where he had received a bribe, or had acted from some corrupt motive or other. If the President had received a bribe, without the privity or knowledge of the Senate, from a foreign power, and, under the influence of that bribe, had address enough with the Senate, by artifices and misrepresentations, to seduce their consent to a pernicious treaty,—if it appeared afterwards that this was the case, would not that Senate be as competent to try him as any other persons whatsoever? Would they not exclaim against his villany? Would they not feel a particular resentment against him, for being made the instrument of his treacherous purposes? In this situation, if any objection could be made against the Senate as a proper tribunal, it might more properly be made by the President himself, lest their resentment should operate too strongly, rather than by the public, on the ground of a supposed partiality. The President must certainly be punishable for giving false information to the Senate. He is to regulate all intercourse with foreign powers, and it is his duty to impart to the Senate every material intelligence he receives. If it should appear that he has not given them full information, but has concealed important intelligence which he ought to have communicated, and by that means induced them to enter into measures injurious to their country, and which they would not have consented to had the true state of things been disclosed to them,—in this case, I ask whether, upon an impeachment for a misdemeanor upon such an account, the Senate would probably favor him. With respect to the impeachability of the Senate, that is a matter of doubt.

There have been no instances of impeachment for legislative misdemeanors; and we shall find, upon examination, that the inconveniences resulting from such impeachments would more than preponderate the advantages. There is no greater honor in the world than being the representative of a free people. There is no trust on which the happiness of the people has a greater dependence. Yet who ever heard of impeaching a member of the legislature for any legislative misconduct? It would be a great check on the public business, if a member of the Assembly was liable to punishment for his conduct as such. Unfortunately, it is the case, not only in other countries, but even in this, that division and differences in opinion will continually arise. On many questions there will be two or more parties. These often judge with little charity of each other, and attribute every opposition to their own system to an ill motive. We know this very well from experience; but, in my opinion, this constant suspicion is frequently unjust. I believe, in general, both parties really think themselves right, and that the majority of each commonly act with equal innocence of intention. But, with the usual want of charity in these cases, how dangerous would it be to make a member of the legislature liable to impeachment! A mere difference of opinion might be interpreted, by the malignity of party, into a deliberate, wicked action.

It therefore appears to me at least very doubtful whether it would be proper to render the Senate impeachable at all especially as, in the branches of executive government, where their concurrence is required, the President is the primary agent, and plainly responsible, and they, in fact, are but a council to validate proper, or restrain improper, conduct in him; but if a senator is impeachable, it could only be for corruption, or some other wicked motive, in which case, surely those senators who had acted from upright motives would be competent to try him.

14

JAMES MADISON, OBSERVATIONS ON JEFFERSON'S DRAFT OF A CONSTITUTION FOR VIRGINIA
15 Oct. 1788

Papers 11:291–92

(See vol. 1, ch. 17, no. 25)

15

JAMES WILSON, LEGISLATIVE DEPARTMENT, LECTURES ON LAW
1791

Works 1:425–26

The doctrine of impeachments is of high import in the constitutions of free states. On one hand, the most powerful magistrates should be amenable to the law: on the other hand, elevated characters should not be sacrificed merely on account of their elevation. No one should be secure while he violates the constitution and the laws: every one should be secure while he observes them.

Impeachments were known in Athens. They were prosecuted for great and publick offences, by which the commonwealth was brought into danger. They were not referred to any court of justice, but were prosecuted before the popular assembly, or before the senate of five hundred.

Among the ancient Germans also, we discover the traces of impeachments: for we are informed by Tacitus, in his masterly account of the manners of that people, that it was allowed to present accusations, and to prosecute capital offences, before the general assembly of the nation.

An impeachment is described, by the law of England, to be, a presentment to the most high and supreme court of criminal jurisdiction, by the most solemn grand inquest of the kingdom.

It is evident that, in England, impeachments, according to this description, could not exist before the separation of the two houses of parliament. Previous to that era, the national council was accustomed to inquire into the conduct of the different executive officers, and to punish them for malversation in office, or what are called high misdemeanors. The king himself was not exempted from such inquiry and punishment: for it had not yet become a maxim—that the king can do no wrong.

Prosecutions of this nature were not, like those of ordinary crimes, intrusted to the management of an individual: they were conducted by the national council themselves; who acted, improperly enough, in the double character of accusers and judges. Upon the separation of the two houses, it became an obvious improvement, that the power of trying those high misdemeanors should belong to the house of lords, and that the power of conducting the prosecution should belong to the house of commons. In consequence of this improvement, the inconsistent characters of judge and accuser were no longer acted by the same body.

We find the commons appearing as the grand inquest of the nation, about the latter end of the reign of Edward the third. They then began to exhibit accusations for crimes and misdemeanors, against offenders who were thought to be out of the reach of the ordinary power of the law. In the fiftieth year of that reign, they preferred impeachments against many delinquents. These impeachments were tried by the lords.

In the United States and in Pennsylvania, impeachments are confined to political characters, to political crimes and misdemeanors, and to political punishments. The president, vice president, and all civil officers of the United States; the governour and all other civil officers under this commonwealth, are liable to impeachment; the officers of the United States, for treason, bribery, or other high crimes and misdemeanors; the officers of this commonwealth, for any misdemeanor in office. Under both constitutions, judgments, in cases of impeachment, shall not extend further than to removal from office, and disqualification to hold any office of honour, trust, or profit.

16

LUTHER MARTIN, IMPEACHMENT TRIAL OF JUSTICE SAMUEL CHASE, SENATE
23 Feb. 1804

Annals 14:429–32, 436

We have been told by an honorable Manager, (Mr. Campbell,) that the power of trying impeachments was lodged in the Senate with the most perfect propriety; for two reasons—the one, that the person impeached would be tried before those who had given their approbation to his appointment to office. This certainly was not the reason by which the framers of the Constitution were influenced, when they gave this power to the Senate. Who are the officers liable to impeachment? The President, the Vice President, and all civil officers of Government. In the election of the two first, the Senate have no control, either as to nomination or approbation. As to other civil officers, who hold their appointments during good behavior, it is extremely probable that, though they were approved by one Senate, yet from lapse of time, and the fluctuations of that body, an officer may be impeached before a Senate, not one of whom had sanctioned his appointment, not one of whom, perhaps, had he been nominated after their election, would have given him their sanction.

This, then, could not have been one of the reasons for thus placing the power over *these* officers. But as a second reason, he assigned, that, if any other inferior tribunal had been entrusted with the trial of impeachments, the members might have an interest in the conviction of an officer, thereby to have him removed in order to obtain his place; but, that no Senator could have such inducement.

. . . . .

I see two honorable members of this Court, (Messrs. Dayton and Baldwin,) who were with me in Convention, in 1787, who as well as myself, perfectly knew why this power was invested in the Senate. It was because, among all our speculative systems, it was thought this power could no where be more properly placed, or where it would be less likely to be abused. A sentiment, sir, in which I perfectly concurred, and I have no doubt but the event of this trial will show that we could not have better disposed of that power.

. . . . .

Will it be pretended, for I have heard such a suggestion, that the House of Representatives have a right to impeach *every citizen indiscriminately?* For *what* shall they impeach them? For *any* criminal act? Is the House of Representatives, then, to constitute a grand jury to receive information of a criminal nature against all our citizens, and *thereby to deprive them of a trial by jury?* This was never intended by the Constitution?

The President, Vice President, and other civil officers, can only be impeached. They only in that case are deprived of a trial by jury; they, when they accept their offices, accept them on those terms, and, as far as relates to the tenure of their offices, relinquish that privilege; they, therefore, cannot complain. Here, it appears to me, the framers of the Constitution have so expressed themselves as to leave not a single doubt on this subject.

In the first article, section the third, of the Constitution, it is declared that, judgment in all cases of impeachment, shall not extend further than removal from office, and disqualification to hold any office of honor, trust, or profit, under the United States. This clearly evinces, that no persons but those *who hold offices* are liable to impeachment. They are to lose their offices; and, having misbehaved themselves in such manner as to lose their offices, are, with propriety, to be rendered ineligible thereafter.

. . . . .

The truth is, the framers of the Constitution, for many · reasons, which influenced them, did not think proper to place the officers of Government in the power of the two branches of the Legislature, further than the tenure of their office. Nor did they choose to permit the tenure of their offices to depend upon the passions or prejudices of jurors. The very clause in the Constitution, of itself, shows that it was intended the persons impeached and removed from office might still be indicted and punished for the same offence, else the provision would have been not only nugatory, but a reflection on the enlightened body who framed the Constitution; since no person ever could have

dreamed that a conviction on impeachment and a removal from office, in consequence, for one offence, could prevent the same person from being indicted and punished for another and different offence.

. . . . .

I again repeat, that as the framers of the Constitution of the United States did not insert in their Constitution such a clause as is inserted in the constitution of Pennsylvania, it is the strongest proof that they did not mean a judge or other officer should be displaced by an address of any portion of the Legislature, but only according to the Constitutional provisions.

17

WILLIAM RAWLE, A VIEW OF THE CONSTITUTION OF THE UNITED STATES 210–19
1829 (2d ed.)

Impeachments are thus introduced as a known definite term, and we must have recourse to the *common law of England* for the definition of them.

In England, the practice of impeachments by the house of commons before the house of lords, has existed from very ancient times. Its foundation is, that a subject entrusted with the administration of public affairs, may sometimes infringe the rights of the people, and be guilty of such crimes as the ordinary magistrates either dare not or cannot punish. Of these, the representatives of the people or house of commons cannot judge, because they and their constitutents are the persons injured, and can therefore only accuse. But the ordinary tribunals would naturally be swayed by the authority of so powerful an accuser. That branch of the legislature which represents the people, therefore, brings the charge before the other branch, which consists of the nobility, who are said not to have the same interests, or the same passions as the popular assembly.

Such is the English theory, and it well suits a government in which there are three distinct and independent interests, and in which the crown, possessing the power of appointing the high officers, who are most frequently the subjects of impeachments, has also the sole power to carry on or withdraw prosecutions in the ordinary courts. For no misconduct, however flagrant, committed by such men, could the people obtain redress, if the monarch inclined to refuse it, unless a mode of proceeding had been invented which did not require his assent, and which he could not control, and therefore, as heretofore observed, he cannot defeat the inquiry by a previous pardon, although in the exercise of another branch of his prerogative, he may delay it by adjourning or proroguing the session of the parliament.

The difference between the two governments has no doubt already occurred to the reader. Our ordinary tribunals are not dependent on the pleasure of him who appoints the judges, nor are they to be influenced by the authority of the accuser in a case of this sort more than in any other, for with us the people are considered as the accusers in all cases whatever. In England, the king is the accuser, (except in the instance now under consideration,) and all offences are charged to have been committed against his peace, his crown and dignity.

Still less are the weight and influence of any man, however exalted his station, or great his wealth, likely to deter our judges from an impartial administration of justice.

Yet although the reasons are not equally cogent, they will be found on examination sufficient to warrant the introduction of the system into our code.

We shall now proceed to consider—

1. The necessity or utility of impeachments.
2. The necessity or utility of erecting a separate tribunal for the trial of impeachments.
3. The propriety of rendering the senate such a tribunal.
4. The persons liable to be impeached.
5. The constitution of the court, its mode of proceeding, and the extent and effect of its judgments.

1. The delegation of important trusts, affecting the higher interests of society, is always from various causes liable to abuse. The fondness frequently felt for the inordinate extension of power, the influence of party and of prejudice, the seductions of foreign states, or the baser appetite for illegitimate emolument, are sometimes productive of what are not unaptly termed political offences, which it would be difficult to take cognizance of in the ordinary course of judicial proceedings.

2. The involutions and varieties of vice are too many, and too artful to be anticipated by positive law, and sometimes too subtle and mysterious to be fully detected in the limited period of ordinary investigation. As progress is made in the inquiry, new facts are discovered which may be properly connected with others already known, but would not form sufficient subjects of separate prosecution. On these accounts a peculiar tribunal seems both useful and necessary. A tribunal of a liberal and comprehensive character, confined as little as possible to strict forms, enabled to continue its session as long as the nature of the case may require, qualified to view the charge in all its bearings and dependencies, and to appreciate on sound principles of public policy the defence of the accused; the propriety of such a separate tribunal seems to be plain, but not upon the assumed ground that the judges of the supreme court would not possess sufficient fortitude to perform the duty, or sufficient credit and authority to reconcile the people to their decisions.

3. To compose this court of persons wholly distinct from the other branches of government—to form a permanent body for this single purpose—and to keep them always collected at the seat of government for the possible occurrence of an impeachment, would be as inconvenient as to appoint and collect such a body from time to time, when an impeachment is determined on.

On a review of all the departments of government provided by the Constitution, none will be found more suitable to exercise this peculiar jurisdiction than the senate.

Although like the accusers, they are representatives of the people, yet they are by a degree more removed, and hold their stations for a longer term. They are therefore more independent of the people, and being chosen with the knowledge that they may, while in office, be called upon to exercise this high function, they bring with them the confidence of their constituents that they will faithfully execute it, and the implied compact on their own parts that it shall be honestly discharged. Precluded from ever becoming accusers themselves, it is their duty not to lend themselves to the animosities of party or the prejudices against individuals, which may sometimes unconsciously induce the house of representatives to the acts of accusation. Habituated to comprehensive views of the great political relations of the country, they are naturally the best qualified to decide on those charges which may have any connexion with transactions abroad, or great political interests at home, and although we cannot say, that like the English house of lords they form a distinct body, wholly uninfluenced by the passions, and remote from the interests of the people, yet we can discover in no other division of the government a greater probability of impartiality and independence.

Nor does it form a solid objection in point of principle, that in this peculiar instance, a part of the legislative body should be admitted to exercise judicial power. In some degree all legislative bodies necessarily possess such a power. We have seen that for sufficient cause they may expel any of their own members—they may try and punish others for attempts to corrupt, bribe, or intimidate them, and they may punish for what are technically termed contempts committed in their presence, in all which they act judicially. But it is sufficient, to close the subject, that the people at large have concluded that this power would be best deposited in this body.

4. From the reasons already given, it is obvious, that the only persons liable to impeachment, are those who are or have been in public office. All executive and judicial officers, from the president downwards, from the judges of the supreme court to those of the most inferior tribunals, are included in this description. But in the year 1796, a construction was given to the Constitution, founded, it is believed, merely on its phraseology, by which a member of the senate was held not to be liable to impeachment. Their deliberations, after the arguments of counsel, being held in private, we can only infer from those arguments, that the term officers of the United States, as used in the Constitution, was held by a majority of the senate, not to include members of the senate, and on the same principle, members of the house of representatives would also be excluded from this jurisdiction.

An amendment to the Constitution in this respect would perhaps be useful. A breach of duty is as reprehensible in a legislator as in an executive or judicial officer, and if this peculiar jurisdication possesses so much value in respect to the two latter, it is difficult to conceive why the public should not have the benefit of it in regard to the former.

No apprehensions of partiality in favour of one of their own body need to be carried so far as to require the substitution of another tribunal. In England, where there is not a greater portion of public virtue than here, peers are necessarily impeached before peers, and members of the house of commons have been frequently the subjects of impreachment. Judges are liable to trial for every offence before their brethren, and it is in no case to be presumed, that a fair and full administration of justice would be wanting. Of great public delinquencies the people do not long remain in ignorance. If the offences of a member of the house of representatives were culpably passed over by his brethren, the people by the recurrence of the periodical election would soon be enabled to substitute others to prefer the accusation, and, being sensible of this, the house would be slow to expose themselves to the reproach of their constituents, and the loss of public confidence, by omitting to do their duty. The senate is obliged to receive and decide on the charge, and to the strongest moral obligations is added that of an oath or affirmation. It is not probable that the effect of these united impulses would be counteracted by other considerations, which would in themselves be criminal.

5. The legitimate causes of impeachment have been already briefly noticed. They can only have reference to public character and official duty. The words of the text are *treason, bribery, and other high crimes and misdemeanors.* The treason contemplated must be against the United States. In general those offences which may be committed equally by a private person as a public officer, are not the subjects of impeachment. Murder, burglary, robbery, and indeed all offences not immediately connected with office, except the two expressly mentioned, are left to the ordinary course of judicial proceeding, and neither house can regularly inquire into them, except for the purpose of expelling the member. But the ordinary tribunals as we shall see, are not precluded, either before or after an impeachment, from taking cognizance of the public and official delinquency.

We have hitherto had but three instances of impeachment, the first of which has already been noticed. As no decision was given on the merits, it is impossible to say whether the charges, which were chiefly founded on a conspiracy to invade the territories of the king of Spain, with whom the United States were at peace, and to excite the Creek and Cherokee Indians to concur in the outrage, would have been deemed by the senate sufficient, if proved, to support the impeachment. The second, on which a constitutional conviction took place, was against a judge of a district court, and purely for official misconduct. The third was against a judge of the supreme court, and was also a charge of official misconduct. It terminated in an acquittal, there not being a constitutional majority against him on any one article.

As articles of impeachment can only be exhibited by the house of representatives, if it should happen that the senate in the course of their executive functions or otherwise, became apprized of unlawful acts committed by a public officer, and in their opinions, meriting at least a public inquiry, it would be their duty to communicate the evidence they possessed, whether actual or presumptive, to the house of representatives, but the bare communication is all that would be consistent with their duty. They would cautiously avoid to recommend or suggest an impeachment, and the same would be the course pursued by the president.

Articles of impeachment need not to be drawn up with the precision and strictness of indictments. They must however be distinct and intelligible. No one is bound to answer to a charge so obscure and ambiguous that it cannot be understood. Additional articles may be exhibited, perhaps at any stage of the prosecution; certainly before the defendant has put in his answer or plea.

No precise number of senators is required to constitute the court, but no person can be convicted without the concurrence of two-thirds of the members present. The vice president being the president of the senate, presides on the trial, except when the president of the United States is tried. As the vice president succeeds to the functions and emoluments of the president of the United States whenever a vacancy happens in the latter office, it would be inconsistent with the implied purity of a judge that a person under a probable bias of such a nature should participate in the trial—and it would follow that he ought wholly to retire from the court. It is not stated in the Constitution whether the president of the senate is on the trial of an impeachment restricted, as in legislative cases, to the casting vote. As he is constituted one of the judges by being appointed to preside without any restriction, the fair inference would be, that he is entitled to vote like the other judges, but on the trial last mentioned of a judge of the Supreme Court, the vote of the vice president does not appear in the printed journal.

The defendant is entitled to the benefit of counsel—but it is not necessary that he should be personally present; the trial may proceed in his absence if he has had due notice to appear.

The consultations of the senate, as well upon incidental points as on the main questions, are conducted in private, but the judgment is rendered in public.

The judgment is of a limited and peculiar nature—it extends no further than to removal from office, and disqualification to hold and enjoy any office of honour, trust, or profit, under the United States.

Herein we may perceive the importance and utility of this system under our regulations. In England impeachments may be prosecuted for capital crimes and the court may award capital punishment, of which many instances occur in the history of that kingdom. Lord Strafford in the reign of Charles I. and Lord Stafford in the reign of Charles II. were beheaded on the sentences of the court which decided without the aid of a jury, and both of them have been considered rather as victims to the spirit of the times, than as merited oblations to justice. But with us, although the party accused may be found guilty of the highest crime, his life is not in danger before this tribunal, and in no cases are his liberty and property affected: indictment, trial, judgment, and punishment, still await him according to the usual course of law.

Why then, it may be asked, has this system been introduced, and why, if the firmness and integrity of the ordinary tribunals cannot be overpowered by any supposed influence of character, wealth, or office, have we deemed it expedient to copy from a foreign nation an institution for which there is not the same necessity, and which we do not allow altogether to produce the same effects? One answer is, that the sentence which this court is authorized to impose cannot regularly be pronounced by the courts of law. They can neither remove nor disqualify the person convicted, and therefore the obnoxious officer might be continued in power, and the injury sustained by the nation be renewed or increased, if the executive authority were perverse, tyrannical, or corrupt: but by the sentence which may be given by the senate, not only the appointment made by the executive is superseded and rendered void, but the same individual may be rendered incapable of again abusing an office to the injury of the public. It is therefore right and proper that the president should be disabled from granting a pardon, and restoring the offender to his former competency; but there is no restraint on his pardoning when a conviction in the common course ensues, for such pardon extends only to the punishment which is then pronounced, and does not affect the sentence of the senate.

We may perceive in this scheme one useful mode of removing from office him who is unworthy to fill it, in cases where the people, and sometimes the president himself would be unable to accomplish that object. A commission granted during good behaviour can only be revoked by this mode of proceeding. But the express words of the Constitution also extend to the president and vice president, who partake of the legislative capacity, and are chosen by the people. When the corrective jurisdiction is thus applied; when it reaches all judicial officers, all civil officers appointed by the president during pleasure, and involves in its grasp the vice president and the president himself, it is difficult to conceive that it was intended to exempt men whose treachery to their country might be productive of the most serious disasters, because they do not come precisely within a verbal description supposed to be exclusively applicable to those who, except in the two instances of specific enumeration, receive commissions from the president. A member of either house of the legislature betraying his trust and guilty of the most culpable acts of an official nature is, under the decision of the senate, liable, indeed, to expulsion, but not to impeachment; liable to the ordinary course of legal proceedings, but not to disqualification. Yet as from the judgment of this high tribunal there is no appeal; as the decision which has been given in the case adverted to is a judicial one, and probably will be held binding on themselves on all future occasions, we must now receive it as the settled construction of the Constitution.

18

JOSEPH STORY, COMMENTARIES ON THE
CONSTITUTION 2:§§ 758–69, 771–78,
780–803, 810–11
1833

§ 758. That there is great force in this reasoning [of *Federalist*, no. 65] all persons of common candour must allow; that it is in every respect satisfactory and unanswerable, has been denied, and may be fairly questioned. That part of it, which is addressed to the trial at law by the same judges might have been in some degree obviated by confiding the jurisdiction at law over the offence (as in fact it is now confided) to an inferior tribunal, and excluding any judge, who sat at the impeachment, from sitting in the court of trial. Still, however, it cannot be denied, that even in such a case the prior judgment of the Supreme Court, if an appeal to it were not allowable, would have very great weight upon the minds of inferior Judges. But that part of the reasoning, which is addressed to the importance of numbers in giving weight to the decision, and especially that, which is addressed to the public confidence and respect, which ought to follow upon a decision, are entitled to very great weight. It is fit, however, to give the answer to the whole reasoning by the other side in the words of a learned commentator, who has embodied it with no small share of ability and skill. The reasoning "seems," says he, "to have forgotten, that senators may be discontinued from their seats, merely from the effect of popular disapprobation, but that the judges of the Supreme Court cannot. It seems also to have forgotten, that whenever the president of the United States is impeached, the constitution expressly requires, that the chief justice of the Supreme Court shall preside at the trial. Are all the confidence, all the firmness, and all the impartiality of that court, supposed to be concentred in the chief justice, and to reside in his breast only? If that court could not be relied on for the trial of impeachments, much less would it seem worthy of reliance for the determination of any question between the United States and a particular state; much less to decide upon the life and death of a person, whose crimes might subject him to impeachment, but whose influence might avert a conviction. Yet the courts of the United States, are by the constitution regarded, as the proper tribunals, where a party, convicted upon an impeachment, may receive that condign punishment, which the nature of his crimes may require; for it must not be forgotten, that a person, convicted upon an impeachment, will nevertheless be liable to indictment, trial, judgment, and punishment according to law, &c. The question, then, might be retorted; can it be supposed, that the senate, a part of whom must have been either *particeps criminis* with the person impeached, by advising the measure, for which he is to be tried, or must have joined the opposition to that measure, when proposed and debated in the senate, would be a more independent, or a more unprejudiced tribunal, than a court, composed of judges, holding their offices during good behaviour; and who could neither be presumed to have participated in the crime, nor to have prejudged the criminal?"

§ 759. This reasoning also has much force in it; but in candour also it must be admitted to be not wholly unexceptionable. That part, which is addressed to the circumstance of the chief justice's presiding at the trial of the president of the United States, was (as we shall hereafter see) not founded on any supposition, that the chief justice would be superior in confidence, and firmness, and impartiality, to the residue of the judges, (though in talents and public respect, and acquirements, he might fairly be presumed their superior;) but on the necessity of excluding the vice president from the chair, when he might have a manifest interest, which would destroy his impartiality. That part, which is addressed to the supposition of the senators being *particeps criminis,* is still more exceptionable; for it is not only incorrect to affirm, that the senators *must* be, in such a predicament, but in all probability the senators would, in almost all cases, be without any participation in the offence. The offences, which would be generally prosecuted by impeachment, would be those only of a high character, and belonging to persons in eminent stations,—such as a head of department, a foreign minister, a judge, a vice president, or a president. Over the conduct of such persons the senate could ordinarily have no control; and a corrupt combination with them, in the discharge of the duties of their respective offices, could scarcely be presumed. Any of these officers might be bribed, or commit gross misdemeanours, without a single senator having the least knowledge, or participation in the offence. And, indeed, very few of the senators could, at any time, be presumed to be in habits of intimate personal confidence, or connexion with many of these officers. And so far, as public responsibility is concerned, or public confidence is required, the tenure of office of the judges would have no strong tendency to secure the former, or to assuage public jealousies, so as to peculiarly encourage the latter. It is, perhaps, one of the circumstances, most important in the discharge of judicial duties, that they rarely carry with them any strong popular favour, or popular influence. The influence, if any, is of a different sort, arising from dignity of life and conduct, abstinence from political contests, exclusive devotion to the advancement of the law, and a firm administration of justice; circumstances, which are felt more by the profession, than they can be expected to be praised by the public.

§ 760. Besides; it ought not to be overlooked, that such an additional accumulation of power in the judicial department would not only furnish pretexts for clamour against it, but might create a general dread of its influence, which could hardly fail to disturb the salutary effects of its ordinary functions. There is nothing, of which a free people are so apt to be jealous, as of the existence of political functions, and political checks, in those, who are not appointed by, and made directly responsible to themselves. The judicial tenure of office during good behaviour,

though in some respects most favourable for an independent discharge of these functions and checks, is at the same time obnoxious to some strong objections, as a remedy for impeachable offences.

§ 761. There are, however, reasons of great weight, besides those, which have been already alluded to, which fully justify the conclusion, that the Supreme Court is not the most appropriate tribunal to be invested with authority to try impeachments.

§ 762. In the first place, the nature of the functions to be performed. The offences, to which the power of impeachment has been, and is ordinarily applied, as a remedy, are of a political character. Not but that crimes of a strictly legal character fall within the scope of the power, (for, as we shall presently see, treason, bribery, and other high crimes and misdemeanours are expressly within it;) but that it has a more enlarged operation, and reaches, what are aptly termed, political offences, growing out of personal misconduct, or gross neglect, or usurpation, or habitual disregard of the public interests, in the discharge of the duties of political office. These are so various in their character, and so indefinable in their actual involutions, that it is almost impossible to provide systematically for them by positive law. They must be examined upon very broad and comprehensive principles of public policy and duty. They must be judged of by the habits, and rules, and principles of diplomacy, of departmental operations and arrangements, of parliamentary practice, of executive customs and negotiations, of foreign, as well as of domestic political movements; and in short, by a great variety of circumstances, as well those, which aggravate, as those, which extenuate, or justify the offensive acts, which do not properly belong to the judicial character in the ordinary administration of justice, and are far removed from the reach of municipal jurisprudence. They are duties, which are easily understood by statesmen, and are rarely known to judges. A tribunal, composed of the former, would therefore be far more competent, in point of intelligence and ability, than the latter, for the discharge of the functions, all other circumstances being equal. And surely, in such grave affairs, the competency of the tribunal to discharge the duties in the best manner is an indispensable qualification.

§ 763. In the next place, it is obvious, that the strictness of the forms of proceeding in cases of offences at common law are ill adapted to impeachments. The very habits growing out of judicial employments; the rigid manner, in which the discretion of judges is limited, and fenced in on all sides, in order to protect persons accused of crimes by rules and precedents; and the adherence to technical principles, which, perhaps, distinguishes this branch of the law, more than any other, are all ill adapted to the trial of political offences in the broad course of impeachments. And it has been observed with great propriety, that a tribunal of a liberal and comprehensive character, confined, as little as possible, to strict forms, enabled to continue its session as long, as the nature of the law may require, qualified to view the charge in all its bearings and dependencies, and to appropriate on sound principles of public policy the defence of the accused, seems indispensable to the value of the trial. The history of impeachments, both in England and America, justifies the remark. There is little technical in the mode of proceeding; the charges are sufficiently clear, and yet in a general form; there are few exceptions, which arise in the application of the evidence, which grow out of more technical rules, and quibbles. And it has repeatedly been seen, that the functions have been better understood, and more liberally and justly expounded by statesmen, than by mere lawyers. An illustrious instance of this sort is upon record in the case of the trial of Warren Hastings, where the question, whether an impeachment was abated by a dissolution of parliament, was decided in the negative by the house of lords, as well as the house of commons, against what seemed to be the weight of professional opinion.

§ 764. In the next place, the very functions, involving political interests and connexions, are precisely those, which it seems most important to exclude from the cognizance and participation of the judges of the Supreme Court. Much of the reverence and respect, belonging to the judicial character, arise from the belief, that the tribunal is impartial, as well as enlightened; just, as well as searching. It is of very great consequence, that judges should not only be, in fact, above all exception in this respect; but that they should be generally believed to be so. They should not only be pure; but, if possible, above suspicion. Many of the offences, which will be charged against public men, will be generated by the heats and animosities of party; and the very circumstances, that judges should be called to sit, as umpires, in the controversies of party, would inevitably involve them in the common odium of partizans, and place them in public opinion, if not in fact, at least in form, in the array on one side, or the other. The habits, too, arising from such functions, will lead them to take a more ardent part in public discussions, and in the vindication of their own political decisions, than seems desirable for those, who are daily called upon to decide upon the private rights and claims of men, distinguished for their political consequence, zeal, or activity, in the ranks of party. In a free government, like ours, there is a peculiar propriety in withdrawing, as much as possible, all judicial functionaries from the contests of mere party strife. With all their efforts to avoid them, from the free intercourse, and constant changes in a republican government, both of men and measures, there is, at all times, the most imminent danger, that all classes of society will be drawn into the vortex of politics. Whatever shall have a tendency to secure, in tribunals of justice, a spirit of moderation and exclusive devotion to juridical duties is of inestimable value. What can more surely advance this object, than the exemption of them from all participation in, and control over, the acts of political men in their official duties? Where, indeed, those acts fall within the character of known crimes at common law, or by positive statute, there is little difficulty in the duty, because the rule is known, and equally applies to all persons in and out of office; and the facts are to be tried by a jury, according to the habitual course of investigation in common cases. The remark of Mr. Woodeson on this subject is equally just and appro-

priate. After having enumerated some of the cases, in which impeachments have been tried for political offences, he adds, that from these "it is apparent, how little the ordinary tribunals are calculated to take cognizance of such offences, or to investigate and reform the general polity of the state."

§ 765. In the next place, the judges of the Supreme Court are appointed by the executive; and will naturally feel some sympathy and attachment for the person, to whom they owe this honour, and for those, whom he selects, as his confidential advisers in the departments. Yet the president himself, and those confidential advisers, are the very persons, who are eminently the objects to be reached by the power of impeachment. The very circumstance, that some, perhaps a majority of the court, owe their elevation to the same chief magistrate, whose acts, or those of his confidential advisers, are on trial, would have some tendency to diminish the public confidence in the impartiality and independence of the tribunal.

§ 766. But, in the next place, a far more weighty consideration is, that some of the members of the judicial department may be impeached for malconduct in office; and thus, that spirit, which, for want of a better term, has been called the corporation spirit of organized tribunals and societies, will naturally be brought into play. Suppose a judge of the Supreme Court should himself be impeached; the number of his triers would not only be diminished; but all the attachments, and partialities, or it may be the rivalries and jealousies of peers on the same bench, may be, or (what is practically almost as mischievous) may be suspected to be put in operation to screen or exaggerate the offence. Would any person soberly decide, that the judges of the Supreme Court would be the safest and the best of all tribunals for the trial of a brother judge, taking human feelings, as they are, and human infirmity, as it is? If not, would there not be, even in relation to inferior judges, a sense of indulgence, or a bias of opinion, upon certain judicial acts and practices, which might incline their minds to undue extenuation, or to undue harshness? And if there should be, in fact, no danger from such a source, is there not some danger, under some circumstances, that a jealousy of the operations of judicial tribunals over judicial offences, would create in the minds of the community a broad distinction in regard to convictions and punishments, between them and merely political offences? Would not the power of impeachment cease to possess its just reverence and authority, if such a distinction should prevail; and especially, if political victims rarely escaped, and judicial officers as rarely suffered? Can it be desirable thus to create any tendency in the public mind towards the judicial department, which may impair its general respect and daily utility?

§ 767. Considerations of this sort cannot be overlooked in inquiries of this nature; and if to some minds they may not seem wholly satisfactory, they, at least, establish, that the Supreme Court is not a tribunal for the trial of impeachment, wholly above all reasonable exceptions. But if, to considerations of this sort, it is added, that the common practice of free governments, and especially of England, and of the states composing the Union, has been, to confide this power to one department of the legislative body, upon the accusation of another; and that this has been found to work well, and to adjust itself to the public feelings and prejudices, to the dignity of the legislature, and to the tranquillity of the state, the inference in its favour cannot but be greatly strengthened and confirmed.

§ 768. To those, who felt difficulties in confiding to the Supreme Court alone the trial of impeachments, the scheme might present itself, of uniting that court with the senate jointly for this purpose. To this union many of the objections already stated, and especially those, founded on the peculiar functions of the judicial department, would apply with the same force, as they do to vesting the Supreme Court with the exclusive jurisdiction. In some other respects there would result advantages from the union; but they would scarcely overbalance the disadvantages. If the judges, compared with the whole body of the senate, were few in number, their weight would scarcely be felt in that body. The habits of co-operation in common daily duties would create among the senators an habitual confidence, and sympathy with each other; and the same habits would produce a correspondent influence among the judges. There would, therefore, be two distinct bodies, acting together *pro re nata,* which were in a great measure strangers to each other, and with feelings, pursuits, and modes of reasoning wholly distinct from each other. Great contrariety of opinion might naturally be presumed under such circumstances to spring up, and, in all probability, would become quite marked in the action of the two bodies. Suppose, upon an impeachment, the senators should be on one side, and the judges on the other; suppose a minority composed of all the judges, and a considerable number of the senators; or suppose a majority made by the co-operation of all the judges; in these, and many other cases, there might be no inconsiderable difficulty in satisfying the public mind, as to the result of the impeachment. Judicial opinion might go urgently one way, and political character and opinion, as urgently another way. Such a state of things would have little tendency to add weight, or dignity to the court, in the opinion of the community. And perhaps a lurking suspicion might pervade many minds, that one body, or the other, had possessed an undue preponderance of influence in the actual decision. Even jealousies and discontents might grow up in the bosoms of the competent bodies themselves, from their own difference of structure, and habits, and occupations, and duties. The practice of governments has not hitherto established any great value, as attached to the intermixture of different bodies for single occasions, or temporary objects.

§ 769. A third scheme might be, to entrust the trial of impeachments to a special tribunal, constituted for that sole purpose. But whatever arguments may be found in favour of such a plan, there will be found to be correspondent objections and difficulties. It would tend to increase the complexity of the political machine, and add a new spring to the operations of the government, the utility of which would be at least questionable, and might clog its just movements. A court of this nature would be attended with heavy expenses; and might, in practice, be subject to many casualties and inconveniences. It must consist either of permanent officers, stationary at the seat of government, and of course entitled to fixed and regular stipends; or of national officers, called to the duties for the occasion, though previously designated by office, or rank; or of officers of the state governments, selected when the impeachment was actually depending. Now, either of these alternatives would be found full of embarrassment and intricacy, when an attempt should be made to give it a definite form and organization. The court, in order to be efficient and independent, ought to be numerous. It ought to possess talents, experience, dignity, and weight of character, in order to obtain, or to hold, the confidence of the nation. What national officers, not belonging to either of the great departments of the government, legislative, executive, or judicial, could be found, embracing all these requisite qualifications? And if they could be, what compensation is to be made to them, in order to maintain their characters and importance, and to secure their services? If the court is to be selected from the state functionaries, in what manner is this to be accomplished? How can their acceptance, or performance of the duties, be either secured, or compelled? Does it not at once submit the whole power of impeachment to the control of the state governments, and thus surrender into their hands all the means of making it efficient and satisfactory? In political contests it cannot be supposed, that either the states, or the state functionaries, will not become partisans, and deeply interested in the success, or defeat of measures, in the triumph, or the ruin of rivals, or opponents. Parties will naturally desire to screen a friend, or overwhelm an adversary; to secure the predominance of a local policy, or a state party; and if so, what guarantee is there for any extraordinary fidelity, independence, or impartiality, in a tribunal so composed, beyond all others? Descending from such general inquiries to more practical considerations, it may be asked, how shall such a tribunal be composed? Shall it be composed of state executives, or state legislators, or state judges, or of a mixture of all, or a selection from all? If the body is very large, it will become unwieldy, and feeble from its own weight. If it be a mixture of all, it will possess too many elements of discord and diversities of judgment, and local and professional opinion. If it be homogeneous in its character, as if it consist altogether of one class of men, as of the executives of all the states, or the judges of the Supreme Courts of all the states, can it be supposed, (even if an equality in all other respects could be certainly obtained,) that persons, selected mainly by the states for local and peculiar objects, could best administer the highest and most difficult functions of the national government?

. . . . .

§ 771. A scheme somewhat different from either of the foregoing has been recommended by a learned commentator, drawn from the Virginia constitution, by which, in that state, all impeachments are to be tried in the courts of law, "according to the laws of the land;" and by the state laws the facts, as in other cases, are to be tried by a jury. But the objections to this course would be very serious, not only from the considerations already urged, but from the difficulty of impanneling a suitable jury for such purposes. From what state or states is such a jury to be drawn? How is it to be selected, or composed? What are to be the qualifications of the jurors? Would it be safe to entrust the political interests of a whole people to a common panel? Would any jury in times of party excitement by found sufficiently firm to give a true verdict, unaffected by the popularity or odium of the measure, when the nation was the accuser? These questions are more easily put, than they can be satisfactorily answered. And, indeed, the very circumstance, that the example of Virginia has found little favour in other states, furnishes decisive proof, that it is not deemed better than others, to which the national constitution bears the closest analogy.

§ 772. When the subject was before the state conventions, although here and there an objection was started against the plan, three states only formally proposed any amendment. Virginia and North-Carolina recommended, "that some tribunal, other than the senate, be provided for trying impeachments of *senators*," leaving the provision in all other respects, as it stood. New-York alone recommended an amendment, that the senate, the judges of the Supreme Court, and the first or senior judge of the highest state court of general or ordinary common law jurisdiction in each state should constitute a court for the trial of impeachments. This recommendation does not change the posture of a single objection. It received no support elsewhere; and the subject has since silently slept without any effort to revive it.

§ 773. The conclusion, to which, upon a large survey of the whole subject, our judgments are naturally led, is, that the power has been wisely deposited with the senate. . . .

§ 774. The remaining parts of the clause of the constitution now under consideration will not require an elaborate commentary. The first is, that the senate, when sitting as a court of impeachment, "shall be on oath or affirmation;" a provision, which, as it appeals to the conscience and integrity of the members by the same sanctions, which apply to judges and jurors, who sit in other trials, will commend itself to all persons, who deem the highest trusts, rights, and duties, worthy of the same protection and security, at least, as those of the humblest order. It would, indeed, be a monstrous anomaly, that the highest officers might be convicted of the worst crimes, without any sanction being interposed against the exercise of the most vindictive passions; while the humblest individual has a right to demand an oath of fidelity from those, who are his peers, and his triors. In England, however, upon the trial of impeachments, the house of lords are not under oath; but only make a declaration upon their honour. This is a strange anomaly, as in all civil and criminal trials by a jury, the jurors are under oath; and there seems no reason, why a sanction equally obligatory upon the consciences of the triors should not exist in trials for capital or other offences before every other tribunal. What is there in the honour of a peer, which necessarily raises it above the honour of a commoner? The anomaly is rendered still more glaring by the fact, that a peer cannot give testimony, as a witness, except on oath; for, here, his honour is not trusted. The maxim of the law, in such a case,

is *in judicio non creditur, nisi juratis*. Why should the obligation of a judge be less solemn, than the obligation of a witness? The truth is, that it is a privilege of power, conceded in barbarous times, and founded on feudal sovereignty, more than on justice, or principle.

§ 775. The next provision is: "When the president of the United States is tried, the chief justice shall preside." The reason of this clause has been already adverted to. It was to preclude the vice president, who might be supposed to have a natural desire to succeed to the office, from being instrumental in procuring the conviction of the chief magistrate. Under such circumstances, who could be deemed more suitable to preside, than the highest judicial magistrate of the Union. His impartiality and independence could be as little suspected, as those of any person in the country. And the dignity of his station might well be deemed an adequate pledge for the possession of the highest accomplishments.

§ 776. It is added, "And no person shall be convicted, without the concurrence of two thirds of the members present." Although very numerous objections were taken to the constitution, none seems to have presented itself against this particular quorum required for a conviction; and yet it might have been fairly thought to be open to attack on various sides from its supposed theoretical inconvenience and incongruity. It might have been said with some plausibility, that it deserted the general principles even of courts of justice, where a mere majority make the decision; and, of all legislative bodies, where a similar rule is adopted; and, that the requisition of two thirds would reduce the power of impeachment to a mere nullity. Besides; upon the trial of impeachments in the house of lords the conviction of acquittal is by a mere majority; so that there is a failure of any analogy to support the precedent.

§ 777. It does not appear from any authentic memorials, what were the precise grounds, upon which this limitation was interposed. But it may well be conjectured, that the real grounds were, to secure an impartial trial, and to guard public men from being sacrificed to the immediate impulses of popular resentment or party predominance. In England, the house of lords, from its very structure and hereditary independence, furnishes a sufficient barrier against such oppression and injustice. Mr. Justice Blackstone has remarked, with manifest satisfaction, that the nobility "have neither the same interests, nor the same passions, as popular assemblies;" and, that "it is proper, that the nobility should judge, to insure justice to the accused; as it is proper, that the people should accuse, to insure justice to the commonwealth." Our senate is, from the very theory of the constitution, founded upon a more popular basis; and it was desirable to prevent any combination of a mere majority of the states to displace, or to destroy a meritorious public officer. If a mere majority were sufficient to convict, there would be danger, in times of high popular commotion or party spirit, that the influence of the house of representatives would be found irresistible. The only practicable check seemed to be, the introduction of the clause of two thirds, which would thus require an union of opinion and interest, rare, except in cases where guilt was manifest, and innocence scarcely presumable. Nor could the limitation be justly complained of; for, in common cases, the law not only presumes every man innocent, until he is proved guilty; but unanimity in the verdict of the jury is indispensable. Here, an intermediate scale is adopted between unanimity, and a mere majority. And if the guilt of a public officer cannot be established to the satisfaction of two thirds of a body of high talents and acquirements, which sympathizes with the people, and represents the states, after a full investigation of the facts, it must be, that the evidence is too infirm, and too loose to justify a conviction. Under such circumstances, it would be far more consonant to the notions of justice in a republic, that a guilty person should escape, than that an innocent person should become the victim of injustice from popular odium, or party combinations.

§ 778. At the distance of forty years, we may look back upon this reasoning with entire satisfaction. The senate has been found a safe and effective depositary of the trial of impeachments. During that period but four cases have occurred, requiring this high remedy. In three there have been acquittals; and in one a conviction. Whatever may have been the opinions of zealous partisans at the times of their occurrence, the sober judgment of the nation sanctioned these results, at least, on the side of the acquittals, as soon as they became matters of history, removed from the immediate influences of the prosecutions. The unanimity of the awards of public opinion, in its final action on these controversies, has been as great, and as satisfactory, as can be attributed to any, which involve real doubt, or enlist warm prejudices and predilections on either side. No reproach has ever reached the senate for its unfaithful discharge of these high functions; and the voice of a state has rarely, if ever, displaced a single senator for his vote on such an occasion. What more could be asked in the progress of any government? What more could experience produce to justify confidence in the institution?

. . . . .

§ 780. It is obvious, that, upon trials on impeachments, one of two courses must be adopted in case of a conviction; either for the court to proceed to pronounce a full and complete sentence of punishment for the offence according to the law of the land in like cases, pending in the common tribunals of justice, superadding the removal from office, and the consequent disabilities; or, to confine its sentence to the removal from office and other disabilities. If the former duty be a part of the constitutional functions of the court, then, in case of an acquittal, there cannot be another trial of the party for the same offence in the common tribunals of justice, because it is repugnant to the whole theory of the common law, that a man should be brought into jeopardy of life or limb more than once for the same offence. A plea of acquittal is, therefore, an absolute bar against any second prosecution for the same offence. If the court of impeachments is merely to pronounce a sentence of removal from office and the other disabilities; then it is indispensable, that provision should be made, that the common tribunals of justice should be at liberty to entertain jurisdiction of the offence, for the purpose of inflicting, the common punishment applicable to unofficial offenders. Otherwise, it might be matter of

extreme doubt, whether, consistently with the great maxim above mentioned, established for the security of the life and limbs and liberty of the citizen, a second trial for the same offence could be had, either after an acquittal, or a conviction in the court of impeachments. And if no such second trial could be had, then the grossest official offenders might escape without any substantial punishment, even for crimes, which would subject their fellow citizens to capital punishment.

§ 781. The constitution, then, having provided, that judgment upon impeachments shall not extend further, than to removal from office, and disqualification to hold office, (which, however afflictive to an ambitious and elevated mind, would be scarcely felt, as a punishment, by the profligate and the base,) has wisely subjected the party to trial in the common criminal tribunals, for the purpose of receiving such punishment, as ordinarily belongs to the offence. Thus, for instance, treason, which by our laws is a capital offence, may receive its appropriate punishment; and bribery in high officers, which otherwise would be a mere disqualification from office, may have the measure of its infamy dealt out to it with the same unsparing severity, which attends upon other and humbler offenders.

§ 782. In England, the judgment upon impeachments is not confined to mere removal from office; but extends to the whole punishment attached by law to the offence. The house of lords, therefore, upon a conviction, may, by its sentence, inflict capital punishment; or perpetual banishment; or forfeiture of goods and lands; or fine and ransom; or imprisonment; as well as removal from office, and incapacity to hold office, according to the nature and aggravation of the offence.

§ 783. As the offences, to which the remedy of impeachment has been, and will continue to be principally applied, are of a political nature, it is natural to suppose, that they will be often exaggerated by party spirit, and the prosecutions be sometimes dictated by party resentments, as well as by a sense of the public good. There is danger, therefore, that in cases of conviction the punishment may be wholly out of proportion to the offence, and pressed as much by popular odium, as by aggravated crime. From the nature of such offences, it is impossible to fix any exact grade, or measure, either in the offences, or the punishments; and a very large discretion must unavoidably be vested in the court of impeachments, as to both. Any attempt to define the offences, or to affix to every grade of distinction its appropriate measure of punishment, would probably tend to more injustice and inconvenience, than it would correct; and perhaps would render the power at once inefficient and unwieldy. The discretion, then, if confided at all, being peculiarly subject to abuse, and connecting itself with state parties, and state contentions, and state animosities, it was deemed most advisable by the convention, that the power of the senate to inflict punishment should merely reach the right and qualifications to office; and thus take away the temptation in factious times to sacrifice good and great men upon the altar of party. History had sufficiently admonished them, that the power of impeachment had been thus mischievously and inordinately applied in other ages; and it was not safe to disregard those lessons, which it had left for our instruction, written not unfrequently in blood. Lord Strafford, in the reign of Charles the First, and Lord Stafford, in the reign of Charles the Second, were both convicted, and punished capitally by the house of lords; and both have been supposed to have been rather victims to the spirit of the times, than offenders meriting such high punishments. And other cases have occurred, in which whatever may have been the demerits of the accused, his final overthrow has been the result of political resentments and hatreds, far more than of any desire to promote public justice.

§ 784. There is wisdom, and sound policy, and intrinsic justice in this separation of the offence, at least so far, as the jurisdiction and trial are concerned, into its proper elements, bringing the political part under the power of the political department of the government, and retaining the civil part for presentment and trial in the ordinary forum. A jury might well be entrusted with the latter; while the former should meet its appropriate trial and punishment before the senate. If it should be asked, why separate trials should thus be successively had; and why, if a conviction should take place in a court of law, that court might not be entrusted with the power to pronounce a removal from office, and the disqualification to office, as a part of its sentence, the answer has been already given in the reasoning against vesting any court of law with merely political functions. In the ordinary course of the administration of criminal justice, no court is authorized to remove, or disqualify an offender, as a part of its regular judgment. If it results at all, it results as a consequence, and not as a part of the sentence. But it may be properly urged, that the vesting of such a high and delicate power, to be exercised by a court of law at its discretion, would, in relation to the distinguished functionaries of the government, be peculiarly unfit and inexpedient. What could be more embarrassing, than for a court of law to pronounce for a removal upon the mere ground of political usurpation, or malversation in office, admitting of endless varieties, from the slightest guilt up to the most flagrant corruption? Ought a president to be removed from office at the mere will of a court for political misdemeanours? Is not a political body, like the senate, from its superior information in regard to executive functions, far better qualified to judge, how far the public weal might be promoted by such a punishment in a given case, than a mere juridical tribunal? Suppose the senate should still deem the judgment irregular, or unjustifiable, how is the removal to take effect, and how is it to be enforced? A separation of the removing power altogether from the appointing power might create many practical difficulties, which ought not, except upon the most urgent reasons, to be introduced into matters of government. Without attempting to maintain, that the difficulties would be insuperable, it is sufficient to show, that they might be highly inconvenient in practice.

§ 785. It does not appear from the Journal of the Convention, that the provision thus limiting the sentence upon impeachments to removal and disqualification from office, attracted much attention, until a late period of its deliberations. The adoption of it was not, however, without some difference of opinion; for it passed only by the vote of seven states against three. The reasons, on which this opposition was founded, do not appear; and in the state conventions no doubt of the propriety of the provision seems to have been seriously entertained.

§ 786. In order to complete our review of the constitutional provisions on the subject of impeachments, it is necessary to ascertain, who are the persons liable to be impeached; and what are impeachable offences. By some strange inadvertence, this part of the constitution has been taken from its natural connexion, and with no great propriety arranged under that head, which embraces the organization, and rights, and duties of the executive department. To prevent the necessity of again recurring to this subject, the general method prescribed in these commentaries will, in this instance, be departed from, and the only remaining provision on impeachments be here introduced.

§ 787. The fourth section of the second article is as follows: "The president, vice-president, and all civil officers of the United States, shall be removed from office on impeachment for, and conviction of, treason, bribery, or other high crimes and misdemeanours."

§ 788. From this clause it appears, that the remedy by impeachment is strictly confined to civil officers of the United States, including the president and vice-president. In this respect, it differs materially from the law and practice of Great-Britain. In that kingdom, all the king's subjects, whether peers or commoners, are impeachable in parliament; though it is asserted, that commoners cannot now be impeached for capital offences, but for misdemeanours only. Such kind of misdeeds, however, as peculiarly injure the commonwealth by the abuse of high offices of trust, are the most proper, and have been the most usual grounds for this kind of prosecution in parliament. There seems a peculiar propriety, in a republican government at least, in confining the impeaching power to persons holding office. In such a government all the citizens are equal, and ought to have the same security of a trial by jury for all crimes and offences laid to their charge, when not holding any official character. To subject them to impeachment would not only be extremely oppressive and expensive, but would endanger their lives and liberties, by exposing them against their wills to persecution for their conduct in exercising their political rights and privileges. Dear as the trial by jury justly is in civil cases, its value, as a protection against the resentment and violence of rulers and factions in criminal prosecutions, makes it inestimable. It is there, and there only, that a citizen, in the sympathy, the impartiality, the intelligence, and incorruptible integrity of his fellows, impanelled to try the accusation, may indulge a well-founded confidence to sustain and cheer him. If he should choose to accept office, he would voluntarily incur all the additional responsibility growing out of it. If impeached for his conduct, while in office, he could not justly complain, since he was placed in that predicament by his own choice; and in accepting office he submitted to all the consequences. Indeed, the moment it was decided, that the judgment upon impeachments should be limited to removal and disqualification from office, it followed, as a natural result, that it ought not to reach any but officers of the United States. It seems to have been the original object of the friends of the national government to confine it to these limits; for in the original resolutions proposed to the convention, and in all the subsequent proceedings, the power was expressly limited to national officers.

§ 789. Who are "civil officers," within the meaning of this constitutional provision, is an inquiry, which naturally presents itself; and the answer cannot, perhaps, be deemed settled by any solemn adjudication. The term "civil" has various significations. It is sometimes used in contradistinction to *barbarous*, or *savage*, to indicate a state of society reduced to order and regular government. Thus, we speak of civil life, civil society, civil government, and civil liberty; in which it is nearly equivalent in meaning to *political*. It is sometimes used in contradistinction to *criminal*, to indicate the private rights and remedies of men, as members of the community, in contrast to those, which are public, and relate to the government. Thus, we speak of civil process and criminal process, civil jurisdiction and criminal jurisdiction. It is sometimes used in contradistinction to *military* or *ecclesiastical*, to *natural* or *foreign*. Thus, we speak of a civil station, as opposed to a military or ecclesiastical station; a civil death, as opposed to a natural death; a civil war, as opposed to a foreign war. The sense, in which the term is used in the constitution, seems to be in contradistinction to *military*, to indicate the rights and duties relating to citizens generally, in contradistinction to those of persons engaged in the land or naval service of the government. It is in this sense, that Blackstone speaks of the laity in England, as divided into three distinct states; the civil, the military, and the maritime; the two latter embracing the land and naval forces of the government. And in the same sense the expenses of the civil list of officers are spoken of, in contradistinction to those of the army and navy.

§ 790. All officers of the United States, therefore, who hold their appointments under the national government, whether their duties are executive or judicial, in the highest or in the lowest departments of the government, with the exception of officers in the army and navy, are properly civil officers within the meaning of the constitution, and liable to impeachment. The reason for excepting military and naval officers is, that they are subject to trial and punishment according to a peculiar military code, the laws, rules, and usages of war. The very nature and efficiency of military duties and discipline require this summary and exclusive jurisdiction; and the promptitude of its operations are not only better suited to the notions of military men; but they deem their honour and their reputation more safe in the hands of their brother officers, than in any merely civil tribunal. Indeed, in military and naval affairs it is quite clear, that the senate could scarcely possess competent knowledge or experience to decide upon the acts of military men; so much are these acts to be governed by mere usage, and custom, by military discipline, and military discretion, that the constitution has wisely committed the whole trust to the decision of courts-martial.

§ 791. A question arose upon an impeachment before the senate in 1799, whether a senator was a civil officer of the United States, within the purview of the constitution; and it was decided by the senate, that he was not; and the like principle must apply to the members of the house of representatives. This decision, upon which the senate itself was greatly divided, seems not to have been quite satisfactory (as it may be gathered) to the minds of some learned commentators. The reasoning, by which it was sustained in the senate, does not appear, their deliberations having been private. But it was probably held, that "civil officers of the United States" meant such, as derived their appointment from, and under the national government, and not those persons, who, though members of the government, derived their appointment from the states, or the people of the states. In this view, the enumeration of the president and vice president, as impeachable officers, was indispensable; for they derive, or may derive, their office from a source paramount to the national government. And the clause of the constitution, now under consideration, does not even affect to consider them officers of the United States. It says, "the president, vice-president, and *all civil officers* (not all *other* civil officers) shall be removed," &c. The language of the clause, therefore, would rather lead to the conclusion, that they were enumerated, as contradistinguished from, rather than as included in the description of, civil officers of the United States. Other clauses of the constitution would seem to favour the same result; particularly the clause, respecting appointment of officers of the United States by the executive, who is to "commission all the officers of the United States;" and the 6th section of the first article, which declares, that "no person, *holding any office under the United States*, shall be a member of either house during *his continuance in office;*" and the first section of the second article, which declares, that "no senator or representative, or *person holding an office of trust or profit* under the United States, shall be appointed an elector." It is far from being certain, that the convention itself ever contemplated, that senators or representatives should be subjected to impeachment; and it is very far from being clear, that such a subjection would have been either politic or desirable.

§ 792. The reasoning of the Federalist on this subject, in answer to some objections to vesting the trial of impeachments in the senate, does not lead to the conclusion, that the learned author thought the senators liable to impeachment. Some parts of it would rather incline the other way. "The convention might *with propriety*," it is said, "have mediated the punishment of the executive for a deviation from the instructions of the senate, or a want of integrity in the conduct of the negotiations committed to him. They might also have had in view the punishment of a few leading individuals in the senate, who should have prostituted their influence in that body, as the mercenary instruments of foreign corruption. But they could not with more, or with equal propriety, have contemplated the impeachment and punishment of two-thirds of the senate, consenting to an improper treaty, *than of a majority of that,* or of the *other branch of the legislature,* consenting to a pernicious or unconstitutional law; *a principle, which I believe has never been admitted into any government,*" &c. "And yet, what reason is there, that a majority of the house of representatives, sacrificing the interests of the society by an unjust and tyrannical act of legislation, should escape with impunity, more than two-thirds of the senate sacrificing the same interests in an injurious treaty with a foreign power? The truth is, that in all such cases, it is essential to the freedom, and to the necessary independence of the deliberations of the body, *that the members of it should be exempt from punishment for acts done in a collective capacity;* and the security to the society must depend on the care, which is taken, to confide the trust to proper hands; to make it their interest to execute it with fidelity; and to make it as difficult, as possible, for them to combine in any interest, opposite to that of the public good." And it is certain, that in some of the state conventions the members of congress were admitted by the friends of the constitution, not to be objects of the impeaching power.

§ 793. It may be admitted, that a breach of duty is as reprehensible in a legislator, as in an executive, or judicial officer; but it does not follow, that the same remedy should be applied in each case; or that a remedy applicable to the one may not be unfit, or inconvenient in the other. Senators and representatives are at short periods made responsible to the people, and may be rejected by them. And for personal offences, not purely political, they are responsible to the common tribunals of justice, and the laws of the land. If a member of congress were liable to be impeached for conduct in his legislative capacity, at the will of a majority, it might furnish many pretexts for an irritated and predominant faction to destroy the character, and intercept the influence of the wisest and most exalted patriots, who were resisting their oppressions, or developing their profligacy. It is, therefore, with great reason urged, that a legislator should be above all fear and influence of this sort in his public conduct. The impeachment of a legislator, for his official acts, has hitherto been unacknowledged, as matter of right, in the annals of England and America. A silence of this sort is conclusive, as to the state of public opinion in relation to the impolicy and danger of conferring the power.

§ 794. The next inquiry is, what are impeachable offences? They are "treason, bribery, or other high crimes and misdemeanours." For the definition of treason, resort may be had to the constitution itself; but for the definition of bribery, resort is naturally and necessarily had to the common law; for that, as the common basis of our jurisprudence, can alone furnish the proper exposition of the nature and limits of this offence. The only practical question is, what are to be deemed high crimes and misdemeanours? Now, neither the constitution, nor any statute of the United States has in any manner defined any crimes, except treason and bribery, to be high crimes and misdemeanours, and as such impeachable. In what manner, then, are they to be ascertained? Is the silence of the statute book to be deemed conclusive in favour of the party, until congress have made a legislative declaration and enumeration of the offences, which shall be deemed high crimes and misdemeanours? If so, then, as has been truly remarked, the power of impeachment, except as to the two expressed cases, is a complete nullity; and the party is wholly dispunishable, however enormous may be his corruption or criminality. It will not be sufficient to say,

that in the cases, where any offence is punished by any statute of the United States, it may, and ought to be, deemed an impeachable offence. It is not every offence, that by the constitution is so impeachable. It must not only be an offence, but a *high* crime and misdemeanour. Besides; there are many most flagrant offences, which, by the statutes of the United States, are punishable only, when committed in special places, and within peculiar jurisdictions, as, for instance, on the high seas, or in forts, navyyards, and arsenals ceded to the United States. Suppose the offence is committed in some other, than these privileged places, or under circumstances not reached by any statute of the United States, would it be impeachable?

§ 795. Again, there are many offences, purely political, which have been held to be within the reach of parliamentary impeachments, not one of which is in the slightest manner alluded to in our statute book. And, indeed, political offences are of so various and complex a character, so utterly incapable of being defined, or classified, that the task of positive legislation would be impracticable, if it were not almost absurd to attempt it. What, for instance, could positive legislation do in cases of impeachment like the charges against Warren Hastings, in 1788? Resort, then, must be had either to parliamentary practice, and the common law, in order to ascertain, what are high crimes and misdemeanours; or the whole subject must be left to the arbitrary discretion of the senate, for the time being. The latter is so incompatible with the genius of our institutions, that no lawyer or statesman would be inclined to countenance so absolute a despotism of opinion and practice, which might make that a crime at one time, or in one person, which would be deemed innocent at another time, or in another person. The only safe guide in such cases must be the common law, which is the guardian at once of private rights and public liberties. And however much it may fall in with the political theories of certain statesmen and jurists, to deny the existence of a common law belonging to, and applicable to the nation in ordinary cases, no one has as yet been bold enough to assert, that the power of impeachment is limited to offences positively defined in the statute book of the Union, as impeachable high crimes and misdemeanours.

§ 796. The doctrine, indeed, would be truly alarming, that the common law did not regulate, interpret, and control the powers and duties of the court of impeachment. What, otherwise, would become of the rules of evidence, the legal notions of crimes, and the application of principles of public or municipal jurisprudence to the charges against the accused? It would be a most extraordinary anomaly, that while every citizen of every state, originally composing the Union, would be entitled to the common law, as his birth-right, and at once his protector and guide; as a citizen of the Union, or an officer of the Union, he would be subjected to no law, to no principles, to no rules of evidence. It is the boast of English jurisprudence, and without it the power of impeachment would be an intolerable grievance, that in trials by impeachment the law differs not in essentials from criminal prosecutions before inferior courts. The same rules of evidence, the same legal notions of crimes and punishments prevail. For impeachments are not framed to alter the law; but to carry it into more effectual execution, where it might be obstructed by the influence of too powerful delinquents, or not easily discerned in the ordinary course of jurisdiction, by reason of the peculiar quality of the alleged crimes. Those, who believe, that the common law, so far as it is applicable, constitutes a part of the law of the United States in their sovereign character, as a nation, not as a source of jurisdiction, but as a guide, and check, and expositor in the administration of the rights, duties, and jurisdiction conferred by the constitution and laws, will find no difficulty in affirming the same doctrines to be applicable to the senate, as a court of impeachments. Those, who denounce the common law, as having any application or existence in regard to the national government, must be necessarily driven to maintain, that the power of impeachment is, until congress shall legislate, a mere nullity, or that it is despotic, both in its reach, and in its proceedings. It is remarkable, that the first congress, assembled in October, 1774, in their famous declaration of the rights of the colonies, asserted, "that the respective colonies are entitled to the common law of England;" and "that they are entitled to the benefit of such of the English statutes, as existed at the time of their colonization, and which they have by experience respectively found to be applicable to their several local and other circumstances." It would be singular enough, if, in framing a national government, that common law, so justly dear to the colonies, as their guide and protection, should cease to have any existence, as applicable to the powers, rights, and privileges of the people, or the obligations, and duties, and powers of the departments of the national government. If the common law has no existence, as to the Union, as a rule or guide, the whole proceedings are completely at the arbitrary pleasure of the government, and its functionaries in all its departments.

§ 797. Congress have unhesitatingly adopted the conclusion, that no previous statute is necessary to authorize an impeachment for any official misconduct; and the rules of proceeding, and the rules of evidence, as well as the principles of decision, have been uniformly regulated by the known doctrines of the common law and parliamentary usage. In the few cases of impeachment, which have hitherto been tried, no one of the charges has rested upon any statutable misdemeanours. It seems, then, to be the settled doctrine of the high court of impeachment, that though the common law cannot be a foundation of a jurisdiction not given by the constitution, or laws, that jurisdiction, when given, attaches, and is to be exercised according to the rules of the common law; and that, what are, and what are not high crimes and misdemeanours, is to be ascertained by a recurrence to that great basis of American jurisprudence. The reasoning, by which the power of the house of representatives to punish for contempts, (which are breaches of privileges, and offences not defined by any positive laws,) has been upheld by the Supreme Court, stands upon similar grounds; for if the house had no jurisdiction to punish for contempts, until the acts had been previously defined, and ascertained by positive law, it is clear, that the process of arrest would be illegal.

§ 798. In examining the parliamentary history of impeachments, it will be found, that many offences, not easily definable by law, and many of a purely political character, have been deemed high crimes and misdemeanours worthy of this extraordinary remedy. Thus, lord chancellors, and judges, and other magistrates, have not only been impeached for bribery, and acting grossly contrary to the duties of their office; but for misleading their sovereign by unconstitutional opinions, and for attempts to subvert the fundamental laws, and introduce arbitrary power. So, where a lord chancellor has been thought to have put the great seal to an ignominious treaty; a lord admiral to have neglected the safe-guard of the sea; an ambassador to have betrayed his trust; a privy counsellor to have propounded, or supported pernicious and dishonourable measures; or a confidential adviser of his sovereign to have obtained exorbitant grants, or incompatible employments;—these have been all deemed impeachable offences. Some of the offences, indeed, for which persons were impeached in the early ages of British jurisprudence, would now seem harsh and severe; but perhaps they were rendered necessary by existing corruptions, and the importance of suppressing a spirit of favouritism, and court intrigue. Thus, persons have been impeached for giving bad counsel to the king; advising a prejudicial peace; enticing the king to act against the advice of parliament; purchasing offices; giving medicine to the king without advice of physicians; preventing other persons from giving counsel to the king, except in their presence; and procuring exorbitant personal grants from the king. But others, again, were founded in the most salutary public justice; such as impeachments for malversations and neglects in office; for encouraging pirates; for official oppression, extortions, and deceits; and especially for putting good magistrates out of office, and advancing bad. One cannot but be struck, in this slight enumeration, with the utter unfitness of the common tribunals of justice to take cognizance of such offences; and with the entire propriety of confiding the jurisdiction over them to a tribunal capable of understanding, and reforming, and scrutinizing the polity of the state, and of sufficient dignity to maintain the independence and reputation of worthy public officers.

§ 799. Another inquiry, growing out of this subject, is, whether, under the constitution, any acts are impeachable, except such, as are committed under colour of office; and whether the party can be impeached therefor, after he has ceased to hold office. A learned commentator seems to have taken it for granted, that the liability to impeachment extends to all, who have been, as well as to all, who are in public office. Upon the other point his language is as follows: "The legitimate causes of impeachment have been already briefly noticed. They can have reference only to public character, and official duty. The words of the text are, 'treason, bribery, and other high crimes and misdemeanours.' The treason contemplated must be against the United States. In general, those offences, which may be committed equally by a private person, as a public officer, are not the subjects of impeachment. Murder, burglary, robbery, and indeed all offences not immediately connected with office, except the two expressly mentioned, are left to the ordinary course of judicial proceeding; and neither house can regularly inquire into them, except for the purpose of expelling a member."

§ 800. It does not appear, that either of these points has been judicially settled by the court having, properly, cognizance of them. In the case of William Blount, the plea of the defendant expressly put both of them, as exceptions to the jurisdiction, alleging, that, at the time of the impeachment, he, Blount, was not a senator, (though he was at the time of the charges laid against him,) and that he was not charged by the articles of impeachment with having committed any crime, or misdemeanour, in the execution of any civil office held under the United States; nor with any malconduct in a civil office, or abuse of any public trust in the execution thereof. The decision, however, turned upon another point, viz., that a senator was not an impeachable officer.

§ 801. As it is declared in one clause of the constitution, that "judgment, in cases of impeachment, shall not extend further, than a removal from office, and disqualification to hold any office of honour, trust, or profit, under the United States;" and in another clause, that "the president, vice president, and all civil officers of the United States, shall be removed from office on impeachment for, and conviction of, treason, bribery, or other high crimes or misdemeanours;" it would seem to follow, that the senate, on the conviction, were bound, in all cases, to enter a judgment of removal from office, though it has a discretion, as to inflicting the punishment of disqualification. If, then, there must be a judgment of removal from office, it would seem to follow, that the constitution contemplated, that the party was still in office at the time of the impeachment. If he was not, his offence was still liable to be tried and punished in the ordinary tribunals of justice. And it might be argued with some force, that it would be a vain exercise of authority to try a delinquent for an impeachable offence, when the most important object, for which the remedy was given, was no longer necessary, or attainable. And although a judgment of disqualification might still be pronounced, the language of the constitution may create some doubt, whether it can be pronounced without being coupled with a removal from office. There is also much force in the remark, that an impeachment is a proceeding purely of a political nature. It is not so much designed to punish an offender, as to secure the state against gross official misdemeanors. It touches neither his person, nor his property; but simply divests him of his political capacity.

§802. The other point is one of more difficulty. In the argument upon Blount's impeachment, it was pressed with great earnestness, that there is not a syllable in the constitution, which confines impeachments to official acts, and it is against the plainest dictates of common sense, that such restraint should be imposed upon it. Suppose a judge should countenance, or aid insurgents in a meditated conspiracy or insurrection against the government. This is not a judicial act; and yet it ought certainly to be impeachable. He may be called upon to try the very persons, whom he has aided. Suppose a judge or other officer to receive a bribe not connected with his judicial office; could he be entitled to any public confidence? Would not these reasons for his removal be just as strong, as if it were a case of an official bribe? The argument on the other side was, that the power of impeachment was strictly confined to civil officers of the United States, and this necessarily implied, that it must be limited to malconduct in office.

§ 803. It is not intended to express any opinion in these commentaries, as to which is the true exposition of the constitution on the points above stated. They are brought before the learned reader, as matters still *sub judice*, the final decision of which may be reasonably left to the high tribunal, constituting the court of impeachment, when the occasion shall arise.

. . . . .

§ 810. Having thus gone through the whole subject of impeachments, it only remains to observe, that a close survey of the system, unless we are egregiously deceived, will completely demonstrate the wisdom of the arrangements made in every part of it. The jurisdiction to impeach is placed, where it should be, in the possession and power of the immediate representatives of the people. The trial is before a body of great dignity, and ability, and independence, possessing the requisite knowledge and firmness to act with vigour, and to decide with impartiality upon the charges. The persons subjected to the trial are officers of the national government; and the offences are such, as may affect the rights, duties, and relations of the party accused to the public in his political or official character, either directly or remotely. The general rules of law and evidence, applicable to common trials, are interposed, to protect the party against the exercise of wanton oppression, and arbitrary power. And the final judgment is confined to a removal from, and disqualification for, office; thus limiting the punishment to such modes of redress, as are peculiarly fit for a political tribunal to administer, and as will secure the public against political injuries. In other respects the offence is left to be disposed of by the common tribunals of justice, according to the laws of the land, upon an indictment found by a grand jury, and a trial by a jury of peers, before whom the party is to stand for his final deliverance, like his fellow citizens.

§ 811. In respect to the impeachment of the president, and vice president, it may be remarked, that they are, upon motives of high state policy, made liable to impeachment, while they yet remain in office. In England the constitutional maxim is, that the king can do no wrong. His ministers and advisers may be impeached and punished; but he is, by his prerogative, placed above all personal amenability to the laws for his acts. In some of the state constitutions, no explicit provision is made for the impeachment of the chief magistrate; and in Delaware and Virginia, he was not (under their old constitutions) impeachable, until he was out of office. So that no immediate remedy in those states was provided for gross malversations and corruptions in office; and the only redress lay in the elective power, followed up by prosecutions after the party had ceased to hold his office. Yet cases may be imagined, where a momentary delusion might induce a majority of the people to re-elect a corrupt chief magistrate; and thus the remedy would be at once distant and uncertain. The provision in the constitution of the United States, on the other hand, holds out a deep and immediate responsibility, as a check upon arbitrary power; and compels the chief magistrate, as well as the humblest citizen, to bend to the majesty of the laws.

SEE ALSO:

Impeachments in England, Hinds' Precedents of the House of Representatives, 3:ch. 43, House Doc. no. 7, 93d Cong., 1st sess. (1973)

Boston Gazette, Impeachment of Public Officers, 4 Jan. 1768, Quincy's Rep. 583–84

Records of the Federal Convention, Farrand 1:78, 90–92, 244, 247, 292–93; 2:46, 120, 136, 145, 154, 159, 164, 172, 178–79, 187, 337, 344, 367–68, 435, 493, 495, 499, 545, 547, 572, 575–76, 600

Federal Farmer, no. 3, 10 Oct. 1787, Storing 2.8.33

Thomas McKean, Pennsylvania Ratifying Convention, 11 Dec. 1787, Elliot 2:534–35

Debate in South Carolina House of Representatives, 16 Jan. 1788, Elliot 4:263

Thomas Jefferson to John Rutledge, 2 Feb. 1788, Papers 12:556–57

Debate in North Carolina Ratifying Convention, 24 July 1788, Elliot 4:34–37

Pennsylvania Constitution of 1790, art. 4, Thorpe 5:3097

Tennessee Constitution of 1796, art. 4, secs. 1–4, Thorpe 6:3418–19

Senate, Impeachment of William Blount, 24 Dec., 3–5, 7–11, 14 Jan. 1799, Annals 8:2247–2319

St. George Tucker, Blackstone's Commentaries 1:App. 336–38, 347–48 (1803)

Impeachment of Judge John Pickering, 1803, House Doc. no. 7, 93d Cong., 1st sess. (1973) 129–31

Senate, Trial of Samuel Chase, 5 Jan.–1 Mar. 1804, Annals 14:81–669

Louisiana Constitution of 1812, art. 5, secs. 1–3, Thorpe 3:1388

Indiana Constitution of 1816, art. 3, secs. 23–24, Thorpe 2:1062

Illinois Constitution of 1818, art. 2, secs. 22–23, Thorpe 2:975

Tennessee Constitution of 1834, art. 5. secs. 1–5, Thorpe 6:3434

Article 1, Section 3, Clauses 1 and 2

The Senate of the United States shall be composed of two Senators from each State, chosen by the Legislature thereof, for six Years; and each Senator shall have one vote.

Immediately after they shall be assembled in Consequence of the first Election, they shall be divided as equally as may be into three Classes. The Seats of the Senators of the first Class shall be vacated at the Expiration of the second Year, of the second Class at the Expiration of the fourth Year, and of the third Class at the Expiration of the sixth Year, so that one third may be chosen every second Year; and if Vacancies happen by Resignation, or otherwise, during the Recess of the Legislature of any State, the Executive thereof may make temporary Appointments until the next Meeting of the Legislature, which shall then fill such Vacancies.

1

GEORGE READ TO JOHN DICKINSON
17 Jan. 1787

(See vol. 1, ch. 12, no. 13)

2

CREDENTIALS OF DELAWARE'S DELEGATES TO THE
FEDERAL CONVENTION
3 Feb. 1787
Farrand 3:574–75

His Excellency Thomas Collins, Esquire, President, Captain General, and Commander in Chief of the Delaware State; To all to whom these Presents shall come, Greeting. Know Ye, that among the Laws of the said State, passed by the General Assembly of the same, on the third day of February, (Seal) in the Year of our Lord One thousand seven hundred and Eighty seven, it is thus inrolled.

In the Eleventh Year of the Independence of the Delaware State

An Act appointing Deputies from this State to the Convention proposed to be held in the City of Philadelphia for the Purpose of revising the Federal Constitution.

Whereas the General Assembly of this State are fully convinced of the Necessity of revising the Federal Constitution, and adding thereto such further Provisions, as may render the same more adequate to the Exigencies of the Union; And Whereas the Legislature of Virginia have already passed an Act of that Commonwealth, appointing and authorizing certain Commissioners to meet, at the city of Philadelphia, in May next, a Convention of Commissioners or Deputies from the different States: And this State being willing and desirous of co-operating with the Commonwealth of Virginia, and the other States in the Confederation, in so useful a design.

Be it therefore enacted by the General Assembly of Delaware, that George Read, Gunning Bedford, John Dickinson, Richard Bassett and Jacob Broom, Esquires, are hereby appointed Deputies from this State to meet in the Convention of the Deputies of other States, to be held at the City of Philadelphia on the Second day of May next: And the said George Read, Gunning Bedford, John Dickinson, Richard Bassett and Jacob Broom, Esquires, or any three of them, are hereby constituted and appointed Deputies from this State, with Powers to meet such Deputies as may be appointed and authorized by the other States to assemble in the saie Convention at the City aforesaid, and to join with them in devising, deliberating on, and discussing, such Alterations and further Provisions as may be necessary to render the Foederal Constitution adequate to the Exigencies of the Union; and in reporting such Act or Acts for that purpose to the United States in Congress Assembled, as when agreed to by them, and duly confirmed by the several States, may effectually provide for the same: So always and Provided, that such Alterations or further Provisions, or any of them, do not extend to that part of the Fifth Article of the Confederation of the said States, finally ratified on the first day of March, in the Year One thousand seven hundred and eighty one, which declares that "In determining Questions in the United States in Congress Assembled each State shall have one Vote."

And be it enacted, that in Case any of the said Deputies hereby nominated, shall happen to die, or to resign his or their Appointment, the President or Commander in Chief with the Advice of the Privy Council, in the Recess of the General Assembly, is hereby authorized to supply such Vacancies

3

RECORDS OF THE FEDERAL CONVENTION

[1:20; Virginia Plan, 29 May]

5. Resold. that the members of the second branch of the National Legislature ought to be elected by those of the first, out of a proper number of persons nominated by the individual Legislatures, to be of the age of   years at least; to hold their offices for a term sufficient to ensure their independency, to receive liberal stipends, by which they may be compensated for the devotion of their time to public service; and to be ineligible to any office established by a particular State, or under the authority of the United States, except those peculiarly belonging to the functions of the second branch, during the term of service, and for the space of   after the expiration thereof.

[1:35; Madison, 30 May]

The following Resolution being the 2d. of those proposed by Mr. Randolph was taken up. viz—"that the rights of suffrage in the National Legislature ought to be proportioned to the quotas of contribution, or to the number of free inhabitants, as the one or the other rule may seem best in different cases."

Mr. Madison observing that the words "or to the number of free inhabitants." might occasion debates which would divert the Committee from the general question whether the principle of representation should be changed, moved that they might be struck out.

Mr. King observed that the quotas of contribution which would alone remain as the measure of representation, would not answer; because waving every other view of the matter, the revenue might hereafter be so collected by the general Govt. that the sums respectively drawn from the States would not appear; and would besides be continually varying.

Mr. Madison admitted the propriety of the observation, and that some better rule ought to be found.

Col. Hamilton moved to alter the resolution so as to read "that the rights of suffrage in the national Legislature ought to be proportioned to the number of free inhabitants. Mr. Spaight 2ded. the motion.

It was then moved that the Resolution be postponed, which was agreed to.

Mr. Randolph and Mr. Madison then moved the following resolution—"that the rights of suffrage in the national Legislature ought to be proportioned"

It was moved and 2ded. to amend it by adding "and not according to the present system"—which was agreed to.

It was then moved and 2ded. to alter the resolution so as to read "that the rights of suffrage in the national Legislature ought not to be according to the present system."

It was then moved & 2ded. to postpone the Resolution moved by Mr. Randolph & Mr. Madison, which being agreed to;

Mr. Madison, moved, in order to get over the difficulties, the following resolution—"that the equality of suffrage established by the articles of Confederation ought not to prevail in the national Legislature, and that an equitable ratio of representation ought to be substituted" This was 2ded. by Mr. Govr. Morris, and being generally relished, would have been agreed to; when,

Mr. Reed moved that the whole clause relating to the point of Representation be postponed; reminding the Come. that the deputies from Delaware were restrained by their commission from assenting to any change of the rule of suffrage, and in case such a change should be fixed on, it might become their duty to retire from the Convention.

Mr. Govr. Morris observed that the valuable assistance of those members could not be lost without real concern, and that so early a proof of discord in the convention as a secession of a State, would add much to the regret; that the change proposed was however so fundamental an article in a national Govt. that it could not be dispensed with.

Mr. Madison observed that whatever reason might have existed for the equality of suffrage when the Union was a federal one among sovereign States, it must cease when a national Governt. should be put into the place. In the former case, the acts of Congs. depended so much for their efficacy on the cooperation of the States, that these had a weight both within & without Congress, nearly in proportion to their extent and importance. In the latter case, as the acts of the Genl. Govt. would take effect without the intervention of the State legislatures, a vote from a small State wd. have the same efficacy & importance as a vote from a large one, and there was the same reason for different numbers of representatives from different States, as from Counties of different extents within particular States. He suggested as an expedient for at once taking the sense of the members on this point and saving the Delaware deputies from embarrassment, that the question should be taken in Committee, and the clause on report to the House be postponed without a question there. This however did not appear to satisfy Mr. Read.

By several it was observed that no just construction of the Act of Delaware, could require or justify a secession of her deputies, even if the resolution were to be carried thro' the House as well as the Committee. It was finally agreed however that the clause should be postponed: it being understood that in the event the proposed change of representation would certainly be agreed to, no objection or difficulty being started from any other quarter than from Delaware.

The motion of Mr. Read to postpone being agreed to

The Committee then rose. The Chairman reported progress, and the House having resolved to resume the subject in Committee tomorrow,

[1:51; Madison, 31 May]

The Committee proceeded to Resolution 5, "that the second, (or senatorial) branch of the National Legislature ought to be chosen by the first branch out of persons nominated by the State Legislatures."

Mr. Spaight contended that the 2d. branch ought to be chosen by the State Legislatures and moved an amendment to that effect.

Mr. Butler apprehended that the taking so many powers out of the hands of the States as was proposed, tended to destroy all that balance and security of interests among the States which it was necessary to preserve; and called on Mr. Randolph the mover of the propositions, to explain the extent of his ideas, and particularly the number of members he meant to assign to this second branch.

Mr. Randf. observed that he had at the time of offering his propositions stated his ideas as far as the nature of general propositions required; that details made no part of the plan, and could not perhaps with propriety have been introduced. If he was to give an opinion as to the number of the second branch, he should say that it ought to be much smaller than that of the first; so small as to be exempt from the passionate proceedings to which numerous assemblies are liable. He observed that the general object was to provide a cure for the evils under which the U. S. laboured; that in tracing these evils to their origin every man had found it in the turbulence and follies of democracy: that some check therefore was to be sought for agst. this tendency of our Governments: and that a good Senate seemed most likely to answer the purpose.

Mr. King reminded the Committee that the choice of the second branch as proposed (by Mr. Spaight) viz. by the State Legislatures would be impracticable, unless it was to be very numerous, or *the idea of proportion* among the States was to be disregarded. According to this *idea*, there must be 80 or 100 members to entitle Delaware to the choice of one of them.—Mr. Spaight withdrew his motion.

Mr. Wilson opposed both a nomination by the State Legislatures, and an election by the first branch of the national Legislature, because the second branch of the latter, ought to be independent of both. He thought both branches of the National Legislature ought to be chosen by the people, but was not prepared with a specific proposition. He suggested the mode of chusing the Senate of N. York. to wit of uniting several election districts, for one branch, in chusing members for the other branch, as a good model.

Mr. Madison observed that such a mode would destroy the influence of the smaller States associated with larger ones in the same district; as the latter would chuse from within themselves, altho' better men might be found in the former. The election of Senators in Virga. where large & small counties were often formed into one district for the purpose, had illustrated this consequence Local partiality, would often prefer a resident within the County or State, to a candidate of superior merit residing out of it. Less merit also in a resident would be more known throughout his own State.

Mr. Sherman favored an election of one member by each of the State Legislatures,

Mr. Pinkney moved to strike out the "nomination by the State Legislatures." On this question.

Massts. no. Cont. no. N. Y. no. N. J. no. Pena. no. Del. divd. Va. no. N. C. no. S. C. no Georg no. [Ayes—0; noes—9; divided—1.]

On the whole question for electing by the first branch out of nominations by the State Legislatures, Mass. ay. Cont. no. N. Y. no. N. Jersey. no. Pena. no. Del. no. Virga. ay. N. C. no. S. C. ay. Ga. no. [Ayes—3; noes—7.]

So the clause was disagreed to & a chasm left in this part of the plan.

[1:58; Pierce, 31 May]

Mr. Butler called on Govr. Randolph to point out the number of Men necessary for the Senate, for on a knowledge of that will depend his opinion of the style and manner of appointing the first branch.

Mr. Randolph said he could not then point out the exact number of Members for the Senate, but he would observe that they ought to be less than the House of Commons. He was for offering such a check as to keep up the balance, and to restrain, if possible, the fury of democracy. He thought it would be impossible for the State Legislatures to appoint the Senators, because it would not produce the check intended. The first branch of the foederal Legislature should have the appointment of the Senators, and then the check would be compleat.

Butler said that until the number of the Senate could be known it would be impossible for him to give a vote on it.

Mr. Wilson was of opinion that the appointment of the 2d branch ought to be made by the people provided the mode of election is as he would have it, and that is to divide the union into districts from which the Senators should be chosen. He hopes that a foederal Government may be established that will insure freedom and yet be vigorous.

Mr. Maddison thinks the mode pointed out in the original propositions the best.

Mr. Butler moved to have the proposition relating to the first branch postponed, in order to take up another,—which was that the second branch of the Legislature consist of blank.

Mr. King objected to the postponement for the reasons which he had offered before.

Mr. Sherman was of opinion that if the Senate was to be appointed by the first branch and out of that Body that it would make them too dependent, and thereby destroy the end for which the Senate ought to be appointed.

Mr. Mason was of opinion that it would be highly improper to draw the Senate out of the first branch; that it would occasion vacancies which would cost much time, trouble, and expence to have filled up,—besides which it would make the Members too dependent on the first branch.

Mr. Chs. Pinckney said he meant to propose to divide the Continent into four Divisions, out of which a certain number of persons shd. be nominated, and out of that nomination to appoint a Senate.

I was myself of opinion that it would be right first to know how the Senate should be appointed, because it would determine many Gentlemen how to vote for the choice of Members for the first branch,—it appeared clear to me that unless we established a Government that should carry at least some of its principles into the mass of the people, we might as well depend upon the present confederation. If the influence of the States is not lost in some part of the new Government we never shall have any thing like a national institution. But in my opinion it will be right to shew the sovereignty of the State in one branch of the Legislature, and that should be in the Senate.

[1:150; Madison, 7 June]

The Clause providing for ye appointment of the 2d branch of the national Legislature, having lain blank since the last vote on the mode of electing it, to wit, by the 1st. branch, Mr. Dickenson now moved "that the members of the 2d. branch ought to be chosen by the individual Legislatures."

Mr. Sherman seconded the motion; observing that the particular States would thus become interested in supporting the National Governmt. and that a due harmony between the two Governments would be maintained. He admitted that the two ought to have separate and distinct jurisdictions, but that they ought to have a mutual interest in supporting each other.

Mr. Pinkney. If the small States should be allowed one Senator only, the number will be too great, there will be 80 at least.

Mr. Dickenson had two reasons for his motion. 1. because the sense of the States would be better collected through their Governments; than immediately from the people at large. 2. because he wished the Senate to consist of the most distinguished characters, distinguished for their rank in life and their weight of property, and bearing as strong a likeness to the British House of Lords as possible; and he thought such characters more likely to be selected by the State Legislatures, than in any other mode. The greatness of the number was no objection with him. He hoped there would be 80 and twice 80. of them. If their number should be small, the popular branch could not be [ba]lanced by them. The legislature of a numerous people ought to be a numerous body.

Mr. Williamson, preferred a small number of Senators, but wished that each State should have at least one. He suggested 25 as a convenient number. The different modes of representation in the different branches, will serve as a mutual check.

Mr. Butler was anxious to know the ratio of representation before he gave any opinion.

Mr. Wilson. If we are to establish a national Government, that Government ought to flow from the people at large. If one branch of it should be chosen by the Legislatures, and the other by the people, the two branches will rest on different foundations, and dissentions will naturally arise between them. He wished the Senate to be elected by the people as well as the other branch, and the people might be divided into proper districts for the purpose & moved to postpone the motion of Mr. Dickenson, in order to take up one of that import.

Mr Morris 2ded. him.

Mr. Read proposed "that the Senate should be appointed by the Executive Magistrate out of a proper number of persons to be nominated by the individual legislatures." He said he thought it his duty, to speak his mind frankly. Gentlemen he hoped would not be alarmed at the idea. Nothing short of this approach towards a proper model of Government would answer the purpose, and he thought it best to come directly to the point at once.—His proposition was not seconded nor supported.

Mr. Madison, if the motion (of Mr. Dickenson) should be agreed to, we must either depart from the doctrine of proportional representation; or admit into the Senate a very large number of members. The first is inadmissable, being evidently unjust. The second is inexpedient. The use of the Senate is to consist in its proceeding with more coolness, with more system, & with more wisdom, than the popular branch. Enlarge their number and you communicate to them the vices which they are meant to correct. He differed from Mr. D. who thought that the additional number would give additional weight to the body. On the contrary it appeared to him that their weight would be in an inverse ratio to their number. The example of the Roman Tribunes was applicable. They lost their influence and power, in proportion as their number was augmented. The reason seemed to be obvious: They were appointed to take care of the popular interests & pretensions at Rome, because the people by reason of their numbers could not act in concert; were liable to fall into factions among themselves, and to become a prey to their aristocratic adversaries. The more the representatives of the people therefore were multiplied, the more they partook of the infirmaties of their constituents, the more liable they became to be divided among themselves either from their own indiscretions or the artifices of the opposite factions, and of course the less capable of fulfilling their trust. When the weight of a set of men depends merely on their personal characters; the greater the number the greater the weight. When it depends on the degree of political authority lodged in them the smaller the number the greater the weight. These considerations might perhaps be combined in the intended Senate; but the latter was the material one.

Mr. Gerry. 4 modes of appointing the Senate have been mentioned. 1. by the 1st. branch of the National Legislature. This would create a dependence contrary to the end proposed. 2. by the National Executive. This is a stride towards monarchy that few will think of. 3. by the people. the people have two great interests, the landed interest, and the commercial including the stockholders. To draw both branches from the people will leave no security to the latter interest; the people being chiefly composed of the landed interest, and erroneously, supposing, that the other interests are adverse to it. 4 by the Individual Legislatures. The elections being carried thro' this refinement, will be most likely to provide some check in favor of the commercial interest agst. the landed; without which oppression will take place, and no free Govt. can last long when that is the case. He was therefore in favor of this last.

Mr. Dickenson. The preservation of the States in a certain degree of agency is indispensible. It will produce that collision between the different authorities which should be wished for in order to check each other. To attempt to abolish the States altogether, would degrade the Councils of our Country, would be impracticable, would be ruinous. He compared the proposed National System to the Solar System, in which the States were the planets, and ought to be left to move freely in their proper orbits. The Gentleman from Pa. (Mr. Wilson) wished he said to extinguish these planets. If the State Governments were excluded from all agency in the national one, and all power drawn from the people at large, the consequence would be that the national Govt. would move in the same direction as the State Govts. now do, and would run into all the same mischiefs. The reform would only unite the 13 small streams into one great current pursuing the same course without any opposition whatever. He adhered to the opinion that the Senate ought to be composed of a large number, and that their influence from family weight & other causes would be increased thereby. He did not admit that the Tribunes lost their weight in proportion as their no. was augmented and gave a historical sketch of this institution. If the reasoning of (Mr. Madison) was good it would prove that the number of the Senate ought to be reduced below ten, the highest no. of the Tribunitial corps.

Mr. Wilson. The subject it must be owned is surrounded with doubts and difficulties. But we must surmount them. The British Governmt. cannot be our model. We have no materials for a similar one. Our manners, our laws, the abolition of entails and of primogeniture, the whole genius of the people, are opposed to it. He did not see the danger of the States being devoured by the Nationl. Govt. On the contrary, he wished to keep them from devouring the national Govt. He was not however for extinguishing these planets as was supposed by Mr. D.—neither did he on the other hand, believe that they would warm or enlighten the Sun. Within their proper orbits they must still be suffered to act for subordinate purposes for which their existence is made essential by the great extent of our Country. He could not comprehend in what manner the landed interest wd. be rendered less predominant in the Senate, by an election through the medium of the Legislatures than by the people themselves. If the Legislatures, as was now complained, sacrificed the commercial to the landed interest, what reason was there to expect such a choice from them as would defeat their own views. He was for an election by the people in large districts which wd. be most likely to obtain men of intelligence & uprightness; subdividing the districts only for the accomodation of voters.

Mr. Madison could as little comprehend in what manner family weight, as desired by Mr. D. would be more certainly conveyed into the Senate through elections by the State Legislatures, than in some other modes. The true question was in what mode the best choice wd. be made? If an election by the people, or thro' any other channel than the State Legislatures promised as uncorrupt & impartial a preference of merit, there could surely be no necessity for an appointment by those Legislatures. Nor was it apparent that a more useful check would be derived thro' that channel than from the people thro' some other. The great evils complained of were that the State Legislatures run into schemes of paper money &c, whenever solicited by the people, & sometimes without even the sanction of the people. Their influence then, instead of checking a like propensity in the National Legislature, may be expected to promote it. Nothing can be more contradictory than to say that the Natl. Legislature witht. a proper check will follow the example of the State legislatures, & in the same breath, that the State Legislatures are the only proper check.

Mr. Sharman opposed elections by the people in districts, as not likely to produce such fit men as elections by the State Legislatures.

Mr. Gerry insisted that the commercial & monied interest wd. be more secure in the hands of the State Legislatures, than of the people at large. The former have more sense of character, and will be restrained by that from injustice. The people are for paper money when the Legislatures are agst. it. In Massts. the County Conventions had declared a wish for a *depreciating* paper that wd. sink itself. Besides, in some States there are two Branches in the Legislature, one of which is somewhat aristocratic. There wd. therefore be so far a better chance of refinement in the choice. There seemed, he thought to be three powerful objections agst. elections by districts 1. It is impracticable; the people can not be brought to one place for the purpose; and whether brought to the same place or not, numberless frauds wd. be unavoidable. 2. small States forming part of the same district with a large one, or large part of a large one, wd. have no chance of gaining an appointment for its citizens of merit. 3 a new source of discord wd. be opened between different parts of the same district.

Mr. Pinkney thought the 2d. branch ought to be permanent & independent, & that the members of it wd. be rendered more so by receiving their appointment from the State Legislatures. This mode wd. avoid the rivalships & discontents incident to the election by districts. He was for dividing the States into three classes according to their respective sizes, & for allowing to the 1st. class three members—to the 2d. two. & to the 3d. one.

On the question for postponing Mr. Dickinson's motion referring the appointment of the Senate to the State Legislatures, in order to consider Mr. Wilson's for referring it to the people.

Mass. no. Cont. no. N. Y. no. N. J. no. Pa. ay Del. no. Md. no. Va. no. N. C. no. S. C. no. Geo. no. [Ayes—1; noes—10.]

Col. Mason. whatever power may be necessary for the Natl. Govt. a certain portion must necessarily be left in the States. It is impossible for one power to pervade the extreme parts of the U. S. so as to carry equal justice to them. The State Legislatures also ought to have some means of defending themselves agst. encroachments of the Natl. Govt. In every other department we have studiously endeavored to provide for its self-defence. Shall we leave the States along unprovided with the means for this purpose? And what better means can we provide than the giving them some share in, or rather to make them a constituent part of, the Natl. Establishment. There is danger on both sides no doubt; but we have only seen the evils arising on the side of the State Govts. Those on the other side remain to be displayed. The example of Cong: does not apply. Congs. had no power to carry their acts into execution as the Natl. Govt. will have.

On Mr. Dickinson's motion for an appointment of the Senate by the State-Legislatures.

Mass. ay. Ct. ay. N. Y. ay. Pa. ay Del. ay. Md. ay. Va. ay N. C. ay. S. C. ay. Geo. ay. [Ayes—10; noes—0.]

[1:156; Yates, 7 June]

Mr. Rutledge moved to take into consideration the mode of electing the second branch of the national legislature.

Mr. Dickinson thereupon moved, *that the second branch of the national legislature be chosen by the legislatures of the individual states.* He observed, that this mode will more intimately connect the state governments with the national legislature—it will also draw forth the first characters either as to family or talent, and that it ought to consist of a considerable number.

Mr. Wilson against the motion, because the two branches thus constituted, cannot agree, they having different views and different sentiments.

Mr. Dickinson is of opinion that the mode by him proposed, like the British house of lords and commons, whose powers flow from different sources, are mutual checks on each other, and will thus promote the real happiness and security of the country—a government thus established would harmonize the whole, and like the planetary system, the national council like the sun, would illuminate the whole—the planets revolving round it in perfect order; or like the union of several small streams, would at last form a respectable river, gently flowing to the sea.

Mr. Wilson. The state governments ought to be preserved—the freedom of the people and their internal good police depends on their existence in full vigor—but such a government can only answer local purposes—That it is not possible a general government, as despotic as even that of the Roman emperors, could be adequate to the government of the whole without this distinction. He hoped that the national government would be independent of state governments, in order to make it vigorous, and therefore moved that the above resolution be postponed, and that the convention in its room adopt the following resolve: *That the second branch of the national legislature be chosen by districts, to be formed for that purpose.*

Mr. Sherman supposes the election of the national legislature will be better vested in the state legislatures, than by the people, for by pursuing different objects, persons may be returned who have not one tenth of the votes.

Mr. Gerry observed, that the great mercantile interest and of stockholders, is not provided for in any mode of election—they will however be better represented if the state legislatures choose the second branch.

Question carried against the postponement—10 states against 1.

Mr. Mason then spoke to the general question—observing on the propriety, that the second branch of the national legislature should flow from the legislature of each state, to prevent the encroachments on each other and to harmonize the whole.

The question put on the first motion, and carried unanimously. Adjourned to to-morrow morning.

[1:160; Mason, 7 June]

[Mason:] At a time when our government is approaching to dissolution, when some of its principles have been found utterly inadequate to the purposes for which it was established, and it is evident that without some material alterations it can not much longer subsist, it must give real concern to every man who has his country's interest at heart to find such a difference of sentiment and opinion in an assembly of the most respectable and confidential characters in America, appointed for the special purpose of revising and amending the federal constitution, so as to obtain and preserve the important objects for which it was instituted—the protection, safety and happiness of the people. We all agree in the necessity of new regulations; but we differ widely in our opinions of what are the safest and most effectual. Perhaps this contrariety of sentiment arises from our not thoroughly considering the peculiar circumstances, situation, character and genius of the people of America, differing materially from that of any other nation. The history of other nations has been minutely investigated, examples have been drawn from and arguments founded on the practice of countries very dissimilar to ours. The treaties, leagues, and confederacies between different sovereign, independent powers have been urged as proofs in support of the propriety and justice of the single and equal representation of each individual State in the American Union; and thence conclusions have been drawn that the people of these United States would refuse to adopt a government founded more on an equal representation of the people themselves, than on the distinct representation of each separate, individual State. If the different States in our Union always had been as now substantially and in reality distinct, sovereign and independent, this kind of reasoning would have great force; but if the premises on which it is founded are mere assumptions not founded on facts, or at best upon facts to be found only upon a paper of yesterday, and even these contradictory to each other, no satisfactory conclusions can be drawn from them.

[1:201; Madison, 11 June]

Mr. Sharman moved that a question be taken whether each State shall have one vote in the 2d. branch. Every thing he said depended on this. The smaller States would never agree to the plan on any other principle than an equality of suffrage in this branch. Mr. Elsworth seconded the motion. On the question for allowing each State one vote in the 2d. branch.

Massts. no. Cont. ay. N. Y. ay. N. J. ay. Pa. no. Del. ay. Md. ay. Va. no. N. C. no. S. C. no. Geo. no. [Ayes—5; noes—6.]

Mr. Wilson & Mr. Hamilton moved that the right of suffrage in the 2d. branch ought to be according to the same rule as in the 1st. branch.

On this question for making the ratio of representation the same in the 2d. as in the 1st. branch it passed in the affirmative: Massts. ay. Cont. no. N. Y. no. N. J. no. Pa. ay. Del. no. Md. no. Va. ay. N. C. ay. S. C. ay. Geo. ay. [Ayes—6; noes—5.]

[1:218; Madison, 12 June]

Mr. Spaight moved to fill the blank for the duration of the appointmts. to the 2d branch of the National Legislature with the words "7 years.

Mr. Sherman thought 7 years too long. He grounded his opposition he said on the principle that if they did their duty well, they would be reelected. And if they acted amiss, an earlier opportunity should be allowed for getting rid of them. He preferred 5 years which wd. be between the terms of 1st branch & of the executive

Mr. Pierce proposed 3 years. 7 years would raise an alarm. Great mischiefs had arisen in England from their septennial act which was reprobated by most of their patriotic Statesmen.

Mr. Randolph was for the term of 7 years. The Democratic licentiousness of the State Legislatures proved the necessity of a firm Senate. The object of this 2d. branch is to controul the democratic branch of the Natl. Legislature. If it be not a firm body, the other branch being more numerous, and coming immediately from the people, will overwhelm it. The Senate of Maryland constituted on like principles had been scarcely able to stem the popular torrent. No mischief can be apprehended, as the concurrence of the other branch, and in some measure, of the Executive, will in all cases be necessary. A firmness & independence may be the more necessary also in this branch, as it ought to guard the Constitution agst. encroachments of the Executive who will be apt to form combinations with the demagogues of the popular branch.

Mr. Madison, considered 7 years as a term by no means too long. What we wished was to give to the Govt. that stability which was every where called for, and which the enemies of the Republican form alleged to be inconsistent with its nature. He was not afraid of giving too much stability by the term of seven years. His fear was that the popular branch would still be too great an overmatch for it. It was to be much lamented that we had so little direct experience to guide us. The Constitution of Maryland was the only one that bore any analogy to this part of the plan. In no instance had the Senate of Maryd. created just suspicions of danger from it. In some instances perhaps it may have erred by yielding to the H. of Delegates. In every instance of their opposition to the measures of the H. of D. they had had with them the suffrages of the most enlightened and impartial people of the other States as well as of their own. In the States where the Senates were chosen in the same manner as the other branches, of the Legislature, and held their seats for 4 years, the institution was found to be no check whatever agst. the instabilities of the other branches. He conceived it to be of great importance that a stable & firm Govt. organized in the republican form should be held out to the people. If this be not done, and the people be left to judge of this species of Govt. by ye. operations of the defective systems under which they now live, it is much to be feared the time is not distant when, in universal disgust, they will renounce the blessing which they have purchased at so dear a rate, and be ready for any change that may be proposed to them.

On the question for "seven years", as the term for the 2d. branch

Massts. divided. (Mr. King. Mr. Ghorum ay—Mr. Gerry, Mr. Strong, no.) Cont. no. N. Y. divd. N. J. ay. Pa. ay Del. ay. Md. ay. Va. ay. N. C. ay. S. C. ay. Geo. ay. [Ayes—8; noes—1; divided—2.]

[1:235; Report of the Committee of the Whole, Madison, 13 June]

4. Resd. that the members of the second branch of the Natl. Legislature ought to be chosen by the individual Legislatures, to be of the age of 30 years at least, to hold thier offices for a term sufficient to ensure their independency, namely, seven years, to receive fixed stipends by which they may be compensated for the devotion of their time to public service to be paid out of the National Treasury; to be ineligible to any office established by a particular State, or under the authority of the U. States, (except those peculiarly belonging to the functions of the second branch) during the term of service, and under the Natl. Govt. for the space of one year after its expiration.

. . . . .

8. Resolved that the right of suffrage in the 2d. branch of the National Legislature ought to be according to the rule established for the first.

[1:289, 291; Madison, 18 June]

[Hamilton:] No temporary Senate will have firmness en'o' to answer the purpose. The Senate (of Maryland) which seems to be so much appealed to, has not yet been sufficiently tried. Had the people been unanimous & eager, in the late appeal to them on the subject of a paper emission they would have yielded to the torrent. Their acquiescing in such an appeal is a proof of it.—Gentlemen differ in their opinions concerning the necessary checks, from the different estimates they form of the human passions. They suppose Seven years a sufficient period to give the Senate an adequate firmness, from not duly considering the amazing violence & turbulence of the democratic spirit. When a great object of Govt. is pursued, which seizes the popular passions, they spread like wild fire, and become irresistable. He appealed to the gentlemen from the N. England States whether experience had not there verified the remark.

. . . . .

III. The Senate to consist of persons elected to serve during good behaviour; their election to be made by electors chosen for that purpose by the people: in order to this the States to be divided into election districts. On the death, removal or resignation of any Senator his place to be filled out of the district from which he came.

[1:300; Yates, 18 June]

[Hamilton:]—*(Here Mr. H. produced his plan, a copy whereof is hereunto annexed)* to consist of two branches—and I would give them the unlimited power of passing *all laws* without exception. The assembly to be elected for three years by the people in districts—the senate to be elected by electors to be chosen for that purpose by the people, and to remain in office during life.

[1:309; Hamilton, 18 June]

The aristocracy ought to be entirely separated; their power should be permanent, and they should have the *caritas liberorum.*

They should be so circumstanced that they can have no interest in a change—as to have an effectual weight in the constitution.

Their duration should be the earnest of wisdom and stability.

'Tis essential there should be a permanent will in a community.

Vox populi, vox Dei.

Source of government—the unreasonableness of the people—separate interests—debtors and creditors, &c.

There ought to be a principle in government capable of resisting the popular current.

No periodical duration will come up to this.

This will always imply hopes and fears.

Creature and Creator.

Popular assemblies governed by a few individuals.

These individuals seeing their dissolution approach, will sacrifice.

The principle of representation will influence.

The most popular branch will acquire an influence over the other.

The other may check in ordinary cases, in which there is no strong public passion; but it will not in cases where there is—the cases in which such a principle is most necessary.

☞ Suppose duration seven years, and rotation.

One-seventh will have only one year to serve.

One-seventh ——————— two years.

One-seventh ——————— three years.

One-seventh ——————— four years.

A majority will look to a dissolution in four years by instalments.

[1:404; Madison, 25 June]

[Charles Pinckney:] No position appears to me more true than this; that the General Govt. can not effectually exist without reserving to the States the possession of their local rights.—They are the instruments upon which the Union must frequently depend for the support & execution of their powers, however immediately operating upon the people, and not upon the States.

Much has been said about the propriety of abolishing the distinction of State Governments, & having but one general System. Suffer me for a moment to examine this question.

(The residue of this speech was not furnished) like the above by Mr. Pinckeney.

The mode of constituting the 2d. branch being under consideration

The word "national" was struck out and "United States" inserted.

Mr. Ghorum, inclined to a compromise as to the rule of proportion. He thought there was some weight in the objections of the small States. If Va. should have 16 votes & Delre. with several other States together 16. those from

Virga. would be more likely to unite than the others, and would therefore have an undue influence. This remark was applicable not only to States, but to Counties or other districts of the same State. Accordingly the Constitution of Massts. had provided that the representatives of the larger districts should not be in an exact ratio to their numbers. And experience he thought had shewn the provision to be expedient.

Mr. Read. The States have heretofore been in a sort of partnership. They ought to adjust their old affairs before they open a new account. He brought into view the appropriation of the common interest in the Western lands, to the use of particular States. Let justice be done on this head; let the fund be applied fairly & equally to the discharge of the general debt, and the smaller States who had been injured would listen then perhaps to those ideas of just representation which had been held out.

Mr. Ghorum. did not see how the Convention could interpose in the case. Errors he allowed had been committed on the Subject. But Congs. were now using their endeavors to rectify them. The best remedy would be such a Government as would have vigor enough to do justice throughout. This was certainly the best chance that could be afforded to the smaller States.

Mr. Wilson. the question is shall the members of the 2d. branch be chosen by the Legislatures of the States? When he considered the amazing extent of country—the immense population which is to fill it, the influence which the Govt. we are to form will have, not only on the present generation of our people & their multiplied posterity, but on the whole Globe, he was lost in the magnitude of the object. The project of Henry the 4th. & his Statesmen was but the picture in miniature of the great portrait to be exhibited. He was opposed to an election by the State Legislatures. In explaining his reasons it was necessary to observe the twofold relation in which the people would stand. 1. as Citizens of the Gen'l Gov't. 2. as Citizens of their particular State. The Genl. Govt. was meant for them in the first capacity; the State Govts. in the second. Both Govts. were derived from the people—both meant for the people—both therefore ought to be regulated on the same principles. The same train of ideas which belonged to the relation of the Citizens to their State Govts. were applicable to their relations to the Genl. Govt. and in forming the latter, we ought to proceed, by abstracting as much as possible from the idea of State Govts. With respect to the province & objects of the Gen'l Govt. they should be considered as having no existence. The election of the 2d. branch by the Legislatures, will introduce & cherish local interests & local prejudices. The Genl. Govt. is not an assemblage of States, but of individuals for certain political purposes—it is not meant for the States, but for the individuals composing them: the *individuals* therefore not the *States,* ought to be represented in it: A proportion in this representation can be preserved in the 2d. as well as in the 1st. branch; and the election can be made by electors chosen by the people for that purpose. He moved an amendment to that effect, which was not seconded.

Mr. Elseworth saw no reason for departing from the mode contained in the Report. Whoever chooses the member, he will be a citizen of the State he is to represent & will feel the same spirit and act the same part whether he be appointed by the people or the Legislature. Every State has its particular views & prejudices, which will find their way into the general councils, through whatever channel they may flow. Wisdom was one of the characteristics which it was in contemplation to give the second branch. Would not more of it issue from the Legislatures; than from an immediate election by the people. He urged the necessity of maintaining the existence & agency of the States. Without their co-operation it would be impossible to support a Republican Govt. over so great an extent of Country. An army could scarcely render it practicable. The largest States are the Worst Governed. Virga. is obliged to acknowledge her incapacity to extend her Govt. to Kentucky. Masts can not keep the peace one hundred miles from her capitol and is now forming an army for its support. How long Pena. may be free from a like situation can not be foreseen. If the principles & materials of our Govt. are not adequate to the extent of these single States; how can it be imagined that they can support a single Govt. throughout the U. States. The only chance of supporting a Genl. Govt. lies in engrafting it on that of the individual States.

Docr. Johnson urged the necessity of preserving the State Govts—which would be at the mercy of the Genl. Govt. on Mr. Wilson's plan.

Mr. Madison thought it wd. obviate difficulty if the present resol: were postponed. & the 8th. taken up. which is to fix the right of suffrage in the 2d. branch.

Docr. Williamson professed himself a friend to such a system as would secure the existence of the State Govts. The happiness of the people depended on it. He was at a loss to give his vote, as to the Senate until he knew the number of its members. In order to ascertain this, he moved to insert these words after "2d. branch of Natl. Legislature"—"who shall bear such proportion to the nol of the 1st. branch as 1 to   " He was not seconded.

Mr. Mason. It has been agreed on all hands that an efficient Govt. is necessary that to render it such it ought to have the faculty of self-defence, that to render its different branches effectual each of them ought to have the same power of self defence. He did not wonder that such an agreement should have prevailed in these points. He only wondered that there should be any disagreement about the necessity of allowing the State Govts. the same self-defence. If they are to be preserved as he conceived to be essential, they certainly ought to have this power, and the only mode left of giving it to them, was by allowing them to appoint the 2d. branch of the Natl. Legislature.

Mr. Butler observing that we were put to difficulties at every step by the uncertainty whether an equality or a ratio of representation wd. prevail finally in the 2d. branch. moved to postpone the 4th. Resol: & to proceed to the Resol: on that point. Mr. Madison seconded him.

On the question

Massts. no. Cont. no. N. Y. ay. N. J. no. Pa. no. Del. no. Md. no. Va. ay. N. C. no. S. C. ay. Geo. ay. [Ayes—4; noes—7.]

On a question to postpone the 4 and take up the 7. Resol: Ays—Mard. Va. N. C. S. C. Geo.—Noes. Mas. Ct. N. Y. N. J. Pa. Del:

On the question to agree "that the members of 2d. branch be chosen by the indivl. Legislatures"

Masts. ay. Cont. ay. N. Y. ay. N. J. ay. Pa. no. Del. ay. Md. ay. Va. no. N. C. ay. S. C. ay. Geo. ay. [Ayes—9; noes—2.]

On a question on the clause requiring the age of 30 years at least"—it was agreed to unanimously:

On a question to strike out—the words "sufficient to ensure their independency" after the word "tmer" it was agreed to.

That the 2d. branch hold their offices for term of seven years", considered.

Mr. Ghorum suggests a term of "4 years", ¼ to be elected every year.

Mr. Randolph. supported the idea of rotation, as favorable to the wisdom & stability of the Corps. which might possibly be always sitting, and aiding the executive. And moves after "7 years" to add, "to go out in fixt proportion" which was agreed to.

Mr Williamson. suggests "6 years," as more convenient for Rotation than 7 years.

Mr Sherman seconds him.

Mr Reed proposed that they sd. hold their offices "during good" behaviour. Mr. R. Morris seconds him.

Genl. Pinkney proposed "4 years". A longer term wd. fix them at the seat of Govt. They wd. acquire an interest there, perhaps transfer their property & lose sight of the States they represent. Under these circumstances the distant States wd. labour under great disadvantages.

Mr. Sherman moved to strike out "7 years" in order to take questions on the several propositions. On the question to strike out "seven"

Masts. ay. Cont. ay. N. Y. ay. N. J. ay. Pa. no. Del. no. Md. divd. Va. no. N. C. ay. S. C. ay. Geo. ay. [Ayes—7; noes—3; divided—1.]

On the question to insert "6 years, which failed 5 Sts. being ay. 5. no. & 1: divided.

Masts. no. Cont. ay. N. Y. no. N. J. no. Pa. ay. Del. ay. Md. divd. Va. ay. N. C. ay. S. C. no. Geo. no.

On a motion to adjourn, the votes were 5 for 5 agst. it & 1 divided.—Con. N. J. Pa.—Del. Va.—ay—Masts. N. Y. N. C. S. C. Geo: no. Maryd. divided.

On the question for "5 years" it was lost

Masts. no. Cont. ay. N. Y. no. N. J. no. Pa. ay. Del. ay. Md. divd. Va. ay. N. C. ay. S. C. No. Geo. No. [Ayes—5; noes—5; divided—1.]

Adjd.

[1:421; Madison, 26 June]

The duration of the 2d. branch under consideration.

Mr. Ghorum moved to fill the blank with "six years". one third of the members to go out every second year.

Mr Wilson 2ded. the motion.

Genl. Pinkney opposed six years in favor of four years. The States he said had different interests. Those of the Southern, and of S. Carolina in particular were different from the Northern. If the Senators should be appointed for a long term, they wd. settle in the State where they exercised their functions; and would in a little time be rather the representatives of that than of the State appoint'g them.

Mr. Read movd. that the term be nine years. This wd. admit of a very convenient rotation, one third going out triennially. He wd. still prefer "during good behaviour," but being little supported in that idea, he was willing to take the longest term that could be obtained.

Mr. Broome 2ded. the motion

Mr. Madison. In order to judge of the form to be given to this institution, it will be proper to take a view of the ends to be served by it. These were first to protect the people agst. their rulers: secondly to protect the people agst. the transient impressions into which they themselves might be led. A people deliberating in a temperate moment, and with the experience of other nations before them, on the plan of Govt. most likely to secure their happiness, would first be aware, that those chargd. with the public happiness, might betray their trust. An obvious precaution agst. this danger wd. be to divide the trust between different bodies of men, who might watch & check each other. In this they wd. be governed by the same prudence which has prevailed in organizing the subordinate departments of Govt. where all business liable to abuses is made to pass thro' separate hands, the one being a check on the other. It wd. next occur to such a people, that they themselves were liable to temporary errors, thro' want of information as to their true interest, and that men chosen for a short term, & employed but a small portion of that in public affairs, might err from the same cause. This reflection wd. naturally suggest that the Govt. be so constituted, as that one of its branches might have an oppy. of acquiring a competent knowledge of the public interests. Another reflection equally becoming a people on such an occasion, wd. be that they themselves, as well as a numerous body of Representatives, were liable to err also, from fickleness and passion. A necessary fence agst. this danger would be to select a portion of enlightened citizens, whose limited number, and firmness might seasonably interpose agst. impetuous counsels. It ought finally to occur to a people deliberating on a Govt. for themselves, that as different interests necessarily result from the liberty meant to be secured, the major interest might under sudden impulses be tempted to commit injustice on the minority. In all civilized Countries the people fall into different classes havg. a real or supposed difference of interests. There will be creditors & debtors, farmers, merchts. & manufacturers. There will be particularly the distinction of rich & poor. It was true as had been observd. (by Mr Pinkney) we had not among us those hereditary distinctions, of rank which were a great source of the contests in the ancient Govts. as well as the modern States of Europe, nor those extremes of wealth or poverty which characterize the latter. We cannot however be regarded even at this time, as one homogeneous mass, in which every thing that affects a part will affect in the same manner the whole. In framing a system which we wish to last for ages, we shd. not lose sight of the changes which ages will produce. An increase of population will of necessity increase the proportion of those who will labour under all the hardships of life, & secretly sigh for a more equal distribution of its blessings. These may in time outnumber those who are placed above the feelings of indigence. According to the equal laws of suffrage, the power will slide into the hands of the former. No agrarian attempts have yet been made in this Country, but symptoms of a leveling spirit, as we have understood, have sufficiently appeared in a certain quarters to give notice of the future danger. How is this danger to be guarded agst. on republican principles? How is the danger in all cases of interested co-alitions to oppress the minority to be guarded agst.? Among other means by the establishment of a body in the Govt. sufficiently respectable for its wisdom & virtue, to aid on such emergencies, the preponderance of justice by throwing its weight into that scale. Such being the objects of the second branch in the proposed Govt. he thought a considerable duration ought to be given to it. He did not conceive that the term of nine years could threaten any real danger; but in pursuing his particular ideas on the subject, he should require that the long term allowed to the 2d. branch should not commence till such a period of life as would render a perpetual disqualification to be re-elected little inconvenient either in a public or private view. He observed that as it was more than probable we were now digesting a plan which in its operation wd. decide forever the fate of Republican Govt we ought not only to provide every guard to liberty that its preservation cd. require, but be equally careful to supply the defects which our own experience had particularly pointed out.

Mr. Sherman. Govt. is instituted for those who live under it. It ought therefore to be so constituted as not to be dangerous to their liberties. The more permanency it has the worse if it be a bad Govt. Frequent elections are necessary to preserve the good behavior of rulers. They also tend to give permanency to the Government, by preserving that good behavior, because it ensures their re-election. In Connecticut elections have been very frequent, yet great stability & uniformity both as to persons & measures have been experienced from its original establishmt. to the present time; a period of more than 130 years. He wished to have provision made for steadiness & wisdom in the system to be adopted; but he thought six or four years would be sufficient. He shd. be content with either.

Mr. Read wished it to be considered by the small States that it was their interest that we should become one people as much as possible, that State attachments shd. be extinguished as much as possible, that the Senate shd. be so constituted as to have the feelings of citizens of the whole.

Mr. Hamilton. He did not mean to enter particularly into the subject. He concurred with Mr. Madison in thinking we were now to decide for ever the fate of Republican Government; and that if we did not give to that form due stability and wisdom, it would be disgraced & lost among ourselves, disgraced & lost to mankind for ever. He acknowledged himself not to think favorably of Republican Government; but addressed his remarks to those who did think favorably of it, in order to prevail on them to tone their Government as high as possible. He professed himself to be as zealous an advocate for liberty as any man whatever, and trusted he should be as willing a martyr to

it though he differed as to the form in which it was most eligible.—He concurred also in the general observations of (Mr. Madison) on the subject, which might be supported by others if it were necessary. It was certainly true that nothing like an equality of property existed: that an inequality would exist as long as liberty existed, and that it would unavoidably result from that very liberty itself. This inequality of property constituted the great & fundamental distinction in Society. When the Tribunitial power had levelled the boundary between the *patricians* & *plebians* what followed? The distinction between rich & poor was substituted. He meant not however to enlarge on the subject. He rose principally to remark that (Mr. Sherman) seemed not to recollect that one branch of the proposed Govt. was so formed, as to render it particularly the guardians of the poorer orders of citizens; nor to have adverted to the true causes of the stability which had been exemplified in Cont. Under the British system as well as the federal, many of the great powers appertaining to Govt. particularly all those relating to foreign Nations were not in the hands of the Govt there. Their internal affairs also were extremely simple, owing to sundry causes many of which were peculiar to that Country. Of late the Governmt. had entirely given way to the people, and had in fact suspended many of its ordinary functions in order to prevent those turbulent scenes which had appeared elsewhere. He asks Mr S. whether the State at this time, dare impose & collect a tax on ye people? To those causes & not to the frequency of elections, the effect, as far as it existed ought to be chiefly ascribed.

Mr. Gerry. wished we could be united in our ideas concerning a permanent Govt. All aim at the same end, but there are great differences as to the means. One circumstance He thought should be carefully attended to. There were not ¹⁄₁₀₀₀ part of our fellow citizens who were not agst. every approach towards Monarchy. Will they ever agree to a plan which seems to make such an approach. The Convention ought to be extremely cautious in what they hold out to the people. Whatever plan may be proposed will be espoused with warmth by many out of respect to the quarter it proceeds from as well as from an approbation of the plan itself. And if the plan should be of such a nature as to rouse a violent opposition, it is easy to foresee that discord & confusion will ensue, and it is even possible that we may become a prey to foreign powers. He did not deny the position of Mr. Madison that the majority will generally violate justice when they have an interest in so doing; But did not think there was any such temptation in this Country. Our situation was different from that of G. Britain: and the great body of lands yet to be parcelled out & settled would very much prolong the difference. Notwithstanding the symtoms of injustice which had marked many of our public Councils, they had not proceeded so far as not to leave hopes, that there would be a sufficient sense of justice & virtue for the purpose of Govt. He admitted the evils arising from a frequency of elections: and would agree to give the Senate a duration of four or five years. A longer term would defeat itself. It never would be adopted by the people.

Mr. Wilson did not mean to repeat what had fallen from

others, but wd. add an observation or two which he believed had not yet been suggested. Every nation may be regarded in two relations 1 to its own citizens. 2 to foreign nations. It is therefore not only liable to anarchy & tyranny within but has wars to avoid & treaties to obtain from abroad. The Senate will probably be the depositary of the powers concerning the latter objects. It ought therefore to be made respectable in the eyes of foreign nations. The true reason why G. Britain has not yet listened to a commercial treaty with us has been, because she had no confidence in the stability of efficacy of our Government. 9 years with a rotation, will provide these desirable qualities; and give our Govt. an advantage in this respect over Monarchy itself. In a monarchy much must alway depend on the temper of the man. In such a body, the personal character will be lost in the political. He wd. add another observation. The popular objection agst. appointing any public body for a long term was that it might by gradual encroachments prolong itself first into a body for life, and finally become a hereditary one. It would be a satisfactory answer to this objection that as ⅓ would go out triennially, there would be always three divisions holding their places for unequal terms, and consequently acting under the influence of different views, and different impulses—On the question for 9 years. ⅓ to go out triennially

Massts no. Cont. no. N. Y. no. N. J. no. Pa. ay. Del. ay. Md. no. Va. ay. N. C. no. S. C. no. Geo. no. [Ayes—3; noes—8.]

On the question for 6 years ⅓ to go out biennially Massts. ay. Cont. ay. N. Y. no. N. J. no. Pa. ay. Del. ay. Md. ay. Va. ay. N. C. ay. S. C. no. Geo. no. [Ayes—7; noes—4.]

[1:468; Madison, 29 June]

Mr. Elseworth moved that the rule of suffrage in the 2d. branch be the same with that established by the articles of confederation". He was not sorry on the whole he said that the vote just passed, had determined against this rule in the first branch. He hoped it would become a ground of compromise with regard to the 2d. branch. We were partly national; partly federal. The proportional representation in the first branch was conformable to the national principle & would secure the large States agst. the small. An equality of voices was conformable to the federal principle and was necessary to secure the Small States agst. the large. He trusted that on this middle ground a compromise would take place. He did not see that it could on any other. And if no compromise should take place, our meeting would not only be in vain but worse than in vain. To the Eastward he was sure Massts. was the only State that would listen to a proposition for excluding the States as equal political Societies, from an equal voice in both branches. The others would risk every consequence rather than part with so dear a right. An attempt to deprive them of it, was at once dutting the body of America in two, and as he supposed would be the case, somewhere about this part of it. The large States he conceived would notwithstanding the equality of votes, have an influence that would maintain their superiority. Holland, as had been admitted (by Mr. Madison) had, notwithstanding a like

equality in the Dutch Confederacy, a prevailing influence in the public measures. The power of self-defence was essential to the small States. Nature had given it to the smallest insect of the creation. He could never admit that there was no danger of combinations among the large States. They will like individuals find out and avail themselves of the advantage to be gained by it. It was true the danger would be greater, if they were contiguous and had a more immediate common interest. A defensive combination of the small States was rendered more difficult by their greater number. He would mention another consideration of great weight. The existing confederation was founded on the equality of the States in the article of suffrage: was it meant to pay no regard to this antecedent plighted faith. Let a strong Executive, a Judiciary & Legislative power be created; but Let not too much be attempted; by which all may be lost. He was not in general a half-way man, yet he preferred doing half the good we could, rather than do nothing at all. The other half may be added, when the necessity shall be more fully experienced.

Mr. Baldwin would have wished that the powers of the General Legislature had been defined, before the mode of constituting it had been agitated. He should vote against the motion of Mr. Elseworth, tho' he did not like the Resolution as it stood in the Report of the Committee of the whole. He thought the second branch ought to be the representation of property, and that in forming it therefore some reference ought to be had to the relative wealth of their Constituents, and to the principles on which the Senate of Massts. was constituted. He concurred with those who thought it wd. be impossible for the Genl. Legislature to extend its cares to the local matters of the States.

[1:474; Yates, 29 June]

[Ellsworth:] I now move the following amendment to the resolve—*that in the second branch each state have an equal vote.* I confess that the effect of this motion is, to make the general government *partly federal and partly national.* This will secure tranquility, and still make it efficient; and it will meet the objections of the larger states. In taxes they will have a proportional weight in the first branch of the general legislature—If the great states refuse this plan, we will be for ever separated. Even in the executive the larger states have ever had great influence.—The provinces of Holland ever had it. If all the states are to exist they must necessarily have an equal vote in the general government. Small communities when associating with greater, can only be supported by an equality of votes. I have always found in my reading and experience, that in all societies the governors are ever gradually rising into power.

The large states, although they may not have a common interest for combination, yet they may be partially attached to each other for mutual support and advancement. This can be more easily effected than the union of the remaining small states to check it; and ought we not to regard antecedent plighted faith to the confederation already entered into, and by the terms of it declared to be perpetual? And it is not yet obvious to me that the states will depart from this ground. When in the hour of common danger we united as equals, shall it now be urged by some that we must depart from this principle when the danger is over? Will the world say that this is just? We then associated as free and independent states, and were well satisfied—To perpetuate that independence, I wish to establish a national legislature, executive and judiciary, for under these we shall I doubt not preserve peace and harmony—nor should I be surprised (although we made the general government the most perfect in our opinion,) that it should hereafter require amendment—But at present this is as far as I possibly can go—If this convention only chalk out lines of a good government we shall do well.

Mr. Baldwin. It appears to be agreed that the government we should adopt ought to be energetic and formidable, yet I would guard against the danger of becoming too formidable. The second branch ought not to be elected as the first. Suppose we take the example of the constitution of Massachusetts, as it is commended for its goodness: There the first branch represents the people, and the second its property.

Mr. Madison. I would always exclude inconsistent principles in framing a system of government. The difficulty of getting its defects amended are great and sometimes insurmountable. The Virginia state government was the first which was made, and though its defects are evident to every person, we cannot get it amended. The Dutch have made four several attempts to amend their system without success. The few alterations made in it were by tumult and faction, and for the worse. If there was real danger, I would give the smaller states the defensive weapons—But there is none from that quarter. The great danger to our general government *is the great southern and northern interests of the continent, being opposed to each other. Look to the votes in congress, and most of them stand divided by the geography of the country, not according to the size of the states.*

Suppose the first branch granted money, may not the second branch, from state views, counteract the first? In congress, the single state of Delaware prevented an embargo, at the time that all the other states thought it absolutely necessary for the support of the army. Other powers, and those very essential, besides the legislative, will be given to the second branch—such as the negativing all state laws. I would compromise on this question, if I could do it on correct principles, but otherwise not—if the old fabric of the confederation must be the ground-work of the new, we must fail.

[1:482; Madison, 30 June]

The motion of Mr. Elseworth resumed for allowing each State an equal vote in ye 2d branch

Mr. Wilson did not expect such a motion after the establishment of ye. contrary principle in the 1st. branch; and considering the reasons which would oppose it, even if an equal vote had been allowed in the 1st. branch. The Gentleman from Connecticut (Mr. Elseworth) had pronounced that if the motion should not be acceded to, of all the States North of Pena. one only would agree to any Genl. Government. He entertained more favorable hopes of Connt. and of the other Northern States. He hoped the alarms exceeded their cause, and that they would not abandon a Country to which they were bound by so many strong and endearing ties. But should the deplored event happen, it would neither stagger his sentiments nor his duty. If the minority of the people of America refuse to coalesce with the majority on just and proper principles, if a separation must take place, it could never happen on better grounds. The votes of yesterday agst. the just principle of representation, were as 22 to 90 of the people of America. Taking the opinions to be the same on this point, and he was sure if there was any room for change it could not be on the side of the majority, the question will be shall less than ¼ of the U. States withdraw themselves from the Union, or shall more than ¾ renounce the inherent, indisputable, and unalienable rights of men, in favor of the artificial systems of States. If issue must be joined, it was on this point he would chuse to join it, The gentleman from Connecticut in supposing that the preponderancy secured to the majority in the 1st. branch had removed the objections to an equality of votes in the 2d. branch for the security of the minority narrowed the case extremely. Such an equality will enable the minority to controul in all cases whatsoever, the sentiments and interests of the majority. Seven States will controul six: seven States according to the estimates that had been used, composed $^{24}/_{90}$. of the whole people. It would be in the power then of less than ½ to overrule ⅔ whenever a question should happen to divide the States in that manner. Can we forget for whom we are forming a Government? Is it for *men,* or for the imaginary beings called *States?* Will our honest Constituents be satisfied with metaphysical distinctions? Will they, ought they to be satisfied with being told that the one third, compose the greater number of states. The rule of suffrage ought on every principle to be the same in the 2d. as in the 1st. branch. If the Government be not laid on this foundation, it can be neither solid nor lasting, any other principle will be local, confined & temporary. This will expand with the expansion, and grow with the growth of the U. States.— Much has been said of an imaginary combination of three States. Sometimes a danger of monarchy, sometimes of aristocracy has been charged on it. No explanation however of the danger has been vouchsafed. It would be easy to prove both from reason & history that rivalships would be more probable than coalitions; and that there are no coinciding interests that could produce the latter. No answer has yet been given to the observations of (Mr. Madison) on this subject. Should the Executive Magistrate be taken from one of the large States would not the other two be thereby thrown into the scale with the other States? Whence then the danger of monarchy? Are the people of the three large States more aristocratic than those of the small ones? Whence then the danger of aristocracy from their influence? It is all a mere illusion of names. We talk of States, till we forget what they are composed of. Is a real & fair majority, the natural hot-bed of aristocracy? It is a part of the definition of this species of Govt. or rather of tyranny, that the smaller number governs the greater. It is true that a majority of States in the 2d. branch can not carry a law agst. a majority of the people in the 1st. But this removes half only of the objection. Bad Governts. are of two sorts. 1. that which does too little. 2. that which does too much: that which fails thro' weakness; and that which destroys thro' oppression. Under which of these evils do the U. States at present groan? under the weakness and inefficiency of its Governt. To remedy this weakness we have been sent to this Convention. If the motion should be agreed to, we shall leave the U. S. fettered precisely as heretofore; with the additional mortification of seeing the good purposes of ye fair representation of the people in the 1st. branch, defeated in 2d. Twenty four will still controul sixty six. He lamented that such a disagreement should prevail on the point of representation, as he did not foresee that it would happen on the other point most contested, the boundary between the Genl. & the local authorities. He thought the States necessary & valuable parts of a good system.

Mr. Elseworth. The capital objection of Mr. Wilson "that the minority will rule the majority" is not true. The power is given to the few to save them from being destroyed by the many. If an equality of votes had been given to them in both branches, the objection might have had weight. Is it a novel thing that the few should have a check on the many? Is it not the case in the British Constitution the wisdom of which so many gentlemen have united in applauding? Have not the House of Lords, who form so small a proportion of the nation a negative on the laws, as a necessary defence of their peculiar rights agst the encroachmts of the Commons. No instance of a Confederacy has existed in which an equality of voices has not been exercised by the members of it. We are running from one extreme to another. We are razing the foundations of the building. When we need only repair the roof. No salutary measure has been lost for want of *a majority of the States,* to favor it. If security be all that the great States wish for the 1st. branch secures them. The danger of combinations among them is not imaginary. Altho' no particular abuses could be foreseen by him, the possibility of them would be sufficient to alarm him. But he could easily conceive cases in which they might result from such combinations. Suppose that in pursuance of some commercial treaty or arrangement, three or four free ports & no more were to be established would not combinations be formed in favor of Boston, Philada. & & some port in Chesapeak? A like concert might be formed in the appointment of the great officers. He appealed again to the obligations of the federal pact which was still in force, and which had been entered into with so much solemnity, persuading himself that some regard would still be paid to the plighted faith under which each State small as well as great, held an equal right of suffrage in the general Councils. His remarks were not the result of partial or local views. The State he represented (Connecticut) held a middle rank.

Mr. Madison. did justice to the able and close reasoning of Mr. E. but must observe that it did not always accord with itself. On another occasion, the large States were described by him as the Aristocratic States, ready to oppress the small. Now the small are the House of Lords requiring a negative to defend them agst the more numerous Commons. Mr. E. had also erred in saying that no instance had existed in which confederated States had not retained to themselves a perfect equality of suffrage. Passing over the German system in which the K. of Prussia has nine voices,

he reminded Mr. E. of the Lycian confederacy, in which the component members had votes proportioned to their importance, and which Montesquieu recommends as the fittest model for that form of Government. Had the fact been as stated by Mr. E. it would have been of little avail to him, or rather would have strengthened the arguments agst. him; The History & fate of the several Confederacies modern as well as Antient, demonstrating some radical vice in their structure. In reply to the appeal of Mr. E. to the faith plighted in the existing federal compact, he remarked that the party claiming from others an adherence to a common engagement ought at least to be guiltless itself of a violation. Of all the States however Connecticut was perhaps least able to urge this plea. Besides the various omissions to perform the stipulated acts from which no State was free, the Legislature of that State had by a pretty recent vote *positively refused* to pass a law for complying with the Requisitions of Congs. and had transmitted a copy of the vote to Congs. It was urged, he said, continually that an equality of votes in the 2d. branch was not only necessary to secure the small, but would be perfectly safe to the large ones whose majority in the 1st. branch was an effectual bulwark. But notwithstanding this apparent defence, the Majority of States might still injure the majority of people. 1. they could *obstruct* the wishes and interests of the majority. 2. they could *extort* measures, repugnant to the wishes & interest of the majority. 3. They could *impose* measures adverse thereto; as the 2d branch will probly exercise some great powers, in which the 1st will not participate. He admitted that every peculiar interest whether in any class of citizens, or any description of States, ought to be secured as far as possible. Wherever there is danger of attack there ought be given a consitutional power of defence. But he contended that the States were divided into different interests not by their difference of size, but by other circumstances; the most material of which resulted partly from climate, but principally from the effects of their having or not having slaves. These two causes concurred in forming the great division of interests in the U. States. It did not lie between the large & small States: it lay between the Northern & Southern. and if any defensive power were necessary, it ought to be mutually given to these two interests. He was so strongly impressed with this important truth that he had been casting about in his mind for some expedient that would answer the purpose. The one which had occurred was that instead of proportioning the votes of the States in both branches, to their respective numbers of inhabitants computing the slaves in the ratio of 5 to 3. they should be represented in one branch according to the number of free inhabitants only; and in the other according to the whole no. counting the slaves as if free. By this arrangement the Southern Scale would have the advantage in one House, and the Northern in the other. He had been restrained from proposing this expedient by two considerations; one was his unwillingness to urge any diversity of interests on an occasion when it is but too apt to arise of itself—the other was the inequality of powers that must be vested in the two branches, and which wd. destroy the equilibrium of interests.

Mr. Elseworth assured the House that whatever might be thought of the Representatives of Connecticut the State was entirely federal in her disposition. He appealed to her great exertions during the War, in supplying both men & money. The muster rolls would show she had more troops in the field than Virga. If she had been delinquent, it had been from inability, and not more so than other States.

Mr. Sherman. Mr. Madison had animadverted on the delinquency of the States, when his object required him to prove that the Constitution of Congs. was faulty. Congs. is not to blame for the faults of the States. Their measures have been right, and the only thing wanting has been, a further power in Congs. to render them effectual.

Mr. Davy was much embarrassed and wished for explanations. The Report of the Committee allowing the Legislatures to choose the Senate, and establishing a proportional representation in it, seemed to be impracticable. There will according to this rule be ninety members in the outset, and the number will increase as new States are added. It was impossible that so numerous a body could possess the activity and other qualities required in it. Were he to vote on the comparative merits of the report as it stood, and the amendment, he should be constrained to prefer the latter. The appointment of the Senate by electors chosen by the people for that purpose was he conceived liable to an insuperable difficulty. The larger Counties or districts thrown into a general district, would certainly prevail over the smaller Counties or districts, and merit in the latter would be excluded altogether. The report therefore seemed to be right in referring the appointment to the Legislatures, whose agency in the general System did not appear to him objectionable as it did to some others. The fact was that the local prejudices & interests which could not be denied to exist, would find their way into the national Councils whether the Representatives should be chosen by the Legislatures or by the people themselves. On the other hand, if a proportional representation was attended with insuperable difficulties, the making the Senate the Representative of the States, looked like bringing us back to Congs. again, and shutting out all the advantages expected from it. Under this view of the subject he could not vote for any plan for the Senate yet proposed. He thought that in general there were extremes on both sides. We were partly federal, partly national in our Union. And he did not see why the Govt. might not in some respects operate on the States, in others on the people.

Mr Wilson admitted the question concerning the number of Senators, to be embarrassing. If the smallest States be allowed one, and the others in proportion, the Senate will certainly be too numerous. He looked forward to the time when the smallest States will contain 100,000 souls at least. Let there be then one Senator in each for every 100,000 souls, and let the States not having that no. of inhabitants be allowed one. He was willing himself to submit to this temporary concession to the small States: and threw out the idea as a ground of compromise.

Docr. Franklin The diversity of opinions turns on two points. If a proportional representation takes place, the small States contend that their liberties will be in danger. If an equality of votes is to be put in its place, the large States say their money will be in danger. When a broad table is to be made, and the edges of planks do not fit the artist takes a little from both, and makes a good joint. In like manner here both sides must part with some of their demands, in order that they may join in some accomodating proposition. He had prepared one which he would read, that it might lie on the table for consideration. The proposition was in the words following"

"That the Legislatures of the several States shǎll choose & send an equal number of Delegates, namely   who are to compose the 2d. branch of the General Legislature—

That in all cases or questions wherein the Sovereignty of individual States may be affected, or whereby their authority over their own Citizens may be diminished, or the authority of the General Government within the several States augmented, each State shall have equal suffrage.

That in the appointment of all Civil Officers of ye. Genl. Govt. in the election of whom the 2d. branch may by the Constitution have part, each State shall have equal suffrage.

That in fixing the salaries of such officers, and in all allowances for public services, and generally in all appropriations & dispositions of money to be drawn out of the General Treasury; and in all laws for supplying that Treasury, the Delegates of the several States shall have suffrage in proportion to the Sums which their respective States do actually contribute to the treasury "Where a ship had many owners this was the rule of deciding on her expedition. He had been one of the ministers from this Country to France during the joint war and wd. have been very glad if allowed a vote in distributing the money to carry it on."

Mr. King observed that the simple question was whether each State should have an equal vote in the 2d. branch; that it must be apparent to those gentlemen who liked neither the motion for this equality, nor the report as it stood, that the report was as susceptible of melioration as the motion; that a reform would be nugatory & nominal only if we should make another Congress of the proposed Senate: that if the adherence to an equality of votes was fixed & unalterable, there could not be less obstinacy on the other side, & that we were in fact cut insunder already, and it was in vain to shut our eyes against it: that he was however filled with astonishment that if we were convinced that every *man* in America was secured in all his rights, we should be ready to sacrifice this substantial good to the phantom of *State* sovereignty: that his feelings were more harrowed & his fears more agitated for his Country than he could express, that he conceived this to be the last opportunity of providing for its liberty & happiness: that he could not therefore but repeat his amazement that when a just Governt. founded on a fair representation of the *people* of America was within our reach, we should renounce the blessing, from an attachment to the ideal freedom & importance of *States*: that should this wonderful illusion continue to prevail, his mind was prepared for every event, rather than sit down under a Govt. founded in a vicious principle of representation and which must be as shortlived as it would be unjust. He might prevail on himself to accede to some such expedient as had been hinted by Mr. Wilson: but he never could listen to an equality of votes as proposed in the motion.

Mr. Dayton. When assertion is given for proof, and terror substituted for argument, he presumed they would have no effect however eloquently spoken. It should have been shewn that the evils we have experienced have proceeded from the equality now objected to: and that the seeds of dissolution for the State Governments are not sown in the Genl. Government. He considered the system on the table as a novelty, an amphibious monster; and was persuaded that it never would be recd. by the people.

Mr. Martin wd. never confederate if it could not be done on just principles

Mr Madison would acquiesce in the concession hinted by Mr. Wilson, on condition that a due independence should be given to the Senate. The plan in its present shape makes the Senate absolutely dependent on the States. The Senate therefore is only another edition of Congs. He knew the faults of that Body & had used a bold language agst. it. Still he wd. preserve the State rights, as carefully as the trials by jury.

Mr. Bedford, contended that there was no middle way between a perfect consolidation and a mere confederacy of the States. The first is out of the question, and in the latter they must continue if not perfectly, yet equally sovereign. If political Societies possess ambition avarice, and all the other passions which render them formidable to each other, ought we not to view them in this light here? Will not the same motives operate in America as elsewhere? If any gentleman doubts it let him look at the votes. Have they not been dictated by interest, by ambition? Are not the large States evidently seeking to aggrandize themselves at the expense of the small? They think no doubt that they have right on their side, but interest had blinded their eyes. Look at Georgia. Though a small State at present, she is actuated by the prospect of soon being a great one. S. Carolina is actuated both by present interest & future prospects. She hopes too to see the other States cut down to her own dimensions. N. Carolina has the same motives of present & future interest. Virga. follows. Maryd. is not on that side of the Question. Pena. has a direct and future interest. Massts has a decided and palpable interest in the part she takes. Can it be expected that the small States will act from pure disinterestedness. Look at G. Britain. Is the Representation there less unequal? But we shall be told again that that is the rotten part of the Constitution. Have not the boroughs however held fast their constitutional rights? and are we to act with greater purity than the rest of mankind. An exact proportion in the Representation is not preserved in any one of the States. Will it be said that an inequality of power will not result from an inequality of votes. Give the opportunity, and ambition will not fail to abuse it. The whole history of mankind proves it. The three large States have a common interest to bind them together in commerce. But whether a combination as we suppose, or a competition as others suppose, shall take place among them, in either case, the smaller States must be ruined. We must like Solon make such a Governt. as

the people will approve. Will the smaller States ever agree to the proposed degradation of them. It is not true that the people will not agree to enlarge the powers of the present Congs. The Language of the people has been that Congs. ought to have the power of collecting an impost, and of coercing the States when it may be necessary. On The first point they have been explicit & in a manner, unanimous in their declarations. And must they not agree to this & similar measures if they ever mean to discharge their engagements. The little States are willing to observe their engagements, but will meet the large ones on no ground but that of the Confederation. We have been told with a dictatorial air that this is the last moment for a fair trial in favor of a good Governmt. It will be the last indeed if the propositions reported from the Committee go forth to the people. He was under no apprehensions. The Large States dare not dissolve the confederation. If they do the small ones will find some foreign ally of more honor and good faith, who will take them by the hand and do them justice. He did not mean by this to intimidate or alarm. It was a natural consequence; which ought to be avoided by Enlarging the federal powers not annihilating the federal system. This is what the people expect. All agree in the necessity of a more efficient Govt. and why not make such an one; as they desire.

Mr. Elseworth,. Under a National Govt. he should participate in the National Security, as remarked by (Mr. King) but that was all. What he wanted was domestic happiness. The Natl. Govt. could not descend to the local objects on which this depended. It could only embrace objects of a general nature. He turned his eyes therefore for the preservation of his rights to the State Govts. From these alone he could derive the greatest happiness he expects in this life. His happiness depends on their existence, as much as a newborn infant on its mother for nourishment. If this reasoning was not satisfactory, he had nothing to add that could be so.

Mr. King was for preserving the States in a subordinate degree, and as far as they could be necessary for the purposes stated by Mr. Elsewth. He did not think a full answer had been given to those who apprehended a dangerous encroachment on their jurisdictions. Expedients might be devised as he conceived that would give them all the security the nature of things would admit of. In the establishment of Societies the Constitution was to the Legislature what the laws were to individuals. As the fundamental rights of individuals are secured by express provisions in the State Constitutions; why may not a like security be provided for the Rights of States in the National Constitution. The articles of Union between Engld. & Scotland furnish an example of such a provision in favor of sundry rights of Scotland. When that Union was in agitation, the same language of apprehension which has been heard from the smaller States, was in the mouths of the Scotch patriots. The articles however have not been violated and the Scotch have found an increase of prosperity & happiness. He was aware that this will be called a mere *paper security*. He thought it a sufficient answer to say that if fundamental articles of compact, are no sufficient defence against physical power, neither will there be any safety agst. it if there be no compact. He could not sit down, without taking some notice of the language of the honorable gentleman from Delaware (Mr Bedford). It was not he that had uttered a dictatorial language. This intemperance had marked the honorable gentleman himself. It was not he who with a vehemence unprecedented in that House, had declared himself ready to turn his hopes from our common Country, and court the protection of some foreign hand—This too was the language of the Honbl member, himself. He was grieved that such a thought had entered into his heart. He was more grieved that such an expression had dropped from his lips. The gentleman cd. only excuse it to himself on the score of passion. For himself whatever might be his distress, he wd. never court relief from a foreign power.

[1:510; Madison, 2 July]

On the question for allowing each State one vote in the Second branch as moved by Mr. Elseworth,

Massts. no. Cont. ay. N. Y. ay. N. J. ay. Pa. no. Del. ay. Md. ay. Mr. Jenifer being not present Mr. Martin alone voted Va. no. N. C. no. S. C. no. Geo. divd. Mr. Houston no Mr Baldwin ay [Ayes—5; noes—5; divided—1.]

Mr. Pinkney thought an equality of votes in the 2d. branch inadmissable. At the same time candor obliged him to admit that the large States would feel a partiality for their own Citizens & give them a preference, in appointments: that they might also find some common points in their commercial interests, and promote treaties favorable to them. There is a real distinction the Northern & Southn. interests. N. Carola. S. Carol: & Geo. in their Rice & Indigo had a peculiar interest which might be sacrificed. How then shall the larger States be prevented from administering the Genl. Govt. as they please, without being themselves unduly subjected to the will of the smaller? By allowing them some but not a full proportion. He was extremely anxious that something should be done, considering this as the last appeal to a regular experiment. Congs. have failed in almost every effort for an amendment of the federal System. Nothing has prevented a dissolution of it, but the appointmt. of this Convention; & he could not express his alarms for the consequences of such an event. He read his motion to form the States into classes, with an apportionment of Senators among them, (see art. 4 of his plan.)

General Pinkney. was willing the motion might be considered. He did not entirely approve it. He liked better the motion of Dr. Franklin (which see Saturday June 30). Some compromise seemed to be necessary: the States being exactly divided on the question for an equality of votes in the 2d. branch. He proposed that a Committee consisting of a member from each State should be appointed to devise & report some compromise.

Mr: L. Martin had no objection to a Commitment, but no modifications whatever could reconcile the Smaller States to the least diminution of their equal Sovereignty.

Mr. Sharman. We are now at a full stop, and nobody he supposed meant that we shd. break up without doing something. A Committee he thought most likely to hit on some expedient.

Mr. Govr. Morris. thought a Come. advisable as the Convention had been equally divided. He had a stronger reason also. The mode of appointing the 2d. branch tended he was sure to defeat the object of it. What is this object? to check the precipitation, changeableness, and excesses of the first branch. Every man of observation had seen in the democratic branches of the State Legislatures, precipitation—in Congress changeableness. in every department excesses agst. personal liberty private property & personal safety. What qualities are necessary to constitute a check in this case? *Abilities* and *virtue*, are equally necessary in both branches. Something more then is wanted. 1. the Checking branch must have a personal interest in checking the other branch. one interest must be opposed to another interest. Vices as they exist, must be turned agst. each other. 2. It must have great personal property, it must have the aristocratic spirit; it must love to lord it thro' pride, pride is indeed the great principle that actuates both the poor & the rich. It is this principle which in the former resists, in the latter abuses authority. 3. It should be independent. In Religion the Creature is apt to forget its Creator. That it is otherwise in political affairs. The late debates here are an unhappy proof. The aristocratic body, should be as independent & as firm as the democratic. If the members of it are to revert to a dependence on the democratic choice. The democratic scale will preponderate. All the guards contrived by America have not restrained the Senatorial branches of the Legislatures from a servile complaisance to the democratic. If the 2d. branch is to be dependent we are better without it. To make it independent, it should be for life. It will then do wrong, it will be said. He believed so: He hoped so. The Rich will strive to establish their dominion & enslave the rest. They always did. They always will. The proper security agst them is to form them into a separate interest. The two forces will then controul each other. Let the rich mix with the poor and in a Commercial Country, they will establish an Oligarchy. Take away commerce, and the democracy will triumph. Thus it has been all the world over. So it will be among us. Reason tells us we are but men: and we are not to expect any particular interference of Heaven in our favor. By thus combining & setting apart, the aristocratic interest, the popular interest will be combined agst. it. There will be a mutual check and mutual security. 4. An independence for life, involves the necessary permanency. If we change our measures no body will trust us: and how avoid a change of measures, but by avoiding a change of men. Ask any man if he confides in Congs. if he confides in the State of Pena. if he will lend his money or enter into contract? He will tell you no. He sees no stability. He can repose no confidence. If G. B. were to explain her refusal to treat with us, the same reasoning would be employed.—He disliked the exclusion of the 2d. branch from holding offices. It is dangerous. It is like the imprudent exclusion of the military officers during the war, from civil appointments. It deprives the Executive of the principal source of influence. If danger be apprehended from the Executive what a lift-handed way is this of obviating it? If the son, the brother or the friend can be appointed, the danger may be even increased, as the disqualified father &c. can then boast of a disinterestedness which he does not possess. Besides shall the best, the most able, the most virtuous citizens not be permitted to hold offices? Who then are to hold them? He was also agst. paying the Senators. They will pay themselves if they can. If they can not they will be rich and can do without it. of such the 2d. branch ought to consist; and none but such can compose it if they are not to be paid—He contended that the Executive should appoint the Senate & fill up vacancies. This gets rid of the difficulty in the present question. You may begin with any ratio you please; it will come to the same thing. The members being independt. & for life, may be taken as well from one place as from another.—It should be considered too how the scheme could be carried through the States. He hoped there was strength of mind eno' in this House to look truth in the face. He did not hesitate therefore to say that loaves & fishes must bribe the Demagogues. They must be made to expect higher offices under the general than the State Govts. A Senate for life will be a noble bait. Without such captivating prospects, the popular leaders will oppose & defeat the plan. He perceived that the 1st. branch was to be chosen by the people of the States: the 2d. by those chosen by the people. Is not here a Govt. by the States. A Governt. by Compact between Virga. in the 1st. & 2d. branch; Massts. in the 1st & 2d. branch &c. This is going back to mere treaty. It is no Govt. at all. It is altogether dependent—on the States, and will act over again the part which Congs. has acted. A firm Governt. alone can protect our liberties. He fears the influence of the rich. They will have the same effect here as elsewhere if we do not by such a Govt. keep them within their proper sphere. We should remember that the people never act from reason alone. The rich will take advantage of their passions and make these the instruments for oppressing them. The Result of the Contest will be a violent aristocracy, or a more violent despotism. The schemes of the Rich will be favored by the extent of the Country. The people in such distant parts can not communicate & act in concert. They will be the dupes of those who have more Knowledge & intercourse. The only security agst. encroachments will be a select & sagacious body of men, instituted to watch agst. them on all sides. He meant only to hint these observations, without grounding any motion on them

Mr. Randolph favored the commitment though he did not expect much benefit from the expedient. He animadverted on the warm & rash language of Mr. Bedford on Saturday; reminded the small States that if the large States should combine some danger of which he did not deny there would be a check in the revisionary power of the Executive, and intimated that in order to render this still more effectual, he would agree that in the choice of the Executive each State should have an equal vote. He was persuaded that two such opposite bodies as Mr. Morris had planned could never long co-exist. Dissentions would arise as has been seen even between the Senate and H. of Delegates in Maryland, appeals would be made to the people; and in a little time commotions would be the result—He was far from thinking the large States could subsist of themselves any more than the small; an avulsion would involve the whole in ruin, and he was determined to pursue such a scheme of Government as would secure us agst. such a calamity.

Mr. Strong was for the Commitment; and hoped the mode of constituting both branches would be referred. If they should be established on different principles, contentions would prevail and there would never be a concurrence in necessary measures.

Docr. Williamson. If we do not concede on both sides, our business must soon be at an end. He approved of the commitment, supposing that as the Come. wd. be a smaller body, a compromise would be pursued with more coolness

Mr. Wilson objected to the Committee, because it would decide according to that very rule of voting which was opposed on one side. Experience in Congs. had also proved the inutility of Committees consisting of members from each State

Mr. Lansing wd. not oppose the Commitment, though expecting little advantage from it.

Mr. Madison opposed the commitment. He had rarely seen any other effect than delay from *such* Committees in Congs. Any scheme of compromise that could be proposed in the Committee might as easily be proposed in the House; and the report of the Committee when it contained merely the *opinion* of the Come. would neither shorten the discussion, nor influence the decision of the House.

Mr. Gerry was for the commitmt. Something must be done, or we shall disappoint not only America, but the whole world. He suggested a consideration of the State we should be thrown into by the failure of the Union. We should be without an Umpire to decide controversies and must be at the mercy of events. What too is to become of our treaties—what of our foreign debts, what of our domestic? We must make concessions on both sides. Without these the constitutions of the several States would never have been formed.

On the question "for commiting" generally

Massts. ay. Cont. ay. N. Y. ay. N. J. no. P. ay. Del. no. Md. ay. Va. ay. N. C. ay. S. C. ay. Geo. ay. [Ayes—9; noes—2.]

On the question for commiting "to a member from each State"

Massts. ay. Cont. ay. N. Y. ay. N. J. ay. Pa. no. Del. ay. Md. ay. Va. ay. N. C. ay. S. C. ay. Geo—ay. [Ayes—10; noes—1.]

The Committee elected by ballot, were Mr. Gerry, Mr. Elseworth, Mr. Yates, Mr. Patterson. Dr. Franklin, Mr. Bedford, Mr. Martin, Mr. Mason, Mr. Davy. Mr. Rutlidge, Mr. Baldwin.

That time might be given to the Committee, and to such as chose to attend to the celebrations on the anniversary of Independence, the Convention adjourned till Thursday.

[1:526; Madison, 5 July]

Mr. Gerry delivered in from the Committee appointed on Monday last the following Report.

"The Committee to whom was referred the 8th Resol. of the Report from the Committee of the whole House, and so much of the 7th. as has not been decided on submit the following Report: That the subsequent propositions be recommended to the Convention on condition that both shall be generally adopted. 1. that in the 1st. branch of the Legislature each of the States now in the Union shall be allowed 1 member for every 40,000 inhabitants of the description reported in the 7th Resolution of the Come. of the whole House: that each State not containing that number shall be allowed 1 member: that all bills for raising or appropriating money, and for fixing the Salaries of the Officers of the Governt. of the U. States shall originate in the 1st branch of the Legislature, and shall not be altered or amended by the 2d branch: and that no money shall be drawn from the public Treasury, but in pursuance of appropriations to be originated in the 1st branch" II. that in the 2d branch each State shall have an equal vote"

Mr. Ghorum observed that as the report consisted of propositions mutually conditional he wished to hear some explanations touching the grounds on which the conditions were estimated.

Mr. Gerry. The Committee were of different opinions as well as the Deputations from which the Come. were taken, and agreed to the Report merely in order that some ground of accommodation might be proposed. Those opposed to the equality of votes have only assented conditionally; and if the other side do not generally agree will not be under any obligation to support the Report.

Mr. Wilson. thought the Committee had exceeded their powers.

Mr. Martin was for taking the question on the whole report.

Mr. Wilson was for a division of the question: otherwise it wd. be a leap in the dark.

Mr. Madison could not regard the exclusive privilege of originating money bills as any concession on the side of the small States. Experience proved that it had no effect. If seven States in the upper branch wished a bill to be originated, they might surely find some member from some of the same States in the lower branch who would originate it. The restriction as to amendments was of as little consequence. Amendments could be handed privately by the Senate to members in the other house. Bills could be negatived that they might be sent up in the desired shape. If the Senate should yield to the obstinacy of the 1st. branch the use of that body as a check would be lost. If the 1st. branch should yield to that of the Senate, the privilege would be nugatory. Experience had also shewn both in G. B. and the States having a similar regulation that it was a source of frequent & obstinate altercations. These considerations had produced a rejection of a like motion on a former occasion when judged by its own merits. It could not therefore be deemed any concession on the present, and left in force all the objections which had prevailed agst. allowing each State an equal voice. He conceived that the Convention was reduced to the alternative of either departing from justice in order to conciliate the smaller States, and the minority of the people of the U. S. or of displeasing these by justly gratifying the larger States and the majority of the people. He could not himself hesitate as to the option he ought to make. The Convention with justice & the majority of the people on their side, had nothing to fear. With injustice and the minority on their side they had every thing to fear. It was in vain to purchase concord in the Convention on terms which would perpetuate discord among their Constituents. The Convention ought to pursue a plan which would bear the test of examination, which would be espoused & supported by the enlightened and impartial part of America, & which they could themselves vindicate & urge. It should be considered that altho' at first many may judge of the system recommended, by their opinion of the Convention, yet finally all will judge of the Convention by the system. The merits of the system alone can finally & effectually obtain the public suffrage. He was not apprehensive that the people of the small States would obstinately refuse to accede to a Govt. founded on just principles, and promising them substantial protection. He could not suspect that Delaware would brave the consequences of seeking her fortunes apart from the other States, rather than submit to such a Govt: much less could he suspect that she would pursue the rash policy of courting foreign support, which the warmth of one of her representatives (Mr. Bedford) had suggested, or if she shd. that any foreign nation wd. be so rash as to hearken to the overture. As little could he suspect that the people of N. Jersey notwithstanding the decided tone of the gentlemen from that State, would choose rather to stand on their own legs, and bid defiance to events, than to acquiesce under an establishment founded on principles the justice of which they could not dispute, and absolutely necessary to redeem them from the exactions levied on them by the commerce of the neighbouring States. A review of other States would prove that there was as little reason to apprehend an inflexible opposition elsewhere. Harmony in the Convention was no doubt much to be desired. Satisfaction to all the States, in the first instance still more so. But if the principal States comprehending a majority of the people of the U. S. should concur in a just & judicious plan, he had the firmest hopes that all the other States would by degrees accede to it.

Mr. Butler said he could not let down his idea of the people. of America so far as to believe they, would from mere respect to the Convention adopt a plan evidently unjust. He did not consider the privilege concerning money bills as of any consequence. He urged that the 2d. branch ought to represent the States according to their property.

Mr. Govr. Morris. thought the form as well as the matter of the Report objectionable. It seemed in the first place to render amendments impracticable. In the next place, it seemed to involve a pledge to agree to the 2d. part if the 1st. shd. be agreed to. He conceived the whole aspect of it to be wrong. He came here as a Representative of America; he flattered himself he came here in some degree as a Representative of the whole human race; for the whole human race will be affected by the proceedings of this Convention. He wished gentlemen to extend their views beyond the present moment of time; beyond the narrow limits of place from which they derive their political origin. If he were to believe some things which he had heard, he should suppose that we were assembled to truck and bargain for our particular States. He can—not descend to think that any gentlemen are really actuated by these views. We must look forward to the effects of what we do. These alone ought to guide us. Much has been said of the sentiments of the people. They were unknown. They could not be known. All that we can infer is that if the plan we recommend be reasonable & right; all who have reasonable minds and sound intentions will embrace it, notwithstanding what had been said by some Gentlemen. Let us suppose that the larger States shall agree; and that the smaller refuse; and let us trace the consequences. The opponents of the system in the smaller States will no doubt make a party, and a noise for a time, but the ties of interest, of kindred, & of common habits which connect them with the other States will be too strong to be easily broken. In N. Jersey particularly he was sure a great many would follow the sentiments of Pena. & N. York. This Country must be united. If persuasion does not unite it, the sword will. He begged that this consideration might have its due weight. The scenes of horror attending civil commotion can not be described, and the conclusion of them will be worse than the term of their continuance. The stronger party will then make traytors of the weaker; and the Gallows & Halter will finish the work of the sword. How far foreign powers would be ready to take part in the confusions he would not say. Threats that they will be invited have it seems been thrown out. He drew the melancholy picture of foreign intrusions as exhibited in the History of Germany, and urged it as a standing lesson to other nations. He trusted that the Gentlemen who may have hazarded such expressions, did not entertain them till they reached their own lips. But returning to the Report he could not think it in any respect calculated for the public good. As the 2d. branch is now constituted, there will be constant disputes & appeals to the States which will undermine the Genl. Government & controul & annihilate the 1st branch. Suppose that the Delegates from Massts. & Rho I. in the upper House disagree, and that the former are out-voted. What Results? they will immediately declare that their State will not abide by the decision, and make such representations as will produce that effect—The same may happen as to Virga. & other States. Of what avail then will be what is on paper. State attachments, and State importance have been the bane of this Country. We cannot annihilate; but we may perhaps take out the teeth of the serpents. He wished our ideas to be enlarged to the true interest of man, instead of being circumscribed within the narrow compass of a particular Spot. And after all how little can be the motive yielded by selfishness for such a policy. Who can say whether he himself, much less whether his children, will the next year be an inhabitant of this or that State.

Mr. Bedord. He found that what he had said as to the small States being taken by the hand, had been misunderstood; and he rose to explain. He did not mean that the small States would court the aid & interposition of foreign powers. He meant that they would not consider the federal compact as dissolved untill it should be so by the acts of the large States. In this case the consequence of the breach of faith on their part, and the readiness of the small States to fulfill their engagements, would be that for-

eign nations having demands on this Country would find it their interest to take the small States by the hand, in order to do themselves justice. This was what he meant. But no man can foresee to what extremities the small States may be driven by oppression. He observed also in apology that some allowance ought to be made for the habits of his profession in which warmth was natural & sometimes necessary. But is there not an apology in what was said by (Mr. Govr. Morris) that the sword is to unite: by Mr. Ghorum that Delaware must be annexed to Penna. and N. Jersey divided between Pena. and N. York. To hear such language without emotion, would be to renounce the feelings of a man and the duty of a citizen— As to the propositions of the Committee, the lesser States have thought it necessary to have a security somewhere. This has been thought necessary for the Executive Magistrate of the proposed Govt. who has a sort of negative on the laws; and is it not of more importance that the States should be protected, than that the Executive branch of the Govt. shd. be protected. In order to obtain this, the smaller States have conceded as to the constitution of the first branch, and as to money bills. If they be not gratified by correspondent concessions as to the 2d. branch is it to be supposed they will ever accede to the plan; and what will be the consequence if nothing should be done! The condition of the U. States requires that something should be immediately done. It will be better that a defective plan should be adopted, than that none should be recommended. He saw no reason why defects might not be supplied by meetings 10, 15 or 20 years hence.

Mr. Elseworth said he had not attended the proceedings of the Committee, but was ready to accede to the compromise they had reported. Some compromise was necessary; and he saw none more convenient or reasonable.

Mr. Williamson hoped that the expressions of individuals would not be taken for the sense of their colleagues, much less of their States which was not & could not be known. He hoped also that the meaning of those expressions would not be misconstrued or exaggerated. He did not conceive that (Mr. Govr. Morris) meant that the sword ought to be drawn agst. the smaller States. He only pointed out the probable consequences of anarchy in the U. S. A similar exposition ought to be given of the expressions (of Mr. Ghorum). He was ready to hear the Report discussed; but thought the propositions contained in it, the most objectionable of any he had yet heard.

Mr. Patterson said that he had when the Report was agreed to in the Come. reserved to himself the right of freely discussing it. He acknowledged that the warmth complained of was improper; but he thought the Sword & the Gallows as little calculated to produce conviction. He complained of the manner in which Mr. M—& Mr. Govr. Morris had treated the small States.

Mr. Gerry. Tho' he had assented to the Report in the Committee, he had very material objections to it. We were however in a peculiar situation. We were neither the same Nation nor different Nations. We ought not therefore to pursue the one or the other of these ideas too closely. If no compromise should take place what will be the consequence. A secession he foresaw would take place; for some gentlemen seem decided on it; two different plans will be proposed, and the result no man could foresee. If we do not come to some agreement among ourselves some foreign sword will probably do the work for us.

Mr. Mason. The Report was meant not as specific propositions to be adopted, but merely as a general ground of accomodation. There must be some accomodation on this point, or we shall make little further progress in the work. Accomodation was the object of the House in the appointment of the Committee; and of the Committee in the Report they had made. And however liable the Report might be to objections, he though[t] it preferable to an appeal to the world by the different sides, as had been talked of by some Gentlemen. It could not be more inconvenient to any gentleman to remain absent from his private affairs, than it was for him: but he would bury his bones in this city rather than expose his Country to the Consequences of a dissolution of the Convention without any thing being done.

[1:549; Madison, 7 July]

"Shall the clause allowing each State one vote in the 2d. branch. stand as part of the Report"? being taken up—

Mr. Gerry. This is the critical question. He had rather agree to it than have no accomodation. A Governt. short of a proper national plan if generally acceptable, would be preferable to a proper one which if it could be carried at all, would operate on discontented States. He thought it would be best to suspend the question till the Comme. yesterday appointed, should make report.

Mr. Sherman Supposed that it was the wish of every one that some Genl. Govt. should be established. An equal vote in the 2d. branch would, he thought, be most likely to give it the necessary vigor. The small States have more vigor in their Govts. than the large ones, the more influence therefore the large ones have, the weaker will be the Govt. In the large States it will be most difficult to collect the real & fair sense of the people. Fallacy & undue influence will be practiced with most success: and improper men will most easily get into office. If they vote by States in the 2d. branch, and each State has an equal vote, there must be always a majority of States as well as a majority of the people on the side of public measures, & the Govt. will have decision and efficacy. If this be not the case in the 2d. branch there may be a majority of the States agst. public measures, and the difficulty of compelling them to abide by the public determination, will render the Government feebler than it has ever yet been.

Mr. Wilson was not deficient in a conciliating temper, but firmness was sometimes a duty of higher obligation. Conciliation was also misapplied in this instance. It was pursued here rather among the Representatives, than among the Constituents; and it wd. be of little consequence, if not established among the latter; and there could be little hope of its being established among them if the foundation should not be laid in justice and right.

On Question shall the words stand as part of the Report?

Massts. divd. Cont. ay. N. Y. ay. N. J. ay. Pa. no. Del. ay.

Md. ay. Va. no. N. C. ay. S. C. no. Geo. divd. [Ayes—6; noes—3; divided—2.]

(Note. several votes were given here in the affirmative or were divd. because another final question was to be taken on the whole report.)

Mr. Gerry thought it would be proper to proceed to enu[m]erate & define the powers to be vested in the Genl. Govt. before a question on the report should be taken as to the rule of representation in the 2d. branch.

Mr. Madison, observed that it wd. be impossible to say what powers could be safely & properly vested in the Govt. before it was known, in what manner the States were to be represented in it. He was apprehensive that if a just representation were not the basis of the Govt. it would happen, as it did when the articles of Confederation were depending, that every effectual prerogative would be withdrawn or withheld, and the New Govt. wd. be rendered as impotent and as short lived as the old.

Mr. Patterson would not decide whether the privilege concerning money bills were a valuable consideration or not: But he considered the mode & rule of representation in the 1st. branch as fully so, and that after the establishment of that point, the small States would never be able to defend themselves without an equality of votes in the 2d. branch. There was no other ground of accommodation. His resolution was fixt. He would meet the large States on that Ground and no other. For himself he should vote agst. the Report, because it yielded too much.

Mr. Govr. Morris. He had no resolution unalterably fixed except to do what should finally appear to him right. He was agst. the Report because it maintained the improper Constitution of the 2d. branch. It made it another Congress, a mere whisp of straw. It had been sd. (by Mr. Gerry) that the new Governt. would be partly national, partly federal; that it ought in the first quality to protect individuals; in the second, the States. But in what quality was it to protect the aggregate interest of the whole. Among the many provisions which had been urged, he had seen none for supporting the dignity and splendor of the American Empire. It had been one of our greatest misfortunes that the great objects of the nation had been sacrificed constantly to local views; in like manner as the general interests of States had been sacrificed to those of the Counties. What is to be the check in the Senate? none; unless it be to keep the majority of the people from injuring particular States. But particular States ought to be injured for the sake of a majority of the people, in case their conduct should deserve it. Suppose they should insist on claims evidently unjust, and pursue them in a manner detrimental to the whole body. Suppose they should give themselves up to foreign influence. Ought they to be protected in such cases. They were originally nothing more than colonial corporations. On the declaration of Independence, a Governmt. was to be formed. The small States aware of the necessity of preventing anarchy, and taking advantage of the moment, extorted from the large ones an equality of votes. Standing now on that ground, they demand under the new system greater rights as men, than their fellow Citizens of the large States. The proper answer to them is that the same necessity of which they formerly took advantage does not now exist, and that the large States are at liberty now to consider what is right, rather than what may be expedient We must have an efficient Govt. and if there be an efficiency to the local Govts. the former is impossible. Germany alone proves it. Notwithstanding their common diet, notwithstanding the great prerogatives of the Emperor as head of the Empire, and his vast resources as sovereign of his particular dominions, no union is maintained: foreign influence disturbs every internal operation, & there is no energy whatever in the general Governmt. Whence does this proceed? From the energy of the local authorities; from its being considered of more consequence to support the Prince of Hesse, than the Happiness of the people of Germany. Do Gentlemen wish this to be ye case here. Good God, Sir, is it possible they can so delude themselves. What if all the Charters & Constitutions of the States were thrown into the fire, and all their demagogues into the ocean. What would it be to the happiness of America. And will not this be the case here if we pursue the train in wch. the business lies. We shall establish an Aulic Council without an Emperor to execute its decrees. The same circumstances which unite the people here, unite them in Germany. They have there a common language, a common law, common usages and manners—and a common interest in being united; yet their local jurisdictions destroy every tie. The case was the same in the Grecian States. The United Netherlands are at this time torn in factions. With these examples before our eyes shall we form establishments which must necessarily produce the same effects. It is of no consequence from what districts the 2d. branch shall be drawn, if it be so constituted as to yield an asylum agst. these evils. As it is now constituted he must be agst. its being drawn from the States in equal portions. But [still] he was ready to join in devising such an amendment of the plan, as will be most likely to secure our liberty & happiness.

Mr. Sherman & Mr. Elseworth moved to postpone the Question on the Report from the Committee of a member from each State, in order to wait for the Report from the come. of 5 last appointed.—

[2:3; Madison, 14 July]

Mr. Rutledge proposed to reconsider the two propositions touching the originating of money bills in the first & the equality of votes in the second branch.

Mr. Sherman was for the question on the whole at once. It was he said a conciliatory plan, it had been considered in all its parts, a great deal of time had been spent on it, and if any part should now be altered, it would be necessary to go over the whole ground again.

Mr. L. Martin urged the question on the whole. He did not like many parts of it. He did not like having two branches, nor the inequality of votes in the 1st. branch. He was willing however to make trial of the plan, rather than do nothing.

Mr. Wilson traced the progress of the Report through its several stages, remarking yt when on the question concerning an equality of votes, the House was divided, our Constituents had they voted as their representatives did, would have stood as ⅔ agst. the equality, and ⅓ only in favor of it. This fact would ere long be known, and it will appear that this fundamental point has been carried by ⅓ agst. ⅔. What hopes will our Constituents entertain when they find that the essential principles of justice have been violated in the outset of the Governmt. As to the privilege of originating money bills, it was not considered by any as of much moment, and by many as improper in itself. He hoped both clauses wd. be reconsidered. The equality of votes was a point of such critical importance, that every opportunity ought to be allowed, for discussing and collecting the mind of the Convention on it.

Mr. L. Martin denies that there were ⅔ agst. the equality of votes. The States that please to call themselves large, are the weekest in the Union. Look at Masts. Look at Virga. Are they efficient States? He was for letting a separation take place if they desired it. He had rather there should be two Confederacies, than one founded on any other principle than an equality of votes in the 2d branch at least.

Mr Wilson was not surprised that those who say that a minority does more than the majority should say that that minority is stronger than the majority. He supposed the next assertion will be that they are richer also, though he hardly expected it would be persisted in when the States shall be called on for taxes & troops—

Mr. Gerry also animadverted on Mr. L. Martins remarks on the weakness of Masts. He favored the reconsideration with a view not of destroying the equality of votes; but of providing that the States should vote per capita. which he said would prevent the delays & inconveniences that had been experienced in Congs. and would give a national aspect & Spirit to the management of business. He did not approve of a reconsideration of the clause relating to money bills. It was of great consequence. It was the corner stone of the accomodation. If any member of the Convention had the exclusive privilege of making propositions, would any one say that it would give him no advantage over other members. The Report was not altogether to his mind. But he would agree to it as it stood rather than throw it out altogether.

The reconsideration being tacitly agreed to

Mr. Pinkney moved that instead of an equality of votes the States should be represented in the 2d branch as follows: N. H. by. 2. members. Mas 4. R. I. 1. Cont. 3. N. Y. 3. N. J. 2. Pa. 4. Del 1. Md. 3. Virga. 5. N. C. 3. S. C. 3. Geo. 2. making in the whole 36.

Mr. Wilson seconds the motion

Mr. Dayton. The smaller States can never give up their equality. For himself he would in no event yield that security for their rights.

Mr. Sherman urged the equality of votes not so much as a security for the small States; as for the State Govts. which could not be preserved unless they were represented & had a negative in the Genl. Government. He had no objection to the members in the 2d b. voting per capita, as had been suggested by (Mr. Gerry)

Mr Madison concurred in the motion of Mr. Pinkney as a reasonable compromise.

Mr. Gerry said he should like the motion, but could see no hope of success. An accomodation must take place, and it was apparent from what had been seen that it could not do so on the ground of the motion. He was utterly against a partial confederacy, leaving other States to accede or not accede; as had been intimated.

Mr. King said it was always with regret that he differed from his colleagues, but it was his duty to differ from (Mr Gerry) on this occasion. He considered the proposed Government as substantially and formally, a General and National Government over the people of America. There never will be a case in which it will act as a federal Government on the States and not on the individual Citizens. And is it not a clear principle that in a free Govt. those who are to be the objects of a Govt. ought to influence the operations of it? What reason can be assigned why the same rule of representation sd. not prevail in the 2d. branch as in the 1st.? He could conceive none. On the contrary, every view of the subject that presented itself, seemed to require it. Two objections had been raised agst. it, drawn 1. from the terms of the existing compact. 2. from a supposed danger to the smaller States.—As to the first objection he thought it inapplicable. According to the existing confederation, the rule by which the public burdens is to be apportioned is *fixed*, and must be pursued. In the proposed Govermt. it cannot be fixed, because indirect taxation is to be substituted. The Legislature therefore will have full discretion to impose taxes in such modes & proportions as they may judge expedient. As to the 2d. objection, he thought it of as little weight. The Genl. Govert. can never wish to intrude on the State Governts. There could be no temptation. None had been pointed out. In order to prevent the interference of measures which seemed most likely to happen, he would have no objection to throwing all the State debts into the federal debt, making one aggregate debt of about 70,000,000, of dollars, and leaving it to be discharged by the Genl. Govt.—According to the idea of securing the State Govts. there ought to be three distinct legislative branches. The 2d. was admitted to be necessary, and was actually meant, to check the 1st. branch, to give more wisdom, system, & stability to the Govt. and ought clearly as it was to operate on the people to be proportioned to them. For the third purpose of securing the States, there ought then to be a 3d. branch, representing the States as such and guarding by equal votes their rights & dignities. He would not pretend to be as thoroughly acquainted with his immediate Constituents as his colleagues, but it was his firm belief that Masts. would never be prevailed on to yield to an equality of votes. In N. York (he was sorry to be obliged to say any thing relative to that State in the absence of its representatives, but the occasion required it), in N. York he had seen that the most powerful argument used by the considerate opponents to the grant of the Impost to Congress, was pointed agst. the viccious constitution of Congs. with regard to representation & suffrage. He was sure that no Govt. could last that was not founded on just principles. He preferred the doing of nothing, to an allowance of an equal vote to all the States.

It would be better he thought to submit to a little more confusion & convulsion, than to submit to such an evil. It was difficult to say what the views of different Gentlemen might be. Perhaps there might be some who thought no Governmt. co-extensive with the U. States could be established with a hope of its answering the purpose. Perhaps there might be other fixed opinions incompatible with the object we were pursing. If there were, he thought it but candid that Gentlemen would speak out that we might understand one another.

Mr. Strong. The Convention had been much divided in opinion. In order to avoid the consequences of it, an accomodation had been proposed. A Committee had been appointed; and though some of the members of it were averse to an equality of votes, a Report has been made in favor of it. It is agreed on all hands that Congress are nearly at an end. If no Accommodation takes place, the Union itself must soon be dissolved. It has been suggested that if we can not come to any general agreement the principal States may form & recommend a scheme of Government. But will the small States in that case ever accede it. Is it probable that the large States themselves will under such circumstances embrace and ratify it. He thought the small States had made a considerable concession in the article of money bills, and that they might naturally expect some concessions on the other side. From this view of the matter he was compelled to give his vote for the Report taken all together.

Mr Madison expressed his apprehensions that if the proper foundation of Governmt was destroyed, by substituting an equality in place of a proportional Representation, no proper superstructure would be raised. If the small States really wish for a Government armed with the powers necessary to secure their liberties, and to enforce obedience on the larger members as well as on themselves he could not help thinking them extremely mistaken in their means. He reminded them of the consequences of laying the existing confederation on improper principles. All the principal parties to its compilation, joined immediately in mutilating & fettering the Governmt. in such a manner that it has disappointed every hope placed on it. He appealed to the doctrine & arguments used by themselves on a former occasion. It had been very properly observed by (Mr. Patterson) that Representation was an expedient by which the meeting of the people themselves was rendered unnecessary; and that the representatives ought therefore to bear a proportion to the votes which their constituents if convened, would respectively have. Was not this remark as applicable to one branch of the Representation as to the other? But it had been said that the Governt. would in its operation be partly federal, partly national; that altho' in the latter respect the Representatives of the people ought to be in proportion to the people: yet in the former it ought to be according to the number of States. If there was any solidity in this distinction he was ready to abide by it, if there was none it ought to be abandoned. In all cases where the Genl. Govert. is to act on the people, let the people be represented and the votes be proportional. In all cases where the Governt. is to act on the States as such, in like manner as Congs. now act on them, let the States be represented & the votes be equal. This was the true ground of compromise if there was any ground at all. But he denied that there was any ground. He called for a single instance in which the Genl. Govt. was not to operate on the people individually. The practicability of making laws, with coercive sanctions, for the States as political bodies, had been exploded on all hands. He observed that the people of the large States would in some way or other secure to themselves a weight proportioned to the importance accruing from their superior numbers. If they could not effect it by a proportional representation in the Govt. they would probably accede to no Govt. which did not in great measure depend for its efficacy on their voluntary cooperation; in which case they would indirectly secure their object. The existing confederacy proved that where the acts of the Genl. Govt. were to be executed by the particular Govts the latter had a weight in proportion to their importance. No one would say that either in Congs. or out of Congs. Delaware had equal weight with Pensylva. If the latter was to supply ten times as much money as the former, and no compulsion could be used, it was of ten times more importance, that she should furnish voluntarily the supply. In the Dutch Confederacy the votes of the Provinces were equal. But Holland, which supplies about half the money, governed the whole republic. He enumerated the objections agst an equality of votes in the 2d. branch, notwithstanding the proportional representation in the first. 1. the minority could negative the will of the majority of the people. 2. they could extort measures by making them a condition of their assent to other necessary measures. 3. they could obtrude measures on the majority by virtue of the peculiar powers which would be vested in the Senate. 4. the evil instead of being cured by time, would increase with every new State that should be admitted, as they must all be admitted on the principle of equality. 5. the perpetuity it would give to the preponderance of the Northn. agst. the Southn. Scale was a serious consideration. It seemed now to be pretty well understood that the real difference of interests lay, not between the large & small but between the N. & Southn. States. The institution of slavery & its consequences formed the line of discrimination. There were 5 States on the South, 8 on the Northn. side of this line. Should a proportl. representation take place it was true, the N. side would still outnumber the other: but not in the same degree, at this time; and every day would tend towards an equilibrium.

Mr. Wilson would add a few words only. If equality in the 2d. branch was an error that time would correct, he should be less anxious to exclude it being sensible that perfection was unattainable in any plan: but being a fundamental and a perpetual error, it ought by all means to be avoided. A vice in the Representation, like an error in the first concoction, must be followed by disease, convulsions, and finally death itself. The justice of the general principle of proportional representation has not in argument at least been yet contradicted. But it is said that a departure from it so far as to give the States an equal vote in one branch of the Legislature is essential to their preservation. He had considered this position maturely, but could not

see its application. That the States ought to be preserved he admitted, But does it follow that an equality of votes is necessary for the purpose? Is there any reason to suppose that if their preservation should depend more on the large than on the small States, the security of the States agst. the Genl. Government would be diminished? Are the large States less attached to their existence, more likely to commit suicide, than the small? An equal vote then is not necessary as far as he can conceive: and is liable, among other objections to this insuperable one: The great fault of the existing Confederacy is its inactivity. It has never been a complaint agst. Congs. that they governed overmuch. The complaint has been that they have governed too little. To remedy this defect we were sent here. Shall we effect the cure by establishing an equality of votes, as is proposed? no; this very equality carries us directly to Congress: to the system which it is our duty to rectify. The small States cannot indeed act, by virtue of this equality, but they may controul the Govt. as they have done in Congs. This very measure is here prosecuted by a minority of the people of America. Is then the object of the Convention likely to be accomplished in this way? Will not our Constituents say? we sent you to form an efficient Govt and you have given us one more complex indeed, but having all the weakness of the former Governt. He was anxious for uniting all the States under one Governt. He knew there were some respectable men who preferred three confederacies, united by offensive & defensive alliances. Many things may be plausibly said, some things may be justly said, in favor of such a project. He could not however concur in it himself; but he thought nothing so pernicious as bad first principles.

Mr. Elseworth asked two questions one of Mr. Wilson, whether he had ever seen a good measure fail in Congs. for want of a majority of States in its favor? He had himself never known such an instance: the other of Mr. Madison whether a negative lodged with a majority of the States even the smallest, could be more dangerous than the qualified negative proposed to be lodged in a single Executive Magistrate, who must be taken from some one State?

Mr. Sherman, signified that his expectation was that the Genl. Legislature would in some cases act on the *federal principle*, of requiring quotas. But he thought it ought to be empowered to carry their own plans into execution, if the States should fail to supply their respective quotas.

On the question for agreeing to Mr Pinkney's motion for allowing N. H. 2. Mas. 4. &c—it passed in the negative

Mas. no. Mr. King ay. Mr. Ghorum absent. Cont. no. N. J. no. Pa. ay. Del. no. Md. ay. Va. ay. N. C. no. S. C. ay Geo. no. [Ayes—4; noes—6.]

[2:17; Madison, 16 July]

Mr. Randolph. The vote of this morning (involving an equality of suffrage in 2d. branch) had embarrassed the business extremely. All the powers given in the Report from the Come. of the whole, were founded on the supposition that a Proportional representation was to prevail in both branches of the Legislature—When he came here this morning his purpose was to have offered some propositions that might if possible have united a great majority of votes, and particularly might provide agst. the danger suspected on the part of the smaller States, by enumerating the cases in which it might lie, and allowing an equality of votes in such cases. But finding from the preceding vote that they persist in demanding an equal vote in all cases, that they have succeeded in obtaining it, and that N. York if present would probably be on the same side, he could not but think we were unprepared to discuss this subject further. It will probably be in vain to come to any final decision with a bare majority on either side. For these reasons he wished the Convention might adjourn, that the large States might consider the steps proper to be taken in the present solemn crisis of the business, and that the small States might also deliberate on the means of conciliation.

Mr. Patterson, thought with Mr. R. that it was high time for the Convention to adjourn that the rule of secrecy ought to be rescinded, and that our Constituents should be consulted. No conciliation could be admissible on the part of the smaller States on any other ground than that of an equality of votes in the 2d. branch. If Mr Randolph would reduce to form his motion for an adjournment sine die, he would second it with all his heart.

Genl. Pinkney wished to know of Mr R. whether he meant an adjournment sine die, or only an adjournment for the day. If the former was meant, it differed much from his idea He could not think of going to S. Carolina, and returning again to this place. Besides it was chimerical to suppose that the States if consulted would ever accord separately, and beforehand.

Mr. Randolph, had never entertained an idea of an adjournment sine die; & was sorry that his meaning had been so readily & strangely misinterpreted. He had in view merely an adjournment till tomorrow in order that some conciliatory experiment might if possible be devised and that in case the smaller States should continue to hold back, the larger might then take such measures, he would not say what, as might be necessary.

Mr. Patterson seconded the adjournment till tomorrow, as an opportunity seemed to be wished by the larger States to deliberate further on conciliatory expedients.

On the question for adjourning till tomorrow, the States were equally divided.

Mas. no. Cont. no. N. J. ay. Pa. ay. Del. no. Md. ay. Va. ay. N. C. ay. S. C. no. Geo. no. So it was lost. [Ayes—5; noes—5.]

Mr. Broome thought it his duty to declare his opinion agst. an adjournment sine die, as had been urged by Mr. Patterson. Such a measure he thought would be fatal. Something must be done by the Convention tho' it should be by a bare majority.

Mr. Gerry observed that Masts. was opposed to an adjournment, because they saw no new ground of compromise. But as it seemed to be the opinion of so many States that a trial shd be made, the State would now concur in the adjournmt.

Mr. Rutledge could see no need of an adjournt. because he could see no chance of a compromise. The little States were fixt. They had repeatedly & solemnly declared themselves to be so. All that the large States then had to do, was

to decide whether they would yield or not. For his part he conceived that altho' we could not do what we thought best, in itself, we ought to do something. Had we not better keep the Govt. up a little longer, hoping that another Convention will supply our omissions, than abandon every thing to hazard. Our Constituents will be very little satisfied with us if we take the latter course.

Mr. Randolph & Mr. King renewed the motion to adjourn till tomorrow.

On the question Mas. ay. Cont. no. N. J. ay. Pa. ay. Del. no. Md. ay. Va. ay. N. C. ay. S. C. ay. Geo. divd. [Ayes—7; noes—2; divided—1.]

Adjourned

On the morning following before the hour of the Convention a number of the members from the larger States, by common agreement met for the purpose of consulting on the proper steps to be taken in consequence of the vote in favor of an equal Representation in the 2d. branch, and the apparent inflexibility of the smaller States on that point—Several members from the latter States also attended. The time was wasted in vague conversation on the subject, without any specific proposition or agreement. It appeared indeed that the opinions of the members who disliked the equality of votes differed so much as to the importance of that point, and as to the policy of risking a failure of any general act of the Convention by inflexibly opposing it. Several of them supposing that no good Governnt could or would be built on that foundation, and that as a division of the Convention into two opinions was unavoidable it would be better that the side comprising the principal States, and a majority of the people of America, should propose a scheme of Govt. to the States, than that a scheme should be proposed on the other side, would have concurred in a firm opposition to the smaller States, and in a separate recommendation, if eventually necessary. Others seemed inclined to yield to the smaller States, and to concur in such an Act however imperfect & exceptionable, as might be agreed on by the Convention as a body, tho' decided by a bare majority of States and by a minority of the people of the U. States. It is probable that the result of this consultation satisfied the smaller States that they had nothing to apprehend from a Union of the larger, in any plan whatever agst. the equality of votes in the 2d. branch.

[2:94; Madison, 23 July]

Mr. Govr. Morris & Mr. King moved that the representation in the second branch consist of _____ members from each State, who shall vote per capita.

Mr Elseworth said he had alway approved of voting in that mode.

Mr. Govr. Morris moved to fill the *blank* with *three*. He wished the Senate to be a pretty numerous body. If two members only should be allowed to each State, and a majority be made a quorum the power would be lodged in 14 members, which was too small a number for such a trust.

Mr Ghorum preferred two to three members for the blank. A small number was most convenient for deciding on peace & war &c. which he expected would be vested in the 2d. branch. The number of States will also increase. Kentucky, Vermont, the province of Mayne & Franklin will probably soon be added to the present number. He presumed also that some of the largest States would be divided. The strenghth of the general Govt. will lie not in the largeness, but in the smallness of the States.

Col. Mason thought 3 from each State including new States would make the 2d. branch too numerous. Besides other objections, the additional expence ought always to form one, where it was not absolutely necessary.

Mr. Williamson. If the number be too great, the distant States will not be on an equal footing with the nearer States. The latter can more easily send & support their ablest Citizens. He approved of the voting per capita.

On the question for filling the blank with *"three"*

N. H. no. Mas. no. Cont. no. Pa. ay. Del. no. Va. no. N. C. no. S. C. no. Geo. no. [Ayes—1; noes—8.]

On question for filling it with "two." Agreed to nem-con,

Mr. L Martin was opposed to voting per Capita, as departing from the idea of the *States* being represented in the 2d. branch.

Mr. Carroll, was not struck with any particular objection agst. the mode; but he did not wish so hastily to make so material an innovation.

On the question on the whole motion viz. the 2d. b."to consist of 2 members from each State and to vote per capita."

N. H. ay. Mas. ay. Ct. ay. Pa. ay. Del. ay. Md. no. Va. ay. N. C. ay: S. C. ay. Geo. ay. [Ayes—9; noes—1.]

[2:231; Madison, 9 Aug.]

Mr. Wilson objected to vacancies in the Senate being supplied by the Executives of the States. It was unnecessary as the Legislatures will meet so frequently. It removes the appointment too far from the people; the Executives in most of the States being elected by the Legislatures. As he had always thought the appointment of the Executives by the Legislative department wrong: so it was still more so that the Executive should elect into the Legislative department.

Mr. Randolph though it necessary in order to prevent inconvenient chasms in the Senate. In some States the Legislatures meet but once a year. As the Senate will have more power & consist of a smaller number than the other House, vacancies there will be of more consequence. The Executives might be safely trusted he thought with the appointment for so short a time.

Mr. Elseworth. It is only said that the Executive *may* supply vacancies. When the Legislative meeting happens to be near, the power will not be exerted. As there will be but two members from a State vacancies may be of great moment.

Mr. Williamson. Senators may resign or not accept. This provision is therefore absolutely necessary.

On the question for striking out "vacancies shall be supplied by Executives"

N. H. no. Mas. no. Ct. no. N. J. no. Pa. ay. Md. divd. Va. no. N. C. no. S. C. no. Geo. no. [Ayes—1; noes—8; divided—1.]

Mr. Williamson moved to insert after "vacancies shall be supplied by the Executives", the following words "unless other provision shall be made by the Legislature" (of the State).

Mr Elseworth. He was willing to trust the Legislature, or the Executive of a State, but not to give the former a discretion to refer appointments for the Senate to whom they pleased.

Question on Mr Williamson's motion

N. H. no. Mas. no. Ct. no. N. J. no. Pa. no. Md. ay. Va. no. N- C. ay. S. C. ay- Geo. ay. [Ayes—4; noes—6.]

Mr. Madison in order to prevent doubts whether resignations could be made by Senators, or whether they could refuse to accept, moved to strike out the words after "vacancies". & insert the words "happening by refusals to accept, resignations or otherwise may be supplied by the Legislature of the State in the representation of which such vacancies shall happen, or by the Executive thereof until the next meeting of the Legislature"

Mr. Govr. Morris this is absolutely necessary. otherwise, as members chosen into the Senate are disqualified from being appointed to any office by sect. 9. of this art: it will be in the power of a Legislature by appointing a man a Senator agst. his consent, to deprive the U. S. of his services.

The motion of Mr. Madison was agreed to nem. con.

Mr. Randolph called for a division of the Section, so as to leave a distinct question on the last words, "each member shall have one vote". He wished this last sentence to be postponed until the reconsideration should have taken place on sect. 5. Art. IV. concerning money bills. If that section should not be reinstated his plan would be to vary the representation in the Senate.

Mr. Strong concurred in Mr. Randolphs ideas on this point

Mr. Read did not consider the section as to money bills of any advantage to the larger States and had voted for striking it out as being viewed in the same light by the larger States. If it was considered by them as of any value, and as a condition of the equality of votes in the Senate, he had no objection to its being re-instated.

Mr. Wilson—Mr. Elseworth & Mr. Madison urged that it was of no advantage to the larger States. and that it might be a dangerous source of contention between the two Houses. All the principal powers of the Natl. Legislature had some relation to money.

Docr. Franklin, considered the two clauses, the originating of money bills, and the equality of votes in the Senate, as essentially connected by the compromise which had been agreed to.

Col. Mason said this was not the time for discussing this point. When the originating of money bills shall be reconsidered, he thought it could be demonstrated that it was of essential importance to restrain the right to the House of Representatives the immediate choice of the people.

Mr. Williamson. The State of N. C. had agreed to an equality in the Senate, merely in consideration that money bills should be confined to the other House: and he was surprised to see the smaller States forsaking the condition on which they had received their equality.

Question on the Section 1. down to the last sentence
N. H ay. Mas. no. Ct. ay. N. J. ay. Pa. no- Del. ay. Md. ay. Virga ay N. C. no. S. C. divd. Geo. ay. [Ayes—7; noes—3; divided—1.]

Mr. Randolph moved that the last sentence "each member shall have one vote." be postponed

It was observed that this could not be necessary; as in case the section as to originating bills should not be reinstated, and a revision of the Constitution should ensue, it wd. still be proper that the members should vote per capita. A postponement of the preceding sentence allowing to each State 2 members wd. have been more proper.

Mr. Mason, did not mean to propose a change of this mode of voting per capita in any event. But as there might be other modes proposed, he saw no impropriety in postponing the sentence. Each State may have two members, and yet may have unequal votes. He said that unless the exclusive originating of money bills should be restored to the House of Representatives, he should, not from obstinacy, but duty and conscience, oppose throughout the equality of Representation in the Senate.

Mr. Govr. Morris. Such declarations were he supposed, addressed to the smaller States in order to alarm them for their equality in the Senate, and induce them agst. their judgments, to concur in restoring the section concerning money bills. He would declare in his turn that as he saw no prospect of amending the Constitution of the Senate & considered the Section relating to money bills as intrinsically bad, he would adhere to the section establishing the equality at all events.

Mr. Wilson. It seems to have been supposed by some that the section concerning money bills is desirable to the large States. The fact was that two of those States (Pa. & Va) had uniformly voted agst. it without reference to any other part of the system.

Mr. Randolph, urged as Col. Mason had done that the sentence under consideration was connected with that relating to money bills, and might possibly be affected by the result of the motion for reconsidering the latter. That the postponement was therefore not improper.

Question for postponing "each member shall have one vote."
N. H. divd. Mas. no. Ct. no. N. J. no. Pa. no. Del. no. Md. no. Va. ay. N. C. ay. S. C. no. Geo. no. [Ayes—2; noes—8; divided—1.]

The words were then agreed to as part of the section.

Mr. Randolph then gave notice that he should move to reconsider this whole Sect: 1. Art. V. as connected with the 5. Sect. art. IV. as to which he had already given such notice.

[2:291; Madison, 14 Aug.]

Mr Madison. If the H. of Reps. is to be chosen *biennially*—and the Senate to be *constantly* dependent on the Legislatures which are chosen *annually*, he could not see any chance for that stability in the Genl Govt. the want of which was a principal evil in the State Govts. His fear was that the organization of the Govt supposing the Senate to be really independt. for six years, would not effect our purpose. It was nothing more than a combination of the peculiarities of two of the State Govts. which separately had been found insufficient. The Senate was formed on the model of that of Maryld. The Revisionary check, on that of N. York. What the effect of A union of these provisions might be, could not be foreseen. The enlargement of the sphere of the Government was indeed a circumstance which he thought would be favorable as he had on several occasions undertaken to show. He was however for fixing at least two extremes not to be exceeded by the Natl. Legislre. in the payment of themselves.

4

"JOHN DEWITT," NO. 4
Fall 1787
Storing 4.3.16

Like the performance of a fine painter, the Senate is the subject of the piece painted.—The people with their priviledges, to an attentive observer, may be seen in the back ground, composing an insignificant part of the drapery, but their existence depends upon the freshness of the colours.—Frequent handling, a little exposure, and the smallest inroads of time upon these shades, will soon destroy them, and they will no longer be considered a part of the composition. If this is true—if in any future period, however distant, we are to be governed by One Branch, it surely behoves us to provide for an equal voice in that Branch, that our respective influence shall bear some small proportion to our respective contributions and numbers: Whereas in this System, equality is totally disregarded. Five pounds in the Senate has an equal voice with fifty, and about five hundred thousand of the inhabitants the same number of votes with the remaining three millions. Where then is the probability the rights of the people will find equal security? Is it not demonstrable that your burthens will be great in proportion as your influence in that body that imposes them is small? As it respects this Commonwealth [of Massachusetts], infinitely better would be our situation in a representation in the British Parliament. The terms offered us by our enemies to place us as we stood in 1763, bear no comparison in their consequences, to those which would flow from the exercise of the powers of this Government by the Senate, as now constructed. If the same proportion in numbers and property had been observed in this Branch as in the House of Representatives (and no reason why it was not hath yet appeared, excepting what the celebrated Southern gentleman is pleased to term a *"necessary compromise between contending interests"*) however successful they might be hereafter in arrogating all the powers of government to themselves, or however severe in executing them, still one gleam of hope with the spirit of consolation would be found in the breast of the subject, that his grievances were proportionate to those of his neighbours; but in the present case, even this satisfaction is denied him—the uncertainty is not left him—his reason instanter convinces him it is not so.

5

James Wilson, State House Speech
6 Oct. 1787
Pamphlets 158–59

Perhaps there never was a charge made with less reason, than that which predicts the institution of a baneful aristocracy in the foederal senate. This body branches into two characters, the one legislative, and the other executive. In its legislative character, it can effect no purpose without the co-operation of the house of representatives: and in its executive character, it can accomplish no object, without the concurrence of the president. Thus fettered, I do not know any act which the senate can of itself perform: and such dependence necessarily precludes every idea of influence and superiority. But I will confess, that in the organization of this body, a compromise between contending interests is discernible: and when we reflect how various are the laws, commerce, habits, population, and extent of the confederated states, this evidence of mutual concession and accommodation ought rather to command a generous applause, than to excite jealousy and reproach. For my part, my admiration can only be equalled by my astonishment, in beholding so perfect a system formed from such heterogenous materials.

6

James Madison to Thomas Jefferson
24 Oct. 1787

(See vol. 1, ch. 17, no. 22)

7

A Democratic Federalist
26 Nov. 1787
Jensen 2:294–98

The examination of the principle of liberty and civil polity is one of the most delightful exercises of the rational faculties of man. Hence the pleasure we feel in a candid, unimpassioned investigation of the grounds and probable consequences of the new frame of government submitted to the people by the Federal Convention. The various doubts, which the subject has created, will lead us to consider it the more by awakening our minds to that attention with which every freeman should examine the intended constitutions of his country.

Several zealous defenders of liberty in America, and some of them of the *first* reputation, have differed from the bulk of the nation in their speculative opinions on the best constitution for a legislative body. In Pennsylvania this question has formed *the line of division* between two parties, in each of which are to be found men of sound judgment and very general knowledge. As this diversity of opinion has not arisen from any peculiarity in our situation or circumstances, it must have been produced by the imperfections of our political researches and by the fallibility of the human mind, ever liable to unfavorable influence even from laudable and necessary passions. The sincere and zealous friend of liberty is naturally in love with a refined democracy, beautiful and perfect as a theory, and adapted to the government of the purest beings; and he views with jealousy, apprehension and dislike not only *real* deviations from democratic principles, but *the appearance* of aristocracy. Hence the idea of an *upper* house (a term erroneously adopted from the British constitution) has been disagreeable and even alarming to many, who were equally friends to perfect and real liberty and to an effective government. Among the various regulations and arrangements of the new Federal Constitution the *peculiar* ground on which the Senate is placed is on this account the most striking and perhaps estimable. A careful comparison of our *second* branch, as proposed by the Convention, with the upper house in the British constitution, will show, I hope, that there is something like *a middle ground* on which the wise and good of both opinions may meet and unite.

The ancestors of the upper house in England originally derived all their power from the feudal system. Possessed by lawless force of extensive domains, which, after a certain period, became hereditary in their families, they established a permanent power through *the military service* of their tenants, for upon those terms were all the lands of the kingdom once held under them. When the address and spirit of the people, exerted upon every proper occasion, obtained for them the interesting privileges of holding in their families also the tenanted estates of the lords, and of alienating their tenancies to such as would perform the conditions on which they were held—when, by the extinction of the families of some of the barons, their tenants remained in possession of their lands—when by the increase of the property, the knowledge and the power of the tenants (or Commons of England) and from other favorable circumstances, the people of that country obtained a portion of that independence which Providence intended for them, such of their nobles as stood the shock, which fell from these circumstances on their order, were formed into a separate independent body. They claimed an absolute right to act in their proper persons, and not by representatives, in the formation of the laws. Being from their wealth, their hereditary power to legislate and judge, and their extraordinary learning in those times, perfectly independent of the rest of the nation, they have often been useful in checking the encroachments of the crown, and the precipitation and inadvertence of the people. In that country they have really held *the balance* between the king and the Commons. But though such a balance may be proper in a royal government, it does not appear necessary *merely in that view* in a genuine republic—which ought to be a government of laws. Yet there are striking and capital advantages resulting from a second, not an *upper* house, if they can be obtained without departing, in our practice, from the real principles of liberty. The arts and influence of popular and unworthy men; too hasty, careless, incautious and passionate proceedings; breaches of wholesome order and necessary form are evils we must wish to avoid, if to be effected without the hazard of greater. Let us examine how far the *peculiar* constitution of our federal Senate will give us the advantages of a second legislative branch without subjecting us to the dangers usually apprehended from such bodies, that the sincere friends of freedom and mankind in America, if there is no longer reason for their differing upon a point of speculation may harmonize and unite.

The federal Senate, from the nature of our governments, will not be hereditary, nor will they possess, like the British barons, a power originally usurped by lawless violence and supported by military tenants. They will not necessarily have even an influential property, for they will have a greater number of fellow citizens, as rich as themselves; and no qualification of wealth exists in the Constitution at present, nor can it be introduced without the consent of *three-fourths of the people of the Union.* It cannot be apprehended, that the people at large of these free commonwealths will consent to disqualify themselves for the senatorial office, which God and the Constitution have intended they should fill. The members of the Senate should certainly be men of very general information, but through the goodness of Providence, numbers will be found in every state, equally well qualified in that respect to execute a trust for which two persons only will be necessary. Instead of their possessing all the knowledge of the state, an equal proportion will be found in some of the members of the House of Representatives, and even a greater share of it will often adorn persons in private walks of life. They will have no distinctions of rank, for the persons over whom a Senator might be weak enough to affect a superiority will be really equal to him and may in a short time change situations with him. The Senator will again become a private citizen and the citizen may become a Senator—nay more—a president of the Senate or President of the Union. The upper house in England have an interest different and separate from the people and, whether in the execution of their office or not, are a distinct body of men, a superior order. Many little circumstances tend to favor and promote this unjust and preposterous distinction. If an ambassador is sent to their court by France or Spain, he is a nobleman of his own country, and a nobleman must be sent from England in return, which operates as a deprivation of the rights of every well-qualified commoner in the kingdom. This is a hardship, which *cannot* arise from our second branch, but exists in Britain not only in the case particularized, but in regard to many other employments of honor and profit. But a greater and more essential distinction between the upper house in England and our federal Senate yet remains. The members of the former claim and possess all their powers and honors in their *own* right, their own *hereditary* right, while the new Constitution renders our Senate merely a *representative* body without one distinction in favor of the

birth, rank, wealth or power of the Senators or their fathers. There has arisen out of the particular nature of our affairs, a *peculiar* happiness in the formation of this body. The federal Senate are *the representatives of the sovereignties of their respective states.* A second branch, *thus constituted,* is a novelty in the history of the world. Instead of an hereditary upper house, the American Confederacy has created a body, the temporary representatives of their component sovereignties, dignified only by their being the immediate delegates and guardians of sovereign states selected from the body of the people for that purpose, and for no reasons, but their possessing the qualifications necessary for their station. We find then in this body, none of the evils of aristocracy apprehended by those who have drawn their reasonings from an erroneous comparison with the upper house of Britain, and all the benefits of a second branch, without hazarding the rights of the people in the smallest particular. As our federal Representatives and state legislatures will be composed of men, who, the moment before their election, were a part of the people and who on the expiration of their time, will return to the same private situations, so the members of our federal Senate will be elected from out of the body of the people, without one qualification being made necessary, but mere citizenship, and at the expiration of their term will again be placed in private life. The Senate, therefore, will be as much a democratic body as the House of Representatives, with this advantage, that they will be elected by the state legislatures to whom, on account of their superior wisdom and virtue, the people at large will have previously committed the care of their affairs.

The plan of federal government proposed by the Convention has another merit of essential consequence to our national liberties. Under the old Confederation, the people at large had no voice in the election of their rulers. The collected wisdom of the state legislatures will hereafter be exercised in the choice of the Senate, but our federal Representatives will be chosen *by the votes of the people themselves.* The Electors of the President and Vice President of the Union may also, by laws of the separate states, be put on the same footing.

The separation of the judicial power from the legislative and executive has been justly deemed one of the most inestimable improvements in modern polity; yet no country has ever completely accomplished it in their actual practice. The British peers are criminal judges in cases of impeachment, and are a court of appeal in civil cases. The power of impeachment, vested in our federal Representatives, and the right to hear those cases, which is vested in the Senate, can produce no punishment in person or property, *even on conviction.* Their whole judicial power lies within a narrow compass. They can take no cognizance of a private citizen and can only declare any dangerous public officer no longer worthy to serve his country. To punish him for his crimes, in body or estate, is not within their constitutional powers. They must consign him to a jury and a court, with whom the deprivation of his office is to be no proof of guilt.

The size of the Senate has been considered by some, as an objection to that body. Should this appear of any importance it is fortunate that there are reasons to expect an addition to their number. The legislature of Virginia have taken measures preparatory to the erection of their western counties into a separate state, from which another good consequence will follow, that the free persons, which will remain within the Dominion of Virginia, will perhaps be nearly or quite as well represented in the Senate as Pennsylvania or Massachusetts. Should Vermont, at some future time, be also introduced into the Union, a further addition to the number of our Senators will take place. If therefore there is any importance in the objection to the size of our federal Senate, or if any such objection prevails in the minds of the people, it is in a way of being removed.

The executive powers of the Union are separated in a higher degree from the legislative than in any government now existing in the world. As a check upon the President, the Senate may disapprove of the officers he appoints, but no person holding *any office* under the United States can be a member of the federal legislature. How differently are things circumstanced in the two houses in Britain where an officer of any kind, naval, military, civil or ecclesiastical, may hold a seat in either house.

This is a most enlightened time, but more especially so in regard to matters of government. The divine right of kings, the force of ecclesiastical obligations in civil affairs, and many other gross errors, under which our forefathers have lain in darker ages of the world, are now done away. The natural, indefeasible and unalienable rights of mankind form the more eligible ground on which we now stand.

The United States are in this respect *"the favored of Heaven."* The Magna Charta, Bill of Rights, and common law of England furnished in 1776 a great part of the materials out of which were formed our several state constitutions. *All these* were more or less recognized in the old Articles of Confederation.

On this solid basis is reared the fabric of our new federal government. These taken together form THE GREAT WHOLE OF THE AMERICAN CONSTITUTIONS, the fairest fabric of liberty that ever blessed mankind, immovably founded on a solid rock, whose mighty base is laid at the center of the earth.

8

LUTHER MARTIN, MARYLAND HOUSE OF DELEGATES
29 Nov. 1787
Farrand 3:151–54

It must be remembered that in forming the Confederacy the State of Virginia proposed, and obstinately contended (tho unsupported by any other) for representation according to Numbers: and the second resolve now brought forward by an Honourable Member from that State was formed in the same spirit that characteriz'd its representatives in their endeavours to increase its powers and influ-

ence in the Federal Government. These Views in the larger States, did not escape the observation of the lesser and meetings in private were formed to counteract them: the subject however was discuss'd with coolness in Convention, and hopes were formed that interest might in some points be brought to Yield to reason, or if not, that at all events the lesser States were not precluded from introducing a different System; and particular Gentlemen were industriously employed in forming such a System at those periods in which Convention were not sitting.

At length the Committee of Detail brought forward their Resolutions which gave to the larger States the same inequality in the Senate that they now are proposed to have in the House of Representatives—Virginia, Pennsylvania and Massachusetts would have one half—all the Officers and even the President were to be chosen by the Legislative: so that these three States might have usurped the whole power.

. . . . .

When the principles of opposition were thus formed and brought forward by the 2d. S: respecting the manner of representation, it was urged by a Member of Pennsylvania, that nothing but necessity had induced the larger States to give up in forming the Confederacy, the Equality of Representation according to numbers—That all governments flowed from the People and that their happiness being the end of governments they ought to have an equal Representation. On the contrary it was urged by the unhappy Advocates of the Jersey System that all people were equally Free, and had an equal Voice if they could meet in a general Assembly of the whole. But because one Man was stronger it afforded no reason why he might injure another, nor because ten leagued together, they should have the power to injure five; this would destroy all equality. That each State when formed, was in a State of Nature as to others, and had the same rights as Individuals in a State of Nature—If the State Government had equal Authority, it was the same as if Individuals were present, because the State Governments originated and flowed from the Individuals that compose the State, and the Liberty of each State was what each Citizen enjoyed in his own State and no inconvenience had yet been experienced from the inequality of representation in the present Federal Government. Taxation and representation go hand and hand, on the principle alone that, none should be taxed who are not represented; But as to the Quantum, those who possess the property pay only in proportion to the protection they receive—The History of all Nations and sense of Mankind shew, that in all former Confederacies every State had an equal voice. Moral History points out the necessity that each State should vote equally—In the Cantons of Switzerland those of Be[r]ne & Lucerne have more Territory than all the others, yet each State has an equal voice in the General Assembly. The Congress in forming the Confederacy adopted this rule on the principle of Natural right—Virginia then objected. This Federal Government was submitted to the consideration of the Legislatures of the respective States and all of them proposed some amendments; but not one that this part should be altered. Hence we are in possession of the General

Voice of America on this subject. When baffled by reason the larger States positively refused to yield—the lesser refused to confederate, and called on their opponents to declare that security they could give to abide by any plan or form of Government that could now be devised. The same reasons that now exist to abolish the old, might be urged hereafter to overthrow the New Government, and as the methods of reform prescribed by the former were now utterly disregarded, as little ceremony might be used in discarding the latter—It was further objected that the large States would be continually increasing in numbers, and consequently their influence in the National Assembly would increase also: That their extensive Territories were guaranteed and we might be drawn out to defend the enormous extent of those States, and encrease and establish that power intended in time to enslave ourselves—Threats were thrown out to compel the lesser States to confederate—They were told this would be the last opportunity that might offer to prevent a Dissolution of the Union, that once dissolve that Band which held us together and the lesser States had no security for their existence, even for a moment—The lesser States threatened in their turn they would not lay under the imputation of refusing to confederate on equitable conditions; they threatened to publish their own offers and the demands of others, and to appeal to the World in Vindication of their Conduct.

At this period there were eleven States represented in Convention on the question respecting the manner of appointing Delegates to the House of Representatives—Massachusetts, Pensylvania, Virginia, North Carolina, South Carolina and Georgia adopted it as now handed to the consideration of the People.—Georgia now insignificant, with an immense Territory, looked forward to future power and Aggrandizement, Connecticut, New York, Jersey, and Delaware were against the Measure and Maryland was unfortunately divided—On the same question respecting the Senate, perceiving the lesser States would break up Convention altogether, if the influence of that branch was likewise carried against them, the Delegates of Georgia differed in sentiment not on principle but on expediency, and fearing to lose every thing if they persisted, they did not therefore vote being divided. Massachusetts, Pensylvania, Virginia, North Carolina, and South Carolina were in the affirmative, and New York, Connecticut, Jersey, Delaware & Maryland were in the Negative. Every thing was now at a stand and little hopes of agreement, the Delegates of New York had left us determined not to return, and to hazard every possible evil, rather than to Yield in that particular; when it was proposed that a conciliating Committee should be formed of one member from each State—Some Members positively refused to lend their names to this measure others compromised, and agreed that if the point was relinquished by the larger States as to the Senate—they would sign the proposed Constitution and did so, not because they approved it but because they thought something ought to be done for the Public—Neither General Washington nor Franklin shewed any disposition to relinquish the superiority of influence in the Senate. I now proposed Convention should adjourn for

consideration of the subject, and requested leave to take a Copy of their proceedings, but it was denied, and the Avenue thus shut to information and reflection—

9

LUTHER MARTIN, GENUINE INFORMATION
1788
Storing 2.4.17, 34–37, 42

These propositions [the Virginia Plan], Sir, were *acceded to* by a *majority of the members of the committee*—a system by which the *large States were to have not only an inequality of suffrage in the first branch*, but also *the same inequality* in the *second branch*, or senate; however, it was not designed the second branch should consist of the same *number* as the first. It was proposed that the senate should consist of *twenty-eight members*, formed on the following scale—Virginia to send *five*, Pennsylvania and Massachusetts each *four*, South-Carolina, North-Carolina, Maryland, New-York, and Connecticut *two* each, and the States of New-Hampshire, Rhode-Island, Jersey, Delaware, and Georgia each of them *one;* upon this plan, the three large States, Virginia, Pennsylvania and Massachusetts, would have *thirteen* senators out of *twenty-eight*, almost *one half of the whole number*—Fifteen senators were to be a quorum to proceed to business; those *three States* would, therefore, have *thirteen* out of that quorum. Having this inequality *in each branch* of the legislature, it must be evident, Sir, that *they would make what laws they pleased, however injurious or disagreeable to the other States*, and that *they would always prevent the other States from making any laws, however necessary and proper, if not agreeable to the view of those three States—*

. . . . .

Thus, Sir, on this *great* and *important* part of the system, the convention being equally divided, five States for the measure, five against, and one divided, there was a total stand, and we did not seem very likely to proceed any further. At length it was proposed, that a select committee should be balloted for, composed of a member from each State, which committee should endeavour to devise some mode of *conciliation* or *compromise;* I had the honor to be on that committee; we met and discussed the subject of difference; the *one side* insisted on the *inequality* of suffrage in *both branches*, the *other* insisted on the *equality* in both; each party was tenacious of their sentiments, when it was found that nothing could induce us to yield the inequality in both branches; they at length proposed by way of compromise, if *we* would *accede* to their wishes as to the *first* branch, *they* would *agree* to the equal representation in the *second*. To this it was answered, that there was no merit in the proposal, it was only consenting, after they had struggled to put *both their feet on our necks*, to take *one of them off*, provided we would consent to let them *keep the other on*, when they knew at the same time, that they could not put *one foot* on *our necks*, unless *we would consent to it*, and that by being permitted to keep on that one foot, they should *afterwards be able to place the other foot on whenever they pleased.*

They were also called on to inform us what *security* they could give us should we agree to this compromise, that they would *abide* by the plan of government formed upon it, *any longer* than it *suited their interest,* or they found it *expedient.*—"The States have a *right* to an equality of representation. This *is secured to us* by our *present* articles of confederation, *we* are in *possession* of this right; *it is now* to be *torn from us.* What security can you give us, that, when you get the *power* the *proposed system* will give you, when you have *men* and *money,* that you will not *force from the* States that *equality* of suffrage in the *second branch,* which you *now* deny to be their right, and *only give up* from *absolute necessity?* Will you tell us we ought to trust you because you *now enter into a solemn compact with us?* This you have done *before,* and *now* treat it with the *utmost contempt.* Will you *now* make an appeal to the Supreme Being, and call on him to guarantee your observance of this compact? The *same* you have *formerly done* for your observance of the articles of confederation, which you are *now violating* in the most *wanton* manner!

The same reasons which you *now* urge for destroying our *present* federal government, may be urged for *abolishing the system* which you now propose to adopt; and as the *method prescribed* by the *articles* of confederation is *now totally disregarded* by you, as *little regard* may be shewn by you to the *rules prescribed* for the amendment of the *new system,* whenever having obtained power by the government, you shall *hereafter* be pleased either to *discard it entirely,* or so to *alter it* as to give *yourselves* all that *superiority* which *you* have *now contended* for, and to *obtain which* you have shewn yourselves disposed to *hazard the union.*"—Such, Sir, was the language used on that occasion, and they were told that as we could not *possibly* have a stronger tie on them for their observance of the new system than we had for their observance of the articles of confederation, which had proved *totally insufficient,* it would be *wrong* and *imprudent* to *confide in them.* It was further observed, that the inequality of the representation would be *daily increasing*—That many of the States whose territory was confined, and whose population was at this time large in proportion to their territory, would probably twenty, thirty, or forty years hence, have no more representatives than at the introduction of the government, whereas the States having extensive territory, where lands are to be procured cheap, would be daily encreasing in the number of their inhabitants, not only from propagation, but from the *emigration* of the inhabitants of the *other States,* and would have soon double, or perhaps treble the number of representatives that they are to have at first, and thereby enormously *increase* their *influence* in the national councils. However, the *majority* of the select committee at length agreed to a series of propositions by way of compromise, part of which related to the representation in the first branch nearly as the system is now published: and part of them to the second branch securing in that equal representation, and reported them as a compromise upon the *express terms* that they were *wholly* to be *adopted* or *wholly to be rejected;* upon this compromise, a great number of the members so far engaged themselves, that if the system was progressed upon agreeable to the terms of compromise, they would lend it their names, by signing it, and would not actively oppose it, if their States should appear inclined to adopt it—Some, however, in which number was myself, who joined in the report, and agreed to proceed upon those principles, and see *what kind of a system* would *ultimately* be formed upon it, yet reserved to themselves in the most *explicit manner* the right of *finally* giving a *solemn dissent* to the system, if it was thought by them *inconsistent* with the *freedom* and *happiness* of their country—This, Sir, will account why the members of the convention so *generally* signed their names to the system; not because they thought it a *proper one;* not because they *thoroughly approved,* or were *unanimous* for it; but because they thought it *better* than the system attempted to be forced upon them. This report of the select committee was after long dissention adopted by a majority of the convention, and the system was proceeded in accordingly—I believe near a fortnight, perhaps more, was spent in the discussion of this business, during which, we were on the verge of dissolution, scarce held together by the strength of an hair, though the public papers were announcing our extreme unanimity.

Mr. Speaker, I think it my duty to observe, that during this *struggle* to prevent the *large* States from having *all power* in their hands, which had nearly terminated in a dissolution of the convention: it did not appear to me, that either of those illustrious characters the Honorable Mr. *Washington,* or the President of the State of Pennsylvania, were disposed to favour the claims of the *smaller States,* against the *undue superiority* attempted by the *large States;* on the contrary, the Honorable President of Pennsylvania, was a *member* of the *committee* of *compromise,* and there *advocated* the *right* of the *large States* to an *inequality* in *both branches,* and only *ultimately conceded* it in the *second branch* on the *principle of conciliation,* when it was found no other terms would be accepted. This, Sir, I think it my duty to mention, for the *consideration of those* who endeavour to *prop up a dangerous* and *defective* system by *great names;* soon after this period, the Honourable Mr. *Yates* and Mr. *Lansing* of New-York, left us; they had uniformly opposed the system, and I *believe,* despairing of getting a *proper one* brought forward, or of *rendering any real service,* they returned no more.

. . . . .

To prove . . . that the senate *as constituted* could not be a *security* for the *protection* and *preservation* of the *State* governments, and that the *senators* could not be justly considered the *representatives* of the *States as States,* it was observed, that upon *just principles of representation,* the *representative* ought to *speak* the sentiments of his *constituents,* and ought to *vote* in the *same manner* that his *constituents* would do (as far as he can judge) provided his constituents were acting in *person,* and had the same knowledge and information with himself; and therefore that the *representative* ought to be *dependant* on his *constituents,* and *answerable* to them; that the connexion between the *representative* and the *represented,* ought to be as *near* and as *close* as possible; according to these principles, Mr. Speaker, in this State it is provided by *its constitution,* that the representatives in Congress, shall be chosen *annually,* shall be *paid* by the *State,* and shall be subject to *recall* even within the year; so *cautiously* has our *constitution* guarded against an *abuse* of the trust reposed in our representatives in the federal government; whereas by the *third* and *sixth* sections of the *first* article of this new system, the senators are to be chosen for *six* years instead of being chosen *annually;* instead of being paid by their *States* who send them, *they* in conjunction with the other branch, are to *pay themselves* out of the treasury of the United States; and are not liable to be *recalled* during the period for which they are chosen: Thus, Sir, for *six years* the *senators* are rendered totally and absolutely *independent* of *their States,* of *whom* they ought to be the *representatives,* without any *bond* or *tie* between them: During that time they may join in measures *ruinous* and *destructive* to *their States,* even such as should *totally annihilate* their *State governments,* and their States *cannot recall them,* nor *exercise any controul over them.*

10

DEBATE IN MASSACHUSETTS RATIFYING CONVENTION
19 Jan. 1788
Elliot 2:45–48

Col. JONES (of Bristol) objected to the length of time. If men continue in office four or six years, they would forget their dependence on the people, and be loath to leave their places. Men elevated so high in power, they would fall heavy when they came down.

Mr. AMES observed, that an objection was made against the Constitution, because the senators are to be chosen for *six years.* It has been said, that they will be removed too far from the control of the people, and that, to keep them in proper dependence, they should be chosen annually. It is necessary to premise, that no argument against the new plan has made a deeper impression than this, that it will produce a consolidation of the states. This is an effect which all good men will deprecate. For it is obvious, that, if state powers are to be destroyed, the representation is too small. The trust, in that case, would be too great to be confided to so few persons. The objects of legislation would be so multiplied and complicated, that the government would be unwieldy and impracticable. The state governments are essential parts of the system, and the defence of this article is drawn from its tendency to their preservation. The *senators* represent the *sovereignty of the states;* in the other house, individuals are represented. The Senate may not originate bills. It need not be said that they are principally to direct the affairs of wars and treaties. They are in the quality of ambassadors of the states, and it will not be denied that some permanency in their office is necessary to a discharge of their duty. Now, if they were chosen yearly, how could they perform their trust? If they

would be brought by that means more immediately under the influence of the people, then they will represent the state legislatures less, and become the representatives of individuals. This belongs to the other house. The absurdity of this, and its repugnancy to the federal principles of the Constitution, will appear more fully, by supposing that they are to be chosen by the people at large. If there is any force in the objection to this article, this would be proper. But whom, in that case, would they represent?—Not the legislatures of the states, but the people. This would totally obliterate the federal features of the Constitution. What would become of the state governments, and on whom would devolve the duty of defending them against the encroachments of the federal government? A consolidation of the states would ensue, which, it is conceded, would subvert the new Constitution, and against which this very article, so much condemned, is our best security. Too much provision cannot be made against a consolidation. The state governments represent the wishes, and feelings, and local interests, of the people. They are the safeguard and ornament of the Constitution; they will protract the period of our liberties; they will afford a shelter against the abuse of power, and will be the natural avengers of our violated rights.

A very effectual *check* upon the power of the Senate is provided. A third part is to retire from office every two years. By this means, while the senators are seated for six years, they are admonished of their responsibility to the state legislatures. If one third new members are introduced, who feel the sentiments of their states, they will awe that third whose term will be near expiring. This article seems to be an excellence of the Constitution, and affords just ground to believe that it will be, in practice as in theory, a *federal* republic.

Afternoon.—The third section respecting the *construction of the Senate* under debate,—

Col. JONES said his objections still remained—that *senators* chosen for so long a time will forget their duty to their constituents. We cannot, said he, recall them. The choice of representatives was too long; the Senate was much worse; it is, said he, a bad precedent, and is unconstitutional.

Mr. KING said, as the Senate preserved the equality of the states, their appointment is equal. To the objection to this branch, that it is chosen for too long a period, he observed, if the principle of classing them is considered, although it appears long, it will not be found so long as it appears. One class is to serve two years, another four years, and another *six years;* the average, therefore, is four years. The senators, said Mr. K., will have a powerful check in those men who wish for their seats, who will watch their whole conduct in the general government, and will give the alarm in case of misbehavior. And the state legislatures, if they find their delegates erring, can and will instruct them. Will not this be a check? When they hear the voice of the people solemnly dictating to them their duty, they will be bold men indeed to act contrary to it. These will not be *instructions* sent them in a private letter, which can be put in their pockets; they will be public instructions, which all the country will see, and they will be hardy men indeed to violate them. The honorable gentleman said, the powers to control the Senate are as great as ever was enjoyed in any government; and that the members, therefore, will be found not to be chosen for too long a time. They are, says he, to assist the executive in the designation and appointment of officers; and they ought to have time to mature their judgments. If for a shorter period, how can they be acquainted with the rights and interests of nations, so as to form advantageous treaties? To understand these rights is the business of education. Their business being naturally different, and more extensive, than the other branch, they ought to have different qualifications; and their duration is not too long for a right discharge of their duty.

Dr. TAYLOR said, he hoped the honorable gentleman did not mean to deceive us, by saying, that the Senate are not to be chosen for six years; for they really are to be chosen for six years; and as to the idea of classing, he did not know who, when chosen for that time, would go out at a shorter. He remarked on Mr. King's idea of checks, and observed, that such indeed were the Articles of Confederation, which provide for delegates being chosen annually; for rotation, and the right of recalling. But in this, they are to be chosen for six years; but a shadow of rotation provided for, and no power to recall; and concluded by saying, that if they are once chosen, they are chosen forever.

Mr. STRONG mentioned the difficulty which attended the construction of the Senate in the Convention; and that a committee, consisting of one delegate from each state, was chosen to consider the subject, who reported as it now stands; and that Mr. Gerry was on the committee from Massachusetts.

Mr. GERRY rose, and informed the president that he was then preparing a letter on the subject in debate; and would set the matter in its true light; and which he wished to communicate. This occasioned considerable conversation, which lasted until the Convention adjourned.

11

JAMES MADISON, FEDERALIST, NO. 62,
415–22
27 Feb. 1788

I. The qualifications proposed for senators, as distinguished from those of representatives, consist in a more advanced age, and a longer period of citizenship. A senator must be thirty years of age at least; as a representative, must be twenty-five. And the former must have been a citizen nine years; as seven years are required for the latter. The propriety of these distinctions is explained by the nature of the senatorial trust; which requiring greater extent of information and stability of character, requires at the same time that the senator should have reached a period of life most likely to supply these advantages; and

which participating immediately in transactions with foreign nations, ought to be exercised by none who are not thoroughly weaned from the prepossessions and habits incident to foreign birth and education. The term of nine years appears to be a prudent mediocrity between a total exclusion of adopted citizens, whose merit and talents may claim a share in the public confidence; and an indiscriminate and hasty admission of them, which might create a channel for foreign influence on the national councils.

II. It is equally unnecessary to dilate on the appointment of senators by the state legislatures. Among the various modes which might have been devised for constituting this branch of the government, that which has been proposed by the convention is probably the most congenial with the public opinion. It is recommended by the double advantage of favouring a select appointment, and of giving to the state governments such an agency in the formation of the federal government, as must secure the authority of the former; and may form a convenient link between the two systems.

III. The equality of representation in the senate is another point, which, being evidently the result of compromise between the opposite pretensions of the large and the small states, does not call for much discussion. If indeed it be right that among a people thoroughly incorporated into one nation, every district ought to have a *proportional* share in the government; and that among independent and sovereign states bound together by a simple league, the parties however unequal in size, ought to have an *equal* share in the common councils, it does not appear to be without some reason, that in a compound republic partaking both of the national and federal character, the government ought to be founded on a mixture of the principles of proportional and equal representation. But it is superfluous to try by the standards of theory, a part of the constitution which is allowed on all hands to be the result not of theory, but "of a spirit of amity, and that mutual deference and concession which the peculiarity of our political situation rendered indispensable." A common government with powers equal to its objects, is called for by the voice, and still more loudly by the political situation of America. A government founded on principles more consonant to the wishes of the larger states, is not likely to be obtained from the smaller states. The only option then for the former lies between the proposed government and a government still more objectionable. Under this alternative the advice of prudence must be, to embrace the lesser evil; and instead of indulging a fruitless anticipation of the possible mischiefs which may ensue, to contemplate rather the advantageous consequences which may qualify the sacrifice.

In this spirit it may be remarked, that the equal vote allowed to each state, is at once a constitutional recognition of the portion of sovereignty remaining in the individual states, and an instrument for preserving that residuary sovereignty. So far the equality ought to be no less acceptable to the large than to the small states; since they are not less solicitous to guard by every possible expedient against an improper consolidation of the states into one simple republic.

Another advantage accruing from this ingredient in the

constitution of the senate, is the additional impediment it must prove against improper acts of legislation. No law or resolution can now be passed without the concurrence first of a majority of the people, and then of a majority of the states. It must be acknowledged that this complicated check on legislation may in some instances be injurious as well as beneficial; and that the peculiar defence which it involves in favour of the smaller states would be more rational, if any interests common to them, and distinct from those of the other states, would otherwise be exposed to peculiar danger. But as the larger states will always be able by their power over the supplies to defeat unreasonable exertions of this prerogative of the lesser states; and as the facility and excess of law-making seem to be the diseases to which our governments are most liable, it is not impossible that this part of the constitution may be more convenient in practice than it appears to many in contemplation.

IV. The number of senators and the duration of their appointment come next to be considered. In order to form an accurate judgment on both these points, it will be proper to enquire into the purposes which are to be answered by a senate; and in order to ascertain these it will be necessary to review the inconveniencies which a republic must suffer from the want of such an institution.

First. It is a misfortune incident to republican government, though in a less degree than to other governments, that those who administer it, may forget their obligations to their constituents, and prove unfaithful to their important trust. In this point of view, a senate, as a second branch of the legislative assembly, distinct from, and dividing the power with, a first, must be in all cases a salutary check on the government. It doubles the security to the people, by requiring the concurrence of two distinct bodies in schemes of usurpation or perfidy, where the ambition or corruption of one, would otherwise be sufficient. This is a precaution founded on such clear principles, and now so well understood in the United States, that it would be more than superfluous to enlarge on it. I will barely remark that as the improbability of sinister combinations will be in proportion to the dissimilarity in the genius of the two bodies; it must be politic to distinguish them from each other by every circumstance which will consist with a due harmony in all proper measures, and with the genuine principles of republican government.

Secondly. The necessity of a senate is not less indicated by the propensity of all single and numerous assemblies, to yield to the impulse of sudden and violent passions, and to be seduced by factious leaders, into intemperate and pernicious resolutions. Examples on this subject might be cited without number; and from proceedings within the United States, as well as from the history of other nations. But a position that will not be contradicted need not be proved. All that need be remarked is that a body which is to correct this infirmity ought itself be free from it, and consequently ought to be less numerous. It ought moreover to possess great firmness, and consequently ought to hold its authority by a tenure of considerable duration.

Thirdly. Another defect to be supplied by a senate lies in a want of due acquaintance with the objects and principles of legislation. It is not possible that an assembly of men

called for the most part from pursuits of a private nature, continued in appointment for a short time, and led by no permanent motive to devote the intervals of public occupation to a study of the laws, the affairs and the comprehensive interests of their country, should, if left wholly to themselves, escape a variety of important errors in the exercise of their legislative trust. It may be affirmed, on the best grounds, that no small share of the present embarrassments of America is to be charged on the blunders of our governments; and that these have proceeded from the heads rather than the hearts of most of the authors of them. What indeed are all the repealing, explaining and amending laws, which fill and disgrace our voluminous codes, but so many monuments of deficient wisdom; so many impeachments exhibited by each succeeding, against each preceding session; so many admonitions to the people of the value of those aids which may be expected from a well constituted senate?

A good government implies two things; first, fidelity to the object of government, which is the happiness of the people; secondly, a knowledge of the means by which that object can be best attained. Some governments are deficient in both these qualities: Most governments are deficient in the first. I scruple not to assert that in the American governments, too little attention has been paid to the last. The federal constitution avoids this error; and what merits particular notice, it provides for the last in a mode which increases the security for the first.

Fourthly. The mutability in the public councils, arising from a rapid succession of new members, however qualified they may be, points out in the strongest manner, the necessity of some stable institution in the government. Every new election in the states, is found to change one half of the representatives. From this change of men must proceed a change of opinions; and from a change of opinions, a change of measures. But a continual change even of good measures is inconsistent with every rule of prudence, and every prospect of success. The remark is verified in private life, and becomes more just as well as more important, in national transactions.

To trace the mischievous effects of a mutable government would fill a volume. I will hint a few only, each of which will be perceived to be a source of innumerable others.

In the first place it forfeits the respect and confidence of other nations, and all the advantages connected with national character. An individual who is observed to be inconstant to his plans, or perhaps to carry on his affairs without any plan at all, is marked at once by all prudent people as a speedy victim to his own unsteadiness and folly. His more friendly neighbours may pity him; but all will decline to connect their fortunes with his; and not a few will seize the opportunity of making their fortunes out of his. One nation is to another what one individual is to another; with this melancholy distinction perhaps, that the former with fewer of the benevolent emotions than the latter, are under fewer restraints also from taking undue advantage of the indiscretions of each other. Every nation consequently whose affairs betray a want of wisdom and stability, may calculate on every loss which can be sustained from the more systematic policy of its wiser neighbours. But the best instruction on this subject is unhappily conveyed to America by the example of her own situation. She finds that she is held in no respect by her friends; that she is the derision of her enemies; and that she is a prey to every nation which has an interest in speculating on her fluctuating councils and embarrassed affairs.

The internal effects of a mutable policy are still more calamitous. It poisons the blessings of liberty itself. It will be of little avail to the people that the laws are made by men of their own choice, if the laws be so voluminous that they cannot be read, or so incoherent that they cannot be understood; if they be repealed or revised before they are promulged, or undergo such incessant changes that no man who knows what the law is to-day can guess what it will be to-morrow. Law is defined to be a rule of action; but how can that be a rule, which is little known and less fixed?

Another effect of public instability is the unreasonable advantage it gives to the sagacious, the enterprising and the moneyed few, over the industrious and uninformed mass of the people. Every new regulation concerning commerce or revenue, or in any manner affecting the value of the different species of property, presents a new harvest to those who watch the change, and can trace its consequences; a harvest reared not by themselves but by the toils and cares of the great body of their fellow citizens. This is a state of things in which it may be said with some truth that laws are made for the *few* not for the *many*.

In another point of view great injury results from an unstable government. The want of confidence in the public councils damps every useful undertaking; the success and profit of which may depend on a continuance of existing arrangements. What prudent merchant will hazard his fortunes in any new branch of commerce, when he knows not but that his plans may be rendered unlawful before they can be executed? What farmer or manufacturer will lay himself out for the encouragement given to any particular cultivation or establishment, when he can have no assurance that his preparatory labors and advances will not render him a victim to an inconstant government? In a word no great improvement or laudable enterprise, can go forward, which requires the auspices of a steady system of national policy.

But the most deplorable effect of all is that diminution of attachment and reverence which steals into the hearts of the people, towards a political system which betrays so many marks of infirmity, and disappoints so many of their flattering hopes. No government any more than an individual will long be respected, without being truly respectable, nor be truly respectable without possessing a certain portion of order and stability.

12

JAMES MADISON, FEDERALIST, NO. 63, 422–31
1 Mar. 1788

A fifth desideratum illustrating the utility of a Senate, is the want of a due sense of national character. Without a select and stable member of the government, the esteem of foreign powers will not only be forfeited by an unenlightened and variable policy, proceeding from the causes already mentioned; but the national councils will not possess that sensibility to the opinion of the world, which is perhaps not less necessary in order to merit, than it is to obtain, its respect and confidence.

An attention to the judgment of other nations is important to every government for two reasons: The one is, that independently of the merits of any particular plan or measure, it is desireable on various accounts, that it should appear to other nations as the offspring of a wise and honorable policy: The second is, that in doubtful cases, particularly where the national councils may be warped by some strong passion, or momentary interest, the presumed or known opinion of the impartial world, may be the best guide that can be followed. What has not America lost by her want of character with foreign nations? And how many errors and follies would she not have avoided, if the justice and propriety of her measures had in every instance been previously tried by the light in which they would probably appear to the unbiassed part of mankind?

Yet however requisite a sense of national character may be, it is evident that it can never be sufficiently possessed by a numerous and changeable body. It can only be found in a number so small, that a sensible degree of the praise and blame of public measures may be the portion of each individual; or in an assembly so durably invested with public trust, that the pride and consequence of its members may be sensibly incorporated with the reputation and prosperity of the community. The half-yearly representatives of Rhode-Island, would probably have been little affected in their deliberations on the iniquitous measures of that state, by arguments drawn from the light in which such measures would be viewed by foreign nations, or even by the sister states; whilst it can scarcely be doubted, that if the concurrence of a select and stable body had been necessary, a regard to national character alone, would have prevented the calamities under which that misguided people is now labouring.

I add as a *sixth* defect, the want in some important cases of a due responsibility in the government to the people, arising from that frequency of elections, which in other cases produces this responsibility. This remark will perhaps appear not only new but paradoxical. It must nevertheless be acknowledged, when explained, to be as undeniable as it is important.

Responsibility in order to be reasonable must be limited to objects within the power of the responsible party; and in order to be effectual, must relate to operations of that power, of which a ready and proper judgment can be formed by the constituents. The objects of government may be divided into two general classes; the one depending on measures which have singly an immediate and sensible operation; the other depending on a succession of well chosen and well connected measures, which have a gradual and perhaps unobserved operation. The importance of the latter description to the collective and permanent welfare of every country needs no explanation. And yet it is evident, that an assembly elected for so short a term as to be unable to provide more than one or two links in a chain of measures, on which the general welfare may essentially depend, ought not to be answerable for the final result, any more than a steward or tenant, engaged for one year, could be justly made to answer for places or improvements, which could not be accomplished in less than half a dozen years. Nor is it possible for the people to estimate the *share* of influence which their annual assemblies may respectively have on events resulting from the mixed transactions of several years. It is sufficiently difficult at any rate to preserve a personal responsibility in the members of a *numerous* body, for such acts of the body as have an immediate, detached and palpable operation on its constituents.

The proper remedy for this defect must be an additional body in the legislative department, which, having sufficient permanency to provide for such objects as require a continued attention, and a train of measures, may be justly and effectually answerable for the attainment of those objects.

Thus far I have considered the circumstances which point out the necessity of a well constructed senate, only as they relate to the representatives of the people. To a people as little blinded by prejudice, or corrupted by flattery, as those whom I address, I shall not scruple to add, that such an institution may be sometimes necessary, as a defence to the people against their own temporary errors and delusions. As the cool and deliberate sense of the community ought in all governments, and actually will in all free governments ultimately prevail over the views of its rulers; so there are particular moments in public affairs, when the people stimulated by some irregular passion, or some illicit advantage, or misled by the artful misrepresentations of interested men, may call for measures which they themselves will afterwards be the most ready to lament and condemn. In these critical moments, how salutary will be the interference of some temperate and respectable body of citizens, in order to check the misguided career, and to suspend the blow meditated by the people against themselves, until reason, justice and truth, can regain their authority over the public mind? What bitter anguish would not the people of Athens have often escaped, if their government had contained so provident a safeguard against the tyranny of their own passions? Popular liberty might then have escaped the indelible reproach of decreeing to the same citizens, the hemlock on one day, and statues on the next.

It may be suggested that a people spread over an extensive region, cannot like the crouded inhabitants of a small district, be subject to the infection of violent passions; or to the danger of combining in the pursuit of unjust measures. I am far from denying that this is a distinction of peculiar importance. I have on the contrary endeavoured in a former paper, to shew that it is one of the principal recommendations of a confederated republic. At the same time this advantage ought not to be considered as superseding the use of auxiliary precautions. It may even be remarked that the same extended situation which will exempt the people of America from some of the dangers incident to lesser republics, will expose them to the inconveniency of remaining for a longer time, under the influence of those misrepresentations which the combined industry of interested men may succeed in distributing among them.

It adds no small weight to all these considerations, to recollect, that history informs us of no long lived republic which had not a senate. Sparta, Rome and Carthage are in fact the only states to whom that character can be applied. In each of the two first there was a senate for life. The constitution of the senate in the last, is less known. Circumstantial evidence makes it probable that it was not different in this particular from the two others. It is at least certain that it had some quality or other which rendered it an anchor against popular fluctuations; and that a smaller council drawn out of the senate was appointed not only for life; but filled up vacancies itself. These examples, though as unfit for the imitation, as they are repugnant to the genius of America, are notwithstanding, when compared with the fugitive and turbulent existence of other antient republics, very instructive proofs of the necessity of some institution that will blend stability with liberty. I am not unaware of the circumstances which distinguish the American from other popular governments, as well antient as modern; and which render extreme circumspection necessary in reasoning from the one case to the other. But after allowing due weight to this consideration, it may still be maintained that there are many points of similitude which render these examples not unworthy of our attention. Many of the defects as we have seen, which can only be supplied by a senatorial institution, are common to a numerous assembly frequently elected by the people, and to the people themselves. There are others peculiar to the former, which require the controul of such an institution. The people can never wilfully betray their own interests: But they may possibly be betrayed by the representatives of the people; and the danger will be evidently greater where the whole legislative trust is lodged in the hands of one body of men, than where the concurrence of separate and dissimilar bodies is required in every public act.

The difference most relied on between the American and other republics, consists in the principle of representation, which is the pivot on which the former move, and which is supposed to have been unknown to the latter, or at least to the antient part of them. The use which has been made of this difference, in reasonings contained in former papers, will have shewn that I am disposed neither to deny its existence nor to undervalue its importance. I feel the less restraint therefore in observing that the position concerning the ignorance of the antient government on the subject of representation is by no means precisely true in the latitude commonly given to it. Without entering into a disquisition which here would be misplaced, I will refer to a few known facts in support of what I advance.

In the most pure democracies of Greece, many of the executive functions were performed not by the people themselves, but by officers elected by the people, and *representing* the people in their *executive* capacity.

Prior to the reform of Solon, Athens was governed by nine Archons, annually *elected by the people at large*. The degree of power delegated to them seems to be left in great obscurity. Subsequent to that period, we find an assembly first of four and afterwards of six hundred members, annually *elected by the people;* and *partially* representing them in their *legislative* capacity; since they were not only associated with the people in the function of making laws; but had the exclusive right of originating legislative propositions to the people. The senate of Carthage also, whatever might be its power or the duration of its appointment, appears to have been *elective* by the suffrages of the people. Similar instances might be traced in most if not all the popular governments of antiquity.

Lastly in Sparta, we meet with the Ephori, and in Rome with the Tribunes; two bodies, small indeed in number, but annually *elected by the whole body of the people*, and considered as the *representatives* of the people, almost in their *plenipotentiary* capacity. The Cosmi of Crete were also annually *elected by the people;* and have been considered by some authors as an institution analogous to those of Sparta and Rome; with this difference only that in the election of that representative body, the right of suffrage was communicated to a part only of the people.

From these facts, to which many others might be added, it is clear that the principle of representation was neither unknown to the antients, nor wholly overlooked in their political constitutions. The true distinction between these and the American Governments lies *in the total exclusion of the people in their collective capacity* from any share in the *latter*, and not in the *total exclusion of representatives of the people*, from the administration of the *former*. The distinction however thus qualified must be admitted to leave a most advantageous superiority in favor of the United States. But to ensure to this advantage its full effect, we must be careful not to separate it from the other advantage, of an extensive territory. For it cannot be believed that any form of representative government, could have succeeded within the narrow limits occupied by the democracies of Greece.

In answer to all these arguments, suggested by reason, illustrated by examples, and enforced by our own experience, the jealous adversary of the constitution will probably content himself with repeating, that a senate appointed not immediately by the people, and for the term of six years, must gradually acquire a dangerous preeminence in the government, and finally transform it into a tyrannical aristocracy.

To this general answer the general reply ought to be sufficient; that liberty may be endangered by the abuses of liberty, as well as by the abuses of power; that there are numerous instances of the former as well as of the latter;

and that the former rather than the latter is apparently most to be apprehended by the United States. But a more particular reply may be given.

Before such a revolution can be effected, the senate, it is to be observed, must in the first place corrupt itself; must next corrupt the state legislatures, must then corrupt the house of representatives, and must finally corrupt the people at large. It is evident that the senate must be first corrupted, before it can attempt an establishment of tyranny. Without corrupting the state legislatures, it cannot prosecute the attempt, because the periodical change of members would otherwise regenerate the whole body. Without exerting the means of corruption with equal success on the house of representatives, the opposition of that co-equal branch of the government would inevitably defeat the attempt; and without corrupting the people themselves, a succession of new representatives would speedily restore all things to their pristine order. Is there any man who can seriously persuade himself, that the proposed senate can, by any possible means within the compass of human address, arrive at the object of a lawless ambition, through all these obstructions?

If reason condemns the suspicion, the same sentence is pronounced by experience. The constitution of Maryland furnishes the most apposite example. The senate of that state is elected, as the federal senate will be, indirectly by the people; and for a term less by one year only, than the federal senate. It is distinguished also by the remarkable prerogative of filling up its own vacancies within the term of its appointment: and at the same time, is not under the controul of any such rotation, as is provided for the federal senate. There are some other lesser distinctions, which would expose the former to colorable objections that do not lie against the latter. If the federal senate therefore really contained the danger which has been so loudly proclaimed, some symptoms at least of a like danger ought by this time to have been betrayed by the senate of Maryland; but no such symptoms have appeared. On the contrary the jealousies at first entertained by men of the same description with those who view with terror the correspondent part of the federal constitution, have been gradually extinguished by the progress of the experiment; and the Maryland constitution is daily deriving from the salutary operations of this part of it, a reputation in which it will probably not be rivalled by that of any state in the union.

But if any thing could silence the jealousies on this subject, it ought to be the British example. The senate there, instead of being elected for a term of six years, and of being unconfined to particular families or fortunes, is an hereditary assembly of opulent nobles. The house of representatives, instead of being elected for two years and by the whole body of the people, is elected for seven years; and in very great proportion, by a very small proportion of the people. Here unquestionably ought to be seen in full display, the aristocratic usurpations and tyranny, which are at some future period to be exemplified in the United States. Unfortunately however for the antifederal argument the British history informs us, that this hereditary assembly has not even been able to defend itself against the continual encroachments of the house of representatives; and that it no sooner lost the support of the monarch, than it was actually crushed by the weight of the popular branch.

As far as antiquity can instruct us on this subject, its examples support the reasoning which we have employed. In Sparta the Ephori, the annual representatives of the people, were found an overmatch for the senate for life, continually gained on its authority, and finally drew all power into their own hands. The tribunes of Rome, who were the representatives of the people, prevailed, it is well known, in almost every contest with the senate for life, and in the end gained the most complete triumph over it. This fact is the more remarkable, as unanimity was required in every act of the tribunes, even after their number was augmented to ten. It proves the irresistable force possessed by that branch of a free government, which has the people on its side. To these examples might be added that of Carthage, whose senate, according to the testimony of Polybius, instead of drawing all power into its vortex, had at the commencement of the second punic war, lost almost the whole of its original portion.

Besides the conclusive evidence resulting from this assemblage of facts, that the federal senate will never be able to transform itself, by gradual usurpations, into an independent and aristocratic body; we are warranted in believing that if such a revolution should ever happen from causes which the foresight of man cannot guard against, the house of representatives with the people on their side will at all times be able to bring back the constitution to its primitive form and principles. Against the force of the immediate representatives of the people, nothing will be able to maintain even the constitutional authority of the senate, but such a display of enlightened policy, and attachment to the public good, as will divide with that branch of the legislature, the affections and support of the entire body of the people themselves.

13

BRUTUS, NO. 16
10 Apr. 1788
Storing 2.9.200–201

The term for which the senate are to be chosen, is in my judgment too long, and no provision being made for a rotation will, I conceive, be of dangerous consequence.

It is difficult to fix the precise period for which the senate should be chosen. It is a matter of opinion, and our sentiments on the matter must be formed, by attending to certain principles. Some of the duties which are to be performed by the senate, seem evidently to point out the propriety of their term of service being extended beyond the period of that of the assembly. Besides as they are designed to represent the aristocracy of the country, it seems fit they should possess more stability, and so continue a longer period than that branch who represent the democ-

racy. The business of making treaties and some other which it will be proper to commit to the senate, requires that they should have experience, and therefore that they should remain some time in office to acquire it.—But still it is of equal importance that they should not be so long in office as to be likely to forget the hand that formed them, or be insensible of their interests. Men long in office are very apt to feel themselves independent [and] to form and pursue interests separate from those who appointed them. And this is more likely to be the case with the senate, as they will for the most part of the time be absent from the state they represent, and associate with such company as will possess very little of the feelings of the middling class of people. For it is to be remembered that there is to be a *federal city,* and the inhabitants of it will be the great and the mighty of the earth. For these reasons I would shorten the term of their service to four years. Six years is a long period for a man to be absent from his home, it would have a tendency to wean him from his constituents.

A rotation in the senate, would also in my opinion be of great use. It is now probable that senators once chosen for a state will, as the system now stands, continue in office for life. The office will be honorable if not lucrative. The persons who occupy it will probably wish to continue in it, and therefore use all their influence and that of their friends to continue in office.—Their friends will be numerous and powerful, for they will have it in their power to confer great favors; besides it will before long be considered as disgraceful not to be re-elected. It will therefore be considered as a matter of delicacy to the character of the senator not to return him again.—Every body acquainted with public affairs knows how difficult it is to remove from office a person who is [has?] long been in it. It is seldom done except in cases of gross misconduct. It is rare that want of competent ability procures it. To prevent this inconvenience I conceive it would be wise to determine, that a senator should not be eligible after he had served for the period assigned by the constitution for a certain number of years; perhaps three would be sufficient. A farther benefit would be derived from such an arrangement; it would give opportunity to bring forward a greater number of men to serve their country, and would return those, who had served, to their state, and afford them the advantage of becoming better acquainted with the condition and politics of their constituents. It farther appears to me proper, that the legislatures should retain the right which they now hold under the confederation, of recalling their members. It seems an evident dictate of reason, that when a person authorises another to do a piece of business for him, he should retain the power to displace him, when he does not conduct according to his pleasure. This power in the state legislatures, under confederation, has not been exercised to the injury of the government, nor do I see any danger of its being so exercised under the new system. It may operate much to the public benefit.

14

DEBATE IN NEW YORK RATIFYING CONVENTION
24–25 June 1788
Elliot 2:286–97, 301–9, 316–22

[*24 June*]

G. LIVINGSTON: First, they would possess legislative powers coëxtensive with those of the House of Representatives except with respect to originating revenue laws; which, however, they would have power to reject or amend, as in the case of other bills. Secondly, they would have an importance, even exceeding that of the representative house, as they would be composed of a smaller number, and possess more firmness and system. Thirdly, their consequence and dignity would still further transcend those of the other branch, from their longer continuance in office. These powers, Mr. Livingston contended, rendered the Senate a dangerous body.

He went on, in the second place, to enumerate and animadvert on the powers with which they were clothed in their judicial capacity, and in their capacity of council to the President, and in the forming of treaties. In the last place, as if too much power could not be given to this body, they were made, he said, a council of appointment, by whom ambassadors and other officers of state were to be appointed. These are the powers, continued he, which are vested in this small body of twenty-six men; in some cases, to be exercised by a bare quorum, which is fourteen; a majority of which number, again, is eight. What are the checks provided to balance this great mass of power? Our present Congress cannot serve longer than three years in six: they are at any time subject to recall. These and other checks were considered as necessary at a period which I choose to honor with the name of *virtuous*. Sir, I venerate the spirit with which every thing was done at the trying time in which the Confederation was formed. America had then a sufficiency of this virtue to resolve to resist perhaps the first nation in the universe, even unto bloodshed. What was her aim? Equal liberty and safety. What ideas had she of this equal liberty? Read them in her Articles of Confederation. True it is, sir, there are some powers wanted to make this glorious compact complete. But, sir, let us be cautious that we do not err more on the other hand, by giving power too profusely, when, perhaps, it will be too late to recall it. Consider, sir, the great influence which this body, armed at all points, will have. What will be the effect of this? Probably a security of their reëlection, as long as they please. Indeed, in my view, it will amount nearly to an appointment for life. What will be their situation in a federal town? Hallowed ground! Nothing so unclean as state laws to enter there, surrounded, as they will be, by an impenetrable wall of adamant and gold, the wealth of the whole country flowing into it. [Here a member, who did not fully understand, called out to know what WALL the gentleman meant; on which he turned, and replied,

"A wall of gold—of adamant, which will flow in from all parts of the continent." At which flowing metaphor, a great laugh in the house.] The gentleman continued: Their attention to their various business will probably require their constant attendance. In this Eden will they reside with their families, distant from the observation of the people. In such a situation, men are apt to forget their dependence, lose their sympathy, and contract selfish habits. Factions are apt to be formed, if the body becomes permanent. The senators will associate only with men of their own class, and thus become strangers to the condition of the common people. They should not only return, and be obliged to live with the people, but return to their former rank of citizenship, both to revive their sense of dependence, and to gain a knowledge of the country. This will afford opportunity to bring forward the genius and information of the states, and will be a stimulus to acquire political abilities. It will be the means of diffusing a more general knowledge of the measures and spirit of the administration. These things will confirm the people's confidence in government. When they see those who have been high in office residing among them as private citizens, they will feel more forcibly that the government is of their own choice. The members of this branch having the idea impressed on their minds, that they are soon to return to the level whence the suffrages of the people raised them,—this good effect will follow: they will consider their interests as the same with those of their constituents, and that they legislate for themselves as well as others. They will not conceive themselves made to receive, enjoy, and rule, nor the people solely to earn, pay, and submit.

Mr. Chairman, I have endeavored, with as much perspicuity and candor as I am master of, shortly to state my objections to this clause. I would wish the committee to believe that they are not raised for the sake of opposition, but that I am very sincere in my sentiments in this important investigation. The Senate, as they are now constituted, have little or no check on them. Indeed, sir, too much is put into their hands. When we come to that part of the system which points out their powers, it will be the proper time to consider this subject more particularly.

I think, sir, we must relinquish the idea of safety under this government, if the time for services is not further limited, and the power of recall given to the state legislatures. I am strengthened in my opinion by an observation made yesterday, by an honorable member from New York, to this effect—"that there should be no fear of corruption of the members in the House of Representatives; especially as they are, in two years, to return to the body of the people." I therefore move that the committee adopt the following resolution, as an amendment to this clause:—

> "*Resolved*, That no person shall be eligible as a senator for more than six years in any term of twelve years, and that it shall be in the power of the legislatures of the several states to recall their senators, or either of them, and to elect others in their stead, to serve for the remainder of the time for which such senator or senators, so recalled, were appointed."

Hon. Mr. LANSING. I beg the indulgence of the committee, while I offer some reasons in support of the motion just made; in doing which, I shall confine myself to the point, and shall hear with attention, and examine with candor, the objections which may be opposed to it.

The representation of the United States, by the proposed system, is vested in two bodies. On the subject of one of these, we have debated several days, and now come to the organization and powers of the other. I believe it was undoubtedly the intention of the framers of this Constitution to make the lower house the proper, peculiar representative of the interests of the people; the Senate, of the sovereignty of the states.

Some very important powers are given to the latter, to be executed without the concurrence of the representative house. Now, if it was the design of the plan to make the Senate a kind of bulwark to the independence of the states, and a check to the encroachments of the general government, certainly the members of this body ought to be peculiarly under the control, and in strict subordination to the state who delegated them. In proportion to their want of dependence, they will lose their respect for the power from whom they receive their existence, and, consequently, will disregard the great object for which they are instituted. The idea of rotation has been taken from the articles of the old Confederation. It has thus far, in my opinion, operated with great advantage. The power of recall, too, has been an excellent check, though it has, in fact, never been exercised. The thing is of so delicate a nature, that few men will step forward to move a recall, unless there is some strong ground for it.

Sir, I am informed by gentlemen who have been conversant in public affairs, and who have had seats in Congress, that there have been, at different times, violent parties in that body—an evil that a change of members has contributed, more than any other thing, to remedy. If, therefore, the power of recall should be never exercised, if it should have no other force than that of a check to the designs of the bad, and to destroy party spirit, certainly no harm, but much good, may result from adopting the amendment. If my information be true, there have been parties in Congress which would have continued to this day, if the members had not been removed. No inconvenience can follow from placing the powers of the Senate on such a foundation as to make them feel their dependence. It is only a check calculated to make them more attentive to the objects for which they were appointed. Sir, I would ask, Is there no danger that the members of the Senate will sacrifice the interest of their state to their own private views? Every man in the United States ought to look with anxious concern to that body. Their number is so exceedingly small, that they may easily feel their interests distinct from those of the community. This smallness of number also renders them subject to a variety of accidents, that may be of the highest disadvantage. If one of the members is sick, or if one or both are prevented occasionally from attending, who are to take care of the interests of their state?

Sir, we have frequently observed that deputies have been appointed for certain purposes, who have not punctually attended to them, when it was necessary. Their private concerns may often require their presence at home. In what manner is this evil to be corrected? The amendment provides a remedy. It is the only thing which can give the states a control over the Senate. It will be said, there is a power in Congress to compel the attendance of absent members; but will the members from the other states be solicitous to compel such attendance, except to answer some particular view, or promote some interest of their own? If it be the object of the senators to protect the sovereignty of their several states, and if, at any time, it be the design of the other states to make encroachments on the sovereignty of any one state, will it be for their interest to compel the members from this state to attend, in order to oppose and check them? This would be strange policy indeed.

A number of other reasons might be adduced on this point; but those which have been advanced are sufficient, I imagine, to convince the committee that such a provision is necessary and proper. If it be not adopted, the interests of any one state may be easily sacrificed to the ambition of the others, or to the private advantage of individuals.

Mr. R. R. LIVINGSTON. The amendment appears to have in view two objects—that a rotation shall be established in the Senate, and that its members shall be subject to recall by the state legislatures. It is not contended that six years are too long a time for the senators to remain in office. Indeed, this cannot be objected to, when the purposes for which this body is instituted are considered. They are to form treaties with foreign nations. This requires a comprehensive knowledge of foreign politics, and an extensive acquaintance with characters, whom, in this capacity, they have to negotiate with, together with such an intimate conception of our best interests, relative to foreign powers, as can only be derived from much experience in this business. What singular policy, to cut off the hand which has just qualified itself for action! But, says the gentleman, as they are the representatives of the states, those states have a control. Will this principle hold good? The members of the lower house are the representatives of the people. Have the people any power to recall them? What would be the tendency of the power contended for? Clearly this: The state legislatures, being frequently subject to factious and irregular passions, may be unjustly disaffected and discontented with their delegates; and a senator may be appointed one day and recalled the next. This would be a source of endless confusion. The Senate are indeed designed to represent the state governments; but they are also the representatives of the United States, and are not to consult the interest of any one state alone, but that of the Union. This could never be done, if there was a power of recall; for sometimes it happens that small sacrifices are absolutely indispensable for the good and safety of the confederacy; but, if a senator should presume to consent to these sacrifices, he would be immediately recalled. This reasoning turns on the idea that a state, not being able to comprehend the interest of the whole, would, in all instances, adhere to her own, even to the hazard of the Union.

I should disapprove of this amendment, because it would open so wide a door for faction and intrigue, and afford such scope for the arts of an evil ambition. A man might go to the Senate with an incorruptible integrity, and the strongest attachment to the interest of his state. But if he deviated, in the least degree, from the line which a prevailing *party* in a popular assembly had marked for him, he would be immediately recalled. Under these circumstances, how easy would it be for an ambitious, factious demagogue to misrepresent him, to distort the features of his character, and give a false color to his conduct! How easy for such a man to impose upon the public, and influence them to recall and disgrace their faithful delegate! The general government may find it necessary to do many things which some states might never be willing to consent to. Suppose Congress should enter into a war to protect the fisheries, or any of the northern interests; the Southern States, loaded with their share of the burden which it would be necessary to impose, would condemn their representatives in the Senate for acquiescing in such a measure. There are a thousand things which an honest man might be obliged to do, from a conviction that it would be for the general good, which would give great dissatisfaction to his constituents.

Sir, all the arguments drawn from an imaginary prospect of corruption have little weight with me. From what source is this corruption to be derived? One gentleman tells you that this dreadful Senate is to be surrounded by a wall of adamant—of gold, and that this wall is to be a liquid one, and to flow in from all quarters. Such arguments as these seem rather the dreamings of a distempered fancy, than the cool, rational deductions of a deliberate mind. Whence is this corruption to be derived? Are the people to corrupt the senators with their own gold? Is *bribery* to enter the *federal city*, with the amazing influx of adamant the gentleman so pathetically contemplates? Are not Congress to publish, from time to time, an account of their receipts and expenditures? Can there be any appropriation of money by the Senate, without the concurrence of the Assembly? And can we suppose that a majority of both houses can be corrupted? At this rate we must suppose a miracle indeed.

But to return: The people are the best judges who ought to represent them. To dictate and control them, to tell them whom they shall not elect, is to abridge their natural rights. This rotation is an absurd species of ostracism—a mode of proscribing eminent merit, and banishing from stations of trust those who have filled them with the greatest faithfulness. Besides, it takes away the strongest stimulus to public virtue—the hope of honors and rewards. The acquisition of abilities is hardly worth the trouble, unless one is to enjoy the satisfaction of employing them for the good of one's country. We all know that experience is indispensably necessary to good government. Shall we, then, drive experience into obscurity? I repeat that this is an absolute abridgment of the people's rights.

As to the Senate's rendering themselves perpetual, or establishing such a power as to prevent their being removed, it appears to me chimerical. Can they make interest with their legislatures, who are themselves varying every year, sufficient for such a purpose? Can we suppose two senators will be able to corrupt the vhole legislature of this state? The idea, I say, is chimerical. The thing is impossible.

Hon. Mr. LANSING. The objects of this amendment are, first, to place the senators in such a situation of dependence on their several state legislatures, as will induce them to pay a constant regard to the good of their constituents; secondly, to oblige them to return, at certain periods, to their fellow-citizens, that, by mingling with the people, they may recover that knowledge of their interests, and revive that sympathy with their feelings, which power and an exalted station are too apt to efface from the minds of rulers.

It has been urged that the senators should be acquainted with the interests of the states in relation to each other, and to foreign powers, and that they should remain in office, in order to acquire extensive political information. If these were the only objects, the argument would extend to the rendering their dignity perpetual—an idea which probably none of the gentlemen will consent to; but, if one third of the senators go out every two years, cannot those who succeed them acquire information from the remaining members, with respect to the relative interests of the states? It is to be presumed that the Senate will be composed of the best-informed men, and that no such men will be incapable of comprehending the interests of the states either singly or collectively. If it be the design of representation that the sense and spirit of the people's interests and feelings should be carried into the government, it is obvious that this design can be accomplished in no way so perfectly as by obliging our rulers, at certain periods, to relinquish their offices and rank. The people cannot be represented by men who are perpetually separated from them.

It is asked, Why not place the senators in the same situation as the representatives? or, Why not give the people a power of recall? Because, sir, this is impracticable, and contrary to the first principles of representative government. There is no regular way of collecting the people's sentiments. But a power in the state legislatures to recall their senators, is simple and easy, and will be attended with the highest advantages.

An honorable gentleman, who has spoken largely on the preceding question, has acknowledged that a variety of views, and great diversity of sentiment, prevailed in the federal Convention; that particularly there was a difference of interest between the navigating and non-navigating states. The same opposition of interests will probably ever remain; and the members of Congress will retain the same disposition to regard as their principal object the genuine good of their respective states. If they do not, if they presume to sacrifice the fundamental advantages of their state, they betray the confidence reposed in them, and violate their duty. I wish gentlemen would uniformly adhere to the distinction between the grand design of the House of Representatives and that of the Senate. Does not one represent the individuals, the people of a state, and the other its collective sovereignty? This distinction is properly noticed, when it is convenient and useful to the gentlemen's argument; but when it stands in their way, it is easily passed by and disregarded.

Sir, it is true there have been no instances of the success of corruption under the old Confederation; and may not this be attributed to the power of recall, which has existed from its first formation? It has operated effectually, though silently. It has never been exercised, because no great occasion has offered. The power has by no means proved a discouragement to individuals, in serving their country. A seat in Congress has always been considered a distinguished honor, and a favorite object of ambition: I believe no public station has been sought with more avidity. If this power has existed for so many years, and through so many scenes of difficulty and danger, without being exerted, may it not be rationally presumed that it never will be put in execution, unless the indispensable interest of a state shall require it? I am perfectly convinced that, in many emergencies, mutual concessions are necessary and proper; and that, in some instances, the smaller interests of the states should be sacrificed to great national objects. But when a delegate makes such sacrifices as tend to political destruction, or to reduce sovereignty to subordination, his state ought to have the power of defeating his design, and reverting to the people. It is observed, that the appropriation of money is not in the power of the Senate alone; but, sir, the exercise of certain powers, which constitutionally and necessarily involve the disposal of money, belongs to the Senate: they have, therefore, a right of disposing of the property of the United States. If the Senate declare war, the lower house must furnish the supplies.

It is further objected to this amendment, that it will restrain the people from choosing those who are most deserving of their suffrages, and will thus be an abridgment of their rights. I cannot suppose this last inference naturally follows. The rights of the people will be best supported by checking, at a certain point, the current of popular favor, and preventing the establishment of an influence which may leave to elections little more than the form of freedom. The Constitution of this state says, that no man shall hold the office of sheriff or coroner beyond a certain period. Does any one imagine that the rights of the people are infringed by this provision? The gentlemen, in their reasoning on the subject of corruption, seem to set aside experience, and to consider the Americans as exempt from the common vices and frailties of human nature. It is unnecessary to particularize the numerous ways in which public bodies are accessible to corruption. The poison always finds a channel, and never wants an object. Scruples would be impertinent, arguments would be in vain, checks would be useless, if we were certain our rulers would be good men; but for the virtuous government is not instituted: its object is to restrain and punish vice; and all free constitutions are formed with two views—to deter the governed from crime, and the governors from tyranny.

The CHANCELLOR [Robert R. Livingston] rose only to correct an error which had appeared in the course of the debate. It had been intimated that the Senate had a right to declare war. This was a mistake. The power could not be exercised except by the whole legislature; nor, indeed, had the Senate a right alone to appoint a single federal officer. The President, with the advice and consent of the Senate, made these appointments. He believed that the power of recall would have a tendency to bind the senators too strongly to the interests of their respective states; and for that reason he objected to it. It will destroy, said he, that spirit of independence and free deliberation which ought to influence the senator. Whenever the interests of a state clash with those of the Union, it will oblige him to sacrifice the great objects of his appointment to local attachments. He will be subjected to all the caprices, the parties, the narrow views, and illiberal politics, of the state governments, and become a slave to the ambitions and factions at home.

These observations, continued the chancellor, are obvious inferences from a principle which has been already explained—that the state legislatures will be ever more or less incapable of comprehending the interests of the Union. They cannot perceive the propriety, or feel the necessity, of certain great expedients in politics, which may seem, in their immediate operation, to injure the private interests of the members.

Hon. R. MORRIS. I am happy, Mr. Chairman, to perceive that it is a principle on all sides conceded, and adopted by this committee, that an energetic federal government is essential to the preservation of our Union; and that a constitution for these states ought to unite firmness and vigor in the national operations, with the full security of our rights and liberties. It is our business, then, to examine whether the proposed Constitution be agreeable to this description. I am pretty well convinced that, on this examination, the system will be found capable of accomplishing these purposes; but if the event of our deliberations should be different, I hope we shall not adopt any amendments which will defeat their own design. Let us be cautious, that, in our eager pursuit of the great object, we do not run into those errors which disfigure the old Confederation. We may render useless all our provisions for security, by urging and straining them too far: we may apply checks which may have a direct tendency to impede the most salutary operations of the government, and ultimately deprive it of the strength and vigor necessary to preserve our national freedom. I fear the proposed amendment, were it adopted, would have such an effect. My reason has been anticipated by my honorable colleague. It is, that it would create a slavish subjection to the contracted views and prevailing factions of the state governments, or, in its exercise, would deprive the national council of its members in many difficult emergencies, and thus throw the Union into disorder, take away the means of defence, and expose it an easy prey to its enemies.

The gentlemen, in all their zeal for liberty, do not seem to see the danger to be apprehended from foreign power; they consider that all the danger is derived from a fancied tyrannical propensity in their rulers; and against this they are content to provide. I am sorry their views are so confined and partial. An extensive and liberal survey of the subject should teach us that vigor in the government is as necessary to the protection of freedom, as the warmest attachment to liberty in the governors. Sir, if the proposed amendment had been originally incorporated in the Constitution, I should consider it as a capital objection: I believe it would have ultimately defeated the very design of our Union.

. . . . .

Hon. Mr. HAMILTON. In the commencement of a revolution which received its birth from the usurpations of tyranny, nothing was more natural than that the public mind should be influenced by an extreme spirit of jealousy. To resist these encroachments, and to nourish this spirit, was the great object of all our public and private institutions. The zeal for liberty became predominant and excessive. In forming our Confederation, this passion alone seemed to actuate us, and we appear to have had no other view than to secure ourselves from despotism. The object certainly was a valuable one, and deserved our utmost attention; but, sir, there is another object, equally important, and which our enthusiasm rendered us little capable of regarding: I mean a principle of *strength* and *stability* in the organization of our government, and *vigor* in its operations. This purpose could never be accomplished but by the establishment of some select body, formed particularly upon this principle. There are few positions more demonstrable than that there should be, in every republic, some permanent body to correct the prejudices, check the intemperate passions, and regulate the fluctuations, of a popular assembly. It is evident that a body instituted for these purposes must be so formed as to exclude, as much as possible, from its own character, those infirmities, and that mutability, which it is designed to remedy. It is, therefore, necessary that it should be small, that it should hold its authority during a considerable period, and that it should have such an independence in the exercise of its powers, as will divest it, as much as possible, of local prejudices. It should be so formed as to be the centre of political knowledge, to pursue always a steady line of conduct, and to reduce every irregular propensity to system. Without this establishment, we may make experiments without end, but shall never have an efficient government.

It is an unquestionable truth, that the body of the people, in every country, desire sincerely its prosperity; but it is equally unquestionable, that they do not possess the discernment and stability necessary for systematic government. To deny that they are frequently led into the grossest errors by misinformation and passion, would be a flattery which their own good sense must despise. That branch of administration, especially, which involves our political relation with foreign states, a community will ever be incompetent to. These truths are not often held up in public assemblies; but they cannot be unknown to any who hear me.

From these principles it follows that there ought to be two distinct bodies in our government—one which shall be immediately constituted by and peculiarly represent the people, and possess all the popular features; another formed upon the principle and for the purposes before explained. Such considerations as these induced the Convention who formed your state Constitution to institute a Senate upon the present plan. The history of ancient and modern republics had taught them that many of the evils which these republics suffered arose from the want of a certain balance and mutual control indispensable to a wise administration; they were convinced that popular assemblies were frequently misguided by ignorance, by sudden impulses, and the intrigues of ambitious men, and that some firm barrier against these operations was necessary: they, therefore, instituted your Senate, and the benefits we have experienced have fully justified their conceptions.

Now, sir, what is the tendency of the proposed amendment? To take away the stability of government by depriving the Senate of its permanency; to make this body subject to the same weakness and prejudices which are incident to popular assemblies, and which it was instituted to correct; and, by thus assimilating the complexion of the two branches, destroy the balance between them. The amendment will render the senator a slave to all the capricious humors among the people. It will probably be here suggested, that the legislatures, not the people, are to have the power to recall. Without attempting to prove that the legislatures must be, in a great degree, the image of the multitude, in respect to federal affairs, and that the same prejudices and factions will prevail, I insist that, in whatever body the power of recall is vested, the senator will perpetually feel himself in such a state of vassalage and dependence, that he never can possess that firmness which is necessary to the discharge of his great duty to the Union.

Gentlemen, in their reasoning, have placed the interests of the several states, and those of the United States, in contrast; this is not a fair view of the subject; they must necessarily be involved in each other. What we apprehend is, that some sinister prejudice, or some prevailing passion, may assume the form of a genuine interest. The influence of these is as powerful as the most permanent conviction of the public good; and against this influence we ought to provide. The local interests of a state ought, in every case, to give way to the interests of the Union; for when a sacrifice of one or the other is necessary, the former becomes only an apparent partial interest, and should yield, on the principle that the small good ought never to oppose the great one. When you assemble from your several counties in the legislature, were every member to be guided only by the apparent interest of his country, government would be impracticable. There must be a perpetual accommodation and sacrifice of local advantage to general expediency; but the spirit of a mere popular assembly would rarely be actuated by this important principle. It is therefore absolutely necessary that the Senate should be so formed as to be unbiased by false conceptions of the real interests or undue attachment to the apparent good of their several states.

Gentlemen indulge too many unreasonable apprehensions of danger to the state governments; they seem to suppose that, the moment you put men into a national council, they become corrupt and tyrannical, and lose all affection for their fellow-citizens. But can we imagine that the senators will ever be so insensible of their own advantage as to sacrifice the genuine interest of their constituents? The state governments are essentially necessary to the form and spirit of the general system. As long, therefore, as Congress have a full conviction of this necessity, they must, even upon principles purely national, have as firm an attachment to the one as to the other. This conviction can never leave them, unless they become madmen. While the Constitution continues to be read, and its principles known, the states must, by every rational man, be considered as essential, component parts of the Union; and therefore the idea of sacrificing the former to the latter is wholly inadmissible.

The objectors do not advert to the natural strength and resources of state governments, which will ever give them an important superiority over the general government. If we compare the nature of their different powers, or the means of popular influence which each possesses, we shall find the advantage entirely on the side of the states. This consideration, important as it is, seems to have been little attended to. The aggregate number of representatives throughout the states may be two thousand. The personal influence will, therefore, be proportionably more extensive than that of one or two hundred men in Congress. The state establishments of civil and military officers of every description, infinitely surpassing in number any possible correspondent establishments in the general government, will create such an extent and complication of attachments, as will ever secure the predilection and support of the people. Whenever, therefore, Congress shall meditate any infringement of the state constitutions, the great body of the people will naturally take part with their domestic representatives. Can the general government withstand such a united opposition? Will the people suffer themselves to be stripped of their privileges? Will they suffer their legislatures to be reduced to a shadow and name? The idea is shocking to common sense.

From the circumstances already explained, and many others which might be mentioned, results a complicated, irresistible check, which must ever support the existence and importance of the state governments. The danger, if any exists, flows from an opposite source. The probable evil is, that the general government will be too dependent on the state legislatures, too much governed by their prejudices, and too obsequious to their humors; that the states, with every power in their hands, will make encroachments on the national authority, till the Union is weakened and dissolved.

Every member must have been struck with an observation of a gentleman from Albany. Do what you will, says he, local prejudices and opinions will go into the government. What! shall we then form a constitution to cherish and strengthen these prejudices? Shall we confirm the distemper, instead of remedying it? It is undeniable that there must be a control somewhere. Either the general interest is to control the particular interests, or the contrary. If the former, then certainly the government ought to be so framed, as to render the power of control efficient to all intents and purposes; if the latter, a striking absurdity follows: the controlling powers must be as numerous as the varying interests, and the operations of government must therefore cease; for the moment you accommodate these different interests, which is the only way to set the government in motion, you establish a general controlling power. Thus, whatever constitutional provisions are made

to the contrary, every government will be at last driven to the necessity of subjecting the partial to the universal interest. The gentlemen ought always, in their reasoning, to distinguish between the real, genuine good of a state, and the opinions and prejudices which may prevail respecting it. The latter may be opposed to the general good, and consequently ought to be sacrificed; the former is so involved in it, that it never can be sacrificed. Sir, the main design of the Convention, in forming the Senate, was to prevent fluctuations and cabals. With this view, they made that body small, and to exist for a considerable period. Have they executed this design too far? The senators are to serve six years. This is only two years longer than the senators of this state hold their places. One third of the members are to go out every two years; and in six, the whole body will be changed. Prior to the revolution, the representatives in the several colonies were elected for different periods—for three years, for seven years, &c. Were those bodies ever considered as incapable of representing the people, or as too independent of them? There is one circumstance which will have a tendency to increase the dependence of the senators on the states, in proportion to the duration of their appointments. As the state legislatures are in continual fluctuation, the senator will have more attachments to form, and consequently a greater difficulty of maintaining his place, than one of shorter duration. He will, therefore, be more cautious and industrious to suit his conduct to the wishes of his constituents.

Sir, when you take a view of all the circumstances which have been recited, you will certainly see that the senators will constantly look up to the state governments with an eye of dependence and affection. If they are ambitious to continue in office, they will make every prudent arrangement for this purpose, and, whatever may be their private sentiments or politics, they will be convinced that the surest means of obtaining a reëlection will be a uniform attachment to the interests of their several states.

The gentlemen, to support their amendment, have observed that the power to recall, under the old government, has never been exercised. There is no reasoning in this. The experience of a few years, under peculiar circumstances, can afford no probable security that it never will be carried into execution with unhappy effects. A seat in Congress has been less an object of ambition; and the arts of intrigue, consequently, have been less practised. Indeed, it has been difficult to find men who were willing to suffer the mortifications to which so feeble a government, and so dependent a station, exposed them.

Sir, if you consider but a moment the purposes for which the *Senate* was instituted, and the nature of the business which they are to transact, you will see the necessity of giving them duration. They, together with the President, are to manage all our concerns with foreign nations; they must understand all their interests, and their political systems. This knowledge is not soon acquired; but a very small part is gained in the closet. Is it desirable, then, that new and unqualified members should be continually thrown into that body? When public bodies are engaged in the exercise of general powers, you cannot judge of the propriety of their conduct, but from the result of their systems. They may be forming plans which required time and diligence to bring to maturity. It is necessary, therefore, that they should have a considerable and fixed duration, that they may make their calculations accordingly. If they are to be perpetually fluctuating, they can never have that responsibility which is so important in republican governments. In bodies subject to frequent changes, great political plans must be conducted by members in succession. A single assembly can have but a partial agency in them, and, consequently, cannot properly be answerable for the final event. Considering the Senate, therefore, with a view to responsibility, duration is a very interesting and essential quality. There is another view in which duration in the Senate appears necessary. A government changeable in its policy must soon lose its sense of national character, and forfeit the respect of foreigners. Senators will not be solicitous for the reputation of public measures, in which they had but a temporary concern, and will feel lightly the burden of public disapprobation, in proportion to the number of those who partake of the censure. Our political rivals will ever consider our mutable counsels as evidence of deficient wisdom, and will be little apprehensive of our arriving at any exalted station in the scale of power.

Such are the internal and external disadvantages which would result from the principle contended for. Were it admitted, I am fully persuaded, sir, that prejudices would govern the public deliberations, and passions rage in the counsels of the Union. If it were necessary, I could illustrate my subject by historical facts. I could travel through an extensive field of detail, and demonstrate that wherever the fatal principle, of the head suffering the control of the members, has operated, it has proved a fruitful source of commotions and disorder.

This, sir, is the first fair opportunity that has been offered of deliberately correcting the errors in government. Instability has been a prominent and very defective feature in most republican systems. It is the first to be seen, and the last to be lamented, by a philosophical inquirer. It has operated most banefully in our infant republics. It is necessary that we apply an immediate remedy, and eradicate the poisonous principle from our government. If this be not done, sir, we shall feel, and posterity will be convulsed by, a painful malady.

The Hon. Mr. LANSING said, he had very closely attended to the arguments which had been advanced on the subject; but, however strongly and ingenuously they had been urged, he confessed they had not had a tendency to change his sentiments. The principles which the gentleman had laid down, with respect to a division of the legislature, and the necessity of a balance, he admitted. If he had been inclined to dispute the expediency of two distinct branches in the government, he should not now be taking up the time of the committee in a contest respecting the form and powers of these two branches. He granted, therefore, that there ought to be two houses, to afford a mutual check. The gentleman seemed disposed to render the federal government entirely independent, and to prevent the possibility of its ever being influenced by the interests of the several states; and yet he had acknowledged

them to be necessary, fundamental parts of the system. Where, then, was the check? The states, having no constitutional control, would soon be found unnecessary and useless, and would be gradually extinguished. When this took place, the people would lose their liberties, and be reduced from the condition of citizens to that of subjects. It had been remarked, that there were more than two thousand state representatives throughout the Union, and that the number of civil and military officers on the state establishments would far exceed those of the United States; and these circumstances, it has been said, would create such an attachment and dependence on the state governments, as would give them a superiority over the general government. But, said he, were the states arrayed in all the powers of sovereignty? Could they maintain armies? Had they the unlimited power of taxation? There was no comparison, he said, between the powers of the two governments. The circumstances the gentleman had enumerated, which seemed to be in favor of the states, only proved that the people would be under some advantages to discern the encroachments of *Congress,* and to take the alarm; but what would this signify? The gentleman did not mean that his principles should encourage rebellion: what other resource had they? None, but to wait patiently till the long terms of their senators were expired, and then elect other men. All the boasted advantages enjoyed by the states were finally reduced to this. The gentleman had spoken of an enmity which would subsist between the general and state governments: what, then, would be the situation of both? His wish, he said, was to prevent any enmity, by giving the states a constitutional and peaceable mode of checking maladministration, by recalling their senators, and not driving them into hostilities, in order to obtain redress.

The Hon. Mr. SMITH observed, that, when he had the honor to address the committee on the preceding question of the *representation,* he stated to them his idea, that it would be impossible, under the new Constitution as it stands, to have such a genuine representation of the people as would itself form a check in the government; that therefore it became our duty to provide checks of another nature. The honorable gentleman from New York had made many pertinent observations on the propriety of giving stability to the Senate. The general principles laid down, he thought, were just. He only disputed the inferences drawn from them, and their application to the proposed amendments. The only question was, whether the checks attempted in the amendment were incompatible with that stability which, he acknowledged, was essential to good government. Mr. Smith said he did not rise to enter at present into the debate at large. Indisposition compelled him to beg leave of the committee to defer what he had to offer to them till the succeeding day.

[25 June]

The Hon. Mr. HAMILTON. There are two objects in forming systems of government—*safety* for the people, and *energy* in the administration. When these objects are united, the certain tendency of the system will be to the public welfare. If the latter object be neglected, the people's security will be as certainly sacrificed as by disregarding the former. Good constitutions are formed upon a comparison of the liberty of the individual with the strength of government: if the tone of either be too high, the other will be weakened too much. It is the happiest possible mode of conciliating these objects, to institute one branch peculiarly endowed with sensibility, another with knowledge and firmness. Through the opposition and mutual control of these bodies, the government will reach, in its operations, the perfect balance between liberty and power. The arguments of the gentlemen chiefly apply to the former branch—the House of Representatives. If they will calmly consider the different nature of the two branches, they will see that the reasoning which justly applies to the representative house, will go to destroy the essential qualities of the Senate. If the former is calculated perfectly upon the principles of caution, why should you impose the same principles upon the latter, which is designed for a different operation? Gentlemen, while they discover a laudable anxiety for the safety of the people, do not attend to the important distinction I have drawn. We have it constantly held up to us, that, as it is our chief duty to guard against tyranny, it is our policy to form all the branches of government for this purpose.

Sir, it is a truth sufficiently illustrated by experience, that when the *people* act by their representatives, they are commonly *irresistible*. The gentleman admits the position, that stability is essential to the government, and yet enforces principles which, if true, ought to banish stability from the system. The gentleman observes, that there is a fallacy in my reasoning, and informs us that the legislatures of the states, not the people, are to appoint the senators. Does he reflect that they are the immediate agents of the people, that they are so constituted as to feel all their prejudices and passions, and to be governed, in a great degree, by their misapprehensions? Experience must have taught him the truth of this. Look through their history: what factions have arisen from the most trifling causes! What intrigues have been practised for the most illiberal purposes! Is not the state of Rhode Island, at this moment, struggling under difficulties and distresses, for having been led blindly by the spirit of the multitude? What is her legislature but the picture of a *mob*? In this state, we have a senate, possessed of the proper qualities of a permanent body. Virginia, Maryland, and a few other states, are in the same situation. The rest are either governed by a single democratic assembly, or have a senate constituted entirely upon democratic principles. These have been more or less embroiled in factions, and have generally been the image and echo of the multitude. It is difficult to reason on this point, without touching on certain delicate chords. I could refer you to periods and conjunctures when the people have been governed by improper passions, and led by factious and designing men. I could show that the same passions have infected their representatives. Let us beware that we do not make the state legislatures a vehicle in which the evil humors may be conveyed into the national system. To prevent this, it is necessary that the *Senate* should be so formed, as in some measure to check the *state governments*, and preclude the communication of the false impressions which they receive from the people. It has been often repeated, that the legislatures of the states can have only a partial and confined view of national affairs; that they can form no proper estimate of great objects which are not in the sphere of their interests. The observation of the gentleman, therefore, cannot take off the force of argument.

Sir, the senators will constantly be attended with a reflection, that their future existence is absolutely in the power of the states. Will not this form a powerful check? It is a reflection which applies closely to their feelings and interests; and no candid man, who thinks deliberately, will deny that it would be alone a sufficient check. The legislatures are to provide the mode of electing the President, and must have a great influence over the electors. Indeed, they convey their influence, through a thousand channels, into the general government. Gentlemen have endeavored to show that there will be no clashing of local and general interests: they do not seem to have sufficiently considered the subject. We have, in this state, a duty of sixpence per pound on salt, and it operates lightly and with advantage; but such a duty would be very burdensome to some of the states. If Congress should, at any time, find it convenient to impose a salt tax, would it not be opposed by the Eastern States? Being themselves incapable of feeling the necessity of the measure, they could only feel its apparent injustice. Would it be wise to give the New England States a power to defeat this measure, by recalling their senators who may be engaged for it? I beg the gentlemen once more to attend to the distinction between the real and the apparent interests of the states. I admit that the aggregate of individuals constitute the government; yet every state is not the government; every petty district is not the government. Sir, in our state legislatures, a *compromise* is frequently necessary between the interests of counties: the same must happen, in the general government, between states. In this, the few must yield to the many; or, in other words, the particular must be sacrificed to the general interest. If the members of Congress are too dependent on the state legislatures, they will be eternally forming secret combinations from local views. This is reasoning from the plainest principles. Their interest is interwoven with their dependence, and they will necessarily yield to the impression of their situation. Those who have been in Congress have seen these operations. The first question has been, How will such a measure affect my constituents, and, consequently, how will the part I take affect my reëlection? This consideration may be in some degree proper; but to be dependent from day to day, and to have the idea perpetually present, would be the source of numerous evils. *Six years,* sir, is a period short enough for a proper degree of dependence. Let us consider the peculiar state of this body, and see under what impressions they will act. *One third* of them are to go out at the end of two years, *two thirds* at four years, and the *whole* at six years. When one year is elapsed, there is a number who are to hold their places for one year, others for three, and others for five years. Thus there will not only be a constant and frequent change of members, but there will be some whose office is near the point of expiration, and who, from this circumstance, will have a lively sense of their dependence. The *biennial* change of members is an excellent invention for increasing the difficulty of combination. Any scheme of usurpation will lose, every two years, a number of its oldest advocates, and their places will be supplied by an equal number of new, unaccommodating, and virtuous men. When two principles are equally important, we ought, if possible, to reconcile them, and sacrifice neither. We think that safety and permanency in this government are completely reconcilable. The state governments will have, from the causes I have described, a sufficient influence over the Senate, without the check for which the gentlemen contend.

It has been remarked, that there is an inconsistency in our admitting that the *equal vote in the Senate* was given to secure the rights of the states, and at the same time holding up the idea that their interests should be sacrificed to those of the Union. But the committee certainly perceive the distinction between the rights of a state and its interests. The rights of a state are defined by the Constitution, and cannot be invaded without a violation of it; but the interests of a state have no connection with the Constitution, and may be, in a thousand instances, constitutionally sacrificed. A uniform tax is perfectly constitutional; and yet it may operate oppressively upon certain members of the Union. The gentlemen are afraid that the state governments will be abolished. But, sir, their existence does not depend upon the laws of the United States. Congress can no more abolish the state governments, than they can dissolve the Union. The whole Constitution is repugnant to it, and yet the gentlemen would introduce an additional useless provision against it. It is proper that the influence of the states should prevail to a certain extent. But shall the individual states be the judges how far? Shall an unlimited power be left them to determine in their own favor? The gentlemen go into the extreme: instead of a wise government, they would form a fantastical Utopia. But, sir, while they give it a plausible, popular shape, they would render it impracticable. Much has been said about factions. As far as my observation has extended, factions in Congress have arisen from attachment to *state prejudices*. We are attempting, by this Constitution, to abolish factions, and to unite all parties for the general welfare. That a man should have the power, in private life, of recalling his agent, is proper; because, in the business in which he is engaged, he has no other object but to gain the approbation of his principal. Is this the case with the senator? Is he simply the agent of the state? No. He is an agent for the Union, and he is bound to perform services necessary to the good of the whole, though his state should condemn them.

Sir, in contending for a rotation, the gentlemen carry their zeal beyond all reasonable bounds. I am convinced that no government, founded on this feeble principle, can operate well: I believe also that we shall be singular in this proposal. We have not felt the embarrassments resulting from rotation that other states have; and we hardly know the strength of their objection to it. There is no probability that we shall ever persuade a majority of the states to agree to this amendment. The gentlemen deceive themselves; the amendment would defeat their own design. When a man knows he must quit his station, let his merit be what it may, he will turn his attention chiefly to his own emolument: nay, he will feel temptations, which few other situations furnish, to perpetuate his power by unconstitutional usurpations. Men will pursue their interests. It is as easy to change human nature as to oppose the strong current of the selfish passions. A wise legislator will gently divert the channel, and direct it, if possible, to the public good.

It has been observed, that it is not possible there should be in a state only two men qualified for senators. But, sir, the question is not, whether there may be no more than two men; but whether, in certain emergencies, you could find two equal to those whom the amendment would discard. Important negotiations, or other business to which they shall be most competent, may employ them at the moment of their removal. These things often happen. The difficulty of obtaining men capable of conducting the affairs of a nation in dangerous times, is much more serious than the gentlemen imagine.

As to corruption, sir, admitting, in the *President*, a disposition to corrupt, what are the instruments of bribery? It is said he will have in his *disposal* a great number of *offices*. But how many offices are there, for which a man would relinquish the senatorial dignity? There may be some in the judicial, and some in other principal departments. But there are few whose respectability can, in any measure, balance that of the office of senator. Men who have been in the Senate once, and who have a reasonable hope of a reëlection, will not be easily bought by offices. This reasoning shows that a *rotation* would be productive of many *disadvantages:* under particular circumstances, it might be extremely inconvenient, if not fatal to the prosperity of our country.

The Hon. Mr. Smith. Few observations have fallen from the gentleman which appear to be new. He supposes *factions* cannot exist in the Senate without the knowledge of the state legislatures, who may, at the expiration of their office, elect other men. I believe, sir, that factions may prevail to a considerable degree without being known. Violent factions have sometimes taken place in Congress, respecting foreign matters, of which the public are ignorant. Some things have happened which are not proper to be divulged. So it by no means appears probable that the clashing of state interests will be the only cause of parties in the government. It has also been observed that the Senate has the check of the House of Representatives. The gentlemen are not accurate in stating this matter. The Senate is vested with certain great exclusive powers; and in the exercise of these powers, factions may as probably take place as in any transactions whatever. The honorable member further remarks that, from the intimate connection between the state legislatures and the people, the former will be the image of the latter, and subject to the same passions and prejudices. Now, I will ask every candid man if this is a true position. Certainly, it cannot be supposed that a small body of men, selected from the people for the purpose of making laws, will be incapable of a calm and deliberate view of political subjects. Experience has not proved that our legislatures are commonly guilty of errors arising from this source. There always has been, and ever will be, a considerable proportion of moderate and well-informed men among them. Though factions have prevailed, there are no instances of tumultuous proceedings; no instances to prove that they are not capable of wise deliberations. It is perhaps useless for me to continue this discussion, in order to answer arguments which have been answered before. I shall not, therefore, trouble the committee any more at present.

15

DEBATE IN NORTH CAROLINA RATIFYING CONVENTION
25 July 1788
Elliot 4:37–41

Mr. CABARRUS wished to be informed of the reason why the *senators* were to be elected for so long a time.

Mr. IREDELL. Mr. Chairman, I have waited for some time in hopes that a gentleman better qualified than myself would explain this part. Every objection to every part of this Constitution ought to be answered as fully as possible.

I believe, sir, it was the general sense of all America, with the exception only of one state, in forming their own state constitutions, that the legislative body should be divided into two branches, in order that the people might have a double security. It will often happen that, in a single body, a bare majority will carry exceptionable and pernicious measures. The violent faction of a party may often form such a majority in a single body, and by that means the particular views or interests of a part of the community may be consulted, and those of the rest neglected or injured. Is there a single gentleman in this Convention, who has been a member of the legislature, who has not found the minority in the most important questions to be often right? Is there a man here, who has been in either house, who has not at some times found the most solid advantages from the coöperation or opposition of the other? If a measure be right, which has been approved of by one branch, the other will probably confirm it; if it be wrong, it is fortunate that there is another branch to oppose or amend it. These principles probably formed one reason for the institution of a Senate, in the form of government before us. Another arose from the peculiar nature of that government, as connected with the government of the particular states.

The general government will have the protection and management of the general interests of the United States. The local and particular interests of the different states are left to their respective legislatures. All affairs which concern this state only are to be determined by our representatives coming from all parts of the state; all affairs which concern the Union at large are to be determined by representatives coming from all parts of the Union. Thus, then, the general government is to be taken care of, and the state governments to be preserved. The former is done by a numerous representation of the people of each state, in proportion to its importance. The latter is effected by giving each state an equal representation in the Senate. The people will be represented in one house, the state legislatures in the other.

Many are of the opinion that the power of the Senate is too great; but I cannot think so, considering the great weight which the House of Representatives will have. Several reasons may be assigned for this. The House of Representatives will be more numerous than the Senate. They will represent the immediate interests of the people. They will originate all money bills, which is one of the greatest securities in any republican government. The respectability of their constituents, who are the free citizens of America, will add great weight to the representatives; for a power derived from the people is the source of all real honor, and a demonstration of confidence which a man of any feeling would be more ambitious to possess, than any other honor or any emolument whatever. There is, therefore, always a danger of such a house becoming too powerful, and it is necessary to counteract its influence by giving great weight and authority to the other. I am warranted by well-known facts in my opinion that the representatives of the people at large will have more weight than we should be induced to believe from a slight consideration.

The British government furnishes a very remarkable instance to my present purpose. In that country, sir, is a king, who is hereditary—a man, who is not chosen for his abilities, but who, though he may be without principles or abilities, is by birth their sovereign, and may impart the vices of his character to the government. His influence and power are so great, that the people would bear a great deal before they would attempt to resist his authority. He is one complete branch of the legislature—may make as many peers as he pleases, who are immediately members of another branch; he has the disposal of almost all offices in the kingdom, commands the army and navy, is head of the church, and has the means of corrupting a large proportion of the representatives of the people, who form the third branch of the legislature. The House of Peers, which forms the second branch, is composed of members who are hereditary, and, except as to money bills, (which they are not allowed either to originate or alter,) hath equal authority with the other house. The members of the House of Commons, who are considered to represent the people, are elected for seven years, and they are chosen by a small proportion of the people, and, I believe I may say, a large majority of them by actual corruption. Under these circumstances, one would suppose their influence, compared to that of the king and the lords, was very inconsiderable. But the fact is, that they have, by degrees, increased their power to an astonishing degree, and, when they think proper to exert it, can command almost any thing they please. This great power they enjoy, by having the name of representatives of the people, and the exclusive right of originating money bills. What authority, then, will our representatives not possess, who will really represent the people, and equally have the right of originating money bills?

The manner in which our Senate is to be chosen gives us an additional security. Our senators will not be chosen by a king, nor tainted by his influence. They are to be chosen by different legislatures in the Union. Each is to choose two. It is to be supposed that, in the exercise of this power, the utmost prudence and circumspection will be observed. We may presume that they will select two of the most respectable men in the state, two men who had given the strongest proofs of attachment to the interests of their country. The senators are not to hold estates for life in the legislature, nor to transmit them to their children. Their families, friends, and estates, will be pledges for their fidelity to their country. Holding no office under the United States, they will be under no temptation of that kind to forget the interest of their constituents. There is every probability that men elected in this manner will, in general, do their duty faithfully. It may be expected, therefore, that they will coöperate in every laudable act, but strenuously resist those of a contrary nature. To do this to effect, their station must have some permanency annexed to it.

As the representatives of the people may probably be more popular, and it may be sometimes necessary for the Senate to prevent factious measures taking place, which may be highly injurious to the real interests of the public, the Senate should not be at the mercy of every popular clamor. Men engaged in arduous affairs are often obliged to do things which may, for the present, be disapproved of, for want of full information of the case, which it is not in every man's power immediately to obtain. In the mean time, every one is eager to judge, and many to condemn; and thus many an action is for a time unpopular, the true policy and justice of which afterwards very plainly appear. These observations apply even to acts of legislation concerning domestic policy: they apply much more forcibly to the case of foreign negotiations, which will form one part of the business of the Senate. I hope we shall not be involved in the labyrinths of foreign politics. But it is necessary for us to watch the conduct of European powers, that we may be on our defence and ready in case of an attack. All these things will require a continued attention; and, in order to know whether they were transacted rightly or not, it must take up a considerable time.

A certain permanency in office is, in my opinion, useful for another reason. Nothing is more unfortunate for a nation than to have its affairs conducted in an irregular manner. Consistency and stability are necessary to render the laws of any society convenient for the people. If they were to be entirely conducted by men liable to be called away soon, we might be deprived, in a great measure, of their utility; their measures might be abandoned before they were fully executed, and others, of a less beneficial tendency, substituted in their stead. The public also would be deprived of that experience which adds so much weight to the greatest abilities.

The business of a senator will require a great deal of knowledge, and more extensive information than can be acquired in a short time. This can be made evident by facts well known. I doubt not the gentlemen of this house, who have been members of Congress, will acknowledge that they have known several instances of men who were members of Congress, and were there many months before they knew how to act, for want of information of the real state of the Union. The acquisition of full information of this kind must employ a great deal of time; since a general knowledge of the affairs of all the states, and of the relative situation of foreign nations, would be indispensable. Responsibility, also, would be lessened by a short duration; for many useful measures require a good deal of time, and continued operations, and no man should be answerable for the ill success of a scheme which was taken out of his hands by others.

For these reasons, I hope it will appear that six years are not too long a duration for the Senate. I hope, also, it will be thought that, so far from being injurious to the liberties and interest of the public, it will form an additional security to both, especially when the next clause is taken up, by which we shall see that one third of the Senate is to go out every second year, and two thirds must concur in the most important cases; so that, if there be only one honest man among the two thirds that remain, added to the one third which has recently come in, this will be sufficient to prevent the rights of the people being sacrificed to any unjust ambition of that body.

I was in hopes some other gentleman would have explained this paragraph, because it introduces an entire change in our system; and every change ought to be founded on good reasons, and those reasons made plain to the people. Had my abilities been greater, I should have answered the objection better. I have, however, done it in the best manner in my power, and I hope the reasons I have assigned will be satisfactory to the committee.

16

CHARLES PINCKNEY TO JAMES MADISON
28 Mar. 1789
Documentary History 5:168–69

Are you not, to use a full expression, abundantly convinced that the theoretical nonsense of an election of the members of Congress by the people in the first instance, is clearly and practically wrong.—that it will in the end be the means of bringing our councils into contempt & that the legislature are the only proper judges of who ought to be elected?— —

Are you not fully convinced that the Senate ought at least to be double their number to make them of consequence & to prevent their falling into the same comparative state of insignificance that the state Senates have, merely from their smallness?—

17

ROGER SHERMAN TO JOHN ADAMS
July 1789

Adams Works 5:440–41

It appears to me the senate is the most important branch in the government, for aiding and supporting the executive, securing the rights of the individual states, the government of the United States, and the liberties of the people. The executive magistrate is to execute the laws. The senate, being a branch of the legislature, will naturally incline to have them duly executed, and, therefore, will advise to such appointments as will best attain that end. From the knowledge of the people in the several states, they can give the best information as to who are qualified for office; and though they will, as you justly observe, in some degree lessen his responsibility, yet their advice may enable him to make such judicious appointments, as to render responsibility less necessary. The senators being eligible by the legislatures of the several states, and dependent on them for reëlection, will be vigilant in supporting their rights against infringement by the legislature or executive of the United States; and the government of the Union being federal, and instituted by the several states for the advancement of their interests, they may be considered as so many pillars to support it, and, by the exercise of the state governments, peace and good order may be preserved in places most remote from the seat of the federal government, as well as at the centre. And the municipal and federal rights of the people at large will be regarded by the senate, they being elected by the immediate representatives of the people, and their rights will be best secured by a due execution of the laws. What temptation can the senate be under to partiality in the trial of officers of whom they had a voice in the appointment? Can they be disposed to favor a person who has violated his trust and their confidence?

The other evils you mention, that may result from this power, appear to me but barely possible. The senators will doubtless be in general some of the most respectable citizens in the states for wisdom and probity, superior to mean and unworthy conduct, and instead of undue influence, to procure appointments for themselves or their friends, they will consider that a fair and upright conduct will have the best tendency to preserve the confidence of the people and of the states. They will be disposed to be diffident in recommending their friends and kindred, lest they should be suspected of partiality; and the other members will feel the same kind of reluctance, lest they should be thought unduly to favor a person, because related to a member of their body; so that their friends and relations would not stand so good a chance for appointment to offices, according to their merit, as others.

The senate is a convenient body to advise the president, from the smallness of its numbers. And I think the laws would be better framed and more duly administered, if the executive and judiciary officers were in general members of the legislature, in case there should be no interference as to the time of attending to their several duties. This I have learned by experience in the government in which I live, and by observation of others differently constituted. I see no principles in our constitution that have any tendency to aristocracy, which, if I understand the term, is a government by nobles, independent of the people, which cannot take place, in either respect, without a total subversion of the constitution. As both branches of Congress are eligible from the citizens at large, and wealth is not a requisite qualification, both will commonly be composed of members of similar circumstances in life. And I see no reason why the several branches of the government should not maintain the most perfect harmony, their powers being all directed to one end, the advancement of the public good.

18

ST. GEORGE TUCKER,
BLACKSTONE'S COMMENTARIES
1:APP. 195–97, 215–25
1803

The election of representatives we have seen, is by a mode strictly popular. Had the distinction of states been entirely done away, there could have been no good reason assigned, perhaps, why the elections of senators should not have been assimilated thereto, at least in respect to numbers, since in a government where all parts are equal, no preference under any pretext whatsoever ought to be allowed to any one part, over the rest. Why then should Rhode Island and Delaware have as many representatives in the senate as Virginia and Massachusetts, which contain ten times their respective numbers? It has been answered, the senate are chosen to represent the states in their sovereign capacity, as moral bodies, who as such, are all equal; the smallest republic, as a sovereign state, being equal to the most powerful monarchy upon earth. As states, then, Rhode Island and Delaware are entitled to an equal weight in council on all occasions, where that weight does not impose a burthen upon the other states in the union. Now as the relation between taxation and representation, in one branch of the legislature, was fixed by an invariable standard, and as that branch of the legislature possesses the exclusive right of originating bills on the subject of revenue, the undue weight of the smaller states is guarded against, effectually, in the imposition of burdens. In all other cases their interests, as states, are equal, and deserve equal attention from the confederate government. This could no way be so effectually provided for, as in giving them equal weight in the second branch of the legislature, and in the executive whose province it is to make treaties, &c. . . . Without this equality, somewhere, the union could not, under any possible view, have been considered as an equal alliance between equal states. The disparity which must have prevailed, had the apportionment of representation been the same in the senate as in the other house, would have been such as to have submitted the smaller states to the most debasing dependence. I cannot, therefore, but regard this particular in the constitution, as one of the happiest traits in it, and calculated to cement the union equally with any other provision that it contains.

This body is not, like the former, dissolved at the end of the period for which it's members were elected; it is a permanent, perpetual body; the members, indeed, are liable to a partial change every two years, the senate being divided into three classes, one of which is vacated every second year, so that a total change in the members may be made in six years, but cannot possibly be effected, without the intervention of death, in less time. . . . According to the arrangements of the classes actually made, both the senators from the same state shall never vacate their seats at the same time; a provision which certainly has it's advantages, as no state is thereby in danger of being not represented at any time.

This mode of constituting the senate, seems liable to some important objections. The perpetuity of the body is favorable to every stride it may be disposed to make towards extending it's own power and influence in the government: a tendency to be discovered in all bodies, however constituted, and to which no effectual check can be opposed, but frequent dissolutions and elections. It is no satisfactory answer to this objection, that the members are removable, though the body itself be perpetual. The change, even were the members ineligible a second time, would be too gradual, to effect any counterpoise to this prevailing principle.

It has been insisted that the perpetuity of this body, is the only security to be found in the constitution against that instability of councils and of measures which has marked the proceedings of those states, where no such check is provided by the constitution. To which it may be answered, that every newly established government must be a government of experiment. . . . The design of a machine may appear correct, the model perfect, and adapted to all the purposes which the original inventor proposed: yet a thousand defects may be discovered when the actual application of it's powers is made, and, many useful improvements, in time, become obvious, to the eyes of a far less skilful mechanic. Their success and perfection must, however, still depend upon actual experiment, and that experiment may suggest still further improvement. Are we to reject these because they did not occur to the first projector, though evidently growing out of his original design? Or, if on the other hand we have unwarily adopted that as an improvement, which experiment shall evince to be a defect, shall we be so wedded to error as to persist in the practice of it, for no better reason than that we have once fallen into it.

. . . . .

II. We are now to draw a parallel between the house of lords, and the senate of the United States, as a second constituent part of the national legislature; and could the parallel between them end there, it might have been said, that all the branches of our political legislature, were, like a well chosen jury, *omni exceptione maiores.*

The house of lords are to be considered in two distinct points of view. . . . First, as representing a distinct order of men, with exclusive privileges annexed to their individual capacity, and secondly, as representing the nation.

1. As to the necessity of a distinct order of men in a state, with exclusive privileges annexed to the individual capacity, the author of the commentaries observes, "That the distinction of rank and honours is necessary in every well governed state, in order to reward such as are eminent for their public services, in a manner the most desirable to individuals, and yet without burthen to the community; exciting thereby an ambitious, yet laudable ardor, and generous emulation, in others. A spring of action, which however dangerous or invidious in a mere republic, will certainly be attended with good effects under a monarchy. And since titles of nobility are thus expedient in the state, it is also expedient that their owners should form an independent and separate branch of the legislature. If they were confounded with the mass of the people, and like them only had a vote in electing representatives their privileges would soon be borne down and overwhelmed by the popular torrent, which would effectually level all distinctions."

The conclusion which evidently arises from the former part of this quotation, "that no mere republic can ever be a well governed state," inasmuch as honours and titles, the necessity of which, is here so pointedly urged, are dangerous and invidious in such a government, may be proved to be false, both from reasoning and example. But it will be time enough to controvert our author's conclusion, when the truth of the principle upon which it is founded is established. The British constitution, with him, is somewhat like the bed of *Procrustes;* principles must be limited, extended, narrowed, or enlarged, to fit it. If they are not susceptible of so convenient a modification, they are to be wholly rejected. . . . But to return:

The vital principle of mixt governments is the distinction of orders, possessing, both collectively and individually, different rights, privileges or prerogatives. In an absolute monarchy, a confirmed aristocracy, or a pure democracy, this distinction cannot be found. There being no distinction of orders, there can be no contention about rights, in either of these forms of government, so long as the government remains in the full vigour of its constitution. When either of these three forms of government departs from its intrinsic nature, unless it assumes one of the other instead thereof, it becomes a mixt government. . . . And this mixture may consist in the combination of monarchy with aristocracy, as in Poland; or with democracy, as in France, under it's late constitution, as modelled by the national assembly, and ratified by the king; or, in the blending of the aristocratic and democratic forms, as was the case with the Roman republic after the establishment of the tribunes; or of all three, as in the British constitution. The existence of either of these combinations are said to form the constitution of the state, in all the governments of the world, except those of America, and France under it's late constitution; in these the constitution creates the powers that exist: In all others, the existing powers determine the nature of the constitution. To preserve those existing powers in their full tone and vigour, respectively, it may be necessary that each should possess an independent share in the supreme legislature, for the reasons assigned by the author of the commentaries; but this no more proves the necessity of the order, in a well governed state, than the necessity of wings to the human body would be proved, by a critical dissertation, on the structure, size, and position, of those of the fabulous deities of antiquity.

Our author considers those rewards which constitute a separate order of men, as attended with no burthen to the community; nothing can be more false than such a supposition. If the distinction be personal, only, it must be created at the expence of the personal degradation of the rest of the community, during the life of the distinguished person. If hereditary, this degradation is entailed upon the people: personal distinctions cannot be supported without power, or without wealth; these are the true supporters of the arms of nobility; take them away, the shield falls to the ground, and the pageantry of heraldry is trodden under foot. What character is less respected in England, than a poor Scotch lord, who is not one of the sixteen peers of that kingdom? That lord in his own clan, possesses comparative wealth and power sufficient among his humble dependents, to be looked up to as a Cr[o]esus in wealth, and a Caesar in authority.

"A titled nobility," says a late distinguished English writer, "is the most undisputed progeny of feudal barbarism. Titles had in all nations denoted offices; it was reserved for Gothic Europe, to attach them to ranks. Yet this conduct admits explanation, for with them offices were hereditary, and hence the titles denoting them became hereditary too. These distinctions only serve to unfit the nobility for obedience, and the people for freedom; to keep alive the discontent of the one and to perpetuate the servility of the other; to deprive the one of the moderation that sinks them into citizens, and to rob the other of the spirit that exalts them into freemen. The possession of honours by the multitude, who have inherited, but not acquired them, engrosses and depreciates these incentives and rewards of virtue." If these are the genuine fruits of that laudable ardour, and generous emulation, which give life and vigour to the community, and sets all the wheels of government in motion, heaven protect those whom it encounters in it's progress.

But is there no stimulous to that laudable ardour and generous emulation which the commentator speaks of, to be found in a pure democracy, which may compensate for the absence of ranks and honors? Yes. VIRTUE; that principle which actuated the Bruti, a Camillus, and a Cato in the Roman republic, a Timoleon, an Aristides, and an Epaminondas among the Greeks, with thousands of their fellow citizens whose names are scarcely yet lost in the wreck of time. That principle whose operation we have seen in our own days and in our own country, and of which, examples will be quoted by posterity so long as the remembrance of American liberty shall continue among

men. . . . "Virtue," says Montesquieu, "in a republic is a most simple thing; it is a love of the republic. Love of the republic in a democracy is a love of the democracy: love of the democracy is that of equality. The love of equality in a democracy limits ambition to the sole desire, to the sole happiness, of doing greater services to our own country than the rest of our fellow citizens. . . . But all cannot render equal services: hence distinctions arise here from the principle of equality, even when it seems to be removed, by signal services, or superior abilities."

This distinction, the only one which is reconcileable to the genius and principle of a pure republic, is, if we may reason from effect to cause, the most powerful incentive to good government that can animate the human heart, with this advantage over those hereditary honors for which the commentator is so zealous an advocate, that the ambition excited by the former must of necessity be directed to the public good, whilst the latter springing from self love, alone, may exist in the breast of a Caesar or a Cataline. A Franklin, or a Washington, need not the pageantry of honours, the glare of titles, nor the pre-eminence of station to distinguish them. Their heads like the mountain pine are seen above the surrounding trees of the forest, but their roots engross not a larger portion of the soil.

Equality of rights, in like manner, precludes not that distinction which superiority in virtue introduces among the citizens of a republic. Washington in retirement was equal, and only equal, in rights, to the poorest citizen of the state. Yet in the midst of that retirement the elevation of his character was superior to that of any prince in the universe, and the lustre of it far transcended the brightest diadem.

But even were it conceded that distinctions of rank and honours were necessary to good government, it would by no means follow that they should be hereditary; the same laudable ardour which leads to the acquisition of honor, is not necessary to the preservation of its badges; and these are all which it's hereditary possessors, in general, regard. Had nature in her operations shewn that the same vigour of mind and activity of virtue which manifests itself in a father, descends unimpaired to his son, and from him to latest posterity, in the same order of succession, that his estate may be limited to, some appearance of reason in favour of hereditary rank and honors might have been offered. But nature in every place, and in every age, has contradicted, and still contradicts this theory. The sons of Junius Brutus were traitors to the republic; the emperor Commodus was the son of Antoninus the philosopher; and Domitian was at once the son of Vespasian, and the brother of Titus.

If what has been said be a sufficient answer to the necessity of the distinction of ranks and honours to the well government of a state, the commentator himself hath afforded an unanswerable argument against their expedience in a republic, by acknowledging them to be both dangerous and invidious in such a government. And herewith agrees the author of the Spirit of Laws, who informs us, that the principle of a democracy is corrupted, when the spirit of equality is extinct. The same admirable writer gives us a further reason why so heterogeneous a mixture ought not to have a place in any government where the freedom and happiness of the people is thought an object worthy the attention of the government. "A nobility," says he, "think it an honour to obey a king, but consider it as the lowest infamy to share the power with the people."

We are indebted to the same author, for the following distinguished features of aristocracy: "If the reigning families observe the laws, aristocracy is a monarchy with several monarchs: but when they do not observe them, it is a despotic state governed by a great many despotic princes. In this case the republic consists only in respect to the nobles, and among them only. It is in the governing body; and the despotic state is in the body governed. The extremity of corruption is when the power of the nobles becomes hereditary; they can hardly then have any moderation." Such is the picture of that order of men who are elevated above the people by the distinctions of rank and honours. When the subjects of a monarchy, they are the pillars of the throne, as the commentator stiles them; or, according to Montesquieu, the tools of the monarch. . . . When rulers, as in an aristocracy, they are the despots of the people. . . . In a mixed government, they are the political Janizaries of the state, supporting and insulting the throne by turns, but still threatening and enslaving the people.

In America the senate are not a distinct order of individuals, but, the second branch of the national legislature, taken collectively. They have no privileges, but such as are common to the members of the house of representatives, and of the several state legislatures: we have seen that these privileges extend only to an exemption from personal arrests, in certain cases, and that it is utterly lost, in cases of treason, felony, or breach of the peace. They are more properly the privileges of the constituents, than of the members, since it is possible that a state might have no representative, and the United States no legislature, if the members might be restrained from attending their duty, by process issued at the suit of a creditor, or other person who might suppose he had cause of action against them. In England the privileges of the peerage are in some instances an insult to the morals of the people, the honour of a peer, on several occasions, being equipollent with the oath of a commoner. The exemption from personal arrests in civil cases is extended as well to his servant, as to the lord of parliament; to the injury of creditors, and the no small encouragement of fraud and knavery. And the statutes of *scandalum magnatum* hang *in terrorem* over the heads of those who dare to scrutinize, or to question the reality of those superior endowments which the law ascribes, to the immaculate character of a peer or peeress of the realm. Happy for America that her constitution and the genius of her people, equally secure her against the introduction of such a pernicious and destructive class of men.

Secondly. We shall now consider the British house of lords, as representing the nation.

The superior degree of wisdom which is to be found in aristocracies, forms the principal argument in favour of this branch of the British legislature. Let us examine how far this requisite to national councils, is to be attained by the constitution of that house.

1. The house of lords is composed either of new made peers, or of such to whom that honor has been transmitted by hereditary right; we may admit, though the fact will hardly justify it, that the new made peers have a chance of being selected for their superior wisdom; nay that this is universally the case; the portion of wisdom thus acquired, even in the creative reign of George the third, could never be sufficient to counterbalance the large majority of hereditary peers, who affect to hold in great contempt the talents and learning of their new created brethren. The wisdom of this body rests then upon the chance of natural talents, with the advantages of education to improve and mature them. As to the latter, should we admit that a child, who, from the moment he is capable of making any observation, sees himself treated as a superior being, would have the same stimulus to improve, as one who is taught to consider the road to science as the only one which leads to distinction, no advantage could be claimed in favour of the hereditary legislator, unless it should be proved that the benefits of education are necessarily confined to that class of men. . . . The question rests then solely upon the mode by which the nobility become legislators, and here every argument against the transmission of talents and virtue in hereditary succession, recurs with accumulated force, the chance of this inheritance being confined by the laws to the eldest son.

The senate of the United States, as we have seen, is composed of individuals selected for their probity, attachment to their country, and talents, by the legislatures of the respective states. They must be citizens of the states for which they are chosen. . . . their merits must be known, must have been distinguished, and respected. Age must have matured the talents, and confirmed the virtues which dawned with childhood, or shine forth with youth. Principles must have been manifested, and conduct have evinced their rectitude, energy, and stability. . . . Equivocation of character can scarcely obtain admittance where the trust is important, elections rare, and limited to an individual, or, at most, to two. The whole number of senators are at present limited to thirty-two. . . . it is not probable that they will ever exceed fifty. . . . A late writer has observed, that an assembly of Newtons, if they exceeded a hundred, would be a mob. The British house of peers consists of twice that number at the least, and may be encreased, at the will of the prince, to any number. . . . The senators of America have the interest of a state to promote, or to defend. A British house of peers has the privileges of the order, the interests of the corporation of aristocracy, to advance. Their wisdom, their exertions, are directed to their own personal aggrandizement. . . . Those of an American senator can scarcely find an object, except the good of the nation, or of the individual state which he represents. A peer holds himself responsible to no one for his conduct; a senator is responsible to his constituents, and if he abuses their confidence, will be sure to be displaced, whilst the former hugs himself in the security and stability of his station. I say nothing of the bench of bishops. The independence of that body has been too frequently questioned to render them respectable, even in the eyes of their own nation, as a part of the legislature.

A member of the house of lords, may make another lord his proxy, to vote for him in his absence; a privilege which he is supposed to derive from sitting there in his own right; and not as one of the representatives of the nation. He may likewise, by leave of parliament enter his protest against any measure, analogous to which we have seen that the yeas and nays of either house of congress shall be called, if one fifth part of the members present concur therein.

The lord chancellor, or any other person appointed by the king's commission is speaker of the house of lords; and if none be so appointed, the house of lords may elect; and if the speaker be a lord of parliament he may also give his opinion upon any question which the speaker of the commons cannot. . . . The vice president of the United States is in like manner speaker of the senate, but he is prohibited from voting unless the senate be equally divided. The necessity of providing for the case of a vacancy in the office of president doubtless gave rise to the creation of this officer: and for want of something else for him to do, whilst there is a president in office, he seems to have been placed, with no very great propriety, in the chair of the senate. An idea probably originating from the tendency which we have sometimes discovered, to imitate the model of the British constitution. The casting vote, which this officer is entrusted with, (as was before observed,) is a very important trust, and ought to have been so modified as to leave the exercise of it, to as few cases as possible. . . . If a measure originates in the senate, indeed, it would seem to be less dangerous, to permit the exercise of this casting vote, than where it was made use of, to negative a measure, perhaps unanimously adopted by the other house, and upon which the senate have been divided merely from the absence of some of it's members. This has actually happened once, on a very important occasion, as we have seen, and may happen again, on others equally interesting to the rights of the citizen.

19

JOSEPH STORY, COMMENTARIES ON THE CONSTITUTION
2:§§ 697, 699–710
1833

---

§ 697. Another and most important advantage arising from this ingredient is, the great difference, which it creates in the elements of the two branches of the legislature; which constitutes a great desideratum in every practical division of the legislative power. In fact, this divison (as has been already intimated) is of little or no intrinsic value,

unless it is so organised, that each can operate, as a real check upon undue and rash legislation. If each branch is substantially framed upon the same plan, the advantages of the division are shadowy and imaginative; the visions and speculations of the brain, and not the waking thoughts of statesmen, or patriots. It may be safely asserted, that for all the purposes of liberty, and security, of stable laws, and of solid institutions, of personal rights, and of the protection of property, a single branch is quite as good, as two, if their composition is the same, and their spirits and impulses the same. Each will act, as the other does; and each will be led by the same common influence of ambition, or intrigue, or passion, to the same disregard of the public interests, and the same indifference to, and prostration of private rights. It will only be a duplication of the evils of oppression and rashness, with a duplication of obstructions to effective redress. In this view, the organization of the senate becomes of inestimable value. It represents the voice, not of a district, but of a state; not of one state, but of all; not of the interest of one state, but of all; not of the chosen pursuits of a predominant population in one state, but of all the pursuits in all the states.

. . . . .

§ 699. No system could, in this respect, be more admirably contrived to ensure due deliberation and inquiry, and just results in all matters of legislation. No law or resolution can be passed without the concurrence, first of a majority of the people, and then of a majority of the states. The interest, and passions, and prejudices of a district are thus checked by the influence of a whole state; the like interests, and passions, and prejudices of a state, or of a majority of the states, are met and controlled by the voice of the people of the nation. It may be thought, that this complicated system of checks may operate, in some instances, injuriously, as well as beneficially. But if it should occasionally work inequally, or injuriously, its general operation will be salutary and useful. The disease most incident to free governments is the facility and excess of lawmaking; and while it never can be the permanent interest of either branch to interpose any undue restraint upon the exercise of all fit legislation, a good law had better occasionally fail, rather than bad laws be multiplied with a heedless and mischievous frequency. Even reforms, to be safe, must, in general, be slow; and there can be little danger, that public opinion will not sufficiently stimulate all public bodies to changes, which are at once desirable, and politic. All experience proves, that the human mind is more eager and restless for changes, than tranquil and satisfied with existing institutions. Besides; the large states will always be able, by their power over the supplies, to defeat any unreasonable exertions of this prerogative by the smaller states.

§ 700. This reasoning, which theoretically seems entitled to great weight, has, in the progress of the government, been fully realized. It has not only been demonstrated, that the senate, in its actual organization, is well adopted to the exigencies of the nation; but that it is a most important and valuable part of the system, and the real balance-wheel, which adjusts, and regulates its movements. The other auxiliary provisions in the same clause, as to the mode of appointment and duration of office, will be found to conduce very largely to the same beneficial end.

§ 701. Secondly; the mode of appointment of the senators. They are to be chosen by the legislature of each state. Three schemes presented themselves, as to the mode of appointment; one was by the legislature of each state; another was by the people thereof; and a third was by the other branch of the national legislature, either directly, or out of a select nomination. The last scheme was proposed in the convention, in what was called the Virginia scheme, one of the resolutions, declaring, "that the members of the *second* branch (the senate) ought to be elected by those of the *first* (the house of representatives) out of a proper number nominated by the individual legislatures" (of the states.) It met, however, with no decided support, and was negatived, no state voting in its favour, nine states voting against it, and one being divided. The second scheme, of an election by the people in districts, or otherwise, seems to have met with as little favour. The first scheme, that of an election by the legislature, finally prevailed by an unanimous vote.

§ 702. The reasoning, by which this mode of appointment was supported, does not appear at large in any contemporary debates. But it may be gathered from the imperfect lights left us, that the main grounds were, that it would immediately connect the state governments with the national government, and thus harmonize the whole into one universal system; that it would introduce a powerful check upon rash legislation, in a manner not unlike that created by the different organizations of the house of commons, and the house of lords in Great Britain; and that it would increase public confidence by securing the national government from undue encroachments on the powers of the states. The Federalist notices the subject in the following brief and summary manner, which at once establishes the general consent to the arrangement, and the few objections, to which it was supposed to be obnoxious. "It is unnecessary to dilate on the appointment of senators by the state legislatures. Among the various modes, which might have been devised for constituting this branch of the government, that which has been proposed by the convention is probably the most congenial with the public opinion. It is recommended by the double advantage of favouring a select appointment, and of giving to the state governments such an agency in the formation of the federal government, as must secure the authority of the former, and may form a convenient link between the two systems." This is very subdued praise; and indicates more doubts, than experience has, as yet, justified.

§ 703. The constitution has not provided for the manner, in which the choice shall be made by the state legislatures, whether by a joint, or by a concurrent vote; the latter is, where both branches form one assembly, and give a united vote numerically; the former is, where each branch gives a separate and independent vote. As each of the state legislatures now consists of two branches, this is a very important practical question. Generally, but not universally, the choice of senators is made by a concurrent vote. Another question might be suggested, whether the executive

constitutes a part of the legislature for such a purpose, in cases where the state constitution gives him a qualified negative upon the laws. But this has been silently and universally settled against the executive participation in the appointment.

§ 704. Thirdly; the number of senators. Each state is entitled to two senators. It is obvious, that to ensure competent knowledge and ability to discharge all the functions entrusted to the senate, (of which more will be said hereafter,) it is indispensable, that it should consist of a number sufficiently large to ensure a sufficient variety of talents, experience, and practical skill, for the discharge of all their duties. The legislative power alone, for its enlightened and prudent exercise, requires (as has been already shown) no small share of patriotism, and knowledge, and ability. In proportion to the extent and variety of the labours of legislation, there should be members, who should share them, in order, that there may be a punctual and perfect performance of them. If the number be very small, there is danger, that some of the proper duties will be overlooked, or neglected, or imperfectly attended to. No human genius, or industry, is adequate to all the vast concerns of government, if it be not aided by the power and skill of numbers. The senate ought, therefore, on this account alone, to be somewhat numerous, though it need not, and indeed ought not, for other reasons, to be as numerous, as the house. Besides; numbers are important to give to the body a sufficient firmness to resist the influence, which the popular branch will ever be solicitous to exert over them. A very small body is more easy to be overawed, and intimidated, and controlled by external influences, than one of a reasonable size, embracing weight of character, and dignity of talents. Numbers alone, in many cases, confer power; and what is of not less importance, they present more resistance to corruption and intrigue. A body of five may be bribed, or overborne, when a body of fifty would be an irresistible barrier to usurpation.

§ 705. In addition to this consideration, it is desirable, that a state should not be wholly unrepresented in the national councils by mere accident, or by the temporary absence of its representative. If there be but a single representative, sickness or casualty may deprive the state of its vote on the most important occasions. It was on this account, (as well as others,) that the confederation entitled each state to send not less than *two*, nor more than *seven* delegates. In critical cases, too, it might be of great importance to have an opportunity of consulting with a colleague or colleagues, having a common interest and feeling for the state. And if it be not always in the strictest sense true, that in the multitude of counsel there is safety; there is a sufficient foundation in the infirmity of human nature to make it desirable to gain the advantage of the wisdom, and information, and reflection of other independent minds, not labouring under the suspicion of any unfavourable bias. These reasons may be presumed to have had their appropriate weight in the deliberations of the convention. If more than one representative of a state was to be admitted into the senate, the least practicable ascending number was that adopted. At that time a single representative of each state would have made the body too small for all the purposes of its institution, and all the objects before explained. It would have been composed but of thirteen; and supposing no absences, which could not ordinarily be calculated upon, seven would constitute a majority to decide all the measures. Twenty-six was not, at that period, too large a number for dignity, independence, wisdom, experience, and efficiency. And, at the present moment, when the states have grown to twenty-four, it is found, that forty-eight is a number quite small enough to perform the great national functions confided to it, and to embody the requisite skill and ability to meet the increased exigencies, and multiplied duties of the office. There is probably no legislative body on earth, whose duties are more various, and interesting, and important to the public welfare; and none, which calls for higher talents, and more comprehensive attainments, and more untiring industry, and integrity.

§ 706. In the convention there was a considerable diversity of opinion, as to the number, of which the senate should consist, and the apportionment of the number among the states. When the principle of an equality of representation was decided, the only question seems to have been, whether each state should have three, or two members. Three was rejected by a vote of nine states against one; and two inserted by a vote of nine states against one. It does not appear, that any proposition was ever entertained for a less number than two; and the silence of all public discussion on this subject seems to indicate, that the public opinion decidedly adopted the lowest number under the confederation to be the proper number, if an equality of representation was to be admitted into the senate. Whatever may be the future increase of states in the Union, it is scarcely probable, that the number will ever exceed that, which will fit the senate for the best performance of all its exalted functions. The British house of lords, at this moment, probably exceeds any number, which will ever belong to the American senate; and yet, notwithstanding the exaggerated declamation of a few ardent minds, the sober sense of the nation has never felt, that its number was either a burthen, or an infirmity inherent in the constitution.

§ 707. Fourthly; the term of service of the senators. It is for six years; although, as will be presently seen, another element in the composition of that body is, that one third of it is changed every two years.

What would be the most proper period of office for senators, was an inquiry, admitting of a still wider range of argument and opinion, than what would be the most proper for the members of the house of representatives. The subject was confessedly one full of intricacy, and doubt, upon which the wisest statesmen might well entertain very different views, and the best patriots might well ask for more information, without, in the slightest degree, bringing into question their integrity, their love of liberty, or their devotion to a republican government. If, in the present day, the progress of public opinion, and the lights of experience, furnish us with materials for a decided judgment, we ought to remember, that the question was then free to debate, and the fit conclusion was not easily

to be seen, or justly to be measured. The problem to be solved by the great men of that day was, what organization of the legislative power, in a republican government, is best adapted to give permanency to the Union, and security to public liberty. In the convention, a great diversity of judgment was apparent among those, whose purity and patriotism were above all suspicion, and whose talents and public services were equally unquestionable. Various propositions were entertained; that the period of service of senators should be during good behaviour; for nine years; for seven years; for six years; for five years; for four years; for three years. All these propositions successively failed, except that for seven years, which was eventually abandoned for six years with the additional limitation, that one third should go out biennially.

§ 708. No inconsiderable array of objections was brought to bear against this prolonged term of service of the senators beyond that fixed for the members of the house of representatives, both in the convention, and before the people, when the constitution was under their advisement. Perhaps some of those objections still linger in the minds of many, who entertain a general jealousy of the powers of the Union; and who easily persuade themselves on that account, that power should frequently change hands in order to prevent corruption and tyranny. The perpetuity of a body (it has been said) is favourable to every stride it may be disposed to make towards extending its own power and influence in the government. Such a tendency is to be discovered in all bodies, however constituted, and to which no effectual check can be opposed, but frequent dissolutions and elections. The truth of this remark may be admitted; but there are many circumstances, which may justly vary its force and application. While, on the one hand, perpetuity in a body may be objectionable, on the other hand, continual fluctuations may be no less so, with reference to its duties and functions, its powers, and its efficiency. There are dangers arising from too great frequency in elections, as well as from too small. The path of true wisdom is probably best attained by a moderation, which avoids either extreme. It may be said of too much jealousy, and of too much confidence, that, when either is too freely admitted into public councils, it betrays like treason.

§ 709. It seems paradoxical to assert, (as has been already intimated,) but it is theoretically, as well as practically true, that a deep-felt responsibility is incompatible with great frequency of elections. Men can feel little interest in power, which slips away almost as soon, as it is grasped; and in measures, which they can scarcely do more than begin, without hoping to perfect. Few measures have an immediate and sensible operation, exactly according to their wisdom or policy. For the most part, they are dependent upon other measures, or upon time, and gradual intermixtures with the business of life, and the general institutions of society. The first superficial view may shock popular prejudices, or errors; while the ultimate results may be as admirable and excellent, as they are profound and distant. Who can take much interest in weaving a single thread into a measure, which becomes an evanescent quantity in the main fabric, whose texture requires constant skill, and many adaptations from the same hand, before its perfection can be secured, or even be prophesied?

§ 710. The objections to the senatorial term of office all resolve themselves into a single argument, however varied in its forms, or illustrations. That argument is, that political power is liable to be abused; and that the great security for public liberty consists in bringing home responsibility, and dependence in those, who are entrusted with office; and frequent expressions of public opinion in the choice of officers. If the argument is admitted in its most ample scope, it still leaves the question open to much discussion, what is the proper period of office, and how frequent the elections should be. This question must, in its nature, be complicated; and may admit, if it does not absolutely require, different answers, as applicable to different functionaries. Without wandering into ingenious speculations upon the topic in its most general form, our object will be to present the reasons, which have been, or may be relied on, to establish the sound policy and wisdom of the duration of office of the senators as fixed by the constitution. In so doing, it will become necessary to glance at some suggestions, which have already occurred in considering the organization of the other branch of the legislature. It may be proper, however, to premise, that the whole reasoning applies to a moderate duration only in office; and that it assumes, as its basis, the absolute necessity of short limitations of office, as constituting indispensable checks to power in all republican governments. It would almost be useless to descant upon such a basis, because it is universally admitted in the United States as a fundamental principle of all their constitutions of government.

SEE ALSO:

Records of the Federal Convention, Farrand 1:28, 31–32, 39–40, 46, 55, 148–49, 158–60, 193, 206, 211, 221–22, 225, 227, 228, 230, 300, 395–96, 412–18, 430–32, 460, 477, 480, 494–502, 507, 509, 516–20, 523–25, 535, 553–56; 2:1–2, 12, 14, 85, 120–31, 133, 135, 141–42, 154–55, 165, 243, 566, 591

James Wilson, Pennsylvania Ratifying Convention, 4 Dec. 1787, Elliot 2:476–78

Federal Farmer, no. 11, 10 Jan. 1788, Storing 2.8.147

Federal Farmer, no. 12, 12 Jan. 1788, Storing 2.8.164

Charles Pinckney, South Carolina Legislature, 16 Jan. 1788, Elliot 4:256–57

Elbridge Gerry to Vice President of Massachusetts Convention, 21 Jan. 1788, Farrand 3:264–67

John Dickinson, Letters of Fabius, no. 8, May 1788, Pamphlets 206–7

Debate in New York Ratifying Convention, 24–25 June 1788, Elliot 2:297–300, 310–25

James Iredell, Answers to Mr. Mason's Objections to the New Constitution, 1788, Pamphlets 337–42

E. C. E. Genet, Extracts from Yates's Secret Diary, 1808, Farrand 3:413–16

James Kent, Commentaries 1:210–14 (1826)

William Rawle, A View of the Constitution of the United States 36–37, 38–40 (2d ed. 1829)

James Madison to James Hillhouse, May 1830, Writings 4:77

Jared Sparks to James Madison, 30 March 1831, Farrand 3:497–98

James Madison to Jared Sparks, 8 Apr. 1831, Farrand 3:498–500

Joseph Story, Commentaries on the Constitution, 2:§§ 691–95 (1833)

Article 1, Section 3, Clause 3

No Person shall be a Senator who shall not have attained to the Age of thirty Years, and been nine Years a Citizen of the United States, and who shall not, when elected, be an Inhabitant of that State for which he shall be chosen.

1. Records of the Federal Convention

2. Joseph Story, Commentaries on the Constitution (1833)

1

RECORDS OF THE FEDERAL CONVENTION

[1:228; Journal, 13 June]

4 Resolved that the Members of the second Branch of the national Legislature ought to be chosen by the individual Legislatures.

to be of the age of thirty years at least.

[1:428; Madison, 26 June]

Col. Mason. He did not rise to make any motion, but to hint an idea which seemed to be proper for consideration. One important object in constituting the Senate was to secure the rights of property. To give them weight & firmness for this purpose, a considerable duration in office was thought necessary. But a longer term than 6 years, would be of no avail in this respect, if needy persons should be appointed. He suggested therefore the propriety of annexing to the office a qualification of property. He thought this would be very practicable; as the rules of taxation would supply a scale for measuring the degree of wealth possessed by every man.

[2:235; Madison, 9 Aug.]

Mr. Govr. Morris moved to insert 14 instead of 4 years citizenship as a qualification for Senators; urging the danger of admitting strangers into our public Councils. Mr. Pinkney 2ds. him

Mr. Elseworth. was opposed to the motion as discouraging meritorious aliens from emigrating to this Country.

Mr. Pinkney. As the Senate is to have the power of making treaties & managing our foreign affairs, there is peculiar danger and impropriety in opening its door to those who have foreign attachments. He quoted the jealousy of the Athenians on this subject who made it death for any stranger to intrude his voice into their legislative proceedings.

Col. Mason highly approved of the policy of the motion. Were it not that many not natives of this Country had acquired great merit during the revolution, he should be for restraining the eligibility into the Senate, to natives.

Mr. Madison was not averse to some restrictions on this subject; but could never agree to the proposed amendment. He thought any restriction however in the *Constitution* unnecessary, and improper. unnecessary; because the Natl. Legislre. is to have the right of regulating naturalization, and can by virtue thereof fix different periods of residence as conditions of enjoying different privileges of Citizenship: Improper: because it will give a tincture of illiberality to the Constitution: because it will put it out of the power of the Natl Legislature even by special acts of naturalization to confer the full rank of Citizens on meritorious strangers & because it will discourage the most desirable class of people from emigrating to the U. S. Should the proposed Constitution have the intended effect of giving stability & reputation to our Govts. great numbers of respectable Europeans; men who love liberty and wish to partake its blessings, will be ready to transfer their fortunes hither. All such would feel the mortification of being marked with suspicious incapacitations though they sd. not covet the public honors. He was not apprehensive that any dangerous number of strangers would be appointed by the State Legislatures, if they were left at liberty to do so: nor that foreign powers would make use of strangers as instruments for their purposes. Their bribes would be expended on men whose circumstances would rather stifle than excite jealousy & watchfulness in the public.

Mr. Butler was decidely opposed to the admission of foreigners without a long residence in the Country. They bring with them, not only attachments to other Countries; but ideas of Govt. so distinct from ours that in every point of view they are dangerous. He acknowledged that if he himself had been called into public life within a short time after his coming to America, his foreign habits opinions & attachments would have rendered him an improper agent in public affairs. He mentioned the great strictness observed in Great Britain on this subject.

Docr. Franklin was not agst. a reasonable time, but should be very sorry to see any thing like illiberality inserted in the Constitution. The people in Europe are friendly to this Country. Even in the Country with which we have been lately at war, We have now & had during the war, a great many friends not only among the people at large but in both Houses of Parliament. In every other Country in Europe all the people are our friends. We found in the Course of the Revolution, that many strangers served us faithfully—and that many natives took part agst. their Country. When foreigners after looking about for some other Country in which they can obtain more happiness, give a preference to ours, it is a proof of attachment which ought to excite our confidence & affection.

Mr. Randolph did not know but it might be problematical whether emigrations to this Country were on the whole useful or not: but he could never agree to the motion for disabling them for 14 years to participate in the public honours. He reminded the Convention of the language held by our patriots during the Revolution, and the principles laid down in all our American Constitutions. Many foreigners may have fixed their fortunes among us under the faith of these invitations. All persons under this description with all others who would be affected by such a regulation, would enlist themselves under the banners of hostility to the proposed System. He would go as far as seven years, but no further.

Mr. Wilson said he rose with feelings which were perhaps peculiar; mentioning the circumstance of his not being a native, and the possibility, if the ideas of some gentlemen should be pursued, of his being incapacitated from holding a place under the very Constitution which he had shared in the trust of making. He remarked the illiberal complexion which the motion would give to the System, & the effect which a good system would have in inviting meritorious foreigners among us, and the discouragement & mortification they must feel from the degrading discrimination, now proposed. He had himself experienced this mortification. On his removal into Maryland, he found himself, from defect of residence, under certain legal incapacities, which never ceased to produce chagrin, though he assuredly did not desire & would not have accepted the offices to which they related. To be appointed to a place may be matter of indifference. To be incapable of being appointed, is a circumstance grating, and mortifying.

Mr. Govr. Morris. The lesson we are taught is that we should be governed as much by our reason, and as little by our feelings as possible. What is the language of Reason on this subject? That we should not be polite at the expense of prudence. There was a moderation in all things. It is said that some tribes of Indians, carried their hospitality so far as to offer to strangers their wives and daughters. Was this a proper model for us? He would admit them to his house, he would invite them to his table, would provide for them comfortable lodgings; but would not carry the complaisance so far as, to bed them with his wife. He would let them worship at the same altar, but did not choose to make Priests of them. He ran over the privileges which emigrants would enjoy among us, though they should be deprived of that of being eligible to the great offices of Government; observing that they exceeded the privileges allowed to foreigners in any part of the world; and that as every Society from a great nation down to a club had the right of declaring the conditions on which new members should be admitted, there could be no room for complaint. As to those philosophical gentlemen, those Citizens of the World, as they called themselves, He owned he did not wish to see any of them in our public Councils. He would not trust them. The men who can shake off their attachments to their own Country can never love any other. These attachments are the wholesome prejudices which uphold all Governments, Admit a Frenchman into your Senate, and he will study to increase the commerce of France: An Englishman, he will feel an equal bias in favor of that of England. It has been said that The Legislatures will not chuse foreigners, at least improper ones. There was no knowing what Legislatures would do. Some appointments made by them, proved that every thing ought to be apprehended from the cabals practised on such occasions. He mentioned the case of a foreigner who left this State in disgrace, and worked himself into an appointment from another to Congress.

Question on the motion of Mr. Govr. Morris to insert 14 in place of 4 years

N. H. ay. Mas. no. Ct. no. N. J. ay. Pa. no. Del. no. Md. no. Va. no. N. C. no. S. C. ay. Geo. ay. [Ayes—4; noes—7.]

On 13 years, moved Mr. Govr. Morris

N. H. ay. Mas. no. Ct. no. N. J. ay. Pa. no Del. no. Md. no. Va. no. N. C. no. S. C. ay. Geo. ay. [Ayes—4; noes—7.]

On 10 years moved by Genl Pinkney

N. H. ay. Mas. no. Ct. no. N. J. ay. Pa. no. Del. no. Md. no. Va. no. N. C. no. S. C. ay. Geo. ay. [Ayes—4; noes—7.]

Dr. Franklin reminded the Convention that it did not follow from an omission to insert the restriction in the Constitution that the persons in question wd. be actually chosen into the Legislature.

Mr. Rutlidge. 7 years of Citizenship have been required for the House of Representatives. Surely a longer time is requisite for the Senate, which will have more power.

Mr. Williamson. It is more necessary to guard the Senate in this case than the other House. Bribery & Cabal can be more easily practised in the choice of the Senate which is to be made by the Legislatures composed of a few men, than of the House of Represents. who will be chosen by the people.

Mr. Randolph will agree to 9 years with the expectation that it will be reduced to seven if Mr. Wilson's motion to reconsider the vote fixing 7 years for the House of Representatives should produce a reduction of that period.

On a question for 9 years

N. H. ay. Mas. no. Ct. no. N. J. ay. Pa. no. Del. ay. Md.

no. Va. ay. N. C. divd. S. C. ay. Geo. ay. [Ayes—6; noes—4; divided—1.]

The term "Resident" was struck out, & "inhabitant" inserted nem. con.

Art. V Sect. 3. as amended agreed to nem. con.

[2:242; King, 9 Aug.]

G Morris

Liberal & illiberal—The terms are indefinite—The Indians are the most liberal, because when a Stranger comes among them they offer him yr. wife & Daughters for his carnal amusement—

It is said yt. we threw open our Doors—invited the oppressed of all Countries to come & find an Asylum in America—This is true we invited them to come and worship in our Temple but we never invited them to become Priests at our Altar—We shd. cherish the love of our country—This is a wholesome prejudice and is in favor of our Country—Foreigners will not learn our laws & Constitution under 14 yrs.—7yrs must be applied to learn to be a Shoe Maker—14 at least are necessary to learn to be an Amer. Legislator—Again—that period will be requisite to eradicate the Affections of Education and native Attachments—

Franklin—I am agt. the Term of 14 yrs—it looks illiberal—we have many good Friends in Engld. & other parts of Europe—they ought not to be excluded—Wilson—agt. the motion of 14 yrs—

[2:243; McHenry, 9 Aug.]

Governeur Morris proposed insted of 4 years 14. He would have confined the members he said to natives—but for its appearance and the effects it might have against the system.

Mr. *Mason* had the same wishes, but he could not think of excluding those foreigners who had taken a part and borne with the country the dangers and burdenths of the war.

Mr. Maddison was against such an invidious distinction. The matter might be safely intrusted to the respective legislatures. Doctor Franklin was of the same opinion. Mr. Willson expressed himself feelingly on the same side. It might happen, he said, that he who had been thought worthy of being trusted with the framing of the Constitution, might be excluded from it. He had not been born in this country. He considered such exclusing as one of the most galling chains which the human mind could experience, It was wrong to deprive the government of the talents virtue and abilities of such foreigners as might chuse to remove to this country. The corrup of other countries would not come here. Those who were tired in opposing such corruptions would be drawn hither, etc. etc.

[2:248; Madison, 10 Aug.]

Mr. Pinkney—The Committee as he had conceived were instructed to report the proper qualifications of property for the members of the Natl. Legislature; instead of which they have referred the task to the Natl. Legislature itself. Should it be left on this footing, the first Legislature will meet without any particular qualifications of property; and if it should happen to consist of rich men they might fix such such qualifications as may be too favorable to the rich; if of poor men, an opposite extreme might be run into. He was opposed to the establishment of an undue aristocratic influence in the Constitution but he thought it essential that the members of the Legislature, the Executive, and the Judges—should be possessed of competent property to make them independent & respectable. It was prudent when such great powers were to be trusted to connect the tie of property with that of reputation in securing a faithful administration. The Legislature would have the fate of the Nation put into their hands. The President would also have a very great influence on it. The Judges would have not only important causes between Citizen & Citizen but also where foreigners are concerned. They will even be the Umpires between the U. States and individual States as well as between one State & another. Were he to fix the quantum of property which should be required, he should not think of less than one hundred thousand dollars for the President, half of that sum for each of the Judges, and in like proportion for the members of the Natl. Legislature. He would however leave the sums blank. His motion was that the President of the U. S. the Judges, and members of the Legislature should be required to swear that they were respectively possessed of a clear unincumbered Estate to the amount of——in the case of the President, &c &c—

Mr. Rutlidge seconded the motion; observing, that the Committee had reported no qualifications because they could not agree on any among themselves, being embarrassed by the danger on one side of displeasing the people by making them high, and on the other of rendering them nugatory by making them low.

Mr. Elseworth. The different circumstances of different parts of the U. S. and the probable difference between the present and future circumstances of the whole, render it improper to have either *uniform* or *fixed* qualifications. Make them so high as to be useful in the S. States, and they will be inapplicable to the E. States. Suit them to the latter, and they will serve no purpose in the former. In like manner what may be accommodated to the existing State of things among us, may be very inconvenient in some future state of them. He thought for these reasons that it was better to leave this matter to the Legislative discretion than to attempt a provision for it in the Constitution.

Doctr Franklin expressed his dislike of every thing that tended to debase the spirit of the common people. If honesty was often the companion of wealth, and if poverty was exposed to peculiar temptation, it was not less true that the possession of property increased the desire of more property— Some of the greatest rogues he was ever acquainted with, were the richest rogues. We should remember the character which the Scripture requires in Rulers, that they should be men hating covetousness— This Constitution will be much read and attended to in Europe, and if it should betray a great partiality to the rich— will not only hurt us in the esteem of the most liberal and enlightened men

there, but discourage the common people from removing to this Country.

The Motion of Mr. Pinkney was rejected by so general a *no*, that the States were not called.

Mr Madison was opposed to the Section as vesting an improper & dangerous power in the Legislature. The qualifications of electors and elected were fundamental articles in a Republican Govt. and ought to be fixed by the Constitution. If the Legislature could regulate those of either, it can by degrees subvert the Constitution. A Republic may be converted into an aristocracy or oligarchy as well by limiting the number capable of being elected, as the number authorised to elect. In all cases where the representatives of the people will have a personal interest distinct from that of their Constituents, there was the same reason for being jealous of them, as there was for relying on them with full confidence, when they had a common interest. This was one of the former cases. It was as improper as to allow them to fix their own wages, or their own privileges. It was a power also, which might be made subservient to the views of one faction agst. another. Qualifications founded on artifical distinctions may be devised, by the stronger in order to keep out partizans of a weaker faction.

Mr. Elseworth, admitted that the power was not unexceptionable; but he could not view it as dangerous. Such a power with regard to the electors would be dangerous because it would be much more liable to abuse.

Mr. Govr. Morris moved to strike out "with regard to property" in order to leave the Legislature entirely at large.

Mr. Williamson. This could surely never be admitted. Should a majority of the Legislature be composed of any particular description of men, of lawyers for example, which is no improbable supposition, the future elections might be secured to their own body.

Mr. Madison observed that the British Parliamt. possessed the power of regulating the qualifications both of the electors, and the elected; and the abuse they had made of it was a lesson worthy of our attention. They had made the changes in both cases subservient to their own views, or to the views of political or Religious parties.

Question on the motion to strike out with regard to property

N. H. no. Mas. no. Ct. ay. N. J. ay. Pa. ay. Del. no. Md. no. Va. no. N. C. no. S. C. no. Geo- ay. [Ayes—4; noes—7.]

Mr Rutlidge was opposed to leaving the power to the Legislature– He proposed that the qualifications should be the same as for members of the State Legislatures.

Mr. Wilson thought it would be best on the whole to let the Section go out. A uniform rule would probably be never fixed by the Legislature. and this particular power would constructively exclude every other power of regulating qualifications–

On the question for agreeing to Art– VI– sect– 2d

N. H. ay. Mas. ay. Ct. no. N. J. no. Pa. no. Md. no. Va. no. N. C. no S. C. no. Geo. ay- [Ayes—3; noes—7.]

2

JOSEPH STORY, COMMENTARIES ON THE
CONSTITUTION 2:§§ 726–30
1833

§ 726. As the nature of the duties of a senator require more experience, knowledge, and stability of character, than those of a representative, the qualification in point of age is raised. A person may be a representative at twenty-five; but he cannot be a senator until thirty. A similar qualification of age was required of the members of the Roman senate. It would have been a somewhat singular anomaly in the history of free governments, to have found persons actually exercising the highest functions of government, who, in some enlightened and polished countries, would not be deemed to have arrived at an age sufficiently mature to be entitled to all the private and municipal privileges of manhood. In Rome persons were not deemed at full age until twenty-five; and that continues to be the rule in France, and Holland, and other civil law countries; and in France, by the old law, in regard to marriage full age was not attained until thirty. It has since been varied, and the term diminished.

§ 727. The age of senators was fixed in the constitution at first by a vote of seven states against four; and finally, by an unanimous vote. Perhaps no one, in our day, is disposed to question the propriety of this limitation; and it is, therefore, useless to discuss a point, which is so purely speculative. If counsels are to be wise, the ardour, and impetuosity, and confidence of youth must be chastised by the sober lesson of experience; and if knowledge, and solid judgment, and tried integrity, are to be deemed indispensable qualifications for senatorial service, it would be rashness to affirm, that thirty years is too long a period for a due maturity and probation.

§ 728. The next qualification is citizenship. The propriety of some limitation upon admissions to office, after naturalization, cannot well be doubted. The senate is to participate largely in transactions with foreign governments; and it seems indispensable, that time should have elapsed sufficient to wean a senator from all prejudices, resentments, and partialities, in relation to the land of his nativity, before he should be entrusted with such high and delicate functions. Besides; it can scarcely be presumed, that any foreigner can have acquired a thorough knowledge of the institutions and interests of a country, until he has been permanently incorporated into its society, and has acquired by the habits and intercourse of life the feelings and the duties of a citizen. And if he has acquired the requisite knowledge, he can scarcely feel that devoted attachment to them, which constitutes the great security for fidelity and promptitude in the discharge of official duties. If eminent exceptions could be stated, they would furnish no safe rule; and should rather teach us to fear our being misled by brilliancy of talent, or disinterested patriotism, into a confidence, which might betray, or an acquiescence, which might weaken, that jealousy of foreign influence, which is one of the main supports of republics. In the convention it was at first proposed, that the limitation should be four years; and it was finally altered by a vote of six states against four, one being divided, which was afterwards confirmed by a vote of eight states to three. . . .

§ 729. The only other qualification is, that the senator shall, when elected, be an inhabitant of the state, for which he is chosen. This scarcely requires any comment; for it is manifestly proper, that a state should be represented by one, who, besides an intimate knowledge of all its wants and wishes, and local pursuits, should have a personal and immediate interest in all measures touching its sovereignty, its rights, or its influence. The only surprise is, that provision was not made for his ceasing to represent the state in the senate, as soon as he should cease to be an inhabitant. There does not seem to have been any debate in the convention on the propriety of inserting the clause, as it now stands.

§ 730. In concluding this topic, it is proper to remark, that no qualification whatsoever of property is established in regard to senators, as non had been established in regard to representatives. Merit, therefore, and talent have the freest access open to them into every department of office under the national government. Under such circumstances, if the choice of the people is but directed by a suitable sobriety of judgment, the senate cannot fail of being distinguished for wisdom, for learning, for exalted patriotism, for incorruptible integrity, and for inflexible independence.

SEE ALSO:

Records of the Federal Convention, Farrand 2:121–26

Article 1, Section 3, Clauses 4 and 5

The Vice President of the United States shall be President of the Senate, but shall have no Vote, unless they be equally divided.

The Senate shall chuse their other Officers, and also a President pro tempore, in the Absence of the Vice President, or when he shall exercise the Office of President of the United States.

1

RECORDS OF THE FEDERAL CONVENTION

[2:495; Journal, 4 Sept.]

SECT. 3. The Vice President shall be ex officio, President of the Senate, except when they sit to try the impeachment of the President, in which case the Chief Justice shall preside, and excepting also when he shall exercise the powers and duties of President, in which case, and in case of his absence, the Senate shall chuse a President pro tempore—The Vice President when acting as President of the Senate shall not have a vote unless the House be equally divided

[2:536; Madison, 7 Sept.]

Section 3. (see Sepr. 4). "The vice President shall be ex officio President of the Senate"

Mr. Gerry opposed this regulation. We might as well put the President himself at the head of the Legislature. The close intimacy that must subsist between the President & vice-president makes it absolutely improper. He was agst. having any vice President.

Mr Govr Morris. The vice president then will be the first heir apparent that ever loved his father—If there should be no vice president, the President of the Senate would be temporary successor, which would amount to the same thing.

Mr Sherman saw no danger in the case. If the vice-President were not to be President of the Senate, he would be without employment, and some member by being made President must be deprived of his vote, unless when an equal division of votes might happen in the Senate, which would be but seldom.

Mr. Randolph concurred in the opposition to the clause.

Mr. Williamson, observed that such an officer as vice-President was not wanted. He was introduced only for the sake of a valuable mode of election which required two to be chosen at the same time.

Col: Mason, thought the office of vice-President an encroachment on the rights of the Senate; and that it mixed too much the Legislative & Executive, which as well as the Judiciary departments, ought to be kept as separate as possible. He took occasion to express his dislike of any reference whatever of the power to make appointments to either branch of the Legislature. On the other hand he was averse to vest so dangerous a power in the President alone. As a method for avoiding both, he suggested that a privy Council of six members to the president should be established; to be chosen for six years by the Senate, two out of the Eastern two out of the middle, and two out of the Southern quarters of the Union, & to go out in rotation two every second year; the concurrence of the Senate to be required only in the appointment of Ambassadors, and in making treaties. which are more of a legislative nature. This would prevent the constant sitting of the Senate which he thought dangerous, as well as keep the departments separate & distinct. It would also save the expence of constant sessions of the Senate. He had he said always considered the Senate as too unwieldy & expensive for appointing officers, especially the smallest, such as tide waiters &c. He had not reduced his idea to writing, but it could be easily done if it should be found acceptable.

On the question shall the vice President be ex officio President of the Senate?

N— H. ay— Mas. ay— Ct. ay. N. J. no. Pa. ay. Del. ay— Mas— no. Va ay— N— C— abst S. C. ay— Geo. ay. [Ayes—8; noes—2; absent—1.]

[2:574; Committee of Style, 7 Sept.]

SECT. 3. The Vice President shall be ex officio, President of the Senate, except when they sit to try the impeachment of the President, in which case the Chief Justice shall preside, and excepting also when he shall exercise the powers and duties of President, in which case, and in case of his absence, the Senate shall chuse a President pro tempore—The Vice President when acting as President of the Senate shall not have a vote unless the House be equally divided

. . . . .

(c) The Vice-President of the United States shall be, ex officio, President of the senate, but shall have no vote, unless they be equally divided.

[2:612; Madison, 14 Sept.]

"Ex officio" struck out of the same section as superfluous; nem: con:

2

A NATIVE OF VIRGINIA, OBSERVATIONS UPON THE
PROPOSED PLAN OF FEDERAL GOVERNMENT
1788
Monroe Writings 1:361

The Vice-President has been introduced from the State Government of New York. This useful, though surely inoffensive officer, has been made by some objectors the bugbear of the Constitution. It is a strong proof of want of argument in the enemies to it, when they hold up this officer as dangerous. He is elected by the same persons as the President, and in the same manner. He presides in the Senate, but has no vote except when they are divided. This is the only power incident to his office whilst he continues Vice-President; and he is obviously introduced into the government to prevent the ill-consequences which might otherwise happen from the death or removal of the President. This is the purpose for which a similar officer has been introduced into the Constitution of New-York.

3

DEBATE IN NORTH CAROLINA RATIFYING
CONVENTION
24–25 July 1788
Elliot 4:26–27, 42

[24 July]

Mr. CALDWELL. Mr. Chairman, I am sorry to be objecting, but I apprehend that all the legislative powers granted by this Constitution are not vested in a Congress consisting of the Senate and the House of Representatives, because the Vice-President has a right to put a check on it. This is known to every gentleman in the Convention. How can all the legislative powers granted in that Constitution be vested in the Congress, if the Vice-President is to have a vote in case the Senate is equally divided? I ask for information, how it came to be expressed in this manner, when this power is given to the Vice-President.

Mr. MACLAINE declared, that he did not know what the gentleman meant.

Mr. CALDWELL said, that the Vice-President is made a part of the legislative body, although there was an express declaration, that all the legislative powers were vested in the Senate and House of Representatives, and that he would be glad to know how these things consisted together.

Mr. MACLAINE expressed great astonishment at the gentleman's criticism. He observed, that the Vice-President had only a casting vote in case of an equal division in the Senate—that a provision of this kind was to be found in all deliberative bodies—that it was highly useful and expedient—that it was by no means of the nature of a check which impedes or arrests, but calculated to prevent the operation of the government from being impeded—that, if the gentleman could show any legislative power to be given to any but the two houses of Congress, his objection would be worthy of notice.

Some other gentlemen said, they were dissatisfied with Mr. Maclaine's explanation—that the Vice-President was not a member of the Senate, but an officer of the United States, and yet had a legislative power, and that it appeared to them inconsistent—that it would have been more proper to have given the casting vote to the President.

His excellency, Gov. JOHNSTON, added to Mr. Maclaine's reasoning, that it appeared to him a very good and proper regulation—that, if one of the Senate was to be appointed Vice-President, the state which he represented would either lose a vote if he was not permitted to vote on every occasion, or if he was, he might, in some instances, have two votes—that the President was already possessed of the power of preventing the passage of a law by a bare majority; yet laws were said not to be made by the President, but by the two houses of Congress exclusively.

[25 July]

[Mr. MACLAINE.] Mr. Chairman, I will state to the committee the reasons upon which this officer was introduced. I had the honor to observe to the committee, before, the causes of the particular formation of the Senate—that it was owing, with other reasons, to the *jealousy* of the states, and, particularly, to the extreme jealousy of the lesser states of the power and influence of the larger members of the confederacy. It was in the Senate that the several political interests of the states were to be preserved, and where all their powers were to be perfectly balanced. The commercial jealousy between the Eastern and Southern States had a principal share in this business. It might happen, in important cases, that the voices would be equally divided. Indecision might be dangerous and inconvenient to the public. It would then be necessary to have some person who should determine the question as impartially as possible. Had the Vice-President been taken from the representation of any of the states, the vote of that state would have been under local influence in the second. It is true he must be chosen from some state; but, from the nature of his election and office, he represents no one state in particular, but all the states. It is impossible that any officer could be chosen more impartially. He is, in consequence of his election, the creature of no particular district or state, but the officer and representative of the Union. He must possess the confidence of the states in a very great degree, and consequently be the most proper person to decide in cases of this kind. These, I believe, are the principles upon which the Convention formed this officer.

4

JOSEPH STORY, COMMENTARIES ON THE CONSTITUTION 2:§§ 732–33, 735–39
1833

§ 732. The original article, as first reported, authorized the senate to choose its own president, and other officers; and this was adopted in the convention. But the same draft authorized the president of the senate, in case of the removal, death, resignation, or disability of the president, to discharge his duties. When at a late period of the convention it was deemed advisable, that there should be a vice president, the propriety of retaining him, as presiding officer of the senate, seems to have met with general favour, eight states voting in the affirmative, and two only in the negative.

§ 733. Some objections have been taken to the appointment of the vice president to preside in the senate. It was suggested in the state conventions, that the officer was not only unnecessary, but dangerous; that it is contrary to the usual course of parliamentary proceedings to have a presiding officer, who is not a member; and that the state, from which he comes, may thus have two votes, instead of one. It has also been coldly remarked by a learned commentator, that "the necessity of providing for the case of a vacancy in the office of president doubtless gave rise to the creation of that officer; and for want of something else for him to do, whilst there is a president in office, he seems to have been placed, with no very great propriety, in the chair of the senate."

. . . . .

§ 735. There is no novelty in the appointment of a person to preside, as speaker, who is not a constituent member of the body, over which he is to preside. In the house of lords in England the presiding officer is the lord chancellor, or lord keeper of the great seal, or other person appointed by the king's commission; and if none such be so appointed, then it is said, that the lords may elect. But it is by no means necessary, that the person appointed by the king should be a peer of the realm or lord of parliament. Nor has this appointment by the king ever been complained of, as a grievance, nor has it operated with inconvenience or oppression in practice. It is on the contrary deemed an important advantage, both to the officer, and to the house of peers, adding dignity and weight to the former, and securing great legal ability and talent in aid of the latter. This consideration alone might have had some influence in the convention. The vice president being himself chosen by the states, might well be deemed, in point of age, character, and dignity, worthy to preside over the deliberations of the senate, in which the states were all assembled and represented. His impartiality in the discharge of its duties might be fairly presumed; and the employment would not only bring his character in review before the public; but enable him to justify the public confidence, by performing his public functions with independence, and firmness, and sound discretion. A citizen, who was deemed worthy of being one of the competitors for the presidency, could scarcely fail of being distinguished by private virtues, by comprehensive acquirements, and by eminent services. In all questions before the senate he might safely be appealed to, as a fit arbiter upon an equal division, in which case alone he is entrusted with a vote.

§ 736. But the strong motive for this appointment was of another sort, founded upon state jealousy, and state equality in the senate. If the speaker of the senate was to be chosen from its own members, the state, upon whom the choice would fall, might possess either more or less, than its due share of influence. If the speaker were not allowed to vote, except where there was an equal division, independent of his own vote, then the state might lose its own voice; if he were allowed to give his vote, and also a casting vote, then the state might, in effect, possess a double vote. Either alternative would of itself present a predicament sufficiently embarrassing. On the other hand, if no casting vote were allowed in any case, then the indecision and inconvenience might be very prejudicial to the public interests, in case of an equality of votes. It might give rise to dangerous feuds, or intrigues, and create sectional and state agitations. The smaller states might well suppose, that their interests were less secure, and less guarded, than they ought to be. Under such circumstances, the vice president would seem to be the most fit arbiter to decide, because he would be the representative, not of one state only, but of all; and must be presumed to feel a lively interest in promoting all measures for the public good. This reasoning appears to have been decisive in the convention, and satisfactory to the people. It establishes, that there was a manifest propriety in making the arrangement conducive to the harmony of the states, and the dignity of the general government. And as the senate possesses the power to make rules for its own proceedings, there is little danger, that there can ever arise any abuse of the presiding power. The danger, if any, is rather the other way, that the presiding power will be either silently weakened, or openly surrendered, so as to leave the office little more, than the barren honour of a place, without influence and without action.

§ 737. A question, involving the authority of the vice president, as presiding officer in the senate, has been much discussed in consequence of a decision recently made by that officer. Hitherto the power of preserving order during the deliberations of the senate in all cases, where the rules of the senate did not specially prescribe another mode, had been silently supposed to belong to the vice president, as an incident of office. It had never been doubted, much less denied, from the first organization of the senate; and its existence had been assumed, as an inherent quality, constitutionally delegated, subject only to such rules, as the senate should from time to time prescribe. In the winter session of 1826, the vice president decided in effect, that, as president of the senate, he had no power of preserving order, or of calling any member to order, for words spoken in the course of debate, upon his own authority, but only so far, as it was given, and regulated by the rules of the senate. This was a virtual surrender of the presiding power (if not universally, at least in that case) into the hands of the senate; and disarmed the officer even of the power of self-protection from insult or abuse, unless the senate should choose to make provision for it. If, therefore, the senate should decline to confer the power of preserving order, the vice president might become a mere pageant and cipher in that body. If, indeed, the vice president had not this power *virtute officii*, there was nothing to prevent the senate from confiding it to any other officer chosen by itself. Nay, if the power to preside had not this incident, it was difficult to perceive, what other incident it had. The power to put questions, or to declare votes, might just as well, upon similar reasoning, be denied, unless it was expressly conferred. The power of the senate to prescribe rules could not be deemed omnipotent. It must be construed with reference to, and in connexion with the power to preside; and the latter, according to the common sense of mankind, and of public bodies, was always understood to include the power to keep order; upon the clear ground, that the grant of a power includes the authority to make it effectual, and also of self-preservation.

§ 738. The subject at that time attracted a good deal of discussion; and was finally, as a practical inquiry, put an end to in 1828, by a rule made by the senate, that "every question of order shall be decided by the president without debate, subject to appeal to the senate." But still the question, as one of constitutional right and duty, liable to be regulated, but not to be destroyed by the senate, deserves, and should receive, the most profound investigation of every man solicitous for the permanent dignity and independence of the vice presidency.

§ 739. The propriety of entrusting the senate with the choice of its other officers, and also of a president pro tempore in the absence of the vice president, or when he exercises the office of president, seems never to have been questioned; and indeed is so obvious, that it is wholly unnecessary to vindicate it. Confidence between the senate and its officers, and the power to make a suitable choice, and to secure a suitable responsibility for the faithful discharge of the duties of office, are so indispensable for the public good, that the provision will command universal assent, as soon as it is mentioned. It has grown into a general practice for the vice president to vacate the senatorial chair a short time before the termination of each session, in order to enable the senate to choose a president pro tempore, who might already be in office, if the vice president in the recess should be called to the chair of state. The practice is founded in wisdom and sound policy, as it immediately provides for an exigency, which may well be expected to occur at any time; and prevents the choice from being influenced by temporary excitements or intrigues, arising from the actual existence of a vacancy. As it is useful in peace to provide for war; so it is likewise useful in times of profound tranquillity to provide for political agitations, which may disturb the public harmony.

SEE ALSO:

Records of the Federal Convention, Farrand 2:129, 134, 141, 155, 165

James McHenry, Maryland House of Delegates, 28 Nov. 1787, Farrand 3:147

James Kent, Commentaries 1:214 (1826)

William Rawle, A View of the Constitution of the United States 37 (2d ed. 1829)

Article 1, Section 4, Clause 1

The Times, Places and Manner of holding Elections for Senators and Representatives, shall be prescribed in each State by the Legislature thereof; but the Congress may at any time by Law make or alter such Regulations, except as to the Places of chusing Senators.

1

RECORDS OF THE FEDERAL CONVENTION

[2:239; Madison, 9 Aug.]

Art. VI. sect. 1. taken up.

[ARTICLE VI, SECT. 1. "The times and places and manner of holding the elections of the members of each House shall be prescribed by the Legislature of each State; but their provisions concerning them may, at any time, be altered by the Legislature of the United States."]

Mr. Madison — & Mr. Govr. Morris moved to strike out "each House" & to insert "the House of Representatives"; the right of the Legislatures to regulate the times & places &c. in the election of Senators being involved in the right of appointing them, which was disagreed to.

Division of the question being called, it was taken on the first part down to "but their provisions concerning &c"

The first part was agreed to nem. con.

Mr. Pinkney & Mr. Rutlidge moved to strike out the remaining part viz "but their provisions concerning them may at any time be "altered by the Legislature of the United States." The States they contended could & must be relied on in such cases.

Mr Ghorum. It would be as improper take this power from the Natl. Legislature, as to Restrain the British Parliament from regulating the circumstances of elections, leaving this business to the Counties themselves—

Mr Madison. The necessity of a Genl. Govt. supposes that the State Legislatures will sometimes fail or refuse to consult the common interest at the expense of their local conveniency or prejudices. The policy of referring the appointment of the House of Representatives to the people and not to the Legislatures of the States, supposes that the result will be somewhat influenced by the mode, This view of the question seems to decide that the Legislatures of the States ought not to have the uncontrouled right of regulating the times places & manner of holding elections. These were words of great latitude. It was impossible to foresee all the abuses that might be made of the discretionary power. Whether the electors should vote by ballot or vivâ voce, should assemble at this place or that place; should be divided into districts or all meet at one place, shd all vote for all the representatives; or all in a district vote for a number allotted to the district; these & many other points would depend on the Legislatures. and might materially affect the appointments. Whenever the State

248

Legislatures had a favorite measure to carry, they would take care so to mould their regulations as to favor the candidates they wished to succeed. Besides, the inequality of the Representation in the Legislatures of particular States, would produce a like inequality in their representation in the Natl. Legislature, as it was presumable that the Counties having the power in the former case would secure it to themselves in the latter. What danger could there be in giving a controuling power to the Natl. Legislature? Of whom was it to consist? 1. of a Senate to be chosen by the State Legislatures. If the latter therefore could be trusted, their representatives could not be dangerous. 2. of Representatives elected by the same people who elect the State Legislatures; surely then if confidence is due to the latter, it must be due to the former. It seemed as improper in principle—though it might be less inconvenient in practice, to give to the State Legislatures this great authority over the election of the Representatives of the people in the Genl. Legislature, as it would be to give to the latter a like power over the election of their Representatives in the State Legislatures.

Mr. King. If this power be not given to the Natl. Legislature, their right of judging of the returns of their members may be frustrated. No probability has been suggested of its being abused by them. Altho this scheme of erecting the Genl. Govt. on the authority of the State Legislatures has been fatal to the federal establishment, it would seem as if many gentlemen, still foster the dangerous idea.

Mr. Govr. Morris—observed that the States might make false returns and then make no provisions for new elections

Mr. Sherman did not know but it might be best to retain the clause, though he had himself sufficient confidence in the State Legislatures. The motion of Mr. P. & Mr. R. did not prevail

The word "respectively" was inserted after the word "State"

On the motion of Mr Read the word "their" was struck out, & "regulations in such cases" inserted in place of "provisions concerning them". the clause then reading— "but regulations, in each of the foregoing cases may at any time, be made or altered by the Legislature of the U. S. This was meant to give the Natl. Legislature a power not only to alter the provisions of the States, but to make regulations in case the States should fail or refuse altogether.

Art. VI. Sect. 1—as thus amended was agreed to nem. con.

Adjourned.

2

FEDERAL FARMER, NO. 3
10 Oct. 1787
Storing 2.8.25

The branches of the legislature are essential parts of the fundamental compact, and ought to be so fixed by the people, that the legislature cannot alter itself by modifying the elections of its own members. This, by a part of Art. 1. Sect. 4. the general legislature may do, it may evidently so regulate elections as to secure the choice of any particular description of men.—It may make the whole state one district—make the capital, or any places in the state, the place or places of election—it may declare that the five men (or whatever the number may be the state may chuse) who shall have the most votes shall be considered as chosen— In this case it is easy to perceive how the people who live scattered in the inland towns will bestow their votes on different men—and how a few men in a city, in any order or profession, may unite and place any five men they please highest among those that may be voted for—and all this may be done constitutionally, and by those silent operations, which are not immediately perceived by the people in general.—I know it is urged, that the general legislature will be disposed to regulate elections on fair and just principles:—This may be true—good men will generally govern well with almost any constitution: but why in laying the foundation of the social system, need we unnecessarily leave a door open to improper regulations?—This is a very general and unguarded clause, and many evils may flow from that part which authorises the congress to regulate elections—Were it omitted, the regulations of elections would be solely in the respective states, where the people are substantially represented; and where the elections ought to be regulated, otherwise to secure a representation from all parts of the community, in making the constitution, we ought to provide for dividing each state into a proper number of districts, and for confining the electors in each district to the choice of some men, who shall have a permanent interest and residence in it; and also for this essential object, that the representative elected shall have a majority of the votes of those electors who shall attend and give their votes.

3

VOX POPULI, NO. 1
29 Oct. 1787
Storing 4.4.2–6

By this clause, the *time, place* and *manner* of choosing representatives is *wholly* at the disposal of Congress.

Why the Convention, who formed the proposed Constitution, wished to invest Congress with such a power, I am by no means capable of saying; or why the good people of this commonwealth should delegate such a power to them, is no less hard to determine.—But as the subject is open for discussion, I shall make a little free inquiry into the matter.

And, first. What national advantage is there to be acquired by giving them such a power?

The only advantage which I have heard proposed by it is, to prevent a partial representation of the several states in Congress; "for if the time, manner and place were left wholly in the hands of the state legislatures, it is probable they would not make provision by appointing time, manner and place for election; in which case there *could* be no election, and consequently the federal government weakened."

But *this* provision is by no means sufficient to prevent an evil of *that* nature; for will any reasonable man suppose, that when the legislature of any state, who are annually chosen, are so corrupt as to break thro' *that* government which they have formed, and refuse to appoint time, place and manner of choosing representatives—I say, can any person suppose, that a state, so corrupt, would not be full as likely to neglect, or even refuse, to choose representatives at the time and place and in the manner prescribed by Congress? Surely they would.—So it could answer no good national purpose on *that* account; and I have not heard any other national advantage proposed thereby.

We will now proceed, in the next place, to consider *why* the people of this commonwealth should vest Congress with such a power.—

No one proposes that it would be any advantage to the people of this state; therefore, it must be considered as a matter of indifference, except there is an opportunity for its operating to *their* disadvantage: in which case, I conceive it ought to be disapprobated.

Whether there is danger of its operating to the good people's disadvantage, shall now be the subject of our inquiry.—

Supposing Congress should direct, that the representatives of this commonwealth should be chosen all in one town, (Boston, for instance) on the first day of March—would not that be a very injurious institution to the good people of this commonwealth?—Would not there be at least nine-tenths of the landed interest of this commonwealth intirely unrepresented? Surely one may reasonably imagine there would. What, then, would be the case if Congress should think proper to direct, that the elections should be held at the north-west, south-west or north-east part of the state, the last day of March? How many electors would there attend the business?—And it is a little remarkable, that any gentleman should suppose, that Congress could possibly be in any measure as good judges of the time, place and manner of elections as the legislatures of the several respective states.

4

DEBATE IN PENNSYLVANIA RATIFYING CONVENTION
28 Oct., 11 Nov. 1787
Elliot 2:440–41, 535

[*28 Oct.*]

[James Wilson:] Mr. President, the only proof that is attempted to be drawn from the work itself, is that which has been urged from the fourth section of the first article. I will read it: "The times, places, and manner, of holding elections for senators and representatives, shall be prescribed in each state by the legislature thereof; but the Congress may at any time, by law, make or alter such regulations, except as to the places of choosing senators."

And is this a proof that it was intended to carry on this government after the state governments should be dissolved and abrogated? This clause is not only a proper, but necessary one. I have already shown what pains have been taken in the Convention to secure the preservation of the state governments. I hope, sir, that it was no crime to sow the seed of self-preservation in the federal government; without this clause, it would not possess self-preserving power. By this clause, the times, places, and manner of holding elections, shall be prescribed in each state, by the legislature thereof. I think it highly proper that the federal government should throw the exercise of this power into the hands of the state legislatures; but not that it should be placed there entirely without control.

If the Congress had it not in their power to make regulations, what might be the consequences? Some states might make no regulations at all on the subject. And shall the existence of the House of Representatives, the immediate representation of the people in Congress, depend upon the will and pleasure of the state governments? Another thing may possibly happen; I don't say it will; but we were obliged to guard even against possibilities, as well as probabilities. A legislature may be willing to make the necessary regulations; yet the minority of that legislature may, by absenting themselves, break up the house, and prevent the execution of the intention of the majority. I have supposed the case, that some state governments may make no regulations at all; it is possible, also, that they may make improper regulations. I have heard it surmised by the opponents of this Constitution, that the Congress may order the election for Pennsylvania to be held at Pittsburg, and thence conclude that it would be improper for them to have the exercise of the power. But suppose, on the other hand, that the assembly should order an election to be held at Pittsburg; ought not the general government to have the power to alter such improper election of one of its own constituent parts? But there is an additional reason still that shows the necessity of this provisionary clause. The members of the Senate are elected by the state legislatures. If those legislatures possessed, uncontrolled, the power of prescribing the times, places, and manner, of electing members of the House of Representatives, the members of one branch of the general legislature would be the tenants at will of the electors of the other branch; and the general government would lie prostrate at the mercy of the legislatures of the several states.

[*11 Nov.*]

[Thomas McKean:] Fourth. "That the Congress may by law deprive the electors of a fair choice of their representatives, by fixing improper times, places, and modes of election."

Every House of Representatives are of necessity to be the judges of the elections, returns, and qualifications of its own members. It is therefore their province, as well as duty, to see that they are fairly chosen, and are the legal members; for this purpose, it is proper they should have it in their power to provide that the times, places, and manner of election should be such as to insure free and fair elections.

Annual *Congresses* are expressly secured; they have only a power given to them to take care that the *elections* shall be at convenient and suitable times and places, and conducted in a proper manner; and I cannot discover why we may not intrust these particulars to the representatives of the United States with as much safety as to those of individual states.

In some states the electors vote *viva voce,* in others by ballot. They ought to be uniform, and the elections held on the same day throughout the United States, to prevent corruption or undue influence. Why are we to suppose that Congress will make a bad use of this power, more than the representatives in the several states?

5

BRUTUS, NO. 4
29 Nov. 1787
Storing 2.9.51–54

By section 4, article 1, the Congress are authorized, at any time, by law, to make, or alter, regulations respecting the time, place, and manner of holding elections for senators and representatives, except as to the places of choosing senators. By this clause the right of election itself, is, in a great measure, transferred from the people to their rulers.—One would think, that if any thing was necessary to be made a fundamental article of the original compact, it would be, that of fixing the branches of the legislature, so as to put it out of its power to alter itself by modifying the election of its own members at will and pleasure. When a people once resign the privilege of a fair election, they clearly have none left worth contending for.

It is clear that, under this article, the foederal legislature may institute such rules respecting elections as to lead to the choice of one description of men. The weakness of the representation, tends but too certainly to confer on the

rich and *well-born,* all honours; but the power granted in this article, may be so exercised, as to secure it almost beyond a possibility of controul. The proposed Congress may make the whole state one district, and direct, that the capital (the city of New-York, for instance) shall be the place for holding the election; the consequence would be, that none but men of the most elevated rank in society would attend, and they would as certainly choose men of their own class; as it is true what the *Apostle Paul* saith, that "no man ever yet hated his own flesh, but nourisheth and cherisheth it."—They may declare that those members who have the greatest number of votes, shall be considered as duly elected; the consequence would be that the people, who are dispersed in the interior parts of the state, would give their votes for a variety of candidates, while any order, or profession, residing in populous places, by uniting their interests, might procure whom they pleased to be chosen—and by this means the representatives of the state may be elected by one tenth part of the people who actually vote. This may be effected constitutionally, and by one of those silent operations which frequently takes place without being noticed, but which often produces such changes as entirely to alter a government, subvert a free constitution, and rivet the chains on a free people before they perceive they are forged. Had the power of regulating elections been left under the direction of the state legislatures, where the people are not only nominally but substantially represented, it would have been secure; but if it was taken out of their hands, it surely ought to have been fixed on such a basis as to have put it out of the power of the foederal legislature to deprive the people of it by law. Provision should have been made for marking out the states into districts, and for choosing, by a majority of votes, a person out of each of them of permanent property and residence in the district which he was to represent.

If the people of America will submit to a constitution that will vest in the hands of any body of men a right to deprive them by law of the privilege of a fair election, they will submit to almost any thing. Reasoning with them will be in vain, they must be left until they are brought to reflection by feeling oppression—they will then have to wrest from their oppressors, by a strong hand, that which they now possess, and which they may retain if they will exercise but a moderate share of prudence and firmness.

I know it is said that the dangers apprehended from this clause are merely imaginary, that the proposed general legislature will be disposed to regulate elections upon proper principles, and to use their power with discretion, and to promote the public good. On this, I would observe, that constitutions are not so necessary to regulate the conduct of good rulers as to restrain that of bad ones.—Wise and good men will exercise power so as to promote the public happiness under any form of government. If we are to take it for granted, that those who administer the government under this system, will always pay proper attention to the rights and interests of the people, nothing more was necessary than to say who should be invested with the powers of government, and leave them to exercise it at will and pleasure. Men are apt to be deceived both with respect to their own dispositions and those of others. Though this truth is proved by almost every page of the history of nations, to wit, that power, lodged in the hands of rulers to be used at discretion, is almost always exercised to the oppression of the people, and the aggrandizement of themselves; yet most men think if it was lodged in their hands they would not employ it in this manner.—Thus when the prophet *Elisha* told *Hazael,* "I know the evil that thou wilt do unto the children of Israel; their strong holds wilt thou set on fire, and their young men, wilt thou slay with the sword, and wilt dash their children, and rip up their women with child." Hazael had no idea that he ever should be guilty of such horrid cruelty, and said to the prophet, "Is thy servant a dog that he should do this great thing." Elisha answered. "The Lord hath shewed me that thou shalt be king of Syria." The event proved, that Hazael only wanted an opportunity to perpetrate these enormities without restraint, and he had a disposition to do them, though he himself knew it not.

6

CORNELIUS
18 Dec. 1787
Storing 4.10.10

By this Federal Constitution, each House is to be the judge, not only of the elections, and returns, but also of the *qualifications* of its members; and that, without any other rule than such as they themselves may prescribe. This power in Congress, I take to be equal to that of a negative on elections in general. And the freedom of elections being taken away, where is the security or liberty that is reserved to the citizens under this federal government? But as if this were a light thing, and the liberties of the people not sufficiently cramped by their election being thus exposed to a negative, at the pleasure of each House; the Congress are also vested with the power of prescribing, not only the times and manner of holding elections for Senators; but, the times, manner and *places* of holding elections for Representatives. There is undoubtedly, some interesting and important design in the Congress being, by the Constitution, thus particularly vested with this discretionary power of controuling elections. Will it be urged that, as to such particular times and *places* for holding elections as may be most convenient for the several States, the Congress will be more competent judges than the citizens themselves, or their respective legislatures? This, surely, will not be pretended. The end then of placing this power in the hands of the Congress, cannot have been, the greater convenience of the citizens who are interested and concerned in those elections. But whatever may have been the *design,* it is easy to see that a very interesting and important use may be made of this power; and I can conceive of but one reason why it should be vested in the Congress; particularly as it relates to the *places* of holding elections for Representatives. This power being vested in the Con-

gress, may enable them, from time to time, to throw the elections into such particular parts of the several States where the dispositions of the people shall appear to be the most subservient to the wishes and views of that honourable body; or, where the interests of the major part of the members may be found to lie. Should it so happen (as it probably may) that the major part of the Members of Congress should be elected in, and near the seaport towns; there would, in that case, naturally arise strong inducements for fixing the places for holding elections in such towns, or within their vicinity. This would effectually exclude the distant parts of the several States, and the bulk of the landed interest, from an equal share in that government, in which they are deeply interested.

7

TIMOTHY PICKERING TO CHARLES TILLINGHAST
24 Dec. 1787
Life 2:356–57

The capital error of all these objectors, and which reduces all their reasoning to mere sophistry, is their assuming for granted that our *Federal* rulers will *necessarily have interests separate from those of the people,* and exercise the powers of government not only *arbitrarily* but *wantonly.* But, Sir, on what do they ground such wild surmises? Why, they tell you that Congress will have power to regulate the elections of Senators and Representatives, and that, possessing this power, they will exercise it to deprive the people of the freedom of election. The "Federal Farmer" says, "The general legislature *may* so regulate elections, as to secure the choice of any particular description of men; it may make the whole State one district; make the capital, or any places in the State, the place or places of election," and so forth, in the same chimerical strain. But does he, does any man of common sense, really believe that the Congress will ever be guilty of so wanton an exercise of power? Will the immediate Representatives of the people, in Congress, ever consent to so oppressive a regulation? For whose benefit would they do it? Would not the first attempt certainly exclude themselves? And would not the State legislatures, at their next election of Senators, as certainly reject every one who should give his assent to such a law? and if the President did not firmly give his qualified negative to it, would he ever again be placed in the chair of government? What other oppressive regulation can they make, which will not immediately, or in a short time, affect *them* in common with their fellow-citizens? What, then, have we to fear on this head? But will no advantage arise from the *controlling* power of Congress? Yes, certainly. I say a *controlling,* because a candid interpretation of that section in the Constitution will show that it is intended and expected, that the times, places, and modes of electing Senators and Representatives should be regulated by the State legislatures; but that, if any particular State government should be refractory, and, in the pride of sovereignty, or influenced by any other motive, should either make no such regulations or improper ones, then the Congress will have power to make such regulations as will ensure to the *people* their rights of election and establish a *uniformity in the mode of constituting the members of the Senate and House of Representatives.* If we give a loose to our imaginations, we may suppose that the State governments *may* abuse their power, and regulate these elections in such manner as would be highly inconvenient to the people, and injurious to the common interests of the States. And, if such abuses should be attempted, will not the *people* rejoice that Congress have a *constitutional* power of correcting them?

8

LUTHER MARTIN, GENUINE INFORMATION
1788
Storing 2.4.43

But even this provision *apparently* for the *security* of the *State governments, inadquate* as it is, is *entirely left* at the *mercy* of the general government, for by the fourth section of the first article, it is *expressly provided,* that the *Congress* shall have a power to *make* and *alter* all regulations concerning the *time* and *manner* of *holding elections for senators;* a provision, *expressly looking forward to,* and *I have no doubt designed for the utter extinction and abolition of all State governments;* nor will this, I believe, be doubted by any person, when I inform you that some of the warm advocates and patrons of the system in convention, *strenuously opposed* the *choice* of the senators by the *State legislatures, insisting* that the *State governments ought not to be introduced in any manner* so as to be *component parts of,* or *instruments for carrying into execution,* the general government: Nay, so far were the friends of the system from pretending that they meant it, or considered it as a *federal* system, that on the question being proposed, "that a union of the States, merely federal, ought to be the sole object of the exercise of the powers vested in the convention;" it was negatived by a majority of the members, and it was resolved, "that a *national* government ought to be formed"—afterwards the word *"national"* was struck out by them, because they thought the *word* might tend to *alarm:* and although *now,* they who *advocate* the system, pretend to call themselves *federalists,* in convention the distinction was quite the reverse; those who *opposed* the system, were *there* considered and styled the *federal party,* those who *advocated* it, the *antifederal.*

9

FEDERAL FARMER, NO. 12
12 Jan. 1788
Storing 2.8.161–65

I think we are all sufficiently acquainted with the progress of elections to see, that the regulations, as to times, places, and the manner merely of holding elections, may, under the constitution, easily be made useful or injurious. It is important then to enquire, who has the power to make regulations, and who ought to have it. By the constitution, the state legislatures shall prescribe the times, places, and manner of holding elections, but congress may make or alter such regulations. Power in congress merely to alter those regulations, made by the states, could answer no valuable purposes; the states might make, and congress alter them *ad infinitum:* and when the state should cease to make, or should annihilate its regulations, congress would have nothing to alter. But the states shall make regulations, and congress may make such regulations as the clause stands: the true construction is, that when congress shall see fit to regulate the times, places, and manner of holding elections, congress may do it, and state regulations, on this head, must cease; for if state regulations could exist, after congress should make a system of regulations, there would, or might, be two incompatible systems of regulations relative to the same subject.

It has been often urged, that congress ought to have power to make these regulations, otherwise the state legislatures, by neglecting to make provision for elections, or by making improper regulations, may destroy the general government. It is very improbable that any state legislature will adopt measures to destroy the representation of its own constituents in congress, especially when the state must, represented in congress or not, pay its proportion of the expence of keeping up the government, and even of the representatives of the other states, and be subject to their laws. Should the state legislatures be disposed to be negligent, or to combine to break up congress, they have a very simple way to do it, as the constitution now stands— they have only to neglect to chuse senators, or to appoint the electors of the president, and vice-president: there is no remedy provided against these last evils: nor is it to be presumed, that if a sufficient number of state legislatures to break up congress, should, by neglect or otherwise, attempt to do it, that the people, who yearly elect those legislatures, would elect under the regulations of congress. These and many other reasons must evince, that it was not merely to prevent an annihilation of the federal government that congress has power to regulate elections.

It has been urged also, that the state legislatures chuse the federal senators, one branch, and may injure the people, who chuse the other, by improper regulations; that therefore congress, in which the people will immediately have one, the representative branch, ought to have power to interfere in behalf of the people, and rectify such improper regulations. The advocates have said much about the opponents dwelling upon possibilities; but to suppose the people will find it necessary to appeal to congress to restrain the oppressions of the state legislatures, is supposing a possibility indeed. Can any man in his senses suppose that the state legislatures, which are so numerous as almost to be the people themselves, all branches of them depending yearly, for the most part, on the elections of the people, will abuse them in regulating federal elections, and make it proper to transfer the power to congress, a body, one branch of which is chosen once in six years by these very legislatures, and the other biennially, and not half so numerous as even the senatorial branches in those legislatures?

Senators are to be chosen by the state legislatures, where there are two branches the appointment must be, I presume, by a concurrent resolution, in passing which, as in passing all other legislative acts each branch will have a negative; this will give the senatorial branch just as much weight in the appointment as the democratic: the two branches form a legislature only when acting separately, and therefore, whenever the members of the two branches meet, mix and vote individually in one room, for making an election, it is expressly so directed by the constitutions. If the constitution, by fixing the choice to be made by the legislatures, has given each branch an equal vote, as I think it has, it cannot be altered by any regulations.

On the whole, I think, all general principles respecting electors ought to be carefully established by the constitution, as the qualifications of the electors and of elected: the number of the representatives, and the inhabitants of each given district, called on to chuse a man from among themselves by a majority of votes; leaving it to the legislature only so to regulate, from time to time, the extent of the districts so as to keep the representatives proportionate to the number of inhabitants in the several parts of the country; and so far as regulations as to elections cannot be fixed by the constitution, they ought to be left to the state legislatures, they coming far nearest to the people themselves; at most, congress ought to have power to regulate elections only where a state shall neglect to make them.

10

Debate in Massachusetts Ratifying Convention
16–17, 21 Jan. 1788
Elliot 2:22–35

[*16 Jan.*]

Mr. PIERCE, (from Partridgefield,) after reading the 4th section, wished to know the opinion of gentlemen on it, as Congress appeared thereby to have a power to regulate the *time, place, and manner* of holding elections. In respect to the manner, said Mr. P., suppose the legislature of this state should prescribe that the choice of the federal rep-

resentatives should be in the same manner as that of governor,—a majority of all the votes in the state being necessary to make it such,—and Congress should deem it an improper *manner*, and should order that it be as practised in several of the Southern States, where the highest number of votes make a choice;—have they not power by this section to do so? Again, as to the *place*, continues Mr. P., may not Congress direct that the election for Massachusetts shall be held in Boston? and if so, it is possible that, previous to the election, a number of the electors may meet, agree upon the eight delegates, and propose the same to a few towns in the vicinity, who, agreeing in sentiment, may meet on the day of election, and carry their list by a major vote. He did not, he said, say that this would be the case; but he wished to know if it was not a possible one. As the federal representatives, who are to form the democratical part of the general government, are to be a check on the representatives of the sovereignty, the senate, he thought the utmost caution ought to be used to have their elections as free as possible. He observed that, as men have ever been fond of power, we must suppose they ever will continue so; and concluded by observing, that our caution ought in the present case to be greater, as, by the proposed Constitution, no qualification of property was required in a representative; and it might be in the power of some people thereby to choose a bankrupt for a representative, in order to give such representatives employment, or that he might make laws favorable to such a description of the people.

Gen. PORTER (from Hadley) endeavored to obviate the objections of Mr. Pierce, by showing the almost *impossibility* of Congress making a law whereby eight men could be elected, as Mr. Pierce had supposed; and he thought it equally impossible for the people to choose a person to take care of their property, who had none himself.

Mr. BISHOP rose, and observed that, by the 4th section, Congress would be enabled to control the elections of representatives. It has been said, says he, that this power was given in order that refractory states may be made to do their duty. But if so, sir, why was it not so mentioned? If that was the intention, he asked why the clause did not run thus: "The times, places, and manner of holding elections for senators and representatives, shall be prescribed in each state by the legislature thereof; but," *if any state shall refuse or neglect so to do,* "Congress may," &c. This, he said, would admit of no prevarication. I am, says Mr. B., for giving Congress as much power to do good as possible. It has been said, Mr. President, that the conduct of Rhode Island, in recalling its delegates from Congress, has demonstrated the necessity of such a power being lodged in Congress. I have been informed by people belonging to Rhode Island, sir, that that state never has recalled her delegates from Congress. I do not believe it has. And I call upon the gentleman who mentioned it to authenticate the fact.

The Hon. Mr. KING rose, and assured the Convention that the state of Rhode Island did, by a solemn resolution, some time since, recall its delegates from Congress.

The Hon. Mr. GORHAM confirmed what Mr. K. had said, and added, that, during the session of the federal

Convention, when seven states only were represented in Congress, application was made by two companies for the purchase of lands, the sale of which would have sunk seven or eight millions of dollars of the Continental debt, and the most pressing letters were sent on to Rhode Island to send on its delegates; but that state refused: the consequence was, the contract could not then be made.

Mr. BISHOP confessed himself convinced of the fact. He proceeded to observe, that, if the states shall refuse to do their duty, then let the power be given to Congress to oblige them to do it. But if they do their duty, Congress ought not to have the power to control elections. In an uncontrolled representation, says Mr. B., lies the security of freedom; and he thought by these clauses, that that freedom was sported with. In fact, says he, the moment we give Congress this power, the liberties of the yeomanry of this country are at an end. But he trusted they would never give it; and he felt a consolation from the reflection.

The 4th section, which provides that the state legislatures shall prescribe the time, place, and manner of holding elections, and that Congress may at any time make or alter them, except in those of senators, [*though not in regular order,*] under deliberation.

The Hon. Mr. STRONG followed Mr. Bishop, and pointed out the necessity there is for the 4th section. The power, says he, to regulate the elections of our federal representatives must be lodged somewhere. I know of but two bodies wherein it can be lodged—*the legislatures of the several states, and the general Congress.* If the legislative bodies of the states, who must be supposed to know at what time, and in what place and manner, the elections can best be held, should so appoint them, it cannot be supposed that Congress, by the power granted by this section, will alter them; but if the legislature of a state should refuse to make such regulations, the consequence will be, that the representatives will not be chosen, and the general government will be dissolved. In such case, can gentlemen say that a power to remedy the evil is not necessary to be lodged somewhere? And where can it be lodged but in Congress? I will consider its advantage in another respect. We know, sir, that a negligence in the appointment of rulers is the characteristic of all nations. In this state, and since the establishment of our present constitution, the first officers of government have been elected by less than one tenth part of the electors of the state. We also know that our town meetings, for the choice of officers, are generally attended by an inconsiderable part of the qualified voters. People attend so much to their private interest, that they are apt to neglect this right. Nations have lost their liberties by neglecting their privileges; consequently Congress ought to have an interposing power to awaken the people when thus negligent. Even supposing, sir, the provisional clause suggested by the worthy gentleman from Norton should be added, would not Congress then be the judges whether the elections in the several states were constitutional and proper? If so, it will then stand on the same ground it now does. It appears evident that there must be a general power to regulate general elections. Gentlemen have said, the proposed Constitution was in some places ambiguous. I wish they would point out the particular instances of ambiguity; for my part, I think the whole of it is expressed in the plain, common language of mankind. If any parts are not so explicit as they could be, it cannot be attributed to any design; for I believe a great majority of the men who formed it were sincere and honest men.

Mr. BISHOP said the great difficulty with him was, that the power given by the 4th section was unlimited; and he did not yet see that any advantage would arise from its being so.

Mr. CABOT, (of Beverly,) not having spoken upon the question of biennial elections of representatives, begged leave to revert to that subject, so far as to add to what had been said by others, that we should consider the particular business which that body will be frequently called upon to transact, especially in the way of revenue. We should consider that, on a question of supplies of money to support a war, or procure a treaty, it will be impossible for those representatives to judge of the expediency or inexpediency of such supplies, until they shall have had time to become acquainted with the general system of federal politics, in its connection or relation to foreign powers; because upon the situation of those must depend the propriety or impropriety of granting supplies. If to this be added a due attention to the easiest way of raising such supplies, it must appear that biennial elections are as frequent as is consistent with using the power of the representatives for the benefit of their constituents.

Mr. C. then turned to the 4th section, now under debate, and said, It gives me pain to see the anxiety of different gentlemen concerning this paragraph under consideration, as it evinces a conviction in their minds of what I believe to be true—*that a free and equal representation is the best, if not the only foundation upon which a free government can be built;* and, consequently, that the greatest care should be taken in laying it. I am, sir, one of *the people;* such I shall continue; and, with their feelings, I hold "that the *right* of electing persons to represent the *people* in the federal government, is an important and sacred right." The opinions that have been offered upon the manner in which the exercise of this right is provided for by the 4th section, satisfies me that we are all solicitous for the same end, and that we only differ as to the means of attaining it; and for my own part, I confess that I prize the 4th section as highly as any in the Constitution; because I consider the *democratic* branch of the national government, the branch chosen immediately for the people, as intended to be a *check* on the *federal* branch, which latter is not an immediate representation of the people of America, and is not chosen by them, but is a representation of the sovereignty of the individual states, and its members delegated by the several state legislatures; and if the state legislatures are suffered to regulate conclusively the elections of the democratic branch, they may, by such an interference, first weaken, and at last destroy, that check; they may at first diminish, and finally annihilate, that control of the general government, which the people ought always to have through their immediate representatives. As one of the *people,* therefore, I repeat, that, in my mind, the 4th section is to be as highly prized as any in the Constitution.

Mr. PARSONS contended for vesting in Congress the

powers contained in the 4th section, not only as those powers were necessary for preserving the union, but also for securing to the people their equal rights of election. He considered the subject very fully; but we are able to give our readers very imperfectly the heads of his speech. In the Congress, not only the sovereignty of the states is represented in the Senate, but, to balance their power, and to give the people a suitable and efficient check upon them, the federal representatives are introduced into Congress. The legislatures of the several states are the constituents of the Senate, and the people are the constituents of the Representatives. These two branches, therefore, have different constituents, and as they are designed as mutual checks upon each other, and to balance the legislative powers, there will be frequent struggles and contentions between them. The Senate will wish to control, depress, and render inefficient the Representatives; the same disposition in the Representatives towards the Senate, will produce the like exertions on their part. The Senate will call upon their constituents, the legislatures, for aid; the Representatives will look up to the people for support. If, therefore, the power of making and altering the regulations defined in this section, is vested absolutely in the legislature, the Representatives will very soon be reduced to an undue dependence upon the Senate, because the power of influencing and controlling the election of the representatives of the people, will be exerted without control by the constituents of the senators. He further observed, that there was much less danger in trusting these powers in Congress, than in the state legislatures. For if the federal representatives wished to introduce such regulations as would secure to them their places, and a continuance in office, the federal Senate would never consent, because it would increase the influence and check of the Representatives; and, on the other hand, if the Senate were aiming at regulations to increase their own influence by depressing the Representatives, the consent of the latter would never be obtained; and no other regulations would ever obtain the consent of both branches of the legislature, but such as did not affect their neutral rights and the balance of government; and those regulations would be for the benefit of the people. But a state legislature, under the influence of their senators, who would have their fullest confidence, or under the influence of ambitious or popular characters, or in times of popular commotion, and when faction and party spirit run high, would introduce such regulations as would render the rights of the people insecure and of little value. They might make an unequal and partial division of the states into districts for the election of representatives, or they might even disqualify one third of the electors. Without these powers in Congress, the people can have no remedy; but the 4th section provides a remedy, a controlling power in a legislature, composed of senators and representatives of twelve states, without the influence of our commotions and factions, who will hear impartially, and preserve and restore to the people their equal and sacred rights of election. Perhaps it then will be objected, that from the supposed opposition of interests in the federal legislature, they may never agree upon any regulations; but regulations necessary for the interests of the people can never be opposed to the interests of either of the branches of the federal legislature; because that the interests of the people require that the mutual powers of that legislature should be preserved unimpaired, in order to balance the government. Indeed, if the Congress could never agree on any regulations, then certainly no objection to the 4th section can remain; for the regulations introduced by the state legislatures will be the governing rule of elections, until Congress can agree upon alterations.

Mr. WIDGERY insisted that we had a right to be jealous of our rulers, who ought never to have a power which they could abuse. The 4th section ought to have gone further; it ought to have had the provision in it mentioned by Mr. Bishop; there would then be a mutual check. And he still wished it to be further explained. The worthy gentleman contested the similitude made by the honorable gentleman from Newburyport, between the power to be given to Congress by the 4th section, to compel the states to send representatives, and the power given to the legislatures by our own constitution, to oblige towns to send representatives to the General Court, by observing that the case was materially different; as, in the latter, if any town refuses to send representatives, a power of *fining* such towns only is given. It is in vain, said Mr. Widgery, to say that rulers are not subject to passions and prejudices. In the late General Court, of which I was a member, I would willingly have deprived the three western counties from sending delegates to this house, as I *then* thought it necessary. But, sir, what would have been the consequence? A large part of the state would have been deprived of their dearest privileges. I mention this, sir, to show the force of passion and prejudice.

The Hon. Mr. WHITE said, we ought to be jealous of rulers. All the godly men we read of have failed; nay, he would not trust a "flock of Moseses." If we give up this section, says he, there is nothing left. Suppose the Congress should say that none should be electors but those worth 50 or a £100 sterling, cannot they do it? Yes, said he, they can; and if any lawyer (alluding to Mr. Parsons) can beat me out of it, I will give him ten guineas.

Col. JONES (of Bristol) thought, by this power to regulate elections, Congress might keep themselves in to all duration.

The Rev. Mr. PERLEY wished Mr. Gerry might be asked some questions on this section. [But Mr. Gerry was not in the house.]

Mr. J. C. JONES said, it was not right to argue the *possibility of the abuse of any measure* against its adoption. The power granted to Congress by the 4th section, says he, is a *necessary* power; it will provide against *negligence* and *dangerous designs*. The senators and representatives of this state, Mr. President, are now chosen by a small number of electors; and it is likely we shall grow equally negligent of our federal elections; or, sir, a state may *refuse* to send to Congress its representatives, as Rhode Island has done. Thus we see its necessity.

To say that the power may be abused, is saying what will apply to all *power*. The federal representatives will represent *the people*; they will be *the people*; and it is not *probable* they will abuse themselves. Mr. J. concluded with repeating, that the arguments against this power could be urged against any power whatever.

Dr. JARVIS. Many gentlemen have inferred from the right of regulating elections, by the 4th section, being invested in the federal head, that the powers of wresting this essential privilege from the people would be equally delegated. But it appeared to him, he said, that there is a very material distinction in the two cases; for, however possible it may be that this controlling authority may be abused, it by no means followed that Congress, in any situation, could strip the people of their right to a direct representation. If he could believe in this, he should readily join in sentiment with gentlemen on the other side of the house, that this section alone would be a sufficient objection to the Constitution itself. The right of election, founded on the principle of equality, was, he said, the basis on which the whole superstructure was erected; this right was inherent in the people; it was unalienable in its nature, and it could not be destroyed without presuming a power to subvert the Constitution, of which this was the principal; and by recurring to the 2d section, it would appear that *"representatives and direct taxes shall be apportioned among the several states according to their respective numbers;"* it equally appeared that 30,000 inhabitants were entitled to send a representative, and that wherever this number was found, they would have a right to be represented in the federal legislature. If it was argued that Congress might abuse their power, and, by varying the places of election, distress the people, it could only be observed, that such a wanton abuse could not be supposed; but, if it could go to the annihilation of the right, he contended the people would not submit. He considered the Constitution as an elective democracy, in which the sovereignty still rested in the people, and he by no means could believe that this article was so alarming in its nature, or dangerous in its tendency, as many gentlemen had supposed.

Mr. HOLMES, in reply to Dr. Jarvis, said, the worthy gentleman's superstructure must fall to the ground; for the Constitution does not provide that every 30,000 shall send a representative, but that it shall not exceed one for every 30,000.

[17 Jan.]

Hon. Mr. TURNER. Mr. President, I am pleased with the ingenuity of some gentlemen in defence of this section. I am so impressed with the love of our liberty, so dearly bought, that I heartily acquiesce to compulsory laws, for the people ought to be obliged to attend to their interest. But I do not wish to give Congress a power which they can abuse; and I wish to know whether such a power is not contained in this section? I think it is. I now proceed, sir, to the consideration of an idea, that Congress may alter the place for choosing representatives in the general Congress: they may order that it may be at the extremity of a state, and, by their influence, may there prevail that persons may be chosen, who otherwise would not; by reason that a part of the qualified voters, in part of the state, would be so incommoded thereby, as to be debarred from their right as much as if they were bound at home. If so,

such a circumstance would militate against the Constitution, which allows every man to vote. Altering the *place* will put it so far in the power of Congress, as that the representatives chosen will not be the true and genuine representatives of the people, but creatures of the Congress; and so far as they are so, so far are the people deprived of their rights, and the choice will be made in an irregular and unconstitutional manner. When this alteration is made by Congress, may we not suppose whose reëlection will be provided for? Would it not be for those who were chosen before? The great law of self-preservation will prevail. It is true, they might, one time in a hundred, provide for a friend; but most commonly for themselves. But, however honorable the Convention may be who proposed this article, I think it is a genuine power for Congress to perpetuate themselves—a power that cannot be unexceptionably exercised in any case whatever. Knowing the numerous arts that designing men are prone to, to secure their election and perpetuate themselves, it is my hearty wish that a rotation may be provided for. I respect and revere the Convention who proposed this Constitution. In order that the power given to Congress may be more palatable, some gentlemen are pleased to hold up the idea, that we may be blessed with sober, solid, upright men in Congress. I wish that we may be favored with such rulers; but I fear they will not all, if most, be the best moral or political characters. It gives me pain, and I believe it gives pain to others, thus to characterize the country in which I was born. I will endeavor to guard against any injurious reflections against my fellow-citizens. But they must have their true characters; and if I represent them wrong, I am willing to make concessions. I think that the operation of paper money, and the practice of privateering, have produced a gradual decay of morals; introduced pride, ambition, envy, lust of power; produced a decay of patriotism, and the love of commutative justice; and I am apprehensive these are the invariable concomitants of the luxury in which we are unblessedly involved, almost to our total destruction. In the lower ranks of people, luxury and avarice operate to the want of public duty and the payment of debts. These demonstrate the necessity of an energetic government. As people become more luxurious, they become more incapacitated for governing themselves. And are we not so? Alike people, alike prince. But suppose it should so happen, that the administrators of this Constitution should be preferable to the corrupt mass of the people, in point of manners, morals, and rectitude; power will give a keen edge to the principles I have mentioned. Ought we not, then, to put all checks and controls on governors for the public safety? Therefore, instead of giving Congress powers they may not abuse, we ought to withhold our hands from granting such as must be abused if exercised. This is a general observation. But to the point; at the time of the restoration, the people of England were so vexed and worn down by the *anarchical* and confused state of the nation, owing to the commonwealth not being well digested, that they took an opposite career; they run mad with loyalty, and would have given Charles any thing he could have asked. Pardon me, sir, if I say I feel the want of an energetic government, and the dangers to which this dear country is reduced, as much as any citizen of the United States; but I cannot prevail on myself to adopt a government which wears the face of power, without examining it. Relinquishing a *hair's breadth* in a constitution, is a great deal; for by small degrees has liberty, in all nations, been wrested from the hands of the people. I know great powers are necessary to be given to Congress, but I wish they may be well guarded.

Judge SUMNER, remarking on Gen. Thompson's frequent exclamation of *"O my country!"* expressed from an apprehension that the Constitution would be adopted, said, that expression might be used with great propriety, should this Convention reject it. The honorable gentleman then proceeded to demonstrate the necessity of the 4th section; the absurdity of the supposition that Congress would remove the places of election to remote parts of the states; combated the idea that Congress would, when chosen, act as bad as possible; and concluded by asking, if a war should take place, (and it was supposable,) if France and Holland should send an army to collect the millions of livres they have lent us in the time of our distresses, and that army should be in possession of the seat of government of any particular state, (as was the case when Lord Cornwallis ravaged Carolina,) and that the state legislature could not appoint electors,—is not a power to provide for such elections necessary to be lodged in the general Congress?

Mr. WIDGERY denied the statement of Dr. Jarvis (that every 30,000 persons can elect one representative) to be just, as the Constitution provides that the number *shall not exceed* one to every 30,000; it did not follow, he thought, that the 30,000 shall elect one. But, admitting that they have a right to choose one,—we will suppose Congress should order an election to be in Boston in January, and from the scarcity of money, &c., not a fourth part could attend; would not three quarters of the people be deprived of their right?

Rev. Mr. WEST. I rise to express my astonishment at the arguments of some gentlemen against this section. They have only started *possible* objections. I wish the gentlemen would show us that what they so much deprecate is *probable*. Is it probable that we shall choose men to ruin us? Are we to object to all governments? and because power *may* be abused, shall we be reduced to anarchy and a state of nature? What hinders our state legislatures from abusing their powers? They may violate the Constitution; they may levy taxes oppressive and intolerable, to the amount of all our property. An argument which proves too much, it is said, proves nothing. Some say Congress may remove the place of elections to the state of South Carolina. This is inconsistent with the words of the Constitution, which says, *"that the elections, in each state, shall be prescribed by the legislature thereof,"* &c., and that representation be apportioned according to numbers; it will frustrate the end of the Constitution, and is a reflection on the gentlemen who formed it. Can we, sir, suppose them so wicked, so vile, as to recommend an article so dangerous? Surely, gentlemen who argue these *possibilities*, show they have a very weak cause. That we may all be free from passions, prepossessions, and party spirit, I sincerely hope; otherwise, reason will have

no effect. I hope there are none here but who are open to conviction, as it is the surest method to gain the suffrage of our consciences. The honorable gentleman from Scituate has told us that the people of England, at the restoration, *on account of the inconveniences of the confused state of the commonwealth, run mad with loyalty.* If the gentleman means to apply this to us, we ought to adopt this Constitution; for if the people are *running mad* after an energetic government, it is best to stop now, as by this rule they may run farther, and get a worse one; therefore the gentleman's arguments turn right against himself. Is it possible that imperfect men can make a perfect constitution? Is it possible that a frame of government can be devised by such weak and frail creatures, but what must savor of that weakness? Though there are some things that I do not like in this Constitution, yet I think it necessary it should be adopted. For may we not rationally conclude, that the persons we shall choose to administer it will be, in general, good men?

Gen. THOMPSON. Mr. President, I have frequently heard of the abilities of the learned and reverend gentleman last speaking, and now I am witness to them; but, sir, one thing surprises me: it is, to hear the worthy gentleman insinuate that our federal rulers would undoubtedly be *good men*, and that, therefore, we have little to fear from their being intrusted with all power. This, sir, is quite contrary to the common language of the clergy, who are continually representing mankind as reprobate and deceitful, and that we really grow worse and worse day after day. I really believe we do, sir, and I make no doubt to prove it before I sit down, and from the Old Testament. When I consider the man that slew the lion and the bear, and that he was a man after *God's own heart*,—when I consider his son, blessed with *all wisdom*, and the errors they fell into,—I extremely doubt the infallibility of human nature. Sir, I suspect my own heart, and I shall suspect our rulers.

Dr. HOLTON thought this paragraph necessary to a complete system of government. [*But the honorable gentleman spoke so low that he could not be heard distinctly throughout.*]

Capt. SNOW. It has been said, Mr. President, that there is too much power delegated to Congress by the section under consideration. I doubt it; I think power the hinge on which the whole Constitution turns. Gentlemen have talked about Congress moving the place of election from Georgia to the Mohawk River; but I never can believe it. I will venture to conjecture we shall have some honest men in our Congress. We read that there were two who brought a *good report*—Caleb and Joshua. Now, if there are but two in Congress who are honest men, and Congress should attempt to do what the gentlemen say they will, (which will be *high treason*,) they will bring a *report* of it; and I stand ready to leave my wife and family, sling my knapsack, travel westward, to cut their heads off. I, sir, since the war, have had commerce with six different nations of the globe: I have inquired in what estimation America is held; and if I may believe good, honest, credible men, I find this country held in the same light, by foreign nations, as a well-behaved negro is in a gentleman's family. Suppose, Mr. President, I had a chance to make a good voyage, but I tie my captain up to such strict orders, that he can go to no other island to sell my cargo, although there is a certainty of his doing well; the consequence is, he returns, but makes a bad voyage, because he had not power enough to act his judgment; (for honest men do right.) Thus, sir, Congress cannot save us from destruction, because we tie their hands, and give them no power; (I think people have lost their privileges by not improving them;) and I like this power being vested in Congress as well as any paragraph in the Constitution; for, as the man is accountable for his conduct, I think there is no danger. Now, Mr. President, to take all things into consideration, something more must be said to convince me to the contrary.

[Several other gentlemen went largely into the debate on the 4th section, which those in favor of it demonstrated to be necessary; first, as it may be used to correct a negligence in elections; secondly, as it will prevent the dissolution of the government by designing and refractory states; thirdly, as it will operate as a check, in favor of the people, against any designs of the federal Senate, and their constituents, the state legislatures, to deprive the people of their right of election; and fourthly, as it provides a remedy for the evil, should any state, by invasion, or other cause, not have it in its power to appoint a place, where the citizens thereof may meet to choose their federal representatives. Those against it urged that the power is unlimited and unnecessary.]

[*21 Jan.*]

Mr. AMES rose to answer several *objections*. He would forbear, if possible, to go over the ground which had been already well trodden. The fourth section had been, he said, well discussed, and he did not mean to offer any formal argument or new observations upon it. It had been said, the power of regulating *elections* was given to Congress. He asked, if a motion was brought forward in Congress, on that particular, subjecting the states to any inconvenience, whether it was probable such a motion could obtain. It had been also said, that our federal legislature would endeavor to perpetuate themselves in office; and that the love of power was predominant. Mr. Ames asked how the gentlemen prevailed on themselves to trust the state legislature. He thought it was from a degree of confidence that was placed in them. At present we trust Congress with power; nay, we trust the representatives of Rhode Island and Georgia. He thought it was better to trust the general government than a foreign state. Mr. A. acknowledged he came with doubts of the fourth section. Had his objections remained, he would have been obliged to vote against the Constitution; but now he thought, if all the Constitution was as clear as this section, it would meet with little opposition.

Judge DANA. This section, Mr. President, has been subject to much dispute and difficulty. I did not come here approving of every paragraph of this Constitution. I supposed this clause dangerous; it has been amply discussed; and I am now convinced that this paragraph is much better as it stands, than with the amendment, which is, that Congress be restricted in the appointing of *"time, place, &c.,"* unless when the state legislatures refuse to make

them. I have altered my opinion on this point; these are my reasons:—It is apparent, the intention of the Convention was to set Congress on a different ground; that a part should proceed directly from the people, and not from their substitutes, the legislatures; therefore the legislature ought not to control the elections. The legislature of Rhode Island has lately formed a plan to alter their representation to corporations, which ought to be by numbers. Look at Great Britain, where the injustice of this mode is apparent. Eight tenths of the people there have no voice in the elections. A borough of but two or three cottages has a right to send two representatives to *Parliament*, while Birmingham, a large and populous manufacturing town, lately sprung up, cannot send one. The legislature of Rhode Island are about adopting this plan, in order to deprive the towns of Newport and Providence of their weight, and that thereby the legislature may have a power to counteract the will of a majority of the people.

Mr. COOLEY (of Amherst) thought Congress, in the present instance, would, from the powers granted by the Constitution, have authority to control elections, and thereby endanger liberty.

Dr. TAYLOR wished to ask the gentleman from Newburyport, whether the two branches of Congress could not agree to play into each other's hands; and, by making the *qualifications* of electors £100 by their power of regulating elections, fix the matters of elections so as to keep themselves in.

Hon. Mr. KING rose to pursue the inquiry why the *"place and manner"* of holding elections were omitted in the section under debate. It was to be observed, he said, that, in the Constitution of Massachusetts and other states, the *manner and place* of elections were provided for; the manner was by ballot, and the places, towns; for, said he, we happened to settle originally in townships. But it was different in the Southern States: he would mention an instance. In Virginia, there are but fifteen or twenty towns, and seventy or eighty counties; therefore no rule could be adopted to apply to the whole. If it was practicable, he said, it would be necessary to have a district the fixed place; but this is liable to exceptions; as a district that may now be fully settled, may in time be scarcely inhabited; and the back country, now scarcely inhabited, may be fully settled. Suppose this state thrown into eight *districts,* and a member apportioned to each; if the numbers increase, the representatives and districts will be increased. The matter, therefore, must be left subject to the regulation of the state legislature, or the general government. Suppose the state legislature, the circumstances will be the same. It is truly said, that our representatives are but a part of the Union; that they may be subject to the control of the rest; but our representatives make a ninth part of the whole; and if any authority is vested in Congress, it must be in our favor. But to the subject. In Connecticut they do not choose by numbers, but by corporations. Hartford, one of their largest towns, sends no more delegates than one of their smallest corporations, each town sending two, except latterly, when a town was divided. The same rule is about to be adopted in Rhode Island. The inequality of such representation, where every corporation would have an equal right to send an equal number of representatives, was apparent. In the Southern States, the inequality is greater. By the constitution of South Carolina, the city of Charleston has a right to send thirty representatives to the General Assembly; the whole number of which amounts to two hundred. The back parts of Carolina have increased greatly since the adoption of their constitution, and have frequently attempted an alteration of this unequal mode of representation; but the members from Charleston, having the balance so much in their favor, will not consent to an alteration; and we see that the delegates from Carolina in Congress have always been chosen by the delegates of the city. The representatives, therefore, from that state, will not be chosen *by the people*, but will be the representatives of a faction of that state. If the general government cannot control in this case, how are the people secure? The idea of the honorable gentleman from Douglass, said he, transcends my understanding; for the power of control given by this section extends to the *manner* of election, not the *qualifications* of the electors. The qualifications are age and residence, and none can be preferable.

11

Rufus King, Massachusetts Ratifying
Convention
Jan. 1788
Life 1:304–5

The time, place, and manner of electing Representatives must in the first instance be prescribed by the State Legislatures, but the Congress may make or alter the regulations on the subject: possibly Mr. Gerry may ground his objection upon this authority's being vested in Congress. We wish to submit our remarks on this clause to your candid consideration. We agree and have always contended that the people ought always to enjoy the exclusive right of appointing their Reps. but we also hold it an important principle, that as it is of consequence to the Freedom of the people that they should possess the right of Election, so it is essential to the preservation and existence of the Government, that the people should be bound to exercise it. For this reason in the Constitution of Massachusets not only the persons are clearly designated and their qualifications ascertained, who may vote for Representatives, but the Genl. Court have a right to compel the Electors to exercise their right of Election and thereby to preserve the Government from Dissolution.

If the time, place and manner of Electing Representatives to the General Court was left entirely to the several Towns in the commonwealth, and if the constitution gave no power to the Genl. Court to require and compel the towns to elect Representatives, there wd. be a manifest defect in the Constitution, which, agreeably to the Course of human affairs, might in a short period subvert the Government. Town after Town from disaffection or other

motives might refuse to elect Representatives; counties and larger districts might combine against sending members to the General Court, and in this silent manner the Govt. might be wholly destroyed. If these remarks are just, as applying to this State and prove the propriety of vesting, as the Constitution has done, a power in the Genl. Court to compel the Electors to exercise their right of Election, they are equally just in Relation to Congress, and equally prove the propriety of vesting in that assembly a power to compel the Electors of the federal Representatives to exercise their rights, and for that purpose, if necessary, to make Regulations concerning the time, place and manner of electing members of the H. of Reps.

It may be said that the State Legislatures are more capable of regulating this Subject than the Congress; that Congress may fix improper places, inconvenient Times, and a manner of electing contrary to the usual practice of the several States. It is not a very probable supposition that a law of this nature shd. be enacted by Congress: but let the supposition be ever so probable, as applied to Congress, it is thirteen times more probable that some one of the States may make these inconvenient Regulations as that Congress should enact them. Congress will be interested to preserve the United States entire and to prevent a dismemberment. The individual States may some of them grow rich and powerful; and, as the great members of the antient Confederacies have heretofore done, they may be desirous of becoming wholly independent of the Union, and therefore may either omit to form any Regulations or Laws concerning the Time, place and manner of electing federal Rep. or they may fix on improper places, inconvenient Times, & a manner of electing wholly disagreeable to the people. Should either of these cases take place, and no power be vested in Congress to revise their Laws, or to provide other Regulations, the Union might be dismembered and dissolved without a constitutional power to prevent it. But this revisionary power being vested in Congress, the States will make wise and prudent regulations on the subject of Elections; they will do all that is necessary to keep up a Representation of the People, because they know that in case of omission the Congress will make the necessary provision for this Object. (R. Island was required by Cong. (and refused) to send delegates.)

12

Charles Cotesworth Pinckney,
South Carolina House of Representatives
18 Jan. 1788
Elliot 4:302–4

There will be no necessity, as the honorable gentleman has strangely supposed, for all the freeholders in the state to meet at Charleston to choose five members for the House of Representatives; for the State may be divided into five election districts, and the freeholders in each election district may choose one representative. These freeholders need not all meet at the same place in the district; they may ballot in their particular parishes and counties on the same day, and the ballots may be thence carried into a central part of the district, and opened at the same time; and whoever shall appear to have a majority of the votes of the freeholders of the whole district will be one of the five representatives for this state. But if any state should attempt to fix a very inconvenient time for the election, and name (agreeably to the ideas of the honorable gentleman) only one place in the state, or even one place in one of the five election districts, for the freeholders to assemble to vote, and the people should dislike this arrangement, they can petition the general government to redress this inconvenience, and to fix times and places of election of representatives in the state in a more convenient manner; for, as this house has a right to fix the times and places of election, in each parish and county, for the members of the House of Representatives of this state, so the general government has a similar right to fix the times and places of election, in each state, for the members of the general House of Representatives. Nor is there any real danger to be apprehended from the exercise of this power, as it cannot be supposed that any state will consent to fix the election at inconvenient seasons and places in any other state lest she herself should hereafter experience the same inconvenience; but it is absolutely necessary that Congress should have this superintending power, lest, by the intrigues of a ruling faction in a state, the members of the House of Representatives should not really represent the people of the state, and lest the same faction, through partial state views, should altogether refuse to send representatives of the people to the general government. The general government has not the same authority with regard to the members of the Senate. It would have been improper to have intrusted them with it; for such a power would, in some measure, have authorized them to fix the times and places when and where the state legislatures should convene, and would tend to destroy that necessary check which the general and state governments will have on each other. The honorable gentleman, as if he was determined to object to every part of the Constitution, though he does not approve of electing representatives immediately by the people, or at least cannot conceive how it is to be effected, yet objects to the constitution of the Senate, because the senators are to be elected by the state legislatures, and not immediately by the people. When the Constitution says the people shall elect, the gentleman cries out. "It is chimerical!—the election will be merely virtual." When the Constitution determines that the state legislatures are to elect, he exclaims, "The people's rights are invaded!—the election should be immediately by them, and not by their representatives." How, then, can we satisfy him, as he is determined to censure, in this Constitution, that mode of election which he so highly approves in the old Confederation? The reason why our present state Constitution, made in 1778, changed the mode of electing senators from the mode prescribed by our first constitution, passed in 1776, was because, by the first, the senators were elected by this house, and therefore, being their

mere creatures, they could not be supposed to have that freedom of will as to form a proper check on its proceedings; whereas, in the general Constitution, the House of Representatives will be elected immediately by the people, and represent them and their personal rights individually; the Senate will be elected by the state legislatures, and represent the states in their political capacity; and thus each branch will form a proper and independent check on the other, and the legislative powers will be advantageously balanced.

13

ALEXANDER HAMILTON, FEDERALIST, NO. 59, 397–403
22 Feb. 1788

The natural order of the subject leads us to consider in this place, that provision of the Constitution which authorises the national Legislature to regulate in the last resort the election of its own members. It is in these words— "The *times, places* and *manner* of holding elections for Senators and Representatives, shall be prescribed in each State by the Legislature thereof; but the Congress may at any time by law, make or alter *such regulations* except as to *places* of choosing senators." This provision has not only been declaimed against by those who condemn the Constitution in the gross; but it has been censured by those, who have objected with less latitude and greater moderation; and in one instance, it has been thought exceptionable by a gentleman who has declared himself the advocate of every other part of the system.

I am greatly mistaken, notwithstanding, if there be any article in the whole plan more completely defensible than this. Its propriety rests upon the evidence of this plain proposition, that *every government ought to contain in itself the means of its own preservation.* Every just reasoner will at first sight, approve an adherence to this rule, in the work of the Convention; and will disapprove every deviation from it, which may not appear to have been dictated by the necessity of incorporating into the work some particular ingredient, with which a rigid conformity to the rule was incompatible. Even in this case, though he may acquiesce in the necessity; yet he will not cease to regard a departure from so fundamental a principle, as a portion of imperfection in the system which may prove the seed of future weakness and perhaps anarchy.

It will not be alledged that an election law could have been framed and inserted into the Constitution, which would have been always applicable to every probable change in the situation of the country; and it will therefore not be denied that a discretionary power over elections ought to exist somewhere. It will, I presume, be as readily conceded, that there were only three ways, in which this power could have been reasonably modified and disposed, that it must either have been lodged wholly in the National

Legislature, or wholly in the State Legislatures, or primarily in the latter, and ultimately in the former. The last mode has with reason been preferred by the Convention. They have submitted the regulation of elections for the Foederal Government in the first instance to the local administrations; which in ordinary cases, and when no improper views prevail, may be both more convenient and more satisfactory; but they have reserved to the national authority a right to interpose, whenever extraordinary circumstances might render that interposition necessary to its safety.

Nothing can be more evident, than that an exclusive power of regulating elections for the National Government, in the hands of the State Legislatures, would leave the existence of the Union entirely at their mercy. They could at any moment annihilate it, by neglecting to provide for the choice of persons to administer its affairs. It is to little purpose to say that a neglect or omission of this kind, would not be likely to take place. The constitutional possibility of the thing, without an equivalent for the risk, is an unanswerable objection. Nor has any satisfactory reason been yet assigned for incurring that risk. The extravagant surmises of a distempered jealousy can never be dignified with that character. If we are in a humour to presume abuses of power, it is as fair to presume them on the part of the State Governments, as on the part of the General Government. And as it is more consonant to the rules of a just theory to intrust the Union with the care of its own existence, than to transfer that care to any other hands; if abuses of power are to be hazarded, on the one side, or on the other, it is more rational to hazard them where the power would naturally be placed, than where it would unnaturally be placed.

Suppose an article had been introduced into the Constitution, empowering the United States to regulate the elections for the particular States, would any man have hesitated to condemn it, both as an unwarrantable transposition of power, and as a premeditated engine for the destruction of the State governments? The violation of principle in this case would have required no comment; and to an unbiassed observer, it will not be less apparent in the project of subjecting the existence of the National Government, in a similar respect to the pleasure of the State governments. An impartial view of the matter cannot fail to result in a conviction, that each, as far as possible, ought to depend on itself for its own preservation.

As an objection to this position, it may be remarked, that the Constitution of the national Senate, would involve in its full extent the danger which it is suggested might flow from an exclusive power in the State Legislatures to regulate the foederal elections. It may be alledged, that by declining the appointment of Senators they might at any time give a fatal blow to the Union; and from this, it may be inferred, that as its existence would be thus rendered dependent upon them in so essential a point, there can be no objection to entrusting them with it, in the particular case under consideration. The interest of each State, it may be added, to maintain its representation in the national councils, would be a complete security against an abuse of the trust.

This argument though specious, will not upon examination be found solid. It is certainly true, that the State Legislatures, by forbearing the appointment of Senators, may destroy the National Government. But it will not follow, that because they have the power to do this in one instance, they ought to have it in every other. There are cases in which the pernicious tendency of such a power may be far more decisive, without any motive, equally cogent with that which must have regulated the conduct of the Convention, in respect to the construction of the Senate, to recommend their admission into the system. So far as that construction may expose the Union to the possibility of injury from the State Legislatures, it is an evil; but it is an evil, which could not have been avoided without excluding the States, in their political capacities, wholly from a place in the organization of the National Government. If this had been done, it would doubtless have been interpreted into an entire dereliction of the foederal principle; and would certainly have deprived the State governments of that absolute safe-guard, which they will enjoy under this provision. But however wise it may have been, to have submitted in this instance to an inconvenience, for the attainment of a necessary advantage, or a greater good, no inference can be drawn from thence to favor an accumulation of the evil, where no necessity urges, nor any greater good invites.

It may easily be discerned also, that the National Government would run a much greater risk from a power in the State Legislatures over the elections of its House of Representatives, than from their power of appointing the members of its Senate. The Senators are to be chosen for the period of six years; there is to be a rotation, by which the seats of a third part of them are to be vacated, and replenished every two years; and no State is to be entitled to more than two Senators: A quorum of the body is to consist of sixteen members. The joint result of these circumstances would be, that a temporary combination of a few States, to intermit the appointment of Senators, could neither annul the existence nor impair the activity of the body: And it is not from a general or permanent combination of the States, that we can have any thing to fear. The first might proceed from sinister designs in the leading members of a few of the State Legislatures; the last would suppose a fixed and rooted disaffection in the great body of the people; which will either never exist at all, or will in all probability proceed from an experience of the inaptitude of the General Government to the advancement of their happiness; in which event no good citizen could desire its continuance.

But with regard to the Foederal House of Representatives, there is intended to be a general election of members once in two years. If the State Legislatures were to be invested with an exclusive power of regulating these elections, every period of making them would be a delicate crisis in the national situation; which might issue in a dissolution of the Union, if the leaders of a few of the most important States should have entered into a previous conspiracy to prevent an election.

I shall not deny that there is a degree of weight in the observation, that the interest of each State to be represented in the foederal councils will be a security against the abuse of a power over its elections in the hands of the State Legislatures. But the security will not be considered as complete, by those who attend to the force of an obvious distinction between the interest of the people in the public felicity, and the interest of their local rulers in the power and consequence of their offices. The people of America may be warmly attached to the government of the Union at times, when the particular rulers of particular States, stimulated by the natural rivalship of power and by the hopes of personal aggrandisement, and supported by a strong faction in each of those States, may be in a very opposite temper. This diversity of sentiment, between a majority of the people and the individuals who have the greatest credit in their councils, is exemplified in some of the States, at the present moment, on the present question. The scheme of separate confederacies, which will always multiply the chances of ambition, will be a never failing bait to all such influential characters in the State administrations as are capable of preferring their own emolument and advancement to the public weal; with so effectual a weapon in their hands as the exclusive power of regulating elections for the National Government a combination of a few such men, in a few of the most considerable States, where the temptation will always be the strongest, might accomplish the destruction of the Union, by seizing the opportunity of some casual dissatisfaction among the people (and which perhaps they may themselves have excited) to discontinue the choice of members for the Foederal House of Representatives. It ought never to be forgotten, that a firm Union of this country, under an efficient government, will probably be an encreasing object of jealousy to more than one nation of Europe; and that enterprises to subvert it will sometimes originate in the intrigues of foreign powers, and will seldom fail to be patronised and abetted by some of them. Its preservation therefore ought in no case, that can be avoided, to be committed to the guardianship of any but those, whose situation will uniformly beget an immediate interest in the faithful and vigilant performance of the trust.

14

ALEXANDER HAMILTON, FEDERALIST, NO. 60,
403–10
23 Feb. 1788

We have seen that an incontroulable power over the elections for the federal government could not without hazard be committed to the state legislatures. Let us now see what would be the dangers on the other side; that is, from confiding the ultimate right of regulating its own elections to the union itself. It is not pretended, that this right would ever be used for the exclusion of any state from its share in the representation. The interest of all would in this respect at least be the security of all. But it is alledged that it

might be employed in such a manner as to promote the election of some favourite class of men in exclusion of others; by confining the places of election to particular districts, and rendering it impracticable to the citizens at large to partake in the choice. Of all chimerical suppositions, this seems to be the most chimerical. On the one hand no rational calculation of probabilities would lead us to imagine, that the disposition, which a conduct so violent and extraordinary would imply, could ever find its way into the national councils; and on the other, it may be concluded with certainty, that if so improper a spirit should ever gain admittance into them, it would display itself in a form altogether different and far more decisive.

The improbability of the attempt may be satisfactorily inferred from this single reflection, that it could never be made without causing an immediate revolt of the great body of the people,—headed and directed by the state governments. It is not difficult to conceive that this characteristic right of freedom may, in certain turbulent and factious seasons, be violated in respect to a particular class of citizens by a victorious and overbearing majority; but that so fundamental a privilege, in a country so situated and so enlightened, should be invaded to the prejudice of the great mass of the people, by the deliberate policy of the government; without occasioning a popular revolution, is altogether inconceivable and incredible.

In addition to this general reflection, there are considerations of a more precise nature, which forbid all apprehension on the subject. The dissimilarity in the ingredients, which will compose the national government; and still more in the manner in which they will be brought into action in its various branches must form a powerful obstacle to a concert of views, in any partial scheme of elections. There is sufficient diversity in the state of property, in the genius, manners, and habits of the people of the different parts of the union to occasion a material diversity of disposition in their representatives towards the different ranks and conditions in society. And though an intimate intercourse under the same government will promote a gradual assimilation, of temper and sentiment, yet there are causes as well physical as moral, which may in a greater or less degree permanently nourish different propensities and inclinations in this particular. But the circumstance, which will be likely to have the greatest influence in the matter, will be the dissimilar modes of constituting the several component parts of the government. The house of representatives being to be elected immediately by the people; the senate by the state legislatures; the president by electors chosen for that purpose by the people; there would be little probability of a common interest to cement these different branches in a predilection for any particular class of electors.

As to the senate it is impossible that any regulation of "time and manner," which is all that is proposed to be submitted to the national government in respect to that body, can affect the spirit which will direct the choice of its members. The collective sense of the state legislatures can never be influenced by extraneous circumstances of that sort: A consideration, which alone ought to satisfy us that the discrimination apprehended would never be attempted. For what inducement could the senate have to concur in a preference, in which itself would not be included? Or to what purpose would it be established in reference to one branch of the legislature; if it could not be extended to the other? The composition of the one would in this case counteract that of the other. And we can never suppose that it would embrace the appointments to the senate, unless we can at the same time suppose the voluntary cooperation of the state legislatures. If we make the latter supposition, it then becomes immaterial where the power in question is placed; whether in their hands or in those of the union.

But what is to be the object of this capricious partiality in the national councils? Is it to be exercised in a discrimination between the different departments of industry, or between the different kinds of property, or between the different degrees of property? Will it lean in favor of the landed interest, or the monied interest, or the mercantile interest, or the manufacturing interest? Or to speak in the fashionable language of the adversaries of the Constitution; will it court the elevation of the "wealthy and the well born" to the exclusion and debasement of all the rest of the society?

If this partiality is to be exerted in favor of those who are concerned in any particular description of industry or property, I presume it will readily be admitted that the competition for it will lie between landed men and merchants. And I scruple not to affirm, that it is infinitely less likely, that either of them should gain an ascendant in the national councils, than that the one or the other of them should predominate in all the local councils. The inference will be, that a conduct tending to give an undue preference to either is much less to be dreaded from the former than from the latter.

The several states are in various degrees addicted to agriculture and commerce. In most, if not all of them, agriculture is predominant. In a few of them, however, commerce nearly divides its empire, and in most of them has a considerable share of influence. In proportion as either prevails, it will be conveyed into the national representation, and for the very reason that this will be an emanation from a greater variety of interests, and in much more various proportions, than are to be found in any single state, it will be much less apt to espouse either of them, with a decided partiality, than the representation of any single state.

In a country consisting chiefly of the cultivators of land[,] where the [rules] of an equal representation obtain[,] the landed interest must upon the whole preponderate in the government. As long as this interest prevails in most of the state legislatures, so long it must maintain a correspondent superiority in the national senate, which will generally be a faithful copy of the majorities of those assemblies. It cannot therefore be presumed that a sacrifice of the landed to the mercantile class will ever be a favorite object of this branch of the federal legislature. In applying thus particularly to the senate a general observation suggested by the situation of the country, I am governed by the consideration, that the credulous votaries of state power, cannot upon their own principles suspect that the state legislatures would be warped from their duty by any external influence. But as in reality the same situation must have the same effect in the primitive composition at least of the federal house of representatives; an improper byass towards the mercantile class is as little to be expected from this quarter or from the other.

In order perhaps to give countenance to the objection at any rate, it may be asked, is there not danger of an opposite byass in the national government, which may dispose it to endeavour to secure a monopoly of the federal administration to the landed class? As there is little likelihood that the supposition of such a byass will have any terrors for those who would be immediately injured by it, a laboured answer to this question will be dispensed with. It will be sufficient to remark, first, that for the reasons elsewhere assigned, it is less likely that any decided partiality should prevail in the councils of the union than in those of any of its members. Secondly that there would be no temptation to violate the constitution in favor of the landed class, because that class would in the natural course of things enjoy as great a preponderancy as itself could desire. And thirdly that men accustomed to investigate the sources of public prosperity, upon a large scale, must be too well convinced of the utility of commerce, to be inclined to inflict upon it so deep a wound as would result from the entire exclusion of those who would best understand its interest from a share in the management of them. The importance of commerce in the view of revenue alone must effectually guard it against the enmity of a body which would be continually importuned in its favour by the urgent calls of public necessity. I the rather consult brevity in discussing the probability of a preference founded upon a discrimination between the different kinds of industry and property; because, as far as I understand the meaning of the objectors, they contemplate a discrimination of another kind. They appear to have in view, as the objects of the preference with which they endeavour to alarm us, those whom they designate by the description of the "wealthy and the well born." These, it seems, are to be exalted to an odious pre-eminence over the rest of their fellow citizens. At one time however their elevation is to be a necessary consequence of the smallness of the representative body; at another time it is to be effected by depriving the people at large of the opportunity of exercising their right of suffrage in the choice of that body.

But upon what principle is the discrimination of the places of election to be made in order to answer the purpose of the meditated preference? Are the wealthy and the well born, as they are called, confined to particular spots in the several states? Have they by some miraculous instinct or foresight set apart in each of them a common place of residence? Are they only to be met with in the towns or cities? Or are they, on the contrary, scattered over the face of the country as avarice or chance may have happened to cast their own lot, or that of their predecessors? If the latter is the case, (as every intelligent man knows it to be*) is it not evident that the policy of confin-

*Particularly in the Southern States and in this State.

ing the places of elections to particular districts would be as subversive of its own aim as it would be exceptionable on every other account? The truth is that there is no method of securing to the rich the preference apprehended, but by prescribing qualifications of property either for those who may elect, or be elected. But this forms no part of the power to be conferred upon the national government. Its authority would be expressly restricted to the regulation of the *times,* the *places,* and the *manner* of elections. The qualifications of the persons who may choose or be chosen, as has been remarked upon another occasion, are defined and fixed in the constitution; and are unalterable by the legislature.

Let it however be admitted, for argument sake, that the expedient suggested might be successful; and let it at the same time be equally taken for granted that all the scruples which a sense of duty or an apprehension of the danger of the experiment might inspire, were overcome in the breasts of the national rulers; still, I imagine, it will hardly be pretended, that they could ever hope to carry such an enterprise into execution, without the aid of a military force sufficient to subdue, the resistance of the great body of the people. The improbability of the existence of a force equal to that object, has been discussed and demonstrated in different parts of these papers; but that the futility of the objection under consideration may appear in the strongest light, it shall be conceded for a moment that such a force might exist; and the national government shall be supposed to be in the actual possession of it. What will be the conclusion? With a disposition to invade the essential rights of the community, and with the means of gratifying that disposition, is it presumable that the persons who were actuated by it would amuse themselves in the ridiculous task of fabricating election laws for securing a preference to a favourite class of men? Would they not be likely to prefer a conduct better adapted to their own immediate aggrandisement? Would they not rather boldly resolve to perpetuate themselves in office by one decisive act of usurpation, than to trust to precarious expedients, which in spite of all the precautions that might accompany them, might terminate in the dismission, disgrace and ruin of their authors? Would they not fear that citizens not less tenacious than conscious of their rights would flock from the remotest extremes of their respective states to the places of election, to overthrow their tyrants, and to substitute men who would be disposed to avenge the violated majesty of the people?

15

ALEXANDER HAMILTON, FEDERALIST, NO. 61,
410–14
26 Feb. 1788

The more candid opposers of the provision respecting elections contained in the plan of the Convention, when pressed in argument, will sometimes concede the propriety of that provision; with this qualification however that it ought to have been accompanied with a declaration that all elections should be had in the counties where the electors resided. This say they, was a necessary precaution against an abuse of the power. A declaration of this nature, would certainly have been harmless: So far as it would have had the effect of quieting apprehensions, it might not have been undesirable. But it would in fact have afforded little or no additional security against the danger apprehended; and the want of it will never be considered by an impartial and judicious examiner as a serious, still less, as an insuperable objection to the plan. The different views taken of the subject in the two preceding papers must be sufficient to satisfy all dispassionate and discerning men, that if the public liberty should ever be the victim of the ambition of the national rulers, the power under examination at least will be guiltless of the sacrifice.

If those who are inclined to consult their jealousy only would exercise it in a careful inspection of the several State Constitutions, they would find little less room for disquietude and alarm from the latitude which most of them allow in respect to elections, than from the latitude which is proposed to be allowed to the National Government in the same respect. A review of their situation, in this particular, would tend greatly to remove any ill impressions which may remain in regard to this matter. But as that review would lead into lengthy and tedious details, I shall content myself with the single example of the State in which I write. The Constitution of New-York makes no other provision for *locality* of elections, than that the members of the Assembly shall be elected in the *counties,* those of the Senate in the great districts into which the State is or may be divided; these at present are four in number, and comprehend each from two to six counties. It may readily be perceived that it would not be more difficult to the Legislature of New-York to defeat the suffrages of the citizens of New-York by confining elections to particular places, than to the Legislature of the United States to defeat the suffrages of the citizens of the Union, by the like expedient. Suppose for instance, the city of Albany was to be appointed the sole place of election for the county and district of which it is a part, would not the inhabitants of that city speedily become the only electors of the members both of the Senate and Assembly, for that county and district? Can we imagine that the electors who reside in the remote subdivisions of the county of Albany, Saratoga, Cambridge, &c. or in any part of the county of Montgomery, would take the trouble to come to the city of Albany to give their votes for members of the Assembly or Senate, sooner than they would repair to the city of New-York to participate in the choice of the members of the Foederal House of Representatives? The alarming indifference discoverable in the exercise of so invaluable a privilege under the existing laws, which afford every facility to it, furnishes a ready answer to this question. And, abstracted from any experience on the subject, we can be at no loss to determine that when the place of election is at an *inconvenient distance* from the elector, the effect upon his conduct will be the same whether that distance be twenty miles or twenty thousand miles. Hence it must appear that objections to the particular modification of the foederal power of regulating elections will in substance apply with equal force to the modification of the like power in the Constitution of this State; and for this reason it will be impossible to acquit the one and to condemn the other. A similar comparison would lead to the same conclusion in respect to the Constitutions of most of the other States.

If it should be said that defects in the State Constitutions furnish no apology for those which are to be found in the plan proposed; I answer, that as the former have never been thought chargeable with inattention to the security of liberty, where the imputations thrown on the latter can be shown to be applicable to them also, the presumption is that they are rather the cavilling refinements of a predetermined opposition, than the well founded inferences of a candid research after truth. To those who are disposed to consider, as innocent omissions in the State Constitutions, what they regard as unpardonable blemishes in the plan of the Convention, nothing can be said; or at most they can only be asked to assign some substantial reason why the representatives of the people in a single State should be more impregnable to the lust of power or other sinister motives, than the representatives of the people of the United States? If they cannot do this, they ought at least to prove to us, that it is easier to subvert the liberties of three millions of people, with the advantage of local governments to head their opposition, than of two hundred thousand people, who are destitute of that advantage. And in relation to the point immediately under consideration, they ought to convince us that it is less probable a predominant faction in a single State, should, in order to maintain its superiority, incline to a preference of a particular class of electors, than that a similar spirit should take possession of the representatives of thirteen States spread over a vast region, and in several respects distinguishable from each other by a diversity of local circumstances, prejudices and interests.

Hitherto my observations have only aimed at a vindication of the provision in question, on the ground of theoretic propriety, on that of the danger of placing the power elsewhere, and on that of the safety of placing it in the manner proposed. But there remains to be mentioned a positive advantage which will result from this disposition, and which could not as well have been obtained from any other: I allude to the circumstance of uniformity in the time of elections for the Foederal House of Representatives. It is more than possible, that this uniformity may be found by experience to be of great importance to the public welfare; both as a security against the perpetuation of the same spirit in the body; and as a cure for the diseases of faction. If each State may choose its own time of election, it is possible there may be at least as many different periods as there are months in the year. The times of election in the several States as they are now established for local purposes, vary between extremes as wide as March and November. The consequence of this diversity would be, that there could never happen a total dissolution or renovation of the body at one time. If an improper spirit of any kind should happen to prevail in it, that spirit would be apt to infuse itself into the new members as they come forward in succession. The mass would be likely to remain nearly the same; assimilating constantly to itself its gradual accretions. There is a contagion in example which few men have sufficient force of mind to resist. I am inclined to think that treble the duration in office, with the condition of a total dissolution of the body at the same time, might be less formidable to liberty, than one third of that duration, subject to gradual and successive alterations.

Uniformity in the time of elections seems not less requisite for executing the idea of a regular rotation in the Senate; and for conveniently assembling the Legislature at a stated period in each year.

It may be asked, why then could not a time have been fixed in the Constitution? As the most zealous adversaries of the plan of the Convention in this State, are in general not less zealous admirers of the Constitution of the State, the question may be retorted, and it may be asked, why was not a time for the like purpose fixed in the Constitution of this State? No better answer can be given, than that it was a matter which might safely be entrusted to legislative discretion, and that if a time had been appointed, it might upon experiment have been found less convenient than some other time. The same answer may be given to the question put on the other side. And it may be added, that the supposed danger of a gradual change being merely speculative, it would have been hardly adviseable upon that speculation to establish, as a fundamental point, what would deprive several States of the convenience of having the elections for their own governments, and for the National Government, at the same epoch.

16

DEBATE IN VIRGINIA RATIFYING CONVENTION
4–5, 9, 14 June 1788
Elliot 3:9–11, 60, 175–76, 366–67

[*4 June*]

MR. NICHOLAS. There is another objection which has been echoed from one end of the continent to the other—that Congress may alter the time, place, and manner of holding elections; that they may direct the place of elections to be where it will be impossible for those who have a right to vote, to attend; for instance, that they may order the freeholders of Albemarle to vote in the county of Princess Anne, or *vice versa;* or regulate elections, otherwise, in such a manner as totally to defeat their purpose, and lay them entirely under the influence of Congress. I flatter myself, that, from an attentive consideration of this power, it will clearly appear that it was essentially necessary to give it to Congress, as, without it, there could have been no security for the general government against the state legislatures. What, Mr. Chairman, is the danger apprehended in this case? If I understand it right, it must be, that Congress might cause the elections to be held in the most inconvenient places, and at so inconvenient a time, and in such a manner, as to give them the most undue influence over the choice, nay, even to prevent the elections from being held at all,—in order to perpetuate themselves. But what would be the consequence of this measure? It would be this, sir,—that Congress would cease to exist; it would destroy the Congress itself; it would absolutely be an act of suicide; and therefore it can never be expected. This alteration, so much apprehended, must be made by law; that is, with the concurrence of both branches of the legislature. Will the House of Representatives, the members of which are chosen only for two years, and who depend on the people for their reëlection, agree to such an alteration? It is unreasonable to suppose it.

But let us admit, for a moment, that they will: what would be the consequence of passing such a law? It would be, sir, that, after the expiration of the two years, at the next election they would either choose such men as would alter the law, or they would resist the government. An enlightened people will never suffer what was established for their security to be perverted to an act of tyranny. It may be said, perhaps, that resistance would then become vain; Congress are vested with the power of raising an army; to which I say, that if ever Congress shall have an army sufficient for their purpose, and disposed to execute their unlawful commands, before they would act under this disguise, they would pull off the mask, and declare themselves absolute. I ask, Mr. Chairman, is it a novelty in our government? Has not our state legislature the power of fixing the time, places, and manner of holding elections? The possible abuse here complained of never can happen as long as the people of the United States are virtuous. As long as they continue to have sentiments of freedom and independence, should the Congress be wicked enough to harbor so absurd an idea as this objection supposes, the people will defeat their attempt by choosing other representatives, who will alter the law. If the state legislature, by accident, design, or any other cause, would not appoint a place for holding elections, then there might be no election till the time was past for which they were to have been chosen; and as this would eventually put an end to the Union, it ought to be guarded against; and it could only be guarded against by giving this discretionary power, to the Congress, of altering the time, place, and manner of holding the elections. It is absurd to think that Congress will exert this power, or change the time, place, and manner established by the states, if the states will regulate them properly, or so as not to defeat the purposes of the Union. It is urged that the state legislature ought to be fully and exclusively possessed of this power. Were this the case, it might certainly defeat the government. As the powers vested by this plan in Congress are taken from the state legislatures, they would be prompted to throw every obstacle in the way of the general government. It was then necessary that Congress should have this power.

Another strong argument for the necessity of this power is, that, if it was left solely to the states, there might have been as many times of choosing as there are states. States having solely the power of altering or establishing the time of election, it might happen that there should be no Congress. Not only by omitting to fix a time, but also by the elections in the states being at thirteen different times, such intervals might elapse between the first and last election, as to prevent there being a sufficient number to form a house; and this might happen at a time when the most urgent business rendered their session necessary; and by this power, this great part of the representation will be always kept full, which will be a security for a due attention to the interest of the community; and also the power of Congress to make the times of elections uniform in all the states, will destroy the continuance of any cabal, as the whole body of representatives will go out of office at once.

[5 *June*]

Mr. HENRY. What can be more defective than the clause concerning the elections? The control given to Congress over the time, place, and manner of holding elections, will totally destroy the end of suffrage. The elections may be held at one place, and the most inconvenient in the state; or they may be at remote distances from those who have a right of suffrage: hence nine out of ten must either not vote at all, or vote for strangers; for the most influential characters will be applied to, to know who are the most proper to be chosen. I repeat, that the control of Congress over the *manner*, &c., of electing, well warrants this idea. The natural consequence will be, that this democratic branch will possess none of the public confidence; the people will be prejudiced against representatives chosen in such an injudicious manner. The proceedings in the northern conclave will be hidden from the yeomanry of this country. We are told that the yeas and nays shall be taken, and entered on the journals. This, sir, will avail nothing: it may be locked up in their chests, and concealed forever from the people; for they are not to publish what parts they think require secrecy: they *may* think, and *will think*, the whole requires it. Another beautiful feature of this Constitution is, the publication from time to time of the receipts and expenditures of the public money.

[9 *June*]

Mr. HENRY. I shall make a few observations to prove that the power over elections, which is given to Congress, is contrived by the federal government, that the people may be deprived of their proper influence in the government, by destroying the force and effect of their suffrages. Congress is to have a discretionary control over the time, place, and manner of elections. The representatives are to be elected, consequently, when and where they please. As to the time and place, gentlemen have attempted to obviate the objection by saying, that the time is to happen once in two years, and that the place is to be within a particular district, or in the respective counties. But how will they obviate the danger of referring the *manner* of election to Congress? Those illumined genii may see that this may not endanger the rights of the people; but in my unenlightened understanding, it appears plain and clear that it will impair the popular weight in the government. Look at the Roman history. They had two ways of voting—the one by tribes, and the other by centuries. By the former, numbers prevailed; in the latter, riches preponderated. According to the mode prescribed, Congress may tell you that they

267

have a right to make the vote of one gentleman go as far as the votes of a hundred poor men. The power over the manner admits of the most dangerous latitude. They may modify it as they please. They may regulate the number of votes by the quantity of property, without involving any repugnancy to the Constitution. I should not have thought of this trick or contrivance, had I not seen how the public liberty of Rome was trifled with by the mode of voting by centuries, whereby one rich man had as many votes as a multitude of poor men. The plebeians were trampled on till they resisted. The patricians trampled on the liberties of the plebeians till the latter had the spirit to assert their right to freedom and equality. The result of the American mode of election may be similar.

[14 June]

Mr. MONROE wished that the honorable gentleman, who had been in the federal Convention, would give information respecting the clause concerning elections. He wished to know why Congress had an ultimate control over the time, place, and manner, of elections of representatives, and the time and manner of that of senators, and also why there was an exception as to the place of electing senators.

Mr. MADISON. Mr. Chairman, the reason of the exception was, that, if Congress could fix the place of choosing the senators, it might compel the state legislatures to elect them in a different place from that of their usual sessions, which would produce some inconvenience, and was not necessary for the object of regulating the elections. But it was necessary to give the general government a control over the time and manner of choosing the senators, to prevent its own dissolution.

With respect to the other point, it was thought that the regulation of time, place, and manner, of electing the representatives, should be uniform throughout the continent. Some states might regulate the elections on the principles of equality, and others might regulate them otherwise. This diversity would be obviously unjust. Elections are regulated now unequally in some states, particularly South Carolina, with respect to Charleston, which is represented by thirty members. Should the people of any state by any means be deprived of the right of suffrage, it was judged proper that it should be remedied by the general government. It was found impossible to fix the time, place, and manner, of the election of representatives, in the Constitution. It was found necessary to leave the regulation of these, in the first place, to the state governments, as being best acquainted with the situation of the people, subject to the control of the general government, in order to enable it to produce uniformity, and prevent its own dissolution. And, considering the state governments and general governments as distinct bodies, acting in different and independent capacities for the people, it was thought the particular regulations should be submitted to the former, and the general regulations to the latter. Were they exclusively under the control of the state governments, the general government might easily be dissolved. But if they be regulated properly by the state legislatures, the congressional control will very probably never be exercised. The power

appears to me satisfactory, and as unlikely to be abused as any part of the Constitution.

17

DEBATE IN NEW YORK RATIFYING CONVENTION
25–26 June 1788
Elliot 2:325–29

[25 June]

Mr. JONES rose, and observed, that it was a fact universally known, that the present Confederation had not proved adequate to the purposes of good government. Whether this arose from the want of powers in the federal head, or from other causes, he would not pretend to determine. Some parts of the proposed plan appeared to him imperfect, or at least not satisfactory. He did not think it right that Congress should have the power of prescribing or altering the time, place, and manner of holding elections. He apprehended that the clause might be so construed as to deprive the states of an essential right, which, in the true design of the Constitution, was to be reserved to them. He therefore wished the clause might be explained, and proposed, for the purpose, the following amendment:—

> "*Resolved,* as the opinion of this committee, that nothing in the Constitution, now under consideration, shall be construed to authorize the Congress to make or alter *any regulations,* in any state, respecting the times, places, or manner of holding elections for senators or representatives, unless the legislature of such state shall neglect or refuse to make laws or regulations for the purpose, or, from any circumstance, be incapable of making the same, and then only until the legislature of such state shall make provision in the premises."

The Hon. Mr. JAY said that, as far as he understood the ideas of the gentleman, he seemed to have doubts with respect to this paragraph, and feared it might be misconstrued and abused. He said that every government was imperfect, unless it had a power of preserving itself. Suppose that, by design or accident, the states should *neglect to appoint representatives;* certainly there should be some constitutional remedy for this evil. The obvious meaning of the paragraph was, that, if this neglect should take place, Congress should have power, by law, to support the government, and prevent the dissolution of the Union. He believed this was the design of the federal Convention.

The Hon. R. MORRIS suggested, that, so far as the people, distinct from their legislatures, were concerned in the operation of the Constitution, it was absolutely necessary that the existence of the general government should not depend, for a moment, on the will of the state legislatures.

The power of perpetuating the government ought to belong to their federal representatives; otherwise, the right of the people would be essentially abridged.

His excellency, Governor CLINTON, rose, just to notice the attempt that had been made to influence the committee by fear, and to introduce gloomy reflections upon the situation of the state. This had been done in heightened colors, and, he thought, in an indelicate manner. He said, he had observed also, in the course of the debates, that a distinction had been kept up between the state legislatures and the representatives of the people, and also between the legislatures and the senators. He did not think these distinctions warrantable. They were distinctions which would never appear in operation, while the government was well administered. It was true, he said, the representatives of the people, and the senators, might deviate from their duty, and express a will distinct from that of the people, or that of the legislatures; but any body might see that this must arise from corruption. Congress, in all its branches, was to speak the will of the people, and that will was law, and must be uniform. The distinction, therefore, of the honorable gentleman could have no proper weight in the discussion of this question.

Mr. JAY did not think the gentleman had taken up the matter right. The *will of the people* certainly ought to be the law, but the only question was, How was this will to be expressed:—whether the will of the people, with respect to the time, place, and manner of holding elections, ought to be expressed by the general government, or by the state legislatures.

Mr. M. SMITH proposed the following addition to Mr. Jones's motion:—

> "And that each state shall be divided into as many districts as the representatives it is entitled to, and that each representative shall be chosen by a majority of votes."

But on suggestion that this motion was ill timed, it was withdrawn for the present.

[*26 June*]

Mr. SMITH again moved the additional amendment proposed the preceding day; when the Hon. Mr. DUANE called on him to explain the motives which induced his proposal.

Mr. SMITH expressed his surprise that the gentleman should want such an explanation. He conceived that the amendment was founded on the fundamental principles of representative government. As the Constitution stood, the whole state might be a single district for election. This would be improper. The state should be divided into as many districts as it sends representatives. The whole number of representatives might otherwise be taken from a small part of the state, and the bulk of the people, therefore, might not be fully represented. He would say no more at present on the propriety of the amendment. The principle appeared to him so evident, that he hardly knew how to reason upon it, until he heard the arguments of the gentlemen in opposition.

Mr. DUANE. I will not examine the merits of the measure the gentleman recommends. If the proposed mode of election be the best, the legislature of this state will undoubtedly adopt it. But I wish the gentleman to prove that his plan will be practicable, and will succeed. By the Constitution of this state, the representatives are apportioned among the counties, and it is wisely left to the people to choose whom they will, in their several counties, without any further division into districts. Sir, how do we know the proposal will be agreeable to the other states? Is every state to be compelled to adopt our ideas on all subjects? If the gentleman will reflect, I believe he will be doubtful of the propriety of these things. Will it not seem extraordinary that any one state should presume to dictate to the Union? As the Constitution stands, it will be in the power of each state to regulate this important point. While the legislatures do their duty, the exercise of their discretion is sufficiently secured. Sir, this measure would carry with it a presumption which I should be sorry to see in the acts of this state. It is laying down, as a principle, that whatever may suit our interest or fancy should be imposed upon our sister states. This does not seem to correspond with that moderation which I hope to see in all the proceedings of this Convention.

Mr. SMITH. The gentleman misunderstands me. I did not mean the amendment to operate on the other states: they may use their discretion. The amendment is in the negative. The very design of it is to enable the states to act their discretion, without the control of Congress. So the gentleman's reasoning is directly against himself.

If the argument had any force, it would go against proposing any amendment at all; because, says the gentleman, it would be dictating to the Union. What is the object of our consultations? For my part, I do not know, unless we are to express our sentiments of the Constitution before we adopt it. It is only exercising the privilege of freemen; and shall we be debarred from this? It is said, it is left to the discretion of the states. If this were true, it would be all we contend for. But, sir, Congress can alter as they please any mode adopted by the states. What discretion is there here? The gentleman instances the Constitution of New York, as opposed to my argument. I believe that there are now gentlemen in this house, who were members of the Convention of this state, and who were inclined for an amendment like this. It is to be regretted that it was not adopted. The fact is, as your Constitution stands, a man may have a seat in your legislature, who is not elected by a majority of his constituents. For my part, I know of no principle that ought to be more fully established than the right of election by a majority.

Mr. DUANE. I neglected to make one observation which I think weighty. The mode of *election* recommended by the gentleman must be attended with great embarrassments. His idea is, that a *majority* of all the votes should be necessary to return a member.

I will suppose a state divided into *districts*. How seldom will it happen that a majority of a district will unite their votes in favor of one man! In a neighboring state, where they have this mode of election, I have been told that it rarely happens that more than one half unite in a choice. The consequence is, they are obliged to make provision, by a previous election, for *nomination,* and another election for appointment; thus suffering the inconvenience of a double election. If the proposition was adopted, I believe we should be seldom represented—the election must be lost. The gentleman will, therefore, I presume, either abandon his project, or propose some remedy for the evil I have described.

Mr. SMITH. I think the example the gentleman adduces is in my favor. The states of Massachusetts and Connecticut have regulated elections in the mode I propose; but it has never been considered inconvenient, nor have the people ever been unrepresented. I mention this to show that the thing has not proved impracticable in those states. If not, why should it in New York?

After some further conversation, Mr. LANSING proposed the following modification of Mr. Smith's motion—

"And that nothing in this Constitution shall be construed to prevent the legislature of any state to pass laws, from time to time, to divide such state into any convenient districts as the state shall be entitled to elect representatives for Congress, nor to prevent such legislature from making provision, that the electors in each district shall choose a citizen of the United States, who shall have been an inhabitant of the district, for the term of one year immediately preceding the time of his election, for one of the representatives of such state."

18

DEBATE IN NORTH CAROLINA RATIFYING CONVENTION
25 July 1788
Elliot 4:50–72

Mr. SPENCER. Mr. Chairman, it appears to me that this clause, giving this control over the time, place, and manner, of holding elections, to Congress, does away the right of the people to choose the representatives every second year, and impairs the right of the state legislatures to choose the senators. I wish this matter to be explained.

Gov. JOHNSTON. Mr. Chairman, I confess that I am a very great admirer of the new Constitution, but I cannot comprehend the reason of this part. The reason urged is, that every government ought to have the power of continuing itself, and that, if the general government had not this power, the state legislatures might neglect to regulate elections, whereby the government might be discontinued. As long as the state legislatures have it in their power not to choose the senators, this power in Congress appears to me altogether useless, because they can put an end to the general government by refusing to choose senators. But I do not consider this such a blemish in the Constitution as

that it ought, for that reason, to be rejected. I observe that every state which has adopted the Constitution, and recommended amendments, has given directions to remove this objection; and I hope, if this state adopts it, she will do the same.

Mr. SPENCER. Mr. Chairman, it is with great reluctance that I rise upon this important occasion. I have considered with some attention the subject before us. I have paid attention to the Constitution itself, and to the writings on both sides. I considered it on one side as well as on the other, in order to know whether it would be best to adopt it or not. I would not wish to insinuate any reflections on those gentlemen who formed it. I look upon it as a great performance. It has a great deal of merit in it, and it is, perhaps, as much as any set of men could have done. Even if it be true, what gentlemen have observed, that the gentlemen who were delegates to the Federal Convention were not instructed to form a new constitution, but to amend the Confederation, this will be immaterial, if it be proper to be adopted. It will be of equal benefit to us, if proper to be adopted in the whole, or in such parts as will be necessary, whether they were expressly delegated for that purpose or not. This appears to me to be a reprehensible clause; because it seems to strike at the state legislatures, and seems to take away that power of elections which reason dictates they ought to have among themselves. It apparently looks forward to a consolidation of the government of the United States, when the state legislatures may entirely decay away.

This is one of the grounds which have induced me to make objections to the new form of government. It appears to me that the state governments are not sufficiently secured, and that they may be swallowed up by the great mass of powers given to Congress. If that be the case, such power should not be given; for, from all the notions which we have concerning our happiness and well-being, the state governments are the basis of our happiness, security, and prosperity. A large extent of country ought to be divided into such a number of states as that the people may conveniently carry on their own government. This will render the government perfectly agreeable to the genius and wishes of the people. If the United States were to consist of ten times as many states, they might all have a degree of harmony. Nothing would be wanting but some cement for their connection. On the contrary, if all the United States were to be swallowed up by the great mass of powers given to Congress, the parts that are more distant in this great empire would be governed with less and less energy. It would not suit the genius of the people to assist in the government. Nothing would support government, in such a case as that, but military coercion. Armies would be necessary in different parts of the United States. The expense which they would cost, and the burdens which they would render necessary to be laid upon the people, would be ruinous. I know of no way that is likely to produce the happiness of the people, but to preserve, as far as possible, the existence of the several states, so that they shall not be swallowed up.

It has been said that the existence of the state governments is essential to that of the general government, because they choose the senators. By this clause, it is evident that it is in the power of Congress to make any alterations, except as to the place of choosing senators. They may alter the time from six to twenty years, or to any time; for they have an unlimited control over the time of elections. They have also an absolute control over the election of the representatives. It deprives the people of the very mode of choosing them. It seems nearly to throw the whole power of election into the hands of Congress. It strikes at the mode, time, and place, of choosing representatives. It puts all but the place of electing senators into the hands of Congress. This supersedes the necessity of continuing the state legislatures. This is such an article as I can give no sanction to, because it strikes at the foundation of the governments on which depends the happiness of the states and the general government. It is with reluctance I make the objection. I have the highest veneration for the characters of the framers of this Constitution. I mean to make objections only which are necessary to be made. I would not take up time unnecessarily. As to this matter, it strikes at the foundation of every thing. I may say more when we come to that part which points out the mode of doing without the agency of the state legislatures.

Mr. IREDELL. Mr. Chairman, I am glad to see so much candor and moderation. The liberal sentiments expressed by the honorable gentleman who spoke last command my respect. No time can be better employed than in endeavoring to remove, by fair and just reasoning, every objection which can be made to this Constitution. I apprehend that the honorable gentleman is mistaken as to the extent of the operation of this clause. He supposes that the control of the general government over elections looks forward to a consolidation of the states, and that the general word *time* may extend to twenty, or any number of years. In my humble opinion, this clause does by no means warrant such a construction. We ought to compare other parts with it. Does not the Constitution say that representatives shall be chosen every second year? The right of choosing them, therefore, reverts to the people every second year. No instrument of writing ought to be construed absurdly, when a rational construction can be put upon it. If Congress can prolong the election to any time they please, why is it said that representatives shall be chosen every second year? *They must be chosen every second year;* but whether in the month of March, or January, or any other month, may be ascertained, at a future time, by regulations of Congress. The word *time* refers only to the particular month and day within the two years. I heartily agree with the gentleman, that, if any thing in this Constitution tended to the annihilation of the state government, instead of exciting the admiration of any man, it ought to excite the resentment and execration. No such wicked intention ought to be suffered. But the gentlemen who formed the Constitution had no such object; nor do I think there is the least ground for that jealousy. The very existence of the general government depends on that of the state governments. The state legislatures are to choose the senators. Without a Senate there can be no Congress. The state legislatures are also to direct the manner of choosing the President. Unless, therefore, there are state legislatures to direct that

manner, no President can be chosen. The same observation may be made as to the House of Representatives, since, as they are to be chosen by the electors of the most numerous branch of each state legislature, if there are no state legislatures, there are no persons to choose the House of Representatives. Thus it is evident that the very existence of the general government depends on that of the state legislatures, and of course, that their continuance cannot be endangered by it.

An occasion may arise when the exercise of this ultimate power in Congress may be necessary; as, for instance, if a state should be involved in war, and its legislature could not assemble, (as was the case of South Carolina, and occasionally of some other states, during the late war;) it might also be useful for this reason—lest a few powerful states should combine, and make regulations concerning elections which might deprive many of the electors of a fair exercise of their rights, and thus injure the community, and occasion great dissatisfaction. And it seems natural and proper that every government should have in itself the means of its own preservation. A few of the great states might combine to prevent any election of representatives at all, and thus a majority might be wanting to do business; but it would not be so easy to destroy the government by the non-election of senators, because one third only are to go out at a time, and all the states will be equally represented in the Senate. It is not probable this power would be abused; for, if it should be, the state legislatures would immediately resent it, and their authority over the people will always be extremely great. These reasons induce me to think that the power is both necessary and useful. But I am sensible great jealousy has been entertained concerning it; and as perhaps the danger of a combination, in the manner I have mentioned, to destroy or distress the general government, is not very probable, it may be better to incur the risk, than occasion any discontent by suffering the clause to continue as it now stands. I should, therefore, not object to the recommendation of an amendment similar to that of other states—that this power in Congress should only be exercised when a state legislature neglected or was disabled from making the regulations required.

Mr. SPENCER. Mr. Chairman, I did not mean to insinuate that designs were made, by the honorable gentlemen who composed the Federal Constitution, against our liberties. I only meant to say that the words in this place were exceeding vague. It may admit of the gentleman's construction; but it may admit of a contrary construction. In a matter of so great moment, words ought not to be so vague and indeterminate. I have said that the states are the basis on which the government of the United States ought to rest, and which must render us secure. No man wishes more for a federal government than I do. I think it necessary for our happiness; but at the same time, when we form a government which must entail happiness or misery on posterity, nothing is of more consequence than settling it so as to exclude animosity and a contest between the general and individual governments. With respect to the mode here mentioned, they are words of very great extent. This clause provides that a Congress may at any time alter such regulations, except as to the places of choosing senators. These words are so vague and uncertain, that it must ultimately destroy the whole liberty of the United States. It strikes at the very existence of the states, and supersedes the necessity of having them at all. I would therefore wish to have it amended in such a manner as that the Congress should not interfere but when the states refused or neglected to regulate elections.

Mr. BLOODWORTH. Mr. Chairman, I trust that such learned arguments as are offered to reconcile our minds to such dangerous powers will not have the intended weight. The House of Representatives is the only democratical branch. This clause may destroy representation entirely. What does it say? "The times, places, and manner, of holding elections for senators and representatives, shall be prescribed in each state by the legislature thereof; but the Congress may at any time, by law, make or alter such regulations, except as to the places of choosing senators." Now, sir, does not this clause give an unlimited and unbounded power to Congress over the times, places, and manner, of choosing representatives? They may make the time of election so long, the place so inconvenient, and the manner so oppressive, that it will entirely destroy representation. I hope gentlemen will exercise their own understanding on this occasion, and not let their judgment be led away by these shining characters, for whom, however, I have the highest respect. This Constitution, if adopted in its present mode, must end in the subversion of our liberties. Suppose it takes place in North Carolina; can farmers elect them? No, sir. The elections may be in such a manner that men may be appointed who are not representatives of the people. This may exist, and it ought to be guarded against. As to the place, suppose Congress should order the elections to be held in the most inconvenient place in the most inconvenient district; could every person entitled to vote attend at such a place? Suppose they should order it to be laid off into so many districts, and order the election to be held within each district, yet may not their power over the manner of election enable them to exclude from voting every description of men they please? The democratic branch is so much endangered, that no arguments can be made use of to satisfy my mind to it. The honorable gentleman has amused us with learned discussions, and told us he will condescend to propose amendments. I hope the representatives of North Carolina will never swallow the Constitution till it is amended.

Mr. GOUDY. Mr. Chairman, the invasion of these states is urged as a reason for this clause. But why did they not mention that it should be only in cases of invasion? But that was not the reason, in my humble opinion. I fear it was a combination against our liberties. I ask, when we give them the purse in one hand, and the sword in another, what power have we left? It will lead to an aristocratical government, and establish tyranny over us. We are freemen, and we ought to have the privileges of such.

Gov. JOHNSTON. Mr. Chairman, I do not impute any impure intentions to the gentlemen who formed this Constitution. I think it unwarrantable in any one to do it. I believe that were there twenty conventions appointed, and as many constitutions formed, we never could get men more able and disinterested than those who formed this; nor a constitution less exceptionable than that which is now before you. I am not apprehensive that this article will be attended with all the fatal consequences which the gentleman conceives. I conceive that Congress can have no other power than the states had. The states, with regard to elections, must be governed by the articles of the Constitution; so must Congress. But I believe the power, as it now stands, is unnecessary. I should be perfectly satisfied with it in the mode recommended by the worthy member on my right hand. Although I should be extremely cautious to adopt any constitution that would endanger the rights and privileges of the people, I have no fear in adopting this Constitution, and then proposing amendments. I feel as much attachment to the rights and privileges of my country as any man in it; and if I thought any thing in this Constitution tended to abridge these rights, I would not agree to it. I cannot conceive that this is the case. I have not the least doubt but it will be adopted by a very great majority of the states. For states who have been as jealous of their liberties as any in the world have adopted it, and they are some of the most powerful states. We shall have the assent of all the states in getting amendments. Some gentlemen have apprehensions that Congress will immediately conspire to destroy the liberties of their country. The men of whom Congress will consist are to be chosen from among ourselves. They will be in the same situation with us. They are to be bone of our bone and flesh of our flesh. They cannot injure us without injuring themselves. I have no doubt but we shall choose the best men in the community. Should different men be appointed, they are sufficiently responsible. I therefore think that no danger is to be apprehended.

Mr. M'DOWALL. Mr. Chairman, I have the highest esteem for the gentleman who spoke last. He has amused us with the fine characters of those who formed that government. Some were good, but some were very imperious, aristocratical, despotic, and monarchical. If parts of it are extremely good, other parts are very bad.

The freedom of election is one of the greatest securities we have for our liberty and privileges. It was supposed by the member from Edenton, that the control over elections was only given to Congress to be used in case of invasion. I differ from him. That could not have been their intention, otherwise they could have expressed it. But, sir, it points forward to the time when there will be no state legislatures—to the consolidation of all the states. The states will be kept up as boards of elections. I think the same men could make a better constitution; for good government is not the work of a short time. They only had their own wisdom. Were they to go now, they would have the wisdom of the United States. Every gentleman who must reflect on this must see it. The adoption of several other states is urged. I hope every gentleman stands for himself, will act according to his own judgment, and will pay no respect to the adoption by the other states. It may embarrass us in some political difficulties, but let us attend to the interest of our constituents.

Mr. IREDELL answered, that he stated the case of invasion as only one reason out of many for giving the ultimate control over elections to Congress.

Mr. DAVIE. Mr. Chairman, a consolidation of the states is said by some gentlemen to have been intended. They insinuate that this was the cause of their giving this power of elections. If there were any seeds in this Constitution which might, one day, produce a consolidation, it would, sir, with me, be an insuperable objection, I am so perfectly convinced that so extensive a country as this can never be managed by one consolidated government. The Federal Convention were as well convinced as the members of this house, that the state governments were absolutely necessary to the existence of the federal government. They considered them as the great massy pillars on which this political fabric was to be extended and supported; and were fully persuaded that, when they were removed, or should moulder down by time, the general government must tumble into ruin. A very little reflection will show that no department of it can exist without the state governments.

Let us begin with the House of Representatives. Who are to vote for the federal representatives? Those who vote for the state representatives. If the state government vanishes, the general government must vanish also. This is the foundation on which this government was raised, and without which it cannot possibly exist.

The next department is the Senate. How is it formed? By the states themselves. Do they not choose them? Are they not created by them? And will they not have the interest of the states particularly at heart? The states, sir, can put a final period to the government, as was observed by a gentleman who thought this power over elections unnecessary. If the state legislatures think proper, they may refuse to choose senators, and the government must be destroyed.

Is not this government a nerveless mass, a dead carcase, without the executive power? Let your representatives be the most vicious demons that ever existed; let them plot against the liberties of America; let them conspire against its happiness,—all their machinations will not avail if not put in execution. By whom are their laws and projects to be executed? By the President. How is he created? By electors appointed by the people under the direction of the legislatures—by a union of the interest of the people and the state governments. The state governments can put a *veto*, at any time, on the general government, by ceasing to continue the executive power. Admitting the representatives or senators could make corrupt laws, they can neither execute them themselves, nor appoint the executive. Now, sir, I think it must be clear to every candid mind, that no part of this government can be continued after the state governments lose their existence, or even their present forms. It may also be easily proved that all federal governments possess an inherent weakness, which continually tends to their destruction. It is to be lamented that all governments of a federal nature have been short-lived.

Such was the fate of the Achaean league, the Amphictyonic council, and other ancient confederacies; and this opinion is confirmed by the uniform testimony of all history. There are instances in Europe of confederacies subsisting a considerable time; but their duration must be attributed to circumstances exterior to their government. The Germanic confederacy would not exist a moment, were it not for fear of the surrounding powers, and the interest of the emperor. The history of this confederacy is but a series of factions, dissensions, bloodshed, and civil war. The confederacies of the Swiss, and United Netherlands, would long ago have been destroyed, from their imbecility, had it not been for the fear, and even the policy, of the bordering nations. It is impossible to construct such a government in such a manner as to give it any probable longevity. But, sir, there is an excellent principle in this proposed plan of federal government, which none of these confederacies had, and to the want of which, in a great measure, their imperfections may be justly attributed—I mean the principle of representation. I hope that, by the agency of this principle, if it be not immortal, it will at least be long-lived. I thought it necessary to say this much to detect the futility of that unwarrantable suggestion, that we are to be swallowed up by a great consolidated government. Every part of this federal government is dependent on the constitution of the state legislatures for its existence. The whole, sir, can never swallow up its parts. The gentleman from Edenton (Mr. Iredell) has pointed out the reasons of giving this control over elections to Congress, the principle of which was, to prevent a dissolution of the government by designing states. If all the states were equally possessed of absolute power over their elections, without any control of Congress, danger might be justly apprehended where one state possesses as much territory as four or five others; and some of them, being thinly peopled now, will daily become more numerous and formidable. Without this control in Congress, those large states might successfully combine to destroy the general government. It was therefore necessary to control any combination of this kind.

Another principal reason was, that it would operate, in favor of the people, against the ambitious designs of the federal Senate. I will illustrate this by matter of fact. The history of the little state of Rhode Island is well known. An abandoned faction have seized on the reins of government, and frequently refused to have any representation in Congress. If Congress had the power of making the law of elections operate throughout the United States, no state could withdraw itself from the national councils, without the consent of a majority of the members of Congress. Had this been the case, that trifling state would not have withheld its representation. What once happened may happen again; and it was necessary to give Congress this power, to keep the government in full operation. This being a federal government, and involving the interests of several states, and some acts requiring the assent of more than a majority, they ought to be able to keep their representation full. It would have been a solecism, to have a government without *any means* of self-preservation. The Confederation is the only instance of a government without such means, and is a nerveless system, as inadequate to every purpose of government as it is to the security of the liberties of the people of America. When the councils of America have this power over elections, they can, in spite of any faction in any particular state, give the people a representation. Uniformity in matters of election is also of the greatest consequence. They ought all to be judged by the same law and the same principles, and not to be different in one state from what they are in another. At present, the manner of electing is different in different states. Some elect by ballot, and others *viva voce*. It will be more convenient to have the manner uniform in all the states. I shall now answer some observations made by the gentleman from Mecklenburg. He has stated that this power over elections gave to Congress power to lengthen the time for which they were elected. Let us read this clause coolly, all prejudice aside, and determine whether this construction be warrantable. The clause runs thus: "The times places, and manner, of holding elections for senators and representatives, shall be prescribed in each state by the legislature thereof; but the Congress may at any time, by law, make or alter such regulations, except as to the place of choosing senators." I take it as a fundamental principle, which is beyond the reach of the general or individual governments to alter, that the representatives shall be chosen every second year, and that the tenure of their office shall be for two years; that senators be chosen every sixth year, and that the tenure of their office be for six years. I take it also as a principle, that the electors of the most numerous branch of the state legislatures are to elect the federal representatives. Congress has ultimately no power over elections, but what is primarily given to the state legislatures. If Congress had the power of prolonging the time, &c., as gentlemen observe, the same powers must be completely vested in the state legislatures. I call upon every gentleman candidly to declare, whether the state legislatures have the power of altering the time of elections for representatives from two to four years, or senators from six to twelve; and whether they have the power to require any other qualifications than those of the most numerous branch of the state legislatures; and also whether they have any other power over the manner of elections, any more than the mere mode of the act of choosing; or whether they shall be held by sheriffs, as contradistinguished from any other officer; or whether they shall be by votes, as contradistinguished from ballots, or any other way. If gentlemen will pay attention, they will find that, in the latter part of this clause, Congress has no power but what was given to the states in the first part of the same clause. They may alter the manner of holding the election, but cannot alter the tenure of their office. They cannot alter the nature of the elections; for it is established, as fundamental principles, that the electors of the most numerous branch of the state legislature shall elect the federal representatives, and that the tenure of their office shall be for two years; and likewise, that the senators shall be elected by the legislatures, and that the tenure of their office shall be for six years. When gentlemen view the clause accurately, and see that Congress have only the same power which was in the state legislature, they will not be alarmed. The learned doctor on my right (Mr. Spencer) has also said that Congress might lengthen the time of

elections. I am willing to appeal to grammatical construction and punctuation. Let me read this, as it stands on paper. [Here he read the clause different ways, expressing the same sense.] Here, in the first part of the clause, this power over elections is given to the states, and in the latter part the same power is given to Congress, and extending only to the time of *holding*, the place of *holding*, and the manner of *holding*, the elections. Is this not the plain, literal, and grammatical construction of the clause? Is it possible to put any other construction on it, without departing from the natural order, and without deviating from the general meaning of the words, and every rule of grammatical construction? Twist it, torture it, as you may, sir, it is impossible to fix a different sense upon it. The worthy gentleman from New Hanover, (whose ardor for the liberty of his country I wish never to be damped,) has insinuated that high characters might influence the members on this occasion. I declare, for my own part, I wish every man to be guided by his own conscience and understanding, and by nothing else. Every man has not been bred a politician, nor studied the science of government; yet, when a subject is explained, if the mind is unwarped by prejudice, and not in the leading-strings of other people, gentlemen will do what is right. Were this the case, I would risk my salvation on a right decision.

Mr. CALDWELL. Mr. Chairman, those things which can be may be. We know that, in the British government, the members of Parliament were eligible only for three years. They determined they might be chosen for seven years. If Congress can alter the time, manner, and place, I think it will enable them to do what the British Parliament once did. They have declared that the elections of senators are for six years, and of representatives for two years. But they have said there was an exception to this general declaration, viz., that Congress can alter them. If the Convention only meant that they should alter them in such a manner as to prevent a discontinuation of the government, why have they not said so? It must appear to every gentleman in this Convention, that they can alter the elections to what time they please. And if the British Parliament did once give themselves the power of sitting four years longer than they had a right to do, Congress, having a standing army, and the command of the militia, may, with the same propriety, make an act to continue the members for twenty years, or even for their natural lives. This construction appears perfectly rational to me. I shall therefore think that this Convention will never swallow such a government, without securing us against danger.

Mr. MACLAINE. Mr. Chairman, the reverend gentleman from Guilford has made an objection which astonishes me more than any thing I have heard. He seems to be acquainted with the history of England, but he ought to consider whether his historical references apply to this country. He tells us of triennial elections being changed to septennial elections. This is an historical fact we well know, and the occasion on which it happened is equally well known. They talk as loudly of constitutional rights and privileges in England as we do here, but they have no written constitution. They have a common law,—which has been altered from year to year, for a very long period,—

Magna Charta, and bill of rights. These they look upon as their constitution. Yet this is such a constitution as it is universally considered Parliament can change. Blackstone, in his admirable Commentaries, tells us that the power of the Parliament is transcendent and absolute, and can do and undo every thing that is not naturally impossible. The act, therefore, to which the reverend gentleman alludes, was not unconstitutional. Has any man said that the legislature can deviate from this Constitution? The legislature is to be guided by the Constitution. They cannot travel beyond its bounds. The reverend gentleman says, that, though the representatives are to be elected for two years, they may pass an act prolonging their appointment for twenty years, or for natural life, without any violation of the Constitution. Is it possible for any common understanding or sense to put this construction upon it? Such an act, sir, would be a palpable violation of the Constitution: were they to attempt it, sir, the country would rise against them. After such an unwarrantable suggestion as this, any objection may be made to this Constitution. It is necessary to give power to the government. I would ask that gentleman who is so much afraid it will destroy our liberties, why he is not as much afraid of our state legislature; for they have much more power than we are now proposing to give this general government. They have an unlimited control over the purse and sword; yet no complaints are made. Why is he not as much afraid that our legislature will call out the militia to destroy our liberties? Will the militia be called out by the general government to enslave the people—to enslave their friends, their families, themselves? The idea of the militia being made use of, as an instrument to destroy our liberties, is almost too absurd to merit a refutation. It cannot be supposed that the representatives of our general government will be worse men than the members of our state government. Will we be such fools as to send our greatest rascals to the general government? We must be both fools as well as villains to do so.

Gov. JOHNSTON. Mr. Chairman, I shall offer some observations on what the gentleman said. A parallel has been drawn between the British Parliament and Congress. The powers of Congress are all circumscribed, defined, and clearly laid down. So far they may go, but no farther. But, sir, what are the powers of the British Parliament? They have no written constitution in Britain. They have certain fundamental principles and legislative acts, securing the liberty of the people; but these may be altered by their representatives, without violating their constitution, in such manner as they may think proper. Their legislature existed long before the science of government was well understood. From very early periods, you find their Parliament in full force. What is their Magna Charta? It is only an act of Parliament. Their Parliament can, at any time, alter the whole or any part of it. In short, it is no more binding on the people than any other act which has passed. The power of the Parliament is, therefore, unbounded. But, sir, can Congress alter the Constitution? They have no such power. They are bound to act by the Constitution. They dare not recede from it. At the moment that the time for which they are elected expires, they may be removed. If they make bad laws, they will be re-

moved; for they will be no longer worthy of confidence. The British Parliament can do every thing they please. Their bill of rights is only an act of Parliament, which may be, at any time, altered or modified, without a violation of the constitution. The people of Great Britain have no constitution to control their legislature. The king, lords, and commons, can do what they please.

Mr. CALDWELL observed, that whatever nominal powers the British Parliament might possess, yet they had infringed the liberty of the people in the most flagrant manner, by giving themselves power to continue four years in Parliament longer than they have been elected for—that though they were only chosen for three years by their constituents, yet they passed an act that representatives should, for the future, be chosen for seven years—that this Constitution would have a dangerous tendency—that this clause would enable them to prolong their continuance in office as long as they pleased—and that, if a constitution was not agreeable to the people, its operation could not be happy.

Gov. JOHNSTON replied, that the act to which allusion was made by the gentleman was not unconstitutional; but that, if Congress were to pass an act prolonging the terms of elections of senators or representatives, it would be clearly unconstitutional.

Mr. MACLAINE observed, that the act of Parliament referred to was passed on urgent necessity, when George I. ascended the throne, to prevent the Papists from getting into Parliament; for parties ran so high at that time, that Papists enough might have got in to destroy the act of settlement which excluded the Roman Catholics from the succession to the throne.

Mr. SPENCER. The gentleman from Halifax said, that the reason of this clause was, that some states might be refractory. I profess that, in my opinion, the circumstances of Rhode Island do not appear to apply. I cannot conceive the particular cause why Rhode Island should not send representatives to Congress. If they were united in one government, is it presumed that they would waive the right of representation? I have not the least reason to doubt they would make use of the privilege. With respect to the construction that the worthy member put upon the clause, were that construction established, I would be satisfied; but it is susceptible of a different explanation. They may alter the mode of election so as to deprive the people of the right of choosing. I wish to have it expressed in a more explicit manner.

Mr. DAVIE. Mr. Chairman, the gentleman has certainly misconceived the matter, when he says "that the circumstances of Rhode Island do not apply." It is a fact well known of which, perhaps, he may not be possessed, that the state of Rhode Island has not been regularly represented for several years, owing to the character and particular views of the prevailing party. By the influence of this faction, who are in possession of the state government, the people have been frequently deprived of the benefit of a representation in the Union, and Congress often embarrassed by their absence. The same evil may again result from the same cause; and Congress ought, therefore, to possess constitutional power to give the people an opportunity of electing representatives, if the states neglect or refuse to do it. The gentleman from Anson has said, "that this clause is susceptible of an explanation different from the construction I put upon it." I have a high respect for his opinion, but that alone, on this important occasion, is not satisfactory: we must have some *reasons* from him to support and sanction this opinion. He is a professional man, and has held an office many years, the nature and duties of which would enable him to put a different construction on this clause, if it is capable of it.

This clause, sir, has been the occasion of much groundless alarm, and has been the favorite theme of declamation out of doors. I now call upon the gentlemen of the opposition to show that it contains the mischiefs with which they have alarmed and agitated the public mind, and I defy them to support the construction they have put upon it by one single plausible reason. The gentleman from New Hanover has said, in objection to this clause, "that Congress may appoint the most inconvenient place in the most inconvenient district, and make the manner of election so oppressive as entirely to destroy representation." If this is considered as possible, he should also reflect that the state legislatures may do the same thing. But this can never happen, sir, until the whole mass of the people become corrupt, when all parchment securities will be of little service. Does that gentleman, or any other gentleman who has the smallest acquaintance with human nature or the spirit of America, suppose that the people will passively relinquish privileges, or suffer the usurpation of powers unwarranted by the Constitution? Does not the right of electing representatives revert to the people every second year? There is nothing in this clause that can impede or destroy this reversion; and although the particular time of year, the particular place in a county or a district, or the particular mode in which elections are to be held, as whether by vote or ballot, be left to Congress to direct, yet this can never deprive the people of the *right* or *privilege* of election. He has also added, "that the democratical branch was in danger from this clause;" and, with some other gentlemen, took it for granted that an aristocracy must arise out of the general government. This, I take it, from the very nature of the thing, can never happen. Aristocracies grow out of the combination of a few powerful families, where the country or people upon which they are to operate are immediately under their influence; whereas the interest and influence of this government are too weak, and too much diffused, ever to bring about such an event. The confidence of the people, acquired by a wise and virtuous conduct, is the only influence the members of the federal government can ever have. When aristocracies are formed, they will arise within the individual states. It is therefore absolutely necessary that Congress should have a constitutional power to give the people at large a representation in the government, in order to break and control such dangerous combinations. Let gentlemen show when and how this aristocracy they talk of is to arise out of this Constitution. Are the first members to perpetuate themselves? Is the Constitution to be attacked by such absurd assertions as these, and charged with defects with which it has no possible connection?

Mr. BLOODWORTH. Mr. Chairman, the gentleman has mistaken me. When we examine the gentleman's arguments, they have no weight. He tells us that it is not probable "that an aristocracy can arise." I did not say that it would. Various arguments are brought forward in support of this article. They are vague and trifling. There is nothing that can be offered to my mind which will reconcile me to it while this evil exists—while Congress have this control over elections. It was easy for them to mention that this control should only be exerted when the state would neglect, or refuse, or be unable in case of invasion, to regulate elections. If so, why did they not mention it expressly?

It appears to me that some of their general observations imply a contradiction. Do they not tell us that there is no danger of a consolidation? that Congress can exist no longer than the states—the massy pillars on which it is said to be raised? Do they not also tell us that the state governments are to secure us against Congress? At another time, they tell us that it was unnecessary to secure our liberty by giving them power to prevent the state governments from oppressing us. We know that there is a corruption in human nature. Without circumspection and carefulness, we shall throw away our liberties. Why is this general expression used on this great occasion? Why not use expressions that were clear and unequivocal? If I trust my property with a man and take security, shall I then barter away my rights?

Mr. SPENCER. Mr. Chairman, this clause may operate in such a manner as will abridge the liberty of the people. It is well known that men in power are apt to abuse it, and extend it if possible. From the ambiguity of this expression, they may put such construction upon it as may suit them. I would not have it in such a manner as to endanger the rights of the people. But it has been said that this power is necessary to preserve their existence. There is not the least doubt but the people will keep them from losing their existence, if they shall behave themselves in such a manner as will merit it.

Mr. MACLAINE. Mr. Chairman, I thought it very extraordinary that the gentleman who was last on the floor should say that Congress could do what they please with respect to elections, and be warranted by this clause. The gentleman from Halifax (Mr. Davie) has put that construction upon it which reason and common sense will put upon it. Lawyers will often differ on a point of law, but people will seldom differ about so very plain a thing as this. The clause enables Congress to alter such regulations as the states shall have made with respect to elections. What would he infer from this? What is it to alter? It is to alter the time, place, and manner, established by the legislatures, if they do not answer the purpose. Congress ought to have power to perpetuate the government, and not the states, who might be otherwise inclined. I will ask the gentleman—and I wish he may give me a satisfactory answer—if the whole is not in the power of the people, as well when the elections are regulated by Congress, as when by the states. Are not both the agents of the people, amenable to them? Is there any thing in this Constitution which gives them the power to perpetuate the sitting members? Is there any such strange absurdity? If the legislature of this state has the power to fix the time, place, and manner, of holding elections, why not place the same confidence in the general government? The members of the general government, and those of the state legislature, are both chosen by the people. They are both from among the people, and are in the same situation. Those who served in the state legislature are eligible, and may be sent to Congress. If the elections be regulated in the best manner in the state government, can it be supposed that the same man will lose all his virtue, his character and principles, when he goes into the general government, in order to deprive us of our liberty?

The gentleman from New Hanover seems to think it possible Congress will so far forget themselves as to point out such improper seasons of the year, and such inconvenient places for elections, as to defeat the privilege of the democratic branch altogether. He speaks of inconsistency in the arguments of the gentlemen. I wish he would be consistent himself. If I do not mistake the politics of that gentleman, it is his opinion that Congress had sufficient power under the Confederation. He has said, without contradiction, that we should be better without the Union than with it; that it would be better for us to be by ourselves than in the Union. His antipathy to a general government, and to the Union, is evidently inconsistent with his predilection for a federal democratic branch. We should have no democratic part of the government at all, under such a government as he would recommend. There is no such part in the old Confederation. The body of the people had no agency in that system. The members of the present general government are selected by the state legislatures, and have the power of the purse, and other powers, and are not amenable to the people at large. Although the gentleman may deny my assertions, yet this argument of his is inconsistent with his other assertions and doctrines. It is impossible for any man in his senses to think that we can exist by ourselves, separated from our sister states. Whatever gentlemen may pretend to say on this point, it must be a matter of serious alarm to every reflecting mind, to be disunited from the other states.

Mr. BLOODWORTH begged leave to wipe off the assertion of the gentleman; that he could not account for any expression which he might drop among a laughing, jocose people, but that it was well known he was for giving power to Congress to regulate the trade of the United States; that he had said that Congress had exercised power not given them by the Confederation, and that he was accurate in the assertion; that he was a freeman, and was under the control of no man.

Mr. MACLAINE replied, that he meant no aspersions; that he only meant to point out a fact; that he had committed mistakes himself in argument, and that he supposed the gentleman not more infallible than other people.

Mr. J. TAYLOR wished to know why the states had control over the place of electing senators, but not over that of choosing the representatives.

Mr. SPAIGHT answered, that the reason of that reservation was to prevent Congress from altering the places for holding the legislative assemblies in the different states.

Mr. JAMES GALLOWAY. Mr. Chairman, in the beginning I found great candor in the advocates of this government, but it is not so towards the last. I hope the gentleman from Halifax will not take it amiss, if I mention how he brought the motion forward. They began with dangers. As to Rhode Island being governed by a faction, what has that to do with the question before us? I ask, What have the state governments left for them, if the general government is to be possessed of such extensive powers, without control or limitation, without any responsibility to the states? He asks, How is it possible for the members to perpetuate themselves? I think I can show how they can do it. For instance, where they to take the government as it now stands organized. We send five members to the House of Representatives in the general government. They will go, no doubt, from or near the seaports. In other states, also, those near the sea will have more interest, and will go forward to Congress; and they can, without violating the Constitution, make a law continuing themselves, as they have control over the place, time, and manner, of elections. This may happen; and where the great principles of liberty are endangered, no general, indeterminate, vague expression ought to be suffered. Shall we pass over this article as it is now? They will be able to perpetuate themselves as well as if it had expressly said so.

Mr. STEELE. Mr. Chairman, the gentleman has said that the five representatives which this state shall be entitled to send to the general government, will go from the seashore. What reason has he to say they will go from the seashore? The time, place, and manner, of holding elections are to be prescribed by the legislatures. Our legislature is to regulate the first election, at any event. They will regulate it as they think proper. They may, and most probably will, lay the state off into districts. Who are to vote for them? Every man who has a right to vote for a representative to our legislature will ever have a right to vote for a representative to the general government. Does it not expressly provide that the electors in each state shall have the qualifications requisite for the most numerous branch of the state legislature? Can they, without a most manifest violation of the Constitution, alter the qualifications of the electors? The power over the manner of elections does not include that of saying who shall vote:—the Constitution expressly says that the qualifications which entitle a man to vote for a state representative. It is, then, clearly and indubitably fixed and determined *who* shall be the electors; and the power over the manner only enables them to determine *how* these electors shall elect—whether by ballot, or by vote, or by any other way. Is it not a maxim of universal jurisprudence, of reason and common sense, that an instrument or deed of writing shall be so construed as to give validity to all parts of it, if it can be done without involving any absurdity? By construing it in the plain, obvious way I have mentioned, all parts will be valid. By the way, gentlemen suggest the most palpable contradiction, and absurdity will follow. To say that they shall go from the sea-shore, and be able to perpetuate themselves, is a most extravagant idea. Will the members of Congress deviate from their duty without any prospect of advantage to themselves? What interest can they have to make the place of elections inconvenient? The judicial power of that government is so well constructed as to be a check. There was no check in the old Confederation. Their power was, in principle and theory, transcendent. If the Congress make laws inconsistent with the Constitution, independent judges will not uphold them, nor will the people obey them. A universal resistance will ensue. In some countries, the arbitrary disposition of rulers may enable them to overturn the liberties of the people; but in a country like this, where every man is his own master, and where almost every man is a freeholder, and has the right of election, the violations of a constitution will not be passively permitted. Can it be supposed that in such a country the rights of suffrage will be tamely surrendered? Is it to be supposed that 30,000 free persons will send the most abandoned wretch in the district to legislate for them in the general legislature? I should rather think they would choose men of the most respectable characters.

19

JAMES IREDELL, PROPOSED AMENDMENT, NORTH
CAROLINA RATIFYING CONVENTION
1 Aug. 1788
Elliot 4:249

---

4. The Congress shall not alter, modify, or interfere in the times, places, or manner, of holding elections for senators and representatives, or either of them, except when the legislature of any state shall neglect, refuse, or be disabled by invasion or rebellion, to prescribe the same.

20

HOUSE OF REPRESENTATIVES, AN AMENDMENT TO
ART. 1, SEC. 4, CL. 1
21 Aug. 1789
Annals 1:768–73

MR. BURKE.—The majority of this House may be inclined to think all our propositions unimportant, as they seemed to consider that upon which the ayes and noes were just now called. However, to the minority they are important; and it will be happy for the Government, if the majority of our citizens are not of their opinion; but be this as it may, I move you, sir, to add to the articles of amendment the following: "Congress shall not alter, modify, or interfere in the times, places, or manner of holding elections of Senators, or Representatives, except when any State shall refuse or neglect, or be unable, by invasion or rebellion, to make such election."

Mr. AMES thought this one of the most justifiable of all the powers of Congress; it was essential to a body representing the whole community, that they should have power to regulate their own elections, in order to secure a representation from every part, and prevent any improper regulations, calculated to answer party purposes only. It is a solecism in politics to let others judge for them, and is a departure from the principles upon which the constitution was founded.

Mr. LIVERMORE said, this was an important amendment, and one that had caused more debate in the Convention of New Hampshire than any other whatever. The gentleman just up said it was a solecism in politics, but he could cite an instance in which it had taken place. He only called upon gentlemen to recollect the circumstance of Mr. SMITH's (of South Carolina) election, and to ask if that was not decided by the State laws? Was not his qualification as a member of the Federal Legislature determined upon the laws of South Carolina? It was not supposed by the people of South Carolina, that the House would question a right derived by their representative from their authority.

Mr. MADISON.—If this amendment had been proposed at any time either in the Committee of the whole or separately in the House, I should not have objected to the discussion of it. But I cannot agree to delay the amendments now agreed upon, by entering into the consideration of propositions not likely to obtain the consent of either two-thirds of this House or three-fourths of the State Legislatures. I have considered this subject with some degree of attention, and, upon the whole, am inclined to think the constitution stands very well as it is.

Mr. GERRY was sorry that gentlemen objected to the time and manner of introducing this amendment, because it was too important in its nature to be defeated by want of form. He hoped, and he understood it to be the sense of the House, that each amendment should stand upon its own ground; if this was, therefore, examined on its own merits, it might stand or fall as it deserved, and there would be no cause for complaint on the score of inattention.

His colleague (Mr. AMES) objected to the amendment, because he thought no Legislature was without the power of determining the mode of its own appointment; but he would find, if he turned to the constitution of the State he was a representative of, that the times, places, and manner of choosing members of their Senate and Council were prescribed therein.

Why, said he, are gentlemen desirous of retaining this power? Is it because it gives energy to the Government? It certainly has no such tendency; then why retain a clause so obnoxious to almost every State? But this provision may be necessary in order to establish a Government of an arbitrary kind, to which the present system is pointed in no very indirect manner: in this way, indeed, it may be useful. If the United States are desirous of controlling the elections of the people, they will in the first place, by virtue of the powers given them by the 4th sect. of the 1st art. abolish the mode of balloting; then every person must publicly announce his vote, and it would then frequently happen that he would be obliged to vote for a man, or "the friend of a man" to whom he was under obligations. If the Government grows desirous of being arbitrary, elections will be ordered at remote places, where their friends alone will attend. Gentlemen will tell me that these things are not to be apprehended; but if they say that the Government has the power of doing them, they have no right to say the Government will never exercise such powers, because it is presumable that they will administer the constitution at one time or another with all its powers: and whenever that time arrives, farewell to the rights of the people, even to elect their own representatives.

Mr. STONE called upon gentlemen to show what confederated Government had the power of determining on the mode of their own election. He apprehended there were none; for the representatives of States were chosen by the States in the manner they pleased. He was not afraid that the General Government would abuse this power, and as little afraid that the States would; but he thought it was in the order of things that the power should vest in the States respectively, because they can vary their regulations to accommodate the people in a more convenient manner than can be done in any general law whatever. He thought the amendment was generally expected, and therefore, on the principles of the majority, ought to be adopted.

Mr. SMITH (of South Carolina) said, he hoped it would be agreed to; that eight States had expressed their desires on this head, and all of them wished the General Government to relinquish their control over the elections. The eight States he alluded to were New Hampshire, Massachusetts, New York, Pennsylvania, Maryland, Virginia, North Carolina, and South Carolina.

Mr. CARROLL denied that Maryland had expressed the desire attributed to her.

Mr. FITZSIMONS.—The remark was not just as it respected Pennsylvania.

Mr. SMITH (of South Carolina) said, the Convention of Maryland appointed a committee to recommend amendments, and among them was the one now under consideration.

Mr. STONE replied there was nothing of the kind noticed on the journals of that body.

Mr. SMITH (of South Carolina) did not know how they came into the world, but he had certainly seen them. As to Pennsylvania, there was a very considerable minority, he understood one-third, who had recommended the amendment. Now, taking all circumstances into consideration, it might be fairly inferred that a majority of the United States were in favor of this amendment. He had studied to make himself acquainted with this particular subject, and all that he had ever heard in defence of the power being exercised by the General Government was, that it was necessary, in case any State neglected or refused to make provision for the election. Now these cases were particularly excepted by the clause proposed by his honorable colleague; and therefore he presumed there was no good argument against it.

Mr. SEDGWICK moved to amend the motion, by giving the power to Congress to alter the times, manner, and places of holding elections, provided the States made improper ones; for as much injury might result to the Union from improper regulations, as from a neglect or refusal to make any. It is as much to be apprehended that the States may abuse their powers, as that the United States may make an improper use of theirs.

Mr. AMES said, that inadequate regulations were equally injurious as having none, and that such an amendment as was now proposed would alter the constitution; it would vest the supreme authority in places where it was never contemplated.

Mr. SHERMAN observed, that the Convention were very unanimous in passing this clause; that it was an important provision, and if it was resigned it would tend to subvert the Government.

Mr. MADISON was willing to make every amendment that was required by the States, which did not tend to destroy the principles and the efficacy of the constitution; he conceived that the proposed amendment would have that tendency, he was therefore opposed to it.

Mr. SMITH (of South Carolina) observed, that the States had the sole regulation of elections, so far as it respected the President. Now he saw no good reason why they should be indulged in this, and prohibited from the other. But the amendment did not go so far; it admitted that the General Government might interfere whenever the State Legislature refused or neglected; and it might happen that the business would be neglected without any design to injure the administration of the General Government; it might be that the two branches of the Legislature could not agree, as happened he believed in the Legislature of New York, with respect to their choice of Senators at their late session.

Mr. TUCKER objected to Mr. SEDGWICK's motion of amendment, because it had a tendency to defeat the object of the proposition brought forward by his colleague, (Mr. BURKE.) The General Government would be the judge of inadequate or improper regulations; of consequence they might interfere in any or every law which the States might pass on that subject.

He wished that the State Legislatures might be left to themselves to perform every thing they were competent to, without the guidance of Congress. He believed there was no great danger, but they knew how to pursue their own good, as well when left to their discretion, as they would under the direction of a superior. It seemed to him as if there was a strong propensity in this Government to take upon themselves the guidance of the State Governments, which to his mind implied a doubt of their capacity to govern themselves; now his judgment was convinced that the particular State Governments could take care of themselves, and deserved more to be trusted than this did, because the right of the citizen was more secure under it.

It had been supposed by some States, that electing by districts was the most convenient mode of choosing members to this House; others have thought that the whole State ought to vote for the whole number of members to be elected for that State. Congress might, under like impressions, set their regulations aside. He had heard that many citizens of Virginia (which State was divided into eleven districts) supposed themselves abridged of nine-tenths of their privilege by being restrained to the choice of one man instead of ten, the number that State sends to this House.

With respect to the election of Senators, the mode is fixed; every State but New York has established a precedent; there is, therefore, but little danger of any difficulty on this account. As to New York, she suffers by her want of decision; it is her own loss; but probably they may soon decide the point, and then no difficulty can possibly arise hereafter. From all these considerations, he was induced to hope Mr. SEDGWICK's motion would be negatived, and his colleague's agreed to.

Mr. GOODHUE hoped the amendment never would obtain. Gentlemen should recollect there appeared a large majority against amendments, when the subject was first introduced, and he had no doubt but that majority still existed. Now, rather than this amendment should take effect, he would vote against all that had been agreed to. His greatest apprehensions were, that the State Governments would oppose and thwart the general one to such a degree as finally to overturn it. Now, to guard against this evil, he wished the Federal Government to possess every power necessary to its existence.

Mr. BURKE was convinced there was a majority against him; but, nevertheless, he would do his duty, and propose such amendments as he conceived essential to secure the rights and liberties of his constituents. He begged permission to make an observation or two, not strictly in order; the first was on an assertion that had been repeated more than once in this House, "That this revolution or adoption of the new constitution was agreeable to the public mind, and those who opposed it at first are now satisfied with it." I believe, sir, said he, that many of those gentlemen who agreed to the ratification without amendments, did it from principles of patriotism, but they knew at the same time that they parted with their liberties; yet they had such reliance on the virtue of a future Congress, that they did not hesitate, expecting that they would be restored to them unimpaired, as soon as the Government commenced its operations, conformably to what was mutually understood at the sealing and delivering up of those instruments.

It has been supposed that there is no danger to be apprehended from the General Government of an invasion of the rights of election. I will remind gentlemen of an instance in the Government of Holland. The patriots in that country fought no less strenuously for that prize than the people of America; yet, by giving to the States General powers not unlike those in this constitution, their right of representation was abolished. That they once possessed it is certain, and that they made as much talk about its importance as we do; but now the right has ceased, all vacancies are filled by the men in power. It is our duty, therefore, to prevent our liberties from being fooled away in a similar manner; consequently we ought to adopt the clause which secures to the General Government every thing that ought to be required.

Mr. MADISON observed, that it was the State Governments in the Seven United Provinces which had assumed to themselves the power of filling vacancies, and not the General Government; therefore the gentleman's application did not hold.

The question on Mr. SEDGWICK's motion for amending Mr. BURKE's proposition was put and lost.

The question was then put on Mr. BURKE's motion, [ayes—23; noes—28].

SEE ALSO:

Records of the Federal Convention, Farrand 2:135, 139, 141, 153, 155, 165, 229, 567, 613

James McHenry, Maryland House of Delegates, 29 Nov. 1787, Farrand 3:148

St. George Tucker, Blackstone's Commentaries 1:App. 191–94 (1803)

James Kent, Commentaries 217–18 (1826)

Joseph Story, Commentaries on the Constitution, 2:§§ 813–26 (1833)

Article 1, Section 4, Clause 2

The Congress shall assemble at least once in every Year, and such Meeting shall be on the first Monday in December, unless they shall by Law appoint a different Day.

1

WILLIAM BLACKSTONE, *Commentaries* 1:144–49
1765

There is also no doubt but these great councils were held regularly under the first princes of the Norman line. Glanvil, who wrote in the reign of Henry the second, speaking of the particular amount of an amercement in the sheriff's court, says, it had never yet been ascertained by the general assise, or assembly, but was left to the custom of particular counties. Here the general assise is spoken of as a meeting well known, and it's statutes or decisions are put in a manifest contradistinction to customs, or the common law. And in Edward the third's time an act of parliament, made in the reign of William the conqueror, was pleaded in the case of the abbey of St Edmund's-bury, and judicially allowed by the court.

Hence it indisputably appears, that parliaments, or general councils, are coeval with the kingdom itself. How those parliaments were constituted and composed, is another question, which has been matter of great dispute among our learned antiquarians; and, particularly, whether the commons were summoned at all; or, if summoned, at what period they began to form a distinct assembly. But it is not my intention here to enter into controversies of this sort. I hold it sufficient that it is generally agreed, that in the main the constitution of parliament, as it now stands, was marked out so long ago as the seventeenth year of king John, *A.D.*1215, in the great charter granted by that prince; wherein he promises to summon all arch-bishops, bishops, abbots, earls, and greater barons, personally; and all other tenants in chief under the crown, by the sheriff and bailiffs; to meet at a certain place, with forty days notice, to assess aids and scutages when necessary. And this constitution has subsisted in fact at least from the year 1266, 49 Hen. III: there being still extant writs of that date, to summon knights, citizens, and burgesses to parliament. I proceed therefore to enquire wherein consists this constitution of parliament, as it now stands, and has stood for the space of five hundred years. And in the prosecution of this enquiry, I shall consider, first, the manner and time of it's assembling: secondly, it's constituent parts: thirdly, the laws and customs relating to parliament, considered as one aggregate body: fourthly and fifthly, the laws and customs relating to each house, separately and distinctly taken: sixthly, the methods of proceeding, and of making statutes, in both houses: and lastly, the manner of the parliament's adjournment, prorogation, and dissolution.

I. As to the manner and time of assembling. The parliament is regularly to be summoned by the king's writ or letter, issued out of chancery by advice of the privy council, at least forty days before it begins to sit. It is a branch of the royal prerogative, that no parliament can be convened by it's own authority, or by the authority of any, except the king alone. And this prerogative is founded upon very good reason. For, supposing it had a right to meet spontaneously, without being called together, it is impossible to conceive that all the members, and each of the houses, would agree unanimously upon the proper time and place of meeting: and if half of the members met, and half absented themselves, who shall determine which is really the legislative body, the part assembled, or that which stays away? It is therefore necessary that the parliament should be called together at a determinate time and place; and highly becoming it's dignity and independence, that it should be called together by none but one of it's own constituent parts; and, of the three constituent parts, this office can only appertain to the king; as he is a single person, whose will may be uniform and steady; the first person in the nation, being superior to both houses in dignity; and the only branch of the legislature that has a separate existence, and is capable of performing any act at a time when no parliament is in being. Nor is it an exception to this rule that, by some modern statutes, on the demise of a king or queen, if there be then no parliament in being, the last parliament revives, and is to sit again for six months, unless dissolved by the successor: for this revived parliament must have been originally summoned by the crown.

It is true, that by a statute, 16 Car. I. c. 1. it was enacted, that if the king neglected to call a parliament for three years, the peers might assemble and issue out writs for the choosing one; and, in case of neglect of the peers, the constituents might meet and elect one themselves. But this, if ever put in practice, would have been liable to all the inconveniences I have just now stated; and the act itself was esteemed so highly detrimental and injurious to the royal prerogative, that it was repealed by statute 16 Car. II. c.1. From thence therefore no precedent can be drawn.

It is also true, that the convention-parliament, which restored king Charles the second, met above a month before his return; the lords by their own authority, and the commons in pursuance of writs issued in the name of the keepers of the liberty of England by authority of parliament: and that the said parliament sat till the twenty ninth of December, full seven months after the restoration; and enacted many laws, several of which are still in force. But this was for the necessity of the thing, which supersedes all law; for if they had not so met, it was morally impossible that the kingdom should have been settled in peace. And the first thing done after the king's return, was to pass an act declaring this to be a good parliament, notwithstanding the defect of the king's writs. So that, as the royal prerogative was chiefly wounded by their so meeting, and as the king himself, who alone had a right to object, consented to wave the objection, this cannot be drawn into an example in prejudice of the rights of the crown. Besides we should also remember, that it was at that time a great doubt among the lawyers, whether even this healing act made it a good parliament; and held by very many in the negative: though it seems to have been too nice a scruple.

It is likewise true, that at the time of the revolution, *A.D.* 1688, the lords and commons by their own authority, and upon the summons of the prince of Orange, (afterwards king William) met in a convention and therein disposed of the crown and kingdom. But it must be remembered, that this assembling was upon a like principle of necessity as at the restoration; that is, upon an apprehension that king James the second had abdicated the government, and that the throne was thereby vacant: which apprehension of theirs was confirmed by their concurrent resolution, when they actually came together. An in such a case as the palpable vacancy of a throne, it follows *ex necessitate rei*, that the form of the royal writs must be laid aside, otherwise no parliament can ever meet again. For, let us put another possible case, and suppose, for the sake of argument, that the whole royal line should at any time fail, and become extinct, which would indisputably vacate the throne: in this situation it seems reasonable to presume, that the body of the nation, consisting of lords and commons, would have a right to meet and settle the government; otherwise there must be no government at all. And upon this and no other principle did the convention in 1688 assemble. The vacancy of the throne was precedent to their meeting without any royal summons, not a consequence of it. They did not assemble without writ, and then make the throne vacant; but the throne being previously vacant by the king's abdication, they assembled without writ, as they must do if they assembled at all. Had the throne been full, their meeting would not have been regular; but, as it was really empty, such meeting became absolutely necessary. And accordingly it is declared by statute 1 W & M. st. 1. c. 1. that this convention was really the two houses of parliament, notwithstanding the want of writs or other defects of form. So that, notwithstanding these two capital exceptions, which were justifiable only on a principle of necessity, (and each of which, by the way, induced a revolution in the government) the rule laid down is in general certain, that the king, only, can convoke a parliament.

And this by the antient statutes of the realm, he is bound to do every year, or oftener, if need be. Not that he is, or ever was, obliged by these statutes to call a *new* parliament every year; but only to permit a parliament to sit annually for the redress of grievances, and dispatch of business, *if need be*. These last words are so loose and vague, that such of our monarchs as were enclined to govern without parliaments, neglected the convoking them, sometimes for a very considerable period, under pretence that there was no need of them. But, to remedy this, by the statute 16 Car. II. c. 1. it is enacted, that the fitting and holding of parliaments shall not be intermitted above three years at the most. And by the statute 1 W. & M. st. 2. c. 2. it is declared to be one of the rights of the people, that for redress of all grievances, and for the amending, strengthening, and preserving the laws, parliaments ought to be held *frequently*. And this indefinite *frequency* is again reduced to a certainty by statute 6 W. & M. c. 2. which enacts, as the statute of Charles the second had done before, that a new parliament shall be called within three years after the determination of the former.

2

DECLARATION OF INDEPENDENCE
4 July 1776
Tansill 23

—He has called together legislative bodies at places unusual, uncomfortable, and distant from the depository of their public Records, for the sole purpose of fatiguing them into compliance with his measures.—He has dissolved Representative Houses repeatedly, for opposing with manly firmness his invasions on the rights of the people.—He has refused for a long time, after such dissolutions, to cause others to be elected; whereby the Legislative powers, incapable of Annihilation, have returned to the People at large for their exercise; the State remaining in the mean time exposed to all the dangers of invasion from without, and convulsions within.

3

RECORDS OF THE FEDERAL CONVENTION

[2:163; *Committee of Detail, IX*]
To meet on the 1st Monday every December—

[2:177; *Madison, 6 Aug.*]
The Legislature shall meet on the first Monday in December in every year.

[2:193; *Journal, 7 Aug.*]
It was moved and seconded to add the following words to the last clause of the third article
"unless a different day shall be appointed by law"
which passed in the affirmative [Ayes—8; noes—2.]
It was moved and seconded to strike out the word "December" and to insert the word "May" in the third article
which passed in the negative. [Ayes—2; noes—8.]
. . . . .
It was moved and seconded to amend the last clause of the third article to read as follows namely
"The Legislature shall meet at least once in every year; and such meeting shall be on the first monday in December unless a different day shall be appointed by law"
which passed in the affirmative

[2:197; *Madison, 7 Aug.*]
Mr Madison wished to know the reasons of the Come for fixing by ye. Constitution the time of Meeting for the Legislature; and suggested, that it be required only that one meeting at least should be held every year leaving the time to be fixed or varied by law.

Mr. Govr. Mor[ris] moved to strike out the sentence. It was improper to tie down the Legislature to a particular time, or even to require a meeting every year. The public business might not require it.

Mr. Pinckney concurred with Mr Madison

Mr. Ghorum. If the time be not fixed by the Constitution, disputes will arise in the Legislature; and the States will be at a loss to adjust thereto, the times of their elections. In the N. England States, the annual time of meeting had been long fixed by their Charters and Constitutions, and no inconveniency had resulted. He thought it necessary that there should be one meeting at least every year as a check on the Executive department.

Mr. Elseworth was agst. striking out the words. The Legislature will not know till they are met whether the public interest required their meeting or not. He could see no impropriety in fixing the day, as the Convention could judge of it as well as the Legislature.

Mr. Wilson thought on the whole it would be best to fix the day.

Mr. King could not think there would be a necessity for a meeting every year. A great vice in our system was that of legislating too much. The most numerous objects of legislation belong to the States. Those of the Natl. Legislature were but few. The chief of them were commerce & revenue. When these should be once settled, alterations would be rarely necessary & easily made.

Mr Madison thought if the time of meeting should be fixed by a law it wd. be sufficiently fixed & there would be no difficulty then as had been suggested, on the part of the States in adjusting their elections to it. One consideration appeared to him to militate strongly agst. fixing a time by the Constitution. It might happen that the Legislature might be called together by the public exigencies & finish their Session but a short time before the annual period. In this case it would be extremely inconvenient to reassemble so quickly & without the least necessity. He thought one annual meeting ought to be required; but did not wish to make two unavoidable.

Col. Mason thought the objections against fixing the time insuperable; but that an annual meeting ought to be required as essential to the preservation of the Constitution. The extent of the Country will supply business. And if it should not, the Legislature, besides *legislative,* is to have *inquisitorial* powers, which can not safely be long kept in a State of suspension.

Mr. Sherman was decided for fixing the time, as well as for frequent meetings of the Legislative body. Disputes and difficulties will arise between the two Houses, & between both & the States, if the time be changeable—frequent meetings of Parliament were required at the Revolution in England as an essential safeguard of liberty. So also are annual meetings in most of the American charters and constitutions. There will be business eno' to require it. The Western Country, and the great extent and varying state of our affairs in general will supply objects.

Mr. Randolph was agst. fixing any day irrevocably; but as there was no provision made any where in the Constitution for regulating the periods of meeting, and some precise time must be fixed, untill the Legislature shall make provision, he could not agree to strike out the words altogether. Instead of which he moved to add the words following—"unless a different day shall be appointed by law."

Mr. Madison 2ded. the motion, & on the question

N. H. no. Mas. ay. Ct. no. Pa. ay. Del. ay. Md. ay. Va. ay. N. C. ay. S. C. ay. Geo. ay. [Ayes—8; noes—2.]

Mr. Govr. Morris moved to strike out Decr. & insert May. It might frequently happen that our measures ought to be influenced by those in Europe, which were generally planned during the Winter and of which intelligence would arrive in the Spring.

Mr. Madison 2ded. the motion. he preferred May to Decr. because the latter would require the travelling to & from the Seat of Govt. in the most inconvenient seasons of the year.

Mr. Wilson. The Winter is the most convenient season for business.

Mr. Elseworth. The summer will interfere too much with private business, that of almost all the probable members of the Legislature being more or less connected with agriculture.

Mr Randolph. The time is of no great moment now, as the Legislature can vary it. On looking into the Constitutions of the States, he found that the times of their elections with which the elections of the Natl. Representatives would no doubt be made to co-incide, would suit better with Decr than May. And it was advisable to render our innovations as little incommodious as possible.

On question for "May" instead of "Decr."

N- H. no. Mas. no. Ct. no. Pa. no. Del. no. Md. no. Va. no. N. C. no. S. C. ay. Geo. ay. [Ayes—2; noes—8.]

4

JOSEPH STORY, COMMENTARIES ON THE
CONSTITUTION 2:§§ 827–28
(1833)

---

§ 827. . . . This clause, for the first time, made its appearance in the revised draft of the constitution near the close of the convention; and was silently adopted, and, so far as can be perceived, without opposition. Annual parliaments had been long a favourite opinion and practice with the people of England; and in America, under the colonial governments, they were justly deemed a great security to public liberty. The present provision could hardly be overlooked by a free people, jealous of their rights; and therefore the constitution fixed a constitutional period, at which congress should assemble in every year, unless some other day was specially prescribed. Thus, the legislative discretion was necessarily bounded; and annual sessions were placed equally beyond the power of faction, and of party, of power, and of corruption. In two of the states a more frequent assemblage of the legislature was known to exist. But it was obvious, that from the nature of their duties, and the distance of their abodes, the members of congress ought not to be brought together at shorter periods, unless upon the most pressing exigencies. A provision, so universally acceptable, requires no vindication, or commentary.

§ 828. Under the British constitution, the king has the sole right to convene, and prorogue, and dissolve parliament. And although it is now usual for parliament to assemble annually, the power of prorogation may be applied at the king's pleasure, so as to prevent any business from being done. And it is usual for the king, when he means, that parliament should assemble to do business, to give notice by proclamation accordingly; otherwise a prorogation is of course on the first day of the session.

SEE ALSO:

Records of the Federal Convention, Farrand 2:206, 565, 592

Article 1, Section 5, Clauses 1–4

Each House shall be the Judge of the Elections, Returns and Qualifications of its own Members, and a Majority of each shall constitute a Quorum to do Business; but a smaller Number may adjourn from day to day, and may be authorized to compel the Attendance of absent Members, in such Manner, and under such Penalties as each House may provide.

Each House may determine the Rules of its Proceedings, punish its Members for disorderly Behaviour, and, with the Concurrence of two thirds, expel a Member.

Each House shall keep a Journal of its Proceedings, and from time to time publish the same, excepting such Parts as may in their Judgment require Secrecy; and the Yeas and Nays of the Members of either House on any question shall, at the Desire of one fifth of those Present, be entered on the Journal.

Neither House, during the Session of Congress, shall, without the Consent of the other, adjourn for more than three days, nor to any other Place than that in which the two Houses shall be sitting.

1. Junius, no. 18, 29 July 1769
2. *Brass Crosby's Case*, 95 Eng. Rep. 1005 (C.P. 1771)
3. Maryland Constitution of 1776, art. 12
4. Declaration of Independence, 4 July 1776, in 1.4.2, no. 2
5. Massachusetts Constitution of 1780, pt. 2, ch. 1, sec. 3, arts. 10, 11
6. Articles of Confederation, art. 9, 1 Mar. 1781
7. Records of the Federal Convention
8. Cornelius, 18 Dec. 1787, in 1.4.1, no. 6
9. Debate in Massachusetts Ratifying Convention, 19 Jan. 1788
10. Debate in Virginia Ratifying Convention, 14–15 June 1788
11. George Mason, Virginia Ratifying Convention, 14, 16 June 1788
12. Debate in North Carolina Ratifying Convention, 26 July 1788
13. House of Representatives, Contested Election, 22 May 1789
14. Thomas Jefferson, Constitutionality of Residence Bill of 1790, 15 July 1790
15. James Wilson, Legislative Department, Lectures on Law, 1791
16. Senate, Contested Election of Mr. Gallatin, 20–22, 28 Feb. 1794
17. House of Representatives, Evidence in Contested Elections, 6 Dec. 1797
18. House of Representatives, Breach of Privilege, 2, 8, 12 Feb. 1798
19. St. George Tucker, Blackstone's Commentaries (1803)
20. William Rawle, A View of the Constitution of the United States (2d ed. 1829)
21. Joseph Story, Commentaries on the Constitution (1833)
22. Benjamin F. Butler, Punishment by the House of Representatives No Bar to an Indictment, 25 June 1834

1

JUNIUS, NO. 18
29 July 1769
Cannon 97

You cannot but know, Sir, that what was Mr. Wilkes's case yesterday may be your's or mine tomorrow, and that consequently the common right of every subject of the realm is invaded by it. Professing therefore to treat of the constitution of the house of commons, and of the laws and customs relative to that constitution, you certainly were guilty of a most unpardonable omission in taking no notice of a right and privilege of the house, more extraordinary and more arbitrary than all the others they possess put together. If the expulsion of a member, not under any legal disability, of itself creates in him an incapacity to be elected, I see a ready way marked out, by which the majority may at any time remove the honestest and ablest men who happen to be in opposition to them. To say that they *will not* make this extravagant use of their power, would be a language unfit for a man so learned in the laws as you are. By your doctrine, Sir, they *have* the power, and laws you know are intended to guard against what men *may* do, not to trust to what they *will* do.

2

BRASS CROSBY'S CASE
95 Eng. Rep. 1005 (C.P. 1771)

Lord Chief Justice de Grey.—If either myself, or any of my brothers on the Bench, had any doubt in this case, we should certainly have taken some time to consider, before we had given our opinions; but the case seems so very clear to us all, that we have no reason for delay.

The writ by which the lord-mayor is now brought before us, is a habeas corpus at common law, for it is not signed per statutum; it is called a prerogative writ for the King; or a remedial writ; and this writ was properly advised by the counsel for his Lordship, because all the Judges (including Holt) agreed, that such a writ as the present case required, is not within the statute: this is a writ by which the subject has a right of remedy to be discharged out of custody, if he hath been committed, and is detained contrary to law; therefore the Court must consider, whether the authority committing is a legal authority; if the commitment is made by those who have authority to commit, this Court cannot discharge or bail the party committed, nor can this Court admit to bail, one charged or committed in execution. Whether the authority committing the lord-mayor, is a legal authority or not, must be adjudged by the return of the writ now before the Court; the return states the commitment to be by the House of Commons,

for a breach of privilege, which is also stated in the return; and this breach of privilege or contempt is, as the counsel has truly described it, threefold; discharging a printer in custody of a messenger by order of the House of Commons; signing a warrant for the commitment of the messenger, and holding him to bail; that is, treating a messenger of the House of Commons as acting criminally, in the execution of the orders of that House. In order to see whether that House has authority to commit, see Co. 4 Inst. 23. Such an assembly must certainly have such authority, and it is legal because necessary: Lord Coke says they have a judicial power; each member has a judicial seat in the House, he speaks of matters of judicature of the House of Commons. 4 Inst. 23. The House of Commons, without doubt, have power to commit persons examined at their Bar touching elections, when they prevaricate or speak falsely; so they have for breaches of privilege, so they have in many other cases. Thomas Long gave the Mayor of Westbury 4*l.* to be elected a burgess; he was elected, and the mayor was fined and imprisoned, and Long removed. Arthur Hall, a member, was sent to the Tower, for publishing the conferences of the House. 4 Inst. 23. This power of committing must be inherent in the House of Commons, from the very nature of its institution, and therefore is part of the law of the land; they certainly always could commit in many cases: in matters of elections, they can commit sheriffs, mayors, officers, witnesses, &c. and it is now agreed that they can commit generally for all contempts. All contempts are either punishable in the Court contemned, or in some higher Court; now the Parliament has no Superior Court; therefore the contempts against either House can only be punished by themselves. The stat. 1 Jac. 1, cap. 13, sect. 3, sufficiently proves, that they have power to punish, it is in these words, viz. "Provided always, that this Act, or any thing therein contained, shall not extend to the diminishing of any punishment to be hereafter by censure in Parliament inflicted upon any person which hereafter shall make, or procure to be made, any such arrest as is aforesaid." So that it is most clear, the Legislature have recognized this power of the House of Commons. In the case of *The Aylesbury men*, the counsel admitted, Lord Chief Justice Holt owned, and the House of Lords acknowledged, that the House of Commons had power to commit for contempt and breach of privilege. Indeed, it seems, they must have power to commit for any crime, because they have power to impeach for any crime. When the House of Commons adjudge any thing to be a contempt, or a breach of privilege, their adjudication is a conviction, and their commitment in consequence, is execution; and no Court can discharge or bail a person that is in execution by the judgment of any other Court. The House of Commons therefore having an authority to commit, and that commitment being an execution, the question is, what can this Court do? It can do nothing when a person is in execution, by the judgment of a Court having a competent jurisdiction; in such case, this Court is not a Court of Appeal.

It is objected; 1, that the House of Commons are mistaken, for that they have not this power, this authority; 2, that supposing they have, yet in this case they have not used it rightly and properly; and 3, that the execution of their orders was irregular. In order to judge, I will consider the practice of the Courts in common and ordinary cases. I do not find any case where the Courts have taken cognizance of such execution, or of commitments of this kind; there is no precedent of Westminster-Hall interfering in such a case. In *Sir J. Paston's case,* 13 Rep. there is a case recited from the Year-Book, where it is held that every Court shall determine of the privilege of that Court; besides, the rule is, that the Court of remedy must judge by the same [law] as the Court which commits: now this Court cannot take cognizance of a commitment by the House of Commons, because it cannot judge by the same law; for the law by which the Commons judge of their privileges is unknown to us. If the Court of Common Pleas should commit a person for a contempt, the Court of King's Bench would not inquire into the legality or particular cause of commitment, if a contempt was returned; yet in some cases the Court of King's Bench is a Court of inquiry, but in this case is only co-ordinate with this Court. In the case of *Chambers,* Cro. Car. 168, Chambers was brought up by habeas corpus out of the Fleet; and it was returned, that he was committed by virtue of a decree in the Star-Chamber, by reason of certain words he used at the council-table, &c. for which he was censured to be committed to the Fleet, till he made his submission at the council-table, and paid a fine of 2000*l.* and at the Bar he prayed to be delivered, because the sentence was not warranted by any law or statute: for the Statute 3 Hen. 7, which is the foundation of the Court of Star-Chamber, doth not give them any authority to punish for words only. But all the Court informed him, that the Court of Star-Chamber was not erected by the Stat. 3 Hen. 7, but was a Court many years before, and one of the most high and honourable Courts of Justice; and to deliver one who was committed by the decree of one of the Courts of Justice, was not the usage of this Court, and therefore he was remanded. The Courts of B. R. or C. B. never discharged any person committed for contempt, in not answering in the Court of Chancery, if the return was for a contempt; if the Admiralty Court commits for a contempt, or one be taken up and committed on an excommunicato expiendo, this Court never discharges the persons committed. Formerly, when many abuses were committed, and the people could not obtain a remedy, the subject was not contented with the ancient habeas corpus, but did not complain of the Courts for refusing them what they could not by law grant them; instead of that, they sought redress by petition to the Throne. In Chief Justice Wilmot's time, a person was brought by habeas corpus before this Court, who had been committed by the Court of Chancery of Durham; that Court being competent, and having jurisdiction, the man was not discharged, but recommitted. How then can we do any thing in the present case, when the law by which the lord-mayor is committed, is different from the law by which he seeks to be relieved? He is committed by the law of Parliament, and yet he would have redress from the common law; the law of Parliament is only known to Parliament-men, by experience in the House. Lord Coke says, Every man looks for it, but few can find it. The House of Commons only know how to act within their own limits; we are not a Court of Appeal; we do not know certainly the jurisdiction of the House of Commons; we cannot judge of the laws and privileges of the House, because we have no knowledge of those laws and privileges; we cannot judge of the contempts thereof, we cannot judge of the punishment therefore.

I wish we had some code of the law of Parliament; but till we have such a code, it is impossible we should be able to judge of it. Perhaps a contempt in the House of Commons, in the Chancery, in this Court, and in the Court of Durham, may be very different; therefore we cannot judge of it, but every Court must be sole judge of its own contempts. Besides, as the Court cannot go out of the return of this writ, how can we inquire into the truth of the fact, as to the nature of the contempt? We have no means of trying whether the lord-mayor did right or wrong: this Court cannot summon a jury to try the matter; we cannot examine into the fact; here are no parties in litigation before the Court: we cannot call in any body; we cannot hear any witnesses, or depositions of witnesses; we cannot issue any process; we are even now hearing ex parte, and without any counsel on the contrary side. Again, if we could determine upon the contempts of any other Court, so might the other Courts of Westminster-Hall; and what confusion would then ensue! none of us knowing the law by which persons are committed by the House of Commons. If three persons were committed for the same breach of privilege, and applied severally to different Courts, one Court perhaps would bail, another Court discharge, a third re-commit.

Two objections have been made, which I own have great weight; because they hold forth, if pursued to all possible cases, consequences of most important mischief. 1st, it is said, that if the rights and privileges of Parliament are legal rights, for that very reason the Court must take notice of them, because they are legal. And 2dly, if the law of Parliament is part of the law of the land, the Judges must take cognizance of one part of the law of the land, as well as of the other. But these objections will not prevail. There are two sorts of privileges which ought never to be confounded; personal privilege, and the privilege belonging to the whole collective body of that assembly. For instance, it is the privilege of every individual member, not to be arrested; if he was arrested, before the Stat. 12 & 13 W. 3, the method in Westminster-Hall was, to discharge him by writ of privilege under the Great Seal, which was in the nature of a supersedeas to the proceedings; and as soon as it came into the Court of B. R. and was pleaded there, then it became a record, and the pleading concluded, si Curia domini Regis placitum praedictum cognoscere velit aut debeat. The Stat. 11 & 12 W. 3, has altered this, and there is now no occasion to plead the privilege of a member of Parliament. 2 Stran. 985, *Holiday & Al.* versus *Colonel Pitt.* There is a great difference between matters of privilege coming incidentally before the Court, and being the point itself directly before the Court; in the first case the Court will take notice of them, because it is necessary, in order to prevent a failure of justice; as in *Lord Banbury's case,* where the Court of King's Bench determined against the determination of the House of Lords; but in that case they considered the legality and validity of the letters patent, without regarding the other right of a seat in the House of Lords, with which the Court did not concern themselves. The counsel at the Bar have not cited one case where any Court of this Hall ever determined a matter of privilege which did not come incidentally before them. If a question is to be determined in this Court touching a descent, whereby property is to be determined, and which depends upon legitimacy; that is, whether the father and mother were married lawfully; this Court must determine by the bishop's certificate; but in some cases, where the legitimacy of marriage does not come in question, but cohabitation only for a great length of time, which is evidence of a marriage, comes in question, this Court will determine according to the verdict of a jury, although the Courts of Westminster-Hall go by a different rule from the Spiritual Courts. But the present case differs much from those which the Court will determine; because it does not come incidentally before us, but is brought before us directly, and is the whole point in question; and to determine it, we must supersede the judgment and determination of the House of Commons, and a commitment in execution of that judgment.

Another objection has been made, which likewise holds out to us, if pursued in all its possible cases, some dreadful consequences; and that is, the abuses which may be made by jurisdictions from which there is no appeal, and for which abuses there is no remedy: but this is unavoidable; and it is better to leave some Courts to the obligation of their oaths. In the case of a commitment by this Court or the King's Bench, there is no appeal. Suppose the Court of B. R. sets an excessive fine upon a man for a misdemeanor; there is no remedy, no appeal to any other Court. We must depend upon the discretion of some Courts. A man not long ago was sentenced to stand in the pillory, by this Court of Common Pleas, for a contempt. Some may think this very hard, to be done without a trial by jury; but it is necessary. Suppose the Courts should abuse their jurisdiction, there can be no remedy for this: it would be a public grievance; and redress must be sought from the Legislature. The laws can never be a prohibition to the Houses of Parliament; because, by law, there is nothing superior to them. Suppose they also, as well as the Courts of Law, should abuse the powers which the constitution has given them, there is no redress, it would be a public grievance. The constitution has provided checks to prevent its happening; it must be left at large; it was wise to leave it at large: some persons, some Courts, must be trusted with discretionary powers; and though it is possible, it is in the highest degree improbable, that such abuses should ever happen, and the very supposal is answered by Serjeant Hawkins, in the place cited at the Bar. As for the case of the Chancery committing for crimes, that is a different thing, because the Chancery has no criminal jurisdiction; but if that Court commits for contempts, the persons committed will not be discharged by any other Court. Many authorities may be drawn from the reign of Charles, but those were in times of contest. At present, when the House of Commons commits for contempt, it is very nec-

essary to state what is the particular breach of privilege; but it would be a sufficient return, to state the breach of privilege generally: this doctrine is fortified by the opinion of all the Judges, in the case of Lord Shaftesbury, and I never heard this decision complained of till 1704; though they were times of heat, the Judges could have no motive in their decision, but a regard to the laws: the Houses disputed about jurisdiction, but the Judges were not concerned in the dispute. As for the present case, I am perfectly satisfied, that if Lord Holt himself were to have determined it, the lord-mayor would be remanded. In the case of Mr. Murray, the Judges could not hesitate concerning the contempt by a man who refused to receive his sentence in a proper posture: all the Judges agreed, that he must be remanded, because he was committed by a Court having competent jurisdiction: Courts of Justice have no cognizance of the Acts of the Houses of Parliament, because they belong ad aliud examen. I have the most perfect satisfaction in my own mind in that determination. Sir Martin Wright, who felt a generous and distinguished warmth for the liberty of the subject; Mr. Justice Denison, who was so free from connections and ambition of every kind; and Mr. Justice Foster, who may be truly called the magna charta of liberty of persons, as well as fortunes; all these revered Judges concurred in this point: I am therefore clearly and with full satisfaction of opinion, that the lord-mayor must be remanded.

Gould Justice.—I entirely concur in opinion with my Lord Chief Justice, that this Court hath no cognizance of contempts or breach of privilege of the House of Commons: they are the only judges of their own privileges; and that they may be properly called judges, appears in 4 Inst. 47, where my Lord Coke says, an alien cannot be elected of the Parliament, because such a person can hold no place of judicature. Much stress has been laid upon an objection, that the warrant of the Speaker is not conformable to the order of the House, and yet no such thing appears upon the return, as has been pretended. The order says that the lord-mayor shall be taken into the custody of the serjeant or his deputy; it does not say, by the serjeant or his deputy. This Court cannot know the nature and power of the proceedings of the House of Commons; it is founded on a different law; the lex et consuetudo Parliamenti, is known to Parliament-men only. *Trewynnard's case*, Dier 59, 60. When matters of privilege come incidentally before the Court, it is obliged to determine them to prevent a failure of justice. It is true this Court did, in the instance alluded to by the counsel at the Bar, determine upon the privilege of Parliament in the case of a libel; but then that privilege was promulged and known; it existed in records and law-books, and was allowed by Parliament itself; but even in that case, we now know that we were mistaken, for the House of Commons have since determined, that privilege does not extend to matters of libel. The cases produced respecting the High Commission Court, &c. are not to the present purpose, because those Courts had not a legal authority; the resolution of the House of Commons is an adjudication, and every Court must judge of its own contempts.

Blackstone Justice.—I concur in opinion, that we cannot

discharge the lord-mayor; the present case is of great importance, because the liberty of the subject is materially concerned. The House of Commons is a Supreme Court, and they are judges of their own privileges and contempts, more especially with respect to their own members: here is a member committed in execution by the judgment of his own House. All Courts, by which I mean to include the two Houses of Parliament, and the Courts of Westminster-Hall, can have no controul in matters of contempt. The sole adjudication of contempts, and the punishment thereof, in any manner, belongs exclusively, and without interfering, to each respective Court. Infinite confusion and disorder would follow, if Courts could by writ of habeas corpus, examine and determine the contempts of others. This power to commit results from the first principles of justice; for if they have power to decide; they ought to have power to punish: no other Court shall scan the judgment of a Superior Court, or the principal seat of justice; as I said before, it would occasion the utmost confusion, if every Court of this Hall should have power to examine the commitments of the other Courts of the Hall, for contempts; so that the judgment and commitment of each respective Court, as to contempts, must be final, and without controul. It is a confidence, that may, with perfect safety and security, be reposed in the Judges, and the Houses of Parliament. The Legislature since the Revolution (see 9 & 10 W. 3, c. 15) have created many new contempts. The objections which are brought of abusive consequences prove too much, because they are applicable to all Courts of dernier resort: et ab abusu ad usum non valent consequentia, is a maxim of law as well as of logic. General convenience must always outweight partial inconvenience; even supposing (which, in my conscience, I am far from supposing) that in the present case the House has abused its power. I know, and am sure, that the House of Commons are both able and well inclined to do justice. How preposterous is the present murmur and complaint! the House of Commons have this power only in common with all the Courts of Westminster-Hall: and if any persons may be safely trusted with this power, they must surely be the Commons, who are chosen by the people; for their privileges and powers are the privileges and powers of the people. There is a great fallacy in my brother Glynn's whole argument, when he makes the question to be, whether the House have acted according to their rights or not? Can any good man think of involving the Judges in a contest with either House of Parliament, or with one another? and yet this manner of putting the question would produce such a contest. The House of Commons is the only judge of its own proceedings: Holt differed from the other Judges in this point, but we must be governed by the eleven, and not by the single one. It is a right inherent in all Supreme Courts: the House of Commons have always exercised it. Little nice objections of particular words and forms, and ceremonies of execution, are not to be regarded in the acts of the House of Commons; it is our duty to presume the orders of that House, and their execution, are according to law. The habeas corpus in *Murray's case* was at common law. I concur intirely with my Lord Chief Justice.

Nares Justice.—I shall ever entertain a most anxious concern for whatever regards the liberty of the subject; I have not the vanity to think I can add any thing to the weight of the arguments used by my Lord Chief Justice and my brothers: I have attended with the utmost industry, to every case and argument that has been produced, and most heartily and readily concur with my Lord Chief Justice and my brothers.

The lord-mayor was remanded to the Tower.

3

MARYLAND CONSTITUTION OF 1776, ART. 12
Thorpe 3:1693

That the House of Delegates may punish, by imprisonment, any person who shall be guilty of a contempt in their view, by any disorderly or riotous behavior, or by threats to, or abuse of their members, or by any obstruction to their proceedings. They may also punish, by imprisonment, any person who shall be guilty of a breach of privilege, by arresting on civil process, or by assaulting any of their members, during their sitting, or on their way to, or return from the House of Delegates, or by any assault of, or obstruction to their officers, in the execution of any order or process, or by assaulting or obstructing any witness, or any other person, attending on, or on their way to or from the House, or by rescuing any person committed by the House: and the Senate may exercise the same power, in similar cases.

4

DECLARATION OF INDEPENDENCE
4 July 1776

(See 1.4.2, no. 2)

5

MASSACHUSETTS CONSTITUTION OF 1780,
PT. 2, CH. 1, SEC. 3, ARTS. 10, 11
Thorpe 3:1899

ART. X. . . . They [the house of representatives] shall have authority to punish by imprisonment every person, not a member, who shall be guilty of disrespect to the house, by any disorderly or contemptuous behavior in its presence; or who, in the town where the general court is sitting, and during the time of its sitting, shall threaten harm to the body or estate of any of its members, for anything said or done in the house; or who shall assault any of them therefor; or who shall assault or arrest any witness, or other person, ordered to attend the house, in his way in going or returning; or who shall rescue any person arrested by the order of the house.

And no member of the house of representatives shall be arrested, or held to bail on mesne process, during his going unto, returning from, or his attending the general assembly.

ART. XI. The senate shall have the same powers in the like cases; and the governor and council shall have the same authority to punish in like cases: *Provided,* That no imprisonment, on the warrant or order of the governor, council, senate, or house of representatives, for either of the above-described offences, be for a term exceeding thirty days.

6

ARTICLES OF CONFEDERATION, ART. 9
1 Mar. 1781

The congress of the united states shall have power to adjourn to any time within the year, and to any place within the united states, so that no period of adjournment be for a longer duration than the space of six Months, and shall publish the Journal of their proceedings monthly, except such parts thereof relating to treaties, alliances or military operations, as in their judgment require secrecy; and the yeas and nays of the delegates of each state on any question shall be entered on the Journal, when it is desired by any delegate; and the delegates of a state, or any of them, at his or their request shall be furnished with a transcript of the said Journal, except such parts as are above excepted, to lay before the legislatures of the several states.

7

RECORDS OF THE FEDERAL CONVENTION

[2:251; Madison, 10 Aug.]

Mr. Ghorum contended that less than a Majority in each House should be made of Quorum, otherwise great delay might happen in business, and great inconvenience from the future increase of numbers.

Mr. Mercer was also for less than a majority. So great a number will put it in the power of a few by seceding at a critical moment to introduce convulsions, and endanger the Governmt. Examples of secession have already happened in some of the States. He was for leaving it to the Legislature to fix the Quorum, as in Great Britain, where the requisite number is small & no inconveniency has been experienced.

Col. Mason. This is a valuable & necessary part of the plan. In this extended Country, embracing so great a diversity of interests, it would be dangerous to the distant parts to allow a small number of members of the two Houses to make laws. The Central States could always take care to be on the Spot and by meeting earlier than the distant ones, or wearying their patience, and outstaying them, could carry such measures as they pleased. He admitted that inconveniences might spring from the secession of a small number: But he had also known good produced by an apprehension of it. He had known a paper emission prevented by that cause in Virginia. He thought the Constitution as now moulded was founded on sound principles, and was disposed to put into it extensive powers. At the same time he wished to guard agst abuses as much as possible. If the Legislature should be able to reduce the number at all, it might reduce it as low as it pleased & the U. States might be governed by a Juncto— A majority of the number which had been agreed on, was so few that he feared it would be made an objection agst. the plan.

Mr. King admitted there might be some danger of giving an advantage to the Central States; but was of opinion that the public inconveniency on the other side was more to be dreaded.

Mr. Govr. Morris moved to fix the quorum at 33 members in the H. of Reps. & 14 in the Senate. This is a majority of the present number, and will be a bar to the Legislature: fix the number low and they will generally attend knowing that advantage may be taken of their absence. the Secession of a small number ought not to be suffered to break a quorum. Such events in the States may have been of little consequence. In the national Councils, they may be fatal. Besides other mischiefs, if a few can break up a quorum, they may sieze a moment when a particular part of the Continent may be in need of immediate aid, to extort, by threatening a secession, some unjust & selfish measure.

Mr. Mercer 2ded. the motion

Mr. King said he had just prepared a motion which instead of fixing the numbers proposed by Mr. Govr Morris as Quorums, made those the lowest numbers, leaving the Legislature at liberty to increase them or not. He thought the future increase of members would render a majority of the whole extremely cumbersome.

Mr. Mercer agreed to substitute Mr. Kings motion in place of Mr. Morris's.

Mr. Elseworth was opposed to it. It would be a pleasing ground of confidence to the people that no law or burden could be imposed on them, by a few men. He reminded the movers that the Constitution proposed to give such a discretion with regard to the number of Representatives that a very inconvenient number was not to be apprehended. The inconveniency of secessions may be guarded agst by giving to each House an authority to require the attendance of absent members.

Mr. Wilson concurred in the sentiments of Mr. Elseworth.

Mr. Gerry seemed to think that some further precautions than merely fixing the quorum might be necessary.

He observed that as 17 wd. be a majority of a quorum of 33, and 8 of 14, questions might by possibility be carried in the H. of Reps. by 2 large States, and in the Senate by the same States with the aid of two small ones.—He proposed that the number for a quorum in the H. of Reps. should not exceed 50 nor be less than 33. leaving the intermediate discretion to the Legislature.

Mr. King. as the quorum could not be altered witht. the concurrence of the President by less than ⅔ of each House, he thought there could be no danger in trusting the Legislature.

Mr Carrol this will be no security agst. a continuance of the quorums at 33 & 14. when they ought to be increased.

On question on Mr Kings motion "that not less than 33 in the H. of Reps. nor less than 14 in the Senate shd. constitute a Quorum, which may be increased by a law, on additions of members in either House."

N. H. no. Mas. ay. Ct. no. N. J. no. Pa. no. Del. ay. Md. no. Va. no. N. C. no. S. C. no. Geo. no. [Ayes—2; noes—9.]

Mr. Randolph & Mr. Madison moved to add to the end of Art. VI Sect 3, "and may be authorized to compel the attendance of absent members in such manner & under such penalties as each House may provide." Agreed to by all except Pena—which was divided

Art: VI. Sect. 3. Agreed to as amended Nem. con. . . .

Mr. Madison observed that the right of expulsion (Art. VI. Sect. 6.) was too important to be exercised by a bare majority of a quorum: and in emergencies of faction might be dangerously abused. He moved that "with the concurrence of ⅔" might be inserted between may & expel.

Mr. Randolph & Mr. Mason approved the idea.

Mr Govr Morris. This power may be safely trusted to a majority. To require more may produce abuses on the side of the minority. A few men from factious motives may keep in a member who ought to be expelled.

Mr. Carrol thought that the concurrence of ⅔ at least ought to be required.

On the question for requiring ⅔ in cases of expelling a member.

N. H. ay– Mas. ay. Ct. ay– N. J– ay. Pa. divd. Del. ay. Md. ay. Va. ay. N– C. ay– S. C. ay. Geo. ay. [Ayes—10; noes—0; divided—1.]

Art. VI– Sect– 6– as thus amended agreed to nem. con. . . .

Mr. Govr Morris urged that if the yeas & nays were proper at all any individual ought to be authorized to call for them: and moved an amendment to that effect.—The small States may otherwise be under a disadvantage, and find it difficult. to get a concurrence of ⅕

Mr. Randolph 2ded. ye motion.

Mr. Sherman had rather strike out the yeas & nays altogether. they never have done any good, and have done much mischief. They are not proper as the reasons governing the voter never appear along with them.

Mr Elseworth was of the same opinion

Col. Mason liked the Section as it stood. it was a middle way between two extremes.

Mr Ghorum was opposed to the motion for allowing a single member to call the yeas & nays, and recited the abuses of it, in Massts. 1 in stuffing the journals with them on frivolous occasions. 2 in misleading the people who never know the reasons determining the votes.

The motion for allowing a single member to call the yeas & nays was disagd. to nem– con–

Mr. Carrol & Mr. Randolph moved to strike out the words "each House" and to insert the words "the House of Representatives" in sect– 7. art– 6. and to add to the Section the words "and any member of the Senate shall be at liberty to enter his dissent"

Mr. Govr Morris & Mr Wilson observed that if the minority were to have a right to enter their votes & reasons, the other side would have a right to complain, if it were not extended to them: & to allow it to both, would fill the Journals, like the records of a Court, with replications, rejoinders &c–

Question on Mr Carrols motion to allow a member to enter his dissent

N. H– no. Mas. no. Cont. no. N. J. no. Pa. no. Del. no. Md. ay. Va. ay. N. C. no. S. C. ay. Geo. no. [Ayes—3; noes—8.]

Mr Gerry moved to strike out the words "when it shall be acting in its legislative capacity" in order to extend the provision to the Senate when exercising its peculiar authorities and to insert "except such parts thereof as in their judgment require secrecy" after the words "publish them".—(It was thought by others that provision should be made with respect to these when that part came under consideration which proposed to vest those additional authorities in the Senate.)

On this question for striking out the words "when acting in its Legislative capacity"

N. H. divd. Mas ay. Ct. no. N. J. no. Pa. no. Del. ay. Md. ay. Va. ay– N. C. ay. S. C– ay. Geo. ay– [Ayes—7; noes—3; divided—1.]

[2:259; Madison, 11 Aug.]

Mr Madison & Mr. Rutlidge moved "that each House shall keep a journal of its proceeding, & shall publish the same from time to time; except such part of the proceedings of the Senate, when acting not in its Legislative capacity as may be judged by that House to require secrecy."

Mr. Mercer. This implies that other powers than legislative will be given to the Senate which he hoped would not be given.

Mr. Madison & Mr. R's motion. was disagd. to by all the States except Virga.

Mr. Gerry & Mr. Sharman moved to insert after the words "publish them" the following "except such as relate to treaties & military operations." Their object was to give each House a discretion in such cases.—On this question

N. H– no. Mas– ay. Ct. ay. N– J. no. Pa. no. Del– no. Va. no. N. C. no. S. C. no. Geo. no. [Ayes—2; noes—8.]

Mr. Elseworth. As the clause is objectionable in so many shapes, it may as well be struck out altogether. The Legislature will not fail to publish their proceedings from time to time—The people will call for it if it should be improperly omitted.

Mr. Wilson thought the expunging of the clause would be very improper. The people have a right to know what their Agents are doing or have done, and it should not be in the option of the Legislature to conceal their proceedings. Besides as this is a clause in the existing confederation, the not retaining it would furnish the adversaries of the reform with a pretext by which weak & suspicious minds may be easily misled.

Mr. Mason thought it would give a just alarm to the people to make a conclave of their Legislature.

Mr. Sherman thought the Legislature might be trusted in this case if in any.

Question on 1st. part of the Section, down to *"publish them"* inclusive: Agreed to nem. con.

Question on the words to follow, to wit "except such parts thereof as may in their Judgment require secrecy." N. H. divd. Mas. ay. Ct. ay. N. J– ay. Pa. no. Del– no. Md. no. Va. ay– N. C. ay. S. C. no. Geo. ay–[Ayes—6; noes—4; divided—1.]

The remaining part as to yeas and nays.—agreed to nem. con. . . .

[Art. 6, sec. 8: "Neither House, without the consent of the other, shall adjourn for more than three days, nor to any other place than that at which the two Houses are sitting. But this regulation shall not extend to the Senate, when it shall exercise the powers mentioned in the   article."]

Mr. King remarked that the section authorized the 2 Houses to adjourn to a new place. He thought this inconvenient. The mutability of place had dishonored the federal Govt. and would require as strong a cure as we could devise. He thought a law at least should be made necessary to a removal of the Seat of Govt.

Mr Madison viewed the subject in the same light, and joined with Mr. King in a motion requiring a law.

Mr. Governr. Morris proposed the additional alteration by inserting the words "during the Session" &c".

Mr. Spaight. this will fix the seat of Govt at N. Y. The present Congress will convene them there in the first instance, and they will never be able to remove; especially if the Presidt. should be Northern Man.

Mr Govr Morris. such a distrust is inconsistent with all Govt.

Mr. Madison supposed that a central place for the Seat of Govt. was so just and wd. be so much insisted on by the H. of Representatives, that though a law should be made requisite for the purpose, it could & would be obtained. The necessity of a central residence of the Govt wd be much greater under the new than old Govt The members of the new Govt wd. be more numerous. They would be taken more from the interior parts of the States: they wd. not, like members of ye present Congs. come so often from the distant States by water. As the powers & objects of the new Govt. would be far greater yn. heretofore, more private individuals wd. have business calling them to the seat of it, and it was more necessary that the Govt should be in that position from which it could contemplate with the most equal eye, and sympathize most equally with, every part of the nation. These considerations he supposed would extort a removal even if a law were made necessary. But in order to quiet suspicions both within & without doors, it might not be amiss to authorize the 2

Houses by a concurrent vote to adjourn at their first meeting to the most proper place, and to require thereafter, the sanction of a law to their removal. The motion was accordingly moulded into the following form: "the Legislature shall at their first assembling determine on a place at which their future sessions shall be held; neither House shall afterwards, during the session of the House of Reps. without the consent of the other, adjourn for more than three days, nor shall they adjourn to any other place than such as shall have been fixt by law"

Mr. Gerry thought it would be wrong to let the Presidt check the will of the 2 Houses on this subject at all.

Mr Williamson supported the ideas of Mr. Spaight

Mr Carrol was actuated by the same apprehensions

Mr. Mercer. it will serve no purpose to require the two Houses at their first Meeting to fix on a place. They will never agree.

After some further expressions from others denoting an apprehension that the seat of Govt. might be continued at an improper place if a law should be made necessary to a removal, and the motion above stated with another for recommitting the section had been negatived, the Section was left in the shape it which it was reported, as to this point. The words "during the session of the legislature" were prefixed to the 8th section—and the last sentence "But this regulation shall not extend to the Senate when it shall exercise the powers mentioned in the   article" struck out. The 8th section as amended was then agreed to.

[2:300; Madison, 15 Aug.]

Mr. Carrol– when the negative to be overruled by ⅔ only was agreed to, the *quorum* was not fixed. He remarked that as a majority was now to be the quorum, 17, in the larger, and 8 in the smaller house might carry points. The Advantage that might be taken of this seemed to call for greater impediments to improper laws. He thought the controuling power however of the Executive could not be well decided, till it was seen how the formation of that department would be finally regulated. He wished the consideration of the matter to be postponed.

Mr. Ghorum saw no end to these difficulties and postponements. Some could not agree to the form of Government before the powers were defined. Others could not agree to the powers till it was seen how the Government was to be formed. He thought a majority as large a quorum as was necessary. It was the quorum almost every where fixt in the U. States.

[2:305, Madison, 16 Aug.]

Mr. Carroll reminded the Convention of the great difference of interests among the States, and doubts the propriety in that point of view of letting a majority be a quorum.

[2:613; Madison, 14 Sept.]

Art. 1. Sect. 5. "Each House shall keep a Journal of its proceedings, and from time to time publish the same, excepting such parts as may in their judgment require secrecy."

Col: Mason & Mr. Gerry moved to insert after the word "parts" the words "of the proceedings of the Senate" so as to require publication of all the proceedings of the House of Representatives.

It was intimated on the other side that cases might arise where secrecy might be necessary in both Houses—Measures preparatory to a declaration of war in which the House of Reps. was to concur, were instanced.

On the question, it passed in the negative

N. H. no. (Rh. I. ab:.) Mas. no. Con: no. (N. Y. abs) N. J. no. Pen. ay. Del–no. Mary. ay. Virg. no. N. C. ay. S. C. divd. Geor. no [Ayes—3; noes—7; divided—1.]

8

CORNELIUS
18 Dec. 1787
Storing 4.10.10

(See 1.4.1, no. 6)

9

DEBATE IN MASSACHUSETTS RATIFYING CONVENTION
19 Jan. 1788
Elliot 2:52

Dr. TAYLOR wished to know the meaning of the words "from time to time," in the third paragraph. Does it mean, says he, from year to year, from month to month, or from day to day?

The Hon. Mr. KING rose, and explained the term.

Mr. WIDGERY read the paragraph, and said, by the words, "except such parts as may require secrecy," Congress might withhold the whole *journals* under this pretence, and thereby the people be kept in ignorance of their doings.

The Hon. Mr. GORHAM exposed the absurdity of any public body *publishing* all their *proceedings*. Many things in great bodies are to be kept secret, and records must be brought to maturity before published. In case of treaties with foreign nations, would it be policy to inform the world of the extent of the powers to be vested in our ambassador, and thus give our enemies opportunity to defeat our negotiations? There is no provision in the constitution of this state, or of Great Britain, for any publication of the kind; and yet the people suffer no inconveniency. The printers, no doubt, will be interested to obtain the journals as soon as possible for publication, and they will be published in a book, by Congress, at the end of every session.

Rev. Mr. PERLEY described the alarms and anxiety of the people at the commencement of the war, when the whole country, he said, cried with one voice, "Why don't General Washington march into Boston, and drive out the tyrants?" But, said he, Heaven gave us a commander who knew better than to do this. The reverend gentleman said, he was acquainted with the Roman history, and the Grecian too, and he believed there never was, since the creation of the world, a greater general than Washington, except, indeed, Joshua, who was inspired by the Lord of Hosts, the God of the armies of Israel. Would it, he asked, have been prudent for that excellent man, General Washington, previous to the American army's taking possession of Dorchester Heights, to have published to the world his intentions of doing so? No, says he, it would not.

10

DEBATE IN VIRGINIA RATIFYING CONVENTION
14–15 June 1788
Elliot 3:367–68, 460

[*14 June*]

Mr. MONROE wished to hear an explanation of the clause which prohibits either house, during the session of Congress, from adjourning for more than three days without the consent of the other. He asked if it was proper or right, that the members of the lower house should be dependent on the Senate. He considered that it rendered them in some respect dependent on the senators, as it prevented them from returning home, or adjourning, without their consent; and, as this might increase their influence unduly, he thought it improper.

Mr. MADISON wondered that this clause should meet with a shadow of objection. It was possible, he observed, that the two branches might not agree concerning the time of adjournment, and this possibility suggested the power given the President of adjourning both houses to such time as he should think proper, in case of their disagreement. That it would be very exceptionable to allow the senators, or even the representatives, to adjourn, without the consent of the other house, at any season whatsoever, without any regard to the situation of public exigencies. That it was possible, in the nature of things, that some inconvenience might result from it; but that it was as well secured as possible.

Gov. RANDOLPH observed, that the Constitution of Massachusetts was produced as an example, in the grand Convention, in favor of this power given to the President If, said his excellency, he be honest, he will do what is right. if dishonest, the representatives of the people will have the power of impeaching him.

Mr. GEORGE MASON apprehended the loose expression of "publication from time to time" was applicable to any time. It was equally applicable to monthly and septennial periods. It might be extended ever so much. The reason urged in favor of this ambiguous expression was, that there might be some matters which require secrecy. In matters relative to military operations and foreign negotiations, secrecy was necessary sometimes; but he did not conceive that the receipts and expenditures of the public money ought ever to be concealed. The people, he affirmed, had a right to know the expenditures of their money; but that this expression was so loose, it might be concealed forever from them, and might afford opportunities of misapplying the public money, and sheltering those who did it. He concluded it to be as exceptionable as any clause, in so few words, could be.

Mr. LEE (of Westmoreland) thought such trivial argument as that just used by the honorable gentleman would have no weight with the committee. He conceived the expression to be sufficiently explicit and satisfactory. It must be supposed to mean, in the common acceptation of language, short, convenient periods. It was as well as if it had said one year, or a shorter term. Those who would neglect this provision would disobey the most pointed directions. As the Assembly was to meet next week, he hoped gentlemen would confine themselves to the investigation of the principal parts of the Constitution.

[15 June]

Mr. GEORGE NICHOLAS said it was a better direction and security than was in the state government. No appropriation shall be made of the public money but by law. There could not be any misapplication of it. Therefore, he thought, instead of censure it merited applause; being a cautious provision, which few constitutions, or none, had ever adopted.

Mr. CORBIN concurred in the sentiments of Mr. Nicholas on this subject.

Mr. MADISON thought it much better than if it had mentioned any specified period; because, if the accounts of the public receipts and expenditures were to be published at short, stated periods, they would not be so full and connected as would be necessary for a thorough comprehension of them, and detection of any errors. But by giving them an opportunity of publishing them from time to time, as might be found easy and convenient, they would be more full and satisfactory to the public, and would be sufficiently frequent. He thought, after all, that this provision went farther than the constitution of any state in the Union, or perhaps in the world.

Mr. MASON replied, that, in the Confederation, the public proceedings were to be published monthly, which was infinitely better than depending on men's virtue to publish them or not, as they might please. If there was no such provision in the Constitution of Virginia, gentlemen ought to consider the difference between such a full representation, dispersed and mingled with every part of the community, as the state representation was, and such an inadequate representation as this was. One might be safely trusted, but not the other.

Mr. MADISON replied, that the inconveniences which had been experienced from the Confederation, in that respect, had their weight with him in recommending this in preference to it; for that it was impossible, in such short intervals, to adjust the public accounts in any satisfactory manner.

11

GEORGE MASON, VIRGINIA RATIFYING CONVENTION
14, 16 June 1788
Papers 3:1078, 1079

[14 June]

I have doubts on another point. The fifth section, of the first article, provides, "that each house shall keep a journal of its proceedings, and *from time to time* publish the same, excepting such parts as may, in their judgment, require secrecy." This enables them to keep the negotiations about treaties secret. Under this veil they may conceal *any* thing and *every* thing. Why not insert words that would exclude ambiguity and danger? The words of the confederation, that defective system, are, in this respect, more eligible. What are they? In the last clause of the ninth article it provides, "that congress shall publish the journal of their proceedings monthly, except such parts thereof relating to treaties, alliances, or military operations, as in their judgment require secrecy." The proceedings by that system are to be published monthly, except certain exceptions. These are proper guards. It is not so here. On the contrary they may conceal what they please. Instead of giving information, they will produce suspicion. You cannot discover the advocates of their iniquitous acts. This is an additional defect of responsibility. Neither house can adjourn without the consent of the other for more than three days. This is no parliamentary rule. It is untrodden ground, and appears to me liable to much exception.

[16 June]

The senators are chosen for six years. They are not recallable for those six years, and are re-eligible at the end of the six years. It stands on a very different ground from the confederation. By that system they were only elected for one year, might be recalled, and were incapable of re-election. But in the new constitution, instead of being elected for one, they are chosen for six years. They cannot be recalled in all that time for any misconduct, and at the end of that long term may again be elected. What will be the operation of this? Is it not probable, that those gentlemen who will be elected senators will fix themselves in the federal town, and become citizens of that town more than of our state? They will purchase a good seat in or near the town, and become inhabitants of that place. Will it not be then in the power of the senate to worry the house of representatives into any thing? They will be a continually existing body. They will exercise those machinations and contrivances, which the many have always to fear from the few. The house of representatives is the only check on the senate, with their enormous powers. But by that clause you give them the power of worrying the house of representatives into a compliance with any measure. The senators living at the spot will feel no inconvenience from long sessions, as they will vote themselves handsome pay, without incurring any additional expences. Your representatives are on a different ground, from their shorter continuance in office. The gentlemen from Georgia are six or seven hundred miles from home, and wish to go home. The senate taking advantage of this, by stopping the other house from adjourning, may worry them into any thing. These are my doubts, and I think the provision not consistent with the usual parliamentary modes.

12

DEBATE IN NORTH CAROLINA RATIFYING
CONVENTION
26 July 1788
Elliot 4:72–73

Mr. STEELE observed, that he had heard objections to the 3d clause of this section, with respect to the periodical publication of the Journals, the entering the yeas and nays on them, and the suppression of such parts as required secrecy—that he had no objection himself, for that he thought the necessity of publishing their transactions was an excellent check, and that every principle of prudence and good policy pointed out the necessity of not publishing such transactions as related to military arrangements and war—that this provision was exactly similar to that which was in the old Confederation.

Mr. GRAHAM wished to hear an explanation of the words "from time to time," whether it was a short or a long time, or how often they should be obliged to publish their proceedings.

Mr. DAVIE answered, that they would be probably published after the rising of Congress, every year—that if they sat two or three times, or oftener, in the year, they might be published every time they rose—that there could be no doubt of their publishing them as often as it would be convenient and proper, and that they would conceal nothing but what it would be unsafe to publish. He further observed, that some states had proposed an amendment, that they should be published annually; but he thought it very safe and proper as it stood—that it was the sense of the Convention that they should be published at the end of every session. The gentleman from Salisbury had said, that in this particular it resembled the old Confederation. Other gentlemen have said there is no similarity at all. He therefore wished the difference to be stated.

Mr. IREDELL remarked, that the provision in the clause under consideration was similar in meaning and substance to that in the Confederation—that in time of war it was absolutely necessary to conceal the operations of government; otherwise no attack on an enemy could be premeditated with success, for the enemy could discover our plans soon enough to defeat them—that it was no less imprudent to divulge our negotiations with foreign powers, and the most salutary schemes might be prevented by imprudently promulgating all the transactions of the government indiscriminately.

Mr. J. GALLOWAY wished to obviate what gentlemen had said with regard to the similarity of the old Confederation to the new system, with respect to the publication of their proceedings. He remarked, that, at the desire of one member from any state, the yeas and nays were to be put on the Journals, and published by the Confederation; whereas, by this system, the concurrence of one fifth was necessary.

To this it was answered, that the alteration was made because experience had showed, when any two members could require the yeas and nays, they were taken on many trifling occasions; and there was no doubt one fifth would require them on every occasion of importance.

13

HOUSE OF REPRESENTATIVES, CONTESTED ELECTION
22 May 1789
Annals 1:397–408

Resolved, That it appears to this House, upon full and mature consideration, that the said WILLIAM SMITH had been seven years a citizen of the United States, at the time of his election.

Mr. SMITH.—As the House are inclined to hear the observations I have to make, I shall begin with admitting the facts stated in the memorial of Doctor Ramsay, hoping the House will excuse the egotism into which I am unavoidably drawn. I was born in Charleston, South Carolina, of a family whose ancestors were among the first settlers of that colony, and was sent to England for my education when I was but twelve years of age. In 1774, I was sent to Geneva, to pursue my studies, where I resided until 1778. In November, that year, I went to Paris, where I resided upwards of two months in the character of an American gentleman. Immediately on my arrival there, I waited on Doctor Franklin, Mr. Adams, and Mr. A. Lee, the commissioners from Congress to the court of France, as a citizen of America, and was received as such by them. In January, 1779, I left Paris for London, whither I went to procure the means of embarking for America, from the gentleman who had been appointed my guardian by my father when I was first sent to Europe in 1770, and from whom alone I had any hope of obtaining such means. But in this endeavor, I was disappointed, and remained some time in England, with the hope of receiving remittances from Charleston. Here again my expectation was defeated. The rapid depreciation of the continental money rendered the negotiation of money transactions extremely difficult, and thus I remained till the fall of Charleston. I took this opportunity of studying the law, but could not be called to the bar, because I had not taken the oath of allegiance to Great Britain, which is a necessary qualification. After the surrender of Charleston, the whole State of South Carolina, fell into the hands of the enemy, and it was impossible at that time to return. No sooner, however, did I acquire the means, and an opportunity offered, than I prepared myself to go back to America. I quitted London for that purpose in October or November, 1782, not in a vessel bound to Charleston, then a British garrison, and which I certainly should have done, had I considered myself a British subject, and which would have been most convenient, as there were vessels constantly going from London to Charleston; but I travelled to Ostend, and there embarked in a neutral vessel bound to St. Kitt's, from whence it was my intention to proceed to a Danish island, and thence to some American port in North Carolina or Georgia, from whence I could reach the American camp. In the beginning of January, 1783, I sailed from Ostend, but was detained a considerable time by contrary winds, and in the middle of the month of February, was shipwrecked on the coast of England, and was obliged to return to London in order to procure another passage. These circumstances unavoidably prevented my return to Charleston, until some time in November, 1783.

On my arrival at Charleston, I was received by my countrymen as a citizen of the State of South Carolina, and elected by their free suffrage a member of the Legislature in November, 1784. In the August following I was chosen, by the Governor and Council, a member of the Privy Council, and this election was confirmed by the Legislature the October following. In September, the same year, I was elected one of the Wardens of the City of Charleston. In November, 1786, I was again elected into the Legislature; again in November, 1788; I was elected at the same time that I was elected to the House of Representatives of the United States, the September preceding having been chosen again a Warden of the city.

After having stated these facts, he went on adverting to the laws referred to in the report of the committee, which, he said, he conceived to be applicable to the present case.

In September, 1779, a question was discussed in the Legislature of South Carolina, respecting the young men who were sent abroad for their education, and it was determined there it was most for the interest of the State, that they should be allowed to continue in Europe till they were twenty-two years of age; after which the law provided they should be doubly taxed if they did not return. This law might fairly be supposed to recognise the citizenship of all the young men in a similar predicament with himself. It allowed them all to be absent until they were twenty-two years of age; but even after that period it did not deprive them of the right of citizenship; it only subjected them to the penalty of a double tax. This he contended was a sort of compact with him, that if he chose to be absent after that time, he should suffer a certain penalty, which, in its own nature, implied that his citizenship remained; but before he attained that age, South Carolina was in such a situation that her best friends were compelled to be absent, and take refuge in distant countries. It was not till some time after that the friends of the American cause began to assemble in that State; the absentee law, therefore, never operated on him, and he never was doubly taxed.

In February, 1782, the Legislature met at Jacksonburg, and discriminated between friend and foe, between American and British subjects, by disposing of the estates of the latter, and banishing them; from an inspection of the law passed at that time, it would be evident in what light they viewed him. He had landed property in the State, but was himself in England; yet they did not attempt to confiscate his property, or subject him to an amercement. The absentee law was his safeguard, he had the permission of the State to be abroad.

If the Legislature in 1782 recognised as citizens some of those persons whose estates were confiscated for adhering to Great Britain, and for being disaffected to America *a fortiori*, did it not recognise as a citizen one whose estate was not forfeited, who had not been deemed worthy of punishment, and who had been absent under the sanction of the law?

By the constitution of South Carolina it appears, that no person was eligible to a seat in the Legislature until he had resided three years, nor to a seat in the Privy Council until he had resided five years in the State. He had a seat in both those bodies before he had resided two years in the State of South Carolina, and no objection was ever made on that score. He could not have been qualified for either, had not the people of South Carolina deemed his residence in that State, such a residence as gained him a qualification; or had they not supposed the qualification required in the constitution applied only to new comers and new citizens, for whom that residence was necessary to wean them from their local prejudices and national habits, and to attach them to the commonwealth. Had they not, in short, supposed him to have been a citizen during the revolution, and attached to his native State by every tie which could bind an individual to any country. Three years residence was either not required of him, or his former residence was deemed within the meaning of the constitution.

An act to confer the right of citizenship on aliens was passed March 26, 1784. For the purpose of possessing the subordinate rights of citizenship, such as an exemption from the alien duty, a residence of one year, and taking the oath of allegiance, was sufficient. To confer a right of voting at elections, a person must have been admitted a citizen two years prior to his voting; but for the higher privileges of a citizen, being eligible to offices of trust, to a seat in the Legislature and Privy Council, the alien must have been naturalized by law. Now, in November, 1784, he was elected into the Legislature, and took his seat without objection in January, 1785, and was elected into the Privy Council, October, 1785; all without being naturalized by law.

In October, 1785, when he was elected to the Council, his election was opposed, but the objection now brought forward was not then made; and the memorialist himself, who was a member of the Legislature, voted in favor of the choice; though, unquestionably, unless he was considered by the Legislature as a citizen before he returned to Charleston, nothing had afterwards occurred to make him so, and the alien act of 1784 positively required a naturalization by act of Assembly to give him a qualification.

The constitution of South Carolina is silent as to citizenship, but allowed any person to vote at elections who had resided a year in the State, and paid a certain tax; to be a member of the Assembly he must have resided three, and to be a Privy Counsellor five years previous to his election, but nothing was said about citizenship. The act of 1784, however, expressly defined who should and who should not be deemed citizens; and, consequently, all persons who did not become citizens must have been held to be aliens, and considered so, till they had conformed to the alien act of 1784. Now, as he was admitted to offices of trust, to which aliens were not admissible, and as he was admitted to them without having the rights of citizenship conferred upon him, in pursuance of that act, it followed clearly, that the people of South Carolina and the Legislature acknowledged him to be a citizen by virtue of the revolution.

He went on to observe, that, from the doctrine laid down by the memorialist, it was difficult to ascertain when he did become a citizen of South Carolina. When he was admitted to the bar in 1784, he did no act which made him a citizen, the bare act of taking an oath of qualification to an office could not convert an alien to a citizen. The constitution seemed to imply a mere residence of a year, by giving a right to vote, gave a right of citizenship; if that were the case, and if his residence prior to the revolution was considered such a residence as the constitution required, then he was a citizen, by virtue of the constitution, after having resided a year in Carolina. Now, it was clear, his residence prior to the war was deemed such a residence as the constitution required; because he was admitted to vote and admitted to a seat in the Legislature and Council by right of such residence, not having had the requisite residence since the war, and yet being deemed qualified. If, therefore, that part of the constitution which gave a right of voting, in consequence of a year's residence and paying a certain tax, virtually conferred citizenship, by giving a right to vote, (and it appeared absurd that a right to vote should be given to persons not citizens,) and if, also, his residence, prior to the revolution, was deemed a sufficient residence, then he was a citizen by virtue of the constitution.

The points that seemed most to be relied upon by the memorialist were:

1st. That residence was actually necessary to confer citizenship, or, in other words, that a person could not become a citizen of a country, till he has resided in it.

2d. That a person could not become a citizen till he was of age to choose his country.

In answer to the first, he denied that residence in the country was absolutely necessary. Was it to be supposed, he asked, that when a man sent his son into another country for his education and improvement, the son was thereby to lose any political benefits which might, during such temporary absence, accrue to his country? If his father had lived a few years longer, would there have arisen any question on this subject? Would he not, though absent, have acquired, according to the petitioner's own positions, a right of citizenship? And should his death, at such an early period, not be deemed a sufficient misfortune for him, without using that as a pretence for making him an alien? Those who represented him in Carolina as his

guardians, who were *in loco parentis,* were residents in Carolina at the declaration of independence.

His property was in Carolina, his money in the treasury, assisting to carry on the war. The declaration of independence affected him as much, though at Geneva, as it did those in Carolina; his happiness, that of his dearest connexions, his property, were deeply interested in it: his fate was so closely connected with that of Carolina, that any revolution in Carolina was a revolution to him. Though a minor, as soon as he heard of the independence of America, he considered himself an American citizen.

If a person could not become a citizen of a country without residing in it, what should be said of those gentlemen who had been in Europe during the war, and were now in high office in America? Several of them went to Europe before the war, were there at the declaration of independence, and did not return to America till after the war, or about the close of it. When did their citizenship commence? According to the petitioner, they could not become citizens of America until they returned to America, and took an oath of allegiance to the States; but Congress employed them in offices of great confidence, before they had returned to America, or taken such oath. Congress, therefore, considered them citizens, by virtue of the revolution.

It had been said, that Carolina had called on her young men to come to her assistance. This was not the true state of the case. Carolina thought that her young men who were abroad for their education, should not be taken from their studies till they were twenty-two years of age, and doubly taxed them after that. His guardian wrote to him that he had permission of the Legislature to be absent till he was twenty-two, and that he should be doubly taxed after that age.

It has been also said, that Carolina tendered an oath, to discover who were friends, and who were enemies. In March, 1778, the Legislature of South Carolina passed an act to oblige every free male inhabitant of that State, above sixteen years of age, to take an oath of allegiance to the State. As there were notoriously many persons then in the State who were inimical to its liberties, such a step was necessary to give a reasonable cause for obliging them to quit the country. With that view, the oath was generally tendered only to those who were suspected or known not to be friendly to the cause. He had been informed by several persons, who were zealous partisans, and then in Carolina, that they had never taken any oath of allegiance, and that it had not been required of them on this occasion.

The act directed, that those who did not take it, should quit the State; and, if they returned, should be dealt with as traitors, and suffer death. Let us examine whether this act can, in any respect, apply to the present question. 1st, It particularly mentioned "inhabitants of the State of South Carolina." It could not, therefore, apply to persons who were abroad. 2dly, It directed that the oath should be taken before a justice of peace in Carolina; this could not, therefore, extend to a person then at Geneva. 3dly, It was directed to be taken in one month after the passing of the act; and it was not possible that I should hear of the existence of such an act in less than three months. 4thly, It was directed, that if the persons refused to take it, they should quit the State; but I was already out of it. 5thly, Those who refused to take it, were prevented from acquiring or conveying property, and rendered incapable of exercising any profession. But on my return to Carolina, I took peaceable possession of my estate, part of which consisted of lands and houses, which had been mine since the year 1770; and I was immediately admitted to the exercise of the profession for which I was educated. 6thly, The act directed, that if any person returned to Carolina, after having refused to take the oath, he should be put to death as a traitor; and, yet, on my return, never having taken the oath, I was elected a member of the Legislature, and a Privy Counsellor; and, instead of being deemed a criminal myself, I acted as Attorney General to punish others; and yet the petitioner, in one of his late publications, lays great stress on the applicability of this act.

2dly, There could be no doubt that a minor might be a citizen, from the very words of the constitution, which admitted a person to be a member of the House of Representatives at twenty-five, and yet required a citizenship of seven years. This was of itself a sufficient refutation of every thing contained in the petition on this head. The constitution acknowledged that a person might be a citizen at eighteen; if so, there was no reason why a person might not be one at sixteen or fourteen.

Mr. LEE said, the committee had now to determine, whether Mr. SMITH was a citizen of South Carolina during his absence from home, or not. If the laws of that State recognised him as such, the question was determined, because this House could not dispute a fact of that kind. From the reference that has been made to the constitution and laws of South Carolina, and the circumstances which took place under them, with respect to Mr. SMITH, it was convincing that he was acknowledged there to be a citizen in consequence of the revolution.

Mr. THATCHER thought the examination had been full; the facts stated in the memorial were admitted; but, nevertheless, it appeared from other facts, that Mr. SMITH was received and respected as a citizen of that standing which the constitution required. He had considered the subject maturely, and was now ready for the decision.

The petition of Dr. Ramsay was again read, in which he stated, "That citizenship with the United States is an adventitious character to every person possessing it, who is now thirty years of age; and that it can, in no case, have been acquired but in one of the following modes: 1st, By birth or inheritance. 2dly, By having been a party to the late revolution. 3dly, By taking an oath of fidelity to some of the States. 4thly, By tacit consent. 5thly, By adoption: and that Mr. SMITH cannot have acquired the character of a citizen in either of these modes, seven years ago. He cannot be a citizen by birth or inheritance, for he was born in 1758, in South Carolina, while a British colony; and his parents were both dead many years before the declaration of independence; his birthright and inheritance can, therefore, be no other than that of a British subject; for no man can be born a citizen of a Government which did

not exist at the time of his being born; nor can parents leave to their children any other political character than that which they themselves possessed."

After going on to state his reasons why Mr. SMITH could not have acquired citizenship in any of the other modes, he proceeds to say, that he "conceives that birth and residence in this country, before the revolution, could not confer citizenship on Americans who were absent when independence was declared, while they were absent, and anterior to their returning and joining their country under its new and independent Government: for, on that supposition, many persons hostile to these States must be admitted citizens; those who have been born for thirteen years before the declaration of independence, within the posts of our northwestern frontiers, which are unjustly detained from us by the British, would be citizens. Our East India trade would be laid open to the numerous natives of this country, who are now dispersed over Europe and the West Indies. If birth and residence within the limits of the United States before the revolution conferred the rights of citizenship, persons of the aforesaid description, who have neither done nor hazarded any thing for our independence, might trade to the East Indies as citizens of the United States, from the circumstance of their having been born, in this country thirty or forty years ago, and, after having glutted our market with extravagant importations, carry the whole profits of their commerce to their present residence in foreign countries. These, and many other dangerous consequences, would, as your petitioner apprehends, follow from the establishment of a precedent, by which it was acknowledged, that a native of this country might be a citizen of the United States before he lived under their Government."

Mr. MADISON.—I think the merit of the question is now to be decided, whether the gentleman is eligible to a seat in this House or not; but it will depend on the decision of a previous question, whether he had been seven years a citizen of the United States or not.

From an attention to the facts which have been adduced, and from a consideration of the principles established by the revolution, the conclusion I have drawn is, that Mr. SMITH was, on the declaration of independence, a citizen of the United States; and unless it appears that he has forfeited his right, by some neglect or overt act, he had continued a citizen until the day of his election to a seat in this House. I take it to be a clear point, that we are to be guided, in our decision, by the laws and constitution of South Carolina, so far as they can guide us; and where the laws do not expressly guide us, we must be guided by principles of a general nature, so far as they are applicable to the present case.

It were to be wished, that we had some law adduced, more precisely defining the qualities of a citizen or an alien; particular laws of this kind have obtained in some of the States; if such a law existed in South Carolina, it might have prevented this question from ever coming before us; but since this has not been the case, let us settle some general principle before we proceed to the presumptive proof arising from public measures under the law, which tend to give support to the inference drawn from such principles.

It is an established maxim, that birth is a criterion of allegiance. Birth, however, derives its force sometimes from place, and sometimes from parentage; but, in general, place is the most certain criterion; it is what applies in the United States; it will, therefore, be unnecessary to investigate any other. Mr. SMITH founds his claim upon his birthright; his ancestors were among the first settlers of that colony.

It is well known to many gentlemen on this floor, as well as to the public, that the petitioner is a man of talents, one who would not lightly hazard his reputation in support of visionary principles: yet I cannot but think he has erred in one of the principles upon which he grounds his charge. He supposes, when this country separated from Great Britain, the tie of allegiance subsisted between the inhabitants of America and the King of that nation, unless, by some adventitious circumstance, the allegiance was transferred to one of the United States. I think there is a distinction which will invalidate his doctrine in this particular, a distinction between that primary allegiance which we owe to that particular society of which we are members, and the secondary allegiance we owe to the sovereign established by that society. This distinction will be illustrated by the doctrine established by the laws of Great Britain, which were the laws of this country before the revolution. The sovereign cannot make a citizen by any act of his own; he can confer denizenship; but this does not make a man either a citizen or subject. In order to make a citizen or subject, it is established, that allegiance shall first be due to the whole nation; it is necessary that a national act should pass to admit an individual member. In order to become a member of the British empire, where birth has not endowed the person with that privilege, he must be naturalized by an act of Parliament.

What was the situation of the people of America, when the dissolution of their allegiance took place by the declaration of independence? I conceive that every person who owed this primary allegiance to the particular community in which he was born, retained his right of birth, as a member of a new community; that he was consequently absolved from the secondary allegiance he had owed to the British sovereign. If he were not a minor, he became bound, by his own act, as a member of the society who separated with him from a submission to a foreign country. If he were a minor, his consent was involved in the decision of that society to which he belonged by the ties of nature. What was the allegiance, as a citizen of South Carolina, he owed to the King of Great Britain? He owed his allegiance to him as a King of that society to which, as a society, he owed his primary allegiance. When that society separated from Great Britain, he was bound by that act, and his allegiance transferred to that society, or the sovereign which that society should set up; because it was through his membership of the society of South Carolina that he owed allegiance to Great Britain.

This reasoning will hold good, unless it is supposed that the separation which took place between these States and Great Britain, not only dissolved the union between those countries, but dissolved the union among the citizens themselves: that the original compact, which made them altogether one society, being dissolved, they could not fall into pieces, each part making an independent society; but must individually revert into a state of nature; but I do not conceive that this was, of necessity, to be the case; I believe such a revolution did not absolutely take place. But in supposing that this was the case, lies the error of the memorialist. I conceive the colonies remained as a political society, detached from their former connexion with another society, without dissolving into a state of nature; but capable of substituting a new form of Government in the place of the old one, which they had, for special considerations, abolished. Suppose the State of South Carolina should think proper to revise her constitution, abolish that which now exists, and establish another form of Government: surely this would not dissolve the social compact. It would not throw them back into a state of nature. It would not dissolve the union between the individual members of that society. It would leave them in perfect society, changing only the mode of action, which they are always at liberty to arrange. Mr. SMITH being then, at the declaration of independence, a minor, but being a member of that particular society, he became, in my opinion, bound by the decision of the society, with respect to the question of independence and change of Government; and if afterwards he had taken part with the enemies of his country, he would have been guilty of treason against that Government to which he owed allegiance, and would have been liable to be prosecuted as a traitor.

If it be said, that very inconvenient circumstances would result from this principle, that it would constitute all those persons who are natives of America, but who took part against the revolution, citizens of the United States, I would beg leave to observe, that we are deciding a question of right, unmixed with the question of expediency, and must, therefore, pay a proper attention to this principle. But I think it can hardly be expected by gentlemen that the principle will operate dangerously. Those who left their country, to take part with Britain, were of two descriptions—minors, or persons of mature age. With respect to the latter, nothing can be inferred with respect to them from the decision of the present case; because they had the power of making an option between the contending parties; whether this was a matter of right or not is a question which need not be agitated in order to settle the case before us. Then, with respect to those natives who were minors at the revolution, and whose case is analogous to Mr. SMITH's, if we are bound by the precedent of such a decision as we are about to make, and it is declared that they owe a primary allegiance to this country, I still think we are not likely to be inundated with such characters; so far as any of them took part against us, they violated their allegiance, and opposed our laws; so, then, there can be only a few characters, such as were minors at the revolution, and who have never violated their allegiance by a foreign connexion, who can be affected by the decision of the present question. The number, I admit, is large who might be acknowledged citizens on my principles; but there will very few be found daring enough to face the laws of the country they have violated, and against which they have committed high treason.

So far as we can judge by the laws of Carolina, and the practice and decision of that State, the principles I have adduced are supported; and I must own, that I feel myself at liberty to decide, that Mr. SMITH was a citizen at the declaration of independence, a citizen at the time of his election, and, consequently, entitled to a seat in this Legislature.

Mr. BOUDINOT expressed an apprehension, that the principle supported by the gentleman from Virginia would tend to injure the State of New Jersey very considerably. He was afraid it would be construed to embrace all the natives of America who had deserted their country's cause during the late war; and, on this account, he was against deciding in favor of the proposed resolution, though he believed Mr. SMITH to be fairly and constitutionally entitled to a seat in that House.

Mr. JACKSON.—I differ widely from the gentleman from Virginia (Mr. MADISON) on the subject of allegiance and the social compact, and hold the principles advanced by him exceedingly dangerous to many of the States, and, in particular, to the one I have the honor to represent. The situation of America, at the time of the revolution, was not properly to be compared to a people altering their mode or form of Government. Nor were there two allegiances due, one to the community here, another to that of Great Britain. We were all on a footing; and I contend the principle is right, in some degree, of a total reversion to a state of nature amongst individuals, and to a mere parental or patriarchal authority, where the heads had families dependent on them; the former, or individual, pursued that line which appeared right in his own eyes, and the cause which he thought just; and, in the latter case, the children followed the will of the father, who chose for them, as the person who brought them into life, and whose fortunes they were to inherit. I conceive the whole allegiance or compact to have been dissolved. Many of the States were a considerable period without establishing constitutions or forms of Government, and during that period we were in a little better state than that of nature; and then it was, that every man made his election for an original compact, or tie, which, by his own act, or that of his father for him, he became bound to submit to. And what, sir, would otherwise be the result? And if the gentleman's doctrines of birth were to be supported, those minors who, with British bayonets, have plundered and ravaged, nay, cruelly butchered their more virtuous neighbors—the sons of the most inveterate traitors, whose names deservedly sounded in every bill of confiscation; and the minors, sons of those who sheltered themselves under the shade of the British King, and supported his armies, if not with arms, with the resources of war, until the hour of danger was over—those, I say, after the blood of thousands has been spilt in the establishment of our Government, can now come forward and sneer at the foolish patriots, who endured every hardship of a seven years' war, to secure to them the freedom and property they had no hand in defending. Sir, did we fight for this? Was it for this the soldier watched his numerous nights, and braved the inclemency of the sea-sons? Will he submit, after having gained his point at the expense of property and the loss of constitution, to have those sentiments established? If he will, he has fought to little purpose indeed.

Sir, I again contend, that when the revolution came on, we were all alike with respect to allegiances, and all under the same social tie. An Englishman born did not conceive himself more liable to be condemned for treason than an American, had the enemy succeeded; nor would there have been any distinction in the laws on coming to a trial. But, sir, how should this primary allegiance be known to belong to the less, or American community, where the majority did not prevail. In Georgia, the majority were opposed to American measures; agreeably to the gentleman's reasoning, the minors must have been all on the British side; and yet many of them, on arriving to years of discretion, behaved well and valiantly with us. To corroborate this, sir, I will remark, that, for a considerable period, we had no general or federal Government, or form of constitution, and yet were in arms. I would ask what state we were in then? Neighbor was against neighbor, and brother against brother. But, sir, the gentleman says, the hardened minor will not return. Sir, experience has proved the contrary. The Middle and Eastern States, except Pennsylvania, New Jersey, and New York, never had the enemy long with them; there was not the same trial of men, and they knew not the audacity of those villains. After having received their equivalent for, in many cases, feigned losses, from the British crown, they are daily returning and pushing into office. It is necessary we should guard against them. Britain, although humiliated, yet has a longing eye upon this country; she has yet posts in it. Although it is improbable that so many of these people will get into Congress as to form a corrupt majority, yet they have ambition and resentment enough to attempt it. At this moment, sir, in Georgia, are some of the most daring bringing ejectments for estates which their fathers had deservedly forfeited, although themselves had imbrued their hands in the blood of their fellow citizens.

Now, to the present case: Highly as I regard the gentleman (Mr. SMITH) as a valuable member, and esteem his abilities, I can only form my opinion on the leave given him by the State to be absent. If that principle is introduced into the resolution, I will vote in favor of Mr. SMITH's eligibility; but if not, I must decline voting.

Which he accordingly did when the question was put.

Mr. TUCKER hoped that the yeas and nays would be taken on this question, not because he had any doubt in his own mind of Mr. SMITH's right to a seat, but because he had been solicited by Dr. Ramsay to have the yeas and nays taken.

YEAS.—Messrs. Baldwin, Benson, Boudinot, Cadwalader, Carroll, Clymer, Coles, Contee, Fitzsimons, Floyd, Gilman, Goodhue, Heister, Huntington, Lawrence, Lee, Leonard, Livermore, Madison, Moore, Muhlenburg, Page, Van Rensselaer, Seney, Schureman, Scott, Sinnickson, Smith, of Maryland, Sturgis, Sylvester, Thatcher, Trumbull, Tucker, Vining, White, and Wynkoop. Jonathan Grout voted in the negative.

14

THOMAS JEFFERSON, CONSTITUTIONALITY OF
RESIDENCE BILL OF 1790
15 July 1790
Papers 17:195–96

Every man, and every body of men on earth, possesses the righ[t] of self-government: they recieve it with their being from the hand of nature. Individuals exercise it by their single will: collections of men, by that of their majority; for the law of the *majority* is the natural law of every society of men. When a certain description of men are to transact together a particular business, the times and places of their meeting and separating depend on their own will; they make a part of the natural right of self-government. This, like all other natural rights, may be abridged or modified in it's exercise, by their own consent, or by the law of those who depute them, if they meet in the right of others: but so far as it is not abridged or modified, they retain it as a natural right, and may exercise it in what form they please, either exclusively by themselves, or in association with others, or by others altogether, as they shall agree.

Each house of Congress possesses this natural right of governing itself, and consequently of fixing it's own times and places of meeting, so far as it has not been abridged by the law of those who employ them, that is to say, by the Constitution. This act manifestly considers them as possessing this right of course, and therefore has no where given it to them. In the several different passages where it touches this right, it treats it as an existing thing, not as one called into existence by them. To evince this, every passage of the constitution shall be quoted, where the right of adjournment is touched; and it will be seen that no one of them pretends to give that right; that on the contrary every one is evidently introduced either to enlarge the right where it would be too narrow, to restrain it where, in it's natural and full exercise, it might be too large and lead to inconvenience, to defend it from the latitude of it's own phrases, where these were not meant to comprehend it, or to provide for it's exercise by others where they cannot exercise it themselves.

"A majority of each house shall constitute a quorum to do business; but a *smaller number* may adjourn from day to day, and may be authorised to compel the attendance of absent members." Art. 1. sect. 5. A majority of every collection of men being naturally necessary to constitute it's will, and it being frequently to happen that a majority is not assembled, it was necessary to enlarge the natural right, by giving to "a *smaller number* than a majority" a right to compel the attendance of the absent members, and in the mean time to adjourn from day to day. This clause then does not pretend to give to a majority a right which it knew that majority would have of themselves, but to a number *less than a majority* a right which it knew that lesser number would not have of themselves.

"Neither house, during the session of Congress, shall, without the consent of the other, adjourn for more than three days, nor to any other place than that in which the two houses shall be sitting." Ibid. Each house exercising separately it's natural right to meet when and where it should think best, it might happen that the two houses would separate either in time or place, which would be inconvenient. It was necessary therefore to keep them together by restraining their natural right of deciding on separate times and places, and by requiring a concurrence of will.

But as it might happen that obstinacy, or a difference of object might prevent this concurrence, it goes on to take from them, in that instance, the right of adjournment altogether, and to transfer it to another, by declaring Art. 2. sect. 3. that "in case of disagreement between the two houses with respect to the time of adjournment the President may adjourn them to such time as he shall think proper."

These clauses then do not import a gift, to the two houses, of a general right of adjournment, which it was known they would have without that gift, but to restrain or abrogate the right it was known they would have, in an instance where, exercised in it's full extent, it might lead to inconvenience, and to give that right to another who would not naturally have had it. It also gives to the President a right, which he otherwise would not have had, "to convene both houses, or either of them, on extraordinary occasions," thus substituting the will of another, where they are not in a situation to exercise their own.

15

JAMES WILSON, LEGISLATIVE DEPARTMENT,
LECTURES ON LAW
1791
Works 1:420–22

Each house may not only punish, but, with the concurrence of two thirds, it may expel a member. This regulation is adopted by the constitution of Pennsylvania: "but," it is added, "not a second time for the same cause." The reason for the addition evidently is—that the member, who has offended, cannot be an object of a second expulsion, unless, since the offence given and punished by the first expulsion, he has been either reelected by his former constituents, or elected by others. In both cases, his election is a proof, that, in the opinion of his constituents, he either has not offended at all, or has been already sufficiently punished for his offence. The language of each opinion is, that he ought not to be expelled again: and the language of the constituents is a law to the house.

. . . . .

The constitution of the United States directs, that each house shall keep a journal of its proceedings, and, from time to time, publish them, except such parts as may require secrecy: it directs further, that the yeas and nays of the members of either house, on any question, shall, at the desire of one fifth of those present, be entered on the journal. The constitution of Pennsylvania goes still further upon these points: it directs, that the journals shall be published weekly; that the yeas and nays shall be entered on them, at the desire of any two members; and that the doors of each house, and of committees of the whole, shall be open, unless when the business shall be such as ought to be kept secret.

That the conduct and proceedings of representatives should be as open as possible to the inspection of those whom they represent, seems to be, in republican government, a maxim, of whose truth or importance the smallest doubt cannot be entertained. That, by a necessary consequence, every measure, which will facilitate or secure this open communication of the exercise of delegated power, should be adopted and patronised by the constitution and laws of every free state, seems to be another maxim, which is the unavoidable result of the former. For these reasons, I feel myself necessarily and unavoidably led to consider the additional regulations made, upon this subject, by the constitution of Pennsylvania, as improvements upon those made by the constitution of the United States. The regulation—that the doors of each house, and of committees of the whole, shall be open—I view as an improvement highly beneficial both in its nature and in its consequence—both to the representatives and to their constituents. "In the house of commons," says Sir William Blackstone, "the conduct of every member is subject to the future censure of his constituents, and therefore should be openly submitted to their inspection." But I forbear to enter more largely into this interesting topick.

16

SENATE, CONTESTED ELECTION OF MR. GALLATIN
20–22, 28 Feb. 1794
Annals 4:48–55, 57

[*20 Feb.*]

Mr. GALLATIN accordingly rose and recapitulated the facts stated in the written paper which he had presented to the PRESIDENT, commenting on each of them as he proceeded. He proved that he had been an inhabitant of the United States for thirteen years, and was one before the Peace of 1783, and before the Confederation. He quoted the laws previous thereto respecting aliens, and also the British statutes, and he maintained that they were all done away by the Revolution. He conceived himself a citizen in common with the other citizens of the United States, from the time of his first qualifying after his arrival and attachment to the country. He concluded by saying, he would reserve the remainder of his defence until after he should hear the counsel on behalf of the petitioners.

Mr. Lewis commenced his speech by observing, that he appeared there on behalf of Conrad Laub, and other respectable men, who complained of the unconstitutionality of admitting Mr. GALLATIN to a seat in the Senate. He was glad to find, by the gentleman's expressions, that the ground of debate had been narrowed into so small a compass, and he would therefore take him up from the argument where he had left off speaking, that of his being a citizen in common of the United States, from the time of his qualifying in Massachusetts or Virginia. But in Virginia two oaths are required, and they must be taken in a Court, not before a Magistrate, to entitle a man to citizenship. He must also be possessed of a certain quantity of property and be a resident for two years. It appears Mr. G. did not remain in Virginia more than two months. [Here Mr. Lewis read the law of Virginia of the 20th October, 1783.] On this law Mr. L. argued that Mr. G. had not gone through the necessary qualifications to entitle him to citizenship there; and he observed, that he admired the gentleman's candor in not insisting on it here. In this State he had certainly not qualified himself agreeably to the law. Under these circumstances, Mr. L. for his part could never admit of the gentleman's right to citizenship so far back as to entitle him to the suffrage of a vote for a seat in the Senate, &c.

The mischievous consequences of permitting such innovations, he represented in strong terms; and he called to the recollection of the Senate, the conduct of ancient and modern Governments on this question. One of the ancient Republics made it death for an alien to intermeddle in their politics. The sentiments of antiquity, and those of men in modern days, proved the justice of these conclusions.

With regard to the arguments of the gentleman respecting his being entitled to be a citizen of the Union, or of any individual State of it, because he had qualified himself to be citizen of one of them, Mr. L. said, was a mere bubble, for surely the gentleman was not one of the mass of citizens at the accomplishment of Independence.

The doctrine of the old law, which the gentleman says was done away by the Revolution, in respect to aliens, may have been so with regard to the British King; it was still, however, virtually in force against the gentleman. But supposing it to be done away, how do the Constitutions of the different States stand on this head? Is it not implied by all of them, that certain oaths, residence, and property, make the requisites to form citizenship? In Massachusetts, a foreigner is not a citizen without he complies with those terms. [Here he quoted p. 70 of the small volume of the Laws of Massachusetts. He also cited the act in favor of John Jarvis and others; also, p. 104 of the same book, and p. 191 and 192.] From these he maintained, that no such wild idea was ever contemplated by either the law of Massachusetts or Virginia, as to admit foreigners or persons from other States to citizenship, immediately on their entrance within their limits.

The situation of the sitting member, with respect to the Constitution and laws of Pennsylvania, he had little doubt was similar to what he had mentioned in regard to the other States, although he would not assert it as a fact. [He read the 42d section, and also in p. 43 of the Law of Pennsylvania, 13th of March, 1789, a proviso which contains some precautions requiring records to be kept by the Master of the rolls of the persons admitted to citizenship.] The same principle pervades all the States as well as it does the Constitution of the United States. The absurdity of applying it in any other sense, was severely pictured by Mr. L., and to admit the idea advanced by the sitting member, was as inadmissible as it was novel. In support of what he wished to impress on the minds of the Senate, Mr. L. quoted the 1st vol. of the Journals of Congress in 1774 and 1775, p. 28 and 29. He then recurred to *Blackstone*, vol. 1, p. 63, 64, and 69; also 73 and 79.

It was not his intention to quote the Parliamentary Laws of England in support of any thing, but such parts of their Common Law as could be got over. That Common Law of England which was imported by our ancestors, and handed down to them by the People, not the Parliament. The People had made the Common Law, from time to time. The Saxons, Normans, &c., were all concerned in making and improving it, until it had finally reached that degree of perfection in which it was given to us by our ancestors, and it was founded in wisdom and justice.

Mr. L. next quoted, first *Blackstone*, 402, which was one of the British laws that had never been admitted in this country, and which, he hoped, never would, viz: that wherein the distinction is drawn between the Commoner and the Peer, an oath being required of the Commoner, upon all occasions, and no more than *"upon my honor,"* from a Peer, except in giving evidence in civil or criminal trials.

Mr. L. concluded, by saying that the difficulties which stood between Mr. GALLATIN and his seat, were insurmountable and could not be removed without showing a law of Massachusetts, Virginia, &c., repealing those laws in regard to the qualification of citizens, which he had mentioned, but which repeal he was certain did not exist. He therefore stated, that to insist upon the gentleman's right to a seat, was both novel and absurd. These were his opinions, which he had given in a perfectly extempore way, not having been allowed time, nor expecting to meet the subject on the new ground which it had this day taken in the Senate.

[*21 Feb.*]

Mr. GALLATIN commenced his defence by laying down the principles on which he intended to argue. His was a very serious situation, for a person to be placed in, who had been so long in America, and who had mingled with the inhabitants in the common cause, that he should afterwards be called before so solemn a tribunal, with an intention to wrest from him his right of citizenship. He confessed, that on this occasion his feelings were deeply interested, particularly as the manner of the counsel for the prosecutors was so personal, and went not only to deny him a seat in the Senate of the United States, but even to contest his citizenship, and denounce him as being yet an alien.

This was a matter of consequence to many thousands as well as himself, who have long considered themselves in possession of all the privilege of denizens, and yet may be deprived of their rights, if the doctrines of the counsel for the prosecutors should obtain any sanction from the body who were now to judge of its merits.

Mr. G. entered into a series of observations on the various points of law, &c., which had been adduced by Mr. LEWIS, and he particularly remarked, that the Common Law of England was entirely inapplicable to the subject under consideration. He read the laws of Virginia respecting naturalization, &c., from which he insisted that he had long since become a citizen of the United States. He also quoted 1st *Blackstone*, p. 374, and *Viner's Abridgment*, vol. ii. p. 266, respecting the different acceptations of denizen and citizen, and he went back so far as the British statutes in 1740, to show the intention of the old Government was to naturalize all persons who would go and reside in the Colonies. He next mentioned the act of Pennsylvania, of 31st of August, 1778, and commented on the principles generally entertained by most writers on the subjects of allegiance and citizenship. *Blackstone*, 266, &c.

An alien is a man born out of the allegiance of the King. But allegiance in England is not an allegiance to the country or to society, as it is understood in this country.

In order to explain the principle of reciprocity, he observed, that when the two crowns of England and Scotland were united under James, the inhabitants of Scotland became naturalized in England, as if they had been natural-born subjects of that country. The allegiance in Britain was personal to the King, and it has there this remarkable quality, that by the British laws allegiance can never be shaken off.

This country, before the Revolution, owed allegiance to the King, but that was destroyed by the Declaration of Independence, and then the inhabitants of the States became mutually citizens of every State reciprocally; and they continued so until such time as the States made laws of their own afterwards respecting naturalization.

As soon as separate Governments existed, allegiance was due to each, and here the allegiance was a reality, it was to the Government and to society, whereas in Britain it is merely fictitious, being only to one man.

Every man who took an active part in the American Revolution, was a citizen according to the great laws of reason and of nature, and when afterwards positive laws were made, they were retrospective in regard to persons under this predicament, nor did those posterior laws invalidate the rights which they enjoy under the Confederation.

Mr. G. here mentioned his having been an inhabitant of Massachusetts, before October, 1780, and he also observed, that the law passed in that State was decisive against the Common Law of England.

In quoting the laws of Massachusetts, which were passed in 1785, and afterwards, for naturalizing John Gardner, and James Martin, he remarked that they clearly implied that even a natural born subject, who had not acted in the Revolution, and an absentee, was not entitled to citizenship. He likewise took notice of the case of Mr. WILLIAM SMITH, of South Carolina, against whose election as a Representative in Congress, a petition was presented by Doctor Ramsay, although the decision of South Carolina on that subject was exactly the reverse of Massachusetts.

In speaking of the difficulties that occurred in explaining the terms citizen and alien, he ran over a number of cases, and asked whether if a person had arrived in the United States during the war, from Nova-Scotia, or elsewhere, and had taken an active part against the enemy, would he not be better entitled to the right of a citizen, than even those who afterwards subscribed to the acts? The counsel for the prosecutors had admitted that a person who had been one of the mass of the people, at the Declaration of Independence, was a citizen. On the same principle, until a law passes to disprove that a man who was active in the Revolution previous to the Treaty of Peace, was a citizen, he must be one *ipso facto*.

Mr. G. next read a quotation from the 1st vol. of *Woodison*, p. 382, an English writer, who acknowledged that all persons were aliens at the recognition of Independence, and that is a more liberal construction than the counsel for the petitioners would admit of, for by his construction, our sailors, &c., ought to be naturalized, lest they be alarmed by the British.

The new Constitution of the United States requires certain qualifications for members of Congress, &c., but it does not deprive persons of their rights who were actually citizens before this Constitution was ratified that made the States the United States. They were united by consent before, and consequently he was one of the people before the United States existed.

He went on to read from the Constitution of Massachusetts, and several other States, sundry clauses in support of his reasoning, and recapitulated the several heads of Mr. L.'s arguments, to each of which he replied.

Mr. G. said, that Mr. Lewis was unfortunate in producing the law of Pennsylvania, for, by proving too much, he had proved nothing, for the 42d sec. of the Constitution is retrospective, and by acknowledging the Articles of Confederation to be the supreme law of the land, persons who were reciprocally citizens before, are still left in full possession of the right.

So far from any dangerous consequences arising on my construction of citizenship, said he, I think it must be evident, that there is more danger and absurdity in the counsel's own constructions. For, in remarking on the policy of nations, we find even slaves have been enfranchised by the great Republics in times of common danger. The policy of America should be to make citizenship as easy as possible, for the purpose of encouraging population; even during the British dominion that was a principle laid down, and afterwards it was attempted to be varied; it is made one of the principal subjects of complaint in the Declaration of Independence, where it is expressly said, that the King endeavored to prevent the population of these States, by having laws made to obstruct the naturalization of foreigners.

If there was any dangerous consequences to be apprehended from the former regulations on this subject, they are all remedied by the new Constitution.

Therefore, no ill consequence or absurdity can follow. The author of the Federalist supports this principle in vol. ii, p. 54, for he says, that it is a construction scarcely avoidable, that citizens of each of the States are mutually so in all of them.

The first words in the Constitution, "We, the People," furnished another argument in support of Mr. G.'s principles, which he turned to great advantage, still drawing an inference to show that Mr. L.'s construction of the subject was most liable to difficulties and to mischievous consequences.

He concluded by observing, that if there was any disfranchising clauses in the Constitution of the United States, tending to deprive citizens of antecedent rights, all such clauses must be construed favorably, and were evidently on his side. With regard to a sentence that had been added, by the advice of counsel, to the affidavit of Pelatiah Webster, he made some remarks which tended to establish his own personal character, which he trusted would be found, when traced back to his nativity, to stand the test; and that his right to a seat in the Senate would also stand upon an equally just foundation.

Mr. Lewis denied having ever seen the affidavit of Mr. Webster, until it was shown him at the time the examination before the Committee was going forward.

Mr. GALLATIN recriminated, that the clause of which he took notice, was not in the affidavit when Mr. Webster brought it to the Committee, and that he had permitted it to be added with great reluctance. It was only the recital of a few words which passed between Mr. G. and Mr W. in jest, some years since, wherein Mr. G. had ironically said his name was Sidney, probably alluding to some essays that had appeared in the newspapers under that signature, which have been generally attributed to the pen of another gentleman in this State.

Mr. JACKSON, in order to bring the merits of the subject directly before the Senate, said he would move a resolution, that would have that effect; but upon Mr. LEWIS's observing, that he had not yet closed his arguments, and at the instance of Mr. BUTLER, from South Carolina, who said he would second Mr. JACKSON's motion hereafter, it was withdrawn for the present.

Ordered, That the further consideration thereof be postponed until to-morrow.

[*22 Feb.*]

The Senate resumed the consideration of the report of the committee on the petition of Conrad Laub, and others, respecting the election of Mr. GALLATIN to be a Senator of the United States.

The greater part of the day was taken up by Mr. Lewis's pleadings, wherein he entered into a very extensive field of reasoning, and quoted a great number of authorities, in support of the principles on which he had set out last Thursday, and to prove that in the true sense of the Constitution of the United States, as well as of that of the State of Pennsylvania, Mr. GALLATIN was not duly qualified for the office of a Senator, and therefore, he trusted that the honorable Senate, upon mature reflection, would vacate his seat.

Mr. GALLATIN closed his defence in a short speech, wherein he quoted *Vattel*. p. 167, and explained the 42d section of the Constitution of Pennsylvania, the liberal construction of which, he said, was in his favor, and the construction contended for by the counsel, absurd. He finished by reading a passage from *Lord Bacon's* works, to show that where there is any doubt in the laws, it should operate in favor of the defendant, and he accordingly made no doubt but that the Senate would validate his election.

[*28 Feb.*]

On motion to adopt the resolution as follows:

> "*Resolved*, That the election of ALBERT GALLA-TIN to be a Senator of the United States was void, he not having been a citizen of the United States the term of years required as a qualification to be a Senator of the United States:"

It passed in the affirmative—yeas 14, nays 12, as follows:

YEAS.—Messrs. Bradford, Cabot, Ellsworth, Foster, Frelinghuysen, Hawkins, Izard, King, Livermore, Mitchell, Morris, Potts, Strong, and Vining.

NAYS.—Messrs. Bradley, Brown, Burr, Butler, Edwards, Gunn, Jackson, Langdon, Martin, Monroe, Robinson, and Taylor.

17

HOUSE OF REPRESENTATIVES, EVIDENCE IN CONTESTED ELECTIONS
6 Dec. 1797
Annals 7:683–86

Mr. SITGREAVES did not understand the object which the mover of these resolutions had in view. He knew not whether he meant to confine the operation of his rule to the present House of Representatives only, or to all future Houses. From the language of the first resolution he judged the latter was his intention. As it was his opinion, therefore, that any attempt of theirs to bind future Houses would be perfectly nugatory, he should move to strike out the words from, "If it be," to "given," (in the first clause.) This resolution will then confine the operation of the rule to the elections which may take place during the fifth Congress. By the Constitution every House was to judge of the elections and returns of its own members. It was not in the power of any House to prescribe rules for a succeeding one, for this reason the rules which governed a preceding House were always revised by the succeeding one. If they were to prescribe rules which were to be binding on future Houses, it could only be done by an act of the whole Legislature, which would certainly be exceptionable, as it would give to the President and Senate a power over the rules for governing their proceedings, which, by the Constitution, they were alone the judges of. He thought his ideas on this subject correct; if they were, he doubted not the motion which he had made would be agreed to.

Mr. HARPER said, if the idea of the gentleman last up was correct, his motion would doubtless be acceded to, though he did not go far enough, because, in that case he should have moved to have struck out the whole clause; because, if the rules proposed were not to have a permanent effect, they would be perfectly nugatory. But he apprehended his friend had not attended to a distinction which he thought a plain one. It was this: the power to establish rules for the taking of evidence, and that of judging of the evidence after it was taken. This House could not say it would admit members under such and such disqualifications, but an agreement to the mode of taking evidence was very different from the qualifications themselves. It was essentially necessary that Legislative and Judicial powers should be kept distinct, yet it was not thought an interference with the Judicial authority for the Legislature to direct the mode of taking evidence in certain cases. Nothing could be more clear than this distinction. It could not be said, therefore, that because the whole Legislature directed the mode of taking evidence in cases of contested election, that the President and Senate interfered with the Constitutional direction that every House should be the judge of its own rules. He was of opinion that a law was necessary, and a law of permanent nature, to which he could see no reasonable objection. He allowed that it would be unconstitutional for the President or Senate to interfere with their rules or elections, but when they came to make a law which was to operate upon the whole community, their interference was necessary and proper. If these ideas were sound, and he thought they were, the proposed amendment would be rejected.

Mr. N. SMITH said the motion now before them was founded upon an idea that permanent rules could not be made for taking evidence in cases of contested elections. He had frequently heard it said that rules could not be made to be binding any longer than whilst the House existed which formed them. For himself he never conceived this opinion to be correct. That it was highly important that permanent regulations should be made on the subject in question, every one must admit. It became of importance, therefore, to know whether it had the power of making them. When he spoke of permanent rules he would not be understood to mean that any rules should be longer permanent than until the time came when the House of Representatives should wish to rescind them.

The idea which led to the conclusion of the gentleman from Pennsylvania was this: that every new Congress occasioned a new House of Representatives; that whenever the members were newly elected there was a new House of Representatives. He did not believe this doctrine to be correct. The House of Representatives, in his opinion, always existed; and there was no period at which it could be said there was not a House of Representatives in being. He never believed it was broken in pieces once in two years; for when the time of one set of members expired, that of another set commenced; so that it was the nature of a corporation, which always existed. He did not think there had been four Houses of Representatives since the commencement of the present Government, but that the whole had been one uninterrupted House. He thought this was the view which the Constitution gave of the subject, as it spoke of it always as a permanent body. In the same way the President and Senate were permanent. If this were not the case, and every election made a new House, there was a time when the Senate was only two-thirds of a Senate (when one-third went out of office.) This idea, therefore, could not be right. There was no difficulty, therefore, in forming permanent rules, since they were made to govern the House and not the individual members. With respect to those things which each branch of Government had the power of doing for itself, each could establish its own rules; but what related to the whole Government must be the act of the whole. The gentleman from Pennsylvania had said that each House had the power of judging of its own elections. This, he apprehended, did not refer to different Houses of Representatives, but to the House of Representatives and the Senate, as each House was always considered by the Constitution as a permanent body. He was, therefore, opposed to the amendment.

Mr. NICHOLAS believed this was a subject in which they should never advance far enough to come to a decision. Very long and very plausible arguments might be adduced on both sides of the question, which would produce different effects on those who heard them; but, he thought the question before them might be acted upon, without coming to a question on that point. He supposed, if any case of contested election came before the House, and the evidence was taken in such a way as to ascertain the truth, they should be at liberty to proceed to the examination of the case; and, therefore, all that was wanting, was to call in the power of the General Legislature to authorize the attendance of witnesses to deliver their testimony. Let that testimony be taken upon established and acknowledged rules, which satisfy every man's mind, and it will carry conviction with it, that it is proper. The necessity of adopting some mode of this kind was evident, as it was a great grievance that persons disputing elections had to come there to learn the mode of doing it, before they could proceed to take evidence. Indeed, it was putting the power of sending members to that House in the hands of returning officers. He had no doubt that the Constitution gave them power to make a law on the subject; if necessary the necessity of the case would show the reasonableness of it; but he did not know that a law was requisite; he thought a rule of the House to the effect he had mentioned, would cure the evil complained of.

Mr. SEWALL believed, that the great difficulty on the subject arose from in the form which it presented itself, which had introduced the question, whether that House was a perpetual body, or not. He must confess that he differed in opinion altogether from the gentleman from Connecticut, (Mr. N. SMITH,) that this House was a perpetual body. He thought the Constitution had shown, that though there was always a House of Representatives, yet, that every House had only two years duration; but, he believed, in determining the real object of this motion, there was no necessity for coming to a decision on this point.

18

HOUSE OF REPRESENTATIVES, BREACH OF PRIVILEGE
2, 8, 12 Feb. 1798
Annals 7:961–62, 973–78, 997–1002

[2 Feb.]

Mr. VENABLE, from the Committee of Privileges, made the following report:

The Committee of Privileges, to whom was referred a resolution on the 30th of January, charging Matthew Lyon with disorderly behaviour, with instructions to inquire into the whole matter thereof, and to report the same, with their opinion thereon, to the House, having examined several witnesses on oath touching the subject, report: That, during the sitting of the House of Representatives on the 30th day of January, 1798, the tellers of the House being engaged in counting the ballots for Managers of the impeachment against William Blount, the Speaker had left his Chair, and many members their seats, as is usual on such occasions; the Speaker was sitting in one of the member's seats, next to the bar of the House, and several members near him, of whom Mr. Griswold was one.

Mr. Lyon was standing without the bar of the House, leaning on the same, and holding a conversation with the Speaker. He spoke loud enough to be heard by all those who were near him, as if he intended to be heard by them. The subject of his conversation was, the conduct of the Representatives of the State of Connecticut, (of whom Mr. Griswold was one.) Mr. Lyon declared that they acted in opposition to the interests and opinion of nine-tenths of their constituents; that they were pursuing their own private views, without regarding the interests of the people; that they were seeking offices, which they were willing to accept, whether yielding $9,000 or $1,000. He further observed that the people of that State were blinded or deceived by those Representatives; that they were permitted to see but one side of the question in politics, being lulled asleep by the opiates which the members from that State administered to them; with other expressions equally tending to derogate from the political integrity of the Representatives of Connecticut.

On Mr. Lyon's observing, that if he should go into Connecticut, and manage a press there six months, although the people of that State were not fond of revolutionary principles, he could effect a revolution, and turn out the present Representatives—Mr. Griswold replied to these remarks, and, amongst other things, said, "If you go into Connecticut, you had better wear your wooden sword," or words to that effect, alluding to Mr. Lyon's having been cashiered in the army.

Mr. Lyon did not notice the allusion at this time, but continued the conversation on the same subject. Mr. Griswold then left his seat, and stood next to Mr. Lyon, leaning on the bar, being outside the same.

On Mr. Lyon's saying he knew the people of Connecticut well, having lived among them many years—that he had frequent occasion to fight them in his own district, and that he never failed to convince them—Mr. Griswold asked, if he fought them with his wooden sword, on which Mr. Lyon spat in his face.

The Committee having attentively considered the foregoing state of facts, and having heard Mr. Lyon in his defence, are of opinion that his conduct in this transaction was highly indecorous, and unworthy of a member of this House.

They, therefore, recommend the adoption of the resolution submitted to their consideration by the House, in the words following, to wit:

"*Resolved,* That Matthew Lyon, a member of this House, for a violent attack and gross indecency, committed upon the person of Roger Griswold, another member, in the presence of the House while sitting, be for this disorderly behaviour expelled therefrom."

[*8 Feb.*]

Mr. LYON. Again, I say, Mr. Chairman, I am very extraordinarily situated. Evidence has been introduced into this House to induce the members to believe that I left Colonel Warner's regiment with dishonor; that I am a person of disrepute; that I have been in the habit of receiving insult with impunity. Here I am, three hundred and fifty miles from home, and from the evidence who are able to show the contrary. Had I a reasonable opportunity, I could prove, by the Lieutenant Colonel, who is now General Safford, and several other officers of that regiment, that when I left it, I left it with the regret of much the greater part of the officers and all the soldiers—I mention the Lieutenant Colonel because Colonel Warner is not living. My certificate of having settled my accounts, which is at home, would prove my having done my duty well.

I could prove my having taken my musket and marched to the lines every day, during the siege of Burgoyne. I should not have mentioned this circumstance, had not the SPEAKER mentioned his having done so when Paymaster.

I could also prove, that when an officer offered me an insult, I chastised him before the officers of that regiment.

[Mr. CHAMPLIN asked whether the gentleman said he had chastised an officer, or would chastise him?

Mr. LYON answered that he had chastised him.]

I could prove that I took the commission in Colonel Warner's regiment when I was driven from my plantation by Burgoyne's invasion; that I resigned my appointment, and left the regiment for the care of my family, for preferment, for honor, for superior office, and to serve the people of the State of Vermont.

I could prove, had I opportunity, that I was immediately appointed Deputy Secretary of the State, Paymaster of the troops of Vermont, assistant to the Treasurer, assistant to the Commissioner of Loans, and Captain of the Militia, besides being called on to act as private Secretary to the Governor.

I could also prove that within two years from the time of that resignation, I was appointed Secretary to the Governor and Council, a Member of the Legislature, Clerk of the House of Assembly, one of a Committee for the Collection and Revision of the Laws, and to a number of other offices under the authority of that State, besides a considerable number of offices in the municipal establishment of the town in which I lived, as well as my promotion to the command of a regiment, and all this before I formed a connexion with one of the most respectable families in that State. I could prove also, that I have been a member of the Legislature of Vermont, except two years, ever since; that I have been appointed to many other offices in which I did not think proper to serve, such as Auditor of the Treasurer's Accounts, and Judge of the County where I live.

By these things, and my standing in this House, I could prove that I have always been respected in the country I represent, and where I have lived these twenty-four years.

The free electors of my district have given me a preference to a gentleman of very great respectability, one who has served six years with unimpeachable fidelity in this House, and is now Chief Justice of the State of Vermont; yet evidence has been adduced in order to show that I am a person of disrepute.

As to my being in the habit of receiving insult with impunity—for which it seems Mr. CHIPMAN's testimony was introduced—were I allowed to call testimony from Vermont, I could very easily prove so much on this head, as, perhaps, to prove, in the minds of some gentlemen, that respectability which, in every other respect, attaches to my character. Among other things, I could prove that the gentleman from Vermont who was called to give testimony against me, has, with the politeness peculiar to a certain country which I will not now name, insulted me and received due chastisement from me for it.

Mr. HARPER called to order. The gentleman from Vermont had already spoken very improperly of witnesses, and he now spoke in a very reprehensible way of Mr. CHIPMAN. He hoped he would be admonished.

Mr. OTIS differed in opinion from the gentleman from South Carolina. If the gentleman thought it would be of service to him to inform the committee that he had chastised an officer in the face of his regiment, or beaten a Judge of the Supreme Court, he was right in stating the circumstances.

Mr. HARPER said, if he wished to see the gentleman disgrace himself, and the House, he should not object to this mode of proceeding; but he did not.

Mr. LYON. It would be folly in me to state anything to this committee, that I cannot prove. Nor should I have mentioned that circumstance, had I not been charged with receiving injuries with impunity. I never did receive injuries with impunity; nor did I come here to do so. I would sooner leave the world. Mr. L. then proceeded:

Were I to be allowed time to bring forward testimony from Vermont, I could prove that my character, as a man of spirit, stands on such ground in my country, that I had no need to defend it, by entering into a squabble with such a Chief Justice in court time.

If the proof of these things be considered of importance, I hope I shall be allowed time to send to Vermont to obtain it—for my own part, I cannot so consider it. I must think that the House of Representatives ought never to have taken up the matter of the difference between Mr. GRISWOLD and myself, circumstanced as it was; and that if the House thought otherwise, the due submission to their authority, which I have always stood ready to pay, and the sorrow which I have expressed, and am continually expressing, for my misapprehension, might serve as some mitigation of an offence against the dignity of this House, which I never could have knowingly been guilty of.

Mr. CHAMPLIN rose and said, it was expressly declared by the Constitution, "that each House may determine the rules of its proceedings, punish its members for disorderly behaviour, and, with the concurrence of two-thirds, expel a member," and he thought they were called upon to exercise this Constitutional power of expulsion in the present instance, by the respect due not only to themselves as legislators, but to their constituents; and as they valued the reputation of the National Legislature, both at home and abroad, as they regarded the *American* character, uninfluenced by the spirit of party, without taking into view the relative characters of the person who offered, and the person who received, the insult, without attending to the infinite distance there was between the *one* and the *other*—they were bound to give their votes, upon the present occasion, under the influence only of an high sense of duty and of honor. And under these impressions, he said, he had attentively and impartially considered all the circumstances of the present case, as they had appeared in evidence; and he found it was fully proved that an offence of a gross and injurious nature had been committed by the member from Vermont, (Mr. LYON,) against the person of the member from Connecticut, (Mr. GRISWOLD;) that the conversation which produced the altercation between them, originated with the member from Vermont; that it was a violent and groundless attack upon the public character of the member from Connecticut; inasmuch as he was represented to be regardless of the public good, and actuated entirely by selfish, sordid views; that this indecent attack upon his political integrity was repelled by a retort, that the occasion fully justified; that in consequence of this retort, the member from Vermont committed, within those walls, and whilst the House was sitting, the gross indecency stated by the Committee of Privileges, and of which the very SPEAKER of the House was an eyewitness; and that the member from Connecticut, whose cheek glowed with indignation, and whose arm was nerved by the desire of vengeance, recollecting the place in which he stood, and the respect due from him to that House, repressed his resentment. Mr. C. then observed, that the passions of some men, had their feelings been thus outraged by the member from Vermont, would have made him expiate the injury upon the spot. For the outrage committed by him bid defiance to order and decorum, tended to degrade the members of that House from the rank of men, and to reduce them to a level with the meanest reptile that crawled upon the earth. He was therefore compelled to declare, that, in his opinion, nothing short of

a vote that would deprive the member from Vermont of a seat in it could vindicate the honor of that House, which had been deeply wounded through one of its members. He was aware, he said, that the punishment of expulsion was a severe one. And there was no *man*, who had the feelings appropriate to *that character*, and whose mind was formed of common materials, but would be deeply affected by it. It must fix a stain upon the man who suffered it, for a gross and scandalous offence, that the waters of the ocean could not wash away. It should, however, be recollected that it was no further disgraceful, than as an unquestionable evidence of the gross indecency that gave occasion to it. And if a sacred regard to justice, to the representative character they sustained, and to their own honor, required that they should inflict that punishment upon a member of that House, they ought not to start at the effects of it. For if the member from Vermont should be compelled to return to his constituents, loaded with the opprobrium necessarily attached, in the present instance, to the punishment contemplated, they would have only to regret the disgraceful circumstance, the painful necessity, that had led to it. They would have discharged their duties, and the honor and dignity of the House would be preserved.

Mr. S. SMITH said, he did not wish to enter into a discussion of the subject before them. The committee had heard the evidence upon this subject very fully, and he doubted not every one was in full possession of the facts relative to it, and competent to come to a decision. To go into a discussion of the subject, therefore, would only be an unnecessary consumption of time, as it would not, he apprehended, change the opinion of any one. He hoped, therefore, the question would be taken without debate.

Mr. R. WILLIAMS did not mean to introduce a debate upon this subject, but merely to state the reasons which had induced him in the select committee, and which would induce him in this committee, and in the House, to vote against this report. He was as fully impressed as any gentleman with the necessity of preserving the dignity and honor of the House, and perfectly agreed with gentlemen as to the propriety of an attention to order and decorum in all their proceedings. But it appeared to him that there was a previous consideration necessary.

It was necessary first to consider how far the powers of the House extended with respect to punishing its members, and whether certain acts should be considered as done in the House or out of it. When these general principles were settled, it would be easily ascertained how far this power would extend in the present case. He was of opinion that the powers of the House should be cautiously extended. This, he thought, would be the opinion of every member of the committee, when they considered the nature and principles upon which our laws were founded, amongst which it is a principal feature that the makers of a law shall not have the execution of it; another is, that all offences shall be declared by law, before any person shall be charged with committing them. The laws are published, and judges are bound down by rule, and every man knows the law; but how is it in the present case? The House of Representatives is the injured party, the members are the judges, the jurors, and the executioners. He did not mention this because he thought the power of punishing its members was improperly placed in their own body; he mentioned it only to show that the power was liable to abuse from giving too much way to passion in their proceedings.

Having made these remarks, he would state why he thought the House had not the power to expel the member from Vermont. He did not believe that a member of the Legislature could be expelled for any act done out of the House, except it rendered him infamous. Mere lewdness, and breaches of morality committed out of the House, the House could not take cognizance of. A member, out of the House, may do things which may render him very disagreeable society, yet he may come into the House and behave very orderly. His constituents might have known, when they elected him, that he was subject to such behaviour, yet they might have sufficient confidence in him as a representative on that floor; but if any member acted so as to disturb the peace and order of the House, they had, doubtless, a right to turn him out.

Having mentioned what he conceived to be the powers of the House, he would consider whether the act done by the member from Vermont could be considered as done in the House, or in violation of its rules. If he could persuade himself that it was done when the House was in order, in violation of its rules, he should have no hesitation in saying that the member ought to be expelled; since he should take no notice of the offensive words which had been mentioned in justification, for though this circumstance might have considerable weight with some gentlemen, it would have none with him. In the rules for the regulation of the proceedings of the House, it was declared that, whenever the House meets, the SPEAKER should take the Chair at the hour to which the House adjourned. But where, he asked, was the SPEAKER, when the act complained of was committed, and what was the situation of the House at the time? He did not mean to say that the SPEAKER or any other member was not doing his duty, but to show that the House was not in order. The SPEAKER had left his seat, and was in that of another member; and the members were passing to and from different parts of the House. So that if even it could be considered in such a situation as that the rules of the House would apply to it, some allowance ought to be made to members who might think differently. But certainly no motion could have been stated to the House in this situation.

If the House had been organized, the SPEAKER could not have suffered such conversation as has been stated to have taken place before him. A breach of order, in such a situation of things, therefore, could not deserve expulsion. Besides, this transaction happened without the bar of the House, which, according to the practice which had existed since he had a seat there, was never considered as within the House, as no member who was standing there, when any question was taken, was permitted to vote. And he thought there was a great difference between a disorderly act done in the House and one done out of it. Two members walking without the bar of the House might insult each other in a variety of ways without disturbing the business of the House, and, in such a case, he did not think they would be liable to be expelled. If this were so, it might be said members could not walk together; he did not see this, for though he would not agree to an expulsion in such a case, he should think it proper to punish the offender.

Mr. W. thought the Constitution was clear on this subject. A bare majority may punish a member but the Constitution has declared that two-thirds of the members present are necessary to expel a member. The power of expulsion is the highest punishment the House can inflict; indeed, it is a punishment which not only goes to the person and character of the member himself, but it also affects all the citizens of a large district of country—his constituents. Being, therefore, so serious a power, as he before stated, it ought not to be extended. The House had no power over members out of the House. If two members were to quarrel and insult each other out of the House, the House could take no cognizance of the affair, except on a complaint made, and, in that case, the offender could not be expelled but might be punished. Suppose, for instance, a member of the House and an individual who is not a member were to quarrel out of the House, could the member come to the House and complain of the individual who is not a member? Certainly not, since the House had no power over that individual. Nor would a member be protected from arrest and process, were he to commit any violent act out of the House which should make him liable to such a process. He mentioned these instances to show that the House had not a right to extend their privileges, but only to protect them.

These were the reasons, Mr. W. said, which induced him to think the member from Vermont ought not to be expelled; not because he approved of his conduct, or that the insult which he states to have been offered to him, as warranting the improper manner in which he resented it; not because the House had not the power to expel its members, but because it was not in such a situation at the time as to authorize an expulsion for the offence, and that, therefore, the person offending did not know that any such consequence as an expulsion could be the punishment to which he was liable. But, though he was against an expulsion, he should be in favor of such a punishment as the House would have deemed proper, if the offence had been committed without the walls of the House.

Mr. W. said, there was another circumstance which ought to be noticed. No application was made for the punishment of this offence by the person offended; but it was taken up as a breach of the order of the House.

. . . . .

The question on the resolution as amended was about to be put, when

Mr. GALLATIN said he knew how late in the day it was, and therefore his remarks should not be long; but as he considered there was a point of view in which the subject had not been placed, he wished to say a few words before the question was taken.

Of the fact itself he had no remarks to make; the evidence was direct, and all could draw their inferences from it. Nor did he consider it very material whether the insult arose from provocation or not, because he did not think that any provocation could justify an indecency of that nature.

But it appeared to him that gentlemen who expressed so much sensibility on the occasion, had confined themselves wholly to the indecency committed within the walls of the House, without taking any notice of the nature of the punishment proposed to be inflicted. It was on that part of the subject, and on that alone, he meant to make some observations.

Our Government, he said, was a Government by representation. The people of the United States had not vested power with a sparing hand; they had given all power out of their hands, but they had guarded against the abuse of it. They had said this power shall not be exercised but by persons appointed by ourselves. This being the case, said Mr. G., we, the representatives of the people, have only a limited power over individual representatives in our body. It is true the Constitution has given us the power of expulsion, but under as much caution as power could be given. It is guarded by making it necessary to have a vote of two-thirds of the members present—the same caution which was laid upon the Senate with respect to treaties. He conceived that the power of expulsion had not been given for the purpose of indulging our sensibility; for the purpose of impairing the principle of representation, but for the purpose of enforcing that principle; and two cases might exist in which the power of expulsion, lodged in that House, might be considered as a safeguard to the principle of representation. These two cases were, when the House discovered a person to be disqualified by some infamous conduct from voting, and when a member pertinaciously interrupted and prevented public business from being carried on.

As to the first case, he could not suppose that any man would ever be sent to that House who had been guilty of any crime that would disqualify him from holding his seat, if the people who sent him knew it at the time; but if any such crime should be afterwards committed, or be discovered to have been heretofore committed, then the House has a right to expel and send such a member back to his constituents. The present case, every one will allow, does not fall within this rule. The charge against the member from Vermont is a gross indecency, which shows a want of manners—a want of good breeding. There could be no doubt the act was highly indecent; but it did not show a corruption of heart. It may disqualify him from associating with some gentlemen on this floor; but, said Mr. G., we do not come here to associate as individuals, but to deliberate upon legislative subjects in our representative capacity. We may, if we please, associate together, or we may let it alone. He did not think himself compelled to associate with any member of this House whose society he did not like.

This was not then one of those cases which discovered a corruption of heart, that would disqualify a man from giving a vote on a legislative subject, though it might show the person to be disqualified for polite society. He would go on to the other case, which was said to be a good reason for expulsion. He allowed that cases might exist, in which

a man might so far persist in interrupting the business of that House, by his disorderly behaviour, as to render it necessary, in order that the business might proceed, that he should be expelled. This led him to inquire whether this was the case under consideration, and whether the business of the House had been interrupted by the act in question.

When he put questions to the witnesses in relation to the order of the House, at the time the act complained of took place, he did it not with a view of lessening the offence itself. He did not mean to inquire whether the member from Vermont had committed a less degree of indecency, because the House was in one situation, than it would have been if it had been in another; but his object was to show, that the public business had not been interrupted, and that the House was in a situation in which it could not have been interrupted. It was true the SPEAKER had, in the morning, taken the Chair, and the House had not adjourned; but it must also be allowed, that the House was not at that time organized. What was the business before the House? A committee of two members were counting the votes for managers of an impeachment. Were they interrupted; or could they be interrupted by an incident of this kind? He was sure they were not interrupted. If, then, the public business was not interrupted, and if the fact was not of that nature which showed a corruption of heart, he did not think it would be proper to expel the member from Vermont.

He saw, indeed, that it was unpleasant for some gentlemen to sit in the House with the member from Vermont. He allowed it was an evil; but what is the evil, he asked, on the other side? It is this: They all knew that a new election could not take place in the State of Vermont for several weeks. He remembered, from the contested election which was formerly before the House from that State, that twelve days notice is requisite before writs can be issued; a certain time would be required to bring the votes to the Governor; the necessary notice, a new election, ascertaining the return, the notification to the member elected, and the time necessary for his journey hither, would take up many weeks; and by the laws of that State, if there be not a majority on the first vote, a new election will be necessary; so that it may be pretty certainly said, that if the present member was expelled, one-half of the State of Vermont would be deprived of a representation on that floor for the remainder of the session. And shall we, said Mr. G., in order to gratify our sensibilities, deprive one-half of that State, for a number of weeks, and perhaps for the whole session, of its representation? He was not willing to do so, and therefore should vote against the resolution.

He knew that other gentlemen on that floor had as great regard for the principle of representation as he; therefore, he supposed, they had considered this subject already, and made up their minds upon it. When he stated these reasons he did not doubt they had weight upon the minds of other gentlemen. For his part, however, he was more apprehensive of depriving Vermont of its representation, than of any other consideration arising from the subject.

He thought gentlemen had laid too much stress on this indecency, as it affected the Legislature of the United

States. However disagreeable the act was in itself, he did not think because a member sent there by the people of Vermont does an improper act, that it could attach disgrace and indelible infamy to the House itself, nor did he see how it could affect any other person besides the member from Vermont himself.

There seemed to be a great desire, very loudly expressed, that the question should be taken before the committee rose; but Mr. SEWALL and Mr. RUTLEDGE, both appearing to have a desire to speak on the subject, and it being near four o'clock, the committee rose and had leave to sit again.

Just before the committee rose, the Chairman informed the committee he had received a letter from Mr. CHIPMAN, of the Senate, in consequence of what had fallen from Mr. LYON, in his defence of yesterday. The letter was requested to be read, and was as follows:

SIR: I feel it my duty, in this public manner, to vindicate myself against an unwarranted attack on my character, by Mr. Lyon, yesterday, in the House of Representatives. I learn that he there asserted that he had once chastised me publicly for an affront which I had given him. This assertion of Mr. Lyon is without foundation; it is false. Nor can I conjecture to what circumstance Mr. Lyon could have alluded, unless it might be a ludicrous transaction, which took place at Westminster, in the State of Vermont, in the beginning of the year 1780, the circumstances of which I beg leave to relate: The Legislature of Vermont were in session at that place; Mr. Lyon attended as a member; I attended on business. The House of Representatives requested me, though not a member, to examine and report my opinion concerning certain debts due from persons whose estates had been confiscated. I had made a report accordingly, at some part of which Mr. Lyon took offence. One morning Mr. Lyon called at Mr. Bradley's room, in which I was then doing business. No person was in the room but Mr. Bradley, Mr. Lyon, and myself. Mr. Bradley and I sat writing at the opposite sides of the table; Mr. Lyon took a seat by the table at the side of Mr. Bradley, and entered into a conversation upon the subject of the report above mentioned. He soon discovered himself to be somewhat irritated, and in a very rude and pointed manner declared that no man who had a spark of honesty could have reported as I had done. Attacked in this rude manner, I retorted, in a passion, that he was an ignorant Irish puppy.

Mr. Lyon rose in a violent passion, grasped at my hair, that was turned back with a comb, which he broke in the grasp. I was at that moment mending a pen; I instantly rose, intending to revenge the insult with the knife in my hand; but Mr. Bradley had seized Mr. Lyon from behind, round the arms, and drew him back a little; upon which, Mr. Lyon, bearing himself in Mr. Bradley's arms, threw his feet upon the table to kick across. The awkward appearance of Mr. Lyon at this moment, and the grimaces of his countenance, provoked me to laugh. I dropt the penknife, seized

Mr. Lyon's feet, and, in this manner, with the help of Mr. Bradley, who still kept his hold, carried him across the room, and laid him on his back in a corner. Mr. Bradley and I returned to our seats, laughing very merrily at the scene. In the meantime, Mr. Lyon rose from his corner, stood a short time in apparent agitation, and without uttering a word. At length he turned upon his heel, with these expressions: "Damn it, I will not be mad"—forced a laugh, and left the room. Nothing ever afterwards passed between Mr. Lyon and myself upon this subject. I therefore repeat, that Mr. Lyon's assertion is wholly without foundation.

I ask pardon for the trouble I have given the House upon this business.

And am, with respect, &c.,

NATHANIEL CHIPMAN.

The Chairman of the Committee upon the report of the Committee of Privileges.

[12 Feb.]

Mr. RUTLEDGE denied that any similar outrage had ever been committed in that House like the present, though the gentleman from Virginia had spoken of something analogous. It was true, a challenge had been sent by a member of the Senate to a member of that House; but this was not at all comparable to the present offence. Mr. R. thought the punishment by expulsion was the only punishment which could be adopted, as nothing short of it would be effectual.

Mr. FINDLEY said, the question before the committee was a question of *indecency,* and not of *crime;* and he wished, for the sake of decency, so much had not been said upon it. In forming the Constitution there had been a distinction made between punishment and expulsion. Expulsion was evidently the highest punishment which the House could inflict, but no one could say indecency was the highest crime. He never understood, either at the time the Constitution was formed, or since, that expulsion was intended to be applied to anything but crimes—for what would be a subject of impeachment in other bodies where impeachments could be brought. This was not, therefore, an opinion formed upon the spur of the occasion. Mr. F. said, he knew of an instance of this kind, which happened in another Legislative body, upon which a committee was appointed to consider it; but they never made a report, but held their decision *in terrorem* over the offending member. He thought, if a similar course had been taken in this matter, it would have been preferable to spending so much time in debate upon it.

Mr. SEWALL rose to reply to what fell from Mr. GALLATIN on Friday, with respect to the two cases which he pointed out, as coming under the rule for expulsion, and referred to the law of Parliament in England to show that this doctrine was ill founded. He said no district of country ought to have it in its power to send a man among them as a legislator for the United States, who should be hateful to two-thirds of the House. The Constitution had defined no particular cases in which the power of expulsion should be exercised; the House was therefore left at liberty to use it according to its discretion. And, if it were to be abused, instead of punishment, it might become the highest honor to the person expelled, as, if the House were become so corrupt as to expel a person without just cause, it might awaken the people to a sense of the necessity of changing their representatives.

Mr. S. said, it was a new doctrine that the business of the House should actually be interrupted, before a person should be deemed an offender against its rules. It was necessary to look at the consequence of actions, and refer to what might have been the case if Mr. GRISWOLD had resented the affront upon the spot.

Mr. S. spoke of the importance of this decision as a precedent; and of the danger to be apprehended from the conduct of Mr. LYON in future, if the present outrage was suffered to pass without exemplary punishment, and that it would be necessary to come armed to the House, in order to guard themselves against him.

Mr. SHEPARD spoke again upon this subject. If the member from Vermont were not expelled, he supposed it would break up the present session, without doing any business; that it would divide the States against each other, and finally end in a civil war.

Mr. PINCKNEY said, in order to insure perfect freedom of debate, it was necessary to repress every personal violence in the first instance. In considering this question, he considered it as fixing a rule for their government in future; and he thought, if it were so considered, (and no reference had to the dispute which had produced the discussion,) there would be a pretty unanimous opinion that an offence of this kind ought to be punished by expulsion. He thought a member thus violently offending the rules of the House, should be immediately deprived of the power of the people in that House; and it was on this ground that he moved for the immediate commitment of the member from Vermont to the care of the Sergeant-at-Arms, when the offence was first made known to the House, not only for the security of his person, but for immediate punishment. As the Constitution gave the House a power to expel a member for disorderly conduct, he thought this case came clearly within the rule. In some cases of offence there might appear mitigating circumstances, but there were none in this. The conduct of the member since the transaction was committed had been such as to convince the House that he felt no compunction for what he had done.

Mr. LIVINGSTON rose to entreat gentlemen, as they valued the respectability of the House, the good opinion of their constituents, and the public Treasury, that they would suffer this business to come to a conclusion. Their constituents, he was certain, had long been tired of the discussion. Nearly twenty days, which had cost as many thousand dollars to the country, had been consumed in this business. Gentlemen rose to express their abhorrence of abuse in abusive terms, and their hatred of indecent acts with indecency. The simple question before the House was, what degree of punishment was proper to be inflicted upon the member from Vermont. [The CHAIRMAN informed Mr. L. he was mistaken in saying twenty days had been consumed in this business; it had been before the House only fourteen.] Mr. L. said it was in a fair way for being twenty.

Mr. COIT was sorry to hurt the feelings of the gentleman last up by saying anything on the subject, but having been considered as an advocate of Mr. LYON, he would make a few observations upon the subject. He did not himself think that this vote ought to have been taken without discussion. If, indeed, it had only been necessary to have inquired how does this man generally vote? then no discussion was necessary; but he could not consider that this was the only inquiry necessary to be made. With respect to the fact, nothing need be said; every one allowed it to be brutal, indecent, and unmannerly. The Constitution gave the House the power of expulsion for disorderly conduct. It has been said, this disorder must be committed within the House; but he found nothing of this sort in the Constitution. He had no doubt himself that the House was in session at the time. It had been attempted to show that there was a provocation for the offence; but an inquiry into this matter turned wholly against the gentleman from Vermont, as his previous abuse of the whole representation of Connecticut was a sufficient ground for the retort which was drawn from his colleague. It appeared, therefore, to him, that to retain amongst them a man of this description was to retain a man who would produce nothing but disorder and confusion in their proceedings. His letter of apology did not say that this was a transaction of heat, and that he was sorry for it, but that he was sorry the House had thought it necessary to take cognizance of it; and his defence before the Committee of the Whole was far from being contrite; it was, indeed, an attack upon the witnesses, in order to invalidate their testimony. He hoped the resolution would be agreed to.

19

ST. GEORGE TUCKER,
BLACKSTONE'S COMMENTARIES
1:APP. 200–205, N. §
1803

What further powers or privileges the several houses of congress may constitutionally possess, has now become a question of no small importance. The great Bacon observes, "that as exception strengthens the force of a law, in cases not excepted, so enumeration weakens it, in cases not enumerated." The powers vested in congress, the privileges of the members, and of each house, are severally enumerated in the constitution; not made exceptions from general powers, not enumerated. Consequently it would appear that they were not capable of extension, beyond the letter of the constitution itself. The twelfth article of the amendments to the constitution seems also not to favour a constructive extension of the powers of the federal government, or any department thereof; yet a case has occurred, which shews that the house of representatives have put a different construction on their powers. . . . On the 28th day of December, 1795, on information given by several members in their places (not upon oath,) of an attempt to corrupt them made by one Robert Randall, it was "resolved, that Mr. Speaker do issue his warrant directed to the serjeant at arms attending this house, commanding him to take into custody, wherever to be found, the body of the said Robert Randall, and the same in his custody to keep, subject to the further order and direction of the house.

"A warrant, pursuant to the said resolution, was accordingly prepared, signed by Mr. Speaker under his seal, attested by the clerk, and delivered to the serjeant, with order forthwith to execute the same, and make due return thereof to the house." The next day Randall was brought before the house in custody. He was detained in custody from that time to the 6th day of January, when a motion was made and seconded, that the house do come to the following resolution:

"Whereas any attempt to influence the conduct of this house, or its members, on subjects appertaining to their legislative functions, by motives other than the public advantage, is a high contempt of this house, and a breach of its privileges: and whereas it does appear to this house, by the information on oath of sundry members, and by the proceedings thereon had before the house, that Robert Randall did attempt to influence the conduct of the said members, in a matter relating to their legislative functions, to wit, the sale of a large portion of the public property, by motives of private emolument to the said members, other than, and distinct from the public advantage: therefore,

"Resolved, That the said Robert Randall has thereby committed a high contempt of this house, and a breach of its privileges.

"The previous question thereon was called for by five members, to wit . . . shall the main question, to agree to the said resolution, be now put?

"And on the question . . . shall the said main question be now put?

"It passed in the negative.

"A motion was then made and seconded, that the house do come to the following resolution:

"Resolved, that it appears to this house, that Robert Randall has been guilty of a contempt to, and a breach of the privileges of this house, by attempting to corrupt the integrity of its members, in the manner laid to his charge.

"And on the question thereupon,

"It was resolved in the affirmative, } Yeas, 78.
Nays, 17.

"Another motion was then made and seconded, that the house do come to the following resolution:

"Resolved, that the said Robert Randall be brought to the bar, reprimanded by the speaker, and committed to the custody of the serjeant at arms, until the further order of this house.

"And on the question thereupon,

"It was resolved in the affirmative.

"Pursuant thereto, the said Robert Randall was brought to the bar in custody, reprimanded by Mr. Speaker, and

remanded in custody of the serjeant at arms, until further order of the house.

"The 13th of January, the house proceeded to consider the petition of Robert Randall, praying to be released from the imprisonment to which he is subject, by the order of this house, which lay on the table: whereupon,

"Resolved, That Robert Randall be discharged from the custody of the serjeant at arms, upon the payment of fees.". . . Proceedings of the house of representatives of the U. States, in the case of Robert Randall and Charles Whitney. . . . Published by order of the house of representatives.

Upon these proceedings a few remarks may not be deemed impertinent in this place.

1. By the amendments to the constitution, no person shall be deprived of life, liberty, or property, without due process of law.

Due process of law as described by sir Edward Coke 1, is by indictment or presentment of good and lawful men, where such deeds be done in due manner, or by writ original of the common law. Due process of law must then be had before a judicial court, or a judicial magistrate. The judicial power of the United States is vested in one supreme court, and such inferior tribunals, as congress may establish, and extends to all cases in law and equity, arising under the constitution, &c. In the distribution of the powers of government, the legislative powers were vested in congress . . . the executive powers (except in the instances particularly enumerated,) in the president and senate. The judicial powers (except in the cases particularly enumerated in the first article) in the courts: the word *the,* used in defining the powers of the executive, and of the judiciary, is, with these exceptions, co-extensive in it's signification with the word *all:* for all the powers granted by the constitution are either legislative, executive, or judicial; to keep them for ever separate and distinct, except in the cases positively enumerated, has been uniformly the policy, and constitutes one of the fundamental principles of the American governments.

2. It will be urged, perhaps, that the house of representatives of the United States is, like a British house of commons, a judicial court: to which the answer is, it is neither established as such by the constitution (except in respect to its own members,) nor has it been, nor can it be so established by authority of congress; for all the courts of the United States must be composed of judges commissioned by the president of the United States, and holding their offices during good behaviour, and not by the unstable tenure of biennial elections.

3. The amendments to the constitution expressly provide, "that no warrant shall issue but upon probable cause supported by oath or affirmation." The speaker's warrant for apprehending Randall was not supported by either: for the word affirmation must be understood as such a solemn asseveration by persons religiously scrupulous of swearing, as amounts in judicial proceedings to an oath, in point of obligation and penal consequences, and not to a bare assertion, however positive, made in any other manner. That the information of the members was made in the solemn manner before mentioned, or that their oath

was dispensed with on account of religious scruples, cannot be presumed, since they were all sworn to their several declarations on the fourth of January, and not before.

4. The amendments to the constitution expressly provide, that no person shall be held to answer to a capital, or otherwise infamous crime, unless on presentment, or indictment of a grand jury. Randall's offence was certainly an infamous crime, for which he deserved exemplary punishment. On the twenty-ninth of December, being brought to the bar in custody, it was demanded of him, whether he did admit or deny the truth of the charge against him; to which he answered, that he was not prepared to admit or deny the same. On the fourth of January, being again brought to the bar in custody, it was demanded of him by Mr. Speaker what he had to say in his defence; to which he answered, that he was not guilty. Here then Randall was held to answer for an infamous crime, without indictment or presentment of a grand jury.

5. The constitution provides, that the trial of all crimes, except in cases of impeachment, shall be by a jury.

After the prisoner had pleaded not guilty, and made an application to the house that the informations might be sworn to, the house (after some preliminary proceedings) "resumed the hearing of his trial, and made some progress therein;" the next day they resumed it; and resolved to "proceed to a final decision on the said case" the next day.

6. The amendments to the constitution provide, that in all criminal prosecutions, the accused shall enjoy the right to a public trial by an impartial jury of the state and district where the crime shall have been committed.

On the sixth of January the house proceeded to a final decision on the case of Robert Randall.

Five members of the house were his accusers, triers, and judges: four of these voted him guilty; the fifth voted with the minority; whether, as not conceiving him guilty, or as not conceiving the house to be a proper tribunal to condemn him, (both questions being blended in the resolution), does not appear. . . . Was this a trial by an impartial jury? Again,

By the amendments to the constitution, the jury should be from the state and district in which the crime was committed. The triers were composed of members, *huc undique collatis.*

20

WILLIAM RAWLE, A VIEW OF THE CONSTITUTION
OF THE UNITED STATES 46–48
1829 (2d ed.)

Both the senate and house of representatives possess the usual powers to judge of the elections, returns and qualifications of their own members, and to punish them for disorderly behaviour, which may be carried to the extent of expulsion, provided two-thirds concur.

It has not yet been precisely settled what must be the disorderly behaviour to incur punishment, nor what kind of punishment is to be inflicted; but it cannot be doubted that misbehaviour out of the walls of the house or within them, when it is not in session, would not fall within the meaning of the Constitution.

Expulsion may, however, be founded on criminal conduct committed in any place, and either before or after conviction in a court of law.

But a power extending beyond their own precincts, and affecting others than their own members, has been exercised by both houses, and has been decided in the supreme court to be constitutional.

It is a maxim in the practical application of government, that the public functionaries should be supported in the full exercise of the powers intrusted to them. Attempts to bribe or to intimidate them constitute offences against the public. They amount to more than contempts or breaches of privilege against the legislative bodies, and they undoubtedly subject the offenders to the usual course of prosecution and punishment in the courts of law. But this liability does not exclude the immediate jurisdiction of the legislative body, which is supported by strong considerations of public policy. The people are entitled to the utmost purity and integrity in the conduct of their representatives. The house is a guardian of the public interests in this respect. It is its duty to make immediate inquiry as to any attempt to assail the freedom or corrupt the integrity of any of its members. From the duty to inquire arises the right to punish; it needs not to be devolved on the ordinary tribunals. It is true that no power to this effect is expressly given by the Constitution, nor does the judicial or criminal power given to the courts of the United States in any part, expressly extend to the infliction of punishment for such offences. But it is not therefore to be inferred that no such power exists any where. If the courts of the United States would possess it by implication, there is no reason for refusing it to the legislative body itself, unless it should be discovered to be wholly inconsistent with the construction or nature of that body, or with some clause in the Constitution. But the reverse of the first position is the truth. It would be inconsistent with the nature of such a body to deny it the power of protecting itself from injury or insult. If its deliberations are not perfectly free, its constituents are eventually injured. This power has never been denied in any country, and is incidental to the nature of all legislative bodies. If it possesses such a power in the case of an immediate insult, or disturbance preventing the exercise of its ordinary functions, it is impossible to deny it in other cases, which although less immediate or less violent, partake of the same character, by having a tendency to impair the firm and honest discharge of public duties.

Those clauses in the Constitution which provide that the trial of all crimes shall be by jury, in the state and district where the offence has been committed, are ever to be held sacred—but it would be doing violence to them to carry them further than the plain meaning, that trial by jury shall be preserved in criminal prosecutions in the ordinary courts; otherwise it would be impossible to support the jurisdiction given to the senate in cases of impeachment, wherein no trial by jury takes place. It appears then that this implied power of punishing what are termed contempts and infringements of the privileges of the houses, is in reality the useful institution of a summary jurisdiction for the punishment of offences substantially committed against the people, and that it is correctly deduced from the Constitution.

21

JOSEPH STORY, COMMENTARIES ON THE
CONSTITUTION 2:§§ 831–36, 838–46
1833

§ 831. It is obvious, that a power must be lodged somewhere to judge of the elections, returns, and qualifications of the members of each house composing the legislature; for otherwise there could be no certainty, as to who were legitimately chosen members, and any intruder, or usurper, might claim a seat, and thus trample upon the rights, and privileges, and liberties of the people. Indeed, elections would become, under such circumstances, a mere mockery; and legislation the exercise of sovereignty by any self-constituted body. The only possible question on such a subject is, as to the body, in which such a power shall be lodged. If lodged in any other, than the legislative body itself, its independence, its purity, and even its existence and action may be destroyed, or put into imminent danger. No other body, but itself, can have the same motives to preserve and perpetuate these attributes; no other body can be so perpetually watchful to guard its own rights and privileges from infringement, to purify and vindicate its own character, and to preserve the rights, and sustain the free choice of its constituents. Accordingly, the power has always been lodged in the legislative body by the uniform practice of England and America.

§ 832. The propriety of establishing a rule for a quorum for the despatch of business is equally clear; since otherwise the concerns of the nation might be decided by a very small number of the members of each body. In England, where the house of commons consists of nearly six hundred members, the number of forty-five constitutes a quorum to do business. In some of the state constitutions a particular number of the members constitutes a quorum to do business; in others, a majority is required. The constitution of the United States has wisely adopted the latter course; and thus, by requiring a majority for a quorum, has secured the public from any hazard of passing laws by surprise, or against the deliberate opinion of a majority of the representative body.

§ 833. It may seem strange, but it is only one of many proofs of the extreme jealousy, with which every provision in the constitution of the United States was watched and scanned, that though the ordinary quorum in the state legislatures is sometimes less, and rarely more, than a major-

ity; yet it was said, that in the congress of the United States more than a majority ought to have been required; and in particular cases, if not in all, more than a majority of a quorum should be necessary for a decision. Traces of this opinion, though very obscure, may perhaps be found in the convention itself. To require such an extraordinary quorum for the decision of questions would, in effect, be to give the rule to the minority, instead of the majority; and thus to subvert the fundamental principle of a republican government. If such a course were generally allowed, it might be extremely prejudicial to the public interests in cases, which required new laws to be passed, or old ones modified, to preserve the general, in contradistinction to local, or special interests. If it were even confined to particular cases, the privilege might enable an interested minority to screen themselves from equitable sacrifices to the general weal; or, in particular cases, to extort undue indulgences. It would also have a tendency to foster and facilitate the baneful practice of secession, a practice, which has shown itself even in states, where a majority only is required, which is subversive of all the principles of order and regular government, and which leads directly to public convulsions, and the ruin of republican institutions.

§ 834. But, as a danger of an opposite sort required equally to be guarded against, a smaller number is authorized to adjourn from day to day, thus to prevent a legal dissolution of the body, and also to compel the attendance of absent members. Thus, the interests of the nation, and the despatch of business, are not subject to the caprice, or perversity, or negligence of the minority. It was a defect in the articles of confederation, sometimes productive of great public mischief, that no vote, except for an adjournment, could be determined, unless by the votes of a majority of the states; and no power of compelling the attendance of the requisite number existed.

§ 835. . . . No person can doubt the propriety of the provision authorizing each house to determine the rules of its own proceedings. If the power did not exist, it would be utterly impracticable to transact the business of the nation, either at all, or at least with decency, deliberation, and order. The humblest assembly of men is understood to possess this power; and it would be absurd to deprive the councils of the nation of a like authority. But the power to make rules would be nugatory, unless it was coupled with a power to punish for disorderly behaviour, or disobedience to those rules. And as a member might be so lost to all sense of dignity and duty, as to disgrace the house by the grossness of his conduct, or interrupt its deliberations by perpetual violence or clamour, the power to expel for very aggravated misconduct was also indispensable, not as a common, but as an ultimate redress for the grievance. But such a power, so summary, and at the same time so subversive of the rights of the people, it was foreseen, might be exerted for mere purposes of faction or party, to remove a patriot, or to aid a corrupt measure; and it has therefore been wisely guarded by the restriction, that there shall be a concurrence of two thirds of the members, to justify an expulsion. This clause, requiring a concurrence of two thirds, was not in the original draft of the constitution, but it was inserted by a vote of ten states, one being divided. A like general authority to expel, exists in the British house of commons; and in the legislative bodies of many of the states composing the Union.

§ 836. What must be the disorderly behaviour, which the house may punish, and what punishment, other than expulsion, may be inflicted, do not appear to have been settled by any authoritative adjudication of either house of congress. A learned commentator supposes, that members can only be punished for misbehaviour committed during the session of congress, either within, or without the walls of the house; though he is also of opinion, that expulsion may be inflicted for criminal conduct committed in any place. He does not say, whether it must be committed during the session of congress or otherwise. In July, 1797, William Blount was expelled from the senate, for "a high misdemeanour, entirely inconsistent with his public trust and duty as a senator." The offence charged against him was an attempt to seduce an American agent among the Indians from his duty, and to alienate the affections and confidence of the Indians from the public authorities of the United States, and a negotiation for services in behalf of the British government among the Indians. It was not a statuteable offence; nor was it committed in his official character; nor was it committed during the session of congress; nor at the seat of government. Yet by an almost unanimous vote he was expelled from that body; and he was afterwards impeached (as has been already stated) for this, among other charges. It seems, therefore, to be settled by the senate upon full deliberation, that expulsion may be for any misdemeanour, which, though not punishable by any statute, is inconsistent with the trust and duty of a senator. In the case of John Smith (a senator) in April, 1808, the charge against him was for participation in the supposed treasonable conspiracy of Colonel Burr. But the motion to expel him was lost by a want of the constitutional majority of two thirds of the members of the senate. The precise ground of the failure of the motion does not appear; but it may be gathered from the arguments of his counsel, that it did not turn upon any doubt, that the power of the senate extended to cases of misdemeanour, not done in the presence or view of the body; but most probably it was decided upon some doubt as to the facts. It may be thought difficult to draw a clear line of distinction between the right to inflict the punishment of expulsion, and any other punishment upon a member, founded on the time, place, or nature of the offence. The power to expel a member is not in the British house of commons confined to offences committed by the party as a member, or during the session of parliament; but it extends to all cases, where the offence is such, as, in the judgment of the house, unfits him for parliamentary duties.

. . . . .

§ 838. This clause [1.5.3] in its actual form did not pass in the convention without some struggle and some propositions of amendment. The first part finally passed by an unanimous vote; the exception was carried by a close vote of six states against four, one being divided; and the remaining clause, after an ineffectual effort to strike out "one fifth," and insert in its stead, "if every member present," was finally adopted by an unanimous vote. The object of the whole clause is to ensure publicity to the proceedings of the legislature, and a correspondent responsibility of the members to their respective constituents. And it is founded in sound policy and deep political foresight. Intrigue and cabal are thus deprived of some of their main resources, by plotting and devising measures in secrecy. The public mind is enlightened by an attentive examination of the public measures; patriotism, and integrity, and wisdom obtain their due reward; and votes are ascertained, not by vague conjecture, but by positive facts. Mr. Justice Blackstone seems, indeed, to suppose, that votes openly and publicly given are more liable to intrigue and combination, than those given privately and by ballot. "This latter method," says he, "may be serviceable to prevent intrigues and unconstitutional combinations. But it is impossible to be practised with us, at least in the house of commons, where every member's conduct is subject to the future censure of his constituents, and therefore should be openly submitted to their inspection."

§ 839. The history of public assemblies, or of private votes, does not seem to confirm the former suggestion of the learned author. Intrigue and combination are more commonly found connected with secret sessions, than with public debates, with the workings of the ballot box, than with the manliness of *viva voce* votes. At least, it may be questioned, if the vote by ballot has, in the opinion of a majority of the American people, obtained any decisive preference over *viva voce* voting, even at elections. The practice in New England is one way, and at the South another way. And as to the votes of representatives and senators in congress, no man has yet been bold enough to vindicate a secret or ballot vote, as either more safe, or more wise, more promotive of independence in the members, or more beneficial to their constituents. So long as known and open responsibility is valuable as a check, or an incentive among the representatives of a free people, so long a journal of their proceedings, and their votes, published in the face of the world, will continue to enjoy public favour, and be demanded by public opinion. When the people become indifferent to the acts of their representatives, they will have ceased to take much interest in the preservation of their liberties. When the journals shall excite no public interest, it will not be matter of surprise, if the constitution itself is silently forgotten, or deliberately violated.

§ 840. The restriction of calls of the yeas and nays to one fifth is founded upon the necessity of preventing too frequent a recurrence to this mode of ascertaining the votes, at the mere caprice of an individual. A call consumes a great deal of time, and often embarrasses the just progress of beneficial measures. It is said to have been often used to excess in the congress under the confederation; and even under the present constitution it is notoriously used, as an occasional annoyance, by a dissatisfied minority, to retard the passage of measures, which are sanctioned by the approbation of a strong majority. The check, therefore, is not merely theoretical; and experience shows, that it has been resorted to, at once to admonish, and to control members, in this abuse of the public patience and the public indulgence.

§ 841. . . . It is observable, that the duration of each session of congress, (subject to the constitutional termination of their official agency,) depends solely upon their own will and pleasure, with the single exception, as will be presently seen, of cases, in which the two houses disagree in respect to the time of adjournment. In no other case is the president allowed to interfere with the time and extent of their deliberations. And thus their independence is effectually guarded against any encroachment on the part of the executive. Very different is the situation of parliament under the British constitution; for the king may, at any time, put an end to a session by a prorogation of parliament, or terminate the existence of parliament by a dissolution, and a call of a new parliament. It is true, that each house has authority to adjourn itself separately; and this is commonly done from day to day, and sometimes for a week or a month together, as at Christmas and Easter, or upon other particular occasions. But the adjournment of one house is not the adjournment of the other. And it is usual, when the king signifies his pleasure, that both, or either of the houses should adjourn themselves to a certain day, to obey the king's pleasure, and adjourn accordingly; for otherwise a prorogation would certainly follow.

§ 842. Under the colonial governments, the undue exercise of the same power by the royal governors constituted a great public grievance, and was one of the numerous cases of misrule, upon which the declaration of independence strenuously relied. It was there solemnly charged against the king, that he had called together legislative [colonial] bodies at places, unusual, uncomfortable, and distant from the repository of the public records; that he had dissolved representative bodies, for opposing his invasions of the rights of the people; and after such dissolutions, he had refused to reassemble them for a long period of time. It was natural, therefore, that the people of the United States should entertain a strong jealousy on this subject, and should interpose a constitutional barrier against any such abuse by the prerogative of the executive. The state constitutions generally contain some provision on the same subject, as a security to the independence of the legislature.

§ 842. [sic] These are all the powers and privileges, which are expressly vested in each house of congress by the constitution. What further powers and privileges they incidentally possess has been a question much discussed, and may hereafter be open, as new cases arise, to still further discussion. It is remarkable, that no power is conferred to punish for any contempts committed against either house; and yet it is obvious, that, unless such a power, to some extent, exists by implication, it is utterly impossible for either house to perform its constitutional functions. For instance, how is either house to conduct its own deliberations, if it may not keep out, or expel intruders? If it may not require and enforce upon strangers silence and decorum in its presence? If it may not enable its own members to have free ingress, egress, and regress to its own hall of legislation? And if the power exists, by implication, to require the duty, it is wholly nugatory, unless it draws after it the incidental authority to compel obedi-

ence, and to punish violations of it. It has been suggested by a learned commentator, quoting the language of Lord Bacon, that, as exception strengthens the force of a law in cases not excepted, so enumeration weakens it in cases not enumerated; and hence he deduces the conclusion, that, as the power to punish contempts is not among those enumerated, as belonging to either house, it does not exist. Now, however wise or correct the maxim of Lord Bacon is in a general sense, as a means of interpretation, it is not the sole rule. It is no more true, than another maxim of a directly opposite character, that where the end is required, the means are, by implication, given. Congress are required to exercise the powers of legislation and deliberation. The safety of the rights of the nation require this; and yet, because it is not expressly said, that congress shall possess the appropriate means to accomplish this end, the means are denied, and the end may be defeated. Does not this show, that rules of interpretation, however correct in a general sense, must admit of many qualifications and modifications in their application to the actual business of human life and human laws? Men do not frame constitutions of government to suspend its vital interests, and powers, and duties, upon metaphysical doubts, or ingenious refinements. Such instruments must be construed reasonably, and fairly, according to the scope of their purposes, and to give them effect and operation, not to cripple and destroy them. They must be construed according to the common sense applied to instruments of a like nature; and in furtherance of the fundamental objects proposed to be attained; and according to the known practice and incidents of bodies of a like nature.

§ 843. We may resort to the common law to aid us in interpreting such instruments, and their powers; for that law is the common rule, by which all our legislation is interpreted. It is known, and acted upon, and revered by the people. It furnishes principles equally for civil and criminal justice, for public privileges, and private rights. Now, by the common law, the power to punish contempts of this nature belongs incidentally to courts of justice, and to each house of parliament. No man ever doubted, or denied its existence, as to our colonial assemblies in general, whatever may have been thought, as to particular exercises of it. Nor is this power to be viewed in an unfavourable light. It is a privilege, not of the members of either house; but, like all other privileges of congress, mainly intended as a privilege of the people, and for their benefit. Mr. Justice Blackstone has, with great force, said, that "laws, without a competent authority to secure their administration from disobedience and contempt, would be vain and nugatory. A power, therefore, in the supreme courts of justice to suppress such contempts, &c., results from the first principles of judicial establishments, and must be an inseparable attendant upon every superior tribunal." . . .

§ 844. This subject has of late undergone a great deal of discussion both in England and America; and has finally received the adjudication of the highest judicial tribunals in each country. In each country upon the fullest consideration the result was the same, viz. that the power did exist, and that the legislative body was the proper and exclusive forum to decide, when the contempt existed, and when there was a breach of its privileges; and, that the power to punish followed, as a necessary incident to the power to take cognizance of the offence. The judgment of the Supreme Court of the United States, in the case alluded to, contains so elaborate and exact a consideration of the whole argument on each side, that it will be far more satisfactory to give it in a note, as it stands in the printed opinion, than to hazard, by any abridgment, impairing the just force of the reasoning.

§ 845. This is not the only case, in which the house of representatives has exerted the power to arrest, and punish for a contempt committed within the walls of the house. The power was exerted in the case of Robert Randall, in December, 1795, for an attempt to corrupt a member: in 1796, in the case of ———, a challenge given to a member, which was held a breach of privilege; and in May, 1832, in the case of Samuel Houston, for an assault upon a member for words spoken in his place, and afterwards printed, reflecting on the character of Houston. In the former case, the house punished the offence by imprisonment; in the latter, by a reprimand by the speaker. So in 1800, in the case of William Duane, for a printed libel against the senate, the party was held guilty of a contempt, and punished by imprisonment. Nor is there any thing peculiar in the claim under the constitution of the United States. The same power has been claimed, and exercised repeatedly, under the state governments, independent of any special constitutional provision, upon the broad ground stated, by Mr. Chief Justice Shippen, that the members of the legislature are legally, and inherently possessed of all such privileges, as are necessary to enable them, with freedom and safety, to execute the great trust reposed in them by the body of the people, who elected them.

§ 846. The power to punish for contempts, thus asserted both in England and America, is confined to punishment during the session of the legislative body, and cannot be extended beyond it. It seems, that the power of congress to punish cannot, in its utmost extent, proceed beyond imprisonment; and then it terminates with the adjournment, or dissolution of that body. Whether a fine may not be imposed, has been recently made a question in a case of contempt before the house of lords; upon which occasion Lord Chancellor Brougham expressed himself in the negative, and the other law lords, Eldon and Tenterden, in the affirmative; but the point was not then solemnly decided. It had, however, been previously affirmed by the house of lords in the case of *Rex* v. *Flower*, (8 T. R. 314,) in case of a libel upon one of the Bishops. Lord Kenyon then said, that in ascertaining and punishing for a contempt of its privileges, the house acted in a judicial capacity.

22

BENJAMIN F. BUTLER, PUNISHMENT BY THE HOUSE OF REPRESENTATIVES NO BAR TO AN INDICTMENT
25 June 1834
2 Ops. Atty. Gen. 655

SIR: In answer to the question submitted to me on the memorial of General Houston, who appears to have been indicted, convicted, and fined in the criminal court of this District, for an assault on the person of a member of the House of Representatives, after having been previously punished by that House for the same act, as a contempt and breach of privilege, I have the honor to state that, in my opinion, the proceedings of the House constituted no bar to the subsequent indictment and conviction. The fifth amendment to the constitution of the United States, which provides that no person "shall be subject, for the *same offence*, to be twice put in jeopardy of life or limb," does not apply to cases of this sort. Courts, and other bodies which have the power of punishing for contempts, are invested with that power, and are supposed to employ it, for the purpose of protecting themselves in the due exercise of their appropriate functions, and not for the purpose of vindicating the general law of the land, which may also have been violated by the same act. Technically, therefore, General Houston has not been twice tried for the *same offence*. The act committed by him was one and the same, and it constituted but one indictable offence; and he was, therefore, liable to only one conviction on *indictment*. But, if this act was also a breach of the privileges of the House of Representatives, and a contempt of the House, they had the right to punish him for the contempt independently of the action of the criminal court; and so *vice versa*.

SEE ALSO:

Thomas Jefferson to John Adams, 16 May 1777, Papers 2:19
John Jay to George Washington, 26 Apr. 1779, Correspondence 1:209–10
Records of the Federal Convention, Farrand 2:140, 141, 142, 155, 156, 158, 165–66, 245–46, 257, 258, 264, 566–67, 568, 592–93
House of Representatives, Defeat of the Army under General St. Clair, 27 Mar., 13 Nov. 1792, Annals 3:490–93, 679–84
General St. Clair Investigation, 1792, Schlesinger & Bruns, Congress Investigates: A Documented History, 1792–1974, 1:3 (1975)
House of Representatives, Treaty with Morocco, 27, 30 Dec. 1793, Annals 4:149–52
House of Representatives, Robert Randall—Case of Bribery, 30–31 Dec., 1795, 1, 5–7 Jan. 1796, Annals 5:179–83, 185–95, 210–29
House of Representatives, On Expelling Matthew Lyon, 22 Feb. 1799, Annals 9:2959–62, 2972–73
Senate, Breach of Privilege, 5 Mar. 1800, Annals 10:68–93
Hinds' Precedents of the House of Representatives, Dec. 1805, § 635

House of Representatives, General Wilkinson, 7–8, 12–13 Jan. 1808, Annals 17:1333–57, 1377–78, 1411–33, 1434–40, 1441–58, 1459–60

Senate, Case of John Smith, 5–6, 8–9 Apr. 1808, Annals 17:187–93, 208–14, 237–42, 324

House of Representatives, General Wilkinson, 18 Dec. 1810, Annals 22:435–38, 439–40, 441, 444–49

Investigation of the Burning of Washington, 1814, Schlesinger & Bruns, *supra*, 1:247

Investigation of Andrew Jackson's Invasion of Florida, 1818, *id.* 1:338

House of Representatives, Case of Colonel Anderson, 8–10,

12–13 Jan. 1818, Annals 31:592–94, 605–6, 611–16, 625–28, 653–58, 661–62, 667–70, 695–702, 706–10, 713–18

Hinds' Precedents of the House of Representatives, Dec. 1821, § 638

Id., Mar. 1822, § 654

James Kent, Commentaries 1:220, 221 (1826)

John C. Calhoun—The Rip Rap Imbroglio, 1826, Schlesinger & Bruns, *supra*, 1:481

The Second Bank of the United States, 1832, *id.*, 1:591

Indian Rations and Sam Houston's Trial, 1832, *id.*, 1:668

Article 1, Section 6, Clause 1

The Senators and Representatives shall receive a Compensation for their Services, to be ascertained by Law, and paid out of the Treasury of the United States. They shall in all Cases, except Treason, Felony and Breach of the Peace, be privileged from Arrest during their Attendance at the Session of their respective Houses, and in going to and returning from the same; and for any Speech or Debate in either House, they shall not be questioned in any other Place.

1. Bill of Rights, sec. 9, 1 W. & M., 2d sess., c. 2, 16 Dec. 1689.
2. *Holiday* v. *Pitt*, 93 Eng. Rep. 984 (K.B. 1734)
3. William Blackstone, Commentaries (1765)
4. Thomas Jefferson, Bill for Giving the Members of the General Assembly an Adequate Allowance, 12 Dec. 1778
5. Articles of Confederation, art. 5, 1 Mar. 1781
6. John Adams to John Jebb, 21 Aug. 1785
7. Records of the Federal Convention
8. Vermont Constitution of 1786, ch. 1, art. 16
9. A Georgian, 15 Nov. 1787
10. Cornelius, 11–18 Dec. 1787
11. Debate in Massachusetts Ratifying Convention, 19 Jan. 1788
12. Luther Martin, Genuine Information, 1788
13. *Bolton* v. *Martin*, 1 Dall. 296 (C.P. Phila. 1788)
14. *Geyer's Lessee* v. *Irwin*, 4 Dall. 107 (Pa.S.Ct. 1790)
15. James Madison, Militia Bill, House of Representatives, 16 Dec. 1790
16. James Wilson, Legislative Department, Lectures on Law, 1791
17. House of Representatives, Reduction of Salaries, 27 Jan. 1795
18. Thomas Jefferson (and James Madison), Protest to the Virginia House of Delegates, 1797
19. *Coxe* v. *McClenachan*, 3 Dall. 478 (Pa. 1798)
20. Kentucky Constitution of 1799, art. 2, sec. 24
21. Charles Pinckney, Breach of Privilege, Senate, 5 Mar. 1800
22. *Coffin* v. *Coffin*, 4 Mass. 1 (1803)
23. *Hurst's Case*, 4 Dall. 387 (C.C.D.Pa. 1804)
24. Joseph Story, Commentaries on the Constitution, (1833)

1

BILL OF RIGHTS, SEC. 9
1 W. & M., 2d sess., c. 2, 16 Dec. 1689

9. That the freedom of speech, and debates or proceedings in parliament, ought not to be impeached or questioned in any court or place out of parliament.

2

HOLIDAY V. PITT
93 Eng. Rep. 984 (K.B. 1734)

After the matter had been spoken to in B. R. it was adjourned to Serjeants-Inn, to be argued before all the Judges. And the counsel for Mr. Pitt applied themselves to three points. 1. To shew that there was a privilege redeundo after a dissolution, as well as after prorogation, which was not disputed. 2. To shew that Mr. Pitt was arrested within that time of privilege. And 3. That this application for his discharge by way of motion was proper.

As to the first point: it was said, that all privilege arises by prescription time out of mind, and no new privilege can be created but by Act of Parliament. Sir Robert Atkins in his treatise of the Power of Parliament 38, 39. That prorogations are modern, in comparison with the antiquity of Parliaments; and it was not till the time of Henry 8 that the present frequent prorogations were made. Formerly two or three new Parliaments were summoned in one year, and dissolved; and therefore the privilege redeundo (which it is agreed there is) must be after a dissolution as well as a prorogation. It is the duty of members to stay the whole session; and in 6 H. 8, c. 16, departing before the end of the session is a loss of wages; and in 4 Inst. 44, there are many instances of informations by the Attorney General for departing from Parliament. In Scobel's Memorials 88, it is mentioned to be a privilege, eundo morando et redeundo for themselves and servants, which is likewise mentioned page 103, 108, and in Dewe's Journal 414, Dodderidge's Preface to the Opinions of Learned Antiquaries, and Sir R. Atkins 38, 39. So in the article of wages, they were paid for some days after the dissolution; 4 Inst. 46, wages are due for every day, veniendo, morando et exinde ad propria redeundo, and the 35 H. 8, c. 11, gives them for as many days as may be reasonably taken up in coming and returning. In the Register 192 a. there is a writ to the sheriff to levy 19*l.* 4*s.* pro expensis militum veniendo ad Parliamentum, ibidem morando, et exinde ad propria redeundo, pro 48 diebus.

Another authority to shew that equal privilege subsists in returning as in coming, was from Charta de Foresta, c. 11, Quicunque Archiepiscopus, episcopus, comes vel baro veniens ad nos ad mandatum nostrum, transierit per forestam nostram, liceat ei capere unam bestiam vel duas per visum forestarii si praesens fuerit; sin autem, faciat cornare, ne videatur hoc furtive facere. Hoc idem liceat eis redeundo facere sicut praedictum est. And 4 Inst. 308, was cited to prove that the words veniens ad nos ad mandatum nostrum, were to be understood of coming to Parliament.

Another argument was drawn from 1 Jac. 1, c. 3, which was made to cure an inconvenience arising from this privilege as to members taken in execution out of the time of privilege, and to give the plaintiff a new writ of execution, when the time of privilege was over.

It may be objected, that these are not rights inherent in the Commons, but what flow from the grace and favour of the Crown, and on the beginning of a Parliament is asked by the Speaker as such. To which it is answered, that this is done rather by way of recognition, and keeping up their right, than acknowledging it as a favour. And it appears in Dewe's Journal 122, and Sir R. Atkins 40, that Mr. Onslow, who was elected Speaker in 1566, neglected on his being presented to Queen Elizabeth to demand this freedom from arrests; and it was resolved that such demand was not necessary, and the privilege subsisted notwithstanding.

They likewise compared this to the case of witnesses, who are protected eundo et redeundo. 1 Mod. 66. 2 Roll. Abr. 272. The same as to the parties to the suit; and Rastal, tit. Privilege, uses the words in the writ for wages, et exinde ad propria redeundo. And this returning has never been very nicely scanned, so as to require a man to go the direct road. Bro. Privilege 4, allows that the protection is not forfeited by the plea of extra viam, because it may be he went to buy a horse, victuals, or other necessaries for his journey. Neither is the law so strict in point of time, as to require the party to set out immediately after the trial is over; and for that was cited the case of *Hatch* against *Blisset*, vide Trin. 13 Ann. in B. R. She had a trial at Winchester Assizes, which was over on Friday at four in the afternoon: she staid there till after dinner on Saturday, and in the evening at seven was arrested going home to Portsmouth, which is twenty miles: and the Court held, that she ought to be discharged, her protection not being expired, and a little deviation or loitering would not alter it.

The statute 12 & 13 W. 3, c. 3, was also mentioned, as taking notice of this privilege of freedom from arrests, and as making no distinction between a prorogation and a dissolution.

2. The next point was to shew that Colonel Pitt was arrested within this time of privilege; and for this were cited 2 Lev. 72. 1 Brownl. 91, which speak of it as subsisting for forty days after the Parliament. And in the Irish Acts 3 Ed. 4 (which were generally transcripts of laws enacted here) it is expressly recited to have continuance for forty days before and after the Parliament finished. However this point was not much insisted on, it appearing that the House of Commons had always avoided determining this question, and had left it at large to a convenient time, of which themselves were the Judges: and therefore in the case of Mr. Martin in 1586, who was arrested twenty days

before the meeting of the Parliament, the question was put whether the House would limit the time, and resolved they would not; but they held that the twenty days were within a convenient time, and that therefore Mr. Martin should be discharged. Scobel 109, 110.

It doth not appear, they ever entered into the consideration of the nearness or distance of each gentleman's borough; but hold the same general rule, as it is done in testes and returns of writs at common law; which are the same near, as in the remotest counties.

This gentleman was arrested two days after the dissolution, before he had time to settle his private affairs and prepare for his journey. And the cases before cited of parties to a suit and witnesses were again relied on, to shew there was no occasion for him to set out immediately upon his return.

3. The third point (and indeed the only one the Court doubted of) was whether he could be discharged by motion. And for this Nalson's Collections, vol. 2, page 450, was cited, where it is said, that privilege of Parliament is a restraint to the proceedings of Inferior Courts. That the Courts of Westminster-Hall are bound to take notice of this privilege, and allow the time out of the Statute of Limitations. That it is ex necessitate, else he must lie till the next Parliament, which may be sooner or later. That for expedition many things are now done in a summary way by motion, for which formerly the party used to be put to his audita querela; and in the case cited of *Hatch* v. *Blisset*, she was discharged by motion. So on 7 Ann. c. 12, the servants of ambassadors are every day discharged on motion; and yet there are exceptions in that Act, as to merchants and traders, which might be very proper for special pleading. And the statute 29 Car. 2, c. 7, against arrests upon Sundays was mentioned where no doubt the party would be discharged on motion.

The counsel for the plaintiffs offered very little on the two first points; but applied themselves chiefly to the last, to shew that the discharge ought not to be on motion, and mentioned the case in Salk. 544, where it was held, that an attorney must plead his privilege: and Carth. 131, as to the Act of Oblivion. That the proper way would be to bring his writ of privilege, the suggestions whereof might be pleaded to, and this great point determined upon record. If there be no addition in an outlawry, it is bad; but must be avoided by writ of error. And wherever it has been intended to give a power of discharging on motion, it is mentioned particularly, as to bankrupts and seamen.

There was nothing said upon the argument by the Judges at Serjeants'-Inn. But the last day of the term the Chief Justice declared, that all the Judges were of opinion Mr. Pitt was intitled to privilege redeundo for a convenient time, and that within that time he was arrested.

And as to the third point he declared, that there was great doubt amongst the Judges; who however did all agree, that if a writ of privilege was procured, that would remove all difficulties: and therefore the rule was enlarged till next term without prejudice to the question, whether it could be done by way of motion or writ.

Early in the next term a petition was presented to the Lord Chancellor, with an affidavit to verify it. And upon presenting it, his Lordship said, that in so untrodden a path as this, he should be very careful what he did; and as it was not his business to draw the writ, he expected Mr. Pitt's counsel should prepare one, and send him and the Master of the Rolls a copy of it: which was done, from Pryn's 4th vol. of Parliamentary Writs, 722, 755, 759, 776, 784, and a day appointed to speak to it before them both. There were no counsel attended on behalf of the plaintiffs, the main point being determined against them. But several objections being taken to the manner of verifying the petition, and to the draft of the writ, the matter was put off, with an intimation that it was hardly probable any determination would be made within the term; and therefore recommending it to Mr. Pitt's counsel, whether they would not try what they could do in B. R. upon their motion, before the term was over. Upon this the petition was withdrawn, and mention made to the Judges of the King's Bench, that their opinion was desired upon the motion.

Whereupon the evening before the end of the term, the Judges all met again at Serjeants'-Inn. And the last day of the term the Chief Justice delivered their opinions.

That all the Judges, except the Chief Baron Reynolds, and Baron Thompson, were of opinion, that Mr. Pitt ought to be discharged on motion: that the Chief Baron did not say it would be wrong to do so, but was doubtful; and as for Mr. Baron Thompson he was strongly against it.

As what is to be done is therefore clearly the opinion of ten Judges, I will briefly state the ground they go upon. For that purpose they have taken two things into consideration. 1. How the law stood before the 12 & 13 W. 3, c. 3, and, 2. Whether that has altered the law, and how far.

As to the first we think that before the Statute 12 & 13 W. 3, the method in Westminster-Hall was, to discharge by writ of privilege, which was in nature of a supersedeas to the proceedings, and the pleading concluded, si curia Domini Regis placitum praed' cognoscere velit aut debeat. 1 Pryn's Register 660.

And as to the Statute 12 & 13 W. 3, we think it has made two alterations. 1. That it has taken away the old plea of privilege; and, 2. By making the arrest irregular and illegal.

The Act was designed to abridge the privilege, and to give leave to proceed after a prorogation. Then comes an enacting clause with negative words, that the body of a member shall not be arrested during the time of privilege. The old plea therefore of not proceeding is taken away, for it is made lawful to proceed, and he cannot plead to the process though irregularly arrested; agreeable to what was held in the case of *Widrington* v. *Charlton*, Hil. 11 Ann. in an appeal. If he cannot take advantage of this the old way, there is no other left but by motion; and it being rendered illegal to arrest the body, it is an irregular execution of the process. In *Sir Richard Temple's case* in 1 Sid. 192, and 1 Keb. 727, the Judges told Sir Richard he must shew his return, or writ of privilege. Here the defendant has complied with the first part, by producing the original return. In *Lord Banbury's case* in Salk. 512, it is said, they would not proceed to try his peerage by motion; but I have seen a manuscript report of that case, where Holt says, if there had been no dispute of the identity of the person, and the summons to Parliament had been shewn, he would have discharged him on motion. There was *My Lord Mordington's case* in C. B. in my Lord King's time: and he being a Scotch peer was arrested, and the Act of Union having given them the privilege of English peers, he was discharged upon motion.

In the present case here is matter of record produced to warrant the discharge, and if we have proper evidence, why should not the remedy be speedily applied?

It is certainly so, as mentioned at the Bar, that ambassadors' servants, and persons arrested on a Sunday, are discharged on motion. There are many writs in Rastal for discharging jurors, and witnesses, and yet it is done every day by motion; and those writs only prove, that it may be done another way. And the inclination of Courts to discharge on motion has been so great, that the party arrested may apply to the Court under whose protection he is, or the Court out of which the process issues, which ever happens to sit first.

And if in *Blisset's case* the Court above took notice of the privilege of the Court of Nisi Prius, and discharged her; what reason is there we should not pay the same regard to a superior privilege?

There must be a rule to discharge the defendant out of the custody of the marshal.

3

WILLIAM BLACKSTONE, COMMENTARIES 1:159–61
1765

The *privileges* of parliament are likewise very large and indefinite; which has occasioned an observation, that the principal privilege of parliament consisted in this, that it's privileges were not certainly known to any but the parliament itself. And therefore when in 31 Hen. VI the house of lords propounded a question to the judges touching the privilege of parliament, the chief justice, in the name of his brethren, declared, "that they ought not to make answer to that question; for it hath not been used aforetime that the justices should in any wise determine the privileges of the high court of parliament; for it is so high and mighty in his nature, that it may make law; and that which is law, it may make no law; and the determination and knowledge of that privilege belongs to the lords of parliament, and not to the justices". Privilege of parliament was principally established, in order to protect it's members not only from being molested by their fellow-subjects, but also more especially from being oppressed by the power of the crown. If therefore all the privileges of parliament were once to be set down and ascertained, and no privilege to be allowed but what was so defined and determined, it were easy for the executive power to devise some new case, not within the line of privilege, and under pretence thereof to harass any refractory member and violate the freedom of parliament. The dignity and independence of the two houses are therefore in great measure preserved by keeping their privileges indefinite. Some however of the more notorious privileges of the members of either house are, privilege of speech, of person, of their domestics, and of their lands and goods. As to the first, privilege of speech, it is declared by the statute 1 W. & M. st. 2. c. 2. as one of the liberties of the people, "that the freedom of speech, and debates, and proceedings in parliament, ought not to be impeached or questioned in any court or place out of parliament." And this freedom of speech is particularly demanded of the king in person, by the speaker of the house of commons, at the opening of every new parliament. So likewise are the other privileges, of person, servants, lands and goods; which are immunities as antient as Edward the confessor, in whose laws we find this precept. *"Ad synodos venientibus, sive summoniti sint, sive per se quid agendum habuerint, sit summa pax:"* and so too, in the old Gothic constitutions, *"extenditur haec pax et securitas ad quatuordecim dies, convocato regni senatu."* This includes not only privilege from illegal violence, but also from legal arrests, and seisures by process from the courts of law. To assault by violence a member of either house, or his menial servants, is a high contempt of parliament, and there punished with the utmost severity. It has likewise peculiar penalties annexed to it in the courts of law, by the statutes 5 Hen. IV. c. 6. and 11 Hen. VI. c. 11. Neither can any member of either house be arrested and taken into custody, nor served with any process of the courts of law; nor can his menial servants be arrested; nor can any entry be made on his lands; nor can his goods be distrained or seised; without a breach of the privilege of parliament. These privileges however, which derogate from the common law, being only indulged to prevent the member's being diverted from the public business, endure no longer than the session of parliament, save only as to the freedom of his person: which in a peer is for ever sacred and inviolable; and in a commoner for forty days after every prorogation, and forty days before the next appointed meeting; which is now in effect as long as the parliament subsists, it seldom being prorogued for more than fourscore days at a time. But this privilege of person does not hold in crimes of such public malignity as treason, felony, or breach of the peace; or rather perhaps in such crimes for which surety of the peace may be required. As to all other privileges which obstruct the ordinary course of justice, they cease by the statutes 12 W. III. c. 3. and 11 Geo. II. c. 24. immediately after the dissolution or prorogation of the parliament, or adjournment of the houses for above a fortnight; and during these recesses a peer, or member of the house of commons, may be sued like an ordinary subject, and in consequence of such suits may be dispossessed of his lands and goods. In these cases the king has also his prerogative: he may sue for his debts, though not arrest the person of a member, during the sitting of parliament; and by statute 2 & 3 Ann. c. 18. a member may be sued during the sitting of parliament for any misdemesnor or breach of trust in a public office. Likewise, for the benefit of commerce, it is provided by statute 4 Geo. III. c. 33, that any trader, having privilege of parliament, may be served with legal process for any just debt, (to the amount of 100*l*.) and unless he makes satisfaction within two months, it shall be deemed an act of bankruptcy; and that commissions of bankrupt may be issued against such privileged traders, in like manner as against any other.

4

THOMAS JEFFERSON, BILL FOR GIVING THE MEMBERS OF THE GENERAL ASSEMBLY AN ADEQUATE ALLOWANCE
12 Dec. 1778
Papers 2:231–32

Whereas it is just that the members of General assembly, delegated by the people to transact for them the legislative business, should, while attending that business, have their reasonable sustenance defrayed, dedicating to the public service their time and labors freely and without account: and it is also expedient that the public councils should not be deprived of the aid of good and able men, who might be deterred from entering into them by the insufficiency of their private fortunes to bear the extraordinary expences they must necessarily incur:

And it being inconsistent with the principles of civil liberty, and contrary to the natural rights of the other members of the society, that any body of men therein should have authority to enlarge their own powers, prerogatives, or emoluments without restraint, the said General assembly cannot at their own will increase the allowance which their members are to draw from the public treasury for their expences while on assembly; but to enable them so to do, an application to the body of the people has become necessary:

And such application having been accordingly made to the freeholders of the several counties, and they having thereupon consented that the said allowance shall be enlarged, and authorized and instructed their members to enlarge the same for themselves and the members of all future assemblies, to   pounds of nett tobacco by the day for attendance on assembly, and to   lbs of like tobacco for every mile they must necessarily travel going to or from the same, together with their ferriages, to be paid in money out of the public treasury at such rate as shall be estimated by the court of appeals at their session next before the meeting of every session of assembly, governing themselves in the said estimate by the worth of the said tobacco, and the competence of the same to defray the necessary expences of travelling and attendance:

Be it therefore enacted by the General assembly by express authority and instruction from the body of the people that the allowance to the several members of the present and of all future general assemblies shall be of   pounds of tobacco by the day for attendance on the said assemblies,   lbs of the like tobacco for every mile they must necessarily travel going to or from the same, together

with their ferriages; to be paid to them in money out of the public treasury at such rate as shall be estimated by the court of appeals at their session next before the meeting of each respective session of assembly, governing themselves in the said estimate by the worth of the said tobacco and the competence of the same to defray the necessary expences of travelling and attendance.

5

ARTICLES OF CONFEDERATION, ART. 5
1 Mar. 1781

Freedom of speech and debate in Congress shall not be impeached or questioned in any Court, or place out of Congress, and the members of Congress shall be protected in their persons from arrests and imprisonments, during the time of their going to and from, and attendance on Congress, except for treason, felony, or breach of the peace.

6

JOHN ADAMS TO JOHN JEBB
21 Aug. 1785
Works 9:532–36

As I had the misfortune, the other day, not to agree fully with you in opinion concerning the 36th article of the Constitution of Pennsylvania, I beg leave to state to you my objections against it, and then to ask you if there is not some weight in them.

My first objection is, that it is not intelligible. It is impossible to discover what is meant by "offices of profit." Does it mean that there can be no necessity for, nor use in, annexing either salary, fees, or perquisites, to public offices? and that all who serve the public should have no pay from the public, but should subsist themselves and families out of their own private fortunes, or their own labor in their private profession, calling, trade, or farm? This seems to be the sense of it, and in this sense it may make its court to the Quakers and Moravians, Dunkers, Mennonites, or other worthy people in Pennsylvania, that is to say, to their prejudices, and it will recommend itself to whatever there is of popular malignity and envy, and of vulgar avarice, in every country. But it is founded in error and mischief. For public offices in general require the whole time, and all the attention of those who hold them. They can have no time nor strength of body or mind for their private professions, trades, or farms. They must then starve with their families unless they have ample fortunes. But would you make it a law that no man should hold an office who had not a private income sufficient for the subsistence and prospects of himself and family? What would be the consequence of this? All offices would be monopolized by the rich; the poor and the middling ranks would be excluded, and an aristocratic despotism would immediately follow, which would take by fraud and intrigue at first, and by open avowed usurpation soon, whatever they pleased for their compensation.

My second objection to the article is, that it is inconsistent. After seeming to require that offices should have no emoluments, it stumbles at its own absurdity and adds: "But if any man is called into public service to the prejudice of his private affairs, he has a right to a reasonable compensation." Is not this contrary to the doctrine that there can be no use in offices of profit? Are not the profits of offices intended as a reasonable compensation for time, labor, and neglect and prejudice of private affairs? If you look into the salaries and fees of offices in general, that is, into the legal profits, you will find them, not only in America, but in France, Holland, nay in England, far from being extravagant. You will find them but a moderate and reasonable compensation for their unavoidable expenses and the prejudice to their private affairs. It is not the legal profit, but the secret perquisites, the patronage, and the abuse, which is the evil. And this is what I complain of in the article, that it diverts the attention, jealousy, and hatred of the people from the perquisites, patronage, and abuse, which is the evil, to the legal, honest profit of the office, which is a blessing.

3. The dependence and servility in the possessors and expectants, and the faction, contention, corruption, and disorder among the people, do not proceed from the legal profits of offices, which are known to all, but from the perquisites, patronage, and abuses, which are known only to a few.

4. Nor is it by any means a good rule, that whenever an office, through increase of fees or otherwise, becomes so profitable as to occasion many to apply for it, the profit ought to be lessened by the legislature.

We are so fond of being seen and talked of, we have such a passion for the esteem and confidence of our fellow-men, that wherever applications for office are permitted by the laws and manners, there will be many to apply, whether the profits are large or small, or none at all. If the profits are none, all the rich will apply, that is to say, all who can live upon their own incomes; all others will be excluded, because, if they labor for the public, themselves and families must starve. By this means an aristocracy or oligarchy of the rich will be formed, which will soon put an end by their arts and craft to this self-denying system. If many apply, all applications should be forbidden, or, if they are permitted, a choice should be made of such out of the multitude as will be contented with legal profits, without making advantage of patronage and perquisites.

I do not mean by this, that the legal profits should be very great. They should afford a decent support, and should enable a man to educate and provide for his family as decent and moderate men do in private life; but it would be unjust as well as impolitic in the public, to call men of the best talents and characters from professions and occupations where they might provide for their fami-

lies plentifully, and let them spend their lives in the service of the public, to the impoverishment and beggary of their posterity.

I have given you this trouble, because I think these to be fundamental errors in society. Mankind will never be happy nor their liberties secure, until the people shall lay it down as a fundamental rule to make the support and reward of public offices a matter of justice and not gratitude. Every public man should be honestly paid for his services; then justice is done to him. But he should be restrained from every perquisite not known to the laws, and he should make no claims upon the gratitude of the public, nor ever confer an office within his patronage, upon a son, a brother, a friend, upon pretence that he is not paid for his services by the profits of his office. Members of parliament should be paid, as well as soldiers and sailors.

I know very well that the word "disinterested" turns the heads of the people by exciting their enthusiasm. But although there are disinterested men, they are not enough in any age or any country to fill all the necessary offices, and therefore the people may depend upon it, that the hypocritical pretence of disinterestedness will be set up to deceive them, much oftener than the virtue will be practised for their good. It is worth while to read the lives of the Roman Catholic saints; your St. Ignatius Loyolas, your St. Bernards, and hundreds of others. It was always disinterestedness, which enabled them to excite enthusiasm among the people, and to command their purses to any amount, in order to establish their wild and pernicious institutions. The cry of gratitude has made more men mad, and established more despotism in the world, than all other causes put together. Every throne has been erected on it, and every mitre has sprung out of it; so has every coronet; and whenever any man serves the public without pay, a cry of gratitude is always set up, which pays him, or his cousins or sons, ten times as much as he ever deserved. Let government, then, be founded in justice; and let all claims upon popular gratitude be watched with a jealous eye. Hang well and pay well, conveys to my understanding infinitely more sense and more virtue than this whole article of the Pennsylvania Constitution.

I have long wanted to communicate with some of the enlightened friends of liberty here upon some parts of our constitutions, and I know of none who merits the character better. If you are willing, I will take some future opportunity to write you a few thoughts upon some other things. Meantime, let this remain between ourselves, if you please.

7

RECORDS OF THE FEDERAL CONVENTION

[1:20; *Madison, 29 May*]

4. Resd. that the members of the first branch of the National Legislature ought . . . to receive liberal stipends by

which they may be compensated for the devotion of their time to public service. . . .

5. Resold. that the members of the second branch of the National Legislature ought . . . to receive liberal stipends, by which they may be compensated for the devotion of their time to public service. . . .

[1:215; Madison, 12 June]

The words "liberal compensation for members" being considd. Mr. Madison moves to inset the words "& fixt." He observed that it would be improper to leave the members of the Natl. legislature to be provided for by the State Legisls: because it would create an improper dependence; and to leave them to regulate their own wages, was an indecent thing, and might in time prove a dangerous one. He thought wheat or some other article of which the average price throughout a reasonable period precedn'g might be settled in some convenient mode, would form a proper standard.

Col. Mason seconded the motion; adding that it would be improper for other reasons to leave the wages to be regulated by the States. 1. the different States would make different provision for their representatives, and an inequality would be felt among them, whereas he thought they ought to be in all respects equal. 2. the parsimony of the States might reduce the provision so low that as had already happened in choosing delegates to Congress, the question would be not who were most fit to be chosen, but who were most willing to serve.

On the question for inserting the words "and fixt."

Massts. no Cont. no. N. Y. ay. N. J. ay. Pa. ay. Del. ay. Md. ay. Va. ay. N. C. ay. S. C. no. Geo. ay. [Ayes—8; noes—3.]

Doctr. Franklyn said he approved of the amendment just made for rendering the salaries as fixed as possible; but disliked the word "liberal". He would prefer the word moderate if it was necessary to substitute any other. He remarked the tendency of abuses in every case, to grow of themselves when once begun. and related very pleasantly the progression in ecclesiastical benefices, from the first departure from the gratuitous provision for the Apostles, to the establishment of the papal system. The word "liberal" was struck out nem. con.

On the motion of Mr. Pierce, that the wages should be paid out of the National Treasury, Massts. ay. Ct. no. N. Y. no. N. J. ay. Pa. ay. Del. ay Md. ay. Va. ay. N. C. ay. S. C. no. G. ay. [Ayes—8; noes—3.]

Question on the clause relating to term of service & compensation of 1st. branch

Massts. ay. Ct. no. N. Y. no. N. J. ay. Pa. ay. Del. ay. Md. ay. Va. ay. N. C. ay. S. C. no. Geo. ay. [Ayes—8; noes—3.]

. . . . .

Mr. Butler & Mr. Rutledge proposed that the members of the 2d. branch should be entitled to no salary or compensation for their services. on the question

Masts. divd. Cont. ay. N. Y. no. N. J. no. P. no. Del. ay. Md. no Va. no. N. C. no. S. C. ay. Geo. no. [Ayes—3; noes—7; divided—1.]

It was then moved & agreed that the clauses respecting the stipends & ineligibility of the 2d. branch be the same as, of the 1st. branch: Con: disagreeing to the ineligibility.

[1:371; Madison, 22 June]

The clause in Resol. 3 "to receive fixed stipends to be paid out of the Nationl. Treasury" considered.

Mr. Elseworth, moved to substitute payment by the States out of their own Treasurys: observing that the manners of different States were very different in the Stile of living and in the profits accruing from the exercise of like talents. What would be deemed therefore a reasonable compensation in some States, in others would be very unpopular, and might impede the system of which it made a part.

Mr. Williamson favored the idea. He reminded the House of the prospect of new States to the Westward. They would be poor—would pay little into the common Treasury—and would have a different interest from the old States. He did not think therefore that the latter ought to pay the expences of men who would be employed in thwarting their measures & interests.

Mr. Ghorum, wished not to refer the matter to the State Legislatures who were always paring down salaries in such a manner as to keep out of offices men most capable of executing the functions of them. He thought also it would be wrong to fix the compensations by the constitution, because we could not venture to make it as liberal as it ought to be without exciting an enmity agst. the whole plan. Let the Natl. Legisl: provide for their own wages from time to time; as the State Legislatures do. He had not seen this part of their power abused, nor did he apprehend an abuse of it.

Mr. Randolph feared we were going too far, in consulting popular prejudices. Whatever respect might be due to them, in lesser matters, or in cases where they formed the permanent character of the people, he thought it neither incumbent on nor honorable for the Convention, to sacrifice right & justice to that consideration. If the States were to pay the members of the Natl. Legislature, a dependence would be created that would vitiate the whole System. The whole nation has an interest in the attendance & services of the members. The Nationl. Treasury therefore is the proper fund for supporting them.

Mr. King, urged the danger of creating a dependence on the States by leavg. to them the payment of the members of the Natl. Legislature. He supposed it wd. be best to be explicit as to the compensation to be allowed. A reserve on that point, or a reference to the Natl. Legislature of the quantum, would excite greater opposition than any sum that would be actually necessary or proper.

Mr. Sherman contended for referring both the quantum and the payment of it to the State Legislatures.

Mr. Wilson was agst. fixing the compensation as circumstances would change and call for a change of the amount. He thought it of great moment that the members of the Natl. Govt. should be left as independent as possible of the State Govts. in all respects.

Mr. Madison concurred in the necessity of preserving the compensations for the Natl. Govt. independent on the

State Govts. but at the same time approved of *fixing* them by the constitution, which might be done by taking a standard which wd. not vary with circumstances. He disliked particularly the policy suggested by Mr. Williamson of leaving the members from the poor States beyond the Mountains, to the precarious & parsimonious support of their constituents. If the Western States hereafter arising should be admitted into the Union, they ought to be considered as equals & as brethren. If their representatives were to be associated in the Common Councils, it was of common concern that such provisions should be made as would invite the most capable and respectable characters into the service.

Mr. Hamilton apprehended inconveniency from *fixing* the wages. He was strenuous agst. making the National Council dependent on the Legislative rewards of the States. Those who pay are the masters of those who are paid. Payment by the States would be unequal as the distant States would have to pay for the same term of attendance and more days in travelling to & from the seat of the Govt. He expatiated emphatically on the difference between the feelings & views of the *people*—& the *Governments* of the States arising from the personal interest & official inducements which must render the latter unfriendly to the Genl. Govt.

Mr. Wilson moved that the salaries of the 1st. branch *"be ascertained by the National Legislature,"* and be paid out of the Natl. Treasury.

Mr. Madison, thought the members of the Legisl. too much interested to ascertain their own compensation. It wd. be indecent to put their hands into the public purse for the sake of their own pockets.

On this question Mas. no. Con. no. N. Y. divd. N. J. ay. Pa. ay. Del. no. Md. no. Va. no. N. C. no S. C. no Geo. divd. [Ayes—2; noes—7; divided—2.]

On the question for striking out "Natl. Treasury" as moved by Mr. Elseworth

Mr. Hamilton renewed his opposition to it. He pressed the distinction between State Govts. & the people. The former wd. be the rivals of the Gen'l Govt. The State legislatures ought not therefore to be the pay masters of the latter.

Mr. Elesworth. If we are jealous of the State Govts. they will be so of us. If on going home I tell them we gave the Gen: Govt. such powers because we cd. not trust you.— will they adopt it. & witht. yr. approbation it is a nullity.

Masts. ay. Cont. ay. N. Y. divd. N. J. no. Pena. no. Del. no. Md. no. Va. no, N. C. ay. S. C. ay. Geo. divd. [Ayes—4; noes—5; divided—2.]

On a question for substituting "adequate compensation" in place of "fixt Stipends" it was agreed to nem. con. the friends of the latter being willing that the practicability of *fixing* the compensation should be considered hereafter in forming the details.

It was then moved by Mr. Butler that a question be taken on both points jointly; to wit "adequate compensation to be paid out of the Natl. Treasury." It was objected to as out of order, the parts having been separately decided on. The Presidt. referd. the question of order to the House, and it was determined to be in order. Con. N. J. Del. Md. N. C. S. C.—ay—N. Y. Pa. Va. Geo. no—Mass: divided. The question on the sentence was then postponed by S. Carolina in right of the State.

[1:426; Madison, 26 June]

"To receive fixt stipends by which they may be compensated for their services". considered

General Pinkney proposed "that no Salary should be allowed". As this (the Senatorial) branch was meant to represent the wealth of the Country, it ought to be composed of persons of wealth; and if no allowance was to be made the wealthy alone would undertake the service. He moved to strike out the Clause.

Doctr: Franklin seconded the motion. He wished the Convention to stand fair with the people. There were in it a number of young men who would probably be of the Senate. If lucrative appointments should be recommended we might be chargeable with having carved out places for ourselves.

On the question.—

Masts. Connecticut Pa. Md. S. Carolina Ay. N. Y. N. J. Del. Virga. N. C. Geo. no.

Mr. Williamson moved to change the expression into these words towit. "to receive a compensation for the devotion of their time to the public Service". The motion was seconded by Mr. Elseworth. And was agreed to by all the States except S. Carola. It seemed to be meant only to get rid of the word "fixt" and leave greater room for modifying the provision on this point.

Mr. Elseworth moved to strike out "to be paid out of the natl. Treasury" and insert "to be paid by their respective States". If the Senate was meant to strengthen the Govt. it ought to have the confidence of the States. The States will have an interest in keeping up a representation and will make such provision for supporting the members as will ensure their attendance.

Mr. Madison, considered this a departure from a fundamental principle, and subverting the end intended by allowing the Senate a duration of 6 years. They would if this motion should be agreed to, hold their places during pleasure; during the pleasure of the State Legislatures. One great end of the institution was, that being a firm, wise and impartial body, it might not only give stability to the Genl. Govt. in its operations on individuals, but hold an even balance among different States. The motion would make the Senate like Congress, the mere Agents & Advocates of State interests & views, instead of being the impartial umpires & Guardians of justice and general Good. Congs. had lately by the establishment of a board with full powers to decide on the mutual claims between the U. States & the individual States, fairly acknowledged themselves to be unfit for discharging this part of the business referred to them by the Confederation.

Mr. Dayton considered the payment of the Senate by the States as fatal to their independence. he was decided for paying them out of the Natl Treasury.

On the question for payment of the Senate to be left to the States as moved by Mr. Elseworth

Massts. no. Cont. ay. N. Y. ay. N. J. ay. Pa. no. Del. no. Md. no. Va. no. N. C. no. S. C. ay. Geo. ay. [Ayes—5; noes—6.]

Col. Mason. He did not rise to make any motion, but to hint an idea which seemed to be proper for consideration. One important object in constituting the Senate was to secure the rights of property. To give them weight & firmness for this purpose, a considerable duration in office was thought necessary. But a longer term than 6 years, would be of no avail in this respect, if needy persons should be appointed. He suggested therefore the propriety of annexing to the office a qualification of property. He thought this would be very practicable; as the rules of taxation would supply a scale for measuring the degree of wealth possessed by every man.

A question was then taken whether the words "to be paid out of the public treasury." should stand"

Masts. ay. Cont no. N. Y. no. N. J. no. Pa. ay. Del. ay. Md. ay. Va. ay. N. C. no. S. C. no. Geo. no. [Ayes—5; noes—6.]

[2:290; Madison, 14 Aug.]

Mr. Elseworth said that in reflecting on this subject he had been satisfied that too much dependence on the States would be produced by this mode of payment. He moved to strike out and insert "that they should" be paid out of the Treasury of the U.S. an allowance not exceeding (blank) dollars per day or the present value thereof,

Mr. Govr Morris, remarked that if the members were to be paid by the States it would throw an unequal burden on the distant States, which would be unjust as the Legislature was to be a national Assembly. He moved that the payment be out of the Natl. Treasury; leaving the quantum to the discretion of the Natl. Legislature. There could be no reason to fear that they would overpay themselves.

Mr. Butler contended for payment by the States; particularly in the case of the Senate, who will be so long out of their respective States, that they will lose sight of their Constituents unless dependent on them for their support.

Mr Langdon was agst. payment by the States. There would be some difficulty in fixing the sum; but it would be unjust to oblige the distant States to bear the expence of their members in travelling to and from the Seat of Govt.

Mr Madison. If the H. of Reps. is to be chosen *biennially*—and the Senate to be *constantly* dependent on the Legislatures which are chosen *annually*, he could not see any chance for that stability in the Genl Govt. the want of which was a principal evil in the State Govts. His fear was that the organization of the Govt supposing the Senate to be really independt. for six years, would not effect our purpose. It was nothing more than a combination of the peculiarities of two of the State Govts. which separately had been found insufficient. The Senate was formed on the model of that of Maryld. The Revisionary check, on that of N. York. What the effect of A union of these provisions might be, could not be foreseen. The enlargement of the sphere of the Government was indeed a circumstance which he thought would be favorable as he had on several occasions undertaken to show. He was however for

fixing at least two extremes not to be exceeded by the Natl. Legislre. in the payment of themselves.

Mr. Gerry. There are difficulties on both sides. The observation of Mr. Butler has weight in it. On the other side, the State Legislatures may turn out the Senators by reducing their salaries. Such things have been practised.

Col. Mason. It has not yet been noticed that the clause as it now stands makes the House of Represents. also dependent on the State Legislatures; so that both Houses will be made the instruments of the politics of the States whatever they may be.

Mr. Broom could see no danger in trusting the Genl. Legislature with the payment of themselves. The State Legislatures had this power, and no complaint had been made of it—

Mr. Sherman was not afraid that the Legislature would make their own wages too high; but too low, so that men ever so fit could not serve unless they were at the same time rich. He thought the best plan would be to fix a moderate allowance to be paid out of the Natl. Treasy. and let the States make such additions as they might judge fit. He moved that 5 dollars per day be the sum, any further emoluments to be added by the States.

Mr. Carrol had been much surprised at seeing this clause in the Report. The dependence of both houses on the State Legislatures is compleat; especially as the members of the former are eligible to State offices. The States can now say: if you do not comply with our wishes, we will starve you: if you do we will reward you. The new Govt. in this form was nothing more than a second edition of Congress in two volumes, instead of one, and perhaps with very few amendments—

Mr Dickenson took it for granted that all were convinced of the necessity of making the Genl. Govt. independent of the prejudices, passions, and improper views of the State Legislatures. The contrary of This was effected by the section as it stands. On the other hand, there were objections agst taking a permanent standard as Wheat which had been suggested on a former occasion, as well as against leaving the matter to the pleasure of the Natl. Legislature. He proposed that an Act should be passed every 12 years by the Natl. Legislre settling the quantum of their wages. If the Genl. Govt. should be left dependent on the State Legislatures, it would be happy for us if we had never met in this Room.

Mr. Elseworth was not unwilling himself to trust the Legislature with authority to regulate their own wages, but well knew that an unlimited discretion for that purpose would produce strong, tho' perhaps not insuperable objections. He thought changes in the value of money, provided for by his motion in the words, "or the present value thereof."

Mr. L. Martin. As the Senate is to represent the States, the members of it ought to be paid by the States—

Mr. Carrol. The Senate was to represent & manage the affairs of the whole, and not to be the advocates of State interests. They ought then not to be dependent on nor paid by the States.

On the question for paying the Members of the Legislature out of the Natl Treasury, ÷

N. H. ay. Mas. no. Ct. ay. N. J. ay. Pa. ay. Del. ay. Md. ay. Va. ay. N. C. ay. S. C. no. Geo. ay. [Ayes—9; noes—2.]

Mr. Elsworth moved that the pay be fixed at 5 dollrs. or the present value thereof per day during their attendance & for every thirty miles in travelling to & from Congress.

Mr. Strong preferred 4 dollars, leaving the Sts at liberty to make additions

On question for fixing the pay at 5 dollars.

N. H. no. Mas. no. Ct. ay. N. J. no. Pa. no. Del. no. Md. no. Va. ay. N. C. no. S. C. no. Geo. no. [Ayes—2; noes—9.]

Mr. Dickenson proposed that the wages of the members of both houses sd. be required to be the same.

Mr. Broome seconded him.

Mr Ghorum. this would be unreasonable. The Senate will be detained longer from home, will be obliged to remove their families, and in time of war perhaps to sit constantly. Their allowance should certainly be higher. The members of the Senates in the States are allowed more, than those of the other house.

Mr Dickenson withdrew his motion

It was moved & agreed to amend the Section by adding—"to be ascertained by law"

The Section (Art VI. sec. 10) as amended– agreed to nem. con.

[2:502; *Madison, 4 Sept.*]

Mr. Pinkney moved a clause declaring "that each House should be judge of the privilege of its own members." Mr Govr. Morris 2ded. the motion

Mr. Randolph & Mr. Madison expressed doubts as to the propriety of giving such a power, & wished for a postponement.

Mr Govr. Morris thought it so plain a case that postponement could be necessary.

Mr. Wilson thought the power involved, and the express insertion of it needless. It might beget doubts as to the power of other public bodies, as Courts &c. Every Court is the judge of its own privileges.

Mr Madison distinguished between the power of Judging of privileges previously & duly established, and the effect of the motion which would give a discretion to each House as to the extent of its own privileges. He suggested that it would be better to make provision for ascertaining by *law*, the privileges of each House, than to allow each House to decide for itself. He suggested also the necessity of considering what privileges ought to be allowed to the Executive.

8

VERMONT CONSTITUTION OF 1786, CH. 1, ART. 16
Thorpe 6:3753

The freedom of deliberation, speech, and debate, in the legislature, is so essential to the rights of the people, that it cannot be the foundation of any accusation or prosecution, action or complaint, in any other court or place whatsoever.

9

A GEORGIAN
15 Nov. 1787
Storing 5.9.6

Art. 1, sect. 6. What advantage can it be to Congress to have the power to pay themselves? and yet it may be very detrimental to the states. May they not do as the members of a certain state assembly did, spend most of the money raised by the taxes in paying themselves? And why is their salary not fixed? for who can say how the senators or representatives may incline to live? perhaps much better than we can afford to pay. Also, is it meant by this section that a member, either of the senate or representatives, is not to account for his acts to his constituents? If so, this is contrary to the idea entertained by freemen who delegate their power for a limited time. That the representative should be called on by his constituents to answer and give his reasons for his measures is one of the firmest barriers to liberty. Therefore I would propose this section to read thus:

"Art. I., sect. 6. The senators and representatives shall receive a compensation for their services, not exceeding five dollars per day, during their attendance and going to and coming from Congress, to be paid out of the treasury of their respective states. They shall in all cases, except treason, felony, and breach of the peace, be privileged from arrest, during their attendance at the sessions of their respective houses, and in going to and returning from the same. And for any speech or debate in either house they shall not be questionable in any other place, except when they shall be called upon for that purpose by their constituents."

10

CORNELIUS
11–18 Dec. 1787
Storing 4.10.8–9

The Congress are to have *power to levy and collect taxes, duties, imposts and excises,* at their discretion; and out of this revenue, to make themselves such compensation for their services as they may think proper.

Is it altogether certain, that a body of men elected for so long a term,—rendered thus independent, and most of them placed at the distance of some hundreds of miles from their constituents, will pay a more faithful regard to their interest, and set an example of economy, more becoming the circumstances of this country, than they would do, if they were annually elected, subject to some kind of instructions, and liable to be recalled, in case of male administration? Have the several states, in the estimation of the compilers of this Constitution, been hitherto, so parsimonious and unjust in paying their delegates, that they have rendered themselves unfit to contract with their Senators and Representatives, respecting a compensation for their service? If so, what may we suppose will be considered as a just compensation, when this honourable Body shall set their own pay, and be accountable to none but themselves?

It will probably be urged, "Our State Legislature set their own pay; and why should not Congress do the same."

If the cases are similar, the reasoning may be good; but there is a wide difference between them. The members of our State legislature are annually elected—they are subject to instructions—they are chosen within small circles—they are sent but a small distance from their respective homes: Their conduct is constantly known to their constituents. They frequently see, and are seen, by the men whose servants they are. While attending the duties of their office, their connexions in general, are with men who have been bred to economy, and whose circumstances require them to live in a frugal style. They are absent from their respective homes but a few days, or weeks, at most. They return, and mix with their neighbours of the lowest rank, see their poverty, and feel their wants.—On the contrary: The members of Congress are to be chosen for a term of years. They are to be subject to no instructions. They are to be chosen within large circles: They will be unknown to a very considerable part of the constituents, and their constituents will be not less unknown to them. They will be far removed, and long detained, from the view of their constituents. Their general conduct will be unknown. Their chief connections will be with men of the first rank in the United States, who have been bred in affluence at least, if not in the excess of luxury. They will have constantly before them the enchanting example of Ambassadors, other publick Ministers, and Consuls from foreign courts, who, both from principles of policy, and private ambition, will live in the most splendid and costly style. Men are naturally enough inclined to vie with each other. Let any body of men whatever be placed, from year to year, in circumstances like these; let them have the unlimitted controul of the property of the United States; and let them feel themselves vested, at the same time, with a constitutional right, out of this property to make themselves such compensation as they may think fit: And then, let any one judge, whether they will long retain the same ideas, and feel themselves under equal restraints as to fixing their own pay, with the members of our state legislature. This part of the Constitution, I conceive to be calculated, not only to enhance the expense of the federal government to a degree that will be truely burdensome; but also, to increase that luxury and extravagance, in general, which threatens the ruin of the United States; and that, to which the Eastern States in particular, are wholly unequal.

11

DEBATE IN MASSACHUSETTS RATIFYING CONVENTION
19 Jan. 1788
Elliot 2:52–54

Dr. TAYLOR. Mr. President, it has hitherto been customary for the gentlemen of Congress to be *paid* by the several state legislatures out of the state treasury. As no state has hitherto failed paying its delegates, why should we leave the good old path? Before the revolution it was considered as a grievance that the governors, &c., received their pay from Great Britain. They could not, in that case, feel their dependence on the people, when they received their appointments and salaries from the crown. I know not why we should not pay them now, as well as heretofore.

Gen. PORTER. Have not delegates been retained from Congress, which is virtually recalling them, because they have not been paid? Has not Rhode Island failed to pay their delegates? Should there not be an equal charge throughout the United States, for the payment of the delegates, as there is in this state for the payment of the members of this Convention, met for the general good? Is it not advantageous to the people at large, that the delegates to this Convention are paid out of the public treasury? If any inconvenience, however, can be shown to flow from this plan, I should be glad to hear it.

Hon. Mr. SEDGWICK hoped gentlemen would consider that the federal officers of government would be responsible for their conduct; and, as they would regard their reputations, will not assess exorbitant *wages*. In Massachusetts, and in every other state, the legislatures have power to provide for their own payment; and, he asked, have they ever established it higher than it ought to be? But, on the contrary, have they not made it extremely inconsiderable? The commons of Great Britain, he said, have the power to assess their own wages; but for two centuries they have never exercised it. Can a man, he asked, who has the least respect for the good opinion of his fellow-countrymen, go home to his constituents, after having robbed them by voting himself an exorbitant salary? This principle will be a most powerful check; and in respect to economy, the power lodged as it is in this section will be more advantageous to the people than if retained by the state legislatures. Let us see what the legislature of Massachusetts have done; they vote the *salaries* of the delegates to Congress, and they have voted them such as have enabled them to live in style suited to the dignity of a respectable state; but these *salaries* have been four times as much, for the same time, as they ever voted themselves. Therefore, concluded the honorable gentleman, if left to themselves to provide for their own payment, as long as they wish for the good opinion of mankind, they will assess no more than they really deserve, as a compensation for their services.

Hon. Mr. KING said, if the arguments on the 4th section against an undue control, in the state legislatures, over the federal representatives, were in any degree satisfactory, they are so on this.

Gen. THOMPSON. Mr. President, the honorable gentleman means well, and is honest in his sentiments; it is all alike. When we see matters at large, and what it all is, we will know what to do with it.

Mr. PARSONS. In order that the general government should preserve itself, it is necessary it should preserve justice between the several states. Under the Confederation, the power of this section would not be just; for each state has a right to send seven members to Congress, though some of them do not pay one tenth as much of the public expenses as others. It is a mere federal government of states, neither equal nor proportionate. If gentlemen would use the same candor that the honorable gentleman from Topsham (Gen. Thompson) does, considering all the parts as connected with others, the Constitution would receive a better discussion.

12

LUTHER MARTIN, GENUINE INFORMATION
1788
Storing 2.4.42

To prove . . . that the senate *as constituted* could not be a *security* for the *protection* and *preservation* of the *State* governments, and that the *senators* could not be justly considered the *representatives* of the *States* as *States*, it was observed, that upon *just principles of representation*, the *representative* ought to *speak* the sentiments of his *constituents*, and ought to *vote* in the *same manner* that his *constituents* would do (as far as he can judge) provided his constituents were acting in *person*, and had the same knowledge and information with himself; and therefore that the *representative* ought to be *dependant* on his *constituents*, and answerable to them; that the connexion between the *representative* and the *represented*, ought to be as *near* and as *close* as possible; according to these principles, Mr. Speaker, in this State it is provided by *its constitution*, that the representatives in Congress, shall be chosen *annually*, shall be *paid* by the *State*, and shall be subject to *recall* even within the year; so *cautiously* has our *constitution* guarded against an *abuse* of the trust reposed in our representatives in the federal government; whereas by the *third* and *sixth* sections of the *first* article of this new system, the senators are to be chosen for *six* years instead of being chosen *annually;* instead of being paid by their *States* who send them, *they* in conjunction with the other branch, are to *pay themselves* out of the treasury of the United States; and are not liable to be *recalled* during the period for which they are chosen: Thus, Sir, for *six years* the *senators* are rendered totally and absolutely *independent* of *their States*, of *whom* they ought to

be the *representatives*, without any *bond* or *tie* between them: During that time they may join in measures *ruinous* and *destructive* to *their States*, even such as should *totally annihilate* their *State governments*, and their States *cannot recall them*, nor *exercise any controul over them*.

13

BOLTON V. MARTIN
1 Dall. 296 (C.P. Phila. 1788)

On the 6th of September, the President delivered the opinion of the court.

SHIPPEN, President.—The question in this case, is, whether a member of convention, residing in a distant county, could legally, and consistently with the privileges of such a deliberative assembly, be arrested or served with a summons, or other process, out of this court, issued to compel his appearance to a civil action, while he remained in the city of Philadelphia attending the duties of that office?

The members of convention, elected by the people, and assembled for a great national purpose, ought to be considered, in reason, and from the nature as well as dignity of their office, as invested with the same or equal immunities with the members of General Assembly, met in their ordinary legislative capacity: and in this light, I shall consider them.

The Assembly of Pennsylvania being the legislative branch of our government, its members are legally and inherently possessed of all such privileges, as are necessary to enable them, with freedom and safety, to execute the great trust reposed in them by the body of the people who elected them. As this is a parliamentary trust, we must necessarily consider the law of Parliament, in that country from whence we have drawn our other laws. That part of the law of Parliament, which respects the privileges of its members, was principally established to protect them from being molested by their fellow-subjects, or oppressed by the power of the crown, and to prevent their being diverted from the public business. The parliament, in general, is the sole and exclusive judge and expositor of its own privileges: but, in certain cases, it will happen, that they come necessarily and incidentally before the courts of law, and then they must likewise judge upon them.

The origin of these privileges is said by Selden to be as ancient as Edward the Confessor. For a long time, however, after the conquest, we find very little, either in the books of law, or history, upon this subject. If there were then any regular parliaments, their members held their privileges by a very precarious tenure. There appears, indeed, in the reigns of *Henry IV.* and *Henry VI.* to have been some provisions made by acts of Parliament, to protect the members from illegal and violent attacks upon their persons. In the reign of *Edward IV.*, there has been a case cited to show, that the judges determined that a menial servant of a member of parliament, though privileged from actual arrest, might yet be impleaded. Although it were fairly to be inferred from the case, that the privilege of the servant was equal to the privilege of the member himself, yet a case determined at so early a period, when the rights and privileges of parliament were so little ascertained and defined, cannot have the same weight as more modern authorities.

Upon an attentive perusal of the statute of 12 & 13 *Wm. III., c.* 3; I think, no other authority will be wanting to show what the law was upon this subject, before the passing of that act. From the whole frame of that statute, it appears clearly to be the sense of the legislature, that, before that time, members of parliament were privileged from arrests, and from being served with any process out of the courts of law, not only during the sitting of parliament, but during the recess within the time of privilege; which was a reasonable time *eundo ct redeundo.* The design of this act was not to meddle with the privileges which the members enjoyed during the sitting of parliament (those seem to have been held sacred), but it enacts, that after the dissolution or prorogation of parliament, or after adjournment of both houses, for above the space of fourteen days, any person might commence and prosecute any action against a member of parliament, provided the person of the member be not arrested during the time of privilege. The manner of bringing the action against a member of the house of commons is directed to be by *summons* and *distress infinite,* to compel a common appearance; but even this was not to be done, until after the dissolution, prorogation or adjournment. The act further directs, that where any plaintiff shall, by reason of privilege of parliament, be stayed from prosecuting any suit commenced, such plaintiff shall not be barred by the statute of limitations, or nonsuited, dismissed, or his suit discontinued for want of prosecution, but shall, upon the rising of parliament, be at liberty to proceed. So that before the rising of parliament, and during the actual sitting of it, it appears, not only that, generally, a suit could not be commenced, but, if it had been commenced before, it could not be prosecuted during that time. One exception, as to commencing the action, appears to have been made by the judges, agreeable to the spirit and apparent intention of the act; which is, that in order to prevent a member of parliament from taking advantage of the statute of limitations, by reason of his privilege, an *original* might be filed against him; but that original must lie dormant, during the sitting of parliament, no process could issue upon it to compel an appearance; nor until this act passed, could it have been done at any time, after the rising of parliament, during the time of privilege.

This construction of the act is so obvious, that, upon any other, almost all the provisions in it would have been nugatory; and it fully accounts for the seeming doubt in *Col. Pitt's case* in Strange, whether he should be discharged on common bail, or be discharged altogether; it being after the dissolution of parliament, the plaintiff had a right, by the act, to commence a suit against him; and therefore, it seemed, at first, that he should only be discharged on common bail; but as he had commenced his suit by *arresting his person,* before his time of privilege expired, the judges,

that they might not seem to countenance the arrest, discharged him entirely.

If it were possible to doubt of this being the true construction of the act of 12 & 13 *Wm. III.,* it is made still clearer, by the act of 2 & 3 *Ann. c.* 18, which directs that any action may be commenced against a member of parliament employed in the revenue, or other place of public trust, even during the sitting of parliament, for any misdemeanor, breach of trust, or penalty, relating to such public trust, provided his person be not arrested. This act was made for this single purpose, and would have been likewise nugatory, if an action could have been brought before, against any member of parliament, during the sitting of the house.

Black. Com. 165 was cited, to show, that a member of parliament might be sued for his debts, though not arrested, during the sitting of parliament. This will appear to be expressly confined to actions at the suit of the King, under a particular provision in the statute of *Wm. III.,* and, by the strongest implication, shows, that it could not be done at the suit of a private person. A little higher, in the same page, a general position of Judge Blackstone will be found, which fully reaches the case in question. "Neither (says he) can any member of either house be arrested, or taken into custody, nor served with any process of the courts of law, nor his servants arrested, &c., without a breach of the privilege of parliament."

In the case before us, the defendant appears to have been served with a *summons* out of this court, during the time of the actual sitting of the Convention. Whether we take the law to be, as it stood in England before, and at the time of passing the act of *Wm. III.,* or as it stood after the passing that act, down to the 10th of *Geo. III.,* about six years before our revolution, it is clear, that no member of parliament, other than those particularly excepted, could be arrested or served with any process out of the courts of law, during the sitting of parliament.

We cannot but consider our members of assembly, as they have always considered themselves, entitled by law, to the same privileges. They ought not to be diverted from the public business by law-suits, brought against them during the sitting of the house; which, though not attended with the arrest of their persons, might yet oblige them to attend to those law-suits, and to bring witnesses from a distant county, to a place whither they came, perhaps solely, on account of that public business.

14

Geyer's Lessee v. Irwin
4 Dall. 107 (Pa.S.Ct. 1790)

By the Court: A member of the general assembly is, undoubtedly, privileged from arrest, summons, citation, or other civil process, during his attendance on the public business confided to him. And, we think, that upon principle, his suits cannot be forced to a trial and decision, while the session of the legislature continues.

But every privileged person must, at a proper time, and in a proper manner, claim the benefit of his privilege. The judges are not bound, judicially, to notice a right of privilege, nor to grant it without a claim. In the present instance, neither the defendant, nor his attorney, suggested the privilege, as an objection to the trial of the cause: and this amounts to a waiver, by which the party is forever concluded.

We are, therefore, unanimously of opinion, that the judgment cannot now be set aside, or opened.

15

JAMES MADISON, MILITIA BILL, HOUSE OF
REPRESENTATIVES
16 Dec. 1790
Papers 13:323

Mr. Madison moved, to strike out that part which related to the members of Congress, with their officers and servants attending either house, and to insert the members of the House of Representatives, whilst travelling to, attending at, or returning from the session of Congress, and the members of the Senate in similar circumstances, or in case of a separate session of the Senate. He did not see any reason for a total exemption from the service of the militia, and it was a principle with him, that on every occasion where an exception was made in favour of the framers of a law, that exception should not be extended or carried beyond what is evidently proper and necessary. Now to exempt the members of Congress at all times is unnecessary, because during the recess of the houses, they may be at liberty to pursue their ordinary avocations, and participate in the duties and exercises of their fellow-citizens. They ought ever to bear a share of the burthens they lay on others, in order that their acts may not slide into an abuse of the power vested in them.

. . . . .

Mr. Madison thought it an important principle, and one that ought in general to be attended to—That all laws should be made to operate as much on the law makers as upon the people; the greatest security for the preservation of liberty, is for the government to have a sympathy with those on whom the laws act, and a real participation and communication of all their burthens and grievances. Whenever it is necessary to exempt any part of the government from sharing in these common burthens, that necessity ought not only to be palpable, but should on no account be exceeded. He thought the amendment, together with the constitution, provided on this occasion for all that was necessary, and that the clause as it stood at present, went beyond that necessity.

16

JAMES WILSON, LEGISLATIVE DEPARTMENT,
LECTURES ON LAW
1791
Works 1:421

The members of the national legislature, and those also of the legislature of Pennsylvania, shall not, for any speech or debate in either house, be questioned in any other place. In England, the freedom of speech is, at the opening of every new parliament, particularly demanded of the king in person, by the speaker of the house of commons. The liberal provision, which is made, by our constitutions, upon this subject, may be justly viewed as a very considerable improvement in the science and the practice of government. In order to enable and encourage a representative of the publick to discharge his publick trust with firmness and success, it is indispensably necessary, that he should enjoy the fullest liberty of speech, and that he should be protected from the resentment of every one, however powerful, to whom the exercise of that liberty may occasion offence.

When it is mentioned, that the members shall not be questioned in any *other* place; the implication is strong, that, for their speeches in either house, they may be questioned and censured by that house, in which they are spoken. Besides; each house, both in the United States and in Pennsylvania, has an express power given it to "punish its members for disorderly behaviour." Under the protection of privilege, to use indecency or licentiousness of language, in the course of debate, is disorderly behaviour, of a kind peculiarly base and ungentlemanly.

17

HOUSE OF REPRESENTATIVES, REDUCTION OF
SALARIES
27 Jan. 1795
Annals 4:1136–45

Mr. CLAIBORNE: We now have fairly before us a proposition that contemplates a redress of these grievances, which, since the adoption of the present form of Government, have been a subject of grievous complaint and heartburning amongst the citizens of the United States. Many of them and, I believe, a very great majority, conceive that the exorbitant salaries established to the Legislative, Executive, Judiciary, and their assistants, are not consistent with, or can possibly contribute to the existence or well-being of a Republican Government, which, in its nature, holds out the idea of equality and justice, but which, in the present mode of administration, cannot fail to have a direct opposite tendency, inasmuch as the very profuse salaries that all who have the good fortune to get places under the pay and influence of the present Administration, if they make a prudent use of them, must ultimately enrich and place them in a situation so far above the vast bulk of the citizens, whose industrious fingers are not permitted a single dip into those very coffers which have been swelled by filching a little from that hard-gotten pittance already far inadequate to the necessary but very ordinary subsistence of their families, as at last to endanger the very existence or shadow of this glorious and dear-bought Government, that has already raised the drooping and once-dejected heads of the poor American citizens, who now glory more in having thrown off that subordination that was assumed and exercised over them under the late detestable Monarchical Government, by their rulers, or public officers, than even in their lives and fortunes. Men begin to know the inherent rights of human nature. They have dipped into and tasted a little of the sweets of political regeneration, and, amongst all classes of your citizens, you may discover a zeal that amounts to enthusiasm, that lives and burns and grows almost to a prodigy. Instances are not wanting, sir, to evince that thousands of those who were not fond of this Government at its adoption, are now, on all occasions, ready to step forth in its support, and the laws that are passed consistent therewith. But this does, by no means, argue that they will submit forever to repeated abuses of the Government, which may ultimately tend to its overthrow; and exorbitant salaries, with other profuse appropriations of the public money, at a time when the nation is groaning under an immense weight of foreign and domestic debt, which, (calculating upon the blessings of peace, and, of course, a very increasing revenue, not reasonably to be calculated on so long a time,) it is agreed on all hands will take a term not less than thirty-two years to extinguish. They conceive this to be one of those abuses, and, vested with the rights of freemen, closely interwoven with the obligations of good citizens and lovers of their country, have ventured, by divers ways, to suggest their disapprobation thereof, in hope that its glaring impropriety would be taken up and removed, as far as the present situation of our finances and the public good will admit. It is true, they have not come forward in the Constitutional mode, by petition, &c., but no member in this House will, I presume, say that they have not heard the loud clamors and complaints of the people on this subject. But perhaps I shall be answered that I am not charged with their petitions to make the proposition, and, if I was, that the people are not proper judges whether the salaries complained of are more than adequate, and to prove that some of them have not been so, I shall be told that the allowances to two of your most valuable officers have been so inadequate as to drive them out of your service. To this, I answer, that many other officers, with as large families, and a much less salary, have not abandoned your service—and why, sir? Permit me to answer, because they have probably proportioned their style of living to their quantum of salary, which prudence dictates, or custom has established, through all ranks of your citizens; else whence comes it that twenty-five thousand dollars per annum is not too much for the PRESIDENT OF THE UNITED STATES? Five thousand dollars is enough for the Vice President, two thousand one hundred and ninety for a member of Congress; and the salaries of many of your valuable officers, who have families, and devote their whole time to your service, are as low as five hundred dollars per annum. Here I shall again be told, that the price of house-rent, and every other necessary of life, has increased, and may continue to increase, so as to drive all your officers out of your service. To this, I beg leave to answer, that, if you continue such high salaries, or increase them, as in some instances it is asked, and because of the present enhanced price of the necessaries of life, I think the evil will increase in proportion to the immense sum of money that you throw into circulation, for a redundancy of that, or any thing else, will always diminish the value; and, if the present custom of disbursing the public money is persisted in, the whole wealth of the United States must shortly centre in and about Philadelphia! But, sir, by the adoption of public economy, we may shortly become able to obviate this great evil, and make our disbursements more diffusive, by paying out money to those who have demands upon your justice, distributed over the United States, if any but those who reside around the Seat of Government have any demand upon your justice or goodness. I am apprised that the proposition is a very unpopular one here, and that many will perhaps knit their brows at me; but, sir, when I entered into public life, it was without any cringing views. I meant not to court smiles, or fear frowns, and I had no doubt but I should meet my share of both. When I gain the former by proper conduct, I have pleasure in it; when the latter by improper conduct, I am sorry for it. But it will be much to be lamented if ever we see the day when the people shall be suffered to complain from year to year of any grievance, and their Representatives shall be ashamed, or afraid, to make those grievances known, or ask redress, lest they be laughed out of countenance, or lose favor at Court. But so hardy am I, if you prefer that expression, that, while I have the honor of a seat in this House, none of those considerations shall ever deter me from stepping forth in their behalf; but, be the result of this proposition what it may, I now warn you against evils that *may* come, as you have been heretofore warned of evils that *have* come, for the obligations of power and submission are reciprocal. It is as much your duty to pass wholesome laws, as it is the duty of the people to obey them. And now, having done my duty, I shall take my seat, content to abide the result, but hope a committee will be appointed.

Mr. NICHOLAS declared that he would be very willing to vote for the appointment of such a committee, if he could see any good purpose to be derived from it, or if the gentleman who laid the resolution on the table could give him any information that tended to prove its expediency. For his own part, he had but a small family, and of that he had left one-half behind him in Virginia, yet he found that his allowance as a member of the Legislature was barely sufficient for supporting this half of his family, though he lived with as much economy as he ever had done in his life. He was certain that he should not take one shilling of public money home with him to Virginia. He requested gentlemen to remember that it was not the present Congress who had given six dollars per day to themselves, but that it had been fixed by their predecessors, and fixed at a time when living was fifty per cent cheaper than it is now.

Mr. BOUDINOT observed, that he should not have troubled the Committee on this question, had it not been for several considerations particularly applicable to himself. He was as impartial on the present debate as any member on the floor. After the close of this session of Congress, he never expected to receive a farthing of public money again, and therefore no interest of his own could sway his judgment improperly to object against the resolution on the table. He had been among the number of those members who originally were for fixing the compensation of members of Congress at a less sum than six dollars; not because he thought it beyond the amount of their expenses, but, from an idea of the then deranged state of the finances, and that, if sacrifices were to be made, they should begin with this House. He appealed to his uniform conduct for six years past, to prove that he had always opposed an increase of salaries or other public expenses, when the interest of the Union did not require it. He did not doubt that the gentleman who brought forward this resolution thought he was doing his duty in advocating it; and Mr. B. thought it was equally the duty of the Committee to be convinced that they were not wasting their time in unnecessarily proceeding in business, without having some foundation for rational inquiry. The gentleman had declared that he was led to bring forward the resolution, not from any conviction of his own, for he knew not the officer to whom he could point his finger and say, that he had a greater salary than he deserved, but it was from the voice of the people, who were discontented and clamorous on the subject of large salaries, and particularly the compensation to members of Congress. Mr. B. said, for his own part, he did not believe these objections arose from the voice of the people. Had the gentleman offered any evidence of this to the Commitee? That he believed it himself, Mr. B. did not doubt; but this ought not to be sufficient evidence to the Committee. There was none on the table. Not a single petition had come forward to the House on this subject. There was nothing in the complexion of our Government that prevented the application of the people to their Representatives, if they were dissatisfied. They had frequently rechosen the same members, who voted for this compensation. From whence, then, arose the evidence of the public voice, being clamorous against the compensation of the members of Congress?

Mr. B. did not doubt but there were uninformed individuals, who might object to six dollars per day; but he was confident that the well-informed among the citizens of the United States, and those who reflected on the subject, would think (at the present day at least) it was not more than would barely pay the reasonable expenses of gentlemen who attended to their duty here in a proper manner. Almost every article of consumption was from twenty to thirty per cent. higher now than it was at the commencement of the Government.

The Constitution of the United States, as the act of the people and the public voice, contemplated a compensation to the members of Congress. Did not this mean something more than the bare discharge of their expenses? Yet Congress had not gone beyond it.

When Congress sat at New York, Mr. B. said that he was in a situation more favorable in point of expense than any gentleman on the floor, who did not reside in that city. He boarded with a near relation, and was in a manner in his own family; and, although he paid the usual price of boarding as at other places, yet there were a thousand nameless small articles which saved him many advances. He was within sixteen miles of his own family, from whence he received many things that prevented his laying out money. During three sessions, he kept an exact and faithful account of his expenditures, and, at the end of that time, the balance was but 43s. 4d.; but on which side of the question his memory did not allow him to say. At present, he was also under very peculiar advantages, yet he was confident that, at the end of the session, he should not have any balance in his favor from his compensation as a member. Mr. B. appealed to every gentleman's own knowledge, and particularly to the gentleman who made the motion, if he thought that what he received would more than pay his expenses.

Gentlemen were often crying out against an Aristocracy in this country; yet measures of this kind tended to establish one, by reducing the compensation of members, so that no citizen but the rich and affluent could attend as a Representative in Congress. This certainly was the most effectual way of bringing about a dangerous Aristocracy in the United States. Should not men of abilities, though in the middle walks of life, be encouraged to come forward and yield their services to their country, without being dependent on any person or set of men whatever? Is it not sufficient that their time and talents are given to the public? Must they pay their expenses too?

Mr. B. was aware that the resolution proposed related to the officers of Government as well as members of Congress, but he had confined his remarks to the last, as the part of the subject he was best acquainted with. He begged gentlemen to look around and point out the public officer who received more than a reasonable reward for his services. Professional men, of the first abilities, were absolutely necessary to carry on the public business; and could any one, fit for his office, be shown who could not do full as well, if not much better, in the exercise of his profession in private life, than he did in the public service, if pecuniary matters were his only object? In short, (Mr. B. said,) this House was placed between Scylla and Charybdis. The public officers were complaining, and even resigning, for want of sufficient compensation for their services; on the other hand, an attempt was now made to reduce their salaries still lower, on the supposed clamors of the people. Mr. B. did not believe they could be denominated those of the people; neither did he see any evidence of the fact. He did not consider the complaints of a few individuals as the public voice. Ought not the gentlemen to come forward with some kind of calculations or estimates to have shown that certain salaries were too high, or more than the services performed were entitled to? This had not been done;

but the Committee were urged, at this important moment, to proceed to an inquiry, which every gentleman on the floor already knew as well as he could do by the most labored investigation. He therefore concluded that, to agree to the resolution, would be a waste of the short time that yet remained of the session, and an unwise measure. Mr. B. would have contented himself with joining the Committee in a silent vote on this subject, but he thought the observations made in support of the measure ought to receive some answer, if not to convince the Committee, yet to satisfy their constituents that there could exist no necessity for a present inquiry of this nature.

Mr. CLAIBORNE begged leave to remind the House that he had never asserted the salaries were too high. His motion went only to appointing a committee for an inquiry whether the salaries were so or not.

Mr. W. SMITH said, that the resolution was, in its present shape, so extremely vague, that one did not know how to give it a definition or a vote. Different objects were lumped together. If, by an inquiry, the gentleman meant to examine into the wages of members of this House, it was quite needless to appoint a committee, because every member can at this moment speak for himself. But Mr. S. did not consider the present time as the most proper for beginning to reduce salaries, when, within the last twelve months, there had been three resignations, viz: the Secretary of State, the Secretary of War, and the Secretary of the Treasury, and all chiefly for one reason, the smallness of the salary. I have no doubt (said Mr. S.) of there being complaints, and, if the salary was reduced to three dollars per day, there would be still complaints, as we see is the case with the members of the Legislature of Pennsylvania. He only wished that the Committee would rise, and he should then vote in the House that they might not have leave to sit again. The mover of this resolution had mentioned the danger of meeting with reproaches from the people, who thought their salaries too high. Mr. S. saw very little in this matter, because the people who railed at the salary of six dollars per day, were only anxious to get in themselves, and embraced this topic as an expedient of ousting those members whom they wanted to succeed.

Mr. GOODHUE wished to ask Mr. CLAIBORNE one question, "Whether he found himself growing rich?"

Mr. SEDGWICK saw no occasion for rising because the Committee were perfectly competent at this moment to determine the question.

Mr. RUTHERFORD was for reducing the salaries by one dollar per day, and one dollar every twenty-five miles that the members had to travel. This would be a reduction of one hundred dollars per day, which would be much better bestowed upon the innocent widow of the veteran who had fallen in the service of his country.

Mr. PAGE said, that he did not think the resolution as it was worded, was a proper subject for discussion in that place; for the House, and not a committee, could properly resolve that committees should be appointed. However, as the resolution had been submitted by the House to the consideration of the Committee of the Whole, it must be examined; but, as to the object of it, that he thought was more properly before the Committee, as proposed by the

resolution; for, as I have remarked on other occasions, if, instead of discussing a question fully, and collecting the sense of all the members in a Committee of the Whole, it be referred to a committee of one member from each State, that committee might be unanimous in favor of a resolution, against which, eighteen members from Virginia, and a proportionate number from other States, might vote; or, by the weight of that committee, the resolution might be carried, which could not have passed had it been fully and freely discussed in the House. Here, then, my colleague's question should be examined, as I cannot say (as has been said by one of them) that I had no hand in fixing the salaries and pay of the officers of Government and members of Congress, having actually voted at New York for them as they now stand. I think I may with propriety, give my opinion respecting it. And I am clearly of opinion, sir, that the question arises from a misapprehension of the subject to which it is applied; for there cannot be a greater mistake than to suppose that parsimony in a Republic is necessary to its support. A certain degree of economy is so; but parsimony, applied to the salaries of public officers, and the Representatives in particular, may be ruinous to the interests of a Republic. Should the salaries be so low that men of small fortunes cannot afford to serve their country, it must be deprived of their assistance, and we must accept of the services of the rich, who, to have their wills, though low, will serve even without pay; or, the State will be served by artful demagogues, by ready, designing men, who may, in pursuit of profit as well as popularity, cut out places for themselves and friends, producing at length confusion and anarchy, or, at least, such a bungling system of legislation as will cost more time and money to rectify their blunders than the most extravagant salaries could amount to. What true Republican could wish to exclude from a seat in Congress a physician, lawyer, merchant, farmer, or any other person possessed of such well-known abilities and virtues as to attract the attention and respect of a district which might wish to intrust its interests to him as a Representative? Or, rather, who ought not to desire that, as all offices are open to all, that the son of the poorest citizen might be enabled, if qualified, to fill a seat here or elsewhere, to do it without sacrificing his private interest? Is it reasonable to expect that men should sacrifice domestic ease and the interests of their families to serve their country? It is not just to require it. Human nature, except on great and trying occasions, cannot obey such a requisition. My colleague says that he is not a man of fortune; but, has he not a profession by which he can make more than by his attendance on this House? If not, he has not a right to require such a sacrifice of any other person's time and talents. The Constitution, far from requiring any thing like it, demands that compensation shall be made for all services; and who will desire less for services than a mere subsistence for a person whilst actually employed in such service? I am sure that less than the present pay of members of Congress would not, in their present situation, be a subsistence. I recollect that, when the House of Representatives were debating, in the first session, at New York, whether their daily pay should be four, five, or six dollars, I affirmed

ARTICLE 1, SECTION 6, CLAUSE 1, NO. 17

that the expences of the members where I boarded required that it should be six, that the State of Virginia having once allowed her Delegates to Congress eight dollars, and never less than six, when she bore the whole expense, could not object to her Representatives receiving that sum, when divided, as it was, amongst the States, and spread out over the various duties and taxes of the United States. I asked those, as I might ask my colleague now, who of our constituents could calculate what he would save by any proposed reduction of our pay? I have long suspected, sir, that Republics have lost more by parsimony than they were aware of, and that a misapprehension of some practices in ancient Republics has been artfully kept up, so as to favor Aristocracy and Monarchy. The British Parliament has now no pay; but have they been as independent as their countrymen wished them under the British Government?

The Upper House of the Legislature, which was also the Supreme Court and Privy Council, had a moderate salary, and would never consent to have it raised, that it might be no object to men of small fortunes. But we are told that there is discontent amongst some of our constituents respecting the high salaries of certain officers of Government, as well as of the members of Congress. I am sorry to hear it; but I hope that when they reconsider the subject of their complaint, they will find that it was founded on mistaken ideas of what is the real interest of a Government like this. I believe such a dissatisfaction is subsiding. I know that I was informed that some of my constituents had objected to my re-election on account of my votes at New York for high salaries; but I was re-elected by a great majority of votes in a district of ten counties, and have been again elected by a district composed of six other counties—that county in which I was born, and have always resided, being the only one which made a part of the former district of ten—and yet I have heard no complaints respecting our six dollars: on the contrary, I have been often told they were a moderate compensation. Had my constituents furnished me with intructions to vote for a reduction of it, I should have obeyed them. Had they sent by me remonstrances, such as my colleague says may be heaped upon your table, I should have laid them there; but I should never again ask them for a seat in the House. I should wish to retire.

In reply to the member who had objected to the pay of the SPEAKER, and the difference between the pay of members of the two Houses, Mr. P. said, that whoever would consider the duty of the SPEAKER; his long confinement to the Chair; his painful attention to every word spoken in the House, and his responsibility for the correctness of the Journals—an examination of which must take up much of his time—would surely not think his pay too great. As to the difference between the pay of a Senator and Representative, he had voted for it, from a belief that a Senator having more services to perform than a Representative, had a right to more pay. The Senate not only have to originate bills as this House has, and to revise and amend bills sent from hence, and often to correct the careless errors they contain, but to make themselves acquainted with the Law of Nations, and to be prepared to judge of Treaties;

and also of offences brought before them by impeachments. When the Senators may have gone through the labors of a long session, and the Representatives are returning home, they may be called upon to consider certain nominations to offices, or certain Treaties; and at another time to try certain impeachments. Besides all this, the age of a Senator must be such, by the Constitution, that it is probable that his family is larger, and his pursuits in life more fixed and profitable than those of a Representative, who may be elected when only twenty-five, and therefore his services must require higher compensation. As to the PRESIDENT and VICE PRESIDENT's salaries, I voted for a larger sum than was allowed to either, and thought that the disproportion between them was too great. With respect to the judges, I still think their salaries too small, and so should every one think who will consider the vast importance of their office; the labor of both mind and body which it requires; the laborious course of study through which a man must have gone to be qualified for it, and the lucrative employment such an one must have given up to undertake it. In short, I do not recollect a salary which I think too high. And I must repeat it, that I do not think that large salaries in a Republic can injure it; but that small, inadequate salaries may overturn a Republic.

I am sorry that the question has been brought before us respecting our own pay this session because the elections in Virginia are not over; it would become us much better another session, if re-elected, to reduce it, than to do so when we may be left out. Besides, if I vote for a reduction. I may be suspected of courting popularity; and, if against it, of despising the opinions of my constituents, if they have adopted those which some members tell us prevail amongst their constituents. I do not like to be in such a dilemma, nor to have my independence unnecessarily tried. I wish, as the question is before us, that it may be fully debated here, and even referred to the further consideration of a select committee; because I think the opinions even of a single member and his district should be treated with respect; and that when they have been fairly proved to be founded in error, there will be an end of complaints, and an acquiescence in the decision of this House.

Mr. GILLESPIE proposed an amendment, the scope of which was, that a committee should be appointed to examine and report whether any and what alterations were necessary in the act fixing salaries to the officers under Government. He suggested this amendment from no motive whatever but what was fair. There had been, and there still was, a degree of clamor upon the subject, and it was the duty of the House to pay attention to the voice of the public, whether right or wrong. If, upon investigation, it should appear that the salaries were not higher than they ought to be, then the report of the Committee would be the best method for stopping the public clamor.

Mr. CLAIBORNE hoped that the Committee would not rise, but decide the point. He trusted that no gentleman would again point at him, and say that that the motion came out of his brain. There was not one officer under Government whom he would point out and say, that such an officer had too high a salary. He had expectations that this discussion, by bringing forward the observations of several gentlemen, would in some degree satisfy the people, and that there would be no more pointing out with a finger and saying, *"There goes a six-dollars-a-day man."*

Another member observed, that it was the duty of the House to attend to the voice of their constituents, and for this reason, he should vote for a Committee. He would mention what he had always considered as a most odious distinction, the additional dollar per day, which is to be paid to the Senate from and after the 4th of March next. [The reader will observe, that by the act, members of the Senate were to have seven dollars per day, but the additional dollar was not to commence till the lapse of six years, when all the Senators of the first Congress had gone out.] There was another thing for which he never could see any reason, and that was the giving of twelve dollars per day to the SPEAKER.

Mr. GILES was perfectly convinced that the allowance to the members is small enough already. The saving of a dollar per day suggested by Mr. RUTHERFORD, would be but little, and it was beginning at the worst of resources. The pay ought to be such as would bring persons of middling circumstances into the House; persons neither too high in life nor too low. If the pay was greatly reduced, none but very rich people could afford to give their attendance, and if too high, a seat in the House might be an object to persons of an opposite description. Formerly the State of Virginia allowed eight dollars per day to the members of its Legislature. This sum had since been reduced to six dollars. Mr. G. mentioned this to show that in the practice of individual States, there might be found a precedent for the allowance to members of Congress. He was for voting directly. Mr. G. said, that there was a country from which America had copied a great deal, and very often too much; a country which still had a very pernicious influence in the United States. The members of the British House of Commons received no wages, while the officers of State had immense salaries. It was, however understood, that the British House of Commons were very well paid for the trouble of their attendance. Mr. G. did not wish to see scenes of that kind in this country.

18

THOMAS JEFFERSON (AND JAMES MADISON), PROTEST
TO THE VIRGINIA HOUSE OF DELEGATES
1797
Works 8:322–23, 325–27

That in order to give to the will of the people the influence it ought to have, and the information which may enable them to exercise it usefully, it was a part of the common law, adopted as the law of this land, that their representatives, in the discharge of their functions, should be free from the cognizance or coercion of the co-ordinate branches, Judiciary and Executive; and that their communications with their constituents should of right, as of duty also, be free, full, and unawed by any: that so necessary has this intercourse been deemed in the country from which they derive principally their descent and laws, that the correspondence between the representative and constituent is privileged there to pass free of expense through the channel of the public post, and that the proceedings of the legislature have been known to be arrested and suspended at times until the Representatives could go home to their several counties and confer with their constituents.

. . . . .

That when circumstances required that the ancient confederation of this with the sister States, for the government of their common concerns, should be improved into a more regular and effective form of general government, the same representative principle was preserved in the new legislature, one branch of which was to be chosen directly by the citizens of each State, and the laws and principles remained unaltered which privileged the representative functions, whether to be exercised in the State or General Government, against the cognizance and notice of the co-ordinate branches, Executive and Judiciary; and for its safe and convenient exercise, the intercommunication of the representative and constituent has been sanctioned and provided for through the channel of the public post, at the public expense.

. . . . .

That the grand jury is a part of the Judiciary, not permanent indeed, but in office, *pro hac vice* and responsible as other judges are for their actings and doings while in office: that for the Judiciary to interpose in the legislative department between the constituent and his representative, to control them in the exercise of their functions or duties towards each other, to overawe the free correspondence which exists and ought to exist between them, to dictate what communications may pass between them, and to punish all others, to put the representative into jeopardy of criminal prosecution, of vexation, expense, and punishment before the Judiciary, if his communications, public or private, do not exactly square with their ideas of fact or right, or with their designs of wrong, is to put the legislative department under the feet of the Judiciary, is to leave us, indeed, the shadow, but to take away the substance of representation, which requires essentially that the representative be as free as his constituents would be, that the same interchange of sentiment be lawful between him and them as would be lawful among themselves were they in the personal transaction of their own business; is to do away the influence of the people over the proceedings of their representatives by excluding from their knowledge, by the terror of punishment, all but such information or misinformation as may suit their own views; and is the more vitally dangerous when it is considered that grand jurors are selected by officers nominated and holding their places at the will of the Executive . . . ; and finally, is to give to the Judiciary, and through them to the Executive, a complete preponderance over the legislature rendering ineffectual that wise and cautious distribution of powers made by the constitution between the three branches, and subordinating to the other two that branch which most immediately depends on the people themselves, and is responsible to them at short periods.

19

COXE V. MCCLENACHAN
3 Dall. 478 (Pa. 1798)

JUDGMENT having been obtained against McClenachan, a *ca. sa.* issued, to September term last, and was returned *non est inventus*. The plaintiff then issued a *scire facias* against Huston, the special bail, which was returnable to the present term; and within the first four days of the term, McClenachan was surrendered in discharge of his bail, when a motion was made for leave to enter an *exoneretur*. But the defendant, being a member of the congress, which was in session at the time of his surrender, presented a memorial to the court, demanding, as his privilege, to be discharged from the custody of the sheriff; and it was agreed, that the motion for an *exoneretur*, on behalf of the bail, as well as the motion for a discharge, on behalf of the defendant, should be argued together, upon rules to show cause.

Ingersoll and *Dallas* contended, that both the rules ought to be made absolute. 1st. The defendant would be entitled to his privilege, even if he were in execution; and his being surrendered by his bail, places him in custody at the suit of the plaintiff. Had the defendant been arrested, before he was entitled to privilege, he could not have been held in custody, after his privilege; but, in the present case, he was never in custody until the session of congress had actually commenced. The following authorities were cited on this point: Const. Art. I., § 6; 1 Bl. Com. 64, 66; 11 Vin. Abr. 36; 12 & 13 Wm. III., c. 3; 11 Geo. II., c. 24; 10 Geo. III., c. 50; 3 Com. Dig. 310; 5 T. R. 686; 1 Jac. I., c. 13; 4 Com. Dig. 336.

2d. An *exoneretur* ought to be entered on the bail-piece. Indulgence is always shown to bail, where no injury is produced to the plaintiff. If the defendant had been taken on the *ca. sa.*, or if he had been surrendered, before congress assembled, he would now have been entitled to his privilege; so that the plaintiff has suffered nothing by the delay. The general rule is, that the bail may surrender within the first four days of the term to which the *scire facias* is returnable. Sherid. Pr. 377, 381; 4 Burr. 2134. And if the bail is prevented from making a surrender, by any legal bar, even arising from matter *ex post facto*, he shall be entitled to an *exoneretur*. 1 Burr. 339, 340; Sell. 180; 2 Str. 1217; 1 Burr. 339, 340; Doug. 45; Sell. 183. Whether, therefore, the bail could, or could not, surrender the defendant, after the time that privilege had occurred, the present application is equally well founded. But to place the case on the fairest footing, the bail will consent on the

principles recognised in 1 Str. 419, to remain responsible for surrendering the defendant, within four days after the sessions of congress, provided that time is allowed to make the surrender.

E. Tilghman and *Ross*, the plaintiff's counsel, having considered the proposition, for allowing further time to make the surrender, agreed to it; and THE COURT declared their approbation of the compromise, as affording a good precedent for future cases of a similar kind.

Tilghman then acknowledged, that he thought the privilege of congress extended to arrests on judicial, as well as mesne, process; but controverted the doctrine, that a person arrested before he had privilege, was entitled to be discharged, in consequence of privilege afterwards acquired.

20

KENTUCKY CONSTITUTION OF 1799, ART. 2, SEC. 24
Thorpe 3:1280

The members of the general assembly shall, in all cases, except treason, felony, breach or surety of the peace, be privileged from arrest during their attendance at the sessions of their respective houses, and in going to and returning from the same; and for any speech or debate in either house, they shall not be questioned in any other place.

21

CHARLES PINCKNEY, BREACH OF PRIVILEGE, SENATE 5 Mar. 1800
Annals 10:72, 74

The remainder of the clause respecting privilege is so express on the subjects of privilege from arrest, government of members, and expulsion, that every civil officer in the United States, and every man who has the least knowledge, cannot misunderstand them. I assert that it was the design of the Constitution, and that not only its spirit, but letter, warrant me in the assertion, that it never was intended to give Congress, or either branch, any but specified, and those very limited, privileges indeed. They well knew how oppressively the power of undefined privileges had been exercised in Great Britain, and were determined no such authority should ever be exercised here. They knew that in free countries very few privileges were necessary to the undisturbed exercise of legislative duties, and those few only they determined that Congress should possess; they never meant that the body who ought to be the purest and the least in want of shelter from the operation of laws equally affecting all their fellow citizens, should be able to avoid them; they therefore not only intended, but did confine their privileges within the narrow limits mentioned in the Constitution.

. . . Let us inquire, why the Constitution should have been so attentive to each branch of Congress, so jealous of their privileges, and have shewn so little to the President of the United States in this respect. . . . No privilege of this kind was intended for your Executive, nor any except that which I have mentioned for your Legislature. The Convention which formed the Constitution well knew that this was an important point, and no subject had been more abused than privilege. They therefore determined to set the example, in merely limiting privilege to what was necessary, and no more.

22

COFFIN v. COFFIN
4 Mass. 1 (1803)

Parsons, C. J.: The twenty-first article of the declaration of rights declares that "The freedom of deliberation, speech and debate in either house of the legislature is so essential to the rights of the people, that it cannot be the foundation of any accusation or prosecution, action or complaint in any other court or place whatsoever." On this article the defendant relies for his justification. And if it were competent to the judge on the trial to declare his opinion of the true intent and meaning of it, it must be competent for this court to decide whether his opinion was or was not legal: or the defendant can have no relief by his motion; unless the court are to decide without enquiry or authority, that the opinion was against law. But I know of no action within the jurisdiction of a court, and regularly before it, in which it will not be the duty of the judges to decide all matters of law arising in it, so far as the court is competent to decide on them, according to their own apprehension of the law. Otherwise they will have no jurisdiction of legal questions; or they must act as ministerial agents, deciding according to the will of others.

In considering this article, it appears to me that the privilege secured by it is not so much the privilege of the house as an organized body, as of each individual member composing it, who is entitled to this privilege, even against the declared will of the house. For he does not hold this privilege at the pleasure of the house; but derives it from the will of the people, expressed in the constitution, which is paramount to the will of either or both branches of the legislature. In this respect the privilege here secured resembles other privileges attached to each member by another part of the constitution, by which he is exempted from arrests on *mesne* (or original) process, during his

going to, returning from, or attending the general court. Of these privileges, thus secured to each member, he cannot be deprived, by a resolve of the house, or by an act of the legislature.

These privileges are thus secured, not with the intention of protecting the members against prosecutions for their own benefit, but to support the rights of the people, by enabling their representatives to execute the functions of their office without fear of prosecutions, civil or criminal. I therefore think that the article ought not to be construed strictly, but liberally, that the full design of it may be answered. I will not confine it to delivering an opinion, uttering a speech, or haranguing in debate; but will extend it to the giving of a vote, to the making of a written report, and to every other act resulting from the nature, and in the execution, of the office: and I would define the article, as securing to every member exemption from prosecution, for every thing said or done by him, as a representative, in the exercise of the functions of that office; without enquiring whether the exercise was regular according to the rules of the house, or irregular and against their rules. I do not confine the member to his place in the house; and I am satisfied that there are cases, in which he is entitled to this privilege, when not within the walls of the representatives' chamber.

He cannot be exercising the functions of his office as member of a body, unless the body be in existence. The house must be in session, to enable him to claim this privilege: and it is in session, notwithstanding occasional adjournments, for short intervals for the convenience of its members. If a member therefore be out of the chamber, sitting in committee, executing the commission of the house, it appears to me that such member is within the reason of the article, and ought to be considered within the privilege. The body of which he is a member, is in session, and he, as a member of that body, is in fact discharging the duties of his office. He ought therefore to be protected from civil or criminal prosecutions for every thing said or done by him in the exercise of his functions, as a representative in committee, either in debating, in assenting to, or in draughting a report. Neither can I deny the member his privilege, when executing the duties of his office, in a convention of both houses, although the convention should be holden in the senate chamber.

To this construction of the article it is objected, that a private citizen may have his character basely defamed, without any pecuniary recompense or satisfaction. The truth of the objection is admitted. But he may have other compensation awarded to him by the house, who have power, as a necessary incident, to demand of any of its members a retraction, or apology, of or for any thing he has said, while discharging the duties of his office, either in the house, in committee, or in a convention of the two houses, on pain of expulsion. But if it is allowed that the remedy is inadequate, then a private benefit must submit to the publick good. The injury to the reputation of a private citizen is of less importance to the commonwealth, than the free and unreserved exercise of the duties of a representative, unawed by the fear of legal prosecutions.

A more extensive construction of the privileges of the members secured by this article, I cannot give; because it could not be supported by the language, or the manifest intent of the article. When a representative is not acting as a member of the house, he is not entitled to any privileges above his fellow citizens; nor are the rights of the people affected if he is placed on the same ground, on which his constituents stand. He is secured the liberty of travelling to the house, of attending his duties there, of exercising the functions of his office as a member, and of returning home. But so careful were the people in providing that the privileges, which they, for their own benefit, had secured to their representatives, should not unreasonably prejudice the rights of private citizens; that a member may be arrested upon execution in a civil suit, in cases where he could not be lawfully arrested on original, or *mesne* process. And that offences against law may be duly and seasonably punished, this privilege is not extended to arrests on criminal prosecutions, in any case where by law the member may be prosecuted as a criminal.

If this very liberal construction of the twenty-first article be just; if it be warranted by its language; if it be consonant to its manifest intent and design, the question before the court lies in a narrow compass.

Was *Coffin*, the defendant, in speaking the defamatory words, executing the duties of his office? Or, in other language, was he acting as a representative? If he was, he is entitled to the privilege he claims: If he was not, but was acting as a private citizen, as a private citizen he must answer.

Upon information given by the plaintiff to *Russell*, a member, he had moved a resolution providing for the choice of another notary for *Nantucket;* and on *Russell's* stating that his information was from a respectable person from that place the resolution had passed; the house had proceeded to other business; and the subject matter of the resolution, or of the information, was not in fact before the house; although it is certain that any member might have moved to rescind the resolution. *Russell*, his brother member, was in the passage way, conversing with several gentlemen: the defendant came to him, and enquired the name of *Russell's* informant, who, he had declared, was a respectable gentleman from *Nantucket*. Was this inquiry, thus made, the act of a representative, discharging his duty, or of a private citizen to gratify his curiosity? It was the former, say the defendant's counsel. Whether it was or not, certainly it was innocent. But to pursue the evidence: the defendant was answered: whatever was his motive, he had received the information. If upon it, he intended again to call up the resolution, he might have done it. But no motion, for that purpose, was ever made. He then utters to *Russell* the defamatory words. What part of his legislative duty was he now performing? It is said that he might apprehend that the plaintiff was a candidate for the office of notary; and that his motive might be to dissuade *Russell* from giving him his vote. But there is no evidence that the defendant supposed the plaintiff to be a candidate, and it is in evidence that the plaintiff was not a candidate. It is also apparent that the defendant believed that

Russell was not ignorant of the indictment against the plaintiff, and of his acquittal. I cannot therefore assign to the defendant any other motive for his indiscreet language, but to correct *Russell* for giving to the plaintiff the appellation of a respectable gentleman; and to justify the correction by asserting that an honourable acquittal, by the verdict of a jury, is not evidence of innocence. It is not therefore possible for me to presume that the defendant, in using thus publickly, the defamatory words, even contemplated that he was in the discharge of any official duty. This enquiry by the defendant, and his replies might have been made, for all the purposes intended by him, in *State-Street*, or in any other place, as well as in the representatives' chamber: and it is not easy for me to conceive that any language or conduct of a representative must be considered as official, merely because he chooses the representatives' chamber for the scene.

But it has been urged, that the privilege must extend to a representative giving information to a brother member, on any subject before the house; or which may be expected to come before the house; for the information may be necessary to enable the member informed to discharge his official duty with ability and propriety. Without remarking the essential distinction between a man's seeking information on subjects relating to his office, and his actual execution of its functions: and without observing the extreme difficulty of supposing that defamatory words, maliciously uttered, can ever be considered as useful information: I do clearly admit, that a representative will certainly be entitled to his privilege in all cases, where he shall give information in the discharge of his official duty; although the manner may be irregular, and against the rules of the house. But when a representative pleads his privilege, to entitle himself to it, it must appear that some language or conduct of his, in the character of a representative, is the foundation of the prosecution, for in no other character can he claim the privilege.

But in actions for defamatory words against a member, he may, in cases to which his privilege does not extend, defend himself like any other citizen, by proving that the words were spoken for a justifiable purpose, not maliciously, nor with a design to defame the character of any man. And this defence will avail every man charged with slander, although it may be that the words uttered are not true. I do not therefore consider any citizen, who is a representative, answerable in a prosecution for defamation, where the words charged were uttered in the execution of his official duty although they were spoken maliciously: or where they were not uttered in the execution of his official duty, if they were not spoken maliciously with an intent to defame the character of any person. And I do consider a representative holden to answer for defamatory words, spoken maliciously, and not in discharging the functions of his office. But to consider every malicious slander, uttered by a citizen, who is a representative, as within his privilege, because it was uttered in the walls of the representatives' chamber to another member, but not uttered in executing his official duty, would be to extend the privilege farther than was intended by the people, or than is consistent with sound policy; and would render the representatives' chamber a sanctuary for calumny: an effect, which never has been, and I confidently trust, never will be endured by any house of representatives of *Massachusetts.*

It has been said, that although the judge at the trial had no other information of the nature and extent of the defendant's privileges but what he derived from the constitution; yet that since the trial, on the first of March instant, the house passed a resolution declaratory of the privileges of its members, to which declaration we are obliged to conform in our judgments: because the house is to judge exclusively of its own privileges.

That the house is to judge exclusively of its privileges; for certain intents and purposes, is very certain: but if it is to exclude courts of law from judging of the privileges of its members in every case, the consequences would be unfortunate to the members. If a member, in any action pleads his privilege, he submits it to the judgment of the court; and if it be allowed, it is by virtue of the judgment of the court. All therefore, which the court could do, upon such a hypothesis, would be to reject the plea, lest, in judging of it, it should invade the privileges of the house.

The resolution declares that words spoken by any member, within the walls of the house, relative to any subject under their consideration, either in their separate capacity, or in a convention of both branches of the legislature, whether the member speaking such words addresses himself in debate to the chair or deliberates or advises with another member respecting such subject, are alone and exclusively cognizable by the house; and that for any other tribunal to take cognizance of words thus spoken would be a violation of the twenty-first article of the constitution. And the words relied on for the defendant are, *"whether the member speaking such words addressed himself to the chair, or deliberates or advises with another member respecting such subject."*

As it is admitted by the defendants counsel that this court is competent to construe the twenty-first article, in order to decide whether the facts in the case bring the defendant within it; so also it is admitted that the court is competent to construe this resolution for the same purpose. The resolution, judging from the face of it, does not appear to be an act of the house in any case of contempt on trial before it; but to be a general declaration of the privileges secured to the members by the twenty-first article of the constitution; because it is declared that an invasion of these privileges would be a violation of that article. I consider the house therefore as defining the constitutional privileges of its members, relating to words spoken by them. In this declaration, the words must be spoken on a subject before the house, and either addressed to the chair, or by one member to another by way of deliberation and advice on the same subject. In either case the words must be spoken officially, although in the latter case they may be spoken in a disorderly and irregular manner. The house has not therefore claimed any privileges for its members, when prosecuted for slander, unless the words charged were spoken officially in the character of a representative. This inference is inevitable, unless it should be

unreasonably concluded that one member could deliberate or advise with another member, on a subject before the house, having abandoned his official duty, and acting as a private citizen. Whether I do, or do not allow to the resolution, thus passed, the force of law: I am satisfied that it claims no privileges, but what are secured to the members by the constitution, of which, as far as it extends, it is in affirmance. The resolution does not therefore, in my opinion, aid the defendant; for it appears, from the facts in the case, that the defamatory words, charged on the defendant, were not spoken by him on a subject before the house, either in an address to the chair, or by way of deliberation or advice with another member.

It has been urged that a declaration of privileges made by the house, whether those privileges do, or do not belong to it, has the force of law, and is obligatory, in all cases, or the courts of justice. A declaration of that nature is not now before us; for I am satisfied that the house has all the privileges claimed by its resolution. Whenever a declaration shall be made by the house, claiming privileges not belonging to it in the opinion of the judges of a court of law, let the judges then decide the question. The merits of it must depend on a careful consideration of the constitution, with a due regard to the privileges and prerogatives of the house resulting from it. On this subject I give no opinion; but from the observations I have already made, it may not be improper to declare, that if it had appeared to me that the words charged on the defendant, had been officially spoken by him without the walls of the representatives' chamber, either in a convention of the two houses holden in the senate chamber, or in a committee, while executing the commission of the house then in session, as I am now advised, I would have allowed him his privilege, although by the resolution produced, the house seem to confine its privileges to words spoken within the walls of the representatives' chamber.

But the danger of conflicting jurisdictions has been insisted on with much ability and eloquence, if we should support the present action. I am sensible that where a conflict of final jurisdictions exists in any state, there must be a defect in the laws of that state. In my opinion, this state is not liable to the opprobrium: for I do not conceive that final conflicting jurisdictions here are consistent either with our constitution or statutes.

To introduce examples from the *British* house of commons, cannot much illustrate the subject. The privileges of that house are not derived from any written constitution, but have been acquired by the successful struggles of centuries, directed either against the monarchy or an hereditary aristocracy. The exertions of the commons have generally been popular, because the people were supposed to reap the fruits of them. In this state we have a written constitution, formed by the people, in which they have defined, not only the powers, but the privileges of the house, either by express words, or by necessary implication. A struggle for privileges, in this state, would be a contest against the people, to wrest from them what they have not chosen to grant. And it may be added that the grant of privileges is a restraint on the rights of private citizens, which cannot be further restrained but by some constitutional law. These principles are perfectly consistent with the resolution of the house, which is not a claim of any further privileges not granted by the constitution; but a description of some, and only of some privileges there granted.

I consider the house of representatives, not only as an integral branch of the legislature, and as an essential part of the two houses in convention, but also as a court having final and exclusive cognizance of all matters within its jurisdiction, for the purposes for which it was vested with jurisdiction. It has jurisdiction of the election of its members; of the choice of its officers; of its rules of proceeding; and of all contempts against the house, either in its presence, or by violating the constitutional privileges of its *members*. When the house is proceeding as a court, it has, exclusively, authority to decide whether the matter before it be, or be not within its jurisdiction, without the legal controul of any other court. As to contempts, the house proceeds against the offender to punish the contempt. Courts of law proceed to punish offences against the state, and to redress private wrongs. The same act may be a contempt against the house, an offence against the state, and an injury to an individual: and in all these respects, proceedings may be had against the offender.

When the house decides in a question of election, it can conclusively decide on the right of voting claimed by any elector, so far as is necessary to settle the election. But an elector, illegally deprived of his right of voting, may demand redress for this wrong against the selectmen by a suit at law. This was decided in the cases of *Gardner* and of *Kilham against the selectmen of Salem:* where the only defence set up was that the plaintiffs had no right to vote. Upon this question the judgments of both courts, however rendered, could be executed without any interference. Let me illustrate the subject by supposing a case or two. A member is assaulted in the town, in which the house is in session, and is cruelly beaten, for words spoken in the house in the execution of his duty. The house may proceed against the assailant for a contempt: and cannot the member prosecute him at law for damages? And may not the grand jury indict him for a breach of the peace? And neither can the proceedings of a court of law controul the proceedings of the house, nor can the proceedings of the house controul the courts of law. The judgments of each court, whatever may be the result, can be executed without any interference. Suppose a publick officer indicted for extortion, and upon trial acquitted at law; cannot he afterwards be convicted by the senate on an impeachment? Both judgments may be executed without interference. The courts of law proceed to punish the offender, and he is acquitted. The power of the senate is censorial, and exercised to preserve purity in office. If it should be supposed that the senate cannot proceed after an acquittal at law, it should be remembered that, by the express provision of the constitution, courts of law may proceed after a conviction in senate; and in the proceedings at law the jury may acquit: and it could not have been intended to place the senate as subordinate to a court of law. The true design of that provision was a mere cautionary declaration that the proceedings in the senate were not to *punish* of-

fenders against the state, but for a different end. And I would add that, in the present case, if the house, of which the defendant was a member, had proceeded against the plaintiff for a contempt in suing this action; whatever had been the result of its proceedings, this court could not have interfered, or granted any relief, until the sentence had been performed. And as this judgment could not have affected those proceedings, so neither could those proceedings have controuled the authority of this court. The two courts are independent and have each exclusive cognizance of the matters within its jurisdiction: and although the transaction animadverted on may be the same, yet the proceedings are for different purposes, and the judgments of both courts may be executed without any interference. There cannot therefore be any conflict of jurisdictions.

Extreme cases of the abuse of power, either in the house of representatives, or in this court, may be imagined; but they are not to be argued from, to influence legal decisions.

Since the argument of this cause, I have examined the subject with as much attention as I have been able to give to it, amidst all the business of the court pressing on us, with a strong disposition to guard the privileges of the house, and of its members, because their privileges are essential to the rights of the people, and ought to be supported, by every good citizen, according to their true limits.

From this examination I am satisfied that, whatever may be our decision of the question, it is within our jurisdiction thus brought before us; and that no breach of the privileges of the house, or a conflict with its jurisdiction can result from our determination.

I am convinced, after much consideration, that the facts presented by the case do not entitle the defendant to the privilege, which he claims; and that, for this cause, the verdict ought not to be set aside.

Under this impression, to give a different opinion would be a desertion of a solemn duty, and a gross prevarication with my own conscience.

In this opinion of the *chief justice*, the other judges, *viz. Sedgwick, Sewall, Thacher* and *Parker* severally declared their full and entire concurrence.

23

HURST'S CASE
4 Dall. 387 (C.C.D.Pa 1804)

On the affidavit of *Timothy Hurst*, it appeared, that he had come from his residence at New York, to attend the trial of *Hurst* v. *Hurst* (in which he was a party) at the present term; that after his arrival he had been subpoenaed as a witness, in the case, of *W. Hurst* v. *Rodney*, which was, also, upon the trial list; that yesterday (the 13th of November) while he was at his lodgings, in *Hardy's* tavern, he had been arrested by the sheriff upon a *ca. sa.* issuing from the supreme Court of Pennsylvania; and that he had come to Philadelphia, and was remaining here, at the time of the arrest, only upon the business of his suit, and in obedience to the subpoena.

Ingersoll upon these facts, moved, that Hurst should be discharged from the custody of the sheriff. And he argued, in support of the motion, 1st. That the application was properly addressed to this Court, and not to the Supreme Court. 2d. That a discharge from the *ca. sa.* by order of the court, without the consent, or concurrence, of the plaintiff, would not operate as a satisfaction of the debt; and another execution might afterwards be taken out. 3d. That the discharge by a competent Court, would excuse and protect the sheriff, in an action for an escape. *Barnes* 2. *Ld. Raym.* 1524. *Bac. Abr.* 631. 5 *T. Rep.* 686. 5 *Bac. Abr.* 617. 673. 1 *H. Bl.* 636. *Tidd Pr.* 61, 2. *Stra.* 990. 1 *Dall. Rep.* 356. 3 *Dall.* 478. *Dy.* 60. *a.*

Rawle, in opposition to the discharge, insisted, that, under the circumstances of this case, Hurst was neither privileged as a witness, nor as a party. 1st. Not as a witness. The arrest was made at the lodgings of the defendant: but although a witness is privileged, while he is going from home, while he is actually attending, the Court, and while he is returning to his home; he is not privileged while he is at home. 2d. Not as a party. If the privilege of a party is not limited to the same times and places, as the privilege of a witness, its extent is indefinite, and its operation unequal. Is a suitor in this Court, residing in Georgia, protected from arrest, as soon as he receives the notice of trial, in his own state, and in every state, through which he passes, on his journey to Philadelphia? Again: Is every resident citizen of Philadelphia, who has a suit depending, privileged during the trial term, not only while actually attending the Court, but while at home, with his family? And if not, why should a non-resident suitor be protected at his lodgings, which are his home? There is, indeed, a distinction between the cases, favourable to the witness; for, a witness is under an absolute obligation to attend the Court; but a party may prosecute his suit by an attorney, without personal attendance. Besides, the sheriff will be bound to show a regular discharge, in an action for an escape; and if the Supreme Court should adhere to the rule in *Starret's* case, the order of this Court will not be a justification. 1 *Brownl.* 15. *Barn.* 200. 5 *T. Rep.* 686. 2. *Cha. Ca.* 69. *T. Raym.* 100. 2 *Ld. Raym.* 1524. 6 *Com. Dig.* 89. 88. *Woods Inst.* 478. 2 *Bro. Abr.* 159. *Tit. Priv. pl.* 37.

Washington, justice. I will not examine the powers of the Supreme Court of the state, upon the present occasion. It is enough to assertain, that the power of this Court is competent to the object proposed. If, indeed, any injury would be done either to the plaintiff in the suit, or to the sheriff (both of whom have acted innocently, and without knowledge of the facts, on which the claim of privilege arises) by our interposition, we might be induced to pause upon the subject. But, as to the plaintiff, it is clear, that he may renew his execution, whenever the privilege ceases: And, as to the sheriff, the order of a Court of competent jurisdiction, touching the subject matter, must be a conclusive justification in every other court, acting upon sound principles of law and justice.

To decide the principal question, therefore, I find it necessary to go no further, than to state, that I think the witness was, in this case, privileged, while he was at his lodgings. The subpoena was in force; and the arrest of the witness at that place, has all the effects which could be produced by an arrest in the streets while coming to, or going from, the Court.

Peters, justice. I concur in the sentiments, that have been expressed by the presiding judge; and add, as my separate opinion, that the party is intitled to be discharged, upon both the grounds of privilege.

A special order of discharge was, accordingly, made, and filed; at the instance of *Dallas,* who appeared for the sheriff.

24

JOSEPH STORY, COMMENTARIES ON THE CONSTITUTION 2:§§ 849–63
1833

§ 849. In respect to compensation, there is, at present, a marked distinction between the members of the British parliament, and the members of congress; the former not being, at present, entitled to any pay. Formerly, indeed, the members of the house of commons were entitled to receive wages from their constituents; but the last known case is that of Andrew Marvell, who was a member from Hull, in the first parliament after the restoration of Charles the Second. Four shillings sterling a day used to be allowed for a knight of the shire; and two shillings a day for a member of a city or borough; and this rate was established in the reign of Edward the Third. And we are told, that two shillings a day, the allowance to a burgess, was so considerable a sum, in these ancient times, that there are many instances, where boroughs petitioned to be excused from sending members to parliament, representing, that they are engaged in building bridges or other public works, and, therefore, unable to bear so extraordinary an expense. It is believed, that the practice in America during its colonial state was, if not universally, at least generally, to allow a compensation to be paid to members; and the practice is believed to be absolutely universal, under the state constitutions. The members are not, however, always paid out of the public treasury; but the practice still exists, constitutionally, or by usage, in some of the states, to charge the amount of the compensation fixed by the legislature upon the constituents, and levy it in the state tax. That has certainly been the general course in the state of Massachusetts; and it was probably adopted from the ancient practice in England.

§ 850. Whether it is, on the whole, best to allow to members of legislative bodies a compensation for their services, or whether their services should be considered merely honorary, is a question admitting of much argument on each side; and it has accordingly found strenuous advocates, and opponents, not only in speculation, but in practice. It has been already seen, that in England none is now allowed, or claimed; and there can be little doubt, that public opinion is altogether in favour of their present course. On the other hand, in America an opposite opinion prevails among those, whose influence is most impressive with the people on such subjects. It is not surprising, that under such circumstances, there should have been a considerable diversity of opinion manifested in the convention itself. The proposition to allow compensation out of the public treasury, to members of the house of representatives, was originally carried by a vote of eight states against three; and to the senators by a vote of seven states against three, one being divided. At a subsequent period, a motion to strike out the payment out of the public treasury was lost by a vote of four states in the affirmative, and five in the negative, two being divided; and the whole proposition, as to representatives, was (as amended) lost by a vote of five states for it, and five against it, one being divided. And as to senators, a motion was made, that they should be paid by their respective states, which was lost, five states voting for it, and six against it; and then the proposition to pay them out of the public treasury was lost by a similar vote. At a subsequent period a proposition was reported, that the compensation of the members of both houses should be made by the state, in which they were chosen; and ultimately the present plan was agreed to by a vote of nine states against two. Such a fluctuation of opinion exhibits in a strong light the embarrassing considerations, which surrounded the subject.

§ 851. The principal reasons in favour of a compensation may be presumed to have been the following. In the first place, the advantage, it secured, of commanding the first talents of the nation in the public councils, by removing a virtual disqualification, that of poverty, from that large class of men, who, though favoured by nature, might not be favoured by fortune. It could hardly be expected, that such men would make the necessary sacrifices in order to gratify their ambition for a public station; and if they did, there was a corresponding danger, that they might be compelled by their necessities, or tempted by their wants, to yield up their independence, and perhaps their integrity, to the allurements of the corrupt, or the opulent. In the next place, it would, in a proportionate degree, gratify the popular feeling by enlarging the circle of candidates, from which members might be chosen, and bringing the office within the reach of persons in the middle ranks of society, although they might not possess shining talents; a course best suited to the equality found, and promulgated in a republic. In the next place, it would make a seat in the national councils, as attractive, and perhaps more so, than in those of the state, by the superior emoluments of office. And in the last place, it would be in conformity to a long and well settled practice, which embodied public sentiment, and had been sanctioned by public approbation.

§ 852. On the other hand, it might be, and it was, probably, urged against it, that the practice of allowing compensation was calculated to make the office rather more a matter of bargain and speculation, than of high political ambition. It would operate, as an inducement to vulgar and groveling demagogues, of little talent, and narrow means, to defeat the claims of higher candidates, than themselves; and with a view to the compensation alone to engage in all sorts of corrupt intrigues to procure their own election. It would thus degrade these high trusts from being deemed the reward of distinguished merit, and strictly honorary, to a mere traffic for political office, which would first corrupt the people at the polls, and then subject their liberties to be bartered by their venal candidate. Men of talents in this way would be compelled to degradation, in order to acquire office, or would be excluded by more unworthy, or more cunning candidates, who would feel, that the labourer was worthy of his hire. There is no danger, that the want of compensation would deter men of suitable talents and virtues, even in the humbler walks of life, from becoming members; since it could scarcely be presumed, that the public gratitude would not, by other means, aid them in their private business, and increase their just patronage. And if, in a few cases, it should be otherwise, it should not be forgotten, that one of the most wholesome lessons to be taught in republics was, that men should learn suitable economy and prudence in their private affairs; and that profusion and poverty were, with a few splendid exceptions, equally unsafe to be entrusted with the public rights and interests, since, if they did not betray, they would hardly be presumed willing to protect them. The practice of England abundantly showed, that compensation was not necessary to bring into public life the best talents and virtues of the nation. In looking over her list of distinguished statesmen, of equal purity and patriotism, it would be found, that comparatively few had possessed opulence; and many had struggled through life with the painful pressure of narrow resources, the *res augustae domi*.

§ 853. It does not become the commentator to say, whether experience has as yet given more weight to the former, than to the latter reasons. Certain it is, that the convention, in adopting the rule of allowing a compensation, had principally in view the importance of securing the highest dignity and independence in the discharge of legislative functions, and the justice, as well as duty of a free people, possessing adequate means, to indemnify those, who were employed in their service, against all the sacrifices incident to their station. It has been justly observed, that the principle of compensation to those, who render services to the public, runs through the whole constitution.

§ 854. If it be proper to allow a compensation for services to the members of congress, there seems the utmost propriety in its being paid out of the public treasury of the United States. The labour is for the benefit of the nation, and it should properly be remunerated by the nation. Besides; if the compensation were to be allowed by the states, or by the constitutents of the members, if left to their discretion, it might keep the latter in a state of slavish dependence, and might introduce great inequalities in the allowance. And if it were to be ascertained by congress, and paid by the constitutents, there would always be danger, that the rule would be fixed to suit those, who were the least enlightened, and the most parsimonious, rather than those, who acted upon a high sense of the dignity and the duties of the station. Fortunately, it is left for the decision of congress. The compensation is "to be ascertained by law;" and never addresses itself to the pride, or the parsimony, the local prejudices, or local habits of any part of the Union. It is fixed with a liberal view to the national duties, and is paid from the national purse. If the compensation had been left, to be fixed by the state legislature, the general government would have become dependent upon the governments of the states; and the latter could almost, at their pleasure, have dissolved it. Serious evils were felt from this source under the confederation, by which each state was to maintain its own delegates in congress; for it was found, that the states too often were operated upon by local considerations, as contradistinguished from general and national interests.

§ 855. The only practical question, which seems to have been farther open upon this head, is, whether the compensation should have been ascertained by the constitution itself, or left, (as it now is,) to be ascertained from time to time by congress. If fixed by the constitution, it might, from the change of the value of money, and the modes of life, have become too low, and utterly inadequate. Or it might have become too high in consequence of serious changes in the prosperity of the nation. It is wisest, therefore, to have it left, where it is, to be decided by congress from time to time, according to their own sense of justice, and a large view of the national resources. There is no danger, that it will ever become excessive, without exciting general discontent, and then it will soon be changed from the reaction of public opinion. The danger rather is, that public opinion will become too sensitive upon this subject; and refuse to allow any addition to what may be at the time a very moderate allowance. In the actual practice of the government, this subject has rarely been stirred without producing violent excitements at the elections. This alone is sufficient to establish the safety of the actual exercise of the power by the bodies, with which it is lodged, both in the state and national legislatures. It is proper, however, to add, that the omission to provide some constitutional mode of fixing the pay of members of congress, without leaving the subject to their discretion, formed in some minds a strong objection to the constitution.

§ 856. The next part of the clause regards the privilege of the members from arrest, except for crimes, during their attendance at the sessions of congress, and their going to, and returning from them. This privilege is conceded by law to the humblest suitor and witness in a court of justice; and it would be strange, indeed, if it were denied to the highest functionaries of the state in the discharge of their public duties. It belongs to congress in common with all other legislative bodies, which exist, or have existed in America, since its first settlement, under every variety of government; and it has immemorially constituted a privilege of both houses of the British parliament. It seems absolutely indispensable for the just exercise of the legislative power in every nation, purporting to possess a free constitution of government; and it cannot be surrendered without endangering the public liberties, as well as the private independence of the members.

§ 857. This privilege from arrest, privileges them of course against all process, the disobedience to which is punishable by attachment of the person, such as a *subpoena ad respondendum, aut testificandum,* or a summons to serve on a jury; and (as has been justly observed) with reason, because a member has superior duties to perform in another place. When a representative is withdrawn from his seat by a summons, the people, whom he represents, lose their voice in debate and vote, as they do in his voluntary absence. When a senator is withdrawn by summons, his state loses half its voice in debate and vote, as it does in his voluntary absence. The enormous disparity of the evil admits of no comparison. The privilege, indeed, is deemed not merely the privilege of the member, or his constituents, but the privilege of the house also. And every man must at his peril take notice, who are the members of the house returned of record.

§ 858. The privilege of the peers of the British parliament to be free from arrest, in civil cases, is for ever sacred and inviolable. For other purposes, (as for common process,) it seems, that their privilege did not extend, but from the teste of the summons to parliament, and for twenty days before and after the session. But that period has now, as to all common process but arrest, been taken away by statute. The privilege of the members of the house of commons from arrest is for forty days after every prorogation, and for forty days before the next appointed meeting, which in effect is as long, as the parliament lasts, it seldom being prorogued for more than four score days, at a time. In case of a dissolution of parliament, it does not appear, that the privilege is confined to any precise time; the rule being, that the party is entitled to it for a convenient time, *redeundo.*

§ 859. The privilege of members of parliament formerly extended also to their servants and goods, so that they could not be arrested. But so far, as it went to obstruct the ordinary course of justice in the British courts, it has since been restrained. In the members of congress, the privilege is strictly personal, and does not extend to their servants or property. It is also, in all cases confined to a reasonable time, *eundo, morando, et redeundo,* instead of being limited by a precise number of days. It was probably from a survey of the abuses of privilege, which for a long time defeated in England the purposes of justice, that the constitution has thus marked its boundary with a sedulous caution.

§ 860. The effect of this privilege is, that the arrest of the member is unlawful, and a trespass *ab initio,* for which he may maintain an action, or proceed against the aggressor by way of indictment. He may also be discharged by motion to a court of justice, or upon a writ of *habeas corpus;* and the arrest may also be punished, as a contempt of the house.

§ 861. In respect to the time of going and returning, the law is not so strict in point of time, as to require the party to set out immediately on his return; but allows him time to settle his private affairs, and to prepare for his journey. Nor does it nicely scan his road, nor is his protection forfeited, by a little deviation from that, which is most direct; for it is supposed, that some superior convenience or necessity directed it. The privilege from arrest takes place by force of the election, and before the member has taken his seat, or is sworn.

§ 862. The exception to the privilege is, that it shall not extend to "treason, felony, or breach of the peace." These words are the same as those, in which the exception to the privilege of parliament is usually expressed at the common law, and was doubtless borrowed from that source. Now, as all crimes are offences against the peace, the phrase "breach of the peace" would seem to extend to all indictable offences, as well those, which are, in fact, attended with force and violence, as those, which are only constructive breaches of the peace of the government, inasmuch as they violate its good order. And so in truth it was decided in parliament, in the case of a seditious libel, published by a member, (Mr. Wilkes,) against the opinion of Lord Camden and the other judges of the Court of Common Pleas; and, as it will probably now be thought, since the party spirit of those times has subsided, with entire good sense, and in furtherance of public justice. It would be monstrous, that any member should protect himself from arrest, or punishment for a libel, often a crime of the deepest malignity and mischief, while he would be liable to arrest, for the pettiest assault, or the most insignificant breach of the peace.

§ 863. The next great and vital privilege is the freedom of speech and debate, without which all other privileges would be comparatively unimportant, or ineffectual. This privilege also is derived from the practice of the British parliament, and was in full exercise in our colonial legislatures, and now belongs to the legislature of every state in the Union, as matter of constitutional right. In the British parliament it is a claim of immemorial right, and is now farther fortified by an act of parliament; and it is always particularly demanded of the king in person by the speaker of the house of commons, at the opening of every new parliament. But this privilege is strictly confined to things done in the course of parliamentary proceedings, and does not cover things done beyond the place and limits of duty. Therefore, although a speech delivered in the house of commons is privileged, and the member cannot be questioned respecting it elsewhere; yet, if he publishes his speech, and it contains libellous matter, he is liable to an action and prosecution therefor, as in common cases of libel. And the same principles seem applicable to the privilege of debate and speech in congress. No man ought to have a right to defame others under colour of a performance of the duties of his office. And if he does so in the actual discharge of his duties in congress, that furnishes no reason, why he should be enabled through the medium of the press to destroy the reputation, and invade the repose of other citizens. It is neither within the scope of his duty, nor in furtherance of public rights, or public policy. Every citizen has as good a right to be protected by the laws from malignant scandal, and false charges, and defamatory imputations, as a member of congress has to utter them in his seat. If it were otherwise, a man's character might be taken away without the possibility of redress, either by the malice, or indiscretion, or overweening self-conceit of a member of congress. It is proper, however, to apprise the learned reader, that it has been recently denied in congress by very distinguished lawyers, that the privilege of speech and debate in congress does not extend to publication of his speech. And they ground themselves upon an important distinction arising from the actual differences between English and American legislation. In the former, the publication of the debates is not strictly lawful, except by license of the house. In the latter, it is a common right, exercised and supported by the direct encouragement of the body. This reasoning deserves a very attentive examination.

SEE ALSO:

Stroud's Case, 3 How. St. Tr. 235 (1629)

Barnard v. *Mordaunt*, 96 Eng. Rep. 939 (C.P. 1754)

Lord Mansfield, 1770, Potter's Dwarris on Statutes 601

Hatsell's Precedents in the House of Commons 1:206–7 (1776)

Vermont Constitution of 1786, ch. 1, art. 16, Thorpe 6:3753

Records of the Federal Convention, Farrand 1:210, 211, 221, 369–70, 377–79, 383, 418, 433–34; 2:129, 135, 140, 141, 142, 156, 166, 282–83, 334, 567, 568, 593

James McHenry, Maryland House of Delegates, 29 Nov. 1787, Farrand 3:148

Luther Martin, Maryland House of Delegates, 29 Nov. 1787, Farrand 3:155

Debate in Massachusetts Ratifying Convention, 19 Jan. 1788, Elliot 2:52–54

James Iredell, Amendments to the Constitution Proposed at North Carolina Ratifying Convention, 1 Aug. 1788, Elliot 4:249

House of Representatives, An Amendment to Art. 1, sec. 6, par. 1, 14 Aug. 1789, Annals 1:728–29

James Wilson, On Crimes, Lectures on Law (1791), Works 2:618, 619

United States v. *Cooper*, 4 Dall. 341 (C.C.D.Pa. 1800)

St. George Tucker, Blackstone's Commentaries 1:App. 198–99 (1803)

Blight v. *Fisher*, 3 Fed. Cas. 704, Case no. 1,542 (C.C.D.N.J. 1809)

William Rawle, A View of the Constitution of the United States 179–82 (2d ed. 1829)

Article 1, Section 6, Clause 2

No Senator or Representative shall, during the Time for which he was elected, be appointed to any civil Office under the Authority of the United States, which shall have been created, or the Emoluments whereof shall have been encreased during such time; and no Person holding any Office under the United States, shall be a Member of either House during his Continuance in Office.

1

RECORDS OF THE FEDERAL CONVENTION

[1:379; Yates, 22 June]

[Resolved that the members of the first branch of the National Legislature . . . to be ineligible to any office established by a particular State, or under the authority of the U. States, . . . during the term of service, and under the national Government for the space of one year after its expiration.]

Mr. Gorham. I move that after the words, *and under the national government for one year after its expiration,* be struck out.

Mr. King for the motion. It is impossible to carry the system of exclusion so far; and in this instance we refine too much by going to *utopian* lengths. It is a mere cobweb.

Mr. Butler. We have no way of judging of mankind but by experience. Look at the history of the government of Great Britain, where there is a very flimsy exclusion—Does it not ruin their government? A man takes a seat in parliament to get an office for himself or friends, or both; and this is the great source from which flows its great venality and corruption.

Mr. Wilson. I am for striking out the words moved for. Strong reasons must induce me to disqualify a good man from office. If you do, you give an opportunity to the dependent or avaricious man to fill it up, for to them offices are objects of desire. If we admit there may be cabal and intrigue between the executive and legislative bodies, the exclusion of one year will not prevent the effects of it. But we ought to hold forth every honorable inducement for men of abilities to enter the service of the public.—This is truly a republican principle. Shall talents, which entitle a man to public reward, operate as a punishment? While a member of the legislature, he ought to be excluded from any other office, but no longer. Suppose a war breaks out and a number of your best military characters were members; must we lose the benefit of their services? Had this been the case in the beginning of the war, what would have been our situation?—and what has happened may happen again.

Mr. Madison. Some gentlemen give too much weight and others too little to this subject. If you have no exclusive clause, there may be danger of creating offices or augmenting the stipends of those already created, in order to gratify some members if they were not excluded. Such an instance has fallen within my own observation. I am therefore of opinion, that no office ought to be open to a member, which may be created or augmented while he is in the legislature.

Mr. Mason. It seems as if it was taken for granted, that all offices will be filled by the executive, while I think many will remain in the gift of the legislature. In either case, it is necessary to shut the door against corruption. If otherwise, they may make or multiply offices, in order to fill them. Are gentlemen in earnest when they suppose that this exclusion will prevent the first characters from coming forward? Are we not struck at seeing the luxury and venality which has already crept in among us? If not checked we shall have ambassadors to every petty state in Europe—

the little republic of *St. Marino* not excepted. We must in the present system remove the temptation. I admire many parts of the British constitution and government, but I detest their corruption.—Why has the power of the crown so remarkably increased the last century? A stranger, by reading their laws, would suppose it considerably diminished; and yet, by the sole power of appointing the increased officers of government, corruption pervades every town and village in the kingdom. If such a restriction should abridge the right of election, it is still necessary, as it will prevent the people from ruining themselves; and will not the same causes here produce the same effects? I consider this clause as the corner-stone on which our liberties depend—and if we strike it out we are erecting a fabric for our destruction.

Mr. Gorham. The corruption of the English government cannot be applied to America. This evil exists there in the venality of their boroughs: but even this corruption has its advantage, as it gives stability to their government. We do not know what the effect would be if members of parliament were excluded from offices. The great bulwark of our liberty is the frequency of elections, and their great danger is the septennial parliaments.

Mr. Hamilton. In all general questions which become the subjects of discussion, there are always some truths mixed with falsehoods. I confess there is danger where men are capable of holding two offices. Take mankind in general, they are vicious—their passions may be operated upon. We have been taught to reprobate the danger of influence in the British government, without duly reflecting how far it was necessary to support a good government. We have taken up many ideas upon trust, and at last, pleased with our own opinions, establish them as undoubted truths. Hume's opinion of the British constitution confirms the remark, that there is always a body of firm patriots, who often shake a corrupt administration. Take mankind as they are, and what are they governed by? Their passions. There may be in every government a few choice spirits, who may act from more worthy motives. One great error is that we suppose mankind more honest than they are. Our prevailing passions are ambition and interest; and it will ever be the duty of a wise government to avail itself of those passions, in order to make them subservient to the public good—for these ever induce us to action. Perhaps a few men in a state, may, from patriotic motives, or to display their talents, or to reap the advantage of public applause, step forward; but if we adopt the clause we destroy the motive. I am therefore against all exclusions and refinements, except only in this case; that when a member takes his seat, he should vacate every other office. It is difficult to put any exclusive regulation into effect. We must in some degree submit to the inconvenience.

The question was then put for striking out—4 ayes—4 noes—3 states divided. New-York of the number.

[1:386; Madison, 23 June]

Genl. Pinkney moves to strike out the ineligibility of members of the 1st. branch to offices established "by a particular State." He argued from the inconveniency to which such a restriction would expose both the members of the 1st. branch, and the States wishing for their services; from the smallness of the object to be attained by the restriction.

It wd. seem from the ideas of some that we are erecting a Kingdom to be divided agst. itself, he disapproved such a fetter on the Legislature.

Mr. Sherman seconds the motion. It wd. seem that we are erecting a Kingdom at war with itself. The Legislature ought not to be fettered in such a case. on the question

Masts. no. Cont. ay. N. Y. ay. N. J. ay. Pa. no. Del. no. Md. ay. Va. ay. N. C. ay. S. C. ay. Geo. ay [Ayes—8; noes—3.]

Mr. Madison renewed his motion yesterday made & waved to render the members of the 1st. branch "ineligible during their term of service, & for one year after—to such offices only as should be established, or the emoluments thereof, augmented by the Legislature of the U. States during the time of their being members." He supposed that the unnecessary creation of offices, and increase of salaries, were the evils most experienced, & that if the door was shut agst. them, it might properly be left open for the appointt. of members to other offices as an encouragmt. to the Legislative service.

Mr. Alex: Martin seconded the motion.

Mr. Butler. The amendt. does not go far eno' & wd. be easily evaded

Mr. Rutledge, was for preserving the Legislature as pure as possible, by shutting the door against appointments of its own members to offices, which was one source of its corruption.

Mr. Mason. The motion of my colleague is but a partial remedy for the evil. He appealed to him as a witness of the shameful partiality of the Legislature of Virginia to its own members. He enlarged on the abuses & corruption in the British Parliament, connected with the appointment of its members. He cd. not suppose that a sufficient number of Citizens could not be found who would be ready, without the inducement of eligibility to offices, to undertake the Legislative service. Genius & virtue it may be said, ought to be encouraged. Genius, for aught he knew, might, but that virtue should be encouraged by such a species of venality, was an idea, that at least had the merit of being new.

Mr. King remarked that we were refining too much in this business; and that the idea of preventing intrigue and solicitation of offices was chimerical. You say that no member shall himself be eligible to any office. Will this restrain him from availing himself of the same means which would gain appointments for himself, to gain them for his son, his brother, or any other object of his partiality. We were losing therefore the advantages on one side, without avoiding the evils on the other.

Mr. Wilson supported the motion. The proper cure he said for corruption in the Legislature was to take from it the power of appointing to offices. One branch of corruption would indeed remain, that of creating unnecessary offices, or granting unnecesary salaries, and for that the amendment would be a proper remedy. He animadverted on the impropriety of stigmatizing with the name of venality the laudable ambition of rising into the honorable offices of the Government; an ambition most likely to be felt in the early & most incorrupt period of life, & which all wise & free Govts. had deemed it sound policy, to cherish, not to check. The members of the Legislature have perhaps the hardest & least profitable task of any who engage in the service of the state. Ought this merit to be made a disqualification?

Mr. Sherman, observed that the motion did not go far enough. It might be evaded by the creation of a new office, the translation to it of a person from another office, and the appointment of a member of the Legislature to the latter. A new Embassy might be established to a new court & an ambassador taken from another, in order to *create* a vacancy for a favorite member. He admitted that inconveniencies lay on both sides. He hoped there wd. be sufficient inducements to the public service without resorting to the prospect of desireable offices, and on the whole was rather agst. the motion of Mr. Madison.

Mr. Gerry thought there was great weight in the objection of Mr. Sherman. He added as another objection agst. admitting the eligibility of members in any case that it would produce intrigues of ambitious men for displacing proper officers, in order to create vacancies for themselves. In answer to Mr. King he observed that although members, if disqualified themselves might still intrigue & cabal for their sons, brothers &c, yet as their own interest would be dearer to them, than those of their nearest connections, it might be e[x]pected they would go greater lengths to promote it.

Mr. Madison had been led to this motion as a middle ground between an eligibility in all cases, and an absolute disqualification. He admitted the probable abuses of an eligibility of the members, to offices, particularly within the gift of the Legislature He had witnessed the partiality of such bodies to their own members, as had been remarked of the Virginia assembly by his colleague (Col. Mason). He appealed however to him in turn to vouch another fact not less notorious in Virginia, that the backwardness of the best citizens to engage in the legislative service gave but too great success to unfit characters. The question was not to be viewed on one side only. The advantages & disadvantages on both ought to be fairly compared. The objects to be aimed at were to fill all offices with the fittest—characters, & to draw the wisest & most worthy citizens into the Legislative service. If on one hand, public bodies were partial to their own members; on the other they were as apt to be misled by taking characters on report, or the authority of patrons and dependents. All who had been concerned in the appointment of strangers on these recommendations must be sensible of this truth. Nor wd. the partialities of such Bodies be obviated by disqualifying their own members. Candidates for office would hover round the seat of Govt. or be found among the residents there, and practise all the means of courting the favor of the members. A great proportion of the appointments made by the States were evidently brought about in this way. In the general Govt. the evil must be still greater, the characters of distant states, being much less known throughout the U. States than those of the distant parts of the same State. The elections by Congress had generally turned on men living at the seat of the fedl. Govt. or in its neighbourhood.—As to the next object, the impulse to the Legislative service, was evinced by experience to be in general too feeble with those best qualified for it. This inconveniency wd. also be more felt in the Natl. Govt. than in the State Govts as the sacrifices reqd. from the distant members wd. be much greater, and the pecuniary provisions, probably, more disproporti[on]ate. It wd. therefore be impolitic to add fresh objections to the Legislative service by an absolute disqualification of its members. The point in question was whether this would be an objection with the most capable citizens. Arguing from experience he concluded that it would. The Legislature of Virga would probably have been without many of its best members, if in that situation, they had been ineligible to Congs. to the Govt. & other honorable offices of the State.

Mr. Butler thought Characters fit for office wd. never be unknown.

Col. Mason. If the members of the Legislature are disqualified, still the honors of the State will induce those who aspire to them, to enter that service, as the field in which they can best display & improve their talents, & lay the train for their subsequent advancement.

Mr. Jenifer remarked that in Maryland, the Senators chosen for five years, cd. hold no other office & that this circumstance gained them the greatest confidence of the people.

On the question for agreeing to the motion of Mr. Madison. Massts. divd. Ct. ay. N. Y. no. N. J. ay. Pa. no. Del. no. Md. no. Va. no. N. C. no. S. C. no. Geo. no. [Ayes—2; noes—8; divided—1.]

Mr. Sherman movd. to insert the words "and incapable of holding" after the words "eligible to offices" wch. was agreed to without opposition.

The word "established" & the words "Natl. Govt." were struck out of Resolution 3d;

Mr. Spaight called for a division of the question, in consequence of which it was so put, as that it turned in the first member of it, "on the ineligibility of the members *during the term for which they were elected*"—whereon the States were, Massts. divd. Ct. ay. N. Y. ay. N. J. ay. Pa. no. Del. ay. Md. ay. Va. ay. N. C. ay. S. C. ay. Geo. no. [Ayes—8; noes—2; divided—1.]

On the 2d. member of the sentence extending ineligibility of members to one year after the term for which they were elected Col. Mason thought this essential to guard agst—evasions by resignations, and stipulations for office to be fulfilled at the expiration of the legislative term. Mr. Gerry had known such a case. Mr. Hamilton. Evasions cd. not be prevented ÷ as by proxies—by friends holding for a year. and them opening the way &c. Mr. Rutledge admitted the possibility of evasions but was for controuling them as possible. Mas. no. Ct. no. N. Y. ay. N. J. no. Pa. divd. Del. ay. Mard. ay. Va. no N. C. no. S. C. ay. Geo no [Ayes—4; noes—6; divided—1.]

[1:428; Madison, 26 June]

Mr. Butler moved to strike out the the ineligibility of Senators to *State offices*.

Mr. Williamson seconded the motion.

Mr. Wilson remarked the additional dependence this wd. create in the Senators on the States. The longer the time he observed allotted to the officer, the more compleat will be the dependance, if it exists at all.

Genl. Pinkney was for making the States as much as could be conveniently done a part of the Genl. Gov't: If the Senate was to be appointed by the States, it ought in pursuance of the same idea to be paid by the States: and the States ought not to be barred from the opportunity of calling members of it into offices at home. Such a restriction would also discourage the ablest men from going into the Senate.

Mr. Wiliamson moved a resolution so penned as to admit of the two following questions. 1. whether the members of the Senate should be ineligible to & incapable of holding offices *under the U. States*

2. whether &c. under the *particular States.*

On the question to postpone in order to consider Williamson's Resoln: Masts. no. Cont. ay. N. Y. no. N. J. no. Pa. ay. Del. ay. Md. ay. Va. ay. N. C. ay. S. C. ay. Geo. ay. [Ayes—8; noes—3.]

Mr. Gerry & Mr. Madison—move to add to Mr. Williamsons 1. quest: "and for 1 year thereafter." On this amendt.

Masts. no. Cont. ay N. Y. ay. N. J. no. P. no. Del. ay. Md. ay. Va. ay. N. C. ay. S. C. ay. Geo. no. [Ayes—7; noes—4.]

On Mr. Will—son's 1 Question as amended. vz. inelig: & incapable &c. &c. for 1 year &c. agd. unanimously.

On the 2. question as to ineligibility &c. to State offices. Mas. ay. Ct. no. N. Y. no. N. J. no. P. ay. Del. no. Md. no. Va. ay. N. C. no. S. C. no. Geo. no. [Ayes—3; noes—8.]

[1:518; Yates, 2 July]

[G. Morris:] You intend also that the second branch shall be incapable of holding any office in the general government.—It is a dangerous expedient. They ought to have every inducement to be interested in your government. Deprive them of this right, and they will become inattentive to your welfare. The wealthy will ever exist; and you never can be safe unless you gratify them as a body, in the pursuit of honor and profit. Prevent them by positive institutions, and they will proceed in some left-handed way. A son may want a place—you mean to prevent him from promotion—They are not to be paid for their services—they will in some way pay themselves; nor is it in your power to prevent it. It is good policy that men of property be collected in one body, to give them one common influence in your government. Let vacancies be filled up as they happen, by the executive. Besides it is of little consequence, on this plan, whether the states are equally represented or not. If the state governments have the division of many of the loaves and fishes, and the general government few, it cannot exist. This senate would be one of the *baubles* of the general government. If you choose them for *seven* years, whether chosen by the people or the states; whether by equal suffrage or in any other proportion, how will they be a check? They will still have local and state prejudices.—A government by compact is

no government at all. You may as well go back to your congressional federal government, where, in the character of ambassadors, they may form treaties for each state.

[2:283; Madison, 14 Aug.]

Mr. Pinkney argued that the making the members ineligible to offices was *degrading* to them, and the more improper as their election into the Legislature implied that they had the confidence of the people; that it was *inconvenient*, because the Senate might be supposed to contain the fittest men. He hoped to see that body become a School of Public Ministers, a nursery of Statesmen: that it was *impolitic*, because the Legislature would cease to be a magnet to the first talents and abilities. He moved to postpone the section in order to take up the following proposition viz—"the members of each House shall be incapable of holding any office under the U.S. for which they or any of others for their benefit receive any salary, fees, or emoluments of any kind—and the acceptance of such office shall vacate their seats respectively"

Genl. Mifflin 2ded. the motion

Col. Mason ironically proposed to strike out the whole section, as a more effectual expedient for encouraging that exotic corruption which might not otherwise thrive so well in the American Soil—for compleating that Aristocracy which was probably in the contemplation of some among us. and for inviting into the Legislative service, those generous & benevolent characters who will do justice to each other's merit, by carving out offices & rewards for it. In the present state of American morals & manners, few friends it may be thought will be lost to the plan, by the opportunity of giving premiums to a mercenary & depraved ambition.

Mr Mercer. It is a first principle in political science, that whenever the rights of property are secured, an aristocracy will grow out of it. Elective Governments also necessarily become aristocratic, because the rulers being few can & will draw emoluments for themselves from the many. The Governments of America will become aristocracies. They are so already. The public measures are calculated for the benefit of the Governors, not of the people. The people are dissatisfied & complain. They change their rulers, and the public measures are changed, but it is only a change of one scheme of emolument to the rulers, for another. The people gain nothing by it, but an addition of instability & uncertainty to their other evils.—Governmts. can only be maintained by *force* or *influence*. The Executive has not *force*, deprive him of influence by rendering the members of the Legislature ineligible to Executive offices, and he becomes a mere phantom of authority. The Aristocratic part will not even let him in for a share of the plunder. The Legislature must & will be composed of wealth & abilities, and the people will be governed by a Junto. The Executive ought to have a Council, being members of both Houses. Without such an influence, the war will be between the aristocracy & the people. He wished it to be between the Aristocracy & the Executive. Nothing else can protect the people agst. those speculating Legislatures which are now plundering them throughout the U. States.

Mr. Gerry read a Resolution of the Legislature of Massts. passed before the Act of Congs. recommending the Convention, in which her deputies were instructed not to depart from the rotation established in the 5th. art: of Confederation, nor to agree in any case to give to the members of Congs. a capacity to hold offices under the Government. This he said was repealed in consequence of the Act of Congs. with which the State thought it proper to comply in an unqualified manner. The Sense of the State however was still the same. He could not think with Mr. Pinkney that the disqualification was degrading. Confidence is the road to tyranny. As to Ministers & Ambassadors few of them were necessary. It is the opinion of a great many that they ought to be discontinued, on our part; that none may be sent among us, & that source of influence be shut up. If the Senate were to appoint Ambassadors as seemed to be intended, they will multiply embassies for their own sakes. He was not so fond of those productions as to wish to establish nurseries for them. If they are once appointed, the House of Reps. will be obliged to provide salaries for them, whether they approve of the measures or not. If men will not serve in the Legislature without a prospect of such offices, our situation is deplorable indeed. If our best Citizens are actuated by such mercenary views, we had better chuse a single despot at once. It will be more easy to satisfy the rapacity of one than of many. According to the idea of one Gentleman (Mr. Mercer) our Government it seems is to be a Govt. of plunder. In that case it certainly would be prudent to have but one rather than many to be employed in it. We cannot be too circumspect in the formation of this System. It will be examined on all sides and with a very suspicious eye. The People who have been so lately in arms agst. G. B. for their liberties, will not easily give them up. He lamented the evils existing at present under our Governments, but imputed them to the faults of those in office, not to the people. The misdeeds of the former will produce a critical attention to the opportunities afforded by the new system to like or greater abuses. As it now stands it is as compleat an aristocracy as ever was framed If great powers should be given to the Senate we shall be governed in reality by a Junto as has been apprehended. He remarked that it would be very differently constituted from Congs 1. there will be but 2 deputies from each State, in Congs. there may be 7. and are generally 5.—2. they are chosen for six years. those of Congs. annually. 3. they are not subject to recall; those of Congs. are. 4. In Congs. 9 *states* are necessary for all great purposes—here 8 *persons* will suffice. Is it to be presumed that the people will ever agree to such a system? He moved to render the members of the H. of Reps. as well as of the Senate ineligible not only during, but for one year after the expiration of their terms.—If it should be thought that this will injure the Legislature by keeping out of it men of abilities who are willing to serve in other offices it may be required as a qualification for other offices, that the Candidate shall have served a certain time in the Legislature.

Mr Govr. Morris. Exclude the officers of the army & navy, and you form a band having a different interest from & opposed to the civil power: you stimulate them to despise & reproach those "talking Lords who dare not face the foe". Let this spirit be roused at the end of a war, before your troops shall have laid down their arms, and though the Civil authority be "entrenched in parchment to the teeth" they will cut their way to it. He was agst. rendering the members of the Legislature ineligible to offices. He was for rendering them eligible agn. after having vacated their Seats by accepting office. Why should we not avail ourselves of their services if the people chuse to give them their confidence. There can be little danger of corruption either among the people or the Legislatures who are to be the Electors. If they say, we see their merits, we honor the men, we chuse to renew our confidence in them, have they not a right to give them a preference; and can they be properly abridged of it.

Mr. Williamson; introduced his opposition to the motion by referring to the question concerning "money bills". That clause he said was dead. Its ghost he was afraid would notwithstanding haunt us. It had been a matter of conscience with him, to insist upon it as long as there was hope of retaining it. He had swallowed the vote of rejection, with reluctance. He could not digest it. All that was said on the other side was that the restriction was not *convenient*. We have now got a House of Lords which is to originate money-bills. To avoid another *inconveniency*, we are to have a whole Legislature at liberty to cut out offices for one another. He thought a self-denying ordinance for ourselves would be more proper. Bad as the Constitution has been made by expunging the restriction on the Senate concerning money bills he did not wish to make it worse by expunging the present Section. He had scarcely seen a single corrupt measure in the Legislature of N– Carolina, which could not be traced up to office hunting.

Mr Sherman. The Constitution shd. lay as few temptations as possible in the way of those in power. Men of abilities will increase as the Country grows more populous and, and the means of education are more diffused.

Mr. Pinkney– No State has rendered the members of the Legislature ineligible to offices. In S– Carolina the Judges are eligible into the Legislature. It cannot be supposed then that the motion will be offensive to the people. If the State Constitutions should be revised he believed restrictions of this sort wd be rather diminished than multiplied.

Mr. Wilson could not approve of the Section as it stood, and could not give up his judgment to any supposed objections that might arise among the people. He considered himself as acting & responsible for the welfare of millions not immediately represented in this House. He had also asked himself the serious question what he should say to his constituents in case they should call upon him to tell them why he sacrificed his own Judgment in a case where they authorized him to exercise it? Were he to own to them that he sacrificed it in order to flatter their prejudices, he should dread the retort: did you suppose the people of Penna. had not good sense enough to receive a good Government? Under this impression he should certainly follow his own Judgment which disapproved of the section. He would remark in addition to the objections urged agst. it. that as one branch of the Legislature was to be appointed by the Legislatures of the States, the other by the people of the States, as both are to be paid by the States, and to be appointable to State offices; nothing seemed to be wanting to prostrate the Natl. Legislature, but to render its members ineligible to Natl offices, & by that means take away its power of attracting those talents which were necessary to give weight to the Governt. and to render it useful to the people. He was far from thinking the ambition which aspired to Offices of dignity and trust, an ignoble or culpable one. He was sure it was not politic to regard it in that light, or to withold from it the prospect of those rewards, which might engage it in the career of public service. He observed that the State of Penna. which had gone as far as any State into the policy of fettering power, had not rendered the members of the Legislature ineligible to offices of Govt.

Mr Elsworth did not think the mere postponement of the reward would be any material discouragement of merit. Ambitious minds will serve 2 years or 7 years in the Legislature for the sake of qualifying themselves for other offices. This he thought a sufficient security for obtaining the services of the ablest men in the Legislature, although whilst members they should be ineligible to Public offices. Besides, merit will be most encouraged, when most impartially rewarded. If rewards are to circulate only within the Legislature, merit out of it will be discouraged.

Mr. Mercer was extremely anxious on this point. What led to the appointment of this Convention? The corruption & mutability of the Legislative Councils of the States. If the plan does not remedy these, it will not recommend itself: and we shall not be able in our private capacities to support & enforce it: nor will the best part of our Citizens exert themselves for the purpose.—It is a great mistake to suppose that the paper we are to propose will govern the U. States? It is The men whom it will bring into the Governt. and interest in maintaining it that is to govern them. The paper will only mark out the mode & the form— Men are the substance and must do the business. All Govt. must be by force or influence. It is not the King of France—but 200,000 janisaries of power that govern that Kingdom. There will be no such force here; influence then must be substituted; and he would ask whether this could be done, if the members of the Legislature should be ineligible to offices of State; whether such a disqualification would not determine all the most influential men to stay at home, and & prefer appointments within their respective States.

Mr. Wilson was by no means satisfied with the answer given by Mr. Elseworth to the argument as to the discouragement of merit. The members must either go a second time into the Legislature, and disqualify themselves—or say to their Constituents, we served you before only from the mercenary view of qualifying ourselves for offices, and haveg answered this purpose we do not chuse to be again elected.

Mr. Govr. Morris put the case of a war, and the Citizen the most capable of conducting it, happening to be a member of the Legislature. What might have been the conse-

quence of such a regulation at the commencement, or even in the Course of the late contest for our liberties?

On question for postponing in order to take up Mr. Pinkneys motion, it was lost.

N– H– ay– Mas. no. Ct no. N. J– no. Pa ay. Del. ay. Md. ay. Va. ay. N. C. no. S– C. no. Geo. divd. [Ayes—5; noes—5; divided—1.]

Mr Govr Morris moved to insert, after "office", except offices in the army or navy: but in that case their offices shall be vacated

Mr. Broome 2ds. him

M. Randolph had been & should continue uniformly opposed to the striking out of the clause; as opening a door for influence & corruption. No arguments had made any impression on him, but those which related to the case of war, and a co-existing incapacity of the fittest commanders to be employed. He admitted great weight in these, and would agree to the exception proposed by Mr. Govr. Morris.

Mr. Butler & Mr Pinkney urged a general postponemt. of 9 Sect. art. VI till it should be seen what powers would be vested in the Senate, when it would be more easy to judge of the expediency of allowing the Officers of State to be chosen out of that body.—A general postponement was agreed to nem. con.

[2:489; Madison, 3 Sept.]

Mr. Pinkney moved to postpone the Report of the Committee of Eleven (see Sepr. 1) in order to take up the following,

"The members of each House shall be incapable of holding any office under the U— S— for which they or any other for their benefit, receive any salary, fees or emoluments of any kind, and the acceptance of such office shall vacate their seats respectively." He was strenuously opposed to an ineligibility of members to office, and therefore wished to restrain the proposition to a mere incompatibility. He considered the eligibility of members of the Legislature to the honorable offices of Government, as resembling the policy of the Romans, in making the temple of virtue the road to the temple of fame.

On this question

N. H. no. Mas. no. Ct no— N— J. no. Pa ay. Md. no Va. no. N. C. ay. S. C—no. Geo. no. [Ayes—2; noes—8.]

Mr King moved to insert the word "created" before the word "during" in the Report of the Committee. This he said would exclude the members of the first Legislature under the Constitution, as most of the Offices wd. then be created.

Mr. Williamson 2ded. the motion, He did not see why members of the Legislature should be ineligible to *vacancies* happening during the term of their election,

Mr Sherman was for entirely incapacitating members of the Legislature. He thought their eligibility to offices would give too much influence to the Executive. He said the incapacity ought at least to be extended to cases where salaries should be *increased,* as well as *created,* during the term of the member. He mentioned also the expedient by which the restriction could be evaded to wit: an existing officer might be translated to an office created, and a member of the Legislature be then put into the office vacated.

Mr Govr. Morris contended that the eligibility of members to office wd. lessen the influence of the Executive. If they cannot be appointed themselves, the Executive will appoint their relations & friends, retaining the service & votes of the members for his purposes in the Legislature. Whereas the appointment of the members deprives him of such an advantage.

Mr. Gerry. thought the eligibility of members would have the effect of opening batteries agst. good officers, in order to drive them out & make way for members of the Legislature.

Mr Gorham was in favor of the amendment. Without it we go further than has been done in any of the States, or indeed any other Country, The experience of the State Governments where there was no such ineligibility, proved that it was not necessary; on the contrary that the eligibility was among the inducements for fit men to enter into the Legislative service

Mr. Randolph was inflexibly fixed against inviting men into the Legislature by the prospect of being appointed to offices.

Mr. Baldwin remarked that the example of the States was not applicable. The Legislatures there are so numerous that an exclusion of their members would not leave proper men for offices. The case would be otherwise in the General Government.

Col: Mason. Instead of excluding merit, the ineligibility will keep out corruption, by excluding office-hunters.

Mr. Wilson considered the exclusion of members of the Legislature as increasing the influence of the Executive as observed by Mr Govr Morris at the same time that it would diminish, the general energy of the Government. He said that the legal disqualification for office would be odious to those who did not wish for office, but did not wish either to be marked by so degrading a distinction—

Mr Pinkney. The first Legislature will be composed of the ablest men to be found. The States will select such to put the Government into operation. Should the Report of the Committee or even the amendment be agreed to, The great offices, even those of the Judiciary Deparment which are to continue for life, must be filled whilst those most capable of filling them will be under a disqualification

On the question on Mr. King's motion

N—H. ay. Mas. ay—Ct. no. N. J. no. Pa. ay. Md. no. Va. ay N—C. ay. S—C. no. Geo—no. [Ayes—5; noes—5.]

The amendment being thus lost by the equal division of the States, Mr Williamson moved to insert the words "created or the emoluments whereof shall have been increased" before the word "during" in the Report of the Committee

Mr. King 2ded. the motion. &

On the question

N—H—ay—Mas—ay—Ct. no. N— J. no. Pa. ay. Md. no. Va. ay. N—C. ay. S. C. no. Geo—divided. [Ayes—5; noes—4; divided—1.]

The last clause rendering a Seat in the Legislature & an office incompatible was agreed to nem: con:

The Report as amended & agreed to is as follows.

"The members of each House shall be ineligible to any Civil office under the authority of the U. States, created, or the emoluments whereof shall have been increased during the time for which they shall respectively be elected—And no person holding any office under the U. S. shall be a member of either House during his continuance in office."

[2:613; Madison, 14 Sept.]

Mr Baldwin observed that the clause. art. 1. sect 6. declaring that no member of Congs, "during the time for which he was elected; shall be appointed to any Civil office under the authority of the U. S. which shall have been created, or the emoluments whereof shall have been increased during such time", would not extend to offices *created by the Constitution;* and the salaries of which would be created, *not increased* by Congs. at their first session— The members of the first Congs consequently might evade the disqualification in this instance.—He was neither seconded nor opposed; nor did any thing further pass on the subject.

2

JAMES WILSON, PENNSYLVANIA RATIFYING CONVENTION
4 Dec. 1787
Elliot 2:475–76, 483–84

It is said, that the House of Representatives will be subject to corruption, and the *Senate* possess the means of corrupting, by the share they have in the appointment to office. This was not spoken in the soft language of attachment to government. It is, perhaps, impossible, with all the caution of legislators and statesmen, to exclude corruption and undue influence entirely from government. All that can be done, upon this subject, is done in the Constitution before you. Yet it behoves us to call out, and add every guard and preventive in our power. I think, sir, something very important, on this subject, is done in the present system; for it has been provided, effectually, that the man that has been bribed by an office shall have it no longer in his power to earn his wages. The moment he is engaged to serve the Senate, in consequence of their gift, he no longer has it in his power to sit in the House of Representatives; for "No representative shall, during the term for which he was elected, be appointed to any civil office, under the authority of the United States, which shall have been created, or the emoluments whereof shall have been increased, during such time." And the following annihilates corruption of that kind: "And no person holding any office under the United States shall be a member of either house during his continuance in office." So the mere acceptance of an office, as a bribe, effectually destroys the end for which it was offered. Was this attended to when it was mentioned that the members of the one house could be bribed by the other? "But the members of the Senate may enrich themselves," was an observation made as an objection to this system.

As the mode of doing this has not been pointed out, I apprehend the objection is not much relied upon. The Senate are incapable of receiving any money, except what is paid them out of the public treasury. They cannot vote to themselves a single penny, unless the proposition originates from the other house. This objection, therefore, is visionary, like the following one—"that pictured group, that numerous host, and prodigious swarm of officers, which are to be appointed under the general government." The gentlemen tell you that there must be judges of the supreme, and judges of the inferior courts, with all their appendages: there will be taxgatherers swarming throughout the land. "O!" say they, "if we could enumerate the offices, and the numerous officers that must be employed every day in collecting, receiving, and comptrolling, the moneys of the United States, the number would be almost beyond imagination."

. . . . .

Another good quality in this Constitution is, that the members of the legislature cannot hold offices under the authority of this government. The operation of this, I apprehend, would be found to be very extensive, and very salutary, in this country, to prevent those intrigues, those factions, that corruption, that would otherwise rise here, and have risen so plentifully in every other country. The reason why it is necessary in England to continue such influence, is, that the crown, in order to secure its own influence against two other branches of the legislature, must continue to bestow places; but those *places produce the opposition* which frequently runs so strong in the British Parliament.

Members who do not enjoy offices combine against those who do enjoy them. It is not from principle that they thwart the ministry in all its operations. No; their language is, Let us turn them out, and succeed to their places. The great source of corruption, in that country, is, that persons may hold offices under the crown, and seats in the legislature, at the same time.

3

LUTHER MARTIN, GENUINE INFORMATION
1788
Storing 2.4.46–48

In the *sixth* section of the *first* article, it is provided, that senators and representatives may be appointed to any civil office under the authority of the United States, except such as shall have been created, or the emoluments of which have been increased during the time for which they were elected: upon this subject. Sir, there was a great diversity of sentiment among the members of the conven-

tion—As the propositions were reported by the committee of the whole house, a senator or representative could not be appointed to *any office* under a *particular State*, or under the *United States*, during the time for which they were chosen, nor to any office under the United States until one year after the expiration of that time.—It was said, and in my opinion justly, that no good reason could be assigned why a senator or representative should be incapacitated to hold an office in *his own* government, since it can only bind him more closely to his State, and attach him the more to its interests, which, as its representative, he is bound to consult and sacredly guard, as far as is consistent with the welfare of the union; and therefore, at most, would only add the additional motive of gratitude for discharging his duty; and according to this idea, the clause which prevented senators or delegates from holding offices in their own States, was rejected by a considerable majority; but, Sir, we sacredly endeavoured to preserve all that part of the resolution which prevented them from being *eligible* to *offices* under the *United States*, as we considered it *essentially necessary* to preserve the *integrity, independence*, and *dignity* of the legislature, and to secure its members from *corruption*.

I was in the number of those who were extremely solicitous to preserve this part of the report; but there was a powerful opposition made by such who wished the members of the legislature to be eligible to offices under the United States—*Three* different times did they attempt to procure an alteration, and *as often* failed, a majority firmly adhering to the resolution as reported by the committee; however, an alteration was at length by dint of perseverance, obtained even within the last twelve days of the convention, for it happened after I left Philadelphia—As to the exception that they cannot be appointed to offices created by themselves, or the emoluments of which are by themselves increased, it is certainly of little consequence, since they may easily evade it by creating new offices, to which may be appointed the persons who fill the offices before created, and thereby vacancies will be made, which may be filled by the members who for that purpose have created the new offices.

It is true, the acceptance of an office vacates their seat, nor can they be re-elected during their continuance in office; but it was said, that the evil would first take place, that the price for the office would be paid before it was obtained; that vacating the seat of the person who was appointed to office, made way for the admission of a new member, who would come there as desirous to obtain an office as him whom he succeeded, and as ready to pay the price necessary to obtain it; in fine, that it would be only driving away the flies who were *filled*, to make room for the those that were *hungry*—And as the system is now reported, the *President* having the power to *nominate* to *all offices*, it must be evident, that there is *no possible security* for the *integrity* and *independence* of the *legislature*, but that they are most *unduly* placed under the *influence* of the *President*, and exposed to *bribery* and *corruption*.

4

FEDERAL FARMER, NO. 13
14 Jan. 1788
Storing 2.8.169–70

In considering the legislators, in relation to the subject before us, two interesting questions particularly arise—1. Whether they ought to be eligible to any offices whatever during the period for which they shall be elected to serve, and even for some time afterwards—and 2. How far they ought to participate in the power of appointments. As to the first, it is true that legislators in foreign countries, or in our state governments, are not generally made ineligible to office: there are good reasons for it; in many countries the people have gone on without ever examining the principles of government. There have been but few countries in which the legislators have been a particular set of men periodically chosen: but the principal reason is, that which operates in the several states, viz. the legislators are so frequently chosen, and so numerous, compared with the number of offices for which they can reasonably consider themselves as candidates, that the chance of any individual member's being chosen, is too small to raise his hopes or expectations, or to have any considerable influence upon his conduct. Among the state legislators, one man in twenty may be appointed in some committee business, &c. for a month or two; but on a fair computation, not one man in a hundred sent to the state legislatures is appointed to any permanent office of profit: directly the reverse of this will evidently be found true in the federal administration. Throughout the United States, about four federal senators, and thirty-three representatives, averaging the elections, will be chosen in a year; these few men may rationally consider themselves as the fairest candidates for a very great number of lucrative offices, which must become vacant in the year, and pretty clearly a majority of the federal legislators, if not excluded, will be mere expectants for public offices. I need not adduce further arguments to establish a position so clear, I need only call to your recollection my observations in a former letter, wherein I endeavoured to shew the fallacy of the argument, that the members must return home and mix with the people. It is said, that men are governed by interested motives, and will not attend as legislators, unless they can, in common with others, be eligible to offices of honor and profit. This will undoubtedly be the case with some men, but I presume only with such men as never ought to be chosen legislators in a free country; an opposite principle will influence good men; virtuous patriots, and generous minds, will esteem it a higher honor to be selected as the guardians of a free people; they will be satisfied with a reasonable compensation for their time and service; nor will they wish to be within the vortex of influence. The valuable effects of this principle of making legislators ineligible to offices for a given time, has never yet been sufficiently attended to or considered: I am assured, that it was established by the convention after long debate, and afterwards, on an unfortunate change of a few members, altered. Could the federal legislators be excluded in the manner proposed, I think it would be an important point gained; as to themselves, they would be left to act much more from motives consistent with the public good.

In considering the principle of rotation I had occasion to distinguish the condition of a legislator from that of mere official man—We acquire certain habits, feelings, and opinions, as men and citizens—others, and very different ones, from a long continuance in office: It is, therefore, a valuable observation in many bills of rights, that rulers ought frequently to return and mix with the people. A legislature, in a free country, must be numerous; it is in some degree a periodical assemblage of the people, frequently formed—the principal officers in the executive and judicial departments, must have more permanency in office. Hence it may be inferred, that the legislature will remain longer uncorrupted and virtuous; longer congenial to the people, than the officers of those departments. If it is not, therefore, in our power to preserve republican principles, for a series of ages, in all the departments of government, we may a long while preserve them in a well formed legislature. To this end we ought to take every precaution to prevent legislators becoming mere officemen; chuse them frequently, make them recallable, establish rotation among them, make them ineligible to offices, and give them as small a share as possible in the disposal of them. Add to this, a legislature, in the nature of things, is not formed for the detail business of appointing officers; there is also generally an impropriety in the same men's making offices and filling them, and a still greater impropriety in their impeaching and trying the officers they appoint. For these, and other reasons, I conclude, the legislature is not a proper body for the appointment of officers in general. But having gone through with the different modes of appointment, I shall endeavour to shew what share in the distribution of the power of appointments the legislature must, from necessity, rather than from propriety, take.

5

DEBATE IN VIRGINIA RATIFYING CONVENTION
14 June 1788
Elliot 3:368–75

Mr. HENRY. Mr. Chairman, our burden should, if possible, be rendered more light. I was in hopes some other gentleman would have objected to this part. The pay of the members is, by the Constitution, to be fixed by themselves, without limitation or restraint. They may therefore indulge themselves in the fullest extent. They may make their compensation as high as they please. I suppose, if they be good men, their own delicacy will lead them to be satisfied with moderate salaries. But there is no security for this, should they be otherwise inclined. I really believe that, if the state legislatures were to fix their pay, no inconvenience would result from it, and the public mind would be better satisfied. But in the same section there is a defect of a much greater consequence. There is no restraint on corruption. They may be appointed to offices without any material restriction, and the principal source of corruption in representatives is the hope or expectation of offices and emoluments. After the first organization of offices, and the government is put in motion, they may be appointed to any existing offices which become vacant, and they may create a multiplicity of offices, in order thereafter to be appointed to them. What says the clause? "No senator or representative shall, during the time for which he was elected, be appointed to any civil office, under the authority of the United States, which shall have been created, or the emoluments whereof shall have been increased, during such time." This is an idea strangely expressed.

He shall not accept of any office created during the time he is elected for, or of any office whereof the emoluments have been increased in that time. Does not this plainly say that, if an office be not created during the time for which he is elected, or if its emoluments be not increased during such time, he may accept of it? I can see it in no other light. If we wish to preclude the enticement to getting offices, there is a clear way of expressing it. If it be better that Congress should go out of their representative offices by accepting other offices, then it ought to be so. If not, we require an amendment in the clause, that it shall not be so. I may be wrong. Perhaps the honorable member may be able to give a satisfactory answer on this subject.

Mr. MADISON. Mr. Chairman, I most sincerely wish to give a proper explanation on this subject, in such a manner as may be to the satisfaction of every one. I shall suggest such considerations as led the Convention to approve of this clause. With respect to the right of ascertaining their own pay, I will acknowledge that their compensations, if practicable, should be fixed in the Constitution itself, so as not to be dependent on Congress itself, or on the state legislatures. The various vicissitudes, or rather the gradual diminution, of the value of all coins and circulating medium, is one reason against ascertaining them immutably; as what may be now an adequate compensation, might, by the progressive reduction of the value of our circulating medium, be extremely inadequate at a period not far distant.

It was thought improper to leave it to the state legislatures, because it is improper that one government should be dependent on another; and the great inconveniences experienced under the old Confederation show the states would be operated upon by local considerations, as contradistinguished from general and national interests. Experience shows us that they have been governed by such heretofore, and reason instructs us that they would be influenced by them again. This theoretic inconvenience of leaving to Congress the fixing their compensations is more than counterbalanced by this in the Confederation—that the state legislatures had a right to determine the pay of the members of Congress, which enabled the states to de-

stroy the general government. There is no instance where this power has been abused. In America, legislative bodies have reduced their own wages lower, rather than augmented them. This is a power which cannot be abused without rousing universal attention and indignation. What would be the consequence of the Virginian legislature raising their pay to four or five pounds each per day? The universal indignation of the people. Should the general Congress annex wages disproportionate to their service, or repugnant to the sense of the community, they would be universally execrated. The certainty of incurring the general detestation of the people will prevent abuse.

It was conceived that the great danger was in creating new offices, which would increase the burdens of the people; and not in a uniform admission of all meritorious characters to serve their country in the old offices. There is no instance of any state constitution which goes as far as this. It was thought to be a mean between two extremes. It guards against abuse by taking away the inducement to create new offices, or increase the emolument of old offices; and it gives them an opportunity of enjoying, in common with other citizens, any of the existing offices which they may be capable of executing. To have precluded them from this, would have been to exclude them from a common privilege to which every citizen is entitled, and to prevent those who had served their country with the greatest fidelity and ability from being on a par with their fellow-citizens. I think it as well guarded as reason requires; more so than the constitution of any other nation.

Mr. NICHOLAS thought it sufficiently guarded, as it prevented the members of the general government from holding offices which they created themselves, or of which they increased the emoluments; and as they could not enjoy any office during their continuance in Congress, to admit them to old offices when they left Congress, was giving them no exclusive privilege, but such as every citizen had an equal right to.

Mr. TYLER was afraid that, as their compensations were not fixed in the Constitution, Congress might fix them so low, that none but rich men could go; by which the government might terminate in an aristocracy. The states might choose men noted for their wealth and influence, and state influence would govern the Senate. This, though not the most capital objection, he thought was considerable, when joined to others of greater magnitude. He thought the gentleman's account of it was by no means satisfactory. A parallel had been drawn between this power in Congress of fixing their compensations, and that of our Assembly fixing the quantum of their salaries. He was of opinion the comparison did not apply, as there was less responsibility in the former than in the latter case. He dreaded that great corruption would take place, and wished to have it amended so as to prevent it.

Mr. GRAYSON. Mr. Chairman, it strikes me that they may fix their wages very low. From what has happened in Great Britain, I am warranted to draw this conclusion. I think every member of the House of Commons formerly had a right to receive twenty shillings, or a guinea, a day. But I believe that this salary is taken away since the days of corruption. The members of the House of Commons, if I recollect rightly, get nothing for their services as such. But there are some noble emoluments to be derived from the minister, and some other advantages to be obtained. Those who go to Parliament form an idea of emoluments. They expect something besides wages. They go in with the wishes and expectations of getting offices. This, sir, may be the case in this government. My fears are increased from the inconveniences experienced under the Confederation.

Most of the great officers have been taken out of Congress, such as ambassadors to foreign courts, &c. A number of offices have been unnecessarily created, and ambassadors have been unnecessarily sent to foreign countries—to countries with which we have nothing to do. If the present Congress exceeded the limits of propriety, though extremely limited with respect to power in the creation of offices, what may not the future Congress do, when they have, by this system, a full scope of creating what offices and annexing what salaries they please? There are but few members in the Senate and lower house. They may all get offices at different times, as they are not excluded from being appointed to existing offices for the time for which they shall have been elected. Considering the corruption of human nature, and the general tendency of mankind to promote their own interest, I think there is great danger. I am confirmed in my opinion from what I have seen already in Congress, and among other nations. I wish this part, therefore, to be amended, by prohibiting any senator or representative from being appointed to any office during the time for which he was elected, and by fixing their emoluments; though I would not object to the Constitution on this account solely, were there no other defect.

Mr. MADISON. Mr. Chairman, let me ask those who oppose this part of the system, whether any alteration would not make it equally, or more liable to objections. Would it be better to fix their compensations. Would not this produce inconveniences? What authorizes us to conclude that the value of coins will continue always the same? Would it be prudent to make them dependent on the state governments for their salaries—on those who watch them with jealous eyes, and who consider them as encroaching, not on the people, but on themselves? But the worthy member supposes that Congress will fix their wages so low, that only the rich can fill the offices of senators and representatives. Who are to appoint them? The rich? No, sir; the people are to choose them. If the members of the general government were to reduce their compensations to a trifle, before the evil suggested could happen, the people could elect other members in their stead, who would alter that regulation. The people do not choose them for their wealth. If the state legislatures choose such men as senators, it does not influence the people at large in their election of representatives. They can choose those who have the most merit and least wealth. If Congress reduce their wages to a trifle, what shall prevent the states from giving a man of merit so much as will be an adequate compensation? I think the evil very remote; and if it were now to happen, the remedy is in our own hands, and may by ourselves be applied.

Another gentleman seems to apprehend infinite mischief from a possibility that any member of Congress may be appointed to an office, although he ceases to be a member the moment he accepts it. What will be the consequence of precluding them from being so appointed? If you have in your country one man whom you could, in time of danger, trust, above all others, with an office of high importance, he cannot undertake it till two years expire if he be a representative, or till six years elapse if a senator. Suppose America was engaged in war, and the man of the greatest military talents and approved fidelity was a member of either house; would it be right that this man, who could lead us to conquer, and who could save his country from destruction, could not be made general till the term of his election expired? Before that time we might be conquered by our enemies. This will apply to civil as well as military officers. It is impolitic to exclude from the service of his country, in any office, the man who may be most capable of discharging its duties, when they are most wanting.

The honorable gentleman said, that those who go to Congress will look forward to offices, as a compensation for their services, rather than salaries. Does he recollect that they shall not fill offices created by themselves? When they go to Congress, the old offices will be filled. They cannot make any probable calculation that the men in office will die, or forfeit their offices. As they cannot get any new offices, one of these contingencies must happen before they can get any office at all. The chance of getting an office is, therefore, so remote, and so very distant, that it cannot be considered as a sufficient reason to operate on their minds to deviate from their duty.

Let any man calculate in his own mind the improbability of a member of the general government getting into an office, when he cannot fill any office newly created, and when he finds all the old offices filled at the time he enters into Congress. Let him view the danger and impolicy of precluding a member of Congress from holding existing offices, and the danger of making one government dependent on another, and he will find that both clauses deserve applause.

The observations made by several honorable members illustrate my opinion, that it is impossible to devise any system agreeable to all. When objections so contradictory are brought against it, how shall we decide? Some gentlemen object to it because they may make their wages too high; others object to it because they may make them too low. If it is to be perpetually attacked by principles so repugnant, we may cease to discuss. For what is the object of our discussion? Truth, sir. To draw a true and just conclusion. Can this be done without rational premises and syllogistic reasoning?

As to the British Parliament, it is nearly as he says. But how does it apply to this case? Suppose their compensations had been appointed by the state governments, or fixed in the Constitution; would it be a safe government for the Union, if its members depended on receiving their salaries from other political bodies at a distance, and fully competent to withhold them? Its existence would, at best, be but precarious. If they were fixed in the Constitution, they might become extremely inadequate, and produce the very evil which gentlemen seem to fear; for then a man of the highest merit could not act unless he were wealthy. This is the most delicate part in the organization of a republican government. It is the most difficult to establish on unexceptionable grounds. It appears to me most eligible as it is. The Constitution has taken a medium between the two extremes, and perhaps with more wisdom than either the British or the state governments, with respect to their eligibility to office. They can fill no new offices created by themselves, nor old ones of which they increased the salaries. If they were excluded altogether, it is possible that other disadvantages might accrue from it, besides the impolicy and injustice of depriving them of a common privilege. They will not relinquish their legislative, in order to accept other offices. They will more probably confer them on their friends and connections. If this be an inconvenience, it is incident to all governments. After having heard a variety of principles developed, I thought that on which it is established the least exceptionable, and it appears to me sufficiently well guarded.

Mr. GRAYSON. Mr. Chairman, I acknowledge that the honorable gentleman has represented the clause rightly as to their exclusion from new offices; but is there any clause to hinder them from giving offices to uncles, nephews, brothers, and other relations and friends? I imagine most of the offices will be created the first year, and then gentlemen will be tempted to carry on this accommodation.

A worthy member has said—what had been often said before—that, suppose a war took place, and the most experienced and able man was unfortunately in either house, he could not be made general, if the proposed amendment was adopted. Had he read the clause, he would have discovered that it did not extend to military offices, and that the restriction extends to civil offices only. No case can exist, with respect to civil offices, that would occasion a loss to the public, if the members of both houses were precluded from holding any office during the time for which they were elected. The old Confederation is so defective in point of power, that no danger can result from creating offices under it; because those who hold them cannot be paid. The power of making paper money will not be exercised. This country is so thoroughly sensible of the impropriety of it, that no attempt will be made to make any more. So that no danger can arise, as they have not power to pay, if they appoint, officers. Why not make this system as secure as that, in this respect? A great number of offices will be created, to satisfy the wants of those who shall be elected. The worthy member says, the electors can alter them. But have the people the power of making honest men be elected? If he be an honest man, and his wages so low that he could not pay for his expenses, he could not serve them if elected. But there are many thirsting after offices more than public good. Political adventurers go up to Congress solely to advance their own particular emoluments. It is so in the British House of Commons. There are two sets always in that house—one, the landed interest, the most patriotic and respectable; the other, a set of dependants and fortune-hunters, who are elected for their own particular interest, and are willing to sell the interest

of their constituents to the crown. The same division may happen among our representatives. This clause might as well not be guarded at all, as in this flimsy manner. They cannot be elected to offices for the terms for which they were elected, and continue to be members of Congress. But as they can create as many offices as they please for the particular accommodation of their friends, it might as well not be guarded at all. Upon the whole, I consider it entirely imperfect.

6

House of Representatives, Plurality of Offices
28 Mar., 1 Apr. 1806
Annals 16:880–91, 923–30

[*28 Mar.*]

The House resolved itself into a Committee of the Whole on the following resolutions submitted some time since by Mr. J. RANDOLPH:

> *Resolved,* That a contractor under the Government of the United States is an officer within the purview and meaning of the Constitution, and, as such, is incapable of holding a seat in this House.
>
> *Resolved,* That the union of a plurality of offices in the person of a single individual, but more especially of the military with the civil authority, is repugnant to the spirit of the Constitution of the United States, and tends to the introducing of an arbitrary government.
>
> *Resolved,* That provision ought to be made, by law, to render any officer, in the Army or Navy of the United States, incapable of holding any civil office under the United States.

The question was taken on these resolutions without debate.

The first was agreed to—ayes 54, noes 37.

The second was agreed to—ayes 75; and

The third was agreed to without a division.

When the Committee rose and reported their agreement to the resolutions.

The House immediately considered the report.

On concurring with the Committee of the Whole in their agreement to the first resolution,

Mr. FISK said he sincerely regretted it was not in his power to vote for this resolution. He regretted there was no such principle in the Constitution as is prescribed. Such a principle not being in the Constitution, he did not conceive it in the power of the House to make the provision. It was not, in his opinion, in their power to say a man should not hold a seat in that House who was not prohibited by the Constitution. It was on this ground only he was against the resolution under consideration.

Mr. J. RANDOLPH.—I think the gentleman from Vermont may in perfect consistence with the principle he has laid down, which I do not mean at present to contest, give his vote in favor of this resolution. He says that this House has not a right to make a disqualification which the Constitution itself does not attach to the tenure of a seat on this floor; that the Constitution draws a line between the qualification and disqualification of a member, and that this House has no right to alter them. What do we propose to do? To add a new disqualification? No; to do that which the Constitution put in our hands, which it not only authorizes but enjoins upon us. The Constitution declares that each House shall be the judge of the qualification of its members. It is clearly, then, the duty of the House to expound what is or is not a disqualification; and we are now only about to declare what is such a disqualification—merely to expound the Constitution on this head. I know some gentlemen are startled at the idea of expounding the Constitution. But do we not do this every day? Is not the passage of every act a declaration on the part of this House that a decision upon it is among their Constitutional powers? Or, in other words, is it not an exposition of the Constitution? So, in this instance, I will suppose a man returned to serve as a member of this House, and that he is declared, for some reason, to be disqualified from holding a seat. This, according to the gentleman, would be expounding the Constitution. We propose doing no more than saying, if the Secretary of State, or Chief Justice, should come here, they cannot hold a seat. We say that an abuse exists under the Constitution, and offer a remedy.

I have heard some quibbling about the meaning of the word "officer." What is the meaning of office? Agency; it is the office of a man's cook to dress his dinner, of a tailor to supply him with clothes; and it is the office of a contractor to fatten on the land—to acquire lordships, demesnes, baronies—extensive territory—by the advantage he derives from holding the public money, in virtue of his contract. But it is asked, if a contractor is an officer? and whether he can be impeached? because, under the Constitution, all civil officers are liable to impeachment. Would you impeach the Marshal of the District of Columbia? It may be answered that you may impeach him, but that you would not probably do so, because that would be breaking a butterfly on the wheel. Would you impeach a deputy postmaster? And yet when the postmaster at New York accepted his appointment, did he not vacate his seat in the Senate? There is no doubt a contractor is an officer *pro tempore*—it is not an office in perpetuity, but created for a time, and for a particular purpose. And I will ask, if it is not more dangerous to the independence of the two Houses to admit commissioners and contractors within their walls than officers with legal salaries and appointments? If we are to admit either, I say, give me the legal officer, with a determinate salary and definite powers, rather than the contractor who may gain thousands and tens of thousands of dollars by a single job. But, if the gentleman from Vermont is of opinion that a contractor is not an officer, under the Constitution, I hope he will join me in another vote, on an amendment which I shall beg leave to offer—this goes only to purge these walls, not those of the other House. I mean an amendment declaring

void all contracts made with members of either House, and on this principle: Between the sessions of the Legislature it is possible for a member to receive a lucrative job, by which he may put thousands in his pocket, and, which being completed in the recess, and there being nobody to take cognizance of it, it will be impossible to apply a remedy. But, I hope this construction, which, so far as relates to our own House, we have an undoubted right to make, will obtain as the true construction of the Constitution.

But it is said that this House, and Houses which may hereafter meet, may give the Constitution a different construction. No doubt of it; and this may operate to the end of time. A former House passed a Sedition law; a subsequent House deemed the law unconstitutional. It is true they did not declare it so, and I am sorry for it; but there is no doubt of the fact. Now, we may pass a Sedition law again to-morrow, and the people rise up against it, and send different members to represent them. The people may again slumber; as long as you keep your hands from their pockets, they will keep their eyes from yours; and, in the same way, this law may be repealed. I can, therefore, see no force in this objection. The courts of justice undertake to expound the Constitution, and shall not the House of Representatives be as competent to do this as any court of justice? I will suppose a case, that of a man condemned under the Sedition law by a tribunal of justice. Suppose men of different principles come on the bench, would they hesitate to reverse the preceding decision of the court? Indisputably not. Here, too, then, we would behold varying and repugnant decisions.

MR. EPPES.—I have no doubt that every objection which can be made to a member of this House holding a civil office during his continuance as a Representative applies with equal force to his holding a lucrative contract. The framers of the Constitution in excluding civil officers from the floor of this House, most certainly intended to prevent any species of dependence which might influence the conduct of the Representative—to prevent his looking up for preferment to the Executive, or being biassed in his vote by Executive favor. A lucrative contract creates the same species of dependence, and every objection which could be urged against an officer, applies with equal force against contractors, who are dependent on the Executive will, and particularly carriers of the mail. While, however, I make this admission, I do not believe we have power to pass this resolution. The words of the Constitution are: "No person holding an office under the United States shall be a member of either House during his continuance in office." These words are plain and clear. Their obvious intention was to have excluded officers and officers only. It would certainly have been equally wise to have excluded contractors, because the reason for excluding officers applies to them with equal force. We are not, however, to inquire what the Constitution ought to have been, but what it is. We cannot legislate on its spirit against the strict letter of the instrument. Our inquiry must be, is he an officer? If an officer, under the words of the Constitution, he is excluded; if not an officer, we cannot exclude him by law. It is true, as has been stated, that, by the Constitution, we are made the judges of the qualifications of our own members. This judgment, however, is confined within very narrow limits. The Constitution prescribes the qualifications of a member. We can neither narrow nor enlarge them by law. Our inquiry can go no further than this: has the Representative the qualifications prescribed by the Constitution? An extensive meaning has been given to the word "office." How far such a construction of the meaning of this word is warranted, I leave for others to decide. That all contractors are not officers, I am certain. A man, for instance, makes a contract with the Government to furnish supplies. He is certainly not an officer, according to the common and known acceptation of that word. He is, however, a contractor, and, under this resolution, excluded from a seat here. A carrier of the mail approaches very near an officer. The person takes an oath, is subject to penalties, the remission of which depend on the Executive. His duties are fixed and prescribed by law. Near, however, as this species of contract approaches to an office, I do not consider that the word "office" in the Constitution can include even this species of contract. I consider the word "office" in the Constitution ought to be construed according to the usual import and meaning of that term; and as I do conscientiously believe that the word "office" and the word "contract" cannot be tortured to mean the same thing, I shall vote against the resolution.

Mr. Alston.—While I am as much opposed as any man to see any holder of public money within these walls, I cannot justify myself in declaring what is or what is not the Constitution. If in any case this ought to be done, this surely should be the last. What is its effect? To deprive a member of his seat on the vote of a bare majority, when the Constitution has declared that "no seat shall be vacated but on the vote of two-thirds of the members." Let this House say so, and what becomes of a contractor, if any such there be within these walls? The decision of the House will be in violation of the Constitution. No man who knows me will imagine that I have any partiality for contractors holding seats within these walls. I have never held a contract, or received a cent of the public money but for my wages as a member of this House. I am, therefore, as disinterested as man can be on this point. If there is a contractor within the meaning of the Constitution, let him be pointed out. I am not certain how I shall vote upon such a proposition. But I will not declare beforehand a particular construction of the Constitution. If I believe the case comes within the Constitution, of which I am not certain, I will vote for clearing the House of such a member. But I will not consent to a majority declaring in this way what they cannot carry into effect. How can this be done? If you cannot get two-thirds of the members of this House to vacate the seat, I ask what becomes of the resolution declaratory of the meaning of the Constitution? But it is idle to pass a declaratory resolution unless it can be carried into effect. One thing I will say, if the mover will modify his resolution so as to impose a penalty on any officer who shall make a contract with a member of Congress, I will give it my consent. For I wish to see no man in these walls dependent on the Government. I still adhere to the prin-

ciple which I set out with, when I entered into public life, for I became a member of the Legislature of the State which I have the honor to represent at the age of twenty-one; but there was no office in the gift of any Government which I would possess. This is a principle to which I strictly adhere, and I do not believe I have any relation on earth who holds an office, numerous as my relatives are.

Mr. J. Clay.—The gentleman says he is willing to vote for the expulsion of any member on this floor who holds public money.

Mr. Alston explained by observing that he had not absolutely said so.

Mr. J. Clay.—If this cannot be done under the Constitution, with what consistency can the gentleman vote for the measure he proposes, as, under the provision of the Constitution alluded to, we have no right to expel a member but for some offence committed by him? The judges of your courts as well as the State courts have assumed the right of expounding the Constitution, inasmuch as they are bound on oath to support it. Are we not bound by the same oath to support it? And have we not, by parity of reasoning, the same right to construe it? Are not gentlemen indeed, by their negative vote, giving the Constitution their own exposition? I have no doubt of our right to expound the Constitution. Let us take things as they are. What is an officer? A man holding a public charge or agency. What is an office? A public charge or agency. Is not a contract an agency? A man contracts to carry letters in the mail. Is not that an agency? So a man contracts as an agent of the Postmaster General to carry letters from Washington to Baltimore; is he not as much an officer as if he resided at Washington or Baltimore? The only difference is, that one is moving and the other stationary. Every officer under the Government is a contractor, inasmuch as he contracts to do certain things for a certain sum of money. I believe, likewise, the converse of the proposition is true, and that contractors are likewise officers.

Mr. Findley said, were this proposition proposed as an amendment to the Constitution, he should vote for it; but for reasons very different from those which had been assigned. He did not believe that every contractor was an officer under the Constitution, for if this was the case, every man who furnished the public with the least article of supply would be an officer—the miller who sold flour for the use of the army, as well as the stationer who supplied the House with paper and quills. Every man who sold anything to the Government must, in this light, be considered as an officer. Would gentleman be disposed to exclude all persons of this description from a seat in this House? Great weight had been attached to that clause in the Constitution which made the two Houses judges of the qualifications of their members; but it was a sufficient answer to this argument to observe, that though the Constitution gives the two Houses the power of judging of the qualifications of their members, it does not give them the power to make those qualifications. He agreed that it was discretionary with each House to expel a member, but then the act could only be effected by a vote of two-thirds of the members. He had always understood, and believed it to be correct, that it was an essential attribute of office for a man to possess some power, to be exercised on behalf of the Government. Now a mere contractor receives no such power; he only enters into an engagement to perform certain specified duties.

Mr. J. RANDOLPH desired that part of the Constitution to be read, which authorizes the expulsion of a member, by which, he said, it would appear that such expulsion could only be made for disorderly behaviour.

The Clerk read the article as follows:

"Each House may determine the rules of its proceedings; punish its members for disorderly behaviour, and, with the concurrence of two-thirds, expel a member."

Mr. G. W. CAMPBELL said he would assign the reasons, on account of which he could not give his vote in favor of the resolution under consideration. It proposed to decide what shall, and what shall not be the true construction of the Constitution as to the term *office*. He was of opinion that it was not competent for that House to put a construction upon the Constitution, except in a particular case under their consideration; and that they could then and then only act upon it. If there were any gentlemen upon the floor of the House who were contractors, and a motion should be made to expel them, he would then be ready to give his vote upon such a motion; but he was not prepared to give a general construction to the Constitution as to the existence of any such case. With regard to the case under consideration, he was not prepared to say whether a contractor was an officer within the meaning of the Constitution. The Constitution declared that no Senator or Representative should be appointed to an office: when, therefore, they were inquiring what constituted an office under the Constitution, it was necessary that they should refer to the Constitution itself, to determine the meaning of the word *office*. It declares, in the third section of the second article, that the President shall commission all the officers of the United States. I am not prepared, said Mr. C., to say that a man is an officer who is not so commissioned under the Constitution. It appears to me that a person must have a commission before he can be considered an officer under the Constitution. Mr. C. said he was clearly of opinion that it would be advisable to make a provision to remedy the evil, and he would cheerfully agree to any measure which would have this effect, as he did consider it extremely indecorous for any man holding a contract and the money of the public to participate in the making of laws for its application.

Mr. R. NELSON said he was sorry that he could not on this occasion, consistent with the oath he had taken to support the Constitution, advocate the resolution under consideration. He agreed that it was highly improper for contractors to hold seats in that House, as there were many cases in which they could not give a free and impartial vote; but in his opinion there was no power to exclude members from a seat, unless that power was contained in the Constitution. He said he would give his idea of the spirit and meaning of the Constitution on this point. They

were bound by its letter—where the letter and the words of it were plain, they were bound strictly to adhere to them; where, from the wording, the meaning was doubtful, or difficult, every member was bound to put that construction which his judgment dictated. But where there was no difficulty, where the words were plain and obvious, he would ever raise his hands against what was called the spirit of the Constitution, or, in other words, giving it a meaning which the words would not bear. If this power existed in the Constitution, it must be found under that section, which declares, that "No Senator or Representative shall, during the time for which he was elected, be appointed to any civil office under the authority of the United States, which shall have been created, or the emoluments of which shall have been increased, during such time; and no person holding any office under the United States shall be a member of either House, during his continuance in office." The question then comes to the single point: Is a contractor an officer under the Constitution? If he is, there is no doubt he may be excluded from a seat in this House; but if he is not, he cannot be excluded. What then is the idea of an officer under the Constitution? It either must be recognised by the Constitution, or some law passed in conformity to it, for no man under the Government has a right without law to create as many offices as he pleases. The Postmaster General has a right to contract for carrying the mail; he may employ for this purpose fifty, five hundred, or five thousand men. Will anybody thence contend that the Postmaster General has the right of creating five thousand offices? Our Constitution has been justly extolled as the freest in the world, and as the best calculated to promote the happiness and security of the people. It has been called free in contradistinction to those despotic governments, where all the offices are held up to sale. Is not this the case with contracts? Are they not uniformly given to the lowest bidder? What government of principle then is this, which proposes to put a construction upon the Constitution, by which offices under the Government shall be thus exposed to sale? But are they in truth officers of the United States, recognised either by the Constitution or laws? No, they are not officers of the United States, they are mere hirelings of the Postmaster General; he has not the power of setting up the Constitution to the highest bidder. If so, it is no longer a free Constitution; it does not deserve the eulogiums which have been so justly passed upon it.

Mr. EARLY.—I would not rise to trouble you were not the yeas and nays to be recorded on this question. I am as fully sensible as the honorable mover of the resolution, or any other gentleman on this floor, of the extreme impropriety, to say the least of it, of persons remaining members of this House who hold a contract under the Government to which any emolument is attached. With him and them I believe, that of all descriptions of appointment, this is the most improper to be blended, where the emoluments are not fixed by law, but rise or fall with circumstances. I am therefore as willing as any person can be to adopt any measure to effect a remedy of this evil, which we possess the Constitutional right of doing. My difficulty on this subject is not the same with that presented to the minds of some gentlemen, that we are not authorized to pass a resolution putting a construction upon the Constitution. On this subject, by the Constitution we are made judges of the qualifications of the members of this House. If so, we are necessarily judges of their disqualification also. One power implies the other. I therefore have no difficulty on this score. The simple question is, in my mind, whether a contractor is an officer under the Constitution? My own opinion is decidedly in the negative—an opinion formed after the most mature reflection. I can appeal to you, sir, that I have sought after truth on this subject with industry; and I can appeal to other members to attest my having contemplated early in the session the offering a resolution as the foundation of a law, to give effect to the object of the gentleman from Virginia to declare void any contract made by any officer under this Government with any member of either House. So far I am prepared to go, if any member shall introduce such a proposition. The passage of such a law will remove the inconvenience which might arise from interfering decisions made in this House at different times, and will prevent the existence of a different rule in the two branches of the Legislature.

Mr. Smilie said he heartily concurred in opinion with those gentlemen who considered an union of a contract with a seat on this floor as highly improper. But that was not the question under consideration. It was simply, how far they were authorized by the Constitution to take the course now recommended. Every man attending to that Constitution, would see that it had two great objects in view. One was to promote the interests of the community: the other to protect the rights of individuals. But these duties were equally sacred. Was it then proper, in maintaining the one, to sacrifice the other? To avoid Scylla but strike on Charybdis? He wished to God the Constitution had excluded contractors; but as it had given them a right in common with the citizens of the United States to a seat on that floor in case they were elected, he could not in conscience do anything which would take away those rights. It did not belong to that House, previous to the existence of a particular case, to make a general declaration. When a particular case was brought forward it would be time enough to take the subject under consideration.

Mr. Bidwell said, before he gave his vote, he would concisely state the reasons which would influence him in giving it. This was not a mere question of policy, but a question that implicated the Constitution. It was their duty to decide, not what the Constitution ought to be, but what it was. However it might or might not conform to their abstract idea, they were nevertheless bound by it. The resolution says a contractor is an officer within the meaning of the Constitution. In elucidating this point, the Constitution must be our guide. The clause of the Constitution relied upon is, that "no person holding any office under the United States, shall be a member of either House during his continuance in office." To say that a contractor is an officer is giving a new signification to the words contractor or officer. He considered both words to be as well understood, and to have as definite meanings as any other words in the English language. There is a Constitutional definition of the word officer in the third section of the second article of the Constitution, which provides that the President "shall commission all the officers of the United States." Here then is a Constitutional definition of what is meant by a person holding an office, viz: a person commissioned by the President. A contractor does not necessarily or even generally hold such a commission. By deciding that a contractor is an officer, it will be decided that no contractor could be appointed without being commissioned by the President. This would be extending the doctrine a length to which it had never been carried. Further, it is provided, that the President, Vice President, and other officers of the Government, shall take an oath to support the Constitution of the United States. Is there any such requisition, or has it been usual to require such an oath from contractors? Under this view of the subject, and conceiving himself bound by the oath which he had taken to support the Constitution, he could not in conscience agree to the resolution, whatever evils it might have for its object to cure.

Mr. Rhea (of Tennessee) said this was an abstract question, in the affirmative of which he was not prepared to vote. There were abstract reasons which induced him to vote against the resolution. He said he was averse to assume from the Constitution of the United States, what was not expressly declared therein.

He was not willing to go on, by a principle of construction, until the Constitution of the United States was made anything or nothing. There was a day when the principle of construction was reprobated, and now, having a seat in this honorable House, he was not willing to revive that principle. He said he was determined to vote against the resolution.

Mr. J. Randolph admitted that this might be, as he was convinced it was with many gentlemen, and hoped it was with all, a question admitting of a fair difference of opinion. It was a question that respected the construction of the Constitution of the United States. The point in issue, whether a contractor is or is not an officer of the United States, had been set aside by being begged. Gentlemen argue as if it was proposed to add a new qualification to holding a seat on this floor, when in truth, no such question existed; the only question was, whether there was an existing disqualification. While I am up, said Mr. R., permit me to say the gentleman from Maryland has, with a peculiar infelicity, abandoned the ground which he had first taken. He says that a contract cannot be an office, because the former are put up to sale; and because no man, under the Constitution, can possess the power of creating an indefinite number of offices. And yet, how are those men who carry the mail or discharge the duties of postmasters appointed, but on the mere *dictum* of the Postmaster General? And how are foreign Ministers appointed? They are not appointed by law. The President nominates as many as he pleases, and is only limited by the money at his disposal. As to the offices under the Postmaster General, as has been alleged, being let to the lowest bidder, I believe it would be difficult to establish the allegation. I understand that that is not the principle on which they have been let out. We are told that a contract is nothing but a bargain. It certainly is a bargain. But suppose the office of Postmaster General, as that seems in this debate to have engaged so much of the attention of gentlemen, should be let to the lowest bidder; would the person that discharged those duties be less an officer of the United States? There is one office which I believe is always let to the lowest bidder—a common executioner. Who is he? The deputy of the sheriff: and *quo ad hoc,* he is as much an officer as the superior who employs him.

What do we propose to do? To give a construction to the Constitution which is to operate on our House only, and which is not to govern the other House. They are as much the judges of the qualifications of their own members, as we are of the qualifications of ours. And although the gentleman from Georgia is unwilling a different principle should obtain in the two Houses; and although I should be glad that a proper principle should be applied to both, and should, therefore, be willing that such a principle should be fixed by law; I am not, therefore, for abandoning that, which we have an indisputable right to do, a right to judge of the qualifications of our own members, in hope of obtaining that which we may never accomplish. But let me ask those gentlemen who profess themselves willing to aid us in framing a law upon this subject, how, on their own principle, a law can be framed to do that by law which cannot, as they say, be done under the Constitution? If the Constitution does not authorize such a step, much less will it be authorized by our laws.

Mr. ELMER said it was perfectly clear to him, that the members of that House were not at liberty to vote for the resolution under consideration. Both common sense and the Constitution forbade considering a contract in the light of an office, and he had never before heard it contended that they were equivalent terms. He would cordially give his vote for any law which could be constitutionally passed, to get rid of speculation and corruption of any sort, but the oath which he had taken to support the Constitution limited his power, which he could not transcend.

Mr. KELLY said he would concisely assign the reasons which would induce him to vote against the resolution. He did not believe an officer and a contractor meant the same things. With regard to the contractors holding a seat on that floor, it might happen that a man might be a contractor without being in the least disqualified from impartially discharging all the duties of a member, as the contract which he formed might be more for the good of others than his own benefit. He, however, allowed that where a person held a seat, and made use of the power it gave him to make a contract, he was highly censurable. Still he was of opinion that it was not in the power of the House to declare the two appointments incompatible, unless the Constitution expressly authorized them. In examining the Constitution he found no such provision. Though it had been attempted to be shown that a contractor and an officer were one and the same, he believed they were very distinct things. A contractor receives no authority from Government; his contract was derived from an officer, and all the power he possessed was derived from him, who was only amenable for the performance of the duty to the person who appointed him. A contractor could not, therefore,

be considered as an officer under the Constitution, amenable to the United States.

Several allusions, said Mr. K., have been made to cases which have occurred under the Postmaster General, but until these shall be particularly pointed out, it will be impossible for us to decide how we are to act. I believe that it does not become this House to pass declaratory acts relative to the Constitution. It ought, in my opinion to stand on its own footing; and every case that is presented ought to be decided, not by a declaratory act, but by the Constitution itself. My colleague says that the judges of the federal as well as State courts take an oath as well as we do, to support the Constitution; and that, notwithstanding they are in the daily habit of construing the Constitution. But there is a wide difference between their deciding particular cases which properly come before them, and this House going into a general declaration without any such particular case. Would the judges undertake to declare the meaning of the Constitution without the existence of a particular case calling for their decision? So that the very thing which the House is about doing, has been invariably avoided by the judges.

Mr. DAWSON observed that when the resolution was offered, he had voted for it, because he approved the principle on which it was founded. He should now be obliged to vote against it, because it tended to curtail the privileges of the House. If a contractor had constitutionally no right to a seat in the House, the proper way was to take up the case and act directly upon it. He believed that such a case did exist, and he was ready to say if there were any members who received money from the public, they ought not to hold a seat on that floor.

The question was then taken by yeas and nays on agreeing to the resolution—yeas 25, nays 86.

[*1 Apr.*]

On motion of Mr. JOHN RANDOLPH, the House took up the report of the Committee of the Whole on sundry resolutions agreed to by them on the 28th ultimo. When the question was put on concurring in the report of the Committee of the Whole in their agreement to the second resolution, as follows:

> 2d. *Resolved*—That the union of a plurality of offices in the person of a single individual, but more especially of the military with the civil authority, is repugnant to the spirit of the Constitution of the United States, and tends to the introducing of an arbitrary Government.

Mr. BIDWELL said, he would very concisely assign his reasons for voting against this resolution. It declares that "the union of a plurality of offices in the person of a single individual, but more especially of the military with the civil authority, is repugnant to the spirit of the Constitution of the United States, and tends to the introducing of an arbitrary Government." It appeared to him that this was not a correct declaration. If the Constitution itself be referred to, it will appear that it recognises an union of civil and military officers in the same person. Such an union is to be found in the First Magistrate of the United States, who exercises the highest Executive civil functions, and is at the same time Commander-in-Chief of the Army and Navy, and of the militia while in actual service. The same principle pervaded the Constitution, he believed, of every State. There was also an union of civil and military authority in several offices, by acts of Congress. This was the case with the marshals in certain cases, and officers who are charged with the superintendence of Territorial affairs. If it were proper, said Mr. B., as I do not think it is, by a vote of this House, to undertake to define the Constitution, it still appears to me that we cannot consistently say that the union of a plurality of offices in the person of a single individual, but more especially of the military with the civil authority, is repugnant to the spirit of the Constitution of the United States. A declaration of that kind would be a vote of censure on the people of the whole United States, for having adopted the Federal Constitution, on the people of the several States, for having adopted their constitutions, and on the Legislatures under both Governments, for having passed laws which authorized such an union.

Mr. J. CLAY said, the objections of the gentleman arose from not having properly considered the nature of the union of civil and military office in the First Magistrate. By the Constitution, the military was placed in strict subordination to the civil power. For this reason the President of the United States had placed under his control all the officers of the Army and Navy. The union contemplated in the resolution before you, said Mr. C., is that which gives the actual discharge of civil powers to an officer who has actual command of your army. I ask if it was ever in the contemplation of the Constitution, that the President should in person head your armies and command your fleets? I believe not. There exists in one of the Territories such an union as is contemplated in the resolution. In Louisiana a person holding the office of Governor, is at the same time Commander-in-Chief of the Army of the United States, in virtue of his appointment of Brigadier General. Will any man pretend to say that an union of offices, such as these, the discharge of whose duties is incompatible, is such an union as is contemplated in the Constitution? No; the union in the Constitution was only intended to give the President a control over the Army and Navy; while this resolution contemplates the positive and actual union of powers in the same person, powers, which at the same time he may be called upon to exercise at different and distant places. To separate these powers is the object of the resolution. I hope the resolution will be agreed to, and the separation take place.

Mr. SMILIE said he did not know that he should have any objection to the third resolution, although he had not made up his mind upon it. But with regard to the resolution under consideration, he could not agree to it. He did not know that there was a right in that House to declare what the Constitution was. The Constitution must speak for itself, and they had no right to supply any deficiency in it. When a particular case occurred they might construe it, but he never heard of an instance where a Legislative body put a construction upon it without the existence of a particular case; nor did he believe they possessed such a power. The resolution declared an union of a plurality of offices in the same person repugnant to the spirit of the Constitution. He did not know where to find that spirit but in the letter of the Constitution. He had looked it carefully over, and had not been able to find a single expression that warranted such an inference. He called on gentlemen to point their finger to a single section of it that justified the inference. If at this rate they continued to supply its defects, he did not know where the thing would end. He himself thought the instrument very defective, yet he never thought himself at liberty to remedy the defects but in the way pointed out in the Constitution. If examined it would be found, as it originally stood, to be extremely defective. In providing for the powers of the Government it had almost entirely overlooked the rights of individuals. These defects excited great objection to the instrument. They were, however, supplied by the first Congress, and gentlemen would find that almost all the amendments which have been incorporated into it, go to secure the rights of individuals. Though these amendments constitute what might be called the marrow of the Constitution, Mr. S. said, he should not have considered himself authorized, if they had not taken place, to remedy the evil in any other than a Constitutional way. But he did not deny that it was a defect in the Constitution, that the military and civil authorities were not kept separate. But the simple question was, had they a right under the Constitution to separate them? He thought not. In every point of view, he said, in which he contemplated the resolution, he thought it one of the most dangerous attacks on the Constitution he had ever heard of.

Mr. J. RANDOLPH.—My friend from Pennsylvania has left me little to say on the question, and indeed I have heard nothing in the shape of argument, or assertion, but what I was prepared to hear, and of which I apprized the House some time ago. It has come out at last from the lips of a man who has prided himself upon being the champion of the Constitution of the United States to-day, although but a few days ago he threatened us with a dissolution of the Union, that the Constitution has no spirit in it. He calls on any man to lay his finger on that spirit. What does the Constitution of the United States say? Does it not guarantee to each State a Republican form of Government? Is there no spirit in this? Is not the Constitution then devised under the influence of a Republican spirit, for the benefit of the people who are governed by it, and not for the exclusive benefit of those who administer it? Will any man pretend to say that a Republic is anything or nothing? And that it is congenial to such a Government that the civil and military authority should be vested in the same hands? Is it not of the very essence of such a Government that the military should be kept in strict subordination to the civil power? And have not your laws, which give to marshals in certain cases a power over the military, been passed to keep the military under such subjection? How is the military to be kept in such subjection, when, according to the usage of the Romans, the leader of an army is the Governor of a province? If the Constitution has no spirit in it, it is a dead, lifeless thing, not worth the protection of any man of sense. But I am happy that it has a spirit, which I trust will save this nation, even if its letter shall be killed.

But we are told that this is a declaratory resolution. Gentlemen may call it a declaratory resolution, or a preamble to the third resolution, whichever they may see fit, but it is the reasoning on which the third resolution is founded. What is it but a declaration on the part of this House, which they have a right to make, that a certain principle is salutary, because it is consonant with the spirit of the Constitution? Is it not agreeable to the spirit of the Constitution that the three great Departments of the Government, Executive, Legislative, and Judicial, should be kept separate and distinct? Is there a man fool-hardy enough to deny the proposition? I believe not. Now, suppose we were about to devise a form of Government for New Orleans and Louisiana, and a member should propose to concentre all the powers of the Government in one and the same body, and a resolution should be laid on the table declaring that whereas an union of Executive, Legislative, and Judicial powers in the same body is repugnant to the spirit of the Constitution, and should go on in the shape of a resolution to apply the remedy—and some man should make the wonderful discovery that the Senate of the United States are constitutionally participators of the Executive power of the Government, and that in case of impeachment they have also Judicial powers, and infer from this that such an union was consonant with the spirit of the Constitution—would not this be a satire on the Constitution as well as those who adopt it?

Suppose all offices in the gift of the Executive Government were united in one man. I do not see, if this is consonant to the spirit of the Constitution, and a man is properly qualified, why he may not unite in himself the powers of all the Departments. The Secretary of War may, on the same principle, be Commander-in-Chief of the Army. No,—it is not because this resolution is a satire upon the people who framed or adopted the Constitution, but because it is a satire, a reproof of which the times call for, that gentlemen are so extremely tender relative to it; and the question now is, whether the House ought, in tenderness to any man, to flinch from the exercise of their Constitutional powers. What would I have said seven years ago to any man who should have told me that the gentleman from Pennsylvania would have been found in opposition to this measure—who should have predicted that the rugged patriot of those days should be softened by Court favor into so accomplished a courtier? It shows that what cannot be done by force or violence, may be by influence. This question may be put into a short compass. It is, whether the Constitution of the United States is a republican Constitution, devised and adopted for the benefit of the people it governs, or a piece of mechanism, to be tortured and twisted in the hands in which chance may throw it, for the benefit of a temporary incumbent. If the case has come to this, that the Chief Justice may be made Commander-in-Chief of the Armies, without the Constitution

being violated, it is time the nation should know their situation.

Mr. SLOAN said he had examined the resolution, and would cordially give his assent to the principle contained in it, provided it were brought forward in the form of an amendment to the Constitution. He thought, with his friend from Pennsylvania, that, as it stood, it was a dangerous attack upon the Constitution. He therefore trusted it would be rejected, and that every similar attempt would be treated in the same manner.

Mr. QUINCY said he would merely observe, that, though it were true that an union of civil and military offices in the same person was repugnant to the spirit of the Constitution, it was not true that an union of different offices in the same person was repugnant to it. They had to-day united two offices in the same person, in the bill relative to the Territory of Michigan. They had heretofore constituted several of the officers of the Government Commissioners of the Sinking Fund. He could see nothing in the Constitution which interfered with a plurality of offices, which in many instances was attended with great practical benefit. As there was therefore in the Constitution nothing explicit against this union, he could not vote for the resolution.

Mr. GREGG said, he believed it was contrary to the spirit of the Constitution, that civil and military offices should be united in the same person; but, he would ask what benefit would result from such a declaration? The power of appointing to office was vested in the President and Senate, who were sworn to support the Constitution. They were, therefore, the judges of the powers with which they were invested. In the exercise of this power, they have actually declared that they do possess it. What does this resolution amount to? If they undertook to declare the President guilty of such a flagrant act as involved a violation of the Constitution, it was their business to impeach him. Mr. G. said, as he could see no good likely to arise from this resolution, he should not vote for it. The practice it referred to was not new, though he had always thought it wrong. He recollected, that, some years since, the Governor of the Northwestern Territory was likewise Superintendent of Indian Affairs and Commander-in-Chief of the Army, for all which appointments he drew pay, though no notice had been taken of it. Other instances of the same kind might be pointed out. He did believe this union was contrary to the spirit of the Constitution—to the true spirit of a republican Government—and if the gentleman from Virginia would bring forward an amendment to the Constitution to prohibit such an union, he would vote for it.

Mr. FINDLEY said he did not understand the language of the spirit of the Constitution. Spirit was altogether an immaterial thing—it was only when connected with the body that they could see it—and with regard to the Constitution, it could only be seen through its letter. How long is it, said Mr. F., since the gentleman from Virginia and myself agreed to unite in the same body both civil, military, and judicial powers? We did so, in forming the first government for the Territory of Orleans. Mr. F. said he was against all such declaratory resolutions. They did not bind Congress, the President, or even the next House of

Representatives. They only contained an expression of opinions where there was no authority. They were sent here to pass laws, and not to make declarations relative to the Constitution.

Mr. RHEA, of Tennessee, said he considered the Constitution as a sacred deposit placed in their hands, and not capable of alteration, except in the way fixed by itself. Every resolution similar to that under consideration operated as an amendment to it, which went to torture and twist it out of its proper shape. He should, therefore, not only vote against this resolution, but against every resolution which appeared to him to have a similar effect.

Mr. J. RANDOLPH.—Six years ago, there could not have been a doubt of the right of this House to pass this resolution—now, the right is disputed. Have we not a right to pass a resolution referring to the Constitution, in order to bring in a law grounded on it? Do we not do this every day? One word as to the appointment of General Wilkinson. Gentlemen are fond of sheltering themselves behind great names. I have no hesitation in saying I think the Executive was wrong in making that appointment. I have no hesitation in saying so here, though gentlemen who join me out of doors are reluctant to make the same declaration on this floor. I do not think, however, the persons who made the appointment as reprehensible as the persons at whose importunate solicitation it was made. I believe that a man of good sense, and of upright intentions, may be induced to do that which his own judgment will afterwards condemn. It is well known, that the antechambers of our great men were crowded with applicants for offices in Louisiana. I have understood that for every office there were at least one hundred and fifty applications. Thus much for the idea which has been thrown out of the existence of a scarcity of characters to supply these offices.

But we are told that we ourselves have done as bad as this, in establishing the temporary government of Louisiana. If gentlemen bring me many more precedents on this subject, I shall be compelled to say that purchase was the greatest curse that ever befell us. What! Shall a temporary system, formed on an emergency, when it was necessary to do something to take the country into our hands, be compared to a deliberate and systematic procedure?

But there is another reason alleged for uniting a plurality of offices in one person, and that is the lowness of salaries. I do not know any spectacle more disgusting to a man of unsophisticated feelings, than that of men hunting, with all the avidity of terriers, after appointments, and the next moment complaining that the salaries attached to their places are too low. Before they get the office they have no objection to the salary, but the moment they are on the saddle, they discover that they have sacrificed their talents to the public good. This is the cant of the whole tribe—the slang of those men whose last object is to live on their own honest exertions, and who are therefore for making a job of Government.

One observation has been made, which shows that the meaning of this resolution has not been properly understood, which relates to the Commissioners of the Sinking Fund. But the Commissioners of the Sinking Fund are not, strictly speaking, officers. The duties they discharge are *ex officio*, in virtue of their holding other high offices, and, as Commissioners, they receive no salary. I will go further, and state that this resolution does not contain any veto on the union of small offices, such as those in the custom-houses, where the compensation attached to each appointment is too small to support the officer, and the duties too inconsiderable to occupy his time; in consequence of which, several small appointments are united in one man, on the true principles of economy. No; this resolution is intended for great cases, such as that which has been alluded to. I believe that the person who made that appointment is himself conscious that it was wrong, and that, so far from entertaining the feelings which gentlemen have imagined, he will feel a sentiment of respect for this House, should they pass it.

Mr. VARNUM considered the resolution as going too far, and said it was a very common thing for two offices to be united in one man. It had been usual to unite the diplomatic character with the military command in our intercourse with the Indians, and a diplomatic character had likewise been given to our naval commander in the Mediterranean. Instances of a plurality of offices in one person were very numerous. If there existed, at present, any case, in which such an union was incompatible with the discharge of official duties, he hoped it would be pointed out; whether there was or was not, he could not say. But where did the responsibility for such appointments lie? Not that House, but the other branch of the Legislature was responsible; for the correct discharge of whose duties they were accountable to the people. Where, then, was the propriety of an interference by the House? If the President made an appointment against the spirit of the Constitution, the people would know it. Was it presumable that if a law was to pass this House, predicated on the resolution under consideration, the other branch of the Legislature would agree to it, after having sanctioned the appointments at which it is levelled? Was this House to sit as a court of censure? The Constitution did not delegate such a power. Our very laws, in various cases, direct the union of office prescribed by the resolution. Ought we not, then, in the first place, to repeal those laws before we pass a resolution in direct hostility to them?

Mr. V. said, he had no hesitation to observe, that the military and civil office should, in general, be kept distinct; but he believed there were cases where it was necessary. He was perfectly willing to leave the responsibility where the Constitution had placed it—in the hands of the President and Senate. With regard to the union of the military office in the cases alluded to, he would not undertake to say whether it was proper or not. He could readily, however, conceive, that the union arose from the most correct motive, as the country was a frontier, which might be menaced with danger, and which might require the united exercise of the military and civil authority to repel it.

Mr. J. CLAY said, he would ask whether the ordinary union of military and civil powers in the Governors of the Territories was such as that contemplated in the resolution? The case of the Governor of Louisiana had been alluded to, where the same person, he believed, received the pay of Governor and Brigadier. Is that the case with the other Governors? He believed gentlemen would not say that it was necessary that the Governor of New Orleans should be a brigadier general in the army; and yet they allowed that to be the most vulnerable point on the frontier. If, then, they say that the union is necessary in one case, they will admit that it ought to be in the other. When the marshal executes the petty military authority with which he is invested, does he receive additional pay? Does the Governor of a State, being commander of the militia, bear any relation to the Governor of Louisiana, holding a high rank in the standing army? Suppose the southern frontier should be invaded, and it should be necessary to call out the army to defend it, where would be the compatibility of these two appointments? The same individual might be called at one and the same time to St. Louis and St. Mary's. He would ask whether it was compatible with the spirit of the Constitution for a man to enjoy a sinecure? and whether one of these offices was not a sinecure, when the discharge of its duties was inconsistent with that of the other?

Mr. Leib said that, viewing the resolution as an abstract proposition, he had no objection to giving it his support; but if was intended as a side attack upon the Administration, he was not prepared to vote for it. Before he was prepared to act on it under this view, he wished for facts which were not before the House. He, therefore, moved a postponement of the resolution till Monday.

The motion to postpone was lost.

The question was then taken on agreeing to the resolution, and decided in the negative—yeas 31, nays 81.

7

Hinds' Precedents of the House of Representatives, sec. 499
Jan. 1818

On January 5, 1818, the Committee on Elections made a report in the case of C. Hammond's contest for the seat of Mr. Samuel Herrick, of Ohio. On the 19th of December, 1810, Mr. Herrick had been appointed attorney of the United States for the district of Ohio, which office he accepted and held until his resignation thereof on the 29th of November, 1817. In October, 1816, he was elected one of the Representatives of the State of Ohio for the Fifteenth Congress. The result of the election was publicly announced on the 7th of January, 1817, in the presence of the senate of that State. On the 15th of September, 1817, the governor executed a certificate of Mr. Herrick's election, according to the law of Ohio, which was received by him on or about the 30th day of the same month. Mr. Herrick, therefore, continued in office almost nine months after the 4th of March and two months after receiving the certificate of his election. Congress met December 1, 1817, and Mr. Herrick took his seat on that day in the House of Representatives.

The Committee on Elections which examined the case consisted of Messrs. John W. Taylor, of New York, John Tyler, of Virginia, Ezekiel Whitman, of Massachusetts, Orsamus C. Merrill, of Vermont, Solomon Strong, of Massachusetts, John L. Boss, jr., of Rhode Island, and Henry Shaw, of Massachusetts. Their report, which seems to have been unanimous, examined very carefully whether or not the sixth section of Article I of the Constitution had been violated. After referring to the cases of John P. Van Ness and Philip Barton Key and certain English precedents the report proceeds to a very full consideration of the status of a Member-elect of the House:

Persons elected to the House of Commons become at one time members for certain purposes and at another time for other purposes. Thus immediately upon executing the indenture of return by the sheriff or other returning officer, the person elected becomes entitled to the privilege of franking, although the day at which the Parliament is made returnable may not have arrived. Yet he is not a member, for he may thereafter be a candidate for election in another district at any time before the Parliament is made returnable and the return actually filed in the Crown office. From the time last mentioned he becomes a member so far that he can not be a candidate for another district, but yet he may thereafter hold an office incompatible with membership, and upon resigning his office he may immediately qualify and take his seat in the House. It has often been decided by their committee of elections that a person holding an office incompatible with membership is, nevertheless, capable of prosecuting his claim to a [seat]. After examination of all the parliamentary registers, histories, and journals within our reach we have found no case where a person elected to the House of Commons was brought in on a call of the House before he had voluntarily appeared, qualified, and taken his seat, nor do we find any instance of a person having been expelled until after such time.

A very particular case occurred on the 10th of February, 1620. Sir John Leech having been elected a member of the House of Commons, and appearing to take the oaths of supremacy and allegiance, was asked whether he had not already sat in the House that Parliament in violation of the statute. He confessed that on the Wednesday morning previous he did sit in the House a quarter of an hour, being unsworn. For this offense Sir John was not expelled, but it was resolved that he was disabled to serve in the House, and a new writ of election was issued to supply the vacancy, in the same manner as if no election and return had taken place. The same course of proceeding has been pursued when a person duly elected and returned comes into the House and refuses to be sworn. Such was the case of Mr. Archdale, in the year 1698, who, being elected and returned, came into the House of Commons and said he was ready to serve if his affirmation of allegiance could be accepted instead of his oath. The House resolved that it could not. Mr. Archdale, still declining to take the oath, was refused admittance to a seat and a new writ was issued to supply his place. This case is more peculiar because a person elected to the House of Commons can not relinquish his right to a seat either before or after qualification otherwise than by accepting an incompatible office. But by refusing to be sworn he may do that indirectly which he is not permitted to do directly. We have seen several similar cases which occurred in the colonial assembly of New York, but not now having access to the journals we are unable to report the particulars.

Persons elected and returned to the House of Commons may be chosen members of committees before they appear and qualify. But it is allowed for a reason similar to that which, in courts of law, permits a declaration to be filed de bene esse before the defendant appears in court. In both cases the act is conditional; and it is ineffectual unless the condition of appearance be performed.

The practice of this House, which does not allow the appointment of persons to be members of committees until they shall have been sworn and shall have taken their seats, is obviously more reasonable and convenient than the other. It was decided as early as the first session of the Second Congress, in the case of John F. Mercer, who was chosen to supply a vacancy in the representation of the State of Maryland, occasioned by the resignation of William Pinckney, that a Representative-elect might decline his election before taking his seat and before the first session of the Congress to which he was elected. We do not find that the question has since been agitated, although similar cases have often occurred. Our rule in this particular is different from that of the House of Commons; it is also better, for it makes our theory conform to what is fact in both countries, that the act of becoming in reality a Member of the House depends wholly upon the will of the person elected and returned. Election of itself does not constitute membership, although the period may have arrived at which the Congressional term commences. This is evident from the consideration that all the votes given at an election may not be returned by a returning officer in season to be counted, whereby a person not elected may be returned and take the seat of one who was duly elected. Neither does a return necessarily confer membership, for if he in whose favor it be made should be prevented taking a seat at the organization of a House of Representatives, he might find upon presenting himself to qualify that his return had been superseded by the admission of another person into the seat for which he was returned.

At an election held in the State of Georgia in October, 1804, Thomas Spalding was duly chosen a Representative to the Ninth Congress, but because the votes of three counties were not returned to the governor within twenty days after the election, Cowles Mead received a certificate and took his seat. Mr. Spalding afterwards presented his petition. The House vacated Mr. Mead's seat and admitted Mr. Spalding.

In April, 1814, Doctor Willoughby was elected a Representative of the State of New York to the Fourteenth Congress; but by reason of a clerical error of certain inspectors in returning certificates of votes to the office of the county clerk, General Smith was declared duly elected, and a certificate of election was accordingly delivered to him; but he, having omitted to take a seat at the commencement of the session, was, on the ninth day thereafter, declared not entitled, and thereupon Doctor Willoughby was admitted in his seat.

Several other cases might be cited where persons were returned who never in fact became Members, and where others became Members who were not returned. Neither do election and return create membership. These acts are nothing more than the designation of the individual, who, when called upon, in the manner prescribed by law, shall be authorized to claim title to a seat. This designation, however, does not confer a perfect right, for a person may be selected by the people destitute of certain qualifications, without which he can not be admitted to a seat. He is, nevertheless, so far the Representative of those who elected him that no vacancy can exist until his disqualification be adjudged by the House. Yet it would be easy to state cases where he would not be permitted for a moment to occupy a seat, notwithstanding the regularity of his election and return. To no practical purpose could he ever have been a Member. So, also, if a person duly qualified be elected and returned and die before the organization of the House of Representatives, we do not think he could be said to have been a Member of that body, which had no existence until after his death. We say which had no existence, for we consider that concept altogether fanciful which represents one Congress succeeding to another as members of the same corporation. It has no foundation either in fact or in the theory of our Government. Each House of Representatives is a distinct legislative body, having no connection with any preceding one. It commences its existence unrestrained by any rules or regulations for the conducting of business, which were established by former Houses, and which were binding upon them. It prescribes its own course of proceeding, elects its officers, and designates their duties. Even joint rules for the government of both Houses of Congress are not binding upon a new House of Representatives, unless expressly established by it. Although the Fourteenth Congress had never assembled the Fifteenth would have met, under the Constitution, clothed with every legislative power, as amply as it was enjoyed by the Thirteenth. The Constitution does not define the time for which Representatives shall be chosen. It is satisfied provided the choice take place at any time in every second year. The rest is left to the discretion of each State. Accordingly, in some States Representatives are usually chosen for one year and seven months, and in other States for a longer time.

The privilege of exemption from arrest, granted by the Constitution to Representatives before a meeting of the House, and after its adjournment, furnishes no argument in favor of their membership at such times. Exemptions from arrest is a privilege as old as the Parliament of England. There it is extended, not only to members, but to their servants, horses, and carriages. Our Constitution adopts the very words of the common law, but restricts the privilege to Members. In both countries the object is the same, not the benefit of the Member, but of the public service. It is an essential incident to the right of being represented, and a consequence of that right. But that membership is not coextensive with the enjoyment of that privilege is manifest from the consideration that such a construction might make the Members of one Congress continue in office, not only after the Congress had expired, but also after the next Congress was actually in session. This construction, therefore, is not only absurd, but it serves to illustrate the fallacy of that suggestion which fancies the Representatives of one Congress succeeding to the seats of their predecessors as members of the same corporate body.

The privilege of franking letters, and of exemption from militia duty, are not granted by the Constitution. They are established by law and liable to be changed at the will of the Government. They have been extended and may be restricted, as public convenience shall require. Previous to the last Congress the privilege of franking was not enjoyed until after the commencement of each session. But as that does not prove negatively that persons elected to the House of Representatives were not Members before that time, so the existing law does not prove affirmatively that they are. It is true that the words "Members of the House of Representatives" are used as descriptive of the persons to whom the privilege is granted, but they certainly were used without intending thereby to express an opinion, much less to decide when membership commences, and probably without in any wise adverting to that inquiry.

The conclusion of the committee was embodied in this resolution:

Resolved, That Samuel Herrick is entitled to a seat in this House.

On March 19 this report, which had been committed to the Committee of the Whole, was considered. Mr. Richard C. Anderson, jr., of Kentucky, spoke at length in opposition to the idea that a Member-elect was not a Member. He said the provision of the Constitution that, "a majority of each House shall constitute a quorum to do business, but a smaller number may adjourn from day to day, and may be authorized to compel the attendance of absent Members," must refer to the first as well as to any subsequent session of Congress, and therefore was the plainest evidence that a person elected might be a Member of the House before he had appeared and taken his seat. Other sections of the Constitution, that giving Representatives privilege from arrest while going to and returning from

the sessions, that prohibiting a Representative from being appointed an elector, and that fixing the age of the Representative at at least 25 years were also evidence of the same thing. If a Member-elect was not a Representative he might be an elector, and thus, in certain contingencies, vote for President once as an elector and again a little later as a Representative on the floor of the House, a situation evidently not contemplated by the Constitution. Also if a Member-elect was not a Representative, a man under 25 years might be chosen provided he would become 25 by the time Congress should meet. But a provision making the eligibility of a Representative depend upon the time of year at which Congress might meet was an evident absurdity.

On March 20, on motion of Mr. Benjamin Adams, of Massachusetts, and by a vote of 67 ayes to 66 noes, the Committee of the Whole inserted the word "not" in the resolution, so it should read that Mr. Herrick was not entitled to the seat.

When this amendment was reported to the House, the House disagreed to it—yeas 74, nays 77. The resolution declaring Mr. Herrick entitled to the seat was then adopted—yeas, 77, nays 70.

8

SENATE, SELECT COMMITTEE REPORT ON AMENDMENT TO CONSTITUTION
1 Mar. 1826

Sen. Doc. no. 52, 19th Cong., 1st sess.

Mr. BENTON, from the Select Committee, to whom was referred the proposition to amend the Constitution of the United States, with respect to the appointment of Senators and Representatives to offices under the Federal Government,

REPORTED:

That, having had recourse to the history of the times in which the Constitution was formed, the Committee find that the proposition now referred to them, had engaged the deliberations of the Federal Convention which framed the Constitution, and of several of the State Conventions which ratified it.

In an early stage of the session of the Federal Convention, it was resolved, as follows:

"Article 6, section 9. The members of each House (of Congress) shall be ineligible to, and incapable of, holding any office under the authority of the United States, during the time for which they shall respectively be elected; and the members of the Senate shall be ineligible to, and incapable of, holding any such office for one year afterwards."—(*Journal of the Federal Convention, page* 219.)

It further appears from the journal, that this clause, in the first draft of the Constitution, was adopted with great unanimity, and that afterwards, in the concluding days of the session, it was altered, and its intention defeated, by a majority of a single vote, in the absence of one of the States by which it had been supported.

Following the Constitution into the State Conventions which ratified it, and the Committee find, that, by the New York Convention, it was recommended, as follows:

"That no Senator or Representative shall, during the time for which he was elected, be appointed to any office under the authority of the United States."

By the Virginia Convention, as follows:

"That the members of the Senate and House of Representatives shall be ineligible to, and incapable of, holding any civil office under the authority of the United States, during the term for which they shall respectively be elected."

By the North Carolina Convention, the same amendment was recommended, in the same words.

In the first session of the first Congress, which was held under the Constitution, a member of the House of Representatives submitted a similar proposition of amendment; and, in the third session of the eleventh Congress, James Madison being President, a like proposition was again submitted, and being referred to a Committee of the House, was reported by them in the following words:

"No Senator or Representative shall be appointed to any civil office, place, or emolument, under the authority of the United States, until the expiration of the Presidential term in which such person shall have served as a Senator or Representative."

Upon the question to adopt this resolution, the vote stood 71 yeas, 40 nays, wanting but three votes of the constitutional number for referring it to the decision of the States.

Having thus shewn, by a reference to the venerable evidence of our early history, that the principle of the amendment now under consideration, has had the support and approbation of the first friends of the Constitution, the Committee will now declare their own opinion in favor of its correctness, and expresses its belief that the ruling principle in the organization of the Federal Government demands its adoption.

That ruling principle requires that the three great branches of the Federal Government, the Executive, Legislative, and Judiciary, should be separate and distinct from each other, not only in contemplation of law, but in point of fact; and, for this end, that each should not only have its independent organization, but that the individuals administering each, should be wholly free from the control and influence of the individuals who administered the others.

To secure this independence on the part of the President, and to prevent the legislative department from starving him into a compliance with their will, by withholding his necessary support, or seducing him into an acquiescence in their views, by tempting his avarice with an augmented salary, (*Fed. No. 77*,) it is provided in the constitution that he shall receive a *fixed* compensation for his services, which shall neither be *increased* nor *diminished* during the term for which he was elected.

To secure the independence of the Legislative Department, and to prevent the Executive from influencing its deliberations, by retaining a set of dependants in the Senate and House of Representatives, always ready, like the placemen in the British Parliament, to support the measures of administration, it was provided, in the same constitution, that persons holding offices under the authority of the United States, should be wholly excluded from the floor of Congress.

The Committee believe that this provision for the independence of the Senate and House of Representatives, though wise and proper as far as it goes, does not go far enough to accomplish the object it had in view. They admit that the presence of office holders in the legislative department would be the bane of honest and independent legislation; and they believe that the presence of office hunters would be equally fatal. The danger to be apprehended from each, is, in effect, the same. The office holder would support the measures of administration for the purpose of saving the office which he had in possession; the office hunter would support the same measures, for the purpose of securing the office which he had in expectation. By either party, the interest of the country would be sacrificed to the views of the Executive; and the appropriate means for preventing this mischief, was, first, to exclude office holders from seats in Congress, and this the constitution has done; and secondly, to prevent Senators and Representatives from taking appointments from the President under whose administration they had served; and this it has omitted to do. The omission was too material to escape the observation of those who were not blind to the defects of the constitution; and their animadversions were too loud and vehement to pass unnoticed by the great advocates for the ratification of that instrument. The authors of the Federalist, in their *No. 55*, felt it to be their duty to meet the objection which grew out of this omission. But even these great men, with their superior abilities, and ardent zeal in the best of causes, could attempt no more than to diminish the quantum of a danger which could not be denied to exist, and to cover, with a brilliant declamation, a part of their beloved constitution which could not be defended. They said:

"Sometimes we are told, that this fund of corruption, (Executive appointments,) is to be exhausted by the President in subduing the virtue of the Senate. Now, the fidelity of the other House is to be the victim. The improbability of such a mercenary and perfidious combination of the several members of the Government, standing on as different foundations as republican principles will well admit, and at the same time accountable to the society over which they are placed, ought alone to quiet this apprehension. But, fortunately, the constitution has provided a still further safeguard. The members of the Congress are rendered ineligible to any civil offices that may be created, or of which the emoluments may be increased, during the term of their election. No offices, therefore, can be dealt out to the existing members but such as may become vacant by ordinary casualties; and to suppose that these would be sufficient to purchase the guardians of the people, selected by the people themselves, is to renounce every rule by which events ought to be calculated, and to substitute an indiscriminate and unbounded jealousy, with which all reasoning must be vain."

The Committee believe that this answer, though specious and confident, was insufficient at the time it was given, and that subsequent events have entirely invalidated it. It was insufficient, because it turned upon the false position that one office could only influence one member, whereas, in the opinion of the Committee, it might influence many; for the danger to be apprehended from this source, lies in the *pursuit,* and not in the *enjoyment* of the office, and many members might be pursuing the same one, at the same time, and all upon the same principle, of devotion to the will of the President and neglect of the interests of their constituents. But whether good or bad at the time it was given, there can be no question about its insufficiency at the present time. The *fact* upon which it rested has ceased to exist. It is no longer true that the President, in dealing out offices to members of Congress, will be limited, as supposed in the Federalist, to the inconsiderable number of places which may become vacant by the ordinary casualties of deaths and resignations; on the contrary, he may now draw, for that purpose, upon the entire fund of the Executive patronage. Construction and legislation have accomplished this change. In the very first year of the constitution, a construction was put upon that instrument which enabled the President to create as many vacancies as he pleased, and at any moment that he thought proper. This was effected by yielding to him the kingly prerogative of dismissing officers without the formality of a trial. The authors of the Federalist had not foreseen this construction; so far from it, they had asserted the contrary, and, arguing logically from the premises, *"that the dismissing power was appurtenant to the appointing power,"* they had maintained, in *No. 77* of that standard work, that, as the consent of the Senate was necessary to the appointment of an officer, so the consent of the same body would be equally necessary to his dismission from office. But this construction was overruled by the first Congress which was formed under the constitution; the power of dismission from office was abandoned to the President alone, and, with the acquisition of this prerogative, the power and patronage of the Presidential office was instantly increased to an indefinite extent, and the argument of the Federalist against the capacity of the President to corrupt the members of Congress, founded upon the small number of places which he could use for that purpose, was totally overthrown. So much for construction. Now for the effects of legislation; and without going into an enumeration of statutes which unnecessarily increase the Executive patronage, the four years' appointment law will alone be mentioned; for, this single act, by vacating almost the entire civil list once in every period of a Presidential term of service, places more offices at the command of the President than were known to the constitution at the time of its adoption, and is, of itself, again sufficient to overthrow the whole of the argument which was used in the Federalist. So completely is this the fact, and so entirely has that argument vanished, that no one

pretends to repeat it now. A new reason is now resorted to; and an improved capacity for discharging the duties of these offices, which a service in Congress is supposed to confer, is the argument now relied upon. But the committee do not yield to this argument the force which is claimed for it. They believe that it ought to be received with great qualification, and limited in its application to a small number of offices of the highest grade, and to such members of either house as actually apply themselves to the discharge of their public duties. The places which impart the faculty of giving counsel to the President, as the Departments of State, Treasury, War and Navy, and those which impose the obligation of treating with foreign powers, as embassies, may be offices of this description; but as for the great mass of places which compose the bulk of Executive patronage, and which require no particular experience in foreign affairs, nor very enlarged knowledge of the science of government, such as those connected with the Army, the Navy, the Judiciary, the Territorial Governments, the Customs, the Land Offices, the Post Offices, the affairs of the Indians, the collection and disbursement of the public revenue, &c. &c. &c. the committee are wholly at a loss to conceive of any additional fitness or capability for discharging their duties which the most laborious service in Congress would confer. But, while they admit that heads of departments and ambassadors to foreign countries might be advantageously taken from the halls of Congress, they believe that it would be invidious to discriminate between the higher and the lower offices, and that any discrimination of this kind which could be made would still leave open the door to that sort of tampering with the independence of members which the purity of the government, and the ruling principle of the constitution, require to be closed up forever. The only discrimination which occurs to the Committee as proper to be made, is the one which has been indicated in most of the propositions to amend the Constitution in this particular, and which consists, in itself, an obvious and essential difference in the nature of the offices, and in the facility of using them for corrupt purposes. This distinction is found in the difference between *civil* and *military* appointments; to the latter of which it is deemed inexpedient to extend the ineligibility of Senators and Representatives, as well on account of the high nature of the service to be performed, as because the occasions for such appointments, (being confined to a state of war,) will rarely occur; and when they do, will be attended with a degree of danger, toil, and privation, which will deprive them of all attraction for that description of politicians, who could be capable of bartering their official independence for the mercenary emoluments and the gilded trappings of office.

But, besides the danger to the independence of Congress, which the committee apprehend from the continued eligibility of Senators and Representatives, to Executive appointments, another evil, equally at war with the intention of the Constitution, and with the rights of the People, may spring from the same source. It was the intention of the Constitution, that Senators and Representatives should be periodically returned, as private citizens, to the mass of their constituents, to have their official conduct reviewed by them, and to receive, at their hands, the approbation or the censure which that conduct might deserve. This return to the people, and accountability to them, constitutes the *responsibility* of the Representative, and affords the only check and control over his conduct, which the constituent can possess. The value of this responsibility was particularly relied upon, and enforced, by the authors of the Federalist, *(No. 57;)* but, if the President may prevent this return of the Senators and Representatives to their constituents: if, more than that, he may take them from their seats, and place them in other offices, far removed from the reach of the People, then the responsibility which the Constitution intended to establish, is not only destroyed, but an unfaithful member, who has sacrificed the rights of the People to the will of the Executive, may be elevated to new honors, enriched with great emoluments, and placed in a condition to defy the resentment of those to whom the Constitution intended to make him accountable.

Considering all which, the Committee have come to the unanimous resolution to submit to the Senate a proposition of amendment to the Constitution of the United States, embracing the principle of this report:

Resolved, by the Senate and House of Representatives of the United States of America in Congress assembled, two-thirds of both Houses concurring, That the following amendment to the Constitution of the United States, be proposed to the Legislatures of the several States which, when ratified by three-fourths of said Legislatures, shall be valid, to all intents and purposes, as part of said Constitution:

No Senator or Representative shall be appointed to any civil office, place, or emolument, under the authority of the United States, until the expiration of the Presidential term in which such person shall have served as a Senator or Representative.

9

WILLIAM WIRT, CONTRACTS WITH MEMBERS OF CONGRESS
18 July 1826
2 Ops. Atty. Gen. 39

SIR: The question which you submit for my opinion is, whether your employment of members of Congress, as assistant counsel to the district attorneys of the United States, be within the prohibitions of the act of April 21, 1808, "concerning public contracts?"

I am entirely satisfied that this sort of engagements was not within the view of Congress when the act was passed; but that the species of contracts which led to its passage were of a different character, as stated in the report of a select committee of the 29th March, 1822, upon the subject of the employment of a Senator of the United States in the examination of certain land offices in Ohio, &c. The practice, too, in several instances stated in that report,

seems to have limited the construction of the act to the specific species of contracts which were known to have led to its enactment. But yet, the language of the law is so broad and so explicit, not only in its positive enactments, but in its exceptions; and its policy, too, is so broad and general, that I cannot discover any satisfactory distinction by which the contracts in question can be withdrawn from its operation.

The first section forbids all contracts between officers of the government and members of Congress. It is true that the language of this section seems, for the most part, to be applicable only to the kind of contracts which produced the law; and had the question rested on this section only, there would have been good ground for confining the operation of the act to those kinds of contracts to which it owes its origin. But the second reflects a larger construction on the first, by excepting from its action a species of contract as far removed from the natural sense of the first section, as the kind of engagements now in question—to wit, the purchase of bills of exchange from members of Congress. The exception proves that Congress intended, by the first section, to use language broad enough to cover the excepted cases; and that hence it was necessary to introduce the positive exception. Now if, as is thus implied by the legislature itself, the first section is broad enough to comprehend the sale of bills of exchange, I see not why it is not broad enough to comprehend the sale of professional services, or any other species of work and labor, in any other art, mystery, or science, as well as that of the law. And again: if the prohibitions do not extend to engagements for professional services with gentlemen of the law, do they extend to engagements with gentlemen of the medical faculty? If not, a member of Congress might be stationed as a surgeon at a military post, on an annual stipend, without any violation of the law.

But let us pursue the inquiry one step further. The second section of the act having expressly excepted from the operation of the law two cases only—to wit, contracts with corporations, and the purchase of bills of exchange—the fourth section uses the following pointed and comprehensive terms: "That if any officer of the United States, in behalf of the United States, shall, directly or indirectly, make or enter into *any contract, bargain, or agreement,* in writing or otherwise, *other than such as are herein excepted,* with any member of Congress, such officer so offending," &c., &c. Now, I think it cannot be denied that an engagement with a gentleman of the bar, whereby, for a valuable consideration, he is to render his professional services in a given case, is *a contract, a bargain, an agreement,* in the legal sense of these terms, (and in none other are they to be regarded;) and it is a bargain, contract, or agreement, other than the two which had been previously excepted by the act. It is, therefore, a contract forbidden expressly by the fourth section of the act.

Should it be objected that this is sticking *in the letter* of the law to the disregard of *its policy,* I cannot accede to the objection.

The policy of the law is to prevent the exercise of executive influence over the members of Congress by the means of contracts; and whether the contract be for the service of a lawyer, a physician, or a mail carrier, an army purveyor, or a turnpike-road maker, it seems to me to be equally within the policy and mischief of the law. The only difference is in the permanency of the engagement; but a succession of single engagements is quite as mischievous as a contract *in solido;* and if the distinction is to be allowed, the law might easily be evaded.

Finally, even if the construction of the law were dubious, yet, as executive officers, it would become us to remember that it is a remedial law, enacted as a bar to executive influence; that, in the construction of all such laws, the rule is to give them a large construction for the advancement of the remedy and the suppression of the mischief; and that it is much safer to err on the side of forbearance, than on that of possible encroachment.

10

JOSEPH STORY, COMMENTARIES ON THE
CONSTITUTION 2:§§ 864–69
1833

§ 864. . . . This clause does not appear to have met with any opposition in the convention, as to the propriety of some provision on the subject, the principal question being, as to the best mode of expressing the disqualifications. It has been deemed by one commentator an admirable provision against venality, though not perhaps sufficiently guarded to prevent evasion. And it has been elaborately vindicated by another with uncommon earnestness. The reasons for excluding persons from offices, who have been concerned in creating them, or increasing their emoluments, are to take away, as far as possible, any improper bias in the vote of the representative, and to secure to the constituents some solemn pledge of his disinterestedness. The actual provision, however, does not go to the extent of the principle; for his appointment is restricted only "during the time, for which he was elected;" thus leaving in full force every influence upon his mind, if the period of his election is short, or the duration of it is approaching its natural termination. It has sometimes been matter of regret, that the disqualification had not been made co-extensive with the supposed mischief; and thus have for ever excluded members from the possession of offices created, or rendered more lucrative by themselves. Perhaps there is quite as much wisdom in leaving the provision, where it now is.

§ 865. It is not easy, by any constitutional or legislative enactments, to shut out all, or even many of the avenues of undue or corrupt influence upon the human mind. The great securities for society—those, on which it must for ever rest in a free government—are responsibility to the people through elections, and personal character, and purity of principle. Where these are wanting, there never can be any solid confidence, or any deep sense of duty. Where these exist, they become a sufficient guaranty against all

sinister influences, as well as all gross offences. It has been remarked with equal profoundness and sagacity, that, as there is a degree of depravity in mankind, which requires a certain degree of circumspection and distrust; so there are other qualities in human nature, which justify a certain portion of esteem and confidence. Republican government presupposes the existence of these qualities in a higher form, than any other. It might well be deemed harsh to disqualify an individual from any office, clearly required by the exigencies of the country, simply because he had done his duty. And, on the other hand, the disqualification might operate upon many persons, who might find their way into the national councils, as a strong inducement to postpone the creation of necessary offices, lest they should become victims of their high discharge of duty. The chances of receiving an appointment to a new office are not so many, or so enticing, as to bewilder many minds; and if they are, the aberrations from duty are so easily traced, that they rarely, or never escape the public reproaches. And if influence is to be exerted by the executive for improper purposes, it will be quite as easy, and in its operation less seen, and less suspected, to give the stipulated patronage in another form, either of office, or of profitable employment, already existing. And even a general disqualification might be evaded by suffering the like patronage silently to fall into the hands of a confidential friend, or a favourite child or relative. A dishonourable traffic in votes, if it should ever become the engine of party or of power in our country, would never be restrained by the slight network of any constitutional provisions of this sort. It would seek, and it would find its due rewards in the general patronage of the government, or in the possession of the offices conferred by the people, which would bring emolument, as well as influence, and secure power by gratifying favourites. The history of our state governments (to go no farther) will scarcely be thought by any ingenuous mind to afford any proofs, that the absence of such a disqualification has rendered state legislation less pure, or less intelligent; or, that the existence of such a disqualification would have retarded one rash measure, or introduced one salutary scruple into the elements of popular or party strife. History, which teaches us by examples, establishes the truth beyond all reasonable question, that genuine patriotism is too lofty in its honour, and too enlightened in its object, to need such checks; and that weakness and vice, the turbulence of faction, and the meanness of avarice, are easily bought, notwithstanding all the efforts to fetter, or ensnare them.

§ 866. The other part of the clause, which disqualifies persons holding any office under the United States from being members of either house during their continuance in office, has been still more universally applauded; and has been vindicated upon the highest grounds of public policy. It is doubtless founded in a deference to state jealousy, and a sincere desire to obviate the fears, real or imaginary, that the general government would obtain an undue preference over the state governments. It has also the strong recommendation, that it prevents any undue influence from office, either upon the party himself, or those, with whom he is associated in legislative deliberations. The universal exclusion of all persons holding office is (it must be admitted) attended with some inconveniences. The heads of the departments are, in fact, thus precluded from proposing, or vindicating their own measures in the face of the nation in the course of debate; and are compelled to submit them to other men, who are either imperfectly acquainted with the measures, or are indifferent to their success or failure. Thus, that open and public responsibility for measures, which properly belongs to the executive in all governments, and especially in a republican government, as its greatest security and strength, is completely done away. The executive is compelled to resort to secret and unseen influence, to private interviews, and private arrangements, to accomplish its own appropriate purposes; instead of proposing and sustaining its own duties and measures by a bold and manly appeal to the nation in the face of its representatives. One consequence of this state of things is, that there never can be traced home to the executive any responsibility for the measures, which are planned, and carried at its suggestion. Another consequence will be, (if it has not yet been,) that measures will be adopted, or defeated by private intrigues, political combinations, irresponsible recommendations, and all the blandishments of office, and all the deadening weight of silent patronage. The executive will never be compelled to avow, or to support any opinions. His ministers may conceal, or evade any expression of their opinions. He will seem to follow, when in fact he directs the opinions of congress. He will assume the air of a dependent instrument, ready to adopt the acts of the legislature, when in fact his spirit and his wishes pervade the whole system of legislation. If corruption ever eats its way silently into the vitals of this republic, it will be, because the people are unable to bring responsibility home to the executive through his chosen ministers. They will be betrayed, when their suspicions are most lulled by the executive, under the disguise of an obedience to the will of congress. If it would not have been safe to trust the heads of departments, as representatives, to the choice of the people, as their constituents, it would have been at least some gain to have allowed them a seat, like territorial delegates, in the house of representatives, where they might freely debate without a title to vote. In such an event, their influence, whatever it would be, would be seen, and felt, and understood, and on that account would have involved little danger, and more searching jealousy and opposition; whereas, it is now secret and silent, and from that very cause may become overwhelming.

§ 867. One other reason in favour of such a right is, that it would compel the executive to make appointments for the high departments of government, not from personal or party favourites, but from statesmen of high public character, talents, experience, and elevated services; from statesmen, who had earned public favour, and could command public confidence. At present, gross incapacity may be concealed under official forms, and ignorance silently escape by shifting the labours upon more intelligent subordinates in office. The nation would be, on the other plan, better served; and the executive sustained by more masculine eloquence, as well as more liberal learning.

§ 868. In the British parliament no restrictions of the former sort exist, and few of the latter, except such as have been created by statute. It is true, that an acceptance of any office under the crown is a vacation of a seat in parliament. This is wise; and secures the people from being betrayed by those, who hold office, and whom they do not choose to trust. But generally, they are re-eligible; and are entitled, if the people so choose, again to hold a seat in the house of commons, notwithstanding their official character. The consequence is, that the ministers of the crown assume an open public responsibility; and if the representation of the people in the house of commons were, as it is under the national government, founded upon a uniform rule, by which the people might obtain their full share of the government, it would be impossible for the ministry to exercise a controlling influence, or escape (as in America they may) a direct palpable responsibility. There can be no danger, that a free people will not be sufficiently watchful over their rulers, and their acts, and opinions, when they are known and avowed; or, that they will not find representatives in congress ready to oppose improper measures, or sound the alarm upon arbitrary encroachments. The real danger is, when the influence of the rulers is at work in secret, and assumes no definite shape; when it guides with a silent and irresistible sway, and yet covers itself under the forms of popular opinion, or independent legislation; when it does nothing, and yet accomplishes every thing.

§ 869. Such is the reasoning, by which many enlightened statesmen have not only been led to doubt, but even to deny the value of this constitutional disqualification. And even the most strenuous advocates of it are compelled so far to admit its force, as to concede, that the measures of the executive government, so far as they fall within the immediate department of a particular officer, might be more directly and fully explained on the floor of the house. Still, however, the reasoning from the British practice has not been deemed satisfactory by the public; and the guard interposed by the constitution has been received with general approbation, and has been thought to have worked well during our experience under the national government. Indeed, the strongly marked parties in the British parliament, and their consequent dissensions have been ascribed to the non-existence of any such restraints; and the progress of the influence of the crown, and the supposed corruptions of legislation, have been by some writers traced back to the same original blemish.

SEE ALSO:

Records of the Federal Convention, Farrand 1:20–21, 210, 211, 217, 219, 228, 229, 370, 375–76, 383–84, 391–94, 419, 434, 435, 513; 2:129, 130, 140, 141–42, 155, 166, 282, 483, 486–87, 568, 593

Luther Martin, Maryland House of Delegates, 29 Nov. 1787, Farrand 3:155

George Nichols, Virginia Ratifying Convention, 4 June 1788, Elliot 3:19–21

Debate in New York Ratifying Convention, 26 June 1788, 2 Elliot 329

House of Representatives, Amendment to the Constitution, 21 Dec. 1810, Annals 22:453–58, 841–42, 897, 898, 899–900, 904–5

Article 1, Section 7, Clause 1

All Bills for raising Revenue shall originate in the House of Representatives; but the Senate may propose or concur with amendments as on other Bills.

1

BILL OF RIGHTS, SEC. 4
1 W. & M., 2d sess., c. 2,
16 Dec. 1689

4. That levying money for or to the use of the crown, by pretence of prerogative, without grant of parliament, for longer time, or in other manner than the same is or shall be granted, is illegal.

2

WILLIAM BLACKSTONE, COMMENTARIES 1:163–64
1765

First, with regard to taxes: it is the antient indisputable privilege and right of the house of commons, that all grants of subsidies or parliamentary aids do begin in their house, and are first bestowed by them; although their grants are not effectual to all intents and purposes, until they have the assent of the other two branches of the legislature. The general reason, given for this exclusive privilege of the house of commons, is, that the supplies are raised upon the body of the people, and therefore it is proper that they alone should have the right of taxing themselves. This reason would be unanswerable, if the commons taxed none but themselves: but it is notorious, that a very large share of property is in the possession of the house of lords; that this property is equally taxable, and taxed, as the property of the commons; and therefore the commons not being the *sole* persons taxed, this cannot be the reason of their having the *sole* right of raising and modelling the supply. The true reason, arising from the spirit of our constitution, seems to be this. The lords being a permanent hereditary body, created at pleasure by the king, are supposed more liable to be influenced by the crown, and when once influenced to continue so, than the commons, who are a temporary elective body, freely nominated by the people. It would therefore be extremely dangerous, to give them any power of framing new taxes for the subject: it is sufficient, that they have a power of rejecting, if they think the commons too lavish or improvident in their grants. But so reasonably jealous are the commons of this valuable privilege, that herein they will not suffer the other house to exert any power but that of rejecting; they will not permit the least alteration or amendment to be made by the lords to the mode of taxing the people by a money bill; under which appellation are included all bills, by which money is directed to be raised upon the subject, for any purpose or in any shape whatsoever; either for the exigencies of government, and collected from the kingdom in general, as the land tax; or for private benefit, and collected in any particular district; as by turnpikes, parish rates, and the like. Yet sir Matthew Hale mentions one case, founded on the practice of parliament in the reign of Henry VI, wherein he thinks the lords may alter a money bill; and that is, if the commons grant a tax, as that of tonnage and poundage, for *four* years; and the lords alter it to a less time, as for *two* years; here, he says, the bill need not be sent back to the commons for their concurrence, but may receive the royal assent without farther ceremony; for the alteration of the lords is consistent with the grant of the commons. But such an experiment will hardly be repeated by the lords, under the present improved idea of the privilege of the house of commons: and, in any case where a money bill is remanded to the commons, all amendments in the mode of taxation are sure to be rejected.

3

STAMP ACT CONGRESS, DECLARATION OF RIGHTS
19 Oct. 1765
Sources 270–71

The members of this congress, sincerely devoted, with the warmest sentiments of affection and duty to his majesty's person and government, inviolably attached to the present happy establishment of the protestant succession, and with minds deeply impressed by a sense of the present and impending misfortunes of the British colonies on this continent; having considered as maturely as time would permit, the circumstances of said colonies, esteem it our indispensable duty to make the following declarations of our humble opinions, respecting the most essential rights and liberties of the colonists, and of the grievances under which they labor, by reason of several late acts of parliament.

1st. That his majesty's subjects in these colonies, owe the same allegiance to the crown of Great Britain, that is owing from his subjects born within the realm, and all due subordination to that august body, the parliament of Great Britain.

2d. That his majesty's liege subjects in these colonies are entitled to all the inherent rights and privileges of his natural born subjects within the kingdom of Great Britain,

3d. That it is inseparably essential to the freedom of a people, and the undoubted rights of Englishmen, that no taxes should be imposed on them, but with their own consent, given personally, or by their representatives.

4th. That the people of these colonies are not, and from their local circumstances, cannot be represented in the house of commons in Great Britain.

5th. That the only representatives of the people of these colonies, are persons chosen therein by themselves; and that no taxes ever have been, or can be constitutionally imposed on them, but by their respective legislatures.

6th. That all supplies to the crown, being free gifts of the people, it is unreasonable and inconsistent with the principles and spirit of the British constitution, for the people of Great Britain to grant to his majesty the property of the colonists.

7th. That trial by jury is the inherent and invaluable right of every British subject in these colonies.

8th. That the late act of parliament entitled, an act for granting and applying certain stamp duties, and other duties in the British colonies and plantations in America, &c., by imposing taxes on the inhabitants of these colonies, and the said act, and several other acts, by extending the jurisdiction of the courts of admiralty beyond its ancient limits, have a manifest tendency to subvert the rights and liberties of the colonists.

9th. That the duties imposed by several late acts of parliament, from the peculiar circumstances of these colonies, will be extremely burthensome and grievous, and from the scarcity of specie, the payment of them absolutely impracticable.

10th. That as the profits of the trade of these colonies ultimately centre in Great Britain, to pay for the manufactures which they are obliged to take from thence, they eventually contribute very largely to all supplies granted there to the crown.

11th. That the restrictions imposed by several late acts of parliament, on the trade of these colonies, will render them unable to purchase the manufactures of Great Britain.

12th. That the increase, prosperity, and happiness of these colonies, depend on the full and free enjoyment of their rights and liberties, and an intercourse, with Great Britain, mutually affectionate and advantageous.

13th. That it is the right of the British subjects in these colonies, to petition the king or either house of parliament.

Lastly, That it is the indispensable duty of these colonies to the best of sovereigns, to the mother country, and to themselves, to endeavor, by a loyal and dutiful address to his majesty, and humble application to both houses of parliament, to procure the repeal of the act for granting and applying certain stamp duties, of all clauses of any other acts of parliament, whereby the jurisdiction of the admiralty is extended as aforesaid, and of the other late acts for the restriction of the American commerce.

4

BENJAMIN RUSH TO CATHERINE MACAULAY
18 Jan. 1769
Letters 1:71

In page 32, you propose that "the representative assembly should not have the power of *imposing taxes* till the subject has been first debated by the senate." Give me leave to observe here that I cannot help thinking that the representative assembly should retain the exclusive right of taxing their country to themselves. They represent the greatest part of the people. They are supposed to be collected from all parts of the commonwealth and are therefore much better acquainted with the circumstances of the country. Besides, they (from their greater number) are naturally supposed to have more property in the state, and therefore have a better right to give it away for the purposes of government.

Perhaps I am wrong in both these observations. If I am, I expect to be rectified by you, madam, who are so well skilled in the science of government. I am but a young scholar in the school of politics, although I have made great progress in the love of liberty; for *this*, let me assure you, madam, was among the first passions that warmed my breast.

5

DELAWARE CONSTITUTION OF 1776, ART. 6
Thorpe 1:563

All money-bills for the support of government shall originate in the house of assembly, and may be altered, amended, or rejected by the legislative council. All other bills and ordinances may take rise in the house of assembly or legislative council, and may be altered, amended, or rejected by either.

6

VIRGINIA CONSTITUTION OF 1776
Thorpe 7:3816

All laws shall originate in the House of Delegates, to be approved of or rejected by the Senate, or to be amended, with consent of the House of Delegates; except money-bills, which in no instance shall be altered by the Senate, but wholly approved or rejected.

7

RECORDS OF THE FEDERAL CONVENTION

[1:233; Madison, 13 June]

Mr. Gerry. moved to restrain the Senatorial branch from originating money bills. The other branch was more immediately the representatives of the people, and it was a maxim that the people ought to hold the purse-strings. If the Senate should be allowed to originate such bills, they wd. repeat the experiment, till chance should furnish a sett of representatives in the other branch who will fall into their snares.

Mr. Butler saw no reason for such a discrimination. We were always following the British Constitution when the reason of it did not apply. There was no analogy between the Ho of Lords and the body proposed to be established. If the Senate should be degraded by any such discriminations, the best men would be apt to decline serving in it in favor of the other branch. And it will lead the latter into the practice of tacking other clauses to money bills.

Mr. Madison observed that the Commentators on the Brit: Const: had not yet agreed on the reason of the restriction on the H. of L. in money bills. Certain it was there could be no similar reason in the case before us. The Senate would be the representatives of the people as well as the 1st. branch. If they sd. have any dangerous influence over it, they would easily prevail on some member of the latter to originate the bill they wished to be passed. As the Senate would be generally a more capable sett of men, it wd. be wrong to disable them from any preparation of the business, especially of that which was most important and in our republics, worse prepared than any other. The Gentleman in pursuance of his principle ought to carry the restraint to the *amendment;* as well as the originating of money bills. Since, an addition of a given sum wd. be equivalent to a distinct proposition of it.

Mr. King differed from Mr. Gerry, and concurred in the objections to the proposition.

Mr. Read favored the proposition, but would not extend the restraint to the case of amendments.

Mr. Pinkney thinks the question premature. If the Senate shd. be formed on the *same* proportional representation as it stands at present, they sd have equal power, otherwise if a different principle sd. be introduced.

Mr. Sherman. As both branches must concur, there can be no danger whichever way the Senate be formed. We establish two branches in order to get more wisdom, which is particularly needed in the finance business—The Senate bear their share of the taxes, and are also the representatives of the people. What a man does by another, he does by himself is a maxim. In Cont. both branches can originate in all cases, and it has been found safe & convenient. Whatever might have been the reason of the rule as to The H. of Lords, it is clear that no good arises from it now even there.

Genl. Pinkney. This distinction prevails in S. C. & has been a source of pernicious disputes between ye. 2 branches. The constitution is now evaded, by informal schedules of amendments handed from ye. Senate to the other House.

Mr. Williamson wishes for a question chiefly to prevent re-discussion. The restriction will have one advantage, it will oblige some members in lower branch to move, & people can then mark him.

On the question for excepting money bills as propd. by Mr. Gerry. Mas. no. Cont. no. N. Y. ay. N. J. no. Del. ay. Md. no. Va. ay. N. C. no. S. C. no. Geo. no. [Ayes—3; noes—7.]

[1:527; Madison, 5 July]

Mr. Madison. could not regard the exclusive privilege of originating money bills as any concession on the side of the small States. Experience proved that it had no effect. If seven States in the upper branch wished a bill to be originated, they might surely find some member from some of the same States in the lower branch who would originate it. The restriction as to amendments was of as little consequence. Amendments could be handed privately by the Senate to members in the other house. Bills could be negatived that they might be sent up in the desired shape. If the Senate should yield to the obstinacy of the 1st. branch the use of that body as a check would be lost. If the 1st. branch should yield to that of the Senate, the privilege would be nugatory. Experience had also shewn both in G. B. and the States having a similar regulation that it was a source of frequent & obstinate altercations. These considerations had produced a rejection of a like motion on a former occasion when judged by its own merits. It could not therefore be deemed any concession on the present, and left in force all the objections which had prevailed agst. allowing each State an equal voice.

. . . . .

Mr. Butler said he could not let down his idea of the people. of America so far as to believe they, would from mere respect to the Convention adopt a plan evidently unjust. He did not consider the privilege concerning money bills as of any consequence. He urged that the 2d. branch ought to represent the States according to their property.

. . . . .

[Mr. Bedford:] . . . As to the propositions of the Committee, the lesser States have thought it necessary to have a security somewhere. This has been thought necessary for the Executive Magistrate of the proposed Govt. who has a sort of negative on the laws; and is it not of more importance that the States should be protected, than that the Executive branch of the Govt. shd. be protected. In order to obtain this, the smaller States have conceded as to the constitution of the first branch, and as to money bills. If they be not gratified by correspondent concessions as to the 2d. branch is it to be supposed they will ever accede to the plan. . . .

[1:543; Madison, 6 July]

The 1st. clause relating to the originating of money bills was then resumed.

Mr. Governr. Morris was opposed to a restriction of this right in either branch, considered merely in itself and as unconnected with the point of representation in the 2d. branch. It will disable the 2d. branch from proposing its own money plans, and giving the people an opportunity of judging by comparison of the merits of those proposed by the 1st. branch.

Mr. Wilson could see nothing like a concession here on the part of the smaller States. If both branches were to say yes or no, it was of little consequence which should say yes or no first, which last. If either was indiscriminately to have the right of originating, the reverse of the Report. would he thought be most proper; since it was a maxim that the least numerous body was the fittest for deliberation; the most numerous for decision. He observed that this discrimination had been transcribed from the British into several American constitutions. But he was persuaded

that on examination of the American experiment, it would be found to be a trifle light as air. Nor could he ever discover the advantage of it in the parliamentary history of G. Britain. He hoped if there was any advantage in the privilege, that it would be pointed out.

Mr. Williamson thought that if the privilege were not common to both branches it ought rather to be confined to the 2d. as the bills in that case would be more narrowly watched, than if they originated with the branch having most of the popular confidence.

Mr. Mason. The consideration which weighed with the Committee was that the 1st. branch would be the immediate representatives of the people, the 2d. would not. Should the latter have the power of giving away the peoples money, they might soon forget the Source from whence they received it. We might soon have an aristocracy. He had been much concerned at the principles which had been advanced by some gentlemen, but had the satisfaction to find they did not generally prevail. He was a friend to proportional representation in both branches; but supposed that some points must be yielded for the sake of accomodation.

Mr. Wilson. If he had proposed that the 2d. branch should have an independent disposal of public money, the observations of (Col. Mason) would have been a satisfactory answer. But nothing could be farther from what he had said. His question was how is the power of the 1st. branch increased or that of the 2d. diminished by giving the proposed privilege to the former? Where is the difference, in which branch it begins if both must concur, in the end?

Mr. Gerry would not say that the concession was a sufficient one on the part of the small States. But he could not but regard it in the light of a concession. It wd. make it a constitutional principle that the 2d. branch were not possessed of the Confidence of the people in money matters, which wd. lessen their weight & influence. In the next place if the 2d. branch were dispossessed of the privilege, they wd. be deprived of the opportunity which their continuance in office 3 times as long as the 1st. branch would give them of make'g three successive essays in favor of a particular point.

Mr. Pinkney thought it evident that the Concession was wholly on one side, that of the large States, the privilege of originating money bills being of no account.

Mr. Govr. Morris had waited to hear the good effects of the restriction. As to the alarm sounded, of an aristocracy, his creed was that there never was, nor ever will be a civilized Society without an Aristocracy. His endeavor was to keep it as much as possible from doing mischief. The restriction if it has any real operation will deprive us of the services of the 2d. branch in digesting and proposing money bills of which it will be more capable than the 1st. branch, It will take away the responsibility of the 2d branch, the great security for good behavior. It will always leave a plea as to an obnoxious money bill that it was disliked, but could not be constitutionally amended; nor safely rejected. It will be a dangerous source of disputes between the two Houses. We should either take the British Constitution altogether or make one for ourselves. The

Executive there has dissolved two Houses as the only cure for such disputes. Will our Executive be able to apply such a remedy? Every law directly or indirectly takes money out of the pockets of the people. Again what use may be made of such a privilege in case of great emergency? Suppose an enemy at the door, and money instantly & absolutely necessary for repelling him, may not the popular branch avail itself of this duress, to extort concessions from the Senate destructive of the Constitution itself. He illustrated this danger by the example of the Long Parliament's expedts. for subverting the H. of Lords: concluding on the whole that the restriction would be either useless or pernicious.

Docr. Franklin did not mean to go into a justification of the Report; but as it had been asked what would be the use of restraining the 2d. branch from medling with money bills, he could not but remark that it was always of importance that the people should know who had disposed of their money, & how it had been disposed of. It was a maxim that those who feel, can best judge. This end would, he thought, be best attained, if money affairs were to be confined to the immediate representatives of the people. This was his inducement to concur in the report. As to the danger or difficulty that might arise from a negative in the 2d. where the people wd. not be proportionally represented, it might easily be got over by declaring that there should be no such Negative: or if that will not do, by declaring that there shall be no such branch at all.

Mr. Martin said that it was understood in the Committee that the difficulties and disputes which had been apprehended, should be guarded agst. in the detailing of the plan.

Mr. Wilson. The difficulties & disputes will increase with the attempts to define & obviate them. Queen Anne was obliged to dissolve her Parliamt. in order to terminate one of these obstinate disputes between the two Houses. Had it not been for the mediation of the Crown, no one can say what the result would have been. The point is still sub judice in England. He approved of the principles laid down by the Honble President (Docr. Franklin) his Colleague, as to the expediency of keeping the people informed of their money affairs. But thought they would know as much, and be as well satisfied, in one way as in the other.

Genl. Pinkney was astonished that this point should have been considered as a concession. He remarked that the restriction to money bills has been rejected on the merits singly considered, by 8 States agst. 3. and that the very States which now called it a concession, were then agst. it as nugatory or improper in itself.

On the question whether the clause relating to money bills in the Report of the Come. consisting of a member from each State, shd. stand as part of the Report—

Massts. dividd. Cont. ay. N. Y. divd. N. J. ay. Pa. no. Del. ay. Md. ay. Va. no. N. C. ay. S. C. no. Geo. divd. [Ayes—5; noes—3; divided—3.]

[2:224; Madison, 8 Aug.]

Mr. Pinkney moved to strike out Sect. 5, As giving no peculiar advantage to the House of Representatives, and

as clogging the Govt. If the Senate can be trusted with the many great powers proposed, it surely may be trusted with that of originating money bills.

Mr. Ghorum. was agst. allowing the Senate to *originate;* but only to *amend.*

Mr. Govr. Morris. It is particularly proper that the Senate shd. have the right of originating money bills. They will sit constantly. will consist of a smaller number. and will be able to prepare such bills with due correctness; and so as to prevent delay of business in the other House.

Col. Mason was unwilling to travel over this ground again. To strike out the section, was to unhinge the compromise of which it made a part. The duration of the Senate made it improper. He does not object to that duration. On the Contrary he approved of it. But joined with the smallness of the number, it was an argument against adding this to the other great powers vested in that body. His idea of an Aristocracy was that it was the governt. of the few over the many. An aristocratic body, like the screw in mechanics, workig. its way by slow degrees, and holding fast whatever it gains, should ever be suspected of an encroaching tendency—The purse strings should never be put into its hands.

Mr Mercer, considered the exclusive power of originating Money bills as so great an advantage, that it rendered the equality of votes in the Senate ideal & of no consequence.

Mr. Butler was for adhering to the principle which had been settled.

Mr. Wilson was opposed to it on its merits, with out regard to the compromise

Mr. Elseworth did not think the clause of any consequence, but as it was thought of consequence by some members from the larger States, he was willing it should stand.

Mr. Madison was for striking it out: considering it as of no advantage to the large States as fettering the Govt. and as a source of injurious altercations between the two Houses.

On the question for striking out "Sect. 5. art. IV"
N. H. no. Mas. no. Ct. no. N. J. ay. Pa. ay. Del. ay. Md. ay. Va. ay. N. C. no. S. C. ay. Geo. ay. [Ayes—7; noes—4.]

[2:230; Madison, 9 Aug.]

Art: IV. sect. 6. Mr. Randolph expressed his dissatisfaction at the disagreement yesterday to sect 5. concerning money bills, as endangering the success of the plan, and extremely objectionable in itself; and gave notice that he should move for a reconsideration of the vote.

Mr. Williamson said he had formed a like intention.

. . . . .

Mr. Randolph called for a division of the Section, so as to leave a distinct question on the last words, "each member shall have one vote". He wished this last sentence to be postponed until the reconsideration should have taken place on sect. 5. Art. IV. concerning money bills. If that section should not be reinstated his plan would be to vary the representation in the Senate.

Mr. Strong concurred in Mr. Randolphs ideas on this point

Mr. Read did not consider the section as to money bills of any advantage to the larger States and had voted for striking it out as being viewed in the same light by the larger States. If it was considered by them as of any value, and as a condition of the equality of votes in the Senate, he had no objection to its being re-instated.

Mr. Wilson—Mr. Elseworth & Mr. Madison urged that it was of no advantage to the larger States, and that it might be a dangerous source of contention between the two Houses. All the principal powers of the Natl. Legislature had some relation to money.

Docr. Franklin, considered the two clauses, the originating of money bills, and the equality of votes in the Senate, as essentially connected by the compromise which had been agreed to.

Col. Mason said this was not the time for discussing this point. When the originating of money bills shall be reconsidered, he thought it could be demonstrated that it was of essential importance to restrain the right to the House of Representatives the immediate choice of the people.

Mr. Williamson. The State of N. C. had agreed to an equality in the Senate, merely in consideration that money bills should be confined to the other House: and he was surprised to see the smaller States forsaking the condition on which they had received their equality.

Question on the Section 1. down to the last sentence

N. H ay. Mas. no. Ct. ay. N. J. ay. Pa. no- Del. ay. Md. ay. Virga ay N. C. no. S. C. divd. Geo. ay. [Ayes—7; noes—3; divided—1.]

Mr. Randolph moved that the last sentence "each member shall have one vote." be postponed

It was observed that this could not be necessary; as in case the section as to originating bills should not be reinstated, and a revision of the Constitution should ensue, it wd. still be proper that the members should vote per capita. A postponement of the preceding sentence allowing to each State 2 members wd. have been more proper.

Mr. Mason, did not mean to propose a change of this mode of voting per capita in any event. But as there might be other modes proposed, he saw no impropriety in postponing the sentence. Each State may have two members, and yet may have unequal votes. He said that unless the exclusive originating of money bills should be restored to the House of Representatives, he should, not from obstinacy, but duty and conscience, oppose throughout the equality of Representation in the Senate.

Mr. Govr. Morris. Such declarations were he supposed, addressed to the smaller States in order to alarm them for their equality in the Senate, and induce them agst. their judgments, to concur in restoring the section concerning money bills. He would declare in his turn that as he saw no prospect of amending the Constitution of the Senate & considered the Section relating to money bills as intrinsically bad, he would adhere to the section establishing the equality at all events.

Mr. Wilson. It seems to have been supposed by some that the section concerning money bills is desirable to the large States. The fact was that two of those States (Pa. & Va) had uniformly voted agst. it without reference to any other part of the system.

Mr. Randolph, urged as Col. Mason had done that the sentence under consideration was connected with that relating to money bills, and might possibly be affected by the result of the motion for reconsidering the latter. That the postponement was therefore not improper.

Question for postponing "each member shall have one vote."

N. H. divd. Mas. no. Ct. no. N. J. no. Pa. no. Del. no. Md. no. Va. ay. N. C. ay. S. C. no. Geo. no. [Ayes—2; noes—8; divided—1.]

The words were then agreed to as part of the section.

Mr. Randolph then gave notice that he should move to reconsider this whole Sect: 1. Art. V. as connected with the 5. Sect. art. IV. as to which he had already given such notice.

[2:262; Madison, 11 Aug.]

Mr. Randolph moved according to notice to reconsider Art: IV: Sect. 5. concerning money-bills which had been struck out. He argued 1. that he had not wished for this privilege whilst a proportional Representation in the Senate was in contemplation. but since an equality had been fixed in that house, the large States would require this compensation at least. 2. that it would make the plan more acceptable to the people, because they will consider the Senate as the more aristocratic body, and will expect that the usual guards agst its influence be provided according to the example in G. Britain. 3. the privilege will give some advantage to the House of Reps. if it extends to the originating only—but still more, if it restrains the Senate from amendg 4. he called on the smaller States to concur in the measure, as the condition by which alone the compromise had entitled them to an equality in the Senate. He signified that he should propose instead of the original Section, a clause specifying that the bills in question should be for the purpose of Revenue, in order to repel ye. objection agst. the extent of the words *"raising money,"* which might happen incidentally, and that the Senate should not so amend or alter as to increase or diminish the sum; in order to obviate the inconveniences urged agst. a restriction of the Senate to a simple affirmative or negative.

Mr. Williamson 2ded. the motion

Mr. Pinkney was sorry to oppose the opportunity gentlemen asked to have the question again opened for discussion, but as he considered it a mere waste of time he could not bring himself to consent to it. He said that notwithstanding what had been said as to the compromise, he always considered this section as making no part of it. The rule of Representation in the 1st. branch was the true condition of that in the 2d. branch.—Several others spoke for & agst. the reconsideration, but without going into the merits—on the Question to reconsider.

N. H. ay. Mas. ay. Ct. ay. N. J. ay. Pa. ay. Del. ay. Md. no. Va. ay. N. C. ay. S. C. divd. Geo. ay. [Ayes—9; noes—1; divided—1.]—Monday was then assigned—

[2:273; Madison, 13 Aug.]

Mr. Randolph moved that the clause be altered so as to read—"Bills for raising money for the *purpose of revenue* or for appropriating the same shall originate in the House of

Representatives and shall not be so amended or altered by the Senate as to increase or diminish the sum to be raised, or change the mode of levying it, or the object of its appropriation."—He would not repeat his reasons, but barely remind the members from the smaller States of the compromise by which the larger States were entitled to this privilege.

Col. Mason. This amendment removes all the objections urged agst. the section as it stood at first. By specifying *purposes of revenue*, it obviated the objection that the Section extended to all bills under which money might incidentally arise. By authorizing amendments in the Senate it got rid of the objections that the Senate could not correct errors of any sort, & that it would introduce into the House of Reps. the practice of tacking foreign matter to money bills: These objections being removed, the arguments in favor of the proposed restraint on the Senate ought to have their full force. 1. the Senate did not represent the *people,* but the *States* in their political character. It was improper therefore that it should tax the people. The reason was the same agst. their doing it; as it had been agst. Congs. doing it. Nor was it in any respect necessary in order to cure the evils of our Republican system. He admitted that notwithstanding the superiority of the Republican form over every other, it had its evils. The chief ones, were the danger of the majority oppressing the minority, and the mischievous influence of demagogues. The Genl. Government of itself will cure these. As the States will not concur at the same time in their unjust & oppressive plans, the general Govt. will be able to check & defeat them, whether they result from the wickedness of the majority, or from the misguidance of demagogues. Again, the Senate is not like the H. of Reps. chosen frequently and obliged to return frequently among the people. They are to be chosen by the Sts for 6 years, will probably settle themselves at the seat of Govt. will pursue schemes for their own aggrandizement—will be able by wearyg out the H. of Reps and taking advantage of their impatience at the close of a long Session, to extort measures for that purpose. If they should be paid as he expected would be yet determined & wished to be so, out of the Natl. Treasury, they will particularly extort an increase of their wages. A bare negative was a very different thing from that of originating bills. The practice in Engld was in point. The House of Lords does not represent nor tax the people, because not elected by the people. If the Senate can originate, they will in the recess of the Legislative Sessions, hatch their mischievous projects, for their own purposes, and have their money bills ready cut & dried, (to use a common phrase) for the meeting of the H. of Reps. He compared the case to Poyning's law—and signified that the House of Reps. might be rendered by degrees like the Parliament of Paris, the mere depository of the decrees of the Senate. As to the compromise so much had passed on that subject that he would say nothing about it. He did not mean by what he had said to oppose the permanency of the Senate. On the contrary he had no repugnance to an increase of it—nor to allowing it a negative, though the Senate was not by its present constitution entitled to it. But in all events he would contend that the pursestrings should be in the hands of the Representatives of the people.

Mr. Wilson was himself directly opposed to the equality of votes granted to the Senate by its present Constitution. At the same time he wished not to multiply the vices of the system. He did not mean to enlarge on a subject which had been so much canvassed, but would remark as an insuperable objection agst. the proposed restriction of money bills to the H. of Reps. that it would be a source of perpetual contentions where there was no mediator to decide them. The Presidt. here could not like the Executive Magistrate in England interpose by a prorogation, or dissolution. This restriction had been found pregnant with altercation in every State where the Constitution had established it. The House of Reps. will insert the other things in money bills, and by making them conditions of each other, destroy the deliberate liberty of the Senate. He stated the case of a Preamble to a money bill sent up by the House of Commons in the reign of Queen Anne, to the H. of Lords, in which the conduct of the displaced Ministry, who were to be impeached before the Lords, was condemned; the Commons thus extorting a premature judgmt. without any hearing of the Parties to be tried, and the H. of Lords being thus reduced to the poor & disgraceful expedient of opposing to the authority of a law a protest on their Journals agst. its being drawn into precedent. If there was any thing like Poynings law in the present case, it was in the attempt to vest the exclusive right of originating in the H. of Reps. and so far he was agst it. He should be equally so if the right were to be exclusively vested in the Senate. With regard to the pursestrings, it was to be observed that the purse was to have two strings, one of which was in the hands of the H. of Reps. the other in those of the Senate. Both houses must concur in untying, and of what importance could it be which untied first, which last. He could not conceive it to be any objection to the senate's preparing the bills, that they would have leisure for that purpose and would be in the habits of business. War, Commerce, & Revenue were the great objects of the Genl. Government. All of them are connected with money. The restriction in favor of the H. of Represts. would exclude the Senate from originating any important bills whatever—

Mr Gerry considered this as a part of the plan that would be much scrutinized. Taxation & representation are strongly associated in the minds of the people, and they will not agree that any but their immediate representatives shall meddle with their purses. In short the acceptance of the plan will inevitably fail, if the Senate be not restrained from originating Money bills.

Mr. Govermr. Morris All the arguments suppose the right to originate money & to tax, to be exclusively vested in the Senate.—The effects commented on may be produced by a Negative only in the Senate. They can tire out the other House, and extort their concurrence in favorite measures, as well by withholding their negative, as by adhering to a bill introduced by themselves.

Mr Madison thought If the substitute offered by Mr. Randolph for the original section is to be adopted it would be proper to allow the Senate at least so to amend as to *diminish* the sums to be raised. Why should they be restrained from checking the extravagance of the other House?—One of the greatest evils incident to Republican Govt. was the spirit of contention & faction. The proposed substitute, which in some respects lessened the objections agst. the section, had a contrary effect with respect to this particular. It laid a foundation for new difficulties and disputes between the two houses. The word *revenue* was ambiguous. In many acts, particularly in the regulations of trade, the object would be twofold. The raising of revenue would be one of them. How could it be determined which was the primary or predominant one; or whether it was necessary that revenue shd: be the sole object, in exclusion even of other incidental effects. When the Contest was first opened with G. B. their power to regulate trade was admitted. Their power to raise revenue rejected. An accurate investigation of the subject afterward proved that no line could be drawn between the two cases. The words *amend or alter*, form an equal source of doubt & altercation. When an obnoxious paragraph shall be sent down from the Senate to the House of Reps it will be called an origination under the name of an amendment. The Senate may actually couch extraneous matter under that name. In these cases, the question will turn on the *degree* of connection between the matter & object of the bill and the alteration or amendment offered to it. Can there be a more fruitful source of dispute, or a kind of dispute more difficult to be settled? His apprehensions on this point were not conjectural. Disputes had actually flowed from this source in Virga. where the Senate can originate no bill. The words "so as to *increase or diminish* the sum to be raised," were liable to the same objections. In levying indirect taxes, which it seemed to be understood were to form the principal revenue of the new Govt. the sum to be raised, would be increased or diminished by a variety of collateral circumstances influencing the consumption, in general, the consumption of foreign or of domestic articles—of this or that particular species of articles, and even by the mode of collection which may be closely connected with the productiveness of a tax.—The friends of the section had argued its necessity from the permanency of the Senate. He could not see how this argumt. applied. The Senate was not more permanent now than in the form it bore in the original propositions of Mr. Randolph and at the time when no objection whatever was hinted agst. its originating money bills. Or if in consequence of a loss of the present question, a proportional vote in the Senate should be reinstated as has been urged as the indemnification the permanency of the Senate will remain the same.—If the right to originate be vested exclusively in the House of Reps. either the Senate must yield agst. its judgment to that House, in which case the Utility of the check will be lost—or the Senate will be inflexible & the H. of Reps must adapt its Money bill to the views of the Senate, in which case, the exclusive right will be of no avail.—As to the Compromise of which so much had been said, he would make a single observation. There were 5 States which had opposed the equality of votes in the Senate. viz. Masts. Penna. Virga. N. Carolina & S. Carola. As a compensation for the sacrifice extorted from them on this head, the exclusive origination of money bills in the other House had been tendered. Of the five States a majority viz. Penna. Virga. & S. Carola, have uniformly voted agst. the proposed compensation, on its own merits, as rendering the plan of Govt. still more objectionable— Massts has been divided. N. Carolina alone has set a value on the compensation, and voted on that principle. What obligation then can the small States be under to concur agst. their judgments in reinstating the section?

Mr. Dickenson. Experience must be our only guide. Reason may mislead us. It was not Reason that discovered the singular & admirable mechanism of the English Constitution. It was not Reason that discovered or ever could have discovered the odd & in the eye of those who are governed by reason, the absurd mode of trial by Jury. Accidents probably produced these discoveries, and experience has give[n] a sanction to them. This is then our guide. And has not experience verified the utility of restraining money bills to the immediate representatives of the people. Whence the effect may have proceeded he could not say; whether from the respect with which this privilege inspired the other branches of Govt. to the H. of Commons, or from the turn of thinking it gave to the people at large with regard to their rights, but the effect was visible & could not be doubted Shall we oppose to this long experience, the short experience of 11 years which we had ourselves, on this subject—As to disputes, they could not be avoided any way. If both Houses should originate, each would have a different bill to which it would be attached, and for which it would contend.—He observed that all the prejudices of the people would be offended by refusing this exclusive privilege to the H. of Repress. and these prejudices shd. never be disregarded by us when no essential purpose was to be served. When this plan goes forth, it will be attacked by the popular leaders. Aristocracy will be the watchword; the Shibboleth among its adversaries. Eight States have inserted in their Constitutions the exclusive right of originating money bills in favor of the popular branch of the Legislature. Most of them however allowed the other branch to amend. This he thought would be proper for us to do.

Mr Randolph regarded this point as of such consequence, that as he valued the peace of this Country, he would press the adoption of it. We had numerous & monstrous difficulties to combat. Surely we ought not to increase them. When the people behold in the Senate, the countenance of an aristocracy; and in the president, the form at least of a little monarch, will not their alarms be sufficiently raised without taking from their immediate representatives, a right which has been so long appropriated to them.—The Executive will have more influence over the Senate, than over the H. of Reps—Allow the Senate to originate in this case, & that influence will be sure to mix itself in their deliberations & plans. The Declaration of War he conceived ought not to be in the Senate composed of 26 men only, but rather in the other House. In the other House ought to be placed the origination of the means of war. As to Commercial regulations which may involve revenue, the difficulty may be avoided by restraining the definition to bills for the *mere* or *sole,* purpose of raising revenue. The Senate will be more likely to be corrupt than the H. of Reps and should therefore have less to do with money matters. His principal object however was to prevent popular objections against the plan, and to secure its adoption.

Mr. Rutlidge. The friends of this motion are not consistent in their reasoning. They tell us, that we ought to be guided by the long experience of G. B. & not our own experience of 11 years: and yet they themselves propose to depart from it. The *H. of Commons* not only have the exclusive right of originating, but the *Lords* are not allowed to alter or amend a money bill. Will not the people say that this restriction is but a mere tub to the whale. They cannot but see that it is of no real consequence; and will be more likely to be displeased with it as an attempt to bubble them, than to impute it to a watchfulness over their rights. For his part, he would prefer giving the exclusive right to the Senate, if it was to be given exclusively at all. The Senate being more conversant in business, and having more leisure, will digest the bills much better, and as they are to have no effect, till examined & approved by the H. of Reps there can be no possible danger. These clauses in the Constitutions of the States had been put in through a blind adherence to the British model. If the work was to be done over now, they would be omitted. The experiment in S. Carolina– where the Senate cannot originate or amend money bills, has shown that it answers no good purpose; and produces the very bad one of continually dividing & heating the two houses. Sometimes indeed if the matter of the amendment of the Senate is pleasing to the other House they wink at the encroachment; if it be displeasing, then the Constitution is appealed to. Every Session is distracted by altercations on this subject. The practice now becoming frequent is for the Senate not to make formal amendments; but to send down a schedule of the alterations which will procure the bill their assent.

Mr. Carrol. The most ingenious men in Maryd. are puzzled to define the case of money bills, or explain the Constitution on that point; tho' it seemed to be worded with all possible plainness & precision. It is a source of continual difficulty & squabble between the two houses.

Mr. McHenry mentioned an instance of extraordinary subterfuge, to get rid of the apparent force of the Constitution

On Question on the first part of the motion as to the exclusive originating of Money bills in the H. of Reps.

N. H. ay. Mas. ay. Ct. no. N. J. no. Pa. no. Del. no. Md. no. Virga. ay. Mr. Blair & Mr. M. no– Mr. R. Col. Mason and Genl. Washinton ay. N. C. ay. S. C. no. Geo no [Ayes—4; noes—7.]

Question on Originating by H. of Reps & *amending* by Senate. as reported, art IV. Sect. 5.

N. H. ay. Mas. ay. Ct. no. N J. no. Pa. no. Del. no. Md. no. Virga. ay. Mr. Blair & Mr. M. no– Mr. R. Col. Mason and Genl. Washington ay. N. C. ay. S. C. no. Geo no [Ayes—4; noes—7.]

Question on Originating by H. of Reps & *amending* by Senate. as reported, Art IV. Sect. 5.

N. H. ay. Mas. ay. Ct. no. N J. no. Pa. no. Del. no. Md. no. Va. ay. N. C. ay S. C. no. Geo. no [Ayes—4; noes—7.]

Question on the last clause of sect: 5—Art: IV—viz "No money shall be drawn from the Public Treasury, but in pursuance of *appropriations* that shall originate in the House of Reps. It passed in the negative

N. H. no. Mas. ay. Con. no N. J no. Pa. no Del no. Md no Va no. N. C. no. S. C. no. Geo. no. [Ayes—1; noes—10.]

[2:297; Madison, 15 Aug.]

Mr. Strong moved to amend the article so as to read— "Each House shall possess the right of originating all bills, except bills for raising money for the purposes of revenue, or for appropriating the same and for fixing the salaries of the officers of the Govt. which shall originate in the House of Representatives; but the Senate may propose or concur with amendments as in other cases"

Col. Mason, 2ds. the motion. He was extremely earnest to take this power from the Senate, who he said could already sell the whole Country by means of Treaties.

Mr Ghorum urged the amendment as of great importance. The Senate will first acquire the habit of preparing money bills, and then the practice will grow into an exclusive right of preparing them.

Mr. Gouvernr. Morris opposed it as unnecessary and inconvenient.

Mr. Williamson–some think this restriction on the Senate essential to liberty—others think it of no importance. Why should not the former be indulged. he was for an efficient and stable Govt: but many would not strengthen the Senate if not restricted in the case of money bills. The friends of the Senate would therefore lose more than they would gain by refusing to gratify the other side. He moved to postpone the subject till the powers of the Senate should be gone over.

Mr. Rutlidge 2ds. the motion.

[2:509; Madison, 5 Sept.]

The (3) clause, Mr. Govr. Morris moved to postpone. It had been agreed to in the Committee on the ground of compromise, and he should feel himself at liberty to dissent to it; if on the whole he should not be satisfied with certain other parts to be settled.—Mr. Pinkney 2ded. the motion

Mr. Sherman was for giving immediate ease to those who looked on this clause as of great moment, and for trusting to their concurrence in other proper measures.

On the question for postponing

N— H— ay— Mas— no. Ct. ay. N— J— ay— Pa. ay— Del. ay. Md ay—Va. no. N— C— ay— S. C ay— Geo ay. [Ayes—9; noes—2.]

. . . . .

Mr King observed that the influence of the Small States in the Senate was somewhat balanced by the influence of the large States in bringing forward the candidates, and also by the Concurrence of the small States in the Committee in the clause vesting the exclusive origination of Money bills in the House of Representatives.

[2:552; Madison, 8 Sept.]

The clause of the report made on the 5th. Sepr. & postponed was taken up, to wit—"All bills for raising revenue shall originate in the House of Representatives; and shall be subject to alterations and amendments by the Senate. No money shall be drawn from the Treasury but in consequence of appropriations made by law."

It was moved to strike out the words "and shall be subject to alterations and amendments by the Senate" and insert the words used in the Constitution of Massachusetts on the same subject—"but the Senate may propose or concur with amendments as in other bills"—which was agreed too nem: con:

On the question On the first part of the clause—"All bills for raising revenue shall originate in the house of Representatives"

N. H. ay. Mas. ay. Ct. ay. N. J. ay Pa. ay. Del. no. Md. no. Va. ay. N. C. ay. S. C. ay. Geo. ay. [Ayes—9; noes—2.]

8

LUTHER MARTIN, GENUINE INFORMATION
1788
Storing 2.4.49–52

The *seventh* section of this article was also the subject of contest—It was thought by many members of the convention, that it was very wrong to confine the origination of all revenue bills to the house of representatives, since the members of the senate will be chosen by the people as well as the members of the house of delegates, if not *immediately*, yet *mediately*, being chosen by the members of the State legislature, which members are elected by the *people*, and that it makes no *real* difference whether we do a thing *in person*, or by a *deputy*, or agent, appointed by *us* for *that purpose*.

That no argument can be drawn from the House of Lords in the British constitution, since they are neither mediately nor immediately the representatives of the people, but are one of the *three estates*, composing that kingdom, having *hereditary right* and *privileges*, *distinct* from, and *independent* of, the *people*.

That it may, and probably will be a future source of dispute and controversy between the two branches, what are, or are not revenue bills, and the more so, as they are not *defined* in the constitution; which controversies may be difficult to settle, and may become serious in their consequences, [there] being no power in the constitution to decide upon, or authorised in cases of absolute necessity to terminate them by a prorogation or dissolution of either of the branches; a remedy provided in the British constitution, where the King has that power, which has been found necessary at times to be exercised in case of violent dissentions between the Lords and Commons on the subject of money bills.

That every regulation of commerce; every law relative to excises, stamps, the post-office, the imposing of taxes, and their collection, the creation of courts and offices; in fine, every law for the union, if enforced by any pecuniary sanctions, as they would tend to bring money into the continental treasury, might and no doubt would be considered a revenue act—That consequently the senate, the members of whom will it may be presumed, be the most select in their choice, and consist of men the most enlightened, and of the greatest abilities, who from the duration of their appointment and the permanency of their body, will probably be best acquainted with the common concerns of the States, and with the means of providing for them, will be rendered almost useless as a part of the legislature; and that they will have but little to do in that capacity, except patiently to wait the proceedings of the house of representatives, and afterwards examine and approve, or propose amendments.

9

THEOPHILUS PARSONS, MASSACHUSETTS RATIFYING CONVENTION
23 Jan. 1788
Elliot 2:92–93

It is objected that it is dangerous to allow the Senate a right of proposing alterations or amendments in money bills; that the Senate may by this power increase the supplies, and establish profuse salaries; that for these reasons the lords in the British Parliament have not this power, which is a great security to the liberties of Englishmen. I was much surprised at hearing this objection, and the grounds upon which it was supported. The reason why the lords have not this power, is founded on a principle in the English constitution, that the commons alone represent the whole property of the nation; and as a money bill is a grant to the king, none can make the grant but those who represent the property of the nation; and the negative of the lords is introduced to check the profusion of the commons, and to guard their own property. The manner of passing a money bill is conclusive evidence of these principles; for, after the assent of the Lords, it does not remain with the clerk of the Parliament, but is returned to the commons, who, by their speaker, present it to the king as the gift of the commons. But every supposed control the Senate, by this power, may have over money bills, they can have without it; for, by private communications with the representatives, they may as well insist upon the increase of the supplies, or salaries, as by official communications. But had not the Senate this power, the representatives might take any foreign matter to a money bill, and compel the Senate to concur, or lose the supplies. This might be done in critical seasons, when the Senate might give way to the encroachments of the representatives, rather than sustain the odium of embarrassing the affairs of the nation; the balance between the two branches of the legislature would, in this way, be endangered, if not destroyed, and the Constitution materially injured. This subject was fully considered by the Convention for forming the constitution of Massachusetts, and the provision made by that body, after mature deliberation, is introduced into the federal Constitution.

10

DEBATE IN VIRGINIA RATIFYING CONVENTION
14 June 1788
Elliot 3:375–78

Mr. GRAYSON objected to the power of the Senate to propose or concur with amendments to money bills. He looked upon the power of proposing amendments to be equal, in principle, to that of originating, and that they were, in fact, the same. As this was, in his opinion, a departure from that great principle which required that the immediate representatives of the people only should interfere with money bills, he wished to know the reasons on which it was founded. The lords in England had never been allowed to intermeddle with money bills. He knew not why the Senate should. In the lower house, said he, the people are represented according to their numbers. In the upper house, the states are represented in their political capacities. Delaware, or Rhode Island, has as many representatives here as Massachusetts. Why should the Senate have a right to intermeddle with money, when the representation is neither equal nor just?

Mr. MADISON. Mr. Chairman, the criticism made by the honorable member is, that there is an ambiguity in the words, and that it is not clearly ascertained where the origination of money bills may take place. I suppose the first part of the clause is sufficiently expressed to exclude all doubts. The gentlemen who composed the Convention divided in opinion concerning the utility of confining this to any particular branch. Whatever it be in Great Britain, there is a sufficient difference between us and them to render it inapplicable to this country. It has always appeared to me to be a matter of no great consequence, whether the Senate had a right of originating or proposing amendments to money bills, or not. To withhold it from them would create disagreeable disputes. Some American constitutions make no difference. Virginia and South Carolina are, I think, the only states where this power is restrained. In Massachusetts, and other states, the power of proposing amendments is vested, unquestionably, in their senates. No inconvenience has resulted from it. On the contrary, with respect to South Carolina, this clause is continually a source of disputes. When a bill comes from the other house, the Senate entirely rejects it, and this causes contentions. When you send a bill to the Senate, without the power of making any alteration, you force them to reject the bill altogether, when it would be necessary and advantageous that it should pass.

The power of proposing alterations removes this inconvenience, and does not appear to me at all objectionable. I should have no objection to their having a right of originating such bills. People would see what was done, and it would add the intelligence of one house to that of the other. It would be still in the power of the other house to obstruct any injudicious measure proposed by them.

There is no landmark or constitutional provision in Great Britain, which prohibits the House of Lords from intermeddling with money bills; but the House of Commons have established this rule. Yet the lords insist on their having a right to originate them, as they possess great property, as well as the commons, and are taxed like them. The House of Commons object to their claim, lest they should too lavishly make grants to the crown, and increase the taxes. The honorable member says that there is no difference between the right of originating bills and proposing amendments. There is some difference, though not considerable. If any grievances should happen in consequence of unwise regulations in revenue matters, the odium would be divided, which will now be thrown on the House of Representatives. But you may safely lodge this power of amending with the Senate. When a bill is sent with proposed amendments to the House of Representatives, if they find the alterations defective, they are not conclusive. The House of Representatives are the judges of their propriety, and the recommendation of the Senate is nothing. The experience of this state justifies this clause. The House of Delegates has employed weeks in forming a money bill; and because the Senate had no power of proposing amendments, the bill was lost altogether, and a new bill obliged to be again introduced, when the insertion of one line by the Senate would have done. Those gentlemen who oppose this clause will not object to it when they recollect that the senators are appointed by the states, as the present members of Congress are appointed; for, as they will guard the political interests of the states in other respects, they will attend to them very probably in their amendments to money bills. I think this power, for these considerations, is useful and necessary.

Mr. GRAYSON still considered the power of proposing amendments to be the same, in effect, as that of originating. The Senate could strike out every word of the bill, except the word *whereas,* or any other introductory word, and might substitute new words of their own. As the state of Delaware was not so large as the county of Augusta, and Rhode Island was still less, and yet had an equal suffrage in the Senate, he could not see the propriety of giving them this power, but referred it to the judgment of the house.

11

HOUSE OF REPRESENTATIVES, DUTIES
15 May 1789
Annals 1:65

Mr. WHITE. The Constitution, having authorized the House of Representatives alone to originate money bills, places an important trust in our hands, which, as their protectors, we ought not to part with. I do not mean to imply that the Senate are less to be trusted than this house; but the Constitution, no doubt for wise purposes, has given the immediate representatives of the people a control over the whole government in this particular, which, for their interest, they ought not to let out of their hands.

Mr. MADISON. The Constitution places the power in the House of originating money bills. The principal reason why the Constitution had made this distinction was, because they were chosen by the people, and supposed to be the best acquainted with their interest and ability. In order to make them more particularly acquainted with these objects, the democratic branch of the legislature consisted of a greater number, and were chosen for a shorter period; that so they might revert more frequently to the mass of the people.

12

JAMES WILSON, LEGISLATIVE DEPARTMENT,
LECTURES ON LAW
1791
Works 1:423–25

In England, all grants of aids by parliament begin in the house of commons. Of that house, this is an ancient, and, now, an indisputable privilege. With regard to it, the commons are so jealous, that, over money bills, they will not suffer the other house to exert any powers, except simply those of concurrence or rejection. From the lords, no alteration or amendment will be received on this delicate subject. The constitutions of the United States and Pennsylvania have, on this head, adopted the parliamentary law of England in part; but they have not adopted it altogether. They have directed, that money bills shall originate in the house of representatives; but they have directed also, that the senate may propose amendments in these, as well as in other bills. It will be proper to investigate the reasons of each part of the direction. This will best be done by tracing the matter historically, and attending to the difference between the institution of the house of lords in England, and that of the senates of the United States and Pennsylvania.

During a considerable time after the establishment of the house of commons as a separate branch of the legislature, it appears, that the members of that house were, with regard to taxes and assessments, governed altogether by the instructions, which they received from their constituents. Each county and borough seems to have directed its representatives, concerning the amount of the rates to which they might give their assent. By adding together the sums contained in those particular directions, it was easy to ascertain, in the house of commons, the sum total, which the commonalty of the kingdom were willing to grant. To the extent of this sum, the commons conceived themselves empowered and directed to go; but no farther.

According to this mode of proceeding, the imposition of taxes produced no interchange of communication between the two houses of parliament. To introduce a money bill, or an amendment to a money bill, into the house of lords—to deliberate upon the bill or amendment in that house—after agreeing to it there, to submit it to the deliberation of the house of commons—all this would have been perfectly nugatory. Let us suppose, that the bill or amendment had undergone the most full and careful examination in the house of lords, who, acting only for themselves, could examine it under every aspect, unfettered by exteriour direction and control: let us suppose it then transmitted to the house of commons, for their concurrence: what could the house of commons do? They could not deliberate upon the bill or the amendment: they could only compare it with their instructions: if they found it consistent with them, they could give, if inconsistent, they must refuse, their consent. The only course, therefore, in which this business could be transacted, was, that the commons should begin by mentioning the sum, which they were empowered to grant, and that what they proposed should be sent to the house of lords, who, upon all the circumstances, might deliberate and judge for themselves.

In this manner, and for these reasons, the house of commons became possessed of this important privilege, which is now justly regarded by them, as one of the strongest pillars of their freedom and power. Once possessed of this privilege, they were far from relinquishing it, when the first reasons for its possession had ceased. Other reasons, stronger than the first, succeeded to them. In the flux of time and things, the revenue and influence of the crown became so great, and the property of the peerage, considered with relation to the general property of the kingdom, became comparatively so small, that it was judged unwise to permit that body to model, or even to alter, the general system of taxation. This is the aspect, under which this subject was viewed in the lecture, to which I have alluded; and I will not repeat now what was observed then.

From this short historical deduction, it appears, that the provision, which we now consider, is far from being so important here, as it is in England. In the United States and in Pennsylvania, both houses of the legislature draw their authority, either immediately, or, at least, not remotely, from the same common fountain. In England, one of the houses acts entirely in its private and separate right.

But though this regulation is by no means so necessary

here, as it is in England; yet it may have its use, so far as it has been adopted into our constitutions. Our houses of representatives are much more numerous than our senates: the members of the former are chosen much more frequently, than are the members of the latter. For these reasons, an information more local and minute may be expected in the houses of representatives, than can be expected in the senates. This minute and local information will be of service, in suggesting and in collecting materials for the laws of revenue. After those materials are collected and prepared, the wisdom and the patriotism of both houses will be employed in forming them into a proper system.

13

JOSEPH STORY, COMMENTARIES ON THE CONSTITUTION 2:§§ 871–77
1833

§ 871. . . . This provision, so far as it regards the right to originate what are technically called "money bills," is, beyond all question, borrowed from the British house of commons, of which it is the ancient and indisputable privilege and right, that all grants of subsidies and parliamentary aids shall begin in their house, and are first bestowed by them, although their grants are not effectual to all intents and purposes, until they have the assent of the other two branches of the legislature. The general reason given for this privilege of the house of commons is, that the supplies are raised upon the body of the people; and therefore it is proper, that they alone should have the right of taxing themselves. And Mr. Justice Blackstone has very correctly remarked, that this reason would be unanswerable, if the commons taxed none but themselves. But it is notorious, that a very large share of property is in possession of the lords; that this property is equally taxed, as the property of the commons; and therefore the commons, not being the sole persons taxed, this cannot be the reason of their having the sole right of raising and modelling the supply. The true reason seems to be this. The lords being a permanent hereditary body, created at pleasure by the king, are supposed more liable to be influenced by the crown, and when once influenced, more likely to continue so, than the commons, who are a temporary elective body, freely nominated by the people. It would, therefore, be extremely dangerous to give the lords any power of framing new taxes for the subject. It is sufficient, that they have a power of rejecting, if they think the commons too lavish or improvident in their grants.

§ 872. This seems a very just account of the matter, with reference to the spirit of the British constitution; though a different explanation has been deduced from a historical review of the power. It has been asserted to have arisen from the instructions from time to time given by the constituents of the commons, (whether county, city, or borough,) as to the rates and assessments, which they were respectively willing to bear and assent to; and from the aggregate it was easy for the commons to ascertain the whole amount, which the commonalty of the whole kingdom were willing to grant to the king. Be this as it may, so jealous are the commons of this valuable privilege, that herein they will not suffer the other house to exert any power, but that of rejecting. They will not permit the least alteration or amendment to be made by the lords to the mode of taxing the people by a money bill; and under this appellation are included all bills, by which money is directed to be raised upon the subject for any purpose, or in any shape whatsoever, either for the exigencies of the government, and collected from the kingdom in general, as the land tax, or for private benefit, and collected in any particular district, as turnpikes, parish rates, and the like. It is obvious, that this power might be capable of great abuse, if other bills were tacked to such money bills; and accordingly it was found, that money bills were sometimes tacked to favourite measures of the commons, with a view to ensure their passage by the lords. This extraordinary use, or rather perversion of the power, would, if suffered to grow into a common practice, have completely destroyed the equilibrium of the British constitution, and subjected both the lords and the king to the power of the commons. Resistance was made from time to time to this unconstitutional encroachment; and at length the lords, with a view to give permanent effect to their own rights, have made it a standing order to reject upon sight all bills, that are tacked to money bills. Thus, the privilege is maintained on one side, and guarded against undue abuse on the other.

§ 873. It will be at once perceived, that the same reasons do not exist in the same extent, for the same exclusive right in our house of representatives in regard to money bills, as exist for such right in the British house of commons. It may be fit, that it should possess the exclusive right to originate money bills; since it may be presumed to possess more ample means of local information, and it more directly represents the opinions, feelings, and wishes of the people; and, being directly dependent upon them for support, it will be more watchful and cautious in the imposition of taxes, than a body, which emanates exclusively from the states in their sovereign political capacity. But, as the senators are in a just sense equally representatives of the people, and do not hold their offices by a permanent or hereditary title, but periodically return to the common mass of citizens; and above all, as direct taxes are, and must be, apportioned among the states according to their federal population; and as all the states have a distinct local interest, both as to the amount and nature of all taxes of every sort, which are to be levied, there seems a peculiar fitness in giving to the senate a power to alter and amend, as well as to concur with, or reject all money bills. The due influence of all the states is thus preserved; for otherwise it might happen, from the overwhelming representation of some of the large states, that taxes might be levied, which would bear with peculiar severity upon the interests, either agricultural, commercial, or manufacturing, of others being the minor states; and thus the equilibrium intended by the constitution, as well of power, as of interest, and influence, might be practically subverted.

§ 874. There would also be no small inconvenience in excluding the senate from the exercise of this power of amendment and alteration; since if any, the slightest modification were required in such a bill to make it either palatable or just, the senate would be compelled to reject it, although an amendment of a single line might make it entirely acceptable to both houses. Such a practical obstruction to the legislation of a free government would far outweigh any supposed theoretical advantages from the possession or exercise of an exclusive power by the house of representatives. Infinite perplexities, and misunderstandings, and delays would clog the most wholesome legislation. Even the annual appropriation bills might be in danger of a miscarriage on these accounts; and the most painful dissensions might be introduced.

§ 875. Indeed, of so little importance has the exclusive possession of such a power been thought in the state governments, that some of the state constitutions make no difference, as to the power of each branch of the legislature to originate money bills. Most of them contain a provision similar to that in the constitution of the United States; and in those states, where the exclusive power formerly existed, as, for instance, in Virginia and South-Carolina, it was a constant source of difficulties and contentions. In the revised constitution of South-Carolina, (in 1790), the provision was altered, so as to conform to the clause in the constitution of the United States.

§ 876. The clause seems to have met with no serious opposition in any of the state conventions; and indeed could scarcely be expected to meet with any opposition, except in Virginia; since the other states were well satisfied with the principle adopted in their own state constitutions; and in Virginia the clause created but little debate.

§ 877. What bills are properly "bills for raising revenue," in the sense of the constitution, has been matter of some discussion. A learned commentator supposes, that every bill, which indirectly or consequentially may raise revenue, is, within the sense of the constitution, a revenue bill. He therefore thinks, that the bills for establishing the post-office, and the mint, and regulating the value of foreign coin, belong to this class, and ought not to have originated (as in fact they did) in the senate. But the practical construction of the constitution has been against his opinion. And, indeed, the history of the origin of the power, already suggested, abundantly proves, that it has been confined to bills to levy taxes in the strict sense of the words, and has not been understood to extend to bills for other purposes, which may incidentally create revenue. No one supposes, that a bill to sell any of the public lands, or to sell public stock, is a bill to raise revenue, in the sense of the constitution. Much less would a bill be so deemed, which merely regulated the value of foreign or domestic coins, or authorized a discharge of insolvent debtors upon assignments of their estates to the United States, giving a priority of payment to the United States in cases of insolvency, although all of them might incidentally bring revenue into the treasury.

SEE ALSO:

Thomas Hedley, 28 June 1610, Proceedings in Parliament, 2:170–97 (1966)

Records of the Federal Convention, Farrand 1:224, 238, 523, 538–39; 2:4, 5, 8, 14, 131, 144, 154, 164, 191, 214, 266, 294, 505, 545, 568, 593, 638

James McHenry, Maryland House of Delegates, 29 Nov. 1787, Farrand 3:148

House of Representatives, Duties on Imports, 16 May 1789, Annals 1:357–62

House of Representatives, Appropriations for 1796, 18 Jan. 1796, Annals 5:253–62

Article 1, Section 7, Clauses 2 and 3

Every Bill which shall have passed the House of Representatives and the Senate, shall, before it become a Law, be presented to the President of the United States; If he approve he shall sign it, but if not he shall return it, with his Objections to that House in which it shall have originated, who shall enter the Objections at large on their Journal, and proceed to reconsider it. If after such Reconsideration two thirds of that House shall agree to pass the Bill, it shall be sent, together with the Objections, to the other House, by which it shall likewise be reconsidered, and if approved by two thirds of that House, it shall become a Law. But in all such Cases the Votes of both Houses shall be determined by yeas and Nays, and the Names of the Persons voting for and against the Bill shall be entered on the Journal of each House respectively. If any Bill shall not be returned by the President within ten Days (Sunday excepted) after it shall have been presented to him, the Same shall be a Law, in like Manner as if he had signed it, unless the Congress by their Adjournment prevent its Return, in which Case it shall not be a Law.

Every Order, Resolution, or Vote to which the Concurrence of the Senate and House of Representatives may be necessary (except on a question of Adjournment) shall be presented to the President of the United States; and before the Same shall take Effect, shall be approved by him, or being disapproved by him, shall be repassed by two thirds of the Senate and House of Representatives, according to the Rules and Limitations prescribed in the Case of a Bill.

---

1. William Blackstone, Commentaries (1765)
2. Declaration of Independence, 4 July 1776
3. Edmund Burke, Letter to the Sheriffs of Bristol, 1777
4. Records of the Federal Convention
5. James Wilson, Pennsylvania Ratifying Convention, 1, 4 Dec. 1787
6. Luther Martin, Genuine Information, 1788
7. Federal Farmer, no. 14, 17 Jan. 1788
8. Alexander Hamilton, Federalist, no. 69, 14 Mar. 1788
9. Alexander Hamilton, Federalist, no. 73, 21 Mar. 1788
10. Impartial Examiner, no. 4, 11 June 1788
11. James Iredell, North Carolina Ratifying Convention, 26 July 1788
12. James Madison, Observations on Jefferson's Draft of a Constitution for Virginia, 15 Oct. 1788
13. Roger Sherman to John Adams, 20 July 1789
14. James Wilson, Comparison of Constitutions, Lectures on Law, 1791
15. James Madison to James K. Tefft, 3 Dec. 1830
16. Joseph Story, Commentaries on the Constitution (1833)

1

WILLIAM BLACKSTONE, COMMENTARIES
1:149–51, 155
1765

It is highly necessary for preserving the ballance of the constitution, that the executive power should be a branch, though not the whole, of the legislature. The total union of them, we have seen, would be productive of tyranny; the total disjunction of them for the present, would in the end produce the same effects, by causing that union, against which it seems to provide. The legislature would soon become tyrannical, by making continual encroachments, and gradually assuming to itself the rights of the executive power. Thus the long parliament of Charles the first, while it acted in a constitutional manner, with the royal concurrence, redressed many heavy grievances and established many salutary laws. But when the two houses assumed the power of legislation, in exclusion of the royal authority, they soon after assumed likewise the reins of administration; and, in consequence of these united powers, overturned both church and state, and established a worse oppression than any they pretended to remedy. To hinder therefore any such encroachments, the king is himself a part of the parliament: and, as this is the reason of his being so, very properly therefore the share of legislation, which the constitution has placed in the crown, consists in the power of *rejecting*, rather than *resolving;* this being sufficient to answer the end proposed. For we may apply to the royal negative, in this instance, what Cicero observes of the negative of the Roman tribunes, that the crown has not any power of *doing* wrong, but merely of *preventing* wrong from being done. The crown cannot begin of itself any alterations in the present established law; but it may approve or disapprove of the alterations suggested and consented to by the two houses. The legislative therefore cannot abridge the executive power of any rights which it now has by law, without it's own consent; since the law must perpetually stand as it now does, unless all the powers will agree to alter it. And herein indeed consists the true excellence of the English government, that all the parts of it form a mutual check upon each other. In the legislature, the people are a check upon the nobility, and the nobility a check upon the people; by the mutual privilege of rejecting what the other has resolved: while the king is a check upon both, which preserves the executive power from encroachments. And this very executive power is again checked, and kept within due bounds by the two houses, through the privilege they have of enquiring into, impeaching, and punishing the conduct (not indeed of the king, which would destroy his constitutional independence; but, which is more beneficial to the public) of his evil and pernicious counsellors. Thus every branch of our civil polity supports and is supported, regulates and is regulated, by the rest; for the two houses naturally drawing in two directions of opposite interest, and the prerogative in another still different from them both, they mutually keep each other from exceeding their proper limits; while the whole is prevented from separation, and artificaly connected together by the mixed nature of the crown, which is a part of the legislative, and the sole executive magistrate. Like three distinct powers in mechanics, they jointly impel the machine of government in a direction different from what either, acting by themselves, would have done; but at the same time in a direction partaking of each, and formed out of all; a direction which constitutes the true line of the liberty and happiness of the community.

. . . . .

These are the constituent parts of a parliament, the king, the lords spiritual and temporal, and the commons. Parts, of which each is so necessary, that the consent of all three is required to make any new law that shall bind the subject. Whatever is enacted for law by one, or by two only, of the three is no statute; and to it no regard is due, unless in matters relating to their own privileges. For though, in the times of madness and anarchy, the commons once passed a vote, "that whatever is enacted or declared for law by the commons in parliament assembled hath the force of law; and all the people of this nation are concluded thereby, although the consent and concurrence of the king or house of peers be not had thereto;" yet, when the constitution was restored in all it's forms, it was particularly enacted by statute 13 Car. II. c. 1. that if any person shall maliciously or advisedly affirm, that both or either of the houses of parliament have any legislative authority without the king, such person shall incur all the penalties of a praemunire.

2

DECLARATION OF INDEPENDENCE
4 July 1776

—He has refused his Assent to Laws, the most wholesome and necessary for the public good.—He has forbidden his Governors to pass Laws of immediate and pressing importance, unless suspended in their operation till his Assent should be obtained; and when so suspended, he has utterly neglected to attend to them.

3

EDMUND BURKE, LETTER TO THE
SHERIFFS OF BRISTOL
1777
Works 1:28

The king's negative to bills is one of the most indisputed of the royal prerogatives; and it extends to all cases whatsoever. I am far from certain, that if several laws which I know had fallen under the stroke of that sceptre, that the public would have had a very heavy loss. But it is not the *propriety* of the exercise which is in question. The exercise itself is wisely forborne. Its repose may be the preservation of its existence; and its existence may be the means of saving the constitution itself, on an occasion worthy of bringing it forth.

4

RECORDS OF THE FEDERAL CONVENTION

[1:97; Madison, 4 June]

First Clause of Proposition 8th relating *to a Council of Revision* taken into consideration.

Mr. Gerry doubts whether the Judiciary ought to form a part of it, as they will have a sufficient check agst. encroachments on their own department by their exposition of the laws, which involved a power of deciding on their Constitutionality. In some States the Judges had actually set aside laws as being agst. the Constitution. This was done too with general approbation. It was quite foreign from the nature of ye. office to make them judges of the policy of public measures. He moves to postpone the clause in order to propose "that the National Executive shall have a right to negative any Legislative act which shall not be afterwards passed by   parts of each branch of the national Legislature.

Mr. King seconds the motion, observing that the Judges ought to be able to expound the law as it should come before them, free from the bias of having participated in its formation.

Mr. Wilson thinks neither the original proposition nor the amendment go far enough. If the Legislative Exētiv & Judiciary ought to be distinct & independent, The Executive ought to have an absolute negative. Without such a Self-defence the Legislature can at any moment sink it into non-existence. He was for varying the proposition in such a manner as to give the Executive & Judiciary jointly an absolute negative

On the question to postpone in order to take Mr. Gerry's proposition into consideration it was agreed to Massts. ay. Cont. no. N. Y. ay. Pa. ay. Del. no. Maryd. no. Virga. no. N. C. ay. S. C. ay. Ga. ay. [Ayes—6; noes—4.]

Mr. Gerry's proposition being now before Committee, Mr. Wilson & Mr. Hamilton move that the last part of it (viz wch. sl. not be afterwds. passed" unless by   parts of each branch of the National legislature) be struck out, so as to give the Executive an absolute negative on the laws. There was no danger they thought of such a power being too much exercised. It was mentioned (by Col: Hamilton) that the King of G. B. had not exerted his negative since the Revolution.

Mr. Gerry sees no necessity for so great a controul over the legislature as the best men in the Community would be comprised in the two branches of it.

Docr. Franklin, said he was sorry to differ from his colleague for whom he had a very great respect, on any occasion, but he could not help it on this. He had had some experience of this check in the Executive on the Legislature, under the proprietary Government of Pena. The negative of the Governor was constantly made use of to extort money. No good law whatever could be passed without a private bargain with him. An increase of his salary, or some donation, was always made a condition; till at last it became the regular practice, to have orders in his favor on the Treasury, presented along with the bills to be signed, so that he might actually receive the former before he should sign the latter. When the Indians were scalping the western people, and notice of it arrived, the concurrence of the Governor in the means of self-defence could not be got, till it was agreed that his Estate should be exempted from taxation. so that the people were to fight for the security of his property, whilst he was to bear no share of the burden. This was a mischievous sort of check. If the Executive was to have a Council, such a power would be less objectionable. It was true the King of G. B. had not, As was said, exerted his negative since the Revolution: but that matter was easily explained. The bribes and emoluments now given to the members of parliament rendered it unnecessary, everything being done according to the will of the Ministers. He was afraid, if a negative should be given as proposed, that more power and money would be demanded, till at last eno' would be gotten to influence & bribe the Legislature into a compleat subjection to the will of the Executive.

Mr. Sherman was agst. enabling any one man to stop the will of the whole. No one man could be found so far above all the rest in wisdom. He thought we ought to avail ourselves of his wisdom in revising the laws, but not permit him to overrule the decided and cool opinions of the Legislature.

Mr. Madison supposed that if a proper proportion of each branch should be required to overrule the objections of the Executive, it would answer the same purpose as an absolute negative. It would rarely if ever happen that the Executive constituted as ours is proposed to be would, have firmness eno' to resist the Legislature, unless backed by a certain part of the body itself. The King of G. B. with all his splendid attributes would not be able to withstand ye. unanimous and eager wishes of both houses of Parliament. To give such a prerogative would certainly be obnoxious to the temper of this country; its present temper at least.

Mr. Wilson believed as others did that this power would seldom be used. The Legislature would know that such a power existed, and would refrain from such laws, as it would be sure to defeat. Its silent operation would therefore preserve harmony and prevent mischief. The case of Pena. formerly was very different from its present case. The Executive was not then as now to be appointed by the people. It will not in this case as in the one cited be supported by the head of a Great Empire, actuated by a different & sometimes opposite interest. The salary too is now proposed to be fixed by the Constitution, or if Dr. F's idea should be adopted all salary whatever interdicted. The requiring a large proportion of each House to overrule the Executive check might do in peaceable times; but there might be tempestuous moments in which animosties may run high between the Executive and Legislative branches, and in which the former ought to be able to defend itself.

Mr. Butler had been in favor of a single Executive Magistrate; but could he have entertained an idea that a compleat negative on the laws was to be given him he certainly should have acted very differently. It had been observed that in all countries the Executive power is in a constant course of increase. This was certainly the case in G. B. Gentlemen seemed to think that we had nothing to apprehend from an abuse of the Executive power. But why might not a Cataline or a Cromwell arise in this Country as well as in others.

Mr. Bedford was opposed to every check on the Legislative, even the Council of Revision first proposed. He thought it would be sufficient to mark out in the Constitution the boundaries to the Legislative Authority, which would give all the requisite security to the rights of the other departments. The Representatives of the People were the best judges of what was for their interest, and ought to be under no external controul whatever. The two branches would produces a sufficient controul within the Legislature itself.

Col. Mason observed that a vote had already passed he found (he was out at the time) for vesting the executive powers in a single person. Among these powers was that of appointing to offices in certain cases. The probable abuses of a negative had been well explained by Dr. F as proved by experience, the best of all tests. Will not the same door be opened here. The Executive may refuse its assent to necessary measures till new appointments shall be referred to him; and having by degrees engrossed all these into his own hands, the American Executive, like the British, will by bribery & influence, save himself the trouble & odium of exerting his negative afterwards. We are Mr. Chairman going very far in this business. We are not indeed constituting a British Government, but a more dangerous monarchy, an elective one. We are introducing a new principle into our system, and not necessary as in the British Govt. where the Executive has greater rights to defend. Do gentlemen mean to pave the way to hereditary Monarchy? Do they flatter themselves that the people will ever consent to such an innovation? If they do I venture to tell them, they are mistaken. The people never will consent. And do gentlemen consider the danger of delay, and the still greater danger of a rejection not for a moment but forever, of the plan which shall be proposed to them. Notwithstanding the oppressions & injustice experienced among us from democracy; the genius of the people is in favor of it, and the genius of the people must be consulted. He could not but consider the federal system as in effect dissolved by the appointment of this Convention to devise a better one. And do gentlemen look forward to the dangerous interval between the extinction of an old, and the establishment of a new Governmt. and to the scenes of confusion which may ensue. He hoped that nothing like a monarchy would ever be attempted in this Country. A hatred to its oppressions had carried the people through the late Revolution. Will it not be eno' to enable the Executive to suspend offensive laws, till they shall be coolly revised, and the objections to them overruled by a greater majority than was required in the first instance. He never could agree to give up all the rights of the people to a single Magistrate. If more than one had been fixed on, greater powers might have been entrusted to the Executive. He hoped this attempt to give such powers would have its weight hereafter as an argument for increasing the number of the Executive.

Docr. Franklin.[1] A Gentleman from S. C. (Mr. Butler) a

[1]Franklin's draft of this speech:

The Steady Course of public Measures is most probably to be expected from a Number.

A single Person's Measures may be good. The Successor, often differs in Opinion of those Measures, & adopts others. Often is ambitious of distinguishing himself, by opposing them, and offering new Projects. One is peaceably dispos'd. Another may be fond of War, &c: Hence foreign States can never have that Confidence, in the Treaties or Friendship of such a Government as in that which is conducted by a Number.

The Single Head may be Sick. Who is to conduct the Public Affairs in that Case? When he dies, who are to conduct, till a new Election?—If a Council why not continue them?—Shall we not be harass'd with Factions for the Election of Successors? become like Poland, weak from our Dissensions?

Consider the present distracted Condition of Holland. They had at first a Stadtholder, the Prince of Orange, a Man of undoubted and great Merit. They found some Inconveniencies however in the Extent of Powers annex'd to that Office, and exercis'd by a single Person. On his Death They resum'd and divided those Powers among the States and Cities. But there has been a constant Struggle since between that Family & the Nation. In the last Century the then Prince of Orange found Means to inflame the Populace against their Magistrates, excite a general Insurrection in which an excellent Minister, *Dewit*, was murdered, all the old Magistrates displac'd, and the Stadtholder re-invested with all the former Powers. In this Century, the Father of the present Stadtholder, having married a British Princess, did, by exciting another Insurrection, force from the Nation a Decree that the Stadtholdership should be thenceforth hereditary in his Family. And now his Son, being suspected of having favour'd England in the late War, and thereby lost the Confidence of the Nation, he is forming an internal Faction to support his Power, & reinstate his Favourite the Duke of Brunswick; and he holds up his Family Alliances with England and Prussia to terrify Opposition. It was this Conduct of the Statholder which induc'd the States to recur to the Protection of France, and put their Troops under a French rather than the Stadtholder's German General the Duke of Brunswick. And this is the Source of all the present Disorders in Holland, which if the Stadtholder has Abilities equal to his Inclinations, will probably after a ruinous & bloody civil War, end in establishing an hereditary Monarchy in his Family.

day or two ago called our attention to the case of the U. Netherlands. He wished the gentleman had been a little fuller, and had gone back to the original of that Govt. The people being under great obligations to the Prince of Orange whose wisdom and bravery had saved them, chose him for the Stadtholder. He did very well. Inconveniences however were felt from his powers; which growing more & more oppressive, they were at length set aside. Still however there was a party for the P. of Orange, which descended to his son who excited insurrections, spilt a great deal of blood, murdered the de Witts, and got the powers revested in the Stadtholder. Afterwards another Prince had power to excite insurrections & to make the Stadtholdership hereditary. And the present Stadthder. is ready to wade thro' a bloody civil war to the establishment of a monarchy. Col. Mason had mentioned the circumstance of appointing officers. He knew how that point would be managed. No new appointment would be suffered as heretofore in Pensa. unless it be referred to the Executive; so that all profitable offices will be at his disposal. The first man, put at the helm will be a good one. No body knows what sort may come afterwards. The executive will be always increasing here, as elsewhere, till it ends in a monarchy

On the question for striking out so as to give Executive an absolute Negative—

Massts. no. Cont. no. N. Y. no. Pa. no. Dl. no. Md. no. Va. no. N. C. no. S. C. no. Georga. no. [Ayes—0; noes—10.]

Mr. Butler moved that the Resoln. be altered so as to read—"Resolved that the National Executive have a power to suspend any legislative act for the term of   ."

Doctr. Franklin seconds the motion.

Mr. Gerry observed that a power of suspending might do all the mischief dreaded from the negative of useful laws; without answering the salutary purpose of checking unjust or unwise ones.

On question "for giving this suspending power". all the States, to wit Massts. Cont. N. Y. Pa. Del. Maryd. Virga. N. C. S. C. Georgia. were *no*.

On a question for enabling *two thirds* of each branch of the Legislature to overrule the revisionary check: it passed in the affirmative sub silentio; and was inserted in the blank of Mr. Gerry's motion.

On the question on Mr. Gerry's motion which gave the Executive alone without the Judiciary the revisionary controul on the laws unles overruled by ⅔ of each branch. Massts. ay. Cont. no. N. Y. ay. Pena. ay. Del. ay. Maryd. no. Va. ay N. C. ay. S. C. ay. Geo. ay. [Ayes—8; noes—2.]

[1:138; Madison, 6 June]

Mr. Wilson moved to reconsider the vote excluding the Judiciary from a share in the revision of the laws, and to add after "National Executive" the words "with a convenient number of the national Judiciary"; remarking the expediency of reinforcing the Executive with the influence of that Department.

Mr. Madison 2ded. the motion. He observed that the great difficulty in rendering the Executive competent to its own defence arose from the nature of Republican Govt.

which could not give to an individual citizen that settled pre-eminence in the eyes of the rest, that weight of property, that personal interest agst. betraying the National interest, which appertain to an hereditary magistrate. In a Republic personal merit alone could be the ground of political exaltation, but it would rarely happen that this merit would be so pre-eminent as to produce universal acquiescence. The Executive Magistrate would be envied & assailed by disappointed competitors: His firmness therefore wd. need support. He would not possess those great emoluments from his station, nor that permanent stake in the public interest which wd. place him out of the reach of foreign corruption: He would stand in need therefore of being controuled as well as supported. An association of the Judges in his revisionary function wd both double the advantage and diminish the danger. It wd. also enable the Judiciary Department the better to defend itself agst. Legislative encroachments. Two objections had been made 1st. that the Judges ought not to be subject to the bias which a participation in the making of laws might give in the exposition of them. 2dly. that the Judiciary Departmt. ought to be separate & distinct from the other great Departments. The 1st. objection had some weight; but it was much diminished by reflecting that a small proportion of the laws coming in question before a Judge wd. be such wherein he had been consulted; that a small part of this proportion wd. be so ambiguous as to leave room for his prepossessions; and that but a few cases wd. probably arise in the life of a Judge under such ambiguous passages. How much good on the other hand wd. proceed from the perspicuity, the conciseness, and the systematic character wch. the Code of laws wd. receive from the Judiciary talents. As to the 2d. objection, it either had no weight, or it applied with equal weight to the Executive & to the Judiciary revision of the laws. The maxim on which the objection was founded required a separation of the Executive as well as of the Judiciary from the Legislature & from each other. There wd. in truth however be no improper mixture of these distinct powers in the present case. In England, whence the maxim itself had been drawn, the Executive had an absolute negative on the laws; and the supreme tribunal of Justice (the House of Lords) formed one of the other branches of the Legislature. In short, whether the object of the revisionary power was to restrain the Legislature from encroaching on the other co-ordinate Departments, or on the rights of the people at large; or from passing laws unwise in their principle, or incorrect in their form, the utility of annexing the wisdom and weight of the Judiciary to the Executive seemed incontestable.

Mr. Gerry thought the Executive, whilst standing alone wd. be more impartial than when he cd. be covered by the sanction & seduced by the sophistry of the Judges

Mr. King. If the Unity of the Executive was preferred for the sake of responsibility, the policy of it is as applicable to the revisionary as to the Executive power.

Mr. Pinkney had been at first in favor of joining the heads of the principal departmts. the Secretary at War, of foreign affairs &—in the council of revision. He had however relinquished the idea from a consideration that these could be called on by the Executive Magistrate whenever he pleased to consult them. He was opposed to an introduction of the Judges into the business.

Col Mason was for giving all possible weight to the revisionary institution. The Executive power ought to be well secured agst. Legislative usurpations on it. The purse & the sword ought never to get into the same hands whether Legislative or Executive.

Mr. Dickinson. Secrecy, vigor & despatch are not the principal properties reqd. in the Executive. Important as these are, that of responsibility is more so, which can only be preserved; by leaving it singly to discharge its functions. He thought too a junction of the Judiciary to it, involved an improper mixture of powers.

Mr Wilson remarked, that the responsibility required belonged to his Executive duties. The revisionary duty was an extraneous one, calculated for collateral purposes.

Mr. Williamson, was for substituting a clause requiring ⅔ for every effective act of the Legislature, in place of the revisionary provision

On the question for joining the Judges to the Executive in the revisionary business Mass. no. Cont. ay. N. Y. ay. N. J. no. Pa. no. Del. no. Md. no. Va. ay. N. C. no. S. C. no. Geo. no. [Ayes—3; noes—8.]

[2:73; Madison, 21 July]

Mr. Wilson moved as an amendment to Resoln:10. that the supreme Natl Judiciary should be associated with the Executive in the Revisionary power". This proposition had been before made, and failed; but he was so confirmed by reflection in the opinion of its utility, that he thought it incumbent on him to make another effort: The Judiciary ought to have an opportunity of remonstrating agst projected encroachments on the people as well as on themselves. It had been said that the Judges, as expositors of the Laws would have an opportunity of defending their constitutional rights. There was weight in this observation; but this power of the Judges did not go far enough. Laws may be unjust, may be unwise, may be dangerous, may be destructive; and yet not be so unconstitutional as to justify the Judges in refusing to give them effect. Let them have a share in the Revisionary power, and they will have an opportunity of taking notice of these characters of a law, and of counteracting, by the weight of their opinions the improper views of the Legislature.—Mr Madison 2ded. the motion

Mr Ghorum did not see the advantage of employing the Judges in this way. As Judges they are not to be presumed to possess any peculiar knowledge of the mere policy of public measures. Nor can it be necessary as a security for their constitutional rights. The Judges in England have no such additional provision for their defence, yet their jurisdiction is not invaded. He thought it would be best to let the Executive alone be responsible, and at most to authorize him to call on Judges for their opinions,

Mr. Elseworth approved heartily of the motion. The aid of the Judges will give more wisdom & firmness to the Executive. They will possess a systematic and accurate knowledge of the Laws, which the Executive can not be expected always to possess. The law of Nations also will frequently come into question. Of this the Judges alone will have competent information.

Mr. Madison considered the object of the motion as of great importance to the meditated Constitution. It would be useful to the Judiciary departmt. by giving it an additional opportunity of defending itself agst: Legislative encroachments; It would be useful to the Executive, by inspiring additional confidence & firmness in exerting the revisionary power: It would be useful to the Legislature by the valuable assistance it would give in preserving a consistency, conciseness, perspicuity & technical propriety in the laws, qualities peculiarly necessary; & yet shamefully wanting in our republican Codes. It would moreover be useful to the Community at large as an additional check agst. a pursuit of those unwise & unjust measures which constituted so great a portion of our calamities. If any solid objection could be urged agst. the motion, it must be on the supposition that it tended to give too much strength either to the Executive or Judiciary. He did not think there was the least ground for this apprehension. It was much more to be apprehended that notwithstanding this co-operation of the two departments, the Legislature would still be an overmatch for them. Experience in all the States had evinced a powerful tendency in the Legislature to absorb all power into its vortex. This was the real source of danger to the American Constitutions; & suggested the necessity of giving every defensive authority to the other departments that was consistent with republican principles.

Mr. Mason said he had always been a friend to this provision. It would give a confidence to the Executive, which he would not otherwise have, and without which the Revisionary power would be of little avail.

Mr. Gerry did not expect to see this point which had undergone full discussion, again revived. The object he conceived of the Revisionary power was merely to secure the Executive department agst. legislative encroachment. The Executive therefore who will best know and be ready to defend his rights ought alone to have the defence of them. The motion was liable to strong objections. It was combining & mixing together the Legislative & the other departments. It was establishing an improper coalition between the Executive & Judiciary departments. It was making Statesmen of the Judges; and setting them up as the guardians of the Rights of the people. He relied for his part on the Representatives of the people as the guardians of their Rights & interests. It was making the Expositors of the Laws, the Legislators which ought never to be done. A better expedient for correcting the laws, would be to appoint as had been done in Pena. a person or persons of proper skill, to draw bills for the Legislature.

Mr. Strong thought with Mr. Gerry that the power of making ought to be kept distinct from that of expounding, the laws. No maxim was better established. The Judges in exercising the function of expositors might be influenced by the part they had taken, in framing the laws.

Mr. Govr. Morris. Some check being necessary on the Legislature, the question is in what hands it should be lodged. On one side it was contended that the Executive alone ought to exercise it. He did not think that an Executive appointed for 6 years, and impeachable whilst in office, wd. be a very effectual check. On the other side it was urged that he ought to be reinforced by the Judiciary department. Agst. this it was objected that Expositors of laws ought to have no hand in making them, and arguments in favor of this had been drawn from England. What weight was due to them might be easily determined by an attention to facts. The truth was that the Judges in England had a great share in ye Legislation. They are consulted in difficult & doubtful cases. They may be & some of them are members of the Legislature. They are or may be members of the privy Council, and can there advise the Executive as they will do with us if the motion succeeds. The influence the English Judges may have in the latter capacity in strengthening the Executive check can not be ascertained, as the King by his influence in a manner dictates the laws. There is one difference in the two Cases however which disconcerts all reasoning from the British to our proposed Constitution. The British Executive has so great an interest in his prerogatives and such powerful means of defending them that he will never yield any part of them. The interest of our Executive is so inconsiderable & so transitory, and his means of defending it so feeble, that there is the justest ground to fear his want of firmness in resisting incroachments. He was extremely apprehensive that the auxiliary firmness & weight of the Judiciary would not supply the deficiency. He concurred in thinking the public liberty in greater danger from Legislative usurpations than from any other source. It had been said that the Legislature ought to be relied on as the proper Guardians of liberty. The answer was short and conclusive. Either bad laws will be pushed or not. On the latter supposition no check will be wanted. On the former a strong check will be necessary: And this is the proper supposition. Emissions of paper money, largesses to the people—a remission of debts and similar measures, will at sometimes be popular, and will be pushed for that reason At other times such measures will coincide with the interests of the Legislature themselves, & that will be a reason not less cogent for pushing them. It might be thought that the people will not be deluded and misled in the latter case. But experience teaches another lesson. The press is indeed a great means of diminishing the evil, yet it is found to be unable to prevent it altogether.

Mr. L. Martin. considered the association of the Judges with the Executive as a dangerous innovation; as well as one which, could not produce the particular advantage expected from it. A knowledge of mankind, and of Legislative affairs cannot be presumed to belong in a higher deger degree to the Judges than to the Legislature. And as to the Constitutionality of laws, that point will come before the Judges in their proper official character. In this character they have a negative on the laws. Join them with the Executive in the Revision and they will have a double negative. It is necessary that the Supreme Judiciary should have the confidence of the people. This will soon be lost, if they are employed in the task of remonstrating agst. popular measures of the Legislature. Besides in what mode & proportion are they to vote in the Council of Revision?

Mr. Madison could not discover in the proposed association of the Judges with the Executive in the Revisionary check on the Legislature any violation of the maxim which requires the great departments of power to be kept separate & distinct. On the contrary he thought it an auxiliary precaution in favor of the maxim. If a Constitutional discrimination of the departments on paper were a sufficient security to each agst. encroachments of the others, all further provisions would indeed be superfluous. But experience had taught us a distrust of that security; and that it is necessary to introduce such a balance of powers and interests, as will guarantee the provisions on paper. Instead therefore of contenting ourselves with laying down the Theory in the Constitution that each department ought to be separate & distinct, it was proposed to add a defensive power to each which should maintain the Theory in practice. In so doing we did not blend the departments together. We erected effectual barriers for keeping them separate. The most regular example of this theory was in the British Constitution. Yet it was not only the practice there to admit the Judges to a seat in the legislature, and in the Executive Councils, and to submit to their previous examination all laws of a certain description, but it was a part of their Constitution that the Executive might negative any law whatever; a part of *their* Constitution which had been universally regarded as calculated for the preservation of the whole. The objection agst. a union of the Judiciary & Executive branches in the revision of the laws, had either no foundation or was not carried far enough. If such a Union was an improper mixture of powers, or such a Judiciary check on the laws, was inconsistent with the Theory of a free Constitution, it was equally so to admit the Executive to any participation in the making of laws; and the revisionary plan ought to be discarded altogether.

Col Mason Observed that the defence of the Executive was not the sole object of the Revisionary power. He expected even greater advantages from it. Notwithstanding the precautions taken in the Constitution of the Legislature, it would so much resemble that of the individual States, that it must be expected frequently to pass unjust and pernicious laws. This restraining power was therefore essentially necessary. It would have the effect not only of hindering the final passage of such laws; but would discourage demagogues from attempting to get them passed. It had been said (by Mr. L. Martin) that if the Judges were joined in this check on the laws, they would have a double negative, since in their expository capacity of Judges they would have one negative. He would reply that in this capacity they could impede in one case only, the operation of laws. They could declare an unconstitutional law void. But with regard to every law however unjust oppressive or pernicious, which did not come plainly under this description, they would be under the necessity as Judges to give it a free course. He wished the further use to be made of the Judges, of giving aid in preventing every improper law. Their aid will be the more valuable as they are in the habit and practice of considering laws in their true principles, and in all their consequences.

Mr. Wilson. The separation of the departments does not require that they should have separate objects but that they should act separately tho' on the same objects. It is necessary that the two branches of the Legislature should be separate and distinct, yet they are both to act precisely on the same object

Mr. Gerry had rather give the Executive an absolute negative for its own defence than thus to blend together the Judiciary & Executive departments. It will bind them together in an offensive and defensive alliance agst. the Legislature, and render the latter unwilling to enter into a contest with them.

Mr. Govr. Morris was surprised that any defensive provision for securing the effectual separation of the departments should be considered as an improper mixture of them. Suppose that the three powers, were to be vested in three persons, by compact among themselves; that one was to have the power of making—another of executing, and a third of judging, the laws. Would it not be very natural for the two latter after having settled the partition on paper, to observe, and would not candor oblige the former to admit, that as a security agst. legislative acts of the former which might easily be so framed as to undermine the powers of the two others, the two others ought to be armed with a veto for their own defence, or at least to have an opportunity of stating their objections agst. acts of encroachment? And would any one pretend that such a right tended to blend & confound powers that ought to be separately exercised? As well might it be said that If three neighbours had three distinct farms, a right in each to defend his farm agst. his neighbours, tended to blend the farms together.

Mr. Ghorum. All agree that a check on the Legislature is necessary. But there are two objections agst. admitting the Judges to share in it which no observations on the other side seem to obviate. the 1st. is that the Judges ought to carry into the exposition of the laws no prepossessions with regard to them. 2d. that as the Judges will outnumber the Executive, the revisionary check would be thrown entirely out of the Executive hands, and instead of enabling him to defend himself, would enable the Judges to sacrifice him.

Mr. Wilson. The proposition is certainly not liable to all the objections which have been urged agst. it. According to (Mr. Gerry) it will unite the Executive & Judiciary in an offensive & defensive alliance agst. the Legislature. According to Mr. Ghorum it will lead to a subversion of the Executive by the Judiciary influence. To the first gentleman the answer was obvious; that the joint weight of the two departments was necessary to balance the single weight of the Legislature. To the 1st. objection stated by the other Gentleman it might be answered that supposing the prepos[ses]sion to mix itself with the exposition, the evil would be overbalanced by the advantages promised by the expedient. To the 2d. objection, that such a rule of voting might be provided in the detail as would guard agst. it.

Mr. Rutlidge thought the Judges of all men the most unfit to be concerned in the revisionary Council. The Judges ought never to give their opinion on a law till it comes before them. He thought it equally unnecessary. The Executive could advise with the officers of State, as of war, finance &c. and avail himself of their information and opinions.

On Question on Mr. Wilson's motion for joining the Judiciary in the Revision of laws it passed in the negative—

Mas. no. Cont. ay. N. J. not present. Pa. divd. Del. no. Md. ay. Va. ay. N. C. no. S. C. no. Geo. divd. [Ayes—3; noes—4; divided—2.]

Resol: 10 giving the Ex. a qualified veto without the amendmt. was then agd. to nem. con.

[2:298; Madison, 15 Aug.]

Mr. Madison moved that all acts before they become laws should be submitted both to the Executive and Supreme Judiciary Departments, that if either of these should object ⅔ of each House, if both should object, ¾ of each House, should be necessary to overrule the objections and give to the acts the force of law.

Mr. Wilson seconds the motion

Mr. Pinkney opposed the interference of the Judges in the Legislative business: it will involve them in parties, and give a previous tincture to their opinions.

Mr. Mercer heartily approved the motion. It as an axiom that the Judiciary ought to be separate from the Legislative but equally so that it ought to be independent of that department. The true policy of the axiom is that legislative usurpation and oppression may be obviated. He disapproved of the Doctrine that the Judges as expositors of the Constitution should have authority to declare a law void. He thought laws ought to be well and cautiously made, and then to be uncontroulable.

Mr. Gerry. This motion comes to the same thing with what has been already negatived.

Question on the motion of Mr Madison

N– H. no. Mass. no. Ct. no. N. J. no. Pa. no. Del. ay. Maryd. ay. Virga. ay. N. C. no. S. C. no. Geo. no. [Ayes—3; noes—8.]

Mr. Govr. Morris regretted that something like the proposed check could not be agreed to. He dwelt on the importance of public Credit, and the difficulty of supporting it without some strong barrier against the instability of legislative Assemblies. He suggested the idea of requiring three fouths of each house to *repeal* laws where the President should not concur. He had no great reliance on the revisionary power as the Executive was now to be constituted (elected by the Congress). The legislature will contrive to soften down the President. He recited the history of paper emissions, and the perseverance of the legislative assemblies in repeating them, with all the distressing effects of such measures before their eyes. Were the National legislature formed, and a war was now to break out, this ruinous expedient would be again resorted to, if not guarded against. The requiring ¾ to repeal would, though not a compleat remedy, prevent the hasty passage of laws, and the frequency of those repeals which destroy faith in the public, and which are among our greatest calamities.—

Mr Dickenson was strongly impressed with the remark of Mr. Mercer as to the power of the Judges to set aside the law. He thought no such power ought to exist. He was

at the same time at a loss what expedient to substitute. The Justiciary of Aragon he observed became by degrees the lawgiver.

Mr. Govr. Morris, suggested the expedient of an absolute negative in the Executive. He could not agree that the Judiciary which was part of the Executive, should be bound to say that a direct violation of the Constitution was law. A controul over the legislature might have its inconveniences. But view the danger on the other side. The most virtuous citizens will often as members of a legislative body concur in measures which afterwards in their private capacity they will be ashamed of. Encroachments of the popular branch of the Government ought to be guarded agst. The Ephori at Sparta became in the end absolute. The Report of the Council of Censors in Pennsylva points out the many invasions of the legislative department on the Executive numerous as the latter is, within the short term of seven years, and in a State where a strong party is opposed to the Constitution, and watching every occasion of turning the public resentments agst. it. If the Executive be overturned by the popular branch, as happened in England, the tyranny of one man will ensue– In Rome where the Aristocracy overturned the throne, the consequence was different. He enlarged on the tendency of the legislative Authority to usurp on the Executive and wished the section to be postponed, in order to consider of some more effectual check than requiring ⅔ only to overrule the negative of the Executive.

Mr Sherman. Can one man be trusted better than all the others if they all agree? This was neither wise nor safe. He disapproved of Judges meddling in politics and parties. We have gone far enough in forming the negative as it now stands.

Mr. Carrol– when the negative to be overruled by ⅔ only was agreed to, the *quorum* was not fixed. He remarked that as a majority was now to be the quorum, 17, in the larger, and 8 in the smaller house might carry points. The Advantage that might be taken of this seemed to call for greater impediments to improper laws. He thought the controuling power however of the Executive could not be well decided, till it was seen how the formation of that department would be finally regulated. He wished the consideration of the matter to be postponed.

Mr. Ghorum saw no end to these difficulties and postponements. Some could not agree to the form of Government before the powers were defined. Others could not agree to the powers till it was seen how the Government was to be formed. He thought a majority as large a quorum as was necessary. It was the quorum almost every where fixt in the U. States.

Mr. Wilson; after viewing the subject with all the coolness and attention possible was most apprehensive of a dissolution of the Govt from the legislature swallowing up all the other powers. He remarked that the prejudices agst the Executive resulted from a misapplication of the adage that the parliament was the palladium of liberty. Where the Executive was really formidable, *King* and *Tyrant*, were naturally associated in the minds of people; not *legislature* and *tyranny*. But where the Executive was not formidable, the two last were most properly associated. After the destruction of the King in Great Britain, a more pure and unmixed tyranny sprang up in the parliament than had been exercised by the monarch. He insisted that we had not guarded agst. the danger on this side by a sufficient self-defensive power either to the Executive or Judiciary department—

Mr Rutlidge was strenuous agst postponing; and complained much of the tediousness of the proceedings.

Mr Elseworth held the same language. We grow more & more skeptical as we proceed. If we do not decide soon, we shall be unable to come to any decision.

The question for postponement passed in the negative: Del: & Maryd only being in the affirmative.

Mr. Williamson moved to change "⅔ of each house" into "¾" as requisite to overrule the dissent of the President. He saw no danger in this, and preferred giving the power to the Presidt. alone, to admitting the Judges into the business of legislation.

Mr. Wilson 2ds. the motion; referring to and repeating the ideas of Mr. Carroll.

On this motion for ¾. instead of two thirds; it passed in the affirmative

N– H– no– Mas. no. Ct. ay N– J. no. Pena. divd. Del– ay. Md. ay. Va. ay. N. C. ay. S. C. ay. Geo. no. [Ayes—6; noes—4; divided—1.]

Mr. Madison, observing that if the negative of the President was confined to *bills;* it would be evaded by acts under the form and name of Resolutions, votes &c—proposed that "or resolve" should be added after *"bill"* in the beginning of sect 13. with an exception as to votes of adjournment &c.

[2:585; Madison, 12 Sept.]

Mr. Williamson moved to reconsider the clause requiring three fourths of each House to overrule the negative of the President, in order to strike out ¾ and insert ⅔. He had he remarked himself proposed ¾ instead of ⅔, but he had since been convinced that the latter proportion was the best. The former puts too much in the power of the President.

Mr. Sherman was of the same opinion; adding that the States would not like to see so small a minority and the President, prevailing over the general voice. In making laws regard should be had to the sense of the people, who are to be bound by them, and it was more probable that a single man should mistake or betray this sense than the Legislature

Mr Govr Morris. Considering the difference between the two proportions numerically, it amounts in one House to two members only; and in the other to not more than five, according to the numbers of which the Legislature is at first to be composed— It is the interest moreover of the distant States to prefer ¾ as they will be oftenest absent and need the interposing check of the President. The excess rather than the deficiency of laws was to be dreaded. The example of N. York shows that ⅔ is not sufficient to answer the purpose.

Mr. Hamilton added his testimony to the fact that ⅔ in N. York had been ineffectual either where a popular ob-

ject, or a legislative faction operated; of which he mentioned some instances.

Mr. Gerry. It is necessary to consider the danger on the other side also. ⅔ will be a considerable, perhaps a proper security. ¾ puts too much in the power of a few men— The primary object of the revisionary check in the President is not to protect the general interest, but to defend his own department. If ¾ be required, a few Senators having hopes from the nomination of the President to offices, will combine with him and impede proper laws. Making the vice-President Speaker increases the danger,

Mr. Williamson was less afraid of too few than of too many laws. He was most of all afraid that the repeal of bad laws might be rendered too difficult by requiring ¾ to overcome the dissent of the President.

Col: Mason had always considered this as one of the most exceptionable parts of the System. As to the numerical argument of Mr. Govr. Morris, little arithmetic was necessary to understand that ¾ was more than ⅔, whatever the numbers of the Legislature might be. The example of New York depended on the real merits of the laws. The Gentlemen citing it, had no doubt given their own opinions. But perhaps there were others of opposite opinions who could equally paint the abuses on the other side. His leading view was to guard against too great an impediment to the repeal of laws.

Mr. Govr. Morris dwelt on the danger to the public interest from the instability of laws, as the most to be guarded against. On the other side there could be little danger. If one man in office will not consent when he ought, every fourth year another can be substituted. This term was not too long for fair experiments. Many good laws are not tried long enough to prove their merit. This is often the case with new laws opposed to old habits. The Inspection laws of Virginia & Maryland to which all are now so much attached were unpopular at first.

Mr. Pinkney was warmly in opposition to ¾ as putting a dangerous power in the hands of a few Senators headed by the President.

Mr. Madison. When ¾ was agreed to, the President was to be elected by the Legislature and for seven years— He is now to be elected by the people and for four years. The object of the revisionary power is twofold. 1. to defend the Executive Rights 2. to prevent popular or factious injustice. It was an important principle in this & in the State Constitutions to check legislative injustice and incroachments. The Experience of the States had demonstrated that their checks are insufficient. We must compare the danger from the weakness of ⅔ with the danger from the strength of ¾. He thought on the whole the former was the greater. As to the difficulty of repeals, it was probable that in doubtful cases the policy would soon take place of limiting the duration of laws so as to require renewal instead of repeal.

The reconsideration being agreed to On the question to insert ⅔ in place of ¾.

N– H– divd. Mas. no. Ct. ay. N– J. ay. Pa. no. Del. no. Md. ay. Mr McHenry no. Va no. Genl. Washington Mr. Blair, Mr. Madison no. Col. Mason, Mr. Randolph ay.

N— C.— ay. S— C. ay. Geo. ay. [Ayes—6; noes—4; divided—1.]

5

JAMES WILSON, PENNSYLVANIA
RATIFYING CONVENTION
1, 4 Dec. 1787
Elliot 2:447–48, 472–73

[*1 Dec.*]

The two branches will serve as checks upon each other; they have the same legislative authorities, except in one instance. Money bills must originate in the House of Representatives. The Senate can pass no law without the concurrence of the House of Representatives; nor can the House of Representatives without the concurrence of the Senate. I believe, sir, that the observation which I am now going to make will apply to mankind in every situation: they will act with more caution, and perhaps more integrity, if their proceedings are to be under the inspection and control of another, than when they are not. From this principle, the proceedings of Congress will be conducted with a degree of circumspection not common in single bodies, where nothing more is necessary to be done than to carry the business through amongst themselves, whether it be right or wrong. In compound legislatures, every object must be submitted to a distinct body, not influenced by the arguments, or warped by the prejudices, of the other; and I believe that the persons who will form the Congress will be cautious in running the risk, *with a bare majority*, of having the negative of the President put on their proceedings. As there will be more circumspection in forming the laws, so there will be more stability in the laws when made. Indeed, one is the consequence of the other; for what has been well considered, and founded in good sense, will in practice be useful and salutary, and, of consequence, will not be liable to be soon repealed. Though two bodies may not possess more wisdom or patriotism than what may be found in a single body, yet they will necessarily introduce a greater degree of precision. An indigested and inaccurate code of laws is one of the most dangerous things that can be introduced into any government. The force of this observation is well known by every gentleman who has attended to the laws of this state. This, sir, is a very important advantage, that will arise from this division of the legislative authority.

I will proceed now to take some notice of a still further restraint upon the legislature—I mean the qualified *negative* of the President. I think this will be attended with very important advantages for the security and happiness of the people of the United States. The President, sir, will not be a stranger to our country, to our laws, or to our wishes. He will, under this Constitution, be placed in office as the President of the whole Union, and will be chosen in such

a manner that he may be justly styled *the man of the people.* Being elected by the different parts of the United States, he will consider himself as not particularly interested for any one of them, but will watch over the whole with paternal care and affection. This will be the natural conduct to recommend himself to those who placed him in that high chair, and I consider it as a very important advantage, that such a man must have every law presented to him, before it can become binding on the United States. He will have before him the fullest information of our situation; he will avail himself not only of records and official communications, foreign and domestic, but he will have also the advice of the executive officers in the different departments of the general government.

If, in consequence of this information and advice, he exercise the authority given to him, the effect will not be lost. He returns his *objections*, together with the bill; and, unless *two thirds* of both branches of the legislature are now found to approve it, it does not become a law. But, even if his objections do not prevent its passing into a law, they will not be useless; they will be kept, together with the law, and, in the archives of Congress, will be valuable and practical materials, to form the minds of posterity for legislation. If it is found that the law operates inconveniently, or oppressively, the people may discover in the President's objections the source of that inconvenience or oppression. Further, sir, when objections shall have been made, it is provided, in order to secure the greatest degree of caution and responsibility, that the *votes* of both houses shall be determined by *yeas* and *nays*, and the names of the persons voting for and against the bill shall be entered in the journal of each house respectively. This much I have thought proper to say, with regard to the distribution of the legislative authority, and the restraints under which it will be exercised.

[*4 Dec.*]

Neither shall I take particular notice of his observation on the *qualified negative* of the President; for he finds no fault with it: he mentions, however, that he thinks it a vain and useless power, because it can never be executed. The reason he assigns for this is, that the king of Great Britain, who has an absolute negative over the laws proposed by Parliament, has never exercised it, at least for many years. It is true, and the reason why he did not exercise it was that, during all that time, the king possessed a negative before the bill had passed through the two houses—a much stronger power than a negative after debate. I believe, since the revolution, at the time of William III., it was never known that a bill disagreeable to the crown passed both houses. At one time, in the reign of Queen Anne, when there appeared some danger of this being effected, it is well known that she created twelve peers, and by that means effectually defeated it. Again: there was some risk, of late years, in the present reign, with regard to Mr. Fox's East India Bill, as it is usually called, that passed through the House of Commons; but the king had interest enough in the House of Peers to have it thrown out; thus it never came up for the royal assent. But that is no reason why this negative should not be exercised here, and exercised with great advantage. Similar powers are known in more than one of the states. The governors of Massachusetts and New York have a power similar to this, and it has been exercised frequently to good effect.

I believe the governor of New York, under this power, has been known to send back five or six bills in a week; and I well recollect that, at the time the funding system was adopted by our legislature, the people in that state considered the negative of the governor as a great security that their legislature would not be able to encumber them by a similar measure. Since that time, an alteration has been supposed in the governor's conduct, but there has been no alteration in his power.

The honorable gentleman from Westmoreland, (Mr. Findley,) by his highly-refined critical abilities, discovers an inconsistency in this part of the Constitution, and that which declares, in section 1, "All legislative powers, herein granted, shall be vested in a Congress of the United States, which shall consist of a Senate and a House of Representatives;" and yet here, says he, is a power of legislation given to the President of the United States, because every bill, before it becomes a law, shall be presented to him. Thus he is said to possess legislative powers. Sir, the Convention observed, on this occasion, strict propriety of language: "If he approve the bill, when it is sent, he shall sign it, but if not, he shall return it;" but no bill passes in consequence of having his assent: therefore, he possesses no legislative authority.

The *effect* of this power, upon this subject, is merely this: if he disapproved a bill, two thirds of the legislature become necessary to pass it into a law, instead of a bare majority. And when two thirds are in favor of the bill, it becomes a law, not by his, but by authority of the two houses of the legislature.

6

LUTHER MARTIN, GENUINE INFORMATION
1788
Storing 2.4.53–54

There were also objections to that part of this section which relates to the *negative* of the *President.*—There were some who thought no good reason could be assigned for giving the President a negative of *any kind*—Upon the principle of a check to the proceedings of the legislature, it was said to be unnecessary; that the two branches having a controul over each others proceedings; and the senate being chosen by the State legislatures, and being composed of members from the *different* States, there would always be a sufficient guard against measures being *hastily* or *rashly* adopted.

That the *President* was not likely to have *more wisdom* or *integrity* than the *senators,* or *any of them,* or to *better know* or *consult* the interest of the States, than *any member* of the

Senate, so as to be entitled to a negative on that principle—And as to the precedent from the British constitution (for we were eternally troubled with arguments and precedents from the British government) it was said it would not apply. The King of Great-Britain there composed *one* of the *three estates* of the kingdom; *he* was possessed of *rights* and *privileges,* as such, *distinct from* the Lords and Commons; *rights* and *privileges* which *descended* to his *heirs,* and were inheritable by them; that for the *preservation* of these it was necessary *he* should have a negative, but that this was not the case with the President of the United States, who was no more than an *officer* of government, the *sovereignty* was not in *him,* but in the *legislature:* And it was further urged, even if he was allowed a negative, it ought not to be of so great extent as that given by the system, since his *single voice* is to countervail the *whole* of *either* branch, and any number *less* than *two-thirds* of the other; however, a majority of the convention was of a different opinion, and adopted it as it now makes a part of the system.

7

FEDERAL FARMER, NO. 14
17 Jan. 1788
Storing 2.8.182

I shall conclude my observations on the organization of the legislature and executive, with making some remarks, rather as a matter of amusement, on the branch, or partial negative, in the legislation:—The third branch in the legislature may answer three valuable purposes, to impede in their passage hasty and intemperate laws, occasionally to assist the senate or people, and to prevent the legislature from encroaching upon the executive or judiciary. In Great Britain the king has a complete negative upon all laws, but he very seldom exercises it. This may be well lodged in him, who possesses strength to support it, and whose family has independent and hereditary interests and powers, rights and prerogatives, in the government, to defend: but in a country where the first executive officer is elective, and has no rights, but in common with the people, a partial negative in legislation, as in Massachusetts and New-York, is, in my opinion, clearly best: in the former state, as before observed, it is lodged in the governor alone; in the latter, in the governor, chancellor, and judges of the supreme court—the new constitution lodges it in the president. This is simply a branch of legislative power, and has in itself no relation to executive or judicial powers. The question is, in what hands ought it to be lodged, to answer the three purposes mentioned the most advantageously? The prevailing opinion seems to be in favour of vesting it in the hands of the first executive magistrate. I will not say this opinion is ill founded. The negative, in one case, is intended to prevent hasty laws, not supported and revised by two-thirds of each of the two branches; in the second, it is to aid the weaker branch; and in the third, to defend the executive and judiciary. To answer these ends, there ought, therefore, to be collected in the hands which hold this negative, firmness, wisdom, and strength; the very object of the negative is occasional opposition to the two branches. By lodging it in the executive magistrate, we give him a share in making the laws, which he must execute; by associating the judges with him, as in New York, we give them a share in making the laws, upon which they must decide as judicial magistrates; this may be a reason for excluding the judges: however, the negative in New-York is certainly well calculated to answer its great purposes: the governor and judges united must possess more firmness and strength, more wisdom and information, than either alone, and also more of the confidence of the people; and as to the balance among the departments, why should the executive alone hold the scales, and the judicial be left defenceless? I think the negative in New-York is found best in practice; we see it there frequently and wisely put upon the measures of the two branches; whereas in Massachusetts it is hardly ever exercised, and the governor, I believe, has often permitted laws to pass to which he had substantial objections, but did not make them; he, however, it is to be observed, is annually elected.

8

ALEXANDER HAMILTON, FEDERALIST, NO. 69,
463–64
14 Mar. 1788

The President of the United States is to have power to return a bill, which shall have passed the two branches of the Legislature, for re-consideration; but the bill so returned is to become a law, if upon that re-consideration it be approved by two thirds of both houses. The King of Great Britain, on his part, has an absolute negative upon the acts of the two houses of parliament. The disuse of that power for a considerable time past, does not affect the reality of its existence; and is to be ascribed wholly to the crown's having found the means of substituting influence to authority, or the art of gaining a majority in one or the other of the two houses, to the necessity of exerting a prerogative which could seldom be exerted without hazarding some degree of national agitation. The qualified negative of the President differs widely from this absolute negative of the British sovereign; and tallies exactly with the revisionary authority of the Council of revision of this State, of which the Governor is a constituent part. In this respect, the power of the President would exceed that of the Governor of New-York; because the former would possess singly what the latter shares with the Chancellor and Judges: But it would be precisely the same with that of the Governor of Massachusetts, whose constitution, as to this article, seems to have been the original from which the Convention have copied.

9

ALEXANDER HAMILTON, FEDERALIST, NO. 73,
494–99
21 Mar. 1788

The first thing that offers itself to our observation, is the qualified negative of the President upon the acts or resolutions of the two Houses of the Legislature; or in other words his power of returning all bills with objections; to have the effect of preventing their becoming laws, unless they should afterwards be ratified by two thirds of each of the component members of the legislative body.

The propensity of the legislative department to intrude upon the rights and to absorb the powers of the other departments, has been already suggested and repeated; the insufficiency of a mere parchment delineation of the boundaries of each, has also been remarked upon; and the necessity of furnishing each with constitutional arms for its own defence, has been inferred and proved. From these clear and indubitable principles results the propriety of a negative, either absolute or qualified, in the executive, upon the acts of the legislative branches. Without the one or the other the former would be absolutely unable to defend himself against the depredations of the latter. He might gradually be stripped of his authorities by successive resolutions, or annihilated by a single vote. And in the one mode or the other, the legislative and executive powers might speedily come to be blended in the same hands. If even no propensity had ever discovered itself in the legislative body, to invade the rights of the executive, the rules of just reasoning and theoretic propriety would of themselves teach us, that the one ought not to be left at the mercy of the other, but ought to possess a constitutional and effectual power of self defence.

But the power in question has a further use. It not only serves as a shield to the executive, but it furnishes an additional security against the enaction of improper laws. It establishes a salutary check upon the legislative body calculated to guard the community against the effects of faction, precipitancy, or of any impulse unfriendly to the public good, which may happen to influence a majority of that body.

The propriety of a negative, has upon some occasions been combated by an observation, that it was not to be presumed a single man would possess more virtue or wisdom, than a number of men; and that unless this presumption should be entertained, it would be improper to give the executive magistrate any species of controul over the legislative body.

But this observation when examined will appear rather specious than solid. The propriety of the thing does not turn upon the supposition of superior wisdom or virtue in the executive: But upon the supposition that the legislative will not be infallible: That the love of power may sometimes betray it into a disposition to encroach upon the rights of the other members of the government; that a spirit of faction may sometimes pervert its deliberations; that impressions of the moment may sometimes hurry it into measures which itself on maturer reflection would condemn. The primary inducement to conferring the power in question upon the executive, is to enable him to defend himself; the secondary one is to encrease the chances in favor of the community, against the passing of bad laws, through haste, inadvertence, or design. The oftener a measure is brought under examination, the greater the diversity in the situations of those who are to examine it, the less must be the danger of those errors which flow from want of due deliberation, or of those missteps which proceed from the contagion of some common passion or interest. It is far less probable, that culpable views of any kind should infect all the parts of the government, at the same moment and in relation to the same object, than that they should by turns govern and mislead every one of them.

It may perhaps be said, that the power of preventing bad laws includes that of preventing good ones; and may be used to the one purpose as well as to the other. But this objection will have little weight with those who can properly estimate the mischiefs of that inconstancy and mutability in the laws, which form the greatest blemish in the character and genius of our governments. They will consider every institution calculated to restrain the excess of law-making, and to keep things in the same state, in which they may happen to be at any given period, as much more likely to do good than harm; because it is favorable to greater stability in the system of legislation. The injury which may possibly be done by defeating a few good laws will be amply compensated by the advantage of preventing a number of bad ones.

Nor is this all. The superior weight and influence of the legislative body in a free government, and the hazard to the executive in a trial of strength with that body, afford a satisfactory security, that the negative would generally be employed with great caution, and that there would oftener be room for a charge of timidity than of rashness, in the exercise of it. A King of Great-Britain, with all his train of sovereign attributes, and with all the influence he draws from a thousand sources, would at this day hesitate to put a negative upon the joint resolutions of the two houses of parliament. He would not fail to exert the utmost resources of that influence to strangle a measure disagreeable to him, in its progress to the throne, to avoid being reduced to the dilemma of permitting it to take effect, or of risking the displeasure of the nation, by an opposition to the sense of the legislative body. Nor is it probable that he would ultimately venture to exert his prerogative, but in a case of manifest propriety, or extreme necessity. All well informed men in that kingdom will accede to the justness of this remark. A very considerable period has elapsed since the negative of the crown has been exercised.

If a magistrate, so powerful and so well fortified as a British monarch, would have scruples about the exercise of the power under consideration, how much greater caution may be reasonably expected in a President of the United States, cloathed for the short period of four years

with the executive authority of a government wholly and purely republican?

It is evident that there would be greater danger of his not using his power when necessary, than of his using it too often, or too much. An argument indeed against its expediency has been drawn from this very source. It has been represented on this account as a power odious in appearance; useless in practice. But it will not follow, that because it might be rarely exercised, it would never be exercised. In the case for which it is chiefly designed, that of an immediate attack upon the constitutional rights of the executive, or in a case in which the public good was evidently and palpably sacrificed, a man of tolerable firmness would avail himself of his constitutional means of defence, and would listen to the admonitions of duty and responsibility. In the former supposition, his fortitude would be stimulated by his immediate interest in the power of his office; in the latter by the probability of the sanction of his constituents; who though they would naturally incline to the legislative body in a doubtful case, would hardly suffer their partiality to delude them in a very plain case. I speak now with an eye to a magistrate possessing only a common share of firmness. There are men, who under any circumstances will have the courage to do their duty at every hazard.

But the Convention have pursued a mean in this business; which will both facilitate the exercise of the power vested in this respect in the executive magistrate, and make its efficacy to depend on the sense of a considerable part of the legislative body. Instead of an absolute negative, it is proposed to give the executive the qualified negative already described. This is a power, which would be much more readily exercised than the other. A man who might be afraid to defeat a law by his single VETO, might not scruple to return it for re-consideration; subject to being finally rejected only in the event of more than one third of each house concurring in the sufficiency of his objections. He would be encouraged by the reflection, that if his opposition should prevail, it would embark in it a very respectable proportion of the legislative body, whose influence would be united with his in supporting the propriety of his conduct, in the public opinion. A direct and categorical negative has something in the appearance of it more harsh, and more apt to irritate, than the mere suggestion of argumentative objections to be approved or disapproved, by those to whom they are addressed. In proportion as it would be less apt to offend, it would be more apt to be exercised; and for this very reason it may in practice be found more effectual. It is to be hoped that it will not often happen, that improper views will govern so large a proportion as two-thirds of both branches of the Legislature at the same time; and this too in defiance of the counterpoising weight of the executive. It is at any rate far less probable, that this should be the case, than that such views should taint the resolutions and conduct of a bare majority. A power of this nature, in the executive, will often have a silent and unperceived though forcible operation. When men engaged in unjustifiable pursuits are aware, that obstructions may come from a quarter which they cannot controul, they will often be restrained, by the bare apprehension of opposition, from doing what they would with eagerness rush into, if no such external impediments were to be feared.

This qualified negative, as has been elsewhere remarked, is in this State vested in a council, consisting of the Governor, with the Chancellor and Judges of the Supreme Court, or any two of them. It has been freely employed upon a variety of occasions, and frequently with success. And its utility has become so apparent, that persons who in compiling the Constitution were violent opposers of it, have from experience become its declared admirers.

I have in another place remarked, that the Convention in the formation of this part of their plan, had departed from the model of the Constitution of this State, in favor of that of Massachusetts—two strong reasons may be imagined for this preference. One is that the Judges, who are to be the interpreters of the law, might receive an improper bias from having given a previous opinion in their revisionary capacities. The other is that by being often associated with the executive they might be induced to embark too far in the political views of that magistrate, and thus a dangerous combination might by degrees be cemented between the executive and judiciary departments. It is impossible to keep the Judges too distinct from every other avocation than that of expounding the laws. It is peculiarly dangerous to place them in a situation to be either corrupted or influenced by the executive.

10

IMPARTIAL EXAMINER, NO. 4
11 June 1788
Storing 5.14.36–37

In monarchy, where the established maxim is, that the king should be respected as a great and transcendent personage, who knows no equal—who in his royal political capacity can commit no *wrong*—to whom no evil can be ascribed—in whom exists the height of perfection—who is supreme above all, and accountable to no earthly being, it is consistent with such a maxim, that the *prince* should form a constituent branch of the legislature, and that his power of rejecting whatever has been passed by the other branches should be distinct, and co-extensive with that of either of those branches in rejecting what has been proposed and consented to by the other. It is necessary that the fundamental laws of the realm should ascribe to the king those high and eminent attributes—that he should possess in himself the sovereignty of the nation; and that the regal dignity should distinguish him, as superior to all his subjects, and in his political character endowed with certain inherent qualities, which cannot be supposed to reside in any other individual within the kingdom: otherwise, that constitutional independence, which the laws meant peculiarly to establish in his person, would not be preserved. To this end the king of England is invested with the sole *executive* authority, and a branch of legislative jurisdiction so far as to pass his *negative* on all proceedings of the other two branches, or to confirm them by his *assent*.

This secures to him the intended superiority in the constitution, and gives him the ascendant in government; else his sovereignty would become a shadow—whilst that doctrine, whereby he is declared to be the *head*, the *beginning* and *end* of the great *body politic*, would prove to be nothing more than mere sound. This two-fold jurisdiction established in the British monarch being founded on maxims extremely different from those, which prevail in the American States, the writer hereof is inclined to hope that he will not be thought singular, if he conceives an impropriety in assimilating the component parts of the American government to those of the British: and as the reasons, which to the founders of the British constitution were motives superior to all others to induce them thus to give the *executive* a controul over the *legislative*, are so far from existing in this country, that every principle of that kind is generally, if not universally, exploded; so it should appear that the same *public spirit*, which pervades the nation, would proclaim the doctrine of prerogative and other peculiar properties of the royal character, as incompatible with the view of these states when they are settling the *form of a republican* government. Is it not therefore sufficient that every branch in the proposed system be distinct and independent of each other—that no one branch might receive any accession of power (by taking part of another) which would tend to overturn the balance and thereby endanger the very *being* of the constitution? Whilst the king of England enjoys all the *regalia*, which are annexed to his crown—whilst he exercises a transcendent dominion over his subjects, the existence whereof is coeval with the first rudiments of their constitution—let the free citizens of America, consulting their true national happiness, wish for no innovation, but what is regulated according to the scale of equal liberty, or which may not destroy that liberty by too great a share of power being lodged in any particular hands;—let this collateral jurisdiction, which constitutes the *royal negative*, be held by kings alone, since with kings it first originated:—Let this remain in its native soil, as most congenial to it; there it will cumber less, and be more productive,—here it will be an exotick, and may poison the *stock*, in which it may be engrafted.

11

JAMES IREDELL, NORTH CAROLINA RATIFYING
CONVENTION
26 July 1788
Elliot 4:73–75

Mr. Chairman, this is a novelty in the Constitution, and is a regulation of considerable importance. Permit me to state the reasons for which I imagine this regulation was made. They are such as, in my opinion, fully justify it.

One great alteration proposed by the Constitution—and which is a capital improvement on the Articles of Confederation—is, that the executive, legislative, and judicial powers should be separate and distinct. The best writers, and all the most enlightened part of mankind, agree that it is essential to the preservation of liberty, that such distinction and separation of powers should be made. But this distinction would have very little efficacy if each power had no means to defend itself against the encroachment of the others.

The British constitution, the theory of which is much admired, but which, however, is in fact liable to many objections, has divided the government into three branches. The king, who is hereditary, forms one branch, the Lords and Commons the two others; and no bill passes into a law without the king's consent. This is a great constitutional support of his authority. By the proposed Constitution, the President is of a very different nature from a monarch. He is to be chosen by electors appointed by the people; to be taken from among the people; to hold his office only for the short period of four years; and to be personally responsible for any abuse of the great trust reposed in him.

In a republican government, it would be extremely dangerous to place it in the power of one man to put an absolute negative on a bill proposed by two houses, one of which represented the people, and the other the states of America. It therefore became an object of consideration, how the executive could defend itself without being a competent part of the legislature. This difficulty was happily remedied by the clause now under our consideration. The executive is not entirely at the mercy of the legislature; nor is it put in the power of the executive entirely to defeat the acts of those two important branches. As it is provided in this clause, if a bare majority of both houses should pass a bill which the President thought injurious to his country, it is in his power—to do what? Not to say, in an arbitrary, haughty manner, that he does not approve of it—but, if he thinks it a bad bill, respectfully to offer his reasons to both houses; by whom, in that case, it is to be reconsidered, and not to become a law unless two thirds of both houses shall concur; which they still may, notwithstanding the President's objection. It cannot be presumed that he would venture to oppose a bill, under such circumstances, without very strong reasons. Unless he was sure of a powerful support in the legislature, his opposition would be of no effect; and as his reasons are to be put on record, his fame is committed both to the present times and to posterity.

The exercise of this power, in a time of violent factions, might be possibly hazardous to himself; but he can have no ill motive to exert himself in the face of a violent opposition. Regard to his duty alone could induce him to oppose, when it was probable two thirds would at all events overrule him. This power may be usefully exercised, even when no ill intention prevails in the legislature. It might frequently happen that, where a bare majority had carried a pernicious bill, if there was an authority to suspend it, upon a cool statement of reasons, many of that majority, on a reconsideration, might be convinced, and vote differ-

ently. I therefore think the method proposed is a happy medium between the possession of an absolute negative, and the executive having no control whatever on acts of legislation; and at the same time that it serves to protect the executive from ill designs in the legislature, it may also answer the purposes of preventing many laws passing which would be immediately injurious to the people at large. It is a strong guard against abuses in all, that the President's reasons are to be entered at large on the Journals, and, if the bill passes notwithstanding, that the yeas and nays are also to be entered. The public, therefore, can judge fairly between them.

12

JAMES MADISON, OBSERVATIONS ON JEFFERSON'S DRAFT OF A CONSTITUTION FOR VIRGINIA 15 Oct. 1788
Papers 11:292–93

Council of Revision. A revisionary power is meant as a check to precipitate, to unjust, and to unconstitutional laws. These important ends would it is conceived be more effectually secured, without disarming the Legislature of its requisite authority, by requiring bills to be separately communicated to the Exec: & Judicy. depts. If either of these object, let ⅔, if both ¾ of each House be necessary to overrule the objection; and if either or both protest agst. a bill as violating the Constitution, let it moreover be suspended, notwithstanding the overruling proportion of the Assembly, until there shall have been a subsequent election of the H. of Ds. and a repassage of the bill by ⅔ or ¾ of both Houses, as the case may be. It sd. not be allowed the Judges or the Ex to pronounce a law thus enacted, unconstitul. & invalid.

In the State Constitutions & indeed in the Fedl. one also, no provision is made for the case of a disagreement in expounding them; and as the Courts are generally the last in making their decision, it results to them, by refusing or not refusing to execute a law, to stamp it with its final character. This makes the Judiciary Dept paramount in fact to the Legislature, which was never intended, and can never be proper.

13

ROGER SHERMAN TO JOHN ADAMS 20 July 1789
Adams Works, 6:438–39

But what I principally have in view, is to submit to your consideration the reasons that have inclined me to think that the qualified negative given to the executive by our constitution is better than an absolute negative. In Great Britain, where there are the rights of the nobility as well as the rights of the common people to support, it may be necessary that the crown should have a complete negative to preserve the balance; but in a republic like ours, wherein is no higher rank than that of common citizens, unless distinguished by appointments to office, what occasion can there be for such a balance? It is true that some men in every society have natural and acquired abilities superior to others, and greater wealth. Yet these give them no legal claim to offices in preference to others, but will doubtless give them some degree of influence, and justly, when they are men of integrity; and may procure them appointments to places of trust in the government. Yet, they having only the same common rights with the other citizens, what competition of interests can there be to require a balance? Besides, while the real estates are divisible among all the children, or other kindred in equal degree, and entails are not admitted, it will operate as an agrarian law, and the influence arising from great estates in a few hands or families will not exist to such a degree of extent or duration as to form a system, or have any great effect.

In order to trace moral effects to their causes, and *vice versa*, it is necessary to attend to principles as they operate on men's minds. Can it be expected that a chief magistrate of a free and enlightened people, on whom he depends for his election and continuance in office, would give his negative to a law passed by the other two branches of the legislature, if he had power? But the qualified negative given to the executive by our constitution, which is only to produce a revision, will probably be exercised on proper occasions; and the legislature have the benefit of the president's reasons in their further deliberations on the subject, and if a sufficient number of the members of either house should be convinced by them to put a negative upon the bill, it would add weight to the president's opinion, and render it more satisfactory to the people. But if two thirds of the members of each house, after considering the reasons offered by the President, should adhere to their former opinion, will not that be the most safe foundation to rest the decision upon? On the whole, it appears to me that the *power* of a complete negative, if given, would be a dormant and useless one, and that the provision in the constitution is calculated to operate with proper weight, and will produce beneficial effects.

The negative vested in the crown of Great Britain has never been exercised since the Revolution, and the great influence of the crown in the legislature of that nation is derived from another source, that of appointment to all offices of honor and profit, which has rendered the power of the crown nearly absolute; so that the nation is in fact governed by the cabinet council, who are the creatures of the crown. The consent of parliament is necessary to give sanction to their measures, and this they easily obtain by the influence aforesaid. If they should carry their points so far as directly to affect personal liberty or private property, the people would be alarmed and oppose their progress; but this forms no part of their system, the principal object of which is *revenue*, which they have carried to an enormous height. Wherever the chief magistrate may ap-

point to offices without control, his government may become absolute, or at least aggressive; therefore the concurrence of the senate is made requisite by our constitution.

14

JAMES WILSON, COMPARISON OF CONSTITUTIONS,
LECTURES ON LAW
1791
Works 1:322–24

Perhaps the qualified negative of the president of the United States on the proceedings of the senate and house of representatives in congress, possesses advantages over an absolute negative, such as that vested in the crown of Great Britain over the proceedings of the lords and commons. To this last, recourse would not be had, unless on occasions of the greatest emergency. A determination not to interpose it without the last necessity, would prevent the exercise of it in many instances, in which it would be proper and salutary. In this manner, it would remain, like a sword always in the scabbard, an instrument, sometimes of distant apprehension, but not of present or practical utility. The exercise of the qualified negative is not an experiment of either dangerous or doubtful issue. A small bias it turns without noise or difficulty. To the operation of a powerful bias, which cannot be safely checked or diverted, it decently and leisurely gives way.

The qualified negative will be highly advantageous in another point of view: it will form an index, by which, from time to time, the strength and height of the current of publick opinions and publick movements may, with considerable exactness, be ascertained. Whenever it is exercised, the votes of all the members of both the houses must be entered on their journals. The single point, that there is a majority, will not be the only one, which will appear: it will be evinced also, how great that majority is. If it consists of less than two thirds of both houses, it seems reasonable, that the dissent of the executive department should suspend a business, which is already so nearly in equilibrio. On the other hand, if, after all the discussion, investigation, and consideration, which must have been employed upon a bill in its different stages, before its presentment to the president of the United States, and after its return from him with his objections to it, two thirds of each house are still of sentiment, that it ought to be passed into a law; this would be an evidence, that the current of publick opinion in its favour is so strong, that it ought not to be opposed. The experiment, though doubtful, ought to be made, when it is called for so long and so loudly.

Besides; the objections of the president, even when unsuccessful, will not be without their use. If the law, notwithstanding all the unfavourable appearances, which accurate political disquisition discovered against it, proves, upon trial, to be beneficial in practice; it will add one to the many instances, in which feeling may be trusted more than argument. If, on the contrary, experience shows the law to be replete with all the inconveniences, which sagacious scrutiny foresaw in its operations, the disease will no sooner appear, than the remedy will be known and applied.

Another advantage, of very general and extensive import, will flow from the qualified negative possessed by the president of the United States. His observations upon the bills and acts of the legislature will, in a series of time, gradually furnish the most valuable and the best adapted materials for composing a practical system of legislation. In every successive period, experience and reasoning will go hand in hand; and will, jointly, produce a collection of accurate and satisfactory knowledge, which could be the separate result of neither.

By the British constitution, the power of judging in the last resort is placed in the house of lords. It is allowed, by an English writer on that constitution, that there is nothing in the formation of the house of lords; nor in the education, habits, character, or professions of the members who compose it; nor in the mode of their appointment, or the right, by which they succeed to their places in it, that suggests any intelligible fitness, in the nature of this regulation. Ecclesiasticks, courtiers, naval and military officers, young men, just of age, born to their elevated station, in other words, placed there by chance, are, for the most part, the members, who compose this important and supreme tribunal. These are the men, authorized and assigned to revise and correct the decisions, pronounced by the sages of the law, who have been raised to the seat of justice on account of their professional eminence, and have employed their lives in the study and practice of the jurisprudence of their country. There is surely something, which, at least in theory, appears very incongruous in this establishment of things. The practical consequences of its impropriety are, in a considerable degree, avoided, by placing in the house of lords some of the greatest law characters in the kingdom; by calling to their assistance the opinions of the judges upon legal questions, which come before the house for its final determination; and by the great deference which those, who are uninformed, naturally pay to those, who are distinguished by their information. After all, however, there is a very improper mixture of legislative and judicial authority vested and blended in the same assembly. This is entirely avoided in the constitution of the United States.

15

JAMES MADISON TO JAMES K. TEFFT
3 Dec. 1830
Writings 9:427

In the year 1828 I recd. from J. V. Bevan sundry numbers of the "Savannah Georgian," containing *continuations* of the notes of Majr. Pierce in the Federal Convention of

1827. They were probably sent on account of a marginal suggestion of inconsistency between language held by me in the Convention with regard to an Executive Veto, and a use made of the power by myself, when in the Executive administration. The inconsistency is done away by the distinction, not averted to, between an *absolute* veto, to which the language was applied, and the *qualified* veto which was exercised.

16

JOSEPH STORY, COMMENTARIES ON THE
CONSTITUTION 2:§§ 878–80, 886–89
1833

§ 878. The next clause respects the power of the president to approve, and negative laws. In the convention there does not seem to have been much diversity of opinion on the subject of the propriety of giving to the president a negative on the laws. The principal points of discussion seem to have been, whether the negative should be absolute, or qualified; and if the latter, by what number of each house the bill should be subsequently passed, in order to become a law; and whether the negative should in either case be exclusively vested in the president alone, or in him jointly with some other department of the government. The proposition of a qualified negative seems to have obtained general, but not universal support, having been carried by the vote of eight states against two. This being settled, the question, as to the number, was at first unanimously carried in the affirmative in favour of two thirds of each house; at a subsequent period it was altered to three fourths by a vote of six states against four, one being divided; and it was ultimately restored to the two thirds, without any apparent struggle. An effort was also made to unite the supreme national judiciary with the executive in revising the laws, and exercising the negative. But it was constantly resisted, being at first overruled by a vote of four states against three, two being divided, and finally rejected by the vote of eight states against three.

§ 879. Two points may properly arise upon this subject. First, the propriety of vesting the power in the president; and secondly, the extent of the legislative check, to prevent an undue exercise of it. The former also admits of a double aspect, viz. whether the negative should be absolute, or should be qualified. An absolute negative on the legislature appears, at first, to be the natural defence, with which the executive magistrate should be armed. But in a free government, it seems not altogether safe, nor of itself a sufficient defence. On ordinary occasions, it may not be exerted with the requisite firmness; and on extraordinary occasions, it may be perfidiously abused. It is true, that the defect of such an absolute negative has a tendency to weaken the executive department. But this may be obviated, or at least counterpoised, by other arrangements in the government; such as a qualified connexion with the senate in making treaties and appointments, by which the latter, being a stronger department, may be led to support the constitutional rights of the former, without being too much detached from its own legislative functions. And the patronage of the executive has also some tendency to create a counteracting influence in aid of his independence. It is true, that in England an absolute negative is vested in the king, as a branch of the legislative power; and he possesses the absolute power of rejecting, rather than of resolving. And this is thought by Mr. Justice Blackstone and others, to be a most important, and indeed indispensable part of the royal prerogative, to guard against the usurpations of the legislative authority. Yet in point of fact this negative of the king has not been once exercised since the year 1692; a fact, which can only be accounted for upon one of two suppositions, either that the influence of the crown has prevented the passage of objectionable measures, or that the exercise of the prerogative has become so odious, that it has not been deemed safe to exercise it, except upon the most pressing emergencies. Probably both motives have alternately prevailed in regard to bills, which were disagreeable to the crown; though, for the last half century, the latter has had the most uniform and decisive operation. As the house of commons becomes more and more the representative of the popular opinion, the crown will have less and less inducement to hazard its own influence by a rejection of any favourite measure of the people. It will be more likely to take the lead, and thus guide and moderate, instead of resisting the commons. And, practically speaking, it is quite problematical, whether a qualified negative may not hereafter in England become a more efficient protection of the crown, than an absolute negative, which makes no appeal to the other legislative bodies, and consequently compels the crown to bear the exclusive odium of a rejection. Be this as it may, the example of England furnishes, on this point, no sufficient authority for America. The whole structure of our government is so entirely different, and the elements, of which it is composed, are so dissimilar from that of England, that no argument can be drawn from the practice of the latter, to assist us in a just arrangement of the executive authority.

§ 880. It has been observed by Mr. Chancellor Kent, with pithy elegance, that the peremptory veto of the Roman Tribunes, who were placed at the door of the Roman senate, would not be reconcileable with the spirit of deliberation and independence, which distinguishes the councils of modern times. The French constitution of 1791, a laboured and costly fabric, on which the philosophers and statesmen of France exhausted all their ingenuity, and which was prostrated in the dust in the course of one year from its existence, gave to the king a negative upon the acts of the legislature, with some feeble limitations. Every bill was to be presented to the king, who might refuse his assent; but if the two following legislatures should successively present the same bill in the same terms, it was then to become a law. The constitutional negative, given to the president of the United States, appears to be more wisely digested, than any of the examples, which have been mentioned.

. . . . .

§ 886. The proposition to unite the Supreme Court with the executive in the revision and qualified rejection of laws, failed, as has been seen, in the convention. Two reasons seem to have led to this result, and probably were felt by the people also, as of decisive weight. The one was, that the judges, who are the interpreters of the law, might receive an improper bias from having given a previous opinion in their revisory capacity. The other was, that the judges, by being often associated with the executive, might be induced to embark too far in the political views of that magistrate; and thus a dangerous combination might, by degrees, be cemented between the executive and judiciary departments. It is impossible to keep the judges too distinct from any other avocation, than that of expounding the laws; and it is peculiarly dangerous to place them in a situation to be either corrupted, or influenced by the executive. To these may be added another, which may almost be deemed a corollary from them, that it would have a tendency to take from the judges that public confidence in their impartiality, independence, and integrity, which seem indispensable to the due administration of public justice. Whatever has a tendency to create suspicion, or provoke jealousy, is mischievous to the judicial department. Judges should not only be pure, but be believed to be so. The moral influence of their judgments is weakened, if not destroyed, whenever there is a general, even though it be an unfounded distrust, that they are guided by other motives in the discharge of their duties than the law and the testimony. A free people have no security for their liberties, when an appeal to the judicial department becomes either illusory, or questionable.

§ 887. The other point of inquiry is, as to the extent of the legislative check upon the negative of the executive. It has been seen, that it was originally proposed, that a concurrence of two thirds of each house should be required; that this was subsequently altered to three fourths; and was finally brought back again to the original number. One reason against the three fourths seems to have been, that it would afford little security for any effectual exercise of the power. The larger the number required to overrule the executive negative, the more easy it would be for him to exert a silent and secret influence to detach the requisite number in order to carry his object. Another reason was, that even, supposing no such influence to be exerted, still, in a great variety of cases of a political nature, and especially such, as touched local or sectional interests, the pride or the power of states, it would be easy to defeat the most salutary measures, if a combination of a few states could produce such a result. And the executive himself might, from his local attachments or sectional feelings, partake of this common bias. In addition to this, the departure from the general rule, of the right of a majority to govern, ought not to be allowed but upon the most urgent occasions; and an expression of opinion by two thirds of both houses in favour of a measure certainly afforded all the just securities, which any wise, or prudent people ought to demand in the ordinary course of legislation; for all laws thus passed might, at any time, be repealed at the mere will of the majority. It was also no small recommendation of the lesser number, that it offered fewer inducements to improper combinations, either of the great states, or the small states, to accomplish particular objects. There could be but one of two rules adopted in all governments, either, that the majority should govern, or the minority should govern. The president might be chosen by a bare majority of electoral votes, and this majority might be by the combination of a few large states, and by a minority of the whole people. Under such circumstances, if a vote of three fourths were required to pass a law, the voice of two thirds of the states and two thirds of the people might be permanently disregarded during a whole administration. The case put may seem strong; but it is not stronger, than the supposition, that two thirds of both houses would be found ready to betray the solid interests of their constituents by the passage of injurious or unconstitutional laws. The provision, therefore, as it stands, affords all reasonable security; and pressed farther, it would endanger the very objects, for which it is introduced into the constitution.

§ 888. But the president might effectually defeat the wholesome restraint, thus intended, upon his qualified negative, if he might silently decline to act after a bill was presented to him for approval or rejection. The constitution, therefore, has wisely provided, that "if any bill shall not be returned by the president within ten days (Sundays excepted) after it shall have been presented to him, it shall be a law, in like manner, as if he had signed it." But if this clause stood alone, congress might, in like manner, defeat the due exercise of his qualified negative by a termination of the session, which would render it impossible for the president to return the bill. It is therefore added, "unless the congress, by their adjournment, prevent its return, in which case it shall not be a law."

§ 889. The remaining clause merely applies to *orders, resolutions, and votes*, to which the concurrence of both houses may be necessary; and as to these, with a single exception, the same rule is applied, as is by the preceding clause applied to *bills*. If this provision had not been made, congress, by adopting the form of an order or resolution, instead of a bill, might have effectually defeated the president's qualified negative in all the most important portions of legislation.

§ 890. It has been remarked by De Lolme, that in most of the ancient free states, the share of the people in the business of legislation was to approve or reject the propositions, which were made to them, and to give the final sanction to the laws. The functions of those persons, or in general, those bodies, who were entrusted with the executive power, was to prepare and frame the laws, and then to propose them to the people. In a word, they possessed that branch of the legislative power, which may be called the *initiative*, that is, the prerogative of putting that power into action. In the first times of the Roman republic, this initiative power was constantly exercised by the Roman senate. Laws were made *populi jussu, ex authoritate senati;* and, even in elections, the candidates were subject to the previous approbation of the senate. In modern times, in the republics of Venice, Berne, and Geneva, the same power is, in fact, exercised by a select assembly, before it can be acted upon by the larger assembly of the citizens, or their representatives. He has added, that this power is very useful, and perhaps even necessary, in states of a republican form, for giving a permanence to the laws, as well as for preventing political disorders and struggles for power. At the same time, he is compelled to admit, that this expedient is attended with inconveniences of little less magnitude, than the evils it is meant to remedy. The inconveniences are certainly great, but there are evils of a deeper character belonging to such a system. The natural, nay, necessary tendency of it is, ultimately to concentrate all power in the *initiative* body, and to leave to the approving body but the shadow of authority. It is in fact, though not in form, an oligarchy. And, so far from its being useful in a republic, it is the surest means of sapping all its best institutions, and overthrowing the public liberties, by corrupting the very fountains of legislation. De Lolme praises it as a peculiar excellence of the British monarchy. America, no less, vindicates it, as a fundamental principle in all her republican constitutions.

SEE ALSO:

Records of the Federal Convention, Farrand 1:28, 93–94, 105–6, 107–9, 109–10, 111–12, 131, 226; 2:71, 132, 135, 146, 160–62, 167, 200, 294–95, 300–302, 303, 304–5, 568–69, 593–94, 608

Debate in North Carolina Ratifying Convention, 30 July 1788, Elliot 4:214

St. George Tucker, Blackstone's Commentaries 1:App. 225–26 (1803)

Article 1, Section 8, Clause 1

The Congress shall have Power To lay and collect Taxes, Duties, Imposts and Excises, to pay the Debts and provide for the common Defence and general Welfare of the United States; but all Duties, Imposts and Excises shall be uniform throughout the United States;

1

CONTINENTAL CONGRESS
15 Feb. 1786
Journals 30:70–76

Congress assembled. Present as before.

The Committee, consisting of Mr. [Rufus] King, Mr. [Charles] Pinckney, Mr. [John] Kean, Mr. [James] Monroe and Mr. [Charles] Pettit, to whom were referred several Reports and Documents concerning the System of General Revenue, recommended by Congress on the 18th of April, 1783; Report—

That in pursuance of the above reference, they have carefully examined the Acts of the several States, relative to the general System of Revenue recommended by Congress on the 18th of April, 1783, and find that the States of Delaware and North Carolina have passed Acts in full conformity with the several parts thereof; the former of which States has inserted a proviso in their Act, restraining the operation thereof until each of the other States shall have made a like and equally extensive grant; that the States of New Hampshire, Massachusetts, Connecticut, New Jersey, Virginia and South Carolina, have each passed Acts complying with that part of the System, which recommends a general impost, but have come to no decision on the other part, which proposes the establishment of funds, supplementary to, and in aid of the general impost; that the State of Pennsylvania has passed an Act complying with the recommendation of the general impost, and in the same act has declared, that their proportion or quota of the supplementary funds, shall be raised and levied on the persons and estates of the inhabitants of that State, in such manner as the Legislature thereof shall, from time to time, direct, with this proviso, that if any of the Annual proportion of the supplementary funds shall be otherwise raised and paid to the United States, then such annual levy or tax shall be discontinued: The Committee conceive that this clause is rather an engagement that Pennsylvania will provide adequate supplementary funds, than an actual establishment thereof; nevertheless, the Act contains a proviso restraining its operation until each of the other States shall have passed Laws in full conformity with the whole of the Revenue System aforesaid: The Committee further find, that the state of Rhode Island has passed an Act on this subject, but so different from the plan recommended, and so wholly insufficient, that it cannot be considered as a compliance with any part of the system submitted for their adoption; that the State of Maryland passed an Act in 1782, and a supplement thereto in 1784, complying with the recommendation of Congress of the 3d of February, 1781, which recommendation is not compatible with, and was relinquished by the resolves of Congress of the 18th of April, 1783; but that neither the State of Maryland, New York nor Georgia, has passed any act in pursuance of the system of the 18th of April, 1783.

From this statement it appears that seven States, viz. New Hampshire, Massachusetts, Connecticut, New Jersey, Virginia, North Carolina and South Carolina, have granted the impost in such manner, that if the other Six States had made similar grants, the plan of the general impost might immediately begin to operate; that two other States, viz. Pennsylvania and Delaware, have also granted the impost, but have connected their grants with provisoes, which will suspend their operation until all the other States shall have passed laws in full conformity with the whole of the revenue system aforesaid; that two only of these nine States, viz. Delaware and North Carolina, have fully acceded to that system in all its parts; and that the four other States, viz. Rhode Island, New York, Maryland and Georgia, have not decided in favour of any part of the system of revenue aforesaid, so long since and so repeatedly presented by Congress for their adoption.

The Committee have thought it their duty candidly to examine the principles of this system, and to discover, if possible, the reasons which have prevented its adoption; they cannot learn that any Member of the Confederacy has stated or brought forward any objections against it, and the result of their impartial enquiries into the nature and operation of the plan, has been a clear and decided opinion, that the system itself is more free from well founded exceptions, and is better calculated to receive the approbation of the several States than any other that the wisdom of Congress can devise.

In the course of this enquiry, it most clearly appeared, that the requisitions of Congress, for eight years past, have been so irregular in their operation, so uncertain in their collection, and so evidently unproductive, that a reliance on them in future as a source from whence moneys are to be drawn to discharge the engagements of the Confederacy, definite as they are in time and amount, would be not less dishonourable to the understandings of those who entertain such confidence, than it would be dangerous to the welfare and peace of the Union: The Committee are therefore seriously impressed with the indispensable obligation that Congress are under, of representing to the immediate and impartial consideration of the several States, the utter impossibility of maintaining and preserving the faith of the federal Government, by temporary requisitions on the States, and the consequent necessity of an early and complete accession of all the States to the revenue system of the 18th of April, 1783.

Although in a business of this magnitude and importance to the respective States, it was natural to expect a due degree of caution, and a thorough investigation of the system recommended, yet the Committee cannot forbear to remark, that this plan has been under reference for nearly three years; that, during that period, numerous changes have taken place in the delegations of every State, but that this system has received the repeated approbation of each successive Congress, and that the urgency of the public engagements at this time, renders it the unquestionable duty of the several States to adopt, without further delay, those measures which alone, in the judgment of the Committee, can preserve the sacred faith of this Confederacy.

The following state of facts must convince the States of the propriety of urging this system with unusual anxiety at this period.

	Dollars 90^{ths}
That the sum necessary to discharge the interest on Loans of the King of France, to the 1st January, 1787, is	240,740.60
For interest on Certificates to Foreign Officers, made payable in France, to the 1st of January, 1787	22,370
For interest on the Spanish Loan, to the 21st March, 1787	48,596.55
For interest on the Dutch Loans, to the 1st June, 1787	265,600
	577,307.25

That although some of the objects of disbursement are in the year 1787, the periods at which they become due, will shew the absolute necessity of an immediate provision for them.

That notwithstanding some of the above sums do not fall due until 1787, yet, exclusive of the same, there will be due on the french and dutch Loans, in that year, 1,252,938 dollars and 57 ninetieths, and during the nine succeeding years, that is, until the year 1797, including the payment of the interest and the partial reimbursements of the Capitals of the french and dutch loans, the average sum of near one million of dollars annually; for the certain obtaining of which, at fixed periods, effectual measures can no longer be delayed. More fully to illustrate this subject, the committee annex a schedule of the french and dutch loans, shewing the periods of their redemption, with the annual interest payable thereon, until their final extinction; in addition to the above foreign demands, the interest on the Spanish loan, and on the debts due to foreign Officers, must be provided for and annually paid: The amount of these annual demands will be greatly increased by adding the annual interest on the domestic debt, the whole of which is not yet liquidated, and the aggregate whereof, will consequently be enlarged beyond its last estimate.

The Committee contemplate, with great satisfaction, the prospect of extinguishing a part of the domestic debt, by the sales of the Western territory of the United States; but a considerable time must elapse before that Country can be surveyed and disposed of; and the domestic Creditors, until that event, must depend for support on the justice of their Country: The revenue system, if adopted, would afford this support, and enable Congress to fulfil the public engagements with their foreign Creditors. The whole product of this system is appropriated for the payment of the principal and interest of the National debt, and no part thereof can be diverted to other purposes.

That it has been the earnest wish of Congress to prevent the vast accumulation of foreign interest that now exists, appears, from their estimates and requisitions of the 27th April, 1784, and 27th September, 1785; and the following abstract, taken from the books of the Treasury, of the amount of moneys brought into the federal treasury in the course of the four last years, viz. between the 1st November, 1781, and the 1st of January, 1786, will show the little success of requisitions, and demonstrate the inadequacy of their products to maintain the federal government, and at the same time to discharge the annual public engagements.

	Dollars 90[ths]
The receipt of taxes from the 1st November, 1781, to 1st November, 1784, amount to	2,025,089.34
From 1st November, 1784, to the 1st January, 1786	432,897.81
Total	2,457,987.25

Thus it is evident, that the sum of 2,457,987 dollars and 25-90ths only, was received in a space of more than four years, when the requisitions, in the most forcible manner, pressed on the States the payment of much larger sums, and for purposes of the highest national importance. It should be here observed, that the receipts of the last fourteen months of the above period, amount

only to 432,897 Dollars and 81-90ths, which is at the rate of 371,052 dollars per annum, a sum short of what is essentially necessary for the bare maintenance of the federal government on the most economical establishment, and in time of profound peace.

The Committee observe with great concern, that the security of the Navigation and Commerce of the Citizens of these States from the Barbary powers, the protection of the frontier inhabitants from the savages, the immediate establishment of military magazines in different parts of the Union, rendered indispensable by the principles of public safety, the maintenance of the federal government at home, and the support of the public servants abroad, each and all, depend upon the contributions of the States under the annual requisitions of Congress. The moneys essentially necessary for these important objects, will so far exceed the sums formerly collected from the States by taxes, that no hope can be indulged of being able, from that source, to make any remittances for the discharge of foreign engagements.

Thus circumstanced, after the most solemn deliberation, and under the fullest conviction that the public embarrassments are such as above represented, and that they are daily increasing, the Committee are of opinion, that it has become the duty of Congress to declare most explicitly, that the crisis has arrived, when the people of these United States, by whose will, and for whose benefit the federal government was instituted, must decide whether they will support their rank as a nation, by maintaining the public faith at home and abroad; or whether, for want of a timely exertion in establishing a general revenue, and thereby giving strength to the confederacy, they will hazard not only the existence of the Union, but of those great and invaluable privileges for which they have so arduously and so honourably contended.

Resolved, That Congress agree to the said report.

And to the end, that Congress may remain wholly acquitted from every imputation of a want of attention to the interest and welfare of those whom they represent,

Resolved, That the requisitions of Congress of the 27th of April, 1784, and the 27th of September, 1785, cannot be considered as the establishment of a system of general revenue, in opposition to that recommended to the several States by the resolves of Congress of the 18th of April, 1783.

Resolved, That the resolves of Congress of the 18th of April, 1783, recommending a system of general revenue, be again presented to the consideration of the Legislatures of the several States, which have not fully complied with the same: That it be earnestly recommended to the Legislatures of New Hampshire, Massachusetts, Connecticut, New Jersey, Pennsylvania, Virginia and South Carolina, which have complied only in part with the said system, completely to adopt the same; and to the Legislatures of the States of Rhode Island, New York, Maryland and Georgia, which have not adopted the said system, either in whole or in part, to pass laws, without further delay, in full conformity with the same. But as it is highly necessary that every possible aid should, in the most expeditious manner, be obtained to the revenue of the United States, it is therefore recommended to the several States, that, in adopting the said system, they enable the United States in Congress assembled, to carry into effect that part which relates to the impost, so soon as it shall be acceded to.

Resolved, That whilst Congress are denied the means of satisfying those engagements which they have constitutionally entered into for the common benefit of the Union, they hold it their duty to warn their Constituents that the most fatal evils will inevitably flow from a breach of public faith, pledged by solemn contract, and a violation of those principles of justice, which are the only solid basis of the honor and prosperity of Nations.

2

JAMES MADISON, PREFACE TO DEBATES IN THE
CONVENTION OF 1787
Farrand 3:547

At the date of the Convention, the aspect & retrospect of the pol: condition of the U. S. could not but fill the pub. mind with a gloom which was relieved only by a hope that so select a Body would devise an adequate remedy for the existing and prospective evils so impressively demanding it

It was seen that the public debt rendered so sacred by the cause in which it had been incurred remained without any provision for its payment. The reiterated and elaborate efforts of Cong. to procure from the States a more adequate power to raise the means of payment had failed. The effect of the ordinary requisitions of Congress had only displayed the inefficiency of the authy. making them; none of the States having duly complied with them, some having failed altogether or nearly so; and in one instance, that of N. Jersey, a compliance was expressly refused; nor was more yielded to the expostulations of members of Congs. deputed to her Legislature than a mere repeal of the law, without a compliance.

3

RECORDS OF THE FEDERAL CONVENTION

[1:243; Madison, 15 June]

[New Jersey Plan:] 2. Resd. that in addition to the powers vested in the U. States in Congress, by the present existing articles of Confederation, they be authorized to pass acts for raising a revenue, by levying a duty or duties on all goods or merchandizes of foreign growth or manufacture, imported into any part of the U. States, by Stamps

on paper, vellum or parchment, and by a postage on all letters or packages passing through the general post-Office, to be applied to such federal purposes as they shall deem proper & expedient; to make rules & regulations for the collection thereof. . . .

[2:305; Madison, 16 Aug.]

Art: VII. Sect. 1. taken up. ["The Legislature of the United States shall have the power to lay and collect taxes, duties, imposts and excises."]

Mr. L. Martin asked what was meant by the Committee of detail in the expression *"duties"* and *"imposts"*. If the meaning were the same, the former was unnecessary; if different, the matter ought to be made clear.

Mr Wilson, *duties* are applicable to many objects to which the word *imposts* does not relate. The latter are appropriated to commerce; the former extend to a variety of objects, as stamp duties &c.

Mr. Carroll reminded the Convention of the great difference of interests among the States, and doubts the propriety in that point of view of letting a majority be a quorum.

Mr. Mason urged the necessity of connecting with the power of levying taxes duties &c, the prohibition in Sect 4 of art VI that no tax should be laid on exports. He was unwilling to trust to its being done in a future article. He hoped the Northn. States did not mean to deny the Southern this security. It would hereafter be as desirable to the former when the latter should become the most populous. He professed his jealousy for the productions of the Southern or as he called them, the staple States. He moved to insert the following amendment: "provided that no tax duty or imposition, shall be laid by the Legislature of the U. States on articles exported from any State"

Mr Sherman had no objection to the proviso here, other than it would derange the parts of the report as made by the Committee, to take them in such an order.

Mr. Rutlidge. It being of no consequence in what order points are decided, he should vote for the clause as it stood, but on condition that the subsequent part relating to negroes should also be agreed to.

Mr. Governeur Morris considered such a proviso as inadmissible any where. It was so radically objectionable, that it might cost the whole system the support of some members. He contended that it would not in some cases be equitable to tax imports without taxing exports; and that taxes on exports would be often the most easy and proper of the two.

Mr. Madison 1. the power of taxing exports is proper in itself, and as the States cannot with propriety exercise it separately, it ought to be vested in them collectively. 2. it might with particular advantage be exercised with regard to articles in which America was not rivalled in foreign markets, as Tobo. &c. The contract between the French Farmers Genl. and Mr. Morris stipulating that if taxes sd. be laid in America on the export of Tobo, they sd. be paid by the Farmers, shewed that it was understood by them, that the price would be thereby raised in America, and consequently the taxes be paid by the European Consumer. 3. it would be unjust to the States whose produce was exported by their neighbours, to leave it subject to be taxed by the latter. This was a grievance which had already filled N. H. Cont. N. Jery. Del: and N. Carolina with loud complaints, as it related to imports, and they would be equally authorized by taxes by the States on exports. 4. The Southn. States being most in danger and most needing naval protection, could the less complain if the burden should be somewhat heaviest on them. 5. we are not providing for the present moment only, and time will equalize the situation of the States in this matter. He was for these reasons, agst the motion

Mr. Williamson considered the clause proposed agst taxes on exports as reasonable and necessary.

Mr. Elseworth was agst. Taxing exports; but thought the prohibition stood in the most proper place, and was agst. deranging the order reported by the Committee

Mr. Wilson was decidedly agst prohibiting general taxes on exports. He dwelt on the injustice and impolicy of leaving N. Jersey Connecticut &c any longer subject to the exactions of their commercial neighbours.

Mr Gerry thought the legislature could not be trusted with such a power. It might ruin the Country. It might be exercised partially, raising one and depressing another part of it.

Mr Govr Morris. However the legislative power may be formed, it will if disposed be able to ruin the Country— He considered the taxing of exports to be in many cases highly politic. Virginia has found her account in taxing Tobacco. All Countries having peculiar articles tax the exportation of them; as France her wines and brandies. A tax here on lumber, would fall on the W. Indies & punish their restrictions on our trade. The same is true of livestock and in some degree of flour. In case of a dearth in the West Indies, we may extort what we please. Taxes on exports are a necessary source of revenue. For a long time the people of America will not have money to pay direct taxes. Seize and sell their effects and you push them into Revolts—

Mr. Mercer was strenuous against giving Congress power to tax exports. Such taxes were impolitic, as encouraging the raising of articles not meant for exportation. The States had now a right where their situation permitted, to tax both the imports and exports of their uncommercial neighbours. It was enough for them to sacrifice one half of it. It had been said the Southern States had most need of naval protection. The reverse was the case. Were it not for promoting the carrying trade of the Northn States, the Southn States could let their trade go into foreign bottoms, where it would not need our protection. Virginia by taxing her tobacco had given an advantage to that of Maryland.

Mr. Sherman. To examine and compare the States in relation to imports and exports will be opening a boundless field. He thought the matter had been adjusted, and that imports were to be subject, and exports not, to be taxed. He thought it wrong to tax exports except it might be such articles as ought not to be exported. The complexity of the business in America would render an equal tax on exports impracticable. The oppression of the uncommercial States was guarded agst. by the power to regulate

trade between the States. As to compelling foreigners, that might be done by regulating trade in general. The Government would not be trusted with such a power. Objections are most likely to be excited by considerations relating to taxes & money. A power to tax exports would shipwreck the whole.

Mr. Carrol was surprised that any objection should be made to an exception of exports from the power of taxation.

It was finally agreed that the question concerning exports shd. lie over for the place in which the exception stood in the report. Maryd. alone voting agst it

Sect: 1. (art. VII) agreed to: Mr. Gerry alone answering no.

[2:392; Madison, 23 Aug.]

The 1st sect. of art: VII being so amended as to read "The Legislature *shall* fulfil the engagements and discharge the debts of the U. S, & shall have the power to lay & collect taxes duties imposts & excises", was agreed to

Mr. Butler expressed his dissatisfaction lest it should compel payment as well to the Blood-suckers who had speculated on the distresses of others, as to those who had fought & bled for their country. He would be ready he said tomorrow to vote for a discrimination between those classes of people, and gave notice that he should move for a reconsideration.

[2:412; Madison, 25 Aug.]

The 1st. clause of 1 sect. of art: VII being reconsidered Col. Mason objected to the term, *"shall"*—fullfil the engagements & discharge the debts &c as too strong. It may be impossible to comply with it. The Creditors should be kept in the same plight. They will in one respect be necessarily and properly in a better. The Government will be more able to pay them. The use of the term *shall* will beget speculations and increase the pestilent practice of stock-jobbing. There was a great distinction between original creditors & those who purchased fraudulently of the ignorant and distressed. He did not mean to include those who have bought Stock in open market. He was sensible of the difficulty of drawing the line in this case, but He did not wish to preclude the attempt. Even fair purchasers, at 4, 5, 6, 8 for 1 did not stand on the same footing with the first Holders, supposing them not to be blameable. The interest they receive even in paper is equal to their purchase money. What he particularly wished was to leave the door open for buying up the securities, which he thought would be precluded by the term "shall" as requiring *nominal payment,* & which was not inconsistent with his ideas of public faith. He was afraid also the word *"shall,"* might extend to all the old continental paper.

Mr Langdon wished to do no more than leave the Creditors in statu quo.

Mr. Gerry said that for himself he had no interest in the question being not possessed of more of the securities than would, by the interest, pay his taxes. He would observe however that as the public had received the value of the literal amount, they ought to pay that value to some body. The frauds on *the soldiers* ought to have been foreseen.

These poor & ignorant people could not but part with their securities. There are other creditors who will part with any thing rather than be cheated of the capital of their advances. The interest of the States he observed was different on this point, some having more, others less than their proportion of the paper. Hence the idea of a scale for reducing its value had arisen. If the public faith would admit, of which he was not clear, he would not object to a revision of the debt so far as to compel restitution to the ignorant & distressed, who have been defrauded. As to Stock-jobbers he saw no reason for the censures thrown on them—They keep up the value of the paper. Without them there would be no market.

Mr. Butler said he meant neither to increase nor diminish the security of the Creditors.

Mr. Randolph moved to postpone the clause in favor of the following "All debts contracted & engagements entered into, by or under the authority of Congs. shall be as valid agst the U. States under this constitution as under the Confederation"

Docr Johnson. The debts are debts of the U— S— of the great Body of America. Changing the Government cannot change the obligation of the U— S— which devolves of course on the New Government. Nothing was in his opinion necessary to be said. If any thing, it should be a mere declaration as moved by Mr. Randolph.

Mr. Govr. Morris, said he never had become a public Creditor that he might urge with more propriety the compliance with public faith. He had always done so and always would, and preferr'd the term "*shall*" as the most explicit. As to *buying up* the debt, the term "*shall*" was not inconsistent with it, if provision be first made for paying the interest: if not, such an expedient was a mere evasion. He was content to say nothing as the New Government would be bound of course—but would prefer the clause with the term "*shall*", because it would create many friends to the plan.

On Mr. Randolph's Motion

N— H— ay— Mas. ay. Ct ay— N. J. ay— Pa. no Del. ay— Maryd. ay Va. ay— N. C— ay— S. C. ay Geo. ay— [Ayes— 10; noes— 1.]

Mr. Sherman thought it necessary to connect with the clause for laying taxes duties &c an express provision for the object of the old debts &c—and moved to add to the 1st. clause of 1st. sect—of art VII "for the payment of said debts and for the defraying the expences that shall be incurred for the common defence and general welfare".

The proposition, as being unnecessary was disagreed to, Connecticut alone, being in the affirmative.

[2:434; *Journal, 28 Aug.*]

And all tonnage, duties, imposts, and excises, laid by the "Legislature shall be uniform throughout the United States"

[2:473; *Journal, 31 Aug.*]

On the question to agree to the following clause of the report

"and all duties, imposts, and excises, laid by the Legislature, shall be uniform throughout the United States"
it passed in the affirmative

[2:493; *Journal, 4 Sept.*]

The Committee of eleven to whom sundry resolutions &ca were referred on the 31st ultimo, report that in their opinion the following additions and alterations should be made to the report before the Convention—viz

The first clause of the first Sect. of the 7th article to read as follows. "The Legislature shall have power to lay and collect taxes, duties, imposts, and excises, to pay the debts and provide for the common defence and general welfare of the United States."

4

FEDERAL FARMER, NO. 3
10 Oct. 1787
Storing 2.8.36–39

A power to lay and collect taxes at discretion, is, in itself, of very great importance. By means of taxes, the government may command the whole or any part of the subject's property. Taxes may be of various kinds; but there is a strong distinction between external and internal taxes. External taxes are impost duties, which are laid on imported goods; they may usually be collected in a few seaport towns, and of a few individuals, though ultimately paid by the consumer; a few officers can collect them, and they can be carried no higher than trade will bear, or smuggling permit—that in the very nature of commerce, bounds are set to them. But internal taxes, as poll and land taxes, excises, duties on all written instruments, etc. may fix themselves on every person and species of property in the community; they may be carried to any lengths, and in proportion as they are extended, numerous officers must be employed to assess them, and to enforce the collection of them. In the United Netherlands the general government has compleat powers, as to external taxation; but as to internal taxes, it makes requisitions on the provinces. Internal taxation in this country is more important, as the country is so very extensive. As many assessors and collectors of federal taxes will be above three hundred miles from the seat of the federal government as will be less. Besides, to lay and collect internal taxes, in this extensive country, must require a great number of congressional ordinances, immediately operating upon the body of the people; these must continually interfere with the state laws, and thereby produce disorder and general dissatisfaction, till the one system of laws or the other, operating upon the same subjects, shall be abolished. These ordinances alone, to say nothing of those respecting the militia, coin, commerce, federal judiciary, etc. etc. will probably soon defeat the operations of the state laws and governments.

Should the general government think it politic, as some administrations (if not all) probably will, to look for a support in a system of influence, the government will take every occasion to multiply laws, and officers to execute them, considering these as so many necessary props for its own support. Should this system of policy be adopted, taxes more productive than the impost duties will, probably, be wanted to support the government, and to discharge foreign demands, without leaving any thing for the domestic creditors. The internal sources of taxation then must be called into operation, and internal tax laws and federal assessors and collectors spread over this immense country. All these circumstances considered, is it wise, prudent, or safe, to vest the powers of laying and collecting internal taxes in the general government, while imperfectly organized and inadequate; and to trust to amending it hereafter, and making it adequate to this purpose? [Is it] not only unsafe but absurd to lodge power in a government before it is fitted to receive it? It is confessed that this power and representation ought to go together. Why give the power first? Why give the power to the few, who, when possessed of it, may have address enough to prevent the increase of representation? Why not keep the power, and, when necessary, amend the constitution, and add to its other parts this power, and a proper increase of representation at the same time? Then men who may want the power will be under strong inducements to let in the people, by their representatives, into the government, to hold their due proportion of this power. If a proper representation be impracticable, then we shall see this power resting in the states, where it at present ought to be, and not inconsiderately given up.

When I recollect how lately congress, conventions, legislatures, and people contended in the cause of liberty, and carefully weighed the importance of taxation, I can scarcely believe we are serious in proposing to vest the powers of laying and collecting internal taxes in a government so imperfectly organized for such purposes. Should the United States be taxed by a house of representatives of two hundred members, which would be about fifteen members for Connecticut, twenty-five for Massachusetts, etc. still the middle and lower classes of people could have no great share, in fact, in taxation. I am aware it is said, that the representation proposed by the new constitution is sufficiently numerous; it may be for many purposes; but to suppose that this branch is sufficiently numerous to guard the rights of the people in the administration of the government, in which the purse and sword is placed, seems to argue that we have forgot what the true meaning of representation is. I am sensible also, that it is said that congress will not attempt to lay and collect internal taxes; that it is necessary for them to have the power, though it cannot probably be exercised.—I admit that it is not probable that any prudent congress will attempt to lay and collect internal taxes, especially direct taxes: but this only proves, that the power would be improperly lodged in congress, and that it might be abused by imprudent and designing men.

I have heard several gentlemen, to get rid of objections to this part of the constitution, attempt to construe the powers relative to direct taxes, as those who object to it would have them; as to these, it is said, that congress will only have power to make requisitions, leaving it to the states to lay and collect them. I see but very little colour for this construction, and the attempt only proves that this part of the plan cannot be defended. By this plan there can be no doubt, but that the powers of congress will be complete as to all kinds of taxes whatever—Further, as to internal taxes, the state governments will have concurrent powers with the general government, and both may tax the same objects in the same year; and the objection that the general government may suspend a state tax, as a necessary measure for the promoting the collection of a federal tax, is not without foundation.

5

An Old Whig, no. 6
Fall 1787
Storing 3.3.32–39

I think it is an observation of Dean Swift, that, in political matters, all men can feel, though all cannot see. Agreeably to this doctrine we find, that the necessity of giving additional powers to Congress is at length *felt* by all men, though it was not foreseen by a great number of the people. As the states, individually could not protect our trade, foreign nations, friends as well as enemies, have combined against it; and at the same time that our trade is more beneficial to any nation in Europe, than the trade of any nation in Europe is to us, because we export provisions and raw materials and receive manufactures in return: we are not suffered to be the carriers of our own produce—foreign bottoms engross the whole of our carrying trade, and we are obliged to pay them for doing that which it is the interest of every people to do for themselves. Our shipwrights are starved, our seamen driven abroad for want of employ, our timber left useless on our hands, our ironworks, once a very profitable branch of business, now almost reduced to nothing, and our money banished from the country. These with the train of concomitant evils which always attend the loss of trade, or a state of trade which is unprofitable, have justly alarmed us all; and I am firmly persuaded that scarcely a man of common sense can be found, that does not wish for an efficient federal government, and lament that it has been delayed so long. Yet at the same time it is a matter of immense consequence, in establishing a government which is to last for ages, and which, if it be suffered to depart from the principles of liberty in the beginning, will in all probability, never return to them, that we consider carefully what sort of government we are about to form. Power is very easily encreased; indeed it naturally grows in every government; but it hardly ever lessens.

The misfortunes under which we have for some time laboured, and which still press us severely, would be in a great measure alleviated, if not wholly removed, by devolving upon Congress the power of regulating trade and laying and collecting duties and imposts. If these powers were once fully vested in Congress, trade would immediately assume a new face, money and people would flow in upon us, and the vast tracts of ungranted lands would be a mine of wealth for many years to come. I am pursuaded, that with this addition to the powers of Congress, we should soon find them sufficient for every purpose; and it is very certain that if we did not find them sufficient, we could easily encrease them. But instead of being contented with this, the late convention by their proposed constitution, seem to have resolved to give the new continental government every kind of power whatsoever, throughout the United States. This power I have already attempted to shew, is not limited by any stipulations in favour of the liberty of the subject, and it is easy to shew, that it will be equally unchecked by any restraint from the individual states. The treasure of the whole continent will be entirely at their command. "The Congress shall have power to levy and collect taxes, duties, imposts and excises." And what are the individual states to do, or how are they to subsist? may they also lay and collect taxes, duties, imposts and excises? If they should, the miserable subject will be like sheep twice shorne; the skin must follow the fleece. But the fact is, that no individual state can collect a penny, unless by the permission of Congress; for the "laws of the United States shall be the supreme law of the land, any thing in the constitution or laws of any state to the contrary, notwithstanding." The laws of the individual states, will be only *Leges sub graviore Lege:* for the power of enacting laws necessarily implies the power of repealing laws; and therefore Congress, being the supreme legislatures, may annul or repeal the laws of the individual states, whenever they please. Not a single source of revenue will remain to any state, which Congress may not stop at their sovereign will and pleasure; for if any state attempt to impose a tax or levy a duty, contrary to the inclination of Congress, they have only to exert their supreme legislative power and the law imposing such tax or duty, is done away in a moment. For instance, it will very soon be found inconvenient to have two sets of excise officers in each town or county in every state, they will be in danger of clashing with each other, it will then be found "necessary and proper for carrying into execution the powers vested by the constitution in the government of the United States, or in some department or officer thereof," to forbid the individual states to levy any more excise. Congress may chuse to impose a stamp-duty. It will be very inconvenient for people to run back and forward to different offices, to procure double stamps, and therefore it will be thought "necessary and proper" to forbid any state to meddle with stamp-duties. The same will be the case with many other taxes. They will be in danger of clashing with each other, if Congress and the several states should happen to lay taxes on the same article. The States therefore individually, will be restrained from imposing any taxes upon such articles as Congress shall think proper to tax. They must

then try to find out other articles for taxation, which Congress have not thought proper to touch. This I fear will be a difficult task: for the expensive court to be maintained by the great president, the pay of the standing army and the numerous crouds of hungry expectants, who have lost their all, and it will be said, have lost it by their zeal for the new constitution, must necessarily employ the sharpest wits among their ablest financiers, to devise every possible mode of taxation; and besides, if an individual state should hit upon a new tax that should happen to be productive, there is no doubt but it would soon be taken from it and appropriated to the use of the United States. The inhabitants of the TEN MILE SQUARE, would find ways and means to dispose of all the money that could possibly be raised in every part of the United States. What then will become of the separate governments? They will be annihilated; absolutely annihilated; for no man will ever submit to the wretchedness and contempt of holding any office under them.

The advocates of the proposed constitution, seem to be aware of the difficulty I have hinted at, and therefore it is, I presume, that in conversation as well as in their publications, we are told that under the proposed constitution, "direct taxation will be unnecessary"; that "it is probable the principal branch of revenue will be duties on imports." Some of those who have used such language in public and private, I believe to be very honest men; and I would therefore ask of them, what security they can give us, that the future government of the continent will in any measure confine themselves to the duties upon imports, or that the utmost penny will not be exacted which can possibly be collected either by direct or indirect taxation? How can they answer for the conduct of our future rulers? We have heard enough of these fair promises for the good behaviour of men in office, to learn to doubt of their fulfilment[;] unless we guard ourselves by much better security, there will be no bounds to the new government. They will not have as much to spare for the separate states to collect as Lazarus picked up of the fragments from the rich man's table. There are mouths at this moment gaping in the United States for all that can possibly be collected;—a confederacy is already formed for dividing the public cake to the last crum; and I wish they may not quarrel for more.

But if I were mistaken in this opinion; if in the language of these gentlemen, "it is probable that the principal branch of the public revenue will be duties on imports";— if it is probable that these with the back lands and the post-office will be sufficient, where was the necessity of being in such haste to grant more;—to grant all without limits or restrictions? Men do not usually give up their whole purse where they can pay with part. Why might we not try at least how far the customs and back lands would go before we give all away from the separate states, without reserving any thing for their support.

The true line of distinction which should have been drawn in describing the powers of Congress, and those of the several states, should have been that between internal and external taxation. I am persuaded that the existence of the several states in their separate capacities, and of the United States in their collective capacity, depends upon the maintaining such distinction. Without the power of imposing duties on foreign commerce and regulating trade, the United States will be weak and contemptible, and, indeed, their union must be speedily dissolved: And on the other hand, if the Legislature of the United States shall possess the powers of internal as well as external taxation, the individual states in their separate capacities, will be less than the shadows of a name.

I observe that the late delegates of Connecticut, in their letter to the Governor, speak of the power of direct taxation as an authority which need not be exercised if each state will "furnish the quota." Yet there is no doubt but they may exercise this power if they choose to do it; and they alone will have the right of judging what quotas the several states shall be required to furnish. They may ask as much as they please, and if the states do not furnish all they ask, they may tax at their pleasure; under these circumstances the power of internal taxation will undoubtedly be exercised by the Continental Legislature. If it be said that it is to be expected that the Congress will exercise this power with moderation, I venture to pronounce that those who indulge such hopes, are not acquainted with the principles of human nature. Independent of the multitudinous expectations which the followers of the proposed Constitution entertain in their own favor, which alone, if gratified, would consume the treasures of two such continents as this; there is a spirit of rivalship in power, which will not suffer two suns to shine in the same firmament, one will speedily darken the other, and the individual states will be as totally eclipsed, as the stars in the meridian blaze of the sun. We have seen too much of this spirit in the several states, under the present loose and futile confederation. A jealousy of the powers of Congress in the separate states, which is founded in the same rivalship of power, and which, however contemptible it may appear, was alike founded in the principles of human nature, may furnish us an exemplary lesson upon this head: And when we verge to the other extreme by vesting all power in Congress, we shall find them equally jealous of any power in the individual states, and equally possessed of the same spirit of rivalship, which heretofore denied the necessary supplies from the states to Congress.—We shall never be able to support the collective powers of the United States in Congress, and the powers of the individual states in their separate capacities, without drawing the line fairly between them. If we leave the states individually to the mercy of the Continental Government, they will be stript of the last penny which is necessary for their support; if we give all powers to one, there will be nothing left for the others. The lust of dominion, where it is indulged, will swallow up the whole.

But I shall be told that if Congress are left to depend upon requisitions from the individual states for any part of the necessary supplies, the same difficulty will remain which has hitherto existed; and I may be asked, what shall we do if the supplies should fall short? I answer that although nothing but a very serious necessity of money for continental purposes will ever procure supplies upon requisition from the separate states, yet when that necessity exists in any degree that is really alarming to the whole community, I do not think that such supplies are to be dispaired of. We have seen many instances of aid being furnished, even voluntarily upon pressing occasions, which should teach us to rely on the exertions of the states upon occasions of real and not mere imaginary necessity. One thing will certainly follow from the Continental Government being restrained to external taxation;—that it will be under the necessity of exercising more oeconomy than it has done, especially during the late war. We have been witnesses of such a profuse expenditure of public money at some periods, as these states could never support. This profusion ought to convince us that if all the treasures of the continent are intrusted to the power of Congress, there is too much reason to fear that the whole will be consumed by them, and nothing left to the individual states; and judging from past experience we may venture to presage that the people will be fleeced without mercy, if no check is maintained upon the power of Congress in the articles of taxation.

We ought to be very fully convinced of an absolute necessity existing before we entrust the whole power of taxation to the hands of Congress; and the moment we do so, we ought by consent to annihilate the individual states; for the powers of the individual states will be as effectually swallowed as a drop of water in the ocean; and the next consequence will be a speedy dissolution of our republican form of government.

6

JAMES WILSON, PENNSYLVANIA
RATIFYING CONVENTION
4 Dec. 1787
Elliot 2:466–68

"The powers of Congress extend to taxation—to direct taxation—to internal taxation—to poll taxes—to excises—to other state and internal purposes." Those who possess the power to tax, possess all other sovereign power. That their powers are thus extensive is admitted; and would any thing short of this have been sufficient? Is it the wish of these gentlemen—if it is, let us hear their sentiments—that the general government should subsist on the bounty of the states? Shall it have the power to contract, and no power to fulfil the contract? Shall it have the power to borrow money, and no power to pay the principal or interest? Must we go on in the track that we have hitherto pursued? And must we again compel those in Europe, who lent us money in our distress, to advance the money to pay themselves interest on the certificates of the debts due to them?

This was actually the case in Holland the last year. Like those who have shot one arrow, and cannot regain it, they have been obliged to shoot another in the same direction, in order to recover the first. It was absolutely necessary, sir, that this government should possess these rights; and why should it not, as well as the state governments? Will this government be fonder of the exercise of this authority than those of the states are? Will the states, who are equally represented in one branch of the legislature, be more opposed to the payment of what shall be required by the future, than what has been required by the present Congress? Will the people, who must indisputably pay the whole, have more objections to the payment of this tax, because it is laid by persons of their own immediate appointment, even if those taxes were to continue as oppressive as they now are? But, under the general power of this system, that cannot be the case in Pennsylvania. Throughout the Union, direct taxation will be lessened, at least in proportion to the increase of the other objects of revenue. In this Constitution, a power is given to Congress to collect imposts, which is not given by the present Articles of the Confederation. A very considerable part of the revenue of the United States will arise from that source; it is the easiest, most just, and most productive mode of raising revenue; and it is a safe one, because it is voluntary. No man is obliged to consume more than he pleases, and each buys in proportion only to his consumption. The price of the commodity is blended with the tax, and the person is often not sensible of the payment. But would it have been proper to rest the matter there? Suppose this fund should not prove sufficient; ought the public debts to remain unpaid, or the exigencies of government be left unprovided for? should our tranquillity be exposed to the assaults of foreign enemies, or violence among ourselves, because the objects of commerce may not furnish a sufficient revenue to secure them all? Certainly, Congress should possess the power of raising revenue from their constituents, for the purpose mentioned in the 8th section of the 1st article; that is, "to pay the debts and provide for the common defence and general welfare of the United States." It has been common with the gentlemen, on this subject, to present us with frightful pictures. We are told of the hosts of tax-gatherers that will swarm through the land; and whenever taxes are mentioned, military force seems to be an attending idea. I think I may venture to predict that the taxes of the general government, if any shall be laid, will be more equitable, and much less expensive, than those imposed by state governments.

I shall not go into an investigation of this subject; but it must be confessed that scarcely any mode of laying and collecting taxes can be more burdensome than the present.

7

BRUTUS, NO. 5
13 Dec. 1787
Storing 2.9.59–63

1st. To detail the particulars comprehended in the general terms, taxes, duties, imposts and excises, would require a volume, instead of a single piece in a news-paper. Indeed it would be a task far beyond my ability, and to which no one can be competent, unless possessed of a mind capable of comprehending every possible source of revenue; for they extend to every possible way of raising money, whether by direct or indirect taxation. Under this clause may be imposed a poll-tax, a land-tax, a tax on houses and buildings, on windows and fire places, on cattle and on all kinds of personal property:—It extends to duties on all kinds of goods to any amount, to tonnage and poundage on vessels, to duties on written instruments, newspapers, almanacks, and books:—It comprehends an excise on all kinds of liquors, spirits, wines, cyder, beer, etc. and indeed takes in duty or excise on every necessary or conveniency of life; whether of foreign or home growth or manufactory. In short, we can have no conception of any way in which a government can raise money from the people, but what is included in one or other of [these] general terms. We may say then that this clause commits to the hands of the general legislature every conceivable source of revenue within the United States. Not only are these terms very comprehensive, and extend to a vast number of objects, but the power to lay and collect has great latitude; it will lead to the passing a vast number of laws, which may affect the personal rights of the citizens of the states, expose their property to fines and confiscation, and put their lives in jeopardy: it opens a door to the appointment of a swarm of revenue and excise officers to prey upon the honest and industrious part of the community, eat up their substance, and riot on the spoils of the country.

2d. We will next enquire into what is implied in the authority to pass all laws which shall be necessary and proper to carry this power into execution.

It is, perhaps, utterly impossible fully to define this power. The authority granted in the first clause can only be understood in its full extent, by descending to all the particular cases in which a revenue can be raised; the number and variety of these cases are so endless, and as it were infinite, that no man living has, as yet, been able to reckon them up. The greatest geniuses in the world have been for ages employed in the research, and when mankind had supposed that the subject was exhausted they have been astonished with the refined improvements that have been made in modern times, and especially in the English nation on the subject—If then the objects of this power cannot be comprehended, how is it possible to understand the extent of that power which can pass all laws which shall be necessary and proper for carrying it into execution? It is truly incomprehensible. A case cannot be conceived of, which is not included in this power. It is well known that the subject of revenue is the most difficult and extensive in the science of government. It requires the greatest talents of a statesman, and the most numerous and exact provisions of the legislature. The command of the revenues of a state gives the command of every thing in it.—He that has the purse will have the sword, and they that have both, have every thing; so that the legislature having every source from which money can be drawn under their direction, with a right to make all laws necessary and proper for drawing forth all the resource of the country, would have, in fact, all power.

Were I to enter into the detail, it would be easy to shew how this power in its operation, would totally destroy all the powers of the individual states. But this is not necessary for those who will think for themselves, and it will be useless to such as take things upon trust, nothing will awaken them to reflection, until the iron hand of oppression compel them to it.

I shall only remark, that this power, given to the federal legislature, directly annihilates all the powers of the state legislatures. There cannot be a greater solecism in politics than to talk of power in a government, without the command of any revenue. It is as absurd as to talk of an animal without blood, or the subsistence of one without food. Now the general government having in their controul every possible source of revenue, and authority to pass any law they may deem necessary to draw them forth, or to facilitate their collection; no source of revenue is therefore left in the hands of any state. Should any state attempt to raise money by law, the general government may repeal or arrest it in the execution, for all their laws will be the supreme law of the land: If then any one can be weak enough to believe that a government can exist without having the authority to raise money to pay a door-keeper to their assembly, he may believe that the state government can exist, should this new constitution take place.

It is agreed by most of the advocates of this new system, that the government which is proper for the United States should be a confederated one; that the respective states ought to retain a portion of their sovereignty, and that they should preserve not only the forms of their legislatures, but also the power to conduct certain internal concerns. How far the powers to be retained by the states shall extend, is the question; we need not spend much time on this subject, as it respects this constitution, for a government without the power to raise money is one only in name. It is clear that the legislatures of the respective states must be altogether dependent on the will of the general legislature, for the means of supporting their government. The legislature of the United States will have a right to exhaust every source of revenue in every state, and to annul all laws of the states which may stand in the way of effecting it; unless therefore we can suppose the state governments can exist without money to support the officers who execute them, we must conclude they will exist no longer than the general legislature choose they should. Indeed the idea of any government existing, in any respect, as an independent one, without any means of support in their own hands, is an absurdity. If therefore, this constitution has in view, what many of its framers and advocates say it has, to secure and guarantee to the separate states the exercise of certain powers of government[,] it certainly ought to have left in their hands some sources of revenue. It should have marked the line in which the general government should have raised money, and set bounds over which they should not pass, leaving to the separate states other means to raise supplies for the support of their governments, and to discharge their respective debts. To this it is objected, that the general government ought to have power competent to the purposes of the union; they are to provide for the common defence, to pay the debts of the United States, support foreign ministers, and the civil establishment of the union, and to do these they ought to have authority to raise money adequate to the purpose. On this I observe, that the state governments have also contracted debts, they require money to support their civil officers, and how this is to be done, if they give to the general government a power to raise money in every way in which it can possibly be raised, with such a controul over the state legislatures as to prohibit them, whenever the general legislature may think proper, from raising any money. It is again objected that it is very difficult, if not impossible, to draw the line of distinction between the powers of the general and state governments on this subject. The first, it is said, must have the power of raising the money necessary for the purposes of the union, if they are limited to certain objects the revenue may fall short of a sufficiency for the public exigencies, they must therefore have discretionary power. The line may be easily and accurately drawn between the powers of the two governments on this head. The distinction between external and internal taxes, is not a novel one in this country, it is a plain one, and easily understood. The first includes impost duties on all imported goods; this species of taxes it is proper should be laid by the general government; many reasons might be urged to shew that no danger is to be apprehended from their exercise of it. They may be collected in few places, and from few hands with certainty and expedition. But few officers are necessary to be imployed in collecting them, and there is no danger of oppression in laying them, because, if they are laid higher than trade will bear, the merchants will cease importing, or smuggle their goods. We have therefore sufficient security, arising from the nature of the thing, against burdensome and intolerable impositions from this kind of tax. But the case is far otherwise with regard to direct taxes; these include poll taxes, land taxes, excises, duties on written instruments, on every thing we eat, drink, or wear; they take hold of every species of property, and come home to every man's house and packet. These are often so oppressive, as to grind the face of the poor, and render the lives of the common people a burden to them. The great and only security the people can have against oppression from this kind of taxes, must rest in their representatives. If they are sufficiently numerous to be well informed of the circumstances, and ability of those who send them, and have a proper regard for the people, they will be secure. The general legislature, as I have shewn in a former paper, will not be thus qualified, and therefore, on this account, ought not to exercise the power of direct taxation. If the power of laying imposts will not be sufficient, some other specific mode of raising a revenue should have been assigned the general government; many may be suggested in which their power may be accurately defined and limited, and it would be much better to give them authority to lay and collect a duty on exports, not to exceed a certain rate per cent, than to have surrendered every kind of resource that the country has, to the complete abolition of the state governments, and which will introduce such an infinite number of laws and ordinances, fines and penalties, courts, and judges, collectors, and excisemen, that when a man can number them, he may enumerate the stars of Heaven.

8

BRUTUS, NO. 6
27 Dec. 1787
Storing 2.9.67–82

The general government is to be vested with authority to levy and collect taxes, duties, and excises; the separate states have also power to impose taxes, duties, and excises, except that they cannot lay duties on exports and imports without the consent of Congress. Here then the two governments have concurrent jurisdiction; both may lay impositions of this kind. But then the general government have supperadded to this power, authority to make all laws which shall be necessary and proper for carrying the foregoing power into execution. Suppose then that both governments should lay taxes, duties, and excises, and it should fall so heavy on the people that they would be unable, or be so burdensome that they would refuse to pay them both—would it not be necessary that the general legislature should suspend the collection of the state tax? It certainly would. For, if the people could not, or would not pay both, they must be discharged from the tax to the state, or the tax to the general government could not be collected.—The conclusion therefore is inevitable, that the respective state governments will not have the power to raise one shilling in any way, but by the permission of the Congress. I presume no one will pretend, that the states can exercise legislative authority, or administer justice among their citizens for any length of time, without being able to raise a sufficiency to pay those who administer their governments.

If this be true, and if the states can raise money only by permission of the general government, it follows that the state governments will be dependent on the will of the general government for their existence.

What will render this power in Congress effectual and sure in its operation is, that the government will have complete judicial and executive authority to carry all their laws into effect, which will be paramount to the judicial and executive authority of the individual states: in vain therefore will be all interference of the legislatures, courts, or magistrates of any of the states on the subject; for they will be subordinate to the general government, and engaged by oath to support it, and will be constitutionally bound to submit to their decisions.

The general legislature will be empowered to lay any tax they chuse, to annex any penalties they please to the breach of their revenue laws; and to appoint as many officers as they may think proper to collect the taxes. They will have authority to farm the revenues and to vest the farmer general, with his subalterns, with plenary powers to collect them, in any way which to them may appear eligible. And the courts of law, which they will be authorized to institute, will have cognizance of every case arising under the revenue laws, the conduct of all the officers employed in collecting them; and the officers of these courts will execute their judgments. There is no way, therefore, of avoiding the destruction of the state governments, whenever the Congress please to do it, unless the people rise up, and, with a strong hand, resist and prevent the execution of constitutional laws. The fear of this, will, it is presumed, restrain the general government, for some time, within proper bounds; but it will not be many years before they will have a revenue, and force, at their command, which will place them above any apprehensions on that score.

How far the power to lay and collect duties and excises, may operate to dissolve the state governments, and oppress the people, it is impossible to say. It would assist us much in forming a just opinion on this head, to consider the various objects to which this kind of taxes extend, in European nations, and the infinity of laws they have passed respecting them. Perhaps, if leisure will permit, this may be essayed in some future paper.

It was observed in my last number, that the power to lay and collect duties and excises, would invest the Congress with authority to impose a duty and excise on every necessary and convenience of life. As the principal object of the government, in laying a duty or excise, will be, to raise money, it is obvious, that they will fix on such articles as are of the most general use and consumption; because, unless great quantities of the article, on which the duty is laid, is used, the revenue cannot be considerable. We may therefore presume, that the articles which will be the object of this species of taxes will be either the real necessaries of life; or if not these, such as from custom and habit are esteemed so. I will single out a few of the productions of our own country, which may, and probably will, be of the number.

Cider is an article that most probably will be one of those on which an excise will be laid, because it is one, which this country produces in great abundance, which is in very general use, is consumed in great quantities, and which may be said too not to be a real necessary of life. An excise on this would raise a large sum of money in the United States. How would the power, to lay and collect an excise on cider, and to pass all laws proper and necessary to carry it into execution, operate in its exercise? It might be necessary, in order to collect the excise on cider, to grant to one man, in each county, an exclusive right of building and keeping cider-mills, and oblige him to give bonds and security for payment of the excise; or, if this was not done, it might be necessary to license the mills, which are to make this liquor, and to take from them security, to account for the excise; or, if otherwise, a great number of officers must be employed, to take account of the cider made, and to collect the duties on it.

Porter, ale, and all kinds of malt-liquors, are articles that would probably be subject also to an excise. It would be necessary, in order to collect such an excise, to regulate the manufactory of these, that the quantity made might be ascertained or otherwise security could not be had for the payment of the excise. Every brewery must then be licensed, and officers appointed, to take account of its product, and to secure the payment of the duty, or excise, before it is sold. Many other articles might be named, which would be objects of this species of taxation, but I refrain from enumerating them. It will probably be said, by those who advocate this system, that the observations already made on this head, are calculated only to inflame the minds of the people, with the apprehension of dangers merely imaginary. That there is not the least reason to apprehend, the general legislature will exercise their power in this manner. To this I would only say, that these kinds of taxes exist in Great Britain, and are severely felt. The excise on cider and perry, was imposed in that nation a few years ago, and it is in the memory of every one, who read the history of the transaction, what great tumults it occasioned.

This power, exercised without limitation, will introduce itself into every corner of the city, and country—It will wait upon the ladies at their toilett, and will not leave them in any of their domestic concerns; it will accompany them to the ball, the play, and the assembly; it will go with them when they visit, and will, on all occasions, sit beside them in their carriages nor will it desert them even at church; it will enter the house of every gentleman, watch over his cellar, wait upon his cook in the kitchen, follow the servants into the parlour, preside over the table, and note down all he eats or drinks; it will attend him to his bedchamber, and watch him while he sleeps; it will take cognizance of the professional man in his office, or his study; it will watch the merchant in the counting-house, or in his store; it will follow the mechanic to his shop, and in his work and will haunt him in his family, and in his bed; it will be a constant companion of the industrious farmer in all his labour, it will be with him in the house, and in the field, observe the toil of his hands, and the sweat of his brow; it will penetrate into the most obscure cottage; and finally, it will light upon the head of every person in the United States. To all these different classes of people, and in all these circumstances, in which it will attend them, the language in which it will address them, will be GIVE! GIVE!

A power that has such latitude, which reaches every person in the community in every conceivable circumstance, and lays hold of every species of property they possess, and which has no bounds set to it, but the discretion of those who exercise it[,] I say, such a power must necessarily, from its very nature, swallow up all the power of the state governments.

I shall add but one other observation on this head, which is this—It appears to me a solecism, for two men, or bodies of men, to have unlimited power respecting the same object. It contradicts the scripture maxim, which saith, "no man can serve two masters," the one power or the other must prevail, or else they will destroy each other, and neither of them effect their purpose. It may be compared to two mechanic powers, acting upon the same body in opposite directions, the consequence would be, if the powers were equal, the body would remain in a state of rest, or if the force of the one was superior to that of the other, the stronger would prevail, and overcome the resistance of the weaker.

But it is said, by some of the advocates of this system, "That the idea that Congress can levy taxes at pleasure, is false, and the suggestion wholly unsupported: that the preamble to the constitution is declaratory of the purposes of the union, and the assumption of any power not necessary to establish justice, &c. to provide for the common defence, &c. will be unconstitutional. Besides, in the very clause which gives the power of levying duties and taxes, the purposes to which the money shall be appropriated, are specified, viz. to pay the debts, and provide for the common defence and general welfare" [Noah Webster]. I would ask those, who reason thus, to define what ideas are included under the terms, to provide for the common defence and general welfare? Are these terms definite, and will they be understood in the same manner, and to apply to the same cases by every one? No one will pretend they will. It will then be matter of opinion, what tends to the general welfare; and the Congress will be the only judges in the matter. To provide for the general welfare, is an abstract proposition, which mankind differ in the explanation of, as much as they do on any political or moral proposition that can be proposed; the most opposite measures may be pursued by different parties, and both may profess, that they have in view the general welfare; and both sides may be honest in their professions, or both may have sinister views. Those who advocate this new constitution declare, they are influenced by a regard to the general welfare; those who oppose it, declare they are moved by the same principle; and I have no doubt but a number on both sides are honest in their professions; and yet nothing is more certain than this, that to adopt this constitution, and not to adopt it, cannot both of them be promotive of the general welfare.

It is as absurd to say, that the power of Congress is limited by these general expressions, "to provide for the common safety, and general welfare," as it would be to say, that it would be limited, had the constitution said they should have power to lay taxes, &c. at will and pleasure. Were this authority given, it might be said, that under it the legislature could not do injustice, or pursue any measures, but such as were calculated to promote the public good, and happiness. For every man, rulers as well as others, are bound by the immutable laws of God and reason, always to will what is right. It is certainly right and fit, that the governors of every people should provide for the common defence and general welfare; every government, therefore, in the world, even the greatest despot, is limited in the exercise of his power. But however just this reasoning may be, it would be found, in practice, a most pitiful restriction. The government would always say, their measures were designed and calculated to promote the public good; and there being no judge between them and the people, the rulers themselves must, and would always, judge for themselves.

There are others of the favourers of this system, who admit, that the power of the Congress under it, with respect to revenue, will exist without limitation, and contend, that so it ought to be.

It is said, "The power to raise armies, to build and equip fleets, and to provide for their support, ought to exist without limitation, because it is impossible to foresee, or to define, the extent and variety of national exigencies, or the correspondent extent and variety of the means which may be necessary to satisfy them.["]

This, it is said, "is one of those truths which, to correct and unprejudiced minds, carries its own evidence along with it. It rests upon axioms as simple as they are universal: the means ought to be proportioned to the end; the person, from whose agency the attainment of any end is expected, ought to possess the means by which it is to be attained" [*Federalist*, no. 23].

This same writer insinuates, that the opponents to the plan promulgated by the convention, manifests a want of candor, in objecting to the extent of the powers proposed to be vested in this government; because he asserts, with an air of confidence, that the powers ought to be unlimited as to the object to which they extend; and that this position, if not self-evident, is at least clearly demonstrated by the foregoing mode of reasoning. But with submission to this author's better judgment, I humbly conceive his reasoning will appear, upon examination, more specious than solid. The means, says the gentleman, ought to be proportioned to the end: admit the proposition to be true it is then necessary to enquire, what is the end of the government of the United States, in order to draw any just conclusions from it. Is this end simply to preserve the general government, and to provide for the common defence and general welfare of the union only? certainly not: for beside this, the state governments are to be supported, and provision made for the managing such of their internal concerns as are allotted to them. It is admitted, "that the circumstances of our country are such, as to demand a compound, instead of a simple, a confederate, instead of a sole government," that the objects of each ought to be pointed out, and that each ought to possess ample authority to execute the powers committed to them. The government then, being complex in its nature, the end it has in view is so also; and it is as necessary, that the state governments should possess the means to attain the ends expected from them, as for the general government. Neither the general government, nor the state governments, ought to be vested with all the powers proper to be exercised for promoting the ends of government. The powers are divided between them—certain ends are to be attained by the one, and other certain ends by the other; and these, taken together, include all the ends of good government. This being the case, the conclusion follows, that each should be furnished with the means, to attain the ends, to which they are designed.

To apply this reasoning to the case of revenue; the general government is charged with the care of providing for the payment of the debts of the United States; supporting the general government, and providing for the defence of the union. To obtain these ends, they should be furnished with means. But does it thence follow, that they should command all the revenues of the United States! Most certainly it does not. For if so, it will follow, that no means will be left to attain other ends, as necessary to the happiness of the country, as those committed to their care. The individual states have debts to discharge; their legislatures and executives are to be supported, and provision is to be made for the administration of justice in the respective states. For these objects the general government has no authority to provide; nor is it proper it should. It is clear then, that the states should have the command of such revenues, as to answer the ends they have to obtain. To say, "that the circumstances that endanger the safety of nations are infinite," and from hence to infer, that all the sources of revenue in the states should be yielded to the general government, is not conclusive reasoning: for the Congress are authorized only to controul in general concerns, and not regulate local and internal ones; and these are as essentially requisite to be provided for as those. The peace and happiness of a community is as intimately connected with the prudent direction of their domestic affairs, and the due administration of justice among themselves, as with a competent provision for their defence against foreign invaders, and indeed more so.

Upon the whole, I conceive, that there cannot be a clearer position than this, that the state governments ought to have an uncontroulable power to raise a revenue, adequate to the exigencies of their governments; and, I presume, no such power is left them by this constitution.

9

ALEXANDER HAMILTON, FEDERALIST, NO. 30, 187–93
28 Dec. 1787

It has been already observed, that the Foederal Government ought to possess the power of providing for the support of the national forces; in which proposition was intended to be included the expence of raising troops, of building and equiping fleets, and all other expences in any wise connected with military arrangements and operations. But these are not the only objects to which the jurisdiction of the Union, in respect to revenue, must necessarily be empowered to extend—It must embrace a provision for the support of the national civil list—for the payment of the national debts contracted, or that may be contracted—and in general for all those matters which will call for disbursements out of the national treasury. The conclusion is, that there must be interwoven in the frame of the government, a general power of taxation in one shape or another.

Money is with propriety considered as the vital principle of the body politic; as that which sustains its life and motion, and enables it to perform its most essential functions. A complete power therefore to procure a regular and adequate supply of it, as far as the resources of the community will permit, may be regarded as an indispensable ingredient in every constitution. From a deficiency in this particular, one of two evils must ensue; either the people must be subjected to continual plunder as a substitute for a more eligible mode of supplying the public wants, or the government must sink into a fatal atrophy, and in a short course of time perish.

In the Ottoman or Turkish empire, the sovereign,

though in other respects absolute master of the lives and fortunes of his subjects, has no right to impose a new tax. The consequence is, that he permits the Bashaws or Governors of provinces to pillage the people without mercy; and in turn squeezes out of them the sums of which he stands in need to satisfy his own exigencies and those of the State. In America, from a like cause, the government of the Union has gradually dwindled into a state of decay, approaching nearly to annihilation. Who can doubt that the happiness of the people in both countries would be promoted by competent authorities in the proper hands, to provide the revenues which the necessities of the public might require?

The present confederation, feeble as it is, intended to repose in the United States, an unlimited power of providing for the pecuniary wants of the Union. But proceeding upon an erroneous principle, it has been done in such a manner as entirely to have frustrated the intention. Congress by the articles which compose that compact (as has been already stated) are authorised to ascertain and call for any sums of money necessary, in their judgment, to the service of the United States; and their requisitions, if conformable to the rule of apportionment, are in every constitutional sense obligatory upon the States. These have no right to question the propriety of the demand—no discretion beyond that of devising the ways and means of furnishing the sums demanded. But though this be strictly and truly the case; though the assumption of such a right be an infringement of the articles of Union; though it may seldom or never have been avowedly claimed; yet in practice it has been constantly exercised; and would continue to be so, as long as the revenues of the confederacy should remain dependant on the intermediate agency of its members. What the consequences of this system have been, is within the knowledge of every man, the least conversant in our public affairs, and has been amply unfolded in different parts of these inquiries. It is this which has chiefly contributed to reduce us to a situation which affords ample cause, both of mortification to ourselves, and of triumph to our enemies.

What remedy can there be for this situation but, in a change of the system, which has produced it? In a change of the fallacious and delusive system of quotas and requisitions? What substitute can there be imagined for this *ignis fatuus* in finance, but that of permitting the national government to raise its own revenues by the ordinary methods of taxation, authorised in every well ordered constitution of civil government? Ingenious men may declaim with plausibility on any subject; but no human ingenuity can point out any other expedient to rescue us from the inconveniences and embarrassments, naturally resulting from defective supplies of the public treasury.

The more intelligent adversaries of the new constitution admit the force of this reasoning; but they qualify their admission by a distinction between what they call *internal* and *external* taxation. The former they would reserve to the State governments; the latter, which they explain into commercial imposts, or rather duties on imported articles, they declare themselves willing to concede to the Foederal Head. This distinction, however, would violate that fun-

damental maxim of good sense and sound policy, which dictates that every POWER ought to be proportionate to its OBJECT; and would still leave the General Government in a kind of tutelage to the State governments, inconsistent with every idea of vigor or efficiency. Who can pretend that commercial imposts are or would be alone equal to the present and future exigencies of the Union? Taking into the account the existing debt, foreign and domestic, upon any plan of extinguishment, which a man moderately impressed with the importance of public justice and public credit could approve, in addition to the establishments, which all parties will acknowledge to be necessary, we could not reasonably flatter ourselves, that this resource alone, upon the most improved scale, would even suffice for its present necessities. Its future necessities admit not of calculation or limitation; and upon the principle, more than once adverted to, the power of making provision for them as they arise, ought to be equally unconfined. I believe it may be regarded as a position, warranted by the history of mankind, that *in the usual progress of things, the necessities of a nation in every stage of its existence will be found at least equal to its resources.*

To say that deficiencies may be provided for by requisitions upon the States, is on the one hand, to acknowledge that this system cannot be depended upon; and on the other hand, to depend upon it for every thing beyond a certain limit. Those who have carefully attended to its vices and deformities as they have been exhibited by experience, or delineated in the course of these papers, must feel an invincible repugnancy to trusting the national interests, in any degree, to its operation. Its inevitable tendency, whenever it is brought into activity, must be to enfeeble the Union and sow the seeds of discord and contention between the Foederal Head and its members, and between the members themselves. Can it be expected that the deficiencies would be better supplied in this mode, than the total wants of the Union have heretofore been supplied, in the same mode? It ought to be recollected, that if less will be required from the States, they will have proportionably less means to answer the demand. If the opinions of those who contend for the distinction which has been mentioned, were to be received as evidence of truth, one would be led to conclude that there was some known point in the oeconomy of national affairs, at which it would be safe to stop, and say, thus far the ends of public happiness will be promoted by supplying the wants of government, and all beyond this is unworthy of our care or anxiety. How is it possible that a government half supplied and always necessitous, can fulfil the purposes of its institution—can provide for the security of—advance the prosperity—or support the reputation of the commonwealth? How can it ever possess either energy or stability, dignity or credit, confidence at home or respectability abroad? How can its administration be any thing else than a succession of expedients temporising, impotent, disgraceful? How will it be able to avoid a frequent sacrifice of its engagements to immediate necessity? How can it undertake or execute any liberal or enlarged plans of public good?

Let us attend to what would be the effects of this situation in the very first war in which we should happen to be engaged. We will presume for argument sake, that the revenue arising from the impost-duties answer the purposes of a provision for the public debt, and of a peace establishment for the Union. Thus circumstanced, a war breaks out. What would be the probable conduct of the government in such an emergency? Taught by experience that proper dependence could not be placed on the success of requisitions: unable by its own authority to lay hold of fresh resources, and urged by considerations of national danger, would it not be driven to the expedient of diverting the funds already appropriated from their proper objects to the defence of the State? It is not easy to see how a step of this kind could be avoided; and if it should be taken, it is evident that it would prove the destruction of public credit at the very moment that it was become essential to the public safety. To imagine that at such a crisis credit might be dispensed with, would be the extreme of infatuation. In the modern system of war, nations the most wealthy are obliged to have recourse to large loans. A country so little opulent as ours, must feel this necessity in a much stronger degree. But who would lend to a government that prefaced its overtures for borrowing, by an act which demonstrated that no reliance could be placed on the steadiness of its measures for paying? The loans it might be able to procure, would be as limited in their extent as burthensome in their conditions. They would be made upon the same principles that usurers commonly lend to bankrupt and fraudulent debtors; with a sparing hand, and at enormous premiums.

It may perhaps be imagined, that from the scantiness of the resources of the country, the necessity of diverting the established funds in the case supposed, would exist; though the national government should possess an unrestrained power of taxation. But two considerations will serve to quiet all apprehension on this head; one is, that we are sure the resources of the community in their full extent, will be brought into activity for the benefit of the Union; the other is, that whatever deficiencies there may be, can without difficulty be supplied by loans.

The power of creating new funds upon new objects of taxation by its own authority, would enable the national government to borrow, as far as its necessities might require. Foreigners as well as the citizens of America, could then reasonably repose confidence in its engagements; but to depend upon a government, that must itself depend upon thirteen other governments for the means of fulfilling its contracts, when once its situation is clearly understood, would require a degree of credulity, not often to be met with in the pecuniary transactions of mankind, and little reconcileable with the usual sharp-sightedness of avarice.

Reflections of this kind, may have trifling weight with men, who hope to see realized in America, the halcyon scenes of the poetic or fabulous age; but to those who believe we are likely to experience a common portion of the vicissitudes and calamities, which have fallen to the lot of other nations, they must appear entitled to serious attention. Such men must behold the actual situation of their country with painful solicitude, and deprecate the evils which ambition or revenge might, with too much facility, inflict upon it.

10

ALEXANDER HAMILTON, FEDERALIST, NO. 31,
193–98
1 Jan. 1788

In disquisitions of every kind there are certain primary truths or first principles upon which all subsequent reasonings must depend. These contain an internal evidence, which antecedent to all reflection or combination commands the assent of the mind. Where it produces not this effect, it must proceed either from some defect or disorder in the organs of perception, or from the influence of some strong interest, or passion, or prejudice. Of this nature are the maxims in geometry, that "The whole is greater than its part; that things equal to the same are equal to one another; that two straight lines cannot inclose a space; and that all right angles are equal to each other." Of the same nature are these other maxims in ethics and politics, that there cannot be an effect without a cause; that the means ought to be proportioned to the end; that every power ought to be commensurate with its object; that there ought to be no limitation of a power destined to effect a purpose, which is itself incapable of limitation. And there are other truths in the two latter sciences, which if they cannot pretend to rank in the class of axioms, are yet such direct inferences from them, and so obvious in themselves, and so agreeable to the natural and unsophisticated dictates of common sense, that they challenge the assent of a sound and unbiassed mind, with a degree of force and conviction almost equally irresistable.

The objects of geometrical enquiry are so intirely abstracted from those pursuits which stir up and put in motion the unruly passions of the human heart, that mankind without difficulty adopt not only the more simple theorems of the science, but even those abstruse paradoxes, which however they may appear susceptible of demonstration, are at variance with the natural conceptions which the mind, without the aid of philosophy, would be led to entertain upon the subject. The INFINITE DIVISIBILITY of matter, or in other words, the INFINITE divisibility of a FINITE thing, extending even to the minutest atom, is a point agreed among geometricians; though not less incomprehensible to common sense, than any of those mysteries in religion, against which the batteries of infidelity have been so industriously levelled.

But in the sciences of morals and politics men are found far less tractable. To a certain degree it is right and useful, that this should be the case. Caution and investigation are a necessary armour against error and imposition. But this untractableness may be carried too far, and may degenerate into obstinacy, perverseness or disingenuity. Though it cannot be pretended that the principles of moral and political knowledge have in general the same degree of certainty with those of the mathematics; yet they have much better claims in this respect, than to judge from the conduct of men in particular situations, we should be disposed to allow them. The obscurity is much oftener in the passions and prejudices of the reasoner than in the subject. Men upon too many occasions do not give their own understandings fair play; but yielding to some untoward bias they entangle themselves in words and confound themselves in subtleties.

How else could it happen (if we admit the objectors to be sincere in their opposition) that positions so clear as those which manifest the necessity of a general power of taxation in the government of the union, should have to encounter any adversaries among men of discernment? Though these positions have been elsewhere fully stated, they will perhaps not be improperly recapitulated in this place, as introductory to an examination of what may have been offered by way of objection to them. They are in substance as follow:

A government ought to contain in itself every power requisite to the full accomplishment of the objects committed to its care, and to the complete execution of the trusts for which it is responsible; free from every other control, but a regard to the public good and to the sense of the people.

As the duties of superintending the national defence and of securing the public peace against foreign or domestic violence, involve a provision for casualties and dangers, to which no possible limits can be assigned, the power of making that provision ought to know no other bounds than the exigencies of the nation and the resources of the community.

As revenue is the essential engine by which the means of answering the national exigencies must be procured, the power of procuring that article in its full extent, must necessarily be comprehended in that of providing for those exigencies.

As theory and practice conspire to prove that the power of procuring revenue is unavailing, when exercised over the States in their collective capacities, the Federal government must of necessity be invested with an unqualified power of taxation in the ordinary modes.

Did not experience evince the contrary, it would be natural to conclude that the propriety of a general power of taxation in the national government might safely be permitted to rest on the evidence of these propositions, unassisted by any additional arguments or illustrations. But we find in fact, that the antagonists of the proposed constitution, so far from acquiescing in their justness or truth, seem to make their principal and most zealous effort against this part of the plan. It may therefore be satisfactory to analize the arguments with which they combat it.

Those of them, which have been most labored with that view, seem in substance to amount to this: "It is not true, because the exigencies of the Union may not be susceptible of limitation, that its power of laying taxes ought to be unconfined. Revenue is as requisite to the purposes of the local administrations as to those of the Union; and the former are at least of equal importance with the latter to the happiness of the people. It is therefore as necessary, that

the State Governments should be able to command the means of supplying their wants, as, that the National Government should possess the like faculty, in respect to the wants of the Union. But an indefinite power of taxation in the *latter* might, and probably would in time deprive the former of the means of providing for their own necessities; and would subject them entirely to the mercy of the national Legislature. As the laws of the Union are to become the supreme law of the land; as it is to have power to pass all laws that may be NECESSARY for carrying into execution, the authorities with which it is proposed to vest it; the national government might at any time abolish the taxes imposed for State objects, upon the pretence of an interference with its own. It might alledge a necessity of doing this, in order to give efficacy to the national revenues: And thus all the resources of taxation might by degrees, become the subjects of foederal monopoly, to the intire exclusion and destruction of the State Governments."

This mode of reasoning appears some times to turn upon the supposition of usurpation in the national government; at other times it seems to be designed only as a deduction from the constitutional operation of its intended powers. It is only in the latter light, that it can be admitted to have any pretensions to fairness. The moment we launch into conjectures about the usurpations of the foederal Government, we get into an unfathomable abyss, and fairly put ourselves out of the reach of all reasoning. Imagination may range at pleasure till it gets bewildered amidst the labyrinths of an enchanted castle, and knows not on which side to turn to extricate itself from the perplexities into which it has so rashly adventured. Whatever may be the limits or modifications of the powers of the Union, it is easy to imagine an endless train of possible dangers; and by indulging an excess of jealousy and timidity, we may bring ourselves to a state of absolute scepticism and irresolution. I repeat here what I have observed in substance in another place that all observations founded upon the danger of usurpation, ought to be referred to the composition and structure of the government, not to the nature or extent of its powers. The State governments, by their original constitutions, are invested with complete sovereignty. In what does our security consist against usurpations from that quarter? Doubtless in the manner of their formation, and in a due dependence of those who are to administer them upon the people. If the proposed construction of the Foederal Government, be found upon an impartial examination of it, to be such as to afford, to a proper extent, the same species of security, all apprehensions on the score of usurpation ought to be discarded.

It should not be forgotten, that a disposition in the State governments to encroach upon the rights of the Union, is quite as probable, as a disposition in the Union to encroach upon the rights of the State Governments. What side would be likely to prevail in such a conflict, must depend on the means which the contending parties could employ towards ensuring success. As in republics, strength is always on the side of the people; and as there are weighty reasons to induce a belief, that the State governments will commonly possess most influence over them, the natural conclusion is, that such contests will be most apt to end to the disadvantage of the Union; and that there is greater probability of encroachments by the members upon the Foederal Head, than by the Foederal Head upon the members. But it is evident, that all conjectures of this kind, must be extremely vague and fallible, and that it is by far the safest course to lay them altogether aside; and to confine our attention wholly to the nature and extent of the powers as they are delineated in the constitution. Every thing beyond this, must be left to the prudence and firmness of the people; who, as they will hold the scales in their own hands, it is to be hoped, will always take care to preserve the constitutional equilibrium between the General and the State Governments. Upon this ground, which is evidently the true one, it will not be difficult to obviate the objections which have been made to an indefinite power of taxation in the United States.

11

Brutus, no. 7
3 Jan. 1788
Storing 2.9.88–92

The idea, that the powers of congress in respect to revenue ought to be unlimited, "because the circumstances which may affect the public safety are not reducible to certain determinate limits," is novel, as it relates to the government of the united states. The inconveniencies which resulted from the feebleness of the present confederation was discerned, and felt soon after its adoption. It was soon discovered, that a power to require money, without either the authority or means to enforce a collection of it, could not be relied upon either to provide for the common defence, the discharge of the national debt, or for support of government. Congress therefore, so early as February 1781, recommended to the states to invest them with a power to levy an impost of five per cent ad valorem, on all imported goods, as a fund to be appropriated to discharge the debts already contracted, or which should hereafter be contracted for the support of the war, to be continued until the debts should be fully and finally discharged. There is not the most distant idea held out in this act, that an unlimited power to collect taxes, duties and excises was necessary to be vested in the united states, and yet this was a time of the most pressing danger and distress. The idea then was, that if certain definite funds were assigned to the union, which were certain in their natures, productive, and easy of collection, it would enable them to answer their engagements, and provide for their defence, and the impost of five per cent was fixed upon for the purpose.

This same subject was revived in the winter and spring of 1783, and after a long consideration of the subject, and many schemes were proposed; the result was, a recommendation of the revenue system of April 1783; this system does not suggest an idea that it was necessary to grant the United States unlimited authority in matters of revenue. A variety of amendments were proposed to this system, some of which are upon the journals of Congress, but it does not appear that any of them proposed to invest the general government with discretionary power to raise money. On the contrary, all of them limit them to certain definite objects, and fix the bounds over which they could not pass. This recommendation was passed at the conclusion of the war, and was founded on an estimate of the whole national debt. It was computed, that one million and an half of dollars, in addition to the impost, was a sufficient sum to pay the annual interest of the debt, and gradually to abolish the principal.—Events have proved that their estimate was sufficiently liberal, as the domestic debt appears upon its being adjusted to be less than it was computed, and since this period a considerable portion of the principal of the domestic debt has been discharged by the sale of the western lands. It has been constantly urged by Congress, and by individuals, ever since, until lately, that had this revenue been appropriated by the states, as it was recommended, it would have been adequate to every exigency of the union. Now indeed it is insisted, that all the treasures of the country are to be under the controul of that body, whom we are to appoint to provide for our protection and defence against foreign enemies. The debts of the several states, and the support of the governments of them are to trust to fortune and accident. If the union should not have occasion for all the money they can raise, they will leave a portion for the state, but this must be a matter of mere grace and favor. Doctrines like these would not have been listened to by any state in the union, at a time when we were pressed on every side by a powerful enemy, and were called upon to make greater exertions than we have any reason to expect we shall ever be again. The ability and character of the convention, who framed the proferred constitution, is sounded forth and reiterated by every declaimer and writer in its favor, as a powerful argument to induce its adoption. But are not the patriots who guided our councils in the perilous times of the war, entitled to equal respect. How has it happened, that none of these perceived a truth, which it is pretended is capable of such clear demonstration, that the power to raise a revenue should be deposited in the general government without limitation? Were the men so dull of apprehension, so incapable of reasoning as not to be able to draw the inference? The truth is, no such necessity exists. It is a thing practicable, and by no means so difficult as is pretended, to limit the powers of the general government in respect to revenue, while yet they may retain reasonable means to provide for the common defence.

It is admitted, that human wisdom cannot foresee all the variety of circumstances that may arise to endanger the safety of nations—and it may with equal truth be added, that the power of a nation, exerted with its utmost vigour, may not be equal to repel a force with which it may be assailed, much less may it be able, with its ordinary resources and power, to oppose an extraordinary and unexpected attack;—but yet every nation may form a rational judgment, what force will be competent to protect and defend it, against any enemy with which it is probable it may have to contend. In extraordinary attacks, every country must rely upon the spirit and special exertions of its inhabitants—and these extraordinary efforts will always very much depend upon the happiness and good order the people experience from a wise and prudent administration of their internal government. The states are as capable of making a just estimate on this head, as perhaps any nation in the world.—We have no powerful nation in our neighbourhood; if we are to go to war, it must either be with the Aboriginal natives, or with European nations. The first are so unequal to a contest with this whole continent, that they are rather to be dreaded for the depredations they may make on our frontiers, than for any impression they will ever be able to make on the body of the country. Some of the European nations, it is true, have provinces bordering upon us, but from these, unsupported by their European forces, we have nothing to apprehend; if any of them should attack us, they will have to transport their armies across the atlantic, at immense expence, while we should defend ourselves in our own country, which abounds with every necessary of life. For defence against any assault, which there is any probability will be made upon us, we may easily form an estimate.

I may be asked to point out the sources, from which the general government could derive a sufficient revenue, to answer the demands of the union. Many might be suggested, and for my part, I am not disposed to be tenacious of my own opinion on the subject. If the object be defined with precision, and will operate to make the burden fall any thing nearly equal on the different parts of the union, I shall be satisfied.

There is one source of revenue, which it is agreed, the general government ought to have the sole controul of. This is an impost upon all goods imported from foreign countries. This would, of itself, be very productive, and would be collected with ease and certainty.—It will be a fund too, constantly encreasing—for our commerce will grow, with the productions of the country; and these, together with our consumption of foreign goods, will encrease with our population. It is said, that the impost will not produce a sufficient sum to satisfy the demands of the general government; perhaps it would not. Let some other then, equally well defined, be assigned them:—that this is practicable is certain, because such particular objects were proposed by some members of Congress when the revenue system of April 1783, was agitated in that body. It was then moved, that a tax at the rate of——— ninetieths of a dollar on surveyed land, and a house tax of half a dollar on a house, should be granted to the United States. I do not mention this, because I approve of raising a revenue in this mode. I believe such a tax would be difficult in its collection, and inconvenient in its operation. But it shews, that it has heretofore been the sense of some of those, who now contend, that the general government should have unlimited authority in matters of revenue, that their authority should be definite and limitted on that head.—My own opinion is, that the objects from which the general government should have authority to raise a revenue, should be of such a nature, that the tax should be raised by simple laws, with few officers, with certainty and

expedition, and with the least interference with the internal police of the states.—Of this nature is the impost on imported goods—and it appears to me that a duty on exports, would also be of this nature—and therefore, for ought I can discover, this would be the best source of revenue to grant the general government. I know neither the Congress nor the state legislatures will have authority under the new constitution to raise a revenue in this way. But I cannot perceive the reason of the restriction. It appears to me evident, that a tax on articles exported, would be as nearly equal as any that we can expect to lay, and it certainly would be collected with more ease and less expence than any direct tax. I do not however, contend for this mode, it may be liable to well founded objections that have not occurred to me. But this I do contend for, that some mode is practicable, and that limits must be marked between the general government, and the states on this head, or if they be not, either the Congress in the exercise of this power, will deprive the state legislatures of the means of their existence, or the states by resisting the constitutional authority of the general government, will render it nugatory.

12

ALEXANDER HAMILTON, FEDERALIST, NO. 34,
209–15
5 Jan. 1788

I flatter myself it has been clearly shewn in my last number, that the particular States, under the proposed Constitution, would have CO-EQUAL authority with the Union in the article of revenue, except as to duties on imports. As this leaves open to the States far the greatest part of the resources of the community, there can be no color for the assertion, that they would not possess means, as abundant as could be desired, for the supply of their own wants, independent of all external control. That the field is sufficiently wide, will more fully appear, when we come to advert to the inconsiderable share of the public expences, for which, it will fall to the lot of the State Governments to provide.

To argue upon abstract principles, that this co-ordinate authority cannot exist, is to set up supposition and theory, against fact and reality. However proper such reasonings might be, to show that a thing *ought not to exist*, they are wholly to be rejected, when they are made use of to prove that it does not exist, contrary to the evidence of the fact itself. It is well known, that in the Roman Republic, the Legislative authority in the last resort, resided for ages in two different political bodies; not as branches of the same Legislature, but as distinct and independent Legislatures, in each of which an opposite interest prevailed; in one, the Patrician—in the other, the Plebeian. Many arguments might have been adduced to prove the unfitness of two such seemingly contradictory authorities, each having power to *annul* or *repeal* the acts of the other. But a man would have been regarded as frantic, who should have attempted at Rome, to disprove their existence. It will readily be understood, that I allude to the COMITIA CENTURIATA, *and* COMITIA TRIBUTA. The former, in which the people voted by Centuries, was so arranged as to give a superiority to the Patrician interest: in the latter, in which numbers prevailed, the Plebeian interest had an entire predominancy. And yet these two Legislatures co-existed for ages, and the Roman Republic attained to the utmost height of human greatness.

In the case particularly under consideration, there is no such contradiction as appears in the example cited, there is no power on either side to annul the acts of the other. And in practice, there is little reason to apprehend any inconvenience; because, in a short course of time, the wants of the States will naturally reduce themselves within *a very narrow compass;* and in the interim, the United States will, in all probability, find it convenient to abstain wholly from those objects, to which the particular States would be inclined to resort.

To form a more precise judgment of the true merits of this question, it will be well to advert to the proportion between the objects that will require a Federal provision in respect to revenue; and those which will require a State provision. We shall discover that the former are altogether unlimited; and, that the latter are circumscribed within very moderate bounds. In pursuing this enquiry, we must bear in mind, that we are not to confine our view to the present period, but to look forward to remote futurity. Constitutions of civil Government are not to be framed upon a calculation of existing exigencies; but upon a combination of these, with the probable exigencies of ages, according to the natural and tried course of human affairs. Nothing therefore can be more fallacious, than to infer the extent of any power, proper to be lodged in the National Government, from an estimate of its immediate necessities. There ought to be a CAPACITY to provide for future contingencies, as they may happen; and, as these are illimitable in their nature, it is impossible safely to limit that capacity. It is true, perhaps, that a computation might be made, with sufficient accuracy to answer the purpose of the quantity of revenue, requisite to discharge the subsisting engagements of the Union, and to maintain those establishments, which for some time to come, would suffice in time of peace. But would it be wise, or would it not rather be the extreme of folly, to stop at this point, and to leave the Government entrusted with the care of the National defence, in a state of absolute incapacity to provide for the protection of the community, against future invasions of the public peace, by foreign war, or domestic convulsions? If, on the contrary, we ought to exceed this point, where can we stop, short of an indefinite power of providing for emergencies as they might arise? Though it is easy to assert, in general terms, the possibility of forming a rational judgment of a due provision against probable dangers; yet we may safely challenge those who make the assertion, to bring forward their data, and may affirm, that they would be found as vague and uncertain, as any that could be produced to establish the probable duration of the world. Observations, confined to the mere prospects

of internal attacks, can deserve no weight, though even these will admit of no satisfactory calculation: But if we mean to be a commercial people, it must form a part of our policy, to be able one day to defend that commerce. The support of a navy, and of naval wars must baffle all the efforts of political arithmetic admitting that we ought to try the novel and absurd experiment in politics, of tying up the hands of the Government from offensive war, founded upon reasons of state: Yet, certainly we ought not to disable it from guarding the community against the ambition or enmity of other Nations. A cloud has been for some time hanging over the European world. If it should break forth into a storm, who can insure us, that in its progress, a part of its fury would not be spent upon us? No reasonable man would hastily pronounce that we are entirely out of its reach. Or if the combustible materials that now seem to be collecting, should be dissipated without coming to maturity; or, if a flame should be kindled, without extending to us, what security can we have, that our tranquility will long remain undisturbed from some other cause, or from some other quarter? Let us recollect, that peace or war, will not always be left to our option; that however moderate or unambitious we may be, we cannot count upon the moderation, or hope to extinguish the ambition of others. Who could have imagined, at the conclusion of the last war, that France and Britain, wearied and exhausted as they both were, would so soon have looked with so hostile an aspect upon each other? To judge from the history of mankind, we shall be compelled to conclude, that the fiery and destructive passions of war, reign in the human breast, with much more powerful sway, than the mild and beneficent sentiments of peace; and, that to model our political systems upon speculations of lasting tranquility, is to calculate on the weaker springs of the human character.

What are the chief sources of expence in every Government? What has occasioned that enormous accumulation of debts with which several of the European Nations are oppressed? The answer, plainly is, wars and rebellions—the support of those institutions which are necessary to guard the body politic, against these two most mortal diseases of society. The expences arising from those institutions, which are relative to the mere domestic police of a State—to the support of its Legislative, Executive and Judicial departments, with their different appendages, and to the internal encouragement of agriculture and manufactures, (which will comprehend almost all the objects of State expenditure) are insignificant, in comparison with those which relate to the National defence.

In the kingdom of Great-Britain, where all the ostentatious apparatus of Monarchy is to be provided for, not above a fifteenth part of the annual income of the nation is appropriated to the class of expences last mentioned; the other fourteen fifteenths are absorbed in the payment of the interest of debts, contracted for carrying on the wars in which that country has been engaged, and in the maintenance of fleets and armies. If on the one hand it should be observed, that the expences incurred in the prosecution of the ambitious enterprizes and vain-glorious pursuits of a Monarchy, are not a proper standard by which to judge of those which might be necessary in a republic; it ought on the other hand to be remarked, that there should be as great a disproportion, between the profusion and extravagance of a wealthy kingdom in its domestic administration, and the frugality and oeconomy, which, in that particular, become the modest simplicity of republican Government. If we balance a proper deduction from one side against that which it is supposed ought to be made from the other, the proportion may still be considered as holding good.

But let us advert to the large debt which we have ourselves contracted in a single war, and let us only calculate on a common share of the events which disturb the peace of nations, and we shall instantly perceive without the aid of any elaborate illustration, that there must always be an immense disproportion between the objects of Federal and State expenditures. It is true that several of the States separately are incumbered with considerable debts, which are an excrescence of the late war. But when these are discharged, the only call for revenue of any consequence, which the State Governments will continue to experience, will be for the mere support of their respective civil lists; to which, if we add all contingencies, the total amount in every State, ought not to exceed two hundred thousand pounds.

In framing a Government for posterity as well as ourselves, we ought in those provisions which are designed to be permanent, to calculate not on temporary, but on permanent causes of expence. If this principle be a just one, our attention would be directed to a provision in favor of the State Governments for an annual sum of about 200,000 pounds; while the exigencies of the Union could be susceptible of no limits, even in imagination. In this view of the subject by what logic can it be maintained, that the local Governments ought to command in perpetuity, an EXCLUSIVE SOURCE of revenue for any sum beyond the extent of 200,000 pounds? To extend its power further, in *exclusion* of the authority of the Union, would be to take the resources of the community out of those hands which stood in need of them for the public welfare, in order to put them in other hands, which could have no just or proper occasion for them.

Suppose then the Convention had been inclined to proceed upon the principle of a repartition of the objects of revenue between the Union and its members, in *proportion* to their comparative necessities; what particular fund could have been selected for the use of the States, that would not either have been too much or too little; too little for their present, and too much for their future wants. As to the line of separation between external and internal taxes, this would leave to the States at a rough computation, the command of two thirds of the resources of the community, to defray from a tenth to a twentieth part of its expences, and to the Union, one third of the resources of the community, to defray from nine tenths to nineteen twentieths of its expences. If we desert this boundary, and content ourselves with leaving to the States an exclusive power of taxing houses and lands, there would still be a great disproportion between the *means* and the *end;* the possession of one third of the resources of the community,

to supply at most one tenth of its wants. If any fund could have been selected and appropriated equal to and not greater than the object, it would have been inadequate to the discharge of the existing debts of the particular States, and would have left them dependent on the Union for a provision for this purpose.

The preceeding train of observations will justify the position which has been elsewhere laid down, that, "A CONCURRENT JURISDICTION in the article of taxation, was the only admissible substitute for an entire subordination, in respect to this branch of power, of the State authority to that of the Union." Any separation of the objects of revenue, that could have been fallen upon, would have amounted to a sacrifice of the great INTERESTS of the Union to the POWER of the individual States. The Convention thought the concurrent jurisdiction preferable to that subordination; and it is evident that it has at least the merit of reconciling an indefinite constitutional power of taxation in the Federal Government, with an adequate and independent power in the States to provide for their own necessities. There remain a few other lights, in which this important subject of taxation will claim a further consideration.

13

ALEXANDER HAMILTON, FEDERALIST, NO. 35,
215–18
5 Jan. 1788

Before we proceed to examine any other objections to an indefinite power of taxation in the Union, I shall make one general remark; which is, that if the jurisdiction of the national government in the article of revenue should be restricted to particular objects, it would naturally occasion an undue proportion of the public burthens to fall upon those objects. Two evils would spring from this source, the oppression of particular branches of industry, and an unequal distribution of the taxes, as well among the several States as among the citizens of the same State.

Suppose, as has been contended for, the foederal power of taxation were to be confined to duties on imports, it is evident that the government, for want of being able to command other resources, would frequently be tempted to extend these duties to an injurious excess. There are persons who imagine that this can never be carried to too great a length; since the higher they are, the more it is alleged they will tend to discourage an extravagant consumption, to produce a favourable balance of trade, and to promote domestic manufactures. But all extremes are pernicious in various ways. Exorbitant duties on imported articles would beget a general spirit of smuggling; which is always prejudicial to the fair trader, and eventually to the revenue itself: They tend to render other classes of the community tributary in an improper degree to the manufacturing classes to whom they give a premature monopoly of the markets: They sometimes force industry out of its more natural channels into others in which it flows with less advantage. And in the last place they oppress the merchant, who is often obliged to pay them himself without any retribution from the consumer. When the demand is equal to the quantity of goods at market, the consumer generally pays the duty; but when the markets happen to be overstocked, a great proportion falls upon the merchant, and sometimes not only exhausts his profits, but breaks in upon his capital. I am apt to think that a division of the duty between the seller and the buyer more often happens than is commonly imagined. It is not always possible to raise the price of a commodity, in exact proportion to every additional imposition laid upon it. The merchant especially, in a country of small commercial capital, is often under a necessity of keeping prices down, in order to [make] a more expeditious sale.

The maxim that the consumer is the payer, is so much oftener true than the reverse of the proposition, that it is far more equitable the duties on imports should go into a common stock, than that they should redound to the exclusive benefit of the importing States. But it is not so generally true as to render it equitable that those duties should form the only national fund. When they are paid by the merchant, they operate as an additional tax upon the importing State; whose citizens pay their proportion of them in the character of consumers. In this view they are productive of inequality among the States; which inequality would be encreased with the encreased extent of the duties. The confinement of the national revenues to this species of imposts, would be attended with inequality, from a different cause between the manufacturing and the non-manufacturing States. The States which can go furthest towards the supply of their own wants, by their own manufactures, will not, according to their numbers or wealth, consume so great a proportion of imported articles, as those States which are not in the same favourable situation; they would not therefore in this mode alone contribute to the public treasury in a ratio to their abilities. To make them do this, it is necessary that recourse be had to excises; the proper objects of which are particular kinds of manufactures. New-York is more deeply interested in these considerations than such of her citizens as contend for limiting the power of the Union to external taxation can be aware of—New-York is an importing State, and is not likely speedily to be to any great extent a manufacturing State. She would of course suffer in a double light from restraining the jurisdiction of the Union to commercial imposts.

So far as these observations tend to inculcate a danger of the import duties being extended to an injurious extreme it may be observed, conformably to a remark made in another part of these papers, that the interest of the revenue itself would be a sufficient guard against such an extreme. I readily admit that this would be the case as long as other resources were open; but if the avenues to them were closed HOPE stimulated by necessity would beget experiments fortified by rigorous precautions and additional penalties; which for a time would have the intended effect, till there had been leisure to contrive expedients to elude these new precautions. The first success would be apt to inspire false opinions; which it might require a long course of subsequent experience to correct. Necessity, especially in politics, often occasions false hopes, false reasonings and a system of measures, correspondently erroneous. But even if this supposed excess should not be a consequence of the limitation of the foederal power of taxation the inequalities spoken of would still ensue, though not in the same degree, from the other causes that have been noticed.

14

LUTHER MARTIN, GENUINE INFORMATION
1788
Storing 2.4.55

By the *eighth* section of this article, Congress is to have power to *lay* and *collect taxes, duties, imposts,* and *excises.*— When we met in convention after our adjournment, to receive the report of the committee of detail, the members of that committee were requested to inform us, what powers were meant to be vested in Congress by the word *duties* in this section, since the word *imposts* extended to duties on goods *imported,* and by another part of the system no duties on *exports* were to be laid: In answer to this inquiry we were informed, that it was meant to give the general government the power of laying *stamp* duties on paper, parchment, and vellum. We then proposed to have the power inserted in *express words,* least disputes hereafter might arise on the subject, and that the meaning might be understood by *all* who were to be *affected* by it; but to this it was objected, because it was said that the word stamp would probably sound *odiously* in the ears of many of the inhabitants, and be a cause of objection. By the power of imposing *stamp duties* the Congress will have a *right* to declare, that *no wills, deeds,* or other *instruments* of writing, shall be *good* and *valid,* without being *stamped*—that without being reduced to *writing,* and being *stamped,* no *bargain, sale, transfer of property,* or *contract* of any kind or nature whatsoever shall be *binding;* and also that no *exemplifications of records, depositions,* or *probates* of any kind shall be received in evidence, unless they have the same solemnity—They may likewise oblige all proceedings of a *judicial* nature to be *stamped* to give them effect—Those stamp duties may be imposed to any amount they please, and under the pretence of *securing* the *collection* of these duties, and to prevent the laws which imposed them from being evaded, the Congress may bring the *decision* of all *questions* relating to the *conveyance, disposition* and *rights of property,* and *every question* relating to *contracts* between man and man into the *courts* of the *general government.*— Their *inferior* courts in the *first* instance and the *superior* court by *appeal.* By the power to lay and collect imposts, they may impose duties on any or *every* article of *commerce* imported into these States to what amount they please. By the power to lay *excises,* a power very odious in its nature, since it authorises officers to go into your *houses*, your *kitchens*, your *cellars*, and to examine into your *private concerns*: the Congress may impose *duties* on every *article* of *use* or *consumption*, on the *food* that we *eat*, on the *liquors* we *drink*, on the *clothes* that we *wear*, the *glass* which *enlighten* our *houses*, or the *hearths* necessary for our *warmth* and *comfort*. By the power to lay and collect taxes, they may proceed to *direct taxation* on *every individual* either by a *capitation* tax on their *heads*, or an *assessment* on their *property*. By this part of the section therefore, the government has a power to lay what duties they please on *goods imported*; to lay what duties they please afterwards on whatever we *use* or *consume*; to impose *stamp duties* to what amount they please, and in whatever case they please: afterwards to impose on the people *direct taxes,* by capitation tax, or by assessment, to what amount they choose, and thus to *sluice* them at *every vein* as long as they have a *drop* of blood, without any controul, limitation, or restraint; while *all the officers* for *collecting* these taxes, stamp duties, imposts, and excises, are to be appointed by the *general government,* under its directions, not accountable to the *States;* nor is there *even* a security that they shall be *citizens* of the *respective States,* in which they are to exercise their offices; at the same time the construction of *every* law *imposing* any and all these taxes and duties, and *directing* the collection of them, and *every question* arising thereon, and on the *conduct* of the *officers* appointed to execute these laws, and to collect these taxes and duties so various in their kinds, are *taken away* from the courts of justice of the *different States,* and *confined* to the courts of the *general government,* there is to be *heard* and *determined* by judges holding their offices under the appointment *not* of the *States,* but of the *general government.*

15

OLIVER ELLSWORTH, CONNECTICUT RATIFYING CONVENTION
7 Jan. 1788
Elliot 2:190–97

Mr. President, this is a most important clause in the Constitution; and the gentlemen do well to offer all the objections which they have against it. Through the whole of this debate, I have attended to the objections which have been made against this clause; and I think them all to be unfounded. The clause is general; it gives the general legislature "power to lay and collect taxes, duties, imposts, and excises, to pay the debts and provide for the common defence and general welfare of the United States." There are three objections against this clause—first, that it is too extensive, as it extends to all the objects of taxation; secondly, that it is partial; thirdly, that Congress ought not to have power to lay taxes at all.

The first objection is, that this clause extends to all the objects of taxation. But though it does extend to all, it does not extend to them exclusively. It does not say that Congress shall have all these sources of revenue, and the states none. All, excepting the impost, still lie open to the states. This state owes a debt; it must provide for the payment of it. So do all the other states. This will not escape the attention of Congress. When making calculations to raise a revenue, they will bear this in mind. They will not take away that which is necessary for the states. They are the head, and will take care that the members do not perish. The state debt, which now lies heavy upon us, arose from the want of powers in the federal system. Give the necessary powers to the national government, and the state will not be again necessitated to involve itself in debt for its defence in war. It will lie upon the national government to defend all the states, to defend all its members, from hostile attacks. The United States will bear the whole burden of war. It is necessary that the power of the general legislature should extend to all the objects of taxation, that government should be able to command all the resources of the country; because no man can tell what our exigencies may be. Wars have now become rather wars of the purse than of the sword. Government must therefore be able to command the whole power of the purse; otherwise a hostile nation may look into our Constitution, see what resources are in the power of government, and calculate to go a little beyond us; thus they may obtain a decided superiority over us, and reduce us to the utmost distress. A government which can command but half its resources is like a man with but one arm to defend himself.

The second objection is, that the impost is not a proper mode of taxation; that it is partial to the Southern States. I confess I am mortified when I find gentlemen supposing that their delegates in Convention were inattentive to their duty, and made a sacrifice of the interests of their constituents. If, however, the impost be a partial mode, this circumstance, high as my opinion of it is, would weaken my attachment to it; for I abhor partiality. But I think there are three special reasons why an impost is the best way of raising a national revenue.

The first is, it is the most fruitful and easy way. All nations have found it to be so. Direct taxation can go but little way towards raising a revenue. To raise money in this way, people must be provident; they must constantly be laying up money to answer the demands of the collector. But you cannot make people thus provident. If you would do any thing to the purpose, you must come in when they are spending, and take a part with them. This does not take away the tools of a man's business, or the necessary utensils of his family: it only comes in when he is taking his pleasure, and feels generous; when he is laying out a shilling for superfluities, it takes twopence of it for public use, and the remainder will do him as much good as the whole. I will instance two facts, which show how easily and insensibly a revenue is raised by indirect taxation. I suppose people in general are not sensible that we pay a tax to the state of New York. Yet it is an incontrovertible fact, that we, the people of Connecticut, pay annually into the treasury of New York more than fifty thousand dollars. Another instance I will mention: one of our common river sloops pays in the West Indies a portage bill of £60. This is a tax which foreigners lay upon us, and we pay it; for a duty laid upon our shipping, which transports our produce to foreign markets, sinks the price of our produce, and operates as an effectual tax upon those who till the ground, and bring the fruits of it to market. All nations have seen the necessity and propriety of raising a revenue by indirect taxation, by duties upon articles of consumption. France raises a revenue of twenty-four millions sterling per annum; and it is chiefly in this way. Fifty millions of livres they raise upon the single article of salt. The Swiss cantons raise almost the whole of their revenue upon salt. Those states purchase all the salt which is to be used in the country: they sell it out to the people at an advanced price; the advance is the revenue of the country. In England, the whole public revenue is about twelve millions sterling per annum. The land tax amounts to about two millions; the window and some other taxes, to about two millions more. The other eight millions are raised upon articles of consumption. The whole standing army of Great Britain could not enforce the collection of this vast sum by direct taxation. In Holland, their prodigious taxes, amounting to forty shillings for each inhabitant, are levied chiefly upon articles of consumption. They excise every thing, not excepting even their houses of infamy.

The experiments, which have been made in our own country, show the productive nature of indirect taxes. The imports into the United States amount to a very large sum. They never will be less, but will continue to increase for centuries to come. As the population of our country increases, the imports will necessarily increase. They will increase, because our citizens will choose to be farmers, living independently on their freeholds, rather than to be manufacturers, and work for a groat a day. I find by calculation that a general impost of 5 per cent. would raise the sum of £245,000 per annum, deducting 8 per cent. for the charges of collecting. A further sum might be deducted for smuggling—a business which is too well understood among us, and which is looked upon in too favorable a light. But this loss in the public revenue will be overbalanced by an increase of importations. And a further sum may be reckoned upon some articles which will bear a higher duty than the one recommended by Congress. Rum, instead of 4d. per gallon, may be set higher without any detriment to our health or morals. In England, it pays a duty of 4s. 6d. the gallon. Now, let us compare this source of revenue with our national wants. The interest of the foreign debt is £130,000 lawful money per annum. The expenses of the civil list are £37,000. There are likewise further expenses for maintaining the frontier posts, for the support of those who have been disabled in the service of the Continent, and some other contingencies, amounting, together with the civil list, to £130,000. This sum, added to the interest of the foreign debt, will be £260,000. The consequence follows, that the avails of the impost will pay the interest of the whole foreign debt, and nearly satisfy those current national expenses. But perhaps it will be said that these paper calculations are overdone, and that the real avails will fall far short. Let me point out, then, what has actually been done. In only three of the states, in Massachusetts, New York, and Pennsylvania, 160 or £180,000 per annum have been raised by impost. From this fact, we may certainly conclude that, if a general impost should be laid, it would raise a greater sum than I have calculated. It is a strong argument in favor of an impost, that the collection of it will interfere less with the internal police of the states than any other species of taxation. It does not fill the country with revenue officers, but is confined to the sea-coast, and is chiefly a water operation. Another weighty reason in favor of this branch of the revenue is, if we do not give it to Congress, the individual states will have it. It will give some states an opportunity of oppressing others, and destroy all harmony between them. If we would have the states friendly to each other, let us take away this bone of contention, and place it, as it ought in justice to be placed, in the hands of the general government.

"But," says an honorable gentleman near me, "the impost will be a partial tax; the Southern States will pay but little in comparison with the Northern." I ask, What reason is there for this assertion? Why, says he, we live in a cold climate, and want warming. Do not they live in a hot climate, and want quenching? Until you get as far south as the Carolinas, there is no material difference in the quantity of clothing which is worn. In Virginia, they have the same course of clothing that we have; in Carolina, they have a great deal of cold, raw, chilly weather; even in Georgia, the River Savannah has been crossed upon the ice. And if they do not wear quite as great a quantity of clothing in those states as with us, yet people of rank wear that which is of a much more expensive kind. In these states, we manufacture one half of our clothing, and all our tools of husbandry; in those, they manufacture none, nor ever will. They will not manufacture, because they find it much more profitable to cultivate their lands, which are exceedingly fertile. Hence they import almost every thing, not excepting the carriages in which they ride, the hoes with which they till the ground, and the boots which they wear. If we doubt of the extent of their importations, let us look at their exports. So exceedingly fertile and profitable are their lands, that a hundred large ships are every year loaded with rice and indigo from the single port of Charleston. The rich return of these cargoes of immense value will be all subject to the impost. Nothing is omitted; a duty is to be paid upon the blacks which they import. From Virginia, their exports are valued at a million sterling per annum: the single article of tobacco amounts to seven or eight hundred thousand. How does this come back? Not in money; for the Virginians are poor, to a proverb, in money. They anticipate their crops: they spend faster than they earn: they are ever in debt. Their rich exports return in eatables, in drinkables, and in wearables. All these are subject to the impost. In Maryland, their exports are as great in proportion as those in Virginia. The imports and exports of the Southern States are quite as great in proportion as those of the Northern. Where, then, exists this partiality, which has been objected? It exists nowhere but in the uninformed mind.

But there is one objection, Mr. President, which is broad enough to cover the whole subject. Says the objector, Congress ought not to have power to raise any money at all.

Why? Because they have the power of the sword; and if we give them the power of the purse, they are despotic. But I ask, sir, if ever there were a government without the power of the sword and the purse? This is not a new-coined phrase; but it is misapplied: it belongs to quite another subject. It was brought into use in Great Britain, where they have a king vested with hereditary power. Here, say they, it is dangerous to place the power of the sword and the purse in the hands of one man, who claims an authority independent of the people: therefore we will have a Parliament. But the king and Parliament together, the supreme power of the nation,—they have the sword and the purse. And they must have both; else, how could the country be defended? For the sword without the purse is of no effect: it is a sword in the scabbard. But does it follow, because it is dangerous to give the power of the sword and purse to an hereditary prince, who is independent of the people, that therefore it is dangerous to give it to the Parliament—to Congress, which is your Parliament—to men appointed by yourselves, and dependent upon yourselves? This argument amounts to this: You must cut a man in two in the middle, to prevent his hurting himself.

But, says the honorable objector, if Congress levies money, they must legislate. I admit it. Two legislative powers, says he, cannot legislate in the same place. I ask, Why can they not? It is not enough to say they cannot. I wish for some reason. I grant that both cannot legislate upon the same object at the same time, and carry into effect laws which are contrary to each other. But the Constitution excludes every thing of this kind. Each legislature has its province; their limits may be distinguished. If they will run foul of each other, if they will be trying who has the hardest head, it cannot be helped. The road is broad enough; but if two men will jostle each other, the fault is not in the road. Two several legislatures have in fact existed and acted at the same time in the same territory. It is in vain to say they cannot exist, when they actually have done it. In the time of the war, we had an army. Who made the laws for the army? By whose authority were offenders tried and executed? Congress. By their authority a man was taken, tried, condemned, and hanged, in this very city. He belonged to the army; he was a proper subject of military law; he deserted to the enemy; he deserved his fate. Wherever the army was, in whatever state, there Congress had complete legislative, judicial, and executive power. This very spot where we now are is a city. It has complete legislative, judicial, and executive powers; it is a complete state in miniature. Yet it breeds no confusion, it makes no schism. The city has not eaten up the state, nor the state the city. But if there be a new city, if it have not had time to unfold its principles, I will instance the city of New York, which is, and long has been, an important part of that state; it has been found beneficial; its powers and privileges have not clashed with the state. The city of London contains three or four times as many inhabitants as the whole state of Connecticut. It has extensive powers of government, and yet it makes no interference with the general government of the kingdom. This Constitution defines the extent of the powers of the general govern-ment. If the general legislature should at any time over-leap their limits, the judicial department is a constitutional check. If the United States go beyond their powers, if they make a law which the Constitution does not authorize, it is void; and the judicial power, the national judges, who, to secure their impartiality, are to be made independent, will declare it to be void. On the other hand, if the states go beyond their limits, if they make a law which is a usurpation upon the general government, the law is void; and upright, independent judges will declare it to be so. Still, however, if the United States and the individual states will quarrel, if they want to fight, they may do it, and no frame of government can possibly prevent it. It is sufficient for this Constitution, that, so far from laying them under a necessity of contending, it provides every reasonable check against it. But perhaps, at some time or other, there will be a contest; the states may rise against the general government. If this do take place, if all the states combine, if all oppose, the whole will not eat up the members, but the measure which is opposed to the sense of the people will prove abortive. In republics, it is a fundamental principle that the majority govern, and that the minority comply with the general voice. How contrary, then, to republican principles, how humiliating, is our present situation! A single state can rise up, and put a *veto* upon the most important public measures. We have seen this actually take place. A single state has controlled the general voice of the Union; a minority, a very small minority, has governed us. So far is this from being consistent with republican principles, that it is, in effect, the worst species of monarchy.

Hence we see how necessary for the Union is a coercive principle. No man pretends the contrary: we all see and feel this necessity. The only question is, Shall it be a coercion of law, or a coercion of arms? There is no other possible alternative. Where will those who oppose a coercion of law come out? Where will they end? A necessary consequence of their principles is a war of the states one against the other. I am for coercion by law—that coercion which acts only upon delinquent individuals. This Constitution does not attempt to coerce sovereign bodies, states, in their political capacity. No coercion is applicable to such bodies, but that of an armed force. If we should attempt to execute the laws of the Union by sending an armed force against a delinquent state, it would involve the good and bad, the innocent and guilty, in the same calamity.

But this legal coercion singles out the guilty individual, and punishes him for breaking the laws of the Union. All men will see the reasonableness of this; they will acquiesce, and say, Let the guilty suffer.

How have the morals of the people been depraved for the want of an efficient government, which might establish justice and righteousness! For the want of this, iniquity has come in upon us like an overflowing flood. If we wish to prevent this alarming evil, if we wish to protect the good citizen in his right, we must lift up the standard of justice; we must establish a national government, to be enforced by the equal decisions of law, and the peaceable arm of the magistrate.

16

DEBATE IN VIRGINIA RATIFYING CONVENTION
5–7, 11–12 June 1788

Elliot 3:57–58, 95–96, 98–100, 114–23, 128–29, 250–55, 263–66, 299–301

[5 June]

[Mr. HENRY:] In this scheme of energetic government, the people will find two sets of tax-gatherers—the state and the federal sheriffs. This, it seems to me, will produce such dreadful oppression as the people cannot possibly bear. The federal sheriff may commit what oppression, make what distresses, he pleases, and ruin you with impunity; for how are you to tie his hands? Have you any sufficiently decided means of preventing him from sucking your blood by speculations, commissions, and fees? Thus thousands of your people will be most shamefully robbed: our state sheriffs, those unfeeling blood-suckers, have, under the watchful eye of our legislature, committed the most horrid and barbarous ravages on our people. It has required the most constant vigilance of the legislature to keep them from totally ruining the people; a repeated succession of laws has been made to suppress their iniquitous speculations and cruel extortions; and as often has their nefarious ingenuity devised methods of evading the force of those laws: in the struggle they have generally triumphed over the legislature.

It is a fact that lands have been sold for five shillings, which were worth one hundred pounds: if sheriffs, thus immediately under the eye of our state legislature and judiciary, have dared to commit these outrages, what would they not have done if their masters had been at Philadelphia or New York? If they perpetrate the most unwarrantable outrage on your person or property, you cannot get redress on this side of Philadelphia or New York; and how can you get it there? If your domestic avocations could permit you to go thither, there you must appeal to judges sworn to support this Constitution, in opposition to that of any state, and who may also be inclined to favor their own officers. When these harpies are aided by excisemen, who may search, at any time, your houses, and most secret recesses, will the people bear it? If you think so, you differ from me. Where I thought there was a possibility of such mischiefs, I would grant power with a niggardly hand; and here there is a strong probability that these oppressions shall actually happen. I may be told that it is safe to err on that side, because such regulations may be made by Congress as shall restrain these officers, and because laws are made by our representatives, and judged by righteous judges: but, sir, as these regulations may be made, so they may not; and many reasons there are to induce a belief that they will not. I shall therefore be an infidel on that point till the day of my death.

[6 June]

[Mr. MADISON:] But the honorable member has satirized, with peculiar acrimony, the powers given to the general government by this Constitution. I conceive that the first question on this subject is, whether these powers be necessary; if they be, we are reduced to the dilemma of either submitting to the inconvenience or losing the Union. Let us consider the most important of these reprobated powers; that of direct taxation is most generally objected to. With respect to the exigencies of government, there is no question but the most easy mode of providing for them will be adopted. When, therefore, direct taxes are not necessary, they will not be recurred to. It can be of little advantage to those in power to raise money in a manner oppressive to the people. To consult the conveniences of the people will cost them nothing, and in many respects will be advantageous to them. Direct taxes will only be recurred to for great purposes. What has brought on other nations those immense debts, under the pressure of which many of them labor? Not the expenses of their governments, but war. If this country should be engaged in war,—and I conceive we ought to provide for the possibility of such a case,—how would it be carried on? By the usual means provided from year to year? As our imports will be necessary for the expenses of government and other common exigencies, how are we to carry on the means of defence? How is it possible a war could be supported without money or credit? And would it be possible for a government to have credit without having the power of raising money? No; it would be impossible for any government, in such a case, to defend itself. Then, I say, sir, that it is necessary to establish funds for extraordinary exigencies, and to give this power to the general government; for the utter inutility of previous requisitions on the states is too well known. Would it be possible for those countries, whose finances and revenues are carried to the highest perfection, to carry on the operations of government on great emergencies, such as the maintenance of a war, without an uncontrolled power of raising money? Has it not been necessary for Great Britain, notwithstanding the facility of the collection of her taxes, to have recourse very often to this and other extraordinary methods of procuring money? Would not her public credit have been ruined, if it was known that her power to raise money was limited? Has not France been obliged, on great occasions, to use unusual means to raise funds? It has been the case in many countries, and no government can exist unless its powers extend to make provisions for every contingency. If we were actually attacked by a powerful nation, and our general government had not the power of raising money, but depended solely on requisitions, our condition would be truly deplorable: if the revenue of this commonwealth were to depend on twenty distinct authorities, it would be impossible for it to carry on its operations. This must be obvious to every member here; I think, therefore, that it is necessary, for the preservation of the Union, that this power shall be given to the general government.

. . . . .

[Mr. NICHOLAS:] We are, in the next place, frightened by two sets of collectors, who, he tells us, will oppress us with impunity. The amount of the sums to be raised of the people is the same, whether the state legislatures lay the taxes for themselves, or for the general government; whether each of them lays and collects taxes for its own exclusive purposes; the manner of raising it only is different. So far as the amount of the imposts may exceed that of the present collections, so much will the burdens of the people be less. Money cannot be raised in a more judicious manner than by imposts; it is not felt by the people; it is a mode which is practised by many nations: nine tenths of the revenues of Great Britain and France are raised by indirect taxes; and were they raised by direct taxes, they would be exceedingly oppressive. At present, the reverse of this proposition holds in this country; for very little is raised by indirect taxes.

The public treasuries are supplied by means of direct taxes, which are not so easy for the people. But the people will be benefited by this change. Suppose the imposts will only operate a reduction of one fifth of the public burdens; then, sir, out of every ten shillings we have now to pay, we shall only have to pay eight shillings: and suppose this to be apportioned so that we pay four shillings to the federal and four shillings to the state collector,—what inconvenience or oppression can arise from it? Would this be as oppressive as the payment of ten shillings to the state collector? Our constituents do not suspect our delegates to the state legislature, but we suspect the members of the future Congress.

But, sir, they tell us this power of direct taxation ought not to be intrusted to the general government, because its members cannot be acquainted with the local situation of the people. Where do the members of the state legislatures get their information? It is by their own experience, and intercourse with the people. Cannot those of the general government derive information from every source from which the state representatives get theirs, so as to enable them to impose taxes judiciously? We have the best security we can wish for: if they impose taxes on the people which are oppressive, they subject themselves and their friends to the same inconvenience, and to the certainty of never being confided in again. And what will be the consequence of laying taxes on improper objects? Will the funds be increased by it? By no means. I may venture to say, the amount of the taxes will diminish in proportion to the difficulty and impropriety of the mode of levying them. What advantage, then, would it be to the members of Congress to render the collection of taxes oppressive to the people? They would be certainly out of their senses to oppress the people without any prospect of emolument to themselves.

[7 June]

[Mr. RANDOLPH:] Is it necessary that the legislative power of the United States should be authorized to levy taxes? A strange question to be agitated in this house, after hearing the delinquency of other states, and even of Virginia herself! Money is the nerve—the life and soul of a government. It is the utmost folly to say that a government could be carried on without this great agent of human affairs. Wars cannot be carried on without a full and uncontrolled discretionary power to raise money in an eligible manner. Nay, sir, government cannot be administered in time of peace without this power. For how is it to be done? It is needless to impress any further on the minds of the gentlemen who hear me the necessity of this power in governments. If so, ought the general government to be more circumscribed in the power of providing for its own safety and existence than any other government? Ought it to depend for the means of its preservation on other bodies? This is actually the case with the Confederation. The power of raising money was nominally vested in that system. In March, 1781, even Maryland, the most backward state then, conceded that Congress should have the power of receiving and demanding their proportionate quotas of the states. This was an acknowledgment of the necessity of vesting a power in Congress to raise such sums as emergencies might require; but the means which were proposed have been found inadequate to compass the end: the propriety of the means is alone disputed. No doubt it is the universal opinion of the people of this commonwealth, that its legislature should have the power of raising money at its own will and pleasure. There are two ways whereby this may be effected—by requisitions, or taxation: there is no other manner; for it surpasses the ingenuity of man to devise any other mode of raising money than by one of these two methods. If the alternative of requisitions be determined upon, as more eligible, it will not avail without coercion. If that of taxation be preferred, it will be sufficient without any coercion. If our legislature were to depend on requisitions for money to answer the ends of government, then, sir, the absurdity and sophistry of the arguments urged in defence of such a mode of procuring money would strike the weakest intellect. If the mere pleasure of individuals were alone to be consulted, if it were left to the choice of your people to pay or not, your treasury would be much poorer than it is; and the advocates of this pernicious policy would perhaps be ashamed of their pertinacity. Suppose, for a moment, the only existing mode of raising a revenue in Virginia to be that of requisitions; suppose your requisitions sent on to every county; say that money is wanted; assume the most pressing language—"We earnestly entreat you; we humbly supplicate and solicit you would furnish us with one thousand or one hundred pounds, to defray the necessary charges of our government!" What would be the result of such applications for voluntary contributions? You would be laughed at for your folly, for thinking human nature could be thus operated upon. From my knowledge of human nature, and of my countrymen, I am perfectly certain this would be the case. The argument will be found good in all cases; it will admit of any extension. I ask any gentleman in this house, if states would comply with what even a few individuals would refuse? Would not the requisitions of Congress meet a similar fate? This, sir, has as often happened as it has been the pleasure of the states to withhold the quotas. Not a shilling has been put into the Continental treasury but with the utmost reluctance. The probable delinquency of other states has been the pretext of noncompliance, with every state. It has been thought hard that our General Assembly should pay when Congress ordered us. Our representatives have been supposed careless of our interest in paying the demands of Congress, while delinquencies happened in other states. Punctuality, sir, instead of being held in that estimation which it really merits, has been looked upon as an improvident expenditure of the substance of the people, and a subjection of the inhabitants to grievances and burdens to which the people of delinquent states were not exposed. This idea has been held in many states, and would hold again. Whosoever depends on the mere right to demand their respective proportions of the states, shows a total ignorance of human actions, and betrays an unacquaintance with the principles of sure policy. The principal ends of all political institutions are the happiness and safety of the community; but a reliance on congressional requisitions would leave the country exposed and open to those who should choose to invade us, or lead to such sedition and confusion among ourselves as must subvert and destroy every object of human society. If requisitions be not faithfully complied with, military coercion seems necessary: coercion, judiciously and moderately used, is proper; but, if severely and cruelly inflicted, begets unconquerable aversion and hatred. If the spirit of resentment actuates individuals, will not states be equally vindictive? What species of military coercion could the general government adopt for the enforcement of obedience to its demands? Either an army sent into the heart of a delinquent state, or blocking up its ports. Have we lived to this, then, that, in order to suppress and exclude tyranny, it is necessary to render the most affectionate friends the most bitter enemies?—set the father against the son, and make the brother slay the brother? Is this the happy expedient that is to preserve liberty? Will it not destroy it? If an army be once introduced to force us, if once marched into Virginia, figure to yourself what the dreadful consequence will be: the most lamentable civil war must ensue. Have we any troops but militia to confront those disciplined bands that would be sent to force our compliance with requisitions? The most virulent railings are vented against the federal executive. We are told that the President can fix himself in the chair of state, establish himself as a monarch, and destroy the liberties of the people.

It has too often happened that powers delegated for the purpose of promoting the happiness of a community have been perverted to the advancement of the personal emoluments of the agents of the people; but the powers of the President are too well guarded and checked to warrant this illiberal aspersion. Let us candidly consider the consequences of the favorite plan of requisitions, and see whether, instead of imaginary or problematical, there be not real, palpable dangers. To compel your obedience, a rapacious army will penetrate into the bosom of your country, carrying destruction and desolation before it. The commander of such an army will be liable to the corruptions and passions incident to other men. If he be possessed of military genius, address, and ambition, he may

procure this army to proclaim him king. Who can tell the result? Who can oppose him with success? Who can say to him, Sir, you shall not be a despot! The reasoning, however inconclusive or illogical it may appear to some, is, in my estimation, more accurate than arguments drawn from the possibility of a President's becoming a tyrant.

Mr. Chairman, I should object to the so-much-admired alternative of gentlemen, were there no other reason than the danger of an army to enforce requisitions, and the danger of its general becoming our master. I will not mention those nations that might be applied to for aid in such a case: it could easily be procured, but the remedy would be worse than the disease. I speak with respect to Virginia alone. Suppose our trade was to be taken into the hands of Congress; they would find little to satisfy their demands. If permitted by other nations, the compensation they could derive from the exclusive control of our trade would be but trivial. Great Britain, France, and Holland, are intimately concerned to carry on trade with us: those nations would disapprove of the measure; and such evasions would be practised on such an occasion as would render it totally ineffectual. If Congress were then to block up our ports, or send an army into our country, Virginia would be in such a horrid situation as would induce her to call for the aid of foreign nations: they have their eyes fixed on us; they watch every opportunity to avail themselves of our divisions. It is their interest we should be weak and divided. Any of them would readily engage in our dissensions; none of them would be displeased at our distractions. But what would be their object in assisting us? On what principles have auxiliaries ever been sent to the aid of a country? Show me an instance (except the conduct of France to America) where auxiliaries have not either attempted or actually made themselves masters of those they assisted. With respect to France, her magnanimity to America is almost unprecedented. She has displayed a degree of disinterestedness and generosity not often exemplified in the annals of mankind. Till France joined us, our troops were not able to withstand the enemy. Yet the fate of many other nations ought to convince us that the assistance of foreigners is the most dangerous and the last experiment that ought to be recurred to. Yet the predilection for retaining the power of direct taxation is not to be overcome.

An expedient, proposed by a gentleman whom I do not now see in the house, (Mr. George Mason,) is, that this power shall be only given to the general government as an alternative after requisitions shall have been refused. The most positive requisitions will be unavailable, and failure will produce war. A formal refusal, or negligent non-compliance with the demands of Congress, under a knowledge of the existence of this execrated alternative, would be a prelude to active opposition. I consider this expedient very little better than the ineffectual mode of simple requisitions. The only difference is, that it gives a little more time to a refractory state to provide itself with arms and foreign alliance, to enable it to oppose the operation of this alternative, and resist federal collectors, as was observed by the honorable gentleman in the chair. The proper time will be picked for the commencement of opposition, and for putting the bayonet to the breasts of their fellow-citizens. Suppose a requisition to be made on Virginia for two hundred thousand pounds: she fails to comply: taxes are then to be collected in the common manner. Is it not probable that the aversion to the exercise of this power by the general government will incite discontented minds to oppose it? Then, sir, the dogs of war are to be let loose, and inconceivable mischief to ensue. If the inability of the people requires an extension of the time of payment, let them be indulged as far as may be consistent with a regard for the public exigencies; but let us not be so infatuated as to choose an expedient which must either be inadequate to the destined purpose, or eventuate in bloodshed and war. Requisitions, sir, however modified, must come within this description; they strike me with horror and disgust. I would as soon see a separation from the Union, and trust to the genius, patriotism, vigilance, and activity—to the morals and natural uprightness—of the people, as ask a government with no other powers than those whereof our present system is possessed. This is an improvement on that system; and if we reject it, we are ruined.

Our credit is depressed and irretrievably gone, without a change of that system which has caused its depression. It is humiliating and disgraceful to recur to loans, situated as we are. It is ruinous on any condition on which our credit could be competent to obtain them; though, under a regular, judicious system of administration, they may be very salutary and beneficial. If some accounts be believed, your ambassador has received from the king of France those stipends which have supported him. Is this honorable? Is it safe for America? Safety, sir, forbids so dishonorable and despicable a conduct as to leave our representatives in a state of absolute dependence on another power. Will not this situation be freely and forcibly represented to him?— "Remember, sir, the bread you eat to-morrow depends on the bounty of the Count de Vergennes!" Is it possible that, in our present circumstances, we can inspire any one with confidence in our engagements? Where, in the hour of distress and calamity, shall Congress be able to borrow money? The present revenues are appropriate to different purposes, and are, from the incompetency of requisitions, inadequate to the public exigencies. Admitting the impost will be sufficiently productive to enable Congress to discharge its engagements, and answer all the demands of government, in case of a war, will not necessity and the fear of danger render it necessary for the general government to divert the revenues, from the usual appropriations, to the defence of the Union? The necessity of such a diversion does not lessen the certainty that the public credit would be destroyed by it. The interest on the public debt could not be paid; foreign and domestic creditors would be disappointed and irritated; and the displeasure of the former might lead to the most serious consequences. What could the general government do, in such a situation, without the power of providing money by taxation? Requisitions would be fruitless and ineffectual; nor could a government, which depended on such a slender and inefficient force, meet with credulity enough any where to trust it. Will you expose the Continental Congress to such a critical distress? Do you consult public liberty by reducing it to an extremity, whereof none can with certainty foretell the dangerous consequences? Is it not laying a train by which liberty is to be blown up? By withholding a necessary power, you may unwarily lay the foundation of usurpation itself.

I conclude with my firm belief, that I show my friendship for Virginia more steadfastly by discarding these requisitions, than by any proposition I could suggest.

The benefits arising from loans are innumerable. Every nation, even the most wealthy and the oldest nations, have found it necessary to recur to loans in time of war. This country has found it so even in time of peace; but on a supposition of war, we *must* borrow money. It will be inevitable. How can Congress have credit to borrow any sum to a considerable amount, on any reasonable conditions, unless it have full scope and complete command over the resources of the Union? Whatever may be the visionary and fanciful conclusions of political skeptics, the credit of a nation will be found to be coëxtensive with its ability. If Congress have an uncontrolled power to raise money as contingencies may render it necessary, it can borrow with ease; but if it have not this power, it is not possible that any confidence can be put in it.

The difficulty of justly apportioning the taxes among the states, under the present system, has been complained of; the rule of apportionment being the value of all lands and improvements within the states. The inequality between the rich lands of James River and the barrens of Massachusetts has been thought to militate against Virginia. If taxes could be laid according to the real value, no inconvenience could follow; but, from a variety of reasons, this value was very difficult to be ascertained; and an error in the estimation must necessarily have been oppressive to a part of the community. But in this new Constitution, there is a more just and equitable rule fixed—a limitation beyond which they cannot go. Representatives and taxes go hand in hand: according to the one will the other be regulated. The number of representatives is determined by the number of inhabitants; they have nothing to do but to lay taxes accordingly. I will illustrate it by a familiar example. At present, before the population is actually numbered, the number of representatives is sixty-five. Of this number, Virginia has a right to send ten; consequently she will have to pay ten parts out of sixty-five parts of any sum that may be necessary to be raised by Congress. This, sir, is the line. Can Congress go beyond the bounds prescribed in the Constitution? Has Congress a power to say that she shall pay fifteen parts out of sixty-five parts? Were they to assume such a power, it would be a usurpation so glaring, that rebellion would be the immediate consequence. Congress is only to say on what subject the tax is to be laid. It is a matter of very little consequence how it will be imposed, since it must be clearly laid on the most productive article in each particular state. I am surprised that such strong objections should have been made to, and such fears and alarms excited by, this power of direct taxation, since experience shows daily that it is neither inconvenient nor oppressive. A collector goes to a man's house; the man pays him with freedom, or makes an apology for his inability to do it then: at a future day, if payment be not made, distress is made, and acquiesced in by the party. What difference is there between this and a tax imposed by Congress? Is it not done by lawful authority? The distinction is between a Virginian and Continental authority. Yet, in both cases, it is imposed by ourselves, through the medium of our representatives. When a tax will come to be laid by Congress, the collector will apply in like manner, and in the same manner receive payment, or an apology; at a future day, likewise, the same consequences will result from a failure. I presume, sir, there is a manifest similarity between the two cases. When gentlemen complain of the novelty, they ought to advert to the singular one that must be the consequence of the requisitions—an army sent into your country to force you to comply. Will not this be the dissolution of the Union, if ever it takes effect? Let us be candid on this subject: let us see if the criterion here fixed be not equal and just. Were the tax laid on one uniform article through the Union, its operation would be oppressive on a considerable part of the people. When any sum is necessary for the general government, every state will immediately know its exact proportion of it, from the number of their people and representatives; nor can it be doubted that the tax will be laid on each state, in the manner that will best accommodate the people of such state, as thereby it will be raised with more facility; for an oppressive mode can never be so productive as the most easy for the people.

The system under consideration is objected to in an unconnected and irregular manner: detached parts are attacked without considering the whole: this, sir, is disingenuous and unreasonable. Ask if the powers be unnecessary. If the end proposed can be obtained by any other means, the powers may be unnecessary. Infallibility was not arrogated by the Convention: they included in the system those powers they thought necessary. If you do not think the ceding those powers indispensable, never give them up. But, I trust, this power of imposing direct taxes has been proved to be essential to the very existence of the Union. The advocates for the national government, circumstanced as they are, with the accession of so many states, never will give their assent to leave it in the power of the states to sacrifice the Union. It has been observed, by an honorable gentleman over the way, (Mr. George Mason,) that there could not be a fellow-feeling between the national representatives and their constituents, and that oppression must be inseparable from their exercise of the power of imposing taxes. I beg leave to remind you of a similar complaint made on a similar occasion. I allude to the Scotch union. If gentlemen cast their eyes to that period, they will find there an instructive similitude between our circumstances and the situation of those people. The advocates for a union with England declared that it would be a foundation of lasting peace, remove all jealousies between them, increase their strength and riches, and enable them to resist more effectually the efforts of the Pretender. These were irresistible arguments, one would be inclined to believe; arguments a priori, which challenge conviction, and which appear perfectly conclusive, since now verified by actual events. Yet the opposers of that union declaimed that the independence of Scotland was

gone; that the peerage of Scotland was degraded; that the people of England would alone be gainers; and that the people of Scotland would be the losers. How are the facts? Both kingdoms have derived great benefits from that union, and the predictions of the advocates for that union have been fully verified. The arguments used on that occasion apply with more cogency to our situation.

. . . . .

Mr. MADISON. Mr. Chairman, in considering this great subject, I trust we shall find that part which gives the general government the power of laying and collecting taxes indispensable, and essential to the existence of any efficient or well-organized system of government: if we consult reason, and be ruled by its dictates, we shall find its justification there: if we review the experience we have had, or contemplate the history of nations, here we find ample reasons to prove its expediency. There is little reason to depend for necessary supplies on a body which is fully possessed of the power of witholding them. If a government depends on other governments for its revenues— if it must depend on the voluntary contributions of its members—its existence must be precarious. A government which relies on thirteen independent sovereignties for the means of its existence, is a solecism in theory and a mere nullity in practice. Is it consistent with reason that such a government can promote the happiness of any people? It is subversive of every principle of sound policy, to trust the safety of a community with a government totally destitute of the means of protecting itself or its members. Can Congress, after the repeated unequivocal proofs it has experienced of the utter inutility and inefficacy of requisitions, reasonably expect that they would be hereafter effectual or productive? Will not the same local interests, and other causes, militate against a compliance? Whoever hopes the contrary must ever be disappointed. The effect, sir, cannot be changed without a removal of the cause. Let each county in this commonwealth be supposed free and independent; let your revenues depend on requisitions of proportionate quotas from them; let application be made to them repeatedly:—is it to be presumed that they would comply, or that an adequate collection could be made from partial compliances? It is now difficult to collect the taxes from them: how much would that difficulty be enhanced, were you to depend solely on their generosity! I appeal to the reason of every gentleman here, whether he is not persuaded that the present Confederation is as feeble as the government of Virginia would be in that case: to the same reason I appeal, whether it be compatible with prudence to continue a government of such manifest and palpable debility.

[11 June]

[Mr. MADISON:] The expedient proposed by the gentlemen opposed to this clause is, that requisitions shall be made, and, if not complied with in a certain time, that then taxation shall be recurred to. I am clearly convinced that, whenever requisitions shall be made, they will disappoint those who put their trust in them. One reason to prevent the concurrent exertions of all the states, will arise from the suspicion, in some states, of delinquency in others. States will be governed by the motives that actuate individuals.

When a tax is in operation in a particular state, every citizen, if he knows the energy of the laws to enforce payment, and that every other citizen is performing his duty, will cheerfully discharge his duty; but were it known that the citizens of one district were not performing their duty, and that it was left to the policy of the government to make them come up with it, the other districts would be very supine and careless in making provisions for payment. Our own experience makes the illustration more natural. If requisitions be made on thirteen different states, when one deliberates on the subject, she will know that all the rest will deliberate upon it also. This, sir, has been a principal cause of the inefficacy of requisitions heretofore, and will hereafter produce the same evil. If the legislatures are to deliberate on this subject, (and the honorable gentleman opposed to this clause thinks their deliberation necessary,) is it not presumable that they will consider peculiar local circumstances? In the general council, on the contrary, the sense of all America would be drawn to a single point. The collective interest of the Union at large will be known and pursued. No local views will be permitted to operate against the general welfare. But when propositions would come before a particular state, there is every reason to believe that qualifications of the requisitions would be proposed; compliance might be promised, and some instant remittances might be made. This will cause delays, which, in the first instance, will produce disappointment. This also will make failures everywhere else. This, I hope, will be considered with the attention it deserves. The public creditors will be disappointed, and more pressing. Requisitions will be made for purposes equally pervading all America; but the exertions to make compliances will probably be not uniform in the states. If requisitions be made for future occasions, for putting the states in a state of military defence, or to repel an invasion, will the exertions be uniform and equal in all the states? Some parts of the United States are more exposed than others. Will the least exposed states exert themselves equally? We know that the most exposed will be the more immediately interested, and will make less sacrifices in making exertions. I beg gentlemen to consider that this argument will apply with most effect to the states which are most defenceless and exposed. The Southern States are most exposed, whether we consider their situation, or the smallness of their population. And there are other circumstances which render them still more vulnerable, which do not apply to the Northern States. They are therefore more interested in giving the government a power to command the whole strength of the Union in cases of emergency. Do not gentlemen conceive this mode of obtaining supplies from the states will keep alive animosities between the general government and particular states? Where the chances of failures are so numerous as thirteen, by the thirteen states, disappointment in the first place, and consequent animosity, must inevitably take place.

Let us consider the alternatives proposed by gentlemen, instead of the power of laying direct taxes. After the states shall have refused to comply, weigh the consequences of the exercise of this power by Congress. When it comes in the form of a punishment, great clamors will be raised among the people against the government; hatred will be excited against it. It will be considered as an ignominious stigma on the state. It will be considered, at least, in this light by the state where the failure is made, and these sentiments will no doubt be diffused through the other states. Now, let us consider the effect, if collectors are sent where the state governments refuse to comply with requisitions. It is too much the disposition of mankind not to stop at one violation of duty. I conceive that every requisition that will be made on my part of America will kindle a contention between the delinquent member and the general government. Is there no reason to suppose divisions in the government (for seldom does any thing pass with unanimity) on the subject of requisitions? The parts least exposed will oppose those measures which may be adopted for the defence of the weakest parts. Is there no reason to presume that the representatives from the delinquent state will be more likely to foster disobedience to the requisitions of the government than study to recommend them to the public?

There is, in my opinion, another point of view in which this alternative will produce great evil. I will suppose, what is very probable, that partial compliances will be made. A difficulty here arises which fully demonstrates its impolicy. If a part be paid, and the rest withheld, how is the general government to proceed? They are to impose a tax; but how shall it be done in this case? Are they to impose it, by way of punishment, on those who have paid, as well as those who have not? All these considerations taken into view (for they are not visionary or fanciful speculations) will, perhaps, produce this consequence: The general government, to avoid those disappointments which I first described, and to avoid the contentions and embarrassments which I last described, will, in all probability, throw the public burdens on those branches of revenue which will be more in their power. They will be continually necessitated to augment the imposts. If we throw a disproportion of the burdens on that side, shall we not discourage commerce and suffer many political evils? Shall we not increase that disproportion on the Southern States, which for some time will operate against us? The Southern States, from having fewer manufactures, will import and consume more. They will therefore pay more of the imposts. The more commerce is burdened, the more the disproportion will operate against them. If direct taxation be mixed with other taxes, it will be in the power of the general government to lessen that inequality. But this inequality will be increased to the utmost extent, if the general government have not this power.

There is another point of view in which this subject affords us instruction. The imports will decrease in time of war. The honorable gentleman who spoke yesterday said that the imposts would be so productive that there would be no occasion of laying taxes. I will submit two observations to him and the committee. First, in time of war, the imposts will be less; and as I hope we are considering a government for a perpetual duration, we ought to provide for every future contingency. At present, our importations bear a full proportion to the full amount of our sales, and to the number of our inhabitants; but when we have inhabitants enough, our imposts will decrease, and as the national demands will increase with our population, our resources will increase as our wants increase. The other consideration which I will submit on this part of the subject is this: I believe that it will be found, in practice, that those who fix the public burdens will feel a greater degree of responsibility, when they are to impose them on the citizens immediately than if they were to say what sum should be paid by the states. If they exceed the limits of propriety, universal discontent and clamor will arise. Let us suppose they were to collect the taxes from the citizens of America; would they not consider their circumstances? Would they not attentively consider what could be done by the citizens at large? Were they to exceed, in their demands, what were reasonable burdens, the people would impute it to the right source, and look on the imposers as odious.

When I consider the nature of the various objections brought against this clause, I should be led to think that the difficulties were such that gentlemen would not be able to get over them, and that the power, as defined in the plan of the Convention, was impracticable. I shall trouble them with a few observations on that point.

It has been said that ten men deputed from this state, and others in proportion from other states, will not be able to adjust direct taxes, so as to accommodate the various citizens in thirteen states.

I confess I do not see the force of this observation. Could not ten intelligent men, chosen from ten districts from this state, lay direct taxes on a few objects in the most judicious manner? It is to be conceived that they would be acquainted with the situation of different citizens of this country. Can any one divide this state into ten districts so as not to contain men of sufficient information? Could not one man of knowledge be found in a district? When thus selected, will they not be able to carry their knowledge into the general council? I may say, with great propriety, that the experience of our own legislature demonstrates the competency of Congress to lay taxes wisely. Our Assembly consists of considerably more than a hundred; yet, from the nature of the business, it devolves on a much smaller number. It is, through their sanction, approved of by all the others. It will be found that there are seldom more than ten men who rise to high information on this subject. Our federal representatives, as has been said by the gentleman, (Mr. Marshall,) who entered into the subject with a great deal of ability, will get information from the state governments. They will be perfectly well informed of the circumstances of the people of the different states, and the mode of taxation that would be most convenient for them, from the laws of the states. In laying taxes, they may even refer to the state system of taxation. Let it not be forgotten that there is a probability that that ignorance which is complained of in some parts of America will be continually diminishing. Let us compare the degree of knowledge which the people had in time past to their present infor-

mation. Does not our own experience teach us that the people are better informed than they were a few years ago? The citizen of Georgia knows more now of the affairs of New Hampshire, than he did, before the revolution, of those of South Carolina. When the representatives from the different states are collected together, to consider this subject, they will interchange their knowledge with one another, and will have the laws of each state on the table. Besides this, the intercourse of the states will be continually increasing. It is now much greater than before the revolution. My honorable friend over the way, (Mr. Monroe,) yesterday, seemed to conceive, as an insuperable objection, that, if land were made the particular object of taxation, it would be unjust, as it would exonerate the commercial part of the community; that, if it were laid on trade, it would be unjust, in discharging the landholders; and that any exclusive selection would be unequal and unfair. If the general government were tied down to one object, I confess the objection would have some force in it. But if this be not the case, it can have no weight. If it should have a general power of taxation, they could select the most proper objects, and distribute the taxes in such a manner as that they should fall in a due degree on every member of the community. They will be limited to fix the proportion of each state, and they must raise it in the most convenient and satisfactory manner to the public.

. . . . .

[Mr. MASON:] That unconditional power of taxation which is given to that government cannot but oppress the people. If, instead of this, a conditional power of taxation be given, in case of refusal to comply with requisitions, the same end will be answered with convenience to the people. This will not lessen the power of Congress; we do not want to lessen the power of Congress unnecessarily. This will produce moderation in the demand, and will prevent the ruinous exercise of that power by those who know not our situation. We shall then have that mode of taxation which is the most easy, and least oppressive to the people, because it will be exercised by those who are acquainted with their condition and circumstances. This, sir, is the great object we wish to secure—that our people should be taxed by those who have a fellow-feeling for them. I think I can venture to assert that the general government will lay such taxes as are the easiest and the most productive in the collection. This is natural and probable.

For example, they may lay a poll tax. This is simply and easily collected, but is of all taxes the most grievous. Why the most grievous? Because it falls light on the rich, and heavy on the poor. It is most oppressive: for if the rich man is taxed, he can only retrench his superfluities; but the consequence to the poor man is, that it increases his miseries. That they will lay the most simple taxes, and such as are easiest to collect, is highly probable, nay, almost absolutely certain. I shall take the liberty, on this occasion, to read you a letter, which will show, at least as far as opinion goes, what sort of taxes will be most probably laid on us, if we adopt this Constitution. It was the opinion of a gentleman of information. It will in some degree establish the fallacy of those reports which have been circulated through the country, and which induced a great many poor, ignorant people to believe that the taxes were to be lessened by the adoption of the proposed government.

[Here Mr. Mason read a letter from Mr. Robert Morris, financier of the United States, to Congress, wherein he spoke of the propriety of laying the following taxes for the use of the United States; viz., six shillings on every hundred acres of land, six shillings per poll, and ninepence per gallon on all spirituous liquors distilled in the country. Mr. Mason declared that he did not mean to make the smallest reflection on Mr. Morris, but introduced his letter to show what taxes would probably be laid.]

He then continued: This will at least show that such taxes were in agitation, and were strongly advocated by a considerable part of Congress. I have read this letter to show that they will lay taxes most easy to be collected, without any regard to our convenience; so that, instead of amusing ourselves with a diminution of our taxes, we may rest assured that they will be increased. But my principal reason for introducing it was, to show that taxes would be laid by those who are not acquainted with our situation, and that the agents of the collection may be consulted upon the most productive and simple mode of taxation. The gentleman who wrote this letter had more information on this subject than we have; but this will show gentlemen that we are not to be eased of taxes. Any of those taxes which have been pointed out by this financier as the most eligible, will be ruinous and unequal, and will be particularly oppressive on the poorest part of the people.

As to a poll tax, I have already spoken of its iniquitous operation, and need not say much of it, because it is so generally disliked in this state, that we were obliged to abolish it last year. As to a land tax, it will operate most unequally. The man who has one hundred acres of the richest land will pay as little as a man who has one hundred acres of the poorest land. Near Philadelphia, or Boston, an acre of land is worth one hundred pounds; yet the possessor of it will pay no more than the man with us whose land is hardly worth twenty shillings an acre. Some landholders in this state will have to pay twenty times as much as will be paid for all the land on which Philadelphia stands; and as to excise, this will carry the exciseman to every farmer's house, who distils a little brandy, where he may search and ransack as he pleases. These I mention as specimens of the kind of tax which is to be laid upon us by those who have no information of our situation, and by a government where the wealthy only are represented. It is urged that no new power is given up to the general government, and that the Confederation had those powers before. That system derived its power from the state governments. When the people of Virginia formed their government, they reserved certain great powers in the bill of rights. They would not trust their own citizens, who had a similarity of interest with themselves, and who had frequent and intimate communication with them. They would not trust their own fellow-citizens, I say, with the

exercise of those great powers reserved in the bill of rights. Do we not, by this system, give up a great part of the rights, reserved by the bill of rights, to those who have no fellow-feeling for the people—to a government where the representatives will have no communication with the people? I say, then, there are great and important powers, which were not transferred to the state government, given up to the general government by this Constitution.

[12 June]

[Mr. PENDLETON:] To come to the great object of direct taxation, more immediately under consideration:—If we find it our interest to be intimately connected with the other twelve states, to establish one common government, and bind in one ligament the strength of thirteen states, we shall find it necessary to delegate powers proportionate to that end; for the delegation of adequate powers in this government is not less necessary than in our state government. To whom do we delegate these powers? To our own representatives. Why should we fear so much greater dangers from our representatives there, than from those we have here? Why make so great a distinction between our representatives here, and in the federal government, where every branch is formed on the same principle—preserving throughout the representative, responsible character? We have trusted our lives, and every thing, to our state representatives. We have particularly committed our purse to them, with unlimited confidence. I never heard any objection to it; I am sure I make none. We ought to contribute our share of fixing the principles of the government. Here the representative character is still preserved. We are to have an equal share in the representation of the general government, should we ratify this Constitution. We have hitherto paid more than our share of taxes for the support of the government, &c. But by this system we are to pay our equal, ratable share only. Where is the danger of confiding in our federal representatives? We must choose those in whom we can put the greatest confidence. They are only to remain two years in office. Will they in that time lose all regard for the principles of honor, and their character, and become abandoned prostitutes of our rights? I have no such fear. When power is in the hands of my representatives, I care not whether they meet here or a hundred miles off.

A gentleman (Mr. Monroe) has said that the power of direct taxation was unnecessary, because the imposts and back lands would be abundantly sufficient to answer all federal purposes. If so, what are we disputing about? I ask the gentleman who made the observation, and this committee, if they believe that Congress will ever lay direct taxes if the other funds are sufficient. It will then remain a harmless power upon paper, and do no injury. If it should be necessary, will gentlemen run the risk of the Union by withholding it? I was sorry to hear the subjects of requisitions and taxation misinterpreted. The latter has been compared to taxation by Great Britain without our own consent. The two cases are by no means similar. The king of Great Britain has not the purse, though he holds the sword. He has no means of using the sword but by requisitions on those who hold the purse. He applied to the British Parliament; and they were pleased to trust him with our money. We declared, as we had a right, that we ought to be taxed by our own representatives, and that therefore their disposing of our money without our consent was unjust. Here requisitions are to be made by one body of our representatives to another. Why should this be the case, when they are both possessed of our equal confidence—both chosen in the same manner, and equally responsible to us?

But we are told that there will be a war between the two bodies equally our representatives, and that the state government will be destroyed, and consolidated into the general government. I stated before, that this could not be so. The two governments act in different manners, and for different purposes—the general government in great national concerns, in which we are interested in common with other members of the Union; the state legislature in our mere local concerns. Is it true, or merely imaginary, that the state legislatures will be confined to the care of bridges and roads? I think that they are still possessed of the highest powers. Our dearest rights,—life, liberty, and property,—as Virginians, are still in the hands of our state legislature. If they prove too feeble to protect us, we resort to the aid of the general government for security. The true distinction is, that the two governments are established for different purposes, and act on different objects; so that, notwithstanding what the worthy gentleman said, I believe I am still correct, and insist that, if each power is confined within its proper bounds, and to its proper objects, an interference can never happen. Being for two different purposes, as long as they are limited to the different objects, they can no more clash than two parallel lines can meet. Both lay taxes, but for different purposes. The same officers may be used by both governments, which will prevent a number of inconveniences. If an invasion, or insurrection, or other misfortune, should make it necessary for the general government to interpose, this will be for the general purposes of the Union, and for the manifest interest of the states.

17

JAMES MADISON TO GEORGE THOMPSON
29 Jan. 1789
Papers 11:433–37

A convenient opportunity offering I take the liberty of adding to the former explanation of my sentiments relating to the *federal* constitution the grounds on wh. I dislike a change of that part of it which authorizes direct taxes. I am led to give you this further trouble, by intimations that the necessity of such a trust in the Union is by many not truly understood; & is a subject on which the reasons in favour of my opinion may with propriety be suggested. Should I judge amiss your candour will excuse the com-

munication: Should I judge aright, your discretion will make a proper use of it.

I approve this part of the Constitution because I think it an essential provision for securing the benefits of the Union: the principal of which are 1st the prevention of contests among the States themselves: 2dly security against danger from foreign Nations.

On the first point, it is evident that there is no way to prevent contests among the States but by establishing justice among them: and equally evident that this cannot be done but by some system that will make each bear it's just share of the public burdens. If some States contribute their quotas and others do not, justice is violated; the violation of justice is the ground of disputes among States as well as among individuals; and as among the latter they produce an appeal to the law, so among the former they produce an appeal to the sword. The question to be considered then is which of the two systems, that of requisitions or that of direct taxes, will best answer the essential purpose of making every State bear it's equitable share of the Common burdens. Shall we put our trust in the system of requisitions, by which each State will furnish or not furnish its share as it may like? Reason tells us this can never succeed. Some States will be more just than others, some less just: Some will be more patriotic; others less patriotic; some will be more, some less immediately concerned in the evil to be guarded against or in the good to be obtained. The States therefore not feeling equal motives will not furnish equal aids: Those who furnish most will complain of those who furnish least. From complaints on one side will spring ill will on both sides; from ill will, quarrels; from quarrels, wars; and from wars a long catalogue of evils including the dreadful evils of disunion and a general confusion. Such is the lesson which reason teaches us. But we have a surer guide in our own experience; which like that of every other confederacy that has tried Requisitions, assures us that they will not be duly complied with; that they will not therefore answer the public exigences; and that they moreover lay the foundation for injustice, for discord and for contention. I need not quote particular instances in proof of what is here advanced. The whole history of requisitions not only during the war but since the peace stamps them with the character which I have given them, and proclaims the necessity of resorting for safety to the other system; the system of direct taxes which the Constitution has substituted.

To say that requisitions ought first to be tried, and if they fail, that direct taxes are then to enforce them, is little better than to yeild the point by the manner of urging it: For it admits that requisitions are not likely to be complied with voluntarily; at the same time that the efficacy of them is so much insisted on: It admits again that direct taxes are practicable, although the argument against them is that the General Government cannot in the nature of things levy them. But surely if they be practicable after the refusal of the State Government to comply with the requisitions, shall have raised prejudices against the general Government, the practicability will be much greater if no such prejudices be thrown in the way. One remark however ought not to be omitted. It is, that every State which chuses to collect it's own quota may always prevent a federal collection by keeping a little beforehand in it's finances and making it's payment at once into the federal Treasury. Another remark deserves to be here made. From the reasoning of many on this subject it would seem as if the question concerning requisitions & direct taxes was, whether direct taxes shall be levied or not. This is by no means the case. If extraordinary aids for the public safety be not necessary, direct taxes will not be necessary. If extraordinary emergences call for such aids, the only question will be whether direct taxes shall be raised by the General Government itself or whether the General Government shall require the State Governments to raise them: or in other words whether they shall be raised in all the States, or be raised in some States, whilst others unjustly withdraw their shoulders from the common burden.

On the 2d point to wit, security against danger from abroad, it is no less evident that Requisitions will fatally deceive us. For the same reason that they will not obtain from the States their respective shares of Contribution and thence become a source of intestine quarrels, they must invite foreign attacks by shewing the inability of the Union to repel them: and when attacks are made, must leave the Union to defend itself, if it be defended at all, as was done during the late war; by a waste of blood, a distruction of property, and outrages on private rights, unknown in any Country which has credit or money to employ the regular means of defence. Whilst the late war was carried on by means of impressed property, &c, the annual expense was estimated at about twenty millions of Dollars; at the same time that thousands of brave Citizens were perishing from the scarcity or quality of the supplies provided in that irregular way: to say nothing of the encouragement given by such a situation to the prolongation of the war. Whereas after the General Government was enabled by the pecuniary aids of France to provide supplies in a regular way, the annual expence was reduced to about eight millions of dollars, the army was well fed, the military operations went on with vigour & the blessings of peace were visibly & happily accelerated. Should another war unfortunately be our lot (and the less our ability to repel it, the more likely it is to happen) what would be the condition of the Union if obliged to depend on Requisitions? There are but two methods by which Nations can carry on a regular plan of self defence, one by raising the necessary supplies by taxes within the year equal to the public expences: The other by borrowing money on the credit of taxes pledged for the future repayment of it. The first method is considered by most, if not all nations, as impossible with the aid of every resource they possess. In the United States, possessed of no resource but duties on trade, and their trade probably at the mercy of an enemy superior on the Seas, the very idea of such a method is chimerical. The only remaining method is that of borrowing. But who could be expected to lend to a Government which depended on the punctuality of a dozen or more Governments for the means of discharging even the annual interest of the loan? No man who will candidly make the case his own, will say that he would chuse to become a creditor of a Government under such circumstances. Even if the

scheme of trying requisitions first, and eventually resorting to direct taxes after a refusal of requisitions, were free from other objections which condemn it, the delay & unpunctuality inseperable from it, would be fatal to it as a Fund for borrowing: Or if loans could be attained at all, it could only be from usurers who would make the public pay threefold for the risk & disappointment apprehended. What would have been the condition of America at any period since the peace, that is under the system of Requisitions, if Great Britain had renewed the war, or an attack had come from any other quarter, and money had become essential for the public safety? How was it to have been obtained? Would requisitions have obtained it from the States? There is not a man accquainted with our affairs who will pretend it. Would they have obtained it in loans from individuals to be repaid out of Requisitions? There is probably not a man within the United States aiming at profit only, who would have trusted his money on such a security; or who would not at least have exacted an interest of 20, 30, or 40 perCent, as an indemnification for the fallen State of public credit. We see then that the article of the Constitution in question is absolutely essential whether we consider it as a means of preserving justice & tranquility among the States, or of preventing or repelling foreign wars.

But besides these general Considerations which affect every part of the Union, there are others which claim the most serious attention of the Southern parts of it, and of Virginia particularly. If direct taxes be prohibited, and no reliance can be placed on requisitions, the inevitable consequence will be, that whenever public exigences arise, the duties will be accumulated on imports, until they shall have yeilded every farthing that can be squeezed out of them. Now who is it that pays duties on imports? Those only who consume them. What parts of the Continent manufacture least and consume imported manufactures most? The Southern parts. It is clearly the interest of the Southern parts therefore, and of Virginia particularly that trade should not be overburdened; but that direct taxes when necessary should come in aid of that fund; since being laid on all the States by an equal rule provided in the Constitution, they tend to equalize the general burden on every part of the Continent. It is truly wonderful that from the same quarter it should be urged, as dangerous to yeild a full power over trade, lest the Northern interest should overburden it with duties; and as proper to make an alteration, that might drive the Government into the necessity of overburdening it.

In another view the Southern States have peculiar reasons for retaining the article of direct taxation. If war ever breaks out against America where will it fall? On the weakest parts. Which are the weakest parts? The Southern parts; particularly Virginia, whose long navigable rivers open a great part of her Country to surprize and devastation whenever an enimy powerful at Sea chuses to invade her. Strike out direct taxation from the list of federal authorities and what will be our situation. The revenue from commerce must in great measure fail along with the security of Commerce. The invaded and plundered part of the Union will be unable to raise money for its defence. And no resource will be left; but under the name of Requisitions to solicit benefactions from the Legislatures of other States, who being not witnesses of our distresses cannot properly feel for us; and being remote from the scene of danger cannot feel for themselves. Is [that a] situation in which any man who loves his Country ought to wish it to be placed? Are these the benefits for which Virginia can wish to stipulate as a return for her concessions in favour of a Union and a General Government? That a Northern State should not be averse to expunge the power of direct taxation may be conceived; because a local interest is not always postponed to the general interest. But that a Southern State should hearken to the measure, and be ready to sacrifice it's local interest as well as the general interest, admits of no rational explanation to which I am competent.

18

JAMES MADISON, IMPORT DUTIES,
HOUSE OF REPRESENTATIVES
9 Apr. 1789
Papers 12:69–73

From what has been suggested by the gentlemen that have spoken on the subject before us, I am led to apprehend we shall be under the necessity of travelling further into an investigation of principles than what I supposed would be necessary or had in contemplation when I offered the propositions before you.

It was my view to restrain the first essay on this subject principally to the object of revenue, and make this rather a temporary expedient than any thing permanent. I see however, that there are strong exceptions against deciding immediately on a part of the plan, which I had the honor to bring forward, as well as against an application to the resources mentioned in the list of articles just proposed by the gentleman from Pennsylvania.

I presume, that however much we may be disposed to promote domestic manufactures, we ought to pay some regard to the present policy of obtaining revenue. It may be remarked also, that by fixing on a temporary expedient for this purpose, we may gain more than we shall lose by suspending the consideration of the other subject, until we obtain fuller information of the state of our manufactures. We have at this time the strongest motives for turning our attention to the point I have mentioned; every gentleman sees that the prospect of our harvest from the spring importations is daily vanishing; and if the committee delay levying and collecting an impost, until a system of protecting duties shall be perfected, there will be no importations of any consequence, on which the law is to operate, because, by that time all the spring vessels will have arrived. Therefore, from a pursuit of this policy, we shall suffer a loss equal to the surplus which might be expected from a system of higher duties.

I am sensible that there is great weight in the observation that fell from the hon. gentleman from South-Carolina, (Mr. Tucker) That it will be necessary on the one hand, to weigh and regard the sentiments of the gentlemen from the different parts of the United States; but on the other hand, we must limit our consideration on this head, and notwithstanding all the deference and respect we pay to those sentiments, we must consider the general interest of the union, for this is as much every gentleman's duty to consider as is the local or state interest—and any system of impost that this committee will adopt, must be founded on the principles of mutual concession.

Gentlemen will be pleased to recollect that those parts of the union which contribute more under one system than the other, are also those parts more thinly planted, and consequently stand most in need of national protection—therefore they will have less reason to complain of unequal burthens.

There is another consideration. The states that are most advanced in population and ripe for manufactures, ought to have their particular interest attended to in some degree. While these states retained the power of making regulations of trade, they had the power to protect and cherish such institutions; by adopting the present constitution they have thrown the exercise of this power into other hands—they must have done this with an expectation, that those interests would not be neglected here.

I am afraid, Sir, on the one hand, that if we go fully into a discussion of the subject, we shall consume more time than prudence would dictate to spare; on the other hand, if we do not develop it and see the principles on which we mutually act, we shall subject ourselves to great difficulties. I beg leave therefore to state the grounds on which my opinion with respect to the matter under consideration is founded, namely, whether our present system should be a temporary or permanent one? In the first place, I own myself the friend to a very free system of commerce, and hold it as a truth, that commercial shackles are generally unjust, oppressive and impolitic—it is also a truth, that if industry and labour are left to take their own course, they will generally be directed to those objects which are the most productive, and this in a more certain and direct manner than the wisdom of the most enlightened legislature could point out. Nor do I think that the national interest is more promoted by such restrictions, than that the interest of individuals would be promoted by legislative interference directing the particular application of its industry. For example, we should find no advantage in saying, that every man should be obliged to furnish himself by his own labor with those accommodations which depend upon the mechanic arts, instead of employing his neighbour, who could do it for him on better terms. It would be of no advantage to the shoemaker to make his own clothes to save the expence of the taylor's bill, nor of the taylor to make his own shoes to save the expence of procuring them from the shoemaker. It would be better policy to suffer each to employ his talent in his own way; the case is the same between the exercise of the arts and agriculture—between the city and the country, and between city and town, each capable of making particular articles in sufficient abundance to supply the other—thus all are benefitted by exchange, and the less this exchange is cramped by government, the greater are the proportions of benefit to each. The same argument holds good between nation and nation, and between parts of the same nation.

In my opinion, it would be proper also, for gentlemen to consider the means of encouraging the great staple of America, I mean agriculture, which I think may justly be stiled the staple of the United States; from the spontaneous productions which nature furnishes, and the manifest preference it has over every other object of emolument in this country. If we compare the cheapness of our land with that of other nations, we see so decided an advantage in that cheapness, as to have full confidence of being unrivaled; with respect to the object of manufacture, other countries may and do rival us; but we may be said to have a monopoly in agriculture. The possession of the soil and the lowness of its price, give us as much a monopoly in this case, as any nation or other parts of the world have in the monopoly of any article whatever; but, with this advantage to us, that it cannot be shared nor injured by rivalship.

If my general principle is a good one, that commerce ought to be free, and labour and industry left at large to find its proper object, the only thing which remains, will be to discover the exceptions that do not come within the rule I have laid down. I agree with the gentleman from Pennsylvania, that there are exceptions, important in themselves and claim the particular attention of the committee: Altho the freedom of commerce would be advantageous to all the world, yet, in some particulars, one nation might suffer, to benefit others, and this ought to be for the general good of society.

If America was to leave her ports perfectly free, and make no discrimination between vessels owned by her citizens and those owned by foreigners, while other nations make this discrimination, it is obvious that such policy would go to exclude American shipping altogether from foreign ports, and she would be materially affected in one of her most important interests; to this we may add another consideration, that by encouraging the means of transporting our productions with facility, we encourage the raising them: and this object, I apprehend, is likely to be kept in view by the general government.

Duties laid on imported articles may have an effect which comes within the idea of national prudence: It may happen that materials for manufactures may grow up without any encouragement for this purpose; it has been the case in some of the states, but in others, regulations have been provided and have succeeded in producing some establishment, which ought not to be allowed to perish, from the alteration which has taken place: It would be cruel to neglect them and divert their industry to other channels, for it is not possible for the hand of man to shift from one employment to another, without being injured by the change. There may be some manufactures, which being once formed, can advance toward perfection without any adventitious aid, while others for want of the fostering hand of government will be unable to go on at all. Legislative attention will therefore be necessary to collect

the proper objects for this purpose, and this will form another exception to my general principle.

I observe that a sumptuary prohibition is within the view of some of the proposed articles and forms another exception; I acknowledge that I do not in general think any great national advantage arises from restrictions passed on this head, because as long as a distinction in point of value subsists, sumptuary duties in some form or other will prevail and take effect.

Another exception is embargoes in time of war; these may necessarily occur and shackle the freedom of commerce; but the reasons for this are so obvious, that it renders any remark unnecessary.

The next exception that occurs, is one on which great stress is laid by some well informed men, and this with great plausibility. That each nation should have within itself, the means of defence independent of foreign supplies: That in whatever relates to the operation of war, no state ought to depend upon a precarious supply from any part of the world: There may be some truth in this remark, and therefore it is proper for legislative attention. I am though, well persuaded that the reasoning on this subject has been carried too far. The difficulties we experienced a few years ago, of obtaining military supplies, ought not to furnish too much in favour of an establishment which would be difficult and expensive; because our *national* character is now established and recognized throughout the world, and the laws of war favor *national* exertion more than intestine commotion, so that there is good reason to believe that when it becomes necessary, we may obtain supplies from abroad as readily as any other nation whatsoever. I have mentioned this because I think I see something among the enumerated articles that seems to favor such policy.

The impost laid on trade for the purpose of obtaining revenue, may likewise be considered as an exception; so far therefore as revenue can be more conveniently and certainly raised by this, than any other method without injury to the community, and its operation will be in due proportion to the consumption, which consumption is generally proportioned to the circumstances of individuals, I think sound policy dictates to use this mean; but it will be necessary to confine our attention at this time peculiarly to the object of revenue, because the other subject involves some intricate questions, to unravel which we perhaps are not prepared. I have no objection to the committees accepting the propositions offered by the gentleman from Pennsylvania, because so far as we can enumerate the proper objects and apply specific duties to them, we conform to the practice prevalent in many of the states, and adopt the most laudable method of collecting revenue, at least preferable to laying a general tax. Whether therefore we consult ease and convenience in collection, or pursuing habits already adopted and approved, specific duties as far as the articles can properly be enumerated is the more eligible mode of obtaining the end in contemplation—upon the whole, as I think some of the propositions may be productive of revenue, and some may protect our domestic manufacture, tho' the latter subject ought not to be confusedly blended with the former, I hope the committee will receive them and let them lay over in order that we may have time to consider how far they are consistent with justice and policy.

19

HOUSE OF REPRESENTATIVES, AMENDMENT TO ARTICLE 1, SEC. 8, CL. 1
22 Aug. 1789
Annals 1:773–77

The House resumed the consideration of the amendments to the constitution.

Mr. TUCKER moved the following as a proposition to be added to the same: "The Congress shall never impose direct taxes but where the moneys arising from the duties, imposts, and excise are insufficient for the public exigencies, nor then until Congress shall have made a requisition upon the States to assess, levy, and pay their respective proportions of such requisitions. And in case any State shall neglect or refuse to pay its proportion, pursuant to such requisition, then Congress may assess, and levy such State's proportion, together with the interest thereon, at the rate of six per cent per annum, from the time of payment prescribed by such requisition."

Mr. PAGE said, that he hoped every amendment to the constitution would be considered separately in the manner this was proposed, but he wished them considered fully; it ought to have been referred to the Committee of eleven, reported upon, and then to the Committee of the whole. This was the manner in which the House had decided upon all those already agreed to; and this ought to be the manner in which this should be decided; he should be sorry to delay what was so nearly completed on any account. The House has but little time to sit, and the subject has to go before the Senate, therefore it requires of us all the expedition we can possibly give it. I would prefer putting a finishing hand to what has been already agreed to, and refer this to the Committee of eleven for their consideration.

Mr. TUCKER.—This proposition was referred to the committee, along with many others in the gross, but the Committee of eleven declined reporting upon it. I understood it to be in any gentleman's power to bring it forward when he thought proper, and it was under this influence that I proposed it, nor do I conceive it to be an improper time. The House is engaged in the discussion of amendments; they have made some progress, and I wish them to go on to complete what they have begun. This may be added without inconvenience, if it meet the sense of the House; but if it does not, I wish my constituents to be acquainted with our decision on the whole subject, and therefore hope it may be decided upon at this time.

Mr. JACKSON.—The gentleman has an undoubted right to bring forward the proposition; but I differ greatly with respect to its propriety. I hope, sir, the experience we have had will be sufficient to prevent us from ever agreeing to a relinquishment of such an essential power. The requisitions of the former Congress were ineffectual to obtain supplies; they remain to this day neglected by several States. If a sense of common danger, if war, and that a war of the noblest kind, a contest for liberty, were not sufficient to stimulate the States to a prompt compliance, when the means were abundant, by reason of the immense quantities of paper medium, can we ever expect an acquiescence to a requisition in future, when the only stimulus is honesty, to enable the confederation to discharge the debts of the late war?

But suppose requisitions were likely to be, in some degree, complied with, (which, by the by, I never can admit,) in every case where a State had neglected or refused to furnish its quota, Congress must come in, assess, and collect it. Now, in every such case, I venture to affirm that jealousies would be excited, discontent would prevail, and civil wars break out. What less can gentlemen picture to themselves, when a Government has refused to perform its obligations, but that it will support its measures by the point of the bayonet.

Without the power of raising money to defray the expenses of Government, how are we to be secure against foreign invasion? What, can a Government exert itself, with its sinews torn from it? We can expect neither strength nor exertion; and without these are acquired and preserved, our union will not be lasting; we shall be rent asunder by intestine commotion, or exterior assault; and when that period arrives, we may bid adieu to all the blessings we have purchased at the price of our fortunes, and the blood of our worthiest heroes.

Mr. LIVERMORE thought this an amendment of more importance than any yet obtained; that it was recommended by five or six States, and therefore ought to engage their most serious consideration. It had been supposed that the United States would not attempt to levy direct taxes; but this was certainly a mistake. He believed nothing but the difficulty of managing the subject would deter them. The modes of levying and collecting taxes pursued by the several States are so various, that it is an insuperable obstacle to an attempt by the General Government.

He was sensible that the requisitions of the former Congress had not been fully complied with, and the defect of the confederation was, that the Government had no powers to enforce a compliance. The proposition now under consideration obviated that difficulty. Suppose one or two States refused to comply, certainly the force of the others could compel them, and that is all that ought to be required; because it is not to be supposed that a majority of the States will refuse, as such an opposition must destroy the Union. He hoped the States would be left to furnish their quotas in a manner the most easy to themselves, as was requested by more than half of the present Union.

Unless something more effectual was done to improve the constitution, he knew his constituents would be dissatisfied. As to the amendments already agreed to, they would not value them more than a pinch of snuff; they went to secure rights never in danger.

Mr. PAGE wished the proposition might be recommitted,

for he was certain there was neither time nor inclination to add it to those already agreed upon.

He observed that the warmest friends to amendments differ in opinion on this subject; many of them have ceased urging it, while others have become strenuous advocates for the reverse. The most judicious and discerning men now declare that the Government ought never to part with this power. For his part, experience had convinced him that no reliance was to be had on requisitions, when the States had treated them with contempt in the hour of danger, and had abundant means of compliance. The public credit stood at this moment in the utmost need of support, and he could not consent to throw down one of its strongest props. He thought there was no danger of an abuse of this power, for the Government would not have recourse to it while the treasury could be supplied from any other source; and when they did, they would be studious of adapting their law to the convenience of the States. He hoped, when the gentleman returned home to New Hampshire, his constituents would give him credit for his exertions, and be better satisfied with the amendments than he now supposed them to be.

Mr. SUMTER felt himself so sensibly impressed with the importance of the subject, that if he apprehended the proposition would not have a fair discussion at this time, he would second the motion of commitment, and had not a doubt but the House would acquiesce in it.

Gentlemen had said that the States had this business much at heart. Yes, he would venture to say more, that if the power was not relinquished by the General Government, the State Governments would be annihilated. If every resource is taken from them, what remains in the power of the States for their support, or for the extinguishment of their domestic debt?

Mr. GERRY thought if the proposition was referred, that it ought to go to a Committee of the whole, for he wished it to have a full and candid discussion. He would have something left in the power of every State to support itself, independent of the United States, and therefore was not satisfied with the amendment proposed. The constitution, in its original state, gives to Congress the power of levying and collecting taxes, duties, imposts, and excise. The fault here is, that every thing is relinquished to the General Government. Now, the amendment gives the same power, with qualification, that there shall have been a previous requisition. This by no means came up to his idea; he thought that some particular revenue ought to be secured to the States, so as to enable them to support themselves.

He apprehended, when this clause in the constitution was under the consideration of the several State conventions, they would not so readily have ratified it, if they had considered it more fully in the point of view in which he had now placed it; but if they had ratified it, it would have been under a conviction that Congress would admit such amendments as were necessary to the existence of the State Governments. At present, the States are divested of every means to support themselves. If they discover a new source of revenue, after Congress shall have diverted all the old ones into their treasury, the rapacity of the General Government can take that from them also. The States

can have recourse to no tax, duty, impost, or excise, but what may be taken from them whenever the Congress shall be so disposed; and yet gentlemen must see that the annihilation of the State Governments will be followed by the ruin of this.

Now, what is the consequence of the amendment? Either the States will or will not comply with the requisitions. If they comply, they voluntarily surrender their means of support; if they refuse, the arms of Congress are raised to compel them, which, in all probability, may lay the foundation for civil war. What umbrage must it give every individual to have two sets of collectors and tax-gatherers surrounding his doors; the people then soured, and a direct refusal by the Legislature, will be the occasion of perpetual discord. He wished to alter this proposition in such a manner as to secure the support of the Federal Government and the State Governments likewise, and therefore wished the amendment referred to a Committee of the whole House.

Mr. TUCKER.—I do not see the arguments in favor of giving Congress this power in so forcible a light as some gentlemen do. It will be to erect an *imperium in imperio,* which is generally considered to be subversive of all Government. At any time that Congress shall exercise this power, it will raise commotions in the States; whereas, the mode of requisitions will operate in so easy a way, by being consonant to the habits of the people, that the supplies will be sooner realized in the treasury by this means than by any other. It will require a length of time to form a uniform system of taxation, that shall operate equally and justly through all the States; though I doubt the possibility of forming such a system. It has been said, that requisitions have not been complied with in former times, but it is to be hoped that there will not be so much difficulty in future. The supplies from the impost will greatly diminish the requisitions; besides, should any of the States refuse to comply, they will be liable to the exercise of the power of Congress in the very heart of their country. This power will be so disagreeable, that the very dread of it will stimulate the States to an immediate and prompt compliance with the requisitions. This amendment has been proposed by several of the States, and by some of the most important ones. For this and other reasons that have been offered on the subject, I hope the amendment will be adopted.

Several methods were proposed for disposing of this question for the present; but the motion for its lying on the table being put and negatived, Mr. PARTRIDGE, referring to his instructions, was solicitous that this amendment should not be too precipitately decided upon, and moved the previous question, which was negatived.

Mr. SEDGWICK said, that he believed his mind was as strongly impressed with the force of the instructions he had received from his constituents, as that of other gentlemen. But, sir, a Government entrusted with the freedom and the very existence of the people, ought surely to possess, in a most ample degree, the means of supporting its own existence; and as we do not know what circumstances we may be in, or how necessary it may be for Congress to exercise this power, I should deem it a violation of the oath I have taken to support the constitution were I now to vote for this amendment.

Mr. SHERMAN remarked, that if Congress should exercise this power, the taxes would be laid by the immediate representatives of the people; neither would it be necessary to adopt one uniform method of collecting direct taxes. The several States might be accommodated by a reference to their respective modes of taxation.

The question upon the paragraph being called for from every part of the House, the yeas and nays were taken.

> YEAS.—Messrs. Burke, Coles, Floyd, Grout, Hathorn, Livermore, Van Rensselaer, Sumter, and Tucker.—9.
> NAYS.—Messrs. Ames, Benson, Brown, Cadwalader, Carroll, Clymer, Fitzsimons, Foster, Gale, Gerry, Gilman, Goodhue, Hartley, Heister, Jackson, Lawrence, Lee, Madison, Matthews, Moore, Muhlenburg, Page, Parker, Partridge, Schureman, Scott, Sedgwick, Seney, Sherman, Sylvester, Sinnickson, Smith, of Maryland, Smith, of South Carolina, Stone, Sturges, Thatcher, Trumbull, Vining, and Wadsworth.—39.

20

JAMES MADISON, THE BANK BILL,
HOUSE OF REPRESENTATIVES
2 Feb. 1791

Papers 13:375–76

The bill did not come within the first power. It laid no tax to pay the debts, or provide for the general welfare. It laid no tax whatever. It was altogether foreign to the subject.

No argument could be drawn from the terms "common defence, and general welfare." The power as to these general purposes, was limited to acts laying taxes for them; and the general purposes themselves were limited and explained by the particular enumeration subjoined. To understand these terms in any sense, that would justify the power in question, would give to Congress an unlimited power; would render nugatory the enumeration of particular powers; would supercede all the powers reserved to the state governments. These terms are copied from the articles of confederation; had it ever been pretended, that they were to be understood otherwise than as here explained?

It had been said that "general welfare" meant cases in which a general power might be exercised by Congress, without interfering with the powers of the States; and that the establishment of a National Bank .was of this sort. There were, he said, several answers to this novel doctrine.

1. The proposed Bank would interfere so as indirectly to defeat a State Bank at the same place. 2. It would directly interfere with the rights of the States, *to prohibit* as well as to establish Banks, and the circulation of Bank Notes. He mentioned a law of Virginia, actually prohibiting the circulation of notes payable to bearer. 3. Interfer-

ence with the power of the States was no constitutional criterion of the power of Congress. If the power was not given, Congress could not exercise it; if given, they might exercise it, altho it should interfere with the laws, or even the constitution of the States. 4. If Congress could incorporate a Bank, merely because the act would leave the States free to establish Banks also; any other incorporations might be made by Congress. They could incorporate companies of manufacturers, or companies for cutting canals, or even religious societies, leaving similar incorporations by the States, like State Banks to themselves: Congress might even establish religious teachers in every parish, and pay them out of the Treasury of the United States, leaving other teachers unmolested in their functions. These inadmissible consequences condemned the controverted principle.

The case of the Bank established by the former Congress, had been cited as a precedent. This was known, he said, to have been the child of necessity. It never could be justified by the regular powers of the articles of confederation. Congress betrayed a consciousness of this in recommending to the States to incorporate the Bank also. They did not attempt to protect the Bank Notes by penalties against counterfeiters. These were reserved wholly to the authority of the States.

21

ALEXANDER HAMILTON, REPORT ON
MANUFACTURES
5 Dec. 1791

Papers 10:302–4

A Question has been made concerning the Constitutional right of the Government of the United States to apply this species of encouragement, but there is certainly no good foundation for such a question. The National Legislature has express authority "To lay and Collect taxes, duties, imposts and excises, to pay the debts and provide for the *Common defence* and *general welfare*" with no other qualifications than that "all duties, imposts and excises, shall be *uniform* throughout the United states, that no capitation or other direct tax shall be laid unless in proportion to numbers ascertained by a census or enumeration taken on the principles prescribed in the Constitution, and that "no tax or duty shall be laid on articles exported from any state." These three qualifications excepted, the power to *raise money* is *plenary*, and *indefinite;* and the objects to which it may be *appropriated* are no less comprehensive, than the payment of the public debts and the providing for the common defence and *"general Welfare."* The terms *"general Welfare"* were doubtless intended to signify more than was expressed or imported in those which Preceded; otherwise numerous exigencies incident to the affairs of a Nation would have been left without a provision. The phrase is as comprehensive as any that could have been used; because it was not fit that the constitutional authority of the Union, to appropriate its revenues shou'd have been restricted within narrower limits than the "General Welfare" and because this necessarily embraces a vast variety of particulars, which are susceptible neither of specification nor of definition.

It is therefore of necessity left to the discretion of the National Legislature, to pronounce, upon the objects, which concern the general Welfare, and for which under that description, an appropriation of money is requisite and proper. And there seems to be no room for a doubt that whatever concerns the general Interests of *learning* of *Agriculture* of *Manufactures* and of *Commerce* are within the sphere of the national Councils *as far as regards an application·of Money.*

The only qualification of the generallity of the Phrase in question, which seems to be admissible, is this—That the object to which an appropriation of money is to be made be *General* and not *local;* its operation extending in fact, or by possibility, throughout the Union, and not being confined to a particular spot.

No objection ought to arise to this construction from a supposition that it would imply a power to do whatever else should appear to Congress conducive to the General Welfare. A power to appropriate money with this latitude which is granted too in *express terms* would not carry a power to do any other thing, not authorised in the constitution, either expressly or by fair implication.

22

HOUSE OF REPRESENTATIVES, POST OFFICE BILL
6–7 Dec. 1791, 3, 5 Jan. 1792

(See 1.8.7, no. 3)

23

HOUSE OF REPRESENTATIVES, RELIEF TO SAVANNAH
28 Dec. 1796
Annals 6:1712, 1717–26

Mr. W. SMITH wished the House to resolve itself into a Committee of the Whole on the resolution, which he had the other day laid upon the table, proposing to afford some relief to the sufferers by the late fire at Savannah. For his part, he said, he could see no reasonable objection which could be made to so benevolent a proposition. A gentleman in the House had got a plan of the ruins of the city; it was, indeed, a most distressful scene. There had never occurred so calamitous an event of the kind in the United States, or which had so strong a claim upon the General Government for relief. He said they had granted

assistance to the sufferers by fire at St. Domingo; and surely if it were justifiable to grant relief to foreigners in distress, it was at least equally so when the objects were our own citizens. If gentlemen had objections to the measure, he wished they would state them. The sum with which he should think of filling up the blank would not be such as to materially affect our finances.

· · · · ·

[Mr. MACON:] The sufferings of the people of Savannah were doubtless very great; no one could help feeling for them. But he wished gentlemen to put their finger upon that part of the Constitution which gave that House power to afford them relief. Many other towns had suffered very considerably by fire. He believed he knew one that had suffered more than Savannah in proportion to its size: he alluded to Lexington in Virginia, as every house in the place was burnt. If the United States were to become underwriters to the whole Union, where must the line be drawn when their assistance might be claimed? Was it when three-fourths or four-fifths of a town was destroyed, or what other proportion? Insurance offices were the proper securities against fire. If the Government were to come forward in one instance, it must come forward in all, since every sufferer's claim stood upon the same footing. The sum which had been given to the sufferers at St. Domingo was to be charged to the French Republic, and that given to Count de Grasse's daughters was in consideration of their father's services. But New York had as great right to come forward and expect relief as Savannah. He felt for the sufferers in all these cases, but he felt as tenderly for the Constitution; he had examined it, and it did not authorize any such grant. He should, therefore, be very unwilling to act contrary to it.

Mr. RUTHERFORD said, he felt a great deal of force on what gentlemen had said. There were two circumstances which were perfectly conclusive in his mind. He saw it our duty to grant relief from humanity and from policy. Savannah was a city of a minor, helpless State; it was a very young State, yet it was a part of the Union, and as such, was as much entitled to protection as any State under such a dire misfortune; and it became Congress to alleviate their great distress. They have lost much; they have, many of them, lost their all. To say we will not assist to relieve, when almost every State in the Union is putting their shoulders to support these people's burden, is wrong. The State of Pennsylvania has done itself immortal honor in the relief it has afforded, and shall we not help to support this part of the family in their distress? This State is a branch of the great family of the Union; it would be, in my idea, extremely inconsistent to neglect them. He hoped the motion would be adopted, and he hoped it would never be said that the General Government refused to provide help in such a poignant distress occurring in one of its principal towns.

Mr. HARTLEY said, that the gentleman from North Carolina [Mr. MACON] had voted against both of the bills which had been referred to. He knew no difference between the Constitution of the United States and that of Pennsylvania, yet a vote in their House had been carried unanimously. He thought the law for the relief of the sufferers of St. Domingo perfectly in point; for, notwithstanding what was said about negotiation, the distress of those people had consumed all the money before the six months were expired. If ever there was a case in which they could grant relief, this was one. The losses at New York and Charleston would bear no comparison with that of Savannah; they were rich and flourishing places, whilst Savannah was a small city of a new State, and the sufferers generally poor. He hoped, therefore, the resolution would be agreed to.

Mr. MOORE said, the laws which had been adduced as precedents were not in point; for the one sum we were to have credit with the French Republic, and the other was in consideration of past services. The distress of the people of Savannah was not an object of legislation; every individual citizen could, if he pleased, show his individual humanity by subscribing to their relief; but it was not Constitutional for them to afford relief from the Treasury. If, however, the principle was adopted, it should be general. Every sufferer had an equal claim. Lexington, in Virginia, contained only one hundred houses, and all except two had been destroyed by fire. He should therefore move to add Lexington to Savannah in the resolution before them; though he would observe, as he did not approve of the principle, he should vote against them both.

Mr. W. SMITH wished gentlemen not to endeavor to defeat the proposition before them by an amendment. He did not think there could be a comparison made between the distress occasioned by a fire in a small town and one in a populous city. The destruction of Savannah was a great loss in a national view, as it would cause a considerable defalcation in the revenue, and probably any money they might advance for the relief of the citizens would be amply compensated, by enabling the city the sooner to resume its former importance in the commercial scale.

Mr. VENABLE did not see the difference between the two cases which was so distinguishable to the gentleman last up. Because Savannah was a commercial city, its distress, according to that gentleman, was indescribable, but when a like scene was exhibited in a small town, it was no longer an object which touched his feelings. His humanity went no where but where commerce was to be found. He asked whether the United States might not as well lose revenue in the first instance, as put money into the people's pockets to pay it with? Humanity was the same every where. A person who lost his all in a village, felt the misfortune as heavily as he who had a like loss in a city, and perhaps more so, since the citizen would have a better opportunity by means of commerce of retrieving his loss. He was against the general principle, as he believed, if acted upon, it would bring such claims upon the Treasury as it would not be able to answer.

Mr. MURRAY thought the gentleman from Virginia [Mr. VENABLE] carried his idea of relief too far. He had no idea that the House, or any Legislature, could undertake to make good individual misfortunes. He was of opinion that the lines which separated individual from national cases, were very observable; the one was happening every day, the other seldom occurred. When a large town is burnt down, and that town is an important Southern frontier

town, it is surely a national calamity, and has a claim upon the humanity of the country. It was true, the claim was not of such a nature as to be brought into a Court of Justice, but it was a calamity in which the whole nation sympathized. It was not only a claim upon the humanity of the nation, but also upon its policy, as, by restoring it to its former situation, it would be able to bear its wonted part in contributing to the revenue of the country, and would continue to carry population, arts, and wealth to that distant part of the Union. In case of war, Savannah was a most important place. It was necessary the Union should have a town in that situation, and he could not consider any money which might now be advanced as given away, but as lent to that town, which might enable it, in a few years, to resume its former situation, whilst the withholding of it might prevent its ever rising from its present ruins.

Mr. KITCHELL was opposed to the amendment and to the resolution itself. He had doubts if even they were to give the citizens 15,000 dollars, as was proposed by the gentleman from South Carolina, whether they should not, instead of service, be doing them an injury; because, if the General Government were only to give this sum, the State Legislatures would proportion their donations accordingly, and probably give much less than they would otherwise have done, if they had not had this example before them. He had doubts as to the constitutionality of the measure; he thought the Constitution did not authorize them to make such a use of public money; however he thought it might be a very flexible instrument; it would bend to every situation, and every situation to that. He thought, in this instance, if we grant money, while we attempt to serve, we shall eventually injure. As to what the gentleman from Virginia says of Lexington, Mr. K. thought it had been fully relieved; however he should vote against both propositions.

Mr. PAGE said, that he was sorry that his colleague had made this amendment, as he had done it with a view to defeat the original resolution. If humanity alone were to direct his vote upon this question, and if the amendment had been proposed more early and singly, he might have voted for it. But that not being the case, it, as well as motives of general policy, influenced him in favor of the original motion. He had reasons which could not apply to the amendment. He should vote against it. He was bound by order to confine himself to the single question before the committee. This is, Shall the amendment be received or not? He declared it as his opinion that the case of Lexington ought not to be connected with that of Savannah, which had been, as stated by the member from South Carolina, materially different. He was restrained by order from entering into the merits of the original resolution, but he thought that he had a right to hint at the motive of policy which would apply to the resolution, and not to the amendment. This was, that Savannah being an important place, it would be wise and politic to prevent its revival from being owing to any other aid than that of the General Government of the United States. It ought not to be under obligations to individuals, or single States, and much less to a foreign Power.

Mr. HARTLEY hoped the amendment would not prevail. If the loss of the people at Lexington had been greater than they could support, they would doubtless have applied to the Legislature of Virginia, but he had not heard of any such application having been made. He agreed with the gentleman last up, that the General Government ought to relieve distresses of this kind.

Mr. MURRAY inquired when the fire happened at Lexington?

Mr. MOORE answered, about nine months ago. He thought it was the duty of the United States first to pay the claims which were made upon them by distressed soldiers and others for past services, who were denied justice because they had passed an act of limitation. If they were to act from generosity, he said that generosity ought to be extended universally. It was a new doctrine that because a sufferer by fire did not live in a commercial city he was not equally entitled to relief with the inhabitants of a city, and that though such persons were called upon to contribute to the losses of others, they could have no redress for their own. This seemed as if favorite spots were to be selected upon which special favor was to be shown. He was opposed to all such humanity.

Mr. CLAIRBORNE was against the amendment, but he hoped the resolution would be agreed to. He was sorry any gentleman should propose an amendment like this, purposely to defeat a motion which would tend to relieve such sufferers as those of Georgia must be. He was not certain whether he could vote upon Constitutional grounds or not. It was a sharp conflict between humanity to that suffering country and the Constitution. If any case could be admissible, he thought this could; it ought to be remembered, that that part of the Union has suffered much. Georgia was a slaughter-pen during the war, besides being continually harassed by the hostile Indians. He thought 15,000 dollars would not be ill-spent, as from motives of policy it would be of more advantage to the United States from the quick return the revenue would gain. Indeed, if Constitutional, he hoped the sum would be made more than proposed. These are your fellow-citizens who are suffering, and if not speedily relieved, the whole interest will be involved. If in order, he would vote that the Committee rise, to enable him and, perhaps, many others, to consult whether relief could be constitutionally granted? He said he felt a great propensity to do it.

The motion was put and negatived.

Mr. HARPER hoped the amendment would be rejected, for the same reason that he hoped all amendments which were brought forward with the same view with which it was produced, viz: to defeat the original motion, might be rejected. He thought every proposition should stand or fall upon its own ground. He wished that of his colleague to do so. Mr. H. insisted upon the dissimilarity of the two cases, and that the distinction of great and small calamity was sufficient to distinguish the two cases. With respect to the constitutionality of affording the relief in question, that had already been determined by the several instances which had been quoted, which were also founded upon humanity. The present case might justly be included under the head of promoting the general welfare of the country. Gentlemen who doubted the constitutionality of the present proceeding, had done the same in the instances alluded to. But, since their doubts had been so frequently overruled, he hoped they should hear no more of them. With respect to the policy of the measure, Savannah, he said, was the only considerable port except Charleston, which the United States had in that quarter. It was situated at the mouth of a river which watered a space of country containing a thousand square miles. The average revenue of this city was $76,000. Was not this an object of importance? Was it not an object to foster, to relieve the distresses of such a place? Many great statesmen had employed themselves in founding cities, and should they not hold out a helping hand to one in distress? Peter the Great founded a city upon a morass, and Louis XIV. attempted to build one in the English channel. He trusted the American Government would have more wisdom than to see one of her's sink for want of a little timely assistance.

The question was put on the amendment and negatived—there being only 26 in favor of it.

Mr. BALDWIN said, he had doubted whether to make any observations on this motion; not that he was insensible to the calamitous situation which had been the cause of it, but from an apprehension that it might be thought he was too strongly affected by it. Though it might be disagreeable to one to give his judgment and urge his opinions, when his own relation to the question was different from that of others, yet some of the reflections might not be useless to those who were to determine it. He was sure it was not a want of disposition to relieve the unhappy sufferers that had or would draw forth an observation on this occasion, but merely doubts as to the powers of the Federal Government in money matters. The use of a written Constitution, and of that provision in it which declared that no money should be drawn from the Treasury but under appropriations made by law, was very manifest from the caution which it gave in the expenditure of public money and in laying burdens on the people; yet he believed it impossible to obtain absolute directions from it in every case. The objection is, that Congress is empowered to raise money only to pay the debts and to provide for the common defence, and the other purposes, exactly as specified in the 8th section. The objection has often been made, but many laws have passed not exactly specified in that section. He mentioned the private acts before alluded to, the law for establishing light-houses, to aid navigation in the improvement of harbors, beacons, buoys, and public piers, establishing trading-houses with the Indians, and some others, to show that though the Constitution was very useful in giving general directions, yet it was not capable of being administered under so rigorous and mechanical a construction as had been sometimes contended for. He begged leave to ask and to urge the question, whether there was no possible accumulation of calamity and distress that might be brought upon some part of the country which would justify the Federal Government in granting some relief? No doubt the usual pressure of private misfortune is relieved by the poor-laws and other acts of the State Governments; but, suppose a State belonging to this Union, the greater part, or, perhaps, the whole, was situated on an island, and that at once, by some of the great causes which we know operate in Nature, by tremendous convulsions and earthquakes, it was to be thrown into such a situation as some parts of the world have been, not only the whole property of the wretched survivors destroyed, but their place no longer habitable, would the Federal Government think they had no powers even to grant them some of their new land as a place of refuge? He was sensible that he had put a case so strong that the bare mention almost seemed improper, and that the mind of no gentleman could follow him to that extent. He only wished to establish the principle that there were possible instances in which it would be the duty of the Federal Government to interpose relief. Whether the present calamity was so great and the distress so pressing, that proper relief was scarcely to be expected from the State where it happened, was a question which he must leave to their determination. He was sure they could not want for inducements from the nature of the scene, or from their own dispositions. He could not wish to heighten the coloring in which it stood before them.

Mr. RUTHERFORD again rose in support of the motion. Is it not clear, he said, that it is the duty of the people at large to come forward at this time and hold up the helping hand to those poor distressed people? He presumed the rising dignity of this great Confederation demanded mutual assistance in distress. If the people are left to recover of themselves from this terrible dilemma, the nation will suffer. It is the duty and the interest of this rising nation to help the people of Georgia; it is a part of this great family, and demands assistance from every member. This idea should be conclusive. But for gentlemen to say the law is to have its full operation at this time, is saying nothing at all; it is pouring cold water upon their distresses; it is as though you were to say to a man that is drowning, stay awhile and we will come and assist you. This would be poor comfort. Policy, humanity, and justice, should prompt the House to the noble action. If one part of a system is injured the whole suffers by it. All the generous feelings of the human heart call aloud for help, and I hope we shall grant it.

Mr. NICHOLAS said, he meant to have given a silent vote upon this subject, and have left other gentlemen to follow their own inclinations in the business; but an attempt had been made to ridicule the opinion which he and others held of the sacredness of the Constitution. In reference to what had fallen from the gentleman from Georgia, he said he had never heard it said that no individual instance could occur which might be an exception to a Constitutional rule. He had never heard that our laws should be so general as to admit of no latitude, or that money should never be expended but for payment of debts or for defence.

Mr. N. said, he was not satisfied with the distinction made on this occasion, viz: that if a few inhabitants of a small town experienced loss by fire they were not entitled to consideration; but, if the same calamity happened in a large city, it had a claim upon them for relief. He wished to know whether they were about to do what ought not to be left undone? There was no case in which they were at liberty to act or not. If they were bound to afford relief then, were they not equally bound at any future period to afford relief in similar cases? If the thing was right and proper, relief ought to be commensurate with the distress, otherwise they did not do their duty. If it was otherwise, the thing was arbitrary and a whim. If he voted for relieving this case he should feel bound to relieve every future distress by fire. When an amendment was lately under consideration, it was said to be improper, because the evil was of less magnitude than the present. It was not so; it was an explanation of the subject. The gentleman from South Carolina said he had not heard of that fire. That gentleman lived near Savannah, and other considerations besides those of humanity might influence his conduct on the present occasion. Gentlemen had said they stood in the same situation as individual States. That opinion, he said, had gone too far. The General Government had no power but what was given to it, but the State Governments had all power for the good of their several States. If the general welfare was to be extended (as it had been insinuated it ought) to objects of charity, it was undefined indeed. Charity was not a proper subject for them to legislate upon; and, if this resolution were to pass, all the power of which they were possessed would not be adequate to raise funds to answer the demands which would be brought against the Treasury.

Mr. GILES said, if the present resolution passed it would make them answerable for all future losses by fire. The small sum of $15,000 was not of any consequence when compared with the establishment of a principle of that House acting upon generosity. He believed that neither the money nor humanity, but the establishment of the principle, was the thing aimed at. The unanimity with which a resolution had passed the Pennsylvania Legislature, was a proof that they believed they had the power to pass such a law. It was said the General Government possessed the authority. The gentleman from Georgia had said that "affairs of men" made it necessary to depart from the strict Constitutional power. For his part, he did not think they ought to attend to what "the affairs of men" or what generosity and humanity required, but what the Constitution and their duty required.

The authority of that House, he said, was specified, beyond which they ought not to go. This was a principle not within the Constitution, but opposed to it.

There had, he said, been several cases introduced. That of the sufferers of St. Domingo was not a case in point. They looked for a reimbursement of the money. He believed it had been repaid. And when the daughters of the Count de Grasse had $4,000 given them, it was thought to be necessary to introduce their father's services as a consideration. His feelings, he said, were not less alive to the calls of humanity than those of other gentlemen; but, by granting the money required, they should go beyond their powers, and do more real injury than good.

Mr. W. SMITH said, that gentlemen had spoken of a sum in contemplation; but the question was not on the sum to be granted; that would be for future consideration, and if gentlemen wished to make it commensurate with the object, they could do so. The present question was, whether any relief should be granted? He wished gentlemen would say whether no case of calamity could exist in which the United States ought to grant relief? He believed every one admitted such a case might occur. The question was, whether this was the case? He trusted it was, since it was an unexampled calamity.

The precedents which had been adduced appeared to be no more strongly warranted than this. First, with respect to the relief granted the sufferers at St. Domingo. In order to make the thing more palatable, it was said that sum should be charged to the French Republic. It was provisional, and the fact was they had not admitted it, and the United States paid it. In reference to the relief granted to the daughters of Count de Grasse: it was said to be for services. Did the daughters perform any services? No, but the father did. But did the Constitution of the United States acknowledge any hereditary claim of this sort? He believed not. This was a mere pretence. It was an act of generosity. Another case occurred to him, which had not been mentioned, viz: the recompense allowed to persons who suffered from the Western insurrection. Was this authorized by the Constitution any more than the present? He believed not.

Gentlemen had said, that the Legislature of Pennsylvania had a right to grant relief. Mr. S. asked, what right they had to grant relief to the people of Georgia more than the Representatives of the United States? These are their own citizens, the people whom they represent, and as such ought to feel for and alleviate their distresses.

A gentleman from Virginia [Mr. MOORE] had said we should not grant the relief to those people because we have not paid our debts. Is this a reason? Will a man say he cannot give to the unfortunate because he is in debt? Were that the case perhaps people of the greatest opulence would be as entitled to excuse as any other. Men in great business are seldom out of debt; but they may with safety be generous and charitable. The claims of those soldiers and other petitioners referred to by that gentleman, ought not to be considered as a debt. No claim, he said, which was justly due, was refused payment. A certain time was set at which all claims were to be brought in, and would have been discharged. Such as were not, except in very particular cases, were rejected. This was a necessary measure, and generally approved of. Then surely those claims which were barred by this act of limitation could not be considered a debt.

This argument, Mr. S. said, would not do: because a man owed a little money, or another chose to say he did, he was not to be charitable. He thought the House fully authorized to grant relief in this case.

In examining different cases, Mr. S. said, he found that of the widow of Major Forsyth, and also that of the orphan children of Major Trueman. Gentlemen would perhaps say that these were cases where the husband and ancestor had rendered services to the United States; and he had no doubt that the ancestors of those sufferers at Savannah, and perhaps the sufferers themselves, had rendered services to the United States. If gentlemen pleased, therefore, the words, "in consideration of services performed," &c. might be inserted.

It has been said, that if the proposed donation was made by Congress, it would lessen the claim of the sufferers upon individual States. He thought differently. He thought it would show that Congress believed their case a hard one, and deserving of attention. But another thing: it was not probable that any of the Legislatures would be in session for some time, except one or two. How, then, were the sufferers to be relieved? The few thousand dollars they had yet got would be a mere bagatelle towards their immense loss. He hoped, therefore, the resolutions would be agreed to.

Mr. COIT said he should vote against this resolution, though he felt as much for the distresses of the people of Savannah as any gentleman in that House. Nor would his objections be on Constitutional grounds. He thought where there were calls of generosity and humanity on the National Treasury sufficiently strong, he should vote for paying attention to them. The present, he said, was a call of humanity from the people of Savannah; the call was loud, and ought to be satisfied by somebody. The question was, whether it was made with propriety to them? He thought not; and that to agree to the resolution would be laying a dangerous precedent. He conceived the instances which had been adduced as precedents for the present case were not in point. The application was from foreigners to the feelings of this Government, which he thought had been attended to with propriety. But, he said, there was an obvious distinction between the two cases. There was no probability that a foreigner would be listened to by a State Legislature. This was a reason which did not apply to this case. Major Forsyth and Major Trueman had died in the service of the United States; their families, therefore, seemed to have a just claim for protection. The Western insurrection was a very different thing: the grant was in consequence of exertions in favor of Government.

Mr. C. said it appeared to him, from a variety of reasons, that this subject would be best left in the hands of the individual States. The greatest difficulty attending this Government was, the providing of money to support its necessary expenses. Considering this, therefore, as a precedent likely to draw great sums from the Treasury, he wished to avoid giving it place.

Mr. W. SMITH said that this sum could not be a serious inconvenience to the Treasury, as gentlemen knew there must be additional revenue provided. Indeed, it might be an advantage to the Treasury, as it might put the people of Savannah in a state of paying revenue, which otherwise would not be the case.

Mr. CLAIBORNE said, the more he heard, the more he found himself in favor of the resolution. By the discussion it had undergone, he was inclined to think it was, perhaps, reconcilable with the Constitution; perhaps it was, he said, for he was not certain. The annual revenue, he said, of that place, was seventy thousand dollars to the United States, besides the great consideration of it as a frontier town. He had compared the advantages and disadvantages with respect to its relief in his own mind, and thought it would be highly consistent with policy to grant relief. It was a place which had been in great distress, and had great struggles with enemies in times past. Can it be possible to suppose that we have not power to assist in erecting that place again, and putting it upon a footing to do good to the United States by a return of her revenue? Certainly not. Would the Committee be willing that Savannah should be erased from the revenue? Are they willing to let it rest, and lose it? This is impossible. Then, surely, it becomes policy to give aid towards its re-erection. Unless the people do receive some aid, it will be a long time before seventy thousand dollars will be again produced from the revenue of that place.

For what purpose was it, Mr. C. asked, that money was spent to erect trading-houses in the back countries? He answered, for the general welfare; for the support of trade, and the increase of the revenue. So will a small sum given towards the relief of this suffering town. If there could be reason to grant money to the widows of Major Forsyth and Major Trueman, there surely must be as much to do this.

24

HYLTON v. UNITED STATES
3 Dall. 171 (1796)

(See 1.9.4, no. 13)

25

THOMAS JEFFERSON TO ALBERT GALLATIN
16 June 1817
Works 12:71–73

You will have learned that an act for internal improvement, after passing both Houses, was negatived by the President. The act was founded, avowedly, on the principle that the phrase in the constitution which authorizes Congress "to lay taxes, to pay the debts and provide for the general welfare," was an extension of the powers specifically enumerated to whatever would promote the general welfare; and this, you know, was the federal doctrine. Whereas, our tenet ever was, and, indeed, it is almost the only landmark which now divides the federalists from the republicans, that Congress had not unlimited powers to provide for the general welfare, but were restrained to those specifically enumerated; and that, as it was never meant they should provide for that welfare but by the exercise of the enumerated powers, so it could not have been meant they should raise money for purposes which the enumeration did not place under their action; consequently, that the specification of powers is a limitation of the purposes for which they may raise money. I think the passage and rejection of this bill a fortunate incident. Every State will certainly concede the power; and this will

be a national confirmation of the grounds of appeal to them, and will settle forever the meaning of this phrase, which, by a mere grammatical quibble, has countenanced the General Government in a claim of universal power. For in the phrase, "to lay taxes, to pay the debts and provide for the general welfare," it is a mere question of syntax, whether the two last infinitives are governed by the first or are distinct and co-ordinate powers; a question unequivocally decided by the exact definition of powers immediately following. It is fortunate for another reason, as the States, in conceding the power, will modify it, either by requiring the federal ratio of expense in each State, or otherwise, so as to secure us against its partial exercise. Without this caution, intrigue, negotiation, and the barter of votes might become as habitual in Congress, as they are in those legislatures which have the appointment of officers, and which, with us, is called "logging," the term of the farmers for their exchanges of aid in rolling together the logs of their newly-cleared grounds.

26

JAMES MADISON TO JOSEPH C. CABELL
30 Oct. 1828
Writings 9:324–25

---

2. A history of that clause, as traced in the printed journal of the Federal Convention, will throw light on the subject.

It appears that the clause, as it originally stood, simply expressed "a power to lay taxes, duties, imposts, and excises," without pointing out the objects; and, of course, leaving them applicable in carrying into effect the other specified powers. It appears, farther, that a solicitude to prevent any constructive danger to the validity of public debts contracted under the superseded form of government, led to the addition of the words "to pay the debts."

This phraseology having the appearance of an appropriation limited to the payment of debts, an express appropriation was added "for the expenses of the Government," &c.

But even this was considered as short of the objects for which taxes, duties, imposts, and excises might be required; and the more comprehensive provision was made by substituting "for expenses of Government" the terms of the old Confederation, viz.: and provide for the common defence and general welfare, making duties and imposts, as well as taxes and excises, applicable not only to payment of debts, but to the common defence and general welfare.

27

JAMES MADISON TO ANDREW STEVENSON
27 Nov. 1830
Letters 4:120–39

I enclose the letter which particularly complies with the object of yours. The view it takes of the origin and innocence of the phrase "common defence and general welfare" is what was taken in the Federalist and in the report of 1799, and, I believe, wherever else I may have had occasion to speak of the clause containing the terms.

I have omitted a vindication of the true punctuation of the clause, because I now take for certain that the original document, signed by the members of the Convention, is in the Department of State, and that it testifies for itself against the erroneous editions of the text in that particular. Should it appear that the document is not there, or that the error had slipped into it, the materials in my hands to which you refer will amount, I think, to a proof outweighing even that authority. It would seem a little strange, if the original Constitution be in the Department of State, that it has hitherto escaped notice. But it is to be explained, I presume, by the fact that it was not among the papers relating to the Constitution left with General Washington, and there deposited by him; but, having been sent from the Convention to the old Congress, lay among the mass of papers handed over on the expiration of the latter to that Department. On your arrival at Washington, you will be able personally, or by a friend having more leisure, to satisfy yourself on these points. . . .

Dear Sir,—I have received your very friendly favor of the 20th instant, referring to a conversation when I had lately the pleasure of a visit from you, in which you mentioned your belief that the terms "common defence and general welfare," in the eighth section of the first article of the Constitution of the United States, were still regarded by some as conveying to Congress a substantive and indefinite power, and in which I communicated my views of the introduction and occasion of the terms, as precluding that comment of them; and you express a wish that I would repeat those views in the answer to your letter.

However disinclined to the discussion of such topics, at a time when it is so difficult to separate, in the minds of many, questions purely constitutional from the party polemics of the day, I yield to the precedents which you think I have imposed on myself, and to the consideration that, without relying on my personal recollections, which your partiality over-values, I shall derive my construction of the passage in question from sources of information and evidence known or accessible to all who feel the importance of the subject, and are disposed to give it a patient examination.

In tracing the history and determining the import of the terms "common defence and general welfare," as found in the text of the Constitution, the following lights are furnished by the printed journal of the Convention which formed it:

The terms appear in the general propositions offered May 29, as a basis for the incipient deliberations, the first of which "Resolved, that the articles of the Confederation ought to be so corrected and enlarged as to accomplish the objects proposed by their institution, namely, common defence, security of liberty, and general welfare." On the day following, the proposition was exchanged for, "Resolved, that a Union of the States merely Federal will not accomplish the objects proposed by the Articles of the Confederation, namely, common defence, security of liberty, and general welfare."

The inference from the use here made of the terms, and from the proceedings on the subsequent propositions, is, that although common defence and general welfare were objects of the Confederation, they were limited objects, which ought to be enlarged by an enlargement of the particular powers to which they were limited, and to be accomplished by a change in the structure of the Union from a form merely Federal to one partly national; and as these general terms are prefixed in the like relation to the several legislative powers in the new charter as they were in the old, they must be understood to be under like limitations in the new as in the old.

In the course of the proceedings between the 30th of May and the 6th of August, the terms common defence and general welfare, as well as other equivalent terms, must have been dropped; for they do not appear in the draught of a Constitution reported on that day by a committee appointed to prepare one in detail, the clause in which those terms were afterward inserted being in the draught simply, "The Legislature of the United States shall have power to lay and collect taxes, duties, imposts, and excises."

The manner in which the terms became transplanted from the old into the new system of Government, is explained by a course somewhat adventitiously given to the proceedings of the Convention.

On the 18th of August, among other propositions referred to the committee which had reported the draught, was one "to *secure* the payment of the public debt;" and

On the same day was appointed a committee of eleven members, (one from each State,) "to consider the necessity and expediency of *the debts of the several States* being assumed by the United States."

On the 21st of August, this last committee reported a clause in the words following: "The Legislature of the United States *shall have power* to fulfil the engagements *which have been* entered into by Congress, and to discharge as well the debts of the United States as the debts incurred by the *several* States *during the late war,* for the *common defence* and *general welfare;*" conforming herein to the eighth of the Articles of Confederation, the language of which is, that "all charges of war, and all other expenses that shall be incurred for the common defence and general welfare, and allowed by the United States in Congress assembled, shall be defrayed out of a common Treasury," &c.

On the 22d of August, the committee of five reported, among other additions to the clause, "*giving power* to lay

453

and collect taxes, imposts, and excises," a clause in the words following, "for payment of the debts and necessary expenses," with a proviso qualifying the duration of revenue laws.

This report being taken up, it was moved, as an amendment, that the clause should read, "The Legislature *shall* fulfil the engagements and discharge the debts of the United States."

It was then moved to strike out "discharge the debts," and insert, "liquidate the claims;" which being rejected, the amendment was agreed to as proposed, viz: "The Legislature *shall* fulfil the engagements and discharge the debts of the United States."

On the 23d of August the clause was made to read, "The Legislature shall fulfil the engagements and discharge the debts of the United States, and shall have the power to lay and collect taxes, duties, imposts, and excises," the two powers relating to taxes and debts being merely transposed.

On the 25th of August the clause was again altered so as to read, "All debts contracted and engagements entered into by, or under the authority of Congress, [the Revolutionary Congress,] shall be as valid under this Constitution as under the Confederation."

This amendment was followed by a proposition, referring to the powers to lay and collect taxes, &c., and to discharge the debts, [*old* debts,] to add, "for payment of *said* debts, and for defraying the *expenses that shall be* incurred *for the common defence and general welfare*." The proposition was disagreed to, one State only voting for it.

September 4, the committee of eleven reported the following modification: "The Legislature shall have power to lay and collect taxes, duties, imposts, and excises, to pay the debts and provide for the common defence and general welfare;" thus retaining the terms of the Article of Confederation, and covering, by the general term "debts," those of the old Congress.

A special provision in this mode could not have been necessary for the debts of the new Congress; for a power to provide money, and a power to perform certain acts, of which money is the ordinary and appropriate means, must of course carry with them a power to pay the expense of performing the acts. Nor was any special provision for debts proposed till the case of the revolutionary debts was brought into view; and it is a fair presumption, from the course of the varied propositions which have been noticed, that but for the old debts, and their association with the terms "common defence and general welfare," the clause would have remained as reported in the first draught of a Constitution, expressing generally, "a power in Congress to lay and collect taxes, duties, imposts, and excises," without any addition of the phrase, "to provide for the common defence and general welfare." With this addition, indeed, the language of the clause being in conformity with that of the clause in the Articles of Confederation, it would be qualified, as in those articles, by the specification of powers subjoined to it. But there is sufficient reason to suppose that the terms in question would not have been introduced but for the introduction of the old debts, with which they happened to stand in a familiar though inoper-

ative relation. Thus introduced, however, they passed undisturbed through the subsequent stages of the Constitution.

If it be asked why the terms "common defence and general welfare," if not meant to convey the comprehensive power which, taken literally, they express, were not qualified and explained by some reference to the particular powers subjoined, the answer is at hand, that although it might easily have been done, and experience shows it might be well if it had been done, yet the omission is accounted for by an inattention to the phraseology, occasioned doubtless by its identity with the harmless character attached to it in the instrument from which it was borrowed.

But may it not be asked with infinitely more propriety, and without the possibility of a satisfactory answer, why, if the terms were meant to embrace not only all the powers particularly expressed, but the indefinite power which has been claimed under them, the intention was not so declared? why, on that supposition, so much critical labour was employed in enumerating the particular powers, and in defining and limiting their extent?

The variations and vicissitudes in the modification of the clause in which the terms "common defence and general welfare" appear, are remarkable, and to be no otherwise explained than by differences of opinion concerning the necessity or the form of a constitutional provision for the debts of the Revolution; some of the members apprehending improper claims for losses by depreciated emissions of bills of credit; others an evasion of proper claims, if not positively brought within the authorized functions of the new Government; and others again considering the past debts of the United States as sufficiently secured by the principle that no change in the Government could change the obligations of the nation. Besides the indications in the journal, the history of the period sanctions this explanation.

But it is to be emphatically remarked, that in the multitude of motions, propositions, and amendments, there is not a single one having reference to the terms "common defence and general welfare," unless we were so to understand the proposition containing them made on August 25, which was disagreed to by all the States except one.

The obvious conclusion to which we are brought is, that these terms, copied from the Articles of Confederation, were regarded in the new as in the old instrument, merely as general terms, explained and limited by the subjoined specifications, and therefore requiring no critical attention or studied precaution.

If the *practice* of the revolutionary Congress be pleaded in opposition to this view of the case, the plea is met by the notoriety that on several accounts the practice of that body is not the expositor of the "Articles of Confederation." These articles were not in force till they were finally ratified by Maryland in 1781. Prior to that event, the power of Congress was measured by the exigencies of the war, and derived its sanction from the acquiescence of the States. After that event, habit and a continued expediency, amounting often to a real or apparent necessity, prolonged the exercise of an undefined authority; which was the more readily overlooked, as the members of the body held their seats during pleasure; as its acts, particularly after the failure of the bills of credit, depended for their efficacy on the will of the States, and as its general impotency became manifest. Examples of departure from the prescribed rule are too well known to require proof. The case of the old Bank of North America might be cited as a memorable one. The incorporating ordinance grew out of the inferred necessity of such an institution to carry on the war, by aiding the finances, which were starving under the neglect or inability of the States to furnish their assessed quotas. Congress was at the time so much aware of the deficient authority, that they recommended it to the State Legislatures to pass laws giving due effect to the ordinance, which was done by Pennsylvania and several other States. In a little time, however, so much dissatisfaction arose in Pennsylvania, where the bank was located, that it was proposed to repeal the law of the State in support of it. This brought on attempts to vindicate the adequacy of the power of Congress to incorporate such an institution. Mr. Wilson, justly distinguished for his intellectual powers, being deeply impressed with the importance of a bank at such a crisis, published a small pamphlet, entitled "Considerations on the Bank of North America," in which he endeavoured to derive the power from the *nature* of the *union* in which the colonies were declared and became independent States; and also from the tenor of the "Articles of Confederation" themselves. But what is particularly worthy of notice is, that with all his anxious search in those articles for such a power, he never glanced at the terms "common defence and general welfare" as a source of it. He rather chose to rest the claim on a recital in the text, "that, for the more convenient management of the *general* interests of the *United* States, delegates shall be annually appointed to meet in Congress, which, he said, implied that the *United* States had *general* rights, *general* powers, and *general* obligations, not derived from *any* particular State, nor from *all* the particular States taken separately, but *resulting* from the *union* of the whole," these general powers not being controlled by the article declaring that each State retained *all* powers not granted by the articles, because "the *individual* States *never* possessed and could not retain a *general* power over the others."

The authority and argument here resorted to, if proving the ingenuity and patriotic anxiety of the author on one hand, show sufficiently on the other that the terms common defence and general welfare could not, according to the known acceptation of them, avail his object.

That the terms in question were not suspected in the Convention which formed the Constitution of any such meaning as has been constructively applied to them, may be pronounced with entire confidence; for it exceeds the possibility of belief, that the known advocates in the Convention for a jealous grant and cautious definition of Federal powers should have silently permitted the introduction of words or phrases in a sense rendering fruitless the restrictions and definitions elaborated by them.

Consider for a moment the immeasurable difference between the Constitution limited in its powers to the enumerated objects, and expounded as it would be by the import claimed for the phraseology in question. The difference is equivalent to two Constitutions, of characters essentially contrasted with each other—the one possessing powers confined to certain specified cases, the other extended to all cases whatsoever; for what is the case that would not be embraced by a general power to raise money, a power to provide for the general welfare, and a power to pass all laws necessary and proper to carry these powers into execution; all such provisions and laws superseding, at the same time, all local laws and constitutions at variance with them? Can less be said, with the evidence before us furnished by the journal of the Convention itself, than that it is impossible that such a Constitution as the latter would have been recommended to the States by all the members of that body whose names were subscribed to the instrument?

Passing from this view of the sense in which the terms common defence and general welfare were used by the framers of the Constitution, let us look for that in which they must have been understood by the Convention, or, rather, by the people, who, through their Conventions, accepted and ratified it. And here the evidence is, if possible, still more irresistible, that the terms could not have been regarded as giving a scope to Federal legislation infinitely more objectionable than any of the specified powers which produced such strenuous opposition, and calls for amendments which might be safeguards against the dangers apprehended from them.

Without recurring to the published debates of those Conventions, which, as far as they can be relied on for accuracy, would, it is believed, not impair the evidence furnished by their recorded proceedings, it will suffice to consult the list of amendments proposed by such of the Conventions as considered the powers granted to the new Government too extensive or not safely defined.

Besides the restrictive and explanatory amendments to the text of the Constitution, it may be observed, that a long list was premised, under the name and in the nature of "declarations of rights;" all of them indicating a jealousy of the Federal powers, and an anxiety to multiply securities against a constructive enlargement of them. But the appeal is more particularly made to the number and nature of the amendments proposed to be made specific and integral parts of the constitutional text.

No less than seven States, it appears, concurred in adding to their ratifications a series of amendments which they deemed requisite. Of these amendments, *nine* were proposed by the Convention of Massachusetts, *five* by that of South Carolina, *twelve* by that of New Hampshire, *twenty* by that of Virginia, *thirty-three* by that of New York, *twenty-six* by that of North Carolina, *twenty-one* by that of Rhode Island.

Here are a majority of the States proposing amendments, in one instance thirty-three by a single State; all of them intended to circumscribe the powers granted to the General Government, by explanations, restrictions, or prohibitions, without including a single proposition from a single State referring to the terms common defence and general welfare; which, if understood to convey the asserted power, could not have failed to be the power most strenuously aimed at, because evidently more alarming in its range than all the powers objected to put together; and that the terms should have passed altogether unnoticed by the many eyes which saw danger in terms and phrases employed in some of the most minute and limited of the enumerated powers, must be regarded as a demonstration that it was taken for granted that the terms were harmless, because explained and limited, as in the "Articles of Confederation," by the enumerated powers which followed them.

A like demonstration that these terms were not understood in any sense that could invest Congress with powers not otherwise bestowed by the constitutional charter, may be found in what passed in the first session of the first Congress, when the subject of amendments was taken up, with the conciliatory view of freeing the Constitution from objections which had been made to the extent of its powers, or to the unguarded terms employed in describing them. Not only were the terms "common defence and general welfare" unnoticed in the long list of amendments brought forward in the outset, but the journals of Congress show that, in the progress of the discussions, not a single proposition was made in either branch of the Legislature which referred to the phrase as admitting a constructive enlargement of the granted powers, and requiring an amendment guarding against it. Such a forbearance and silence on such an occasion, and among so many members who belonged to the part of the nation which called for explanatory and restrictive amendments, and who had been elected as known advocates for them, cannot be accounted for without supposing that the terms "common defence and general welfare" were not at that time deemed susceptible of any such construction as has since been applied to them.

It may be thought, perhaps, due to the subject, to advert to a letter of October 5, 1787, to Samuel Adams, and another of October 16, of the same year, to the Governor of Virginia, from R. H. Lee, in both of which it is seen that the terms had attracted his notice, and were apprehended by him "to submit to Congress every object of human legislation." But it is particularly worthy of remark, that, although a member of the Senate of the United States when amendments of the Constitution were before that house, and sundry additions and alterations were there made to the list sent from the other, no notice was taken of those terms as pregnant with danger. It must be inferred, that the opinion formed by the distinguished member at the first view of the Constitution, and before it had been fully discussed and elucidated, had been changed into a conviction that the terms did not fairly admit the construction he had originally put on them, and therefore needed no explanatory precaution against it.

Allow me, my dear sir, to express on this occasion, what I always feel, an anxious hope that, as our Constitution rests on a middle ground between a form wholly national and one merely federal, and on a division of the powers of Government between the States in their united character and in their individual characters, this peculiarity of the system will be kept in view, as a key to the sound interpretation of the instrument, and a warning against any doctrine that would either enable the States to invalidate the powers of the United States, or confer all power on them.

I close these remarks, which I fear may be found tedious, with assurances of my great esteem and best regards.

Memorandum not used in letter to Mr. Stevenson.

These observations will be concluded with a notice of the argument in favour of the grant of a full power to provide for common defence and general welfare, drawn from the punctuation in some editions of the Constitution.

According to one mode of presenting the text, it reads as follows: "Congress shall have power—To lay and collect taxes, duties, imposts, and excises; to pay the debts and provide for the common defence and general welfare of the United States; but all duties, imposts, and excises, shall be uniform." To another mode, the same with commas *vice* semicolons.

According to the other mode, the text stands thus: "Congress shall have power; To lay and collect taxes, duties, imposts, and excises: To pay the debts and provide for the common defence and general welfare of the United States; but all duties, imposts, and excises shall be uniform throughout the United States."

And from this view of the text, it is inferred that the latter sentence conveys a distinct substantive power to provide for the common defence and general welfare.

Without inquiring how far the text in this form would convey the power in question; or admitting that any mode of presenting or distributing the terms could invalidate the evidence which has been exhibited, that it was not the intention of the general or of the State Coventions to express, by the use of the terms common defence and general welfare, a substantive and indefinite power; or to imply that the general terms were not to be explained and limited by the specified powers succeeding them, in like manner as they were explained and limited in the former Articles of Confederation from which the terms were taken; it happens that the authenticity of the punctuation which preserves the unity of the clause can be as satisfactorily shown, as the true intention of the parties to the Constitution has been shown in the language used by them.

The only instance of a division of the clause afforded by the journal of the Convention is in the draught of a Constitution reported by a committee of five members, and entered on the 12th of September.

But that this must have been an erratum of the pen or of the press, may be inferred from the circumstance, that, in a copy of that report, printed at the time for the use of the members, and now in my possession, the text is so printed as to unite the parts in one substantive clause; an inference favoured also by a previous report of September 4, by a committee of eleven, in which the parts of the clause are united, not separated.

And that the true reading of the Constitution, as it passed, is that which unites the parts, is abundantly attested by the following facts:

1. Such is the form of the text in the Constitution printed at the close of the Convention, after being signed by the members, of which a copy is also now in my possession.

2. The case is the same in the Constitution from the Convention to the old Congress, as printed on their journal of September 28, 1787, and transmitted by that body to the Legislatures of the several States.

3. The case is the same in the copies of the transmitted Constitution, as printed by the ratifying States, several of which have been examined; and it is a presumption that there is no variation in the others.

The text is in the same form in an edition of the Constitution published in 1814, by order of the Senate; as also in the Constitution as prefixed to the edition of the laws of the United States; in fact, the proviso for uniformity is itself a proof of identity of them.

It might, indeed, be added, that in the journal of September 14, the clause to which the proviso was annexed, now a part of the Constitution, viz: "but all duties, imposts, and excises, shall be uniform throughout the United States," is called the "first," of course a "single" clause. And it is obvious that the uniformity required by the proviso implies that what it referred to was a part of the same clause with the proviso, not an antecedent clause altogether separated from it.

Should it be not contested that the original Constitution, in its engrossed or enrolled state, with the names of the subscribing members affixed thereto, presents the text in the same form, that alone must extinguish the argument in question.

If, contrary to every ground of confidence, the text, in its original enrolled document, should not coincide with these multiplied examples, the first question would be of comparative probability of error, even in the enrolled document, and in the number and variety of the concurring examples in opposition to it.

And a second question, whether the construction put on the text, in any of its forms or punctuations, ought to have the weight of a feather against the solid and diversified proofs which have been pointed out, of the meaning of the parties to the Constitution.

Supplement to the letter of November 27, 1830, to A. Stevenson, on the phrase "common defence and general welfare."—On the power of indefinite appropriation of money by Congress.

It is not to be forgotten, that a distinction has been introduced between a power merely to appropriate money to the common defence and general welfare, and a power to employ all the means of giving full effect to objects embraced by the terms.

1. The first observation to be here made is, that an *express* power to appropriate money authorized to be raised, to objects authorized to be provided for, could not, as seems to have been supposed, be at all necessary; and that the insertion of the power "to pay the debts," &c., is not to be referred to that cause. It has been seen, that the particular expression of the power originated in a cautious regard to debts of the United States antecedent to the radical change in the Federal Government; and that, but for that consideration, no particular expression of an appropriating power would probably have been thought of. An express power to raise money, and an express power (for example) to raise an army, would surely imply a power to use the money for that purpose. And if a doubt could possibly arise as to the implication, it would be completely removed by the express power to pass all laws necessary and proper in such cases.

2. But admitting the distinction as alleged, the appropriating power to *all* objects of "common defence and general welfare" is itself of sufficient magnitude to render the preceding views of the subject applicable to it. Is it credible that such a power would have been unnoticed and unopposed in the Federal Convention? in the State Conventions, which contended for, and proposed restrictive and explanatory amendments? and in the Congress of 1789, which recommended so many of these amendments? A power to impose *unlimited taxes* for *unlimited purposes* could never have escaped the sagacity and jealousy which were awakened to the many inferior and minute powers which were criticised and combated in those public bodies.

3. A power to appropriate money, without a power to apply it in execution of the object of appropriation, could have no effect but to lock it up from public use altogether; and if the appropriating power carries with it the power of application and execution, the distinction vanishes. The power, therefore, means nothing, or what is worse than nothing, or it is the same thing with the sweeping power "to provide for the common defence and general welfare."

4. To avoid this dilemma, the consent of the States is introduced as justifying the exercise of the power in the full extent within their respective limits. But it would be a new doctrine, that an extra-constitutional consent of the parties to a Constitution could amplify the jurisdiction of the constituted Government. And if this could not be done by the concurring consents of all the States, what is to be said of the doctrine that the consent of an individual State could authorize the application of money belonging to all the States to its individual purposes? Whatever be the presumption that the Government of the whole would not abuse such an authority by a partiality in expending the public treasure, it is not the less necessary to prove the existence of the power. The Constitution is a limited one, possessing no power not actually given, and carrying on the face of it a distrust of power beyond the distrust indicated by the ordinary forms of free Government.

The peculiar structure of the Government, which combines an equal representation of unequal numbers in one branch of the Legislature, with an equal representation of equal numbers in the other, and the peculiarity which invests the Government with selected powers only, not intrusting it even with every power withdrawn from the local governments, prove not only an apprehension of abuse from ambition or corruption in those administering the Government, but of oppression or injustice from the separate interests or views of the constituent bodies themselves, taking effect through the administration of the Government. These peculiarities were thought to be safeguards due to minorities having peculiar interests or institutions at stake, against majorities who might be tempted by interest or other motives to invade them; and all such minorities, however composed, act with consistency in opposing a latitude of construction, particularly that which has been applied to the terms "common defence and general welfare," which would impair the security intended for minor parties. Whether the distrustful precaution interwoven in the Constitution was or was not in every instance necessary; or how far, with certain modifications, any farther powers might be safely and usefully granted, are questions which were open for those who framed the great Federal Charter, and are still open to those who aim at improving it. But while it remains as it is, its true import ought to be faithfully observed; and those who have most to fear from constructive innovations ought to be most vigilant in making head against them.

But it would seem that a resort to the consent of the State Legislatures, as a sanction to the appropriating power, is so far from being admissible in this case, that it is precluded by the fact that the Constitution has expressly provided for the cases where that consent was to sanction and extend the power of the national Legislature. How can it be imagined that the Constitution, when pointing out the cases where such an effect was to be produced, should have deemed it necessary to be positive and precise with respect to such minute spots as forts, &c., and have left the general effect ascribed to such consent to an argumentative, or, rather, to an arbitrary construction? And here again an appeal may be made to the incredibility that such a mode of enlarging the sphere of federal legislation should have been unnoticed in the ordeals through which the Constitution passed, by those who were alarmed at many of its powers bearing no comparison with that source of power in point of importance.

5. Put the case that money is appropriated to a canal* to be cut within a particular State; how and by whom, it may be asked, is the money to be applied and the work to be executed? By agents under the authority of the General Government? then the power is no longer a mere appropriating power. By agents under the authority of the States? then the State becomes either a branch or a functionary of the Executive authority of the United States; an incongruity that speaks for itself.

6. The distinction between a pecuniary power only, and a plenary power "to provide for the common defence and general welfare," is frustrated by another reply to which it is liable. For if the clause be not a mere introduction to the enumerated powers, and restricted to them, the power to provide for the common defence and general welfare stands as a distinct substantive power, the first on the list of legislative powers; and not only involving all the powers incident to its execution, but coming within the purview of

the clause concluding the list, which expressly declares that Congress may make all laws necessary and proper to carry into execution the *foregoing* powers vested in Congress.

The result of this investigation is, that the terms "common defence and general welfare" owed their induction into the text of the Constitution to their connexion in the "Articles of Confederation," from which they were copied, with the debts contracted by the old Congress, and to be provided for by the new Congress; and are used in the one instrument as in the other, as general terms, limited and explained by the particular clauses subjoined to the clause containing them; that in this light they were viewed throughout the recorded proceedings of the Convention which framed the Constitution; that the same was the light in which they were viewed by the State Conventions which ratified the Constitution, as is shown by the records of their proceedings; and that such was the case also in the first Congress under the Constitution, according to the evidence of their journals, when digesting the amendments afterward made to the Constitution. It equally appears that the alleged power to appropriate money to the "common defence and general welfare" is either a dead letter, or swells into an unlimited power to provide for unlimited purposes, by all the means necessary and proper for those purposes. And it results finally, that if the Constitution does not give to Congress the unqualified power to provide for the common defence and general welfare, the defect cannot be supplied by the consent of the States, unless given in the form prescribed by the Constitution itself for its own amendment.

As the people of the United States enjoy the great merit of having established a system of Government on the basis of human rights, and of giving to it a form without example, which, as they believe, unites the greatest national strength with the best security for public order and individual liberty, they owe to themselves, to their posterity, and to the world, a preservation of the system in its purity, its symmetry, and its authenticity. This can only be done by a steady attention and sacred regard to the chartered boundaries between the portion of power vested in the Government over the whole, and the portion undivested from the several Governments over the parts composing the whole; and by a like attention and regard to the boundaries between the several departments, Legislative, Executive, and Judiciary, into which the aggregate power is divided. Without a steady eye to the landmarks between these departments, the danger is always to be apprehended, either of mutual encroachments and alternate ascendencies incompatible with the tranquil enjoyment of private rights, or of a concentration of all the departments of power into a single one, universally acknowledged to be fatal to public liberty.

And without an equal watchfulness over the great landmarks between the General Government and the particular Governments, the danger is certainly not less, of either a gradual relaxation of the band which holds the latter together, leading to an entire separation, or of a gradual assumption of their powers by the former, leading to a consolidation of all the Governments into a single one.

The two vital characteristics of the political system of the

---

*On more occasions than one, it has been noticed in Congressional debates that propositions appear to have been made in the Convention of 1787 to give to Congress the power of opening canals, and to have been rejected; and that Mr. Hamilton, when contending in his report in favour of a bank for a liberal construction of the powers of Congress, admitted that a canal might be beyond the reach of those powers.

United States are, first, that the Government holds its powers by a charter granted to it by the people; second, that the powers of Government are formed into two grand divisions—one vested in a Government over the whole community, the other in a number of independent Governments over its component parts. Hitherto charters have been written grants of privileges by Governments to the people. Here they are written grants of power by the people to their Governments.

Hitherto, again, all the powers of Government have been, in effect, consolidated into one Government, tending to faction and a foreign yoke among a people within narrow limits, and to arbitrary rule among a people spread over an extensive region. Here the established system aspires to such a division and organization of power as will provide at once for its harmonious exercise on the true principles of liberty over the parts and over the whole, notwithstanding the great extent of the whole; the system forming an innovation and an epoch in the science of Government not less honorable to the people to whom it owed its birth, than auspicious to the political welfare of all others who may imitate or adopt it.

As the most arduous and delicate task in this great work lay in the untried demarkation of the line which divides the general and the particular Governments by an enumeration and definition of the powers of the former, more especially the legislative powers; and as the success of this new scheme of polity essentially depends on the faithful observance of this partition of powers, the friends of the scheme, or rather the friends of liberty and of man, cannot be too often earnestly exhorted to be watchful in marking and controling encroachments by either of the Governments on the domain of the other.

28

JOSEPH STORY, COMMENTARIES ON THE
CONSTITUTION 2:§§ 904–25, 927–30,
946–52, 954–70, 972–76, 988
1833

§ 904. Before proceeding to consider the nature and extent of the power conferred by this clause, and the reasons, on which it is founded, it seems necessary to settle the grammatical construction of the clause, and to ascertain its true reading. Do the words, "to lay and collect taxes, duties, imposts, and excises," constitute a distinct, substantial power; and the words, "to pay debts and provide for the common defence, and general welfare of the United States," constitute another distinct and substantial power? Or are the latter words connected with the former, so as to constitute a qualification upon them? This has been a topic of political controversy; and has furnished abundant materials for popular declamation and alarm. If the former be the true interpretation, then it is obvious, that under colour of the generality of the words to "provide for the common defence and general welfare," the

government of the United States is, in reality, a government of general and unlimited powers, notwithstanding the subsequent enumeration of specific powers; if the latter be the true construction, then the power of taxation only is given by the clause, and it is limited to objects of a national character, "for the common defence and the general welfare."

§ 905. The former opinion has been maintained by some minds of great ingenuity, and liberality of views. The latter has been the generally received sense of the nation, and seems supported by reasoning at once solid and impregnable. The reading, therefore, which will be maintained in these commentaries, is that, which makes the latter words a qualification of the former; and this will be best illustrated by supplying the words, which are necessarily to be understood in this interpretation. They will then stand thus: "The congress shall have power to lay and collect taxes, duties, imposts, and excises, *in order* to pay the debts, and to provide for the common defence and general welfare of the United States;" that is, for the purpose of paying the public debts, and providing for the common defence and general welfare of the United States. In this sense, congress has not an unlimited power of taxation; but it is limited to specific objects,—the payment of the public debts, and providing for the common defence and general welfare. A tax, therefore, laid by congress for neither of these objects, would be unconstitutional, as an excess of its legislative authority. In what manner this is to be ascertained, or decided, will be considered hereafter. At present, the interpretation of the words only is before us; and the reasoning, by which that already suggested has been vindicated, will now be reviewed.

§ 906. The constitution was, from its very origin, contemplated to be the frame of a national government, of special and enumerated powers, and not of general and unlimited powers. This is apparent, as will be presently seen, from the history of the proceedings of the convention, which framed it; and it has formed the admitted basis of all legislative and judicial reasoning upon it, ever since it was put into operation, by all, who have been its open friends and advocates, as well as by all, who have been its enemies and opponents. If the clause, "to pay the debts and provide for the common defence and general welfare of the United States," is construed to be an independent and substantive grant of power, it not only renders wholly unimportant and unnecessary the subsequent enumeration of specific powers; but it plainly extends far beyond them, and creates a general authority in congress to pass all laws, which they may deem for the common defence or general welfare. Under such circumstances, the constitution would practically create an unlimited national government. The enumerated powers would tend to embarrassment and confusion; since they would only give rise to doubts, as to the true extent of the general power, or of the enumerated powers.

§ 907. One of the most common maxims of interpretation is, (as has been already stated,) that, as an exception strengthens the force of a law in cases not excepted, so enumeration weakens it in cases not enumerated. But, how could it be applied with success to the interpretation of the constitution of the United States, if the enumerated powers were neither exceptions from, nor additions to, the general power to provide for the common defence and general welfare? To give the enumeration of the specific powers any sensible place or operation in the constitution, it is indispensable to construe them, as not wholly and necessarily embraced in the general power. The common principles of interpretation would seem to instruct us, that the different parts of the same instrument ought to be so expounded, as to give meaning to every part, which will bear it. Shall one part of the same sentence be excluded altogether from a share in the meaning; and shall the more doubtful and indefinite terms be retained in their full extent, and the clear and precise expressions be denied any signification? For what purpose could the enumeration of particular powers be inserted, if these and all others were meant to be included in the preceding general power? Nothing is more natural or common, than first to use a general phrase, and then to qualify it by a recital of particulars. But the idea of an enumeration of particulars, which neither explain, nor qualify the general meaning, and can have no other effect, than to confound and mislead, is an absurdity, which no one ought to charge on the enlightened authors of the constitution. It would be to charge them either with premeditated folly, or premeditated fraud.

§ 908. On the other hand, construing this clause in connexion with, and as a part of the preceding clause, giving the power to lay taxes, it becomes sensible and operative. It becomes a qualification of that clause, and limits the taxing power to objects for the common defence or general welfare. It then contains no grant of any power whatsoever; but it is a mere expression of the ends and purposes to be effected by the preceding power of taxation.

§ 909. An attempt has been sometimes made to treat this clause, as distinct and independent, and yet as having no real significancy *per se*, but (if it may be so said) as a mere prelude to the succeeding enumerated powers. It is not improbable, that this mode of explanation has been suggested by the fact, that in the revised draft of the constitution in the convention the clause was separated from the preceding exactly in the same manner, as every succeeding clause was, viz. by a semicolon, and a break in the paragraph; and that it now stands, in some copies, and it is said, that it stands in the official copy, with a semicolon interposed. But this circumstance will be found of very little weight, when the origin of the clause, and its progress to its present state are traced in the proceedings of the convention. It will then appear, that it was first introduced as an appendage to the power to lay taxes. But there is a fundamental objection to the interpretation thus attempted to be maintained, which is, that it robs the clause of all efficacy and meaning. No person has a right to assume, that any part of the constitution is useless, or is without a meaning; and *a fortiori* no person has a right to rob any part of a meaning, natural and appropriate to the language in the connexion, in which it stands. Now, the words have such a natural and appropriate meaning, as a qualification of the preceding clause to lay taxes. Why, then, should such a meaning be rejected?

§ 910. It is no sufficient answer to say, that the clause ought to be regarded, merely as containing "general terms, explained and limited, by the subjoined specifications, and therefore requiring no critical attention, or studied precaution;" because it is assuming the very point in controversy, to assert, that the clause is connected with any subsequent specifications. It is not said, to "provide for the common defence, and general welfare, *in manner following, viz.*," which would be the natural expression, to indicate such an intention. But it stands entirely disconnected from every subsequent clause, both in sense and punctuation; and is no more a part of them, than they are of the power to lay taxes. Besides; what suitable application, in such a sense, would there be of the last clause in the enumeration, viz., the clause "to make all laws, necessary and proper for carrying into execution the foregoing powers, &c.?" Surely, this clause is as applicable to the power to lay taxes, as to any other; and no one would dream of its being a mere specification, under the power to provide for the common defence, and general welfare.

§ 911. It has been said [in James Madison's 1800 Report on the Virginia Resolutions] in support of this construction, that in the articles of confederation (art. 8) it is provided, that "all charges of war, and all other expenses, that shall be incurred for the common defence, or general welfare, and allowed by the United States in congress assembled, shall be defrayed out of a common treasury, &c.;" and that "the similarity in the use of these same phrases in these two great federal charters may well be considered, as rendering their meaning less liable to misconstruction; because it will scarcely be said, that in the former they were ever understood to be either a general grant or power, or to authorize the requisition or application of money by the old congress to the common defence and [or] general welfare, except in the cases afterwards enumerated, which explained and limited their meaning; and if such was the limited meaning attached to these phrases in the very instrument revised and remodelled by the present constitution, it can never be supposed, that when copied into this constitution, a different meaning ought to be attached to them." Without stopping to consider, whether the constitution can in any just and critical sense be deemed a revision and remodelling of the confederation, if the argument here stated be of any value, it plainly establishes, that the words ought to be construed, as a qualification or limitation of the power to lay taxes. By the confederation, all expenses incurred for the common defence, or general welfare, are to be defrayed out of a common treasury, to be supplied by requisitions upon the states. Instead of requisitions, the constitution gives the right to the national government directly to lay taxes. So, that the only difference in this view between the two clauses is, as to the mode of obtaining the money, not as to the objects or purposes, to which it is to be applied. If then the constitution were to be construed according to the true bearing of this argument, it would read thus: congress shall have power to lay taxes for "all charges of war, and all other expenses, that shall be incurred for the common defence or general welfare." This plainly makes it a qualification of the taxing power; and not an independent provision, or a general index to the succeeding specifications of power. There is not, however, any solid ground, upon which it can be for a moment maintained, that the language of the constitution is to be enlarged, or restricted by the language of the confederation. That would be to make it speak, what its words do not import, and its objects do not justify. It would be to append it, as a codicil, to an instrument, which it was designed wholly to supercede and vacate.

§ 912. But the argument in its other branch rests on an assumed basis, which is not admitted. It supposes, that in the confederation no expenses, not strictly incurred under some of the subsequent specified powers given to the continental congress, could be properly payable out of the common treasury. Now, that is a proposition to be proved; and is not to be taken for granted. The confederation was not finally ratified, so as to become a binding instrument on any of the states, until March, 1781. Until that period there could be no practice or construction under it; and it is not shown, that subsequently there was any exposition to the effect now insisted on. Indeed, after the peace of 1783, if there had been any such exposition, and it had been unfavourable to the broad exercise of the power, it would have been entitled to less weight, than usually belongs to the proceedings of public bodies in the administration of their powers; since the decline and fall of the confederation was so obvious, that it was of little use to exert them. The states notoriously disregarded the rights and prerogatives admitted to belong to the confederacy; and even the requisitions of congress, for objects most unquestionably within their constitutional authority, were openly denied, or silently evaded. Under such circumstances, congress would have little inclination to look closely to their powers; since, whether great or small, large or narrow, they were of little practical value, and of no practical cogency.

§ 913. But it does so happen, that in point of fact, no such unfavourable or restrictive interpretation or practice was ever adopted by the continental congress. On the contrary, they construed their power on the subject of requisitions and taxation, exactly as it is now contended for, as a power to make requisitions on the states for all expenses, which they might deem proper to incur for the common defence and general welfare; and to appropriate all monies in the treasury to the like purposes. This is admitted to be of such notoriety, as to require no proof. Surely, the practice of that body in questions of this nature must be of far higher value, than the mere private interpretation of any persons in the present times, however respectable. But the practice was conformable to the constitutional authority of congress under the confederation. The ninth article expressly delegates to congress the power "to ascertain the necessary sums to be raised for the service of the United States, and to appropriate and apply the same for defraying the public expenses;" and then provides, that congress shall not "ascertain the sums and expenses necessary for the *defence* and *welfare* of the United States, *or any of them*, &c. unless nine states assent to the same." So that here we have, in the eighth article, a declaration, that "all charges of war and all other expenses, that shall be incurred for the *common defence* or *general* welfare, &c. shall

be defrayed out of a common treasury;" and in the ninth article, an express power to ascertain the necessary sums of money to be raised for the public service; and then, that the necessary sums for the defence and welfare of the United States, (and not of the United States alone, for the words are added,) *or of any of them*, shall be ascertained by the assent of nine states. Clearly therefore, upon the plain language of the articles, the words "common defence and general welfare," in one, and "defence and welfare," in another, and "public service," in another, were not idle words, but were descriptive of the very intent and objects of the power; and not confined even to the defence and welfare of all the states, but extending to the welfare and defence of *any of them*. The power then is, in this view, even larger, than that conferred by the constitution.

§ 914. But there is no ground whatsoever, which authorizes any resort to the confederation, to interpret the power of taxation, which is conferred on congress by the constitution. The clause has no reference whatsoever to the confederation; nor indeed to any other clause of the constitution. It is, on its face, a distinct, substantive, and independent power. Who, then, is at liberty to say, that it is to be limited by other clauses, rather than they to be enlarged by it; since there is no avowed connexion, or reference from the one to the others? Interpretation would here desert its proper office, that, which requires, that "every part of the expression ought, if possible, to be allowed some meaning, and be made to conspire to some common end."

§ 915. It has been farther said [in Madison's 1800 Report], in support of the construction now under consideration, that "whether the phrases in question are construed to authorize every measure relating to the common defence and general welfare, as contended by some; or every measure only, in which there might be an application of money, as suggested by the caution of others; the effect must substantially be the same, in destroying the import and force of the particular enumeration of powers, which follow these general phrases in the constitution. For it is evident, that there is not a single power whatsoever, which may not have some reference to the common defence, or the general welfare; nor a power of any magnitude, which, in its exercise, does not involve, or admit an application of money. The government, therefore, which possesses power in either one, or the other of these extents, is a government without limitations, formed by a particular enumeration of powers; and consequently the meaning and effect of this particular enumeration is destroyed by the exposition given to these general phrases." The conclusion deduced from these premises is, that under the confederation, and the constitution, "congress is authorized to provide money for the common defence and general welfare. In both is subjoined to this authority an enumeration of the cases, to which their powers shall extend. Money cannot be applied to the general welfare otherwise, than by an application of it to some particular measure, conducive to the general welfare. Whenever, therefore, money has been raised by the general authority, and is to be applied to a particular measure, a question arises, whether the particular measure be within the enumerated authorities vested in the congress. If it be, the money requisite for it may be applied to it; if it be not, no such application can be made. This fair and obvious interpretation coincides with, and is enforced by the clause in the constitution, which declares, that no money shall be drawn from the treasury but in consequence of appropriations by law. An appropriation of money to the general welfare would be deemed rather a mockery, than an observance of this constitutional injunction."

§ 916. Stripped of the ingenious texture, by which this argument is disguised, it is neither more nor less, than an attempt to obliterate from the constitution the whole clause, "to pay the debts, and provide for the common defence and general welfare of the United States," as entirely senseless, or inexpressive of any intention whatsoever. Strike them out, and the constitution is exactly what the argument contends for. It is, therefore, an argument, that the words ought not to be in the constitution; because if they are, and have any meaning, they enlarge it beyond the scope of certain other enumerated powers, and this is both mischievous and dangerous. Being in the constitution, they are to be deemed, *vox et preterea nihil*, an empty sound and vain phraseology, a finger-board pointing to other powers, but having no use whatsoever, since these powers are sufficiently apparent without. Now, it is not too much to say, that in a constitution of government, framed and adopted by the people, it is a most unjustifiable latitude of interpretation to deny effect to any clause, if it is sensible in the language, in which it is expressed, and in the place, in which it stands. If words are inserted, we are bound to presume, that they have some definite object, and intent; and to reason them out of the constitution upon arguments *ab inconvenienti*, (which to one mind may appear wholly unfounded, and to another wholly satisfactory,) is to make a new constitution, not to construe the old one. It is to do the very thing, which is so often complained of, to make a constitution to suit our own notions and wishes, and not to administer, or construe that, which the people have given to the country.

§ 917. But what is the argument, when it is thoroughly sifted? It reasons upon a supposed dilemma, upon which it suspends the advocates of the two contrasted opinions. If the power to provide for the common defence and general welfare is an independent power, then it is said, that the government is unlimited, and the subsequent enumeration of powers is unnecessary and useless. If it is a mere appendage or qualification of the power to lay taxes, still it involves a power of general appropriation of the monies so raised, which indirectly produces the same result. Now, the former position may be safely admitted to be true by those, who do not deem it an independent power; but the latter position is not a just conclusion from the premises, which it states, that it is a qualified power. It is not a logical, or a practical sequence from the premises; it is a *non sequitur*.

§ 918. A dilemma, of a very different sort, might be fairly put to those, who contend for the doctrine, that the words are not a qualification of the power to lay taxes, and, indeed, have no meaning, or use *per se*. The words are found in the clause respecting taxation, and as a part of that clause. If the power to tax extends simply to the payment of the debts of the United States, then congress has no power to lay any taxes for any other purpose. If so, then congress could not appropriate the money raised to any other purposes; since the restriction is to taxes for payment of the debts of the United States, that is, of the debts *then existing*. This would be almost absurd. If, on the other hand, congress have a right to lay taxes, and appropriate the money to any other objects, it must be, because the words, "to provide for the common defence and general welfare," authorize it, by enlarging the power to those objects; for there are no other words, which belong to the clause. All the other powers are in distinct clauses, and do not touch taxation. No advocate for the doctrine of a restrictive power will contend, that the power to lay taxes to pay *debts*, authorizes the payment of all debts, which the United States may choose to incur, whether for national or constitutional objects, or not. The words, "to pay debts," are therefore, either antecedent debts, or debts to be incurred "for the common defence and general welfare," which will justify congress in incurring any debts for such purposes. But the language is not confined to the payment of debts for the common defence and general welfare. It is not "to pay the debts" merely; but "to *provide for* the common defence and general welfare." That is, congress may lay taxes to provide means for the common defence and general welfare. So that there is a difficulty in rejecting one part of the qualifying clause, without rejecting the whole, or enlarging the words for some purposes, and restricting them for others.

§ 919. A power to lay taxes for any purposes whatsoever is a general power; a power to lay taxes for certain specified purposes is a limited power. A power to lay taxes for the common defence and general welfare of the United States is not in common sense a general power. It is limited to those objects. It cannot constitutionally transcend them. If the defence proposed by a tax be not the common defence of the United States, if the welfare be not general, but special, or local, as contradistinguished from national, it is not within the scope of the constitution. If the tax be not proposed for the common defence, or general welfare, but for other objects, wholly extraneous, (as for instance, for propagating Mahometanism among the Turks, or giving aids and subsidies to a foreign nation, to build palaces for its kings, or erect monuments to its heroes,) it would be wholly indefensible upon constitutional principles. The power, then, is, under such circumstances, necessarily a qualified power. If it is so, how then does it affect, or in the slightest degree trench upon the other enumerated powers? No one will pretend, that the power to lay taxes would, in general, have superseded, or rendered unnecessary all the other enumerated powers. It would neither enlarge, nor qualify them. A power to tax does not include them. Nor would they, (as unhappily the confederation too clearly demonstrated,) necessarily include a power to tax. Each has its appropriate office and objects; each may exist without necessarily interfering with, or annihilating the other. No one will pretend, that the power to lay a tax necessarily includes the power to declare war, to pass naturalization and bankrupt laws, to coin money, to establish post-offices, or to define piracies and felonies on the high seas. Nor would either of these be deemed necessarily to include the power to tax. It might be convenient; but it would not be absolutely indispensable.

§ 920. The whole of the elaborate reasoning upon the propriety of granting the power of taxation, pressed with so much ability and earnestness, both in and out of the convention, as vital to the operations of the national government, would have been useless, and almost absurd, if the power was included in the subsequently enumerated powers. If the power of taxing was to be granted, why should it not be qualified according to the intention of the framers of the constitution? But then, it is said, if congress may lay taxes for the common defence and general welfare, the money may be appropriated for those purposes, although not within the scope of the other enumerated powers. Certainly it may be so appropriated; for if congress is authorized to lay taxes for such purposes, it would be strange, if, when raised, the money could not be applied to them. That would be to give a power for a certain end, and then deny the end intended by the power. It is added, "that there is not a single power whatsoever, which may not have some reference to the common defence or general welfare; nor a power of any magnitude, which, in its exercise, does not involve, or admit an application of money." If by the former language is meant, that there is not any power belonging, or incident to any government, which has not some reference to the common defence or general welfare, the proposition may be peremptorily denied. Many governments possess powers, which have no application to either of these objects in a just sense; and some possess powers repugnant to both. If it is meant, that there is no power belonging, or incident to a good government, and especially to a republican government, which may not have some reference to those objects, that proposition may, or may not be true; but it has nothing to do with the present inquiry. The only question is, whether a mere power to lay taxes, and appropriate money for the common defence and general welfare, does include all the other powers of government; or even does include the other enumerated powers (limited as they are) of the national government. No person can answer in the affirmative to either part of the inquiry, who has fully considered the subject. The power of taxation is but one of a multitude of powers belonging to governments; to the state governments, as well as the national government. Would a power to tax authorize a state government to regulate the descent and distribution of estates; to prescribe the form of conveyances; to establish courts of justice for general purposes; to legislate respecting personal rights, or the general dominion of property; or to punish all offences against society? Would it confide to congress the power to grant patent rights for intervention; to provide for counterfeiting the public securities and coin; to constitute judicial tribunals with the powers confided by the third article of the constitution; to declare war, and raise armies and navies, and make regulations for their government; to exercise exclusive legislation in the territories of the United States, or in other ceded places; or to make all laws necessary and proper to carry into effect all the powers given

by the constitution? The constitution itself upon its face refutes any such notion. It gives the power to tax, as a substantive power; and gives others, as equally substantive and independent.

§ 921. That the same means may sometimes, or often, be resorted to, to carry into effect the different powers, furnishes no objection; for that is common to all governments. That an appropriation of money may be the usual, or best mode of carrying into effect some of these powers, furnishes no objection; for it is one of the purposes, for which, the argument itself admits, that the power of taxation is given. That it is indispensable for the due exercise of all the powers, may admit of some doubt. The only real question is, whether even admitting the power to lay taxes is appropriate for some of the purposes of other enumerated powers, (for no one will contend, that it will, of itself, reach, or provide for them all,) it is limited to such appropriations, as grow out of the exercise of those powers. In other words, whether it is an incident to those powers, or a substantive power in other cases, which may concern the common defence and the general welfare. If there are no other cases, which concern the common defence and general welfare, except those within the scope of the other enumerated powers, the discussion is merely nominal and frivolous. If there are such cases, who is at liberty to say, that, being for the common defence and general welfare, the constitution did not intend to embrace them? The preamble of the constitution declares one of the objects to be, to provide for the common defence, and to promote the general welfare; and if the power to lay taxes is in express terms given to provide for the common defence and general welfare, what ground can there be to construe the power, short of the object? To say, that it shall be merely auxiliary to other enumerated powers, and not co-extensive with its own terms, and its avowed objects? One of the best established rules of interpretation, one, which common sense and reason forbid us to overlook, is, that when the object of a power is clearly defined by its terms, or avowed in the context, it ought to be construed, so as to obtain the object, and not to defeat it. The circumstance, that so construed the power may be abused, is no answer. All powers may be abused; but are they then to be abridged by those, who are to administer them, or denied to have any operation? If the people frame a constitution, the rulers are to obey it. Neither rulers, nor any other functionaries, much less any private persons, have a right to cripple it, because it is according to their own views inconvenient, or dangerous, unwise or impolitic, of narrow limits, or of wide influence.

§ 922. Besides; the argument itself admits, that "congress is authorized to provide money for the common defence and general welfare." It is not pretended, that, when the tax is laid, the specific objects, for which it is laid, are to be specified, or that it is to be solely applied to those objects. That would be to insert a limitation, no where stated in the text. But it is said, that it must be applied to the general welfare; and that can only be by an application of it to some *particular measure*, conducive to the general welfare. This is admitted. But then, it is added, that this particular measure must be within the enumerated authorities vested in congress, (that is, within some of the powers not embraced in the first clause,) otherwise the application is not authorized. Why not, since it is for the general welfare? No reason is assigned, except, that not being within the scope of those enumerated powers, it is not given by the constitution. Now, the premises may be true; but the conclusion does not follow, unless the words *common defence* and *general welfare* are limited to the specifications included in those powers. So, that after all, we are led back to the same reasoning, which construes the words, as having no meaning *per se*, but as dependent upon, and an exponent of, the enumerated powers. Now, this conclusion is not justified by the natural connexion or collocation of the words; and it strips them of all reasonable force and efficacy. And yet we are told, that "this fair and obvious interpretation coincides with, and is enforced by, the clause of the constitution, which provides, that no money shall be drawn from the treasury, but in consequence of appropriations by law;" as if the clause did not equally apply, as a restraint upon drawing money, whichever construction is adopted. Suppose congress to possess the most unlimited power to appropriate money for the general welfare; would it not be still true, that it could not be drawn from the treasury, until an appropriation was made by some law passed by congress? This last clause is a limitation, not upon the powers of congress, but upon the acts of the executive, and other public officers, in regard to the public monies in the treasury.

§ 923. The argument in favour of the construction, which treats the clause, as a qualification of the power to lay taxes, has, perhaps, never been presented in a more concise or forcible shape, than in an official opinion, deliberately given by one of our most distinguished statesmen [Jefferson]. "To lay taxes to provide for the general welfare of the United States, is," says he, "to lay taxes *for the purpose,* of providing for the general welfare. For the laying of taxes is the *power,* and the general welfare the *purpose,* for which the power is to be exercised. Congress are not to lay taxes *ad libitum,* for any purpose they please; but only to pay the debts, or provide for the welfare of the Union. In like manner they are not to do any thing they please, to provide for the general welfare; but only to lay taxes for that purpose. To consider the latter phrase, not as describing the purpose of the first, but as giving a distinct and independent power to do any act they please, which might be for the good of the Union, would render all the preceding and subsequent enumerations of power completely useless. It would reduce the whole instrument to a single phrase, that of instituting a congress with power to do whatever would be for the good of the United States; and, as they would be the sole judges of the good or evil, it would also be a power to do whatever evil they pleased. It is an established rule of construction, where a phrase will bear either of two meanings, to give that, which will allow some meaning to the other parts of the instrument, and not that, which will render all the others useless. Certainly, no such universal power was meant to be given them. It was intended to lace them up strictly within the enumerated powers, and those, without which, as means, those powers could not be carried into effect."

§ 924. The same opinion has been maintained at different and distant times by many eminent statesmen. It was avowed, and apparently acquiesed in, in the state conventions, called to ratify the constitution: and it has been, on various occasions, adopted by congress, and may fairly be deemed, that which the deliberate sense of a majority of the nation has at all times supported. This, too, seems to be the construction maintained by the Supreme Court of the United States. In the case of *Gibbons* v. *Ogden,* Mr. Chief Justice Marshall, in delivering the opinion of the court, said, "Congress is authorized to lay and collect taxes, &c. to pay the debts, and provide for the common defence and general welfare of the United States. This does not interefere with the power of the states to tax for the support of their own governments; nor is the exercise of that power by the states an exercise of any portion of the power, that is granted to the United States. In imposing taxes for state purposes, they are not doing, what congress is empowered to do. Congress is not empowered to tax for those purposes, which are within the exclusive province of the states. When, then, each government is exercising the power of taxation, neither is exercising the power of the other." Under such circumstances, it is not, perhaps, too much to contend, that it is the truest, the safest, and the most authoritative construction of the constitution.

§ 925. The view thus taken of this clause of the constitution will receive some confirmation, (if it should be thought by any person necessary,) by an historical examination of the proceedings of the convention.

. . . . .

§ 927. Besides; it is impracticable in grammatical propriety to separate the different parts of the latter clause. The words are, "to pay the debts, *and* provide for the common defence," &c. "To pay the debts" cannot be construed, as an independent power; for it is connected with the other by the copulative "and." The payment of the antecedent debts of the United States was already provided for by a distinct article; and the power to pay future debts must necessarily be implied to the extent, to which they could constitutionally be contracted; and would fall within the purview of the enumerated power to pass all laws necessary and proper to carry the powers given by the constitution into effect. If, then, these words were and ought to be read, as a part of the preceding power to lay taxes, and in connexion with it, (as this historical review establishes beyond any reasonable controversy,) they draw the other words, "and provide for the common defence," &c. with them into the same connexion. On the other hand, if the connexion be once admitted, it would be almost absurd to contend, that "to pay the debts" of the United States was a general phrase, which pointed to the subsequent enumerated powers, and was qualified by them; and yet, as a part of the very clause, we are not at liberty to disregard it. The truth is, (as the historical review also proves,) that after it had been decided, that a positive power to pay the public debts should be inserted in the constitution, and a desire had been evinced to introduce some restriction upon the power to lay taxes, in order to allay jealousies and suppress alarms, it was (keeping both objects in view) deemed best to append the power to pay the public debts to the power to lay taxes; and then to add other terms, broad enough to embrace all the other purposes contemplated by the constitution. Among these none were more appropriate, than the words, "common defence and general welfare," found in the articles of confederation, and subsequently with marked emphasis introduced into the preamble of the constitution. To this course no opposition was made, because it satisfied those, who wished to provide positively for the public debts, and those, who wished to have the power of taxation co-extensive with all constitutional objects and powers. In other words, it conformed to the spirit of that resolution of the convention, which authorized congress "to legislate, in all cases, for the general interests of the Union."

§ 928. Having thus disposed of the question, what is the true interpretation of the clause, as it stands in the text of the constitution, and ascertained, that the power of taxation, though general, as to the subjects, to which it may be applied, is yet restrictive, as to the purposes, for which it may be exercised; it next becomes matter of inquiry, what were the reasons, for which this power was given, and what were the objections, to which it was deemed liable.

§ 929. That the power of taxation should be, to some extent, vested in the national government, was admitted by all persons, who sincerely desired to escape from the imbecilities, as well as the inequalities of the confederation. Without such a power, it would not be possible to provide for the support of the national forces by land or sea, or the national civil list, or the ordinary charges and expenses of government. For these purposes at least, there must be a constant and regular supply of revenue. If there should be a deficiency, one of two evils must inevitably ensue; either the people must be subjected to continual arbitrary plunder; or the government must sink into a fatal atrophy. The former is the fate of Turkey under its sovereigns: the latter was the fate of America under the confederation.

§ 930. If, then, there is to be a real, effective national government, there must be a power of taxation co-extensive with its powers, wants, and duties. The only inquiry properly remaining is, whether the resources of taxation should be specified and limited; or, whether the power in this respect should be general, leaving a full choice to the national legislature. The opponents of the constitution strenuously contended, that the power should be restricted; its friends, as strenuously contended, that it was indispensable for the public safety, that it should be general.

. . . . .

§ 946. The language of the constitution is, "Congress shall have power to lay and collect taxes, duties, imposts, and excises," &c. "But all *duties, imposts,* and *excises* shall be uniform throughout the United States." A distinction is here taken between taxes, and duties, imposts, and excises; and, indeed, there are other parts of the constitution respecting the taxing power, (as will presently be more fully seen,) such as the regulations respecting direct taxes, the prohibition of taxes or duties on exports by the United States, and the prohibition of imposts or duties by the states on imports or exports, which require an attention to this distinction.

§ 947. In a general sense, all contributions imposed by the government upon individuals for the service of the state, are called taxes, by whatever name they may be known, whether by the name of tribute, tythe, talliage, impost, duty, gabel, custom, subsidy, aid, supply, excise, or other name. In this sense, they are usually divided into two great classes, those, which are direct, and those, which are indirect. Under the former denomination are included taxes on land, or real property, and under the latter, taxes on articles of consumption. The constitution, by giving the power to lay and collect taxes in general terms, doubtless meant to include all sorts of taxes, whether direct or indirect. But, it may be asked, if such was the intention, why were the subsequent words, *duties, imposts* and *excises,* added in the clause? Two reasons may be suggested; the first, that it was done to avoid all possibility of doubt in the construction of the clause, since, in common parlance, the word *taxes* is sometimes applied in contradistinction to duties, imposts, and excises, and, in the delegation of so vital a power, it was desirable to avoid all possible misconception of this sort; and, accordingly, we find, in the very first draft of the constitution, these explanatory words are added. Another reason was, that the constitution prescribed different rules of laying taxes in different cases, and, therefore, it was indispensable to make a discrimination between the classes, to which each rule was meant to apply.

§ 948. The second section of the first article, which has been already commented on for another purpose, declares, that "*direct* taxes shall be apportioned among the several states, which may be included within this Union, according to their respective numbers." The fourth clause of the ninth section of the same article (which would regularly be commented on in a future page) declares, that "no capitation, or other direct tax, shall be laid, unless in proportion to the census or enumeration herein before directed to be taken." And the clause now under consideration, that "all duties, imposts, and excises shall be uniform throughout the United States." Here, then, two rules are prescribed, the rule of apportionment (as it is called) for *direct* taxes, and the rule of uniformity for *duties, imposts,* and *excises.* If there are any other kinds of taxes, not embraced in one or the other of these two classes, (and it is certainly difficult to give full effect to the words of the constitution without supposing them to exist,) it would seem, that congress is left at full liberty to levy the same by either rule, or by a mixture of both rules, or perhaps by any other rule, not inconsistent with the general purposes of the constitution. It is evident, that "duties, imposts, and excises" are indirect taxes in the sense of the constitution. But the difficulty still remains, to ascertain what taxes are comprehended under this description; and what under the description of *direct* taxes. It has been remarked by Adam Smith, that the private revenue of individuals arises ultimately from three different sources, rent, profit, and wages; and, that every public tax must be finally paid from some one, or all of these different sorts of revenue. He treats all taxes upon land, or the produce of land, or upon houses, or parts, or appendages thereof, (such as hearth taxes and window taxes,) under the head of taxes upon rent; all taxes upon stock, and money at interest, upon other personal property yielding an income, and upon particular employments, or branches of trade and business, under the head of taxes on profits; and taxes upon salaries under the head of wages. He treats capitation taxes and taxes on consumable articles, as mixed taxes, falling upon all or any of the different species of revenue. A full consideration of these different classifications of taxes belongs more properly to a treatise upon political economy, than upon constitutional law.

§ 949. The word "duties" has not, perhaps, in all cases a very exact signification, or rather it is used sometimes in a larger, and sometimes in a narrower sense. In its large sense, it is very nearly an equivalent to taxes, embracing all impositions or charges levied on persons or things. In its more restrained sense, it is often used as equivalent to "customs," which appellation is usually applied to those taxes, which are payable upon goods and merchandise imported, or exported, and was probably given on account of the usual and constant demand of them for the use of kings, states, and governments. In this sense, it is nearly synonymous with "imposts," which is sometimes used in the large sense of taxes, or duties, or impositions, and sometimes in the more restrained sense of a duty on imported goods and merchandise. Perhaps it is not unreasonable to presume, that this narrower sense might be in the minds of the framers of the constitution, when this clause was adopted, since, in another clause, it is subsequently provided, that "No tax or duty shall be laid on articles *exported* from any state;" and, that "No state shall, without the consent of congress, lay any *imposts* or *duties* on *imports* or *exports,* except what may be absolutely necessary for executing its inspection laws." There is another provision, that "No state shall, without the consent of congress, lay any *duty of tonnage,*" &c.; from which, perhaps, it may be gathered, that a tonnage duty, (by which is to be understood, not the ancient custom in England, so called, on wines imported, but a duty on the tonnage of ships and vessels,) was not deemed an *impost,* strictly, but a *duty.* However, it must be admitted, that little certainty can be arrived at from such slight changes of phraseology, where the words are susceptible of various interpretations, and of more or less expansion. The most, that can be done, is, to offer a probable conjecture from the apparent use of words in a connexion, where it is desirable not to deem any one superfluous, or synonymous with the others. A learned commentator has supposed, that the words, "duties and imposts," in the constitution, were probably intended to comprehend every species of tax or contribution, not included under the ordinary terms, "*taxes* and excises." Another learned judge has said, "what is the natural and common, or technical and appropriate, meaning of the words, *duty* and *excise,* it is not easy to ascertain. They present no clear or precise idea to the mind. Different persons will annex different significations to the terms." On the same occasion, another learned judge said, "The term, *duty,* is the most comprehensive, next to the generical term, *tax;* and practically in Great Britain, (whence we take our general ideas of taxes, duties, imposts, excises, customs, &c.) embraces taxes on stamps,

tolls for passage, &c. and is not confined to taxes on importations only."

§ 950. "Excises" are generally deemed to be of an opposite nature to "imposts," in the restrictive sense of the latter term, and are defined to be an inland imposition, paid sometimes upon the consumption of the commodity, or frequently upon the retail sale, which is the last stage before the consumption.

§ 951. But the more important inquiry is, what are direct taxes in the sense of the constitution, since they are required to be laid by the rule of apportionment, and all indirect taxes, whether they fall under the head of "duties, imposts, or excises," or under any other description, may be laid by the rule of uniformity. It is clear, that capitation taxes, or, as they are more commonly called, poll taxes, that is, taxes upon the polls, heads, or persons, of the contributors, are direct taxes, for the constitution has expressly enumerated them, as such. "No capitation, or *other direct* tax, shall be laid," &c. is the language of that instrument.

§ 952. Taxes on lands, houses, and other permanent real estate, or on parts or appurtenances thereof, have always been deemed of the same character, that is, direct taxes. It has been seriously doubted, if, in the sense of the constitution, any taxes are direct taxes, except those on polls or on lands.

. . . . .

§ 954. Having endeavoured to point out the leading distinctions between direct and indirect taxes, and that duties, imposts, and excises, in the sense of the constitution, belong to the latter class, the order of the subject would naturally lead us to the inquiry, why direct taxes are required to be governed by the rule of apportionment; and why "duties, imposts, and excises" are required to be uniform throughout the United States. The answer to the former will be given, when we come to the farther examination of certain prohibitory and restrictive clauses of the constitution on the subject of taxation. The answer to the latter may be given in a few words. It was to cut off all undue preferences of one state over another in the regulation of subjects affecting their common interests. Unless duties, imposts, and excises were uniform, the grossest and most oppressive inequalities, vitally affecting the pursuits and employments of the people of different states, might exist. The agriculture, commerce, or manufactures of one state might be built up on the ruins of those of another; and a combination of a few states in congress might secure a monopoly of certain branches of trade and business to themselves, to the injury, if not to the destruction, of their less favoured neighbours. The constitution throughout all its provisions is an instrument of checks, and restraints, as well as of powers. It does not rely on confidence in the general government to preserve the interests of all the states. It is founded in a wholesome and strenuous jealousy, which, foreseeing the possibility of mischief, guards with solicitude against any exercise of power, which may endanger the states, as far as it is practicable. If this provision, as to uniformity of duties, had been omitted, although the power might never have been abused to the injury of the feebler states of the Union, (a presumption, which history does not justify us in deeming quite safe or certain;) yet it would, of itself, have been sufficient to demolish, in a practical sense, the value of most of the other restrictive clauses in the constitution. New York and Pennsylvania might, by an easy combination with the Southern states, have destroyed the whole navigation of New England. A combination of a different character, between the New England and the Western states, might have borne down the agriculture of the South; and a combination of a yet different character might have struck at the vital interests of manufactures. So that the general propriety of this clause is established by its intrinsic political wisdom, as well as by its tendency to quiet alarms, and suppress discontents.

§ 955. Two practical questions of great importance have arisen upon the construction of this clause, either standing alone, or in connexion with other clauses, and incidental powers, given by the constitution. One is, whether the government has a right to lay taxes for any other purpose, than to raise revenue, however much that purpose may be for the common defence, or general welfare. The other is, whether the money, when raised, can be appropriated to any other purposes, than such, as are pointed out in the other enumerated powers of congress. The former involves the question, whether congress can lay taxes to protect and encourage domestic manufactures; the latter, whether congress can appropriate money to internal improvements. Each of these questions has given rise to much animated controversy; each has been affirmed and denied, with great pertinacity, zeal, and eloquent reasoning; each has become prominent in the struggles of party; and defeat in each has not hitherto silenced opposition, or given absolute security to victory. The contest is often renewed; and the attack and defence maintained with equal ardour. In discussing this subject, we are treading upon the ashes of yet unextinguished fires,—*incedimus per ignes suppositos cineri doloso;*—and while the nature of these Commentaries requires, that the doctrine should be freely examined, as maintained on either side, the result will be left to the learned reader, without a desire to influence his judgment, or dogmatically to announce that belonging to the commentator.

§ 956. First, then, as to the question, whether congress can lay taxes, except for the purposes of revenue. This subject has been already touched, in considering what is the true reading, and interpretation of the clause, conferring the power to lay taxes. If the reading and interpretation, there insisted on, be correct, it furnishes additional means to resolve the question, now under consideration.

§ 957. The argument against the constitutional authority is understood to be maintained on the following grounds, which, though applied to the protection of manufactures, are equally applicable to all other cases, where revenue is not the object. The general government is one of specific powers, and it can rightfully exercise only the powers expressly granted, and those, which may be "necessary and proper" to carry them into effect; all others being reserved expressly to the states, or to the people. It results necessarily, that those, who claim to exercise a power under the constitution, are bound to show, that it is expressly granted, or that it is "necessary and proper," as a means to execute some of the granted powers. No such proof has been offered in regard to the protection of manufactures.

§ 958. It is true, that the eighth section of the first article of the constitution authorizes congress to lay and collect an impost duty; but it is granted, as a tax power, for the sole purpose of revenue; a power, in its nature, essentially different from that of imposing protective, or prohibitory duties. The two are incompatible; for the prohibitory system must end in destroying the revenue from imports. It has been said, that the system is a violation of the spirit, and not of the letter of the constitution. The distinction is not material. The constitution may be as grossly violated by acting against its meaning, as against its letter. The constitution grants to congress the power of imposing a duty on imports for revenue, which power is abused by being converted into an instrument for rearing up the industry of one section of the country on the ruins of another. The violation, then, consists in using a power, granted for one object, to advance another, and that by a sacrifice of the original object. It is in a word a *violation of perversion*, the most dangerous of all, because the most insidious and difficult to resist. Such is the reasoning emanating from high legislative authority. On another interesting occasion, the argument has been put in the following shape. It is admitted, that congress has power to lay and collect such duties, as they may deem necessary for the purposes of revenue, and *within these limits* so to arrange those duties, *as incidentally*, and to that extent to give protection to the manufacturer. But the right is denied to convert, what is here denominated the incidental, into the principal power, and transcending the limits of revenue, to impose an additional duty substantially and exclusively for the purpose of affording that protection. Congress may countervail the regulations of a foreign power, which may be hostile to our commerce; but their authority is denied permanently to prohibit all importation, for the purpose of securing the home market exclusively to the domestic manufacturer; thereby destroying the commerce they were entrusted to regulate, and fostering an interest, with which they have no constitutional power to interfere. To do so, therefore, is a palpable abuse of the taxing power, which was conferred for the purpose of revenue; and if it is referred to the authority to regulate commerce, it is as obvious a perversion of that power, since it may be extended to an utter annihilation of the objects, which it was intended to protect.

§ 959. In furtherance of this reasoning, it has been admitted, that under the power to regulate commerce, congress is not limited to the imposition of duties upon imports for the sole purpose of revenue. It may impose retaliatory duties on foreign powers; but these retaliatory duties must be imposed for the regulation of commerce, not for the encouragement of manufactures. The power to regulate manufactures, not having been confided to congress, they have no more right to act upon it, than they have to interfere with the systems of education, the poor laws, or the road laws, of the states. Congress is empowered to lay taxes for revenue, it is true; but there is no power to encourage, protect, or meddle with manufactures.

§ 960. It is necessary to consider the argument at present, so far as it bears upon the constitutional authority of congress to protect or encourage manufactures; because that subject will more properly come under review, in all its bearings, under another head, viz. the power to regulate commerce, to which it is nearly allied, and from which it is more usually derived. Stripping the argument, therefore, of this adventitious circumstance, it resolves itself into this statement. The power to lay taxes is a power exclusively given to raise revenue, and it can constitutionally be applied to no other purposes. The application for other purposes is an abuse of the power; and, in fact, however it may be in *form* disguised, it is a premeditated usurpation of authority. Whenever money or revenue is wanted for constitutional purposes, the power to lay taxes may be applied to obtain it. When money or revenue is not so wanted, it is not a proper means for any constitutional end.

§ 961. The argument in favour of the constitutional authority is grounded upon the terms and the intent of the constitution. It seeks for the true meaning and objects of the power according to the obvious sense of the language, and the nature of the government proposed to be established by that instrument. It relies upon no strained construction of words; but demands a fair and reasonable interpretation of the clause, without any restrictions not naturally implied in it, or in the context. It will not do to assume, that the clause was intended solely for the purposes of raising revenue; and then argue, that being so, the power cannot be constitutionally applied to any other purposes. The very point in controversy is, whether it is restricted to purposes of revenue. That must be proved; and cannot be assumed, as the basis of reasoning.

§ 962. The language of the constitution is, "Congress shall have power to lay and collect taxes, duties, imposts, and excises." If the clause had stopped here, and remained in this absolute form, (as it was in fact, when reported in the first draft in the convention,) there could not have been the slightest doubt on the subject. The absolute power to lay taxes includes the power in every form, in which it may be used, and for every purpose, to which the legislature may choose to apply it. This results from the very nature of such an unrestricted power. *A fortiori* it might be applied by congress to purposes, for which nations have been accustomed to apply it. Now, nothing is more clear, from the history of commercial nations, than the fact, that the taxing power is often, very often, applied for other purposes, than revenue. It is often applied, as a regulation of commerce. It is often applied, as a virtual prohibition upon the importation of particular articles, for the encouragement and protection of domestic products, and industry; for the support of agriculture, commerce, and manufactures; for retaliation upon foreign monopolies and injurious restrictions; for mere purposes of state policy, and domestic economy; sometimes to banish a noxious article of consumption; sometimes, as a bounty upon an infant manufacture, or agricultural product; sometimes, as a temporary restraint of trade; sometimes, as a suppression of particular employments; sometimes, as a

prerogative power to destroy competition, and secure a monopoly to the government!

§ 963. If, then, the power to lay taxes, being general, may embrace, and in the practice of nations does embrace, all these objects, either separately, or in combination, upon what foundation does the argument rest, which assumes one object only, to the exclusion of all the rest? which insists, in effect, that because revenue may be one object, therefore it is the sole object of the power? which assumes its own construction to be correct, because it suits its own theory, and denies the same right to others, entertaining a different theory? If the power is general in its terms, is it not an abuse of all fair reasoning to insist, that it is particular? to desert the import of the language, and to substitute other and different language? Is this allowable in an especial manner, as to constitutions of government, growing out of the rights, duties, and exigencies of nations, and looking to an infinite variety of circumstances, which may require very different applications of a given power?

§ 964. In the next place, then, is the power to lay taxes, given by the constitution, a general power; or is it a limited power? If a limited power, to what objects is it limited by the terms of the constitution?

§ 965. Upon this subject, (as has been already stated,) three different opinions appear to have been held by statesmen of no common sagacity and ability. The first is, that the power is unlimited; and that the subsequent clause, "to pay the debts, and provide for the common defence and general welfare," is a substantive, independent power. In the view of those, who maintain this opinion, the power, being general, cannot with any consistency be restrained to purposes of revenue.

§ 966. The next is, that the power is restrained by the subsequent clause, so that it is a power to lay taxes in order to pay debts, and to provide for the common defence and general welfare. Is raising revenue the only proper mode to provide for the common defence and general welfare? May not the general welfare, in the judgment of congress, be, in given circumstances, as well provided for, nay better provided for, by prohibitory duties, or by encouragements to domestic industry of all sorts? If a tax of one sort, as on tonnage, or foreign vessels, will aid commerce, and a tax on foreign raw materials will aid agriculture, and a tax on imported fabrics will aid domestic manufactures, and so promote the general welfare; may they not be all constitutionally united by congress in a law for this purpose? If congress can unite them all, may they not sustain them severally in separate laws? Is a tax to aid manufactures, or agriculture, or commerce, necessarily, or even naturally, against the general welfare, or the common defence? Who is to decide upon such a point? Congress, to whom the authority is given to exercise the power? Or any other body, state or national, which may choose to assume it?

§ 967. Besides; if a particular act of congress, not for revenue, should be deemed an excess of the powers; does it follow, that all other acts are so? If the common defence or general welfare can be promoted by laying taxes in any other manner, than for revenue, who is at liberty to say, that congress cannot constitutionally exercise the power for such a purpose? No one has a right to say, that the common defence and general welfare can never be promoted by laying taxes, except for revenue. No one has ever yet been bold enough to assert such a proposition. Different men have entertained opposite opinions on subjects of this nature. It is a matter of theory and speculation, of political economy, and national policy, and not a matter of power. It may be wise or unwise to lay taxes, except for revenue; but the wisdom or inexpediency of a measure is no test of its constitutionality. Those, therefore, who hold the opinion above stated, must unavoidably maintain, that the power to lay taxes is not confined to revenue; but extends to all cases, where it is proper to be used for the common defence and general welfare. One of the most effectual means of defence against the injurious regulations and policy of foreign nations, and which is most commonly resorted to, is to apply the power of taxation to the products and manufactures of foreign nations by way of retaliation; and, short of war, this is found to be practically that, which is felt most extensively, and produces the most immediate redress. How, then, can it be imagined for a moment, that this was not contemplated by the framers of the constitution, as a means to provide for the common defence and general welfare?

§ 968. The third opinion is, (as has been already stated,) that the power is restricted to such specific objects, as are contained in the other enumerated powers. Now, if revenue be not the *sole* and *exclusive* means of carrying into effect all these enumerated powers, the advocates of this doctrine must maintain with those of the second opinion, that the power is not limited to purposes of revenue. No man will pretend to say, that all those enumerated powers have no other objects, or means to effectuate them, than revenue. Revenue may be one mode; but it is not the sole mode. Take the power "to regulate commerce." Is it not clear from the whole history of nations, that laying taxes is one of the most usual modes of regulating commerce? Is it not, in many cases, the best means of preventing foreign monopolies, and mischievous commercial restrictions? In such cases, then, the power to lay taxes is confessedly not for revenue. If so, is not the argument irresistible, that it is not limited to purposes of revenue? Take another power, the power to coin money and regulate its value, and that of foreign coin; might not a tax be laid on certain foreign coin for the purpose of carrying this into effect by suppressing the circulation of such coin, or regulating its value? Take the power to promote the progress of science and useful arts; might not a tax be laid on foreigners, and foreign inventions, in aid of this power, so as to suppress foreign competition, or encourage domestic science and arts? Take another power, vital in the estimation of many statesmen to the security of a republic,—the power to provide for organizing, arming, and disciplining the militia; may not a tax be laid on foreign arms, to encourage the domestic manufacture of arms, so as to enhance our security, and give uniformity to our organization and discipline? Take the power to declare war, and its auxiliary powers; may not congress, for the very object of providing for the effectual exercise of these powers, and securing a permanent domestic manufacture and supply of powder, equipments, and other warlike apparatus, impose a pro-

hibitory duty upon foreign articles of the same nature? If congress may, in any, or all of these cases, lay taxes; then as revenue constitutes, upon the very basis of the reasoning, no object of the taxes, is it not clear, that the enumerated powers require the power to lay taxes to be more extensively construed, than for purposes of revenue? It would be no answer to say, that the power of taxation, though in its nature only a power to raise revenue, may be resorted to, as an implied power to carry into effect these enumerated powers in any effectual manner. That would be to contend, that an *express* power to lay taxes is not co-extensive with an *implied* power to lay taxes; that when the express power is given, it means a power to raise revenue only; but when it is implied, it no longer has any regard to this object. How, then, is a case to be dealt with, of a mixed nature, where revenue is mixed up with other objects in the framing of the law?

§ 969. If, then, the power to lay taxes were admitted to be restricted to cases within the enumerated powers; still the advocates of that doctrine are compelled to admit, that the power must be construed, as not confined to revenue, but as extending to all other objects within the scope of those powers. Where the power is expressly given, we are not at liberty to say, that it is to be implied. Being given, it may certainly be resorted to, as a means to effectuate all the powers, to which it is appropriate; not, because it is to be implied in the grant of those powers; but because it is expressly granted, as a substantive power, and may be used, of course, as an auxiliary to them.

§ 970. So that, whichever construction of the power to lay taxes is adopted, the same conclusion is sustained, that the power to lay taxes is not by the constitution confined to purposes of revenue. In point of fact, it has never been limited to such purposes by congress; and all the great functionaries of the government have constantly maintained the doctrine, that it was not constitutionally so limited.

. . . . .

§ 972. The other question is, whether congress has any power to appropriate money, raised by taxation or otherwise, for any other purposes, than those pointed out in the enumerated powers, which follow the clause respecting taxation. It is said, "raised by taxation or otherwise;" for there may be, and in fact are, other sources of revenue, by which money may, and does come into the treasury of the United States otherwise, than by taxation; as, for instance, by fines, penalties, and forfeitures; by sales of the public lands, and interests and dividends on bank stocks; by captures and prize in times of war; and by other incidental profits and emoluments growing out of governmental transactions and prerogatives. But, for all the common purposes of argument, the question may be treated, as one growing out of levies by taxation.

§ 973. The reasoning, upon which the opinion, adverse to the authority of congress to make appropriations not within the scope of the enumerated powers, is maintained, has been already, in a great measure, stated in the preceding examination of the grammatical construction of the clause, giving the power to lay taxes. The controversy is virtually at an end, if it is once admitted, that the words, "to provide for the common defence and general welfare," are a part and qualification of the power to lay taxes; for then, congress has certainly a right to appropriate money to any purposes, or in any manner, conducive to those ends. The whole stress of the argument is, therefore, to establish, that the words, "to provide for the common defence and general welfare," do not form an independent power, nor any qualification of the power to lay taxes. And the argument is, that they are "mere general terms, explained and limited by the subjoined specifications." It is attempted to be fortified (as has been already seen) by a recurrence to the history of the confederation; to the successive reports and alterations of the tax clause in the convention; to the inconveniencies of such a large construction; and to the supposed impossibility, that a power to make such appropriations for the common defence and general welfare, should not have been, at the adoption of the constitution, a subject of great alarm, and jealousy; and as such, resisted in and out of the state conventions.

§ 974. The argument in favour of the power is derived, in the first place, from the language of the clause, conferring the power, (which it is admitted in its literal terms covers it;) secondly, from the nature of the power, which renders it in the highest degree expedient, if not indispensable for the due operations of the national government; thirdly, from the early, constant and decided maintenance of it by the government and its functionaries, as well as by many of our ablest statesmen from the very commencement of the constitution. So, that it has the language and intent of the text, and the practice of the government to sustain it against an artificial doctrine, set up on the other side.

§ 975. The argument derived from the words and intent has been so fully considered already, that it cannot need repetition. It is summed up with great force in the report of the secretary of the treasury on manufactures, in 1791. . . .

§ 976. But the most thorough and elaborate view, which perhaps has ever been taken of the subject, will be found in the exposition of President Monroe, which accompanied his message respecting the bill for the repairs of the Cumberland Road, (4th of May, 1822.).

. . . . .

§ 988. In regard to the practice of the government, it has been entirely in conformity to the principles here laid down. Appropriations have never been limited by congress to cases falling within the specific powers enumerated in the constitution, whether those powers be construed in their broad, or their narrow sense. And in an especial manner appropriations have been made to aid internal improvements of various sorts, in our roads, our navigation, our streams, and other objects of a national character and importance. In some cases, not silently, but upon discussion, congress has gone the length of making appropria-

tions to aid destitute foreigners, and cities labouring under severe calamities; as in the relief of the St. Domingo refugees, in 1794, and the citizens of Venezuela, who suffered from an earthquake in 1812. An illustration equally forcible, of a domestic character, is in the bounty given in the cod-fisheries, which was strenuously resisted on constitutional grounds in 1792; but which still maintains its place in the statute book of the United States.

SEE ALSO:

Generally 1.8.18
William Blackstone, Commentaries 1:303–10 (1765)
Articles of Confederation, arts. 8 and 9, 1 Mar. 1781
Alexander Hamilton, The Continentalist, no. 6, 4 July 1782, Papers 3:99–102, 103–5
Records of the Federal Convention, Farrand 1:247; 2:135, 142, 157, 167, 211, 352, 356, 366–67, 382, 408, 470, 529–30, 569, 571, 594, 614
Richard Henry Lee to Samuel Adams, 5 Oct. 1787, Letters 2:444–45
Federal Farmer, no. 4, 12 Oct. 1787, Storing 2.8.44
John DeWitt, no. 4, Fall, 1787, Storing 4.3.21–23
A Georgian, 15 Nov. 1787, Storing 5.9.7
James McHenry, Maryland House of Delegates, 29 Nov. 1787, Farrand 3:149
Luther Martin, Maryland House of Delegates, 29 Nov. 1787, Farrand 3:156–57
Thomas McKean, Pennsylvania Ratifying Convention, 11 Dec. 1787, Elliot 2:535–36
Debate in Massachusetts Ratifying Convention, 21–25 Jan. 1788, Elliot 2:57–107
Native of Virginia, Observations upon the Proposed Plan of Federal Government, 1788, Monroe Writings 1:366–67
Debate in New York Ratifying Convention, June–July 1788, Elliot 2:330, 331–34, 340–41, 342–47, 350, 351–52, 361–62, 363–65, 366–70, 373, 377–78, 380–81
Debate in North Carolina Ratifying Convention, 26 July 1788, Elliot 4:75–93
An Act Laying a Duty on Goods, Etc. Imported into the United States, 1 Stat. 24 (1789)
House of Representatives, Public Credit, 23–25 Feb., 22 Apr. 1790, Annals 2:1313, 1318, 1324–26, 1327–28, 1334, 1344, 1348, 1354–55, 1538–39
Hugh Williamson, House of Representatives, 3 Feb. 1792, Annals 3:378–79
Thomas Jefferson to George Washington, 9 Sept. 1792, Works 7:139–41
House of Representatives, Public Credit, 6–7 May 1794, Annals 4:643–46, 652–53
An Act Laying Duties upon Conveyances of Persons, 1 Stat. 373 (1794)
St. George Tucker, Blackstone's Commentaries 1:App. 231–46 (1803)
William Rawle, A View of the Constitution of the United States 79–81 (2d ed. 1829)
James Madison to Professor Davis, 1832, Farrand 3:518
James Madison to John Tyler, 1833, Farrand 3:526–27

Article 1, Section 8, Clause 2

To borrow Money on the credit of the United States;

---

1. William Blackstone, Commentaries (1765)
2. Records of the Federal Convention
3. Luther Martin, Genuine Information, 1788
4. Brutus, no. 8, 10 Jan. 1788
5. Alexander Hamilton, Report on Public Credit, 9 Jan. 1790
6. Benjamin Rush to James Madison, 10 Mar. 1790
7. James Madison, The Bank Bill, House of Representatives, 2 Feb. 1791
8. St. George Tucker, Blackstone's Commentaries (1803)
9. William Rawle, A View of the Constitution of the United States (2d ed. 1829)
10. Joseph Story, Commentaries on the Constitution (1833)

1

WILLIAM BLACKSTONE, COMMENTARIES 1:317
1765

The only advantage, that can result to a nation from public debts, is the encrease of circulation by multiplying the cash of the kingdom, and creating a new species of money, always ready to be employed in any beneficial undertaking, by means of it's transferrable quality; and yet productive of some profit, even when it lies idle and unemployed. A certain proportion of debt seems therefore to be highly useful to a trading people; but what that proportion is, it is not for me to determine. Thus much is indisputably certain, that the present magnitude of our national incumbrances very far exceeds all calculations of commercial benefit, and is productive of the greatest inconveniences. For, first, the enormous taxes, that are raised upon the necessaries of life for the payment of the interest of this debt, are a hurt both to trade and manufactures, by raising the price as well of the artificer's subsistence, as of the raw material, and of course, in a much greater proportion, the price of the commodity itself. Secondly, if part of this debt be owing to foreigners, either they draw out of the kingdom annually a considerable quantity of specie for the interest; or else it is made an argument to grant them unreasonable privileges in order to induce them to reside here. Thirdly, if the whole be owing to subjects only, it is then charging the active and industrious subject, who pays his share of the taxes to maintain the indolent and idle creditor who receives them.

2

RECORDS OF THE FEDERAL CONVENTION

[2:144; Committee of Detail, IV]
Power to borrow Money—

[2:168; Committee of Detail, IX]
. . . To borrow Money, and emit Bills on the Credit of the United States; . . .

[2:182; Madison, 6 Aug.]
To borrow money, and emit bills on the credit of the United States;

[2:303; Journal, 16 Aug.]
It was moved and seconded to strike the words "and emit bills" out of the 8. clause of the 1 section of the 7 article
which passed in the affirmative. [Ayes—9; noes—2.]

[2:569, 594; Committee of Style]
Sect. 1. The Legislature shall have power . . . To borrow money on the credit of the United States;

. . . . .

Sect. 8. The Congress . . . shall have power . . . (b) To borrow money on the credit of the United States.

3

LUTHER MARTIN, GENUINE INFORMATION
1788
Storing 2.4.57

By our original articles of confederation, the Congress have a power to borrow money and emit bills of credit on the credit of the United States; agreeable to which was the *report on this* system as *made* by the *committee of detail*. When we came to this part of the report, a motion was made to strike out the words "to emit bills of credit;" against the motion we urged, that it would be improper to *deprive* the Congress of that *power;* that it would be a novelty unprecedented to establish a government which should not have such authority—That it was impossible to look forward into futurity so far as to decide, that events might not happen that should render the *exercise* of such a power *absolutely* necessary—And that we doubted, whether if a war should take place it would be *possible* for this country to *defend* itself, without having recourse to *paper credit,* in which case there would be a *necessity* of becoming a *prey* to our *enemies,* or *violating* the *constitution* of our government; and that considering the administration of the government would be principally in the hands of the wealthy, there could be little reason to fear an *abuse* of the *power* by an unnecessary or injurious exercise of it—But, Sir, a majority of the convention, being wise beyond every event, and being willing to risque any political evil rather than admit the *idea* of a paper emission, in any *possible* case, refused to *trust* this authority to a government, to which they were *lavishing* the most *unlimited* powers of *taxation,* and to the *mercy* of which they were willing *blindly* to *trust* the *liberty* and *property* of the *citizens* of *every State* in the union; and they *erased* that clause from the system.

4

BRUTUS, NO. 8
10 Jan. 1788
Storing 2.9.93–95

The next powers vested by this constitution in the general government, which we shall consider, are those, which authorise them to "borrow money on the credit of the United States, and to raise and support armies." I take these two together and connect them with the power to lay and collect taxes, duties, imposts and excises, because their extent, and the danger that will arise from the exercise of these powers, cannot be fully understood, unless they are viewed in relation to each other.

The power to borrow money is general and unlimited, and the clause so often before referred to, authorises the passing any laws proper and necessary to carry this into execution. Under this authority, the Congress may mortgage any or all the revenues of the union, as a fund to loan money upon, and it is probably, in this way, they may borrow of foreign nations, a principal sum, the interest of which will be equal to the annual revenues of the country.—By this means, they may create a national debt, so large, as to exceed the ability of the country ever to sink. I can scarcely contemplate a greater calamity that could befal this country, than to be loaded with a debt exceeding their ability ever to discharge. If this be a just remark, it is unwise and improvident to vest in the general government a power to borrow at discretion, without any limitation or restriction.

It may possibly happen that the safety and welfare of the country may require, that money be borrowed, and it is proper when such a necessity arises that the power should be exercised by the general government.—But it certainly ought never to be exercised, but on the most urgent occasions, and then we should not borrow of foreigners if we could possibly avoid it.

The constitution should therefore have so restricted, the exercise of this power as to have rendered it very difficult for the government to practise it. The present confederation requires the assent of nine states to exercise this, and a number of the other important powers of the confederacy—and it would certainly have been a wise provision in this constitution, to have made it necessary that two thirds of the members should assent to borrowing money—when the necessity was indispensible, this assent would always be given, and in no other cause ought it to be.

5

ALEXANDER HAMILTON, REPORT ON
PUBLIC CREDIT
9 Jan. 1790
Papers 6:67–72

In the opinion of the Secretary, the wisdom of the House, in giving their explicit sanction to the proposition which has been stated, ["That an *adequate* provision for the support of the Public Credit, is a matter of high importance to the honor and prosperity of the United States."] cannot but be applauded by all, who will seriously consider, and trace through their obvious consequences, these plain and undeniable truths.

That exigencies are to be expected to occur, in the affairs of nations, in which there will be a necessity for borrowing.

That loans in times of public danger, especially from foreign war, are found an indispensable resource, even to the wealthiest of them.

And that in a country, which, like this, is possessed of little active wealth, or in other words, little monied capital, the necessity for that resource, must, in such emergencies, be proportionably urgent.

And as on the one hand, the necessity for borrowing in particular emergencies cannot be doubted, so on the other, it is equally evident, that to be able to borrow upon *good terms*, it is essential that the credit of a nation should be well established.

For when the credit of a country is in any degree questionable, it never fails to give an extravagant premium, in one shape or another, upon all the loans it has occasion to make. Nor does the evil end here; the same disadvantage must be sustained upon whatever is to be bought on terms of future payment.

From this constant necessity of *borrowing* and *buying dear*, it is easy to conceive how immensely the expences of a nation, in a course of time, will be augmented by an unsound state of the public credit.

To attempt to enumerate the complicated variety of mischiefs in the whole system of the social oeconomy, which proceed from a neglect of the maxims that uphold public credit, and justify the solicitude manifested by the House on this point, would be an improper intrusion on their time and patience.

In so strong a light nevertheless do they appear to the Secretary, that on their due observance at the present critical juncture, materially depends, in his judgment, the individual and aggregate prosperity of the citizens of the United States; their relief from the embarrassments they now experience; their character as a People; the cause of good government.

If the maintenance of public credit, then, be truly so important, the next enquiry which suggests itself is, by what means it is to be effected? The ready answer to which question is, by good faith, by a punctual performance of contracts. States, like individuals, who observe their engagements, are respected and trusted: while the reverse is the fate of those, who pursue an opposite conduct.

Every breach of the public engagements, whether from choice or necessity, is in different degrees hurtful to public credit. When such a necessity does truly exist, the evils of it are only to be palliated by a scrupulous attention, on the part of the government, to carry the violation no farther than the necessity absolutely requires, and to manifest, if the nature of the case admits of it, a sincere disposition to make reparation, whenever circumstances shall permit. But with every possible mitigation, credit must suffer, and numerous mischiefs ensue. It is therefore highly important, when an appearance of necessity seems to press upon the public councils, that they should examine well its reality, and be perfectly assured, that there is no method of escaping from it, before they yield to its suggestions. For though it cannot safely be affirmed, that occasions have never existed, or may not exist, in which violations of the public faith, in this respect, are inevitable; yet there is great reason to believe, that they exist far less frequently than precedents indicate; and are oftenest either pretended through levity, or want of firmness, or supposed through want of knowledge. Expedients might often have been devised to effect, consistently with good faith, what has been done in contravention of it. Those who are most commonly creditors of a nation, are, generally speaking, enlightened men; and there are signal examples to warrant a conclusion, that when a candid and fair appeal is made to them, they will understand their true interest too well to refuse their concurrence in such modifications of their claims, as any real necessity may demand.

While the observance of that good faith, which is the basis of public credit, is recommended by the strongest inducements of political expediency, it is enforced by considerations of still greater authority. There are arguments for it, which rest on the immutable principles of moral obligation. And in proportion as the mind is disposed to contemplate, in the order of Providence, an intimate connection between public virtue and public happiness, will be its repugnancy to a violation of those principles.

This reflection derives additional strength from the nature of the debt of the United States. It was the price of liberty. The faith of America has been repeatedly pledged for it, and with solemnities, that give peculiar force to the obligation. There is indeed reason to regret that it has not hitherto been kept; that the necessities of the war, conspiring with inexperience in the subjects of finance, produced direct infractions; and that the subsequent period has been a continued scene of negative violation, or non-compliance. But a diminution of this regret arises from the reflection, that the last seven years have exhibited an earnest and uniform effort, on the part of the government of the union, to retrieve the national credit, by doing justice to the creditors of the nation; and that the embarrassments of a defective constitution, which defeated this laudable effort, have ceased.

From this evidence of a favorable disposition, given by the former government, the institution of a new one, cloathed with powers competent to calling forth the resources of the community, has excited correspondent expectations. A general belief, accordingly, prevails, that the credit of the United States will quickly be established on the firm foundation of an effectual provision for the existing debt. The influence, which this has had at home, is witnessed by the rapid increase, that has taken place in the market value of the public securities. From January to November, they rose thirty-three and a third per cent, and from that period to this time, they have risen fifty per cent more. And the intelligence from abroad announces effects proportionably favourable to our national credit and consequence.

It cannot but merit particular attention, that among ourselves the most enlightened friends of good government are those, whose expectations are the highest.

To justify and preserve their confidence; to promote the encreasing respectability of the American name; to answer the calls of justice; to restore landed property to its due value; to furnish new resources both to agriculture and commerce; to cement more closely the union of the states; to add to their security against foreign attack; to establish public order on the basis of an upright and liberal policy. These are the great and invaluable ends to be secured, by a proper and adequate provision, at the present period, for the support of public credit.

To this provision we are invited, not only by the general considerations, which have been noticed, but by others of a more particular nature. It will procure to every class of the community some important advantages, and remove some no less important disadvantages.

The advantage to the public creditors from the increased value of that part of their property which constitutes the public debt, needs no explanation.

But there is a consequence of this, less obvious, though not less true, in which every other citizen is interested. It is a well known fact, that in countries in which the national debt is properly funded, and an object of established confidence, it answers most of the purposes of money. Transfers of stock or public debt are there equivalent to payments in specie; or in other words, stock, in the principal transactions of business, passes current as specie. The same thing would, in all probability happen here, under the like circumstances.

The benefits of this are various and obvious.

First. Trade is extended by it; because there is a larger capital to carry it on, and the merchant can at the same time, afford to trade for smaller profits; as his stock, which, when unemployed, brings him in an interest from the government, serves him also as money, when he has a call for it in his commercial operations.

Secondly. Agriculture and manufactures are also promoted by it: For the like reason, that more capital can be commanded to be employed in both; and because the merchant, whose enterprize in foreign trade, gives to them activity and extension, has greater means for enterprize.

Thirdly. The interest of money will be lowered by it; for this is always in a ratio, to the quantity of money, and to the quickness of circulation. This circumstance will enable both the public and individuals to borrow on easier and cheaper terms.

And from the combination of these effects, additional aids will be furnished to labour, to industry, and to arts of every kind.

But these good effects of a public debt are only to be looked for, when, by being well funded, it has acquired an *adequate* and *stable* value. Till then, it has rather a contrary tendency. The fluctuation and insecurity incident to it in an unfunded state, render it a mere commodity, and a precarious one. As such, being only an object of occasional and particular speculation, all the money applied to it is so much diverted from the more useful channels of circulation, for which the thing itself affords no substitute: So that, in fact, one serious inconvenience of an unfunded debt is, that it contributes to the scarcity of money.

This distinction which has been little if at all attended to, is of the greatest moment. It involves a question immediately interesting to every part of the community; which is no other than this—Whether the public debt, by a provision for it on true principles, shall be rendered a *substitute* for money; or whether, by being left as it is, or by being provided for in such a manner as will wound those principles, and destroy confidence, it shall be suffered to continue, as it is, a pernicious drain of our cash from the channels of productive industry.

The effect, which the funding of the public debt, on right principles, would have upon landed property, is one of the circumstances attending such an arrangement,

which has been least adverted to, though it deserves the most particular attention. The present depreciated state of that species of property is a serious calamity. The value of cultivated lands, in most of the states, has fallen since the revolution from 25 to 50 per cent. In those farthest south, the decrease is still more considerable. Indeed, if the representations, continually received from that quarter, may be credited, lands there will command no price, which may not be deemed an almost total sacrifice.

This decrease, in the value of lands, ought, in a great measure, to be attributed to the scarcity of money. Consequently whatever produces an augmentation of the monied capital of the country, must have a proportional effect in raising that value. The beneficial tendency of a funded debt, in this respect, has been manifested by the most decisive experience in Great-Britain.

The proprietors of lands would not only feel the benefit of this increase in the value of their property, and of a more prompt and better sale, when they had occasion to sell; but the necessity of selling would be, itself, greatly diminished. As the same cause would contribute to the facility of loans, there is reason to believe, that such of them as are indebted, would be able through that resource, to satisfy their more urgent creditors.

It ought not however to be expected, that the advantages, described as likely to result from funding the public debt, would be instantaneous. It might require some time to bring the value of stock to its natural level, and to attach to it that fixed confidence, which is necessary to its quality as money. Yet the late rapid rise of the public securities encourages an expectation, that the progress of stock to the desireable point, will be much more expeditious than could have been foreseen. And as in the mean time it will be increasing in value, there is room to conclude, that it will, from the outset, answer many of the purposes in contemplation. Particularly it seems to be probable, that from creditors, who are not themselves necessitous, it will early meet with a ready reception in payment of debts, at its current price.

6

BENJAMIN RUSH TO JAMES MADISON
10 Mar. 1790
Madison Papers 13:97–99

I once knew a Swedish Clergyman in this city, who told me that when he preached in the Country, he always studied his Congregation *first*, and *Afterwards* his sermon. Something like this Should be done by legislators. They should perfectly understand the character of the people whom they represent, and Afterwards suit their laws to their habits and principles. I suspect the present Congress have neglected this important part of their duty. They appear as if they were legislating for British subjects, and for a nation whose whole business was to be, *War*—hence the Sacrifices that are called for of justice—gratitude—and national interest to public Credit. After all the encomiums upon it—what is it? An Ability to borrow money. But for what? Why only for the purpose of carrying on unjust and offensive wars—for where wars are just & necessary—Supplies may always be obtained by annual taxes from a free people. Loans (says Genl: Chatteleaux in his treatise upon national felicity) were introduced into Europe only to enable ambitious kings to carry on wars without the Consent of their subjects. But in a republic, where wars must always be wars of the *whole* people, loans will be rendered unnecessary by taxes equal to the exigencies of the state. Under all the disadvantages of a weak Confederation, and corrupted state Governments the United States during the late war nearly at one time realized this Attribute of a republican Government. Under a Constitution like the present, I am sure the most expensive war might be carried on by annual Contributions provided it met with the Consent of a great majority of the people.

The provision which our Congress is making for future Wars by Acts of Supererogation, reminds me of the Conduct of the Earl of Warrington who in the marriage Settlement of his daughter stipulated for a pension of £500 a year for her in case she should commit Adultery, & be divorced for it from her husband. Our distance from Europe is a Security against four out of five of the chances & causes of War. Besides peace is the business and interest of republics. Why then provide for war, at the annual waste of four millions of dollars a year? especially when this Sum will cut the Sinews of our Country, and thereby render a just war impracticable.

Let us not overvalue public credit. It is to nations, what private Credit, & loan offices are to individuals. It begets debt—extravagance—vice—& bankruptcy. But further—if we mean to negociate loans with Success hereafter, let us not exhaust all the taxable resources of our Country. We shall borrow twice as easily if we pay 3, as if we pay 6 per cent upon our present debt, for the lenders of money depend more upon the Ability, than upon the integrity of all Countries to pay debts, & this Ability will be doubled by paying only 3 per cent.

I sicken every time I contemplate the European Vices that the Secretary's gambling report will necessarily introduce into our infant republic.

In five years, the whole debt if funded at four or even five per cent will probably center in London, or Amsterdam. What difference will it make to the American farmers whether 4 millions of their dollars are sent out of the Country every year to support the dignity of the British parliamt:, or the public Credit of the United States? The wars of the Crusades in my Opinion do not place the human Understanding in a more Absurd point of light, than the present Opinions of your house on the Subject of public Credit. Adieu.

7

JAMES MADISON, THE BANK BILL,
HOUSE OF REPRESENTATIVES
2 Feb. 1791
Papers 13:376

The second clause to be examined is that, which empowers Congress to borrow money.

Is this a bill to borrow money? It does not borrow a shilling. Is there any fair construction by which the bill can be deemed an exercise of the power to borrow money? The obvious meaning of the power to borrow money, is that of accepting it from, and stipulating payment to those who are *able* and *willing* to lend.

To say that the power to borrow involves a power of creating the ability, where there may be the will, to lend, is not only establishing a dangerous principle, as will be immediately shewn, but is as forced a construction, as to say that it involves the power of compelling the will, where there may be the ability, to lend.

8

ST. GEORGE TUCKER, BLACKSTONE'S
COMMENTARIES 1:APP. 246–47
1803

2. Congress have power to borrow money on the credit of the United States; a power inseparably connected with that of raising a revenue, and with the duty of protection which that power imposes upon the federal government. For, though in times of profound peace, it may not be necessary to anticipate the revenues of a state, yet the experience of other nations, as well as our own, must convince us that the burthen and expence of one year, in time of war, may be more than equal to the revenues of ten years. Hence a debt is almost unavoidable, whenever a nation is plunged into a state of war. The least burthensome mode of contracting a debt is by a loan: in case of a maritime war, the revenues arising from duties upon merchandize imported, and upon tonnage, must be greatly diminished. Had not congress a power to borrow money, recourse must be had to direct taxes in the extreme, or to impressments, lotteries, and other miserable and oppressive expedients. A system of revenue being once organized, and the ability of the states to pay their debts, being known, money may easily be procured on loan, to be repaid when all the sources of revenue shall have regained their operation, and flow in their proper channel.

But while we contend for the power, let it not be supposed that it is meant to contend for the abuse of it. When used as a means of necessary defence, it gives energy, vigour and dispatch to all the measures of government; inspires a proper confidence in it, and disposes every citizen to alacrity and promptitude, in the service of his country. By enabling the government punctually to comply with all it's engagements, the soldier is not driven to mutiny for want of his subsistence, nor the officer to resign his commission to avoid the ruin of himself, and his family. By this means also, the pressure and burthen of a war, undertaken for the benefit of posterity, as well as the present generation, may be in some degree alleviated, and a part of the burthen transferred to those who are to share the advantage. On the other hand, where loans are voluntarily incurred, upon the principle that a public debt is a public blessing, or to serve the purposes of aggrandizing a few at the expence of the nation, in general, or of strengthening the hands of government, (or more properly those of a party grasping at power, influence and wealth,) nothing can be more dangerous to the liberty of the citizen, nor more injurious to remotest posterity, as well as to present generations.

Congress had power, under the former articles of confederation, to borrow money upon the credit of the United States, and to pledge their faith for the re-payment. But not possessing any revenue independent of the states, their loans were obtained with difficulty, and, very rarely in time to answer the purposes for which they were intended. The consequences of these, and other corresponding defects in the system, have been too frequently noticed to require a repetition of them in this place.

9

WILLIAM RAWLE, A VIEW OF THE CONSTITUTION OF THE UNITED STATES 81
1829 (2d ed.)

When this Constitution was formed, the United States were considerably indebted to foreign nations, for the expenses of the war, and its own citizens had heavy claims, as well on the Union as on individual states, for services and supplies during the same eventful period. To combine and consolidate these debts, to discharge some and secure the rest, was necessary for the public faith and interest both abroad and at home. But to avail itself of the power of taxation, in order to accomplish such extensive objects at once, would have been injurious to the community. It was foreseen that many public creditors, whether distant or domestic, would be satisfied with the assumption or recognition of the principal and the payment of the interest. By the terms thus introduced, congress received power to make the necessary provisions for such objects. In case of

future exigencies, the expenses of war or the failure of part of the usual revenue; a similar mean of continuing the operations and the character of government is also thus provided.

10

JOSEPH STORY, COMMENTARIES ON THE CONSTITUTION 2:§ 1051
1833

§ 1051. The next, is the power of congress "to borrow money on the credit of the United States." This power seems indispensable to the sovereignty and existence of a national government. Even under the confederation this power was expressly delegated. The remark is unquestionably just, that it is a power inseparably connected with that of raising a revenue, and with the duty of protection, which that power imposes upon the general government. Though in times of profound peace it may not be ordinarily necessary to anticipate the revenues of a state; yet the experience of all nations must convince us, that the burthen and expenses of one year, in time of war, may more than equal the ordinary revenue of ten years. Hence, a debt is almost unavoidable, when a nation is plunged into a state of war. The least burthensome mode of contracting a debt is by a loan. Indeed, this recourse becomes the more necessary, because the ordinary duties upon importations are subject to great diminution and fluctuations in times of war; and a resort to direct taxes for the whole supply would, under such circumstances, become oppressive and ruinous to the agricultural interests of the country. Even in times of peace exigencies may occur, which render a loan the most facile, economical, and ready means of supply, either to meet expenses, or to avert calamities, or to save the country from an undue depression of its staple productions. The government of the United States has, on several occasions in times of profound peace, obtained large loans, among which a striking illustration of the economy and convenience of such arrangements will be found in the creation of stock on the purchase of Louisiana. The power to borrow money by the United States cannot (as has been already seen) in any way be controlled, or interfered with by the states. The granting of the power is incompatible with any restraining or controlling power; and the declaration of supremacy in the constitution is a declaration, that no such restraining or controlling power shall be exercised.

SEE ALSO:

Generally 1.8.5; 1.10.1

Article 1, Section 8, Clause 3

To regulate Commerce with foreign Nations, and among the several
States, and with the Indian Tribes;

COMMERCE

1. Alexander Hamilton, Continentalist, no. 5, 18 Apr. 1782
2. Proposed Amendment to Articles of Confederation, 28 Mar. 1785
3. George Mason to Speaker of Virginia House of Delegates, 28 Mar. 1785
4. James Madison to James Monroe, 7 Aug. 1785
5. Richard Henry Lee to ———, 10 Oct. 1785
6. James Madison, Draft of Resolutions on Foreign Trade, Virginia House of Delegates, 12 Nov. 1785
7. James Madison, Preface to Debates in the Convention of 1787
8. Records of the Federal Convention
9. James Madison, Federalist, no. 42, 22 Jan. 1788
10. Thomas Jefferson to Albert Gallatin, 13 Oct. 1802
11. St. George Tucker, Blackstone's Commentaries (1803)
12. *United States* v. *The William*, 28 Fed. Cas. 614, no. 16,700 (D.Mass. 1808)
13. *Livingston* v. *Van Ingen*, 9 Johns. R. 507 (N.Y. 1812)
14. *Gibbons* v. *Ogden*, 17 Johns. R. 488 (N.Y. 1820), rev'd 9 Wheat. 1, no. 16 *infra*
15. *Corfield* v. *Coryell*, 6 Fed. Cas. 546, no. 3,230 (C.C.E.D.Pa. 1823), in 4.2.1, no. 18
16. *Gibbons* v. *Ogden*, 9 Wheat. 1 (1824)
17. *Brown* v. *Maryland*, 12 Wheat. 419 (1827)
18. James Madison to Joseph C. Cabell, 18 Sept. 1828
19. James Madison to Joseph C. Cabell, 13 Feb. 1829
20. *Willson* v. *Blackbird Creek Marsh Co.*, 2 Pet. 245 (1829)
21. James Madison to Professor Davis, 1832
22. Joseph Story, Commentaries on the Constitution (1833)

1

ALEXANDER HAMILTON, CONTINENTALIST, NO. 5
18 Apr. 1782
Papers 3:75–82

The vesting Congress with the power of regulating trade ought to have been a principal object of the confederation for a variety of reasons. It is as necessary for the purposes of commerce as of revenue. There are some, who maintain, that trade will regulate itself, and is not to be benefitted by the encouragements, or restraints of government. Such persons will imagine, that there is no need of a common directing power. This is one of those wild speculative paradoxes, which have grown into credit among us, contrary to the uniform practice and sense of the most enlightened nations. Contradicted by the numerous institutions and laws, that exist every where for the benefit of trade, by the pains taken to cultivate particular branches and to discourage others, by the known advantages derived from those measures, and by the palpable evils that would attend their discontinuance—it must be rejected by every man acquainted with commercial history. Commerce, like other things, has its fixed principles, according to which it must be regulated; if these are understood and observed, it will be promoted by the attention of government, if unknown, or violated, it will be injured—but it is the same with every other part of administration.

To preserve the ballance of trade in favour of a nation ought to be a leading aim of its policy. The avarice of individuals may frequently find its account in pursuing channels of traffic prejudicial to that ballance, to which the government may be able to oppose effectual impediments. There may, on the other hand, be a possibility of opening new sources, which, though accompanied with great difficulties in the commencement, would in the event amply reward the trouble and expence of bringing them to perfection. The undertaking may often exceed the influence and capitals of individuals; and may require no small assistance, as well from the revenue, as from the authority of the state.

The contrary opinion, which has grown into a degree of vogue among us, has originated in the injudicious attempts made at different times to effect a REGULATION of PRICES. It became a cant phrase among the opposers of these attempts, that TRADE MUST REGULATE ITSELF; by which at first was only meant that it had its fundamental laws, agreeable to which its general operations must be directed; and that any violent attempts in opposition to these would commonly miscarry. In this sense the maxim was reasonable; but it has since been extended to militate against all interference by the sovereign; an extreme as little reconcileable with experience, or common sense, as the practice it was first framed to discredit.

The reasonings of a very ingenious and sensible writer, by being misapprehended, have contributed to this mistake. The scope of his argument is not, as by some supposed, that trade will hold a certain invariable course independent on the aid, protection, care or concern of government; but that it will, in the main, depend upon the comparative industry moral and physical advantages of nations; and that though, for a while, from extraordinary causes, there may be a wrong ballance against one of them, this will work its own cure, and things will ultimately return to their proper level. His object was to combat that excessive jealousy on this head, which has been productive of so many unnecessary wars, and with which the British nation is particularly interested; but it was no part of his design to insinuate that the regulating hand of government was either useless, or hurtful. The nature of a government, its spirit, maxims and laws, with respect to trade, are among those constant moral causes, which influence its general results, and when it has by accident taken a wrong direction, assist in bringing it back to its natural course. This is every where admitted by all writers upon the subject; nor is there one who has asserted a contrary doctrine.

Trade may be said to have taken its rise in England under the auspices of Elizabeth; and its rapid progress there is in a great measure to be ascribed to the fostering care of government in that and succeeding reigns.

From a different spirit in the government, with superior advantages, France was much later in commercial improvements, nor would her trade have been at this time in so prosperous a condition had it not been for the abilities and indefatigable endeavours of the great COLBERT. He laid the foundation of the French commerce, and taught the way to his successors to enlarge and improve it. The establishment of the woolen manufacture, in a kingdom, where nature seemed to have denied the means, is one among many proofs, how much may be effected in favour of commerce by the attention and patronage of a wise administration. The number of useful edicts passed by Louis the 14th, and since his time, in spite of frequent interruptions from the jealous enmity of Great Britain, has advanced that of France to a degree which has excited the envy and astonishment of its neighbours.

The Dutch, who may justly be allowed a pre-eminence in the knowledge of trade, have ever made it an essential object of state. Their commercial regulations are more rigid and numerous, than those of any other country; and it is by a judicious and unremitted vigilance of government, that they have been able to extend their traffic to a degree so much beyond their natural and comparitive advantages.

Perhaps it may be thought, that the power of regulation will be left placed in the governments of the several states, and that a general superintendence is unnecessary. If the states had distinct interests, were unconnected with each other, their own governments would then be the proper and could be the only depositaries of such a power; but as they are parts of a whole with a common interest in trade, as in other things, there ought to be a common direction in that as in all other matters. It is easy to conceive, that many cases may occur in which it would be beneficial to all the states to encourage, or suppress a particular branch of trade, while it would be detrimental to either to attempt it without the concurrence of the rest, and where the experiment would probably be left untried for fear of a want of that concurrence.

No mode can be so convenient as a source of revenue to the United States. It is agreed that imposts on trade, when not immoderate, or improperly laid, is one of the most eligible species of taxation. They fall in a great measure upon articles not of absolute necessity, and being partly transferred to the price of the commodity, are so far imperceptibly paid by the consumer. It is therefore that mode which may be exercised by the foederal government with least exception or disgust. Congress can easily possess all the information necessary to impose the duties with judgment, and the collection can without difficulty be made by their own officers.

They can have no temptation to abuse this power, because the motive of revenue will check its own extremes. Experience has shown that moderate duties are more productive than high ones. When they are low, a nation can trade abroad on better terms—its imports and exports will be larger—the duties will be regularly paid, and arising on a greater quantity of commodities, will yield more in the aggregate, than when they are so high as to operate either as a prohibition, or as an inducement to evade them by illicit practices.

It is difficult to assign any good reason why Congress should be more liable to abuse the powers with which they are intrusted than the state-assemblies. The frequency of the election of the members is a full security against a dangerous ambition, and the rotation established by the confederation makes it impossible for any state, by continuing the same men, who may put themselves at the head of a prevailing faction, to maintain for any length of time an undue influence in the national councils. It is to be presumed, that Congress will be in general better composed for abilities, and as well for integrity as any assembly on the continent.

But to take away any temptation from a cabal to load particular articles, which are the principal objects of commerce to particular states, with a too great proportion of duties, to ease the others in the general distributions of expense; let all the duties whether for regulation or revenue raised in each state be credited to that state and let it in like manner be charged for all the bounties paid within itself for the encouragement of agriculture, manufactures, or trade. This expedient will remove the temptation; for as the quotas of the respective states are to be determined by a standard of land, agreeable to the   article of the confederation, each will have so much the less to contribute otherwise as it pays more on its commerce.

An objection has been made in a late instance to this

principle. It has been urged, that as the consumer pays the duty, those states which are not equally well situated for foreign commerce, and which consume a great part of the imports of their neighbours, will become contributors to a part of their taxes. This objection is rather specious, than solid.

The maxim, that the consumer pays the duty has been admitted in theory with too little reserve; frequently contradicted in practice. It is true, the merchant will be unwilling to let the duty be a deduction from his profits, if the state of the market will permit him to incorporate it with the price of his commodity. But this is often not practicable. It turns upon the quantity of goods at market in proportion to the demand. When the latter exceeds the former, and the competition is among the buyers, the merchant can easily increase his price and make his customers pay the duty. When the reverse is the case, and the competition is among the sellers, he must then content himself with smaller profits, and lose the value of the duty or at least of a part of it. Where a nation has a flourishing and well settled trade this more commonly happens than may be imagined, and it will, many times, be found that the duty is divided between the merchant and the consumer.

Besides this consideration, which greatly diminishes the force of the objection, there is another which intirely destroys it. There is strong reciprocal influence between the prices of all commodities in a state, by which they, sooner or later, attain a pretty exact ballance and proportion to each other. If the immediate productions of the soil rise, the manufacturer will have more for his manufacture, the merchant for his goods; and the same will happen with whatever class the increase of price begins. If duties are laid upon the imports in one state, by which the prices of foreign articles are raised, the products of land and labour within that state will take a proportionable rise; and if a part of those articles are consumed in a neighbouring state, it will have the same influence there as at home. The importing state must allow an advanced price upon the commodities, which it receives in exchange from its neighbor in a ratio to the increased price of the article it sells. To know then which is the gainer or loser, we must examine how the general ballance of trade stands between them. If the importing state takes more of the commodities of its neighbour, than it gives in exchange, that will be the loser by the reciprocal augmentation of prices—it will be the gainer, if it takes less—and neither will gain, or lose, if the barter is carried on upon equal terms. The ballance of trade, and consequently the gain, or loss, in this respect will be governed more by the relative industry and frugality of the parties, than by their relative advantages for foreign commerce.

Between separate nations, this reasoning will not apply with full force, because a multitude of local and extraneous circumstances may counteract the principal; but from the intimate connections of these states, the similitude of governments, situations, customs, manners—political and commercial causes will have nearly the same operation in the intercourse between the states, as in that between the different parts of the same state. If this should be controverted, the objection drawn from the hypothesis of the consumer paying the duty must fall at the same time: For as far as this is true it is as much confined in its application to a state within itself, as the doctrine of a reciprocal proportion of prices.

General principles in subjects of this nature ought always to be advanced with caution; in an experimental analysis there are found such a number of exceptions as tend to render them very doubtful; and in questions which affect the existence and collective happiness of these states, all nice and abstract distinctions should give way to plainer interests and to more obvious and simple rules of conduct.

But the objection which has been urged ought to have no weight on another account. Which are the states, that have not sufficient advantages for foreign commerce, and that will not in time be their own carriers? Connecticut and Jersey are the least maritime of the whole; yet the sound which washes the coast of Connecticut has an easy outlet to the ocean, affords a number of harbours and bays, very commodious for trading vessels. New-London may be a receptacle for merchantmen of almost any burthen and the fine rivers with which the state is intersected, by facilitating the transportation of commodities to and from every part, are extremely favorable both to its domestic and foreign trade. Jersey, by way of Amboy has a shorter communication with the ocean, than the city of New-York. Princes bay, which may serve as an out port to it, will admit and shelter in winter and summer vessels of any size. Egg-harbour on its southern coast is not to be despised. The Delaware may be made as subservient to its commerce as to that of Pennsylvania, Gloucester, Burlington, and Trenton, being all conveniently situated on that river. The United Provinces with inferior advantages of position to either of these states, have for centuries held the first rank among commercial nations.

The want of large trading cities has been sometimes objected as an obstacle to the commerce of these states; but this is a temporary deficiency that will repair itself with the encrease of population and riches. The reason that the states in question have hitherto carried on little foreign trade, is that they have found it equally beneficial to purchase the commodities imported by their neighbours. If the imposts on trade should work an inconvenience to them, it will soon cease by making it their interest to trade abroad.

It is too much characteristic of our national temper to be ingenious in finding out and magnifying the minutest disadvantages, and to reject measures of evident utility even of necessity to avoid trivial and sometimes imaginary evils. We seem not to reflect, that in human society, there is scarcely any plan, however salutary to the whole and to every part, by the share, each has in the common prosperity, but in one way, or another, and under particular circumstances, will operate more to the benefit of some parts, than of others. Unless we can overcome this narrow disposition and learn to estimate measures, by their general tendency, we shall never be a great or a happy people, if we remain a people at all.

2

PROPOSED AMENDMENT TO ARTICLES OF
CONFEDERATION
28 Mar. 1785
Jensen 1:155–56

That the first paragraph of the 9th of the Articles of Confederation be altered so as to read thus—viz

"The United States in Congress Assembled shall have the sole and exclusive right and power of determining, on peace and war, except in the cases mentioned in the sixth Article—of sending and receiving Ambassadors—entering into treaties and alliances—of regulating the trade of the States as well with foreign Nations, as with each other, and of laying such imposts and duties, upon imports and exports, as may be necessary for the purpose; provided that the Citizens of the States, shall in no instance be subjected to pay higher imposts and duties, than those imposed on the subjects of foreign powers; provided also that the Legislative power of the several States shall not be restrained from prohibiting the importation or exportation of any species of goods or commodities whatsoever, provided also that all such duties as may be imposed, shall be collected under the authority and accrue to the use of the State in which the same shall be payable. And provided lastly that every Act of Congress for the above purpose shall have the assent of nine States in Congress assembled—of establishing rules for deciding in all cases, what Captures on Land or Water, shall be legal, and in what manner prizes taken by Land or Naval forces in the service of the United States shall be divided or appropriated of granting Letters of Marque & reprisal in time of peace—appointing Courts for the trial of piracies and felonies, committed on the high seas, and establishing Courts for receiving and determining finally appeals in all cases of Captures, provided that no Member of Congress shall be appointed Judge of any of the said Courts"—

3

GEORGE MASON TO SPEAKER OF VIRGINIA
HOUSE OF DELEGATES
28 Mar. 1785
Papers 2:815–16, 823

The Commissioners were of Opinion, these States ought to have Leave from the United States in Congress assembled, to form a Compact for the Purpose of affording in due Time, and in just Proportion between the two States, naval Protection to such Part of Chesapeake Bay and Potomack River, which may at any Time hereafter, be left

unprovided for by Congress. The Commissioners did not consider themselves authorised to make any Compact on this Subject, and submit the Propriety of the two Governments making a joint Application to Congress, for their Consent to enter into Compact, for the Purpose aforesaid; such Compact, when made, to be laid before Congress, for their Approbation; and to continue, until mutually dissolved by these States, or Congress shall declare that such Compact shall no longer exist.

It also appeared to the Commissioners, that foreign Gold & Silver Coin received in the two States, as the Current Money thereof, shou'd pass at the same Value, according to it's Fineness & Weight; and if the Species of Coin cou'd be regulated at the same nominal Value; it wou'd be of great Convenience to the Commerce & Dealings between the Citizens of the two States.

The Damage on foreign Bills of Exchange, protested, are very different in the two States, and it is obvious that they ought to be the same, and shou'd be considered in all Cases, & to all Purposes, as of equal Rank with Debts upon Contract in Writing, signed by the Party; and it was suggested that fifteen per Ct. shou'd be allowed, without Regard to the time of Negotiation, & legal Interest on the Principal, from the time of Protest. It was also conceived by the Commissioners, that Drafts by the Merchants of either state, upon those of the other; in the Nature of Inland Bills of Exchange, shou'd be subject, by Law, to official Protest, by a Notary Public; and that the Damages, for non-payment, shou'd be the same in both States; and it was thought, that eight per Ct. shou'd be allowed upon Protest, and legal Interest upon the Principal, from the Time of Protest.

It appeared to the Commissioners to be essential to the Commerce & Revenue of the two Governments, that Duties on Imports or Exports (if laid) shou'd be the same in both States.

If these Subjects shou'd be deemed worthy [of] Notice, it may be proper for the two Legislatures, at their annual Meeting in the Autumn, to appoint Commissioners to meet, & communicate the Regulations of Commerce & Duties proposed by each State, and to confer on such Subjects as may concern the commercial Interests of both States. It was suggested that the Number of the said Commissioners shou'd be equal, and not less than three, nor more than five, from each State; and that they shou'd annually meet in the third Week in September, at such Place as they shou'd appoint.

. . . . .

[Enclosure: To the President of the Executive Council of the Commonwealth of Pennsylvania]

In Pursuance of Directions from the Legislatures of Virginia and Maryland, respectively to us given, we beg Leave to represent to the State of Pensylvania, that it is in Contemplation of the said two States to promote the clearing & extending the Navigation of Potomack, from tide-Water, upwards, as far as the same may be found practicable; to open a convenient Road, from the Head of such Navigation, to the Waters running into the Ohio, and to render these Waters navigable, as far as may be necessary & proper; that the said works will require great Expence, which may not be repaid, unless a free Use be secured to the said States, & their Citizens, of the water of the Ohio & it's Branches, as far as the same lie within the Limits of Pensylvania: that as essential Advantages will accrue from such Works to a considerable Portion of the said State, it is thought reasonable that the Legislature thereof shou'd by some previous Act engage, that for the Encouragement of the said Works, all Articles of Produce & Merchandize, which may be conveyed to or from either of the said two States, thro' either of the said Rivers, within the Limits of Pensylvania, to or from any Place without the said Limits, shall pass throughout, free from all Duties, or Tolls whatsoever, other than such Tolls as may be established, & be necessary for reimbursing Expences incurred by the State, or it's Citizens, in clearing, or for defraying the Expence of Preserving the Navigation of the said Rivers. And that no Articles imported into Pensylvania thro' the Channel or Channels or any Part thereof to be opened as aforesaid, and vended or used within the said State, shall be subject to any Duties or Imposts, other than such Articles wou'd be subject to, if imported into the said State thro' any other Channel whatsoever.

We request Sir, that you will take the earliest Opportunity of laying this Representation, on Behalf of the two States, before the Legislature of Pensylvania; and that you will communicate the Result to the Executives of Virginia & Maryland.

By Acts of the Legislatures of Virginia & Maryland for opening the Navigation of the River Potomack above tide-Water, the Citizens of the United States have the same Right of trading thro' the said Water, which the Citizens of Maryland & Virginia enjoy; and we have no Doubt but the Legislature of your State will, agreeably to this Principle, give every Encouragement to Measures, which have for their Object, the Interest & Convenience of their Citizens, and those of the other States in the Union.

4

JAMES MADISON TO JAMES MONROE
7 Aug. 1785
Papers 8:333–36

I received the day before yesterday your favour of the 26th July. I had previously recd. the Report on the proposed change of the 9th. art: of the Confederation, transmitted by Col: Grayson, and in my answer to him offered such ideas on the subject as then occurred. I still think the probability of success or failure ought to weigh much with Congress in every recommendation to the States; of which probability Congress, in whom information from every State centers, can alone properly judge. Viewing in the abstract the question whether the power of regulating trade, to a certain degree at least, ought to be vested in Congress,

it appears to me not to admit of a doubt, but that it should be decided in the affirmative. If it be necessary to regulate trade at all, it surely is necessary to lodge the power, where trade can be regulated with effect, and experience has confirmed what reason foresaw, that it can never be so regulated by the States acting in their separate capacities. They can no more exercise this power separately, than they could separately carry on war, or separately form treaties of alliance or Commerce. The nature of the thing therefore proves the former power, no less than the latter, to be within the reason of the foederal Constitution. Much indeed is it to be wished, as I conceive, that no regulations of trade, that is to say, no restriction or imposts whatever, were necessary. A perfect freedom is the System which would be my choice. But before such a system will be eligible perhaps for the U. S. they must be out of debt; before it will be attainable, all other nations must concur in it. Whilst any one of these imposes on our Vessels seamen &c in their ports, clogs from which they exempt their own, we must either retort the distinction, or renounce not merely a just profit, but our only defence against the danger which may most easily beset us. Are we not at this moment under this very alternative? The policy of G. B. (to say nothing of other nations) has shut against us the channels without which our trade with her must be a losing one; and she has consequently the triumph, as we have the chagrin, of seeing accomplished her prophetic threats, that our independence, should forfeit commercial advantages for which it would not recompence us with any new channels of trade. What is to be done? Must we remain passive victims to foreign politics; or shall we exert the lawful means which our independence has put into our hands, of extorting redress? The very question would be an affront to every Citizen who loves his Country. What then are those means? Retaliating regulations of trade only. How are these to be effectuated? only by harmony in the measures of the States. How is this harmony to be obtained? only by an acquiescence of all the States in the opinion of a reasonable majority. If Congress as they are now constituted, can not be trusted with the power of digesting and enforcing this opinion, let them be otherwise constituted: let their numbers be increased, let them be chosen oftener, and let their period of service be short[e]ned; or if any better medium than Congress can be proposed, by which the wills of the States may be concentered, let it be substituted; or lastly let no regulation of trade adopted by Congress be in force untill it shall have been ratified by a certain proportion of the States. But let us not sacrifice the end to the means: let us not rush on certain ruin in order to avoid a possible danger. I conceive it to be of great importance that the defects of the federal system should be amended, not only because such amendments will make it better answer the purpose for which it was instituted, but because I apprehend danger to its very existence from a continuance of defects which expose a part if not the whole of the empire to severe distress. The suffering part, even when the minor part, can not long respect a Government which is too feeble to protect their interest; But when the suffering part come to be the major part, and they despair of seeing a protecting energy given to the General Government, from what motives is their allegiance to be any longer expected. Should G. B. persist in the machinations which distress us; and seven or eight of the States be hindered by the others from obtaining relief by foederal means, I own, I tremble at the anti-foederal expedients into which the former may be tempted. As to the objection against intrusting Congress with a power over trade, drawn from the diversity of interests in the States, it may be answered. 1. that if this objection had been listened to, no confederation could have ever taken place among the States, 2. that if it ought now to be listened to, the power held by Congress of forming Commercial treaties by which 9 States may indirectly dispose of the Commerce of the residue, ought to be immediately revoked. 3 that the fact is that a case can scarcely be imagined in which it would be the interest of any 2/3ds of the States to oppress the remaining 1/3d. 4. that the true question is whether the commercial interests of the States do not meet in more points than they differ. To me it is clear that they do: and if they do there are so many more reasons for, than against, submitting the commercial interest of each State to the direction and care of the Majority. Put the West India trade alone, in which the interest of every State is involved, into the scale against all the inequalities which may result from any probable regulation by nine States, and who will say that the latter ought to preponderate? I have heard the different interest which the Eastern States have as Carriers pointed out as a ground of caution to the Southern States who have no bottoms of their own agst their concurring hastily in retaliations on G. B. But will the present system of G. B. ever give the Southern States bottoms; and if they are not their own Carriers I shod. suppose it no mark either of folly or incivility to give our custom to our brethren rather than to those who have not yet entitled themselves to the name of friends.

In detailing these sentiments I have nothing more in view than to prov[e] the readiness with which I obey your requests. As far as they are just they must have been often suggested in the discussions of Congress on the subject. I can not even give them weight by saying that I have reason to believe they would be relished in the public Councils of this State. From the trials of which I have been a witness I augur that great difficulties will be encountered in every attempt to prevail on the Legislature to part with power. The thing itself is not only unpalatable, but the arguments which plead for it have not their full force on minds unaccustomed to consider the interests of the State as they are interwoven with those of the Confederacy much less as they may be affected by foreign politics whilst those wch. plead agst. it, are not only specious, but in their nature popular: and for that reason, sure of finding patrons. Add to all this that the mercantile interest which has taken the lead in rousing the public attention of other States, is in this so exclusively occupied in British Commerce that what little weight they have will be most likely to fall into the opposite scale. The only circumstance which promises a favorable hearing to the meditated proposition of Congs. is that the power which it asks is to be exerted agst. G. B, and the proposition will consequently be seconded by the animosities which still prevail in a strong degree agst. her.

5

RICHARD HENRY LEE TO ———
10 Oct. 1785
Letters 2:389

So essential is the difference between the Northern & Southern productions and circumstances relative to Commerce, that it is not easy to adopt any general system that would well accord with all; and the Staple States should be feelingly alive to the proposed plan of vesting powers absolute for the restraint & regulation of Commerce in a Body of representatives whose Constituents are very differently circumstanced—Intrigue and coalit[i]on among the No Staple States, taking advantage of the disunion and inattenti[on] of the South, might fix a ruinous Monopoly upon the trade & productions of the Staple States that have not Ships or Seamen for the Exportation of their valuable productions—You know Sir that the Spirit of Commerce is a Spirit of Avarice, and that whenever the power is given the will certainly follows to monopolise, to engross, and to take every possible advantage. I am free therefore to own that I think it both safest & best to give no such power to Congress, leave it to that Body to point out what is fit to be done in this [line], and founding their plans on principles of moderation and most accordant to the actual state & situation of the different States, to recommend their systems for the general adoption. I am persuaded that this plan would be successful to every good purpose. A contrary one would, I verily believe, be more hurtful, much more hurtful to us, than even the crabbed selfish system of Great Britain.

6

JAMES MADISON, DRAFT OF RESOLUTIONS ON
FOREIGN TRADE, VIRGINIA HOUSE OF DELEGATES
12 Nov. 1785
Papers 8:409–10

1. Resd. that to vest Congs. with authority to regulate the foreign trade of the U. S. wd. add energy & dignity to the federal Govt.
2. Resd. that the unrestrained exercise of the powers possessed by each State over its own commerce may be productive of discord among the parties to the Union; and that Congs. ought to be vested with authority to regulate the same in certain cases.
3. Resd. that in regulating the foreign trade of U. S. Congs. ought to enjoy the right

   1. of prohibiting vessels belonging to any foreign nation from entering into any of the ports of the U. S. such prohibition being Uniform through[ou]t the same: and

2. of imposing duties on the vessels, produce or manufactures of foreign nations, & collecting them in such manner, as to Congs. may seem best; to be appropriated to the establishmt. & support of a marine, & to this purpose alone; unless   States in Congress assd. shall concur, on principles of extreme necessity, in any other appropriation. But Congs. shall notwithstanding, have power to grant drawbacks, & shall not change the application of those duties wch. may arise from their recommendations concerning imposts on imported goods.

4. Resd. that no State ought to be at liberty to impose duties on any goods ware or merchandizes imported by land or water from any other State; but each State ought to be free to prohibit altogether the importation from any other State, of any particular species or description of goods wares or merchandizes, which are at the same time prohibited to be imported from all other places whatsoever.

5. Resd. that to every act of Congs. done in pursuance of the foregoing authorities, and prohibiting foreign vessels, or imposing duties on Cargoes the assent of three fourths of the States in Congs shall be necessary; but the power of appropriating to the marine in the first instance shall be exercised with the assent of nine States.

6. Resd. that no Act of Congs. done in pursuance of the foregoing authorities, shall be in force longer than   years, unless continued by ¾ of the confederated States within one year immediately preceding the expiration of the said period.

7

JAMES MADISON, PREFACE TO DEBATES IN THE
CONVENTION OF 1787

Farrand 3:547–48

The want of authy. in Congs. to regulate Commerce had produced in Foreign nations particularly G. B. a monopolizing policy injurious to the trade of the U. S. and destructive to their navigation; the imbecility and anticipated dissolution of the Confederacy extinguishg. all apprehensions of a Countervailing policy on the part of the U. States.

The same want of a general power over Commerce led to an exercise of this power separately, by the States, wch not only proved abortive, but engendered rival, conflicting and angry regulations. Besides the vain attempts to supply their respective treasuries by imposts, which turned their commerce into the neighbouring ports, and to co-erce a relaxation of the British monopoly of the W. Indn. navigation, which was attemted by Virga. the States having ports for foreign commerce, taxed & irritated the adjoining States, trading thro' them, as N. Y. Pena. Virga. & S—Carolina. Some of the States, as Connecticut, taxed imports as from Massts higher than imports even from G. B. of wch Massts. complained to Virga. and doubtless to other States. In sundry instances of as N. Y. N. J. Pa. & Maryd. the navigation laws treated the Citizens of other States as aliens.

8

RECORDS OF THE FEDERAL CONVENTION

[1:133; Madison, 6 June]

Mr. Sherman. . . . The objects of the Union, he thought were few. . . . 4 regulating foreign commerce, & drawing revenues from it.

[1:243; Madison, 15 June]

2. Resd. that in addition to the powers vested in the U. States in Congress, by the present existing articles of Confederation, they be authorized to . . . pass Acts for the regulation of trade & commerce as well with foreign nations as with each other:

[4:23; Martin, 19 June]

. . . because the States individually are incompetent to the purpose that the United-States should also regulate the Commerce of the United-States foreign & internal, is I believe a matter of general Consent. . . .

[2:374; Madison, 22 Aug.]

[Article 7, Sec. 4: "No tax or duty shall be laid by the Legislature on articles exported from any State; nor on the migration or importation of such persons as the several States shall think proper to admit; nor shall such migration or importation be prohibited."]

Mr Govr. Morris wished the whole subject to be committed including the clauses relating to taxes on exports & to a navigation act. These things may form a bargain among the Northern & Southern States.

Mr. Butler declared that he never would agree to the power of taxing exports.

Mr. Sherman said it was better to let the S. States import slaves than to part with them, if they made that a sine qua non. He was opposed to a tax on slaves imported as making the matter worse, because it implied they were *property.* He acknowledged that if the power of prohibiting the importation should be given to the Genl. Government that it would be exercised. He thought it would be its duty to exercise the power.

Mr. Read was for the commitment provided the clause concerning taxes on exports should also be committed.

Mr. Sherman observed that that clause had been agreed to & therefore could not committed.

Mr. Randolph was for committing in order that some middle ground might, if possible, be found. He could never agree to the clause as it stands. He wd. sooner risk the constitution—He dwelt on the dilemma to which the Convention was exposed. By agreeing to the clause, it would revolt the Quakers, the Methodists, and many others in the States having no slaves. On the other hand, two States might be lost to the Union. Let us then, he said, try the chance of a commitment.

On the question for committing the remaining part of Sect 4 & 5. of art: 7. N. H. no. Mas. abst. Cont. ay N. J. ay Pa. no. Del. no Maryd ay. Va ay. N. C. ay S. C. ay. Geo. ay. [Ayes—7; noes—3; absent—1.]

Mr. Pinkney & Mr. Langdon moved to commit sect. 6. as to navigation act by two thirds of each House.

Mr. Gorham did not see the propriety of it. Is it meant to require a greater proportion of votes? He desired it to be remembered that the Eastern States had no motive to Union but a commercial one. They were able to protect themselves. They were not afraid of external danger, and did not need the aid of the Southn. States.

Mr. Wilson wished for a commitment in order to reduce the proportion of votes required.

Mr. Elsworth was for taking the plan as it is. This widening of opinions has a threatening aspect. If we do not agree on this middle & moderate ground he was afraid we should lose two States, with such others as may be disposed to stand aloof, should fly into a variety of shapes & directions, and most probably into several confederations and not without bloodshed.

On Question for committing 6 sect. as to navigation Act to a member from each State—N. H. ay—Mas. ay. Ct no. N. J. no. Pa. ay Del. ay. Md. ay. Va. ay. N.C. ay. S.C. ay. Geo. ay. [Ayes—9; noes—2.]

[2:449; Madison, 29 Aug.]

Art. VII Sect. 6 by ye. Committee of eleven reported to be struck out (see the 24 instant) being now taken up,

Mr. Pinkney moved to postpone the Report in favor of the following proposition—"That no act of the Legislature for the purpose of regulating the commerce of the U—S. with foreign powers, or among the several States, shall be passed without the assent of two thirds of the members of each House—" —He remarked that there were five distinct commercial interests—1. the fisheries & W. India trade, which belonged to the N. England States. 2. the interest of N. York lay in a free trade. 3. Wheat & flour the Staples of the two Middle States, (N. J. & Penna.)— 4. Tobo. the staple of Maryd. & Virginia & partly of N. Carolina. 5. Rice & Indigo, the staples of S. Carolina & Georgia. These different interests would be a source of oppressive regulations if no check to a bare majority should be provided. States pursue their interests with less scruple than individuals. The power of regulating commerce was a pure concession on the part of the S. States. They did not need. the protection of the N. States at present.

Mr. Martin 2ded. the motion

Genl. Pinkney said it was the true interest of the S. States to have no regulation of commerce; but considering the loss brought on the commerce of the Eastern States by the revolution, their liberal conduct towards the views of South Carolina, and the interest the weak Southn. States had in being united with the strong Eastern States, he thought it proper that no fetters should be imposed on the power of making commercial regulations; and that his constituents though prejudiced against the Eastern States, would be reconciled to this liberality—He had himself, he said, prejudices agst the Eastern States before he came here, but would acknowledge that he had found them as liberal and candid as any men whatever.

Mr. Clymer. The diversity of commercial interests, of necessity creates difficulties, which ought not to be increased by unnecessary restrictions. The Northern & middle States will be ruined, if not enabled to defend themselves against foreign regulations.

Mr. Sherman, alluding to Mr. Pinkney's enumeration of particular interests, as requiring a security agst. abuse of the power; observed that, the diversity was of itself a security. adding that to require more than a majority to decide a question was always embarrassing as had been experienced in cases requiring the votes of nine States in Congress.

Mr. Pinkney replied that his enumeration meant the five minute interests—It still left the two great divisions of Northern & Southern Interests.

Mr. Govr. Morris. opposed the object of the motion as highly injurious— Preferences to american ships will multiply them, till they can carry the Southern produce cheaper than it is now carried- —A navy was essential to security, particularly of the S. States, and can only be had by a navigation act encouraging american bottoms & seamen—In those points of view then alone, it is the interest of the S. States that navigation acts should be facilitated. Shipping he said was the worst & most precarious kind of property. and stood in need of public patronage.

Mr Williamson was in favor of making two thirds instead of a majority requisite, as more satisfactory to the Southern people. No useful measure he believed had been lost in Congress for want of nine votes As to the weakness of the Southern States, he was not alarmed on that account. The sickliness of their climate for invaders would prevent their being made an object. He acknowledged that he did not think the motion requiring ⅔ necessary in itself, because if a majority of Northern States should push their regulations too far, the S. States would build ships for themselves: but he knew the Southern people were apprehensive on this subject and would be pleased with the precaution.

Mr. Spaight was against the motion. The Southern States could at any time save themselves from oppression, by building ships for their own use.

Mr. Butler differed from those who considered the rejection of the motion as no concession on the part of the S. States. He considered the interests of these and of the Eastern States, to be as different as the interests of Russia and Turkey. Being notwitstanding desirous of conciliating the affections of the East: States, he should vote agst. requiring ⅔ instead of a majority.

Col: Mason. If the Govt. is to be lasting, it must be founded in the confidence & affections of the people, and must be so constructed as to obtain these. The *Majority* will be governed by their interests. The Southern States are the *minority* in both Houses. Is it to be expected that they will deliver themselves bound hand & foot to the Eastern

States, and enable them to exclaim, in the words of Cromwell on a certain occasion—"the lord hath delivered them into our hands."

Mr. Wilson took notice of the several objections and remarked that if every peculiar interest was to be secured, *unanimity* ought to be required. The majority he said would be no more governed by interest than the minority—It was surely better to let the latter be bound hand and foot than the former. Great inconveniences had, he contended, been experienced in Congress from the article of confederation requiring nine votes in certain cases.

Mr. Madison. went into a pretty full view of the subject. He observed that the disadvantage to the S. States from a navigation act, lay chiefly in a temporary rise of freight, attended however with an increase of Southn. as well as Northern Shipping—with the emigration of Northern seamen & merchants to the Southern States—& with a removal of the existing & injurious retaliations among the States on each other. The power of foreign nations to obstruct our retaliating measures on them by a corrupt influence would also be less if a majority shd be made competent than if ⅔ of each House shd. be required to legislative acts in this case. An abuse of the power would be qualified with all these good effects. But he thought an abuse was rendered improbable by the provision of 2 branches—by the independence of the Senate, by the negative of the Executive, by the interest of Connecticut & N. Jersey which were agricultural, not commercial States; by the interior interest which was also agricultural in the most commercial States—by the accession of Western States which wd. be altogether agricultural. He added that the Southern States would derive an essential advantage in the general security afforded by the increase of our maritime strength. He stated the vulnerable situation of them all, and of Virginia in particular. The increase of the Coasting trade, and of seamen, would also be favorable to the S. States, by increasing, the consumption of their produce. If the Wealth of the Eastern should in a still greater proportion be augmented, that wealth wd. contribute the more to the public wants, and be otherwise a national benefit.

Mr. Rutlidge was agst. the motion of his colleague. It did not follow from a grant of the power to regulate trade, that it would be abused. At the worst a navigation act could bear hard a little while only on the S. States. As we are laying the foundation for a great empire, we ought to take a permanent view of the subject and not look at the present moment only. He reminded the House of the necessity of securing the West India trade to this country. That was the great object, and a navigation Act was necessary for obtaining it.

Mr. Randolph said that there were features so odious in the Constitution as it now stands, that he doubted whether he should be able to agree to it. A rejection of the motion would compleat the deformity of the system. He took notice of the argument in favor of giving the power over trade to a majority, drawn from the opportunity foreign powers would have of obstructing retaliating measures, if two thirds were made requisite. He did not think there was weight in that consideration— The difference between a majority & two thirds did not afford room for such an

opportunity. Foreign influence would also be more likely to be exerted on the President who could require three fourths by his negative— He did not mean however to enter into the merits. What he had in view was merely to pave the way for a declaration which he might be hereafter obliged to make if an accumulation of obnoxious ingredients should take place, that he could not give his assent to the plan.

Mr Gorham. If the Government is to be so fettered as to be unable to relieve the Eastern States what motive can they have to join in it, and thereby tie their own hands from measures which they could otherwise take for themselves. The Eastern States were not led to strengthen the Union by fear for their own safety. He deprecated the consequences of disunion, but if it should take place it was the Southern part of the Continent that had the most reason to dread them. He urged the improbability of a combination against the interest of the Southern States, the different situations of the Northern & Middle States being a security against it. It was moreover certain that foreign ships would never be altogether excluded especially those of Nations in treaty with us.

On the question to postpone in order to take up Mr. Pinkney's Motion

N— H. no. Mas. no. Ct. no. N. J. no. Pa. no. Del. no. Md. ay. Va ay. N. C. ay— S— C. no— Geo. ay, [Ayes— 4; noes—7.]

The Report of the Committee for striking out sect: 6. requiring two thirds of each House to pass a navigation act was then agreed to, nem: con:

[2:504; McHenry, 4 Sept.]

Upon looking over the constitution it does not appear that the national legislature can *erect light houses* or *clean out or preserve the navigation of harbours*—This expence ought to be borne by commerce—of course by the general treasury into which all the revenue of commerce must come—

Is it proper to declare all the navigable waters or rivers and within the U. S. common high ways? Perhaps a power to restrain any State from demanding tribute from citizens of another State in such cases is comprehended in the power to regulate trade between State and State.

This to be further considered. A motion to be made on the light house etc, to-morrow.

[2:529; McHenry, 6 Sept.]

Spoke to Gov Morris Fitzimmons and Mr Goram to insert a power in the confederation enabling the legislature to erect piers for protection of shipping in winter and to preserve the navigation of harbours—Mr Gohram against. The other two gentlemen for it—Mr Gov: thinks it may be done under the words of the 1 clause 1 sect 7 art. amended—"and provide for the common defence and general welfare."—If this comprehends such a power, it goes to authorise the legisl. to grant exclusive privileges to trading companies etc.

[2:563; Madison, 10 Sept.]

Mr. Randolph took this opportunity to state his objections to the System. They turned . . . —on the want of

485

some particular restraint on Navigation acts—on the power to lay duties on exports

[2:633; McHenry, 15 Sept.]

Maryland moved.

No State shall be prohibited from laying such duties of tonnage as may be sufficient for improving their harbors and keeping up lights, but all acts laying such duties shall be subject to the approbation or repeal of Congress.

Moved to amend it viz. No State without the consent of Congress shall lay a duty of tonnage. Carried in the affirmative

6 ays 4 Noes, 1 divided.

. . . . .

Mr. Mason moved in substance that no navigation act be passed without the concurrence of ⅔ of the members present in each house.

Negatived.

[2:635; King, 15 Sept.]

Mr. Gerry's objections. . . .

The Power given respectg. Commerce will enable the Legislature to create corporations and monopolies

[2:639; Mason, 15 Sept.]

By requiring only a majority to make all commercial and navigation laws, the five Southern States, whose produce and circumstances are totally different from that of the eight Northern and Eastern States, will be ruined, for such rigid and premature regulations may be made as will enable the merchants of the Northern and Eastern States not only to demand an exhorbitant freight, but to monopolize the purchase of the commodities at their own price, for many years, to the great injury of the landed interest, and the impoverishment of the people; and the danger is the greater as the gain on one side will be in proportion to the loss on the other. Whereas requiring two-thirds of the members present in both Houses would have produced mutual moderation, promoted the general interest, and removed an insuperable objection to the adoption of the government.

[2:625, 631; Madison, 25 Sept.]

Mr. Mc.Henry & Mr. Carrol moved that "no State shall be restrained from laying duties of tonnage for the purpose of clearing harbours and erecting light-houses".

Col. Mason in support of this explained and urged the situation of the Chesapeak which peculiarly required expences of this sort.

Mr. Govr. Morris. The States are not restrained from laying tonnage as the Constitution now Stands. The exception proposed will imply the Contrary, and will put the States in a worse condition than the gentleman (Col Mason) wishes.

Mr. Madison. Whether the States are now restrained from laying tonnage duties depends on the extent of the power "to regulate commerce". These terms are vague but seem to exclude this power of the States— They may cer-

tainly be restrained by Treaty. He observed that there were other objects for tonnage Duties as the support of Seamen &c. He was more & more convinced that the regulation of Commerce was in its nature indivisible and ought to be wholly under one authority.

Mr. Sherman. The power of the U. States to regulate trade being supreme can controul interferences of the State regulations when such interferences happen; so that there is no danger to be apprehended from a concurrent jurisdiction.

Mr. Langdon insisted that the regulation of tonnage was an essential part of the regulation of trade, and that the States ought to have nothing to do with it. On motion "that no State shall lay any duty on tonnage without the Consent of Congress"

N. H— ay— Mas. ay. Ct. divd. N. J. ay. Pa. no. Del. ay. Md. ay. Va. no. N— C. no. S— C. ay. Geo. no. [Ayes—6; noes—4; divided—1.]

. . . . .

Col: Mason expressing his discontent at the power given to Congress by a bare majority to pass navigation acts, which he said would not only enhance the freight, a consequence he did not so much regard—but would enable a few rich merchants in Philada N. York & Boston, to monopolize the Staples of the Southern States & reduce their value perhaps 50 Per Ct—moved a further proviso "that no law in nature of a navigation act be passed before the year 1808, without the consent of ⅔ of each branch of the Legislature"

On this motion

N. H. no. Mas— no. Ct no. N— J. no— Pa no. Del. no. Md ay. Va. ay. N. C abst S. C. no— Geo— ay. [Ayes—3; noes—7; absent—1.]

9

JAMES MADISON, FEDERALIST, NO. 42, 283–85
22 Jan. 1788

The defect of power in the existing confederacy, to regulate the commerce between its several members, is in the number of those which have been clearly pointed out by experience. To the proofs and remarks which former papers have brought into view on this subject, it may be added, that without this supplemental provision, the great and essential power of regulating foreign commerce, would have been incompleat, and ineffectual. A very material object of this power was the relief of the States which import and export through other States, from the improper contributions levied on them by the latter. Were these at liberty to regulate the trade between State and State, it must be foreseen that ways would be found out, to load the articles of import and export, during the passage through their jurisdiction, with duties which would fall on the makers of the latter, and the consumers of the former. We may be assured by past experience, that such a practice would be introduced by future contrivances;

and both by that and a common knowledge of human affairs, that it would nourish unceasing animosities, and not improbably terminate in serious interruptions of the public tranquility. To those who do not view the question through the medium of passion or of interest, the desire of the commercial States to collect in any form, an indirect revenue from their uncommercial neighbours, must appear not less impolitic than it is unfair; since it would stimulate the injured party, by resentment as well as interest, to resort to less convenient channels for their foreign trade. But the mild voice of reason, pleading the cause of an enlarged and permanent interest, is but too often drowned before public bodies as well as individuals, by the clamours of an impatient avidity for immediate and immoderate gain.

The necessity of a superintending authority over the reciprocal trade of confederated States has been illustrated by other examples as well as our own. In Switzerland, where the Union is so very slight, each Canton is obliged to allow to merchandizes, a passage through its jurisdiction into other Cantons, without an augmentation of the tolls. In Germany, it is a law of the empire, that the Princes and States shall not lay tolls or customs on bridges, rivers, or passages, without the consent of the Emperor and Diet; though it appears from a quotation in an antecedent paper, that the practice in this as in many other instances in that confederacy, has not followed the law, and has produced there the mischiefs which have been foreseen here. Among the restraints imposed by the Union of the Netherlands, on its members, one is, that they shall not establish imports disadvantageous to their neighbors, without the general permission.

The regulation of commerce with the Indian tribes is very properly unfettered from two limitations in the articles of confederation, which render the provision obscure and contradictory. The power is there restrained to Indians, not members of any of the States, and is not to violate or infringe the legislative right of any State within its own limits. What description of Indians are to be deemed members of a State, is not yet settled; and has been a question of frequent perplexity and contention in the Foederal Councils. And how the trade with Indians, though not members of a State, yet residing within its legislative jurisdiction, can be regulated by an external authority, without so far intruding on the internal rights of legislation, is absolutely incomprehensible. This is not the only case in which the articles of confederation have inconsiderately endeavored to accomplish impossibilities; to reconcile a partial sovereignty in the Union, with compleat sovereignty in the States; to subvert a mathematical axiom, by taking away a part, and letting the whole remain.

10

THOMAS JEFFERSON TO ALBERT GALLATIN
13 Oct. 1802
Works 9:398–99

You know my doubts, or rather convictions, about the unconstitutionality of the act for building piers in the Delaware, and the fears that it will lead to a bottomless expense, & to the greatest abuses. There is, however, one intention of which the act is susceptible, & which will bring it within the Constitution; and we ought always to presume that the real intention which is alone consistent with the Constitution. Altho' the power to regulate commerce does not give a power to build piers, wharves, open ports, clear the beds of rivers, dig canals, build warehouses, build manufacturing machines, set up manufactories, cultivate the earth, to all of which the power would go if it went to the first, yet a power to provide and maintain a navy, is a power to provide receptacles for it, and places to cover & preserve it. In choosing the places where this money should be laid out, I should be much disposed, as far as contracts will permit, to confine it to such place or places as the ships of war may lie at, and be protected from ice; & I should be for stating this in a message to Congress, in order to prevent the effect of the present example. This act has been built on the exercise of the power of building light houses, as a regulation of commerce. But I well remember the opposition, on this very ground, to the first act for building a light house. The utility of the thing has sanctioned the infraction. But if on that infraction we build a 2d, on that 2d a 3d, &c., any one of the powers in the Constitution may be made to comprehend every power of government.

11

ST. GEORGE TUCKER,
BLACKSTONE'S COMMENTARIES
1:APP. 248–54
1803

We have already had occasion to mention the state of foreign commerce, upon the conclusion of the peace with Great-Britain; and the conduct of the government of that nation in excluding our vessels from their ports in the West-India Islands. The proposition made by the state of Virginia to authorise congress to prohibit the importation of the growth or produce of those islands into the United States in British vessels, and even to adopt more energetic measures, by refusing the necessary supplies to those islands, if adopted, would probably have counteracted the designs of that politic nation: but, that fatal want of unanimity among the states, which at that period marked all their councils, defeated the proposal. The boldness of the measure on the part of Great-Britain, evinced a determination to secure her commercial advantages, even at the risk of the existence of her colonies; yet it is not to be imagined that she would have persevered in such a conduct towards her own colonies, if the United States had offered to retaliate her policy, by refusing them provisions, lumber, and other articles of the first necessity, unless they were admitted to send them thither in their own vessels, as well as in those of British subjects. For, independent of the injustice and inhumanity of such a conduct in the predominant state, the prosperity of the sugar colonies must have been of more consequence to Great-Britain, than the whole of the carrying trade between those islands and the United States. True it is, that it was pretended by the British ministry, and their adherents, that Nova Scotia and Canada could supply those islands, with every necessary formerly derived from the United States. But the bare admission of those articles from the United States, in any manner whatsoever, might be relied on as an unequivocal evidence that they had no confidence in the sufficiency of the resources which might be drawn from Canada or Nova Scotia; and experience is said to be strongly in favour of the opinion that those colonies cannot supply the sugar islands, either with provisions or lumber, in any degree proportionate to their necessities. The conduct of Great-Britain in declining any commercial treaty with America, at that time, was unquestionably dictated at first by a knowledge of the inability of congress to extort terms of reciprocity from her; and of that want of unanimity among the states, which, under the existing confederation, was a perpetual bar to any restriction upon her commerce with the whole of the states; and any partial restriction would be sure to fail of effect.

Having repeatedly noticed the defect of the former confederation, in respect to the regulation of the commerce between the several states, and the inconveniences resulting from it, I shall only mention one not yet touched upon: I mean the burthens which might be imposed by some of the states, on others, whose exports, and imports must necessarily pass through them. Thus a duty on salt imported into Virginia, or on tobacco exported from thence, might operate very extensively as a tax upon the citizens of the western parts of North Carolina and Tennessee, to the exclusive emolument of the state of Virginia. So unreasonable an advantage ought not to prevail among members of the same confederacy, and without a power to control it lodged somewhere, it would be impossible that it should not be exerted: the repetition of such exertions could scarcely fail to lay the foundation of irreconcileable jealousies, and animosities among the states. And it was evidently with a view to prevent these inconveniences, that the constitution provides that no state shall, without the consent of congress, lay any imposts, or duties on exports or imports, except what may be absolutely necessary for executing it's inspection laws.

A direct consequence of this power of regulating commerce with foreign nations, and among the several states, is that of establishing ports; or such places of entry, lading, and unlading, as may be most convenient for the merchant on the one hand, and for the easy and effectual collection of the revenue from customs, on the other. In England, this is one of the branches of the royal prerogative, but is vested in the supreme federal legislature, and not in the executive, by the constitution of the United States.

Previous to the revolution the ports of Virginia were co-extensive with her tide waters. The ships anchored wherever their navigators thought proper, and discharged or took on board their cargoes, as suited their own convenience, or contributed to the saving of expence. Nothing could be more favourable to the practice of smuggling; and consequently the revenue was frequently defrauded with impunity. Nothing could be more unfavourable to the internal navigation by small vessels, although few countries possess greater advantages for it's encouragement and promotion. The employment of a considerable number of these, would not only afford a nursery for seamen, but prove an actual mercantile saving to the state, so long as commerce should be carried on in foreign bottoms, as was at that time pretty generally the case. The legislature became sensible of these things, and in the year 1784, (May session, c. 82.) passed an act, whereby ships and other vessels trading to this commonwealth, from foreign parts, being the property of other than citizens of the commonwealth, were obliged to lade, and unlade at certain particular ports, and no where else, within the commonwealth. The number of ports was increased, by the act of 1786. c. 42. and the restrictions as to unlading was extended to all vessels whatsoever, coming into the state; but any vessel built within the United States, and wholly owned by any citizens thereof, was permitted to take in her lading at any port or place within the state. These acts underwent some further amendments by the acts of 1787. c. 3, among which were some wholesome regulations respecting river craft: but these appear to have been considered as repealed, by the act of 1 cong. 1 sess. c. 11. sec. 22 and 23, on the subject of the coasting trade. But the constitutionality of that act may perhaps be questioned, so far as it relates to vessels trading wholly within the limits of any particular state. The policy of the before-mentioned acts of this state, appears to have been well founded: the effects begun to manifest themselves in the production of a greater number of river craft, than had ever been known at any former period. . . . But the acts of congress, for the establishment of ports, having extended the number for foreign ships to fourteen, and even permitted them to proceed as far as the tide-water flows in James' River, Rappahannock, and Potowmac, these salutary regulations in the state laws, have undoubtedly been, in a great measure, frustrated. It seems rather extraordinary, that on a subject of this nature, no regard should have been paid to the former policy of the state legislature, especially, as that policy was evidently favourable to the collection of the revenue arising from the customs.

A distinction between the admission of foreign ships, and those of our own confederacy, into the ports of the state, obviously appears to be proper to be made on other grounds. The navigation of our rivers was found, in the time of the revolutionary war, to be infinitely too familiar to our enemies, in consequence of the privilege before-mentioned, which had so long been enjoyed by the trading ships of Great Britain. A renewal of the same policy will probably produce the same consequences, whenever the occasion will permit. But if these reasons be not sufficiently cogent for restraining foreign ships to a few ports, and those as near to the sea as might be consistent with safety; the promotion of an internal domestic navigation, as a nursery for domestic seamen, appears of itself to be an object of sufficient importance to have engaged the attention of congress to this subject.

Another consequence of the right of regulating foreign commerce, seems to be the power of compelling vessels infected with any contagious disease, or arriving from places usually infected with them, to perform their quarantine. The laws of the respective states, upon this subject, were, by some persons, supposed to have been virtually repealed by the constitution of the United States. But congress have manifested a different interpretation of the operation of that instrument, and had passed several acts for giving aid and effect to the execution of the laws of the several states respecting quarantine. The last act upon the subject, 5. cong. c. 118, enjoins it as a duty upon the collectors, and other officers of the revenue, the masters and crews of the revenue-cutters, and the commanding officers of forts or stations upon the sea-coasts, duly to observe, and aid in the execution of those laws. Upon the like principle, I presume that the act of this commonwealth concerning wrecks, (Edi. 1794. c. 6.) remains in force, until congress shall think proper to pass some law upon that subject. A contrary construction of the operation of the federal constitution in these and other similar cases, upon which congress may be authorised to legislate, but omit doing it, might be productive of infinite inconvenience and disorder.

The right of regulating foreign commerce, draws after it also, the right of regulating the conduct of seamen, employed in the merchant service; and by a continued chain, that of punishing other persons harbouring or secreting them, as well on land, as elsewhere; and the act of 1. cong. 2. sess. c. 29, accordingly makes it penal in any person to harbour or secret any seaman regularly engaged in the service of any ship.

There seems to be one class of laws which respect foreign commerce, over which the states still retain an absolute authority; those, I mean, which relate to the inspection of their own produce, for the execution of which, they may even lay an impost, or duty, as far as may be absolutely necessary for that purpose: of this necessity it seems presumable, they are to be regarded as the sole judges. [C. U. S. Art. 1. Sec. 10.] The article, indeed, is not altogether free from obscurity; but as no controversy hath hitherto arisen upon the subject, it is not my intention to begin one.

But, this power of regulating commerce is qualified by some very salutary restrictions; for the constitution expressly declares, Art. 1. Sec. 9. "That no tax or duty shall be laid on articles exported from any state . . . that no preference shall be given by any regulation of commerce, or revenue, to the ports of one state, over those of another; and that vessels bound to, or from, one state, shall

not be obliged to enter, clear, or pay duties in another." These restrictions are well calculated to suppress those jealousies, which must inevitably have arisen among the states, had any tax or duty been laid upon any particular article of exportation; and, at the same time, to curb any disposition towards partiality in congress, should it at any time be likely to manifest itself.

An amendment to the constitution proposed by the convention of this state, and concurred in by that of North Carolina, was, "That no commercial treaty should be ratified without the concurrence of two-thirds of the whole number of the members of the senate. . . . And, that no navigation law, or law regulating commerce should be passed without the consent of two-thirds of the members present in both houses." It is somewhat remarkable, that the treaty of navigation and commerce concluded with Great Britain in the year 1794, notwithstanding the very general repugnance to it in almost every part of the United States, was, nevertheless, ratified precisely in the manner proposed by the first of these amendments. It appears that a proposition somewhat like the second, viz. "that no treaty should be binding upon the United States, which was not ratified by law," had been made in the general convention at Philadelphia, and rejected. Nevertheless, the experience which we have had upon the subject of treaties, seems to recommend the adoption of some further precautions against the indiscreet use of this extensive power. On this subject we shall say something more hereafter.

The regulation of commerce with the Indian tribes, as distinguished from foreign nations, seems, in some degree, to be founded upon this principle, that those tribes which are not settled within the limits of any particular state, could only be regarded as tributary to the United States in their federal capacity; as to those who reside within the limits of particular states, it was thought necessary to unfetter them from two limitations in the articles of confederation which rendered the provision obscure, and perhaps contradictory. The power is there restrained to Indians not members of any of the states, and is not to violate or infringe the legislative right of any state within its own limits. What description of Indians were to be deemed members of a state, had been a question of frequent contention and perplexity in the federal councils. And how the trade with Indians, though not members of a state, yet residing within its legislative jurisdiction, could be regulated by an external authority, without so far intruding on the internal rights of legislation, seems altogether incomprehensible.

12

UNITED STATES V. THE WILLIAM
28 Fed. Cas. 614, no. 16,700 (D.Mass. 1808)

[DAVIS, District Judge.] It is contended, that congress is not invested with powers, by the constitution, to enact laws, so general and so unlimited, relative to commercial inter-course with foreign nations, as those now under consideration. It is well understood, that the depressed state of American commerce, and complete experience of the inefficacy of state regulations, to apply a remedy, were among the great, procuring causes of the federal constitution. It was manifest, that other objects, of equal importance, were exclusively proper for national jurisdiction; and that under national management and control, alone, could they be advantageously and efficaciously conducted. The constitution specifies those objects. A national sovereignty is created. Not an unlimited sovereignty, but a sovereignty, as to the objects surrendered and specified, limited only by the qualifications and restrictions, expressed in the constitution. Commerce is one of those objects. The care, protection, management and controul, of this great national concern, is, in my opinion, vested by the constitution, in the congress of the United States; and their power is sovereign, relative to commercial intercourse, qualified by the limitations and restrictions, expressed in that instrument, and by the treaty making power of the president and senate. "Congress shall have power to regulate commerce with foreign nations, and among the several states, and with the Indian tribes." Such is the declaration in the constitution. Stress has been laid, in the argument, on the word "regulate," as implying, in itself, a limitation. Power to regulate, it is said, cannot be understood to give a power to annihilate. To this it may be replied, that the acts under consideration, though of very ample extent, do not operate as a prohibition of all foreign commerce. It will be admitted that partial prohibitions are authorized by the expression; and how shall the degree, or extent, of the prohibition be adjusted, but by the discretion of the national government, to whom the subject appears to be committed? Besides, if we insist on the exact and critical meaning of the word "regulate," we must, to be consistent, be equally critical with the substantial term, "commerce." The term does not necessarily include shipping or navigation; much less does it include the fisheries. Yet it never has been contended, that they are not the proper objects of national regulation; and several acts of congress have been made respecting them. It may be replied, that these are incidents to commerce, and intimately connected with it; and that congress, in legislating respecting them, act under the authority, given them by the constitution, to make all laws necessary and proper, for carrying into execution the enumerated powers. Let this be admitted; and are they not at liberty, also, to consider the present prohibitory system, as necessary and proper to an eventual beneficial regulation? I say nothing of the policy of the expedient. It is not within my province. But, on the abstract question of constitutional power, I see nothing to prohibit or restrain the measure.

Further, the power to regulate commerce is not to be confined to the adoption of measures, exclusively beneficial to commerce itself, or tending to its advancement; but, in our national system, as in all modern sovereignties, it is also to be considered as an instrument for other purposes of general policy and interest. The mode of its management is a consideration of great delicacy and importance; but, the national right, or power, under the constitution, to adapt regulations of commerce to other purposes, than the mere advancement of commerce, appears to me unquestionable. Great Britain is styled, eminently, a commercial nation; but commerce is, in fact, a subordinate branch of her national policy, compared with other objects. In ancient times, indeed, shipping and navigation were made subordinate to commerce, as then contemplated. The mart, or staple, of their principal productions, wool, leather and lead, was confined to certain great towns in the island, where foreigners might resort to purchase; and Englishmen were restrained from exporting those commodities, under heavy penalties. It was conceived, that trade thus conducted, would be more advantageous to the country, than if transacted by the English, on the continent. On this idea was made the statute of the staple. 27 Edw. III. (Vide Reeves' Hist. of English Law, 2, 393.) This may appear a strange regulation. It was evidently founded on erroneous views, and Selden, the learned commentator on Fortescue, remarks, "that all acts or attempts, which have been derogatory to trade, have ever been noted to be discouraged and short lived," in that nation. It is well known, how the views of their statesmen, and their commercial laws have changed, since that statute was enacted. The navigation system has long stood prominent. The interests of commerce are often made subservient to those of shipping and navigation. Maritime and naval strength is the great object of national solicitude; the grand and ultimate objects are the defence and security of the country. The situation of the United States, in ordinary times, might render legislative interferences, relative to commerce, less necessary; but the capacity and power of managing and directing it, for the advancement of great national purposes, seems an important ingredient of sovereignty. It was perceived, that, under the power of regulating commerce, congress would be authorized to abridge it, in favour of the great principles of humanity and justice. Hence the introduction of a clause, in the constitution, so framed, as to interdict a prohibition of the slave trade, until 1808. Massachusetts and New York proposed a stipulation, that should prevent the erection of commercial companies, with exclusive advantages. Virginia and North Carolina suggested an amendment, that "no navigation law, or law regulating commerce, should be passed, without the consent of two thirds of the members present, in both houses." These proposed amendments were not adopted, but they manifest the public conceptions, at the time, of the extent of the powers of congress, relative to commerce.

It has been said, in the argument, that the large commercial states, such as New York and Massachusetts, would never have consented to the grant of power, relative to commerce, if supposed capable of the extent now claimed. On this point, it is believed, there was no misunderstanding. The necessity of a competent national government was manifest. Its essential characteristics were considered and well understood; and all intelligent men perceived, that a power to advance and protect the national interests, necessarily involved a power, that might be abused. The Federalist, which was particularly addressed to the people of the state of New York, frankly avows the genuine operation of the powers, proposed to be vested in the general government. "If the circumstances of our country are such, as to demand a compound, instead of a simple, a confederate, instead of a sole, government, the essential point, which will remain to be adjusted, will be to discriminate the objects, as far as it can be done, which shall appertain to the different provinces, or departments, of power; allowing to each the most ample authority for fulfilling those, which may be committed to its charge. Shall the Union be constituted the guardian of the common safety? Are fleets, and armies, and revenues necessary for this purpose? The government of the Union must be empowered, to pass all laws, and to make all regulations which have relation to them. The same must be the case, in respect to commerce, and to every other matter, to which its jurisdiction is permitted to extend." Volume 1, No. 23, p. 146.

If it be admitted that national regulations relative to commerce, may apply it as an instrument, and are not necessarily confined to its direct aid and advancement, the sphere of legislative discretion is, of course, more widely extended; and, in time of war, or of great impending peril, it must take a still more expanded range. Congress has power to declare war. It, of course, has power to prepare for war; and the time, the manner, and the measure, in the application of constitutional means, seem to be left to its wisdom and discretion. Foreign intercourse becomes, in such times, a subject of peculiar interest, and its regulation forms an obvious and essential branch of the federal administration. In the year 1798, when aggressions from France became insupportable, a non-intercourse law, relative to that nation and her dependencies, was enacted; partial hostilities, for a time, prevailed; but no war was declared. I have never understood, that the power of congress to adopt that course of proceeding was questioned. It seems to have been admitted, in the argument, that state necessity might justify a limited embargo, or suspension of all foreign commerce; but if congress have the power, for purposes of safety, of preparation, or counteraction, to suspend commercial intercourse with foreign nations, where do we find them limited as to the duration, more than as to the manner and extent of the measure? Must we understand the nation as saying to their government: "We look to you for protection and security, against all foreign aggressions. For this purpose, we give you the controul of commerce; but, you shall always limit the time, during which this instrument is to be used. This shield of defence you may, on emergent occasions, employ; but you shall always announce to us and to the world, the moment when it shall drop from your hands."

It is apparent, that cases may occur, in which the indefinite character of a law, as to its termination, may be essential to its efficacious operation. In this connexion, I would notice the internal indications, exhibited by the acts themselves, relative to their duration. In addition to the authority given to the president to suspend the acts, upon the contingency of certain events, we have evidence, from the very nature of their provisions, that they cannot be designed to be perpetual. An entire prohibition of exportation, unaccompanied with any restriction on importations,

could never be intended for a permanent system; though the laws, in a technical view, may be denominated perpetual, containing no specification of the time when they shall expire. In illustration of their argument, gentlemen have supposed a strong case; a prohibition of the future cultivation of corn, in the United States. It would not be admitted, I presume, that an act, so extravagant, would be constitutional, though not perpetual, but confined to a single season. And why? Because it would be, most manifestly, without the limits of the federal jurisdiction, and relative to an object, or concern, not committed to its management. If an embargo, or suspension of commerce, of any description, be within the powers of congress, the terms and modifications of the measure must also be within their discretion. If the measure be referred to state necessity, the body that is authorized to determine on the existence of such necessity, must, also, be competent so to modify the means, as to adapt them to the exigency. It is said, that such a law is in contravention of unalienable rights; and we have had quotations from elementary writers, and from the bills of rights of the state constitutions, in support of this position. The doctrines and declarations of those respectable writers, and in those venerable instruments, are not to be slighted; but we are to leave the wide field of general reasonings and abstract principles, and are to consider the construction and operation of an express compact, a government of convention. The general position is incontestible, that all that is not surrendered by the constitution, is retained. The amendment which expresses this, is for greater security; but such would have been the true construction, without the amendment. Still, it remains to be determined, and it is often a question of some difficulty, what is given? By the second article of the confederation, congress were prohibited the exercise of any power not expressly delegated. A similar qualification was suggested, in one of the amendments proposed by the state of New-Hampshire, to the new constitution. The phraseology, indeed, was strengthened; and congress were to be prohibited from the exercise of powers, not expressly and particularly delegated. Such expressions were not adopted. If they had been, as an intelligent writer justly observes, "Congress would be continually exposed, as their predecessors, under the confederation, were, to the alternative of construing the term, expressly, with so much rigour, as to disarm the government of all real authority whatever; or, with so much latitude, as to destroy, altogether the force of the restriction." It is wisely left as it is; and the true sense and meaning of the instrument is to be determined by just construction, guided and governed by good sense and honest intentions. Under the confederation, congress could have no agency relative to foreign commerce, but through the medium of treaties; and, by the ninth article, it was stipulated, that no treaty of commerce should be made, whereby the legislative power of the respective states, should be restrained, from imposing such imposts and duties on foreigners, as their own people were subjected to, "or from prohibiting the exportation of any species of goods or commodities whatsoever." Here we find an express reservation to the state legislatures of the power to pass prohibitory commercial laws, and, as respects exportations, without any limitations. Some of them exercised this power. In Massachusetts, it was carried to considerable extent, with marked determination, but to no sensible good effect. One of the prohibitory acts of that state, passed in 1786, was for the express "encouragement of the agriculture and manufactures in our own country." The other, which was a counteracting law, had no definite limitation, but was to continue in force, until congress should be vested with competent powers, and should have passed an ordinance for the regulation of the commerce of the states. Unless congress, by the constitution, possess the power in question, it still exists in the state legislatures—but this has never been claimed or pretended, since the adoption of the federal constitution; and the exercise of such a power by the states, would be manifestly inconsistent with the power, vested by the people in congress, "to regulate commerce." Hence I infer, that the power, reserved to the states by the articles of confederation, is surrendered to congress, by the constitution; unless we suppose, that, by some strange process, it has been merged or extinguished, and now exists no where.

The propriety of this power, on the present construction, may be further evinced, by contemplating the operation of specific limitations or restrictions, which it might be proposed to apply. Will it be said, that the amendment proposed by Virginia and North Carolina, would be an improvement in the instrument of government? Such a provision might prevent the adoption of exceptionable regulations; but, it would be equally operative in defeating those that would be salutary; and would disable that majority of the nation from deciding on the best means of advancing its prosperity. To avoid such a system, as is now in operation, shall the people expressly provide, as a limitation to the power of regulating commerce, that it shall not extend to a total prohibition; or but for a limited time? Nothing would be gained by such restrictions. A prohibition might still be so nearly total, or extend to such a length of time, without violation of the restriction, as to be equivalent, in practical effect, to the present arrangement. Or will it be said, that the judiciary should then be called upon to decide the law void, though not repugnant to the terms of the restriction, and to consider exceptions from the prohibition, as, in the common case of a fraudulent deed, to be merely colourable? Loose and general restrictions would be ineffective, or, at best, merely directory. If particular and precise, they would evince an indiscreet attempt to anticipate the immense extent and variety of national exigencies, and would not be suitable appendages to a power, which, in its exercise, must depend on contingencies, and, from its nature and object, must be general. A particular mischief or inconvenience, contemplated in framing such limitations, might be avoided; but they would also injuriously fetter the national councils, and prevent the application of adequate provisions for the publick safety and happiness, according to the ever varying emergencies of national affairs. Let us not insist on a security, which the nature of human concerns will not permit. More effectual guards against abuse, more complete security for civil and political liberty, and for private right, are not, perhaps, afforded to any nation than to the peo-

ple of the United States. These views of the national powers are not new. I have only given a more distinct exhibition of habitual impressions, coeval, in my mind, with the constitution. Upon these considerations, I am bound to overrule the objections to the acts in question, which I shall proceed to apply to the cases before the court, believing them to be constitutional laws.

I lament the privations, the interruption of profitable pursuits and manly enterprize, to which it has been thought necessary to subject the citizens of this great community. I respect the merchant and his employment. The disconcerted mariner demands our sympathy. The sound of the axe, and of the hammer, would be grateful music. Ocean, in itself a dreary waste, by the swelling sail and floating steamer, becomes an exhilarating object; and it is painful to perceive, by force of any contingencies, the American stars and stripes vanishing from the scene. Commerce, indeed, merits all the eulogy, which we have heard so eloquently pronounced, at the bar. It is the welcome attendant of civilized man, in all his various stations. It is the nurse of arts; the genial friend of liberty, justice and order; the sure source of national wealth and greatness; the promoter of moral and intellectual improvement; of generous affections and enlarged philanthropy. Connecting seas, flowing rivers, and capacious havens, equally with the fertile bosom of the earth, suggest, to the reflecting mind, the purposes of a beneficent Deity, relative to the destination and employments of man. Let us not entertain the gloomy apprehension, that advantages, so precious, are altogether abandoned; that pursuits, so interesting and beneficial, are not to be resumed. Let us rather cherish a hope, that commercial activity and intercourse, with all their wholesome energies will be revived; and, that our merchants and our mariners will, again, be permitted to pursue their wonted employments, consistently with the national safety, honour and independence!

13

Livingston v. Van Ingen
9 Johns. R. 507 (N.Y. 1812)

Kent, Ch. J. The great point in this cause is, whether the several acts of the legislature which have been passed in favor of the appellants, are to be regarded as constitutional and binding.

This house, sitting in its judicial capacity as a court, has nothing to do with the policy or expediency of these laws. The only question here is, whether the legislature had authority to pass them. If we can satisfy ourselves upon this point, or, rather, unless we are fully persuaded that they are void, we are bound to obey them, and give them the requisite effect.

In the first place, the presumption must be admitted to be extremely strong in favor of their validity. There is no very obvious constitutional objection, or it would not so repeatedly have escaped the notice of the several branches of the government, when these acts were under consideration. There are, in the whole, five different statutes, passed in the years 1798, 1803, 1807, 1808 and 1811, all relating to one subject, and all granting or confirming to the appellants, or one of them, the exclusive privilege of using steam-boats upon the navigable waters of this state. The last act was passed after the right of the appellants was drawn into question, and made known to the legislature, and that act was, therefore, equivalent to a declaratory opinion of high authority, that the former laws were valid and constitutional. The act in the year 1798 was peculiarly calculated to awaken attention, as it was the first act that was passed upon the subject, after the adoption of the federal constitution, and it would naturally lead to a consideration of the power of the state to make such a grant. That act was, therefore, a legislative exposition given to the powers of the state governments, and there were circumstances existing at the time, which gave that exposition singular weight and importance. It was a new and original grant to one of the appellants, encouraging him, by the pledge of an exclusive privilege for twenty years, to engage, according to the language of the preamble to the statute, in the "uncertainty and hazard of a very expensive experiment." The legislature must have been clearly satisfied of their competency to make this pledge, or they acted with deception and injustice towards the individual on whose account it was made. There were members in that legislature, as well as in all the other departments of the government, who had been deeply concerned in the study of the constitution of the *United States*, and who were masters of all the critical discussions which had attended the interesting progress of its adoption. Several of them had been members of the state convention, and this was particularly the case with the exalted character, who at that time was chief magistrate of this state, (Mr. *Jay*,) and who was distinguished, as well in the *council of revision*, as elsewhere, for the scrupulous care and profound attention with which he examined every question of a constitutional nature.

After such a series of statutes, for the last fourteen years, and passed under such circumstances, it ought not to be any light or trivial difficulty that should induce us to set them aside. Unless the court should be able to vindicate itself by the soundest and most demonstrable argument, a decree prostrating all these laws would weaken, as I should apprehend, the authority and sanction of law in general, and impair, in some degree, the public confidence, either in the intelligence or integrity of the government.

But we are not to rest upon presumption alone; we must bring these laws to the test of a severer scrutiny.

If they are void, it must be because the people of this state have alienated to the government of the *United States* their whole original power over the subject matter of the grant. No one can entertain a doubt of a competent power existing in the legislature, prior to the adoption of the federal constitution. The capacity to grant separate and exclusive privileges appertains to every sovereign authority. It is a necessary attribute of every independent government. All our bank charters, turnpike, canal and bridge companies, ferries, markets, &c. are grants of exclusive privileges for beneficial public purposes. These grants may possibly be inexpedient or unwise, but that has nothing to do with the question of constitutional right. The legislative power, in a single, independent government, extends to every proper object of power, and is limited only by its own constitutional provisions, or by the fundamental principles of all government, and the unalienable rights of mankind. In the present case, the grant to the appellants took away no vested right. It interfered with no man's property. It left every citizen to enjoy all the rights of navigation, and all the use of the waters of this state which he before enjoyed. There was, then, no injustice, no violation of first principles, in a grant to the appellants, for a limited time, of the exclusive benefit of their own hazardous and expensive experiments. The first impression upon every unprejudiced mind would be, that there was justice and policy in the grant. Clearly, then, it is valid, unless the power to make it be taken away by the constitution of the *United States*.

We are not called upon to say affirmatively what powers have been granted to the general government, or to what extent. Those powers, whether express or implied, may be plenary and sovereign, in reference to the specified objects of them. They may even be liberally construed in furtherance of the great and essential ends of the government. To this doctrine I willingly accede. But the question here is, not what powers are granted to that government, but what powers are retained by this, and, particularly, whether the states have absolutely parted with their original power of granting such an exclusive privilege, as the one now before us. It does not follow, that because a given power is granted to congress, the states cannot exercise a similar power. We ought to bear in mind certain great rules or principles of construction peculiar to the case of a confederated government, and by attending to them in the examination of the subject, all our seeming difficulties will vanish.

When the people create a single, entire government, they grant at once all the rights of sovereignty. The powers granted are indefinite, and incapable of enumeration. Every thing is granted that is not expressly reserved in the constitutional charter, or necessarily retained as inherent in the people. But when a federal government is erected with only a portion of the sovereign power, the rule of construction is directly the reverse, and every power is reserved to the member that is not, either in express terms, or by necessary implication, taken away from them, and vested exclusively in the federal head. This rule has not only been acknowledged by the most intelligent friends to the constitution, but is plainly declared by the instrument itself. Congress have power to lay and collect taxes, duties and excises, but as these powers are not given exclusively, the states have a concurrent jurisdiction, and retain the same absolute powers of taxation which they possessed before the adoption of the constitution, except the power of laying an impost, which is expressly taken away. This very exception proves that, without it, the states would have retained the power of laying an impost; and it further implies, that in cases not excepted, the authority of the states remains unimpaired.

This principle might be illustrated by other instances of grants of power to congress with a prohibition to the states from exercising the like powers; but it becomes unnecessary to enlarge upon so plain a proposition, as it is removed beyond all doubt by the tenth article of the amendments to the constitution. That article declares that "the powers not delegated to the *United States* by the constitution, nor prohibited by it to the states, are reserved to the states respectively, or to the people." The ratification of the constitution by the convention of this state, was made with the explanation and understanding, that "every power, jurisdiction and right, which was not *clearly* delegated to the general government, remained to the people of the several states, or to their respective state governments." There was a similar provision in the articles of confederation, and the principle results from the very nature of the federal government, which consists only of a defined portion of the undefined mass of sovereign power originally vested in the several members of the union. There may be inconveniences, but generally there will be no serious difficulty, and there cannot well be any interruption of the public peace, in the concurrent exercise of those powers. The powers of the two governments are each supreme within their respective constitutional spheres. They may each operate with full effect upon different subjects, or they may, as in the case of taxation, operate upon different parts of the same object. The powers of the two governments cannot indeed be supreme over each other, for that would involve a contradiction. When those powers, therefore, come directly in contact, as when they are aimed at each other, or at one indivisible object, the power of the state is subordinate, and must yield. The legitimate exercise of the constitutional powers of the general government becomes the supreme law of the land, and the national judiciary is specially charged with the maintenance of that law, and this is the true and efficient power to preserve order, dependence and harmony in our complicated system of government. We have, then, nothing to do in the ordinary course of legislation, with the possible contingency of a collision, nor are we to embarrass ourselves in the anticipation of theoretical difficulties, than which nothing could, in general, be more fallacious. Such a doctrine would be constantly taxing our sagacity, to see whether the law might not contravene some future regulation of commerce, or some moneyed or some military operation of the *United States*. Our most simple municipal provisions would be enacted with diffidence, for fear we might involve ourselves, our citizens and our consciences in some case of usurpation. Fortunately, for the peace and happiness of this country, we have a plainer path to follow. We do not handle a work of such hazardous consequence. We are not always walking *per ignes suppositos cineri doloso.* Our safe rule of construction and of action is this, that if any given power was originally vested in this state, if it has not been exclusively ceded to congress, or if the exercise of it has not been prohibited to the states, we may then go on in the exercise of the power until it comes practically in collision with the actual exercise of some congressional power. When that happens to be the case, the state authority will so far be controlled, but it will still be good in

all those respects in which it does not absolutely contravene the provision of the paramount law.

This construction of the powers of the federal compact has the authority of Mr. *Hamilton*. In the thirty-second number of the *Federalist*, he admits that all the authorities of which the states are not explicitly devested, remain with them in full vigor, and that in all cases in which it was deemed improper that a like authority with that granted to the union should reside in the states, there was the most pointed care in the constitution to insert negative clauses. He further states that there are only three cases of the alienation of the state sovereignty; 1. Where the grant to the general government is, in express terms, exclusive; 2. Where a like power is expressly prohibited to the states; and, 3. Where an authority in the states would be absolutely and totally contradictory and repugnant to one granted to the union; and it must be, he says, an immediate constitutional repugnancy that can, by implication, alienate and extinguish a pre-existing right of sovereignty. The same view of the powers of the federal and state governments, and the same rules of interpretation, were given by him, in the discussions which the constitution underwent in our state convention, and they seem generally, if not unanimously, to have been acquiesced in by the members of that very respectable assembly. (See the *Debates of the New-York Convention*, published by *Francis Childs*.) These opinions may be regarded as the best evidence of the sense of the authors of that instrument, the best test of its principles, and the most accurate cotemporary exposition to which we can recur. For every one acquainted with the history of those times, well knows that the principles of the constitution, in the progress of its adoption through the *United States*, were discussed in the several conventions, and before the public, by men of the most powerful talents, and with the most animated zeal for the public welfare. There were many distinguished individuals, and none more so than the one to whom I have referred, who had bestowed intense thought, not only upon the science of civil government at large, but who had specially and deeply studied the history and nature, the tendency and genius of the federal system of government, of which the *European* confederacies had given us imperfect examples, and to which system, as improved by more skilful artists, the destinies of this country were to be confided. Principles of construction solemnly sanctioned at that day, and flowing from such sources, as to be regarded by us, and by posterity, as coming in the language of truth, and with the force of authority.

I now proceed to apply these general rules to those parts of the constitution which are supposed to have an influence on the present question.

The provision that the citizens of each state shall be entitled to all privileges and immunities of citizens in the several states, has nothing to do with this case. It means only that citizens of other states shall have equal rights with our own citizens, and not that they shall have different or greater rights. Their persons and property must, in all respects, be equally subject to our law. This is a very clear proposition, and the provision itself was taken from the articles of the confederation. The two paragraphs of the

494

constitution by which it is contended that the original power in the state governments to make the grant has been withdrawn, and vested exclusively in the union, are, 1. The power to regulate commerce with foreign nations, and among the several states; and, 2. The power to secure to authors and inventors the exclusive right to their writings and discoveries.

1. *As to the power to regulate commerce.*

This power is not, in express terms, exclusive, and the only prohibition upon the states is, that they shall not enter into any treaty or compact with each other, or with a foreign power, nor lay any duty on tonnage, or on imports or exports, except what may be necessary for executing their inspection laws. Upon the principles above laid down, the states are under no other constitutional restriction, and are, consequently, left in possession of a vast field of commercial regulation; all the internal commerce of the state by land and water remains entirely, and I may say exclusively, within the scope of its original sovereignty. The congressional power relates to external not to internal commerce, and it is confined to the *regulation* of that commerce. To what extent these regulations may be carried, it is not our present duty to inquire. The limits of this power seem not to be susceptible of precise definition. It may be difficult to draw an exact line between those regulations which relate to external and those which relate to internal commerce, for every regulation of the one will, directly or indirectly, affect the other. To avoid doubts, embarrassment and contention on this complicated question, the general rule of interpretation which has been mentioned, is extremely salutary. It removes all difficulty, by its simplicity and certainty. The states are under no other restrictions than those expressly specified in the constitution, and such regulations as the national government may, by treaty, and by laws, from time to time, prescribe. Subject to these restrictions, I contend, that the states are at liberty to make their own commercial regulations. There can be no other safe or practicable rule of conduct, and this, as I have already shown, is the true constitutional rule arising from the nature of our federal system. This does away all color for the suggestion that the steam-boat grant is illegal and void under this clause in the constitution. It comes not within any prohibition upon the states, and it interferes with no existing regulation. Whenever the case shall arise of an exercise of power by congress which shall be directly repugnant and destructive to the use and enjoyment of the appellants' grant, it would fall under the cognizance of the federal courts, and they would, of course, take care that the laws of the union are duly supported. I must confess, however, that I can hardly conceive of such a case, because I do not, at present, perceive any power which congress can lawfully carry to that extent. But when there is no existing regulation which interferes with the grant, nor any pretence of a constitutional interdict, it would be most extraordinary for us to adjudge it void, on the mere contingency of a collision with some future exercise of congressional power. Such a doctrine is a monstrous heresy. It would go, in a great degree, to annihilate the legislative power of the states. May not the legislature declare that no bank paper shall circulate, or be given or received in payment, but what originates from some incorporated bank of our own, or that none shall circulate under the nominal value of one dollar? But suppose congress should institute a national bank, with authority to issue and circulate throughout the union, bank notes, as well below as above that nominal value: this would so far control the state law, but it would remain valid and binding, except as to the paper of the national bank. The state law would be absolute, until the appearance of the national bank, and then it would have a qualified effect, and be good *pro tanto.* So, again, the legislature may declare that it shall be unlawful to vend lottery tickets, unless they be tickets of lotteries authorized by a law of this state, and who will question the validity of the provision? But suppose congress should deem it expedient to establish a national lottery, and should authorize persons in each state to vend the tickets, this would so far control the state prohibition, and leave it in full force as to all other lotteries. The possibility that a national bank, or a national lottery, might be instituted, would be a very strange reason for holding the state laws to be absolutely null and void. It strikes me to be an equally inadmissible proposition, that the state is devested of a capacity to grant an exclusive privilege of navigating a steam-boat, within its own waters, merely because we can imagine that congress, in the plenary exercise of its power to regulate commerce, may make some regulation inconsistent with the exercise of this privilege. When such a case arises, it will provide for itself; and there is, fortunately, a paramount power in the Supreme Court of the *United States* to guard against the mischiefs of collision.

The grant to the appellants may, then, be considered as taken subject to such future commercial regulations as congress may lawfully prescribe. Congress, indeed, has not any direct jurisdiction over our interior commerce or waters. *Hudson* river is the property of the people of this state, and the legislature have the same jurisdiction over it that they have over the land, or over any of our public highways, or over the waters of any of our rivers or lakes. They may, in their sound discretion, regulate and control, enlarge or abridge the use of its waters, and they are in the habitual exercise of that sovereign right. If the constitution had given to congress exclusive jurisdiction over our navigable waters, then the argument of the respondents would have applied; but the people never did, nor ever intended, to grant such a power; and congress have concurrent jurisdiction over the navigable waters no further than may be incidental and requisite to the due regulation of commerce between the states, and with foreign nations.

What has been the uniform, practical construction of this power? Let us examine the code of our statute laws. Our turnpike roads, our toll-bridges, the exclusive grant to run stage-wagons, our laws relating to paupers from other states, our *Sunday* laws, our rights of ferriage over navigable rivers and lakes, our auction licenses, our licenses to retail spirituous liquors, the laws to restrain hawkers and pedlars; what are all these provisions but regulations of internal commerce, affecting as well the intercourse between the citizens of this and other states, as between our own citizens? So we also exercise, to a considerable degree, a concurrent power with congress in the regulation of external commerce. What are our inspection laws relative to the staple commodities of this state, which prohibit the exportation, except upon certain conditions, of flour, of salt provisions, of certain articles of lumber, and of pot and pearl ashes, but regulations of external commerce? Our health and quarantine laws, and the laws prohibiting the importation of slaves, are striking examples of the same kind. So the act relative to the poor, which requires all masters of vessels coming from abroad to report and give security to the mayor of *New-York*, that the passengers, being aliens, shall not become chargeable as paupers, and in case of default, making even the ship or vessel from which the ʼalien shall be landed liable to seizure, is another and very important regulation affecting foreign commerce.

Are we prepared to say, in the face of all these regulations, which form such a mass of evidence of the uniform construction of our powers, that a special privilege for the exclusive navigation by a steam-boat upon our waters, is void, because it may, by possibility, and in the course of events, interfere with the power granted to congress to regulate commerce? Nothing, in my opinion, would be more preposterous and extravagant. Which of our existing regulations may not equally interfere with the power of congress? It is said that a steam-boat may become the vehicle of foreign commerce; and, it is asked, can then the entry of them into this state, or the use of them within it, be prohibited? I answer yes, equally as we may prohibit the entry or use of slaves, or of pernicious animals, or an obscene book, or infectious goods, or any thing else that the legislature shall deem noxious or inconvenient. Our quarantine laws amount to an occlusion of the port of *New-York* from a portion of foreign commerce, for several months in the year; and the mayor is even authorized under those laws to stop all commercial intercourse with the ports of any neighboring state. No doubt these powers may be abused, or exercised in bad faith, or with such jealousy and hostility towards our neighbors, as to call for some explicit and paramount regulation of congress on the subject of foreign commerce, and of commerce between the states. Such cases may easily be supposed, but it is not logical to reason from the abuse against the lawful existence of a power; and until such congressional regulations appear, the legislative will of this state, exercised on a subject within its original jurisdiction, and not expressly prohibited to it by the constitution of the *United States*, must be taken to be of valid and irresistible authority.

14

GIBBONS v. OGDEN

17 Johns. R. 488 (N.Y. 1820),
rev'd 9 Wheat. 1
(no. 16 infra)

PLATT, J. This is an appeal from an order of the Court of Chancery, denying a motion for dissolving an injunction, whereby the steam-boat of the appellant was restrained from running between *Elizabeth-town Point* in *New-Jersey* and the city of *New-York*.

The great question which arose in the case of *Livingston and Fulton* v. *Van Ingen and others*, (9 *Johns. Rep.* 507.) whether this state had the power to grant an exclusive right of navigating its waters with steam-boats, is again raised in this cause. That question was then elaborately and profoundly discussed on appeal in this court; and after mature consideration, this court, by a unanimous decree, decided, that the statutes of this state for granting and securing to *Livingston* and *Fulton*, and their assigns, that exclusive privilege, were constitutional and valid.

Immediately after that decision, many persons who had resisted the claim to such exclusive privilege, yielding obedience to that decree, as settling the question by the highest judicial tribunal of the state, became purchasers of that privilege under *Livingston* and *Fulton*. The respondent, *Aaron Ogden*, stands before this court as an assignee under them, and claims the benefit of his purchase. His right is denied by the appellant; 1st. On the old ground, that the state had no power to grant such exclusive privilege in any case; and, 2dly, That he (the appellant) derives authority to navigate his steam-boats under the act of Congress of the 18th of *February*, 1793, for enrolling and licensing coasting vessels, &c.

As to the first general question, I consider it as no longer open for discussion here. It would be trifling with the rights of individuals, and highly derogatory to the character of the court, if it were now to depart from its former deliberate decision on the very same point.

As to the second ground relied on by the appellant, to wit, the *coasting license,* I am unable to discern how that can vary the merits of the question, as presented in the case of *Livingston* v. *Van Ingen.*

The act of Congress for enrolling and licensing coasting ships, or vessels, &c. enacts, that "no ships or vessels, except such as shall be so enrolled and licensed, shall be deemed ships or vessels of the *United States*, entitled to the privileges of ships or vessels employed in the coasting trade or fisheries." (sect. 1.) And the same act also declares, that every ship or vessel engaged in the coasting trade, &c., and not being so enrolled and licensed, "shall pay the same fees and tonnage in every port of the *United States* at which she may arrive, as ships or vessels not belonging to a citizen or citizens of the *United States;* and if she have on board any articles of foreign growth or manufacture, or distilled spirits other than sea-stores, the ship or vessel, with her tackle and lading, shall be forfeited." (sect. 6.)

From these provisions, and an examination of the various regulations of that statute, and from all the laws of the *United States* on that subject, it appears, that the only design of the federal government, in regard to the enrolling and licensing of vessels, was to establish a criterion of *national character*, with a view to enforce the laws which impose *discriminating duties* on *American* vessels, and those of foreign countries.

The term *"license"* seems not to be used in the sense imputed to it by the counsel for the appellant: that is, a *permit to trade;* or as giving *a right of transit.* Because it is perfectly clear, that such a vessel, coasting from one state to another, would have exactly the same right to trade, and the same right of transit, whether she had the coasting license or not. She does not, therefore, derive her right from the *license;* the only effect of which is, to determine her national character, and the rate of duties which she is to pay.

Whatever may be the abstract right of Congress, to pass laws for regulating trade, which might come in collision, and conflict with the exclusive privilege granted by this state, it is sufficient, now, for the protection of the respondent, that the statute of the *United States* relied on by the appellant, is not of that character.

Whether Congress have the power to authorize the coasting trade to be carried on, in vessels propelled by steam, so as to give a *paramount right,* in opposition to the special license given by this state, is a question not yet presented to us. No such act of Congress yet exists, and it will be time enough to discuss that question when it arises.

I am decidedly of opinion, therefore, that the *coasting license* affords no aid or support to the title of the appellant, to run a steam-boat on our waters, in opposition to the laws of this state.

The real merits of this case fall precisely within the decision of this court, in the case of *Livingston, &c.* v. *Van Ingen.* As a *senator,* I was a party to that decision; and concurred in it, for the reasons which were then assigned by the learned judges who delivered the opinion of the court. Those reasons are before the public: and I have not the vanity to believe, that I could add any thing to their force or perspicuity. I, therefore, deem it my only remaining duty to say, that in my judgment, the decree of his honor the chancellor, in this case, ought to be *affirmed.*

15

CORFIELD v. CORYELL

6 Fed. Cas. 546, no. 3,230 (C.C.E.D.Pa. 1823)

(See 4.2.1, no. 18)

16

GIBBONS v. OGDEN

9 Wheat. 1 (1824)

Mr. Chief Justice MARSHALL delivered the opinion of the Court, and, after stating the case, proceeded as follows:

The appellant contends that this decree is erroneous, because the laws which purport to give the exclusive privilege it sustains, are repugnant to the constitution and laws of the United States.

They are said to be repugnant—

1st. To that clause in the constitution which authorizes Congress to regulate commerce.

2d. To that which authorizes Congress to promote the progress of science and useful arts.

The State of New-York maintains the constitutionality of these laws; and their Legislature, their Council of Revision, and their Judges, have repeatedly concurred in this opinion. It is supported by great names—by names which have all the titles to consideration that virtue, intelligence, and office, can bestow. No tribunal can approach the decision of this question, without feeling a just and real respect for that opinion which is sustained by such authority; but it is the province of this Court, while it respects, not to bow to it implicitly; and the Judges must exercise, in the examination of the subject, that understanding which Providence has bestowed upon them, with that independence which the people of the United States expect from this department of the government.

As preliminary to the very able discussions of the constitution, which we have heard from the bar, and as having some influence on its construction, reference has been made to the political situation of these States, anterior to its formation. It has been said, that they were sovereign, were completely independent, and were connected with each other only by a league. This is true. But, when these allied sovereigns converted their league into a government, when they converted their Congress of Ambassadors, deputed to deliberate on their common concerns, and to recommend measures of general utility, into a Legislature, empowered to enact laws on the most interesting subjects, the whole character in which the States appear, underwent a change, the extent of which must be determined by a fair consideration of the instrument by which that change was effected.

This instrument contains an enumeration of powers expressly granted by the people to their government. It has been said, that these powers ought to be construed strictly. But why ought they to be so construed? Is there one sentence in the constitution which gives countenance to this rule? In the last of the enumerated powers, that which grants, expressly, the means for carrying all others into execution, Congress is authorized "to make all laws which shall be necessary and proper" for the purpose. But this limitation on the means which may be used, is not extended to the powers which are conferred; nor is there one sentence in the constitution, which has been pointed out by the gentlemen of the bar, or which we have been able to discern, that prescribes this rule. We do not, therefore, think ourselves justified in adopting it. What do gentlemen mean, by a strict construction? If they contend only against that enlarged construction, which would extend words beyond their natural and obvious import, we might question the application of the term, but should not controvert the principle. If they contend for that narrow construction which, in support of some theory not to be found in the constitution, would deny to the government those powers which the words of the grant, as usually understood, import, and which are consistent with the general views and objects of the instrument; for that narrow construction, which would cripple the government, and render it unequal to the object for which it is declared to be instituted, and to which the powers given, as fairly understood, render it competent; then we cannot perceive the propriety of this strict construction, nor adopt it as the rule by which the constitution is to be expounded. As men, whose intentions require no concealment, generally employ the words which most directly and aptly express the ideas they intend to convey, the enlightened patriots who framed our constitution, and the people who adopted it, must be understood to have employed words in their natural sense, and to have intended what they have said. If, from the imperfection of human language, there should be serious doubts respecting the extent of any given power, it is a well settled rule, that the objects for which it was given, especially when those objects are expressed in the instrument itself, should have great influence in the construction. We know of no reason for excluding this rule from the present case. The grant does not convey power which might be beneficial to the grantor, if retained by himself, or which can enure solely to the benefit of the grantee; but is an investment of power for the general advantage, in the hands of agents selected for that purpose; which power can never be exercised by the people themselves, but must be placed in the hands of agents, or lie dormant. We know of no rule for construing the extent of such powers, other than is given by the language of the instrument which confers them, taken in connexion with the purposes for which they were conferred.

The words are, "Congress shall have power to regulate commerce with foreign nations, and among the several States, and with the Indian tribes."

The subject to be regulated is commerce; and our constitution being, as was aptly said at the bar, one of enumeration, and not of definition, to ascertain the extent of the power, it becomes necessary to settle the meaning of the word. The counsel for the appellee would limit it to traffic, to buying and selling, or the interchange of commodities, and do not admit that it comprehends navigation. This would restrict a general term, applicable to many objects, to one of its significations. Commerce, undoubtedly, is traffic, but it is something more: it is intercourse. It describes the commercial intercourse between nations, and parts of nations, in all its branches, and is regulated by prescribing rules for carrying on that intercourse. The mind can scarcely conceive a system for regulating commerce between nations, which shall exclude all laws concerning navigation, which shall be silent on the admission of the vessels of the one nation into the ports of the other, and be confined to prescribing rules for the conduct of individuals, in the actual employment of buying and selling, or of barter.

If commerce does not include navigation, the government of the Union has no direct power over that subject, and can make no law prescribing what shall constitute American vessels, or requiring that they shall be navigated by American seamen. Yet this power has been exercised from the commencement of the government, has been exercised with the consent of all, and has been understood by all to be a commercial regulation. All America understands, and has uniformly understood, the word "commerce," to comprehend navigation. It was so understood, and must have been so understood, when the constitution was framed. The power over commerce, including navigation, was one of the primary objects for which the people of America adopted their government, and must have been contemplated in forming it. The convention must have used the word in that sense, because all have understood it in that sense; and the attempt to restrict it comes too late.

If the opinion that "commerce," as the word is used in the constitution, comprehends navigation also, requires any additional confirmation, that additional confirmation is, we think, furnished by the words of the instrument itself.

It is a rule of construction, acknowledged by all, that the exceptions from a power mark its extent; for it would be absurd, as well as useless, to except from a granted power, that which was not granted—that which the words of the grant could not comprehend. If, then, there are in the constitution plain exceptions from the power over navigation, plain inhibitions to the exercise of that power in a particular way, it is a proof that those who made these exceptions, and prescribed these inhibitions, understood the power to which they applied as being granted.

The 9th section of the 1st article declares, that "no preference shall be given, by any regulation of commerce or revenue, to the ports of one State over those of another." This clause cannot be understood as applicable to those laws only which are passed for the purposes of revenue, because it is expressly applied to commercial regulations; and the most obvious preference which can be given to one port over another, in regulating commerce, relates to navigation. But the subsequent part of the sentence is still more explicit. It is, "nor shall vessels bound to or from one State, be obliged to enter, clear, or pay duties, in another." These words have a direct reference to navigation.

The universally acknowledged power of the government to impose embargoes, must also be considered as showing, that all America is united in that construction which comprehends navigation in the word commerce. Gentlemen have said, in argument, that this is a branch of the war-making power, and that an embargo is an instrument of war, not a regulation of trade.

That it may be, and often is, used as an instrument of war, cannot be denied. An embargo may be imposed for the purpose of facilitating the equipment or manning of a fleet, or for the purpose of concealing the progress of an expedition preparing to sail from a particular port. In these, and in similar cases, it is a military instrument, and partakes of the nature of war. But all embargoes are not of this description. They are sometimes resorted to without a view to war, and with a single view to commerce. In such case, an embargo is no more a war measure, than a merchantman is a ship of war, because both are vessels which navigate the ocean with sails and seamen.

When Congress imposed that embargo which, for a time, engaged the attention of every man in the United States, the avowed object of the law was, the protection of commerce, and the avoiding of war. By its friends and its enemies it was treated as a commercial, not as a war measure. The persevering earnestness and zeal with which it was opposed, in a part of our country which supposed its interests to be vitally affected by the act, cannot be forgotten. A want of acuteness in discovering objections to a measure to which they felt the most deep rooted hostility, will not be imputed to those who were arrayed in opposition to this. Yet they never suspected that navigation was no branch of trade, and was, therefore, not comprehended in the power to regulate commerce. They did, indeed, contest the constitutionality of the act, but, on a principle which admits the construction for which the appellant contends. They denied that the particular law in question was made in pursuance of the constitution, not because the power could not act directly on vessels, but because a perpetual embargo was the annihilation, and not the regulation of commerce. In terms, they admitted the applicability of the words used in the constitution to vessels; and that, in a case which produced a degree and an extent of excitement, calculated to draw forth every principle on which legitimate resistance could be sustained. No example could more strongly illustrate the universal understanding of the American people on this subject.

The word used in the constitution, then, comprehends, and has been always understood to comprehend, navigation within its meaning; and a power to regulate navigation, is as expressly granted, as if that term had been added to the word "commerce."

To what commerce does this power extend? The constitution informs us, to commerce "with foreign nations, and among the several States, and with the Indian tribes."

It has, we believe, been universally admitted, that these words comprehend every species of commercial intercourse between the United States and foreign nations. No sort of trade can be carried on between this country and any other, to which this power does not extend. It has been truly said, that commerce, as the word is used in the constitution, is a unit, every part of which is indicated by the term.

If this be the admitted meaning of the word, in its application to foreign nations, it must carry the same meaning throughout the sentence, and remain a unit, unless there be some plain intelligible cause which alters it.

The subject to which the power is next applied, is to commerce "among the several States." The word "among" means intermingled with. A thing which is among others, is intermingled with them. Commerce among the States, cannot stop at the external boundary line of each State, but may be introduced into the interior.

It is not intended to say that these words comprehend that commerce, which is completely internal, which is carried on between man and man in a State, or between different parts of the same State, and which does not extend to or affect other States. Such a power would be inconvenient, and is certainly unnecessary.

Comprehensive as the word "among" is, it may very properly be restricted to that commerce which concerns more States than one. The phrase is not one which would probably have been selected to indicate the completely interior traffic of a State, because it is not an apt phrase for that purpose; and the enumeration of the particular classes of commerce, to which the power was to be extended, would not have been made, had the intention

been to extend the power to every description. The enumeration presupposes something not enumerated; and that something, if we regard the language or the subject of the sentence, must be the exclusively internal commerce of a State. The genius and character of the whole government seem to be, that its action is to be applied to all the external concerns of the nation, and to those internal concerns which affect the States generally; but not to those which are completely within a particular State, which do not affect other States, and with which it is not necessary to interfere, for the purpose of executing some of the general powers of the government. The completely internal commerce of a State, then, may be considered as reserved for the State itself.

But, in regulating commerce with foreign nations, the power of Congress does not stop at the jurisdictional lines of the several States. It would be a very useless power, if it could not pass those lines. The commerce of the United States with foreign nations, is that of the whole United States. Every district has a right to participate in it. The deep streams which penetrate our country in every direction, pass through the interior of almost every State in the Union, and furnish the means of exercising this right. If Congress has the power to regulate it, that power must be exercised whenever the subject exists. If it exists within the States, if a foreign voyage may commence or terminate at a port within a State, then the power of Congress may be exercised within a State.

This principle is, if possible, still more clear, when applied to commerce "among the several States." They either join each other, in which case they are separated by a mathematical line, or they are remote from each other, in which case other States lie between them. What is commerce "among" them; and how is it to be conducted? Can a trading expedition between two adjoining States, commence and terminate outside of each? And if the trading intercourse be between two States remote from each other, must it not commence in one, terminate in the other, and probably pass through a third? Commerce among the States must, of necessity, be commerce with the States. In the regulation of trade with the Indian tribes, the action of the law, especially when the constitution was made, was chiefly within a State. The power of Congress, then, whatever it may be, must be exercised within the territorial jurisdiction of the several States. The sense of the nation on this subject, is unequivocally manifested by the provisions made in the laws for transporting goods, by land, between Baltimore and Providence, between New-York and Philadelphia, and between Philadelphia and Baltimore.

We are now arrived at the inquiry—What is this power?

It is the power to regulate; that is, to prescribe the rule by which commerce is to be governed. This power, like all others vested in Congress, is complete in itself, may be exercised to its utmost extent, and acknowledges no limitations, other than are prescribed in the constitution. These are expressed in plain terms, and do not affect the questions which arise in this case, or which have been discussed at the bar. If, as has always been understood, the sovereignty of Congress, though limited to specified objects, is plenary as to those objects, the power over commerce with foreign nations, and among the several States, is vested in Congress as absolutely as it would be in a single government, having in its constitution the same restrictions on the exercise of the power as are found in the constitution of the United States. The wisdom and the discretion of Congress, their identity with the people, and the influence which their constituents possess at elections, are, in this, as in many other instances, as that, for example, of declaring war, the sole restraints on which they have relied, to secure them from its abuse. They are the restraints on which the people must often rely solely, in all representative governments.

The power of Congress, then, comprehends navigation, within the limits of every State in the Union; so far as that navigation may be, in any manner, connected with "commerce with foreign nations, or among the several States, or with the Indian tribes." It may, of consequence, pass the jurisdictional line of New-York, and act upon the very waters to which the prohibition now under consideration applies.

But it has been urged with great earnestness, that, although the power of Congress to regulate commerce with foreign nations, and among the several States, be co-extensive with the subject itself, and have no other limits than are prescribed in the constitution, yet the States may severally exercise the same power, within their respective jurisdictions. In support of this argument, it is said, that they possessed it as an inseparable attribute of sovereignty, before the formation of the constitution, and still retain it, except so far as they have surrendered it by that instrument; that this principle results from the nature of the government, and is secured by the tenth amendment; that an affirmative grant of power is not exclusive, unless in its own nature it be such that the continued exercise of it by the former possessor is inconsistent with the grant, and that this is not of that description.

The appellant, conceding these postulates, except the last, contends, that full power to regulate a particular subject, implies the whole power, and leaves no residuum; that a grant of the whole is incompatible with the existence of a right in another to any part of it.

Both parties have appealed to the constitution, to legislative acts, and judicial decisions; and have drawn arguments from all these sources, to support and illustrate the propositions they respectively maintain.

The grant of the power to lay and collect taxes is, like the power to regulate commerce, made in general terms, and has never been understood to interfere with the exercise of the same power by the States; and hence has been drawn an argument which has been applied to the question under consideration. But the two grants are not, it is conceived, similar in their terms or their nature. Although many of the powers formerly exercised by the States, are transferred to the government of the Union, yet the State governments remain, and constitute a most important part of our system. The power of taxation is indispensable to their existence, and is a power which, in its own nature, is capable of residing in, and being exercised by, different authorities at the same time. We are accustomed to see it placed, for different purposes, in different hands. Taxa-

tion is the simple operation of taking small portions from a perpetually accumulating mass, susceptible of almost infinite division; and a power in one to take what is necessary for certain purposes, is not, in its nature, incompatible with a power in another to take what is necessary for other purposes. Congress is authorized to lay and collect taxes, &c. to pay the debts, and provide for the common defence and general welfare of the United States. This does not interfere with the power of the States to tax for the support of their own governments; nor is the exercise of that power by the States, an exercise of any portion of the power that is granted to the United States. In imposing taxes for State purposes, they are not doing what Congress is empowered to do. Congress is not empowered to tax for those purposes which are within the exclusive province of the States. When, then, each government exercises the power of taxation, neither is exercising the power of the other. But, when a State proceeds to regulate commerce with foreign nations, or among the several States, it is exercising the very power that is granted to Congress, and is doing the very thing which Congress is authorized to do. There is no analogy, then, between the power of taxation and the power of regulating commerce.

In discussing the question, whether this power is still in the States, in the case under consideration, we may dismiss from it the inquiry, whether it is surrendered by the mere grant to Congress, or is retained until Congress shall exercise the power. We may dismiss that inquiry, because it has been exercised, and the regulations which Congress deemed it proper to make, are now in full operation. The sole question is, can a State regulate commerce with foreign nations and among the States, while Congress is regulating it?

The counsel for the respondent answer this question in the affirmative, and rely very much on the restriction in the 10th section, as supporting their opinion. They say, very truly, that limitations of a power, furnish a strong argument in favour of the existence of that power, and that the section which prohibits the States from laying duties on imports or exports, proves that this power might have been exercised, had it not been expressly forbidden; and, consequently, that any other commercial regulation, not expressly forbidden, to which the original power of the State was competent, may still be made.

That this restriction shows the opinion of the Convention, that a State might impose duties on exports and imports, if not expressly forbidden, will be conceded; but that it follows as a consequence, from this concession, that a State may regulate commerce with foreign nations and among the States, cannot be admitted.

We must first determine whether the act of laying "duties or imposts on imports or exports," is considered in the constitution as a branch of the taxing power, or of the power to regulate commerce. We think it very clear, that it is considered as a branch of the taxing power. It is so treated in the first clause of the 8th section: "Congress shall have power to lay and collect taxes, duties, imposts, and excises;" and, before commerce is mentioned, the rule by which the exercise of this power must be governed, is declared. It is, that all duties, imposts, and excises, shall be uniform. In a separate clause of the enumeration, the power to regulate commerce is given, as being entirely distinct from the right to levy taxes and imposts, and as being a new power, not before conferred. The constitution, then, considers these powers as substantive, and distinct from each other; and so places them in the enumeration it contains. The power of imposing duties on imports is classed with the power to levy taxes, and that seems to be its natural place. But the power to levy taxes could never be considered as abridging the right of the States on that subject; and they might, consequently, have exercised it by levying duties on imports or exports, had the constitution contained no prohibition on this subject. This prohibition, then, is an exception from the acknowledged power of the States to levy taxes, not from the questionable power to regulate commerce.

"A duty of tonnage" is as much a tax, as a duty on imports or exports; and the reason which induced the prohibition of those taxes, extends to this also. This tax may be imposed by a State, with the consent of Congress; and it may be admitted, that Congress cannot give a right to a State, in virtue of its own powers. But a duty of tonnage being a part of the power of imposing taxes, its prohibition may certainly be made to depend on Congress, without affording any implication respecting a power to regulate commerce. It is true, that duties may often be, and in fact often are, imposed on tonnage, with a view to the regulation of commerce; but they may be also imposed with a view to revenue; and it was, therefore, a prudent precaution, to prohibit the States from exercising this power. The idea that the same measure might, according to circumstances, be arranged with different classes of power, was no novelty to the framers of our constitution. Those illustrious statesmen and patriots had been, many of them, deeply engaged in discussions which preceded the war of our revolution, and all of them were well read in those discussions. The right to regulate commerce, even by the imposition of duties, was not controverted; but the right to impose a duty for the purpose of revenue, produced a war as important, perhaps, in its consequences to the human race, as any the world has ever witnessed.

These restrictions, then, are on the taxing power, not on that to regulate commerce; and presuppose the existence of that which they restrain, not of that which they do not purport to restrain.

But, the inspection laws are said to be regulations of commerce, and are certainly recognised in the constitution, as being passed in the exercise of a power remaining with the States.

That inspection laws may have a remote and considerable influence on commerce, will not be denied; but that a power to regulate commerce is the source from which the right to pass them is derived, cannot be admitted. The object of inspection laws, is to improve the quality of articles produced by the labour of a country; to fit them for exportation; or, it may be, for domestic use. They act upon the subject before it becomes an article of foreign commerce, or of commerce among the States, and prepare it for that purpose. They form a portion of that immense mass of legislation, which embraces everything within the territory of a State, not surrendered to the general government: all which can be most advantageously exercised by the States themselves. Inspection laws, quarantine laws, health laws of every description, as well as laws for regulating the internal commerce of a State, and those which respect turnpike roads, ferries, &c., are component parts of this mass.

No direct general power over these objects is granted to Congress; and, consequently, they remain subject to State legislation. If the legislative power of the Union can reach them, it must be for national purposes; it must be where the power is expressly given for a special purpose, or is clearly incidental to some power which is expressly given. It is obvious, that the government of the Union, in the exercise of its express powers, that, for example, of regulating commerce with foreign nations and among the States, may use means that may also be employed by a State, in the exercise of its acknowledged powers; that, for example, of regulating commerce within the State. If Congress license vessels to sail from one port to another, in the same State, the act is supposed to be, necessarily, incidental to the power expressly granted to Congress, and implies no claim of a direct power to regulate the purely internal commerce of a State, or to act directly on its system of police. So, if a State, in passing laws on subjects acknowledged to be within its control, and with a view to those subjects, shall adopt a measure of the same character with one which Congress may adopt, it does not derive its authority from the particular power which has been granted, but from some other, which remains with the State, and may be executed by the same means. All experience shows, that the same measures, or measures scarcely distinguishable from each other, may flow from distinct powers; but this does not prove that the powers themselves are identical. Although the means used in their execution may sometimes approach each other so nearly as to be confounded, there are other situations in which they are sufficiently distinct to establish their individuality.

In our complex system, presenting the rare and difficult scheme of one general government, whose action extends over the whole, but which possesses only certain enumerated powers; and of numerous State governments, which retain and exercise all powers not delegated to the Union, contests respecting power must arise. Were it even otherwise, the measures taken by the respective governments to execute their acknowledged powers, would often be of the same description, and might, sometimes, interfere. This, however, does not prove that the one is exercising, or has a right to exercise, the powers of the other.

The acts of Congress, passed in 1796 and 1799, empowering and directing the officers of the general government to conform to, and assist in the execution of the quarantine and health laws of a State, proceed, it is said, upon the idea that these laws are constitutional. It is undoubtedly true, that they do proceed upon that idea; and the constitutionality of such laws has never, so far as we are informed, been denied. But they do not imply an acknowledgment that a State may rightfully regulate commerce with foreign nations, or among the States; for they do not imply that such laws are an exercise of that power, or enacted with a view to it. On the contrary, they are treated as quarantine and health laws, are so denominated in the acts of Congress, and are considered as flowing from the acknowledged power of a State, to provide for the health of its citizens. But, as it was apparent that some of the provisions made for this purpose, and in virtue of this power, might interfere with, and be affected by the laws of the United States, made for the regulation of commerce, Congress, in that spirit of harmony and conciliation, which ought always to characterize the conduct of governments standing in the relation which that of the Union and those of the States bear to each other, has directed its officers to aid in the execution of these laws; and has, in some measure, adapted its own legislation to this object, by making provisions in aid of those of the States. But, in making these provisions, the opinion is unequivocally manifested, that Congress may control the State laws, so far as it may be necessary to control them, for the regulation of commerce.

The act passed in 1803, prohibiting the importation of slaves into any State which shall itself prohibit their importation, implies, it is said, an admission that the State possessed the power to exclude or admit them; from which it is inferred, that they possess the same power with respect to other articles.

If this inference were correct; if this power was exercised, not under any particular clause in the constitution, but in virtue of a general right over the subject of commerce, to exist as long as the constitution itself, it might now be exercised. Any State might now import African slaves into its own territory. But it is obvious, that the power of the States over this subject, previous to the year 1808, constitutes an exception to the power of Congress to regulate commerce, and the exception is expressed in such words, as to manifest clearly the intention to continue the pre-existing right of the States to admit or exclude, for a limited period. The words are, "the migration or importation of such persons as any of the States, now existing, *shall* think proper to admit, shall not be prohibited by the Congress prior to the year 1808." The whole object of the exception is, to preserve the power to those States which might be disposed to exercise it; and its language seems to the Court to convey this idea unequivocally. The possession of this particular power, then, during the time limited in the constitution, cannot be admitted to prove the possession of any other similar power.

It has been said, that the act of August 7, 1789, acknowledges a concurrent power in the States to regulate the conduct of pilots, and hence is inferred an admission of their concurrent right with Congress to regulate commerce with foreign nations, and amongst the States. But this inference is not, we think, justified by the fact.

Although Congress cannot enable a State to legislate, Congress may adopt the provisions of a State on any subject. When the government of the Union was brought into existence, it found a system for the regulation of its pilots in full force in every State. The act which has been mentioned, adopts this system, and gives it the same validity as if its provisions had been specially made by Congress. But the act, it may be said, is prospective also, and the adoption of laws to be made in future, presupposes the right in the maker to legislate on the subject.

The act unquestionably manifests an intention to leave this subject entirely to the States; until Congress should think proper to interpose; but the very enactment of such a law indicates an opinion that it was necessary; that the existing system would not be applicable to the new state of things, unless expressly applied to it by Congress. But this section is confined to pilots within the "bays, inlets, rivers, harbours, and ports of the United States," which are, of course, in whole or in part, also within the limits of some particular state. The acknowledged power of a State to regulate its police, its domestic trade, and to govern its own citizens, may enable it to legislate on this subject, to a considerable extent; and the adoption of its system by Congress, and the application of it to the whole subject of commerce, does not seem to the Court to imply a right in the States so to apply it of their own authority. But the adoption of the State system being temporary, being only "until further legislative provision shall be made by Congress," shows, conclusively, an opinion that Congress could control the whole subject, and might adopt the system of the States, or provide one of its own.

A State, it is said, or even a private citizen, may construct light houses. But gentlemen must be aware, that if this proves a power in a State to regulate commerce, it proves that the same power is in the citizen. States, or individuals who own lands, may, if not forbidden by law, erect on those lands what buildings they please; but this power is entirely distinct from that of regulating commerce, and may, we presume, be restrained, if exercised so as to produce a public mischief.

These acts were cited at the bar for the purpose of showing an opinion in Congress, that the States possess, concurrently with the Legislature of the Union, the power to regulate commerce with foreign nations and among the States. Upon reviewing them, we think they do not establish the proposition they were intended to prove. They show the opinion, that the States retain powers enabling them to pass the laws to which allusion has been made, not that those laws proceed from the particular power which has been delegated to Congress.

It has been contended by the counsel for the appellant, that, as the word "to regulate" implies in its nature, full power over the thing to be regulated, it excludes, necessarily, the action of all others that would perform the same operation on the same thing. That regulation is designed for the entire result, applying to those parts which remain as they were, as well as to those which are altered. It produces a uniform whole, which is as much disturbed and deranged by changing what the regulating power designs to leave untouched, as that on which it has operated.

There is great force in this argument, and the Court is not satisfied that it has been refuted.

Since, however, in exercising the power of regulating their own purely internal affairs, whether of trading or police, the States may sometimes enact laws, the validity of which depends on their interfering with, and being contrary to, an act of Congress passed in pursuance of the constitution, the Court will enter upon the inquiry, whether the laws of New-York, as expounded by the highest tribunal of that State, have, in their application to this case, come into collision with an act of Congress, and deprived a citizen of a right to which that act entitles him. Should this collision exist, it will be immaterial whether those laws were passed in virtue of a concurrent power "to regulate commerce with foreign nations and among the several States," or, in virtue of a power to regulate their domestic trade and police. In one case and the other, the acts of New-York must yield to the law of Congress; and the decision sustaining the privilege they confer, against a right given by a law of the Union, must be erroneous.

This opinion has been frequently expressed in this Court, and is founded, as well on the nature of the government as on the words of the constitution. In argument, however, it has been contended, that if a law passed by a State, in the exercise of its acknowledged sovereignty, comes into conflict with a law passed by Congress in pursuance of the constitution, they affect the subject, and each other, like equal opposing powers.

But the framers of our constitution foresaw this state of things, and provided for it, by declaring the supremacy not only of itself, but of the laws made in pursuance of it. The nullity of any act, inconsistent with the constitution, is produced by the declaration, that the constitution is the supreme law. The appropriate application of that part of the clause which confers the same supremacy on laws and treaties, is to such acts of the State Legislatures as do not transcend their powers, but, though enacted in the execution of acknowledged State powers, interfere with, or are contrary to the laws of Congress, made in pursuance of the constitution, or some treaty made under the authority of the United States. In every such case, the act of Congress, or the treaty, is supreme; and the law of the State, though enacted in the exercise of powers not controverted, must yield to it.

In pursuing this inquiry at the bar, it has been said, that the constitution does not confer the right of intercourse between State and State. That right derives its source from those laws whose authority is acknowledged by civilized man throughout the world. This is true. The constitution found it an existing right, and gave to Congress the power to regulate it. In the exercise of this power, Congress has passed "an act for enrolling or licensing ships or vessels to be employed in the coasting trade and fisheries, and for regulating the same." The counsel for the respondent contend, that this act does not give the right to sail from port to port, but confines itself to regulating a pre-existing right, so far only as to confer certain privileges on enrolled and licensed vessels in its exercise.

It will at once occur, that, when a Legislature attaches certain privileges and exemptions to the exercise of a right over which its control is absolute, the law must imply a power to exercise the right. The privileges are gone, if the right itself be annihilated. It would be contrary to all reason, and to the course of human affairs, to say that a State is unable to strip a vessel of the particular privileges attendant on the exercise of a right, and yet may annul the right itself; that the State of New-York cannot prevent an enrolled and licensed vessel, proceeding from Elizabeth-town, in New-Jersey, to New-York, from enjoying, in her course, and on her entrance into port, all the privileges conferred by the act of Congress; but can shut her up in her own port, and prohibit altogether her entering the waters and ports of another State. To the Court it seems very clear, that the whole act on the subject of the coasting trade, according to those principles which govern the construction of statutes, implies, unequivocally, an authority to licensed vessels to carry on the coasting trade.

But we will proceed briefly to notice those sections which bear more directly on the subject.

The first section declares, that vessels enrolled by virtue of a previous law, and certain other vessels, enrolled as described in that act, and having a license in force, as is by the act required, "and no others, shall be deemed ships or vessels of the United States, entitled to the privileges of ships or vessels employed in the coasting trade."

This section seems to the Court to contain a positive enactment, that the vessels it describes shall be entitled to the privileges of ships or vessels employed in the coasting trade. These privileges cannot be separated from the trade, and cannot be enjoyed, unless the trade may be prosecuted. The grant of the privilege is an idle, empty form, conveying nothing, unless it convey the right to which the privilege is attached, and in the exercise of which its whole value consists. To construe these words otherwise than as entitling the ships or vessels described, to carry on the coasting trade, would be, we think, to disregard the apparent intent of the act.

The fourth section directs the proper officer to grant to a vessel qualified to receive it, "a license for carrying on the coasting trade;" and prescribes its form. After reciting the compliance of the applicant with the previous requisites of the law, the operative words of the instrument are, "license is hereby granted for the said steam-boat, Bellona, to be employed in carrying on the coasting trade for one year from the date hereof, and no longer."

These are not the words of the officer; they are the words of the legislature; and convey as explicitly the authority the act intended to give, and operate as effectually, as if they had been inserted in any other part of the act, than in the license itself.

The word "license," means permission, or authority; and a license to do any particular thing, is a permission or authority to do that thing; and if granted by a person having power to grant it, transfers to the grantee the right to do whatever it purports to authorize. It certainly transfers to him all the right which the grantor can transfer, to do what is within the terms of the license.

Would the validity or effect of such an instrument be questioned by the respondent, if executed by persons claiming regularly under the laws of New-York?

The license must be understood to be what it purports to be, a legislative authority to the steamboat Bellona, "to be employed in carrying on the coasting trade, for one year from this date."

It has been denied that these words authorize a voyage from New-Jersey to New-York. It is true, that no ports are specified; but it is equally true, that the words used are perfectly intelligible, and do confer such authority as unquestionably, as if the ports had been mentioned. The coasting trade is a term well understood. The law has defined it; and all know its meaning perfectly. The act describes, with great minuteness, the various operations of a vessel engaged in it; and it cannot, we think, be doubted, that a voyage from New-Jersey to New-York, is one of those operations.

Notwithstanding the decided language of the license, it has also been maintained, that it gives no right to trade; and that its sole purpose is to confer the American character.

The answer given to this argument, that the American character is conferred by the enrolment, and not by the license, is, we think, founded too clearly in the words of the law, to require the support of any additional observations. The enrolment of vessels designed for the coasting trade, corresponds precisely with the registration of vessels designed for the foreign trade, and requires every circumstance which can constitute the American character. The license can be granted only to vessels already enrolled, if they be of the burthen of twenty tons and upwards; and requires no circumstance essential to the American character. The object of the license, then, cannot be to ascertain the character of the vessel, but to do what it professes to do—that is, to give permission to a vessel already proved by her enrolment to be American, to carry on the coasting trade.

But, if the license be a permit to carry on the coasting trade, the respondent denies that these boats were engaged in that trade, or that the decree under consideration has restrained them from prosecuting it. The boats of the appellant were, we are told, employed in the transportation of passengers; and this is no part of that commerce which Congress may regulate.

If, as our whole course of legislation on this subject shows, the power of Congress has been universally understood in America, to comprehend navigation, it is a very persuasive, if not a conclusive argument, to prove that the construction is correct; and, if it be correct, no clear distinction is perceived between the power to regulate vessels employed in transporting men for hire, and property for hire. The subject is transferred to Congress, and no exception to the grant can be admitted, which is not proved by the words or the nature of the thing. A coasting vessel employed in the transportation of passengers, is as much a portion of the American marine, as one employed in the transportation of a cargo; and no reason is perceived why such vessel should be withdrawn from the regulating power of that government, which has been thought best fitted for the purpose generally. The provisions of the law respecting native seamen, and respecting ownership, are as applicable to vessels carrying men, as to vessels carrying manufactures; and no reason is perceived why the power over the subject should not be placed in the same hands. The argument urged at the bar, rests on the foundation, that the power of Congress does not extend to navigation, as a branch of commerce, and can only be applied to that subject incidentally and occasionally. But if that foundation be removed, we must show some plain, intelligible distinction, supported by the constitution, or by reason, for

discriminating between the power of Congress over vessels employed in navigating the same seas. We can perceive no such distinction.

If we refer to the constitution, the inference to be drawn from it is rather against the distinction. The section which restrains Congress from prohibiting the migration or importation of such persons as any of the States may think proper to admit, until the year 1808, has always been considered as an exception from the power to regulate commerce, and certainly seems to class migration with importation. Migration applies as appropriately to voluntary, as importation does to involuntary, arrivals; and, so far as an exception from a power proves its existence, this section proves that the power to regulate commerce applies equally to the regulation of vessels employed in transporting men, who pass from place to place voluntarily, and to those who pass involuntarily.

If the power reside in Congress, as a portion of the general grant to regulate commerce, then acts applying that power to vessels generally, must be construed as comprehending all vessels. If none appear to be excluded by the language of the act, none can be excluded by construction. Vessels have always been employed to a greater or less extent in the transportation of passengers, and have never been supposed to be, on that account, withdrawn from the control or protection of Congress. Packets which ply along the coast, as well as those which make voyages between Europe and America, consider the transportation of passengers as an important part of their business. Yet it has never been suspected that the general laws of navigation did not apply to them.

The duty act, sections 23 and 46, contains provisions respecting passengers, and shows, that vessels which transport them, have the same rights, and must perform the same duties, with other vessels. They are governed by the general laws of navigation.

In the progress of things, this seems to have grown into a particular employment, and to have attracted the particular attention of government. Congress was no longer satisfied with comprehending vessels engaged specially in this business, within those provisions which were intended for vessels generally; and, on the 2d of March, 1819, passed "an act regulating passenger ships and vessels." This wise and humane law provides for the safety and comfort of passengers, and for the communication of every thing concerning them which may interest the government, to the Department of State, but makes no provision concerning the entry of the vessel, or her conduct in the waters of the United States. This, we think, shows conclusively the sense of Congress, (if, indeed, any evidence to that point could be required,) that the pre-existing regulations comprehended passenger ships among others; and, in prescribing the same duties, the Legislature must have considered them as possessing the same rights.

If, then, it were even true, that the Bellona and the Stoudinger were employed exclusively in the conveyance of passengers between New-York and New-Jersey, it would not follow that this occupation did not constitute a part of the coasting trade of the United States, and was not protected by the license annexed to the answer. But we cannot perceive how the occupation of these vessels can be drawn into question, in the case before the Court. The laws of New-York, which grant the exclusive privilege set up by the respondent, take no notice of the employment of vessels, and relate only to the principle by which they are propelled. Those laws do not inquire whether vessels are engaged in transporting men or merchandise, but whether they are moved by steam or wind. If by the former, the waters of New-York are closed against them, though their cargoes be dutiable goods, which the laws of the United States permit them to enter and deliver in New-York. If by the latter, those waters are free to them, though they should carry passengers only. In conformity with the law, is the bill of the plaintiff in the State Court. The bill does not complain that the Bellona and the Stoudinger carry passengers, but that they are moved by steam. This is the injury of which he complains, and is the sole injury against the continuance of which he asks relief. The bill does not even allege, specially, that those vessels were employed in the transportation of passengers, but says, generally, that they were employed "in the transportation of passengers, or otherwise." The answer avers, only, that they were employed in the coasting trade, and insists on the right to carry on any trade authorized by the license. No testimony is taken, and the writ of injunction and decree restrain these licensed vessels, not from carrying passengers, but from being moved through the waters of New-York by steam, for any purpose whatever.

The questions, then, whether the conveyance of passengers be a part of the coasting trade, and whether a vessel can be protected in that occupation by a coasting license, are not, and cannot be, raised in this case. The real and sole question seems to be, whether a steam machine, in actual use, deprives a vessel of the privileges conferred by a license.

In considering this question, the first idea which presents itself, is, that the laws of Congress for the regulation of commerce, do not look to the principle by which vessels are moved. That subject is left entirely to individual discretion; and, in that vast and complex system of legislative enactment concerning it, which embraces every thing that the Legislature thought it necessary to notice, there is not, we believe, one word respecting the peculiar principle by which vessels are propelled through the water, except what may be found in a single act, granting a particular privilege to steam boats. With this exception, every act, either prescribing duties, or granting privileges, applies to every vessel, whether navigated by the instrumentality of wind or fire, of sails or machinery. The whole weight of proof, then, is thrown upon him who would introduce a distinction to which the words of the law give no countenance.

If a real difference could be admitted to exist between vessels carrying passengers and others, it has already been observed, that there is no fact in this case which can bring up that question. And, if the occupation of steam boats be a matter of such general notoriety, that the Court may be presumed to know it, although not specially informed by the record, then we deny that the transportation of passengers is their exclusive occupation. It is a matter of general history, that, in our western waters, their principal employment is the transportation of merchandise; and all know, that in the waters of the Atlantic they are frequently so employed.

But all inquiry into this subject seems to the Court to be put completely at rest, by the act already mentioned, entitled, "An act for the enrolling and licensing of steam boats."

This act authorizes a steam boat employed, or intended to be employed, only in a river or bay of the United States, owned wholly or in part by an alien, resident within the United States, to be enrolled and licensed as if the same belonged to a citizen of the United States.

This act demonstrates the opinion of Congress, that steam boats may be enrolled and licensed, in common with vessels using sails. They are, of course, entitled to the same privileges, and can no more be restrained from navigating waters, and entering ports which are free to such vessels, than if they were wafted on their voyage by the winds, instead of being propelled by the agency of fire. The one element may be as legitimately used as the other, for every commercial purpose authorized by the laws of the Union; and the act of a State inhibiting the use of either to any vessel having a license under the act of Congress, comes, we think, in direct collision with that act.

As this decides the cause, it is unnecessary to enter in an examination of that part of the constitution which empowers Congress to promote the progress of science and the useful arts.

The Court is aware that, in stating the train of reasoning by which we have been conducted to this result, much time has been consumed in the attempt to demonstrate propositions which may have been thought axioms. It is felt that the tediousness inseparable from the endeavour to prove that which is already clear, is imputable to a considerable part of this opinion. But it was unavoidable. The conclusion to which we have come, depends on a chain of principles which it was necessary to preserve unbroken; and, although some of them were thought nearly self-evident, the magnitude of the question, the weight of character belonging to those from whose judgment we dissent, and the argument at the bar, demanded that we should assume nothing.

Powerful and ingenious minds, taking, as postulates, that the powers expressly granted to the government of the Union, are to be contracted by construction, into the narrowest possible compass, and that the original powers of the States are retained, if any possible construction will retain them, may, by a course of well digested, but refined and metaphysical reasoning, founded on these premises, explain away the constitution of our country, and leave it, a magnificent structure, indeed, to look at, but totally unfit for use. They may so entangle and perplex the understanding, as to obscure principles, which were before thought quite plain, and induce doubts where, if the mind were to pursue its own course, none would be perceived. In such a case, it is peculiarly necessary to recur to safe and fundamental principles to sustain those principles, and when sustained, to make them the tests of the arguments to be examined.

Mr. Justice JOHNSON. The judgment entered by the Court in this cause, has my entire approbation; but having adopted my conclusions on views of the subject materially different from those of my brethren, I feel it incumbent on me to exhibit those views. I have, also, another inducement: in questions of great importance and great delicacy, I feel my duty to the public best discharged, by an effort to maintain my opinions in my own way.

In attempts to construe the constitution, I have never found much benefit resulting from the inquiry, whether the whole, or any part of it, is to be construed strictly, or literally. The simple, classical, precise, yet comprehensive language, in which it is couched, leaves, at most, but very little latitude for construction; and when its intent and meaning is discovered, nothing remains but to execute the will of those who made it, in the best manner to effect the purposes intended. The great and paramount purpose, was to unite this mass of wealth and power, for the protection of the humblest individual; his rights, civil and political, his interests and prosperity, are the sole *end;* the rest are nothing but the *means.* But the principal of those means, one so essential as to approach nearer the characteristics of an end, was the independence and harmony of the States, that they may the better subserve the purposes of cherishing and protecting the respective families of this great republic.

The strong sympathies, rather than the feeble government, which bound the States together during a common war, dissolved on the return of peace; and the very principles which gave rise to the war of the revolution, began to threaten the confederacy with anarchy and ruin. The States had resisted a tax imposed by the parent State, and now reluctantly submitted to, or altogether rejected, the moderate demands of the confederation. Every one recollects the painful and threatening discussions, which arose on the subject of the five per cent. duty. Some States rejected it altogether; others insisted on collecting it themselves; scarcely any acquiesced without reservations, which deprived it altogether of the character of a national measure; and at length, some repealed the laws by which they had signified their acquiescence.

For a century the States had submitted, with murmurs, to the commercial restrictions imposed by the parent State; and now, finding themselves in the unlimited possession of those powers over their own commerce, which they had so long been deprived of, and so earnestly coveted, that selfish principle which, well controlled, is so salutary, and which, unrestricted, is so unjust and tyrannical, guided by inexperience and jealousy, began to show itself in iniquitous laws and impolitic measures, from which grew up a conflict of commercial regulations, destructive to the harmony of the States, and fatal to their commercial interests abroad.

This was the immediate cause, that led to the forming of a convention.

As early as 1778, the subject had been pressed upon the attention of Congress, by a memorial from the State of New-Jersey; and in 1781, we find a resolution presented to that body, by one of the most enlightened men of his day, affirming, that "it is indispensably necessary, that the United States, in Congress assembled, should be vested with a right of superintending the commercial regulations of every State, that none may take place that shall be partial or contrary to the common interests." The resolution of Virginia, appointing her commissioners, to meet commissioners from other States, expresses their purpose to be, "to take into consideration the trade of the United States, to consider how far an uniform system in their commercial regulations, may be necessary to their common interests and their permanent harmony." And Mr. Madison's resolution, which led to that measure, is introduced by a preamble entirely explicit to this point: "Whereas, the relative situation of the United States has been found, on trial, to require uniformity in their commercial regulations, as the only effectual policy for obtaining, in the ports of foreign nations, a stipulation of privileges reciprocal to those enjoyed by the subjects of such nations in the ports of the United States, for preventing animosities, which cannot fail to arise among the several States, from the interference of partial and separate regulations," &c. "therefore, resolved," &c.

The history of the times will, therefore, sustain the opinion, that the grant of power over commerce, if intended to be commensurate with the evils existing, and the purpose of remedying those evils, could be only commensurate with the power of the States over the subject. And this opinion is supported by a very remarkable evidence of the general understanding of the whole American people, when the grant was made.

There was not a State in the Union, in which there did not, at that time, exist a variety of commercial regulations; concerning which it is too much to suppose, that the whole ground covered by those regulations was immediately assumed by actual legislation, under the authority of the Union. But where was the existing statute on this subject, that a State attempted to execute? or by what State was it ever thought necessary to repeal those statutes? By common consent, those laws dropped lifeless from their statute books, for want of the sustaining power, that had been relinquished to Congress.

And the plain and direct import of the words of the grant, is consistent with this general understanding.

The words of the constitution are, "Congress shall have power to regulate commerce with foreign nations, and among the several States, and with the Indian tribes."

It is not material, in my view of the subject, to inquire whether the article *a* or *the* should be prefixed to the word "power." Either, or neither, will produce the same result: if either, it is clear that the article *the* would be the proper one, since the next preceding grant of power is certainly exclusive, to wit: "to borrow money on the credit of the United States." But mere verbal criticism I reject.

My opinion is founded on the application of the words of the grant to the subject of it.

The "power to regulate commerce," here meant to be granted, was that power to regulate commerce which previously existed in the States. But what was that power? The States were, unquestionably, supreme; and each possessed that power over commerce, which is acknowledged to reside in every sovereign State. The definition and limits of that power are to be sought among the features of international law; and, as it was not only admitted, but insisted on by both parties, in argument, that, *"unaffected by a state of war, by treaties, or by municipal regulations, all commerce among independent States was legitimate,"* there is no necessity to appeal to the oracles of the *jus commune* for the correctness of that doctrine. The law of nations, regarding man as a social animal, pronounces all commerce legitimate in a state of peace, until prohibited by positive law. The power of a sovereign state over commerce, therefore, amounts to nothing more than a power to limit and restrain it at pleasure. And since the power to prescribe the limits to its freedom, necessarily implies the power to determine what shall remain unrestrained, it follows, that the power must be exclusive; it can reside but in one potentate; and hence, the grant of this power carries with it the whole subject, leaving nothing for the State to act upon.

And such has been the practical construction of the act. Were every law on the subject of commerce repealed tomorrow, all commerce would be lawful; and, in practice, merchants never inquire what is permitted, but what is forbidden commerce. Of all the endless variety of branches of foreign commerce, now carried on to every quarter of the world, I know of no one that is permitted by act of Congress, any otherwise than by not being forbidden. No statute of the United States, that I know of, was ever passed to permit a commerce, unless in consequence of its having been prohibited by some previous statute.

I speak not here of the treaty making power, for that is not exercised under the grant now under consideration. I confine my observation to *laws* properly so called. And even where freedom of commercial intercourse is made a subject of stipulation in a treaty, it is generally with a view to the removal of some previous restriction; or the introduction of some new privilege, most frequently, is identified with the return to a state of peace. But another view of the subject leads directly to the same conclusion. Power to regulate *foreign commerce*, is given in the same words, and in the same breath, as it were, with that over the commerce of the States and with the Indian tribes. But the power to regulate *foreign* commerce is necessarily exclusive. The States are unknown to foreign nations; their sovereignty exists only with relation to each other and the general government. Whatever regulations foreign commerce should be subjected to in the ports of the Union, the general government would be held responsible for them; and all other regulations, but those which Congress had imposed, would be regarded by foreign nations as trespasses and violations of national faith and comity.

But the language which grants the power as to one description of commerce, grants it as to all; and, in fact, if ever the exercise of a right, or acquiescence in a construction, could be inferred from contemporaneous and continued assent, it is that of the exclusive effect of this grant.

A right over the subject has never been pretended to in any instance, except as incidental to the exercise of some other unquestionable power.

The present is an instance of the assertion of that kind, as incidental to a municipal power; that of superintending the internal concerns of a State, and particularly of extending protection and patronage, in the shape of a monopoly, to genius and enterprise.

The grant to Livingston and Fulton, interferes with the freedom of intercourse among the States; and on this principle its constitutionality is contested.

When speaking of the power of Congress over navigation, I do not regard it as a power incidental to that of regulating commerce; I consider it as the thing itself; inseparable from it as vital motion is from vital existence.

Commerce, in its simplest signification, means an exchange of goods; but in the advancement of society, labour, transportation, intelligence, care, and various mediums of exchange, become commodities, and enter into commerce; the subject, the vehicle, the agent, and their various operations, become the objects of commercial regulation. Ship building, the carrying trade, and propagation of seamen, are such vital agents of commercial prosperity, that the nation which could not legislate over these subjects, would not possess power to regulate commerce.

That such was the understanding of the framers of the constitution, is conspicuous from provisions contained in that instrument.

The first clause of the 9th section, not only considers the right of controlling personal ingress or migration, as implied in the powers previously vested in Congress over commerce, but acknowledges it as a legitimate subject of revenue. And, although the leading object of this section undoubtedly was the importation of slaves, yet the words are obviously calculated to comprise persons of all descriptions, and to recognise in Congress a power to prohibit, where the States permit, although they cannot permit when the States prohibit. The treaty making power undoubtedly goes further. So the fifth clause of the same section furnishes an exposition of the sense of the Convention as to the power of Congress over navigation: "nor shall vessels bound to or from one State, be obliged to enter, clear, or pay duties in another."

But, it is almost labouring to prove a self-evident proposition, since the sense of mankind, the practice of the world, the contemporaneous assumption, and continued exercise of the power, and universal acquiescence, have so clearly established the right of Congress over navigation, and the transportation of both men and their goods, as not only incidental to, but actually of the essence of, the power to regulate commerce. As to the transportation of passengers, and passengers in a steam boat, I consider it as having been solemnly recognised by the State of New-York, as a subject both of commercial regulation and of revenue. She has imposed a transit duty upon steam boat passengers arriving at Albany, and unless this be done in the exercise of her control over personal intercourse, as incident to internal commerce, I know not on what principle the individual has been subjected to this tax. The subsequent imposition upon the steam boat itself, appears to be but a commutation, and operates as an indirect instead of a direct tax upon the same subject. The passenger pays it at last.

It is impossible, with the views which I entertain of the principle on which the commercial privileges of the people of the United States, among themselves, rests, to concur in the view which this Court takes of the effect of the coasting license in this cause. I do not regard it as the foundation of the right set up in behalf of the appellant. If there was any one object riding over every other in the adoption of the constitution, it was to keep the commercial intercourse among the States free from all invidious and partial restraints. And I cannot overcome the conviction, that if the licensing act was repealed to-morrow, the rights of the appellant to a reversal of the decision complained of, would be as strong as it is under this license. One half the doubts in life arise from the defects of language, and if this instrument had been called an *exemption* instead of a license, it would have given a better idea of its character. Licensing acts, in fact, in legislation, are universally restraining acts; as, for example, acts licensing gaming houses, retailers of spiritous liquors, &c. The act, in this instance, is distinctly of that character, and forms part of an extensive system, the object of which is to encourage American shipping, and place them on an equal footing with the shipping of other nations. Almost every commercial nation reserves to its own subjects a monopoly of its coasting trade; and a countervailing privilege in favour of American shipping is contemplated, in the whole legislation of the United States on this subject. It is not to give the vessel an American character, that the license is granted; that effect has been correctly attributed to the act of her enrolment. But it is to confer on her American privileges, as contradistinguished from foreign; and to preserve the government from fraud by foreigners, in surreptitiously intruding themselves into the American commercial marine, as well as frauds upon the revenue in the trade coastwise, that this whole system is projected. Many duties and formalities are necessarily imposed upon the American foreign commerce, which would be burdensome in the active coasting trade of the States, and can be dispensed with. A higher rate of tonnage also is imposed, and this license entitles the vessels that take it, to those exemptions, but to nothing more. A common register, equally entitles vessels to carry on the coasting trade, although it does not exempt them from the forms of foreign commerce, or from compliance with the 16th and 17th sections of the enrolling act. And even a foreign vessel may be employed coastwise, upon complying with the requisitions of the 24th section. I consider the license, therefore, as nothing more than what it purports to be, according to the 1st section of this act, conferring on the licensed vessel certain privileges in that trade, not conferred on other vessels; but the abstract right of commercial intercourse, stripped of those privileges, is common to all.

Yet there is one view, in which the license may be allowed considerable influence in sustaining the decision of this Court.

It has been contended, that the grants of power to the United States over any subject, do not, necessarily, paralyze the arm of the States, or deprive them of the capacity to act on the same subject. That this can be the effect only of prohibitory provisions in their own constitutions, or in that of the general government. The *vis vitae* of power is still existing in the States, if not extinguished by the constitution of the United States. That, although as to all those grants of power which may be called aboriginal, with relation to the government, brought into existence by the constitution, they, of course, are out of the reach of State power; yet, as to all concessions of powers which previously existed in the States, it was otherwise. The practice of our government certainly has been, on many subjects, to occupy so much only of the field opened to them, as they think the public interests require. Witness the jurisdiction of the Circuit Courts, limited both as to cases and as to amount; and various other instances that might be cited. But the license furnishes a full answer to this objection; for, although one grant of power over commerce, should not be deemed a total relinquishment of power over the subject, but amounting only to a power to assume, still the power of the States must be at an end, so far as the United States have, by their legislative act, taken the subject under their immediate superintendence. So far as relates to the commerce coastwise, the act under which this license is granted, contains a full expression of Congress on this subject. Vessels, from five tons upwards, carrying on the coasting trade, are made the subject of regulation by that act. And this license proves, that this vessel has complied with that act, and been regularly ingrafted into one class of the commercial marine of the country.

It remains, to consider the objections to this opinion, as presented by the counsel for the appellee. On those which had relation to the particular character of this boat, whether as a steam boat or a ferry boat, I have only to remark, that in both those characters, she is expressly recognised as an object of the provisions which related to licenses.

The 12th section of the act of 1793, has these words: "That when the master of any ship or vessel, *ferry boats* excepted, shall be changed," &c. And the act which exempts licensed steam boats from the provisions against alien interests, shows such boats to be both objects of the licensing act, and objects of that act, when employed exclusively within our bays and rivers.

But the principal objections to these opinions arise, 1st. From the unavoidable action of some of the municipal powers of the States, upon commercial subjects.

2d. From passages in the constitution, which are supposed to imply a *concurrent* power in the States in regulating commerce.

It is no objection to the existence of distinct, substantive powers, that, in their application, they bear upon the same subject. The same bale of goods, the same cask of provisions, or the same ship, that may be the subject of commercial regulation, may also be the vehicle of disease. And the health laws that require them to be stopped and ventilated, are no more intended as regulations on commerce, than the laws which permit their importation, are intended to innoculate the community with disease. Their different purposes mark the distinction between the powers brought into action; and while frankly exercised, they can produce no serious collision. As to laws affecting ferries, turnpike roads, and other subjects of the same class, so far from meriting the epithet of commercial regulations, they are, in fact, commercial facilities, for which, by the consent of mankind, a compensation is paid, upon the same principle that the whole commercial world submit to pay light money to the Danes. Inspection laws are of a more equivocal nature, and it is obvious that the constitution has viewed that subject with much solicitude. But so far from sustaining an inference in favour of the power of the States over commerce, I cannot but think that the guarded provisions of the 10th section, on this subject, furnish a strong argument against that inference. It was obvious, that inspection laws must combine municipal with commercial regulations; and, while the power over the subject is yielded to the States, for obvious reasons, an absolute control is given over State legislation on the subject, as far as that legislation may be exercised, so as to affect the commerce of the country. The inferences, to be correctly drawn, from this whole article, appear to me to be altogether in favour of the exclusive grants to Congress of power over commerce, and the reverse of that which the appellee contends for.

This section contains the positive restrictions imposed by the constitution upon State power. The first clause of it, specifies those powers which the States are precluded from exercising, even though the Congress were to permit them. The second, those which the States may exercise with the consent of Congress. And here the sedulous attention to the subject of State exclusion from commercial power, is strongly marked. Not satisfied with the express grant to the United States of the power over commerce, this clause negatives the exercise of that power to the States, as to the only two objects which could ever tempt them to assume the exercise of that power, to wit, the collection of a revenue from imposts and duties on imports and exports; or from a tonnage duty. As to imposts on imports or exports, such a revenue might have been aimed at *directly*, by express legislation, or *indirectly*, in the form of inspection laws; and it became necessary to guard against both. Hence, first, the consent of Congress to such imposts or duties, is made necessary; and as to inspection laws, it is limited to the minimum of expenses. Then, the money so raised shall be paid into the treasury of the United States, or may be sued for, since it is declared to be for their use. And lastly, all such laws may be modified, or repealed, by an act of Congress. It is impossible for a right to be more guarded. As to a tonnage duty, that could be recovered in but one way; and a sum so raised, being obviously necessary for the execution of health laws, and other unavoidable port expenses, it was intended that it should go into the State treasuries; and nothing more was required, therefore, than the consent of Congress. But this whole clause, as to these two subjects, appears to have been introduced *ex abundanti cautela*, to remove every temptation to an attempt to interfere with the powers of Congress over commerce, and to show how far Congress might consent to permit the States to exercise that power. Beyond those limits, even by the consent of Congress, they could not exercise it. And thus, we have the whole effect of the clause. The inference which counsel would deduce from it, is neither necessary nor consistent with the general purpose of the clause.

But instances have been insisted on, with much confidence, in argument, in which, by municipal laws, particular regulations respecting their cargoes have been imposed upon shipping in the ports of the United States; and one, in which forfeiture was made the penalty of disobedience.

Until such laws have been tested by exceptions to their constitutionality, the argument certainly wants much of the force attributed to it; but admitting their constitutionality, they present only the familiar case of punishment inflicted by both governments upon the same individual. He who robs the mail, may also steal the horse that carries it, and would, unquestionably, be subject to punishment, at the same time, under the laws of the State in which the crime is committed, and under those of the United States. And these punishments may interfere, and one render it impossible to inflict the other, and yet the two governments would be acting under powers that have no claim to identity.

It would be in vain to deny the possibility of a clashing and collision between the measures of the two governments. The line cannot be drawn with sufficient distinctness between the municipal powers of the one, and the commercial powers of the other. In some points they meet and blend so as scarcely to admit of separation. Hitherto the only remedy has been applied which the case admits of; that of a frank and candid co-operation for the general good. Witness the laws of Congress requiring its officers to respect the inspection laws of the States, and to aid in enforcing their health laws; that which surrenders to the States the superintendence of pilotage, and the many laws passed to permit a tonnage duty to be levied for the use of their ports. Other instances could be cited, abundantly to prove that collision must be sought to be produced; and when it does arise, the question must be decided how far the powers of Congress are adequate to put it down. Wherever the powers of the respective governments are frankly exercised, with a distinct view to the ends of such powers, they may act upon the same object, or use the same means, and yet the powers be kept perfectly distinct. A resort to the same means, therefore, is no argument to prove the identity of their respective powers.

I have not touched upon the right of the States to grant patents for inventions or improvements, generally, because it does not necessarily arise in this cause. It is enough for all the purposes of this decision, if they cannot exercise it so as to restrain a free intercourse among the States.

17

Brown v. Maryland
12 Wheat. 419 (1827)

Mr. Chief Justice Marshall delivered the opinion of the court:

This is a writ of error to a judgment rendered in the Court of Appeals of Maryland, affirming a judgment of the City Court of Baltimore, on an indictment found in that court against the plaintiffs in error, for violating an act of the legislature of Maryland. The indictment was founded on the second section of that act, which is in these words: "And be it enacted, that all importers of foreign articles or commodities, of dry goods, wares, or merchandise, by bale or package, or of wine, rum, brandy, whiskey and other distilled spirituous liquors, &c., and other persons selling the same by wholesale, bale or package, hogshead, barrel, or tierce, shall, before they are authorized to sell, take out a license, as by the original act is directed, for which they shall pay fifty dollars; and in case of neglect or refusal to take out such license, shall be subject to the same penalties and forfeitures as are prescribed by the original act to which this is a supplement." The indictment charges the plaintiffs in error with having imported and sold one package of foreign dry goods without having license to do so. A judgment was rendered against them on demurrer for the penalty which the act prescribes for the offense; and that judgment is now before this court.

The cause depends entirely on the question, whether the legislature of a state can constitutionally require the importer of foreign articles to take out a license from the state, before he shall be permitted to sell a bale or package so imported.

It has been truly said, that the presumption is in favor of every legislative act, and that the whole burthen of proof lies on him who denies its constitutionality. The plaintiffs in error take the burthen upon themselves, and insist that the act under consideration is repugnant to two provisions in the constitution of the United States:

1. To that which declares that "no state shall, without the consent of Congress, lay any imposts, or duties on imports or exports, except what may be absolutely necessary for executing its inspection laws."

2. To that which declares that Congress shall have power "to regulate commerce with foreign nations, and among the several states, and with the Indian tribes."

1. The first inquiry is into the extent of the prohibition upon states "to lay any imposts or duties on imports or exports." The counsel for the state of Maryland would confine this prohibition to the laws imposing duties on the act of importation or exportation. The counsel for the plaintiffs in error give them a much wider scope.

In performing the delicate and important duty of constructing clauses in the constitution of our country, which involve conflicting powers of the government of the Union, and of the respective states, it is proper to take a view of the literal meaning of the words to be expounded, of their connection with other words, and of the general objects to be accomplished by the prohibitory clause, or by the grant of power.

What, then, is the meaning of the words, "imposts, or duties on imports or exports?"

An impost, or duty on imports, is a custom or a tax levied on articles brought into a country, and is most usually secured before the importer is allowed to exercise his rights of ownership over them, because evasions of the law can be prevented more certainly by executing it while the articles are in its custody. It would not, however, be less an impost or duty on the articles, if it were to be levied on them after they were landed. The policy and consequent practice of levying or securing the duty before, or on entering the port, does not limit the power to that state of things, nor, consequently, the prohibition, unless the true meaning of the clause so confines it. What, then, are "imports?" The lexicons inform us, they are "things imported." If we appeal to usage for the meaning of the word, we shall receive the same answer. They are the articles themselves which are brought into the country. "A duty on imports," then, is not merely a duty on the act of importation, but is a duty on the thing imported. It is not, taken in its literal sense, confined to a duty levied while the article is entering the country, but extends to a duty levied after it has entered the country. The succeeding words of the sentence which limit the prohibition, show the extent in which it was understood. The limitation is, "except what may be absolutely necessary for executing its inspection laws." Now, the inspection laws, so far as they act upon articles for exportation, are generally executed on land, before the article is put on board the vessel; so far as they act upon importations, they are generally executed upon articles which are landed. The tax or duty of inspection, then is a tax which is frequently, if not always, paid for service performed on land, while the article is in the bosom of the country. Yet this tax is an exception to the prohibition on the states to lay duties on imports or exports. The exception was made because the tax would otherwise have been within the prohibition.

If it be a rule of interpretation to which all assent, that the exception of a particular thing from general words, proves that, in the opinion of the law-giver, the thing excepted would be within the general clause had the exception not been made, we know no reason why this general rule should not be as applicable to the constitution as to other instruments. If it be applicable, then this exception in favor of duties for the support of inspection laws, goes far in proving that the framers of the constitution classed taxes of a similar character with those imposed for the purposes of inspection, with duties on imports and exports, and supposed them to be prohibited.

If we quit this narrow view of the subject, and passing from the literal interpretation of the words, look to the objects of the prohibition, we find no reason for withdrawing the act under consideration from its operation.

From the vast inequality between the different states of the confederacy, as to commercial advantages, few subjects were viewed with deeper interest, or excited more irritation, than the manner in which the several states exercised, or seemed disposed to exercise, the power of laying duties on imports. From motives which were deemed sufficient by the statesmen of that day, the general power of taxation, indispensably necessary as it was and jealous as the states were of any encroachment on it, was so far abridged as to forbid them to touch imports or exports, with the single exception which has been noticed. Why are they restrained from imposing these duties? Plainly because, in the general opinion, the interest of all would be best promoted by placing that whole subject under the control of Congress. Whether the prohibition to "lay imposts, or duties on imports or exports," proceeded from an apprehension that the power might be so exercised as to disturb that equality among the states which was generally advantageous, or that harmony between them which it was desirable to preserve, or to maintain unimpaired our commercial connections with foreign nations, or to confer this source of revenue on the government of the Union, or whatever other motive might have induced the prohibition, it is plain that the object would be as completely defeated by a power to tax the article in the hands of the importer the instant it was landed as by a power to tax it while entering the port. There is no difference, in effect, between a power to prohibit the sale of an article and a power to prohibit its introduction into the country. The one would be a necessary consequence of the other. No goods would be imported if none could be sold. No object of any description can be accomplished by laying a duty on importation, which may not be accomplished with equal certainty by laying a duty on the thing imported in the hands of the importer. It is obvious that the same power which imposes a light duty can impose a very heavy one, one which amounts to a prohibition. Questions of power do not depend on the degree to which it may be exercised. If it may be exercised at all, it must be exercised at the will of those in whose hands it is placed. If the tax may be levied in this form by a state, it may be levied to an extent which will defeat the revenue by impost, so far as it is drawn from importations into the particular state. We are told, that such wild and irrational abuse of power is not to be apprehended, and is not to be taken into view when discussing its existence. All power may be abused; and if the fear of its abuse is to constitute an argument against its existence, it might be urged against the existence of that which is universally acknowledged, and which is indispensable to the general safety. The states will never be so mad as to destroy their own commerce, or even to lessen it.

We do not dissent from these general propositions. We do not suppose any state would act so unwisely. But we do not place the question on that ground.

These arguments apply with precisely the same force against the whole prohibition. It might, with the same reason be said, that no state would be so blind to its own interests as to lay duties on importation which would either prohibit or diminish its trade. Yet the framers of our constitution have thought this a power which no state ought to exercise. Conceding, to the full extent which is required, that every state would, in its legislation on this subject, provide judiciously for its own interest, it cannot be conceded that each would respect the interest of others. A duty on imports is a tax on the article, which is paid by the consumer. The great importing states would thus levy a tax on the non-importing states, which would not be less a tax because their interest would afford ample security against its ever being so heavy as to expel commerce from their ports.

This would necessarily produce countervailing measures on the part of those states whose situation was less favorable to importation. For this, among other reasons, the whole power of laying duties on imports was, with a single and slight exception, taken from the states. When we are inquiring whether a particular act is within this prohibition, the question is not, whether the state may so legislate as to hurt itself, but whether the act is within the words and mischief of the prohibitory clause. It has already been shown that a tax on the article in the hands of the importer is within its words; and we think it too clear for controversy, that the same tax is within its mischief. We think it unquestionable, that such a tax has precisely the same tendency to enhance the price of the article as if imposed upon it while entering the port.

The counsel for the state of Maryland insist, with great reason, that if the words of the prohibition be taken in their utmost latitude, they will abridge the power of taxation, which all admit to be essential to the states, to an extent which has never yet been suspected, and will deprive them of resources which are necessary to supply revenue, and which they have heretofore been admitted to possess. These words must therefore be construed with some limitation; and, if this be admitted, they insist, that entering the country is the point of time when the prohibition ceases, and the power of the state to tax commences.

It may be conceded that the words of the prohibition ought not to be pressed to their utmost extent; that in our complex system, the object of the powers conferred on the government of the Union, and the nature of the often conflicting powers which remain in the states, must always be taken into view, and may aid in expounding the words of any particular clause. But, while we admit that sound principles of construction ought to restrain all courts from carrying the words of the prohibition beyond the object the constitution is intended to secure, that there must be a point of time when the prohibition ceases, and the power of the state to tax commences; we cannot admit that this point of time is the instant that the articles enter the country. It is, we think, obvious, that this construction would defeat the prohibition.

The constitutional prohibition on the states to lay a duty on imports—a prohibition which a vast majority of them must feel an interest in preserving—may certainly come in conflict with their acknowledged power to tax persons and property within their territory. The power, and the restriction on it, though quite distinguishable when they do not approach each other, may yet, like the intervening colors between white and black, approach so nearly as to perplex the understanding, as colors perplex the vision in marking the distinction between them. Yet the distinction exists, and must be marked as the cases arise. Till they do arise, it might be premature to state any rule as being universal in its application. It is sufficient for the present to say, generally, that when the importer has so acted upon the thing imported that it has become incorporated and mixed up with the mass of property in the country, it has, perhaps, lost its distinctive character as an import, and has become subject to the taxing power of the state; but while remaining the property of the importer, in his warehouse, in the original form or package in which it was imported, a tax upon it is too plainly a duty on imports to escape the prohibition in the constitution.

The counsel for the plaintiffs in error contend that the importer purchases, by payment of the duty to the United

States, a right to dispose of his merchandise, as well as to bring it into the country; and certainly the argument is supported by strong reason, as well as by the practice of nations, including our own. The object of importation is sale; it constitutes the motive for paying the duties; and if the United States possess the power of conferring the right to sell, as the consideration for which the duty is paid, every principle of fair dealing requires that they should be understood to confer it. The practice of the most commercial nations conforms to this idea. Duties, according to that practice, are charged on those articles only which are intended for sale or consumption in the country. Thus, sea stores, goods imported and re-exported in the same vessel, goods landed and carried over land for the purpose of being re-exported from some other port, goods forced in by stress of weather, and landed, but not for sale, are exempted from the payment of duties. The whole course of legislation on the subject shows that, in the opinion of the legislature, the right to sell is connected with the payment of duties.

The counsel for the defendant in error have endeavored to illustrate their proposition, that the constitutional prohibition ceases the instant the goods enter the country, by an array of the consequences which they suppose must follow the denial of it. If the importer acquires the right to sell by the payment of duties, he may, they say, exert that right when, where, and as he pleases, and the state cannot regulate it. He may sell by retail, at auction, or as an itinerant peddler. He may introduce articles, as gunpowder, which endanger a city, into the midst of its population; he may introduce articles which endanger the public health, and the power of self-preservation is denied. An importer may bring in goods, as plate, for his own use, and thus retain much valuable property exempt from taxation.

These objections to the principle, if well founded, would certainly be entitled to serious consideration. But we think they will be found, on examination, not to belong necessarily to the principle, and, consequently, not to prove that it may not be resorted to with safety, as a criterion by which to measure the extent of the prohibition.

This indictment is against the importer, for selling a package of dry goods in the form in which it was imported, without a license. This state of things is changed if he sells them, or otherwise mixes them with the general property of the state, by breaking up his packages, and traveling with them as an itinerant peddler. In the first case, the tax intercepts the import, as an import, in its way to become incorporated with the general mass of property, and denies it the privilege of becoming so incorporated until it shall have contributed to the revenue of the state. It denies to the importer the right of using the privilege which he has purchased from the United States, until he shall have also purchased it from the state. In the last cases, the tax finds the article already incorporated with the mass of property by the act of the importer. He has used the privilege he had purchased, and has himself mixed them up with the common mass, and the law may treat them as it finds them. The same observations apply to plate, or other furniture used by the importer.

So, if he sells by auction. Auctioneers are persons licensed by the state, and if the importer chooses to employ them, he can as little object to paying for this service as for any other for which he may apply to an officer of the state. The right of sale may very well be annexed to importation, without annexing to it, also, the privilege of using the officers licensed by the state to make sales in a peculiar way.

The power to direct the removal of gunpowder is a branch of the police power, which unquestionably remains, and ought to remain, with the states. If the possessor stores it himself out of town, the removal cannot be a duty on imports, because it contributes nothing to the revenue. If he prefers placing it in a public magazine it is because he stores it there, in his own opinion, more advantageously than elsewhere. We are not sure that this may not be classed among inspection laws. The removal or destruction of infectious or unsound articles is, undoubtedly, an exercise of that power, and forms an express exception to the prohibition we are considering. Indeed, the laws of the United States expressly sanction the health laws of a state.

The principle, then, for which the plaintiffs in error contend, that the importer acquires a right, not only to bring the articles into the country, but to mix them with the common mass of property, does not interfere with the necessary power of taxation which is acknowledged to reside in the states, to that dangerous extent which the counsel for the defendants in error seem to apprehend. It carries the prohibition in the constitution no farther than to prevent the states from doing that which it was the great object of the constitution to prevent.

But if it should be proved that a duty on the article itself would be repugnant to the constitution, it is still argued that this is not a tax upon the article, but on the person. The state, it is said, may tax occupations, and this is nothing more.

It is impossible to conceal from ourselves that this is varying the form, without varying the substance. It is treating a prohibition which is general, as if it were confined to a particular mode of doing the forbidden thing. All must perceive that a tax on the sale of an article, imported only for sale, is a tax on the article itself. It is true, the state may tax occupations generally, but this tax must be paid by those who employ the individual, or is a tax on his business. The lawyer, the physician, or the mechanic, must either charge more on the article in which he deals, or the thing itself is taxed through his person. This the state has a right to do, because no constitutional prohibition extends to it. So, a tax on the occupation of an importer is, in like manner, a tax on importation. It must add to the price of the article, and be paid by the consumer, or by the importer himself, in like manner as a direct duty on the article itself would be made. This the state has not a right to do, because it is prohibited by the constitution.

In support of the argument, that the prohibition ceases the instant that the goods are brought into the country, a comparison has been drawn between the opposite words export and import. As, to export, it is said, means only to carry goods out of the country, so, to import, means only to bring them into it. But, suppose we extend this comparison to the two prohibitions. The states are forbidden to lay a duty on exports, and the United States are forbidden to lay a tax or duty on articles exported from any state. There is some diversity in language, but none is perceivable in the act which is prohibited. The United States have the same right to tax occupations which is possessed by the states. Now, suppose the United States should require every exporter to take out a license, for which he should pay such tax as Congress might think proper to impose; would government be permitted to shield itself from the just censure to which this attempt to evade the prohibitions of the constitution would expose it, by saying that this was a tax on the person, not on the article, and that the legislature had a right to tax occupations? Or, suppose revenue cutters were to be stationed off the coast for the purpose of levying a duty on all merchandise found in vessels which were leaving the United States for foreign countries; would it be received as an excuse for this outrage, were the government to say that exportation meant no more than carrying goods out of the country, and as the prohibition to lay a tax on imports, or things imported, ceased the instant they were brought into the country, so the prohibition to tax articles exported ceased when they were carried out of the country?

We think, then, that the act under which the plaintiffs in error were indicted, is repugnant to that article of the constitution which declares that "no state shall lay any impost or duties on imports or exports."

2. Is it also repugnant to that clause in the constitution which empowers "Congress to regulate commerce with foreign nations, and among the several states, and with the Indian tribes?"

The oppressed and degraded state of commerce previous to the adoption of the constitution can scarcely be forgotten. It was regulated by foreign nations with a single view to their own interests; and our disunited efforts to counteract their restrictions were rendered impotent by want of combination. Congress, indeed, possessed the power of making treaties; but the inability of the federal government to enforce them had become so apparent as to render that power in a great degree useless. Those who felt the injury arising from this state of things, and those who were capable of estimating the influence of commerce on the prosperity of nations, perceived the necessity of giving the control over this important subject to a single government. It may be doubted whether any of the evils proceeding from the feebleness of the federal government contributed more to that great revolution which introduced the present system, than the deep and general conviction that commerce ought to be regulated by Congress. It is not, therefore, matter of surprise, that the grant should be as extensive as the mischief, and should comprehend all foreign commerce and all commerce among the states. To construe the power so as to impair its efficacy, would tend to defeat an object, in the attainment of which the American public took, and justly took, that strong interest which arose from a full conviction of its necessity.

What, then, is the just extent of a power to regulate commerce with foreign nations, and among the several states?

This question was considerd in the case of *Gibbons* v. *Ogden* (9 Wheat. Rep., 1), in which it was declared to be complete in itself, and to acknowledge no limitations other than are prescribed by the constitution. The power is coextensive with the subject on which it acts, and cannot be stopped at the external boundary of a state, but must enter its interior.

We deem it unnecessary now to reason in support of these propositions. Their truth is proved by facts continually before our eyes, and was, we think, demonstrated, if they could require demonstration, in the case already mentioned.

If this power reaches the interior of a state, and may be there exercised, it must be capable of authorizing the sale of those articles which it introduces. Commerce is intercourse; one of its most ordinary ingredients is traffic. It is inconceivable that the power to authorize this traffic, when given in the most comprehensive terms, with the intent that its efficacy should be complete, should cease at the point when its continuance is indispensable to its value. To what purpose should the power to allow importation be given, unaccompanied with the power to authorize a sale of the thing imported? Sale is the object of importation, and is an essential ingredient of that intercourse, of which importation constitutes a part. It is as essential an ingredient, as indispensable to the existence of the entire thing, then, as importation itself. It must be considered as a component part of the power to regulate commerce. Congress has a right, not only to authorize importation, but to authorize the importer to sell.

If this be admitted—and we think it cannot be denied—what can be the meaning of an act of Congress which authorizes importation, and offers the privilege for sale at a fixed price to every person who chooses to become a purchaser? How is it to be construed, if an intent to deal honestly and fairly, an intent as wise as it is moral, is to enter into the construction? What can be the use of the contract? what does the importer purchase, if he does not purchase the privilege to sell?

What would be the language of a foreign government, which should be informed that its merchants, after importing according to law, were forbidden to sell the merchandise imported? What answer would the United States give to the complaints and just reproaches to which such an extraordinary circumstance would expose them? No apology could be received, or even offered. Such a state of things would break up commerce. It will not meet this argument to say that this state of things will never be produced; that the good sense of the states is a sufficient security against it. The constitution has not confided this subject to that good sense. It is placed elsewhere. The question is, where does the power reside? not, how far will it be probably abused? The power claimed by the state is, in its nature, in conflict with that given to Congress; and the greater or less extent in which it may be exercised does not enter into the inquiry concerning its existence.

We think, then, that if the power to authorize a sale exists in Congress, the conclusion that the right to sell is connected with the law permitting importation, as an inseparable incident, is inevitable.

If the principles we have stated be correct, the result to which they conduct us cannot be mistaken. Any penalty inflicted on the importer for selling the article in his character of importer, must be in opposition to the act of Congress which authorizes importation. Any charge on the introduction and incorporation of the articles into and with the mass of property in the country, must be hostile to the power given to Congress to regulate commerce, since an essential part of that regulation, and principal object of it, is to prescribe the regular means for accomplishing that introduction and incorporation.

The distinction between a tax on the thing imported, and on the person of the importer, can have no influence on this part of the subject. It is too obvious for controversy, that they interfere equally with the power to regulate commerce.

It has been contended, that this construction of the power to regulate commerce, as was contended in construing the prohibition to lay duties on imports, would abridge the acknowledged power of a state to tax its own citizens, or their property within its territory.

We admit this power to be sacred; but cannot admit that it may be used so as to obstruct the free course of a power given to Congress. We cannot admit that it may be used so as to obstruct or defeat the power to regulate commerce. It has been observed, that the powers remaining with the states may be so exercised as to come in conflict with those vested in Congress. When this happens, that which is not supreme must yield to that which is supreme. This great and universal truth is inseparable from the nature of things, and the constitution has applied it to the often interfering powers of the general and state governments, as a vital principle of perpetual operation. It results, necessarily, from this principle, that the taxing power of the states must have some limits. It cannot reach and restrain the action of the national government within its proper sphere. It cannot reach the administration of justice in the courts of the Union, or the collection of the taxes of the United States, or restrain the operation of any law which Congress may constitutionally pass. It cannot interfere with any regulation of commerce. If the states may tax all persons and property found on their territory, what shall restrain them from taxing goods in their transit through the state from one port to another, for the purpose of re-exportation? The laws of trade authorize this operation, and general convenience requires it. Or what should restrain a state from taxing any article passing through it from one state to another, for the purpose of traffic? or from taxing the transportation of articles passing from the state itself to another state, for commercial purposes? These cases are all within the sovereign power of taxation, but would obviously derange the measures of Congress to regulate commerce, and affect materially the purpose for which that power was given. We deem it unnecessary to press this argument further, or to give additional illustrations of it, because the subject was taken up, and considered with great attention, in *McCulloch* v. *The State of Maryland* (4 Wheat. Rep., 316), the decision in which case is, we think, entirely applicable to this.

It may be proper to add, that we suppose the principles laid down in this case, to apply equally to importations from a sister state. We do not mean to give any opinion on a tax discriminating between foreign and domestic articles.

We think there is error in the judgment of the Court of Appeals of the State of Maryland, in affirming the judgment of the Baltimore City Court, because the act of the legislature of Maryland, imposing the penalty for which the said judgment is rendered, is repugnant to the constitution of the United States, and, consequently, void. The judgment is to be reversed, and the cause remanded to that court, with instructions to enter judgment in favor of the appellants.

Mr. Justice THOMPSON dissented: It is with some reluctance, and very considerable diffidence, that I have brought myself publicly to dissent from the opinion of the court in this case; and did it not involve an important constitutional question relating to the relative powers of the general and state governments, I should silently acquiesce in the judgment of the court, although my own opinion might not accord with theirs.

The case comes before this court on a writ of error to the Court of Appeals of the state of Maryland, upon a judgment rendered in that court against the defendants. The proceedings in the court below were upon an indictment against the defendants, merchants in the city of Baltimore, trading under the firm of Alexander Brown & Sons, and to recover against them the penalty alleged to have been incurred, for a violation of an act of the legislature of that state, by selling a package of foreign dry goods without having a license for that purpose, as required by said act; and the only question which has been made and argued is, whether the act referred to is in violation of the constitution of the United States.

The act in question was passed on the 23d of February, 1822, and is entitled, "A supplement to the act laying duties on licenses to retailers of dry goods, and for other purposes." By the second section, under which the penalty has been recovered, it is enacted, "that all importers of foreign articles or commodities, of dry goods, wares, or merchandise, by bale or package, or of wine, rum, brandy, whiskey, and other distilled spirituous liquors, &c.; and other persons selling the same by wholesale, bale, or package, hogshead, barrel, or tierce, shall, before they are authorized to sell, take out a license, as by the original act is directed, for which they shall pay fifty dollars; and, in case of neglect or refusal to take out such license, shall be subject to the same penalties and forfeitures as are prescribed by the original act to which this is a supplement."

By the original act, passed in 1819, retail dealers in foreign merchandise are required to take out a license; and the supplemental act requires that wholesale dealers should likewise take out a license to sell. These acts being *in pari materia*, are to be taken together, and their effect and operation manifestly is nothing more than to require retail and wholesale dealers in foreign merchandise to take out a license before they should be authorized to sell such merchandise. The act does not require a license to import, or demand anything more of the importer than is required of any other dealer in the article imported. The license is for selling, and is general, applying to all persons: that all importers, and other persons selling by wholesale, bale, or package, &c., shall, before they are authorized to sell, take out a license, &c.

I understand it to be admitted that these laws, so far as they relate to retail dealers, are not in violation of the constitution of the United States; and, if so, the question resolves itself into the inquiry, whether a distinction in this respect between a retail and wholesale dealer in foreign merchandise, can exist under any sound construction of the constitution.

The parts of the constitution which have been drawn in question on the discussion at the bar, and with which the law in question is supposed to be in conflict, are, that which gives to Congress the power to regulate commerce with foreign nations, and among the several states, and that which declares that no state shall, without the consent of Congress, lay any imposts, or duties on imports or exports, except what may be absolutely necessary for executing its inspection laws.

It is very obvious, that this law can in no manner whatever affect the commercial intercourse between the states; it applies purely to the internal trade of the state of Maryland. The defendants were merchants trading in the city of Baltimore. The indictment describes them as such, and alleges the sale to have been in that place; and nothing appears to warrant an inference that the package of goods sold was not intended for consumption at that place; and the law has no relation whatever to goods intended for transportation to another state. It is proper here to notice, that although the indictment alleges that the defendants did import and sell, yet the district-attorney, in framing the indictment, very properly considered the offense to consist in the selling, and not in the importation without a license. No one will pretend, that if the indictment had only alleged that the defendants did import a package of foreign dry goods without a license, it could have been sustained. The act applies to the importer, and other persons selling by wholesale; and the allegation that the defendants did import, is merely descriptive of the double character in which they were dealing, both as importers and sellers. The indictment would, undoubtedly, have been good, had it merely alleged that the defendants sold the package without a license. So that neither the act, nor the form in which the complaint is presented, makes any discrimination between the importer and any other wholesale dealer in foreign merchandise, but requires both to take out a license to sell; nor does it appear to me that this law in any manner infringes or conflicts with the ·power of Congress to regulate commerce with foreign nations. It is to be borne in mind, that this was a power possessed by the states respectively before the adoption of the constitution, and is not a power growing out of the establishment of the general government. It is to be viewed, therefore, as the surrender of a power antecedently possessed by the states, and the extent of the surrender must receive a fair and reasonable interpretation with reference to the object for which the surrender was made. This was principally with a view to the revenue, and extended only to the external commerce of the United States, and did not em-

brace any portion of the internal trade or commerce of the several states. This is not only the plain and obvious interpretation of the terms used in the constitution, commerce with foreign nations; but such has been the construction adopted by this court. In the case of *Gibbons* v. *Ogden* (9 Wheat. Rep., 194), the court, in speaking of the grant of the power of Congress to regulate commerce, say: "It is not intended to comprehend that commerce which is completely internal, which is carried on between man and man in a state, or between different parts of the same state, and which does not extend to, or affect other states; such a power would be inconvenient, and is certainly unnecessary. The enumeration of the particular classes of commerce to which the power was to be extended, would not have been made had the intention been to extend the power to every description. The enumeration presupposes something not enumerated, and that something, if we regard the language on the subject of the sentence must be the exclusively internal commerce of a state. The genius and character of the whole government seems to be, that its action is to be applied to all the external concerns of the nation, and to those internal concerns which affect the states generally, but not to those which are completely within a particular state, which do not affect other states, and with which it is not necessary to interfere for the purpose of executing some of the general powers of the government. The completely internal commerce of a state, then, may be considered as reserved for the state itself." And, again, (208) "the acknowledged power of a state to regulate its police, its domestic trade, and to govern its own citizens, may enable it to legislate on this subject (commerce) to a considerable extent."

If such be the division of power between the general and state governments in relation to commerce, where is the line to be drawn between internal and external commerce? It appears to me, that no other sound and practical rule can be adopted, than to consider the external commerce as ending with the importation of the foreign article; and the importation is complete as soon as the goods are introduced into the country, according to the provisions of the revenue laws, with the intention of being sold here for consumption, or for the purpose of internal and domestic trade, and the duties paid or secured. And this is the light in which this question has been considered by this and other courts of the United States (5 Cranch, 368; 9 Cranch, 104; 1 Mason, 499). This, it will be perceived, does not embrace foreign merchandise intended for exportation, and not for consumption; nor articles intended for commerce between the states; but such as are intended for domestic trade within the state; and it is to such articles only that the law of Maryland extends. I cannot, therefore, think, that this law at all interferes with the power of Congress to regulate commerce; nor does it, according to my understanding of the constitution, violate that provision, which declares that no state shall, without the consent of Congress, lay any imposts or duties on imports or exports, except what may be absolutely necessary for executing its inspection laws.

The compensation required by this law to be paid for a license to sell, cannot be considered an impost or duty, within the sense and meaning of these terms, as used in the constitution. They refer to the foreign duty, and not to any charge that may grow out of the internal police of the states. It may indirectly fall on the imported articles, and enhance the price in the sale; but even this is not an expense imposed on the importer or other seller, but is borne ultimately by the consumer.

But the broad principle has been assumed on the argument, that the payment of the foreign duty is a purchase of the right and privilege, not only of introducing the goods into the country, but of selling them free from any increased burden imposed by the states; and, unless this principle can be sustained, the law in question is not in violation of the constitution.

The counsel, however, aware that the principle thus broadly laid down, if practically carried out to its full extent, would lead to consequences so obviously untenable, that it would at once show the unsoundness of the principle itself, have limited its application to the first wholesale disposition of the merchandise. Can such a distinction, however, be sustained? There is nothing, certainly, in the letter of the constitution to support it; nor does it fall within reasonable intendment growing out of the nature of the subject-matter of the provision. The prohibition to the states is against laying any impost or duty on imports. It is the merchandise that is exempted from the imposition. The constitution nowhere gives any extraordinary protection to the importer. So that, if the law was confined to the importer only, he could find no exemption from the operation of state laws. Nor is there, according to my judgment, any rational grounds upon which the constitution may be considered as extending such exemption to wholesale, and not to retail dealers. If the payment of the foreign duty is the purchase of the privilege to sell, as well as to introduce the article into the country, where can be the difference whether this privilege is exercised in the one way or the other? The retail merchant often imports his own goods; and why should he be compelled to take out a license to sell, when his neighbor, who imports and sells by wholesale, is exempted. But the distinction is altogether fruitless, and does not effect the object supposed to have been intended, viz., to take from the states the power of imposing burdens upon foreign merchandise, that might tend to lessen or entirely prevent the importation, and thereby diminish the revenue of the United States. It is very evident that no such purpose can be accomplished, by limiting the protection to the first sale. It was admitted, that after the first sale, and the article becomes mixed and incorporated in the general mass of the property of the country, and to be applied to domestic use, it loses this pretended privilege. But everyone knows, that whatever charge or burden is imposed upon the retail sale, affects the wholesale indirectly, as much as if laid directly upon the wholesale. The retail dealer takes this charge into calculation in the purchase from the wholesale merchant, and which, of course, equally affects the importation. Suppose the $50 required to be paid by the wholesale dealer was imposed on the retail merchant, would it not equally affect the importation? It would equally increase the burden, and enhance the expense of the article when it comes into

the hands of the consumer, and on whom all the charges ultimately fall. And if these charges are so increased by the state governments, in any stages of the internal trade, as to check their sale for consumption, it will necessarily affect the importation. So that nothing short of a total exemption from state charges or taxes, under all circumstances, will answer the supposed object of the constitution. And to push the principle to such lengths, would be a restriction upon state authority, not warranted by the constitution.

It certainly cannot be maintained that the states have no authority to tax imported merchandise. But the same principle of discrimination between the wholesale and retail dealer, as to a license to sell, would seem to me, if well-founded, to extend to taxes of every description. And it would present a singular incongruity, to exempt a wholesale merchant from all taxes upon his stock of goods, and subject to taxation the like stock of his neighbor who was selling by retail.

It is laid down in No. 32 of the Federalist (and I believe universally admitted), "that the states, with the sole exception of duties on imports and exports, retain authority to tax in the most absolute and unqualified sense; and any attempt on the part of the national government to abridge them in the exercise of it, would be a violent assumption of power, unwarranted by any article or clause in the constitution." Although an impost or duty may be considered a tax in its most enlarged sense, yet every tax cannot be understood to mean an impost or duty in the sense of the constitution. As here used, it evidently refers to the foreign duty imposed by revenue laws. It would be a singular use of the term impost, to apply it to a tax on real estate; and no one, I presume, would contend that all imported articles upon which the duties have been paid are exempt from all state taxation in the hands of the consumer. And yet this would follow, if duty and tax are, in all respects, synonymous; for the constitution declares, that no state shall lay any duty on imports, viz., the article imported. To avoid these consequences, which are certainly inadmissible, the inhibition to the states must be understood as extending only to foreign duties, and not to taxes imposed by the states, after the imports become articles of internal trade, and for domestic use and consumption; they then become subject to state jurisdiction.

This law seems to have been treated as if it imposed a tax or duty upon the importer, or the importation. It certainly admits of no such construction. It is a charge upon the wholesale dealer, whoever he may be, and to operate upon the sale, and not upon the importation. It requires the purchase of a privilege to sell, and must stand on the same footing as a purchase of a privilege to sell in any other manner, as by retail, at auction, or as hawkers and peddlers, or in whatever way state policy may require. Whether such regulations are wise and politic, is not a question for this court. If the broad principle contended for on the part of the plaintiffs in error—that the payment of the foreign duty is a purchase of the privilege of selling—be well founded, no limit can be set by the states to the exercise of this privilege. The first sale may be made in defiance of all state regulation; and all state laws regulating sales of foreign goods at auction, and imposing a duty thereupon, are unconstitutional, so far, at all events, as the sale may be by bale, package, hogshead, barrel or tierce, &c. And, indeed, if the right to sell follows as an incident to the importation, it will take away all state control over infectious and noxious goods, whilst unsold, in the hands of the importer. The principle, when carried out to its full extent, would inevitably lead to such consequences.

It has been urged with great earnestness upon the court, that if the states are permitted to lay such charges and taxes upon imports, they may be so multiplied and increased as entirely to stop all importations. If this argument presents any serious objection to the law in question, the answer to it, in my judgment, has already been given: that the limitation, as contended for, of state power, will not effect the objects proposed. Whether this additional burden is imposed upon the wholesale or retail dealer, it will equally affect the importation: and nothing short of a total exemption from all taxation and charges of every description, will take from the states the power of legislating so as in some way may indirectly affect the importation.

But arguments drawn against the existence of a power from its supposed abuse are illogical, and generally lead to unsound conclusions. And this is emphatically so when applied to our system of government. It supposes the interest of the people, under the general and state governments, to be in hostility with each other, instead of considering the two governments as parts only of the same system, and forming but one government for the same people, having for its object the same common interest and welfare of all.

If the supposed abuse of a power is a satisfactory objection to its existence, it will equally apply to many of the powers of the general government; and it is as reasonable to suppose that the people would wish to injure or destroy themselves, through the instrumentality of the one government as the other.

The doctrine of the court in the case of *M'Culloch* v. *The State of Maryland* (4 Wheat. Rep., 316), has been urged as having a bearing upon this question unfavorable to the validity of the law. But it appears to me, that that case warrants no such conclusion. It is there admitted, that the power of taxation is an incident of sovereignty, and is co-extensive with that to which it is an incident. And that all subjects, over which the sovereign power of a state extends, are objects of taxation. The Bank of the United States could not be taxed by the states, because it was an instrument employed by the government in the execution of its powers. It was called into existence under the authority of the United States, and of course could not have previously existed as an object of taxation by the states. Not so, however, with respect to imports; they were in existence, and under the absolute jurisdiction and control of the states, before the adoption of the constitution. And it is, therefore, as to them, a question of surrender of power by the states, and to what extent this has been given up to the United States. And it is expressly admitted in that case, that the opinion did not deprive the states of any resources they originally possessed; nor to any tax paid by the real property of the bank in common with the other real property within the state; nor to a tax imposed on the interest which the citizens of Maryland may hold in the institution, in common with other property of the same description throughout the state. But the tax was held unconstitutional, because laid on the operations of the bank, and consequently a tax on the operation of an instrument employed by the government of the Union to carry its powers into execution; and this instrument, created by the government of the Union. But these objections do not apply to the law in question. The government of the Union found the states in the full exercise of sovereign power over imports. It was one of the sources of revenue originally possessed by the states. The law does not purport to act directly upon anything which has been surrendered to the general government, viz., the external commerce of the state. It may operate indirectly upon it to some extent; but cannot be made essentially to impede or retard the operations of the government; not more so than might be effected by a tax on the stock held by individuals in the Bank of the United States. And, indeed, the power of crippling the operations of the government, in the former case, would not be so practicable as in the latter; for it has the whole range of the property of its citizens for taxation and to provide the means for carrying on its measures. So that it would be beyond the reach of the states materially to affect the operations of the general government, by taxing foreign merchandise, should they be disposed so to do.

I am, accordingly, of opinion, that the judgment of the Court of Appeals of Maryland ought to be affirmed.

18

JAMES MADISON TO JOSEPH C. CABELL
18 Sept. 1828
Writings 9:316–40

Your late letter reminds me of our Conversation on the constitutionality of the power in Congs. to impose a tariff for the encouragmt. of Manufactures; and of my promise to sketch the grounds of the confident opinion I had expressed that it was among the powers vested in that Body. I had not forgotten my promise, & had even begun the task of fulfilling it; but frequent interruptions from other causes, being followed by a bilious indisposition, I have not been able sooner to comply with your request. The subjoined view of the subject, might have been advantageously expanded; but I leave that improvement to your own reflections and researches.

The Constitution vests in Congress expressly "the power to lay & collect taxes duties imposts & excises;" and "the power to regulate trade"

That the former Power, if not particularly expressed, would have been included in the latter, as one of the objects of a general power to regulate trade, is not necessarily impugned, as has been alledged, by its being so expressed. Examples of this sort, cannot sometimes be easily avoided, and are to be seen elsewhere in the Constitution. Thus the power "to define & punish offences agst. the law of Nations" includes the power, afterward particularly expressed "to make rules concerning captures &c., from offending Neutrals." So also, a power "to coin money," would doubtless include that of "regulating its value," had not the latter power been expressly inserted. The term taxes, if standing *alone,* would certainly have included, duties, imposts & excises. In another clause it is said, "no tax or duty shall be laid on imports [exports]," &c. Here the two terms are used as synonymous. And in another clause where it is said, "no State shall lay any imposts or duties" &c, the terms imposts & duties are synonymous. Pleonasms, tautologies & the promiscuous use of terms & phrases differing in their shades of meaning, (always to be expounded with reference to the context and under the controul of the general character & manifest scope of the Instrument in which they are found) are to be ascribed sometimes to the purpose of greater caution; sometimes to the imperfections of language; & sometimes to the imperfection of man himself. In this view of the subject, it was quite natural, however certainly the general power to regulate trade might include a power to impose duties on it, not to omit it in a clause enumerating the several modes of revenue authorized by the Constitution. In few cases could the *"ex majori cautela"* occur with more claim to respect.

Nor can it be inferred, as has been ingeniously attempted, that a power to regulate trade does not involve a power to tax it, from the distinction made in the original controversy with G. Britain, between a power to regulate trade with the Colonies & a power to tax them. A power to regulate trade between different parts of the Empire was confessedly *necessary;* and was admitted to lie, as far as that was the case in the British Parliament, the taxing part being at the same time denied to the Parliament, & asserted to be necessarily inherent in the Colonial Legislatures, as sufficient & the only safe depositories of the taxing power. So difficult was it nevertheless to maintain the distinction in practice, that the ingredient of revenue was occasionally overlooked or disregarded in the British regulations; as in the duty on sugar & Molasses imported into the Colonies. And it was fortunate that the attempt at an internal and direct tax in the case of the Stamp Act, produced a radical examination of the subject, before a regulation of trade with a view to revenue had grown into an established Authority. One thing at least is certain, that the main & admitted object of the Parliamentary *regulations* of trade with the Colonies, was the encouragement of *manufactures* in G. B.

But the present question is unconnected, with the former relations between G. B. and her Colonies, which were of a peculiar, a complicated, and, in several respects, of an undefined character. It is a simple question under the Constitution of the U. S. whether "the power to regulate trade with foreign nations" as a distinct & substantive item in the enumerated powers, embraces the object of encouraging by duties restrictions and prohibitions the manufactures & products of the Country? And the affirmative must be inferred from the following considerations:

1. The meaning of the Phrase "to regulate trade" must be sought in the general use of it, in other words in the objects to which the power was generally understood to be applicable, when the Phrase was inserted in the Constn.

2. The power has been understood and used by all commercial & manufacturing Nations as embracing the object of encouraging manufactures. It is believed that not a single exception can be named.

3. This has been particularly the case with G. B., whose commercial vocabulary is the parent of ours. A primary object of her commercial regulations is well known to have been the protection and encouragement of her manufactures

4. Such was understood to be a proper use of the power by the States most prepared for manufacturing industry, while retaining the power over their foreign trade. It was the aim of Virginia herself, as will presently appear, tho' at the time among the least prepared for such a use of her power to regulate trade.

5. Such a use of the power by Cong accords with the intention and expectation of the States in transferring the power over trade from themselves to the Govt. of the U. S. This was emphatically the case in the Eastern, the more manufacturing members of the Confederacy. Hear the language held in the Convention of Massts. p. 84, 86, 136.

By Mr. Dawes an advocate for the Constitution, it was observed: "our manufactures are another great subject which has recd. no encouragement by national Duties on foreign manufactures, and they never can by any authority in the Old Confedn" again "If we wish to *encourage our own manufactures,* to preserve our own commerce, to raise the value of our own lands, we must give Congs. the powers in question.

By Mr. Widgery, an opponent, "All we hear is, that the mercht. & farmer will flourish, & that the mechanic & tradesman are to make their fortunes directly, if the Constitution goes down.

The Convention of Massts. was the only one in N. Engd. whose debates have been preserved. But it cannot be doubted that the sentiment there expressed was common to the other States in that quarter, more especially to Connecticut & Rh Isld., the most thickly peopled of all the States, and having of course their thoughts most turned to the subject of manufactures. A like inference may be confidently applied to N. Jersey, whose debates in Convention have not been preserved. In the populous and manufacturing State of Pa:, a partial account only of the debates having been published, nothing certain is known of what passed in her Convention on this point. But ample evidence may be found elsewhere, that regulations of trade for the encouragement of manufactures, were considered as within the power to be granted to the new Congress, as well as within the scope of the National Policy. Of the States south of Pena., the only two in whose Conventions the debates have been preserved are Virga & N. Carola., and from these no adverse inferences can be drawn. Nor is there the slightest indication that either of the two States farthest South, whose debates in Convention if preserved have not been made public, viewed the encouragement of manufactures as not within the general power over trade to be transferred to the Govt. of the U. S.

6 If Congress have not the power it is annihilated for the nation; a policy without example in any other nation, and not within the reason of the solitary one in our own. The example alluded to is the prohibition of a tax on exports which resulted from the apparent impossibility of raising in that mode a revenue from the States proportioned to the ability to pay it; the ability of some being derived in a great measure, not from their exports, but from their fisheries, from their freights and from commerce at large, in some of its branches altogether external to the U. S.; the profits from all which being invisible & intangible would escape a tax on exports. A tax on imports, on the other hand, being a tax on consumption which is in proportion to the ability of the consumers whencesoever derived was free from that inequality.

7 If revenue be the sole object of a legitimate impost, and the encouragt. of domestic articles be not within the power of regulating trade it wd. follow that no monopolizing or unequal regulations of foreign Nations could be counteracted; that neither the staple articles of subsistence nor the essential implements for the public safety could under any circumstances be ensured or fostered at home by regulations of commerce, the usual & most convenient mode of providing for both; and that the American navigation, tho the source of naval defence, of a cheapening competition in carrying our valuable & bulky articles to Market, and of an independent carriage of them during foreign wars, when a foreign navigation might be withdrawn, must be at once abandoned or speedily destroyed; it being evident that a tonnage duty merely in foreign ports agst. our vessels, and an exemption from such a duty in our ports in favor of foreign vessels, must have the inevitable effect of banishing ours from the Ocean.

To assume a power to protect our navigation, & the cultivation & fabrication of all articles requisite for the Public safety as incident to the war power, would be a more latitudinary construction of the text of the Constitution, than to consider it as embraced by the specified power to regulate trade; a power which has been exercised by all Nations for those purposes; and which effects those purposes with less of interference with the authority & conveniency of the States, than might result from internal & direct modes of encouraging the articles, any of which modes would be authorized as far as deemed "necessary & proper," by considering the Power as an incidental Power.

8 That the encouragement of Manufactures, was an object of the power, to regulate trade, is proved by the use made of the power for that object, in the first session of the first Congress under the Constitution; when among the members present were so many who had been members of the federal Convention which framed the Constitution, and of the State Conventions which ratified it; each of these classes consisting also of members who had opposed & who had espoused, the Constitution in its actual form. It does not appear from the printed proceedings of Congress on that occasion that the power was denied by any of them. And it may be remarked that members from Virga. in particular, as well of the antifederal as the fed-

eral party, the names then distinguishing those who had opposed and those who had approved the Constitution, did not hesitate to propose duties, & to suggest even prohibitions, in favor of several articles of her production. By one a duty was proposed on mineral Coal in favor of the Virginia Coal-Pits; by another a duty on Hemp was proposed to encourage the growth of that article; and by a third a prohibition even of foreign Beef was suggested as a measure of sound policy. (See *Lloyd's Debates*.)

A further evidence in support of the Cons, power to protect & foster manufactures by regulations of trade, an evidence that ought of itself to settle the question, is the uniform & practical sanction given to the power, by the Genl. Govt. for nearly 40 years with a concurrence or acquiescence of every State Govt. throughout the same period; and it may be added thro all the vicissitudes of Party, which marked the period. No novel construction however ingeniously devised, or however respectable and patriotic its Patrons, can withstand the weight of such authorities, or the unbroken current of so prolonged & universal a practice. And well it is that this cannot be done without the intervention of the same authority which made the Constitution. If it could be so done, there would be an end to that stability in Govt. and in Laws which is essential to good Govt. & good Laws; a stability, the want of which is the imputation which has at all times been levelled agst. Republicanism with most effect by its most dexterous adversaries. The imputation ought never therefore to be countenanced, by innovating constructions, without any plea of a precipitancy or a paucity of the constructive precedents they oppose; without any appeal to material facts newly brought to light; and without any claim to a better knowledge of the original evils & inconveniences, for which remedies were needed, the very best keys to the true object & meaning of all laws & constitutions.

And may it not be fairly left to the unbiased judgment of all men of experience & of intelligence, to decide which is most to be relied on for a sound and safe test of the meaning of a Constitution, a uniform interpretation by all the successive authorities under it, commencing with its birth, and continued for a long period, thro' the varied state of political contests, or the opinion of every new Legislature heated as it may be by the strife of parties, or warped as often happens by the eager pursuit of some favourite object; or carried away possibly by the powerful eloquence, or captivating address of a few popular Statesmen, themselves influenced, perhaps, by the same misleading causes. If the latter test is to prevail, every new Legislative opinion might make a new Constitution; as the foot of every new Chancellor would make a new standard of measure.

It is seen with no little surprize, that an attempt has been made, in a highly respectable quarter, and at length reduced to a resolution formally proposed in Congress, to substitute for the power of Congs. to regulate trade so as to encourage manufactures, a power in the several States to do so, with the consent of that Body; and this expedient is derived from a clause in the 10. sect. of Art: I. of the Const; which says: ["No State shall, without the consent of Congress, lay any imposts or duties on imports or exports, except what may be absolutely necessary for executing its inspection laws; and the net produce of all duties and imposts laid by any State on imports and exports shall be for the use of the Treasury of the United States; and all such laws shall be subject to the revision and control of the Congress."]

To say nothing of the clear indications in the Journal of the Convention of 1787, that the clause was intended merely to provide for expences incurred by particular States in their inspection laws, and in such improvements as they might chuse to make in their Harbours & rivers with the sanction of Congs., objects to which the reserved power has been applied in several instances, at the request of Virginia & of Georgia, how could it ever be imagined that any State would wish to tax its own trade for the encouragement of manufactures, if possessed of the authority, or could in fact do so, if wishing it?

A tax on imports would be a tax on its own consumption; and the nett proceeds going, according to the clause, not into its own treasury, but into the treasury of the U. S., the State would tax itself separately for the equal gain of all the other States; and as far as the manufactures so encouraged might succeed in ultimately increasing the Stock in Market, and lowering the price by competition, this advantage also, procured at the sole expence of the State, would be common to all the others.

But the very suggestion of such an expedient to any State would have an air of mockery, when its *experienced* impracticability is taken into view. No one who recollects or recurs to the period when the power over Commerce was in the individual States, & separate attempts were made to tax or otherwise regulate it, needs be told that the attempts were not only abortive, but by demonstrating the necessity of general & uniform regulations gave the original impulse to the Constitutional reform which provided for such regulations.

To refer a State therefore to the exercise of a power as reserved to her by the Constitution, the impossibility of exercising which was an inducement to adopt the Constitution, is, of all remedial devices the last that ought to be brought forward. And what renders it the more extraordinary is that, as the tax on commerce as far as it could be separately collected, instead of belonging to the treasury of the State as previous to the Constn. would be a tribute to the U. S.; the State would be in a worse condition, after the adoption of the Constitution, than before, in relation to an important interest, the improvement of which was a particular object in adopting the Constitution.

Were Congress to make the proposed declaration of consent to State tariffs in favour of State manufactures, and the permitted attempts did not defeat themselves, what would be the situation of States deriving their foreign supplies through the ports of other States? It is evident that they might be compelled to pay, in their consumption of particular articles imported, a tax for the common treasury not common to all the States, without having any manufacture or product of their own to partake of the contemplated benefit.

Of the impracticability of separate regulations of trade,

& the resulting necessity of general regulations, no State was more sensible than Virga. She was accordingly among the most earnest for granting to Congress a power adequate to the object. On more occasions than one in the proceedings of her Legislative Councils, it was recited, "that the relative situation of the States had been found on *trial* to require *uniformity* in their comercial regulations as the *only* effectual policy for obtaining in the ports of foreign nations a stipulation of privileges reciprocal to those enjoyed by the subjects of such nations in the ports of the U. S., for preventing animosities which cannot fail to arise among the several States from the interference of partial & separate regulations; and for *deriving from comerce* such aids to the public *revenue* as it ought to contribute," &c.

During the delays & discouragts. experienced in the attempts to invest Congs. with the necessary powers, the State of Virga. made various trials of what could be done by her individual laws. She ventured on duties & imposts as a source of Revenue; Resolutions were passed at one time to encourage & protect her own navigation & ship-building; and in consequence of complaints & petitions from Norfolk, Alexa. & other places, agst. the monopolizing navigation laws of G. B., particularly in the trade *between the U. S. & the British W. Indies*, she deliberated with a purpose controuled only by the inefficacy of separate measures, on the experiment of forcing a reciprocity by prohibitory regulations of her own. (See Journal of Hs. of Delegates in 1785.)

The effect of her separate attempts to raise revenue by duties on imports, soon appeared in Representations from her Merchts., that the commerce of the State was banished by them into other channels, especially of Maryd., where imports were less burdened than in Virginia. (See do. 1786).

Such a tendency of separate regulations was indeed too manifest to escape anticipation. Among the projects prompted by the want of a federal authy. over Comerce, was that of a concert, first proposed on the part of Maryd. for a uniformity of regulations between the 2 States, and commissioners were appointed for that purpose. It was soon perceived however that the concurrence of Pena. was as necessy. to Maryd. as of Maryd. to Virga., and the concurrence of Pennsylvania was accordingly invited. But Pa. could no more concur witht. N. Y. than Md. witht. Pa. nor N. Y. witht. the concurrence of Boston &c.

These projects were superseded for the moment by that of the Convention at Annapolis in 1786, and forever by the Convn at Pha in 1787, and the Consn. which was the fruit of it.

There is a passage in Mr. Necker's work on the finances of France which affords a signal illustration of the difficulty of collecting, in contiguous communities, indirect taxes when not the same in all, by the violent means resorted to against smuggling from one to another of them. Previous to the late revolutionary war in that Country, the taxes were of very different rates in the different Provinces; particularly the tax on salt which was high in the interior Provinces & low in the maritime; and the tax on Tobacco, which was very high in general whilst in some of the Provinces the use of the article was altogether free. The consequence was that the standing army of Patrols agst smuggling, had swollen to the number of twenty three thousand; the annual arrests of men women & children engaged in smuggling, to five thousand five hundred & fifty; and the number annually arrested on account of Salt & Tobacco alone, to seventeen or eighteen hundred, more than three hundred of whom were consigned to the terrible punishment of the Galleys.

May it not be regarded as among the Providential blessings to these States, that their geographical relations multiplied as they will be by artificial channels of intercourse, give such additional force to the many obligations to cherish that Union which alone secures their peace, their safety, and their prosperity. Apart from the more obvious & awful consequences of their entire separation into Independent Sovereignties, it is worthy of special consideration, that divided from each other as they must be by narrow waters & territorial lines merely, the facility of surreptitious introductions of contraband articles, would defeat every attempt at revenue in the easy and indirect modes of impost and excise; so that whilst their expenditures would be necessarily & vastly increased by their new situation, they would, in providing for them, be limited to direct taxes on land or other property, to arbitrary assessments on invisible funds, & to the odious tax on persons.

You will observe that I have confined myself, in what has been said to the constitutionality & expediency of the power in congress to encourage domestic products by regulations of commerce. In the exercise of the power, they are responsible to their Constituents, whose right & duty it is, in that as in all other cases, to bring their measures to the test of justice & of the general good.

19

JAMES MADISON TO JOSEPH C. CABELL
13 Feb. 1829
Letters 4:14–15

For a like reason, I made no reference to the "power to regulate commerce among the several States." I always foresaw that difficulties might be started in relation to that power which could not be fully explained without recurring to views of it, which, however just, might give birth to specious though unsound objections. Being in the same terms with the power over foreign commerce, the same extent, if taken literally, would belong to it. Yet it is very certain that it grew out of the abuse of the power by the importing States in taxing the non-importing, and was intended as a negative and preventive provision against injustice among the States themselves, rather than as a power to be used for the positive purposes of the General Government, in which alone, however, the remedial power could be lodged.

20

WILLSON v. BLACKBIRD CREEK MARSH CO.
2 Pet. 245 (1829)

Mr. Chief Justice MARSHALL delivered the opinion of the Court.

The defendants in error deny the jurisdiction of this Court, because, they say, the record does not show that the constitutionality of the act of the legislature, under which the plaintiff claimed to support his action, was drawn into question.

Undoubtedly the plea might have stated in terms that the act, so far as it authorized a dam across the creek, was repugnant to the Constitution of the United States; and it might have been safer, it might have avoided any question respecting jurisdiction, so to frame it. But we think it impossible to doubt that the constitutionality of the act was the question, and the only question, which could have been discussed in the state Court. That question must have been discussed and decided.

The plaintiffs sustain their right to build a dam across the creek by the act of assembly. Their declaration is founded upon that act. The injury of which they complain is to a right given by it. They do not claim for themselves any right independent of it. They rely entirely upon the act of assembly.

The plea does not controvert the existence of the act, but denies the capacity to authorize the construction of a dam across a navigable stream, in which the tide ebbs and flows; and in which there was, and of right ought to have been, a certain common and public use in the nature of a highway. This plea draws nothing into question but the validity of the act, and the judgment of the Court must have been in favour of its validity. Its consistency with, or repugnancy to the constitution of the United States, necessarily arises upon these pleadings, and must have been determined. This Court has repeatedly decided in favour of its jurisdiction in such a case. Martin *vs.* Hunter's lessee, Miller *vs.* Nicholls, and Williams vs. Norris, are expressly in point. They establish, as far as precedents can establish any thing, that it is not necessary to state in terms on the record, that the Constitution or a law of the United States was drawn in question. It is sufficient to bring the case within the provisions of the twenty-fifth section of the judicial act, if the record shows that the Constitution or a law or a treaty of the United States must have been misconstrued, or the decision could not be made. Or, as in this case, that the constitutionality of a state law was questioned, and the decision has been in favour of the party claiming under such law.

The jurisdiction of the Court being established, the more doubtful question is to be considered, whether the act incorporating the Black Bird Creek Marsh Company is repugnant to the Constitution, so far as it authorizes a dam across the creek. The plea states the creek to be navigable, in the nature of a highway, through which the tide ebbs and flows.

The act of assembly by which the plaintiffs were authorized to construct their dam, shows plainly that this is one of those many creeks, passing through a deep level marsh adjoining the Delaware, up which the tide flows for some distance. The value of the property on its banks must be enhanced by excluding the water from the marsh, and the health of the inhabitants probably improved. Measures calculated to produce these objects, provided they do not come into collision with the powers of the general government, are undoubtedly within those which are reserved to the states. But the measure authorized by this act stops a navigable creek, and must be supposed to abridge the rights of those who have been accustomed to use it. But this abridgement, unless it comes in conflict with the Constitution or a law of the United States, is an affair between the government of Delaware and its citizens, of which this Court can take no cognizance.

The counsel for the plaintiffs in error insist that it comes in conflict with the power of the United States "to regulate commerce with foreign nations, and among the several states." If Congress had passed any act which bore upon the case, any act in execution of the power to regulate commerce, the object of which was to control state legislation over those small navigable creeks into which the tide flows, and which abound throughout the lower country of the middle and southern states; we should feel not much difficulty in saying that a state law coming in conflict with such act would be void. But Congress has passed no such act. The repugnancy of the law of Delaware to the Constitution is placed entirely on its repugnancy to the power to regulate commerce with foreign nations and among the several states; a power which has not been so exercised as to affect the question.

We do not think that the act empowering the Black Bird Creek Marsh Company to place a dam across the creek, can, under all the circumstances of the case, be considered as repugnant to the power to regulate commerce in its dormant state, or as being in conflict with any law passed on the subject.

21

JAMES MADISON TO PROFESSOR DAVIS
1832
Letters 4:247, 251–54

It deserves particular attention, that the Congress which first met contained sixteen members, eight of them in the House of Representatives, fresh from the Convention which framed the Constitution, and a considerable number who had been members of the State Conventions which had adopted it, taken as well from the party which opposed as from those who had espoused its adoption. Yet it appears from the debates in the House of Representatives, (those in the Senate not having been taken,) that not a doubt was started of the power of Congress to impose duties on imports for the encouragement of domestic manufactures.

. . . . .

The incapacity of the States separately to regulate their foreign commerce was fully illustrated by an experience which was well known to the Federal Convention when forming the Constitution. It was well known that the incapacity gave a primary and powerful impulse to the transfer of the power to a common authority capable of exercising it with effect. . . .

New York, Pennsylvania, Rhode Island, and Virginia, previous to the establishment of the present Constitution, had opportunities of taxing the consumption of their neighbours, and the exasperating effect on them formed a conspicuous chapter in the history of the period. The grievance would now be extended to the inland States, which necessarily receive their foreign supplies through the maritime States, and would be heard in a voice to which a deaf ear could not be turned.

The condition of the inland States is of itself a sufficient proof that it could not be the intention of those who framed the Constitution to *substitute* for a power in Congress to impose a protective tariff, a power merely to permit the States individually to do it. Although the present inland States were not then in existence, it could not escape foresight that it would soon, and from time to time, be the case. Kentucky was then known to be making ready to be an independent State, and to become a member of the Confederacy. What is now Tennessee was marked by decided circumstances for the same distinction. On the north side of the Ohio new States were in embryo under the arrangements and auspices of the Revolutionary Congress, and it was manifest, that within the Federal domain others would be added to the Federal family.

As the anticipated States would be without ports for foreign commerce, it would be a mockery to provide for them a permit to impose duties on imports or exports in favor of manufactures, and the mockery would be the greater as the obstructions and difficulties in the way of their bulky exports might the sooner require domestic substitutes for imports; and a protection for the substitutes, by commercial regulations, which could not avail if not general in their operation and enforced by a general authority. . . .

But those who regard the permission grantable in section ten, article one, to the States to impose duties on foreign commerce, as an intended substitute for a general power in Congress, do not reflect that the object of the permission, qualified as it is, might be less inconsistently explained by supposing it a concurrent or supplemental power, than by supposing it a substituted power.

Finally, it cannot be alleged that the encouragement of manufactures permissible to the States by duties on foreign commerce, is to be regarded as an incident to duties imposed for revenue. Such a view of the section is barred by the fact that revenue cannot be the object of the State, the duties accruing, not to the State, but to the United States. The duties also would even diminish, not increase, the gain of the federal treasury, by diminishing the consumption of imports within the States imposing the duties, and, of course, the aggregate revenue of the United States. The revenue, whatever it might be, could only be regarded as an incident to the manufacturing object, not this to the revenue. . . .

Attempts have been made to show, from the journal of the Convention of 1787, that it was intended to withhold from Congress a power to protect manufactures by commercial regulations. The intention is inferred from the rejection or not adopting of particular propositions which embraced a power to encourage them. But, without knowing the reasons for the votes in those cases, no such inference can be sustained. The propositions might be disapproved because they were in a bad form or not in order; because they blended other powers with the particular power in question; or because the object had been, or would be, elsewhere provided for. No one acquainted with the proceedings of deliberative bodies can have failed to notice the frequent uncertainty of inferences from a record of naked votes. It has been with some surprise, that a failure or final omission of a proposition "to establish public institutions, rewards, and immunities for the promotion of agriculture, commerce, and manufactures," should have led to the conclusion that the Convention meant to exclude from the federal power over commerce regulations encouraging domestic manufactures. (See Mr. Crawford's letter to Mr. Dickerson, in the National Intelligencer of ————.) Surely no disregard of a proposition embracing *public institutions, rewards,* and *immunities* for the *promotion* of *agriculture, commerce,* and *manufactures,* could be an evidence of a refusal to encourage the particular object of manufactures, by the particular mode of duties or restrictions on rival imports. In expounding the Constitution and deducing the intention of its framers, it should never be forgotten, that the great object of the Convention was to provide, by a new Constitution, a remedy for the defects of the existing one; that among these defects was that of a power to regulate foreign commerce; that in all nations this regulating power embraced the protection of domestic manufactures by duties and restrictions on imports; that the States had tried in vain to make use of the power, while it remained with them; and that, if taken from them and transferred to the Federal Government, with an exception of the power to encourage domestic manufactures, the American people, let it be repeated, present the solitary and strange spectacle of a nation disarming itself of a power exercised by every nation as a shield against the effect of the power as used by other nations. Who will say that such considerations as these are not among the best keys that can be applied to the text of the Constitution? and infinitely better keys than unexplained votes cited from the records of the Convention.

22

JOSEPH STORY, COMMENTARIES ON THE
CONSTITUTION 2:§§ 1073–91
1833

§ 1073. A question has been recently made, whether congress have a constitutional authority to apply the power to regulate commerce for the purpose of encouraging and protecting domestic manufactures. It is not denied, that congress may, incidentally, in its arrangements for revenue, or to countervail foreign restrictions, encourage the growth of domestic manufactures. But it is earnestly and strenuously insisted, that, under the colour of regulating commerce, congress have no right permanently to prohibit any importations, or to tax any unreasonably for the purpose of securing the home market to the domestic manufacturer, as they thereby destroy the commerce entrusted to them to regulate, and foster an interest, with which they have no constitutional power to interfere. This opinion constitutes the leading doctrine of several states in the Union at the present moment; and is maintained, as vital to the existence of the Union. On the other hand, it is as earnestly and strenuously maintained, that congress does possess the constitutional power to encourage and protect manufactures by appropriate regulations of commerce; and that the opposite opinion is destructive of all the purposes of the Union, and would annihilate its value.

§ 1074. Under such circumstances, it becomes indispensable to review the grounds, upon which the doctrine of each party is maintained, and to sift them to the bottom; since it cannot be disguised, that the controversy still agitates all America, and marks the divisions of party by the strongest lines, both geographical and political, which have ever been seen since the establishment of the national government.

§ 1075. The reasoning, by which the doctrine is maintained, that the power to regulate commerce cannot be constitutionally applied, as a means, directly to encourage domestic manufactures, has been in part already adverted to in considering the extent of the power to lay taxes. It is proper, however, to present it entire in its present connexion. It is to the following effect.—The constitution is one of limited and enumerated powers; and none of them can be rightfully exercised beyond the scope of the objects, specified in those powers. It is not disputed, that, when the power is given, all the appropriate means to carry it into effect are included. Neither is it disputed, that the laying of duties is, or may be an appropriate means of regulating commerce. But the question is a very different one, whether, under pretence of an exercise of the power to regulate commerce, congress may in fact impose duties for objects wholly distinct from commerce. The question comes to this, whether a power, exclusively for the regulation of commerce, is a power for the regulation of manufactures? The statement of such a question would seem to involve its own answer. Can a power, granted for one purpose, be transferred to another? If it can, where is the limitation in the constitution? Are not commerce and manufactures as distinct, as commerce and agriculture? If they are, how can a power to regulate one arise from a power to regulate the other? It is true, that commerce and manufactures are, or may be, intimately connected with each other. A regulation of one may injuriously or beneficially affect the other. But that is not the point in controversy. It is, whether congress has a right to regulate that, which is not committed to it, under a power, which is committed to it, simply because there is, or may be an intimate connexion between the powers. If this were admitted, the enumeration of the powers of congress would be wholly unnecessary and nugatory. Agriculture, colonies, capital, machinery, the wages of labour, the profits of stock, the rents of land, the punctual performance of contracts, and the diffusion of knowledge would all be within the scope of the power; for all of them bear an intimate relation to commerce. The result would be, that the powers of congress would embrace the widest extent of legislative functions, to the utter demolition of all constitutional boundaries between the state and national governments. When duties are laid, not for purposes of revenue, but of retaliation and restriction, to countervail foreign restrictions, they are strictly within the scope of the power, as a regulation of commerce. But when laid to encourage manufactures, they have nothing to do with it. The power to regulate manufactures is no more confided to congress, than the power to interfere with the systems of education, the poor laws, or the road laws of the states. It is notorious, that, in the convention, an attempt was made to introduce into the constitution a power to encourage manufactures; but it was withheld. Instead of granting the power to congress, permission was given to the states to impose duties, with the consent of that body, to encourage their own manufactures; and thus, in the true spirit of justice, imposing the burthen on those, who were to be benefited. It is true, that congress may, incidentally, when laying duties for revenue, consult the other interests of the country. They may so arrange the details, as indirectly to aid manufactures. And this is the whole extent, to which congress has ever gone until the tariffs, which have given rise to the present controversy. The former precedents of congress are not, even if admitted to be authoritative, applicable to the question now presented.

§ 1076. The reasoning of those, who maintain the doctrine, that congress has authority to apply the power to regulate commerce to the purpose of protecting and encouraging domestic manufactures, is to the following effect. The power to regulate commerce, being in its terms unlimited, includes all means appropriate to the end, and all means, which have been usually exerted under the power. No one can doubt or deny, that a power to regulate trade involves a power to tax it. It is a familiar mode, recognised in the practice of all nations, and was known and admitted by the United States, while they were colonies, and has ever since been acted upon without opposition or question. The American colonies wholly denied the authority of the British parliament to tax them, except as a regulation of commerce; but they admitted this exercise of power, as legitimate and unquestionable. The distinction was with difficulty maintained in practice between laws for the regulation of commerce by way of taxation, and laws, which were made for mere monopoly, or restriction, when they incidentally produced revenue. And it is certain, that the main and admitted object of parliamentary regulations of trade with the colonies was the encouragement of manufactures in Great-Britain. Other nations have, in like manner, for like purposes, exercised the like power. So, that there is no novelty in the use of the power, and no stretch in the range of the power.

§ 1077. Indeed, the advocates of the opposite doctrine admit, that the power may be applied, so as incidentally to give protection to manufactures, when revenue is the principal design; and that it may also be applied to countervail the injurious regulations of foreign powers, when there is no design of revenue. These concessions admit, then, that the regulations of commerce are not wholly for purposes of revenue, or wholly confined to the purposes of commerce, considered *per se*. If this be true, then other objects may enter into commercial regulations; and if so, what restraint is there, as to the nature or extent of the objects, to which they may reach, which does not resolve itself into a question of expediency and policy? It may be admitted, that a power, given for one purpose, cannot be perverted to purposes wholly opposite, or beside its legitimate scope. But what perversion is there in applying a power to the very purposes, to which it has been usually applied? Under such circumstances, does not the grant of the power without restriction concede, that it may be legitimately applied to such purposes? If a different intent had existed, would not that intent be manifested by some corresponding limitation?

§ 1078. Now it is well known, that in commercial and manufacturing nations, the power to regulate commerce has embraced practically the encouragement of manufactures. It is believed, that not a single exception can be named. So, in an especial manner, the power has always been understood in Great-Britain, from which we derive our parentage, our laws, our language, and our notions upon commercial subjects. Such was confessedly the notion of the different states in the Union under the confederation, and before the formation of the present constitution. One known object of the policy of the manufacturing states then was, the protection and encouragement of their manufactures by regulations of commerce. And the exercise of this power was a source of constant difficulty and discontent; not because improper of itself; but because it bore injuriously upon the commercial arrangements of other states. The want of uniformity in the regulations of commerce was a source of perpetual strife and dissatisfaction, of inequalities, and rivalries, and retaliations among the states. When the constitution was framed, no one ever imagined, that the power of protection of manufactures was to be taken away from all the states, and yet not delegated to the Union. The very suggestion would of itself have been fatal to the adoption of the constitution. The manufacturing states would never have acceded to it upon any such terms; and they never could, without the power, have safely acceded to it; for it would have sealed their ruin. The same reasoning would apply to the agricultural states; for the regulation of commerce, with a view to encourage domestic agriculture, is just as important, and just as vital to the interests of the nation, and just as much an application of the power, as the protection or encouragement of manufactures. It would have been strange indeed, if the people of the United States had been solicitous solely to advance and encourage commerce, with a total disregard of the interests of agriculture and manufactures, which had, at the time of the adoption of the constitution, an unequivocal preponderance throughout the Union. It is manifest from contemporaneous documents, that one object of the constitution was, to encourage manufactures and agriculture by this very use of the power.

§ 1079. The terms, then, of the constitution are sufficiently large to embrace the power; the practice of other nations, and especially of Great-Britain and of the American states, has been to use it in this manner; and this exercise of it was one of the very grounds, upon which the establishment of the constitution was urged and vindicated. The argument, then, in its favour would seem to be absolutely irresistible under this aspect. But there are other very weighty considerations, which enforce it.

§ 1080. In the first place, if congress does not possess the power to encourage domestic manufactures by regulations of commerce, the power is annihilated for the whole nation. The states are deprived of it. They have made a voluntary surrender of it; and yet it exists not in the national government. It is then a mere nonentity. Such a policy, voluntarily adopted by a free people, in subversion of some of their dearest rights and interests, would be most extraordinary in itself, without any assignable motive or reason for so great a sacrifice, and utterly without example in the history of the world. No man can doubt, that domestic agriculture and manufactures may be most essentially promoted and protected by regulations of commerce. No man can doubt, that it is the most usual, and generally the most efficient means of producing those results. No man can question, that in these great objects the different states of America have as deep a stake, and as vital interests, as any other nation. Why, then, should the power be surrendered and annihilated? It would produce the most serious mischiefs at home; and would secure the most complete triumph over us by foreign nations. It would introduce and perpetuate national debility, if not national ruin. A foreign nation might, as a conqueror, impose upon us this restraint, as a badge of dependence, and a sacrifice of sovereignty, to subserve its own interests; but that we should impose it upon ourselves, is inconceivable. The achievement of our independence was almost worthless, if such a system was to be pursued. It would be in effect a perpetuation of that very system of monopoly, of encouragement of foreign manufactures, and depression of domestic industry, which was so much complained of during our colonial dependence; and which kept all America in a state of poverty, and slavish devotion to British interests. Under such circumstances, the constitution would be established, not for the purposes avowed in the preamble, but for the exclusive benefit and advancement of foreign nations, to aid their manufactures, and sustain

their agriculture. Suppose cotton, rice, tobacco, wheat, corn, sugar, and other raw materials could be, or should hereafter be, abundantly produced in foreign countries, under the fostering hands of their governments, by bounties and commercial regulations, so as to become cheaper with such aids than our own; are all our markets to be opened to such products without any restraint, simply because we may not want revenue, to the ruin of our products and industry? Is America ready to give every thing to Europe, without any equivalent; and take in return whatever Europe may choose to give, upon its own terms? The most servile provincial dependence could not do more evils. Of what consequence would it be, that the national government could not tax our exports, if foreign governments might tax them to an unlimited extent, so as to favour their own, and thus to supply us with the same articles by the overwhelming depression of our own by foreign taxation? When it is recollected, with what extreme discontent and reluctant obedience the British colonial restrictions were enforced in the manufacturing and navigating states, while they were colonies, it is incredible, that they should be willing to adopt a government, which should, or might entail upon them equal evils in perpetuity. Commerce itself would ultimately be as great a sufferer by such a system, as the other domestic interests. It would languish, if it did not perish. Let any man ask himself, if New-England, or the Middle states would ever have consented to ratify a constitution, which would afford no protection to their manufactures or home industry. If the constitution was ratified under the belief, sedulously propagated on all sides, that such protection was afforded, would it not now be a fraud upon the whole people to give a different construction to its powers?

§ 1081. It is idle to say, that with the consent of congress, the states may lay duties on imports or exports, to favour their own domestic manufactures. In the first place, if congress could constitutionally give such consent for such a purpose, which has been doubted; they would have a right to refuse such consent, and would certainly refuse it, if the result would be what the advocates of free trade contend for. In the next place, it would be utterly impracticable with such consent to protect their manufactures by any such local regulations. To be of any value they must be general, and uniform through the nation. This is not a matter of theory. Our whole experience under the confederation established beyond all controversy the utter local futility, and even the general mischiefs of independent state legislation upon such a subject. It furnished one of the strongest grounds for the establishment of the constitution.

§ 1082. In the next place, if revenue be the sole legitimate object of an impost, and the encouragement of domestic manufactures be not within the scope of the power of regulating trade, it would follow, (as has been already hinted,) that no monopolizing or unequal regulations of foreign nations could be counteracted. Under such circumstances, neither the staple articles of subsistence, nor the essential implements for the public safety, could be adequately ensured or protected at home by our regulations of commerce. The duty might be wholly unnecessary for revenue; and incidentally, it might even check revenue. But, if congress may, in arrangements for revenue, incidentally and designedly protect domestic manufactures, what ground is there to suggest, that they may not incorporate this design through the whole system of duties, and select and arrange them accordingly? There is no constitutional measure, by which to graduate, how much shall be assessed for revenue, and how much for encouragement of home industry. And no system ever yet adopted has attempted, and in all probability none hereafter adopted will attempt, wholly to sever the one object from the other. The constitutional objection in this view is purely speculative, regarding only future possibilities.

§ 1083. But if it be conceded, (as it is,) that the power to regulate commerce includes the power of laying duties to countervail the regulations and restrictions of foreign nations, then, what limits are to be assigned to this use of the power? If their commercial regulations, either designedly or incidentally, do promote their own agriculture and manufactures, and injuriously affect ours, why may not congress apply a remedy coextensive with the evil? If congress have, as cannot be denied, the choice of the means, they may countervail the regulations, not only by the exercise of the *lex talionis* in the same way, but in any other way conducive to the same end. If Great Britain by commercial regulations restricts the introduction of our staple products and manufactures into her own territories, and levies prohibitory duties, why may not congress apply the same rule to her staple products and manufactures, and secure the same market to ourselves? The truth is, that as soon as the right to retaliate foreign restrictions or foreign policy by commercial regulations is admitted, the question, in what manner, and to what extent, it shall be applied, is a matter of legislative discretion, and not of constitutional authority. Whenever commercial restrictions and regulations shall cease all over the world, so far as they favour the nation adopting them it will be time enough to consider, what America ought to do in her own regulations of commerce, which are designed to protect her own industry and counteract such favoritism. It will then become a question, not of power, but of policy. Such a state of things has never yet existed. In fact the concession, that the power to regulate commerce may embrace other objects, than revenue, or even than commerce itself, is irreconcilable with the foundation of the argument on the other side.

§ 1084. Besides; the power is to regulate commerce. And in what manner regulate it? Why does the power involve the right to lay duties? Simply, because it is a common means of executing the power. If so, why does not the same right exist as to all other means equally common and appropriate? Why does the power involve a right, not only to lay duties, but to lay duties for *revenue*, and not merely for the regulation and restriction of commerce, considered *per se?* No other answer can be given, but that revenue is an incident to such an exercise of the power. It flows from, and does not create the power. It may constitute the motive for the exercise of the power, just as any other cause may; as for instance, the prohibition of foreign trade, or the retaliation of foreign monopoly; but it does not constitute the power.

§ 1085. Now, the motive of the grant of the power is not even alluded to in the constitution. It is not even stated, that congress shall have power to promote and encourage domestic navigation and trade. A power to regulate commerce is not necessarily a power to advance its interests. It may in given cases suspend its operations and restrict its advancement and scope. Yet no man ever yet doubted the right of congress to lay duties to promote and encourage domestic navigation, whether in the form of tonnage duties, or other preferences and privileges, either in the foreign trade, or coasting trade, or fisheries. It is as certain, as any thing human can be, that the sole object of congress, in securing the vast privileges to American built ships, by such preferences, and privileges, and tonnage duties, was, to encourage the domestic manufacture of ships, and all the dependent branches of business. It speaks out in the language of all their laws, and has been as constantly avowed, and acted on, as any single legislative policy ever has been. No one ever dreamed, that revenue constituted the slightest ingredient in these laws. They were purely for the encouragement of home manufactures, and home artisans, and home pursuits. Upon what grounds can congress constitutionally apply the power to regulate commerce to one great class of domestic manufactures, which does not involve the right to encourage all? If it be said, that navigation is a part of commerce, that is true. But a power to regulate navigation no more includes a power to encourage the manufacture of ships by tonnage duties, than any other manufacture. Why not extend it to the encouragement of the growth and manufacture of cotton and hemp for sails and rigging; of timber, boards, and masts; of tar, pitch, and turpentine; of iron and wool; of sheetings and shirtings; of artisans and mechanics, however remotely connected with it? There are many products of agriculture and manufactures, which are connected with the prosperity of commerce as intimately, as domestic ship building. If the one may be encouraged, as a primary motive in regulations of commerce, why may not the others? The truth is, that the encouragement of domestic ship building is within the scope of the power to regulate commerce, simply, because it is a known and ordinary means of exercising the power. It is one of many, and may be used like all others according to legislative discretion. The motive to the exercise of a power can never form a constitutional objection to the exercise of the power.

§ 1086. Here, then, is a case of laying duties, an ordinary means used in executing the power to regulate commerce; how can it be deemed unconstitutional? If it be said, that the motive is not to collect revenue, what has that to do with the power? When an act is constitutional, as an exercise of a power, can it be unconstitutional from the motives, with which it is passed? If it can, then the constitutionality of an act must depend, not upon the power, but upon the motives of the legislature. It will follow, as a consequence, that the same act passed by one legislature will be constitutional, and by another unconstitutional. Nay, it might be unconstitutional, as well from its omissions as its enactments, since if its omissions were to favour manufactures, the motive would contaminate the whole law. Such a doctrine would be novel and absurd. It would confuse and destroy all the tests of constitutional rights and authorities. Congress could never pass any law without an inquisition into the motives of every member; and even then, they might be re-examinable. Besides; what possible means can there be of making such investigations? The motives of many of the members may be, nay must be utterly unknown, and incapable of ascertainment by any judicial or other inquiry: they may be mixed up in various manners and degrees; they may be opposite to, or wholly independent of each other. The constitution would thus depend upon processes utterly vague, and incomprehensible; and the written intent of the legislature upon its words and acts, the *lex scripta*, would be contradicted or obliterated by conjecture, and parol declarations, and fleeting reveries, and heated imaginations. No government on earth could rest for a moment on such a foundation. It would be a constitution of sand heaped up and dissolved by the flux and reflux of every tide of opinion. Every act of the legislature must therefore be judged of from its object and intent, as they are embodied in its provisions; and if the latter are within the scope of admitted powers, the act must be constitutional, whether the motive for it were wise, or just, or otherwise. The manner of applying a power may be an abuse of it; but this does not prove, that it is unconstitutional.

§ 1087. Passing by these considerations, let the practice of the government and the doctrines maintained by those, who have administered it, be deliberately examined; and they will be found to be in entire consistency with this reasoning. The very first congress, that ever sat under the constitution, composed in a considerable degree of those, who had framed, or assisted in the discussion of its provisions in the state conventions, deliberately adopted this view of the power. And what is most remarkable, upon a subject of deep interest and excitement, which at the time occasioned long and vehement debates, not a single syllable of doubt was breathed from any quarter against the constitutionality of protecting agriculture and manufactures by laying duties, although the intention to protect and encourage them was constantly avowed. Nay, it was contended to be a paramount duty, upon the faithful fulfilment of which the constitution had been adopted, and the omission of which would be a political fraud, without a whisper of dissent from any side. It was demanded by the people from various parts of the Union; and was resisted by none. Yet, state jealousy was never more alive than at this period, and state interests never more actively mingled in the debates of congress. The two great parties, which afterwards so much divided the country upon the question of a liberal and strict construction of the constitution, were then distinctly formed, and proclaimed their opinions with firmness and freedom. If, therefore, there had been a point of doubt, on which to hang an argument, it cannot be questioned, but that it would have been brought into the array of opposition. Such a silence, under such circumstances, is most persuasive and convincing.

§ 1088. The very preamble of this act (the second passed by congress) is, "Whereas it is necessary for the support of the government, for the discharge of the debts of the United States, and *the encouragement and protection of manu-* *factures,* that duties be laid on goods, wares, and merchandises imported, Be it enacted," &c. Yet, not a solitary voice was raised against it. The right, and the duty, to pass such laws was, indeed, taken so much for granted, that in some of the most elaborate expositions of the government upon the subject of manufactures, it was scarcely alluded to. The Federalist itself, dealing with every shadow of objection against the constitution, never once alludes to such a one; but incidentally commends this power, as leading to beneficial results on all domestic interests. Every successive congress since that time has constantly acted upon the system through all the changes of party and local interests. Every successive executive has sanctioned laws on the subject; and most of them have actively recommended the encouragement of manufactures to congress. Until a very recent period, no person in the public councils seriously relied upon any constitutional difficulty. And even now, when the subject has been agitated, and discussed with great ability and zeal throughout the Union, not more than five states have expressed an opinion against the constitutional right, while it has received an unequivocal sanction in the others with an almost unexampled degree of unanimity. And this too, when in most other respects these states have been in strong opposition to each other upon the general system of politics pursued by the government.

§ 1089. If ever, therefore, contemporaneous exposition, and the uniform and progressive operations of the government itself, in all its departments, can be of any weight to settle the construction of the constitution, there never has been, and there never can be more decided evidence in favour of the power, than is furnished by the history of our national laws for the encouragement of domestic agriculture and manufactures. To resign an exposition so sanctioned, would be to deliver over the country to interminable doubts; and to make the constitution not a written system of government, but a false and delusive text, upon which every successive age of speculatists and statesmen might build any system, suited to their own views and opinions. But if it be added to this, that the constitution gives the power in the most unlimited terms, and neither assigns motives, nor objects for its exercise; but leaves these wholly to the discretion of the legislature, acting for the common good, and the general interests; the argument in its favour becomes as absolutely irresistible, as any demonstration of a moral or political nature ever can be. Without such a power, the government would be absolutely worthless, and made merely subservient to the policy of foreign nations, incapable of self-protection or self-support; with it, the country will have a right to assert its equality, and dignity, and sovereignty among the other nations of the earth.

§ 1089 [*sic*]. In regard to the rejection of the proposition in the convention "to establish *institutions, rewards,* and *immunities* for the promotion of agriculture, commerce, trades, and manufactures," it is manifest, that it has no bearing on the question. It was a power much more broad in its extent and objects, than the power to encourage manufactures by the exercise of another granted power. It might be contended with quite as much plausibility, that the rejection was an implied rejection of the right to encourage commerce, for that was equally within the scope of the proposition. In truth, it involved a direct power to establish *institutions, rewards,* and *immunities* for all the great interests of society, and was, on that account, deemed too broad and sweeping. It would establish a general, and not a limited power of government.

§ 1090. Such is a summary (necessarily imperfect) of the reasoning on each side of this contested doctrine. The reader will draw his own conclusions; and these Commentaries have no further aim, than to put him in possession of the materials for a proper exercise of his judgment.

§ 1091. When the subject of the regulation of commerce was before the convention, the first draft of the constitution contained an article, that "no navigation act shall be passed, without the assent of two thirds of the members present in each house." This article was afterwards recommended in a report of a committee to be stricken out. In the second revised draft it was left out; and a motion, to insert such a restriction to have effect until the year 1808, was negatived by the vote of seven states against three. Another proposition, that no act, regulating the commerce of the United States with foreign powers, should be passed without the assent of two thirds of the members of each house, was rejected by the vote of seven states against four. The rejection was, probably, occasioned by two leading reasons. First, the general impropriety of allowing the minority in a government to control, and in effect to govern all the legislative powers of the majority. Secondly, the especial inconvenience of such a power in regard to regulations of commerce, where the proper remedy for grievances of the worst sort might be withheld from the navigating and commercial states by a very small minority of the other states. A similar proposition was made, after the adoption of the constitution, by some of the states; but it was never acted upon.

SEE ALSO:

Generally 1.9.2; 1.9.5; 1.9.6; 1.10.2; 1.10.3
William Blackstone, Commentaries 1:263–64 (1765)
Records of the Federal Convention, Farrand 2:135, 143, 157, 158, 167, 169, 321, 367, 446, 569, 595
Richard Henry Lee to Edmund Randolph, 16 Oct. 1787, Letters 454–55
Oliver Ellsworth, Landholder, no. 6, Dec. 1787, Essays 161–62
Luther Martin, Genuine Information, 1788, Storing 2.4.67
Pierce Butler to Weedon Butler, 5 May 1788, Farrand 3:303
Alexander Hamilton, New York Ratifying Convention, 20 June 1788, Elliot 2:236
George Mason, Virginia Ratifying Convention, 24 June 1788, Elliot 3:604
Melancton Smith, Proposed Amendment, New York Ratifying Convention, 2 July 1788, Elliot 2:407
Native of Virginia, Observations upon the Proposed Plan of Federal Government, 1788, Monroe Writings 1:367–70
An Act for Registering and Clearing Vessels, Regulating the Coastal Trade, and for Other Purposes, 1 Stat. 55 (1789)
An Act to Authorize the President of the United States to Lay, Regulate and Revoke Embargoes, 1 Stat. 372 (1794)
George Washington, Eighth Annual Address, 7 Dec. 1796, Richardson 1:201–2
An Act to Suspend the Commercial Intercourse between the United States and France, 1 Stat. 565 (1798)
An Act Further to Suspend the Commercial Intercourse between the United States and France, 1 Stat. 613 (1799)
The Ulysses, 24 Fed. Cas. 515, no. 14,330 (C.C.D.Mass. 1800)
The Wilson v. United States, 30 Fed. Cas. 239, no. 17,846 (C.C.D.Va. 1820)
North River Steamboat Co. v. Livingston, 3 Cowen 713 (N.Y. 1825)
James Kent, Commentaries 1:404–13 (1826)
Candler v. Mayor of New York, 1 Wend. 493 (N.Y. 1828)
William Rawle, A View of the Constitution of the United States 81–82, 84 (2d ed. 1829)
The Wave v. Hyer, 29 Fed. Cas. 464, no. 17,300 (C.C.S.D.N.Y. 1831)

INDIANS

1

JAMES MONROE TO JAMES MADISON
15 Nov. 1784
Madison Papers 8:140

At fort Stanwix you were necessarily acquainted with the variance which had taken place between the Indian Commissioners of the U. States, & those of New York as well as of the principles upon which they respectively acted & the extent to which they carried them: as I reach'd N. York about eight days after you had left it & the Ind: Comm'rs were then on the ground & have not since made a stat'ment of their final transactions there. I have nothing new to give you upon that head. The questions wh. appear to me to arise upon the subjects of variance are 1. whether these Indians are to be consider'd as members of the State of N. York, or whether the living simply within the bounds of a State, in the exclusion only of an European power, while they acknowledge no obidience to its laws but hold a country over which they do not extend, nor enjoy the protection nor any of the rights of citizenship within it, is a situation wh. will even in the most qualified sense, admit their being held as members of a State? 2. whether on the other hand this is not a description of those whose manag'ment is committed by the confideration to the US. in Congress assembled? In either event the land held by these Indians, having never been ceded either by N. York or Massachusetts belongs not to the U. States; the only point then in wh. N. York can be reprehensible is, for preceding by a particular [state treaty], the general Treaty. This must be attributed to a suspicion that there exists in Congress a design to injure her. The transaction will necessarily come before us, but will it not be most expedient in the present state of our affairs to form no decision thereon? I know no advantages to be deriv'd from one. If the general treaty hath been obstructed the injury sustain'd in that instance is now without remedy. A decision either way, will neither restore the time we have lost nor remove the impressions wh. this variance hath made with the Indians & in the Court of G. Britain respecting us. If the right of Congress hath been contraven'd shall we not derive greater injury by urging it to the reprehension of New York who holds herself aggriev'd in other respects than by suffering our sense of that delinquency to lay dormant? Our purchases must be made without her bounds & those Indians whose alliance we seek inhabit a country to which she hath no claim.

2

JAMES MADISON TO JAMES MONROE
27 Nov. 1784
Papers 8:156–57

The umbrage given to the Comsrs. of the U. S. by the negociations of N. Y. with the Indians was not altogether unknown to me, though I am less acquainted with the circumstances of it than your letter supposes. The Idea which I at present have of the affair leads me to say that as far as N. Y. may claim a right of treating with Indians for the purchase of lands within her limits, she has the confederation on her side; as far as she may have exerted that right in contravention of the Genl. Treaty, or even unconfidentially with the Comisrs. of Congs. she has violated both duty & decorum. The foederal articles give Congs. the exclusive right of managing all affairs with the Indians not members of any State, under a proviso, that the Legislative authority, of the State within its own limits be not violated. By Indian[s] not members of a State, must be meant those, I conceive who do not live within the body of the Society, or whose Persons or property form no objects of its laws. In the case of Indians of this description the only restraint on Congress is imposed by the Legislative authority of the State. If this proviso be taken in its full latitude, it must destroy the authority of Congress altogether, since no act of Congs. within the limits of a State can be conceived which will not in some way or other encroach upon the authority [of the] States. In order then to give some meaning to both parts of the sentence, as a known rule of interpretation requires, we must restrain this proviso to some particular view of the parties. What was this view? My answer is that it was to save to the States their right of preemption of lands from the Indians. My reasons are. 1. That this was the principal right formerly exerted by the Colonies with regard to the Indians. 2. that it was a right asserted by the laws as well as the proceedings of all of them, and therefore being most familiar, wd. be most likely to be in contemplation of the Parties; 3. that being of most consequence to the States individually, and least inconsistent with the general powers of Congress, it was most likely to be made a ground of Compromise. 4. it has been always said that the proviso came from the Virga. Delegates, who wd naturally be most vigilant over the territorial rights of their Constituents. But whatever may be the true boundary between the authority of Congs. & that of N. Y. or however indiscreet the latter may have been, I join entirely with you in thinking that temperance on the part of the former will be the wisest policy.

3

RECORDS OF THE FEDERAL CONVENTION

[2:321; Journal, 18 Aug.]

To regulate affairs with the Indians as well within as without the limits of the United States

[2:367; Journal, 22 Aug.]

at the end of the 2nd clause, 2 sect. 7 article add

"and with Indians, within the Limits of any State, not subject to the laws thereof"

[2:569; Committee of Style]

To regulate commerce with foreign nations, and among the several States; and with the Indian tribes.

4

JAMES MADISON, FEDERALIST, NO. 42, 284–85
22 Jan. 1788

The regulation of commerce with the Indian tribes is very properly unfettered from two limitations in the articles of confederation, which render the provision obscure and contradictory. The power is there restrained to Indians, not members of any of the States, and is not to violate or infringe the legislative right of any State within its own limits. What description of Indians are to be deemed members of a State, is not yet settled; and has been a question of frequent perplexity and contention in the Foederal Councils. And how the trade with Indians, though not members of a State, yet residing within its legislative jurisdiction, can be regulated by an external authority, without so far intruding on the internal rights of legislation, is absolutely incomprehensible. This is not the only case in which the articles of confederation have inconsiderately endeavored to accomplish impossibilities; to reconcile a partial sovereignty in the Union, with compleat sovereignty in the States; to subvert a mathematical axiom, by taking away a part, and letting the whole remain.

5

SENATE, MESSAGE FROM THE PRESIDENT
17–22 Sept. 1789
Annals 1:80–82, 84

The Senate entered on Executive business.

The following Message was received from the PRESIDENT OF THE UNITED STATES:

Gentlemen of the Senate:

It doubtless is important that all treaties and compacts formed by the United States with other nations, whether civilized or not, should be made with caution, and executed with fidelity.

It is said to be the general understanding and practice of nations, as a check on the mistakes and indiscretions of ministers or commissioners, not to consider any treaty negotiated and signed by such officers, as final and conclusive, until ratified by the sovereign or government from whom they derive their powers. This practice has been adopted by the United States respecting their treaties with European nations, and I am inclined to think it would be advisable to observe it in the conduct of our treaties with the Indians; for, though such treaties being, on their part, made by their chiefs or rulers, need not be ratified by them, yet, being formed on our part by the agency of subordinate officers, it seems to be both prudent and reasonable that their acts should not be binding on the nation until approved and ratified by the Government. It strikes me that this point should be well considered and settled, so that our national proceedings, in this respect, may become uniform, and be directed by fixed and stable principles.

The treaties with certain Indian nations, which were laid before you with my message of the 25th May last, suggested two questions to my mind, viz: 1st, Whether those treaties were to be considered as perfected, and, consequently, as obligatory, without being ratified? If not, then 2dly, Whether both, or either, and which of them, ought to be ratified? On these questions I request your opinion and advice.

You have, indeed, advised me *"to execute and enjoin an observance of"* the treaty with the Wyandots, &c. You, gentlemen, doubtless intended to be clear and explicit; and yet, without further explanation, I fear I may misunderstand your meaning: for if by my *executing* that treaty you mean that I should make it (in a more particular and immediate manner than it now is) the act of Government, then it follows that I am to ratify it. If you mean by my *executing it,* that I am to see that it be carried into effect and operation, then I am led to conclude, either that you consider it as being perfect and obligatory in its present state, and therefore to be executed and observed; or, that you consider it to derive its completion and obligation from the silent approbation and ratification which my proclamation may be construed to imply. Although I am inclined to think that the latter is your intention, yet it certainly is best that all doubts respecting it be removed.

Permit me to observe, that it will be proper for me to be informed of your sentiments relative to the treaty with the Six Nations, previous to the departure of the Governor of the Western Territory; and therefore I recommend it to your early consideration.

GEO. WASHINGTON.

September 17, 1789.

Ordered, That the President's Message be committed to Messrs. CARROLL, KING, and READ.

. . . . .

The Senate entered on Executive business.

Mr. CARROLL, on behalf of the committee appointed yesterday, reported as follows:

The committee, to whom was referred a Message from the President of the United States of the 17th September, 1789, report:

That the signature of treaties with the Indian nations has ever been considered as a full completion thereof, and that such treaties have never been solemnly ratified by either of the contracting parties, as hath been commonly practised among the civilized nations of Europe: wherefore, the committee are of opinion, that the formal ratification of the treaty concluded at Fort Harmar, on the 9th day of January, 1789, between Arthur St Clair, Governor of the Western Territory, on the part of the United States, and the sachems and warriors of the Wyandot, Delaware, Ottawa, Chippewa, Pattiwattima, and Sac nations, is not expedient or necessary; and that the resolve of the Senate of the 8th September, 1789, respecting the said treaty, authorizes the President of the United States to enjoin a due observance thereof.

That, as to the treaty made at Fort Harmar, on the 9th of January, 1789, between the said Arthur St. Clair and the sachems and warriors of the Six Nations, (except the Mohawks,) from particular circumstances affecting a part of the ceded lands, the Senate did not judge it expedient to pass any act concerning the same.

Ordered, That the consideration of the report be postponed until Monday next.

. . . . .

The Senate entered on Executive business.

They proceeded to consider the report of the committee, appointed the 17th, on the President's Message of that date; and,

On motion to postpone the report, to substitute the following, to wit:

Resolved, That the Senate do advise and consent that the President of the United States ratify the treaty concluded at Fort Harmar, on the 9th day of January, 1789, between Arthur St. Clair, Governor of the Western Territory, on the part of the United States, and the sachems and warriors of the Wyandot, Delaware, Ottawa, Chippewa, Pattawattima, and Sac nations.

It passed in the affirmative.

6

GEORGE WASHINGTON, THIRD ANNUAL ADDRESS
25 Oct. 1791
Richardson 1:104–5

In the interval of your recess due attention has been paid to the execution of the different objects which were specially provided for by the laws and resolutions of the last session.

Among the most important of these is the defense and security of the Western frontiers. To accomplish it on the most humane principles was a primary wish.

Accordingly, at the same time that treaties have been provisionally concluded and other proper means used to attach the wavering and to confirm in their friendship the well-disposed tribes of Indians, effectual measures have been adopted to make those of a hostile description sensible that a pacification was desired upon terms of moderation and justice.

Those measures having proved unsuccessful, it became necessary to convince the refractory of the power of the United States to punish their depredations. Offensive operations have therefore been directed, to be conducted, however, as consistently as possible with the dictates of humanity. Some of these have been crowned with full success and others are yet depending. The expeditions which have been completed were carried on under the authority and at the expense of the United States by the militia of Kentucky, whose enterprise, intrepidity, and good conduct are entitled to peculiar commendation.

Overtures of peace are still continued to the deluded tribes, and considerable numbers of individuals belonging to them have lately renounced all further opposition, removed from their former situations, and placed themselves under the immediate protection of the United States.

It is sincerely to be desired that all need of coercion in future may cease and that an intimate intercourse may succeed, calculated to advance the happiness of the Indians and to attach them firmly to the United States.

In order to this it seems necessary—

That they should experience the benefits of an impartial dispensation of justice.

That the mode of alienating their lands, the main source of discontent and war, should be so defined and regulated as to obviate imposition and as far as may be practicable controversy concerning the reality and extent of the alienations which are made.

That commerce with them should be promoted under regulations tending to secure an equitable deportment toward them, and that such rational experiments should be made for imparting to them the blessings of civilization as may from time to time suit their condition.

That the Executive of the United States should be enabled to employ the means to which the Indians have been long accustomed for uniting their immediate interests with the preservation of peace.

And that efficacious provision should be made for inflicting adequate penalties upon all those who, by violating their rights, shall infringe the treaties and endanger the peace of the Union.

A system corresponding with the mild principles of religion and philanthropy toward an unenlightened race of men, whose happiness materially depends on the conduct of the United States, would be as honorable to the national character as conformable to the dictates of sound policy.

7

GEORGE WASHINGTON, SEVENTH ANNUAL ADDRESS
8 Dec. 1795
Richardson 1:182, 185

The termination of the long, expensive, and distressing war in which we have been engaged with certain Indians northwest of the Ohio is placed in the option of the United States by a treaty which the commander of our army has concluded provisionally with the hostile tribes in that region.

In the adjustment of the terms the satisfaction of the Indians was deemed an object worthy no less of the policy than of the liberality of the United States as the necessary basis of durable tranquillity. The object, it is believed, has been fully attained. The articles agreed upon will immediately be laid before the Senate for their consideration.

The Creek and Cherokee Indians, who alone of the Southern tribes had annoyed our frontiers, have lately confirmed their preexisting treaties with us, and were giving evidence of a sincere disposition to carry them into effect by the surrender of the prisoners and property they had taken. But we have to lament that the fair prospect in this quarter has been once more clouded by wanton murders, which some citizens of Georgia are represented to have recently perpetrated on hunting parties of the Creeks, which have again subjected that frontier to disquietude and danger, which will be productive of further expense, and may occasion more effusion of blood. Measures are pursuing to prevent or mitigate the usual consequences of such outrages, and with the hope of their succeeding at least to avert general hostility.

. . . . .

. . . It is necessary that we should not lose sight of an important truth which continually receives new confirmations, namely, that the provisions heretofore made with a view to the protection of the Indians from the violences of the lawless part of our frontier inhabitants are insufficient. It is demonstrated that these violences can now be perpetrated with impunity, and it can need no argument to prove that unless the murdering of Indians can be restrained by bringing the murderers to condign punishment, all the exertions of the Government to prevent destructive retaliations by the Indians will prove fruitless and all our present agreeable prospects illusory. The frequent destruction of innocent women and children, who are chiefly the victims of retaliation, must continue to shock humanity, and an enormous expense to drain the Treasury of the Union.

To enforce upon the Indians the observance of justice it is indispensable that there shall be competent means of rendering justice to them. If these means can be devised by the wisdom of Congress, and especially if there can be added an adequate provision for supplying the necessities of the Indians on reasonable terms (a measure the mention of which I the more readily repeat, as in all the conferences with them they urge it with solicitude), I should not hesitate to entertain a strong hope of rendering our tranquillity permanent. I add with pleasure that the probability even of their civilization is not diminished by the experiments which have been thus far made under the auspices of Government. The accomplishment of this work, if practicable, will reflect undecaying luster on our national character and administer the most grateful consolations that virtuous minds can know.

8

GEORGE WASHINGTON, EIGHTH ANNUAL ADDRESS
7 Dec. 1796
Richardson 1:199

Measures calculated to insure a continuance of the friendship of the Indians and to preserve peace along the extent of our interior frontier have been digested and adopted. In the framing of these care has been taken to guard on the one hand our advanced settlements from the predatory incursions of those unruly individuals who can not be restrained by their tribes, and on the other hand to protect the rights secured to the Indians by treaty—to draw them nearer to the civilized state and inspire them with correct conceptions of the power as well as justice of the Government.

The meeting of the deputies from the Creek Nation at Colerain, in the State of Georgia, which had for a principal object the purchase of a parcel of their land by that State, broke up without its being accomplished, the nation having previous to their departure instructed them against making any sale. The occasion, however, has been improved to confirm by a new treaty with the Creeks their preexisting engagements with the United States, and to obtain their consent to the establishment of trading houses and military posts within their boundary, by means of which their friendship and the general peace may be more effectually secured.

9

JOHNSON & GRAHAM v. M'INTOSH
8 Wheat. 543 (1823)

Mr. Chief Justice MARSHALL delivered the opinion of the court:

The plaintiffs in this cause claim the land, in their declaration mentioned, under two grants, purporting to be made, the first in 1773, and the last in 1775, by the chiefs of certain Indian tribes, constituting the Illinois and the Piankeshaw nations; and the question is, whether this title can be recognized in the courts of the United States?

The facts as stated in the case agreed, show the authority of the chiefs who executed this conveyance, so far as it could be given by their own people; and likewise show that the particular tribes for whom these chiefs acted were in rightful possession of the land they sold. The inquiry, therefore, is, in a great measure, confined to the power of Indians to give, and of private individuals to receive, a title which can be sustained in the courts of this country.

As the right of society to prescribe those rules by which property may be acquired and preserved is not, and cannot be drawn into question; as the title to lands, especially, is and must be admitted to depend entirely on the law of the nation in which they lie; it will be necessary, in pursuing this inquiry, to examine, not singly those principles of abstract justice, which the Creator of all things has impressed on the mind of his creature man, and which are admitted to regulate, in a great degree, the rights of civilized nations, whose perfect independence is acknowledged; but those principles also which our own government has adopted in the particular case, and given us as the rule for our decision.

On the discovery of this immense continent, the great nations of Europe were eager to appropriate to themselves so much of it as they could respectively acquire. Its vast extent offered an ample field to the ambition and enterprise of all; and the character and religion of its inhabitants afforded an apology for considering them as a people over whom the superior genius of Europe might claim an ascendency. The potentates of the old world found no difficulty in convincing themselves that they made ample compensation to the inhabitants of the new, by bestowing on them civilization and Christianity, in exchange for unlimited independence. But, as they were all in pursuit of nearly the same object, it was necessary, in order to avoid conflicting settlements, and consequent war with each other, to establish a principle which all should acknowledge as the law by which the right of acquisition, which they all asserted, should be regulated as between themselves. This principle was that discovery gave title to the government by whose subjects, or by whose authority, it was made, against all other European governments, which title might be consummated by possession.

The exclusion of all other Europeans, necessarily gave to the nation making the discovery the sole right of acquiring the soil from the natives, and establishing settlements upon it. It was a right with which no Europeans could interfere. It was a right which all asserted for themselves, and to the assertion of which, by others, all assented.

Those relations which were to exist between the discoverer and the natives, were to be regulated by themselves. The rights thus acquired being exclusive, no other power could interpose between them.

In the establishment of these relations, the rights of the original inhabitants were, in no instance, entirely disregarded; but were necessarily, to a considerable extent, impaired. They were admitted to be the rightful occupants of the soil, with a legal as well as just claim to retain possession of it, and to use it according to their own discretion; but their rights to complete sovereignty, as independent nations, were necessarily diminished, and their power to dispose of the soil at their own will, to whomsoever they pleased, was denied by the original fundamental principle that discovery gave exclusive title to those who made it.

While the different nations of Europe respected the right of the natives, as occupants, they asserted the ultimate dominion to be in themselves; and claimed and exercised, as a consequence of this ultimate dominion, a power to grant the soil, while yet in possession of the natives. These grants have been understood by all to convey a title to the grantees, subject only to the Indian right of occupancy.

The history of America, from its discovery to the present day, proves, we think, the universal recognition of these principles.

Spain did not rest her title solely on the grant of the Pope. Her discussions respecting boundary, with France, with Great Britain, and with the United States, all show that she placed it on the rights given by discovery. Portugal sustained her claim to the Brazils by the same title.

France, also, founded her title to the vast territories she claimed in America on discovery. However conciliatory her conduct to the natives may have been, she still asserted her right of dominion over a great extent of country not actually settled by Frenchmen, and her exclusive right to acquire and dispose of the soil which remained in the occupation of Indians. Her monarch claimed all Canada and Acadie, as colonies of France, at a time when the French population was very inconsiderable, and the Indians occupied almost the whole country. He also claimed Louisiana, comprehending the immense territories watered by the Mississippi, and the rivers which empty into it, by the title of discovery. The letters patent granted to the Sieur Demonts, in 1603, constitute him Lieutenant-General, and the representative of the King in Acadie, which is described as stretching from the fortieth to the forty-sixth degree of north latitude; with authority to extend the power of the French over that country, and its inhabitants; to give laws to the people; to treat with the natives, and enforce the observance of treaties, and to parcel out and give title to lands, according to his own judgment.

The states of Holland also made acquisitions in America,

and sustained their right on the common principle adopted by all Europe. They allege, as we are told by Smith, in his History of New York, that Henry Hudson, who sailed, as they say, under the orders of their East India Company, discovered the country from the Delaware to the Hudson, up which he sailed to the forty-third degree of north latitude; and this country they claimed under the title acquired by this voyage. Their first object was commercial, as appears by a grant made to a company of merchants in 1614; but in 1621, the States-General made, as we are told by Mr. Smith, a grant of the country to the West India Company, by the name of New Netherlands.

The claim of the Dutch was always contested by the English; not because they questioned the title given by discovery, but because they insisted on being themselves the rightful claimants under that title. Their pretensions were finally decided by the sword.

No one of the powers of Europe gave its full assent to this principle more unequivocally than England. The documents upon this subject are ample and complete. So early as the year 1496, her monarch granted a commission to the Cabots, to discover countries then unknown to Christian people, and to take possession of them in the name of the King of England. Two years afterwards, Cabot proceeded on this voyage, and discovered the continent of North America, along which he sailed as far south as Virginia. To this discovery the English trace their title.

In this first effort made by the English government to acquire territory on this continent, we perceive a complete recognition of the principle which has been mentioned. The right of discovery given by this commission is confined to countries "then unknown to all Christian people;" and of these countries Cabot was empowered to take possession in the name of the King of England, thus asserting a right to take possession, notwithstanding the occupancy of the natives, who were heathens, and at the same time admitting the prior title of any Christian people who may have made a previous discovery.

The same principle continued to be recognized. The charter granted to Sir Humphrey Gilbert, in 1578, authorizes him to discover and take possession of such remote, heathen and barbarous lands as were not actually possessed by any Christian prince or people. This charter was afterwards renewed to Sir Walter Raleigh, in nearly the same terms.

By the charter of 1606, under which the first permanent English settlement on this continent was made, James I. granted to Sir Thomas Gates and others, those territories in America lying on the sea-coast, between the thirty-fourth and forty-fifth degrees of north latitude, and which either belonged to that monarch, or were not then possessed by any other Christian prince or people. The grantees were divided into two companies at their own request. The first, or southern colony, was directed to settle between the thirty-fourth and forty-first degrees of north latitude; and the second, or northern colony, between the thirty-eighth and forty-fifth degrees.

In 1609, after some expensive and not very successful attempts at settlement had been made, a new and more enlarged charter was given by the crown to the first col-

ony, in which the king granted to the "Treasurer and Company of Adventurers of the city of London for the first Colony in Virginia," in absolute property, the lands extending along the sea-coast four hundred miles, and into the land throughout from sea to sea. This charter, which is a part of the special verdict in this cause, was annulled, so far as respected the rights of the company, by the judgment of the Court of King's Bench on a writ of *quo warranto;* but the whole effect allowed to this judgment was to revest in the crown the powers of government, and the title to the land within its limits.

At the solicitation of those who held under the grant to the second or northern colony, a new and more enlarged charter was granted to the Duke of Lenox and others, in 1620, who were denominated the Plymouth Company, conveying to them in absolute property all the lands between the fortieth and forty-eighth degrees of north latitude.

Under this patent, New England has been in a great measure settled. The company conveyed to Henry Rosewell and others, in 1627, that territory which is now Massachusetts; and in 1628, a charter of incorporation, comprehending the powers of government, was granted to the purchasers.

Great part of New England was granted by this company, which, at length, divided their remaining lands among themselves; and, in 1635, surrendered their charter to the crown. A patent was granted to Gorges for Maine, which was allotted to him in the division of property.

All the grants made by the Plymouth Company, so far as we can learn, have been respected. In pursuance of the same principle, the King, in 1664, granted to the Duke of York the country of New England as far south as the Delaware Bay. His Royal Highness transferred New Jersey to Lord Berkeley and Sir George Carteret.

In 1663, the crown granted to Lord Clarendon and others, the country lying between the thirty-sixth degree of north latitude and the river St. Mathes; and, in 1666, the proprietors obtained from the crown a new charter, granting to them that province in the King's dominions in North America which lies from thirty-six degrees thirty minutes north latitude to the twenty-ninth degree, and from the Atlantic Ocean to the South Sea.

Thus has our whole country been granted by the crown while in the occupation of the Indians. These grants purport to convey the soil as well as the right of dominion to the grantees. In those governments which were denominated royal, where the right to the soil was not vested in individuals, but remained in the crown, or was vested in the colonial government, the king claimed and exercised the right of granting lands, and of dismembering the government at his will. The grants made out of the two original colonies, after the resumption of their charters by the crown, are examples of this. The governments of New England, New York, New Jersey, Pennsylvania, Maryland, and a part of Carolina, were thus created. In all of them, the soil, at the time the grants were made, was occupied by the Indians. Yet almost every title within those governments is dependent on these grants. In some instances, the soil was conveyed by the crown unaccompanied by the powers of government, as in the case of the northern neck of Virginia. It has never been objected to this, or to any other similar grant, that the title as well as possession was in the Indians when it was made, and that it passed nothing on that account.

These various patents cannot be considered as nullities; nor can they be limited to a mere grant of the powers of government. A charter intended to convey political power only, would never contain words expressly granting the land, the soil and the waters. Some of them purport to convey the soil alone; and in those cases in which the powers of government, as well as the soil, are conveyed to individuals, the crown has always acknowledged itself to be bound by the grant. Though the power to dismember regal governments was asserted and exercised, the power to dismember proprietary governments was not claimed; and, in some instances, even after the powers of government were revested in the crown, the title of the proprietors to the soil was respected.

Charles II. was extremely anxious to acquire the property of Maine, but the grantees sold it to Massachusetts, and he did not venture to contest the right of that colony to the soil. The Carolinas were originally proprietary governments. In 1721 a revolution was effected by the people, who shook off their obedience to the proprietors, and declared their dependence immediately on the crown. The king, however, purchased the title of those who were disposed to sell. One of them, Lord Carteret, surrendered his interest in the government, but retained his title to the soil. That title was respected till the revolution, when it was forfeited by the laws of war.

Further proofs of the extent to which this principle has been recognized, will be found in the history of the wars, negotiations and treaties which the different nations, claiming territory in America, have carried on and held with each other.

The contests between the cabinets of Versailles and Madrid, respecting the territory on the northern coast of the Gulf of Mexico, were fierce and bloody, and continued until the establishment of a Bourbon on the throne of Spain produced such amicable dispositions in the two crowns as to suspend or terminate them.

Between France and Great Britain, whose discoveries as well as settlements were nearly contemporaneous, contests for the country, actually covered by the Indians, began as soon as their settlements approached each other, and were continued until finally settled in the year 1763, by the treaty of Paris.

Each nation had granted and partially settled the country, denominated by the French, Arcadie, and by the English, Nova Scotia. By the twelfth article of the treaty of Utrecht, made in 1703, His Most Christian Majesty ceded to the Queen of Great Britain, "all Nova Scotia or Acadie, with its ancient boundaries." A great part of the ceded territory was in the possession of the Indians, and the extent of the cession could not be adjusted by the commissioners to whom it was to be referred.

The treaty of Aix la Chapelle, which was made on the principle of the *status ante bellum*, did not remove this subject of controversy. Commissioners for its adjustment were appointed, whose very able and elaborate, though unsuccessful arguments, in favor of the title of their respective sovereigns, show how entirely each relied on the title given by discovery to lands remaining in the possession of Indians.

After the termination of this fruitless discussion, the subject was transferred to Europe, and taken up by the cabinets of Versailles and London. This controversy embraced not only the boundaries of New England, Nova Scotia, and that part of Canada which adjoined those colonies, but embraced our whole western country also. France contended not only that the St. Lawrence was to be considered as the center of Canada, but that the Ohio was within that colony. She founded this claim on discovery, and on having used that river for the transportation of troops, in a war with some southern Indians.

This river was comprehended in the chartered limits of Virginia; but, though the right of England to a reasonable extent of country, in virtue of her discovery of the seacoast, and of the settlements she made on it, was not to be questioned; her claim of all the lands to the Pacific Ocean, because she had discovered the country washed by the Atlantic, might, without derogating from the principle recognized by all, be deemed extravagant. It interfered, too, with the claims of France, founded on the same principle. She therefore sought to strengthen her original title to the lands in controversy, by insisting that it had been acknowledged by France in the fifteenth article of the treaty of Utrecht. The dispute respecting the construction of that article has no tendency to impair the principle that discovery gave a title to lands still remaining in the possession of the Indians. Whichever title prevailed, it was still a title to lands occupied by the Indians, whose right of occupancy neither controverted, and neither had then extinguished.

These conflicting claims produced a long and bloody war, which was terminated by the conquest of the whole country east of the Mississippi. In the treaty of 1763, France ceded and guaranteed to Great Britain, all Nova Scotia, or Acadie, and Canada, with their dependencies; and it was agreed that the boundaries between the territories of the two nations, in America, should be irrevocably fixed by a line drawn from the source of the Mississippi, through the middle of that river and the lakes Maurepas and Ponchartrain, to the sea. This treaty expressly cedes, and has always been understood to cede, the whole country, on the English side of the dividing line, between the two nations, although a great and valuable part of it was occupied by the Indians. Great Britain, on her part, surrendered to France all her pretensions to the country west of the Mississippi. It has never been supposed that she surrendered nothing, although she was not in actual possession of a foot of land. She surrendered all right to acquire the country; and any after attempt to purchase it from the Indians would have been considered and treated as an invasion of the territories of France.

By the twentieth article of the same treaty, Spain ceded Florida, with its dependencies, and all the country she claimed east or south-east of the Mississippi, to Great Britain. Great part of this territory also was in possession of the Indians.

By a secret treaty, which was executed about the same time, France ceded Louisiana to Spain; and Spain has since retroceded the same country to France. At the time both of its cession and retrocession, it was occupied chiefly by the Indians.

Thus, all the nations of Europe, who have acquired territory on this continent, have asserted in themselves, and have recognized in others, the exclusive right of the discoverer to appropriate the lands occupied by the Indians. Have the American states rejected or adopted this principle?

By the treaty which concluded the war of our revolution, Great Britain relinquished all claim, not only to the government, but to the "propriety and territorial rights of the United States," whose boundaries were fixed in the second article. By this treaty, the powers of government, and the right to soil, which had previously been in Great Britain, passed definitively to these states. We had before taken possession of them, by declaring independence; but neither the declaration of independence, nor the treaty confirming it, could give us more than that which we before possessed, or to which Great Britain was before entitled. It has never been doubted, that either the United States, or the several states, had a clear title to all the lands within the boundary lines described in the treaty, subject only to the Indian right of occupancy, and that the exclusive power to extinguish that right was vested in that government which might constitutionally exercise it.

Virginia, particularly, within whose chartered limits the land in controversy lay, passed an act in the year 1779, declaring her "exclusive right of pre-emption from the Indians, of all the lands within the limits of her own chartered territory, and that no person or persons whatsoever, have, or ever had, a right to purchase any lands within the same, from any Indian nation, except only persons duly authorized to make such purchase, formerly for the use and benefit of the colony, and lately for the commonwealth." The act then proceeds to annul all deeds made by Indians to individuals, for the private use of the purchasers.

Without ascribing to this act the power of annulling vested rights, or admitting it to countervail the testimony furnished by the marginal note opposite to the title of the law, forbidding purchases from the Indians, in the revisals of the Virginia statutes, stating that law to be repealed, it may safely be considered as an unequivocal affirmance, on the part of Virginia, of the broad principle which had always been maintained that the exclusive right to purchase from the Indians resided in the government.

In pursuance of the same idea, Virginia proceeded, at the same session, to open her land office, for the sale of that country which now constitutes Kentucky—a country, every acre of which was then claimed and possessed by Indians, who maintained their title with as much persevering courage as was ever manifested by any people.

The states, having within their chartered limits different portions of territory covered by Indians, ceded that territory, generally, to the United States, on conditions expressed in their deeds of cession, which demonstrate the opinion that they ceded the soil as well as jurisdiction, and that in doing so they granted a productive fund to the government of the Union. The lands in controversy lay within the chartered limits of Virginia, and were ceded with the whole country north-west of the river Ohio. This grant contained reservations and stipulations which could only be made by the owners of the soil; and concluded with a stipulation that "all the lands in the ceded territory, not reserved, should be considered as a common fund, for the use and benefit of such of the United States as have become, or shall become, members of the confederation," &c., "according to their usual respective proportions in the general charge and expenditure, and shall be faithfully and *bona fide* disposed of for that purpose, and for no other use or purpose whatsoever."

The ceded territory was occupied by numerous and warlike tribes of Indians; but the exclusive right of the United States to extinguish their title, and to grant the soil, has never, we believe, been doubted.

After these states became independent, a controversy subsisted between them and Spain respecting boundary. By the treaty of 1795, this controversy was adjusted, and Spain ceded to the United States the territory in question. This territory, though claimed by both nations, was chiefly in the actual occupation of Indians.

The magnificent purchase of Louisiana was the purchase from France of a country almost entirely occupied by numerous tribes of Indians, who are in fact independent. Yet any attempt of others to intrude into that country would be considered as an aggression which would justify war.

Our late acquisitions from Spain are of the same character; and the negotiations which preceded those acquisitions recognize and elucidate the principle which has been received as the foundation of all European title in America.

The United States, then, have unequivocally acceded to that great and broad rule by which its civilized inhabitants now hold this country. They hold, and assert in themselves, the title by which it was acquired. They maintain, as all others have maintained, that discovery gave an exclusive right to extinguish the Indian title of occupancy, either by purchase or by conquest; and gave also a right to such a degree of sovereignty as the circumstances of the people would allow them to exercise.

The power now possessed by the government of the United States to grant lands, resided, while we were colonies, in the crown, or its grantees. The validity of the titles given by either has never been questioned in our courts. It has been exercised uniformly over territory in possession of the Indians. The existence of this power must negative the existence of any right which may conflict with, and control it. An absolute title to lands cannot exist, at the same time, in different persons, or in different governments. An absolute, must be an exclusive title, or at least a title which excludes all others not compatible with it. All our institutions recognize the absolute title of the crown, subject only to the Indian right of occupancy, and recognized the absolute title of the crown to extinguish that right. This is incompatible with an absolute and complete title in the Indians.

We will not enter into the controversy, whether agriculturists, merchants, and manufacturers, have a right, on abstract principles, to expel hunters from the territory they possess, or to contract their limits. Conquest gives a title which the courts of the conqueror cannot deny, whatever the private and speculative opinions of individuals may be, respecting the original justice of the claim which has been successfully asserted. The British government, which was then our government, and whose rights have passed to the United States, asserted a title to all the lands occupied by Indians within the chartered limits of the British colonies. It asserted also a limited sovereignty over them, and the exclusive right of extinguishing the title which occupancy gave to them. These claims have been maintained and established as far west as the river Mississippi, by the sword. The title to a vast portion of the lands we now hold, originates in them. It is not for the courts of this country to question the validity of this title, or to sustain one which is incompatible with it.

Although we do not mean to engage in the defense of those principles which Europeans have applied to Indian title, they may, we think, find some excuse, if not justification, in the character and habits of the people whose rights have been wrested from them.

The title by conquest is acquired and maintained by force. The conqueror prescribes its limits. Humanity, however, acting on public opinion, has established, as a general rule, that the conquered shall not be wantonly oppressed, and that their condition shall remain as eligible as is compatible with the objects of the conquest. Most usually they are incorporated with the victorious nation and become subjects or citizens of the government with which they are connected. The new and old members of the society mingle with each other; the distinction between them is gradually lost, and they make one people. Where this incorporation is practicable, humanity demands, and a wise policy requires, that the rights of the conquered to property should remain unimpaired; that the new subjects should be governed as equitably as the old, and that confidence in their security should gradually banish the painful sense of being separated from their ancient connections, and united by force to strangers.

When the conquest is complete, and the conquered inhabitants can be blended with the conquerors or safely governed as a distinct people, public opinion, which not even the conquerer can disregard, imposes these restraints upon him; and he cannot neglect them without injury to his fame, and hazard to his power.

But the tribes of Indians inhabiting this country were fierce savages, whose occupation was war, and whose subsistence was drawn chiefly from the forest. To leave them in possession of their country was to leave the country a wilderness; to govern them as a distinct people was impossible, because they were as brave and as high spirited as they were fierce, and were ready to repel by arms every attempt on their independence.

What was the inevitable consequence of this state of things? The Europeans were under the necessity either of abandoning the country, and relinquishing their pompous claims to it, or of enforcing those claims by the sword, and by the adoption of principles adapted to the condition of a people with whom it was impossible to mix, and who could not be governed as a distinct society, or of remaining in their neighborhood and exposing themselves and their families to the perpetual hazard of being massacred.

Frequent and bloody wars, in which the whites were not always the aggressors, unavoidably ensued. European policy, numbers and skill, prevailed. As the white population advanced, that of the Indians necessarily receded. The country in the immediate neighborhood of agriculturalists became unfit for them. The game fled into thicker and more unbroken forests, and the Indians followed. The soil, to which the crown originally claimed title, being no longer occupied by its ancient inhabitants, was parceled out accordingly to the will of the sovereign power, and taken possession of by persons who claimed immediately from the crown, or mediately, through its grantees or deputies.

That law which regulates, and ought to regulate in general, the relations between the conqueror and conquered, was incapable of application to a people under such circumstances. The resort to some new and different rule, better adapted to the actual state of things, was unavoidable. Every rule which can be suggested will be found to be attended with great difficulty.

However extravagant the pretension of converting the discovery of an inhabited country into conquest may appear, if the principle has been asserted in the first instance, and afterwards sustained; if a country has been acquired and held under it; if the property of the great mass of the community originates in it, it becomes the law of the land, and cannot be questioned. So, too, with respect to the concomitant principle, that the Indian inhabitants are to be considered merely as occupants, to be protected, indeed, while in peace, in the possession of their lands, but to be deemed incapable of transferring the absolute title to others. However this restriction may be opposed to natural right, and to the usages of civilized nations, yet, if it be indispensable to that system under which the country has been settled, and be adapted to the actual condition of the two people, it may, perhaps, be supported by reason, and certainly cannot be rejected by courts of justice.

This question is not entirely new in this court. The case of *Fletcher* v. *Peck* grew out of a sale made by the state of Georgia of a large tract of country within the limits of that state, the grant of which was afterwards resumed. The action was brought by a sub-purchaser, on the contract of sale, and one of the covenants in the deed was, that the state of Georgia was, at the time of sale, seized in fee of the premises. The real question presented by the issue was, whether the seisin in fee was in the state of Georgia, or in the United States. After stating that this controversy between the several states and the United States had been compromised, the court thought it necessary to notice the Indian title, which, although entitled to the respect of all courts until it should be legitimately extinguished, was declared not to be such as to be absolutely repugnant to a seisin in fee on the part of the state.

This opinion conforms precisely to the principle which has been supposed to be recognized by all European governments, from the first settlement of America. The absolute ultimate title has been considered as acquired by discovery, subject only to the Indian title of occupancy, which title the discoverers possessed the exclusive right of acquiring. Such a right is no more incompatible with a seisin in fee than a lease for years, and might as effectually bar an ejectment.

Another view has been taken of this question, which deserves to be considered. The title of the crown, whatever it might be, could be acquired only by a conveyance from the crown. If an individual might extinguish the Indian title for his own benefit, or, in other words, might purchase it, still he could acquire only that title. Admitting their power to change their laws or usages, so far as to allow an individual to separate a portion of their lands from the common stock, and hold it in severalty, still it is a part of their territory, and is held under them, by a title dependent on their laws. The grant derives its efficacy from their will; and, if they choose to resume it, and make a different disposition of the land, the courts of the United States cannot interpose for the protection of the title. The person who purchases lands from the Indians, within their territory, incorporates himself with them, so far as respects the property purchased; holds their title under their protection, and subject to their laws. If they annul the grant, we know of no tribunal which can revise and set aside the proceeding. We know of no principle which can distinguish this case from a grant made to a native Indian, authorizing him to hold a particular tract of land in severalty.

As such a grant could not separate the Indian from his nation, nor give a title which our courts could distinguish from the title of his tribe, as it might still be conquered from, or ceded by his tribe, we can perceive no legal principle which will authorize a court to say that different consequences are attached to this purchase, because it was made by a stranger. By the treaties concluded between the United States and the Indian nations, whose title the plaintiffs claim, the country comprehending the lands in controversy has been ceded to the United States, without any reservation of their title. These nations had been at war with the United States, and had an unquestionable right to annul any grant they had made to American citizens. Their cession of the country, without a reservation of this land, affords a fair presumption that they considered it as of no validity. They ceded to the United States this very property, after having used it in common with other lands, as their own, from the date of their deeds to the time of cession; and the attempt now made is to set up their title against that of the United States.

The proclamation issued by the King of Great Britain, in 1763, has been considered, as we think with reason, as constituting an additional objection to the title of the plaintiffs.

By that proclamation, the crown reserved under its own dominion and protection, for the use of the Indians, "all the land and territories lying to the westward of the sources of the rivers which fall into the sea from the west and north-west," and strictly forbade all British subjects from making any purchases or settlements whatever, or taking possession of the reserved lands.

It has been contended that, in this proclamation, the King transcended his constitutional powers; and the case of *Campbell* v. *Hall* (reported by Cowper) is relied on to support this position.

It is supposed to be a principle of universal law that, if an uninhabited country be discovered by a number of individuals, who acknowledge no connection with, and owe no allegiance to, any government whatever, the country becomes the property of the discoverers, so far at least as they can use it. They acquire a title in common. The title of the whole land is in the whole society. It is to be divided and parceled out according to the will of the society, expressed by the whole body, or by that organ which is authorized by the whole to express it.

If the discovery be made, and possession of the country be taken, under the authority of an existing government, which is acknowledged by the emigrants, it is supposed to be equally well settled that the discovery is made for the whole nation, that the country becomes a part of the nation, and that the vacant soil is to be disposed of by that organ of the government which has the constitutional power to dispose of the national domains, by that organ in which all vacant territory is vested by law.

According to the theory of the British constitution, all vacant lands are vested in the crown, as representing the nation; and the exclusive power to grant them is admitted to reside in the crown, as a branch of the royal prerogative. It has been already shown that this principle was as fully recognized in America as in the island of Great Britain. All the lands we hold were originally granted by the crown; and the establishment of a regal government has never been considered as impairing its right to grant lands within the chartered limits of such colony. In addition to the proof of this principle, furnished by the immense grants, already mentioned, of lands lying within the chartered limits of Virginia, the continuing right of the crown to grant lands lying within that colony was always admitted. A title might be obtained, either by making an entry with the surveyor of a county, in pursuance of law, or by an order of the governor in council, who was the deputy of the King, or by an immediate grant from the crown. In Virginia, therefore, as well as elsewhere in the British dominions, the complete title of the crown to vacant lands was acknowledged.

So far as respected the authority of the crown, no distinction was taken between vacant lands and lands occupied by the Indians. The title, subject only to the right of occupancy by the Indians, was admitted to be in the King, as was his right to grant that title. The lands, then, to which this proclamation referred, were lands which the King had a right to grant, or to reserve for the Indians.

According to the theory of the British constitution, the royal prerogative is very extensive so far as respects the political relations between Great Britain and foreign nations. The peculiar situation of the Indians, necessarily considered in some respects, as a dependent, and in some respects as a distinct people, occupying a country claimed by Great Britain, and yet too powerful and brave not to be dreaded as formidable enemies, required that means should be adopted for the preservation of peace, and that their friendship should be secured by quieting their alarms for their property. This was to be effected by restraining the encroachments of the whites; and the power to do this was never, we believe, denied by the colonies to the crown.

In the case of *Campbell* against *Hall*, that part of the proclamation was determined to be illegal which imposed a tax on a conquered province, after a government had been bestowed upon it. The correctness of this decision cannot be questioned, but its application to the case at bar cannot be admitted. Since the expulsion of the Stuart family, the power of imposing taxes, by proclamation, has never been claimed as a branch of regal prerogative; but the powers of granting, or refusing to grant, vacant lands, and of restraining encroachments on the Indians, have always been asserted and admitted.

The authority of this proclamation, so far as it respected this continent, has never been denied, and the titles it gave to lands have always been sustained in our courts.

In the argument of this cause, the counsel for the plaintiffs have relied very much on the opinions expressed by men holding offices of trust, and on various proceedings in America, to sustain titles to land derived from the Indians.

The collection of claims to lands lying in the western country, made in the first volume of the Laws of the United States, has been referred to; but we find nothing in that collection to support the argument. Most of the titles were derived from persons professing to act under the authority of the government existing at the time; and the two grants under which the plaintiffs claim are supposed, by the person under whose inspection the collection was made, to be void because forbidden by the royal proclamation of 1763. It is not unworthy of remark that the usual mode adopted by the Indians for granting lands to individuals has been to reserve them in the treaty, or to grant them under the sanction of the commissioners with whom the treaty was negotiated. The practice, in such case, to grant to the crown, for the use of the individual, is some evidence of a general understanding that the validity even of such a grant depended on its receiving the royal sanction.

The controversy between the colony of Connecticut and the Mohegan Indians, depended on the nature and extent of a grant made by those Indians, to the colony; on the nature and extent of the reservations made by the Indians in their several deeds and treaties, which were alleged to be recognized by the legitimate authority, and on the violation by the colony of rights thus reserved and secured. We do not perceive, in that case, any assertion of the principle that individuals might obtain a complete and valid title from the Indians.

It has been stated, that in the memorial transmitted from the cabinet of London to that of Versailles, during the controversy between the two nations respecting boundary, which took place in 1755, the Indian right to the soil is recognized. But this recognition was made with reference to their character as Indians, and for the pur-pose of showing that they were fixed to a particular territory. It was made for the purpose of sustaining the claim of His Britannic Majesty to dominion over them.

The opinion of the Attorney and Solicitor-General, Pratt and Yorke, have been adduced to prove, that in the opinion of those great law officers, the Indian grant could convey a title to the soil without a patent emanating from the crown. The opinion of those persons would certainly be of great authority on such a question, and we were not a little surprised, when it was read, at the doctrine it seemed to advance. An opinion so contrary to the whole practice of the crown, and to the uniform opinions given on all other occasions by its great law officers, ought to be very explicit, and accompanied by the circumstances under which it was given and to which it was applied, before we can be assured that it is properly understood. In a pamphlet, written for the purpose of asserting the Indian title, styled "Plain Facts," the same opinion is quoted, and is said to relate to purchases made in the East Indies. It is, of course, entirely inapplicable to purchases made in America. Chalmers, in whose collection this opinion is found, does not say to whom it applies; but there is reason to believe, that the author of "Plain Facts" is, in this respect, correct. The opinion commences thus: "In respect to such places as have been, or shall be, acquired, by treaty or grant, from any of the Indian princes or governments, your majesty's letters patent are not necessary." The words "princes or governments" are usually applied to the East Indians, but not to those of North America. We speak of their sachems, their warriors, their chiefmen, their nations or tribes, not of the "princes or governments." The question on which the opinion was given, too, and to which it relates, was whether the King's subjects carry with them the common law wherever they may form settlements. The opinion is given with a view to this point, and its object must be kept in mind while construing its expressions.

Much reliance is also placed on the fact that many tracts are now held in the United States under the Indian title, the validity of which is not questioned.

Before the importance attached to this fact is conceded, the circumstances under which such grants were obtained, and such titles are supported, ought to be considered. These lands lie chiefly in the eastern states. It is known that the Plymouth Company made many extensive grants, which, from their ignorance of the country, interfered with each other. It is also known that Mason, to whom New Hampshire, and Gorges, to whom Maine was granted, found great difficulty in managing such unwieldy property. The country was settled by emigrants, some from Europe, but chiefly from Massachusetts, who took possession of lands they found unoccupied, and secured themselves in that possession by the best means in their power. The disturbances in England, and the civil war and revolution which followed those disturbances, prevented any interference on the part of the mother country, and the proprietors were unable to maintain their title. In the meantime, Massachusetts claimed the country and governed it. As her claim was adversary to that of the proprietors, she encouraged the settlement of persons made under her authority, and encouraged, likewise, their securing themselves in possession, by purchasing the acquiescence and forbearance of the Indians.

After the restoration of Charles II., Gorges and Mason, when they attempted to establish their title, found themselves opposed by men, who held under Massachusetts and under the Indians. The title of the proprietors was resisted; and though, in some cases, compromises were made, and in some, the opinion of a court was given ultimately in their favor, the juries found uniformly against them. They became wearied with the struggle, and sold their property. The titles held under the Indians were sanctioned by length of possession; but there is no case, so far as we are informed, of a judicial decision in their favor.

Much reliance has also been placed on a recital contained in the charter of Rhode Island, and on a letter addressed to the governors of the neighboring colonies by the King's command, in which some expressions are inserted, indicating the royal approbation of titles acquired from the Indians.

The charter to Rhode Island recites "that the said John Clark and others, had transplanted themselves into the midst of the Indian nations, and were seized and possessed, by purchase and consent of the said natives, to their full content, of such lands," &c. And the letter recites that "Thomas Chifflinch, and others, having, in the right of Major Asperton, a just propriety in the Narragansett country, in New England, by grants from the native princes of that country, and being desirous to improve it into an English colony," &c., "are yet daily disturbed."

The impression this language might make, if viewed apart from the circumstances under which it was employed, will be effaced, when considered in connection with those circumstances.

In the year 1635, the Plymouth Company surrendered their charter to the crown. About the same time, the religious dissensions of Massachusetts expelled from that colony several societies of individuals, one of which settled in Rhode Island, on lands purchased from the Indians. They were not within the chartered limits of Massachusetts, and the English government was too much occupied at home to bestow its attention on this subject. There existed no authority to arrest their settlement of the country. If they obtained the Indian title, there were none to assert the title of the crown. Under these circumstances, the settlement became considerable. Individuals acquired separate property in lands which they cultivated and improved; a government was established among themselves; and no power existed in America which could rightfully interfere with it.

On the restoration of Charles II., this small society hastened to acknowledge his authority, and to solicit his confirmation of their title to the soil, and to jurisdiction over the country. Their solicitations were successful, and a charter was granted to them, containing the recital which has been mentioned.

It is obvious that this transaction can amount to no acknowledgment that the Indian grant could convey a title paramount to that of the crown, or could, in itself, constitute a complete title. On the contrary, the charter of the crown was considered as indispensable to its completion.

It has never been contended that the Indian title amounted to nothing. Their right of possession has never been questioned. The claim of government extends to the complete ultimate title, charged with this right of possession, and to the exclusive power of acquiring that right. The object of the crown was to settle the seacoast of America; and when a portion of it was settled, without violating the rights of others, by persons professing their loyalty, and soliciting the royal sanction of an act, the consequences of which were ascertained to be beneficial, it would have been as unwise as ungracious to expel them from their habitations because they had obtained the Indian title otherwise than through the agency of government. The very grant of a charter is an assertion of the title of the crown, and its words convey the same idea. The country granted is said to be "our island called Rhode Island;" and the charter contains an actual grant of the soil, as well as of the powers of government.

The letter was written a few months before the charter was issued, apparently at the request of the agents of the intended colony, for the sole purpose of preventing the trespasses of neighbors, who were disposed to claim some authority over them. The King, being willing himself to ratify and confirm their title, was, of course, inclined to quiet them in their possession.

This charter, and this letter, certainly sanction a previous unauthorized purchase from Indians, under the circumstances attending that particular purchase, but are far from supporting the general proposition that a title acquired from the Indians would be valid against a title acquired from the crown, or without the confirmation of the crown.

The acts of the several colonial assemblies, prohibiting purchases from the Indians, have also been relied on, as proving that, independent of such prohibitions, Indian deeds would be valid. But we think this fact, at most, equivocal. While the existence of such purchases would justify their prohibition, even by colonies which considered Indian deeds as previously invalid, the fact that such acts have been generally passed, is strong evidence of the general opinion that such purchases are opposed by the soundest principles of wisdom and national policy.

After bestowing on this subject a degree of attention which was more required by the magnitude of the interest in litigation, and the able and elaborate arguments of the bar, than by its intrinsic difficulty, the court is decidedly of opinion that the plaintiffs do not exhibit a title which can be sustained in the courts of the United States, and that there is no error in the judgment which was rendered against them in the District Court of Illinois.

10

CHEROKEE NATION V. GEORGIA
5 Pet. 1 (1831)

MARSHALL, Ch. J., delivered the opinion of the court.— This bill is brought by the Cherokee nation, praying an injunction to restrain the state of Georgia from the execution of certain laws of that state, which, as is alleged, go directly to annihilate the Cherokee as a political society, and to seize for the use of Georgia, the lands of the nation which have been assured to them by the United States, in solemn treaties repeatedly made and still in force.

If courts were permitted to indulge their sympathies, a case better calculated to excite them can scarcely be imagined. A people, once numerous, powerful, and truly independent, found by our ancestors in the quiet and uncontrolled possession of an ample domain, gradually sinking beneath our superior policy, our arts and our arms, have yielded their lands, by successive treaties, each of which contains a solemn guarantee of the residue, until they retain no more of their formerly extensive territory than is deemed necessary to their comfortable subsistence. To preserve this remnant, the present application is made.

Before we can look into the merits of the case, a preliminary inquiry presents itself. Has this court jurisdiction of the cause? The third article of the constitution describes the extent of the judicial power. The second section closes an enumeration of the cases to which it is extended, with "controversies" "between a state or citizens thereof, and foreign states, citizens or subjects." A subsequent clause of the same section gives the supreme court original jurisdiction, in all cases in which a state shall be a party. The party defendant may then unquestionably be sued in this court. May the plaintiff sue in it? Is the Cherokee nation a foreign state, in the sense in which that term is used in the constitution? The counsel for the plaintiffs have maintained the affirmative of this proposition with great earnestness and ability. So much of the argument as was intended to prove the character of the Cherokees as a state, as a distinct political society, separated from others, capable of managing its own affairs and governing itself, has, in the opinion of a majority of the judges, been completely successful. They have been uniformly treated as a state, from the settlement of our country. The numerous treaties made with them by the United States, recognise them as a people capable of maintaining the relations of peace and war, of being responsible in their political character for any violation of their engagements, or for any aggression committed on the citizens of the United States, by any individual of their community. Laws have been enacted in the spirit of these treaties. The acts of our government plainly recognise the Cherokee nation as a state, and the courts are bound by those acts.

A question of much more difficulty remains. Do the Cherokees constitute a *foreign* state in the sense of the constitution? The counsel have shown conclusively, that they are not a state of the Union, and have insisted that, individually, they are aliens, not owing allegiance to the United States. An aggregate of aliens composing a state must, they say, be a foreign state; each individual being foreign, the whole must be foreign.

This argument is imposing, but we must examine it more closely, before we yield to it. The condition of the Indians in relation to the United States is, perhaps, unlike that of any other two people in existence. In general, nations not owing a common allegiance, are foreign to each other. The term *foreign* nation is, with strict propriety, applicable by either to the other. But the relation of the Indians to the United States is marked by peculiar and cardinal distinctions which exist nowhere else. The Indian territory is admitted to compose a part of the United States. In all our maps, geographical treatises, histories and laws, it is so considered. In all our intercourse with foreign nations, in our commercial regulations, in any attempt at intercourse between Indians and foreign nations, they are considered as within the jurisdictional limits of the United States, subject to many of those restraints which are imposed upon our own citizens. They acknowledge themselves, in their treaties, to be under the protection of the United States; they admit, that the United States shall have the sole and exclusive right of regulating the trade with them, and managing all their affairs as they think proper; and the Cherokees in particular were allowed by the treaty of Hopewell, which preceded the constitution, "to send a deputy of their choice, whenever they think fit, to congress." Treaties were made with some tribes, by the state of New York, under a then unsettled construction of the confederation, by which they ceded all their lands to that state, taking back a limited grant to themselves, in which they admit their dependence. Though the Indians are acknowledged to have an unquestionable, and heretofore unquestioned, right to the lands they occupy, until that right shall be extinguished by a voluntary cession to our government; yet it may well be doubted, whether those tribes which reside within the acknowledged boundaries of the United States can, with strict accuracy, be denominated foreign nations. They may, more correctly, perhaps, be denominated domestic dependent nations. They occupy a territory to which we assert a title independent of their will, which must take effect in point of possession, when their right of possession ceases. Meanwhile, they are in a state of pupilage; their relation to the United States resembles that of a ward to his guardian. They look to our government for protection; rely upon its kindness and its power; appeal to it for relief to their wants; and address the president as their great father. They and their country are considered by foreign nations, as well as by ourselves, as being so completely under the sovereignty and dominion of the United States, that any attempt to acquire their lands, or to form a political connection with them, would be considered by all as an invasion of our territory and an act of hostility. These considerations go far to support the opinion, that the framers of our constitution had not the Indian tribes in view, when they opened the courts of the Union to controversies between a state or the citizens thereof and foreign states.

In considering this subject, the habits and usages of the Indians, in their intercourse with their white neighbors, ought not to be entirely disregarded. At the time the constitution was framed, the idea of appealing to an American court of justice for an assertion of right or a redress of wrong, had perhaps never entered the mind of an Indian or of his tribe. Their appeal was to the tomahawk, or to the government. This was well understood by the statesmen who framed the constitution of the United States, and might furnish some reason for omitting to enumerate them among the parties who might sue in the courts of the Union. Be this as it may, the peculiar relations between the United States and the Indians occupying our territory are such, that we should feel much difficulty in considering them as designated by the term foreign state, were there no other part of the constitution which might shed light on the meaning of these words. But we think that in construing them, considerable aid is furnished by that clause in the eighth section of the third [first] article, which empowers congress to "regulate commerce with foreign nations, and among the several states, and with the Indian tribes." In this clause, they are as clearly contradistinguished, by a name appropriate to themselves, from foreign nations, as from the several states composing the Union. They are designated by a distinct appellation; and as this appellation can be applied to neither of the others, neither can the application distinguishing either of the others be, in fair construction, applied to them. The objects to which the power of regulating commerce might be directed, are divided into three distinct classes—foreign nations, the several states, and Indian tribes. When forming this article, the convention considered them as entirely distinct. We cannot assume that the distinction was lost, in framing a subsequent article, unless there be something in its language to authorize the assumption.

The counsel for the plaintiffs contend, that the words "Indian tribes" were introduced into the article, empowering congress to regulate commerce, for the purpose of removing those doubts in which the management of Indian affairs was involved by the language of the ninth article of the confederation. Intending to give the whole power of managing those affairs to the government about to be instituted, the convention conferred it explicitly; and omitted those qualifications which embarrassed the exercise of it, as granted in the confederation. This may be admitted, without weakening the construction which has been intimated. Had the Indian tribes been foreign nations, in the view of the convention, this exclusive power of regulating intercourse with them might have been, and, most probably, would have been, specifically given, in language indicating that idea, not in language contradistinguishing them from foreign nations. Congress might have been empowered "to regulate commerce with foreign nations, including the Indian tribes, and among the several states." This language would have suggested itself to statesmen who considered the Indian tribes as foreign nations, and were yet desirous of mentioning them particularly.

It has been also said, that the same words have not necessarily the same meaning attached to them, when found in different parts of the same instrument; their meaning is controlled by the context. This is undoubtedly true. In common language, the same word has various meanings, and the peculiar sense in which it is used in any sentence, is to be determined by the context. This may not be equally true with respect to proper names. "Foreign nations" is a general term, the application of which to Indian tribes, when used in the American constitution, is, at best, extremely questionable. In one article, in which a power is

given to be exercised in regard to foreign nations generally, and to the Indian tribes particularly, they are mentioned as separate, in terms clearly contradistinguishing them from each other. We perceive plainly, that the constitution, in this article, does not comprehend Indian tribes in the general term "foreign nations;" not, we presume, because a tribe may not be a nation, but because it is not foreign to the United States. When afterwards, the term "foreign state;" is introduced, we cannot impute to the convention, the intention to desert its former meaning, and to comprehend Indian tribes within it, unless the context force that construction on us. We find nothing in the context, and nothing in the subject of the article, which leads to it.

The court has bestowed its best attention on this question, and, after mature deliberation, the majority is of opinion, that an Indian tribe or nation within the United States is not a foreign state, in the sense of the constitution, and cannot maintain an action in the courts of the United States.

A serious additional objection exists to the jurisdiction of the court. Is the matter of the bill the proper subject for judicial inquiry and decision? It seeks to restrain a state from the forcible exercise of legislative power over a neighboring people, asserting their independence; their right to which the state denies. On several of the matters alleged in the bill, for example, on the laws making it criminal to exercise the usual powers of self-government in their own country, by the Cherokee nation, this court cannot interpose; at least, in the form in which those matters are presented.

That part of the bill which respects the land occupied by the Indians, and prays the aid of the court to protect their possession, may be more doubtful. The mere question of right might, perhaps, be decided by this court, in a proper case, with proper parties. But the court is asked to do more than decide on the title. The bill requires us to control the legislature of Georgia, and to restrain the exertion of its physical force. The propriety of such an interposition by the court may be well questioned; it savors too much of the exercise of political power, to be within the proper province of the judicial department. But the opinion on the point respecting parties makes it unnecessary to decide this question.

If it be true, that the Cherokee nation have rights, this is not the tribunal in which those rights are to be asserted. If it be true, that wrongs have been inflicted, and that still greater are to be apprehended, this is not the tribunal which can redress the past or prevent the future. The motion for an injunction is denied.

· · · · ·

BALDWIN, Justice.—As jurisdiction is the first question which must arise in every cause, I have confined my examination of this, entirely to that point, and that branch of it which relates to the capacity of the plaintiffs to ask the interposition of this court. I concur in the opinion of the court, in dismissing the bill, but not for the reasons assigned. In my opinion, there is no plaintiff in this suit; and this opinion precludes any examination into the merits of the bill, or the weight of any minor objections. My judgment stops me at the threshold, and forbids me to examine into the acts complained of.

As the reasons for the judgment of the court seem to me more important than the judgment itself, in its effects on the peace of the country, and the condition of the complainants, and as I stand alone on one question of vital concern to both; I must give my reasons in full. The opinion of this court is of high authority in itself; and the judge who delivers it has a support as strong in moral influence over public opinion, as any human tribunal can impart. The judge, who stands alone in decided dissent on matters of the infinite magnitude which this case presents, must sink under the continued and unequal struggle; unless he can fix himself by a firm hold on the constitution and laws of the country. He must be presumed to be in the wrong, until he proves himself to be in the right. Not shrinking even from this fearful issue, I proceed to consider the only question which I shall ever examine in relation to the rights of Indians to sue in the federal courts, until convinced of my error in my present convictions.

My view of the plaintiffs being a sovereign independent nation or foreign state, within the meaning of the constitution, applies to all the tribes with whom the United States have held treaties; for if one is a foreign nation or state, all others, in like condition, must be so, in their aggregate capacity; and each of their subjects or citizens, aliens, capable of suing in the circuit courts. This case, then, is the case of the countless tribes, who occupy tracts of our vast domain; who, in their collective and individual characters, as states or aliens, will rush to the federal courts, in endless controversies, growing out of the laws of the states or of congress.

In the spirit of the maxim *obsta principiis*, I shall first proceed to the consideration of the proceedings of the old congress, from the commencement of the revolution up to the adoption of the constitution; so as to ascertain whether the Indians were considered and treated with, as tribes of savages, or independent nations, foreign states, on an equality with any other foreign state or nation, and whether Indian affairs were viewed as those of foreign nations, and in connection with this view, refer to the acts of the federal government on the same subject.

In 1781 (1 Laws U.S. 586), a department for foreign affairs was established, to which was intrusted all correspondence and communication with the ministers or other officers of foreign powers, to be carried on through that office; also with the governors and presidents of the several states; and to receive the applications of all foreigners, letters of sovereign powers, plans of treaties, conventions, &c., and other acts of congress relative to the department of foreign affairs; and all communications, as well to as from the United States in congress assembled, were to be made through the secretary, and all papers on the subject of foreign affairs to be addressed to him. The same department was established under the present constitution in 1789, and with the same exclusive control over all the foreign concerns of this government with foreign states or princes. (2 Laws U.S. 6, 7.) In July 1775, congress estab-

lished a department of Indian affairs, to be conducted under the superintendence of commissioners. (1 Ibid. 597.) By the ordinance of August 1786, for the regulation of Indian affairs, they were placed under the control of the war department (Ibid. 614); continued there by the act of August 1789 (2 Ibid. 32, 33), under whose direction they have ever since remained. It is clear, then, that neither the old nor new government did ever consider Indian affairs, the regulation of our intercourse or treaties with them, as forming any part of our foreign affairs or concerns with foreign nations, states or princes.

I will next inquire, how the Indians were considered; whether as independent nations, or tribes with whom our intercourse must be regulated by the law of circumstances. In this examination, it will be found, that different words have been applied to them in treaties and resolutions of congress; nations, tribes, hordes, savages, chiefs, sachems and warriors of the Cherokees, for instance, or the Cherokee nation. I shall not stop to inquire into the effect which a name or title can give to a resolve of congress, a treaty or convention with the Indians, but into the substance of the thing done, and the subject-matter acted on; believing it requires no reasoning to prove, that the omission of the words prince, state, sovereignty or nation, cannot divest a contracting party of these national attributes, which are inherent in sovereign power pre- and self-existing, or confer them, by their use, where all the substantial requisites of sovereignty are wanting.

. . . . .

I now proceed to the instructions which preceded the treaty of Hopewell with the complainants, the treaty, and the consequent proceedings of congress. On the 15th March 1785, commissioners were appointed to treat with the Cherokees and other Indians, southward of them, within the limits of the United States, or who have been at war with them, for the purpose of making peace with them, and of receiving them into the favor and protection of the United States, &c. They were instructed to demand that all prisoners, negroes and other property, taken during the war, be given up; to inform the Indians of the great occurrences of the last war; of the extent of country relinquished by the late treaty of peace with Great Britain; to give notice to the governors of Virginia, North and South Carolina and Georgia, that they may attend, if they think proper; and were authorized to expend $4000 in making presents to the Indians; a matter well understood in making Indian treaties, but unknown, at least, in our treaties with foreign nations, princes or states, unless on the Barbary coast. A treaty was accordingly made, in November following, between the commissioners plentipotentiaries of the United States, of the one part, and the headmen and warriors of all the Cherokees, of the other. The word nation is not used in the preamble, nor any part of the treaty, so that we are left to infer the capacity in which the Cherokees contracted, whether as an independent nation, or foreign state, or a tribe of Indians, from the terms of the treaty, its stipulations and conditions. "The Indians, for themselves and their respective tribes and towns, do acknowledge all the Cherokees to be under the protection of the United States." (Art. 3, 1 Laws U.S. 322.) "The boundary allotted to the Cherokees for their hunting-grounds between the said Indians and the citizens of the United States, within the limits of the United States, is and shall be the following," viz. (as defined in Art. 4.) "For the benefit and comfort of the Indians, and for the prevention of injuries and aggressions on the part of the citizens or Indians, the United States, in congress assembled, shall have the sole and exclusive right of regulating the trade with the Indians, and managing all their affairs in such manner as they shall think proper." (Art. 9.) "That the Indians may have full confidence in the justice of the United States respecting their interests, they shall have the right to send a deputy of their choice, whenever they think fit, to congress." (Art. 12.)

This treaty is, in the beginning, called "article:" the word "treaty" is only to be found in the concluding line, where it is called "this definitive treaty." But article or treaty, its nature does not depend upon the name given it. It is not negotiated between ministers on both sides, representing their nations; the stipulations are wholly inconsistent with sovereignty; the Indians acknowledge their dependent character; hold the lands they occupy as an allotment of hunting-grounds; give to congress the exclusive right of regulating their trade, and managing all their affairs, as they may think proper. So it was understood by congress, as declared by them in their proclamation of 1st September 1788 (1 U.S. Laws 619), and so understood at the adoption of the constitution.

The meaning of the words "deputy to congress" in the twelfth article, may be as a person having a right to sit in that body, as, at that time, it was composed of delegates or deputies from the states, not as at present, representatives of the people of the states; or it may be as an agent or minister. But if the former was the meaning of the parties, it is conclusive to show, that he was not and could not be the deputy of a foreign state, wholly separated from the Union. If he sat in congress as a deputy from any state, it must be one having a political connection with, and within the jurisdiction of, the confederacy; if as a diplomatic agent, he could not represent an independent or sovereign nation, for all such have an unquestioned right to send such agents, when and where they please. The securing the right, by an express stipulation of the treaty; the declared objects in conferring the right, especially, when connected with the ninth article; show beyond a doubt, it was not to represent a foreign state or nation, or one to whom the least vestige of independence or sovereignty as to the United States appertained. There can be no dependence so anti-national, or so utterly subversive, of national existence, as transferring to a foreign government the regulation of its trade, and the management of all their affairs, at their pleasure. The nation or state, tribe or village, headmen or warriors of the Cherokees, call them by what name we please; call the articles they have signed a definitive treaty, or an indenture of servitude; they are not, by its force or virtue, a foreign state, capable of calling into legitimate action the judicial power of this Union, by the exercise of the original jurisdiction of this court, against a sovereign state, a component part of this nation. Unless

the constitution has imparted to the Cherokees a national character, never recognised under the confederation; and which, if they ever enjoyed, was surrendered by the treaty of Hopewell; they cannot be deemed, in this court, plaintiffs in such a case as this.

In considering the bearing of the constitution on their rights, it must be borne in mind, that a majority of the states represented in the convention had ceded to the United States the soil and jurisdiction of their western lands, or claimed it to be remaining in themselves; that congress asserted, as to the ceded, and the states, as to the unceded territory, their right to the soil absolutely, and the dominion in full sovereignty, within their respective limits, subject only to Indian occupancy, not as foreign states or nations, but as dependent on, and appendant to the state governments; that before the convention acted, congress had erected a government in the north-western territory, containing numerous and powerful nations or tribes of Indians, whose jurisdiction was contemned, and whose sovereignty was overturned, if it ever existed, except by permission of the states or congress, by ordaining, that the territorial laws should extend over the whole district; and directing divisions for the execution of civil and criminal process in every part; that the Cherokees were then dependents, having given up all their affairs to the regulation and management of congress, and that all the regulations of congress over Indian affairs, were then in force over an immense territory, under a solemn pledge to the inhabitants, that whenever their population and circumstances would admit, they should form constitutions, and become free, sovereign and independent states, on equal footing with the old component members of the confederation; that by the existing regulations and treaties, the Indian tenure to their land was their allotment as hunting-grounds, without the power of alienation, that the right of occupancy was not individual, that the Indians were forbidden all trade or intercourse with any person, not licensed, or at a post not designated by regulation; that Indian affairs formed no part of the foreign concerns of the government, and that though they were permitted to regulate their internal affairs in their own way, it was not by any inherent right, acknowledged by congress or reserved by treaty, but because congress did not think proper to exercise the sole and exclusive right, declared and asserted in all their regulations from 1775 to 1788, in the articles of confederation, in the ordinance of 1787, and the proclamation of 1788; which the plaintiffs solemnly recognised and expressly granted by the treaty of Hopewell, in 1785, as conferred on congress, to be exercised as they should think proper.

To correctly understand the constitution, then, we must read it with reference to this well-known existing state of our relations with the Indians; the United States asserting the right of soil, sovereignty and jurisdiction, in full dominion; the Indians, occupancy of allotted hunting-grounds.

We can thus expound the constitution, without a reference to the definitions of a state or nation by any foreign writer, hypothetical reasoning, or the dissertations of the Federalist. This would be to substitute individual authority in place of the declared will of the sovereign power of the Union, in a written fundamental law. Whether it is the emanation from the people or the states, is a moot question, having no bearing on the supremacy of that supreme law which, from a proper source, has rightfully been imposed on us by sovereign power. Where its terms are plain, I should, as a dissenting judge, deem it judicial sacrilege to put my hands on any of its provisions, and arrange or construe them according to any fancied use, object, purpose or motive, which, by any ingenious train of reasoning I might bring my mind to believe was the reason for its adoption by the sovereign power, from whose hands it comes to me as the rule and guide to my faith, my reason and judicial oath. In taking out, putting in, or varying the plain meaning of a word or expression, to meet the results of my poor judgment, as to the meaning and intention of the great charter, which alone imparts to me my power to act as a judge of its supreme injunctions, I should feel myself acting upon it by judicial amendments, and not as one of its executors. I will not add unto these things; I will not take away from the words of this book of prophecy; I will not impair the force or obligation of its enactments, plain and unqualified in its terms, by resorting to the authority of names; the decisions of foreign courts; or a reference to books or writers. The plain ordinances are a safe guide to my judgment. When they admit of doubt, I will connect the words with the practice, usages and settled principles of this government, as administered by its fathers, before the adoption of the constitution; and refer to the received opinion and fixed understanding of the high parties who adopted it; the usage and practice of the new government, acting under its authority; and the solemn decisions of this court, acting under its high powers and responsibility; nothing fearing, that in so doing, I can discover some sound and safe maxims of American policy and jurisprudence, which will always afford me light enough to decide on the constitutional powers of the federal and state governments, and all tribunals acting under their authority. They will, at least, enable me to judge of the true meaning and spirit of plain words, put into the forms of constitutional provisions, which this court, in the great case of *Sturges* v. *Crowninshield,* say, "is to be collected chiefly from its words. It would be dangerous in the extreme, to infer from extrinsic circumstances, that a case for which the words of an instrument expressly provide, shall be exempted from its operation. Where words conflict with each other, where the different clauses of an instrument bear upon each other, and would be inconsistent, unless the natural and common import of words be varied, constructions become necessary, and a departure from the obvious meaning of words is justifiable." But the absurdity and injustice of applying the provision to the case, must be so monstrous, that all mankind would, without hesitation, unite in rejecting the application. 4 Wheat. 202–3. In another great case, *Cohens* v. *Virginia,* this court say, "the jurisdiction of this court then, being extended, by the letter of the constitution, to all cases arising under it, or under the laws of the United States, it follows, that those who would withdraw any case of this description from that jurisdiction, must sustain the exemption they claim, on the

spirit and true meaning of the constitution, which spirit and true meaning must be so apparent as to overrule the words which its framers have employed." 6 Wheat. 379–80. The principle of these cases is my guide in this. Sitting here, I shall always bow to such authority; and require no admonition to be influenced by no other, in a case where I am called on to take a part in the exercise of the judicial power over a sovereign state.

Guided by these principles, I come to consider the third clause of the second section of the first article of the constitution; which provides for the apportionment of representatives and direct taxes "among the several states which may be included within this Union, according to their respective numbers, excluding Indians not taxed." This clause embraces not only the old but the new states to be formed out of the territory of the United States, pursuant to the resolutions and ordinances of the old congress, and the conditions of the cession from the states, or which might arise by the division of the old. If the clause excluding Indians not taxed had not been inserted, or should be stricken out, the whole free Indian population of all the states would be included in the federal numbers, co-extensively with the boundaries of all the states included in this Union. The insertion of this clause conveys a clear definite declaration, that there were no independent sovereign nations or states, foreign or domestic, within their boundaries, which should exclude them from the federal enumeration, or any bodies or communities within the states, excluded from the action of the federal constitution, unless by the use of express words of exclusion. The delegates who represented the states in the convention well knew the existing relations between the United States and the Indians, and put the constitution in a shape for adoption, calculated to meet them; and the words used in this clause exclude the existence of the plaintiffs as a sovereign or foreign state or nation, within the meaning of this section, too plainly to require illustration or argument.

The third clause of the eighth article shows most distinctly the sense of the convention in authorizing congress to regulate commerce with the Indian tribes. The character of the Indian communities had been settled by many years of uniform usage, under the old government; characterized by the names of nations, towns, villages, tribes, head-men and warriors, as the writers of resolutions or treaties might fancy; governed by no settled rule, and applying the word nation to the Catawbas as well as the Cherokees. The framers of the constitution have thought proper to define their meaning to be, that they were not foreign nations nor states of the Union, but Indian tribes; thus declaring the sense in which they should be considered, under the constitution, which refers to them as tribes only, in this clause. I cannot strike these words from the book; nor construe Indian tribes, in this part of the constitution, to mean a sovereign state, under the first clause of the second section of the third article. It would be taking very great liberty, in the exposition of a fundamental law, to bring the Indians under the action of the legislative power as tribes, and of the judicial, as foreign states. The power conferred to regulate commerce with the Indian tribes, is the same given to the old congress, by the ninth article of the old confederation, "to regulate trade with the Indians." The raising the word "trade" to the dignity of commerce, regulating it with Indians or Indian tribes, is only a change of words. Mere phraseology cannot make Indians nations, nor Indian tribes, foreign states.

The second clause of the third section of the fourth article of the constitution is equally convincing. "The congress shall have power to dispose of, and make all needful regulations and rules respecting, the territory of the United States." What that territory was, the rights of soil, jurisdiction and sovereignty claimed and exercised by the states and the old congress, has been already seen. It extended to the formation of a government whose laws and process were in force within its whole extent, without a saving of Indian jurisdiction. It is the same power which was delegated to the old congress, and according to the judicial interpretation given by this court in *Gibbons* v. *Ogden*, 9 Wheat. 209, the word "to regulate" implied, in its nature, full power over the thing to be regulated; it excludes, necessarily, the action of all others that would perform the same operation on the same thing. Applying this construction to commerce and territory, leaves the jurisdiction and sovereignty of the Indian tribes wholly out of the question. The power given in this clause is of the most plenary kind. Rules and regulations respecting the territory of the United States—they necessarily include complete jurisdiction. It was necessary to confer it, without limitation, to enable the new government to redeem the pledge given by the old, in relation to the formation and powers of the new states. The saving of "the claims" of "any particular states," is almost a copy of a similar provision, part of the ninth article of the old confederation; thus delivering over to the new congress the power to regulate commerce with the Indian tribes, and regulate the territory they occupied, as the old had done, from the beginning of the revolution.

The only remaining clause of the constitution to be considered is the second clause in the sixth article. "All treaties made, or to be made, shall be the supreme law of the land." In *Chirac* v. *Chirac,* this court declared, that it was unnecessary to inquire into the effect of the treaty with France in 1778, under the old confederation, because the confederation had yielded to our present constitution, and this treaty had been the supreme law of the land. 2 Wheat. 271. I consider the same rule as applicable to Indian treaties, whether considered as national compacts between sovereign powers, or as articles, agreements, contracts, or stipulations on the part of this government, binding and pledging the faith of the nation to the faithful observance of its conditions. They secure to the Indians the enjoyment of the rights they stipulate to give or secure, to their full extent, and in the plenitude of good faith; but the treaties must be considered as the rules of reciprocal obligations. The Indians must have their rights; but must claim them in that capacity in which they received the grant or guarantee. They contracted, by putting themselves under the protection of the United States, accepted of an allotment of hunting-grounds, surrendered and delegated to congress the exclusive regulation of their trade, and the management of all their own affairs, taking no assurance of

their continued sovereignty, if they had any before, but relying on the assurance of the United States that they might have full confidence in their justice respecting their interests; stipulating only for the right of sending a deputy of their own choice to congress. If, then, the Indians claim admission to this court, under the treaty of Hopewell, they cannot be admitted as foreign states, and can be received in no other capacity.

The legislation of congress under the constitution, in relation to the Indians, has been in the same spirit, and guided by the same principles, which prevailed in the old congress, and under the old confederation. In order to give full effect to the ordinance of 1787, in the north-west territory, it was adapted to the present constitution of the United States in 1789 (1 U.S. Stat. 50); applied as the rule for its government to the territory south of the Ohio in 1790, except the sixth article (Ibid. 123); to the Mississippi territory in 1798 (Ibid. 549); and with no exception, to Indiana in 1800 (2 Ibid. 58); to Michigan in 1805 (Ibid. 309); to Illinois in 1809 (Ibid. 514).

In 1802, congress passed the act regulating trade and intercourse with the Indian tribes, in which they assert all the rights exercised over them under the old confederation, and do not alter in any degree their political relations. (2 U.S. Stat. 139.) In the same year, Georgia ceded her lands west of her present boundary to the United States; and by the second article of the convention, the United States ceded to Georgia whatever claim, right or title they may have to the jurisdiction or soil of any lands south of Tennessee, North or South Carolina and east of the line of the cession by Georgia. So that Georgia now has all the rights attached to her by her sovereignty, within her limits, and which are saved to her by the second section of the fourth article of the constitution, and all the United States could cede either by their power over the territory, or their treaties with the Cherokees.

The treaty with the Cherokees, made at Holston, in 1791, contains only one article which has a bearing on the political relations of the contracting parties. In the second article, the Cherokees stipulate "that the said Cherokee nation will not hold any treaty with any foreign power, individual state, or with individuals of any state." (7 U.S. Stat. 39.) This affords an instructive definition of the words nation and treaty. At the treaty of Hopewell, the Cherokees, though subdued and suing for peace, before divesting themselves of any of the rights or attributes of sovereignty which this government ever recognised them as possessing by the consummation of the treaty, contracted in the name of the head-men and warriors of all the Cherokees; but at Holston, in 1791, in abandoning their last remnant of political right, contracted as the Cherokee nation, thus ascending in title as they descended in power, and applying the word treaty to a contract with an individual: this consideration will divest words of their magic.

In thus testing the rights of the complainants as to their national character, by the old confederation, resolutions and ordinances of the old congress, the provisions of the constitution, treaties held under the authority of both, and the subsequent legislation thereon, I have followed the rule laid down for my guide by this court, in *Foster* v. *Neil-*

son, 2 Pet. 307, in doing it "according to the principles established by the political department of the government." "If the course of the nation has been a plain one, its courts would hesitate to pronounce it erroneous. However individual judges may construe them (treaties), it is the province of the court to conform its decisions to the will of the legislature, if that will has been clearly expressed." That the existence of foreign states cannot be known to this court judicially, except by some act or recognition of the other departments of this government is, I think, fully established in the case of *United States* v. *Palmer,* 3 Wheat. 634–5; *The Divina Pastora,* 4 Ibid. 63; and *The Anna,* 6 Ibid. 193.

I shall resort to the same high authority as the basis of my opinion on the powers of the state governments. "By the revolution, the duties as well as the powers of government devolved on the people of (Georgia) New Hampshire. It is admitted, that among the latter were comprehended the transcendent powers of parliament, as well as those of the executive department." *Dartmouth College* v. *Woodward,* 4 Wheat. 651; 4 Ibid. 192; *Green* v. *Biddle,* 8 Ibid. 98; *Ogden* v. *Saunders,* 12 Ibid. 254, &c. "The same principle applies, though with no greater force, to the different states of America; for though they form a confederated government, yet the several states retain their individual sovereignties, and with respect to their municipal regulations, are to each other foreign." *Buckner* v. *Findley,* 2 Pet. 591. The powers of government, which thus devolved on Georgia by the revolution, over her whole territory, are unimpaired by any surrender of her territorial jurisdiction, by the old confederation or the new constitution, as there was in both an express saving, as well as by the tenth article of amendments.

But if any passed to the United States by either, they were retroceded by the convention of 1802. Her jurisdiction over the territory in question is as supreme as that of congress, over what the nation has acquired by cession from the states, or treaties with foreign powers, combining the rights of the state and general government. Within her boundaries, there can be no other nation, community or sovereign power, which this department can judicially recognise as a foreign state, capable of demanding or claiming our interposition, so as to enable them to exercise a jurisdiction incompatible with a sovereignty in Georgia, which has been recognised by the constitution, and every department of this government acting under its authority. Foreign states cannot be created by judicial construction; Indian sovereignty cannot be roused from its long slumber, and awakened to action by our *fiat.* I find no acknowledgment of it by the legislative or executive power. Until they have done so, I can stretch forth no arm for their relief, without violating the constitution. I say this with great deference to those from whom I dissent; but my judgment tells me, I have no power to act, and imperious duty compels me to stop at the portal, unless I can find some authority in the judgments of this court, to which I may surrender my own.

Indians have rights of occupancy to their lands, as sacred as the fee-simple, absolute title of the whites; but they are only rights of occupancy, incapable of alienation, or being held by any other than common right, without permission from the government. 8 Wheat. 592. In *Fletcher* v. *Peck,* this court decided, that the Indian occupancy was not absolutely repugnant to a seisin in fee in Georgia; that she had good right to grant land so occupied; that it was within the state, and could be held by purchasers under a law, subject only to extinguishment of the Indian title. 6 Cranch 88, 142; 9 Ibid. 11. In the case of *Johnson* v. *McIntosh,* 8 Wheat. 543, 571, the nature of the Indian title to lands on this continent, throughout its whole extent, was mostly ably and elaborately considered; leading to conclusions satisfactory to every jurist, clearly establishing that, from the time of discovery under the royal government, the colonies, the states, the confederacy and this Union, their tenure was the same occupancy, their rights occupancy, and nothing more; that the ultimate absolute fee, jurisdiction and sovereignty was in the government, subject only to such rights; that grants vested soil and dominion, and the powers of government, whether the land granted was vacant or occupied by Indians.

By the treaty of peace, the powers of government, and the rights of soil, which had previously been in Great Britain, passed definitively to these states. 8 Wheat. 584. They asserted these rights, and ceded soil and jurisdiction to the United States. The Indians were considered as tribes of fierce savages; a people with whom it was impossible to mix, and who could not be governed as a distinct society. They are not named or referred to in any part of the opinion of the court, as nations or states, and nowhere declared to have any national capacity or attributes of sovereignty, in their relations to the general or state governments. The principles established in this case have been supposed to apply to the rights which the nations of Europe claimed to acquire by discovery, as only relative between themselves, and that they did not assume thereby any rights of soil or jurisdiction over the territory in the actual occupation of the Indians. But the language of the court is too explicit to be misunderstood. "This principle was, that discovery gave title to the government by whose subjects or by whose authority it was made, against all other European governments, which title might be consummated by possession." Those relations which were to subsist between the discoverer and the natives were to be regulated by themselves. The rights thus acquired being exclusive, no other power could interpose between them.

While the different nations of Europe respected the rights of the natives, as occupants, they asserted the ultimate dominion to be in themselves; and claimed and exercised, as a consequence of this ultimate dominion, a power to grant the soil, while yet in the possession of the natives. These grants have been understood by all, to convey a title to the grantees, subject only to the Indian rights of occupancy. The history of America, from its discovery to the present day proves, we think, the universal recognition of these principles. 8 Wheat. 574. I feel it my duty, to apply them to this case. They are in perfect accordance with those on which the governments of the united and individual states have acted in all their changes; they were asserted and maintained by the colonies, before they assumed independence. While dependent themselves on the crown, they exercised all the rights of dominion and sovereignty over the territory occupied by the Indians; and this is the first assertion by them of rights as a foreign state, within the limits of a state. If their jurisdiction within their boundaries has been unquestioned, until this controversy; if rights have been exercised, which are directly repugnant to those now claimed; the judicial power cannot divest the states of rights of sovereignty, and transfer them to the Indians, by decreeing them to be a nation, or foreign state, pre-existing and with rightful jurisdiction and sovereignty over the territory they occupy. This would reverse every principle on which our government have acted for fifty-five years; and force, by mere judicial power, upon the other departments of this government, and the states of this Union, the recognition of the existence of nations and states, within the limits of both, possessing dominion and jurisdiction paramount to the federal and state constitutions. It will be a declaration, in my deliberate judgment, that the sovereign power of the people of the United States and Union must hereafter remain incapable of action over territory to which their rights in full dominion have been asserted with the most rigorous authority, and bow to a jurisdiction hitherto unknown; unacknowledged by any department of the government; denied by all, through all time; unclaimed till now; and now declared to have been called into exercise, not by any change in our constitution, the laws of the Union or the states; but pre-existent and paramount over the supreme law of the land.

I disclaim the assumption of a judicial power so awfully responsible. No assurance or certainty of support in public opinion can induce me to disregard a law so supreme; so plain to my judgment and reason. Those who have brought public opinion to bear on this subject, act under a mere moral responsibility; under no oath, which binds their movements to the straight and narrow line drawn by the constitution. Politics or philanthropy may impel them to pass it; but when their objects can be effectuated only by this court, they must not expect its members to diverge from it, when they cannot conscientiously take the first step, without breaking all the high obligations under which they administer the judicial power of the constitution. The account of my executorship cannot be settled before the court of public opinion, or any human tribunal. None can release the balance which will accrue by the violation of my solemn conviction of duty.

THOMPSON, Justice. *(Dissenting.)*—Entertaining different views of the questions now before us in this case, and having arrived at a conclusion different from that of a majority of the court, and considering the importance of the case and the constitutional principle involved in it; I shall proceed, with all due respect for the opinion of others, to assign the reasons upon which my own has been formed.

In the opinion pronounced by the court, the merits of the controversy between the state of Georgia and the Cherokee Indians have not been taken into consideration. The denial of the application for an injunction has been placed solely on the ground of want of jurisdiction in this court to grant the relief prayed for. It became, therefore, unnecessary to inquire into the merits of the case. But

thinking as I do, that the court has jurisdiction of the case, and may grant relief, at least, in part; it may become necessary for me, in the course of my opinion, to glance at the merits of the controversy; which I shall, however, do very briefly, as it is important only so far as relates to the present application.

Before entering upon the examination of the particular points which have been made and argued, and for the purpose of guarding against any erroneous conclusions, it is proper that I should state, that I do not claim for this court, the exercise of jurisdiction upon any matter properly falling under the denomination of political power. Relief to the full extent prayed by the bill may be beyond the reach of this court. Much of the matter therein contained, by way of complaint, would seem to depend for relief upon the exercise of political power; and as such, appropriately devolving upon the executive, and not the judicial, department of the government. This court can grant relief so far only as the rights of person or property are drawn in question, and have been infringed.

It would very ill become the judicial station which I hold, to indulge in any remarks upon the hardship of the case, or the great injustice that would seem to have been done to the complainants, according to the statement in the bill, and which, for the purpose of the present motion, I must assume to be true. If they are entitled to other than judicial relief, it cannot be admitted, that in a government like ours, redress is not to be had in some of its departments; and the responsibility for its denial must rest upon those who have the power to grant it. But believing as I do, that relief to some extent falls properly under judicial cognisance, I shall proceed to the examination of the case under the following heads. 1. Is the Cherokee nation of Indians a competent party to sue in this court? 2. Is a sufficient case made out in the bill, to warrant this court in granting any relief? 3. Is an injunction the fit and appropriate relief?

1. By the constitution of the United States it is declared (Art. 3, § 2), that the judicial power shall extend to all cases in law and equity, arising under this constitution, the laws of the United States, and treaties made or which shall be made under their authority, &c.; to controversies between two or more states, &c., and between a state or the citizens thereof, and foreign states, citizens or subjects. The controversy in the present case is alleged to be between a foreign state, and one of the states of the Union; and does not, therefore, come within the 11th amendment of the constitution, which declares that the judicial power of the United States shall not be construed to extend to any suit in law or equity commenced or prosecuted against one of the United States, by citizens of another state, or by citizens or subjects of any foreign state. This amendment does not, therefore, extend to suits prosecuted against one of the United States by a foreign state. The constitution further provides, that in all cases where a state shall be a party, the supreme court shall have original jurisdiction. Under these provisions in the constitution, the complainants have filed their bill in this court, in the character of a foreign state, against the state of Georgia; praying an injunction to restrain that state from committing various al-

leged violations of the property of the nation, claimed under the laws of the United States, and treaties made with the Cherokee nation.

That a state of this Union may be sued by a foreign state, when a proper case exists and is presented, is too plainly and expressly declared in the constitution, to admit of doubt; and the first inquiry is, whether the Cherokee nation is a foreign state, within the sense and meaning of the constitution. The terms state and nation are used in the law of nations, as well as in common parlance, as importing the same thing; and imply a body of men, united together, to procure their mutual safety and advantage, by means of their union. Such a society has its affairs and interests to manage; it deliberates, and takes resolutions in common, and thus becomes a moral person, having an understanding and a will peculiar to itself, and is susceptible of obligations and laws. Vattel 1. Nations being composed of men naturally free and independent, and who, before the establishment of civil societies, live together in the state of nature, nations or sovereign states; are to be considered as so many free persons, living together in a state of nature. Vattel 2, § 4. Every nation that governs itself, under what form soever, without any dependence on a foreign power, is a sovereign state. Its rights are naturally the same as those of any other state. Such are moral persons who live together in a natural society, under the law of nations. It is sufficient, if it be really sovereign and independent: that is, it must govern itself by its own authority and laws. We ought, therefore, to reckon in the number of sovereigns those states that have bound themselves to another more powerful, although by an unequal alliance. The conditions of these unequal alliances may be infinitely varied; but whatever they are, provided the inferior ally reserves to itself the sovereignty or the right to govern its own body, it ought to be considered an independent state. Consequently, a weak state, that, in order to provide for its safety, places itself under the protection of a more powerful one, without stripping itself of the right of government and sovereignty, does not cease, on this account, to be placed among the sovereigns who acknowledge no other power. Tributary and feudatory states do not thereby cease to be sovereign and independent states, so long as self-government, and sovereign and independent authority, is left in the administration of the state. Vattel, c. 1, pp. 16, 17.

Testing the character and condition of the Cherokee Indians by these rules, it [is] not perceived how it is possible to escape the conclusion, that they form a sovereign state. They have always been dealt with as such by the government of the United States; both before and since the adoption of the present constitution. They have been admitted and treated as a people governed solely and exclusively by their own laws, usages, and customs, within their own territory, claiming and exercising exclusive dominion over the same; yielding up by treaty, from time to time, portions of their land, but still claiming absolute sovereignty and self-government over what remained unsold. And this has been the light in which they have, until recently, been considered, from the earliest settlement of the country, by the white people. And indeed, I do not understand, that

it is denied by a majority of the court, that the Cherokee Indians form a sovereign state, according to the doctrine of the law of nations; but that, although a sovereign state, they are not considered a foreign state, within the meaning of the constitution.

Whether the Cherokee Indians are to be considered a foreign state or not, is a point on which we cannot expect to discover much light from the law of nations. We must derive this knowledge chiefly from the practice of our own government, and the light in which the nation has been viewed and treated by it. That numerous tribes of Indians, and among others the Cherokee nation, occupied many parts of this country, long before the discovery by Europeans, is abundantly established by history; and it is not denied, but that the Cherokee nation occupied the territory now claimed by them, long before that period. It does not fall within the scope and object of the present inquiry, to go into a critical examination of the nature and extent of the rights growing out of such occupancy, or the justice and humanity with which the Indians have been treated, or their rights respected. That they are entitled to such occupancy, so long as they choose quietly and peaceably to remain upon the land, cannot be questioned. The circumstance of their original occupancy is here referred to, merely for the purpose of showing, that if these Indian communities were then, as they certainly were, nations, they must have been foreign nations, to all the world; not having any connection, or alliance of any description, with any other power on earth. And if the Cherokees were then a foreign nation; when or how have they lost that character, and ceased to be a distinct people, and become incorporated with any other community?

They have never been, by conquest, reduced to the situation of subjects to any conqueror, and thereby lost their separate national existence, and the rights of self-government, and become subject to the laws of the conqueror. Whenever wars have taken place, they have been followed by regular treaties of peace, containing stipulations on each side, according to existing circumstances; the Indian nation always preserving its distinct and separate national character. And notwithstanding we do not recognise the right of the Indians to transfer the absolute title of their lands to any other than ourselves, the right of occupancy is still admitted to remain in them, accompanied with the right of self-government, according to their own usages and customs; and with the competency to act in a national capacity, although placed under the protection of the whites, and owing a qualified subjection, so far as is requisite for public safety. But the principle is universally admitted, that this occupancy belongs to them as a matter of right, and not by mere indulgence. They cannot be disturbed in the enjoyment of it, or deprived of it, without their free consent; or unless a just and necessary war should sanction their dispossession.

In this view of their situation, there is as full and complete recognition of their sovereignty, as if they were the absolute owners of the soil. The progress made in civilization by the Cherokee Indians cannot surely be considered as in any measure destroying their national or foreign character, so long as they are permitted to maintain a separate and distinct government; it is their political condition that constitutes their foreign character, and in that sense must the term foreign be understood, as used in the constitution. It can have no relation to local, geographical or territorial position.

11

JOSEPH STORY, COMMENTARIES ON THE CONSTITUTION 2:§§ 1092–96
1833

§ 1092. The power of congress also extends to regulate commerce with the Indian tribes. This power was not contained in the first draft of the constitution. It was afterwards referred to the committee on the constitution (among other propositions) to consider the propriety of giving to congress the power "to regulate affairs with the Indians, as well within, as without the limits of the United States." And, in the revised draft, the committee reported the clause, "and with the Indian Tribes," as it now stands.

§ 1093. Under the confederation, the continental congress were invested with the sole and exclusive right and power "of regulating the trade and managing all affairs with the Indians, not *members* of any of the states, provided, that the legislative right of any state within its own limits be not infringed or violated."

§ 1094. Antecedently to the American Revolution the authority to regulate trade and intercourse with the Indian tribes, whether they were within, or without the boundaries of the colonies, was understood to belong to the prerogative of the British crown. And after the American Revolution, the like power would naturally fall to the federal government, with a view to the general peace and interests of all the states. Two restrictions, however, upon the power were, by the above article, incorporated into the confederation, which occasioned endless embarrassments and doubts. The power of congress was restrained to Indians, not members of any of the states; and was not to be exercised, so as to violate or infringe the legislative right of any state within its own limits. What description of Indians were to be deemed members of a state was never settled under the confederation; and was a question of frequent perplexity and contention in the federal councils. And how the trade with Indians, though not members of a state, yet residing within its legislative jurisdiction, was to be regulated by an external authority, without so far intruding on the internal rights of legislation, was absolutely incomprehensible. In this case, as in some other cases, the articles of confederation inconsiderately endeavoured to accomplish impossibilities; to reconcile a partial sovereignty in the Union, with complete sovereignty in the states; to subvert a mathematical axiom, by taking away a part, and letting the whole remain. The constitution has wisely disembarrassed the power of these two limitations; and has thus given to congress, as the only safe and proper depositary, the exclusive power, which belonged to the crown in the ante-revolutionary times; a power indispensable to the peace of the states, and to the just preservation of the rights and territory of the Indians. In the former illustrations of this subject, it was stated, that the Indians, from the first settlement of the country, were always treated, as distinct, though in some sort, as dependent nations. Their territorial rights and sovereignty were respected. They were deemed incapable of carrying on trade or intercourse with any foreign nations, or of ceding their territories to them. But their right of self-government was admitted; and they were allowed a national existence, under the protection of the parent country, which exempted them from the ordinary operations of the legislative power of the colonies. During the revolution and afterwards they were secured in the like enjoyment of their rights and property, as separate communities. The government of the United States, since the constitution, have always recognised the same attributes of dependent sovereignty, as belonging to them, and claimed the same right of exclusive regulation of trade and intercourse with them, and the same authority to protect and guarantee their territorial possessions, immunities, and jurisdiction.

§ 1095. The power, then, given to congress to regulate commerce with the Indian tribes, extends equally to tribes living within or without the boundaries of particular states, and within or without the territorial limits of the United States. It is (says a learned commentator) wholly immaterial, whether such tribes continue seated within the boundaries of a state, inhabit part of a territory, or roam at large over lands, to which the United States have no claim. The trade with them is, in all its forms, subject exclusively to the regulation of congress. And in this particular, also, we trace the wisdom of the constitution. The Indians, not distracted by the discordant regulations of different states, are taught to trust one great body, whose justice they respect, and whose power they fear.

§ 1096. It has lately been made a question, whether an Indian tribe, situated within the territorial boundaries of a state, but exercising the powers of government, and national sovereignty, under the guarantee of the general government, is a foreign state in the sense of the constitution, and as such entitled to sue in the courts of the United States. Upon solemn argument, it has been held, that such a tribe is to be deemed politically a state; that is, a distinct political society, capable of self-government; but it is not to be deemed a *foreign state,* in the sense of the constitution. It is rather a domestic dependent nation. Such a tribe may properly be deemed in a state of pupillage; and its relation to the United States resembles that of a ward to a guardian.

12

UNITED STATES V. BAILEY
24 Fed. Cas. 937, no. 14,495 (C.C.D.Tenn. 1834)

OPINION OF THE COURT. The defendant, a white man, has been indicted for the murder of a white man in the state of Tennessee, and within the limits of the Indian country occupied by the Cherokees. A plea to the jurisdiction of the court has been filed, and it becomes the duty of the court to decide the question raised by the plea.

The indictment is found under the first section of the act of congress of 1817 which provides, that "if any Indian, or other person or persons, shall, within the United States, and within any town, district, or territory, belonging to any nation or nations, tribe or tribes of Indians, commit any crime, offence or misdemeanor, which if committed in any place or district of country under the sole and exclusive jurisdiction of the United States, would by the laws of the United States, be punished with death, or any other punishment, every such offender, on being thereof convicted, shall suffer the like punishment, as is provided by the laws of the United States for the like offence, if committed within any place or district of country under the sole and exclusive jurisdiction of the United States." From the provisions of this section no doubt can be entertained, that it was the intention of congress to punish all offences specified; and especially the crime of murder committed in the Indian country, though within the limits of a state; and the jurisdiction of the court must be sustained, unless this act shall be found repugnant to the constitution of the United States. This is a grave question, involving on the one hand the life of a fellow being, and on the other the powers of the federal government. At October term, 1816, of this court, an indictment was found against two Indians for killing Vincent Davis, a white man, on a public road passing through the Cherokee Nation of Indians, ceded by treaty with the Cherokee Nation to the United States. A plea to the jurisdiction being filed in the case, the court decided against the jurisdiction on the ground that there was no law of the United States, which "makes the facts as charged and laid in said indictment a crime, affixes a punishment and declares the court which shall have jurisdiction of it." The failure of this prosecution, it is suggested, led to the passage of the act now called in question.

That the federal government is one of limited powers, is a principle so obvious as not to admit of controversy; though the extent of those powers has given rise to much discussion and wide differences of opinion. It would seem however, to be clear, from the 10th article of the amendments to the constitution which provides, that the powers not delegated to the United States by the constitution, nor prohibited by it to the states, are reserved to the states respectively or to the people; and from other considerations, that the federal government can exercise no powers be-

yond those which are expressly delegated to it. When therefore the validity of an act of congress is called in question, we must look to the constitution for the power to pass such an act. In the present case the power is alleged to be given by the 3d article, in the 8th section of the constitution, which declares, that congress shall have power "to regulate commerce with foreign nations and among the several states, and with the Indian tribes." There is no other clause of the constitution which can have any bearing upon the point under consideration; and if the power is not given by this article, it is given nowhere. On the part of the prosecution it is insisted, that congress had power to pass the law in question; and that laws involving the same principle have been enforced by the courts of the United States. The intercourse law of 1802, and other acts of congress, and Indian treaties are referred to; and the decisions of the supreme court and of the circuit courts of the United States, under these laws, it is contended, sustain this position. Under the power to regulate commerce with the Indian tribes, there is undoubtedly a wide scope for legislation; and that too without extending the power beyond what has been exercised in relation to foreign nations. Acts of non-intercourse have been passed; embargos have been imposed, and other restrictions in a great variety of forms have been enacted, affecting foreign commerce, which are admitted to come within the constitutional powers of congress. So as it regards the Indians, various laws have been passed under the above grant of power. The act of 1802 prohibits all intercourse with the Indians, by the whites, except on certain conditions. Agents and other persons are permitted to reside among them for the advancement of their prosperity; and to facilitate our commercial intercourse with them. The persons of these agents are protected from violence and injustice; and our own citizens are punished for committing violence upon the persons or property of the Indians. All these provisions come clearly within the scope of the power to regulate commerce with the Indian tribes; and substantially the same power has been exercised in regulating commerce with foreign nations. All intercourse with a foreign nation, as before remarked, may be prohibited; or it may be admitted under a license or permit. Our agents abroad are protected, and we punish depredations committed by our own citizens on the persons or property of a foreign people, with whom we are at peace. Thus far it would seem the power may be exercised by congress, both as it relates to foreign nations and our Indian tribes. But the act under consideration asserts a general jurisdiction for the punishment of offences, over the Indian territory, though it be within the limits of a state. To the exercise of this jurisdiction within a territorial government there can be no objection, but the case is wholly different as is regards Indian territory within the limits of any state. In such case the power of congress is limited to the regulation of a commercial intercourse, with such tribes of Indians that exist, as a distinct community, governed by their own laws, and resting for their protection on the faith of treaties and laws of the Union. Beyond this, the power of the federal government, in any of its departments cannot be extended.

It is argued that unless the defendant can be tried under the act of congress, there is no law by which he can be punished. If on this ground the federal government may exercise jurisdiction, where shall its powers be limited? The constitution is no longer the guide, when the government acts from the law of necessity. This law always affords a pretext for usurpation. It exists only in the minds of those who exercise the power, and if followed must lead to despotism. It will not be pretended that congress can ever exercise jurisdiction over such parts of a state, as may not be organized into counties. And yet is not this substantially the case under consideration? A murder has been committed by one white person on another within the Indian territory, which act in no respect is connected with the commerce of the Cherokee Indians, or interferes with their prosperity or safety. That congress have power to inflict punishment on all who violate the laws, which regulate a commercial intercourse with the Indians, who maintain a certain relation to the federal government, is admitted; but because this is a legitimate exercise of power, does it follow that the jurisdiction may be extended without limit? Is the Cherokee territory subject to the jurisdiction of the federal government, to the same extent, as it may exercise over forts and arsenals where a cession of jurisdiction has been made by a state? In the act of 1817, congress seem to have considered their power as unlimited in the one case as in the other, as to the punishment of offences; for they provide that the same punishment shall be inflicted, for the commission of crimes within the Cherokee country, as for the like offences, if committed within any place or district of country under the sole and exclusive jurisdiction of the United States. The Cherokee country can in no sense be considered a territory of the United States, over which the federal government may exercise exclusive jurisdiction; nor has there been any cession of jurisdiction by the state of Tennessee; or any prohibition to its exercise of jurisdiction over this territory, constitutionally, except such as the rights recognized and guaranteed to the Indians by treaties and the laws regulating commerce with them, may impose. But it is not necessary in determining the question of jurisdiction in this case, to decide whether any or what jurisdiction may be exercised by the state of Tennessee over the Cherokee country within her limits. If the state has no jurisdiction, or has failed to exercise it, it does not follow that the federal government has a general and unlimited jurisdiction over the territory; for its powers are delegated, and cannot be assumed to supply any defect of power on the part of the state. It is clear that the state of Tennessee either by failing to exercise jurisdiction or by positive enactment, short of a cession of jurisdiction for purposes specified in the constitution, can neither enlarge nor diminish the powers of congress on the subject. The state of New York, for many years has punished its citizens for crimes committed in the Indian territory within its limits; and the state of Georgia, before its laws were extended over the Cherokee country, within the state, punished its own citizens for offences committed within that territory; and we are not aware that the right of either state to do this has been questioned.

It is not pretended that any provision by treaty, between the Cherokee Nation and the federal government has been made to embrace a case like the present; or that the treaty-making power can be thus exercised. The connection which exists by treaty between the Indian tribes and the federal government, is of a political character; and the enforcement of such stipulations must mainly depend on the executive power. There is nothing, therefore, in the treaties referred to, which can give to this court jurisdiction of the offence charged in the indictment. This prosecution cannot be sustained, except upon the ground that congress may exercise the same general and exclusive jurisdiction over the Cherokee country, as over a territory of the United States. In this view, if one citizen commit a depredation upon the property of another, or do violence to his person, within the boundaries of the Indian lands within a state, he may be arrested and punished under the act of congress. Indeed it would be difficult to prescribe any limit to this legislative power, if it may be extended beyond the objects for which it was given. It is insisted that the word "commerce," as used in the constitution, is not necessarily limited to the purposes of trade; but may well be construed to embrace every species of intercourse, which the federal government may think proper to establish with our Indian nations. That the word "commerce" does refer to trade, would seem to be clear, from its being used in the same sentence in reference to foreign nations; but it is admitted that the "power to regulate commerce with the Indian tribes" confers on congress the right of selecting such means as may be necessary to attain the object of the power. But these means must have a direct relation to the object. Congress have power to establish post offices and post roads, consequently, they have power to protect the mail of the United States, by providing for the punishment of those who violate it. They have power to coin money, and they may provide for the punishment of those who shall counterfeit the coin. They have power to regulate commerce with the Indian tribes, consequently, they may provide by law in what manner this intercourse shall be carried on, and impose penal sanctions for a violation of the law. But may they by reason of this special power, assume a general jurisdiction and prescribe for the punishment of all offences? If this may be done under the power to regulate commerce with the Indian tribes, why may it not be done in all other cases, where a limited power is exercised by congress to effectuate a special object? Congress have power to regulate commerce among the several states; and if the same power, given in the same words, in relation to the Indians, may be exercised as contended, why may not congress legislate on crimes for the states generally? That congress have not this general power, is a proposition too clear for demonstration. The thing itself is so palpable that it is susceptible of no illustration. Who would attempt after reading the federal constititon, to prove by any course of argument, that this is a limited government? The very instrument that gives existence to the government imposes the limitations. And is it not equally clear, that where a special jurisdiction has been given to congress, a general one cannot be exercised? Is not the jurisdiction under consideration special? Does it not relate exclusively to the regulation of commerce, with the Indian tribes? And does not the act in question provide for the punishment of a crime committed by one citizen upon another, wholly disconnected from any intercourse with the Indians? If this be a constitutional provision, the jurisdiction by congress for the punishment of offences in the Indian country, within the boundaries of any state, is without limit. Believing that in the passage of this provision of the act in 1817, congress have transcended their constitutional powers, I feel bound to say so, and consider this part of the act as having no force or effect.

13

UNITED STATES v. CISNA
25 Fed. Cas. 422, no. 14,795 (C.C.D.Ohio 1835)

OPINION OF THE COURT. The defendant, having been indicted at the present term, for stealing a horse within the reservation of the Wyandott tribe of Indians, of the state of Ohio, of the goods and chattels of Henry Jocko, a friendly Indian, filed a demurrer to the indictment, which brings before the court the question, whether they can exercise jurisdiction in the case?

The indictment is founded on the fourth section of the act of congress, "to regulate trade and intercourse with the Indian tribes," passed 30th March, 1802 [2 Stat. 139], which provides: "If any citizen or other person shall go into any town, settlement, or territory belonging or reserved by treaty of the United States to any nation or tribe of Indians, and shall there commit robbery, trespass, or other crime, against the person or property of any friendly Indian or Indians, which would be punishable if committed within the jurisdiction of any state against a citizen of the United States, or, unauthorized by law or with a hostile intention, shall be found on any Indian land, such offender shall forfeit a sum not exceeding one hundred dollars, and be imprisoned not exceeding twelve months; and shall also, when property is taken or destroyed, forfeit and pay to such Indian or Indians, to whom the property taken or destroyed belongs, a sum equal to twice the just value of the property taken or destroyed, &c."

The Wyandott reserve is twelve miles square, and is situated in Crawford county, which for some years has been regularly organized as a county. And at the last session of the legislature of Ohio, a law was passed which declared, "that all white inhabitants, now or hereafter resident in said Wyandott reservation, shall be, and they are hereby made subject to the laws of the state of Ohio for the purpose of taxation, and for all civil, criminal, and military purposes, as other white citizens are now, or hereafter may be, in the different townships in the said county of Crawford, any law or custom to the contrary notwithstanding." Before the passage of this law the legislature had not, by express enactment, extended the jurisdiction of the state

over this reserve; but in the general laws respecting crimes and punishments, it is not excepted from their operation. This reserve is surrounded by a dense white population, and public roads lead through it in various directions. It is admitted to be as much frequented by the white population as any other part of the county; and it would be extremely inconvenient, if not impracticable, for the citizens of the county to avoid entering the reserve in pursuing their ordinary and daily avocations.

On the 9th of January, 1789 [7 Stat. 28], the United States entered into a treaty with the Wyandott and other nations of Indians, in which it was agreed that if any citizen of the United States, or other person not being an Indian, shall settle on their land, such person shall forfeit the protection of the United States, and the Indians were at liberty to punish him or not, as they please. And all citizens or inhabitants of the United States were prohibited from hunting or destroying the game, or even entering on the Indian lands without a passport. Certain stipulations were made for the punishment of offences, such as horse-stealing, robbery, &c., and the Indians agreed to surrender the offenders among their tribes, who were to be punished equally with the citizens of the United States. At the time this treaty was formed, the Wyandott tribe owned a very extensive territory of rich and fertile country; but treaties of cession have been made from time to time, until their territory is restricted to twelve miles square.

By the act of 1802, above referred to, which regulates trade with the Indians, all citizens or residents of the United States are prohibited from entering into the Indian lands without a license, and penalties are provided for hunting on them, or committing depredations upon the property of Indians. Murder, by a white person, of an Indian, is punished with death; traders without license forfeit their merchandize; and a penalty is incurred by purchasing from an Indian a gun, any instrument of husbandry, a horse, or other specified articles of property. Jurisdiction is given to the superior courts in each of the territorial districts, and the circuit courts of the United States, of similar jurisdiction in criminal cases in each district of the United States in which any offender under the intercourse law shall be apprehended, or may be brought for trial. The peculiar relation which a tribe of Indians, that resides within the limits of a state, bears to the federal and state governments, renders every exercise of jurisdiction over their persons and property, by the federal government, a matter of great delicacy and importance. The federal government is one of limited and specific powers. It cannot exercise jurisdiction by implication, but is confined to the special grants of power in the constitution; and in carrying into effect these grants, the most appropriate means should be adopted, and no means beyond what are necessary to give effect to the power, can be legitimately used. All powers not delegated to the federal government, are reserved to the states and the people. The power to regulate commerce with foreign nations and among the several states, and with the Indian tribes, is given to congress in the constitution. And under this and the treaty making power, numerous treaties have been formed and laws enacted, to regulate commercial intercourse with the numerous Indian tribes which live within the federal limits. The validity of these treaties and laws, it is believed, has not been questioned, so far as they act upon the Indian tribes and our own citizens, beyond the boundaries of any state. But serious questions have arisen, and are likely again to arise, between the federal and state authorities, respecting the jurisdiction of the former, under these laws, over the territory of Indians situated within a state sovereignty.

Within this state no collisions on this important subject have occurred; but the principle on which jurisdiction is exercised by the federal government, must be the same, under the same circumstances, in every state. The supreme court of Ohio have not decided whether offences under the state laws, if committed within the Wyandott reserve, by a white person, may be punished; but a circuit court of common pleas have decided that no punishment can be inflicted in such a case. No one can read the laws for the regulation of our intercourse with the Indian tribes, without perceiving that they were designed to operate on and protect communities of Indians, remotely situated from our own population. In the act of 1802 is a provision that it shall not be so construed "as to prevent any trade or intercourse with Indians living on lands surrounded by settlements of the citizens of the United States, and being within the ordinary jurisdiction of the individual states." This provision applied to the condition of Indians at the time the law was passed; and at that time the Wyandott tribe was not only far more numerous than it now is, but its territory was extensive and remote from a white population. They did not reside within the ordinary jurisdiction of any state. The exception was applicable to remnants of tribes which resided in Massachusetts, Connecticut, and other Eastern states. No express provision has been made in treaties or by act of congress, at what period or under what circumstances the power of the federal government to regulate commerce with the Wyandott or any other tribe of Indians, living within a state, shall be terminated.

This is a question whether it shall be decided by the federal or state authorities as important as it is delicate; and it is much to be regretted that some rule on the subject has not been adopted which would prevent collisions of jurisdiction. A concurrent action by the federal and state governments, in regard to this matter, would seem to be the most appropriate method of withdrawing the regulation of the general and substituting that of the local authority. But the federal government has not acted on the subject, and the duty is now imposed upon this court to determine, whether the power to act belongs to the judicial branch of the government.

The question of jurisdiction which is raised by the demurrer is, whether the law under which this indictment has been found, can be carried into effect within the Wyandott reserve. Whether this is properly a judicial question may admit of some controversy. If the period at which the law shall be suspended could be fixed, at the time the state government was organized, there would be no difficulty on the subject. But the Wyandott tribe of Indians

required as much the fostering care and superintending power of the federal government, for the protection of its trade in 1803, when Ohio was admitted into the Union, as for some years prior to that period—and the white population was almost as remote from the Indian settlements as it had been for years; and the state jurisdiction was not extended over the Indians, nor was there any difficulty in giving effect to the intercourse law of 1802. In addition to these considerations, the supreme court have decided, that this law is not necessarily suspended within the limits of a state. If the provisions of the act of 1802 shall not apply to the case before the court, it must be upon the ground that they were unconstitutional when adopted, or have become inoperative by the progress of time and change of circumstances.

The former branch of this enquiry is strictly the exercise of a judicial power; but the latter, in most cases, at least, would seem to belong to the legislative department of the government. So far as it regards the policy of the federal government towards the Indians, within its constitutional powers, it is exclusively a question for the legislature; but as it respects any question of power between the federal and state governments, in whatever form it may arise, the judicial power is competent to decide it. During the whole course of our connection with the Indian tribes, we have recognized in them a power to make treaties, and certain political relations exist growing out of treaties between the federal government and almost every distinct tribe of Indians within our national limits. These relations may be extended by treaties as far as a sound policy, in the discretion of the treaty making power shall admit, where the Indians reside beyond the limits of a state; but within those limits neither the treaty making power nor the legislative power can be exercised so as to abridge the rights of a state.

Congress can exercise no power on this subject, beyond that of regulating commerce with the Indian tribes. The same power is given to congress to regulate commerce with foreign nations and among the several states. Under this investiture of power to regulate commerce with foreign nations, a wide scope of legislation has been exercised. But the regulation of commerce among the several states has been limited principally to certain prohibitions and the equalization of duties. Congress cannot effectually regulate commerce with the Indian tribes, without adopting such provisions by law, as shall preserve those tribes from an indiscriminate commercial intercourse with our own citizens; such is their inferiority in the business of commerce while in an uncivilized state, that their interests would be sacrified, if left to an unrestricted intercourse. It was on this ground that the act of 1802 prohibited white persons from entering upon the Indian territory without a license, and further to give protection to the Indians, government agents were appointed to reside among them, and penal laws were enacted, as has been stated, against citizens of the United States for committing depredations upon the territory, the persons or the property of the Indians. The exercise of the power to prohibit any intercourse with the Indians, except under a license, must be considered within the power to regulate commerce with them, if such regulation could not be effectual short of an intercourse thus restricted. Under the power to regulate commerce with foreign nations, congress have passed non-intercourse, embargo and other laws, which restricted or altogether prohibited any commercial intercourse with those nations; and as the power to regulate commerce with the Indian tribes is given to congress in the same clause of the constitution, and in the same words, it would seem to follow that the power may be exercised to the same extent in the one case as in the other. There is nothing in the condition of the Indians, when under the exclusive jurisdiction of the federal government, nor in the constitution, which can operate against this construction. The power to regulate commerce among the several states is limited by other provisions of the constitution, by the nature of the power and the sovereignty of the states.

The law of 1802 is constitutional, and so the supreme court have decided. That this act had a constitutional operation upon the Wyandott Nation admits of no doubt; and it remains to be considered whether the situation of this tribe has become so changed as to render this law inoperative as to them. The territory of the Wyandotts, as before stated, is limited to twelve miles square, and it is surrounded by a dense white population, which have daily intercourse with the Indians. Stores and taverns are kept within the reservation by the Indians or those connected with them, which are as much resorted to for trade and other purposes, by the surrounding white population, as similar establishments in any other part of the country. The treaties made with this tribe have not been abrogated, and they hold their possessory right to the soil on the same tenure as other tribes with whom treaties have been made. And a sub-agent of the government still resides among them, through whom the government holds its official intercourse with the tribe. The Wyandotts have made rapid advances in the arts of civilization. Many of them are very intelligent; their farms are well improved, and they generally live in good houses. They own property of almost every kind, and enjoy the comforts of life in as high a degree as many of their white neighbors.

On a community of Indians situated in so limited a territory, and mixed up with and surrounded by a white population, which carries on with them almost every kind of commerce incident to their condition, can the acts which regulate intercourse with the Indians operate? For years past, as if by universal consent, they have not been enforced over this territory. They are wholly unsuited to the condition of the Wyandott tribe, and it would be impossible to give them a practical operation. And it may be said that the federal government by restricting the territory of this tribe, and encouraging their advances in civilization, has mainly contributed to produce this state of things.

But it is insisted that the larceny charged in the indictment may be punished under the act of congress cited, as it was committed within the reserve, and on the property of one of the Wyandott Indians. And how does congress derive power to punish this offence, when committed within a state? The answer must be, from the power to regulate commerce with the Indians. But if this tribe of Indians is so situated as to render the exercise of this

power wholly impracticable, must it not of necessity cease? And does not the incident fall with the principal power? If congress had power to punish offences committed on the persons or property of Indians, generally, there could be no objection to the exercise of it without reference to circumstances. But when the power to punish is derived exclusively from the power to regulate commerce, it is perfectly clear, when the power to regulate commerce ceases, the power to punish must also cease. To exercise the power to punish for a violation of a regulation necessary to maintain a commercial intercourse with the Indian tribes, as the Wyandotts are now situated, and within their territory, would be a usurpation of power by the general government, and a direct infringement upon the rights of the states.

This conclusion cannot be resisted. And it is immaterial whether the intercourse law of 1802, has been expressly repealed as to the Wyandotts, or rendered inoperative by the force of circumstances. That the law cannot be enforced in this reserve is clear; and this state of things having been produced by the conjoint acts of the federal and state governments, it may be presumed that the former intended, as to this tribe, to abrogate the law. No other presumption can be raised from a state of facts, wholly incompatible with the provisions of the act. An act may be repealed as well by adopting subsequent and incompatible provisions, as by express enactments. And in this view the act of 1802, so far as it regulates trade with the Wyandott Indians, must be considered as substantially repealed. Has not the state jurisdiction to punish offences committed by its own citizens within the Wyandott reserve? Of this, I can entertain no doubt. Ever since the state government has been organized, it has had power to punish its own citizens for offences committed within its limits; whether within an Indian territory or not; and if there be no constitutional prohibition, the state has power to punish its own citizens for offences committed beyond its own limits. The laws of a state cannot operate extra-territorially; but having jurisdiction over its own citizens, the legislature if not prohibited by the constitution, could make certain acts committed by them beyond its own limits, and without the limits of any organized government, an offence. No process could be issued to arrest an offender beyond the state boundaries, but if he comes voluntarily within the state, he would subject himself to its jurisdiction.

By the first section of an act of the British parliament of the 31st Geo. III., passed in 1803, it is provided, "that from and after the passing of this act, all offences committed within any of the Indian territories, or parts of America not within the limits of either of the said provinces of Lower or Upper Canada, or of any civil government of the United States of America shall be, and shall be deemed to be offences of the same nature, and shall be tried in the same manner and subject to the same punishment as if the same had been committed within the provinces of Lower or Upper Canada." Many years ago, the state of Georgia punished its own citizens for depredations committed upon the Indian territory within the state, and no one has ever questioned the legality of such a procedure. The state of New York has not only punished its own citizens, for offences committed within the Indian reserve in that state, but has extended its jurisdiction in criminal cases, over the Indians. The jurisdiction of the federal government over the Indian territory within a state, under the most favorable circumstances for the exercise of the power is limited to the mere purposes of trade, and cannot prevent a state from punishing its own citizens for offences committed within such territory. The exercise of this power by a state, would not be incompatible with the exercise of the power vested in the federal government. There are many offences, such as counterfeiting the gold and silver coin of the country, the notes of the Bank of the United States, &c. which are punishable as well under the laws of the state as those of the Union.

But as it regards the case under consideration, all objections are obviated by the fact, that the regulations of congress respecting commerce with the Indian tribes, have not been enforced within the Wyandott reserve for years, and cannot for the reasons stated be now enforced. It may be admitted that property stolen in an adjoining state and brought into Ohio, would not subject the offender to a prosecution in this state. The offence having been committed in a distinct sovereignty, could not be punished in Ohio; but such a case would, in no respect, be similar to the one under consideration. The Indian territory within a state cannot be considered as a foreign jurisdiction. Under certain circumstances, it has been decided that a state cannot extend its laws over the Indian territory, within it, and especially when those laws are incompatible with constitutional regulations by the federal government. But the jurisdiction is not foreign. If the state have the fee of the Indian lands, it may dispose of that fee subject to the Indian right of occupancy. And in every other respect may the state exercise a jurisdiction over the territory which shall not be incompatible with the constitutional regulations of the general government.

In the course of the argument by the district attorney, several adjudications of the supreme court, and a decision of the circuit court for the Eastern district of Tennessee, were referred to, as sustaining the jurisdiction in the present case. But the facts in this case are wholly dissimilar from those in the cases referred to, and they are not more so than the principles which apply to those facts. It is gratifying to reflect that the state laws will afford a more ample protection to the Wyandotts, as it regards their property, than the laws of the federal government. For the laws of the state punish with greater severity the offence charged in the indictment, than the laws of congress. And as it respects the Indians, no doubt can exist that their complaints will receive as prompt attention and as adequate redress, as those which are made by citizens of the state.

These considerations cannot enter into the question of jurisdiction; but they show that a decision against the jurisdiction of this court, will not leave the Indians unprotected, or lead to a failure of justice. The demurrer must be sustained.

It being suggested to the court by the district attorney, that prosecutions in the state court would be instituted against the defendant and the others against whom indictments have been found, for similar offences, the court directed the marshall to deliver over the defendants to the state authorities to answer, &c.

SEE ALSO:

William Wirt, Georgia and the Treaty of Indian Spring, 28 July 1828, 2 Ops. Atty. Gen. 110

John Macpherson Berrien, The Cherokees and Their Laws, 10 Mar. 1830, 2 Ops. Atty. Gen. 322

John Macpherson Berrien, Trade with the Cherokees, 21 Dec. 1830, 2 Ops. Atty. Gen. 402

William Johnson, J., separate opinion in *Cherokee Nation* v. *Georgia*, 9 Pet. 1 (1831)

Worcester v. *Georgia*, 6 Pet. 515 (1832)

Article 1, Section 8, Clause 4

To establish an uniform Rule of Naturalization, and uniform Laws on
the subject of Bankruptcies throughout the United States;

CITIZENSHIP

1

WILLIAM BLACKSTONE, COMMENTARIES
1:354, 357–58, 361–62
1765

The first and most obvious division of the people is into aliens and natural-born subjects. Natural-born subjects are such as are born within the dominions of the crown of England, that is, within the ligeance, or as it is generally called, the allegiance of the king; and aliens, such as are born out of it. Allegiance is the tie, or *ligamen*, which binds the subject to the king, in return for that protection which the king affords the subject. The thing itself, or substantial part of it, is founded in reason and the nature of government; the name and the form are derived to us from our Gothic ancestors.

. . . . .

Allegiance, both express and implied, is however distinguished by the law into two sorts or species, the one natural, the other local; the former being also perpetual, the latter temporary. Natural allegiance is such as is due from all men born within the king's dominions immediately upon their birth. For, immediately upon their birth, they are under the king's protection; at a time too, when (during their infancy) they are incapable of protecting themselves. Natural allegiance is therefore a debt of gratitude; which cannot be forfeited, cancelled, or altered, by any change of time, place, or circumstance, nor by any thing but the united concurrence of the legislature. An Englishman who removes to France, or to China, owes the same allegiance to the king of England there as at home, and twenty years hence as well as now. For it is a principle of universal law, that the natural-born subject of one prince cannot by any act of his own, no, not by swearing allegiance to another, put off or discharge his natural allegiance to the former: for this natural allegiance was intrinsic, and primitive, and antecedent to the other; and cannot be devested without the concurrent act of that prince to whom it was first due. Indeed the natural-born subject of one prince, to whom he owes allegiance, may be entangled by subjecting himself absolutely to another; but it is his own act that brings him into these straits and difficulties, of owing service to two masters; and it is unreasonable that, by such voluntary act of his own, he should be able at pleasure to unloose those bands, by which he is connected to his natural prince.

Local allegiance is such as is due from an alien, or stranger born, for so long time as he continues within the king's dominion and protection: and it ceases, the instant such stranger transfers himself from this kingdom to another. Natural allegiance is therefore perpetual, and local temporary only: and that for this reason, evidently founded upon the nature of government; that allegiance is a debt due from the subject, upon an implied contract with the prince, that so long as the one affords protection, so long the other will demean himself faithfully. As therefore the prince is always under a constant tie to protect his natural-born subjects, at all times and in all countries, for this reason their allegiance due to him is equally universal and permanent. But, on the other hand, as the prince affords his protection to an alien, only during his residence in this realm, the allegiance of an alien is confined (in point of time) to the duration of such his residence, and (in point of locality) to the dominions of the British empire.

. . . . .

When I say, that an alien is one who is born out of the king's dominions, or allegiance, this also must be understood with some restrictions. The common law indeed stood absolutely so; with only a very few exceptions: so that a particular act of parliament became necessary after the restoration, for the naturalization of children of his majesty's English subjects, born in foreign countries during the late troubles. And this maxim of the law proceeded upon a general principle, that every man owes natural allegiance where he is born, and cannot owe two such allegiances, or serve two masters, at once. Yet the children of the king's embassadors born abroad were always held to be natural subjects: for as the father, though in a foreign country, owes not even a local allegiance to the prince to whom he is sent; so, with regard to the son also, he was held (by a kind of *postliminium*) to be born under the king of England's allegiance, represented by his father, the embassador. To encourage also foreign commerce, it was enacted by statute 25 Edw. III. st. 2. that all children born abroad, provided *both* their parents were at the time of the birth in allegiance to the king, and the mother had passed the seas by her husband's consent, might inherit as if born in England: and accordingly it hath been so adjudged in behalf of merchants. But by several more modern statutes these restrictions are still farther taken off: so that all children, born out of the king's ligeance, whose *fathers* were natural-born subjects, are now natural-born subjects themselves, to all intents and purposes, without any exception; unless their said fathers were attainted, or banished beyond sea, for high treason; or were then in the service of a prince at enmity with Great Britain.

The children of aliens, born here in England, are, generally speaking, natural-born subjects, and entitled to all the privileges of such. In which the constitution of France differs from ours; for there, by their *jus albinatus*, if a child be born of foreign parents, it is an alien.

A denizen is an alien born, but who has obtained *ex donatione regis* letters patent to make him an English subject: a high and incommunicable branch of the royal prerogative. A denizen is in a kind of middle state between an alien, and natural-born subject, and partakes of both of them. He may take lands by purchase or devise, which an alien may not; but cannot take by inheritance: for his parent, through whom he must claim, being an alien had no inheritable blood, and therefore could convey none to the son. And, upon a like defect of hereditary blood, the issue of a denizen, born *before* denization, cannot inherit to him; but his issue born *after,* may. A denizen is not excused from paying the alien's duty, and some other mercantile burthens. And no denizen can be of the privy council, or either house of parliament, or have any office of trust, civil or military, or be capable of any grant from the crown.

Naturalization cannot be performed but by act of parliament: for by this an alien is put in exactly the same state as if he had been born in the king's ligeance; except only that he is incapable, as well as a denizen, of being a member of the privy council, or parliament, &c. No bill for naturalization can be received in either house of parliament, without such disabling clause in it. Neither can any person be naturalized or restored in blood, unless he hath received the sacrament of the Lord's supper within one month before the bringing in of the bill; and unless he also takes the oaths of allegiance and supremacy in the presence of the parliament.

2

DECLARATION OF INDEPENDENCE
4 July 1776

—He has endeavoured to prevent the population of these States; for that purpose obstructing the Laws for Naturalization of Foreigners; refusing to pass others to encourage their migration hither, and raising the conditions of new Appropriations of Lands.

3

ALEXANDER HAMILTON, A SECOND LETTER FROM PHOCION
Apr. 1784
Papers 3:533–35

By the declaration of Independence on the 4th of July, in the year 1776, acceded to by our Convention on the ninth, the late colony of New-York became an independent state. All the inhabitants, who were subjects under the former government, and who did not withdraw themselves upon the change which took place, were to be considered as citizens, owing allegiance to the new government, This, at least, is the legal presumption; and this was the principle, in fact, upon which all the measures of our public councils have been grounded. Duties have been exacted, and punishments inflicted according to this rule. If any exceptions to it were to be admitted, they could only flow from the *indulgence* of the state to such individuals, as from peculiar circumstances might desire to be permitted to stand upon a different footing.

The inhabitants of the southern district, before they fell under the power of the British army, were as much citizens of the state as the inhabitants of other parts of it. They must, therefore, continue to be such, unless they have been divested of that character by some posterior circumstance. This circumstance must, either be—

Their having, by the fortune of war, fallen under the power of the British army.

Their having forfeited their claim by their own misconduct.

Their having been left out of the compact by some subsequent association of the body of the state, or

Their having been dismembered by treaty.

The first of these circumstances according to the fundamental principles of government, and the constant practice of nations could have no effect in working a forfeiture of their citizenship. To allow it such an effect, would be to convert misfortune into guilt; it would be in many instances, to make the negligence of the society, in not providing adequate means of defence for the several parts, the crime of those parts which were the immediate sufferers by that negligence. It would tend to the dissolution of society, by loosening the ties which bind the different parts together, and justifying those who should for a moment fall under the power of a conqueror, not merely in yielding such a submission as was exacted from them, but in taking a willing, interested and decisive part with him.

It was the policy of the revolution, to inculcate upon every citzen the obligation of renouncing his habitation, property, and every private concern for the service of his country, and many of us have scarcely yet learned to consider it as less than treason to have acted in a different manner. But it is time we should correct the exuberances of opinions propagated through policy, and embraced from enthusiasm; and while we admit, that those who did act so disinterested and noble a part, deserve the applause and, wherever they can be bestowed with propriety the rewards of their country, we should cease to impute indiscriminate guilt to those, who, submitting to the accidents of war, remained with their habi[ta]tions and property. We should learn, that this conduct is tolerated by the general sense of mankind; and that according to that sense, whenever the state recovers the possession of such parts as were for a time subdued, the citizens return at once to all the rights, to which they were formerly entitled.

As to the second head of forfeiture by misconduct, there is no doubt, that all such as remaining within the British lines, did not merely yield an obedience, which they could not refuse, without ruin; but took a voluntary and interested part with the enemy, in carrying on the war, became subject to the penalties of treason. They could not however, by that conduct, make themselves aliens, because though they were bound to pay a temporary and qualified obedience to the conqueror, they could not transfer their eventual allegiance from the state to a foreign power. By becoming aliens too, they would have ceased to be traitors; and all the laws of the state passed during the revolution, by which they are considered and punished as subjects, would have been, by that construction, unintelligible and unjust. The idea indeed of citizens transforming themselves into aliens, by taking part against the state, to which they belong, is altogether of new-invention, unknown and inadmissible in law, and contrary to the nature of the social compact.

But were this not the case, an insurmountable difficulty would still remain, for how shall we ascertain who are aliens or traitors, let us call them which we will. It has been seen that the boundaries of the British lines cannot determine the question; for this would be to say, that the merely falling under the power of the British army, constituted every man a *traitor* or an *alien*. It would be to confound one third of the citizens of the state in promiscuous guilt and degradation, without evidence, or enquiry. It would be to make crimes, which are in their nature personal and individual, aggregate and territorial. Shall we go into an enquiry to ascertain the crime of each person? *This would be a prosecution;* and the treaty forbids all future prosecutions. Shall the Legislature take the map and make a geographical delineation of the rights and disqualifications of its citizens? This would be to measure innocence and guilt, by latitute and longitude. It would be to *condemn* and *punish*, not one man, but thousands for *supposed offences*, without giving them an opportunity of making their defence. God forbid that such an act of barefaced tyranny should ever disgrace our history! God forbid that the body of the people should be corrupt enough to wish it, or even to submit to it!

4

AGRIPPA, NO. 9
28 Dec. 1787
Storing 4.6.34

We come now to the second and last article of complaint against the present confederation, which is, that Congress has not the sole power to regulate the intercourse between us and foreigners. Such a power extends not only to war and peace, but to trade and naturalization. This last article ought never to be given them; for though most of the states may be willing for certain reasons to receive foreigners as citizens, yet reasons of equal weight may induce other states, differently circumstanced, to keep their blood pure. Pennsylvania has chosen to receive all that would come there. Let any indifferent person judge whether that state in point of morals, education, energy is equal to any of the eastern states; the small state of Rhode-Island only excepted. Pennsylvania in the course of a century has acquired her present extent and population at the expense of religion and good morals. The eastern states have, by keeping separate from the foreign mixtures, acquired, their present greatness in the course of a century and an half, and have preserved their religion and morals. They have also preserved that manly virtue which is equally fitted for rendering them respectable in war, and industrious in peace.

5

JAMES MADISON, FEDERALIST, NO. 42, 285–87
22 Jan. 1788

The dissimilarity in the rules of naturalization, has long been remarked as a fault in our system, and as laying a foundation for intricate and delicate questions. In the 4th article of the confederation, it is declared "that the *free inhabitants* of each of these States, paupers, vagabonds, and fugitives from justice excepted, shall be entitled to all privileges and immunities of *free citizens*, in the several States, and *the people* of each State, shall in every other, enjoy all the privileges of trade and commerce, &c." There is a confusion of language here, which is remarkable. Why the terms *free inhabitants*, are used in one part of the article; *free citizens* in another, and *people* in another, or what was meant by superadding "to all privileges and immunities of free citizens,"—"all the privileges of trade and commerce," cannot easily be determined. It seems to be a construction scarcely avoidable, however, that those who come under the denomination of *free inhabitants* of a State, although not citizens of such State, are entitled in every other State to all the privileges of *free citizens* of the latter; that is, to greater privileges than they may be entitled to in their own State; so that it may be in the power of a particular State, or rather every State is laid under a necessity, not only to confer the rights of citizenship in other States upon any whom it may admit to such rights within itself; but upon any whom it may allow to become inhabitants within its jurisdiction. But were an exposition of the term "inhabitants" to be admitted, which would confine the stipulated privileges to citizens alone, the difficulty is diminished only, not removed. The very improper power would still be retained by each State, of naturalizing aliens in every other State. In one State residence for a short term confers all the rights of citizenship. In another qualifications of greater importance are required. An alien therefore legally incapacitated for certain rights in the latter, may by previous residence only in the former, elude his incapacity; and thus the law of one State, be preposterously rendered paramount to the law of another, within the jurisdiction of the other. We owe it to mere casualty, that very

serious embarrassments on this subject, have been hitherto escaped. By the laws of several States, certain descriptions of aliens who had rendered themselves obnoxious, were laid under interdicts inconsistent, not only with the rights of citizenship, but with the privilege of residence. What would have been the consequence, if such persons, by residence or otherwise, had acquired the character of citizens under the laws of another State, and then asserted their rights as such, both to residence and citizenship within the State proscribing them? Whatever the legal consequences might have been, other consequences would probably have resulted of too serious a nature, not to be provided against. The new Constitution has accordingly with great propriety made provision against them, and all others proceeding from the defect of the confederation, on this head, by authorising the general government to establish an uniform rule of naturalization throughout the United States.

6

FEDERAL FARMER, NO. 18
25 Jan. 1788
Storing 2.8.224

The power of naturalization, when viewed in connection with the judicial powers and cases, is, in my mind, of very doubtful extent. By the constitution itself, the citizens of each state will be naturalized citizens of every state, to the general purposes of instituting suits, claiming the benefits of the laws, &c. And in order to give the federal courts jurisdiction of an action, between citizens of the same state, in common acceptation, may not a court allow the plaintiff to say, he is a citizen of one state, and the defendant a citizen of another, without carrying legal fictions so far, by any means, as they have been carried by the courts of King's Bench and Exchequer, in order to bring causes within their cognizance—Further, the federal city and districts, will be totally distinct from any state, and a citizen of a state will not of course be a subject of any of them; and to avail himself of the privileges and immunities of them, must he not be naturalized by congress in them? and may not congress make any proportion of the citizens of the states naturalized subjects of the federal city and districts, and thereby entitle them to sue or defend, in all cases, in the federal courts?

7

HOUSE OF REPRESENTATIVES, CONTESTED ELECTION
22 May 1789
Annals 1:397–408

(See 1.5, no. 13)

8

[*3 Feb.*]

The House then went into a Committee of the whole on the bill establishing an uniform rule of Naturalization. Mr. BALDWIN in the Chair. The first clause enacted, that all free white persons, who have, or shall migrate into the United States, and shall give satisfactory proof, before a magistrate, by oath, that they intend to reside therein, and shall take an oath of allegiance, *and shall have resided in the United States for one whole year*, shall be entitled to all the rights of citizenship, except being capable of holding an office under the State or General Government, which capacity they are to acquire after a residence of two years more.

Mr. TUCKER moved to strike out the words "and shall have resided within the United States for one whole year;" because he conceived it the policy of America to enable foreigners to hold lands, in their own right, in less than one year; he had no objection to extending the term, entitling them to hold an office under Government, to three years. In short, the object of his motion was, to let aliens come in, take the oath, and hold lands without any residence at all.

Mr. HARTLEY said, he had no doubt of the policy of admitting aliens to the rights of citizenship; but he thought some security for their fidelity and allegiance was requisite besides the bare oath; that is, he thought an actual residence of such a length of time as would give a man an opportunity of esteeming the Government from knowing its intrinsic value, was essentially necessary to assure us of a man's becoming a good citizen. The practice of almost every State in the Union countenanced a regulation of this nature; and perhaps it was owing to a wish of this kind, that the States had consented to give this power to the General Government. The terms of citizenship are made too cheap in some parts of the Union; to say, that a man shall be admitted to all the privileges of a citizen, without any residence at all, is what can hardly be expected.

The policy of the old nations of Europe has drawn a line between citizens and aliens: that policy has existed to our knowledge ever since the foundation of the Roman Empire; experience has proved its propriety, or we should have found some nation deviating from a regulation inimical to its welfare. From this it may be inferred, that we ought not to grant this privilege on terms so easy as is moved by the gentleman from South Carolina. If he had gone no further in his motion than to give aliens a right to purchase and hold lands, the objection would not have been so great; but if the words are stricken out that he has moved for, an alien will be entitled to join in the election

of your officers at the first moment he puts his foot on shore in America, when it is impossible, from the nature of things, that he can be qualified to exercise such a talent; but if it was presumable that he was qualified by a knowledge of the candidates, yet we have no hold upon his attachment to the Government.

Mr. SHERMAN thought that the interests of the State where the emigrant intended to reside ought to be consulted, as well as the interests of the General Government. He presumed it was intended by the Convention, who framed the Constitution, that Congress should have the power of naturalization, in order to prevent particular States receiving citizens, and forcing them upon others who would not have received them in any other manner. It was therefore meant to guard against an improper mode of naturalization, rather than foreigners should be received upon easier terms than those adopted by the several States. Now, the regulation provided for in this bill, entitles all free white persons, which includes emigrants, and even those who are likely to become chargeable. It certainly never would be undertaken by Congress to compel the States to receive and support this class of persons; it would therefore be necessary that some clause should be added to the bill to counteract such a general proposition.

Mr. PAGE was of opinion, that the policy of European nations and States respecting naturalization, did not apply to the situation of the United States. Bigotry and superstition, or a deep-rooted prejudice against the Government, laws, religion, or manners of neighboring nations had a weight in that policy, which cannot exist here, where a more liberal system ought to prevail. I think, said he, we shall be inconsistent with ourselves, if, after boasting of having opened an asylum for the oppressed of all nations, and established a Government which is the admiration of the world, we make the terms of admission to the full enjoyment of that asylum so hard as is now proposed. It is nothing to us, whether Jews or Roman Catholics settle amongst us; whether subjects of Kings, or citizens of free States wish to reside in the United States, they will find it their interest to be good citizens, and neither their religious nor political opinions can injure us, if we have good laws, well executed.

Mr. BOUDINOT was against striking out the words, because he would rather choose to alter it from one year to two years, than strike out all that respected the capacity of an alien to be elected into any office. He conceived, that after a person was admitted to the rights of citizenship, he ought to have them full and complete, and not be divested of any part.

Mr. WHITE noticed the inconvenience which would result from permitting an alien to all the rights of citizenship, merely upon his coming and taking an oath that he meant to reside in the United States. Foreign merchants and captains of vessels might by this means evade the additional duties laid on foreign vessels; he thought, therefore, if the words were struck out, that another clause ought to be added, depriving persons of the privilege of citizenship, who left the country and staid abroad for a given length of time.

Mr. LAWRENCE was of opinion, that Congress had nothing more to do than point out the mode by which foreigners might become citizens. The constitution had expressly said how long they should reside among us before they were admitted to seats in the Legislature; the propriety of annexing any additional qualifications is therefore much to be questioned. But this bill is not confined to the qualifications of the General Government only, it descends to those of the State Governments; it may be doubly questioned how far Congress has the power to declare what residence shall entitle an alien to the right of a seat in the State Legislatures.

The reason of admitting foreigners to the rights of citizenship among us is the encouragement of emigration, as we have a large tract of country to people. Now, he submitted to the sense of the committee, whether a term, so long as that prescribed in the bill, would not tend to restrain rather than encourage emigration? It has been said, that we ought not to admit them to vote at our elections. Will they not have to pay taxes from the time they settle amongst us? And is it not a principle that taxation and representation ought to go hand and hand? Shall we then restrain a man from having an agency in the disposal of his own money? It has been also observed, that persons might come and reside amongst us for some time, and then leave the country; he did not doubt that such might be the case, but it was not presumable, that after they had once taken an oath that they meant to reside here, and had become citizens, that they would return as soon as the occasion which required their absence had terminated.

Mr. Madison.—When we are considering the advantages that may result from an easy mode of naturalization, we ought also to consider the cautions necessary to guard against abuses. It is no doubt very desirable that we should hold out as many inducements as possible for the worthy part of mankind to come and settle amongst us, and throw their fortunes into a common lot with ours. But why is this desirable? Not merely to swell the catalogue of people. No, sir, it is to increase the wealth and strength of the community; and those who acquire the rights of citizenship, without adding to the strength or wealth of the community are not the people we are in want of. And what is proposed by the amendment is, that they shall take nothing more than an oath of fidelity, and declare their intention to reside in the United States. Under such terms, it was well observed by my colleague, aliens might acquire the right of citizenship, and return to the country from which they came, and evade the laws intended to encourage the commerce and industry of the real citizens and inhabitants of America, enjoying at the same time all the advantages of citizens and aliens.

I should be exceedingly sorry, sir, that our rule of naturalization excluded a single person of good fame that really meant to incorporate himself into our society; on the other hand, I do not wish that any man should acquire the privilege, but such as would be a real addition to the wealth or strength of the United States.

It may be a question of some nicety, how far we can make our law to admit an alien to the right of citizenship, step by step; but there is no doubt we may, and ought to require residence as an essential.

Mr. Smith, of South Carolina, thought some restraints proper, and that they would tend to raise the Government in the opinion of good men, who are desirous of emigrating; as for the privilege of electing, or being elected, he conceived a man ought to be some time in the country before he could pretend to exercise it. What could he know of the Government the moment he landed? Little or nothing: how then could he ascertain who was a proper person to legislate or judge of the laws? Certainly gentlemen would not pretend to bestow a privilege upon a man which he is incapable of using?

How far the Government may admit a man to the rights of citizenship by progression, is called in question. The Constitution vests in Congress the power to establish a uniform rule of naturalization; it is not various rules they have the power to make, but one complete uniform rule; now, is it one rule, if a man is admitted progressively? It is; because it is only part of a rule, that a man shall be entitled to certain privileges at the end of one year's residence. Another part is to give more in two years, and the whole is completed at the end of three years. The naturalization laws of Carolina proceed upon this plan: they do not there conceive it proper to give the complete right at once; they give citizenship for certain purposes at first, extending them afterwards as the person is fitted to receive them.

The intention of the present motion is, to enable foreigners to come here, purchase and hold lands; but this will go beyond what the mover has required, and therefore it will be better to draught a separate clause, admitting them to purchase and hold lands upon a qualified tenure and pre-emption right, than thus admit them at once to interfere in our politics. The quality of being a freeholder is requisite, in some States, to give a man a title to vote for corporation and parish officers. Now, if every emigrant who purchases a small lot, but for which perhaps he has not paid, becomes in a moment qualified to mingle in their parish or corporation politics, it is possible it may create great uneasiness in neighborhoods which have been long accustomed to live in peace and unity.

Mr. Hartley said, that the subject had employed his thoughts for some time, and that he had made up his mind in favor of requiring a term of residence. The experience of all nations, and the Constitution of most of the States induced the same opinion. An alien has no right to hold lands in any country, and if they are admitted to do it in this, we are authorized to annex to it such conditions as we think proper. If they are unreasonable, they may defeat the object we have in view, but they have no right to complain; yet, considering the circumstances of this country, he was favorable to easy terms of admission, because, he thought, it might be some inducement to foreigners to come and settle among us. It has been remarked, that we must admit those whom we call citizens to all the rights of citizenship at once. This opinion, he presumed, was not well founded; the practice of this country in no instance warrants it. The Constitutions of the several States admit aliens to the privilege of citizenship, step by step; they generally require a residence for a certain time, before they are admitted to vote at elections; some of them annex to it the condition of payment of taxes and other qualifications; but he believed none of the States render a foreigner capable of being elected to serve in a legislative capacity, without a probation of some years. This kind of exception is also contemplated in the Constitution of the United States. It is there required, that a person shall be so many years an inhabitant before he can be admitted to the trust of legislating for the society. He thought, therefore, that this part of the objection is not well supported.

With respect to the policy of striking out the words altogether from the clause, and requiring no residence before a man is admitted to the rights of election, the objections are obvious. If, at any time, a number of people emigrate into a seaport town; for example, from a neighboring colony into the State of New York, will they not, by taking the oath of allegiance, be able to decide the fate of an election contrary to the wishes and inclinations of the real citizens? And are gentlemen disposed to throw such an undue influence into the hands of foreigners? Besides, they will acquire a capacity of evading your revenue laws, intended for the encouragement of the citizens. I have mentioned this example, and might enumerate many others, to point out the impropriety of this policy; but presuming them to be within every gentleman's knowledge, I shall not enlarge upon it.

With respect to the propriety of enabling foreigners to acquire and hold lands on a qualified tenure, I have no objection to such a clause.

Mr. WHITE doubted whether the constitution authorized Congress to say on what terms aliens or citizens should hold lands in the respective States; the power vested by the Constitution in Congress, respecting the subject now before the House, extend to nothing more than making a uniform rule of naturalization. After a person has once become a citizen, the power of Congress ceases to operate upon him; the rights and privileges of citizens in the several States belong to those States; but a citizen of one State is entitled to all the privileges and immunities of the citizens in the several States. Now, if any State in the Union should choose to prohibit its citizens from the privilege of holding real estates, without a residence of a greater number of years than should be thought proper by this House, they could do it, and no authority of the Government, he apprehended, could enforce an obedience to a regulation not warranted by the constitution. So, in the case of elections, if the constitution of a particular State requires four, five, or six years residence, before a man is admitted to acquire a legislative capacity, with respect to the State Government, he must remain there that length of time, notwithstanding you may declare he shall be eligible after a residence of two years; all, therefore, that the House have to do on this subject, is to confine themselves to an uniform rule of naturalization, and not to a general definition of what constitutes the rights of citizenship in the several States.

Mr. JACKSON conceived the present subject to be of high importance to the respectability and character of the American name; the veneration he had for, and the attachment he had to, this country, made him extremely anxious to preserve its good fame from injury. He hoped to see the title of a citizen of America as highly venerated and respected as was that of a citizen of old Rome. I am clearly of opinion, that rather than have the common class of vagrants, paupers, and other outcasts of Europe, that we had better be as we are, and trust to the natural increase of our population for inhabitants. If the motion made by the gentleman from South Carolina, should obtain, such people will find an easy admission indeed to the rights of citizenship; much too easy for the interests of the people of America. Nay, sir, the terms required by the bill on the table are, in my mind, too easy. I think, before a man is admitted to enjoy the high and inestimable privileges of a citizen of America, that something more than a mere residence amongst us is necessary. I think he ought to pass some time in a state of probation, and at the end of the term, be able to bring testimonials of a proper and decent behavior; no man, who would be a credit to the community, could think such terms difficult or indelicate: if bad men should be dissatisfied on this account, and should decline to emigrate, the regulation will have a beneficial effect; for we had better keep such out of the country than admit them into it. I conceive, sir, that an amendment of this kind would be reasonable and proper; all the difficulty will be to determine how a proper certificate of good behaviour should be obtained; I think it might be done by vesting the power in the grand jury or district courts to determine on the character of the man, as they should find it.

Mr. PAGE.—I observed before, Mr. Chairman, that the European policy did not apply to the United States. I gave my reasons for it; they are such as have not been controverted, and I presume cannot.

With respect to the idea of excluding bad men from the rights of citizenship, I look upon it as impracticable; hard terms of admission may exclude good men, but will not keep out one of the wretches alluded to; they will come in various forms, and care little about citizenship. If we make use of the grand jury for this purpose, as proposed by the member from Georgia, (Mr. JACKSON,) we must, to complete the plan, authorize the grand jury to indict such emigrants as are unworthy to become citizens, and expel them. We must add an inquisition, and as it will not be sufficient for our views of having immaculate citizens, we should add censors, and banish the immoral from amongst us. Indeed, sir, I fear, if we go on as is proposed now, in the infancy of our republic, we shall, in time, require a test of faith and politics, of every person who shall come into these States. As to any precautions against admitting strangers to vote at elections, though I think them of less importance than some gentlemen, I object not to them; but contend, that every man, upon coming into the States, and taking the oath of allegiance to the Government, and declaring his desire and intention of residing therein, ought to be enabled to purchase and hold lands, or we shall discourage many of the present inhabitants of Europe from becoming inhabitants of the United States.

Mr. LAWRENCE.—We are authorized to establish a uniform rule of naturalization; but what are the effects resulting from the admission of persons to citizenship, is another concern, and depends upon the constitutions and laws of the States now in operation. I have therefore an objection to that part of the bill which respects the qualification of the members of the State Legislatures. But with respect to residence, before a man is admitted, I am of opinion with the gentleman from Virginia, (Mr. PAGE,) at least it may be questioned, whether any good can result from it, to compensate for the evil it may effect by restraining emigration. The gentleman has said he would admit none but such as would add to the wealth or strength of the nation. Every person who comes among us must do one or the other; if he brings money, or other property with him, he evidently increases the general mass of wealth, and if he brings an able body, his labor will be productive of national wealth, and an addition to our domestic strength. Consequently, every person, rich or poor, must add to our wealth and strength, in a greater or less degree.

Whether there shall be any particular regulation with respect to the character of the man who is to be naturalized, will be an after consideration; but I think it will be sufficient that we are able, by laws, to restrain and regulate the conduct of an individual. Nor do I believe, sir, there is any just ground of apprehension that people will come to this city, from Nova Scotia, or any other part of the world, in bodies of three or four thousand, to turn our elections, or interfere in our politics. And while I am free from these apprehensions, and suppose that the true policy of this country is to make the terms of admission easy, in order to people our country, I shall be against every measure which has a tendency to throw obstacles in the way.

Mr. TUCKER had no object in making his motion, but to enable people to hold lands, who came from abroad to settle in the United States. He was otherwise satisfied with the clause, so far as it made residence a term of admission to the privilege of election; but there was a seeming contradiction in making them freeholders, and, at the same time, excluding them from the performance of duties annexed to that class of citizens. He thought the citizens had a right to require the performance of such duties, by every person who was eligible under their State laws and constitutions. Now, if the motion could be modified in any way to accomplish his object with consistency, he would cheerfully acquiesce therein.

As to the privilege of being elected to office, he was of opinion, the term of three or four years was a term sufficiently short to acquire it in; it was a much easier method of obtaining citizenship, than was practised by other nations: neither would he object to any precaution being introduced into the bill, that had a tendency to prevent the admission of bad men, if such precaution could be devised, consistent with their constitutional power, and could be carried into easy and safe execution. The mode mentioned by the gentleman from Georgia, of a recommendation by the grand jury, or district court, would throw a very great embarrassment into the way of an emigrant's becoming a citizen; but if some more eligible mode can be devised, of making the inhabitants of the United States a select society of good moral men, he was ready to agree to it, yet he almost despaired of its being accomplished.

He had no doubt the Government had a right to make the admission to citizenship progressive, the Constitution pointed out something of this kind, by the different ages and terms of residence they annexed to the right of holding a seat in this House and in the Senate, and of being chosen President. No inhabitant can become President of the United States, unless he has been an inhabitant fourteen years; which plainly infers that he might have been a citizen for other purposes, with a shorter residence. But it goes still further, it enables Congress to dictate the terms of citizenship to foreigners, and to prevent them from being admitted to the full exercise of the rights of citizenship by the General Government; because it declares that no other than a natural born citizen, or a citizen at the time of the adoption of this constitution, shall be eligible to the office of President.

With respect to their interference with the State Governments, he believed it to be improper; and hoped, therefore, that the bill would be confined solely to the objects of the General Government.

Mr. MADISON remarked, that the arguments had extended themselves beyond the simple question before the committee, and called into view matters of considerable importance, but of which, at this time, he did not mean to give an opinion. Whether residence is, or is not, a proper quality to be attached to a citizen, is the question? In his own mind, he had no doubt but residence was a proper pre-requisite, and he was prepared to decide in favor of it.

Mr. SMITH, (S. C.) hoped the question would not be put to-day, as he wished to reflect further on the subject. A variety of observations had been made, which merited the serious attention of the committee; he would suggest another. An alien, in Great Britain, is not permitted to inherit, or hold real estate for his own use; consequently, a citizen of the United States, and a subject of Great Britain, would not be on an equal footing with respect to estates descended to them by inheritance. He thought this, and other weighty observations, would induce the House to postpone the subject till to-morrow.

Mr. SEDGWICK was against the indiscriminate admission of foreigners to the highest rights of human nature, upon terms so incompetent to secure the society from being overrun with the outcasts of Europe; besides, the policy of settling the vacant territory by emigration is of a doubtful nature. He believed, in the United States, the human species might be multiplied by a more eligible and convenient mode, than what seemed to be contemplated by the motion now before the committee. He was well satisfied for himself, that there existed no absolute necessity of peopling it in this way; and, if there was no absolute necessity, he thought Congress might use their discretion, and admit none but reputable and worthy characters; such only were fit for the society into which they were blended. The citizens of America preferred this country, because it is to be preferred; the like principle he wished might be held by every man who came from Europe to reside here; but there was at least some grounds to fear the contrary; their sensations, impregnated with prejudices of education, acquired under monarchical and aristocratical Governments, may deprive them of that zest for pure republicanism, which is necessary in order to taste its beneficence with that gratitude which we feel on the occasion. Some kind of probation, as it has been termed, is absolutely requisite, to enable them to feel and be sensible of the blessing. Without that probation, he should be sorry to see them exercise a right which we have gloriously struggled to attain.

Mr. BURKE thought it of importance to fill the country with useful men, such as farmers, mechanics, and manufacturers, and, therefore, would hold out every encouragement to them to emigrate to America. This class he would receive on liberal terms; and he was satisfied there would be room enough for them, and for their posterity, for five hundred years to come. There was another class of men, whom he did not think useful, and he did not care what impediments were thrown in their way; such as your European merchants, and factors of merchants, who come with a view of remaining so long as will enable them to acquire a fortune, and then they will leave the country, and carry off all their property with them. These people injure us more than they do us good, and, except in this last sentiment, I can compare them to nothing but leeches. They stick to us until they get their fill of our best blood, and then they fall off and leave us. I look upon the privilege of an American citizen to be an honorable one, and it ought not to be thrown away upon such people. There is another class also that I would interdict, that is, the convicts and criminals which they pour out of British jails. I wish sincerely some mode could be adopted to prevent the importation of such; but that, perhaps, is not in our power; the introduction of them ought to be considered as a high misdemeanor.

Mr. STONE had no doubt but an alien might be admitted to the rights of citizenship, step by step; but he questioned the power of the House to say that a man shall be citizen for certain purposes, as it respects the individual State Governments; he concluded that the laws and constitutions of the States, and the constitution and laws of the United States, would trace out the steps by which they should acquire certain degrees of citizenship. Congress may point out a uniform rule of naturalization; but cannot say what shall be the effect of that naturalization, as it respects the particular States. Congress cannot say that foreigners, naturalized under a general law, shall be entitled to privileges which the States withhold from native citizens.

Mr. BOUDINOT.—An exchange of sentiment on this floor I find always tends to throw more light on a subject than is generally to be obtained in any other way. But, as the subject is not yet fully elucidated, I shall be in favor of letting it remain undecided till to-morrow, for which reason, I move the committee to rise.

[*4 Feb.*]

Mr. PAGE wished it delayed until he saw the gentleman from South Carolina (Mr. BURKE) in his place.

Mr. SMITH, (of S. C.) said, he believed the object of his colleague was nothing more than to let foreigners, on easy terms, be admitted to hold lands; that this object could be better effected by introducing a clause to that purpose, and he had no doubt but it would be equally satisfactory to his colleague.

Mr. GOODHUE was against the motion, because it made our citizenship too cheap; after it was decided against, he would move to make the term two years, instead of one, before an alien should be entitled to the privilege of a citizen.

Mr. STONE.—I would let the term of residence be long enough to accomplish two objects, before I would consent to admit a foreigner to have any thing to do with the politics of this country. First, that he should have an opportunity of knowing the circumstances of our Government, and in consequence thereof, shall have admitted the truth of the principles we hold. Second, that he shall have acquired a taste for this kind of Government. And in order that both these things may take place, in such a full manner as to make him worthy of admission into our society, I think a term of four or seven years ought to be required. A foreigner who comes here is not desirous of interfering immediately with our politics; nor is it proper that he should. His emigration is governed by a different principle; he is desirous of obtaining and holding property. I should have no objection to his doing this, from the first moment he sets his foot on shore in America; but it appears to me, that we ought to be cautious how we admit emigrants to the other privileges of citizenship, and that for a reason not yet mentioned; perhaps it may allude to the next generation more than to this, because the present inhabitants, or most of them, have been engaged in a long, hazardous, and expensive war. They have been active in rearing up the present Government, and feel, perhaps, a laudable vanity in having effected what the most sanguine hardly dared to contemplate. There is no danger of these people losing what they so greatly esteem; but the admission of a great number of foreigners to all the places of Government, may tincture the system with the dregs of their former habits, and corrupt what we believe the most pure of all human institutions.

Mr. JACKSON.—It was observed yesterday, Mr. Chairman, that we could not modify or confine our terms of naturalization; that we could not admit an alien to the rights of citizenship progressively. I shall take the liberty of supporting the contrary doctrine, which I contend for, by the reference to the very accurate commentator on the laws of England, *Justice Blackstone*, I, 10.—"Naturalization," says he, "cannot be performed but by an act of Parliament; for by this an alien is put in exactly the same state as if he had been born in the King's legiance, *except* only, that he is incapable, as well as a denizen, of being a member of the Privy Council, or Parliament, holding offices, grants, &c. No bill for naturalization can be received in either House of Parliament without such disabling clause in it." So that here we find, in that nation from which we derive most of our ideas on this subject, not only that citizens are made progressively, but that such a mode is absolutely necessary to be pursued in every act of Parliament for the naturalization of foreigners.

The same learned Judge then goes on to show the attempts that were made to introduce a general system of naturalization, and how they failed; and that, to this day, even of their meritorious naval and military characters they make an exception, as to sitting in Parliament, &c.

and holding grants of land from the Crown, within the Kingdoms of Great Britain and Ireland. After this, I presume, it will not be contended that we cannot found our law on the principle of a progressive and probational naturalization.

With respect to the approbation which a foreigner ought to acquire before he becomes a citizen, I am most clear, and as arguments enough have been used to place it in its strongest point of light, I will not trouble the committee with a repetition; but I believe it essentially necessary to render the American name as honorable as it merits.

Mr. LAWRENCE knew that Congress had power to say on what terms aliens should be admitted to the rights of citizenship, and affix any length of residence they thought proper; so that there was no occasion to bring a commentator on the English law to prove it to him. But he contended, that when the alien was admitted to the right of citizenship, that the law of the United States could not vary any of the effects of that citizenship in the State to which he belonged. He would elucidate this, by referring to the Constitution and practice of this State. No person in New York can be naturalized but by an act of the Legislature; and when he is naturalized, there are certain rights which, perhaps, he cannot exercise, because he is not qualified according to the terms of the Constitution. For example, he may not vote for Representatives in Assembly, unless he has resided six months in the State. Now, the act of Assembly naturalizing him, cannot bestow on him the right of voting, unless he either has before, or shall after, reside in the State for the term of six months. He contended, that the law of the United States could not alter the right of any man to vote after six months' residence in New York, provided he had conformed to the laws of the United States, in remaining one year, as the words, now moved to be struck out, seemed to imply. It is undoubtedly a question of policy, how long a person shall remain here before he is admitted to the rights of a citizen; but as a short term appeared to him to be best, he was for striking out the words proposed.

Mr. JACKSON understood the gentleman yesterday, as having advanced the argument to which he replied; but, if he was mistaken in regard to him, some other gentleman had made the observation, and the authority he adduced would serve to do away any doubts it might have given rise to.

Mr. HUNTINGTON.—The terms of the bill are too indefinite; they require the emigrant to take an oath that he intends to reside in the United States; but how long, and for what purpose, are not ascertained. He may determine to stay here until he accomplishes a particular object; and he may go into the most obscure part of the Union to take this oath. The community certainly will not be benefited by such emigrants, and therefore they ought not to be admitted to the privileges of citizenship. The mode of naturalization, pointed out in this bill, is much too easy. In the State to which I belong, said he, no person could be naturalized, but by an act of the Legislature; the same is the case in several of the other States, and in Britain. He never knew a good inhabitant, who wished to be admitted to the rights of citizenship, but what found this mode sufficiently easy. The term that an emigrant should reside ought to be sufficiently long to give him an opportunity of acquiring a knowledge of the principles of the Government, and of those who are most proper to administer it; otherwise he cannot exercise his privilege with any advantage to himself, or to the community. He therefore wished that the clause might be amended, in such a manner as to leave the naturalization of foreigners to the State Legislatures.

Mr. CLYMER was of opinion, that foreigners ought to be gradually admitted to the rights of citizens; and that a residence for a certain time should entitle them to hold property; but that the higher privileges of citizens, such as electing, or being elected into office, should require a longer term; permitting these rights to be assumed, and exercised at a shorter period, would not operate as any inducement to persons to emigrate; as the great object of emigration is generally with the view of procuring a more comfortable subsistence, or to better the circumstances of the individuals: the exercise of particular privileges was but a secondary consideration. He then observed, that it might be good policy to admit foreigners to purchase and hold lands in fee simple, without ever coming to America; it would, perhaps, facilitate the borrowing of money of Europeans, if they could take mortgages, and be secure. One State (Pennsylvania) had granted this liberty to aliens, and they have experienced no inconvenience therefrom; he wished Congress to pass a similar law, and was convinced it would not be dishonorable.

Mr. STONE gave it as his opinion, that a person, who meant to qualify himself for becoming a citizen of the United States, ought to take the oath of residence and allegiance within six months, and be thereupon entitled to hold property; but that he should not be capable of holding an office, or electing others into one, for seven years.

Mr. BURKE.—Unless some residence is required, it may be attended with confusion. In large cities, like Boston, New York, or Philadelphia, an election may be carried by the votes of the body of sailors who happened to be in port. If the French fleet was here at such a time, and a spirit of party strongly excited, perhaps one of the candidates might get the crews of every ship in the fleet, and after qualifying them, by taking an oath of no definite meaning, carry them up to the hustings, and place himself or his friend on this floor, contrary to the voice of nine-tenths of the city. Even a residence of one year is too short, it ought to be two, three, or four; but seven is too long. Indeed, the whole of this bill seems somehow objectionable; there are some cases also omitted, which may show the necessity of recommitting it.

The case of the children of American parents born abroad ought to be provided for, as was done in the case of English parents, in the 12th year of William III. There are several other cases that ought to be likewise attended to.

Mr. PAGE had given his sentiments yesterday, and was clearly against throwing any obstacles in the way of good men desirous of becoming citizens.

Mr. LEE did not approve of the motion; but was in favor of as short a term as would be consistent, because he apprehended it would tend considerably to encourage emigration.

Mr. SENEY thought Congress had no right to intermeddle with the regulations of the several States, while prescribing a rule of naturalization. If they were disposed to say that two, three, or four years' residence in the United States was proper, before an alien should be eligible to an office under the General Government, they might; but after they have admitted a foreigner to citizenship, he did not believe they were authorized to except him, for two years more, from being capable of election, or appointment to any office, Legislative, Executive, or Judicial, under the State Governments, provided the State laws or constitutions admit him at a shorter period. Nor did he believe Congress could admit foreigners to such privilege so early as two years in States requiring a longer term of probation. He had, however, no objection to foreigners being admitted to hold property, without any previous residence; but he did not like the idea of admitting them to a participation in the Government, without a residence sufficiently long to enable them to understand their duty. As the bill was not satisfactory to his mind, in its present form, he would vote for a recommitment.

Mr. JACKSON had an objection to any persons holding land in the United States without residence, and an intention of becoming a citizen; under such a regulation the whole Western Territory might be purchased up by the inhabitants of England, France, or other foreign nations; the landholders might combine, and send out a large tenantry, and have thereby such an interference in the Government as to overset the principles upon which it is established. It will be totally subversive of the old established doctrine, that allegiance and land go together; a person owing no allegiance to a Sovereign ought not to hold lands under its protection, because he cannot be called upon and obliged to give that support which invasion or insurrection may render necessary. But, with respect to residence and probation, before an alien is entitled to the privilege of voting at elections, I am very clear it is necessary; unless gentlemen mean to render the rank of an American citizen the maygame of the world. Shall stories be told of our citizenship, such as I have read in the Pennsylvania Magazine of the citizenship there? If my memory serves me right, the story runs, that at a contested election in Philadelphia, when parties ran very high, and no stone was left unturned, on either side, to carry the election, most of the ships in the harbor were cleared of their crews, who, ranged under the masters and owners, came before a Magistrate, took the oath of allegiance, and paid half a crown tax to the Collector, as the Constitution required, then went and voted, and decided the contest of the day. On the return of one of the vessels, whose crew had been employed in the affair of the election, they fell in with a shoal of porpoises off Cape Henlopen: "Ha!" said one of them, "what merry company have we got here! I wonder where they are going so cheerfully?" "Going," replied one of his comrades, "why, going to Philadelphia, to be sure, to pay taxes, and vote for Assembly men!" I hope, Mr. Chairman, we have more respect for our situation as citizens, than to expose ourselves to the taunts and jeers of a deriding world, by making that situation too cheap.

Mr. SMITH, (of S. C.) admitted the propriety of recommitting the bill; but he wished some principles to be first established for the direction of the committee; for, at present, he was at a loss to conceive what was the prevailing opinion. Many gentlemen had suggested new ideas, which occasioned new difficulties; he hoped they would settle and remove some of them before they rose. The gentleman from Maryland (Mr. SENEY) has observed, that we have no right to declare upon what terms an alien shall be admitted to the offices of the State Governments; the same argument extends also to the voters. This opinion opens a new field of argument, and entirely changes the system; it ought, therefore, to be decided. For his part, he was of opinion, that an uniform rule of naturalization would extend to make a uniform rule of citizenship pervade the whole Continent, and decide the right of a foreigner to be admitted to elect, or be elected, in any of the States.

He would suggest another idea for consideration. What is to become of those inchoate rights of citizenship, which are not yet completed? Can the Government, by an *ex post facto* law, deprive an alien of the advantage of such an inchoate right?

Mr. SENEY.—The gentleman last up has different ideas of the jurisdiction of the United States from me. He believes we have not only the power of prescribing the qualifications of our own officers, but the officers of every State in the Union; but I conceive, with respect to the latter, we have nothing to do. We can go no further than to prescribe the rule by which it can be determined who are, and who are not citizens; but we cannot say they shall be entitled to privileges in the different States which native citizens are not entitled to, until they have performed the conditions annexed thereto.

Mr. BURKE said, no person ought to be permitted to inherit by descent, in America, unless the same privilege was reciprocated by other nations; perhaps this point would be properly settled by treaty, and it would be well to introduce a provisionary clause to this effect. He was also in favor of admitting foreigners to hold lands on easy terms, if they would come to reside among us; and here he would take an opportunity of doing justice to some of them, as it might be supposed, from what had fallen from various parts of the House, that foreigners, educated under a Monarchy, were inimical to the pure principles of Republicanism. He was convinced that this doctrine was untrue, because he had often remarked, that foreigners made as good citizens of Republics as the natives themselves. Frenchmen, brought up under an absolute Monarchy, evinced their love of liberty in the late arduous struggle; many of them are now worthy citizens, who esteem and venerate the principles of our Revolution. Emigrants from England, Ireland, and Scotland, have not been behind any in the love of this country; so there is but little occasion for the jealousy which appears to be entertained for the preservation of the government.

Mr. CLYMER observed, that though Congress have authority to make a uniform rule of naturalization throughout the States, yet it was not true that it would apply with equal advantage to them all; that it might be proper every where, indeed, that aliens should be admitted, early, to the inferior rights of citizens, but that it would be unsuitable they should be admitted to the higher privileges at the same period, in all the States, however differently circumstanced. In States newly formed, it might be useful to fix a short period; but in the old States, fully peopled, he did not think the longest which had been mentioned too great; for this reason he thought the power of naturalizing should be referred to the States, to make such provision as they pleased, and therefore approved the recommitment; but not till the House had passed on to a following clause, which respects the objects of the bill. When that came under consideration, he thought it might be both a generous and wise policy to make an easy way to the return of those, with exception to one character only, who had been once citizens of the United States, and who would, many of them, gladly again become so; he meant the refugees, who were adding to the wealth and strength of a Power no ways friendly to us, and are actually injuring some of the States by the rivalship they create in the fisheries.

Mr. TUCKER thought the bill must be recommitted; but he did not wish it done till the sense of the House was known on some of the various points that had presented themselves during the debate. With respect to the latter part of the first clause, he agreed with the gentleman from Maryland, (Mr. SENEY,) that we ought to provide a rule of naturalization, without attempting to define the particular privileges acquired thereby under the State Governments. By the Constitution of the United States, the electors of the House of Representatives are to have the qualifications requisite for electors of the most numerous branch of the State Legislatures. He presumed it was to be left to the discretion of the State Constitutions, who were to be the electors of the State Legislatures, and therefore the General Government had no right to interfere therein. The motion he had made for striking out the words, "and shall have resided within the United States for one whole year," not coming up to, or sufficiently explaining his wishes, he would withdraw, and propose to new model the clause, so as to allow aliens to be admitted to so much of the rights of citizenship as to be able to hold lands, upon taking the necessary oaths; but not to elect, or be elected, to any office under the General Government, until they had resided three years within the United States; with a proviso, that the titles to real estates should not be valid, unless they continued to reside for the term of three years in America.

Mr. HARTLEY observed, that the subject was entirely new, and that the committee had no positive mode to enable them to decide; the practice of England, and the regulations of the several States, threw some light on the subject, but not sufficient to enable them to discover what plan of naturalization would be acceptable under a Government like this. Some gentlemen had objected to the bill, without attending to all its parts, for a remedy was therein provided for some of the inconveniences that have been suggested. It was said, the bill ought to extend to the exclusion of those who had trespassed against the laws of foreign nations, or been convicted of a capital offence in any foreign kingdom; the last clause contains a proviso to that effect, and he had another clause ready to present,

providing for the children of American citizens, born out of the United States.

Mr. LIVERMORE thought the bill very imperfect, and that the committee ought to rise, and recommend it to be referred to a select committee; observing, that it was extremely difficult for fifty or sixty persons to arrange and make a system of a variety of motions and observations that had been brought forward.

Mr. SEDGWICK was in favor of the committee rising. He did not recollect an instance wherein gentlemen's ideas had been so various as on this occasion; motions and observations were piled on the back of each other, and the committee, from the want of understanding the subject, had involved themselves in a wilderness of matter, out of which he saw no way to extricate themselves but by the rising of the committee.

Mr. SMITH, (of S. C.,) as a member of the Committee of the whole, wished to take his share of the blame for not understanding the subject; but he thought, nevertheless, that some of the points suggested had been so fully discussed, as to enable them to decide, particularly with respect to residence.

Mr. PAGE did not approve of the rising of the committee, until they had expressed their sense on the point they had had so long under consideration.

Mr. SYLVESTER thought it neither for the honor nor interest of the United States to admit aliens to the rights of citizenship indiscriminately; he was clearly in favor of a term of probation, and that their good behavior should be vouched for. He suggested the idea of lodging the power of admitting foreigners to be naturalized in the District Judges.

Mr. SEDGWICK meant to blame no gentleman, and hoped no gentleman understood him to intend such a thing. He conceived himself as much in fault as any member, because he had not yet turned his attention so seriously to the subject as he ought.

On the question being put, the committee rose and reported, and the bill was recommitted to a committee of ten.

9

COLLET v. COLLET

2 Dall. 294 (C.C.D.Pa. 1792)

BY THE COURT.—The question now agitated, depends upon another question; whether the state of Pennsylvania, since the 26th of March 1790 (when the act of congress was passed), has a right to naturalize an alien? And this must receive its answer from the solution of a third question; whether, according to the constitution of the United States, the authority to naturalize is exclusive or concurrent? We are of opinion then, that the states, individually, still enjoy a concurrent authority upon this subject; but that their individual authority cannot be exercised, so as to contravene the rule established by the authority of the Union. The objection founded on the word *uniform*, and the arguments *ab inconvenienti*, have been carried too far. It is, likewise, declared by the constitution (Art. I., § 8), that all duties, imposts and excises shall be *uniform* throughout the United States; and yet, if express words of exclusion had not been inserted as in a subsequent part of the same article (§ 10), the individual states would still, undoubtedly, have been at liberty, without the consent of congress, to lay and collect duties and imposts. Again, when it is said, that one state ought not to be privileged to admit obnoxious citizens, to the injury of another, it should be recollected, that the state which communicates the infection, must herself be first infected; and in this, as in other cases, we may be assured, that the principle of self-preservation will inculcate every reasonable precaution.

The true reason for investing congress with the power of naturalization has been assigned at the bar. It was to guard against too narrow, instead of too liberal, a mode of conferring the rights of citizenship. Thus, the individual states cannot exclude those citizens, who have been adopted by the United States; but they can adopt citizens upon easier terms, than those which congress may deem it expedient to impose.

But the act of congress itself, furnishes a strong proof that the power of naturalization is concurrent. In the concluding proviso, it is declared, "that no person heretofore proscribed by any state, shall be admitted a citizen aforesaid, except by an act of the legislature of the state, in which such person was proscribed." Here, we find, that congress has not only circumscribed the exercise of its own authority, but has recognised the authority of a state legislature, in one case, to admit a citizen of the United States; which could not be done in any case, if the power of naturalization, either by its own nature, or by the manner of its being vested in the federal government, was an exclusive power.

10

Senate, Contested Election of Mr. Gallatin
20–22 Feb. 1794
Annals 4:48–55, 57

(See 1.5, no. 16)

11

Thomas Paine, Memorial to James Monroe
10 Sept. 1794
Life 5:77–83

I address this memorial to you, in consequence of a letter I received from a friend, 18 Fructidor (September fourth),

in which he says, "Mr. Monroe has told me, that he has no orders [meaning from the American Government] respecting you; but I am sure he will leave nothing undone to liberate you; but, from what I can learn, from all the late Americans, you are not considered either by the Government, or by the individuals, as an American citizen. You have been made a French citizen, which you have accepted, and you have further made yourself a servant of the French Republic; and, therefore, it would be out of character for an American Minister to interfere in their internal concerns. You must therefore either be liberated out of compliment to America, or stand your trial, which you have a right to demand."

This information was so unexpected by me, that I am at a loss how to answer it. I know not on what principle it originates; whether from an idea that I had voluntarily abandoned my citizenship of America for that of France, or from any article of the American Constitution applied to me. The first is untrue with respect to any intention on my part; and the second is without foundation, as I shall show in the course of this memorial.

The idea of conferring honor of citizenship upon foreigners, who had distinguished themselves in propagating the principles of liberty and humanity, in opposition to despotism, war and bloodshed, was first proposed by me to Lafayette, at the commencement of the French Revolution, when his heart appeared to be warmed with those principles. My motive in making this proposal, was to render the people of different nations more fraternal than they had been, or then were. I observed that almost every branch of science had possessed itself of the exercise of this right, so far as it regarded its own institution.

Most of the academies and societies in Europe, and also those of America, conferred the rank of honorary member, upon foreigners eminent in knowledge, and made them, in fact, citizens of their literary or scientific republic, without affecting or anyways diminishing their rights of citizenship in their own country or in other societies: and why the science of government should not have the same advantage, or why the people of one nation should not, by their representatives, exercise the right of conferring the honor of citizenship upon individuals eminent in another nation, without affecting *their* rights of citizenship, is a problem yet to be solved.

I now proceed to remark on that part of the letter, in which the writer says, that *from what he can learn from all the late Americans, I am not considered in America, either by the Government or by the individuals, as an American citizen.*

In the first place I wish to ask, what is here meant by the Government of America? The members who compose the Government are only individuals, when in conversation, and who, most probably, hold very different opinions upon the subject. Have Congress as a body made any declaration representing me, that they now no longer consider me as a citizen? If they have not, anything they otherwise say is no more than the opinion of individuals, and consequently is not legal authority, nor anyways sufficient authority to deprive any man of his citizenship. Besides, whether a man has forfeited his rights of citizenship, is a question not determinable by Congress, but by a court of judicature and a jury; and must depend upon evidence, and the application of some law or article of the Constitution to the case. No such proceeding has yet been had, and consequently I remain a citizen until it be had, be that decision what it may; for there can be no such thing as a suspension of rights in the interim.

I am very well aware, and always was, of the article of the Constitution which says, as nearly I can recollect the words, that "any citizen of the United States, who shall accept any title, place, or office, from any foreign king, prince, or state, shall forfeit and lose his right of citizenship of the United States."*

Had the article said, that *any citizen of the United States who shall be a member of any foreign convention, for the purpose of forming a free constitution, shall forfeit and lose the right of citizenship of the United States,* the article had been directly applicable to me; but the idea of such an article never could have entered the mind of the American Convention, and the present article is altogether foreign to the case with respect to me. It supposes a government in active existence, and not a government dissolved; and it supposes a citizen of America accepting titles and offices under that government, and not a citizen of America who gives his assistance in a convention chosen by the people, for the purpose of forming a government *de nouveau* founded on their authority.

The late Constitution and Government of France was dissolved the tenth of August, 1792. The National Legislative Assembly then in being, supposed itself without sufficient authority to continue its sittings, and it proposed to the departments to elect not another legislative assembly, but a convention for the express purpose of forming a new constitution. When the Assembly were discoursing on this matter, some of the members said, that they wished to gain all the assistance possible upon the subject of free constitutions; and expressed a wish to elect and invite foreigners of any nation to the Convention, who had distinguished themselves in defending, explaining and propagating the principles of liberty.

It was on this occasion that my name was mentioned in the Assembly. (I was then in England.) After this, a deputation from a body of the French people, in order to remove any objection that might be made against my assisting at the proposed convention, requested the Assembly, as their representatives, to give me the title of French citizen; after which, I was elected a member of the Convention, in four different departments, as is already known.

The case, therefore, is, that I accepted nothing from any king, prince or state, nor from any government: for France was without any government, except what arose from common consent, and the necessity of the case. Neither did *I make myself a servant of the French Republic,* as the letter alluded to expresses; for at that time France was not a republic, not even in name. She was altogether a people in a state of revolution.

It was not until the Convention met that France was declared a republic, and monarchy abolished; soon after which a committee was elected, of which I was a member, to form a constitution, which was presented to the Convention [and read by Condorcet, who was also a member] the fifteenth and sixteenth of February following, but was not to be taken into consideration till after the expiration of two months, and if approved of by the Convention, was then to be referred to the people for their acceptance, with such additions or amendments as the Convention should make.

In thus employing myself upon the formation of a constitution, I certainly did nothing inconsistent with the American Constitution. I took no oath of allegiance to France, or any other oath whatever. I considered the citizenship they had presented me with as an honorary mark of respect paid to me not only as a friend to liberty, but as an American citizen. My acceptance of that, or of the deputyship, not conferred on me by any king, prince or state, but by a people in a state of revolution and contending for liberty, required no transfer of my allegiance or of my citizenship from America to France. There I was a real citizen, paying taxes; here, I was a voluntary friend, employing myself on a temporary service.

12

HOUSE OF REPRESENTATIVES, NATURALIZATION BILL
22, 26, 29–31 Dec. 1794, 1, 8 Jan. 1795
Annals 4:1004–9, 1021–23, 1026–27,
1028–32, 1033–38, 1064

[*22 Dec. 1794*]

The House resolved itself into a Committee of the Whole House on the bill to amend the act, entitled "An act to establish an uniform rule of naturalization."

MR. DEXTER after some observations on the importance of the subject before the Committee; and expressing his disapprobation of the facility by which, under the existing law, aliens may acquire citizenship moved that the term of two years in the bill referring to the previous residence should be struck out and a blank left, to be filled up after more mature consideration. This motion was agreed to. Another amendment was proposed by that gentleman, referring particularly to the mercantile foreigners who may wish to acquire citizenship.

MR. PAGE said, that he approved the design of the mover, because he thought nothing more desirable than to see good order, public virtue, and true morality, constituting the character of citizens of the United States; for, without morality, and indeed a general sense of religion, a Republican Government cannot flourish, nay, cannot long exist; since without these, disorders will arise, which the strong arm of powerful Government can alone correct or retrieve. But he should vote against the amendment, because he thought, as his colleague [Mr. MADISON] did, that it would be attended with embarassments to the admission

---

*The actual wording is, "No person holding any office of profit or trust under them [the United States] shall, without the consent of Congress, accept of any present, emolument, office, or title of any kind whatever, from any king, prince, or foreign State."

to the rights of citizenship, which good men ought not to have thrown into their way; and which, too, for his part, he thought might prove insurmountable obstacles to such. Yet they would be no impediment to the views of bad men, or such as he wished to exclude from citizenship, for the best man in the United States might not procure the certificate required by the amendment, if he moved from State to State, staying no where long enough to enable two persons to swear that they had known him to be of such a character as we require, and to have supported it during the length of time which the amendment prescribes. Yet bad men, associating chiefly with men like themselves, regardless of oaths, might procure the requisite certificate. He disliked the amendment on account of its requiring an oath at all. He trusted that a Constitution much admired, and with such wholesome laws, will be an inducement to many good men to become citizens, and that, should bad men come amongst us, they will be discountenanced by the more virtuous class of citizens, and if necessary be punished by the laws. He hoped that good schools would soon be spread all over the States, and hence that good sense and virtue will be so generally diffused amongst us, that emigrants will be unable to corrupt our manners. Even at present, he relied so much on the virtue and discernment of his fellow citizens, the power of the law, and the energy of Government, as to apprehend no danger from emigration into the United States. Mr. P. said, that he knew instances of difficulties which some worthy men had met with in their endeavors to procure such certificates as the amendment proposed. He mentioned one clergyman in Virginia. Even Dr. Griffith, after being nominated Bishop of that State, found it difficult to procure from the Convention the certificate required by the English bishops; because, though hundreds of other persons knew his worthy character, a sufficient number of the members of the Convention had not known it, during the term specified in the certificate required.

Mr. DEXTER's motion was now withdrawn.

Mr. GILES then proposed an amendment the object of which was to impede a return to citizenship of those who should expatriate themselves. He proposed that a special law of the State from which such persons should detach themselves, should be requisite in order to their being reinstated.

Mr. TRACY, after observing, that although he was not in favor of a perpetual allegiance as understood by the British Government, yet he was of opinion that the return of persons who should expatriate themselves ought to be clogged with greater impediments than simply a law of a particular State. If the amendment is a proper one, of which he confessed he had his doubts, he would suggest to the gentleman an addition, by making a law of the General Government also necessary in the case.

Mr. GILES observed that the object of his motion was not by any means to lessen the impediments in the way of a return to citizenship, but the reverse; he should therefore agree to the amendment of the gentleman from Connecticut. The motion was afterwards considered in several points of view, as blending State and Continental legislation, as interfering with the Legislative rights of the State

by some, and as operating in the same manner in respect to the right reserved by the Constitution to the General Government, which is authorized to pass uniform laws of naturalization by others.

Mr. SEDGWICK having stated that his colleague had prepared a motion with regard to the kind of evidence that an applicant should exhibit of the goodness of his moral character and of his attachment to the Government, he requested Mr. GILES to withdraw his motion for the consideration of the other, which he did, and thereupon, Mr. DEXTER moved that no alien should be admitted to the rights of citizenship, but on the oath of two credible witnesses, that in their opinion he was of good moral character and attached to the welfare of this country, which motion was seconded by Mr. SEDGWICK, who added the following observations:

He said that the subject under consideration was certainly of great importance, and opened an extensive field of discussion. The present motion, taken in conjunction with that already adopted, had for its object to embarrass the facility, with which aliens may be admitted to the rights of citizenship. He would submit to the consideration of the committee, some of the leading ideas, which had occurred to his mind on this subject.

America, he said, if her political institutions should on experience be found to be wisely adjusted, and she shall improve her natural advantages, had opened to her view a more rich and glorious prospect than ever was presented to man. She had chosen for herself a Government which left to the citizen as great a portion of freedom as was consistent with a social compact. All believed the preservation of this Government, in its purity, indispensable to the continuance of our happiness. The foundation on which it rested was general intelligence and public virtue; in other words, wisdom to discern, and patriotism to pursue the general good. He had pride, and he gloried in it, in believing his countrymen more wise and virtuous than any other people on earth; hence he believed them better qualified to administer and support a Republican Government. This character of Americans was the result of early education, aided indeed by the discipline of the Revolution. In that part of the country with which he was best acquainted, the education, manners, habits, and institutions, religious and civil, were Republican. The community was divided into corporations, in many respects resembling independent republics, of which almost every man, the qualifications were so small, was a member. They had many important and interesting concerns to transact. They appointed their executive officers, enacted bye laws, raised money for many purposes of use and ornament. Here, then, the citizens early acquired the habits of temperate discussion, patient reasoning, and a capacity of enduring contradiction. Here the means of education and instruction are instituted and maintained; public libraries are purchased and read; these are (said he) the proper schools for the education of Republican citizens; thus are to be planted the seeds of Republicanism. If you will cultivate the plants which are to be reared from these seeds, you will gather an abundant harvest of long continued prosperity.

Much information (he said) might be obtained by the experience of others, if, in despite of it, we were not determined to be guided only by a visionary theory. The ancient Republics of Greece and Rome (said he) see with what jealousy they guarded the rights of citizenship against adulteration by foreign mixture. The Swiss nation, (he said,) in modern times, had not been less jealous on the same subject. Indeed, no example could be found, in the history of man, to authorize the experiment which had been made by the United States. It seemed to have been adopted by universal practice as a maxim, that the Republican character was no way to be formed but by early education. In some instances, to form this character, those propensities which are generally considered as almost irresistible, were opposed and subdued. And shall we (he asked) alone adopt the rash theory, that the subjects of all Governments, Despotic, Monarchical, and Aristocratical, are, as soon as they set foot on American ground, qualified to participate in administering the sovereignty of our country? Shall we hold the benefits of American citizenship so cheap as to invite, nay, almost bribe, the discontented, the ambitious, and the avaricious of every country to accept them?

We had (he said) on this subject not only example, but warning. Will gentlemen (said Mr. S.) recollect the rage of ages, which existed in the country from which we came, between the Saxon, Danish, and Norman emigrants and the natives of the country? The cruelties, the oppressions, the assassinations, in a word the miseries to which this gave birth? Perhaps it might be said that in this instance the emigrants were hostile invaders; but the same events took place in the decline of the Roman empire, between the emigrants who were invited to occupy the vacant frontiers and the ancient inhabitants; although the former ought to have been united to the latter by every principle of affection and gratitude. By these and almost an infinity of other instances, it would not be rash to conclude, that by the undeviating principles of human nature, whenever the inhabitants of one country should be permitted to settle in another, by national affections, an union would be formed, unfriendly not only to the ancient inhabitants, but also to social order. Our own experience was not, he believed, in opposition to the general observation. Although this reasoning was to his mind conclusive against a general and indiscriminate admission of aliens to the rights of citizenship, yet he did not wish it should go to a complete exclusion.

It was said, in support of what was termed our liberal policy, that our country wanted commercial capital; that we had an immense tract of vacant territory; and that we ought not, with the avarice of a miser, to engross to ourselves the exclusive enjoyment of our political treasures.

Mr. SEDGWICK said he had never been convinced, that we ought to make so great a sacrifice of principle for the rapid accumulation of commercial capital. He had never been convinced, that by an improvement of our own resources, it would not accumulate as fast as might be for the public benefit. We heard much of equality. Property was in some sense power; and the possession of immense property generated daring passions which scorned equal-

ity, and with impatience endured the restraints of equal laws. Property was undoubtedly to be protected, as the only sure encouragement of industry, without which we should degenerate into savages. But he had never been convinced that the anxiety with which we wished an accumulation of capital, in the hands of individuals, was founded on correct Republican reflection. The ardent ambition inspired by the possession of great wealth, and the power of gratifying it, which it conferred, had in many instances disturbed the public peace, and in not a few destroyed liberty.

The vacant lands which some with so much avidity wished to see in the occupation of foreigners, he considered as the best capital stock of the future enjoyment of Americans; as an antidote against the poison of luxury; as the nursery of robust and manly virtue, and as a preventive of a numerous class of citizens becoming indigent, and therefore dependent. Whenever the time should arrive, (and may that period be very distant,) when there should no longer be presented to the poor a decent competence and independence, as the effect of industry and economy, (which would generally be the case when lands were no longer to be obtained, on their present easy and reasonable terms,) then that description of men, now perhaps the most happy and virtuous, would become miserable to themselves and a burden to the community. Now the man who entered on the stage of life, without property, had a reasonable assurance, that a few years of industry and economy, would give him independence, competence, and respectability. The prospect gave relish and effect to his labors. He planted himself on the frontiers, and cultivated in his posterity every useful and manly virtue. This was his treasure and it was a glorious one.

Mr. S. said he considered America as in possession of a greater stock of enjoyment than any other people on earth. That it was our duty to husband it with care; yet he could not altogether exclude such virtuous individuals, as might fly here, as to an asylum against oppression. On the one hand, he would not dissipate our treasures with the thoughtless profusion of a prodigal; nor would he, on the other, hoard them, as in the unfeeling grasp of a miser. Our glorious fabric (said he) has been cemented by the richest blood of our country, and may it long continue to shelter us against the blasts of poverty, of anarchy, and of tyranny.

The present (Mr. S. said) he believed the most inauspicious time for the indiscriminate admission of aliens to the rights of citizenship. A war, the most cruel and dreadful which had been known for centuries, was now raging in all those countries from which emigrants were to be expected. The most fierce and unrelenting passions were engaged in a conflict, which shook to their foundations all the ancient political structures in Europe. This contest was supported on the one hand by men who believed personal political distinctions were necessary to the great purpose of security, and on the other by those who thought that society could be protected and individuals secured by a Government with departments, and without checks; neither embracing the principles established here, where, without privileged orders distinct portions of power were to be deposited in different hands, in such manner that it was almost impossible for the mind even to conceive that the different departments should form an union for any mischievous purpose; and altogether impossible to believe that without such concurrence either alone should be capable of executing any wicked design.

Could (he asked) any reasonable man believe, that men who, actuated by such passions, had fought on grounds so opposite, almost equally distant from the happy mean we had chosen, would here mingle in social affections with each other, or with us? That their passions and prejudices would subside as soon as they should set foot in America? or that, possessing those passions and prejudices, they were qualified to make or to be made the governors of Americans?

He believed that the amendment now proposed by his colleague, in conjunction with that which had already succeeded, would on the one hand check the admission of foreigners in such numbers as might be dangerous to our political institutions; and, on the other, that it would not exclude such meritorious individuals as might be willing to serve the apprenticeship which might qualify them to assume the character and discharge the duties of American citizens.

He concluded by saying, that he had always been opposed to the policy of the Government on this subject; that his opposition had not been abated by reflection, but increased by the existing state of things in Europe.

[26 Dec.]

Mr. GILES proposed to amend the intended test of a citizen, by adding, after "two witnesses giving evidence as to his moral character," these words: "attached to a Republican form of Government." He thought this test proper, to prevent those poisonous communications from Europe, of which gentlemen were so much afraid.

Mr. DEXTER preferred saying "attached to the Constitution of the Unitd States."

To this amendment Mr. GILES had little or no objection.

Mr. BOUDINOT did not see the use of either amendment. It was only giving unnecessary trouble. The oath which the person himself must take, was sufficient for expressing his fidelity to the Government of this country.

Mr. NICHOLAS considered both the amendment, and the clause to which it was annexed, as unnecessary; and even if in themselves proper, they were misplaced. He thought both equally superfluous. They should have been inserted in the oath of allegiance of the man himself.

Mr. DAYTON hoped that the whole clause would be rejected. He should be against it, unless the nature of the evidence was referred to a Court of Justice. He foresaw many difficulties arising to poor men in attempting to get two such witnesses. It might suit extremely well with merchants and men of large capital, who had, he supposed, been alluded to the other day, under the title of meritorious emigrants. He was not so anxious for them as for useful laboring people, who, as he thought, would be more likely to do good. This class, however, had never, it was likely, troubled their heads about forms of Government. He further objected to the amendment of the gentleman

from Virginia, that the word Republican was entirely equivocal. This title was assumed by many Governments in Europe, which were upon principles entirely different from ours. Some of them, such as Poland, had been Aristocracies of the most hideous form.

Mr. DEXTER hoped that the amendment of Mr. GILES would not pass, [Mr. GILES had, as before noticed, consented to withdraw it]; not so much for the sake of the principle, as of the language in which it was expressed. The word Republican implied so much, that nobody could tell where to limit it. Why use so hackneyed a word? Many call themselves Republican, who, by this word, mean, pulling down every establishment: they were mere Anarchists.

Mr. HILLHOUSE was equally against the clause and amendment. Mr. DEXTER and Mr. GILES previously declared themselves extremely doubtful whether they should even vote for the clause, when amended in their own way.

Mr. GILES felt himself extremely surprised to hear it asserted on the floor of Congress, that the words "Republican form of Government" meant anything or nothing. He read a passage from the Constitution, whereby a Republican form of Government is guarantied to each of the United States composing the Union. He should, therefore, have imagined, that the words were well understood from one end of the Continent to the other. He did not expect such criticism. He was not sure if he should vote for the clause at all; but if he did so, he should wish the best to be made of it. He then altered his amendment to these words: "attached to the principles of the Government of the United States."

Mr. DAYTON.—With all the ambition of that gentleman [Mr. GILES] to be called a Democrat, both he and Mr. D. would more properly be called Republicans. He again vindicated his assertion as to the equivocal meaning of the word. A Venetian or Genoese might come to this country, and take the oath as proposed, and then excuse himself by saying, "it was the Republican form of my own country which I had in view." One of the best writers on the British Constitution had called that also a Republic.

Mr. MADISON was of opinion, that the word was well enough understood to signify a free Representative Government, deriving its authority from the people, and calculated for their benefit; and thus far the amendment of his colleague was sufficiently proper. Mr. M. doubted whether he himself should, however, vote for the clause, thus amended. It would perhaps be very difficult for many citizens to find two reputable witnesses, who could swear to the purity of their principles for three years back. Many useful and virtuous members of the community may be thrown into the greatest difficulties, by such a procedure. In three years time, a person may have shifted his residence from one end of the Continent to the other. How then was he to find evidence of his behaviour during such a length of time? But he objected to both amendments on a different ground. It was hard to make a man swear that he preferred the Constitution of the United States, or to give any general opinion, because he may, in his own private judgment, think Monarchy or Aristocracy better, and yet be honestly determined to support this Government as he finds it.

Mr. HILLHOUSE then proposed as an amendment, to insert, that "evidence should be produced to the satisfaction of the Court."

Mr. DEXTER mentioned the abuses that have happened in the present form of admitting citizens. He did not comprehend the argument of Mr. DAYTON, that it would be more easy for a rich than for a poor man to get evidences to swear to his having resided in the country. If he had not, the fact was of a notorious nature. It would likewise be as easy for a poor man, as for a rich one, to get an attestation of his character. The point of residence was, in itself, but little. A man may have resided here for a long time, and defrauded the citizens, which would be no recommendation.

Several other gentlemen spoke. The resolution finally passed.

The second resolution produced a long conversation, in the course of which Mr. MURRAY declared, that he was quite indifferent if not fifty emigrants came into this Continent in a year's time. It would be unjust to hinder them, but impolitic to encourage them. He was afraid that, coming from a quarter of the world so full of disorder and corruption, they might contaminate the purity and simplicity of the American character.

The Committee now rose, and had leave to sit again.

[*29 Dec.*]

The motion before the Committee, made by Mr. VENABLE, when they broke off the last discussion, had been to strike the word "moral" out of this amendment: "good moral character." These three words, altogether, were an addition of what was to be attested by the witnesses for a candidate to admission as a citizen.

Mr. DEXTER opened the debate on the amendment of Mr. VENABLE to the amendment, by saying that he wished to hear the reasons for it.

Mr. NICHOLAS said, that he did not make the motion; but his colleague, who had made it, thought that the insertion of the word "moral" gave too strict an air to the sentence. This word might be hereafter implied to mean something relative to religious opinions.

Mr. SEDGWICK remarked, that if no better reason than that advanced by Mr. NICHOLAS could be given for striking out the word "moral," he could not agree to it. Moral is opposed to immoral, but has no particular reference whatever to religion, or whether a man believes anything or nothing. It has no reference to religious opinions. We can everywhere tell, by the common voice of the World, whether a man is moral or not in his life, without difficulty. In some States of the Union adultery is not punishable by law, yet it is everywhere said to be an immoral action. It is too nice to make a distinction between a good character and a good moral character. The word good, itself, is very equivocal in its meaning. It signifies anything, everything, or nothing. A good companion is one thing; a good man, as applied to wealth, conveys a different sense; and so on.

Mr. B. BOURNE considered the amendment itself, and the motion of Mr. VENABLE to strike out the word "moral," as equally useless.

Mr. MURRAY hoped that the word would not be struck out. This would be the greatest slander ever cast upon the American character. It would excite the surprise of foreign nations.

Mr. VENABLE had thought the wording of the phrase too strict; but rather than have any further dispute, he withdrew his motion for striking out the word "moral."

The clause was then read, as amended.

Mr. GILBERT thought that the term of residence, before admitting aliens, ought to be very much longer than mentioned in the bill. The Chairman informed him that the term in the bill was left blank.

Mr. SEDGWICK agreed to the idea of Mr. GILBERT. He wished that a method could be found of permitting aliens to possess and transmit property, without, at the same time, giving them a right to vote. He did not know if the Constitution authorized such a thing.

[*30 Dec.*]

Mr. HILLHOUSE moved as an amendment to the clause before the Committee, that if any citizen of the United States, at any time thereafter, should become a citizen or subject of any other State or country, he should not again be admitted an American citizen. This amendment gave rise to debate.

Mr. MURRAY hoped the amendment would succeed, and that any citizen of the United States who, when out of the United States, elected to be a subject of any foreign Power, should not again be permitted to the rights of complete citizenship; nor did he think it necessary to decide the question which had resulted from the ingenious arguments of his friend from Massachusetts, [Mr. DEXTER,] whether a man can expatriate himself without the express consent of the community or nation of which he is a citizen or subject. It was enough for us to say, that any man who does expatriate himself from the United States, shall not again become a citizen. He could not agree with the gentleman from Massachusetts, in the position, that a man cannot expatriate without the consent of his country. The practice of this country is a direct confutation of this doctrine; and it must be admitted, either that this country has trampled on the most solemn of social and national rights, by its practice, or that a man may leave his country and take on him the obligations of a new allegiance in this country. It seemed to him a position as conformable to sound morals as to political truth, that what a man has no right to offer, another man, or society, cannot rightfully accept. He would infer, that this country had a right to naturalize foreigners, because she has naturalized them; and that this country, by its laws, having accepted the allegiance of an alien, the alien had a right to offer that allegiance. The very proviso to naturalize an alien, without inquiry as to the consent of his own country having been previously obtained, seems to be predicated on the principle for which he contended—that a man has the right to expatriate himself without leave obtained: if he has not, all our laws of this sort, by which we convert an alien into a citizen completely, must be acknowledged to be a violation of the rights of nations. How far a man, after having been naturalized at a period of life when his reason enabled him to choose, and to enter into a solemn obligation, and after he has expressly entered into it, has a right, without the consent of the society, to quit that society, might be another question. After a citizen throws off his allegiance to this country, by leaving it and entering into a new obligation to some other nation, though he may have a right so to do, he has no right to return to his allegiance here without the consent of this society; and it is not a question of right, but of policy, how far we will readmit him to citizenship. When he said that the right of dissolving allegiance must be admitted both to give exercise to a right and to give consistency to our principles and practice, he did not mean that a citizen could throw off his allegiance in this country, but that he must complete the act of dissolution in some other country. Such a principle would belong to the theory of the dissolution, rather than the formation of a civil society; hence appeared to him the strange solecism of that law of Virginia which provides for the throwing off allegiance within the community. The consequences of such a principle are not only destructive to the very form and body of civil society, but are unnatural. They present a civilized being belonging to no civil society on earth; for, in the intermediate state in which he stands, between the allegiance and country he has just disowned, and the allegiance and country to which he may intend to pledge himself, he is in the imaginary state of nature, which is, in reality, an unnatural state, for a being whose every faculty and quality constitutes him a moral agent, surrounded by essential relations, and, of course, impel him to discharge duties of a social nature.

He wished this Government, while it expressly adopted the right of naturalizing aliens, to do and to say nothing that involved a contradiction between its principles and practice. If it accepts the allegiance of an alien, it presupposes that the alien has the right to tender his allegiance; and one clause of the bill expressly requires of the alien an abjuration of his former allegiance, which is certainly proper. In doing this, the bill admits, unequivocally, the right of subjects and citizens to expatriate. The British Government, by a want of conformity between their first principle, as laid down in their law books, and the practice of Parliament, have shown us a singular mixture of old principles which the nation have outgrown. It is a maxim with them, that allegiance cannot be dissolved by any change of time or place, nor by the oath of a subject to any foreign Power; yet they naturalize by act of Parliament. They accept what they declare by their theory of civil law cannot be rightfully offered: nay, for one century the throne of England has presented Monarchs who were foreigners. William of Orange was a Prince, but he was a subject, too, of a foreign Power; and George the First was a member of the Germanic body. There is little danger that citizens, who are worthy of being so, will throw off their allegiance from the United States. The amendment which prohibits their readmission to a participation of all the rights of citizenship, will be a sufficient penalty, if any be necessary. Though they may have a right to expatriate themselves, there cannot be inferred a right of returning; for every body politic must have the right of saying upon what terms they will accept any addition of aliens to their numbers; and the expatriated man, no longer belonging to this society, and being an alien, the Government may choose whether he ever shall enjoy its privileges again.

Mr. BALDWIN expressed the strongest disapprobation at the idea of expatriating all those of our citizens who may have become subjects or citizens of another country. Many of them had been made citizens without any solicitation of their own, and merely as a mark of esteem from the Government under which they lived. They had no design whatever of renouncing their country. Yet the House, all at once, declares them incapable of returning to their former situation.

The amendment was negatived. The Committee rose, the Chairman reported progress, and the House adjourned.

[*31 Dec.*]

Mr. W. SMITH made a motion for striking out the clause under consideration altogether, and leaving exactly as it now stands the law regarding citizens of America, who became citizens of other countries. This was rejected.

After some further discussion, Mr. GILES proposed a new clause, which was in substance, that all such aliens, who had borne any hereditary titles, or titles of nobility in other countries, should make a renunciation of such titles before they can enjoy any right of citizenship. This renunciation is to be made in the Court where they lay claim to a right of citizenship. Mr. G. said, if we did anything to prevent an improper mixture of foreigners with the Americans, this measure seemed to him one that might be useful.

Mr. W. SMITH was entirely opposed to the motion. An attempt of this kind had been made some years ago in the Legislature of one of the States, but dropped again as having been seen to be improper. The mind of the public is completely guarded against the introduction of titles, and they will never be current here. You cannot hinder a man from calling another a Viscount. You cannot declare this a crime.

Mr. S. doubted whether the House had, by the Constitution, any right of making such a law. They were directed not to grant any titles, but their authority did not extend to the taking away of titles from persons who were not born in the country. The Marquis de LAFAYETTE has been distinguished all over the Continent by the title of Marquis. Mr. S. hoped that he would one day be again in America, and then he would very likely be called Marquis again. By this law it would be illegal. The member then went into a long detail on English nobility, and explained the difference between several kinds of titles.

Mr. GILES did not think his motion positively necessary, but it might be useful. It seemed to be a growing practice with some gentlemen in the House to treat the most serious subjects with ridicule. He, for his own part, considered this conduct as highly improper.

Mr. DEXTER was as averse to titles as any man in the House, but he did not like to make laws against them. An alien might as well be obliged to make a renunciation of his connexions with the Jacobin club. The one was fully as abhorrent to the Constitution as the other.

Mr. PAGE highly recommended the motion of his colleague. He mentioned a particular occasion at New York, where the word *honorable* had been applied in Congress to a particular body. He had proposed to strike out this word honorable. He was ridiculed, but he stood to his point, and carried it by a great majority. If the Marquis LAFAYETTE was to return to America, he would behave with the frank manners which became a Republican. The case might be very different with a British Peer with his star and garter, and other baubles of that sort. If he were called My Lord Duke, or My Lord, or any other of these foolish names, it might tickle the ears of some people, and make them like the custom.

Mr. GILES, in reply to Mr. DEXTER, said, that if a thing be implied in the Constitution, where is the harm of expressing it? This is said to be implied in the Constitution, and therefore it is needless to express it. Now this was one of the very best arguments which could be thought of in favor of the motion. At the time when the Constitution was made, nobody could foresee the strange turn which affairs have taken, or that there might be a danger from an inundation of titled fugitives. Indeed, if no better reasoning could be adduced against his motion than that employed by the gentleman from South Carolina, he was not likely to think the worse of it. That gentleman had objected to the adoption of the motion because it agrees with the public mind. He says that the dispositions of the people will of themselves be sufficient to exclude the use of titles. It was certainly no reason against making a law in Congress, that it would exactly meet the wishes of the people. The motion might be useful. Mr. G. hoped that it would pass. Foreigners coming here with titles never will voluntarily renounce them. Mr. G. reminded the House that his proposal went only to the renunciation of titles, when the party concerned wanted to become a citizen.

Mr. W. SMITH said, that the fact was against the gentleman. Foreigners coming to this country had renounced their titles, and called themselves only by their plain names. Why might there not be an interdiction against persons connected with the Jacobin club? Why not forbid the wearing of certain badges of distinction used by Jacobins?

Mr. MADISON approved of the motion. He regarded it as exactly to the business in hand, to exclude all persons from citizenship who would not renounce forever their connexion with titles of nobility. The propriety of the thing would be illustrated by this reflection, that if any titled Orders had existed in America before the Revolution, they would infallibly have been abolished by it.

Mr. GILES said, that the debate had turned upon these people called Jacobins. Both these and the persons with titles were dangerous to the country. Some of the former part of the regulations in this proposed act had an eye to them. He would have more faith in an individual who came forward in an open Court and renounced his connexions with nobility. He was willing to withdraw for the present his motion.

[*1 Jan. 1795*]

Several gentlemen spoke on this subject. As to the granting of privileges to aliens, Mr. MADISON remarked, that there was no class of emigrants from whom so much was to be apprehended as those who should obtain property in shipping. Much greater mischief was to be feared from them than from any influence in votes at an election. If he were disposed to make any distinction of one class of emigrants more than another, as to the length of time before they should be admitted citizens, it would be as to the mercantile people—as these persons may, by possessing themselves of American shipping and seamen, be enabled clandestinely to favor such particular nations in the way of trade as they may think proper.

The House went through the report of the Committee, and agreed to the amendments.

Mr. GILES then rose to make his promised motion as to the exclusion of any foreign emigrant from citizenship who had borne a title of nobility in Europe till he had formally renounced it. He proceeded to observe that, agreeably to the spirit of the Constitution, we ought to have the strongest possible evidence that people of this description have renounced all pretence to a right of this nature, before we admit them into the bosom of society. Moderation had been recommended. He requested gentlemen to observe that he conducted his motion on the strictest principles of moderation. He had, in a former part of this bill, voted for some clauses which were intended to guard the Government against any disturbance from the people called Jacobins, when their principles should run to a dangerous and seditious extreme. The same spirit of candor and moderation which had induced him to vote for a precaution against the attempts of the one party, now led him to propose a precaution against the prejudices of the aristocrats, which were, upon the whole, more hostile to the spirit of the American Constitution than those of their antagonists. He also requested gentlemen to observe that his present motion went not to the invasion of any positive right. It left the individual exactly where it found him, unless he aspired to be an American citizen. Otherwise, he might retain his titles undisturbed as long as he pleased. But if he wanted any promotion of a civil nature in this country, he must rise to it by conforming exactly to the rules laid down by the Constitution itself. That code had declared no titled character admissible to any civil rank. It was not to be supposed that people born and nurtured in the lap of aristocracy would heartily renounce their titles, and become all at once sincere Republicans. It was therefore highly improper that such people should be admitted. If we are allowed to anticipate probabilities, it seems highly probable that we shall soon have a great number of this kind of persons here. A revolution is now going onward, to which there is nothing similar in history. A large portion of Europe has already declared against titles, and where the innovations are to stop, no man can presume to guess. There is at present no law in the United States by which a foreigner can be hindered from voting at elections, or even from coming into this House; and if a great number of these fugitive nobility come over, they may soon acquire considerable influence. The tone of thinking may insensibly change in the course of a few years, and no person can say how far such a matter may spread. After these, and other prefatory remarks, Mr. G. read a resolution, which was in effect as follows:

"And in case any alien applying for admission to citizenship of the United States, shall have borne any title or order of nobility in any Kingdom or State from whence he may come, he must renounce all pretensions to his title before the Court in which such application shall be made; and this renunciation must be registered in the said Court."

Mr. G. observed that previous to the late Revolution the French nobility were, by the lowest calculation, rated at twenty thousand; and as we may conclude on France being successful, a great proportion of these people may be finally expected here.

Mr. DEXTER declared that he was not very anxious against the resolution. He, however, opposed it. He imagined that, by the same mode of reasoning, we might hinder his Holiness the Pope from coming into this country. He entered at some length into the ridicule of certain tenets in the Roman Catholic religion, and said that priestcraft had done more mischief than aristocracy.

Mr. MADISON said that the question was not perhaps so important as some gentlemen supposed; nor of so little consequence as others seem to think it. It is very probable that the spirit of Republicanism will pervade a great part of Europe. It is hard to guess what numbers of titled characters may, by such an event, be thrown out of that part of the world. What can be more reasonable than that when crowds of them come here, they should be forced to renounce everything contrary to the spirit of the Constitution. He did not approve the ridicule attempted to be thrown out on the Roman Catholics. In their religion there was nothing inconsistent with the purest Republicanism. In Switzerland about one-half of the Cantons were of the Roman Catholic persuasion. Some of the most Democratical Cantons were so; Cantons where every man gave his vote for a Representative. Americans had no right to ridicule Catholics. They had, many of them, proved good citizens during the Revolution. As to hereditary titles, they were proscribed by the Constitution. He would not wish to have a citizen who refused such an oath.

Mr. PAGE was for the motion of his colleague. It did not become that House to be afraid of introducing Democratical principles. Titles only give a particular class of men a right to be insolent, and another class a pretence to be mean and cringing. The principle will come in by degrees, and produce mischievous effects here as well as elsewhere. If such men do come here, nothing can be more grateful to a Republican than to see them renounce their titles. This does not amount to any demand of making them renounce their principles. If they do not aspire to be citizens, they may assume as many titles as they think fit. Equality is the basis of good order and society, whereas titles turn everything wrong. Mr. P. said that a scavenger was as necessary to the health of a city as any one of its magistrates. It was proper, therefore, not to lose sight of equality, and to prevent, as far as possible, any opportunities of being insolent. He did not want to see a Duke

come here, and contest an election for Congress with a citizen.

Mr. SEDGWICK was really at a loss to see what end this motion could answer. He agreed with the arguments of Mr. GILES. But the point in view was explicitly provided for already. By taking an oath of citizenship, the individual not only renounces, but solemnly abjures nobility. The title is destroyed when the allegiance is broken by his oath being taken to this Government. This abjuration has destroyed all connexion with the old Government. Why then provide for it a second time?

Mr. GILES said, that by admitting a thing to have been once done, it was admitted that it might be done again. If it had been right to do it once, there could be no harm in repeating it. The member then quoted Mr. DEXTER, who rose and declared that the gentleman had misunderstood him. He spoke for some time, and when he sat down—

Mr. GILES declared himself incapable of comprehending whether Mr. DEXTER was for his motion or against it. He therefore proceeded to reply to Mr. SEDGWICK, whose chief argument had been that the thing was provided for already. He did not suppose that this gentleman would allege the matter to be explicitly provided for. It only could be so by implication; which was a very bad way of making a law, because it gave room for endless disputes. If the thing is in itself right, why refuse to vote directly for it? Why leave it only to be implied? He wished to let foreigners know expressly the ground upon which they stood. Why not tell them at once, and in plain English, you must renounce your titles before you can have the privileges of an American citizen? Mr. G. pressed home this idea more than once. He meant no act of inhospitality to these emigrants. He would deprive them of no right, nor do anything unkind to them. But he was entitled by the spirit of the Constitution to withhold this right from them till they renounced all hereditary titles. This was no incivility. He concluded, by declaring that he would, if supported, call for the yeas and nays on this question. A number of members rose to support this proposal.

Mr. NICHOLAS had no objection to the motion, but that it did not go far enough. The emigrants ought to be obliged to swear not only that they abjured all titles hitherto received, but that they would never accept of any in future. He believed that this would hurt their feelings, and, sympathizing with them, he would not urge a proposal that might add to their distress, but should vote for the motion as it stood.

Mr. LEE was very sorry that the present subject had been so long agitated—he never viewed it as important—but a degree of importance had been now given to it by the calling of the yeas and nays.

Under these circumstances, it appeared to him very well calculated to impress on the public mind, that there was a real danger of the establishment of nobility or aristocratic orders in this country; and that those who voted against this motion were friendly to such a change in our political system: and that those who voted for it were the only true patriots. He trusted so much to the liberality of the mover as to rely that he neither meant unnecessarily to alarm the public mind, nor intended to inflict a stigma on those gentlemen who, entertaining an opinion of the frivolity and inefficacy of the motion, should vote against it. Mr. LEE would therefore impute the motion to the most laudable zeal to guard the public liberty. And on this ground it would be necessary to inquire what was the danger which existed that this provision was intended to protect us from. The gentleman must have felt great alarm, or he would not have introduced it. Mr. L. said, when he looked through the Constitution and Laws of the United States, and particularly when he considered the Constitutions and laws of the respective States, that he could not see the shadow of a foundation to build an alarm upon. As to mere empty names, as to sounds, we must be very corrupt, we must be very ignorant, if we could be alarmed by them. And in this free country every man had a right to call himself by what name or title he pleased: and if the mover thought proper to change his name for any other name, sound, or title, it would neither add to, nor diminish his real worth and importance; it would not give qualities to his heart which he had not before, nor detract from those he had. What were the mischiefs experienced in Europe from privileged orders? they did not flow from the names by which those orders were distinguished; they arose from the exclusive preference and privileges which those orders possessed in political rights, and in property. Without these their titles would have been mere empty gewgaws, ridiculous in the extreme, and unworthy of the acceptance of any man of common sense. Titles then did not produce the mischiefs; but the privileges annexed to titles. Mr. L. had said, in this country every man had a right to call himself by what name or title he pleased; but here no mischief could result from it, because neither political rank nor property could be attached to titles. Every citizen was equal to his fellow-citizen in political rights; and the laws of the respective States had wisely provided that property could not be accumulated in such a degree in the hands of individuals as to give them an improper influence in society. By the equal distribution of estates individuals are prevented from being so rich as to trample upon the necks of their equals. Great accumulations of property are more likely in fact to introduce the effects of aristocracy than the ridiculous names by which individuals may be distinguished. It was a slander upon the fundamental laws and political institutions of our country, to suppose that a few aliens, because they had possessed titles in foreign countries after having renounced their allegiance to those countries, even if they were disposed to do it, could as it were by magic, overturn the established habits of our people, and the liberty of the Government into which they had incorporated themselves. The body of our citizens were too enlightened, too virtuous, for Mr. L. to apprehend any danger from so trivial a cause. If worthy citizens were so corruptible, and so easily corrupted, we must relinquish the idea of ever being fit to maintain a free and Republican Government. But our citizens can distinguish between sound and reality. When we passed the excise law, it was said that the name was odious; but the Legislature, having a proper confidence in the understanding of the community, did not hesitate to pass it; because it was a just

and necessary one. If nobility should ever unfortunately be introduced into this country (to which at present every circumstance is hostile, and which Mr. L. believed impossible, as long as we adhere to our present fundamental laws and virtuous habits) it would be from internal corruption, and not because a few foreigners, who once possessed titles in their native countries, may become citizens of this. They in fact can have no privilege among us in consequence of any foreign title; but must exist in perfect equality in all social rights with the rest of our citizens.

But his colleague objected to the qualities of their hearts. To find out the heart of any man, would be a difficult task. We are liable to be deceived by every description of men. The professions of over-zealous patriots do not always secure us from their treason, or we should not so frequently in history read of Catilines and Caesars, or lately have witnessed the tyranny of Robespierre. All these men were once flaming patriots. And if zealous patriots can turn traitors and tyrants, was it not as possible for the member of a foreign privileged order to become a good citizen? The truth is, professions and abjurations are no certain proofs of the virtue and apprehended patriotism of any man. We are secure from the danger, because every citizen here is equal. No privileged orders exist amongst us, nor can exist, unless the people shall choose to change their present Constitution and Laws, which is not to be expected. Mr. L. said, if he understood his colleague, his strongest reason why a foreign nobleman could not become a good citizen, was the education he had received; the superiority which he had been accustomed to exercise over his fellow men, and the servile court he had been accustomed to receive from them. It was, then, the corrupting relation of lord and vassal, which rendered him an unfit member of an equal Republican Government. Mr. L. feared that this reasoning applied to the existing relation of master and slave in the Southern country, (rather a more degrading one than even that of lord and vassal) would go to prove that the people of that country were not qualified to be members of our free Republican Government. But he knew that this was not the case. Though in that House the members from the State of Virginia held persons in bondage, he was sure that their hearts glowed with a zeal as warm for the equal rights and happiness of men, as gentlemen from other parts of the Union where such degrading distinctions did not exist. He rejoiced, that, notwithstanding the unfavorable circumstances of his country in this respect, the virtue of his fellow-citizens shone forth equal to that of any other part of the nation.

Mr. L. was afraid that the force of his colleague's reasoning might be extended to throw an improper imputation on the virtue of his countrymen, which he was sure could not be intended. But, Mr. L. did not think that the citizens in the South had any right to assume a superiority in political virtue, over their fellow-citizens to the East. He claimed to be equal, not to be behind them was sufficient glory. Mr. L. did not know but the proposition, if it had any effect, which he very much doubted, might collaterally affect the rights to property, which, in the course of time, might devolve to aliens in the countries from which they came, which, he believed, his colleague could not intend.

[8 Jan.]

The bill to establish an uniform system of naturalization, and to repeal the act heretofore passed on that subject, was then read a third time, and passed. The filling up of the blanks in this bill produced a dispute of some length, and from the intricacy in some parts of it, the abridging of it would be a work of difficulty. Several members spoke to the filling up of the blanks, and their arguments sometimes applied equally to all the three clauses before the House. To be intelligible, therefore, it appears necessary in the first place to insert the clauses themselves at length, as in the end filled up. We shall then repeat some of the remarks made on the subject by different gentlemen. The sections of the bill in question were as follows:

1. The alien shall have declared on oath or affirmation, before the Supreme, Superior, District, or Circuit Court of some one of the States, or a Circuit or District Court of the United States, three years at least before his admission, that it was, *bona fide*, his intention to become a citizen of the United States, and to renounce all allegiance and fidelity to any foreign Prince, Potentate, State, or Sovereignty whatever, and particularly by name the Prince, Potentate, State, or Sovereignty whereof such alien may, at the time, be a citizen or subject.

2. He shall, at the time of his application to be admitted, declare on oath or affirmation, before some one of the Courts aforesaid, that he has resided within the United States five years at least, and within the State where such Court is at the time held, one year at least; that he will support the Constitution of the United States; and that he doth renounce and abjure all allegiance and fidelity to every foreign Prince, Potentate, State, or Sovereignty, whatever, and particularly by name the Prince, Potentate, State, or Sovereignty whereof he was before a citizen or subject; which proceedings shall be recorded by the Clerk of the Court.

3. The Court admitting such alien, shall be satisfied that he has resided within the limits, and under the jurisdiction of the United States five years; and it shall further appear to their satisfaction, that during that time he has behaved as a man of a good moral character, attached to the principles of the Constitution of the United States, and well disposed to the good order and happiness of the same.

Some gentlemen having spoke on the propriety of different terms for admission.

Mr. MADISON said, that he feared the House would never see an end of the discussion, if they went on at this rate, for, by descending to discriminate all the qualifications of a citizen, they run the hazard of losing the bill altogether, from the mere waste of time. Ten years were named by Mr. MURRAY to fill up the first blank, and seven years by Mr. HARTLEY. These terms he thought by much too long. This would oblige the friends of the bill to vote against it.

Mr. BALDWIN objected that the law was inconsistent with itself, for a man is not to be admitted as a citizen to vote for ten years, while a residence of nine years may qualify him to be elected a Senator. This differed from the temper of the Constitution.

Mr. S. SMITH said, that the discussion on several parts of the bill in Committee had appeared to him unimportant, that the great object with him was the time of probation. He was for the longest term, that the prejudices which the aliens had imbibed under the Government from whence they came might be effaced, and that they might, by communication and observance of our laws and government, have just ideas of our Constitution and the excellence of its institution before they were admitted to the rights of a citizen. A gentleman from Virgina [Mr. NICHOLAS] had stated that holding a purse with money in it was sufficient to admit strangers to a vote in Maryland; the fact was not so; before an alien can be admitted to the right of suffrage, he must abjure all allegiance to the King of Great Britain, take the oaths to the State, and to support the Government of the United States, and have one year's residence. The gentleman says, that the bill can only embrace the officers of Government and the commercial interest, and fears that the Eastern States wish to exclude the competition that arises from the foreign merchant. He could not see how that jealousy could apply, for it was as rare to see a foreign merchant in New England, as to see a native merchant in Virginia; that if the gentleman thought the place of foreign merchants would be filled from New England, he could foresee no injury, on the contrary a benefit. For, in case of war, you might be assured that they would not act as spies; that there were many merchants from New England in Maryland—that they were good Republicans, good citizens, and always industrious.

Mr. FITZSIMONS thought that ten years were much too long a time for keeping an alien from being a citizen—it would make this class of people enemies to your Government. He was firmly of opinion that emigrants deserved to be encouraged; and to discourage them was an idea which till this day he had never heard either in or out of the House. Nature seems to have pointed out this country as an asylum for the people oppressed in other parts of the world. It would be wrong, therefore, to first admit them here, and then treat them for so long a time so hardly. As to the merchants from this country returning home with their wealth acquired here, it was not the case in Pennsylvania, whatever it might be in Virginia. They very seldom went home again, but married and settled in the country. He also thought the country obliged to them, as it was capable of employing the largest capital which could be brought into it. He knew of no such competition as the gentleman spoke about between the natives and the aliens.

Mr. BOUDINOT reminded the House of a late Proclamation by the PRESIDENT, wherein, among other things, it is said that this country is an asylum to the oppressed of all nations. He was for shortening the period of admission. He saw a great deal in the remark as to the bad policy of admitting people into the country and refusing them for so long a period the rights of citizens.

Several other gentlemen spoke. The bill finally passed.

13

THE CASE OF ISAAC WILLIAMS
27 Feb. 1797

St. George Tucker, Blackstone's Commentaries
1:App. 436–38 (1803)

On the trial of Isaac Williams, in the district court of Connecticut, February 27, 1797, for accepting a commission under the French Republic, and under the authority thereof committing acts of hostility against Great-Britain, the defendant alledged, and offered to prove that he had expatriated himself from the United States, and become a French citizen before the commencement of the war between France and England. This produced a question as to the right of expatriation; when Judge Ellsworth, then chief justice of the United States, is said to have delivered an opinion nearly to the following effect.

"The common law of this country remains the same as it was before the revolution. The present question is to be decided by two great principles; one is, that all the members of a civil community are bound to each other by compact; the other is, that one of the parties to this compact cannot dissolve it by his own act. The compact between our community and it's members is, that the community shall protect it's members, and on the part of the members, that they will at all times be obedient to the laws of the community, and faithful in it's defence. It necessarily results that the member cannot dissolve this compact, without the consent or default of the community. There has been no consent . . . . no default. Express consent is not claimed; but it is argued that the consent of the community is implied, by it's policy . . . . it's conditions . . . . and it's acts. In countries so crouded with inhabitants, that the means of subsistence are difficult to be obtained, it is reason and policy to permit emigration; but our policy is different; for our country is but scarcely settled, and we have no inhabitants to spare.

"Consent has been argued from the condition of the country, because we were in a state of peace. But though we were in peace, the war had commenced in Europe. We wished to have nothing to do with the war; but the war would have something to do with us. It has been extremely difficult for us to keep out of this war; the progress of it has threatened to involve us. It has been necessary for our government to be vigilant in restraining our own citizens from those acts which would involve us in hostilities. The most visionary writers on this subject do not contend for the principle in the unlimited extent, that a citizen may, at any, and at all times, renounce his own, and join himself to a foreign country.

"Consent has been argued from the acts of our government permitting the naturalization of foreigners. When a foreigner presents himself here, we do not inquire what his relation is to his own country; we have not the means of knowing, and the inquiry would be indelicate; we leave him to judge of that. If he embarrasses himself by contracting contradictory obligations, the fault and folly are his own; but this implies no consent of the government that our own citizens should also expatriate themselves. . . . It is, therefore, my opinion, that these facts which the prisoner offers to prove, in his defence, are totally irrelevant," &c. The prisoner was accordingly found guilty, fined and imprisoned.

14

JAMES IREDELL, CHARGE TO GRAND JURY
9 Fed. Cas. 826, no. 5,126 (C.C.D.Pa. 1799)

I. The alien laws, there being two. To these laws, in particular, it has been objected: 1. That an alien ought not to be removed on suspicion, but on proof of some crime. 2. That an alien coming into the country, on the faith of an act stipulating that in a certain time, and on certain conditions, he may become a citizen, to remove him in an arbitrary manner before that time, would be a breach of public faith. 3. That it is inconsistent with the following clause in the constitution (article 1, § 9): "The migration or importation of such persons as any of the states now existing shall think proper to admit, shall not be prohibited by the congress prior to the year one thousand eight hundred and eight, but a tax or duty may be imposed on such importation, not exceeding ten dollars for each person."

With regard to the first objection, viz., "That an alien ought not to be removed on suspicion, but on proof of some crime." It is believed that it never was suggested in any other country, that aliens had a right to go into a foreign country, and stay at their will and pleasure without any leave from the government. The law of nations undoubtedly is, that when an alien goes into a foreign country, he goes under either an express or implied safe conduct. In most countries in Europe, I believe, an express passport is necessary for strangers. Where greater liberality is observed, yet it is always understood that the government may order away any alien whose stay is deemed incompatible with the safety of the country. Nothing is more common than to order away, on the eve of a war, all aliens or subjects of the nation with whom the war is to take place. Why is that done, but that it is deemed unsafe to retain in the country, men whose prepossessions are naturally so strong in favour of the enemy, that it may be apprehended they will either join in arms, or do mischief by intrigue, in his favour? How many such instances took place at the beginning of the war with Great Britain, no body then objecting to the authority of the measure, and the expediency of it being alone in contemplation! In cases like this, it is ridiculous to talk of a crime; because perhaps the only crime that a man can then be charged with, is his being born in another country, and having a strong attachment to it. He is not punished for a crime that he has committed, but deprived of the power of committing one hereafter to which even a sense of patriotism may tempt a warm and misguided mind. Nobody who has ever heard of Major André, that possesses any liberality of mind, but must believe that he did what he thought right at the time, though in my opinion it was a conduct in no manner justifiable. Yet how fatal might his success have proved! If men, therefore, of good character, and held in universal estimation for integrity, can be tempted when a great object is in view, to violate the strict duties of morality, what may be expected from others who have neither character nor virtue, but stand ready to yield to temptations of any kind? The opportunities during a war of making use of men of such a description are so numerous and so dangerous, that no prudent nation would ever trust to the possible good behaviour of many of them. Indeed, most of those who oppose this law seem to admit that as to alien enemies the interposition may be proper, but they contend it is improper, before a war actually takes place, to exercise such an authority, and that as to neutral aliens, it is totally inadmissible. To be sure the two latter instances are not quite so plain; the objection I am considering belongs equally to them all; for if an alien cannot be removed but on conviction of a crime, then an alien enemy ought not to be removed but on conviction of treason, or some other crime showing the necessity of it. If, however, we are not blind to what is evident to all the rest of the world, equal danger may be apprehended from the citizens of a hostile power, before war is actually declared as after, perhaps more, because less suspicion is entertained; and some citizens of a neutral power are equally dangerous with the others. What has given France possession of the Netherlands, Geneva, Switzerland and almost all Italy, and enables her to domineer over so many other countries, lately powerful and completely independent, but that her arts have preceded her arms; the smooth words of amity, peace, and universal love, by seducing weak minds, have led to an unbounded confidence, which has ended in their destruction, and they have now to deplore the infatuation which led them to court a fraternal embrace from a bosom in which a dagger was concealed.

In how many countries, alien friends as to us, dependent upon them, are there warm partisans not nominally French citizens, but completely illuminated with French principles, electrified with French enthusiasm, and ready for any sort of revolutionary mischief! Are we to be guarded against the former and exposed to the latter? No, gentlemen. If with such examples before their eyes, congress had either confined their precaution to a war in form, or to citizens of France only, losing all sense of danger to their country in a regard to nominal distinctions, they would probably justly have deserved the charge of neglecting their country's safety in one of its most essential points, and hereafter the very men who are now clamorous against them for exercising a judicious foresight, might too late have had reason to charge them, (as many former infatuated governments in Europe may now fairly be charged by their miserable deluded fellow-citizens), as the authors of their country's ruin. But those who object to this law seem to pay little regard to considerations of this kind, and to entertain no other fear but that the pres-

ident may exercise this authority for the mere purpose of abusing it. There is no end to arguments or suspicions of this kind. If this power is proper, it must be exercised by somebody. If from the nature of it, it could be exercised by so numerous a body as congress, yet as congress are not constantly sitting, it ought not to be exercised by them alone. If they are not to exercise it, who so fit as the president? What interest can he have in abusing such an authority? But on this occasion, as on others of the like kind, gentlemen think it sufficient to show, not that a power is likely to be abused (which is all that can be prudently guarded against), but that it possibly may, and therefore to guard against the possibility of an abuse of power, the power is not at all to be exercised. The argument would be just as good against his acknowledged powers, as any others, that the legislature may occasionally confide to him. Suppose he should refuse to nominate to any office, or to command the army or navy, or should assign frivolous reasons against every law, so that no law could be passed but with the concurrence of two-thirds of both houses! Suppose congress should raise an army without necessity, lay taxes where there was no occasion for money, declare war from mere caprice, lay wanton and oppressive restraints on commerce, or in a time of imminent danger trifle with the safety of their country, to gain a momentary breath of popularity at the hazard of their country's ruin! All this they may do. Does any man of candour, who does not believe everything they do, wrong, apprehend that any of these things will be done? They have the power to do them because the authority to pass very important and necessary acts of legislation on all those subjects, and in regard to which discretion must be left, unavoidably implies that, as it may be exercised in a right manner, it may, if no principle prevent it, be exercised in a wrong one. If the state legislatures should combine to choose no more senators, they may abolish the constitution without the danger of committing treason. If to prevent a house of representatives being in existence, they should keep no law in being for a similar branch of their own, deeming the abolition of the government of the United States cheaply purchased by such a sacrifice, they may do this. They have the same power over the election of a president and vice president. What is the security against abuse in any of these cases? None, but the precautions taken to procure a proper choice, which, if well exercised, will at least secure the public against a wanton abuse of power, though nothing can secure them absolutely against the common frailty of men, or the possibility of bad men, if accidentally invested with power, carrying it into a dangerous extreme. We must trust some persons, and as well as we can, submit to any collateral evil which may arise from a provision for a great and indispensable good that can only be obtained through the medium of human imperfection. At the same time it may be observed, that in the case of the president, or any executive or judicial officer wantonly abusing his trust, he is liable to impeachment, and there are frequent opportunities of changing the members of the legislature, if their conduct is not acceptable to their constituents.

The clause in the constitution, declaring that the trial of

all crimes, except by impeachment, shall be by jury, can never in reason be extended to amount to a permission of perpetual residence of all sorts of foreigners, unless convicted of some crime, but is evidently calculated for the security of any citizen, a party to the instrument, or even of a foreigner if resident in the country, who, when charged with the commission of a crime against the municipal laws for which he is liable to punishment, can be tried for it in no other manner.

The second objection is, "that an alien coming into the country, on the faith of an act stipulating that in a certain time and on certain conditions, he may become a citizen, to remove him in an arbitrary manner before that time, would be a breach of public faith." With regard to this, it may be observed, that undoubtedly the faith of government ought, under all circumstances, and in all possible situations, to be preserved sacred. If, therefore, in virtue of this law, all aliens from any part of the world had a right to come here, stay the probationary time, and become citizens, the act in question could not be justified, unless it could be shown that a real (not a pretended) overruling public necessity to which all inchoate acts of legislation must forever be subject, occasioned a partial repeal of it. But there are certain conditions, without which no alien can ever be admitted, if he stay ever so long; and one is, that during a limited time (two years in the case of aliens then resident; five in the case of aliens arriving after), he has behaved as a man of a good moral character, attached to the principles of the constitution of the United States, and well disposed to the good order and happiness of the same. If his conduct be different, he is no object of the naturalization law at all, and consequently no implied compact was made with him. If his conduct be conformable to that description, he is no object of the alien law to which the objection is applied, because he is not a person whom the president is empowered to remove, for such a person could not be deemed dangerous to the peace and safety of the United States, nor could there be reasonable grounds to suspect such a man of being concerned in any treasonable or secret machinations against the government, in which cases alone the removal of any alien friend is authorized. Besides, any alien coming to this country must, or ought to know, that this being an independent nation, it has all the rights concerning the removal of aliens which belong by the law of nations to any other; that while he remains in the country in the character of an alien, he can claim no other privilege than such as an alien is entitled to; and consequently, whatever risk he may incur in that capacity, is incurred voluntarily, with the hope that in due time, by his unexceptionable conduct, he may become a citizen of the United States. As there is no end to the ingenuity of man, it has been suggested that such a person, if not a citizen, is a denizen, and therefore cannot be removed as an alien. A denizen in those laws from which we derive our own, means a person who has received letters of denization from the king, and under the royal government such a power might undoubtedly have been exercised. This power of denization is a kind of partial naturalization, giving some, but not all of the privileges of a natural born subject. He may take lands by purchase or devise, but cannot inherit. The issue of a denizen born before denization cannot inherit; but if born after may, the ancestor having been able to communicate to him inheritable blood. But this power of the crown was thought so formidable that it is expressly provided by act of parliament, that no denizen can be a member of the privy council, or of either house of parliament, or have any office of trust, civil or military, or be capable of any grant of lands from the crown. Upon the dissolution of the royal government, the whole authority of naturalization, either whole or partial, belonged to the several states, and this power the people of the states have since devolved on the congress of the United States. Denization, therefore, (in the sense here used,) is a term unknown in our law, since the right was not derived from any general legislative authority, but from a special prerogative of the crown, to which parliamentary restrictions afterwards were applied. So much so, that if an act of parliament had passed, giving certain rights to an alien with restrictions exactly similar to those of a denizen, I imagine he would not have been called a denizen; because the royal authority was not the source from which his rights were derived. As to acts of naturalization themselves, they are liable in England, by an express law to certain limitations, one of which is, that the person naturalized is incapable of being a member of the privy council, or either house of parliament, or of holding offices or grants from the crown. Yet I never heard, nor do I believe that such a person was ever called a denizen; for which, as there is no foundation in precedent, or in the constitution of the United States, I presume it is a distinction without solidity. Fixed principles of law cannot be grounded on the airy imagination of man.

The third objection is, "That it is inconsistent with the following clause in the constitution, viz.: "The migration or importation of such persons as any of the states now existing shall think proper to admit, shall not be prohibited by the congress prior to the year one thousand eight hundred and eight, but a tax or duty may be imposed on said importation not exceeding ten dollars for each person."" I am not satisfied, as to this objection, that it is sufficient to overrule it, to say the words do not express the real meaning, either of those who formed the constitution, or those who established it, although I do verily believe in my own mind, that the article was intended only for slaves, and the clause was expressed in its present manner to accommodate different gentlemen, some of whom could not bear the name slaves, and others had objections to it. But though this probably is the real truth, yet, if in attempting to compromise, they have unguardedly used expressions that go beyond their meaning, and there is nothing but private history to elucidate it, I shall deem it absolutely necessary to confine myself to the written instrument. Other reasons may make the point doubtful, but at present I am inclined to think it must be admitted, that congress, prior to the year 1808, cannot prohibit the migration of free persons to a particular state, existing at the time of the constitution, which such state shall, by law, agree to receive. The states then existing, therefore, till 1808, may (we will say) admit the migration of persons to their own states, without any prohibitory act of congress.—

This they may do upon principles of general policy, and in consistence with all their other duties. The states are expressly prohibited from entering into an engagement or contract with another state, or engaging in war, unless actually invaded, or in such imminent danger, as will not admit of delay. The avenues to foreign connection being thus carefully closed, it will scarcely be contended, that in case of war, a state could, either directly or indirectly, permit the migration of enemies. If they did, the United States could certainly, without any impeachment of the general right of allowing migration, in virtue of their authority to repel invasion, prevent the arrival of such. And as such invasion may be attempted without a formal war, and congress have an express right to protect against invasion, as well as repel it, I presume congress would also have authority to prevent the arrival of any enemies, coming in the disguise of friends, to invade their country. But, admitting the right to permit migration in its full force, the persons migrating on their authority must be subject to the laws of the country, which consist not only of those of the particular state, but of the United States. While aliens, therefore, they must remain in the character of aliens; and, of course, upon the principles I have mentioned, be subject to a power of removal, in certain cases recognized in the law of nations; nor can they cease to be in this situation, until they become citizens of the United States; in which case they must obey the laws of the Union as well as of the particular state they reside in. But, gentlemen argue as if because the states had a right to permit migration, the migrants were under a sort of special protection of the state admitting it, lest the United States, merely to disappoint the purpose of migration, should exercise an arbitrary authority of removal without any cause at all. It would be just as consistent to say, that if such migrant was charged with a murder on the high seas, or in any fort or arsenal of the United States, he should not be tried for it in a court of the United States, lest the court and juries, out of ill will to the state, should combine to procure his conviction and punishment, in all events, to defeat the state law. The two powers may undoubtedly be made compatible, if the legislatures of the particular states, and the government of the United States, do their duty, without which presumption, not an authority given by the constitution can exist. They surely are more compatible than the collateral powers of taxation, which, under each government, go to an unlimited extent, but the very nature of which forbids any other limitation than a sense of moral right and justice. If we skepticize in the manner of some gentlemen on this subject, suppose each legislature should tax to the amount of 19s. in the pound; each has the power; but is such an exercise of it more apprehended than we apprehend an earthquake to swallow us all up at this very moment? All systems of government suppose they are to be administered by men of common sense and common honesty. In our country, as all ultimately depends on the voice of the people, they have it in their power, and it is to be presumed they generally will choose men of this description: but if they will not, the case, to be sure, is without remedy. If they choose fools, they will have foolish laws. If they choose knaves, they will have knavish ones. But this can never be the case until they are generally fools or knaves themselves, which, thank God, is not likely ever to become the character of the American people.

15

ST. GEORGE TUCKER,
BLACKSTONE'S COMMENTARIES
1:App. 184–85, 254–59; 2:App. 90–103
1803

1. Congress being authorized to establish an uniform rule of naturalization, and uniform laws on the subject of bankruptcies throughout the United States, it may well be questioned how far the states can possess any concurrent authority, on these subjects.

If, however, a doubt should arise respecting the former, it might be presumed, that the rights intended to be conferred by this uniform rule of naturalization, should be, in general, confined to such as might be derived from the federal government, without infringing those rights which peculiarly appertain to the states. Thus a person naturalized pursuant to the laws of the United States, would undoubtedly acquire every right that any other citizen possesses, as a citizen of the United States, except such as the constitution expressly denies, or defers the enjoyment of; and such as the constitution or laws of the individual states require on the part of those who are candidates for office under the authority of the states. Five years residence, for example, is required by the laws of Virginia, before any naturalized foreigner is capable of being elected to any office under the state. It is presumable that his being naturalized under the laws of the United States would not supercede the necessity of this qualification.

. . . . .

4. Congress have power to establish an uniform rule of naturalization, and uniform laws on the subject of bankruptcies, throughout the United States.

As to the former of these powers; by the first articles of confederation and perpetual union between the states, it was agreed, that the free inhabitants of each state, paupers, vagabonds, and fugitives from justice excepted, should be entitled to all privileges and immunities of free citizens in the several states; and the people of each state shall, in every other, enjoy all the privileges of trade and commerce, &c. The dissimilarity of the rules of naturalization in the several states, had long been remarked as a fault in the system, and, as combined with this article in the confederation, laid a foundation for intricate and delicate questions. It seems to be a construction scarcely avoidable, that those who come under the denomination of free inhabitants of a state, (although not citizens of such state), were entitled in every other state to all the privileges of free citizens of the latter, that is, to greater privileges than they may be entitled to in their own state: our free negroes, for example, though not entitled to the right of suffrage in Virginia, might, by removing into another state, acquire that right there; and persons of the same description, removing from any other state, into this, might be supposed to acquire the same right here, in virtue of that article, though native-born negroes are undoubtedly incapable of it under our constitution: so that every state was laid under the necessity, not only to confer the rights of citizenship in other states, upon any whom it might admit to such rights within itself, but upon any whom it might allow to become *inhabitants* within its jurisdiction. But were an exposition of the term "inhabitants" to be admitted, which would confine the stipulated privileges to citizens alone, the difficulty would not be removed. The very improper power would still have been retained by each state, of naturalizing in every other state. In one state, residence for a short time conferred all the rights of citizenship; in another, qualifications of greater importance were required: an alien, therefore, legally incapacitated for certain rights in the latter, might, by previous residence only in the former, elude his incapacity; and thus the law of one state, be preposterously rendered paramount to the law of another, within the jurisdiction of such other. By the laws of several states, certain descriptions of aliens, who had rendered themselves obnoxious, and other persons whose conduct had rendered them liable to the highest penalties of the law, were laid under interdicts inconsistent, not only with the rights of citizenship, but with the privileges of residence, beyond the short period allowed by the treaty of peace with Great Britain. We owe it to mere casualty, that very serious embarrassments on this subject have not occurred. The constitution, and the several acts of naturalization passed by congress, have therefore wisely provided against them by this article, and by an explicit declaration contained in the law, that no person heretofore proscribed by any state, shall be admitted a citizen, except by an act of the legislature of the state in which such person was proscribed.

The federal court, consisting of judges Wilson and Blair, of the supreme court, and judge Peters, district judge in Pennsylvania, at a circuit court held for the district of Pennsylvania, in April, 1792; decided, "that the states, individually, still enjoy a concurrent jurisdiction upon the subject of naturalization: but that their individual authority cannot be exercised so as to contravene the rule established by the authority of the union: the true reason for investing congress with the power of naturalization (said the court,) was to guard against too narrow, instead of too liberal a mode of conferring the right of citizenship. Thus the individual states cannot exclude those citizens, who have been adopted by the United States; but they can adopt citizens upon easier terms, than those which congress may deem it expedient to impose."

But this decision seems to have been afterwards doubted by judge Iredel, 2 Dallas, 373. And the act of 5 cong. c. 71. declares, that "no alien shall be admitted to become a citizen of the United States, or of any state, unless in the manner prescribed by that act." And by a subsequent act, passed 7 cong. chapter 28, it is also declared, that any alien, being a free white person, may become a citizen of the United States, or any of them, on the conditions therein mentioned, "and not otherwise." These legislative expositions of the constitution do not accord with the judicial opinion above-mentioned. A very respectable political writer makes the following pertinent remarks upon this subject. "Prior to the adoption of the constitution, the people inhabiting the different states might be divided into two classes: natural born citizens, or those born within the state, and aliens, or such as were born out of it. The first, by their birth-right, became entitled to all the privileges of citizens; the second, were entitled to none, but such as were held out and given by the laws of the respective states prior to their emigration. In the states of Kentucky and Virginia, the privileges of alien friends depended upon the constitution of each state, the acts of their respective legislatures, and the common law; by these they were considered, according to the time of their residence, and their having complied with certain requisitions pointed out by these laws, either as denizens, or naturalized citizens. As denizens, they were placed in a kind of middle state between aliens and natural born citizens; by naturalization, they were put exactly in the same condition that they would have been, if they had been born within the state, except so far as was specially excepted by the laws of each state. The common law has affixed such distinct and appropriate ideas to the terms denization, and naturalization, that they can not be confounded together, or mistaken for each other in any legal transaction whatever. They are so absolutely distinct in their natures, that in England the rights they convey, can not both be given by the same power; the king can make denizens, by his grant, or letters patent, but nothing but an act of parliament can make a naturalized subject. This was the legal state of this subject in Virginia, when the federal constitution was adopted; it declares that congress shall have power to establish an uniform rule of naturalization; throughout the United States; but it also further declares, that the powers not delegated by the constitution to the U. States, nor prohibited by it to the states, are reserved to the states, respectively or to the people. The power of naturalization, and not that of denization, being delegated to congress, and the power of denization not being prohibited to the states by the constitution, that power ought not to be considered as given to congress, but, on the contrary, as being reserved to the states. And as the right of denization did not make a citizen of an alien, but only placed him in a middle state, between the two, giving him local privileges only, which he was so far from being entitled to carry with him into another state, that he lost them by removing from the state giving them, the inconveniences which might result from the indirect communication of the rights of naturalized citizens, by different modes of naturalization prevailing in the several states, could not be apprehended. It might therefore have been extremely impolitic in the states to have surrendered the right of *denization*, as well as that of *naturalization* to the federal government, inasmuch as it might have operated to discourage migration to those states, which have lands to dispose of, and settle; since, it might be a disagreeable alternative to the states, either to permit aliens to hold lands within their territory, or to exclude all who have not yet completed their probationary residence within the

U. States, so as to become naturalized citizens, from purchasing, or holding lands, until they should have acquired all other rights appertaining to that character."

Here, another question presents itself: if the states, individually, possess the right of making denizens of aliens, can a person so made a denizen of a particular state, hold an office under the authority of such state? And I think it unquestionable that each state hath an absolute, and uncontrolable power over this subject, if disposed to exercise it. For every state must be presumed to be the exclusive judge of the qualifications of it's own officers and servants: for this is a part of their sovereignty which they can not be supposed to have intended ever to give up. And if there be nothing in their constitutions, respectively, to the contrary, the legislature may unquestionably, by a general law, limit, or extend such qualifications, so far as they may think proper. The law of Virginia declares, "that all persons other than alien enemies, who shall migrate into this state, and give satisfactory proof by oath or affirmation that they intend to reside therein, and take the legal oath of fidelity to the commonwealth shall be entitled to all the rights, privileges and advantages of citizens, except that they shall not be capable of election or appointment to any office, legislative, executive or judiciary, until an actual residence in the state for five years thereafter; nor until they shall have evinced a permanent attachment to the state, by intermarrying with a citizen thereof, or of some one of the United States, or purchased lands of the value of three hundred dollars therein." Now although the act of congress may operate to repeal this act, so far as relates to the rights of naturalization, or, a state of perfect citizenship, under the constitution and laws of the union; yet, as it respects the rights which the state hath power to grant, such as holding lands, or an office under the sole, and distinct authority of the state, I see no reason to doubt that the law is as valid at this day, as it was before the adoption of the constitution of the United States.

The periods of residence, required by the several acts of congress before an alien can be admitted a citizen, have been various. The act of 1 congress, 2 session, c. 3, required two years only: this period was increased to five years, by the act of 3 congress, c. 85, which was still further extended to fourteen years, by the act of 5 congress, c. 71, but the act of 7 cong., c. 28. has reduced it to five years, again. Any alien who shall have borne any hereditary title; or been of any order of nobility, in any other state, must renounce the same, on oath, at the time of his admission to take the oath of a citizen. A wise provision, the benefit of which it is to be hoped, may reach to the latest posterity.
. . . . .

"It is a principle of universal law, that the natural born subject of one prince cannot by any act of his own, no, not by swearing allegiance to another, put off, or discharge his natural allegiance to the former." Blacks. Com. Vol. I. p. 369.

The positive, and unqualified manner in which the learned commentator advances this to be a principle of universal law, would induce a supposition, that it is a point in which all the writers on the law of nature and nations are perfectly agreed. As my researches have led me to adopt a very different, or, rather, opposite conclusion, it will be the business of this note to examine the subject.

If it be contended that this is a principle of the divine law, I should wish to be informed in which of the books of the old, or new testament it is to be found. The family of the patriarch Jacob voluntarily became subjects to the Egyptian monarch. . . . And four hundred years afterwards, Moses, their prophet, and deliverer, voluntarily abandoned Egypt, his native country, and dwelt among the Midianites; and then he, with the whole of the descendants of Jacob voluntarily departed out of Egypt, under the immediate protection and guidance of Jehovah, himself. . . . David also, the man after God's own heart, abandoned his natural liege lord Saul, and went and dwelt with Achish, king of Gath; and even marched in his army against his native country, and liege lord, until the jealousy of the lords of the Philistines obliged him to turn back. I can not therefore believe that the divine law contains in it any such principle.

Neither can I well conceive how this can be considered as a principle of the law of nature; for according to that law, all men are equal. One man therefore can not owe allegiance to another, in virtue of that law; since there is neither prince nor subject among men according to the principles of it.

Nor yet does this appear to be a principle of the law of nations, though perhaps it may have been the practice of particular nations to prohibit their subjects from migrating to any other: but in this case the prohibition arises from the particular law of the state, and not from the general law and practice of nations towards each other. The law of Solon, which prohibited the Athenians from admitting any person into their commonwealth, except such as were condemned to perpetual banishment from their own country, or else such as removed their whole families to Athens for the convenience of trade, and employment of the arts they professed, was not made so much to keep out foreigners, as to invite them to settle at Athens, by giving them assurance of incorporating them in the body of the commonwealth. . . . For he made no doubt, says Plutarch, but both these sorts of people would make very good subjects, the one because they voluntarily quitted, and the other, because they were forced out of their own country. Plato says that, at Athens it was lawful for every private man, after he had examined the laws and customs of the republic, if he did not approve of them, to quit the city, and retire where he pleased with his effects. By the constitution of the Roman commonwealth, no citizen could forced to leave the commonwealth, or if he pleased, not to leave it, when he was made a member of another which he preferred to it. And therefore Cicero says, that a little before his remembrance, several citizens of Rome, men of credit and fortunes, voluntarily left that, and settled themselves in other commonwealths. And the way, says he, lies open from every state to ours, and from ours to every other. This right he extols in the most emphatic manner. "What noble rights! which by the blessing of heaven have been enjoyed by us and our ancestors, ever since the Roman state begun, that none of us should be forced to leave our country, or stay in it against our wills. This is the immovable foundation of our liberty, that every man is master of his right, and may keep it or resign it, as he pleases." These instances, which are cited by Puffendorf, on this subject, prove at least that this principle was neither to be found in the Athenian or Roman institutions.

The practice among more modern nations is various: among the Muscovites, emigration is not permitted. The citizens of Neufchatel and Valengen, in Switzerland, may quit the country, and carry off their effects in what manner they please; a citizen of Bern may, if he pleases, remove to Fribourg, and reciprocally, a citizen of Fribourg may go and settle in Bern, and he has a right to take all his effects with him. On the other hand it appears from several historical facts, particularly in the history of Switzerland and the neighbouring countries, that the law of nations established there by custom, for some ages past, does not permit a state to receive the subjects of another state into the number of its citizens. This vicious custom, says Vattel, had no other foundation than the slavery to which the people were then reduced. A prince considered his subjects in the rank of his property and riches; he calculated their numbers, as he did his flocks; and to the disgrace of human nature this strange abuse is not yet every where destroyed.

Although Grotius denies that emigrants ought to leave the state in troops or large companies, (an opinion which is controverted by Puffendorf, and Burlamaqui), yet he allows the case to be quite different when a single person leaves his country; it is one thing, says he, to draw water out of a river, and another to divert the course of a part of that river. And Puffendorf expressly says, where there are no laws about the matter (for the laws of different countries differ in this respect), we must be determined by customs arising from the nature of civil subjection. What custom admits of, every subject is supposed at liberty to use. But if this gives no light to the matter, and the compact of subjection makes no mention of it; it must be presumed that every man reserves to himself the liberty to remove at discretion. For when a man enters into a commonwealth, it cannot be supposed that he gives up all care of himself and his fortunes, but rather that by so doing he takes the best expedient to defend and secure both. But because it often happens that the nature of the government does not suit with every private man's circumstances, or he thinks, at least, he can make his fortune with more advantage elsewhere; and since it would be unreasonable to reform and make alterations in the commonwealth at the desire, and for the benefit of only a few private subjects, the only method left is, to give them leave to remove and provide for themselves where they think best. Burlamaqui scruples not to adopt the opinion of Puffendorf, altogether. So that we have the opinion of these four jurists that every man hath a natural right to migrate from one state to another, and that this right can only be restrained under special circumstances, by the state to which he belongs, without imposing upon him an unwarrantable slavery.

Mr. Locke, in his essay on civil government seems to have examined thoroughly the foundation of this pretended right in governments to prohibit the emigration of

their subjects, or citizens. There are no examples, says he, so frequent in history, both sacred and profane, as those of men withdrawing themselves, and their obedience from the jurisdiction they were born under, and the family or community they were bred up in, and setting up new governments in other places: this has been the practice of the world, from its first beginning to this day; nor is it now any more hindrance to the freedom of mankind, that they are born under constituted and antient polities, that have established laws, and set forms of government, than if they were born in the woods, among the unconfined inhabitants that run loose in them. For those who would persuade us, that by being born under any government, we are naturally subjects to it, and have no more any title, or pretence, to the freedom of the state of nature, have no other reason (bating that of paternal power) to produce for it, but only because our fathers, or progenitors passed away their natural liberty, and thereby bound up themselves and their posterity to a perpetual subjection to the government, which they themselves submitted to. 'Tis true, that whatever engagements, or promises, any one has made for himself, he is under the obligation of them, but cannot by any compact whatsoever bind his children, or posterity. For his son, when a man, being altogether as free as the father, any act of the father can no more give away the liberty of the son, than it can of any body else: he may, indeed, annex such conditions to the land he enjoyed, as a subject of any commonwealth, as may oblige his son to be of the community, if he will enjoy those possessions, which were his fathers; because that estate being his father's property he may dispose, or settle it as he pleases. And this has generally given the occasion to mistake in this matter; because commonwealths not permitting any part of their dominions to be dismembered, nor to be enjoyed by any but those of their community, the son cannot ordinarily enjoy the possession of his father, but under the same terms his father did, by becoming a member of the society; whereby he puts himself presently under the government he finds established, as much as any other subject of that commonwealth. And thus the consent of freemen, born under government, which, only, makes them members of it, being given separately in their turn, as each comes of age, and not in a multitude together; people taking no notice of it, and thinking it not done at all, or not necessary, conclude they are naturally subjects, as they are men.

And this mistake, it is evident Sir Matthew Hale has fallen into, when he tells us, that a lawful prince who hath the prior obligation of allegiance, can not lose that interest without his own consent, by his subjects resigning himself to the subjection of another; so that the natural born subject of one prince can not, by swearing allegiance to another prince, put off, or discharge himself from that natural allegiance; for this natural allegiance, says he, was intrinsic, and primitive, and antecedent to the other, and cannot be divested without the concurrent act of that prince to whom it was first due. And the authorities which he brings in support of this opinion clearly prove that he fell into mistake from the very reason assigned by Mr. Locke. For, in the next paragraph he tells us, that there were very many that had been antiently *ad fidem regis An-*

gliae et Franciae, especially before the loss of Normandy: such were the *comes marescallus* that usually lived in England, and *M. de Feynes, manens in Francia,* who were *ad fidem utriusque regis;* but they ordered their homages and fealties so, that they swore or professed allegiance, only to one, viz. [that king in whose dominions they respectively resided;] the homage they performed to the other, [in whose dominions they held lands, but did not reside therein,] being not purely *liege homage,* but rather feudal: and therefore when war happened between the two crowns, *remaneat personaliter quilibet eorum cum eo, cui fecerat ligeanteam; et faciat servitium debitum ei, cum quo non steterat in persona,* namely the service due from the feud, or fee he held: but this did not always satisfy the prince, *cum quo non steterat in persona,* but their possessions were usually seized, and rarely, or not without difficulty restored, without a capitulation to that purpose between the two crowns. And all the cases which he there cites in support of his opinion proceed upon the same ground; namely, the right which each prince exercised to seize the lands and possessions within his dominions, which belonged to the subjects of the other with whom he was at war. Which clearly proves that the right of confiscation thus mutually claimed and exercised, did not proceed upon the ground that the party whose lands were seized had broken his natural allegiance, or that which he might be supposed to owe to the prince in whose dominions he was born; but that feudal obligation, only, which every inferior tenant owed to his superior lord, (whether such a superior were a sovereign prince, or merely a private person) of whom he held his lands. Now this power which a prince might possess over the lands and possessions of a man who never resided within his dominions, can not be construed to give him any right over the person of such a man; neither on the other hand can that prince in whose territories he happens to be born claim any right to detain him therein, merely because he first saw the light there, as Mr. Locke has most clearly shewn; the most that he can do is to prohibit him from carrying his property with him; which if it be lands he can not, and if it be goods, he may not (if the laws of the state forbid) carry away without the consent of the government.

From the whole that we have seen, it appears, that the right of emigration is a right strictly natural; and that the restraints which may be imposed upon the exercise of it, are merely creatures of the *juris positivi,* or municipal laws of a state. And consequently that wherever the laws of any country do not prohibit, they permit emigration, or, as I rather chuse to call it, expatriation. Now I apprehend it is altogether immaterial to us in America, whether the laws of England, France or Spain, permit the subjects of those countries, respectively, to expatriate themselves, inasmuch as I have shewn, or at least endeavoured so to do, that the municipal law of no other country upon earth hath any force, or obligation over the citizens of the United States, as such; or over the citizens of any one state in the union, otherwise, or in any greater degree than the constitution or laws of such particular state may have adopted the same: and then it obtains a force and operation, so far, and so far only, as the act of adoption extends, and not on account of any intrinsic obligation which it might be sup-

posed to possess, or derive from any other source. And, although Virginia has adopted the common law of England, under certain restrictions, yet Virginia by a positive act of her legislature, so long since as the year 1783, declared it to be a natural right which all men have, to relinquish that society in which birth or accident may have thrown them, and seek subsistence and happiness elsewhere, and accordingly pointed out the mode in which any citizen might exercise it. The constitution of Vermont, and the first constitution of Pennsylvania contain similar declarations. Can it then be doubted that the citizens of those states, respectively, possess the right of exercising this natural privilege, whatever may be the laws of the other states in the union? If a doubt exists upon what principle it is founded? perhaps it will be answered, upon the power granted to congress by the constitution to establish an uniform rule of naturalization. I have given an answer to this, in a preceding tract. Perhaps; upon the faith of our treaties with France, England, and other European nations. But those treaties only stipulate for the conduct of the citizens of the United States, so long as they remain such; not, for their conduct after they shall have abandoned that character in the manner which the laws of the respective states permit.

If a person violates the treaties, and remains a citizen, the treaties stipulate that he shall be punished, or be abandoned by the U. States, as a pirate, and robber. But, if before he attaches himself to any other nation, he renounces his character of an American citizen, I cannot see that he is any longer amenable to the United States for his conduct; nor can they be considered as any longer responsible for a conduct which in ninety nine cases out of an hundred, they can by no possibility control, or punish; the parties having forever bidden adieu to their territory and jurisdiction.

. . . . .

Let us now compare the situation and rights of aliens in England with those in America. An alien in England remained the subject of that king or government under which he was born; he migrated to England for the temporary purposes of merchandise, and not of perpetual residence; because, as he continued to be the subject of a foreign power, he was always supposed to retain the *animum revertandi* to his *natural* sovereign; and, consequently, whenever a war broke out between his own nation and that of Great Britain, he was (however attached to the place of his residence, it's laws or government,) considered as an enemy, unless he could obtain a special letter of license from the crown to remain in England; he could not be made a denizen, but by the *special favour* of the crown; nor be naturalized, but by the *like favour* of the supreme legislature, (whose power extends even to an alteration of the constitution itself.) Both these acquisitions must be obtained as a matter of the highest grace and favour, and not of *right.* Yet, under all these circumstances, an *alien,* whose *nation* is in *amity* with England, is clearly and indisputably entitled to the full protection of the laws in every matter that respects his personal liberty, his personal security, and his personal property, as fully and completely as if he had been naturalized by act of parliament, or had acquired all the rights of an Englishman by his birth.

An alien in America, antecedent to the revolution, was entitled to *all* the rights and privileges of an alien in England, and *many more;* to *all* that an alien in England could claim, because, as has been remarked elsewhere, the *common law of England* and every statute of that country *made for the benefit of the subject,* before our ancestors migrated to this country, were, so far as the same were applicable to the nature of their situation, *and for their benefit, brought over hither by them;* and wherever they are not repealed, altered, or amended by the constitutional provisions, or legislative declaration, of the respective states, every beneficial statute and rule of the common law still remains in force. An alien in America was also entitled to *many more rights* than an alien in England. 1st, By the very act of migrating to, and settling in, America, he became *ipso facto* a *denizen,* under the express stipulations of the colonial charters, (all of which, it is believed, contained similar clauses) whereby it was stipulated for the better encouragement of all who would engage in the settlement of the colonies, that they, and every of them that should thereafter be inhabiting the same, should, and might, have all the privileges of free *denizens,* or persons native of England. 2d, By the same act of migrating he had a right to be *naturalized* under the sanction of a *pre-existing* law, made not only for the benefit, but for *the encouragement,* of *all* in a similar situation with himself. The operation of these laws was *immediate,* not *remote;* he became a denizen, as of right, *instantly;* he became naturalized upon payment of the legal fees for his letters of naturalization, and taking the usual oaths.

By the adoption of the constitution of the United States, the rights of aliens to become citizens was by no means intended to be taken away. . . . on the contrary, it is expressly provided, that congress shall have power to establish an *uniform rule of naturalization,* throughout the United States. The dissimilarity in the rules of naturalization, in the several states, was supposed to have laid the foundation for intricate and delicate questions, under that article of the confederation which declares, that the *free inhabitants* of each state, paupers, vagabonds, and fugitives from justice excepted, should be entitled to all privileges and immunities of free citizens in the several states; under which provision, it seems to have been apprehended, that the *free inhabitants* of one state, although *not citzens* thereof, might be entitled to all the privileges of *citizens* in every other: to obviate this and similar inconveniencies, this power of prescribing an uniform rule of naturalization was vested in the federal government. And here we may observe, that congress are authorised to prescribe the *mode* by which aliens may be naturalized, but it never was intended to authorise it to take away the *right.* For, among the acts of misrule alleged against our rejected sovereign, George the third, in the declaration of independence, it is asserted, "that he had endeavoured to prevent the population of these states; for that purpose obstructing the laws for naturalization of foreigners, and refusing to pass others to encourage their migration hither." Every alien coming into the United States, in time of peace, therefore acquired an *inchoate right,* under the constitution, to become a citizen; and when he has, in compliance with the laws,

made the requisite declarations of his intention to become a citizen, and to renounce for ever all allegiance and fidelity to any foreign prince, or state, and particularly that prince or state whereof he was last a citizen or subject, he seems to have acquired a *right,* of which no *subsequent* event can divest him, without violating the principles of political justice, as well as of moral obligation. For the government, in requiring this declaration of renunciation on the part of the alien, previous to his admission to the rights of citizenship, and that at a very considerable period before his right can, by the rule prescribed, be consummated, tacitly engages not to withdraw its protection from him; and much more, not to *betray him,* by sending him back to that sovereign, whose allegiance he had, in the most solemn manner, disclaimed, and whose subject and adherent he could no longer be considered to be, whatever political relations the two nations may thereafter stand in, with respect to each other. If this position be just with respect to those who might, under different circumstances, have been regarded as *alien enemies,* (as being *antecedently* subjects of a power with which the United States may *thereafter* be at war), how much more powerfully will the same reasoning apply in favour of those who can, under no possible view of the case, be considered in that light? And, in fact, nothing could more effectually *discourage* emigration, (no, not even a total incapacity ever to be naturalized,) than such an interpretation of our constitution and laws, as would lay a snare for every foreigner disposed to settle in this country; from whence, upon any personal pique or national quarrel, in which he had no part or share, he might be banished, and sent back to that very sovereign whom he must have offended by making the declarations prescribed by our laws.

Aliens, in the United States, are at present of two kinds. Aliens by birth; and aliens by election. . . . 1. Aliens by birth, are all persons born out of the dominions of the United States, since the fourth day of July, 1776, on which day they declared themselves an independent and sovereign nation, with some few exceptions, viz. 1. In favour of infants, "wheresoever born, whose father, if living, or otherwise, whose mother was a citizen at the time of the birth of such infants; or who migrated hither, their father, if living, or otherwise their mother becoming a citizen of the commonwealth; or who migrated hither without father, or mother," during the continuance of the act of May, 1779, c. 55, declaring who should be deemed citizens, which was repealed October, 1783, c. 16, of that session, so far as relates to the two latter cases; but continued as to the first. 2. Such persons as have obtained a right to citizenship under the existing laws of the state, whether infants, or otherwise. Edi. 1794, c. 110. 3. Such persons as have been naturalized under the act of 1 Cong. 2 Sess. c. 3. 4. Such persons as have, or may acquire the rights of citizenship pursuant to the act of 3 Cong. c. 85, and the children of such persons duly naturalized dwelling within the United States, and being under the age of twenty-one years, at the time of such naturalization; and the children of citizens of the United States, born out of the limits and jurisdiction of the United States. But the same act declares that the right of citizenship shall not descend to persons, whose fathers have never been resident in the United States. . . . All persons born before the fourth day of July, 1776, who were not natural born subjects of the crown of Great-Britain; nor were on that day residents within, or inhabitants of the United States; nor have since that time become citizens of the United States, or some one of them, are also aliens by birth.

2. Aliens by election are all such natural born, or naturalized subjects of the crown of Great-Britain, as were born, or naturalized before the fourth day of July, 1776, and have not since become actual citizens of the United States; or, having been actual citizens, have at any time thereafter during the revolutionary war, voluntarily joined the armies of Great-Britain, and borne arms against the United States, or any of them; or been owner or part owner of any privateer or other vessel of war; or a member of the refugee board of commissioners at New-York; or have acted under their authority; or have been for any other cause proscribed by any state in the union. See V. L. 1779, c. 14 and 55. Oct. 1779, c. 18. Oct. 1783, c. 16, 17. Edi. 1785. 1786, c. 10. 1794, c. 110. L. U. S. 1 Cong. 2 Sess. c. 3. 3 Cong. c. 85.

This distinction between aliens by birth, and those by election, is of importance. Aliens by birth are generally subject to all the incapacities to which aliens are subject by the rules of the common law. Aliens by election (although during the revolutionary war they were subject to many incapacities, and even penalties) are now upon a much more eligible footing; possessing rights, (partly derived from the rules of the common law, and partly from the provisions contained in the treaty of peace in 1783, and the treaty of London in 1794) to which aliens by birth can have no claim, except as they may be derived (under the treaty of 1794) by descent, devise, or purchase, from aliens by election.

Aliens by election may then be shortly described to be those subjects of the crown of Great-Britain on the fourth day of July, 1776, who have elected to remain such, and have not since become, and continued to be, citizens of the United States, or some one of them. These, by the common law, upon the separation of the two countries, were still capable of inheriting and holding lands in the United States, notwithstanding such separation; and on the other hand, the citizens of the United States born before the separation, had the like capacity to inherit, or hold lands in the British dominions. 7 Co. Calvin's case. But it is conceived that upon the death of these *antenati*, as they are called, their lands in both countries, would have been liable to escheat, if their heirs should be *postnati*, or born after the separation. But that is provided against by the treaty of London, 1794, Art. 9, whereby it is agreed, "that British subjects, who THEN held lands in the territories of the United States; and American citizens who *then* held lands in the British dominions, shall continue to hold them according to the nature and tenure of their respective estates, and titles, therein: and might grant, sell or devise the same to whom they please, in like manner as if they were natives; and that neither they, their heirs or assigns, shall, so far as may respect the said lands and the legal remedies incident thereto, be regarded as aliens."

16

GARDNER V. WARD, REPORTED IN KILHAM V. WARD

2 Mass. 236, 244n.a (1806)

This was an action of the case brought by *H. Gardner* against *B. Ward, jun. I. Hathorne, A. Richardson,* and *I. Buffington,* Selectmen of the town of *Salem,* for refusing to receive the plaintiff's vote for Representatives of the town, at a meeting held May 9th, A.D. 1803. At April term the following state of facts was agreed by the parties; and upon them the plaintiff's right to recover in this action was submitted to the court.

"The parties agreed that the plaintiff was born in *Salem* aforesaid, in the year of our Lord 1747, where he lived until May, 1775, following the business of a merchant, and then went with his family to *Newfoundland,* where he resided doing business as a merchant until August 1780, when with his family he went to *St. Eustatia,* and from thence to *St. Christophers,* where he purchased a vessel, in which he returned to *Salem,* in February, 1781. During his absence he left an attorney to transact his business in said *Salem;* and after his return, was owner of parts of several privateers, and engaged in privateering against British ships and vessels until the peace then next following. At the time he offered his vote, as supposed in the writ, his name stood on the list, prepared by the selectmen of *Salem,* as a legal voter in the choice of representatives.

It is further agreed that the proceedings in the probate office, copies of which are hereto annexed, relating to the person or estate of the said *H. Gardner,* are to be taken as part of the case: and that, during the said *Gardner's* residence in *Newfoundland,* he, at sundry times, lent money to American prisoners carried in there: and while at *St. Eustatia,* after its capture, Americans there lodged their effects with said *Gardner,* supposing them as safe as with any British subject, which he safely kept, and restored to the owners.

And if, on the above facts, the court shall be of the opinion that the plaintiff had a right to vote, then the defendants shall be defaulted, and the damages assessed by a jury; but if otherwise, then the plaintiff shall be nonsuit.

Theoph. Parsons for the plaintiff.

N. Dane for the defendants."

The proceedings in the probate office, referred to in the foregoing statement, were,

1st. A certificate from the committee of correspondence, &c. for the town of *Salem,* dated March 2d, 1779, stating that Mr. G. had absented himself from the town, and voluntarily gone to the enemy.

2d. An appointment by the judge of probate of *David Felt* as an agent for the estate of said G.

3d. A warrant of appraisement and a sworn inventory of the real and personal estate of Mr. G. returned by the agent.

This cause was argued at Salem, Nov. Term, 1804, by *Parsons* and *Putman* for the plaintiff, and the attorney general, *Sullivan* and *Dane* for the defendants, and at this term the following opinions were delivered by the judges present.

SEWALL, J. [After a concise recital of the facts, and observing that some circumstances of Mr. G's conduct while abroad, had been introduced by the parties in their statement, which having no very apparent tendency upon the question finally submitted to the court, he should not advert to them, proceeded.]

The question is, generally whether *H. Gardner,* when his vote was rejected by the defendants, had the rights of a legal voter in the town of *Salem,* and a capacity to vote in the election of a representative? And this question, as explained in the argument we have heard upon it, depends altogether upon this enquiry, whether *H. Gardner* was at that time a citizen of the United States, or an alien.

For the defendants it has been argued, 1st. that the plaintiff was, according to the facts stated, an alien by birth, and never has acquired any qualification of citizenship within the U. S.—or 2dly. If by his birth he had that qualification, and might have retained it, yet by his absence in the manner represented, during a part of the revolutionary war, he incurred the disabilities of alienage consequent thereupon, or as the forfeiture and penalty annexed to the offence of absence, in the manner now charged upon him.

For the plaintiff it has been contended that, by his birth and residence, at the commencement of the revolution, and at the treaty of peace, he was a citizen of the U. S. and had never incurred the disabilities or forfeitures supposed by the defendants.

In pursuing this enquiry, it is important to determine, what were the rights of Mr. G., or in what state he must be considered in law, whether as a citizen or an alien, taking the question as not affected by any conduct of Mr. G. nor by any legislative act, appointing certain consequences to the conduct, with which he is now charged:

In determining this question, we are to be governed altogether by the principles of the common law: "and from whatever source these may have been derived, and in whatever form expressed, the substantial part of them is founded in reason and in the nature of government."

I take it then to be established, with a few exceptions not requiring our present notice, that a man, born within the jurisdiction of the common law, is a citizen of the country wherein he is born. By this circumstance of his birth, he is subjected to the duty of allegiance, which is claimed and enforced by the sovereign of his native land; and becomes reciprocally entitled to the protection of that sovereign and to the other rights and advantages, which are included in the term citizenship. The place of birth is coextensive with the dominions of the sovereignty, entitled to the duty of allegiance: and it has been held, that in the event of a partition of these dominions, under distinct sovereignties, the natives remain attached and retain their rights of citizenship, with each portion of the sovereignty; upon this principle, that the right of citizenship in the native soil, and according to the condition of the government

at the time of birth is a natural right, not affected by the after changes in the sovereignty. These doctrines are to be found in the decisions upon *Calvin's* case reported by *Lord Coke.*

To apply these doctrines in the case before us, according to the political revolution in the sovereignty of Mr. G's native land: By his birth he had the rights of citizenship in every part of the dominions of the crown of Great Britain; and especially, in the event of a separation in that portion of them which immediately includes the domicil of his birth. The change of sovereignty there did not, by the course of the common law, divest him of the natural rights of a citizen in his native land. If he has lost or forfeited these rights, it must be by the laws and decrees of the sovereign, to whom he became more immediately a subject, or of whom, in the event of the revolution, he must claim his supposed rights.

This case, in my apprehension of it, must therefore be considered as depending altogether upon the statutes of the government of this state, and perhaps, in some degree, upon those compacts, in which this government is a party, made with the former sovereigns of this country.

The statute of Treason was first cited for the defendants: particularly the description of persons owing allegiance to this state. These are declared to be 1st. All persons abiding within this state, and deriving protection from the laws of the same. 2nd. Persons passing through or having a temporary residence therein, during the time of their residence.

It is remarkable, that in this description, persons born within the territory of the state, those who by the common law owe perpetual fealty and allegiance, are not specified, or are not distinguished from mere residents, and that of *these,* it is not only declared that "they owe allegiance," but also that "they are members of the state."

To give this statute any useful construction, it must be understood to speak, not only of those, who, at the moment when it was enacted, were abiding within the state; but of all who then had, or at any subsequent period should have their abode therein: all these persons are declared to be "members of this state," without any distinction of natives. Upon the ground of this statute it might be argued, contrary to the intention of those who cited it, that Mr. G., wherever his place of birth had been, if, during the complete operation of this statute, he had his abiding place within this state, became thereby a member of the state; that is, acquired a citizenship. For I know of no rule to be employed in distinguishing *members* of this state from *citizens.* This operation of the statute, to confer the rights of citizenship, must be limited to the period preceding the establishment of the constitution of government of the U. S. But in that period Mr. G. according to the state of facts, had his settled abode in his native place within this state, having returned thither in 1781, and there since continued to reside.

It has been argued, however, that whatever, by the common law, had been the privilege of a native, and it may now be said, whatever character any person, entirely a foreigner, might have acquired by the operation of the statute of Treason; yet Mr. G. by the operation of other statutes passed during the revolutionary war, was under a specific disqualification and disability, as a banished, proscribed, or excluded person. And this seems to be the ground ultimately relied upon by the defendants.

Several statutes, supposed to have this effect, have been cited and commented upon at the bar, viz.

1st. "An act to prevent the waste, destruction, and embezzlement of the goods or estates of such persons, who have left the same, and fled to our enemies for protection; and also for payment of their just debts out of their estates."

This act determines nothing, as to the condition or exclusion of the absentees; but only provides for an inventory of their effects, the appointment of an agent to preserve them from embezzlement, &c.

2d. "An act prescribing and establishing an oath of fidelity and allegiance."

This act is equally inconclusive respecting the present question; unless it should be agreed, that the disqualification, and incapacity of becoming a citizen are to be inferred from the power, of excluding certain absentees or persons who have left this state, from the oath of allegiance.

3d. "An act to prevent the return to this state of certain persons therein named and others, who have left this state or either of the United States, and joined the enemies thereof."

This act seems alike inapplicable to the case before us, unless perpetual alienage and incapacity may be inferred from the power of apprehending and transporting certain persons therein named, or having the character therein described. It is not pretended that Mr. G. was included by name in this last act, and whether by description, in this or the act last before cited, might be a question. But I forbear entering upon it, from this consideration. It does not appear in the state of facts, that Mr. G. was ever excluded from the oath of allegiance, according to the provision of the one, or was ever apprehended or transported, pursuant to the provisions of the other, of these two acts. The penalties thereby enacted, whatever may be their extent, have not therefore, attached upon him. It is further observable that this act of 1778 was repealed by the act of March 24, 1784, herein after noticed.

The defendants have appeared to rely more confidently upon the act passed in 1779, entitled, "An act to confiscate the estates of certain persons commonly called absentees." By this act, "every inhabitant of the late province, then state of *Massachusetts*, who had levied war, or conspired to levy war, &c. or who since April 19th, 1775, had withdrawn without the permission of the legislative or executive authority of one of the United States, from any of the said provinces or colonies, into parts or places under the acknowledged authority and dominion of the king of Great Britain, and who had not returned into some one of the United States, been received as a subject thereof, and, if required, taken an oath of allegiance to the United States, shall be deemed to have renounced all allegiance and to have become an alien."

It has been very earnestly and ingeniously argued for the plaintiff, that upon the facts stated, he is not to be considered as a person, who had committed either of the offences described in this act; that his absence from the United States, commencing in May, 1775, was for temporary purposes only; that this construction of it is determined by the circumstances stated, of vessels and other property left by him at *Salem*, of his conduct while abroad, and his return during the continuance of the war; that *Newfoundland*, the place to which Mr. G. first resorted, after he left *Salem*, though "beyond seas, and under the acknowledged dominion of *Great Britain*," was not in a state of hostility with the United States, when Mr. G. arrived there in 1775, but was one of the places excepted by Congress, at the commencement of the revolutionary war.

After a full consideration of the subject, I am not satisfied that this view of the case before us is correct; but I am inclined to the opinion, that Mr. G's absence, in the manner stated in this case, might have been construed a criminal withdrawing of himself, within the intent of the statute under consideration, subjecting him to the penalties thereby enacted, if, at his return within the United States, no other facts, than those now disclosed could have been offered to explain or justify his conduct. *Newfoundland* if not hostile when Mr. G. arrived there, became, at an early period afterwards, a place in open and declared hostility with the United States, and was a place of that description, while Mr. G. continued his residence there, without any effort, which now appears, for a removal therefrom. And he remained there in 1779 when this act passed. But in the application of it, now attempted, another question arises: whether a judgment of alienage, or for the purpose of inflicting the penalties prescribed by this statute, may be now rendered, in this incidental, and, (as to the trial of these facts and their consequences) extrajudicial manner.

This statute, severely penal, and (respecting the facts thereby declared criminal) altogether retrospective, provided a mode of proof to ascertain and convict the persons liable, and who had incurred the forfeitures and disabilities enacted against the offences therein described. The statute required that a complaint should be exhibited "against any person who had offended in the manner therein described, setting forth clearly and plainly the offence such person is charged with," &c.—that notice thereof should be given, and that any person might appear to defend in behalf of the party accused, that a trial should be had, "in the known and ordinary course of the law," and that judgment should be rendered upon the verdict of a jury finding the forfeiture, or, according to the provisions of a subsequent and additional act, upon a default or failure of any person to appear, after notice of the complaint in the manner therein directed.

At the return of Mr. G. to *Salem* in February, 1781, no information had been filed against him, and no judgment, to the purpose or effect of the statute now under consideration, has ever been rendered against him. In the present action then, upon any state of facts, not including the record of a conviction of *Henry Gardner*, can this court adjudge him to have incurred the disability contended for by the defendants, and essential to their defence? In this view of the question, I apprehend that courts of law can admit no other evidence of offences than regular convictions.

The reasonableness of this maxim is an authority for it; but I shall cite *Lord Coke's 2 Inst.* 468. "It is to be understood in acts of parliament, where there be degrees of punishment to be inflicted upon the first, second and third offences, &c. there must be several convictions, that is to say judgments given upon legal proceeding for every several offence; for it appeareth to be no offence, until judgment, by proceeding of law, be given against him."

Upon the application of this statute to the case of Mr. G. it may be further observed, that the penalties of alienage and forfeiture are to be inflicted, not upon a person who had merely withdrawn himself; but to constitute the whole offence, it was requisite by the statute, that he should not have returned, and been received within some one of the United States. The statute has not limited the time of the return and reception, which might do away the crime of withdrawing. I therefore construe it to intend a return and reception before the time of the accusation, or the time to which in its nature it must relate. Upon this construction of the statute, the case of Mr. G. in any view of it, is not within the statute. For, before the accusation, first offered in defence of this action, or any time to which it can relate, that is before the close of the revolutionary war, Mr. G. had returned to *Salem,* his native place, and been there received. I infer his reception from the notoriety of his return and residence there, according to the facts stated, and from the consideration that the statutes for expelling and transporting obnoxious absentees, were then in full force and operation. The forbearance, in this respect, used on that occasion, affords a violent presumption, and is with me satisfactory evidence, that he had upon his return, a favorable reception. Hard indeed must be the case of a man, who, at his return within the country, had been forgiven, or had been able to explain and justify his absence, to be at this day, after a lapse of twenty years, exposed to the severities of this act, because perhaps the proofs of his defence, then satisfactory and tacitly allowed, are no longer in being.

The defendants cited lastly the act of 1784, entitled "An act for repealing two laws of this state, and for asserting the right of this free and sovereign commonwealth, to expel such aliens as may be dangerous to the peace and good order of government." This act passed after the return and reception of Mr. G. within the United States: after he had a settled abode at *Salem* within this state: after he had become a party on the American side in the war against *Great-Britain:* and, I may add, according to my construction of the act against treason, after he had become *a member of the state,* unless excluded by the operation of the statutes already considered. Without recurring therefore to the objection drawn from the constitution of this state, then in operation, which annuls every *ex post facto* law, it is sufficient to say, that this case of Mr. G. could not be within the intentions of the legislature in their act of 1784.

Upon the whole, understanding that, by the common law, a man owes allegiance to the sovereignty of the country wherein he was born, that he has a natural right, which the common law recognizes and preserves, to protection and citizenship from the actual sovereignty of his native country, under every revolution of it, until deprived by an express attainder, or until he shall have incurred a forfeiture of these privileges, upon a regular conviction and judgment of some offence liable thereto; that, in the case of Mr. G. it appears that he is a native of this state, and had his settled abode therein, during a part of the revolutionary war, and at the close of it by the definitive treaty with *Great-Britain;* and that he has never been attainted or convicted of any offence incurring the penalty of alienage, as a disability or exclusion; I conclude him to have been a citizen of this state, at the time his vote was refused by the defendants, and that this action, upon the statement of facts before us, is maintained, in vindication of the plaintiff's rights and capacity as a legal voter within the town of *Salem.*

It may be apprehended that, by the principles of the common law, cited on the subject of alienage, a mutual citizenship of all persons born before the separation of the two countries then under a common sovereign, continues to this day: and that, upon the construction and limited effect, which I have given to the absentee act, as it is called, all who were native inhabitants of this state, but who departed therefrom at the commencement of the revolutionary war, and have remained within the British dominions, are now citizens of the United States. Objections of some importance must be supposed to arise from these inconveniences, in a political view of the subject. But I think that, by recurring to the definitive treaty between the United States and Great Britain, at the close of the war, the apprehension I have suggested may be entirely removed. The definitive treaty established, in a legal sense, the distinct sovereignty of the United States, and their separation from the other dominions of the king of *Great-Britain.* His Britannic majesty thereby acknowledged the United States, formerly the British colonies, to be free, sovereign and independent, and relinquished all claims to the government, and proprietory and territorial rights of the same; and the peace, thereby established, was declared to be between the citizens of the one and the subjects of the other. This relinquishment on the part of *Great-Britain,* and the acceptance of it on the part of the people of the United States, determined their respective claims of allegiance and citizenship. By this compact and event, those natives of the British dominions, who were then settled within, and under the protection of the United States, not being excluded or disqualified, nominally or judicially, by the effect of any special statute or regulation within any state became citizens of the United States, and aliens to their former sovereign; while those, who continued settled within the territories of their former sovereign, and under his protection, adhering to their former allegiance, are, by the same compact, aliens from the new sovereignty recognized by the treaty.

It may not be impertinent however, in this discussion, to observe further, that the right of citizenship throughout the dominions of the native sovereign, which I have supposed to be a principle of the common law, is restored, in a limited degree, by the treaty of *London,* to British subjects and American citizens, who in respect to the titles and tenures of certain real estate, and the legal remedies incident thereto, are not to be regarded as aliens under either sovereignty; a regulation important to the welfare of individuals, in the event of a divided sovereignty, and dictated by the principles of natural justice.

SEDGWICK, J. As this cause has been considered at great length, it has become unnecessary, and perhaps might be deemed improper in me to attend to it, in all the minute particulars. During the able argument which we have heard, I was strongly impressed with an opinion, that the decision must essentially depend on a just construction of the act of the 30th of April, 1779, and the treaty of peace made between the United States and Great Britain in 1783;—and this impression has been strengthened by farther reflection.

The act of April 30th, 1779, was passed before the adoption of the constitution, by a legislature possessing undefined powers, wholly unlimited and unrestrained, so far at least as respected the objects of that law. It is *"an act for confiscating the estates of certain persons commonly called absentees."* The great and leading object of the act is the confiscation of *those estates;* but it also determines, as was necessary, who are those absentees; and how they are to be considered in relation to the state, that is as *aliens.* The preamble asserts the right of every government to command the personal service of all its members, whenever the exigencies of the state shall require it; especially in times of impending or actual invasion; that no member can withdraw himself from the jurisdiction of the government, without justly incurring the forfeiture of all his property, rights and liberties holden under and derived from that constitution of government, to the support of which he hath refused to afford his aid and assistance. It then goes on to state the aggressions of the British government and the resistance of the United States, in which it was the indispensable duty of all to unite; and that nevertheless divers of the members of this, and of the other United States, regardless of their duty towards their country, did withdraw themselves from this and other of the *United States* into parts and places under the acknowledged authority and dominion of the king of *Great Britain;* after this preamble the first section enacts "that every inhabitant and member of the late province, now state of Massachusetts, or any other of the late provinces or colonies, now *United States of America,* who since the 19th of April, A. D. 1775, hath done the acts therein specified, and among them, withdrawn, without the permission of the legislature, or executive authority of this or some other of the said *United States* from any of the said provinces, colonies, or United States, *into parts and places under the acknowledged authority and dominion of the said king of Great Britain,* and who hath not returned into some one of the said United States, and been received as a subject, and, if required, taken an oath of allegiance, shall be held, taken, deemed and adjudged to have freely renounced all civil and political relation to each and every of the said *United States, and be considered as an alien."* The facts agreed bring the plaintiff expressly within this section of the act. He was an inhabitant and member of the late province, then state of *Massachusetts:* for he was born at *Salem* and resided there until the time that he withdrew himself. That was *after the* 19*th day of April,* 1775, viz. in May in the same year. He

then withdrew himself to *Newfoundland, a place under the acknowledged authority of the king of Great Britain:* at the time of the passing of the act, he *had not returned into any of the United States and been received as a subject thereof.* The consequence is irresistible that the facts bring this case within the act, and if they had been ascertained by a judgment, in the manner which the act provided, he must have been subjected to the consequences and *considered as an alien.* This act of 1779 was confirmed, if it was in the power of the legislature to confirm it, by the act passed on the 24th of March, 1784, for repealing two acts of 1778, on the subject of the *absentees* and for asserting the rights of the state to expel such aliens as may be dangerous to the peace and good order of government. This is most manifest from an attention to the preamble and the 2d and 3d sections. As then the facts, which are agreed, bring the plaintiff's case clearly within the act of 1779, it is important, in my opinion, to determine whether by the treaty of peace between the *United States* and *Great-Britain,* he is relieved from the consequences, which might have attached upon him, from the facts which are agreed—that is, *to be considered thereby as an alien.*

The case of the *United States* in their separation from *Great-Britain,* is altogether so singular in its nature; and its effects on the rights, duties and relations of those connected with it, so unprecedented, that very little, if any, light can be thrown upon it by recurrence to authorities. The inhabitants of the provinces, previous to the 4th of July, 1776, were the subjects of the king of *Great-Britain;* and the provinces themselves in some sense at least the colonies of *Great-Britain*—for it was conceded that the mother country possessed power of regulating their commerce. In consequence of various acts of *Great-Britain,* as well legislative as executive, which were by the colonies deemed grievous and oppressive, a war took place which was commenced on the 19th day of April, 1775. As to the justice of this war, various opinions were holden both in *Great-Britain* and *America.* No adjustment having been made, and the applications for that purpose on behalf of the colonies having been rejected; Congress, on the 4th of July, 1776, declared them Independent States, and this declaration having been approved and ratified by them respectively, it has ever since been holden in this country that from that time we were of right, as well as in fact, independent states, and entitled to exercise all the rights of sovereignty. In consequence of this claim the states respectively assumed and exercised the rights of sovereignty, and among other things entered with each other into *"articles of confederation and perpetual union"*—whereby they gave to their representatives in Congress various powers, and among others those of peace, of war and of treaties. Such powers would be of little avail; they could not answer the purposes for which they were intended, unless they were paramount to and controuled the laws of the individual states. By virtue of these powers, Congress, on the 30th of November, 1782, through the medium of their plenipotentiaries, entered into certain provisional articles of peace with *Great-Britain,* which were of the same tenor as the articles of the definitive treaty, which was concluded on the 3d day of September, 1783. Both these treaties have been duly ratified by the governments of the two countries respectively. It has already been said that treaties to effect the purposes for which they are designed, must control all the laws of the states, which are opposed to their stipulations. This is evident from the nature of the thing: but the constitution of the *United States* has not left the establishment of this principle to construction, having expressly provided "that all treaties made or which shall be made under the authority of the United States, shall be the supreme law of the land; and the judges in every state shall be bound thereby, any thing in the constitution or laws of any state to the contrary notwithstanding;" so that if there be any opposition between the treaty and the law, the former must prevail, and the latter, so far as that opposition exists, is repealed. And it cannot be necessary to prove that if the original act of 1779 is repealed, the confirmatory one of 1784 is wholly inoperative. A war existing between two countries united under one sovereign, a mother country and its colonies, they having assumed the character of independent states, is terminated by a peace. The treaty is between the king of the mother country and the states, and between the subjects of the one and the citizens of the other. The plaintiff is a party to this treaty, his rights and interests are involved in it, either as a subject of the king of Great Britain or as a citizen of the United States. Soon after the commencement of hostilities, the next month, being settled as a merchant at *Salem*, the place of his nativity, he removed with his family to *Newfoundland*, from one British colony to another. He did not however abandon all connection with *Salem*; he left there an attorney to transact his business. At *Newfoundland* he did the business of a merchant. It is not stated, nor even pretended that he performed a single act of hostility, and we ought not to presume, without evidence, so harsh a thing, as that he warred against his native country; and especially as disfranchisement is contended for as the consequence of his conduct. *De non apparentibus et non existentibus eadem est ratio.* It is of the highest importance for the security of the rights of individuals to respect this maxim.—What then are we to conclude from the facts agreed between the parties? That the plaintiff during his absence from his native place, was innocent in all things, excepting only that he deprived his country of his personal services during the time of his absence. The case does not stop here. In August, 1780, he left *Newfoundland* and went to the *West-Indies*, and in February 1781, one year and nine months before the provisional articles of peace were executed, and two years and seven months before the definitive treaty was concluded, he returned to *Salem*. And on his return, he entered actively into the war on the part of his country. He was the owner of several parts of privateers, and engaged in privateering against the enemy, and this line of conduct he continued until the peace. He left the country *animo revertendi*, with an intention to return; this is evinced by his having an attorney to transact his business at *Salem*, by his conduct while absent, by his returning during the war, and by his engaging actively in it, on his return—in his absence he is perfectly innocent of every thing active against the United States. He returned and immediately joined his country in *active hostility* against

the enemy. He was received in his native town without reproach and without question. He was there domiciled at the time of the treaty, and there has ever since remained. And shall it now be said that he was not then a citizen, an inhabitant? That he was not of that party with which he was, but of that with which he was not, acting. The treaty on the part of *Great-Britain* stipulates "for and with the people," the "inhabitants," the "citizens" of the *United States*. By these several names are they called in the treaty. And it does seem to me that the facts disclosed show that he was at the time of the treaty one of the people, a citizen of the *United States*, and an inhabitant of *Salem*, there having his domicil. There is nothing which shews he was then a subject of *Great-Britain*. He was then, as has been said, either a subject of the British king, or an American citizen: from the facts, as before observed, it is most clear that he must have been one or the other: and if from the part he was acting, and the business he was *then* engaged in, the place of his domicil and the manner in which he *there* employed himself, he could not be considered as a British subject, he was of course a citizen of the *United States*. Suppose then that the plaintiff's going to *Newfoundland* was an offence for which he might have suffered but for the treaty: yet having previous to the treaty, reunited himself to, and taken part with his countrymen, and it being impossible to consider him at that time, as one with, and for whom the *United States* were contracting as a British subject, he is entitled as a *citizen of the United States* to the benefit of that stipulation in the treaty, *that he should suffer no future loss or damage either in his person, liberty or property, for the part which he took in the war,* and yet the defendants, in their defence, insist that he shall suffer a loss for the part which he did take in the war, the most mortifying and degrading to a generous mind, that of disfranchisement.

Besides the liberal stipulation for the indemnity of all, who had taken a part on either side, to do justice, must be perfectly reciprocal and mutual—that is, wherever it is an indemnity to an American citizen, in any given circumstances, it must be an indemnity also to a British subject. It has already been observed that we, the *United States*, claimed a right to independence from the time we declared it, on the 4th of July 1776. On the other hand, *Great Britain* claimed a supremacy until they gave us independence by the treaty. Till then, she holds that we were her colonies, and that then, and by her act, we became sovereign and independent.—As it respects a vast variety of subjects which might, but which were unnecessary to be mentioned, the American construction is undoubtedly correct, but as respects the construction immediately under consideration, it would I think be extremely erroneous. As to the separation of people into two distinct and independent communities, I think the settled situation and circumstances of individuals at the time of the treaty, ought to determine their relation, and the party to which in future they are to belong. During the war there was a great shifting and fluctuation of opinion and conduct. Men chose sides and changed them, as a sense of interest or a feeling of conscience dictated. Nicely to discriminate and to retribute, as individuals might happen to be within the power of the respective divisions of country, would have been unwise, mischievous and cruel. It was infinitely more liberal to cast the mantle of oblivion over the past, and to *settle men,* as they by their last opinions and conduct had *settled themselves,* and to give them their own choice as to their future connection, as they were then declaring it by their own conduct. This spirit of conciliation, which, on the return of the blessings of peace, ought to prevail, dictated the terms of the treaty. A contrary decision could produce no good, and it could hardly fail of producing great mischief. Suppose we continue to maintain the treaty of peace, and notwithstanding that any person who withdrew himself and voluntarily went to a place under the acknowledged dominion of the king of *Great-Britain,* after the commencement of hostilities, whatever his future conduct might have been and although he might for years have been actively employed against the enemy, and at the time of the peace was engaged in our armies, had by his delinquency, without any prosecution, trial or judgment, *ipso facto,* become and must continue an alien. What would in this case become of reciprocity? *Great-Britain,* until the peace, considered all who were in arms, as equally rebels. She must therefore consider the character of subject or citizen as determined by their situation, circumstances and the part they were acting at *that time.* Take another case—suppose we go back to the declaration of Independence to determine citizenship. A man leaves his country after that declaration, as was the case with many. He joins the British army, and continues to serve in it to the close of the war. Is he an American citizen? If so, and a future war should happen between the *United States* and *Great-Britain,* and the man should be taken, he must be considered as a traitor and punishable for rebellion. Here again there could be no reciprocity, for the principles adopted by the *British* government would not permit her to retaliate in a case similarly circumstanced in relation to itself.

I am, on the whole, clearly of opinion that judgment must be given for the plaintiff.

17

CUSTIS V. LANE
3 Munf. 579 (Va. 1813)

(See 1.8.17, no. 15)

18

UNITED STATES V. GILLIES
25 Fed. Cas. 1321, no. 15,206 (C.C.D.Pa. 1815)

WASHINGTON, Circuit Justice. The court having disposed of the first error assigned in this record, I shall proceed to consider the only remaining question which has been discussed; this is, whether from the facts stated in the special verdict, John Shaw, master of the ship William P. Johnson,

has forfeited his citizenship? If he has, then the judgment below must be reversed, and entered in favour of the United States; otherwise it is to be affirmed.

It appears by the finding of the jury, that Shaw is a citizen of the United States, by birth, and resided therein up to the year 1804, with the exception of two years; that he was abroad from the year 1804, to the present year; whether in England or on the Continent, or whether he was navigating the ocean, is not stated. It is found that he is married, and now has a family in London; but whether he married in England, or in the United States, or whether his family is residing in England, or is there merely on a visit, is not stated. Upon such a case as this, it requires more ingenuity than I possess, to frame an argument to prove, that Shaw has not [sic] forfeited his privileges of a citizen of the United States. It would be like attempting to prove a self-evident proposition. But taking for granted, that the case appeared to be such as the district attorney supposed it to be, and argued upon; that is, that Shaw resided in England from the year 1804, to the year 1815, with his family, having married in that country; I am yet to learn, that an American citizen forfeits that character, or the privileges attached to it, by residing and marrying in a foreign country; though, during a part of the time, war should intervene, between that and his native country, he taking no part therein; unless such character or privileges should be impaired, by some law of his own country. I do not mean to moot the question of expatriation, founded on the self will of a citizen, because it is entirely beside the case before the court. It may suffice for the present to say, that I must be more enlightened upon this subject than I have yet been, before I can admit, that a citizen of the United States can throw off his allegiance to his country, without some law authorising him to do so. It is true, that a man may obtain a foreign domicil, which will impress upon him a national character for commercial purposes, and may expose his property, found upon the ocean, to all the consequences of his new character; in like manner, as if he were, in fact, a subject of the government under which he resides. But he does not, on this account, lose his original character, or cease to be a subject or citizen of the country where he was born, and to which his perpetual allegiance is due. The present case presents no question connected with the subject of domicil, but turns, altogether, upon the construction of a law relative to the navigation system of the United States.

The question, which the case I am supposing suggests is, does an American bottom, lose her privileges as such, on account of the master residing with his family in a foreign country, he being by birth a citizen of the United States? Let the act of congress made upon this subject, answer the question. It declares, that registered vessels of the United States, shall not continue to enjoy the benefits and privileges bestowed upon such vessels, longer than they shall continue to be wholly owned and to be commanded, by a citizen of the United States. The second section of the law, however, declares, that such registered vessel shall cease to enjoy the benefits thereof, if owned in whole or in part, by a citizen of the United States, who usually resides in a foreign country, during the continuance of such residence; unless under certain exceptions. But in respect to the master, no such qualification is to be found in this law, or in any part of our navigation system. Had this latter provision not have been made, in relation to the owner, I cannot perceive upon what principle, the court could have supplied it by construction; but being made by the legislature, it marks the intention of that body, to distinguish between the foreign residence of the owner, and that of the master; and it further proves the sense of congress, as to residence abroad, that it does not, without legislative provision, affect the character or privileges of a citizen.

There is a sound reason for the distinction which the legislature seems to have had in view. The profits of trade, necessarily incorporate themselves with the wealth of the nation where the trade is carried on; and these profits are increased, as the duties upon the trade are diminished. The policy therefore, which dictates discriminating duties, to favour our own merchants, would point out the necessity of applying the system, as well to citizens of the United States, settled abroad, as to other merchants; but the same policy is not applicable to the master of the vessel. If the owner of the vessel which he employs, resides within the United States, it is immaterial where the master resides. It is only necessary, that he should be a citizen of the United States. Judgment affirmed.

19

THE SANTISSIMA TRINIDAD
7 Wheat. 283 (1822)

MR. JUSTICE STORY: What, then, are the consequences which the law attaches to such conduct, so far as they respect the property now under adjudication? It is argued on the part of the libellant, that it presents a *casus foederis*, under our treaty with Spain. The 6th and 14th articles are relied upon for this purpose. The former is, in our judgment, exclusively applicable to the protection and defence of Spanish ships, within our territorial jurisdiction, and provides for the restitution of them, when they have been captured within that jurisdiction. The latter article provides, that no subject of Spain "shall apply for, or take any commission or letter of marque, for arming any ship or ships to act as privateers," against the United States, or their citizens, or their property, from any prince or state with which the United States shall be at war; and that no citizen of the United States "shall apply for, or take any commission or letters of marque, for arming any ship or ships, to act as privateers" against the king of Spain, or his subjects, or their property, from any prince or state with which the said king shall be at war. "And if any person of either nation shall take such commission or letter of marque, he shall be punished as a pirate." In the Spanish counterpart of the treaty, the word "privateers" in the first clause has the corresponding word "*corsarios*;" but in the second clause, no such word is to be found. But it is ob-

vious, that both clauses were intended to receive, and ought to receive, the same construction; and the very terms of the article confine the prohibition to commissions, &c., to privateers. It is not for this court to make the construction of the treaty broader than the apparent intent and purport of the language. There may have existed, and probably did exist, reasons of public policy which forbade an extension of the prohibition to public ships of war. It might well be deemed a breach of good faith in a nation, to enlist in its own service an acknowledged foreigner, and at the same time, subject him by that very act, and its own stipulations, to the penalty of piracy. But it is sufficient for the court, that the language of the treaty does not include the case of a public ship, and we do not perceive that the apparent intention or spirit of any of its provisions, justifies such an interpolation. The question, then, under the Spanish treaty, may be dismissed without further commentary.

This view of the question renders it unnecessary to consider another, which has been discussed at the bar, respecting what is denominated the right of expatriation. It is admitted by Captain Chaytor, in the most explicit manner, that during this whole period, his wife and family have continued to reside at Baltimore; and so far as this fact goes, it contradicts the supposition of any real change of his own domicil. Assuming, for the purposes of argument, that an American citizen may, independently of any legislative act to this effect, throw off his own allegiance to his native country, as to which we give no opinion, it is perfectly clear, that this cannot be done without a *bona fide* change of domicil, under circumstances of good faith. It can never be asserted, as a cover for fraud, nor as a justification for the commission of a crime against the country, or for a violation of its laws, when this appears to be the intention of the act. It is unnecessary to go into a further examination of this doctrine; and it will be sufficient to ascertain its precise nature and limits, when it shall become the leading point of a judgment of the court.

20

CASE OF PHIPPS, REPORTED IN CUMMINGTON v. SPRINGFIELD
2 Pick. 394, 394n. (Mass. 1824)

The opinion alluded to, which was written by the Chief Justice and concurred in by *Putnam* and *Wilde*, Justices, was as follows.

Considering that the same question may arise in controversies respecting property between private litigating parties, we have entertained doubts of the propriety of giving an opinion without the aid of argument by counsel, who might present views to us of importance in the consideration of the subject; but understanding that the public business is embarrassed by the pendency of many applications before the committee on accounts, which depend upon a solution of this question, we have deemed it our duty to yield to the request of the honorable Senate, with the understanding, that if hereafter the rights of suitors shall require a revision of the subject, we shall feel obliged to grant them a hearing, and that the opinion now given will not be binding, if it shall be made to appear that it is incorrect.

The facts stated for our consideration, are, that *George Phipps*, now a pauper, was born in England, and came to this country as a soldier in the British army, under the command of General Burgoyne, that he deserted to the Americans, and has ever since resided in the town of C., within this commonwealth, that he has acquired and held real estate within that town, and has paid taxes therefor, and also for his poll and personal estate. The question presented is, whether by virtue of the treaty of peace in 1783, he is a citizen of the United States, or is still an alien.

We suppose if he were not a citizen before the treaty, he did not become such by the mere force of that instrument. The treaty operated as a relinquishment on the part of Great Britain, of the allegiance claimed by that government from all who had before been the subjects of it, and had by force of the laws of any one of the United States become its citizens or subjects. But it could not confer the rights of citizens upon any who had not before enjoyed them. Thus in the cases of *Gardner* v. *Ward* and *Kilham* v. *Ward,* reported in the second volume of Massachusetts Reports, it was decided that persons born in Massachusetts before the revolution, who had withdrawn to a British Province during the war, and had returned before the ratification of the treaty of peace, retained their citizenship, notwithstanding their absence while hostilities continued; while the same persons, had they remained in the British province until after the treaty, would have been British subjects, because they had chosen to continue their former allegiance, there being but one allegiance before the revolution, and that being to the sovereign of Great Britain. It was considered that Massachusetts had rightfully assumed the rank of a sovereign and independent state, and that she lawfully succeeded to the right of self-government, the sovereignty being in the people as a body politic. All, therefore, who were born within her limits, and who had not been expatriated voluntarily, or by compulsion, had a right to claim the protection of her laws, and owed allegiance to her as their sovereign; but a British subject not born within Massachusetts, would not have become a citizen, from the mere fact that he was here on the ratification of the treaty of peace.

But there are other facts from which, connected with the treaty, citizenship may be deduced in favor of persons born without the territory of Massachusetts.

After the declaration of independence, by Congress, in 1776, each one of the then colonies, parties thereto, became separate and independent states, or sovereignties, with the perfect right of enacting their own laws, and of declaring the terms and principles upon which the duty of allegiance and the right of protection should depend.

Among the earliest exercises of sovereign power by Massachusetts, was that by which the character of a citizen was ascertained, and his duties in relation to the State were prescribed.

The statute of treason, as it is called, was passed in the year 1777, [2 *Mass. Laws,* (edit. 1801,) 1046,] and it enacts, "that all persons, abiding within the State, and deriving protection from the laws of the same, owe allegiance to this State, and are members thereof." It is not required by this statute, that persons thus constituted members of the State, should be born within its territory, it being undoubtedly intended to comprehend within the political family, all persons of whatever country, who should be voluntarily dwelling within the State, making it their home.

If the statute was prospective, and we think it clearly was, it being the policy of the times to invite into the State those who might be able to contribute in their persons and property to maintain its liberty and independence, then the case of the pauper who has given rise to the question, is clearly within its provisions.

The case of prisoners of war would not be embraced by the statute, because their residence was constrained, and indicated no affection towards the country, or its cause. But one who deserted from the army, and voluntarily took up his residence in one of our towns, demeaning himself as a subject and citizen, is such a one as the State chose to adopt as a member, and to whom it offered protection in exchange for allegiance.

The subject of the present inquiry must have left the British army very soon after the passing of the statute before cited, and may be presumed to have accepted the invitation contained in it, to become a member of the State.

He has practically enjoyed all the privileges, and submitted to all the duties of a citizen, for forty-five years. He was with us at the adoption of the constitution of the State, and of the United States, and also when the treaty of peace between the United States and Great Britain was ratified. Probably his citizenship has never been called in question until he became a pauper.

We therefore are of opinion that George Phipps, who is mentioned in the order of the Senate to which this is an answer, is a citizen of Massachusetts, and of the United States.

21

JAMES KENT, *Commentaries* 1:397–98; 2:33–63
1826, 1827

By the constitution of the United States, congress have power to establish an uniform rule of naturalization. It was held, in the Circuit Court of the United States at Philadelphia, in 1792, in *Collet* v. *Collet*, that the state governments still enjoyed a concurrent authority with the United States upon the subject of naturalization, and that though they could not contravene the rule established by congress, or "exclude those citizens who had been made such by that rule, yet that they might adopt citizens upon easier terms than those which congress may deem it expedient to impose." But though this decision was made by two of the judges of the Supreme Court, with the concurrence of the district judge of Pennsylvania, it is obvious, that this opinion was hastily and inconsiderately declared. If the construction given to the constitution in this case was the true one, the provision would be, in a great degree, useless, and the policy of it defeated. The very purpose of the power was exclusive. It was to deprive the states individually of the power of naturalizing aliens according to their own will and pleasure, and thereby giving them the rights and privileges of citizens in every other state. If each state can naturalize upon one year's residence, when the act of congress requires five, of what use is the act of congress, and how does it become an uniform rule?

This decision of the Circuit Court may be considered, as in effect, overruled. In the same Circuit Court, in 1797, Judge Iredell intimated, that if the question had not previously occurred, he should be disposed to think, that the power of naturalization operated exclusively, as soon as it was exercised by congress. And in the Circuit Court of Pennsylvania in 1814, it was the opinion of Judge Washington, that the power to naturalize was exclusively vested in congress. Afterwards, in *Chirac* v. *Chirac*, the chief justice of the United States observed, that it certainly ought not to be controverted, that the power of naturalization was vested exclusively in congress. In *Houston* v. *Moore*, Judge Story mentioned the power in congress to establish an uniform rule of naturalization, as one which was exclusive, on the ground of there being a direct repugnancy or incompatibility in the exercise of it by the states. The weight of authority, as well as of reason, may, therefore, be considered as clearly in favour of this latter construction.

. . . . .

We are next to consider the rights and duties of citizens in their domestic relations, as distinguished from the absolute rights of individuals, of which we have already treated. Most of these relations are derived from the law of nature, and they are familiar to the institutions of every country, and consist of husband and wife, parent and child, guardian and ward, and master and servant. To these may be added, an examination of certain artificial persons created by law, under the well known name of corporations. There is a still more general division of the inhabitants of every country, under the comprehensive title of aliens and natives, and to the consideration of them our attention will be directed in the present lecture.

(1.) Natives are all persons born within the jurisdiction of the United States. If they were resident citizens at the time of the declaration of independence, though born elsewhere, and deliberately yielded to it an express or implied sanction, they became parties to it, and are to be considered as natives; their social tie being coeval with the existence of the nation. If a person was born here before our independence, and before that period voluntarily withdrew into other parts of the British dominions, and never returned; yet, it has been held, that his allegiance accrued to the state in which he was born, as the lawful successor of the king; and that he was to be considered a subject by birth. It was admitted, that this claim of the state to the allegiance of all persons born within its territories prior to our revolution, might subject those persons who adhere to

their former sovereign, to great inconveniences in time of war, when two opposing sovereigns might claim their allegiance; and, under the peculiar circumstances of the case, it was, undoubtedly, a very strong application of the common law doctrine of natural and perpetual allegiance by birth. The inference to be drawn from the discussions in the case of *M'Ilvaine* v. *Coxe*, would seem to be in favour of the more reasonable doctrine, that no *antenatus* ever owed any allegiance to the United States, or to any individual state, provided he withdrew himself from this country before the establishment of our independent government, and settled under the king's allegiance in another part of his dominions, and never afterwards, prior to the treaty of peace, returned and settled here. The United States did not exist as an independent government until 1776; and it may well be doubted whether the doctrine of allegiance by birth be applicable to the case of persons who did not reside here when the revolution took place, and did not, therefore, either by election or tacit assent, become members of the newly created state. The ground of the decision in the latter case was, that the party in question was not only born in New-Jersey, but remained there as an inhabitant until the 4th of October, 1776, when the legislature of that state asserted the right of sovereignty, and the claim of allegiance over all persons then abiding within its jurisdiction. By remaining there after the declaration of independence, and after that statute, the party had determined his right of election to withdraw, and had, by his presumed consent, become a member of the new government, and was, consequently, entitled to protection, and bound to allegiance. The doctrine in the case of *Respublica* v. *Chapman*, goes also to deny the claim of allegiance, in the case of a person who, though born here, were not here and assenting to our new governments, when they were first instituted. The language of that case was, that allegiance could only attach upon those persons who were then inhabitants. When an old government is dissolved, and a new one formed, "all the writers agree," said Ch. J. M'Kean, "that none are subjects of the adopted government who have not freely assented to it." The same principle was declared by the Supreme Court of this state, in *Jackson* v. *White*, and it was held, that though a British subject resided here as a freeholder on the 4th of July, 1776, and on the 16th of July, 1776, when the convention of this state asserted the right of sovereignty, and the claim of allegiance over all persons, was *abiding* here; yet that, under the circumstances, the person in question being a British officer, and a few weeks thereafter placed on his parole, and in December, 1776, joining the British forces, was to be deemed an alien, and as having never changed his allegiance, or elected to become a party to our new government. The doctrine in the case of *Ainslie* v. *Martin*, was contrary also to what had been held by the same court in the cases of *Gardner* v. *Ward*, and *Kilham* v. *Ward*, where it was decided, that persons born in Massachusetts before the revolution, who had withdrawn to a British province before our independence, and returned during the war, retained their citizenship; while the same persons, had they remained in the British province until after the treaty of peace, would have been British subjects, because they had chosen to continue their former allegiance, and there was but one allegiance before the revolution. This principle was asserted by the same court in the case of *Phipps*, and I consider it to be the true and sound law on the subject.

It is the doctrine of the English law, that natural born subjects owe an allegiance, which is intrinsic and perpetual, and which cannot be devested by any act of their own. In the case of *Macdonald*, who was tried for high treason, in 1746, before Lord Ch. J. Lee, and who, though born in England, had been educated in France, and spent his riper years there, his counsel spoke against the doctrine of natural allegiance as slavish, and repugnant to the principles of their revolution. The Court, however, said, it had never been doubted, that a subject born, taking a commission from a foreign prince, and committing high treason, was liable to be punished as a subject for that treason. They held, that it was not in the power of any private subject to shake off his allegiance, and transfer it to a foreign prince; nor was it in the power of any foreign prince, by naturalizing or employing a subject of Great Britain, to dissolve the bond of allegiance between that subject and the crown. Entering into foreign service, without the consent of the sovereign, or refusing to leave such service when required by proclamation, is held to be a misdemeanor at common law.

It has been a question, frequently and gravely argued, both by theoretical writers, and in forensic discussions, whether the English doctrine of perpetual allegiance applies in its full extent to this country. The writers on public law have spoken rather loosely, but generally in favour of the right of a subject to emigrate, and abandon his native country, unless there be some positive restraint by law, or he is at the time in possession of a public trust, or unless his country be in distress, or in war, and stands in need of his assistance. Cicero regarded it as one of the firmest foundations of Roman liberty, that the Roman citizen had the privilege to stay or renounce his residence in the state, at pleasure. The principle which has been declared in some of our state constitutions, that the citizens have a natural and inherent right to emigrate, goes far towards a renunciation of the doctrine of the English common law, as being repugnant to the natural liberty of mankind, provided we are to consider emigration and expatriation, as words intended in those cases to be of synonymous import. But the allegiance of our citizens is due, not only to the local government under which they reside, but primarily to the government of the United States; and the doctrine of final and absolute expatriation requires to be defined with precision, and to be subjected to certain established limitations, before it can be admitted into our jurisprudence, as a safe and practicable principle, or laid down broadly as a wise and salutary rule of national policy. The question has been frequently discussed in the courts of the United States, but it remains still to be definitively settled by judicial decision.

A review of those discussions cannot be uninstructive.

In the case of *Talbot* v. *Janson*, the subject was brought before the Supreme Court of the United States, in 1795. It was contended on one side, that the abstract right of individuals to withdraw from the society of which they were members, was antecedent and superior to the law of society, and recognized by the best writers on public law, and by the usage of nations: that the law of allegiance was derived from the feudal system, by which men were chained to the soil on which they were born, and converted from free citizens, to be the vassals of a lord or superior; that this country was colonized and settled upon the doctrine of the right of emigration; that the right was incontestible, if exercised in due conformity with the moral and social obligations; that the power assumed by the government of the United States of naturalizing aliens, by an oath of allegiance to this country, after a temporary residence virtually implies that our citizens may become subjects of a foreign power by the same means.

The counsel on the other side conceded, that birth gave no property in the man, and that upon the principles of the American government, he might leave his country when he pleased, provided it was done *bona fide*, and with good cause, and under the regulations prescribed by law; and that he actually took up his residence in another country, under an open and avowed declaration of his intention to settle there. This was required by the most authoritative writers on the law of nations; and Heineccius, in particular, required that the emigrant should depart with the design to expatriate, and actually join himself to another state; that though all this be done, it only proved that a man might be entitled to the right of citizenship in two countries, and proving that he had been received by one country, did not prove that his own country had surrendered him; that the locomotive right finally depended upon the consent of the government; and the power of regulating emigration, was an incident to the power of regulating naturalization, and was vested exclusively in Congress; and until they had prescribed the mode and terms, the character and the allegiance of the citizen continued.

The judges of the Supreme Court felt and discovered much embarrassment in the consideration of this delicate and difficult question, and they gave no definitive opinion upon it. One of them observed, that admitting the intention of expatriation had been legally declared, it was necessary that it should have been carried into effect, and that the party should have actually become a subject of the foreign government; that the cause of removal must be lawful, otherwise the emigrant acts contrary to his duty; that though the legislature of a particular state should, by law, specify the lawful causes of expatriation, and prescribe the manner in which it might be effected, the emigration could only affect the local allegiance of the party, and not draw after it a renunciation of the higher allegiance due to the United States; and that an act of Congress was requisite to remove doubts, and furnish a rule of civil conduct on this very interesting subject of expatriation. Another of the judges admitted the right of individual emigration, to be recognised by most of the nations of the world, and that it was a right to be exercised in subordination to the public interest and safety, and ought to be under the regulation of law; that it ought not to be exercised according to a man's will and pleasure, without any restraint; that every man is entitled to claim rights and protection in society, and he is, in his turn, under a solemn obligation to discharge his duty; and no man ought to be permitted to abandon society, and leave his social and political obligations unperformed. Though a person may become naturalized abroad, yet if he has not been legally discharged of his allegiance at home, it will remain, notwithstanding the party may have placed himself in difficulty, by double and conflicting claims of allegiance.

The majority of the Supreme Court gave no opinion upon the question; but the inference, from the discussion, would seem to be, that a citizen could not devest himself of his allegiance, except under the sanction of a law of the United States; and that until some legislative regulations on the subject were prescribed, the rule of the common law must prevail.

In 1797, the same question was brought before the Circuit Court of the United States for the district of Connecticut, in the case of *Isaac Williams,* and Ch. J. Elsworth ruled, that the common law of this country remained as it was before the revolution. The compact between the community and its members was, that the community should protect its members, and that the members should at all times be obedient to the laws of the community, and faithful to its defence. No member could dissolve the compact without the consent or default of the community, and there had been no consent or default on the part of the United States. No visionary writer carried the principle to the extent, that a citizen might, at any, and at all times, renounce his own, and join himself to a foreign country; and no inference of consent could be drawn from the act of the government in the naturalization of foreigners, as we did not inquire into the previous relations of the party, and if he embarrassed himself by contracting contradictory obligations, it was his own folly, or his fault.

The same subject was again brought before the Supreme Court in the case of *Murray* v. *The Charming Betsey,* in the year 1804. It was insisted, upon the argument, that the right of expatriation did exist, and was admitted by all the writers upon general law, but that its exercise must be accompanied by three circumstances, viz. fitness in point of time, fairness of intent, and publicity of the act. The court, however, in giving their opinion, avoided any decision of this great and litigated point, by observing, that "whether a person born within the United States, or becoming a citizen according to the established laws of the country, can devest himself absolutely of that character, otherwise than in such manner as may be prescribed by law, is a question which it was not necessary to decide" Afterwards, in the Circuit Court of the United States, at Philadelphia, Judge Washington observed, that he did not then mean to meet the question, of expatriation, founded on the self-will of a citizen, because it was beside the case before the court; but that he could not admit, that a citizen of the United States could throw off his allegiance to his country without some law authorizing him to do so. This was the doctrine declared also by the Chief Justice of Massachusetts. The question arose again before the Supreme Court of the United States, so late as February, 1822, in the case of *The Santissima Trinidada,* and it was suffered to

remain in the same state of uncertainty. The counsel on the one side insisted, that the party had ceased to be a citizen of the United States, and had expatriated himself, and become a citizen of Buenos Ayres, by the only means in his power, an actual residence in that country, with a declaration of his intention to that effect. The counsel on the other side admitted, that men may remove from their own country in order to better their condition, but it must be done for good cause, and without any fraudulent intent; and that the slavish principle of perpetual allegiance growing out of the feudal system, and the fanciful idea that a man was authorized to change his country and his allegiance at his own will and pleasure, were equally removed from the truth. Mr. Justice Story, in delivering the opinion of the court, waived the decision of the question, by observing, that the court gave no opinion whether a citizen, independent of any legislative act to that effect, could throw off his own allegiance to his native country; that it was perfectly clear it could not be done without a *bona fide* change of domicil, under circumstances of good faith; and that it would be sufficient to ascertain the precise nature and limits of this doctrine of expatriation, when it should become a leading point for the judgment of the court.

From this historical review of the principal discussions in the federal courts on this interesting subject in American jurisprudence, the better opinion would seem to be, that a citizen cannot renounce his allegiance to the United States without the permission of government, to be declared by law; and that, as there is no existing legislative regulation on the case, the rule of the English common law remains unaltered.

There is, however, some relaxation of the old and stern rule of the common law, required and admitted under the liberal influence of commerce. Though a natural born subject cannot throw off his allegiance, and is always amenable for criminal acts against his native country, yet for commercial purposes he may acquire the rights of a citizen of another country, and the place of domicil determines the character of a party as to trade. Thus, in the case of *Scott* v. *Schwartz,* it was decided, in the Exchequer, the 13 Geo. II., that a residence in Russia gave the mariners of a Russian ship the character of Russian mariners, within the meaning of the British navigation act. And in the case of *Wilson* v. *Marryat,* it was decided by the Court of K. B., that a natural born British subject might acquire the character, and be entitled to the privileges of an American citizen for commercial purposes. So, an American citizen may obtain a foreign domicil, which will impress upon him a national character for commercial purposes, in like manner as if he were a subject of the government under which he resided; and yet without losing on that account his original character, or ceasing to be bound by the allegiance due to the country of his birth. The subject who emigrates *bona fide,* and procures a foreign naturalization, may entangle himself in difficulties, and in a conflict of duties, as Lord Hale observed; but it is only in very few cases that the municipial laws would affect him. If there should be war between his parent state and the one to which he has attached himself, he must not arm himself against the parent state; and if he be recalled by his native government, he must return, or incur the pain and penalties of a contempt. Under these disabilities, all the civilized nations of Europe adopt (each according to its own laws) the natural born subjects of other countries.

The French law, as well since as before their revolution, will not allow a natural born subject of France to bear arms, in time of war, in the service of a foreign power, against France; and yet, subject to that limitation, every Frenchman is free to abdicate his country.

(2.) An alien is a person born out of the jurisdiction of the United States. There are some exceptions, however, to this rule, by the ancient English law, as in the case of the children of public ministers abroad, (provided their wives be English women,) for they owe not even a local allegiance to any foreign power. So, also, it is said, that in every case, the children born abroad, of English parents, were capable, at common law, of inheriting as natives, if the father went and continued abroad in the character of an Englishman, and with the approbation of the sovereign. The statute of 25 Edw. III. stat 2, appears to have been made to remove doubts as to the certainty of the common law on this subject, and it declared, that children thereafter born without the ligeance of the king, whose father and mother, at the time of their birth, were natives, should be entitled to the privileges of native subjects, except the children of mothers who should pass the sea without leave of their husbands. The statute of 7 Ann, c. 5. was to the same general effect; but the statute of 4 Geo. II. c. 31. required only that the father should be a natural born subject at the birth of the child, and it applied to all children then born, or thereafter to be born. Under these statutes it has been held, that to entitle a child born abroad to the rights of an English natural born subject, the father must be an English subject; and if the father be an alien, the child cannot inherit to the mother, though she was born under the king's allegiance.

The act of Congress of the 14th of April, 1802, establishing a uniform rule of naturalization, affects the issue of two classes of persons: (1.) By the 4th section, it was declared, that "the children of persons duly naturalized under any of the laws of the United States, or who, previous to the passing of any law on that subject by the government of the United States, may have become citizens of any one of the states, under the laws thereof, being under the age of twenty-one years, at the time of their parents being so naturalized, or admitted to the rights of citizenship, shall, if dwelling in the United States, be considered as citizens of the United States." This provision appears to apply only to the children of persons naturalized, or specially admitted to citizenship; and there is colour for the construction, that it may have been intended to be prospective, and to apply as well to the case of persons *thereafter* to be naturalized, as to those who had previously been naturalized. It applies to all the children of "persons duly naturalized," under the restriction of residence and minority, at the time of the naturalization of the parent. The act applies to the children *of persons* duly naturalized, but does not explicitly state, whether it was intended to apply only to the case where both the parents were duly natural-

ized, or whether it would be sufficient for one of them only to be naturalized, in order to confer, as of course, the right of citizens upon the resident children, being under age. Perhaps it would be sufficient for the father only to be naturalized; for in the supplementary act of the 26th of March, 1804, it was declared, that if any alien, who should have complied with the preliminary steps made requisite by the act of 1802, dies before he is actually naturalized, his *widow* and *children* shall be considered as citizens. This provision shows, that the naturalization of the *father*, was to have the efficient force of conferring the right on his children; and it is worthy of notice, that this last act speaks of *children* at large, without any allusion to residence or minority; and yet, as the two acts are intimately connected, and make but one system, the last act is to be construed with reference to the prior one, according to the doctrine of the case *Ex parte Overington*. (2.) By a subsequent part of the same section, it is declared, that "the children of persons, who now are, or have been, citizens of the United States, shall, though born out of the limits and jurisdiction of the United States, be considered as citizens of the United States: provided that the right of citizenship shall not descend to persons, whose fathers have never resided within the United States." This clause is certainly not prospective in its operation, whatever may be the just construction of the one preceding it. It applied only to the children of persons who *then were*, or *had been* citizens; and consequently the benefit of this provision narrows rapidly by the lapse of time, and the period will soon arrive, when there will be no statute regulation for the benefit of children born abroad, of American parents, and they will be obliged to resort for aid to the dormant and doubtful principles of the English common law. This provision leaves us likewise in doubt, whether the act intended by the words, "children of persons," both the father and mother, in imitation of the statute of 25 Edw. III.; or the father only, according to the more liberal declaration of the statute of 4 Geo. II. This clause differs from the preceding one, in being without any restriction as to the age or residence of the child; and it appears to have been intended for the case of the children of natural born citizens, or of citizens who were original actors in our revolution, and therefore it was more comprehensive and more liberal in their favour. But the whole statute provision is remarkably loose and vague in its terms, and it is lamentably defective in being confined to the case of children of parents who were citizens in 1802, or had been so previously. The former act of 29th January, 1795, was not so; for it declared generally, that "the children of citizens of the United States, born out of the limits and jurisdiction of the United States, shall be considered as citizens of the United States." And when we consider the universal propensity to travel, the liberal intercourse between nations, the extent of commercial enterprise, and the genius and spirit of our municipal institutions, it is quite surprising that the rights of the children of American citizens, born abroad, should, by the existing act of 1802, be left so precarious, and so far inferior in the security which has been given, under like circumstances, by the English statutes.

We proceed next to consider the disabilities, rights and duties of aliens.

An alien cannot acquire a title to real property by descent, or created by other mere operation of law. The law *quae nihil frustra,* never casts the freehold upon an alien heir who cannot keep it. This is a well settled rule of the common law. It is understood to be the general rule, that even a natural born subject cannot take by representation from an alien, because the alien has no inheritable blood through which a title can be deduced. If an alien purchases land, or if land be devised to him, the general rule is, that in these cases, he may take and hold, until an inquest of office has been had; but upon his death, the land would instantly, and of necessity, (as the freehold cannot be kept in abeyance,) without any inquest of office, escheat and vest in the state, because he is incompetent to transmit by hereditary descent. If an alien, according to a case put by Lord Coke, arrives in England, and hath two sons born there, they are of course natural born subjects; and if one of them purchases land, and dies without issue, his brother cannot inherit as his heir, because he must deduce his title by descent, through his father, who had no inheritable blood. But the case, as put by Coke, has been denied to be the law by the majority of the court in *Collingwood* v. *Pace,* and it was there held, that the sons of an alien could inherit to each other, and derive title through the alien father. The elaborate opinion of Lord Ch. B. Hale, was distinguished by his usual learning, though it was rendered somewhat perplexing and obscure by the subtlety of his distinctions, and the very artificial texture of his argument. It is still admitted, however, that a grandson cannot inherit to his grandfather, though both were natural born subjects, provided the intermediate son was an alien, for the grandson must, in that case, represent his father, and he had no inheritable blood to be represented; and the reason why the one brother may inherit from the other, is, that *as to them* the descent is immediate, and they do not take by representation from the father. The law according to Lord Hale, respects only the mediate relation of the brothers as brothers, and not in respect of their father, though it be true that the foundation of their consanguinity is in the father; and it does not look upon the father as such a medium or *nexus* between the brothers, as that his disability should hinder the descent between them. This distinction in the law, which would admit one brother to succeed as heir to the other, though their father be an alien, and yet not admit a son to inherit from his grandfather because his father was an alien, is very subtle. The reason of it is not readily perceived, for the line of succession, and the degrees of consanguinity, must equally, in both cases, be traced through the father. The statute of 11 and 12 Wm. III. c. 6. was made on purpose to cure the disability, and brush away these distinctions, by "enabling natural born subjects to inherit the estate of their ancestors, either lineal or collateral, notwithstanding their father, or mother, or other ancestor, by, from, through, or under whom they might make or derive their title, were aliens." This statute, however, did not go so far as to enable a person to deduce title as heir, from a remote ancestor, through an alien ancestor still living.

The provisions in the statute of Wm. III. is in force in Maryland, as was admitted in the case last referred to, and also in Kentucky; and it was adjudged, in the case of *Palmer* v. *Downer,* to have been adopted, and to be in force in Massachusetts. But it has not been adopted in this state; and, therefore, with us, as well as in those other states where there are no statute regulations on the subject, the rule of law will depend upon the authority of Lord Coke, or the justness and accuracy of the distinctions taken in the greatly contested case of *Collingwood* v. *Page,* and which, according to Sir William Blackstone, was, upon the whole, reasonably decided. The enlarged policy of the present day would naturally incline us to a benignant interpretation of the law of descents, in favour of natural born citizens who were obliged to deduce a title to land from a pure and legitimate source, through an alien ancestor; and Sir Matthew Hale admitted, that the law was very gentle in the construction of the disability of alienism, and rather contracted than extended its severity. If a citizen dies, and his next heir be an alien who cannot take, the inheritance descends to the next of kin who is competent to take, in like manner as if no such alien has ever existed.

The distinctions between the *antenati* and the *postnati,* in reference to our revolution, have been frequently the subject of judicial discussion since the establishment of our independence.

It was declared, in *Calvin's case,* that, "albeit the kingdoms of England and Scotland should, by descent, be divided and governed by several kings; yet all those who were born under one natural obedience, while the realms were united, would remain natural born subjects, and not become aliens by such a matter *ex post facto.* The *postnatus* in such a case would be *ad fidem utriusque regis.*" It was accordingly held, in that case, that the *postnati* of Scotland, born after the union of the two crowns, could inherit lands in England. The community of allegiance, at the time of birth, and at the time of descent, both existed. The principle of the common law contained in that case, that the division of an empire worked no forfeiture of previously vested rights of property, has been frequently acknowledged in our American tribunals, and it rests on solid foundations of justice. The titles of British subjects to lands in the United States, acquired prior to our revolution, remained, therefore, unimpaired. But persons born in England, or elsewhere out of the United States, before the 4th of July, 1776, and who continued to reside out of the United States after that event, have been held to be aliens, and incapable of taking lands subsequently by descent. The right to inherit depends upon the existing state of allegiance at the time of the descent cast; and an English subject, born and always resident abroad, never owed allegiance to a government which did not exist at his birth, and he never became a party to our social compact. The British *antenati* were, consequently, held to be incapable of taking, by subsequent descent, lands in these states, which are governed by the common law. This doctrine was very liberally considered in respect to the period of the American war, in the case of *Den* v. *Brown;* and it was there held, that the British *antenati* were not subject to the disabilities of aliens, as to the acquisition of lands *bona fide* acquired between the date of our independence and that of the treaty of peace in 1783, for the contest for our independence was then pending by an appeal to arms, and remained undecided. But the position was not tenable; and in a case elaborately discussed, and greatly litigated on several grounds, in the Court of Appeals, in Virginia, and afterwards in the Supreme Court of the United States, it was the acknowledged doctrine, that the British *antenati* could not acquire, either by descent or devise, any other than a defeasible title to lands in Virginia, between the date of our independence and that of the treaty of peace in 1783. The line of distinction between aliens and citizens was considered to be coeval with our existence as an independent nation.

It has been very frequently assumed, on the doctrine in *Calvin's case,* that the same principle might not be considered to apply in England, in respect to the American *antenati,* and that they would, on removing within the British dominions, continue to take and inherit lands in England, as natural born subjects; but I apprehend, the assumption has been made without just grounds. It was contrary to the doctrine laid down by Professor Wooddeson, in his lectures, published as early as 1792: and the late case in the King's Bench, of *Doe* v. *Acklam,* seems entirely to explode it. It was decided, that children born in the United States, since the recognition of our independence by Great Britain, of parents born here before that time, and continuing to reside here afterwards, were aliens, and could not inherit lands in England. To entitle a child born out of the allegiance of the crown of England, to be deemed a natural born subject, the father must be a subject at the time of the birth of the child, and the people of the United States ceased to be subjects in the view of the English law, after the recognition of our independence, on the 3d day of September, 1783. If the American *antenati* ceased to be subjects in 1783, they must, of course, have lost their subsequent capacity to take as subjects. The English rule is, to take the date of the treaty of peace in 1783, as the era at which we ceased to be subjects; but our rule is, to refer back to the date of our independence. In the application of that rule, the cases show some difference of opinion. In this state, it has been held, that where an English subject, born abroad, emigrated to the United States, in 1779, and lived and died here, he was to be deemed an alien, and the title to land, which he afterwards acquired by purchase, was protected, not because he was a citizen, but on the ground of the treaty of 1794. In Massachusetts, on the strength of an act passed in 1777, persons born abroad, and coming into that state after 1776, and before 1783, and remaining there voluntarily, were adjudged to be citizens. The Supreme Court, in Connecticut has adopted the same rule, without the aid of any statute, and it was held, that a British soldier, who came over with the British army in 1775, and deserted, and came and settled in Connecticut in 1778, and remained there afterwards, became, of course, a citizen, and ceased to be an alien; and that the United States were enabled to claim as their citizens, all persons who were here voluntarily, at either the period of our independence, or of the treaty of peace. The principle of the case seemed to be, that the treaty of peace operated by way of release from their allegiance of all British subjects who were then domiciled here; for it was admitted, that the rule would not apply to the subjects of any other nation or kingdom, who came to reside here after the declaration of independence, for they would not be within the purview of the treaty. The same principle seems to have been recognised by the chief justice of Massachusetts, in *Ainslie* v. *Martin;* but it may be considered as very much disturbed by the opinion of the judges of the Supreme Court of Massachusetts, in the case of *Phipps,* a pauper, in which they declare, that if a person was not a citizen before the treaty of peace, he did not become such by the mere force of that instrument, and by the mere fact of his being there on the ratification of the treaty. If he was born in Massachusetts, and had returned during the war, though he had withdrawn himself before the date of independence, he was considered as retaining his citizenship. That was the amount of the cases of *Gardner* v. *Ward,* and *Kilham* v. *Ward,* to which the judges referred; and this is the final exposition which has been given to the law on the subject.

Though an alien may purchase land, or take it by devise, yet he is exposed to the danger of being devested of the fee, and of having his lands forfeited to the state, upon an inquest of office found; and if he dies before any such proceeding be had, we have seen that the inheritance cannot descend, but escheats of course. If the alien should undertake to sell to a citizen, yet the prerogative right of forfeiture is not barred by the alienation, and it must be taken to be subject to the right of the government to seize the land. His conveyance is good as against himself, and he may, by a fine, bar persons in reversion and remainder, but the title is still voidable by the sovereign. In Virginia, this prerogative right of seizing lands *bona fide* sold by an alien to a citizen, is abolished by statute; and so it was, to a limited degree, in this state, by an act in 1826. An alien may take a lease for years of a house, for the benefit of trade. According to Lord Coke, none but an alien merchant can lease land at all, and he is restricted to a house, and if he dies before the termination of the lease, the remainder of the term is forfeited to the king, for the law gave him the privilege for habitation only, as necessary to trade, and not for the benefit of his representatives. The force of this rigorous doctrine of the common law is undoubtedly suspended with us, in respect to the subjects of those nations with whom we have commercial treaties; and it is now justly doubted, whether the common law be really so inhospitable, for it is inconsistent with the established maxims of sound policy, and the social intercourse of nations. Foreigners are admitted to the rights of citizenship with us on liberal terms, and as the law requires five, and only five years residence, to entitle them *and their families* to the benefits of naturalization, it would seem to imply a right, in the mean time, to the necessary use of real property; and if it were otherwise, the means would be interdicted which are requisite to render the five years residence secure and comfortable.

Aliens are under the like disabilities as to uses and trusts arising out of real estates. An alien can be seized to the use of another, but the use cannot be executed as against the state, and will be defeated on office found. Nor can an alien be a *cestui que trust* but under the like disability, and the sovereign may, in chancery, compel the execution of the trust.

Aliens are capable of acquiring, holding, and transmitting moveable property, in like manner, as our own citizens, and they can bring suits for the recovery and protection of that property. They may even take a mortgage upon real estate by way of security for a debt, and this I apprehend they may do without any statute permission, for it has been the English law from the early ages. It was so held lately in the Supreme Court of the United States, and that the alien creditor was entitled to come into a court of equity to have the mortgage foreclosed, and the lands sold for the payment of his debt. The question whether the alien in such a case could become a valid purchaser of the mortgaged premises sold at auction at his instance, is left untouched; and as such a privilege is not necessary for his security, and would be in contravention of the general policy of the common law, the better opinion would seem to be, that he could not, in that way, without special provision by statute, become the permanent and absolute owner of the fee.

Even alien enemies, resident in the country, may sue and be sued as in time of peace, for protection to their persons and property is due, and implied from the permission to them to remain, without being ordered out of the country by the President of the United States. The lawful residence does, *pro hac vice*, relieve the alien from the character of an enemy, and entitles his person and property to protection. The effect of war upon the rights of aliens we need not here discuss, as it has been already considered in a former part of this course of lectures, when treating of the law of nations.

During the residence of aliens amongst us, they owe a local allegiance, and are equally bound with natives to obey all general laws for the maintenance of peace, and the preservation of order, and which do not relate specially to our own citizens. This is a principle of justice and of public safety universally adopted; and if they are guilty of any illegal act, or involved in disputes with our citizens, or with each other, they are amenable to the ordinary tribunals of the country. They and their sons are liable to be enrolled in the militia of this state, provided they are seised of any real estate within this state. This is a reasonable duty required of them in consideration of the special benefit which is conferred. It is in the nature of a charge upon their property, and the personal service can be omitted under the penalty of a moderate pecuniary assessment.

If aliens come here, with an intention to make this country their permanent residence, they will have many inducements to become citizens, since they are unable as aliens, to have a stable freehold interest in land, or to hold any civil office, or vote at elections, or take any active share in the administration of the government. There is a convenient and easy mode provided, by which the disabilities of alienism may be removed, and the qualifications of natural born citizens obtained. The terms upon which any alien, being a free white person, can be naturalized, are prescribed by the acts of Congress of the 14th of April,

1802, ch. 28.; the 3d of March, 1813, ch. 184.; and 22d of March, 1816, ch. 32. It is required, that he declare, on oath, before a state court, being a court of record with a seal and clerk, and having common law jurisdiction, or before a circuit or district court of the United States, three years, at least, before his admission, his intention to become a citizen, and to renounce his allegiance to his own sovereign. At the time of his admission, his country must be at peace with the United States, and he must, before one of these courts, take an oath to support the constitution of the United States, and likewise, on oath, renounce and abjure his native allegiance. He must, at the time of his admission, satisfy the court, that he has resided five years, at least, within the United States, and one year, at least, within the state where the court is held; and if he shall have arrived after the peace of 1815, his residence must have been continued for five years next preceding his admission, without being at any time during the five years out of the territory of the United States. The evidence of the time of his arrival within the United States, is to consist of the registry of his arrival made upon his report, or the report of his parent or guardian, before a court of the United States; and the certificate of that report and registry, and of his declared intention to become a citizen, must be produced to the court admitting him; and he must satisfy the court, that during that time, he has behaved as a man of good moral character, attached to the principles of the constitution of the United States, and well disposed to the good order and happiness of the same. He must, at the same time, renounce any title, or order of nobility, if any he hath. The act further provides, that the children of persons duly naturalized, being minors at that time, shall, if dwelling in the United States, be deemed citizens. It is further provided, that if any alien shall die after his report and declaration, and before actual admission as a citizen, his widow and children shall be deemed citizens.

A person thus duly naturalized, becomes entitled to all the privileges and immunities of natural born subjects, except that a residence of seven years is requisite to enable him to hold a seat in congress, and no person, except a natural born citizen, is eligible to the office of governor of this state, or president of the United States.

The laws of Congress on the subject of naturalization, have been subject to great variations. In 1790, only two years' previous residence was required. In 1795, the period was enlarged to five years; and in 1798, to 14 years; and in 1802, it was reduced back to five years, where it still remains. This period of probation has probably been deemed as liberal as was consistent with a due regard to our peace and safety. A moderate previous residence becomes material, to enable aliens to acquire the knowledge and habits proper to make wholesome citizens, who can combine the spirit of freedom with a love of the laws. Strangers, on their first arrival, and before they have had time to acquire property, and form connexions and attachments, are not to be presumed to be acquainted with our political institutions, or to feel pride or zeal in their stability and success.

If an alien dies before he has taken any steps under the

act of naturalization, his personal estate goes according to his will, or if he died intestate, then according to the law of distribution of the place of his domicil, at the time of his death. The stationary place of residence of the party at his death, determines the rule of distribution, and this is a rule of public right, as well as of natural justice. *Mobilia personam sequuntur, immobilia situm.* The unjust and inhospitable rule of the most polished states of antiquity, prevailed in many parts of Europe, down to the middle of the last century; and Vattel expressed his astonishment that there should have remained any vestiges of so barbarous a usage in an age so enlightened. The law, which claimed, for the benefit of the state, the effects of deceased foreigners, who left no heirs, who were natives, existed in France as late as the commencement of their revolution. This rule of the French law, was founded not only on the Roman law, but it was attempted to be justified by the narrow and absurd policy of preventing the wealth of the kingdom from passing into the hands of subjects of other countries. It was abolished by the constitution of the first constituent assembly, in 1791, and foreigners were admitted upon the most liberal terms, and declared capable of acquiring and disposing of property equally with natural born citizens. The treaty of commerce between the United States and France, in 1778, provided against the evil effects of this law, by declaring that the inhabitants of the United States were to be exempted from the *droit d'aubaine,* and might dispose by will of their property, real and personal, *(biens meubles et immeubles,)* and if they died intestate, it was to descend to their heirs, whether residing in France, or elsewhere, and the like privilege was conferred upon Frenchmen dying in this country. The treaties of France with other powers, usually contained the same relaxation of her ancient rule; and though the treaty of 1778 was abolished in 1798, yet, in the renewed treaty of 1801, the same provision was inserted, and under it American citizens in France, and French subjects in the United States, could acquire, hold, and transmit, real as well as personal property, equally as if they were natives, and without the necessity of an act of naturalization, or special permission. This last treaty expired in 1809, and the rights of Frenchmen arising thereafter, were left, like those of other aliens, to be governed by the general law of the land.

The Napoleon code did not pursue the liberal policy of the French constituent assembly of 1791, and it seems to have revived the harsh doctrine of the *Droit D'Aubaine,* under the single exception, that aliens should be entitled to enjoy in France the same civil rights secured to Frenchmen *by treaty* in the country to which the alien belongs. It is not sufficient to create the exemption in favour of the alien, that civil rights are granted to Frenchmen by the local laws of the foreign country, unless that concession be founded upon treaty. The law at present in France is, that a stranger cannot, except by special favour, dispose of his property by will; and when he dies, the sovereign succeeds by right of inheritance to his estate.

British subjects, under the treaty of 1794, between the United States and Great Britain, were confirmed in the titles which they then held to lands in this country, so far as the question of alienism existed; and they were declared competent to sell, devise, and transmit the same, in like manner as if they were natives; and that neither they, nor their heirs or assigns, should, as to those lands, be regarded as aliens. The treaty applied to the title, whatever it might be; but it referred only to titles existing at the time of the treaty, and not to titles subsequently acquired. It was, therefore, a provision of a temporary character, and by the lapse of time it is rapidly becoming unimportant and obsolete.

The legislature of this state, and probably of many other states, are in the practice of annually granting to particular aliens, by name, the privilege of holding real property. In 1825, they passed a general and permanent statute, enabling aliens to take and hold lands in fee, and to sell, mortgage, and devise, but not demise or lease the same, equally, as if they were native citizens, provided the party had previously taken an oath that he was a resident in the United States, and intended always to reside therein, and to become a citizen thereof as soon as he could be naturalized, and that he had taken the incipient measures required by law for that purpose. There are similar statute provisions in favour of aliens in South Carolina, Indiana, Illinois and Missouri; and in Louisiana, Pennsylvania and Ohio, the disability of aliens to take, hold, and transmit real property, seems to be entirely removed. In North Carolina and Vermont, there is even a provision inserted in their constitutions, that every person of good character, who comes into the state, and settles, and takes an oath of allegiance to the same, may thereupon purchase, and by other just means, acquire, hold, and transfer land, and after one year's residence, become entitled to most of the privileges of a natural born subject. These civil privileges, conferred upon aliens, by state authority, are dictated by a just and liberal policy; but they must be taken to be strictly local; and until a foreigner is duly naturalized, according to the act of Congress, he is not entitled in any other state to any other privileges than those which the laws of that state allow to aliens. No other state is bound to admit, nor would the United States admit, any alien to any privileges, to which he is not entitled by treaty, or the laws of nations, or the laws of the United States, or of the state in which he dwells. The article in the constitution of the United States, declaring that citizens of each state were entitled to all the privileges and immunities of citizens in the several states, applies only to natural born or duly naturalized citizens, and if they remove from one state to another, they are entitled to the privileges that persons of the same description are entitled to in the state to which the removal is made, and to none other. If, therefore, for instance, free persons of colour are not entitled to vote in Carolina; free persons of colour emigrating there from a northern state, would not be entitled to vote. The laws of each state ought, and must, govern within its jurisdiction; and the laws and usages of one state cannot be permitted to prescribe qualifications for citizens, to be claimed and exercised in other states, in contravention to their local policy.

The act of Congress confines the description of aliens capable of naturalization to "free white persons." I presume that this excludes the inhabitants of Africa, and their descendants; and it may become a question, to what extent persons of mixed blood, as mulattoes, are excluded, and what shades and degrees of mixture of colour disqualify an alien from application for the benefits of the act of naturalization. Perhaps there might be difficulties also as to the copper-coloured natives of America, or the yellow or tawny races of Asiatics, though I should doubt whether any of them were "white persons" within the purview of the law. It is the declared law of this state, that Indians are not citizens, but distinct tribes, living under the protection of the government, and, consequently, they never can be made citizens under the act of Congress.

Before the adoption of the present constitution of the United States, the power of naturalization resided in the several states; and the constitution of this state, as it was originally passed, required all persons born out of the United States, and naturalized by our legislature, to take an oath abjuring all foreign allegiance and subjection, in all matters, *ecclesiastical* as well as civil. This was intended, and so it operated, to exclude from the benefits of naturalization Roman Catholics who acknowledged the spiritual supremacy of the pope, and it was the result of former fears and prejudices (still alive and active at the commencement of our revolution) respecting the religion of the Romish church, which European history had taught us to believe was incompatible with perfect national independence, or the freedom and good order of civil society. So extremely strong, and so astonishingly fierce and unrelenting, was public prejudice on this subject, in the early part of our colonial history, that we find it declared by law in the beginning of the last century, that every Jesuit and popish priest who should continue in the colony after a given day, should be condemned to perpetual imprisonment; and if he broke prison and escaped, and was retaken, he should be put to death. That law, said Mr. Smith, the historian of the colony as late as the year 1756, was worthy of perpetual duration!

22

OGDEN V. SAUNDERS
12 Wheat. 213 (1827)

(See 1.10.1, no. 19)

23

WILLIAM RAWLE, A VIEW OF THE CONSTITUTION
OF THE UNITED STATES 84–101
1829 (2d ed.)

The power *to establish an uniform system of naturalization* is also an exclusive one.

In the second section of the fourth article it is provided that the citizens of each state, shall be entitled to all privileges and immunities of citizens in the several states, and the same rule had been ambiguously laid down in the articles of confederation. If this clause is retained, and its utility and propriety cannot be questioned, the consequence would be, that if each state retained the power of naturalization, it might impose on all the other states, such citizens as it might think proper. In one state, residence for a short time, with a slight declaration of allegiance, as was the case under the former constitution of Pennsylvania, might confer the rights of citizenship: in another, qualifications of greater importance might be required: an alien, desirous of eluding the latter, might by complying with the requisites of the former, become a citizen of a state in opposition to its own regulations, and thus in fact, the laws of one state become paramount to that of another. The evil could not be better remedied than by vesting the exclusive power in congress.

It cannot escape notice, that no definition of the nature and rights of citizens appears in the Constitution. The descriptive term is used, with a plain indication that its meaning is understood by all, and this indeed is the general character of the whole instrument. Except in one instance, it gives no definitions, but it acts in all its parts, on qualities and relations supposed to be already known. Thus it declares, that no person, except a natural born citizen, or a citizen of the United States at the time of the adoption of this Constitution, shall be eligible to the office of president—that no person shall be a senator who shall not have been nine years a citizen of the United States, nor a representative who has not been such a citizen seven years, and it will therefore be not inconsistent with the scope and tendency of the present essay, to enter shortly into the nature of citizenship.

In a republic the sovereignty resides essentially, and entirely in the people. Those only who compose the people, and partake of this sovereignty are citizens, they alone can elect, and are capable of being elected to public offices, and of course they alone can exercise authority within the community: they possess an unqualified right to the enjoyment of property and personal immunity, they are bound to adhere to it in peace, to defend it in war, and to postpone the interests of all other countries to the affection which they ought to bear for their own.

The citizens of each state constituted the citizens of the United States when the Constitution was adopted. The rights which appertained to them as citizens of those respective commonwealths, accompanied them in the formation of the great, compound commonwealth which ensued. They became citizens of the latter, without ceasing to be citizens of the former, and he who was subsequently born a citizen of a state, became at the moment of his birth a citizen of the United States. Therefore every person born within the United States, its territories or districts, whether the parents are citizens or aliens, is a natural born citizen in the sense of the Constitution, and entitled to all the rights and privileges appertaining to that capacity. It is an error to suppose, as some (and even so great a mind as Locke) have done, that a child is born a citizen of no country and subject of no government, and that he so continues till the age of discretion, when he is at liberty to put himself under what government he pleases. How far the adult possesses this power will hereafter be considered, but surely it would be unjust both to the state and to the infant, to withhold the quality of the citizen until those years of discretion were attained. Under our Constitution the question is settled by its express language, and when we are informed that, excepting those who were citizens, (however the capacity was acquired,) at the time the Constitution was adopted, no person is eligible to the office of president unless he is a natural born citizen, the principle that the place of birth creates the relative quality is established as to us.

The mode by which an alien may become a citizen, has a specific appellation which refers to the same principle. It is descriptive of the operation of law as analogous to birth, and the alien, received into the community by naturalization, enjoys all the benefits which birth has conferred on the other class.

Until these rights are attained, the alien resident is under some disadvantages which are not exactly the same throughout the Union. The United States do not intermeddle with the local regulations of the states in those respects. Thus an alien may be admitted to hold lands in some states, and be incapable of doing so in others. On the other hand, there are certain incidents to the character of a citizen of the United States, with which the separate states cannot interfere. The nature, extent, and duration of the allegiance due to the United States, the right to the general protection and to commercial benefits at home and abroad, derived either from treaties or from the acts of congress, are beyond the control of the states, nor can they increase or diminish the disadvantages to which aliens may, by such measures on the part of the general government, be subjected.

Thus if war should break out between the United States and the country of which the alien resident among us is a citizen or subject, he becomes on general principles an alien enemy, and is liable to be sent out of the country at the pleasure of the general government, or laid under reasonable restraints within it, and in these respects no state can interfere to protect him.

The duration of the quality of citizen, both in the native and in him who is naturalized, is a subject of considerable interest.

The doctrine of indefeasible allegiance has a deeper root in England than in any other country in Europe: the term is indeed almost peculiar to the English law, and in discussing the extent to which they carry it, we shall find it useful to ascend to the source of their government, and the foundation on which this doctrine is placed.

Whatever repugnance may occasionally be felt at the avowal, the present government of England must be considered as founded on conquest, and perhaps it is justly observed by some of their historians, that in scarcely any instance has conquest by foreign arms been pushed to a greater extent than with them.

The reluctance with which a brave and generous nation submitted to the yoke, increased the exasperation, and the tyranny of their conqueror. Their property was almost completely transferred to his military followers, their ancient laws were soon disregarded, although sometimes promised to be restored, and the pure feudal system of tenure was substituted to the ancient allodial estates, or perhaps the imperfect feuds of the Saxons.

With this system the Norman doctrine of allegiance is considered by some to have been introduced, although others trace it up to antecedent periods, but whether the solemn declaration of allegiance was practised in the time of Arthur or of Alfred, whether it were the custom of the Britons or the Angles, the Saxons or the Danes, we have sufficient ground for believing that after the conquest, it was understood to be due only to the king or the ruling chieftain, and not to the nation.

In the conflicts by which the country was distracted after the departure of the Romans, each successful competitor exacted from those he had subdued, an oath of fidelity and submission.

From this practice the usage arose of requiring a similar engagement from their own followers, as they subsequently dispersed themselves through the country and when Harold was overthrown by the Bastard of Normandy, the necessity of exacting it became more obvious, not only from the discontent which his severities excited, but from the impression which the illegitimacy of his birth might make on his subjects.

The oath of fealty and homage necessarily accompanied the numerous grants of land, wrested from its original owners, and bestowed upon his adherents; the oath of allegiance was incorporated with the oath of fealty, and whoever will reflect on the condition of the times will be satisfied that allegiance was not sworn to the nation, but to the individual whose victorious arms had rendered him the ruler of the nation.

Hence certain consequences were understood to flow; the allegiance thus solemnly pledged could not be withdrawn, unless the protection which was implied in return, should be withheld or become impracticable.

If the monarch was driven out by a successful competitor, who took possession of the throne, the allegiance was considered as transferred to him, and the subject who disobeyed the reigning sovereign, was held to violate his oath.

But from this allegiance, either original or transferred, he could not withdraw himself; he was supposed never to cease being the subject of the reigning sovereign. Allegiance equally permanent was held to result from birth. The king could see none but his own subjects within his own domain. Bound as he alleged to protect all, all were bound to be faithful to him. But allegiance sprung from the birth of those only who were born under his dominion. It is observed by Coke, that if enemies were to obtain possession of a town or fort, and have issue there, that issue would not be subjects of the king of England, for they would have no claim to his protection.

If this view of the subject be correct; if allegiance, at least since the Norman Conquest, is to be considered as proceeding from force and not from contract; if it is legally due to the king and not to the society which he governs, we can remain under no difficulty in respect to its inalienable quality according to their laws.

The rights or expectations of the people were seldom taken into account; the king might, by treaty with a foreign power, alienate an entire territory; and its inhabitants, without their previous knowledge or consent, be compelled to serve another sovereign. Thus allegiance was rendered perpetual at the pleasure of the sovereign, not of the people; and the former, not the latter, possessed a sort of property in it; but with us its indefeasible nature rests on better grounds.

The instantaneous result on our political character, from the declaration of independence, was to convert allegiance from compulsion into compact, and while it still remained due to the sovereign, to see that sovereign only in the whole community.

In the native we have observed that it is coeval with life; in him who migrates from another country, it commences as a permanent duty with naturalization; in both it lasts till death, unless it is released by some procedure, mutual on the part of both the state and the individual.

Whether the individual alone may relinquish it, is a question which in this as well as other countries has been often discussed, and on which an opinion cannot be given without diffidence, since it has not yet received a decision in the highest tribunal of our country.

In the first place, we may dispose with little comparative difficulty of the case of the naturalized citizen. His accession is voluntary, and his engagement is neither in its terms nor in its nature limited to any time. He therefore binds himself by contract for his life, and the state,—which differently from the doctrine of the English and other monarchies, cannot afterwards deprive him of the quality thus acquired, which cannot again by its own act, convert him into an alien,—is equally bound for the same term.

This is well expressed by Locke in his treatise on civil government. "He that has once by actual agreement and express declaration given his consent to be of any commonweal, is perpetually and indispensably obliged to be and remain unalterably a subject of it, and can never be again in the liberty of a state of nature, unless by any calamity, the government he was under shall be dissolved, or by some public act it cuts him off from being a member of it."

Under our Constitution the last would be impossible without his own consent, and the citizen can no more dissolve this contract than he can any other of less moment without the consent of the opposite party.

But there are two other classes of citizens, and we must examine whether the same principle can be applied to them. It would, perhaps, be sufficient to say, that if the obligation, to which the naturalized citizen subjects himself, is clearly an obligation for life; that of the native cannot be for a shorter term. Naturalization is but a mode of acquiring the right, subject to the duties of a citizen; it is the factitious substitution of legal form for actual birth, and it can neither exceed nor fall short of the capacities and obligations which birth creates. It would be absurd indeed, if the foreigner was given to understand, that by naturalization he had become bound for life, in the midst of native citizens, none of whom were under the same obligation.

But we need not rest on this postulate. The compact created among the citizens, by the declaration of independence, was well understood by themselves at the moment, not to be of a temporary nature, and in the power of the individual at pleasure to dissolve. It was essential not only to the permanence, but to the formation of the new government, that every one either taking an active part in its establishment, or giving evidence of his consent by remaining within it, should be considered as bound to it, so long as it continued. Their situation at the moment was not that of aliens, who were held by a prior allegiance, while they undertook another. He who thus united himself with the newly-formed state, instantly ceased, in contemplation of our law, to be a subject of Great Britain. He could thereafter, justify no hostile measure against us by alleging his ancient allegiance. What he once owed to that power was now wholly transferred to the new state, with all its qualities and accompaniments, except one. The correlative of protection, could not, as before, be destroyed at pleasure by the receiver of the allegiance. The obligation was mutual and perpetual. If any qualification of it was intended, it would have been expressed, but we do not find in any of the state constitutions, or in that of the United States, the slightest suggestion that the allegiance to be paid to them, was less solemn, less entire, less permanent than that which was previously due to the monarch of Great Britain. Thus the question stands in respect to this class of citizens.

The next inquiry is, whether this contract was confined to the individual or extended also to his issue. So far as relates to the parent, an answer to this question may be found in the mere statement of it. No one can suppose that the parent intended, that while he was a permanent citizen of the state, his children should not partake of the same rights, enjoy the same liberty, and be protected by the same government. Nature itself impresses on the parental mind, a desire to promote the interests of children, and causes it to revolt at the idea of witholding from them what may not only be shared with them, but what also becomes more valuable by being so shared. The pleasing sensation in the parent, of passing from the condition of an oppressed subject, to that of a citizen of a free republic, would surely be impaired by a consideration that his offspring would acquire no birthright in the community of his choice. In respect to him, therefore, we cannot doubt the desire, and have only to examine the power, of fixing the political relations of his descendants. The principle which next presents itself is, that what all the members of the state must have thus understood, must also have been so understood by the state, which is only the collection of those members. The compact so far as relates to the state, of course extends to the individual and to all his descendants, and therefore, as the child is entitled to the benefit of being recognised as a citizen, the state is entitled in its turn, to view the child as under its allegiance. It may however be urged, that an infant cannot bind itself by contract, but if it is necessary to answer the objection, it is sufficient to say that an infant may expressly bind itself for necessaries, as food and raiment, that a contract is always implied where such articles are furnished, and that the reciprocal compact of protection and allegiance, must be ranked among considerations of the highest order and first necessity. The dignity of the subject is however somewhat affected by resting it on a ground so narrow; and when we consider all the obligations cast on a political society by the voluntary formation of it, we may discard the smaller rules of private contract, and more safely rely on the broad basis of the general good, inherent in its nature, and necessary to its self-preservation.

When the child has attained an age sufficiently mature, according to civil institutions, to enable it to determine the choice, it would seem, in consistency with the principles already laid down, that the individual must be allowed a reasonable time to enable him to select the country in which he will reside, and the society to which he will adhere. Of his willingness to continue, no public declaration seems to be requisite. His acts demonstrate his choice; but there would be a great difficulty in fixing the time in which a contrary determination ought to be formed and declared. The law has assigned twenty-one years as the age of discretion; but in whom is the judgment sufficiently ripened at so early a period, to enable him to determine on a subject so momentous, and how long after that period has been reached, shall be allowed for deliberation? These difficulties appear to be almost insuperable, and seem to render the principle itself inadmissible, unless it should be specially provided for by the legislature. But where the adult has for a sufficient length of time, by every external act, manifested his adhesion to the political society in which he was born, there can exist no right in him to shake off his allegiance without the consent of the state, and become a stranger, or in the course of events, an enemy to his country. By his acts he has bound himself as closely as the alien who, seeking to be naturalized, has taken an express oath. The obligations resulting from his birth are rivetted by his voluntary conduct afterwards, and he cannot dispute the indissoluble tie, of which he has thus doubled the effect.

To these positions some objections may be made, which it will be endeavoured to answer.

The leading one is the great act of July 4, 1776, by which two and a half millions of subjects threw off their allegiance to Great Britain, and it is argued that what might be done by them collectively, could be done by them individually; but an obvious fallacy appears in the very statement of this proposition.

When the protection of the crown was withdrawn; when the aspect and the arm of paternal power were converted into virtual exclusion from the pale of the British family; a right of collective resistance was created which, unless similar measures could be exerted against an individual, can never exist in an individual. Our case differed in form only from the cession of territories and their inhabitants already noticed. If either by cession to another or by unmerited severity to those who are nominally retained as subjects, the legitimate protection is thus wholly withdrawn; the dissolution of allegiance is the act of the sovereign, and if assented to by his subjects, is binding on both. It depends therefore upon facts to determine whether the cause of our separation was sufficient, and on these facts no American mind can hesitate.

The treaty of 1783 may be safely referred to in confir-mation of this opinion. In recognising the independence of the United States, the right to declare it on the principles we asserted, may justly be considered as also recognized. Great Britain did not by professing to grant us independence, (a grant which would not have been accepted,) affect to release us from present allegiance; but on the contrary must be considered as retrospectively acknowledging that by her own act she had entitled us to discontinue it.

Another objection arises from the acknowledged right of emigration, of which, with us, no inhabitant is deprived, while, in many other governments, express permission is necessary; but the error of this consists in supposing that emigration implies the dissolution of allegiance.

Emigration in its general sense, merely signifies removal from one place to another; its strict and more appropriate meaning is the removal of a person, his effects and residence: but in no sense does it imply or require that it should take place with a view to become a subject or citizen of another country.

Motives of health or trade, convenience or pleasure, may lead to emigration; but if a deprivation of citizenship were the necessary and immediate consequence, (and unless it is, the argument is without weight,) emigration would often be a cause of terror and sometimes a punishment, instead of a benefit, in which sense the right is considered.

Those who contend for the affirmative of the proposition, must be able to prove that the quality of citizenship ceases at the moment of departure; that if the emigrant returns he cannot be restored to his former rank, without passing through the regular forms of naturalization; that if real estate had descended upon him during his absence, he could not inherit it without the aid of a law in favour of aliens, and that if the country to which he has removed, becomes engaged in war with us, and he did not choose to remain there, he would be liable on his return, to be treated as an alien enemy. In Virginia, what is termed expatriation is authorized by an act of assembly passed in 1792. This is a fair compact which an independent state has a right to make with its citizens, and amounts to a full release of all future claims against the emigrant who, if taken in war against the state, would not be liable to the charge of treason. But the release is effective only so far as relates to the state which grants it. It does not alter his relation to the United States, and it was questioned in the case of Talbot v. Janson how far such a law would be compatible with the Constitution of the United States.

The Virginia act makes no distinction between the time of peace and of war.

Whether the citizen, having formed the unnatural design of aiding the actual enemies of his country, could make use of its legal forms to enable him to commit such a crime with impunity, remains to be decided by the tribunals of that state.

A distinction certainly not unreasonable has been taken between citizenship and allegiance. Perpetual allegiance is a doctrine of less force and efficacy in some countries than in others. It depends on their respective systems of law.

The origin of allegiance in England has been already

described. Its former extension through almost every part of this country is unquestionable, and in many states it continues unimpaired in its qualities and nature.

It is indirectly recognised in the Constitution of the United States, and by the acts of congress, which have been since passed. The indefeasible quality conceived to be incident to it has not yet been decided on by the Supreme Court of the United States; but in the Circuit Courts, Ellsworth, chief justice, declared, that a member of the community cannot dissolve the social compact so as to free himself from our laws, without the consent or the default of the community. And in another case, Washington, J. declared that no citizen can throw off his allegiance to his country without some law authorizing him to do so. But in those countries where the doctrine of allegiance, in the sense we affix to it, does not exist at all, or where it is a part of their law that it may be thrown off in certain cases, our positions do not apply.

It may still further be urged, that the renunciation of all foreign allegiance inserted in the oath of naturalization, implies a power to renounce what is due to us as well as what is due to a foreign state.

If this were found in the Constitution, it might occasion some difficulty; but it is the language of congress, on whom it does not rest to give a binding exposition of the Constitution. It was not required in the first act prescribing the mode of obtaining naturalization, and it was probably introduced from political jealousy, and by way of caution to the new citizen. The necessity of retaining it, is not very perceptible. If a naturalized citizen should commit treason against us, by uniting with a hostile country from which he had emigrated, he would not be more amenable to the law, because of his renunciation, nor less so, if it had never taken place; and it would have no effect in the country which he had left, either by way of aggravation or extenuation of any offence for which he might be responsible to them.

The temporary allegiance, which began with his residence among us, is rendered perpetual by his naturalization, and the renunciation is an useless adjunct.

The last objection which occurs to the author is, that independent of the oath of abjuration, the admission of a foreigner to naturalization among us implies that he may withdraw his allegiance from his native country, and that otherwise in case of war, he would be involved in the hardship of being obliged to commit treason against one or the other: but the satisfactory answer always given to this proposition is, that if the individual chooses to entangle himself in a double allegiance, it is his own voluntary act. He may reside among us without being naturalized, he may enjoy much of the protection, and some of the advantages of a citizen, yet retain, unimpaired even in sensation, his allegiance to his native country till the moment he chooses to leave us. If he determines completely to unite his character and his fortunes with ours, we receive him under the compact already explained, and his temporary allegiance becomes permanently binding.

Another point of considerable moment remains to be noticed. Having shown what a citizen, native or naturalized, may not do by way of withdrawing his allegiance, we will now proceed to show in what cases the state may not withdraw its protection.

Every person has a right to remain within a state as long as he pleases, except the alien enemy, the person charged with crimes in any of the other states, or in a foreign state with whom a treaty to that effect exists, and fugitives from service or labour in any of the states. To the two latter descriptions, no asylum can by the Constitution of the United States, be afforded.

The states are considered as a common family, whose harmony would be endangered, if they were to protect and detain such fugitives, when demanded in one case, by the executive authority of the state, or pursued in the other by the persons claiming an interest in their service.

In the case of alien enemies, the public good is consulted. The right of sending them away, is an incident to the right of carrying on public war. It is not mentioned in the Constitution, but it properly appertains to those who are to conduct the war.

Whoever visits or resides among us, comes under the knowledge that he is liable, by the law of nations, to be sent off, if war breaks out between his country and ours, before he is naturalized. So if there is any treaty in force, by which we are bound to deliver up a fugitive, charged by another nation with the commission of crimes within its territory, every one arriving among us is considered as having knowledge of such compact.

But whatever may be held by certain theoretical writers, there is no foundation for the opinion, that we are bound by the general law of nations, without such compact, to surrender a person charged with a crime in another nation.

The principles by which this conclusion is attained, are as follow. A criminal act, committed within the limits of a nation, is an offence against that nation, and not against any other. It is the duty of a nation to punish offences against itself, but not against others. If the offender escapes, it has no power to pursue him into the territories of another, nor any right, by the general rules of law, to require the other to deliver him up. The nation in which he seeks an asylum, may conscientiously retain and protect him. In legal acceptation, he has been received as an innocent man; he holds this character among us, till he forfeits it by the commission of a crime against us; he is then, on conviction, liable to punishment for such crime, but we cannot punish him for a crime committed in another country.

Nature gives to mankind the right of punishing only for their own defence and safety. Hence it follows, that he can only be punished by those he has offended.

To deliver the fugitive to the nation which claims, in order to punish him, is to assist the punishment, and therefore directly at variance with these principles.

Yet it is not to be inferred, that one state has a right to transfer its criminals to another, and that the latter is bound to receive them. It rests with every independent state to open its doors to the admission of foreigners on such terms only, as it may think proper.

During our colonial dependency, the mother country assumed a privilege of transporting certain classes of her convicted offenders to the provinces, and the want of labourers at first induced us to receive them without complaint.

But it was soon discovered to be an alarming evil, and many of the provinces took measures to oppose it. One of the last acts of the congress under the confederation, was to recommend to the several states to pass proper laws for preventing the transportation of convicted malefactors from foreign countries into the United States. Perhaps the power implied by the 9th section of the 2d article, might be usefully adapted to the regulation of this sort of political commerce, in which, at present, we cannot be gainers, for the United States have no constitutional power to export or banish offenders.

24

SHANKS v. DuPONT
3 Pet. 242 (1830)

STORY, Justice. This was a writ of error to the highest Court of Appeals in law and equity of the state of South Carolina, brought to revise the decision of that Court, in a bill or petition in equity, in which the present defendants were original plaintiffs, and the present plaintiffs were original defendants. From the record of the case it appeared, that the controversy before the Court respected the right to the moiety of the proceeds of a certain tract of land, which had been sold under a former decree in equity, and the proceeds of which had been brought into the registry of the Court. One moiety of the proceeds had been paid over to the original plaintiffs, and the other moiety was now in controversy. The original plaintiffs claimed this moiety also, upon the ground that the original defendants were aliens and incapable of taking the lands by descent from their mother, Ann Shanks, (who was admitted to have taken the moiety of the land by descent from her father, Thomas Scott,) they being British born subjects.

The facts, as they were agreed by the parties, and as they appeared on the record, were as follows:

Thomas Scott, the ancestor and first purchaser, was a native of the colony of South Carolina, and died intestate, seised of the lands in dispute, in 1782. He left surviving him two daughters, Sarah and Ann, who were also born in South Carolina, before the declaration of independence.

Sarah Scott intermarried with Daniel Pepper, a citizen of South Carolina, and resided with him in that state until 1802, when she died, leaving children, the present defendants in error, whose right to her share of the property is conceded.

The British took possession of James Island, on the 11th of February, 1780, and Charleston surrendered to them on the 11th of May, in the same year.

In 1781, Ann Scott was married to Joseph Shanks, a British officer, and at the evacuation of Charleston, in December, 1782, went with him to England, where she remained until her death, in 1801. She left five children, the present plaintiffs in error, British subjects, who claimed in right of their mother, and under the ninth article of the treaty of peace between this country and Great Britain, of the 19th of November, 1794, a moiety of their grandfather's estate in South Carolina.

The decision of the State Court was against this claim, as not within the protection of the treaty, because Mrs. Shanks was an American citizen.

After the elaborate opinions expressed in the case of Inglis vs. The Trustees of the Sailor's Snug Harbour, ante p. 99, upon the question of alienage growing out of the American Revolution, it is unnecessary to do more in delivering the opinion of the Court in the present case, than to state, in a brief manner, the grounds on which our decision is founded.

Thomas Scott, a native of South Carolina, died in 1782, seised of the land in dispute, leaving two daughters surviving him, Sarah, the mother of the defendants in error, and Ann, the mother of the plaintiffs in error. Without question, Sarah took one moiety of the land by descent; and the defendants in error, as her heirs, are entitled to it. The only question is, whether Ann took the other moiety by descent; and if so, whether the plaintiffs in error are capable of taking the same by descent from her.

Ann Scott was born in South Carolina, before the American Revolution; and her father adhered to the American cause, and remained and was at his death a citizen of South Carolina. There is no dispute that his daughter Ann, at the time of the Revolution, and afterwards, remained in South Carolina until December, 1782. Whether she was of age during this time does not appear. If she was, then her birth and residence might be deemed to constitute her by election a citizen of South Carolina. If she was not of age, then she might well be deemed, under the circumstances of this case, to hold the citizenship of her father; for children born in a country, continuing while under age in the family of the father, partake of his national character as a citizen of that country. Her citizenship, then, being prima facie established, (and indeed this is admitted in the pleadings,) has it ever been lost; or was it lost before the death of her father, so that the estate in question was, upon the descent cast, incapable of vesting in her? Upon the facts stated, it appears to us, that it was not lost; and that she was capable of taking it at the time of the descent cast.

The only facts which are brought to support the supposition, that she became an alien before the death of her father, are, that the British captured James Island in February, 1780, and Charleston in May, 1780; that she was then and afterwards remained under the British dominion in virtue of the capture; that in 1781, she married Joseph Shanks, a British officer, and upon the evacuation of Charleston, in December, 1782, she went with her husband, a British subject, to England, and there remained until her death in 1801. Now, in the first place, the capture and possession by the British was not an absolute change of the allegiance of the captured inhabitants. They owed allegiance indeed to the conquerors during their occupation; but it was a temporary allegiance, which did not destroy, but only suspended their former allegiance. It did not annihilate their allegiance to the state of South Carolina, and make them de facto aliens. That could only be by a treaty of peace, which should cede the territory, and them with it; or by a permanent conquest, not disturbed or controverted by arms, which would lead to a like result. Neither did the marriage with Shanks produce that effect; because marriage with an alien, whether a friend or an enemy, produces no dissolution of the native allegiance of the wife. It may change her civil rights, but it does not affect her political rights or privileges. The general doctrine is, that no persons can, by any act of their own, without the consent of the government, put off their allegiance and become aliens. If it were otherwise, then a feme alien would by her marriage become, ipso facto, a citizen, and would be dowable of the estate of her husband; which is clearly contrary to law.

Our conclusion therefore is, that neither of these acts warrant the Court in saying that Ann Shanks had ceased to be a citizen of South Carolina, at the death of her father. This is not, indeed, controverted in the allegations of the parties.

The question then is, whether her subsequent removal with her husband operated as a virtual dissolution of her allegiance, and fixed her future allegiance to the British crown, by the treaty of peace of 1783. Our opinion is that it did. In the first place, she was born under the allegiance of the British crown, and no act of the government of Great Britain ever absolved her from that allegiance. Her becoming a citizen of South Carolina did not, ipso facto, work any dissolution of her allegiance, at least so far as the rights and claims of the British crown were concerned. During the war each party claimed the allegiance of the natives of the colonies as due exclusively to itself. The American states insisted upon the allegiance of all born within the states respectively; and Great Britain asserted an equally exclusive claim. The treaty of peace of 1783 acted upon the state of things as it existed at that period. It took the actual state of things as its basis. All those, whether natives or otherwise, who then adhered to the American states, were virtually absolved from all allegiance to the British crown. All those, who then adhered to the British crown, were deemed and held subjects of that crown. The treaty of peace was a treaty operating between the states on each side, and the inhabitants thereof. In the language of the seventh article, it was a firm and perpetual peace between his Britannic majesty and the said states, "and between the subjects of the one and the citizens of the other." Who were then subjects or citizens, was to be decided by the state of facts. If they were originally subjects of Great Britain and then adhered to her, and were claimed by her as subjects, the treaty deemed them such. If they were originally British subjects, but then adhering to the states, the treaty deemed them citizens. Such, I think, is the natural, and indeed almost necessary meaning of the treaty; it would otherwise follow, that there would continue a double allegiance of many persons; an inconvenience which must have been foreseen, and would cause the most injurious effects to both nations.

It cannot, we think, be doubted, that Mrs. Shanks being then voluntarily under British protection, and adhering to the British side, by her removal with her husband, was deemed by the British government to retain her allegiance, and to be, to all intents and purposes, a British subject. It may be said, that, being sub potestate viri, she had no right to make an election, nor ought she to be bound by an act of removal under his authority or persuasion. If this were a case of a crime alleged against Mrs. Shanks, in connexion with her husband, there might be force in the argument. But it must be considered, that it was at most a mere election of allegiance between two nations, each of which claimed her allegiance. The governments, and not herself, finally settled her national character. They did not treat her as capable by herself of changing or absolving her allegiance; but they virtually allowed her the benefit of her choice, by fixing her allegiance finally on the side of that party to whom she then adhered.

It does not appear to us, that her situation as a feme covert disabled her from a change of allegiance. British femes covert residing here with their husbands at the time of our independence, and adhering to our side until the close of the war, have been always supposed to have become thereby American citizens, and to have been absolved from their antecedent British allegiance. The incapacities of femes covert, provided by the common law, apply to their civil rights, and are for their protection and interest. But they do not reach their political rights, nor prevent their acquiring or losing a national character. Those political rights do not stand upon the mere doctrines of municipal law, applicable to ordinary transactions, but stand upon the more general principles of the law of nations. The case of Martin vs. The Commonwealth, 1 Mass. Rep. 347, turned upon very different considerations. There the question was, whether a feme covert should be deemed to have forfeited her estate for an offence committed with her husband, by withdrawing from the state, &c., under the confiscation act of 1779; and it was held that she was not within the purview of the act. The same remark disposes of the case of Sewell vs. Lee, 9 Mass. Rep. 363, where the Court expressly refused to decide, whether the wife by her withdrawal with her husband became an alien. But in Kelly vs. Harrison, 2 Johns. Cas. 29, the reasoning of the Court proceeds upon the supposition, that the wife might have acquired the same citizenship with her husband, by withdrawing with him from the British dominions.

But if Mrs. Shanks' citizenship was not virtually taken away by her adherence to the British at the peace of 1783, still it must be admitted, that, in the view of the British government, she was at that time, and ever afterwards to the time of her death, and indeed at all antecedent periods, a British subject. At most, then, she was liable to be considered as in that peculiar situation, in which she owed allegiance to both governments, ad utriusque fidem regis. Under such circumstances, the question arises, whether she and her heirs are not within the purview of the ninth article of the treaty with Great Britain of 1794. It appears to us, that they plainly are. The language of that article is, "that British subjects, who now hold lands in the territories of the United States, and American citizens who now hold lands in the dominions of his majesty, shall continue to hold them according to the nature and tenure of their respective estates and titles therein, &c. &c.; and that neither they nor their heirs or assigns shall, so far as respects the said lands, and the legal remedies incident thereto, be regarded as aliens."

Now, Mrs. Shanks was at this time a British subject, and she then held the lands in controversy; she is therefore within the words of the treaty. Why ought she not also to be held within the spirit and intent? It is said, that the treaty meant to protect the rights of British subjects, who were not also American citizens; but that is assuming the very point in controversy. If the treaty admits of two interpretations, and one is limited, and the other liberal; one which will further, and the other exclude private rights; why should not the most liberal expositions be adopted? The object of the British government must have been to protect all her subjects holding lands in America from the disability of alienage, in respect to descents and sales. The class of American loyalists would at least, in her eyes, have been in as much favour as any other. There is nothing in our public policy which is more unfavourable to them than to other British subjects. After the peace of 1783, we had no right or interest in future confiscation; and the effect of alienage was the same in respect to us, whether the British subject was a native of Great Britain or of the colonies. This part of the stipulation then being for the benefit of British subjects, who became aliens by the events of the war; there is no reason, why all persons should not be embraced in it, who sustained the character of British subjects, although we might also have treated them as American citizens. The argument supposes, that because we should treat them as citizens, therefore Great Britain had no right to insist upon their being British subjects within the protection of the treaty. Now, if they were in truth and in fact, upon principles of public and municipal law, British subjects, she has an equal right to require us to recognise them as such. It cannot be doubted that, Mrs. Shanks might have inherited any lands in England, as a British subject, and her heirs might have taken such lands by descent from her. It seems to us, then, that all British born subjects, whose allegiance Great Britain has never renounced, ought, upon general principles of interpretation, to be held within the intent, as they certainly are within the words, of the treaty of 1794.

In either view of this case, and we think both are sustained by principles of public law, as well as of the common law, and by the soundest rules of interpretation applicable to treaties between independent states, the objections taken to the right of recovery of the plaintiffs cannot prevail.

Upon the whole, the judgment of the Court is, that the plaintiffs in error are entitled to the moiety of the land in controversy, which came by descent to their mother, Ann Shanks, and of course to the proceeds thereof; and that the decree of the state Court of Appeals ought to be reversed; and the cause remanded, with directions to enter a decree in favour of the plaintiffs in error.

Mr. Justice JOHNSON, dissenting.

This cause comes up from the state Court of South Carolina.

The question is whether the plaintiffs can inherit to their mother. The objection to their inheriting is, that they are aliens, not born in allegiance to the state of South Carolina, in which the land lies. From the general disability of aliens they would exempt themselves. 1. On the ground that their mother was a citizen born, and in that right, though born abroad, they can inherit under the statute of Edward III 2. That if not protected by that statute, then that their mother was a British subject, and that she and her heirs are protected as to this land by the treaties of 1783 and 1794.

The material facts of their case are, that their mother and her father were natives born of the province of South Carolina, before the declaration of independence; that in 1781, while Charleston and James Island, where the land lies and she and her father resided, were in possession of the British, their mother married their father, a British officer. That the descent was cast in 1782; and in December of that year, when the town was evacuated, she went to England with her husband, and resided there until her death in 1801; in which interval the appellants were born in England.

There is no question about the right of the appellees, if the right of the appellants cannot be maintained.

The first of the grounds taken below, to wit, the statute of Edward III. was not pressed in argument here, and must be regarded as abandoned. The second requires therefore our sole attention.

Was Mrs. Shanks to be regarded as a British subject, within the meaning of our treaties with Great Britain? If so, then the land which was acquired in 1782, has the peculiar incident attached to it of being inheritable by aliens, subjects of Great Britain.

Until the adoption of the federal constitution, titles to land, and the laws of allegiance, were exclusively subjects of state cognizance. Up to the time, therefore, when this descent was cast upon the mother, the state of South Carolina was supreme and uncontrollable on the subject now before us.

By the adoption of the Constitution, the power of the states in this respect was subjected to some modification. But although restrained in some measure from determining who cannot inherit, I consider her power still supreme in determining who can inherit. On this subject her own laws and her own Courts furnish the only rule for governing this or any other tribunal.

By an act of the state passed in 1712, the common law of Great Britain was incorporated into the jurisprudence of South Carolina. In the year 1782, when this descent was cast, it was the law of the land; and it becomes imperative upon these appellants, after admitting that their parent was a native born citizen of South Carolina, daughter of a native born citizen of South Carolina, to show on what ground they can escape from the operation of these leading maxims of common law. Nemo potest exuere patriam;—and proles sequitur sortem paternam.

The unyielding severity with which the Courts of Great

Britain have adhered to the first of these maxims in Dr. Storie's case, furnished by Sir Matthew Hale, and in Aeneas M'Donald's case, to be found in Foster, leaves no ground of complaint for its most ordinary application in the case of descent, and its most liberal application when perpetuating a privilege.

The treaty of peace can afford no ground to the appellants, nor the construction which has extended the provisions of that treaty to the case of escheat; for the question here is not between the alien and the state, but between aliens and other individual claimants. The words of the sixth article of the treaty of 1783 are the same as those in the preliminary treaty of 1782. "There shall be no future confiscations made, or future prosecutions commenced against any person or persons by reason of the part which he or they may have taken in the present war."

Conceding that escheat may be comprised under confiscation; a decision between individuals claiming under no act of force imputable to the state, cannot possibly be considered under that term.

Nor will her case be aided by the following words of that article: to wit, "nor shall any person on that account (the part which he or they may have taken in the present war) suffer any future loss or damage either in person, liberty, or property." The decision of the state Court gives the most liberal extension possible to this provision of the treaty, since it declares that Mrs. Shanks never was precluded by any act of hers from claiming this property. It never entered into the minds of that Court, that the very innocent act of marrying a British officer, was to be tortured into "taking a part in the present war;" nor that following that officer to England and residing there under coverture, was to be imputed to her a cause of forfeiture.

I consider it very important to a clear view of this question, that its constituents or several members should be viewed separately.

The state Court has not pretended to impugn the force of the treaty of 1794, or denied the obligation to concede every right that can be fairly and legally asserted under it; but has only adjudged that the case of the appellants is not one which on legal grounds of construction can be brought within its provision.

The words of the treaty are: "it is agreed that British subjects who now hold lands in the territories of the United States, and American citizens who now hold lands in the dominions of his majesty," shall continue to hold and transmit to their heirs, &c.

The decision of the state Court which we are now reviewing presents two propositions:

1. That Mrs. Shanks was in the year 1782, when the descent was cast, and continued to be in 1794, when the treaty was ratified, a citizen of South Carolina.

2. That she was not a British subject in the sense of the treaty.

As to the first of these two propositions, I consider it as altogether set at rest by the decision itself; it is established by paramount authority; and this Court can no more say that it is not the law of South Carolina, than they could deny the validity of a statute of the state passed in 1780,

declaring that to be her character, and those her privileges.

The only question, therefore, that this Court can pass upon is, whether, being recognised under that character, and possessing those rights, she is still a British subject within the provisions of the treaty.

It is no sufficient answer to this question, that it cannot be denied that Mrs. Shanks was a British subject. She was so in common with the whole American people. The argument therefore proves too much, if it proves any thing; since it leads to the absurdity of supposing that Great Britain was stipulating for the protection of her enemies, and imposing on us an obligation in favour of our own citizens.

It also blends and confounds the national character of those, to separate and distinguish whom was the leading object of the treaty of 1783.

It cannot be questioned that the treaty of 1783 must have left Mrs. Shanks a British subject, or the treaty of 1794 cannot aid her offspring. And the idea of British subject under the latter treaty, will be best explained by reference to its meaning in that of 1783. The two treaties are in pari materia.

The provisions of the third article show that persons who come within the description of "people of the United States," were distinguished from subjects of Great Britain. That article stipulates for a right in the people of the United States to resort to the gulf of St. Lawrence for fishing; a stipulation wholly nugatory, if not distinguishable from subjects of Great Britain.

The fifth article is more explicit in the distinction. It first contains a provision in favour of real British subjects; then one in favour of persons resident in districts in possession of his majesty's arms; and then stipulates that persons of any other description shall have liberty to go to and remain twelve months in the United States to adjust their affairs. These latter must have included the loyalists who had been banished or in any way subjected to punishment, who are explicitly distinguished from real British subjects, and thus classed, in order to avoid the question to whom their allegiance was due, or rather, because, by the same treaty, the king having renounced all claim to their allegiance, could no longer distinguish them as British subjects.

Can those any longer be denominated British subjects whose allegiance the King of Great Britain has solemnly renounced?

I know of no test more solemn or satisfactory than the liability to the charge of treason; not by reason of temporary allegiance, for that is gone with change of domicil; were those who could claim the benefit of the king's renunciation to the colonies, subject to any other than temporary allegiance, while commorant in Great Britain? I say they were not. Their right to inherit is not a sufficient test of that liability as to other nations, for that right results from a different principle, the exemption of a British subject from being disfranchised, while free from crime.

Was Mr[s]. Shanks an individual to whose allegiance the king had renounced his claim?

The commencement of the Revolution found us all indeed professing allegiance to the British crown, but distributed into separate communities; altogether independent of each other, and each exercising within its own limits sovereign powers, legislative, executive, and judicial. We were dependent, it is true, upon the crown of Great Britain, but as to all the world beside, foreign and independent. It lies then at the basis of our Revolution, that when we threw off our allegiance to Great Britain, every member of each body politic stood in the relation of subject to no other power than the community of which he then constituted a member. Those who owed allegiance to the king, as of his province of South Carolina, thenceforward owed allegiance to South Carolina. The Courts of this country all consider this transfer of allegiance as resulting from the declaration of independence; the British from its recognition by the treaty of peace. But as to its effect, the British Courts concur in our view of it. For, in the case of Thomas *vs.* Acklam, 2 B. & C. 229, the language of the British Court is this: "a declaration that a state shall be free, sovereign, and independent, is a declaration that the people composing that state shall no longer be considered as the subjects of that sovereign by whom the declaration is made."

From the previous relations of the colonies and mother country, it is obvious that the declaration of independence must have found many persons resident in the country besides those whose allegiance was marked by the unequivocal circumstance of birth; many native born British subjects voluntarily adhered to the Americans, and many foreigners had, by settlement, pursuits, or principles, devoted themselves to her cause.

Whatever questions may have arisen, as to the national character or allegiance of these; as to the case under review, which is that of a native born citizen of South Carolina, there would be no doubt. And the Courts of that state have put it beyond a doubt, that the Revolution transferred her allegiance to that state.

Whoever will weigh the words "real British subjects," used in the fifth article, and consider the context, can come to but one conclusion: to wit, that it must mean British subjects to whose allegiance the states make no claim. "Estates that have been confiscated belonging to real British subjects" are the words. Now it is notorious, that although, generally speaking, the objects of those confiscations were those to whose allegiance the states laid claim, yet in many instances the estates of British subjects resident in England or this country, or elsewhere, were confiscated, because they were British subjects, on the charge of adhering to the enemy. But if the right of election had ever been contemplated, why should the term real have been inserted. The loyalists were British subjects, and had given the most signal proofs of their election to remain such. What possible meaning can be attached to the term real, unless it raised a distinction to their prejudice? And historically, we know that Great Britain acknowledged their merits by making large provisions for their indemnification; because for them there was no provision made for restoring their property.

It has been argued that the British Courts, in construing the treaty of peace, have recognised this right of election, and the case of Thomas *vs.* Acklam, before cited, is sup-

posed to establish it. But a very little attention to that case will prove the contrary. It is in fact the converse of the present case. Mrs. Thomas was the daughter of Mr. Ludlow, an American citizen born before the Revolution, and was born in America long after the separation. So that her alien character was unquestionable, unless protected by the statute of Geo. II. explaining those of Anne and Edward. The decision of the Court of King's Bench is, that to bring herself within the provisions of the statute, her father must be shown at her birth to have been both a native born and a subject of Great Britain; that by the treaty of peace, the king had renounced all claim to his allegiance, and his subsequent residence in America proved his acceptance of that renunciation.

But when did South Carolina renounce the allegiance of Mrs. Shanks? We have the evidence of the states having acquired it; when did she relinquish it? Or if it be placed on the footing of an ordinary contract, when did South Carolina agree to the dissolution of this contract? Or when did she withdraw her protection, and thus dissolve the right to claim obedience or subjection?

It is true, the treaty of 1794 drops the word real, and stipulates generally for British subjects and American citizens: construing the two treaties as instruments in pari materia. This circumstance is of little consequence; and however we construe it, the argument holds equally good, that the treaty could have been only meant to aid those who needed its aid, not those who were entitled under our own laws to every right which the treaty meant to secure; that is, those whose alien character prevented their holding lands, unless aided by some treaty or statute. Mrs. Shanks was not of this character or description; her right at all times to inherit has been recognised by paramount authority. But it is contended, that it was at her election whether to avail herself of her birthright as a citizen of the state, or her birthright as a subject of Great Britain.

To this there may be several answers given. And, first, the admission of this right would make her case no better under the construction of the treaty; for, having no need of its protection, as has been authentically recognised by the state decision, it cannot be supposed that she was an object contemplated by the treaty; she was not a British subject in the sense of those treaties, especially if the two treaties be construed on the principle of instruments in pari materia.

Secondly, if she had the right of election, at what time did she exercise it? for she cannot claim under her election, and against her election. If she exercised it prior to her father's death, then was she an alien at his death, and could not take even a right of entry by descent, as has been distinctly recognised in Hunter *vs.* Fairfax, 7 Cranch, 619, and I think in some other cases. She then had nothing for the treaty to act upon.

But if her election was not complete until subsequent to her father's death, then it is clearly settled, that taking the oath of allegiance to a foreign sovereign produces no forfeiture, and she still had no need of a treaty to secure her rights to land previously descended to her. If the facts be resorted to, and the Court is called upon to fix the period of her transit, it would be obliged to confine itself to the act of her marrying against her allegiance. It is the only free act of her life stated upon the record, for from thence she continued sub potestate viri; and if she or her descendants were now interested in maintaining her original allegiance, we should hear it contended, and be compelled to admit, that no subsequent act of her life could be imputed to her because of her coverture; and even her marriage was probably during her infancy.

But, lastly, I deny this right of election altogether, as existing in South Carolina, more especially at that time.

I had this question submitted to me on my circuit some years since, and I then leaned in favour of this right of election. But more mature reflection has satisfied me, that I then gave too much weight to natural law and the suggestions of reason and justice; in a case which ought to be disposed of upon the principles of political and positive law, and the law of nations.

That a government cannot be too liberal in extending to individuals the right of using their talents and seeking their fortunes wherever their judgments may lead them, I readily agree. There is no limit short of its own security, to which a wise and beneficent government would restrict its liberality on this subject. But the question now to be decided is of a very different feature; it is not one of expediency, but of right. It is, to what extent may the powers of government be lawfully exercised in restraining individual volition on the subject of allegiance; and what are the rights of the individual when unaffected by positive legislation.

As the common law of Great Britain is the law of South Carolina, it would here perhaps be sufficient to state that the common law altogether denies the right of putting off allegiance. British subjects are permitted, when not prohibited by statute, (as in the case with regard to her citizens,) to seek their fortunes where they please, but always subject to their natural allegiance. And although it is not regarded as a crime to swear allegiance to a foreign state, yet their government stands uncommitted in the subject of the embarrassments in which a state of war between the governments of their natural and that of their adopted allegiance may involve the individual. On this subject the British government acts as circumstances may dictate to her policy. That policy is generally liberal; and as war is the calling of many of her subjects, she has not been rigorous in punishing them even when found with arms in their hands, where there has been no desertion, and no proclamation of recall. The right, however, to withdraw from their natural allegiance is universally denied by the common law.

It is true that, without any act of her own, Mrs. Shanks found herself equally amenable to both governments under the application of this common law principle. But from this only one consequence followed, which is, that so far as related to rights to be claimed or acquired, or duties to be imposed under the laws of either government, she was liable to become the victim of the will or injustice of either.

If we were called upon to settle the claims of the two governments to her allegiance, upon the general principles applicable to allegiance, even as recognised by the contending governments, we should be obliged to decide that the superior claim was in South Carolina. For, although before the Revolution a subordinate state, yet it possessed every attribute of a distinct state; and upon principles of national law, the members of a state or political entity continue members of the state notwithstanding a change of government. The relations between the body politic and its members continue the same. The individual member and the national family remain the same, and every member which made up the body, continues in the eye of other nations in his original relation to that body. Thus we see that the American government is at this day claiming indemnity of France for the acts of those who had expelled the reigning family from the throne, and occupied their place.

But it is obvious, that although the common law be the law of South Carolina, and its principles are hostile to the right of putting off our national allegiance; the constitution and legislative acts of South Carolina, when asserting her independence, must be looked into to determine whether she may not then have modified the rigour of the common law, and substituted principles of greater liberality.

South Carolina became virtually independent on the 4th of June, 1775. The association adopted by her provincial congress on that day, constituted her in effect an independent body politic; and if, in international affairs, the fact of exercising power be the evidence of legally possessing it, there was no want of facts to support the inference there; for officers were deposed, and at one time the most influential men in the state were banished under the powers assumed and exercised under that association. It required the indiscriminate subscription and acquiescence of all the inhabitants of the province, under pain of banishment.

Neither of the Constitutions adopted in 1776 or 1778 contains any definition of allegiance, or designation of the individuals who were held bound in allegiance to the state; but the legislative acts passed under those Constitutions, will sufficiently show the received opinion on which the government acted in its legislation upon this subject.

Neither the ordinance for establishing an oath of abjuration and allegiance, passed February 13th, 1777, nor the act of March 28th, 1778, entitled "an act to oblige every free male inhabitant of this state, above a certain age, to give assurance of fidelity and allegiance to the same," holds out any idea of the right of election. The first requires the oath to be taken by any one to whom it is tendered, and the last requires it to be taken by every male inhabitant above sixteen, under pain of perpetual banishment.

The preamble to the latter act indeed admits that protection and allegiance are reciprocal; but the whole course of its legislation shows that the legislature understands the right of election to belong to the state alone, and an election to withdraw allegiance from the state as a crime in the individual. The eleventh, or penal clause, is very explicit on this subject. It runs thus: "that if any person refusing or neglecting to take the oath prescribed by this act, and withdrawing from this state, shall return to the same, then he shall be adjudged guilty of treason against this state, and shall, upon conviction thereof, suffer death as a traitor."

Now, therefore, where there is no allegiance, there can be no treason.

Since, then, the common law of England was the law of allegiance and of descents in South Carolina, when this descent was cast upon the mother, and since remained unaltered by any positive act of legislation of the only power then possessing the right to legislate on the subject; it follows that the representatives of Mrs. Shanks can derive no benefit from her election; unless the right to elect is inherent and unalienable in its nature, and remains above the legislative control of society, notwithstanding the social compact.

All this doctrine I deny. I have already observed that governments cannot be too liberal in extending the right to individuals; but as to its being unalienable, or unaffected by the social compact, I consider it to be no more so than the right to hold, devise, or inherit the lands or acquisitions of an individual. The right to enjoy, transmit, and inherit the fruits of our own labour, or of that of our ancestors, stands on the same footing with the right to employ our industry wherever it can be best employed; and the obligation to obey the laws of the community on the subject of the right to emigrate, is as clearly to be inferred from the reason and nature of things, as the obligation to use or exercise any other of our rights, powers, or faculties, in subordination to the public good. There is not a writer who treats upon the subject, who does not qualify the exercise of the right to emigrate, much more that of putting off or changing our allegiance, with so many exceptions as to time and circumstances, as plainly to show that it cannot be considered as an unalienable or even perfect right. A state of war, want of inhabitants, indispensable talents, transfer of knowledge and wealth to a rival, and various other grounds, are assigned by writers on public law, upon which a nation may lawfully and reasonably limit and restrict the exercise of individual volition in emigrating or putting off our allegiance. All this shows, that whenever an individual proposes to remove, a question of right or obligation arises between himself and the community, which must be decided on in some mode. And what other mode is there but a reference to the positive legislation or received principles of the society itself? It is therefore a subject for municipal regulation; and the security of the individual lies in exerting his influence to obtain laws which will neither expose the community unreasonably on the one hand, nor restrain one individual unjustly on the other.

Nor have we any thing to complain of in this view of the subject. It is a popular and flattering theory, that the only legitimate origin of government is in compact, and the exercise of individual will. That this is not practically true, is obvious from history; for, excepting the state of Massachusetts, and the United States, there is not perhaps on record an instance of a government purely originating in compact. And even here, probably, not more than one-third of those subjected to the government had a voice in the contract. Women, and children under an age arbitrarily

assumed, are necessarily excluded from the right of assent, and yet arbitrarily subjected. If the moral government of our Maker and our parents is to be deduced from gratuitous benefits bestowed on us, why may not the government that has shielded our infancy claim from us a debt of gratitude to be repaid after manhood? In the course of nature, man has need of protection and improvement long before he is able to reciprocate these benefits. These are purchased by the submission and services of our parents; why then should not those to whom we must be indebted for advantages so indispensable to the development of our powers, be permitted, to a certain extent, to bind us apprentice to the community from which they have been and are to be procured?

If it be answered that this power ought not to be extended unreasonably, or beyond the period when we are capable of acting for ourselves; the answer is obvious,—by what rule is the limit to be prescribed, unless by positive municipal regulation?

It is of importance here, that it should be held in view that we are considering political, not moral obligations. The latter are universal and immutable, but the former must frequently vary according to political circumstances. It is the doctrine of the American Court, that the issue of the revolutionary war settled the point, that the American states were free and independent on the 4th of July, 1776. On that day, Mrs. Shanks was found under allegiance to the state of South Carolina, as a natural born citizen to a community, one of whose fundamental principles was, that natural allegiance was unalienable; and this principle was at no time relaxed by that state, by any express provision, while it retained the undivided control over the rights and liabilities of its citizens.

But it is argued that this lady died long after the right of passing laws of naturalization was ceded to the United States, and the United States have in a series of laws admitted foreigners to the right of citizenship, and imposed an oath which contains an express renunciation of natural and every other kind of allegiance. And so of South Carolina; she had previously passed laws to the same effect. In 1704 she passed a law "for making aliens free of this province," which remained in force until 1784, when it was superseded by the act of the 26th of March, "to confer the right of citizenship on aliens;" to which succeeded that of the 22d of March, 1786, entitled "an act to confer certain rights and privileges on aliens, and for repealing the act therein mentioned."

In both the latter acts the oath of allegiance is required to be taken; and that oath, as prescribed by the act of the 28th of March, 1778, contains an abjuration of allegiance to any other power, and particularly to the King of Great Britain.

These legislative acts, it cannot be denied, do seem to hold out the doctrine of the right to change our allegiance, and do furnish ground for insisting, that it is absurd in a government to deny to its own citizens the right of doing that which it encourages to be done by the citizens of other states.

Most certainly it is [to] be regretted that Congress has not long since passed some law upon the subject, containing a liberal extension of this right to individuals, and prescribing the form and circumstances under which it is to be exercised, and by which the act of expatriation shall be authenticated. A want of liberality in legislating on this subject might involve the government in inconsistency; but the question here is whether, in absence of such declaration of the public will or opinion, Courts of justice are at liberty to fasten upon the government, by inference, a doctrine negatived by the common law, and which is in its nature subject to so many modifications.

I think not. Great Britain exercises the same power either by the king's patent or by legislative enactment; and permanent laws exist in that country which extend the rights of naturalization to men by classes, or by general description. Yet this implication has never been fastened upon her; nor is the doctrine of her common law less sternly adhered to, or less frequently applied, even to the utmost extent of the punishing power of her Courts of justice. In practice she moderates its severities; but in this it is will and policy that guides her, not any relaxation of the restriction upon individual rights.

There is indeed one prominent difficulty hanging over this argument which it is impossible to remove. If it proves any thing, it proves too much; since the inference, if resulting at all, must extend to put off one's allegiance, as well to adopted citizens as to natural born citizens; and to all times and all circumstances. What then is that obligation, that allegiance worth, which may be changed a hundred times a day? or by passing over from one army to another, perhaps in the day of battle? The truth is, it leaves but a shadow of a tie to society, and converts that which is considered as one of the most sacred and solemn obligations that can be entered into, although confirmed by the sanctity of an oath, into nothing but an illusory ground of confidence between individuals and their governments.

The idea brings man back to a state of nature; at liberty to herd with whom he pleases, and connected with society only by the caprice of the moment.

Upon the whole, I am of opinion, that Mrs. Shanks continued, as she was born, a citizen of South Carolina; and of course unprotected by the British treaty.

I have taken a general view of the subject, although it does not appear precisely whether or not Mrs. Shanks had attained an age sufficiently mature to make an election before marriage, or was ever discovert during her life, so as to be able to elect after marriage. I have reasoned on the hypothesis most favourable to her, admitting that she had made an election in authentic form. Nor have I confined myself to authority; since I wished, as far as I was instrumental, to have this question settled on principle. But it does appear to me, that in the case of Coxe vs. M'Ilvaine, this Court has decided against the right of election most expressly; for if ever the exercise of will or choice might be inferred from evidence, it is hardly possible for a stronger case to be made out than that which is presented by the facts in that case.

With regard to state decisions upon this question, I would remark, that it is one so exclusively of state cognizance, that the Courts of the respective states must be held

to be best acquainted with their own law upon it. Though every other state in the Union, therefore, should have decided differently from the state of South Carolina, their decisions could only determine their own respective law upon this subject, and could not weaken that of South Carolina with regard to her own law of allegiance and descents. It does appear singular, that we are here called upon to overrule a decision of the Courts of South Carolina, on a point on which they ought to be best informed, and to decide an individual to be a British subject, to whose allegiance the British Courts have solemnly decided the king has no claim. On this point, the case of Ludlow, in Thomas vs. Acklam, is the case of Mrs. Shanks; it is impossible to distinguish them. The state of South Carolina acknowledges her right to all the benefits of allegiance; the King of Great Britain disavows all claim to her allegiance; and yet we are called upon to declare her a British subject.

I have not had opportunity for examining the decisions of all the states upon this subject, but I doubt not they will generally be found to concur in principle with the Court of South Carolina, except so far as they depend upon local law. This is certainly the case in Massachusetts. The decision in the case of Palmer vs. Downer, does, it is true, admit the right of the election; but besides that that case is very imperfectly, and I may add unauthentically reported, it is most certainly overruled in the subsequent case of Martin vs. Woods.

Before I quit the cause, it may be proper to notice a passage in a book recently published in this country, and which has been purchased and distributed under an act of Congress; I mean Gordon's Digest. There is no knowing what degree of authority it may be supposed to acquire by this act of patronage; but if there is any weight in the argument in favour of expatriation drawn from the acts of Congress on that subject, I presume the argument will at some future time be applied to the doctrines contained in this book. If so, it was rather an unhappy measure to patronise it; since we find in it a multitude of nisi prius decisions, obiter dicta, and certainly some striking misapprehensions, ranged on the same shelf with acts of Congress. On the particular subject now under consideration, art. 1649, we find the following sentence: "Citizens of the United States have a right to expatriate themselves in time of war as well as in time of peace, until restrained by Congress;" and for this doctrine the author quotes Talbot vs. Janson, 3 Dall. and the case of the Santissima Trinidada, 7 Wheat. 348; in both which cases the author has obviously mistaken the argument of counsel for the opinion of the Court; for the Court in both cases expressly waive expressing an opinion, as not called for by the case, since, if conceded, the facts were not sufficient to sustain the defence.

The author also quotes a case from 1 Peters' C. R. which directly negatives the doctrine, and a case from 4 Hall's Law Journal, 462, which must have been quoted to sustain the opposite doctrine. It is the case of the United States vs. Williams, in which the Chief Justice of the United States presided, and in which the right of election is expressly negatived, and the individual who pleaded expatriation is convicted and punished.

25

JOSEPH STORY, COMMENTARIES ON THE CONSTITUTION 3:§§ 1098–99
1833

§ 1098. The propriety of confiding the power to establish an uniform rule of naturalization to the national government seems not to have occasioned any doubt or controversy in the convention. For aught that appears on the journals, it was conceded without objection. Under the confederation, the states possessed the sole authority to exercise the power; and the dissimilarity of the system in different states was generally admitted, as a prominent defect, and laid the foundation of many delicate and intricate questions. As the free inhabitants of each state were entitled to all the privileges and immunities of citizens in all the other states, it followed, that a single state possessed the power of forcing into every other state, with the enjoyment of every immunity and privilege, any alien, whom it might choose to incorporate into its own society, however repugnant such admission might be to their polity, conveniencies, and even prejudices. In effect every state possessed the power of naturalizing aliens in every other state; a power as mischievous in its nature, as it was indiscreet in its actual exercise. In one state, residence for a short time might, and did confer the rights of citizenship. In others, qualifications of greater importance were required. An alien, therefore, incapacitated for the possession of certain rights by the laws of the latter, might, by a previous residence and naturalization in the former, elude at pleasure all their salutary regulations for self-protection. Thus the laws of a single state were preposterously rendered paramount to the laws of all the others, even within their own jurisdiction. And it has been remarked with equal truth and justice, that it was owing to mere casualty, that the exercise of this power under the confederation did not involve the Union in the most serious embarrassments. There is great wisdom, therefore, in confiding to the national government the power to establish a uniform rule of naturalization throughout the United States. It is of the deepest interest to the whole Union to know, who are entitled to enjoy the rights of citizens in each state, since they thereby, in effect, become entitled to the rights of citizens in all the states. If aliens might be admitted indiscriminately to enjoy all the rights of citizens at the will of a single state, the Union might itself be endangered by an influx of foreigners, hostile to its institutions, ignorant of its powers, and incapable of a due estimate of its privileges.

§ 1099. It follows, from the very nature of the power, that to be useful, it must be exclusive; for a concurrent power in the states would bring back all the evils and embarrassments, which the uniform rule of the constitution was designed to remedy. And, accordingly, though there was a momentary hesitation, when the constitution first went into operation, whether the power might not still be exercised by the states, subject only to the control of congress, so far as the legislation of the latter extended, as the supreme law; yet the power is now firmly established to be exclusive. The Federalist, indeed, introduced this very case, as entirely clear, to illustrate the doctrine of an exclusive power by implication, arising from the repugnancy of a similar power in the states. "This power must necessarily be exclusive," say the authors; "because, if each state had power to prescribe a distinct rule, there could be no uniform rule."

SEE ALSO:

Generally 4.2.1
Naturalization Law, 13 Geo. III, c. 21 (1773)
Virginia, Act Declaring Who Shall Be Deemed Citizens of This Commonwealth, 26 June 1779, 10 Hening 129–30
John Jay to Benjamin Franklin, 31 May 1781, Unpublished Papers 2:80–82
Charles Pinckney, Observations on the Plan of Government, 1787, Farrand 3:120
Records of the Federal Convention, Farrand 1:245; 2:144, 158, 167, 182, 445, 483, 486, 489, 569, 570, 595
An Act to Establish an Uniform Rule of Naturalization, 1 Stat. 103 (1790)
Kentucky Constitution of 1792, art. 3, cl. 27, Thorpe 3:1276
An Act to Establish an Uniform Rule of Naturalization, 1 Stat. 414 (1795)
United States v. *Villato*, 28 Fed. Cas. 377, no. 16,622 (C.C.D.Pa. 1797)
House of Representatives, Naturalization Law, 3 May 1798, Annals 8:1570–82
House of Representatives, Alien Enemies, 19 June 1798, Annals 8:1974–78
An Act respecting Alien Enemies, 1 Stat. 577 (1798)
An Act concerning Aliens, 1 Stat. 570 (1798)
Den v. *Brown*, 2 Halstead 305 (N.J. 1799)
An Act to Establish an Uniform Rule of Naturalization, 2 Stat. 153 (1802)
St. George Tucker, Blackstone's Commentaries 2:369–70 (1803)
An Act in Addition to an Act, Etc., 2 Stat. 292 (1804)
Murray v. *Schooner Charming Betsy*, 2 Cranch 64 (1804)
Kilham v. *Ward*, 2 Mass. 236 (1806)
Campbell v. *Gordon*, 6 Cranch 176 (1810)
Louisiana Constitution of 1812, art. 6, secs. 12, 22, Thorpe 3:1389, 1390
Clarke v. *Morey*, 10 Johns. 69 (N.Y. 1813)
Ainslie v. *Martin*, 9 Mass. 454 (1813)
Jackson v. *Decker*, 11 Johns. 418 (N.Y. 1814)
Chirac v. *Chirac*, 2 Wheat. 259 (1817)
House of Representatives, Expatriation, 26, 28 Feb. 1818, Annals: 31:1029–52, 1054–70
Richards v. *McDaniel*, 2 Noll & McCord 351 (S.C. 1820)
Goodell v. *Jackson*, 20 Johns. 693 (N.Y. 1823)

1

WILLIAM BLACKSTONE, COMMENTARIES 2:471–73
1766

X. Bankruptcy; a title which we before lightly touched upon, so far as it related to the transfer of the real estate of the bankrupt. At present we are to treat of it more minutely, as it principally relates to the disposition of chattels, in which the property of persons concerned in trade more usually consists, than in lands or tenements. Let us therefore first of all consider, 1. *Who* may become a bankrupt: 2. What *acts* make a bankrupt: 3. The *proceedings* on a commission of bankrupt: and, 4. In what manner an estate in goods and chattels may be *transferred* by bankruptcy.

1. Who may become a bankrupt. A bankrupt was before defined to be "a trader, who secretes himself, or does certain other acts, tending to defraud his creditors." He was formerly considered merely in the light of a criminal or offender; and in this spirit we are told by sir Edward Coke, that we have fetched as well the name, as the wickedness, of bankrupts from foreign nations. But at present the laws of bankruptcy are considered as laws calculated for the benefit of trade, and founded on the principles of humanity as well as justice; and to that end they confer some privileges, not only on the creditors, but also on the bankrupt or debtor himself. On the creditors; by compelling the bankrupt to give up all his effects to their use, without any fraudulent concealment: on the debtor; by exempting him from the rigor of the general law, whereby his person might be confined at the discretion of his creditor, though in reality he has nothing to satisfy the debt; whereas the law of bankrupts, taking into consideration the sudden and unavoidable accidents to which men in trade are liable, has given them the liberty of their persons, and some pecuniary emoluments, upon condition they surrender up their whole estate to be divided among their creditors.

In this respect our legislature seems to have attended to the example of the Roman law. I mean not the terrible law of the twelve tables; whereby the creditors might cut the debtor's body into pieces, and each of them take his proportionable share: if indeed that law, *de debitore in partes secando*, is to be understood in so very butcherly a light; which many learned men have with reason doubted. Nor do I mean those less inhuman laws (if they may be called so, as *their* meaning is indisputably certain) of imprisoning the debtor's person in chains; subjecting him to stripes and hard labour, at the mercy of his rigid creditor; and sometimes selling him, his wife, and children, to perpetual foreign slavery *trans Tiberim:* an oppression, which produced so many popular insurrections, and secessions to the *mons sacer*. But I mean the law of *cession*, introduced by the christian emperors; whereby if a debtor ceded, or yielded up, all his fortune to his creditors, he was secured from being dragged to a gaol, *"omni quoque corporali cruciatu semoto."* For, as the emperor justly observes, *"inhumanum erat spoliatum fortunis suis in solidum damnari."* Thus far was just and reasonable: but, as the departing from one extreme is apt to produce it's opposite, we find it afterwards enacted, that if the debtor by any unforeseen accident was reduced to low circumstances, and would *swear* that he had not sufficient left to pay his debts, he should not be compelled to cede or give up even that which he had in his possession: a law, which under a false notion of humanity, seems to be fertile of perjury, injustice, and absurdity.

The laws of England, more wisely, have steered in the middle between both extremes: providing at once against the inhumanity of the creditor, who is not suffered to confine an honest bankrupt after his effects are delivered up; and at the same time taking care that all his just debts shall be paid, so far as the effects will extend. But still they are cautious of encouraging prodigality and extravagance by this indulgence to debtors; and therefore they allow the benefit of the laws of bankruptcy to none but actual *traders;* since that set of men are, generally speaking, the only persons liable to accidental losses, and to an inability of paying their debts, without any fault of their own. If persons in other situations of life run in debt without the power of payment, they must take the consequences of their own indiscretion, even though they meet with sudden accidents that may reduce their fortunes: for the law holds it to be an unjustifiable practice, for any person but a tradesman to encumber himself with debts of any considerable value. If a gentleman, or one in a liberal profession, at the time of contracting his debts, has a sufficient fund to pay them, the delay of payment is a species of dishonesty, and a temporary injustice to his creditor: and if, at such time, he has no sufficient fund, the dishonesty and injustice is the greater. He cannot therefore murmur, if he suffers the punishment which he has voluntarily drawn upon himself. But in mercantile transactions the case is far otherwise. Trade cannot be carried on without mutual credit on both sides: the contracting of debts is therefore here not only justifiable, but necessary. And if by accidental calamities, as by the loss of a ship in a tempest, the failure of brother traders, or by the non-payment of persons out of trade, a merchant or tradesman becomes incapable of discharging his own debts, it is his misfortune and not his fault. To the misfortunes therefore of debtors the law has given a compassionate remedy, but denied it to their faults: since, at the same time that it provides for the security of commerce, by enacting that every considerable trader may be declared a bankrupt, for the benefit of his creditors as well as himself, it has also to discourage extravagance declared, that no one shall be capable of being made a bankrupt, but only a *trader;* nor capable of receiving the full benefit of the statutes, but only an *industrious* trader.

2

ABRAHAM BALDWIN, UNIFORM BANKRUPTCY, HOUSE OF REPRESENTATIVES
15 Jan. 1799
Annals 9:2670–71

But it is insisted on, said Mr. B., by some gentlemen, that as the power to pass uniform laws on the subject of bankruptcy is expressly given to Congress by the Constitution, it is their duty to do it; and some go as far as to say that it is not proper for the States to legislate on that subject. He thought there was no great weight in that argument. Congress not having passed such a law for these ten years past, and the States having legislated upon it in their own way, is a sufficient proof that that has not been the understanding of the Constitution.

3

ST. GEORGE TUCKER, BLACKSTONE'S COMMENTARIES
1:APP. 259–60
1803

There are few subjects upon which there is less practical information to be obtained in Virginia, than that of bankruptcies. The English statutes of Bankruptcy have never been regarded as in force, here; and the manner in which the commerce of the colony was conducted, before the revolution, by no means seemed to favour their adoption. In a commercial country, such as England, the necessity of good faith in contracts, and the support of commerce, oblige the legislature to secure for the creditors the persons of bankrupts. It is, however, necessary to distinguish between the fraudulent and the honest bankrupt: the one should be treated with rigor; but the bankrupt, who, after a strict examination, has proved before proper judges, that either the fraud, or losses of others, or misfortunes unavoidable by human prudence, have stripped him of his substance, ought to receive a very different treatment. Let his whole property be taken from him, for the benefit of his creditors; let his debt, if you will, not be considered as cancelled, till the payment of the whole; let him be refused the liberty of leaving his country without leave of his creditors, or of carrying into another nation that industry, which, under a penalty, he should be obliged to employ for their benefit; but what pretence can justify the depriving an innocent, though unfortunate man, of his liberty, as is said to be the practice in some parts of Europe, in order to extort from him the discovery of his fraudulent transactions, after having failed of such a discovery, upon the most rigorous examination of his conduct and affairs!

But, how necessary soever, bankrupt laws may be in great commercial countries, the introduction of them into such as are supported chiefly by agriculture, seems to be an experiment which should be made with great caution. Among merchants and other traders, with whom credit is often a substitute for a capital, and whose only actual property is the gain, which they make by their credit, out of the property of others, a want of punctuality in their contracts, may well be admitted as a ground to suspect fraud, or insolvency. But the farmer has generally a visible capital, the whole of which he can never employ, at the same time, in a productive manner. His want of punctuality may arise from bad crops, unfavourable seasons, low markets, and other causes, which however they may embarrass, endanger not his solvency; his property is incapable of removal, or of that concealment, which fraudulent traders may practise with success; his transactions within the proper line of his occupation are few, and not liable to intricacy; whilst the merchant is perhaps engaged in a dozen different copartnerships, in which his name does not appear, and in speculations which it might require a life to unravel. To expose both to the same rigorous, and summary mode of procedure, would be utterly inconsistent with those maxims of policy, which limit laws to their proper objects, only. And accordingly, we find, that even in England, where the interests of commerce are consulted on all occasions, and where they are never sacrificed, (unless, perhaps, to ambition,) the bankrupt laws cannot affect a farmer, who confines himself to the proper sphere of his occupation; and the bankrupt law of the United States, 6 congress, 1 session, c. 19, is confined to merchants, or other persons, actually using the trade of merchandise, by buying and selling in gross, or by retail, or dealing in exchange as a banker, broker, factor, underwriter, or marine insurer. Whilst the bankrupt laws are confined to such characters, and are resorted to, merely as a necessary regulation of commerce, their effect, in preventing frauds, especially where the parties or their property may lie, or be removed into different states, will probably be so salutary, that the expediency of this branch of the powers of congress, will cease to be drawn in question.

4

UNITED STATES V. FISHER

2 Cranch 358 (1805)

MARSHALL, Ch. J. . . . If the act has attempted to give the United States a preference in the case before the court, it remains to inquire whether the constitution obstructs its operation.

To the general observations made on this subject, it will only be observed, that as the court can never be unmindful of the solemn duty imposed on the judicial department when a claim is supported by an act which conflicts with the constitution, so the court can never be unmindful of its duty to obey laws which are authorised by that instrument.

In the case at bar, the preference claimed by the United States is not prohibited; but it has been truly said that under a constitution conferring specific powers, the power contended for must be granted, or it cannot be exercised.

It is claimed under the authority to make all laws which shall be necessary and proper to carry into execution the powers vested by the constitution in the government of the United States, or in any department or officer thereof.

In construing this clause it would be incorrect and would produce endless difficulties, if the opinion should be maintained that no law was authorised which was not indispensably necessary to give effect to a specified power.

Where various systems might be adopted for that purpose, it might be said with respect to each, that it was not necessary, because the end might be obtained by other means. Congress must possess the choice of means, and must be empowered to use any means which are in fact conducive to the exercise of a power granted by the constitution.

The government is to pay the debt of the union, and must be authorised to use the means which appear to itself most eligible to effect that object. It has consequently a right to make remittances by bills or otherwise, and to take those precautions which will render the transaction safe.

This claim of priority on the part of the United States will, it has been said, interfere with the right of the state sovereignties respecting the dignity of debts, and will defeat the measures they have a right to adopt to secure themselves against delinquencies on the part of their own revenue officers.

But this is an objection to the constitution itself. The mischief suggested, so far as it can really happen, is the necessary consequence of the supremacy of the laws of the United States on all subjects to which the legislative power of congress extends.

5

HARRISON V. STERRY

5 Cranch 289 (1809)

March 15th, 1809. MARSHALL, Ch. J., delivered the opinion of the court, as follows, viz:—The object of this suit is to obtain the direction of the court, for the distribution of certain funds in South Carolina, which were the property of a company trading in England, under the firm of Bird, Savage & Bird, and in America, under the firm of Robert Bird & Co. The United States claim a preference to all other creditors, and their claim will be first considered.

I. Two points have been suggested, as taking this case out of the operation of the preceding decisions of the court respecting the priority to which the United States are entitled. 1. That the contract was made with foreigners, in a foreign country. 2. That the United States have waived their privilege, by proving their debt under the commission of bankruptcy.

1. The words of the act, which entitle the United States to a preference, do not restrain that privilege to contracts made within the United States, or with American citizens. To authorize this court to impose that limitation on them, there must be some principle in the nature of the case which requires it. The court can discern no such principle. The law of the place where a contract is made is, generally speaking, the law of the contract; *i. e.,* it is the law by which the contract is expounded. But the right of priority forms no part of the contract itself. It is extrinsic, and is rather a personal privilege, dependent on the law of the place where the property lies, and where the court sits which is to decide the cause. In the familiar case of the administration of the estate of a deceased person, the assets are always distributed according to the dignity of the debt, as regulated by the law of the country where the representative of the deceased acts, and from which he derives his powers; not by the law of the country where the contract was made. In this country, and in its courts, in a contest respecting property lying in this country, the

United States are not deprived of that priority which the laws give them, by the circumstance that the contract was made in a foreign country, with a person resident abroad.

2. Nor is this priority waived, by proving the debt before the commissioners of the bankrupt. The 62d section of the bankrupt act expressly declares, that "nothing contained in that law shall, in any manner, affect the right of preference to prior satisfaction of debts due to the United States, as secured by any law heretofore passed." There is nothing in the act which restrains the United States from proving their debt under the commission, and the 62d section controls, so far as respects the United States, the operation of those clauses in the law which direct the assignees to distribute the funds of the bankrupt equally among all those creditors who prove their debts under the commission. Omit this section, and the argument of the counsel for the general creditors would be perfectly correct. The coming in as a creditor, under the commission, might then be considered as electing to be classed with other creditors. But the operation of this saving clause is not confined to cases in which the United States decline to prove their debt under the commission. It is universal. It introduces, then, an exception from the general rule laid down in the 29th and 30th sections of the act, and leaves to the United States that right, to full satisfaction of their debts, to the exclusion of other creditors, to which they would be entitled, had they not proved their debt, under the commission.

The priority of the United States is to be maintained in this case, unless some of the creditors can show a title to the property anterior to the time when this priority attaches. The assignment made to Richard Harrison is, it is contended, such a title. To this assignment, several objections have been made.

1st. It is said, that Robert Bird was not authorized to make it, because it is not a transaction within the usual course of trade. But this court is of opinion, that it is such a transaction. The whole commercial business of the company in the United States was necessarily committed to Robert Bird, the only partner residing in this country. He had the command of their funds in America, and could collect or transfer the debts due to them. The assignment under consideration is an act of this character, and is within the power usually exercised by a managing partner. In such a transaction, he had a right to sign the name of both firms, and his act is the act of all the partners.

2d. It is the assignment of a *chose in action;* and is, therefore, to be considered rather as a contract than an actual transfer, and could be of no validity against the several claimants in this case. The authorities cited at bar, especially those from 1 Atkins, and Williams's Law Cases, are conclusive on this point, to prove that equity will support an equitable assignment.

3d. But a third exception has been taken to this instrument, which the court deems a substantial one. It is made under circumstances which expose it to the charge of being a fraud on the bankrupt laws. Considered as the act of Bird, Savage & Bird, it is dated but a few days before their bankruptcy; and considered as the act of Robert Bird & Co., it is but a short time before they stopped payment, and is made at a time when there is much reason to believe, from the face of the deed, as well as from extrinsic circumstances, that such an event was in contemplation.

Money actually advanced upon the credit of this assignment, subsequent to its date, might perhaps be secured by it; but there is no evidence, that any money was actually advanced upon it, and the face of the instrument itself would not encourage such an opinion. It might be caught at, by those who were already creditors, but holds forth no inducements to become creditors. It was impossible for any person viewing it, to judge of the sufficiency of the fund, or of the pre-existing liens on it. This assignment, therefore, under all its circumstances, many of which are not here recited, is no bar to the claim of the United States, or of the attaching-creditors.

This being the case, there exists no obstacle to the priority claimed by the United States, and their debt is to be first satisfied out of the fund to be distributed by the court.

II. The attaching-creditors are next in order. By the bankrupt law of the United States, their priority, as to the funds of the bankrupt, is lost. They can only claim a dividend with other creditors. So far, then, as the effects attached are the effects of the bankrupt, their lien is removed by the bankruptcy. Robert Bird alone has become a bankrupt under the laws of the United States. Consequently, only his private property and his interest in the funds of the company pass to his assignees. This interest is subject to the claim of his copartners, and if, upon a settlement of accounts, Robert Bird should appear to be the creditor or the debtor of the company, his interest would be proportionably enlarged or diminished. But he is not alleged to be either a creditor or a debtor; and of consequence, the court consider his interest as being one undivided third of the fund. This third goes to his assignees.

As the bankrupt law of a foreign country is incapable of operating a legal transfer of property in the United States, the remaining two-thirds of the fund are liable to the attaching-creditors, according to the legal preference obtained by their attachments.

The court thinks it equitable, to order that those creditors who claim under the deed of the 31st of January 1803, and who have not proved their debts under the commission of bankruptcy, should be now admitted to the same dividend out of the estate of the bankrupt as they would have received, if, instead of relying on the deed, they had proved their debts. The assignees, therefore, take this fund subject to that equitable claim, and in making the dividend, those creditors are to receive, in the first instance, so much as will place them on an equal footing with the creditors who have proved their debts under the commission.

With respect to any surplus which may remain of the two-thirds, after satisfying the United States, and the attaching-creditors, it ought to be divided equally among all the creditors, so as to place them on an equal footing with each other. The dividends paid by the British assignees, and those made by the American assignees, being taken into consideration, this residuum is to be so divided between them as to produce equality between the respective creditors.

6

GOLDEN V. PRINCE

10 Fed. Cas. 542, no. 5,509 (C.C.D.Pa. 1814)

WASHINGTON, Circuit Justice. This is an action brought upon a bill of exchange drawn by the defendant, on the 10th of May, 1811, at St. Barts, for value received there, in favour of the plaintiff, on himself, at Philadelphia, 90 days after sight, which was regularly noted for non-acceptance, and protested for non-payment. This action was brought on the 4th of May, 1812; to which the defendant pleaded in bar, his discharge, under a law of this state, passed on the 13th of March, 1812, for the relief of insolvent debtors; obtained provisionally on the 23d of April, and finally, on the 29th of May, 1812. The case agreed, states, that the defendant did not give to the plaintiff, or to any agent of his, notice of the defendant's petition, which was presented on the 20th of April, 1812, although the plaintiff's attorney was informed of the application a few days after it was made; nor has the plaintiff proved his debt under the said proceedings. The act referred to in the plea declares, that a debtor who has conformed to the several regulations of the law, for the purpose of vesting all his property in the assignees, for the benefit of his creditors, and who has received his certificate of discharge from the commissioners, shall be set at large by the sheriff, if he be imprisoned; and that such certificate shall be conclusive evidence of the fact, that such petitioner has been discharged by virtue of that act; and shall be construed to discharge such insolvent from all debts and demands due from him, or for which he was liable, at the date of such certificate, or contract, or originating before that time, though payable afterwards. It is objected to this plea—1. That the act under which the discharge is claimed, having been passed since the year 1789, affords no binding rule for the government of this court:—2. That the law is unconstitutional and void in two respects; as being a bankrupt law—and as being a law impairing the obligation of contracts.

. . . . .

The next question is, whether the law relied upon by the defendant, to bar the present action, is repugnant to the constitution of the United States; and, on that account, is not to be regarded by the court, in this case? We shall reverse the order pursued by the counsel, and consider, in the first place, whether this law is repugnant to the constitution, upon the ground of its impairing the obligation of contracts? It may be proper to premise, that a law may be unconstitutional, and of course void, in relation to particular cases; and yet valid to all intents and purposes, in its application to other cases within the scope of its provisions, but varying from the other in particular circumstances. Thus, a law prospective in its operation, under which a contract afterwards made, may be avoided in a way different from that provided by the parties, would be clearly

constitutional; because the stipulations of the parties, which are inconsistent with such a law, never had a legal existence, and of course could not be impaired by the law. But if the law act retrospectively, as to other contracts, so as to impair their obligation, the law is invalid; or, in milder terms, it affords no rule of decision in these latter cases.

The question then is, whether a law of a state, which declares that a debtor, by delivering up his estate for the benefit of his creditors, shall be for ever discharged from the payment of his debts, due or contracted before the passage of the law;—whether the creditor do any act, or not, in aid of the law; can be set up to bar the right of such creditor to recover his debt, either in a federal or state court? We feel no difficulty in saying that it cannot; because the law is, in its nature and operation, one which, in the case supposed, impairs the obligation of a contract. What is the obligation of a contract? It is to do, or not to do, a certain thing; and this may be either absolutely, or under some condition; immediately, or at some future time, or times; and at some specified place, or generally. A law, therefore, which authorizes the discharge of a contract, by a smaller sum, or at a different time, or in a different manner than the parties have stipulated, impairs its obligation, by substituting for the contract of the parties, one which they never entered into; and to the performance of which, they of course had never consented. The old contract is completely annulled, and a legislative contract imposed upon the parties in lieu of it. That a law which declares a subsisting contract to be void, impairs its obligation, will, we presume, be admitted by all men who can understand the force of the plainest terms; or, if not so, then we should be curious to know by what means the obligation of a contract can be impaired? And if this be the effect of such a law; in what respect does it differ from another, which declares, that a debt consisting of a specified sum, and due at an appointed period of time, shall be discharged at a more distant, or indeed at a different time, or with a smaller sum? The degree of injury to the creditor, may not be so great in the one case as in the other; but the principle is precisely the same. That the framers of the constitution were extremely jealous of the exercise of such a power by the state governments, is apparent from other parts of the section, in which the provision we are examining is found. It would have been a vain thing, to prohibit the state legislatures from passing laws, by which a contract might be annulled, or discharged, by payment of a less sum than is stipulated, if they could emit bills of credit, and make them, or any thing but gold and silver coin, a tender in payment of debts; and, therefore, they are expressly forbid to pass any such laws. And yet, a law, which should make a depreciated paper currency a tender in payment of debts, might be less injurious to the creditor, than one which discharges the debt altogether, upon the payment of perhaps a shilling in the pound, or any other sum less than that stipulated to be paid.

The opinion given upon this last point decides the cause in favour of the plaintiff; and we might well spare ourselves the trouble of examining the other objection made by the plaintiff's counsel to the validity of this law. But, when we observe, from the case under consideration, that a power to pass bankrupt laws is deemed by one state, at least, to be rightfully vested in the state legislature; (for otherwise we must suppose it would not have been exercised;) and when we recollect, that the constitution of the United States contains a grant of other powers to the general government, which may equally with that immediately under consideration be exercised by the state legislatures, if such a right exist in either case; we hold it to be our duty to embrace the first opportunity which presents itself, to express the unhesitating opinion which we entertain upon these great questions, and thus to pave the way for as early a decision of them, as possible, by the supreme national court. No citizen feels a higher respect than we do for the state governments, or would be more cautious in questioning the validity of any laws which their legislatures might think proper to enact. But we should very unfaithfully discharge our duty, were we to remain silent witnesses of designed or unintentional usurpations, by these governments, of powers properly belonging to the general government; when a case comes judicially before us, which demands an expression of our opinion on these subjects. The sooner the limits which separate the two governments are marked by those authorities, which can alone define and establish them, the less danger there will be of serious, if not fatal collisions hereafter, arising respecting essential powers, to which a prescriptive right may be asserted by the one, in opposition to the chartered rights of the other. It is from these considerations that we venture respectfully, yet firmly, to examine the question, whether the power given to congress to pass uniform laws of bankruptcy, be exclusive of such power in the state governments; and whether the latter may exercise it whenever the former has not thought proper to do so.

It would seem, at the first view of this question, that, if an unqualified power be granted to a government to do a particular act, the whole of that power is disposed of, and not a part of it; consequently, that no power over the same subject remains with those who made the grant, either to exercise it themselves, or to part with it to any other government. But, if the application of this principle to the complicated systems of government which prevail in the United States, should be liable to doubt, it will, we presume, be admitted with this qualification; that whenever such a power is given to the general government, the exercise of which by the state governments would be inconsistent with the express grant, the whole of the power is granted, and, consequently, vests exclusively in the general government. In such a case, the people resume the power, which before resided in the state governments as to this subject, without which they could not grant the whole to the general government; and, if resumed, it would seem to follow, that the state governments can in no event exercise the same power, without showing either an express grant of it, or that it is fairly to be deduced from the circumstance upon which the claim is founded. That the exercise of the power to pass bankrupt and naturalization laws by the state governments, is incompatible with the grant of a power to congress to pass uniform laws on the same subjects, is obvious, from the consideration that the

former would be dissimilar and frequently contradictory; whereas the systems are directed to be uniform, which can only be rendered so by the exclusive power in one body to form them.

It was admitted, in the argument of this cause, that whenever congress shall think proper to exercise the power granted to that body, to pass uniform laws of bankruptcy, the state governments cannot legislate upon the same subject. But it was contended, that, if congress shall decline to exercise the power, the right to pass such laws results to the state governments. This conclusion appears to us to beg the whole question in controversy. It resigns all claim to a concurrent right in the state governments, and sets up one which is to arise on a condition, not to be found in the constitution, but which is gratuitously interpolated into it. If, then, this claim of the state legislatures is not founded upon any express grant made to them in the constitution, is it to be deduced from the circumstance of a nonuser of the power by congress? This doctrine appears to us to be as extravagent as it is novel. It has no analogy, that we know of, in legal or political science. It must, in some way or other, be likened to the case of forfeiture, which could not, we conceive, answer the purpose; because, if the power of congress is, upon principles purely legal, divested by an omission to exercise a valid right, it would not of necessity result to the state governments, but would more naturally revert to the people. If the forfeiture be political, then this absurdity would follow, that congress would possess a right to do, by omission, what it must be admitted they could not effect by any direct and positive act:—that is, to delegate to the state governments the power of legislation over a particular subject, of which the people had thought proper not only to deprive the state governments, but to vest exclusively in the national legislature. The inconvenience of dissimilar and discordant rules upon the subjects of bankruptcy and of naturalization, no doubt, suggested to the framers of the constitution, the remedy which that body adopted, of vesting the right to legislate in those cases in the general government; that some uniform system might prevail throughout the United States, if congress should think that any regulations upon those subjects ought at all to be made. Now, it would not only violate the express grant of these powers to congress, but the policy which led the convention to withdraw them from the state governments, if they should be construed to result by implication to the latter, on account of the omission of the former to exercise them.

But let us examine into the reasonableness of this pretension of the state legislatures, and see if the policy which induced the grant of these powers to congress be not effectually answered by the omission of congress to legislate on those subjects as much as if they had done so. Suppose the subject of a bankrupt law to be brought before congress, and the questions to be whether such a system be a wise one under any circumstances, or be at all suitable to the present state of the country; and that body should, in its wisdom, decide negatively on those questions, it would seem to follow, that no bankrupt law ought to exist in the United States, for the reasons which induced the rejection of any plan to establish such a system. In this case, what is congress to do, in order to give effect to this policy? The answer is plain,—reject the bill and do nothing. Then the law of the land would be, that no man is compelled, against his will, to deliver up his property to be distributed amongst his creditors; and, consequently, that he is at all times liable to the payment of his debts, unless discharged by some other legal means. Now, will it be said that the state legislatures, availing themselves of the refusal of congress to act upon this subject, can be at liberty to thwart the very policy which induced it; and pass laws upon the same subject, not only changing the state of the law as congress had constitutionally left it, but impugning the policy which led the convention to deprive the state legislatures of the power altogether, by imposing upon the country at large a variety of systems, instead of one uniform system? To argue, that to prevent such an absurd consequence, congress must legislate upon the subject, is to assert, that in the exercise of a power intended to promote the general good, congress must do some act, which, in its wisdom, it believes will produce a public evil—do wrong that good may come of it—a doctrine, as pernicious in politics as it is wicked in morals. How would state laws upon this subject, and in the case supposed, differ, otherwise than in degree, from similar laws, passed inconsistent with such as congress might think proper to enact upon the same subject? In the one case, the policy and the law of congress might be opposed in part only by the state law. But in the other, the whole policy and law are defeated by inconsistent rules, upon a subject where congress supposed that it was unwise to establish even a uniform rule.

7

GILL V. JACOBS
10 Fed. Cas. 373, no. 5,426 (C.C.D.S.C. 1816)

DRAYTON, District Judge. This was a case of habeas corpus, in which a motion was made to discharge defendant on common bail, he being in the marshal's custody on mesne process issuing from this court, with an order for bail. The plaintiffs are citizens of Philadelphia; and the debt to a considerable amount (upwards of six thousand dollars) was contracted with them there. The defendant having been arrested by process, issuing from the state court of common pleas, has been discharged by the same authority, under the insolvent debtor's act of this state, passed in the year 1759. He therefore contends he should be enlarged on giving common bail, as he has been arrested since he was so discharged. On the part of the plaintiffs it is urged they were not parties to this discharge, not having due notice; nor were they parties to the record. That they have not agreed to receive any portion of the dividends, and, therefore, they ought not to be delayed, or prevented having due relief, under the laws of the United States and the practice of this court.

The case before me being strictly a mercantile contract will be considered as referring to those laws which relate to commerce and merchandise. As respects their principles, it is contended there is a difference between a bankrupt and an insolvent debtor; as the first becomes so by omissions and commissions, as well as by compulsory process; whereas, the latter is so situated, by the effects of a suit at law, and by taking the benefit of an insolvent debtor's act thereupon, for regaining his liberty. This distinction, and the discharge obtained in the state court, appear to be the general grounds on which the argument seems to rest. For bankrupts being exclusively concerned in trade and merchandise, in buying and selling in gross, or by retail; dealing in exchange and in other acts of necessary commercial intercourse; it seems but reasonable they should be protected and controlled by laws more especially for themselves, and which the practice of civilized nations is in the habit of ordaining. Hence a bankrupt law may be very different from an insolvent debtor's act, as a bankrupt law relates to the interest of merchants and traders; where, an insolvent act relates to the general interest of society. If, then, this distinction of interest prevail, can it be said the distinction of rights does not also prevail?

By the eighth section, first article, of the United States constitution, congress have a right "to regulate commerce with foreign nations, and among the several states," also to establish "uniform laws on the subject of bankruptcies throughout the United States." The power, then, of making bankrupt laws no longer remains with the several states; it is vested in the United States government. And how far a transient merchant, indebted in Philadelphia, can plead in this circuit court for the district of South Carolina a discharge under the insolvent debtor's act of South Carolina, obtained in the state court, against a suit instituted in this court, is the question which is now before me. On this point, involving the rights of the United States and individual states, I feel myself delicately situated in deciding the contending claims. More especially, as one of the particular reasons for calling into existence the present constitution of the United States was to equalize the commerce and trade, and the rights and privileges of the American and other merchants and traders throughout the Union, and with foreign nations. Unless, then, the question be considered as having this grand object in view, the merits of this case will be carried back to where they would have been before the passing of the constitution. The lex loci and lex fori of the several states would be brought under special consideration, as having more controlling powers than I think ought to be admitted at this day. Each state would then by such reasoning be deemed to authorize discharges of insolvency according to its own laws, and in mercantile concerns; not by uniform laws resting on the same principles, and promoting the same ends, but sometimes conflicting in points of justice and expediency not only with themselves but with the United States, and the principles of their superintending government.

On the 4th of April, 1800 [2 Stat. 19], a bankrupt law was passed. It was limited to the term of five years; and from thence to the end of the next session of congress thereafter, and no longer. It then expired, and there has never been since any bankrupt law in the United States. What were the reasons which influenced congress not to revive that act, or not to pass a new one, is not for me to say. Although it would appear that the different decisions which take place in the courts of the United States, and in those of the individual states, afford some grounds for the reconsideration of a bankrupt law; as well as the great inconvenience resulting from the want of one to which parties are occasionally subjected, by vexatious suits in different states of the Union against insolvent debtors, after they have obtained insolvent discharges in one of the states. In passing the bankrupt law it is evident congress looked towards bankrupt merchants and traders especially, as respecting the insolvent act of state authorities. For in the sixty-first section of the bankrupt law—5 Smith's Laws U. S. p. 81 [2 Stat. 36]—it is expressly enacted that this act shall not "repeal or annul, or be construed to repeal or annul, the laws of any state now in force, or which may be hereafter enacted, for the relief of insolvent debtors, except so far as the same may respect persons who are or may be clearly within the purview of this act." It is said, however, this act has expired; it does not thence follow that the reasons which gave rise to the exception do not still exist. And so far it does not come within the rule of "cessante ratione, cessata et ipsa lex." If, then, they do exist, I see not why for national and commercial purposes this court should not give them a consideration, although they be not engrafted into a bankrupt law. Under this impression it would seem the distinction taken by the defendant's counsel between a bankrupt law and an insolvent debtor's act has not been improperly introduced.

Among the great features of government, population and credit are to be ranked. As to the population, congress has equalized that by acts of naturalization throughout the United States; but having no bankrupt law, the credit as to provisions for bankrupts, and for securing the rights of their creditors, has not been so equalized, resting at present upon the insolvent acts of individual states, and the discretion and decisions of courts having cognizance. It hence results that foreigners and citizens of different states will look to the government of the United States for some general system, as either emanating from their laws or from their courts; and more particularly when they commence suits in the courts of the United States. The obligation is, therefore, the more imposing upon these courts, having this high responsibility to carry all such suits into effect in as uniform a manner as possible, so far as their authorities will permit, agreeably to the rights and just expectations of individuals, and the confidence so reposed in the United States government.

. . . . .

Upon the whole, without touching any other contested points of the argument (deeming it unnecessary in the opinion I am about to give), the case appears to me to resolve itself into this: That by the constitution of the United States the individual states have given up their rights of legislating as to commerce and bankruptcy; that this right is now solely in possession of the United States government, which, through its laws and judiciary, is bound to watch over and superintend the same; that no

bankrupt law existing at this time does not affect the main question, because the right in government still remains to enact one, or to repose its confidence in the judiciary as to their decision respecting the same, in relation to the state laws; that the courts of the United States by admitting defendants to the benefit of the state insolvent acts, under the superintending and contracting power of the laws of the United States now existing, can and do promote the due ends of justice as relating to bankrupts. But it must be remembered all this is done under the authority of the United States and not under that of state authorities, although in doing so the insolvent acts of the states are referred to as rules of decisions in cases when they apply, as declared by the thirty-fourth section of the judiciary act. Under these impressions I do not think that by insolvent discharges from the courts of this state the insolvent debtor's acts of this state should be allowed to suspend or weaken the lien of process in this court, in the manner contended for in this case. It would be an interference between creditors and debtors, and certainly would tend to impair the obligation of contracts.

8

FARMERS & MECHANICS' BANK V. SMITH
3 Serg. & Rawle 63 (Pa. 1816)

TILGHMAN, C. J. I agree with the counsel for the plaintiff, in considering the act of assembly, on which the question in this case arises, as a bankrupt act. Such, it certainly is, in its nature, although confined in its operation, to a particular part of the state. It has the leading features of a bankrupt law; the discharge from all debts, in consideration of the surrender of the property of the debtor, and it possesses the details usually found in bankrupt laws, for carrying the main design into effect. The validity of this law is contested, as violating the constitution of the *United States* in two respects; 1st, In assuming a power which has been *exclusively* vested in the Congress of the *United States*. 2. In *impairing the obligation of contracts*, contrary to the express prohibition of the 10th sect. of the 1st art. of the constitution.

1. Congress has power, "to establish uniform laws on the subject of bankruptcies, throughout the *United States*," Constitution, art. 1. sect. 8. Hence it is contended, that no state has power to pass a law on the subject of bankruptcy. There would be great strength in this argument, if Congress had exercised their power, by passing a bankrupt law; because then, the uniformity which they were authorized to establish, would be broken in upon, by the act of an individual state. But it is to be considered, whether the power of Congress is *exclusive, even when they do not think proper to exercise it;* for thus the matter is at present circumstanced. Antecedent to the adoption of the Federal constitution, the power of the several states was supreme and unlimited. It follows, therefore, that all power, not trans-

ferred to the *United States*, remains in the states and the people, according to their several constitutions. This would have been the sound construction of the constitution, without amendment. But the jealousy of those, who feared that the federal government would absorb all the power of the states, caused it to be expressly recognized in the 11th and 12th articles of amendment. Supposing, then, that there has been ceded to Congress, the exclusive power to regulate the subject of bankruptcy, whenever they shall think it expedient to exercise it, is it to be inferred, that the states have debarred themselves from all exercise of power on the same subject, when Congress do not think it expedient to act? I can perceive no just ground for the inference. The exercise of this power by the states, under such circumstances, could have no interference with the power delegated to Congress, and it would present a situation of things, very ill suited to the commercial habits of many of the states. For, such are the hazards, to which those who engage in trade and commerce, are unavoidably exposed, that, I believe, it has been found necessary, in all commercial countries, to relieve the unfortunate from the burthen of their debts, upon the surrender of all their property. There seem to be but three cases, in which the several states have no power to legislate. 1. Where they are expressly prohibited. 2. Where exclusive power is expressly vested in the *United States*. 3. Where the power vested in the *United States* is, in its nature, exclusive. The subject of bankruptcy does not fall within the first or second of those cases. And if it falls within the third, it is only during those times in which Congress exercise their power on the same subject. The states are not to be divested of their power by inferences, unless the inferences be inevitable. Now, that is not the case here. On the contrary, the power contended for, on behalf of the states, is in perfect harmony with the power granted to Congress; a power to legislate, on a *subject of necessity*, at a time when Congress do not think it expedient to act. I think the constitution has received a practical construction on this point, although I know that the weighty opinion of Judge WASH-INGTON has lately been pronounced to the contrary, (*Golden v. Prince, April*, 1814, in the Circuit Court of the *United States*, at *Philadelphia*.) But to that opinion, is opposed the strong argument of the Supreme Court of *New York*, in *Livingston v. Van Ingen*, in which it was adopted as a principle, that in cases where power is affirmatively vested in Congress, and not expressly taken away from the states, they may go on to legislate, until their laws come in collision with the acts of Congress. By *practical construction*, however, I do not mean *judicial* decision, but practice sanctioned by general consent. In the same section of the constitution from which Congress derive their power to establish an uniform system on the subject of bankruptcies, they have also given to them the power of fixing the standard of weights and measures. This they have never done, but the states have regulated them at their pleasure, and I believe, without question. In the same section also, there is granted to Congress, the power to provide for organizing, arming, and disciplining the militia; and yet all the states have passed laws on those subjects, much to the public benefit, and in harmony with the acts of Congress. From all these considerations, although I will not say that a case admits of no doubt, in which men of great talents have doubted, yet I have hesitation in giving it as my opinion, that the act of assembly in question is valid, unless it can be brought within the prohibition of the constitution, which relates to the impairing of the obligation of contracts.

2. It cannot be denied, that, taking the words, in their literal, and fullest extent, contracts are impaired by a bankrupt law. But conventions, intended to regulate the conduct of nations, are not to be construed as articles of agreement at common law. It is of little importance to the public, whether a tract of land belongs to *A*, or *B*. In deciding their titles, strict rules of construction may be adhered to—and it is best that they should be adhered to, though sometimes at the expense of justice, because certainty of title is thereby produced, and individual inconvenience is richly compensated by general good. But where multitudes are affected by the construction of an instrument, great regard should be paid to *spirit*, and *intention*. In deciding this question, then, it will be important to consider the situation of the *United States* at the time of framing their present constitution, and the probable intent of the makers. The commercial states had a great preponderance, and it was the interest of *commerce*, which led to the calling of that convention which formed the constitution. It is not going too far, to assume, that a bankrupt law was thought *indispensable;* because it is expressly provided for. Yet, it could hardly be unknown to the members of the convention, that in constructing a system, to pervade part of the union, there would be great difference of opinion, and, probably, great delay. So it has turned out.

It was not until 13 years after the constitution went into operation, that a bankrupt act was passed by Congress. When passed, it continued but five years, and ever since the states have been left to act for themselves. Now, it ought not to be supposed, unless clearly expressed, that the states were to be without bankrupt laws, during those periods in which Congress did not think proper to make them. Especially, as the convention had the matter directly before them, and had given power on the subject to Congress, in express terms. Why were not the states restrained from the exercise of this power, in terms equally express, if it was really the intent to restrain them? It must not be imagined, that it was in contemplation, to cover a *secret meaning* under expressions of general and doubtful import. I presume, it will hardly be contended, that the words, *impairing the obligation of contracts,* are to be understood in their greatest extent. If they are, the consequences are alarming. For, all acts respecting divorce, all acts of limitations, all acts by which private property has been taken for public use, or for the use of chartered companies, for roads, canals, &c., would be void; because, in all those cases, contracts are impaired. It would be questionable too, whether all *insolvent laws*, discharging the person of debtor from imprisonment, would not be void. Because these laws deprive the creditor of one very powerful engine for enforcing payment; an engine which operates on the feelings of friends and relations, and often extorts payment where creditors have no property of their own. So that although the contract is not immediately impaired, yet the means of enforcing it are lessened; and when this is done, subsequently to the making of the contract, it places the creditor on a worse footing than that on which it was by both parties intended that he should stand, when the contract was made. The same remarks will apply to laws giving a stay of execution, after judgment; for by those, contrary to the intent of the parties, the creditor is kept out of his money.

I believe all the states have passed insolvent laws, and Congress has passed one, for the district of Columbia, the validity of which has never been questioned. This act was not made under the express power given to Congress to pass a bankrupt law, (because that was to be *general* and *uniform*, throughout the Union), but under the power vested in them, to legislate for the District of Columbia. Had it been thought that an insolvent law, was the *impairing of a contract*, within the meaning of the constitution, we can hardly suppose, that Congress would have passed one for Columbia, although not prohibited expressly by the constitution; because, to say the least of it, it would have been setting a very bad example.

But, it may be asked, by what rule shall the meaning of these words *"impairing the obligation of contracts,"* be restricted or limited, if they are not taken in their full extent? I confess, that to lay down a rule which would decide all cases, appears to me to be very difficult, perhaps impossible. One may be certain, that particular cases are not within the meaning of a law, without being able to enumerate all the cases that are within it. To attempt such enumerations, is unnecessary and dangerous, lest some should be omitted. It is safer to decide on each case, as it arises. It is probable, that, so far as respects contracts between individuals, the principal mischiefs which the convention meant to remedy, were those which arose, from *tender laws,* and laws by which creditors who sued for their debts, *were compelled to take property upon an appraisement.* Tender laws, are expressly mentioned; yet they would have been included in the general words, for they certainly alter the obligation of the contract. Laws of this kind, impair the contract, by giving an advantage to the debtor, without any consideration in favour of the creditor. Bankrupt laws are essentially different. They afford, in many instances, advantages to both debtor and creditor; the debtor is discharged, on condition of surrendering his property, without delay, for the benefit of his creditors. The creditor is often a great loser. But he is sometimes a gainer, by the means which are offered him of compelling the debtor to a full discovery of his property, and obtaining possession of it, more quickly than in the usual course of law. The bankrupt system has been adopted in countries the most tenacious of the right of creditors, of which *England* and *Holland* are an example, so that without straining, it might be considered as an excepted case, when "laws impairing the obligation of contracts," were mentioned. So it seems to have struck both individuals and public bodies, about the time of the adoption of the Federal Constitution. I well remember, that very soon after its adoption the subject was brought before the legislature of *Maryland,* upon the petition of a gentleman who prayed

to be discharged from his debts on the surrender of his property for the benefit of his creditors. Several members of that legislature had been in the convention by which the Constitution had been recently formed. Doubts were entertained as to the right of the state to pass the law; but the prevailing opinion was in favour of the right, and the petition was granted. From that time to this, *Maryland* has been in the habit of making such laws. I am not exactly informed how many other states have followed her example; but I understand that *Rhode Island* and *New York* are among the number. Judicial decision is not wanting in favour of such right. Judge WASHINGTON, as I have mentioned, is against it. The Supreme Court of *New York* were for it, in the case of *Penniman* v. *Megs,* 9 *Johns.* 325. This Court has never decided directly upon the point; but they have discharged, without bail, where persons have been sued here, who had been discharged from the obligation of their contracts by laws of other states. I refer to the cases of *Hilliard & Pippet* v. *Greenleaf,* 5 *Binn.* 336, *in a note,* and *Boggs, &c.* v. *Teackle,* 5 *Binn.* 332. We are now called upon to decide whether an act of assembly of this Commonwealth be void, because of its violating the Constitution of the *United States.* That this Court possesses the power, and that it is bound in duty to declare a law void, when it violates the Constitution of this state or of the *United States,* has not been denied by the counsel for the plaintiff. It is a point on which I am well satisfied; but at the same time it is certain, that it is a power of high responsibility, and not to be exercised but in cases *free from doubt.* Such has been the opinion frequently expressed by Judges of the highest respectability in different states, and sanctioned by the Supreme Court of the *United States.* I will not pretend to say, that the meaning of that part of the Constitution, on which this question arises, is *clear.* But I may safely say, that it is *doubtful.* According to the established principles of construction, therefore, in doubtful cases, I am of opinion that the law of the state is valid. It follows, that judgment should be entered for the defendant.

9

ADAMS V. STOREY

1 Fed. Cas. 141, no. 66 (C.C.D.N.Y. 1817)

Before LIVINGSTON, Circuit Justice, and VAN NESS, District Judge.

LIVINGSTON, Circuit Justice. This is an action brought on several promissory notes, made or endorsed by the defendant, then residing in Boston, to the plaintiffs, who were then and are yet residents of the same place. The notes are also made payable in Boston, and were dated prior to the passing of the insolvent law hereinafter mentioned. The defendant pleaded the general issue, and on the trial offered in evidence, pursuant to a notice given for that purpose, a discharge by the recorder of the city of

New-York, dated the 13th of November, 1811, which was granted in virtue of an act of the legislature of the state of New-York, entitled "An act for the benefit of insolvent debtors and their creditors," passed the 3d of April of the same year. To the reading of this discharge the plaintiffs objected—but it was admitted. A verdict, however, was taken by consent, for the plaintiffs, subject to the opinion of the court on a case to be made by the parties. If the discharge was improperly admitted, judgment is to be entered on the verdict as it now stands; but if the discharge shall be thought a good bar to the action, the present verdict is to be set aside, and a verdict and judgment thereon entered for the defendant. The defendant, at the time of obtaining his discharge, resided and yet resides in the city of New-York. Few questions have ever been agitated in any court of the United States, since the formation of the federal government, of more extensive consequence, or of more delicacy than those which are now to be decided. When the binding force of an act of the legislature of any state is drawn into question for its supposed repugnancy to the federal constitution, although no court can entertain any doubt of its right to pronounce it invalid, yet it is no more than becoming to proceed with caution, and with more than ordinary deliberation. Presumptions will ever exist in favour of the law, for it will not readily be supposed that any state legislature, who are as much bound by the constitution, and are under the same solemn sanctions as the judges of those courts, to regard it, have either mistaken its meaning, or knowingly transcended their own powers. If, then, by any fair and reasonable interpretation, where the case is at all doubtful, the law can be reconciled with the constitution, it ought to be done, and a contrary course pursued only, where the incompatibility is so great as to render it extremely difficult to give the latter effect, without violating some provision of the former.

The plaintiff's counsel, in support of the verdict, say, that the discharge which was given in evidence can be no bar to the action. They contend that the statute of New-York, under which it was obtained, is a bankrupt law, and as such, is void for its repugnancy to the constitution of the United States; and this position is supported by the broad assertion that every law which discharges the person and property, as well future as in possession of the debtor, is a bankrupt law. But to this definition the court does not assent; for this would be to confound at once almost all the distinctions between these laws, which have been known and recognized in England, from which country we borrow the term, from the first introduction of the system there, in the reign of Henry the Eighth, down to the present time; distinctions which must have been familiar to many of the members of the convention that made the constitution. It is not because these laws may, in some respects, produce the same effects, that they are not to be distinguished from each other. In England the bankrupt system has been confined exclusively to traders, and the creditors of traders; whereas the insolvent laws of this country embrace every class of debtors. It is of no importance whether the debt has been contracted in the way of trade or not, for a person to come within the purview of an insolvent law. So exclusively have bankrupt laws oper-

ated on traders, that it may well be doubted, whether an act of congress subjecting to such a law every description of persons within the United States, would comport with the spirit of the powers vested in them in relation to this subject.

But it is not only in the persons, who are the objects of these laws, that a difference exists, but their general and most important provisions are essentially dissimilar. Under a bankrupt law, the debtor is at once, by operation of law, as soon as he has committed an act of bankruptcy, divested of all his property, which is transferred to assignees in trust for his creditors. All dispositions by the bankrupt himself after this are void; an insolvent, on the contrary, retains the management of his own estate, however he may misbehave towards his creditors at large, and it is rarely, unless on his own application, vested in others. It is of no importance how many acts he may commit, which, under a bankrupt system, would enable his creditors to take from him the control of his property; they can seldom act upon him compulsively under the provisions of an insolvent law, if he be obstinate or dishonest, until he has given what preferences he thinks proper, and is become so poor as to be scarcely worth pursuing. Under the one system the creditors are actors, and under the other the debtor himself originates the proceedings; and if, as is sometimes the case, his creditors may do it, even then his consent is generally indispensable under the provisions of an insolvent system. Other differences, in almost every stage of proceeding, might easily be pointed out, but they are so familiar to the profession, that a bare inspection of the act under which this discharge was obtained, will leave no doubt on the mind of any one to which class it belongs. "The title proclaims it to be an act for the benefit of insolvent debtors and their creditors." The first section gives power to the insolvent himself, who is imprisoned on any civil process issuing under the authority of this state, to present his petition to a proper officer, praying that his estate may be assigned and he discharged from his debts. The residue of the act is principally made up of directions as to the proceedings which are to be observed after the presenting of such petition, until the final discharge of the debtor, all of which differ greatly from the proceedings which take place on the issuing of a commission of bankruptcy. The fourth section declares, that such "discharge shall extend to all debts due from him at the time of the assignment, or contracted for before that time, though payable afterwards." If this be not an insolvent law, the court is at a loss to say to what act this appellation can apply. The opinion which has been expressed on this point would seem to preclude the necessity of inquiring how far this law interferes with the authority given to congress to "establish uniform laws on the subject of bankruptcies;" but as the view which has been taken of the act of this state may be thought incorrect, the court has no objection to consider it, as though it were a bankrupt law. The power to pass laws of this character, it is said, is exclusively vested in congress, and whether they exercise it or not, no state can have a bankrupt law of its own. As a consolidation of the different states into one national sovereignty was neither effected nor intended to be effected by the constitution, it has always been conceded that the state governments retained so much of the power, which they before had, as was not by that instrument exclusively delegated to the United States. It is now indeed one of the amendments to the constitution, that the powers not granted to the United States by the constitution, nor prohibited by it to the states, are reserved to the states respectively or to the people. It is agreed that such exclusive alienation of state sovereignty can only exist in three cases; where, by its terms, it is so, or where a power is conferred on the federal government, and the states are prohibited from exercising a similar authority, or where an authority is granted to the former, to which the exercise of a like power on the part of the different states would be absolutely and totally contradictory and repugnant. It is not pretended that the grant of the power under consideration is exclusive in its terms, or that there is an express prohibition on the states from exercising a like authority; but it is supposed that such exercise would be so totally inconsistent with the one granted to the government of the Union as to be necessarily comprehended in the third class of exclusive delegation. If it be really so, that the passing of a bankrupt law by a state, to operate, as it necessarily must, within its own limits, be absolutely incompatible with the power vested in congress, it would be conceded at once, that such an act would amount to a violation of the constitution of the United States and be void. Let us see whether the counsel have succeeded in establishing this position.

It must be allowed by all, that at the time of making the constitution, each state had a right to pass insolvent and bankrupt laws. As it was desirable, in a country so extensive as the United States, and every part of which was more or less commercial, that the laws relating to bankrupts should be uniform, so also it was an object of great importance that none of the larger commercial states should at any time be without some code on this subject. A system of the first kind, that is, one which should be uniform throughout the Union, could not well be brought about but by delegating the power of rendering it so to congress. Great difficulties however would lay in the way of a statute, whose provisions should pervade the United States; and as these must have been foreseen, the states might be willing and desirous of retaining the right of passing laws of this nature, until congress could agree on a general plan. Nor can the court perceive any contradiction, absurdity, or repugnancy in these several powers existing at the same time in the general and in the state governments; in such subordination, however, that the exercise of the authority vested in the former should, for the time, suspend all exercise of the power which resided in the latter, and operate as a repeal of any laws which might have been previously passed by the several states. It is an uniform rule which congress are to prescribe. But if they furnish none, how is it an interference for each state to legislate for itself? Neither the terms nor spirit of the instrument are thus disturbed. It seems designedly to have been left optional with the general government to exercise this power, that if the embarrassments which lay in their way were insurmountable or very great, they might omit to do it, and thus leave the states to take care of them-

selves. If it had been intended immediately to divest the states of all power on this subject, and to compel congress to act, the terms of the article would have been much more imperative than we find them, and probably it would have been accompanied with a prohibition on the states. No writer on this part of the constitution has gone further than to say that the power of naturalization is exclusive; because, if congress have a right to ordain a general rule, the states can have no right to prescribe a distinct rule. This construction is supposed to follow, not from any inconsistency there would be in each state passing a naturalization act for itself, if congress did not bring into action the power delegated to them, but from the inconvenience to which it might subject some of the states, by imposing upon them as citizens, obnoxious foreigners, who might become naturalized in another state, without any previous residence, or without any regard to character, by the mere formality of taking an oath of allegiance.

If the argument ab inconvenienti applies to the case of naturalization, it has no bearing on that of bankruptcy; for, in this case, each state would be legislating principally for its own citizens, and other states could not be injured by any system it might adopt. But this construction, even in the case of naturalization, where the argument in favor of an exclusive power is much stronger than in that of bankruptcy, has not only been strongly controverted, but is opposed by a judicial decision entitled to no little respect. It is the case of Collet v. Collet, [Case No. 3,001,] in the circuit court of Pennsylvania, in which the three judges, one of whom had been a member of the federal convention, decided, after solemn argument, that the several states still enjoy a concurrent right with congress on this subject, "which, however, cannot, they say, be so exercised as to contravene any rule which congress in their wisdom may establish." The most strenuous advocates for the exclusive exercise of every unqualified power granted to the general government, seem not unwilling to admit the several states to a participation of such power, if it can be exerted consistently with, or without derogating from the express grant to congress. It has not been shown how a bankrupt act, passed by a particular state, can interfere with the exercise of a power residing elsewhere, to promulgate a uniform law for all the states. If similar powers had been granted to the government of the Union, respecting the descent of real estates, the recording of deeds, or the celebration of marriages, will it be said that the several states must have remained without any laws to govern the transmission of landed property, or that no deed could be acknowledged or recorded, nor a valid marriage solemnized, although congress might for years omit to prescribe rules on these subjects? The object of this grant could have been no other than to place somewhere a power to correct the mischiefs which might arise from the different states passing on the same subject, not only dissimilar laws, but such as might be unequal in their operation on the citizens of other states. This end of the grant will be sufficiently and effectually attained, if, when the evil arises, congress bring into action the authority vested in them. From them only can a uniform system emanate; but systems, greatly varying, it is true, all of which, however, may be salutary, may be established without any derogation from or interference with a right residing elsewhere, to introduce uniformity on the same subject. Nay, from these very provisions, however discordant, might be selected materials for the one which it was committed to the general government to form. Neither can the passing of such laws by the states be regarded as a resumption of power by them, in which case, it is said, they should produce an express grant of it. This argument proceeds on the presumption of a previous relinquishment on the part of the states of all right to interfere in this matter, and is thus taking for granted what is the whole question in controversy; for, unless such transfer has been made, which is not admitted, no reassignment of it by the general government can be necessary.

No court of the United States will be suspected of feeling any disposition to countenance encroachments by the state legislature on the legitimate authority of the government of the Union; but in cases of doubt, and where the limits of separation are not very distinctly marked, and especially where the powers exercised leave in full force and unimpaired those given to the general government, the tranquillity and harmony of the Union will be better preserved by allowing to the states a reasonable share of legislation on the subject in dispute, than by strenuously insisting on a total exclusion. Congress themselves must have entertained an opinion, that the different states have this right in the present case; for on no other principle can we account for their leaving the United States so long without a uniform system of bankruptcy. Great and pressing as the call for such a system has been, the obstacles in the way of one that shall be uniform, and in that shape agreeable to all the states, continue to be so numerous, that but little hope is now indulged that any will be soon adopted; but great and serious as these difficulties may be, it would almost be the duty of congress to disregard them, if there existed no where else a power to correct the mischiefs which must necessarily be felt in many of the states from the non-user of this authority. The inference which has been drawn at the bar from this silence or inaction of congress, does not appear correct. It is considered as equivalent to an expression on their part of their sense against the wisdom and policy of all bankrupt laws, and that none ought to exist any where. Keeping in view the power which congress have, on this subject, it is more natural to interpret such silence into a declaration of their opinion of the inexpediency at present of any uniform system, and that the several states still retain the power which has been contended for, and can therefore take care of themselves. This would not be so great an imputation on their wisdom, as to suppose they can entertain an opinion in opposition to the sense of the whole world, that in a commercial state, such laws are mischievous or unnecessary. The opinion of the court, therefore, is, that this law, if a bankrupt law, would not on that account be void.

10

STURGES v. CROWNINSHIELD
4 Wheat. 122 (1819)

MARSHALL, C. J., delivered the opinion of the court.

This case is adjourned from the court of the United States, for the first circuit and the district of Massachusetts, on several points on which the judges of that court were divided, which are stated in the record, for the opinion of this court. The first is:—

Whether, since the adoption of the constitution of the United States, any State has authority to pass a bankrupt law, or whether the power is exclusively vested in the congress of the Unied States?

This question depends on the following clause, in the 8th section of the 1st article of the constitution of the United States.

"The congress shall have power," &c., to "establish a uniform rule of naturalization, and uniform laws on the subject of bankruptcies throughout the United States."

The counsel for the plaintiff contend, that the grant of this power to congress, without limitation, takes it entirely from the several States.

In support of this proposition they argue, that every power given to congress is necessarily supreme; and if, from its nature, or from the words of grant, it is apparently intended to be exclusive, it is as much so as if the States were expressly forbidden to exercise it.

These propositions have been enforced and illustrated by many arguments, drawn from different parts of the constitution. That the power is both unlimited and supreme, is not questioned. That it is exclusive, is denied by the counsel for the defendant.

In considering this question, it must be recollected that, previous to the formation of the new constitution, we were divided into independent States, united for some purposes, but, in most respects, sovereign. These States could exercise almost every legislative power, and, among others, that of passing bankrupt laws.

When the American people created a national legislature, with certain enumerated powers, it was neither necessary nor proper to define the powers retained by the States. These powers proceed, not from the people of America, but from the people of the several States; and remain, after the adoption of the constitution, what they were before, except so far as they may be abridged by that instrument. In some instances, as in making treaties, we find an express prohibition; and this shows the sense of the convention to have been, that the mere grant of a power to congress, did not imply a prohibition on the States to exercise the same power. But it has never been supposed, that this concurrent power of legislation extended to every possible case in which its exercise by the States has not been expressly prohibited. The confusion resulting from such a practice would be endless. The principle laid down by the counsel for the plaintiff, in this respect, is undoubtedly correct. Whenever the terms in which a power is granted to congress, or the nature of the power, require that it should be exercised exclusively by congress, the subject is as completely taken from the state legislatures, as if they had been expressly forbidden to act on it.

Is the power to establish uniform laws on the subject of bankruptcies, throughout the United States, of this description?

The peculiar terms of the grant certainly deserve notice. Congress is not authorized merely to pass laws, the operation of which shall be uniform, but to establish uniform laws on the subject throughout the United States. This establishment of uniformity is, perhaps, incompatible with state legislation, on that part of the subject to which the acts of Congress may extend. But the subject is divisible in its nature into bankrupt and insolvent laws; though the line of partition between them is not so distinctly marked as to enable any person to say, with positive precision, what belongs exclusively to the one, and not the other class of laws. It is said, for example, that laws which merely liberate the person are insolvent laws, and those which discharge the contract, are bankrupt laws. But if an act of congress should discharge the person of the bankrupt, and leave his future acquisitions liable to his creditors, we should feel much hesitation in saying that this was an insolvent, not a bankrupt act; and, therefore, unconstitutional. Another distinction has been stated, and has been uniformly observed. Insolvent laws operate at the instance of an imprisoned debtor; bankrupt laws at the instance of a creditor. But should an act of congress authorize a commission of bankruptcy to issue on the application of a debtor, a court would scarcely be warranted in saying, that the law was unconstitutional, and the commission a nullity.

When laws of each description may be passed by the same legislature, it is unnecessary to draw a precise line between them. The difficulty can arise only in our complex system, where the legislature of the Union possesses the power of enacting bankrupt laws; and those of the States, the power of enacting insolvent laws. If it be determined that they are not laws of the same character, but are as distinct as bankrupt laws and laws which regulate the course of descents, a distinct line of separation must be drawn, and the power of each government marked with precision. But all perceive that this line must be, in a great degree, arbitrary. Although the two systems have existed apart from each other, there is such a connection between them as to render it difficult to say how far they may be blended together. The bankrupt law is said to grow out of the exigencies of commerce, and to be applicable solely to traders; but it is not easy to say who must be excluded from, or may be included within, this description. It is, like every other part of the subject, one on which the legislature may exercise an extensive discretion.

This difficulty of discriminating with any accuracy between insolvent and bankrupt laws, would lead to the opinion, that a bankrupt law may contain those regulations which are generally found in insolvent laws; and that an insolvent law may contain those which are common to a bankrupt law. If this be correct, it is obvious that much inconvenience would result from that construction of the constitution, which should deny to the state legislatures the power of acting on this subject, in consequence of the grant to congress. It may be thought more convenient, that much of it should be regulated by state legislation, and congress may purposely omit to provide for many cases to which their power extends. It does not appear to be a violent construction of the constitution, and is certainly a convenient one, to consider the power of the States as existing over such cases as the laws of the Union may not reach. But be this as it may, the power granted to congress may be exercised or declined, as the wisdom of that body shall decide. If, in the opinion of congress, uniform laws concerning bankruptcies ought not to be established, it does not follow that partial laws may not exist, or that state legislation on the subject must cease. It is not the mere existence of the power, but its exercise, which is incompatible with the exercise of the same power by the States. It is not the right to establish these uniform laws, but their actual establishment, which is inconsistent with the partial acts of the States.

It has been said, that congress has exercised this power; and, by doing so, has extinguished the power of the States, which cannot be revived by repealing the law of congress.

We do not think so. If the right of the States to pass a bankrupt law is not taken away by the mere grant of that power to congress, it cannot be extinguished; it can only be suspended, by the enactment of a general bankrupt law. The repeal of that law cannot, it is true, confer the power on the States; but it removes a disability to its exercise, which was created by the act of congress.

Without entering further into the delicate inquiry respecting the precise limitations which the several grants of power to congress, contained in the constitution, may impose on the state legislatures, than is necessary for the decision of the question before the court, it is sufficient to say, that, until the power to pass uniform laws on the subject of bankruptcies be exercised by congress, the States are not forbidden to pass a bankrupt law, provided it contain no principle which violates the 10th section of the first article of the constitution of the United States.

This opinion renders it totally unnecessary to consider the question whether the law of New York is, or is not, a bankrupt law.

We proceed to the great question on which the cause must depend. Does the law of New York, which is pleaded in this case, impair the obligation of contracts, within the meaning of the constitution of the United States?

This act liberates the person of the debtor, and discharges him from all liability for any debt previously contracted, on his surrendering his property in the manner it prescribes.

In discussing the question whether a State is prohibited from passing such a law as this, our first inquiry is into the meaning of words in common use. What is the obligation of a contract? and what will impair it?

It would seem difficult to substitute words which are more intelligible, or less liable to misconstruction, than those which are to be explained. A contract is an agreement in which a party undertakes to do, or not to do, a particular thing. The law binds him to perform his undertaking, and this is, of course, the obligation of his contract. In the case at bar, the defendant has given his promissory note to pay the plaintiff a sum of money on or before a certain day. The contract binds him to pay that sum on that day; and this is its obligation. Any law which releases a part of this obligation, must, in the literal sense of the word, impair it. Much more must a law impair it which makes it totally invalid, and entirely discharges it.

The words of the constitution, then, are express, and incapable of being misunderstood. They admit of no variety of construction, and are acknowledged to apply to that species of contract, an engagement between man and man, for the payment of money, which has been entered into by these parties. Yet the opinion that this law is not within the prohibition of the constitution, has been entertained by those who are entitled to great respect, and has been supported by arguments which deserve to be seriously considered.

It has been contended, that as a contract can only bind a man to pay to the full extent of his property, it is an implied condition that he may be discharged on surrendering the whole of it.

But it is not true that the parties have in view only the property in possession when the contract is formed, or that its obligation does not extend to future acquisitions. Industry, talents, and integrity, constitute a fund which is as confidently trusted as property itself. Future acquisitions are, therefore, liable for contracts; and to release them from this liability impairs their obligation.

It has been argued, that the States are not prohibited from passing bankrupt laws, and that the essential principle of such laws is to discharge the bankrupt from all past obligations; that the States have been in the constant practice of passing insolvent laws, such as that of New York, and if the framers of the constitution had intended to deprive them of this power, insolvent laws would have been mentioned in the prohibition; that the prevailing evil of the times, which produced this clause in the constitution, was the practice of emitting paper money, of making property which was useless to the creditor a discharge of his debt, and of changing the time of payment by authorizing distant instalments. Laws of this description, not insolvent laws, constituted, it is said, the mischief to be remedied; and laws of this description, not insolvent laws, are within the true spirit of the prohibition.

The constitution does not grant to the States the power of passing bankrupt laws, or any other power; but finds them in possession of it, and may either prohibit its future exercise entirely, or restrain it so far as national policy may require. It has so far restrained it as to prohibit the passage of any law impairing the obligation of contracts. Although, then, the States may, until that power shall be exercised by congress, pass laws concerning bankrupts, yet they cannot constitutionally introduce into such laws a clause which discharges the obligations the bankrupt has entered into. It is not admitted that, without this principle, an act cannot be a bankrupt law; and if it were, that admission would not change the constitution, nor exempt such acts from its prohibitions.

The argument drawn from the omission in the constitution to prohibit the States from passing insolvent laws, admits of several satisfactory answers. It was not necessary, nor would it have been safe, had it even been the intention of the framers of the constitution to prohibit the passage of all insolvent laws, to enumerate particular subjects to which the principle they intended to establish should apply. The principle was the inviolability of contracts. This principle was to be protected in whatsoever form it might be assailed. To what purpose enumerate the particular modes of violation which should be forbidden, when it was intended to forbid all? Had an enumeration of all the laws which might violate contracts been attempted, the provision must have been less complete, and involved in more perplexity than it now is. The plain and simple declaration, that no State shall pass any law impairing the obligation of contracts, includes insolvent laws and all other laws, so far as they infringe the principle the convention intended to hold sacred, and no further.

But a still more satisfactory answer to this argument is, that the convention did not intend to prohibit the passage of all insolvent laws. To punish honest insolvency by imprisonment for life, and to make this a constitutional principle, would be an excess of inhumanity which will not readily be imputed to the illustrious patriots who framed our constitution, nor to the people who adopted it. The distinction between the obligation of a contract, and the remedy given by the legislature to enforce that obligation, has been taken at the bar, and exists in the nature of things. Without impairing the obligation of the contract, the remedy may certainly be modified as the wisdom of the nation shall direct. Confinement of the debtor may be a punishment for not performing his contract, or may be allowed as a means of inducing him to perform it. But the State may refuse to inflict this punishment, or may withhold this means, and leave the contract in full force. Imprisonment is no part of the contract, and simply to release the prisoner does not impair its obligation. No argument can be fairly drawn from the 61st section of the act for establishing a uniform system of bankruptcy, which militates against this reasoning. That section declares, that the act shall not be construed to repeal or annul the laws of any State then in force for the relief of insolvent debtors, except so far as may respect persons and cases clearly within its purview; and in such cases it affords its sanction to the relief given by the insolvent laws of the State, if the creditor of the prisoner shall not, within three months, proceed against him as a bankrupt.

The insertion of this section indicates an opinion in congress, that insolvent laws might be considered as a branch of the bankrupt system, to be repealed or annulled by an act for establishing that system, although not within its purview. It was for that reason only that a provision against this construction could be necessary. The last member of the section adopts the provisions of the State laws so far as they apply to cases within the purview of the act.

This section certainly attempts no construction of the constitution, nor does it suppose any provision in the insolvent laws impairing the obligation of contracts. It leaves them to operate, so far as constitutionally they may, unaffected by the act of congress, except where that act may apply to individual cases.

The argument which has been pressed most earnestly at the bar, is, that although all legislative acts which discharge the obligation of a contract without performance, are within the very words of the constitution, yet an insolvent act, containing this principle, is not within its spirit, because such acts have been passed by colonial and state legislatures from the first settlement of the country, and because we know from the history of the times, that the mind of the convention was directed to other laws, which were fraudulent in their character, which enabled the debtor to escape from his obligation, and yet hold his property; not to this, which is beneficial in its operation.

Before discussing this argument, it may not be improper to premise that, although the spirit of an instrument, especially of a constitution, is to be respected not less than its letter, yet the spirit is to be collected chiefly from its words. It would be dangerous in the extreme to infer from extrinsic circumstances, that a case for which the words of an instrument expressly provide, shall be exempted from its operation. Where words conflict with each other, where the different clauses of an instrument bear upon each other, and would be inconsistent unless the natural and common import of words be varied, construction becomes necessary, and a departure from the obvious meaning of words is justifiable. But if, in any case, the plain meaning of a provision, not contradicted by any other provision in the same instrument, is to be disregarded, because we believe the framers of that instrument could not intend what they say, it must be one in which the absurdity and injustice of applying the provision to the case, would be so monstrous that all mankind would, without hesitation, unite in rejecting the application.

This is certainly not such a case. It is said the colonial and state legislatures have been in the habit of passing laws of this description for more than a century; that they have never been the subject of complaint, and consequently, could not be within the view of the general convention.

The fact is too broadly stated. The insolvent laws of many, indeed, of by far the greater number of the States, do not contain this principle. They discharge the person of the debtor, but leave his obligation to pay in full force. To this the constitution is not opposed.

But, were it even true that this principle had been introduced generally into those laws, it would not justify our varying the construction of the section. Every State in the Union, both while a colony and after becoming independent, had been in the practice of issuing paper money; yet this practice is, in terms, prohibited. If the long exercise of the power to emit bills of credit did not restrain the convention from prohibiting its future exercise, neither can it be said that the long exercise of the power to impair the obligation of contracts, should prevent a similar prohibition. It is not admitted that the prohibition is more express in the one case than in the other. It does not, indeed, extend to insolvent laws by name, because it is not a law by name, but a principle which is to be forbidden; and this principle is described in as appropriate terms as our language affords.

Neither, as we conceive, will any admissible rule of construction justify us in limiting the prohibition under consideration, to the particular laws which have been described at the bar, and which furnished such cause for general alarm. What were those laws?

We are told they were such as grew out of the general distress following the war in which our independence was established. To relieve this distress paper money was issued; worthless lands, and other property of no use to the creditor, were made a tender in payment of debts; and the time of payment, stipulated in the contract, was extended by law. These were the peculiar evils of the day. So much mischief was done, and so much more was apprehended, that general distrust prevailed, and all confidence between man and man was destroyed. To laws of this description therefore, it is said, the prohibition to pass laws impairing the obligation of contracts ought to be confined.

Let this argument be tried by the words of the section under consideration.

Was this general prohibition intended to prevent paper money? We are not allowed to say so, because it is expressly provided, that no State shall "emit bills of credit;" neither could these words be intended to restrain the States from enabling debtors to discharge their debts by the tender of property of no real value to the creditor, because for that subject also particular provision is made. Nothing but gold and silver coin can be made a tender in payment of debts.

It remains to inquire, whether the prohibition under consideration could be intended for the single case of a law directing that judgments should be carried into execution by instalments?

This question will scarcely admit of discussion. If this was the only remaining mischief against which the constitution intended to provide, it would undoubtedly have been, like paper money and tender laws, expressly forbidden. At any rate, terms more directly applicable to the subject, more appropriately expressing the intention of the convention, would have been used. It seems scarcely possible to suppose that the framers of the constitution, if intending to prohibit only laws authorizing the payment of debts by instalment, would have expressed that intention by saying, "no State shall pass any law impairing the obligation of contracts." No men would so express such an intention. No men would use terms embracing a whole class of laws, for the purpose of designating a single individual of that class. No court can be justified in restricting such comprehensive words to a particular mischief to which no allusion is made.

The fair, and we think, the necessary construction of the sentence, requires, that we should give these words their full and obvious meaning. A general dissatisfaction with that lax system of legislation which followed the war of our Revolution, undoubtedly directed the mind of the convention to this subject. It is probable that laws such as those which have been stated in argument, produced the loudest complaints, were most immediately felt. The attention of the convention, therefore, was particularly directed to paper money, and to acts which enabled the debtor to discharge his debt otherwise than was stipulated in the contract. Had nothing more been intended, nothing more would have been expressed. But, in the opinion of the convention, much more remained to be done. The same mischief might be effected by other means. To restore public confidence completely, it was necessary not only to prohibit the use of particular means by which it might be effected, but to prohibit the use of any means by which the same mischief might be produced. The convention appears to have intended to establish a great principle, that contracts should be inviolable. The constitution, therefore, declares, that no State shall pass "any law impairing the obligation of contracts."

If, as we think, it must be admitted that this intention might actuate the convention; that it is not only consistent with, but is apparently manifested by, all that part of the section which respects this subject; that the words used are well adapted to the expression of it; that violence would be done to their plain meaning by understanding them in a more limited sense; those rules of construction, which have been consecrated by the wisdom of ages, compel us to say, that these words prohibit the passage of any law discharging a contract without performance.

By way of analogy, the statutes of limitations, and against usury, have been referred to in argument; and it has been supposed that the construction of the constitution, which this opinion maintains, would apply to them also, and must therefore be too extensive to be correct.

We do not think so. Statutes of limitations relate to the remedies which are furnished in the courts. They rather establish, that certain circumstances shall amount to evidence that a contract has been performed, than dispense with its performance. If, in a State where six years may be pleaded in bar to an action of *assumpsit*, a law should pass declaring that contracts already in existence, not barred by the statute, should be construed to be within it, there could be little doubt of its unconstitutionality.

So with respect to the laws against usury. If the law be, that no person shall take more than six per centum per annum for the use of money, and that, if more be reserved, the contract shall be void, a contract made thereafter reserving seven per cent., would have no obligation in its commencement; but if a law should declare that contracts already entered into, and reserving the legal interest, should be usurious and void, either in the whole or in part, it would impair the obligation of the contract, and would be clearly unconstitutional.

This opinion is confined to the case actually under consideration. It is confined to a case in which a creditor sues in a court, the proceedings of which the legislature, whose act is pleaded, had not a right to control, and to a case where the creditor had not proceeded to execution against the body of his debtor, within the State whose law attempts to absolve a confined insolvent debtor from his obligation. When such a case arises, it will be considered.

It is the opinion of the court, that the act of the State of New York, which is pleaded by the defendant in this cause, so far as it attempts to discharge this defendant from the debt in the declaration mentioned, is contrary to the constitution of the United States, and that the plea is no bar to the action.

11

House of Representatives, The Bankrupt Bill
8, 11 Feb. 1822
Annals 38:971–74, 996–98

[*8 Feb.*]

[Mr. Montgomery] . . . The Convention who framed the National Constitution had the experience of some years before their eyes; the members were witnesses to the results of such discordant legislation in regard to the merchants of the country; they were wise men, and could see that the evil would grow with the growth of our population and commerce, and to guard against it Congress was invested with the power of passing a system of bankruptcy which should be uniform throughout the United States. This in his view was the great reason for the investiture of the power, and the strongest for the expediency of the exercise of it.—

He then remarked that he would consider the question of power with reference to the bill now before the Committee, and endeavor to prove that Congress possessed the power of passing it. (He then read from the 8th section of the first article of the National Constitution, that portion which vests Congress with the power of "establishing an uniform system of bankruptcy throughout the United States.") He said he believed the members of the Convention were wise men, and as such he could not believe that they intended to bring within the scope of the jurisdiction of the national courts the small transactions of handicraftsmen, agriculturists, &c. He could not believe that it was intended to drag them before commissioners of bankruptcy, and finally before a federal court, to adjust the division of an estate, not worth more than one or two hundred dollars. No, he believed, in opposition to many others, that the law ought to be confined to the cases of those classes in society, whose transactions of a mercantile and trading character had furnished the necessity of the system. He then read the second section of the third article of the National Constitution to show that if every class in society were embraced by the terms of the law, their cases would become subjects of cognizance in the federal courts, as being cases governed by a law of the United States. This, in his opinion, was not the intention of the Convention.

He then remarked that the terms bankruptcy and insolvency were both technical terms in the law, the first expressing the condition of a merchant, trader, or broker, &c., who had committed some act, &c., evincive of a disposition to hinder or delay the payment of his debts, and who was entitled, upon a complete surrender of his estate for the benefit of his creditors, to be released from future liability; the second embracing the cases of all the other classes of society who were unable to pay their debts, and who were entitled by sundry statutory provisions to be released from imprisonment, but not from all future liability with reference to their property. The members of the Convention were generally learned in the laws, as well of the States as of Britain; they had a full opportunity of seeing these principles in the form of statutes and digests; they understood them; it is, therefore, a fair conclusion, that, if they had designed to adopt the principles and notion of insolvency, they would have used the term.

He then observed that the term bankruptcy was a technical term in legal science, embracing the persons, acts, proceedings, and results of the bill; that the persons using the term well understood its technical import; and he thought it a fair conclusion that it was used in that sense. He then called the attention of the Committee to one of the rules of construction laid down by Vattel, B. II. chap. 17, section 276. The rule is, that "technical terms, or terms peculiar to the arts and sciences, ought commonly to be interpreted according to the definition given of them by masters of the art, or persons versed in the knowledge of the art or science to which the terms belong." This is the rule; the exceptions, as given by Vattel, are where the writer of a treaty or deed is proved not to understand the art or science; that he is unacquainted with its import, as a technical word, or that he employed it in a vulgar acceptation, &c. Now, as there is no evidence to show that the members of the Convention were ignorant of the science of law; nor any fact or circumstance to justify the inference that they were unacquainted with the import of the word "bankruptcy" as a legal phrase; nor any evidence of its being used in a vulgar sense, the case cannot be taken as falling within the exceptions. The rule, then, is to be applied. He remarked, that it was possible some might say that Vattel was no authority on the question. To this he would answer, that he did not consider the rule as authoritative because it was written by Vattel, but because it was a dictate of good sense, proper to be used in any age, nation, or country, for the purpose of ascertaining the meaning of written instruments.

He then observed that he would endeavor to answer some objections to the power of Congress, as contemplated to be exercised by the passage of the bill, by a gentleman from Virginia, (Mr. STEVENSON.) That gentleman objected that the bill would be an *ex post facto* law, and in violation of the third member of the 9th section of the first article of the National Constitution, which prohibits Congress from passing such laws. To this objection he would answer, 1st. That, if the exposition which he (Mr. M.) had exhibited of the term "bankruptcy" be correct, the prohibition must be considered as a general one, subject to the exception of the power to pass a bankrupt law which should be retroactive in its operations. This is justified by the well known sensible rule, that every part ought to have some operation and effect, if it may be done by any reasonable intendment or construction. 2d. The principles of the bill are not within the terms of the prohibition. Many legal characters are of opinion that the prohibition only relates to criminal matters; but he (Mr. M.) did not believe that the words *ex post facto* ought to be so strictly taken; they are Latin words, which he supposed ought to be rendered "after the fact;" and, as he thought the prohibition precluded Congress from passing laws to render any facts criminal which had happened before the passage of such laws, and were not criminal at the date of the facts; and, also, to prohibit Congress from passing laws to divest individuals of rights dependent upon pre-existing laws and facts. The last idea embraces all that great division of rights, or things in action, which lawyers term actions *ex delicto*. This import of the prohibition is strengthened, by looking into the 10th section of the same article, in which the States are, in like manner, prohibited from passing *ex post facto* laws, and, by the terms of the same prohibitory clause, they are also prohibited from passing laws to impair the obligation of contracts. The latter prohibition secures the rights of the citizens in every thing in action dependent upon contract; and, if the construction above contended for obtains, the other branch of the prohibition secures all the rights dependent upon wrongs; but, if it does not, all the rights of one class, dependent upon the wrongful acts of another, are unprotected. He could not believe that the Convention intended to be thus careful in guarding one great class of rights, and at the same time leave the other great class unprotected. He then remarked, that, under the view of the prohibition to pass *ex post facto* laws just given, no violation could be found in the bill, because, upon examining the bill, it would be found that claims, founded upon torts, were not within its provisions; so that, after the passage of the bill, rights of this class may be enforced as before, and the responsibility will continue as before. The claimants of this class are left to run the race of the law with the others.

The same gentleman had contended that the bill, if passed, would impair the obligation of contracts in releasing debtors from future liability after obtaining certificates of bankruptcy. To this he (Mr M.) answered, 1st. That, if his view of the Constitution was correct, that power was expressly given for the reasons urged by him. 2dly. He contended that the law in force, when contracts are made, must be considered as being in the view of the parties contracting, and must be taken as limiting and fixing the extent of the liability of the obligors: in the cases, then, within the terms of the bill, there was in full force a fundamental rule, under which the liability of the debtors might be determined, upon surrendering up their estates, and so no impairing of the obligation of the contracts, as they ought to have been understood. 3dly. He contended that Congress are not prohibited from passing laws to impair the obligation of contracts. The omission of the prohibition on the part of Congress, when it is so distinctly written, as to the States, affords a strong ground from which to infer that it was intended Congress might exercise it with reference to those cases of contracts, respecting which it might legislate. 4thly. He contended that the humane views of the convention would be marred very much, if not defeated, by confining the operation of the law entirely to cases arising after its passage; and the same may be said of the equal distribution among creditors contemplated by the bill.

[11 Feb.]

[Mr. COLDER] . . . Mr. C. said, he should entirely agree with the gentleman from Virginia, that the power to pass the bill before us—that is to say, a bill discharging the property as well as the person, was expressly given by the Constitution, or that Congress had no power to make such a law. Though he thought the power to pass a bankrupt law might as well be implied from the powers which Congress had to regulate commerce, as the power to grant a bank charter was inferred from any part of the Constitution; yet, he repeated, that he did admit, for the purpose of this argument at least, that there was no such power to pass this law, unless it was expressly given by the letter of the Constitution.

The Constitution has given Congress "power to establish uniform laws on the subject of bankruptcies throughout the United States." Mr. C. said that this phraseology was deserving attention, and seems to have been adopted to convey ideas more extended than the expressions which would be the most likely first to occur for granting a limited power to pass bankrupt laws. Had the Constitution merely said Congress shall have power to establish bankrupt laws, or all bankrupt laws, even then it would be difficult to say that there was any restriction as to the kind of bankrupt law which Congress might pass. But when the power is to pass laws on the subject of bankruptcies, is it not to be understood that Congress have a right to pass every kind of bankrupt law?

Mr. C. said, it seemed to him that this question would be answered by determining the meaning of the word bankrupt, or bankruptcy.

It had been justly said by the gentleman from Virginia, that Blackstone gave us no definition of the word bankrupt. He merely describes those who may become obnoxious to the English bankrupt laws, and points out the consequences of such liability. Neither would the English statutes assist us in our search for a definition. For he who might be a bankrupt at one time, according to the English law, was not so considered at another. Thus, the statute of Henry VIII., which was entitled " a law against such as do make bankrupt," applied to all persons. The statute of Elizabeth confined the application of the bankrupt law to traders. A subsequent statute of James extended it to scriveners. A law of Queen Anne absolved the subsequently acquired property, as well as the person, of a discharged bankrupt—and a statute of George III. extended their then numerous bankrupt laws to bankers, brokers, and factors; so that we cannot appeal to the English statutes for the definition we are in search of, unless we should be willing to admit that the word bankrupt must, at all times, mean whatever the British Parliament shall please to say shall be its signification.

Mr. C. said that we must, in this case, as in all others where the meaning of a word in our language was in question, inquire as to its etymology, its definition by lexicographers, and its use by authors.

The honorable member from Virginia had expressed an aversion to such references, as having an appearance of pedantry. But, Mr. C. said, he knew not in what other channels the inquiry might be pursued, and hoped it would not be thought there was any ostentation in a reference to mere initial books.

Etymology, he admitted, was an uncertain, and often a fallacious, guide to the meaning of words. But where it happened to give a corresponding meaning with that derived from other sources, as in the present case, it might be taken into account. The word bankrupt was probably first applied to money-dealers. They, we may suppose, transacted their business on counters or benches. When they failed, were unable to pay their debts, or absconded, their counters were probably removed, or broken up; and therefore those who had occupied them were said to be bankrupt.

The dictionary definition of bankrupt, as will appear by that of Dr. Johnson, which I now see in the collection of books made for your use in this hall, and which must be admitted to be as of high authority as any other that could be appealed to, defines a bankrupt to be "one indebted beyond the power of payment." This definition evidently implies that, in the opinion of the author, the word bankrupt was not limited in its signification by any statuteable provisions; and we shall see, by again recurring to the statute of Henry VIII., that the word bankrupt had been adopted in our language, and had a precise signification before that statute was passed, and, of course, antecedently to any English statute on the subject. Mr. C. here read an abstract from the statute of Henry VIII., to show that the word bankrupt was not mentioned in the body of the law. That merely provided punishment for those "who craftily obtained the goods of other men, and fled or kept their houses, not minding to pay their debts, but consumed the substance obtained by credit, for their own pleasure against all reason, equity, and good conscience." It is well known that, anciently, there were no titles given to their acts by the Parliament itself. The titles were nothing more than the endorsement of the clerk, in forming which he was determined by the substance of the bill. So, in this case, having found that the act contained provisions against fraudulent and insolvent debtors, he endorsed upon it that it was " a law against such persons as do make bankrupt"—the word bankrupt was not found in any part of the bill. It cannot be doubted, then, that this word, bankrupt, has, at all times, had a meaning independent of legislative enactments, and did mean, and does yet mean, one in debt beyond the power of payment, according to the definition of Johnson; and one who fraudulently avoided payment, according to its application in the title to the statute of Henry VIII. Hence we may derive a definition of bankruptcy; and as Congress have power to establish all laws on that subject, they have power to establish laws which relate to those who are in debt beyond the power of payment, or who fraudulently avoid payment of their debts.

If we have ascertained the meaning of the term bankrupt, there seems an end to the argument on this point. For Congress have power to pass all laws on this subject, as well laws which discharge the subsequently acquired property of the debtor as his person. It cannot, with any reason, be said that Congress has less than plenary powers in this respect; and it would seem absurd to contend that the very general and comprehensive words of the Constitution conveyed to Congress only the lowest grade of authority which a legislative body can exercise on this subject—that is, to exonerate only the person of the debtor.

But, though we should in vain appeal to the statute law of England, or of our own country, for the definition of the term bankrupt, yet we may refer to them to ascertain the sense in which the word was used by the framers of the Constitution; and, when we find that every law which existed in Europe, under the name of a bankrupt law, not only enabled the insolvent debtor to obtain a discharge of his person, but an exoneration of his subsequent acquisitions, can it be supposed that, in our Constitution, the term was used in a more restricted sense than it was used in all contemporaneous laws?

Mr. C. said these considerations had brought his mind to the most satisfactory conclusion, that, by the letter of the Constitution, power was given to Congress to pass the bill now under the consideration of the Committee.

But he would ask the indulgence of the Committee while he attempted to show, by another argument, which appeared to him perfectly conclusive, that Congress had the power in question.

It must be admitted that, previously to the adoption of the Confederation and the present Constitution, the United States were respectively free and independent sovereigns, having all the powers and attributes of sovereignty which ever belonged to any people on earth. They then unquestionably had power, in virtue of their sovereignty, to pass such a law as that on our table, or any other law not forbidden by the laws of God. But it has been determined by an authority, not inferior or subordinate to our own, that the individual States have not now this power. The supreme judicial tribunal, whose decrees cannot be questioned on earth, have said that the States have parted with this power. Where, then, is it gone? If you say that it is not surrendered to Congress, then you must say that a power, which originally belonged to the States, has passed from them, merely in virtue of their having confederated; and yet, strange as it may appear, it must be contended that this power is not vested in the Confederacy, or touched by the instrument of confederation. Sir, said Mr. C., if the power be not in the particular States, nor in the United States, I hope some of the gentlemen who are opposed to the bill will have the goodness to tell us by what process it has been dissipated.

12

OGDEN V. SAUNDERS
12 Wheat. 213 (1827)

(See 1.10.1, no. 19)

13

WILLIAM RAWLE, A VIEW OF THE CONSTITUTION
OF THE UNITED STATES 101–2
1829 (2d ed.)

The power to pass *uniform laws on the subject of bankruptcies*, is contained in the same paragraph. It is held, however, from its nature, not to be completely exclusive.

Until it is exercised, the states are not forbidden to pass bankrupt laws, except so far as they impair the obligation of contracts. When congress enacts a general bankrupt law, the right of the states is suspended, though not extinguished. From the expiration or repeal of the bankrupt law, the ability of the state to exercise the power, qualified as above mentioned, revives. And even while the act of congress is in force, the power of the state continues over such cases as the law does not embrace. Hence the power to pass insolvent laws remains with the state. Bankrupt laws are generally, perhaps properly, considered as confined to the mercantile class, who are more exposed to pecuniary vicissitudes than those who pursue other occupations. Yet as poverty may also assail the latter, it would be hard to exclude them from the humane protection of the state legislatures. But as states are prohibited from passing laws impairing the obligation of contracts, it has been contended that their power to pass insolvent laws is now questionable. The answer to this objection is, that without impairing the obligation of a contract, the remedy to enforce it may be modified as the wisdom of the legislature may direct. Confinement of the debtor may be a punishment for not performing his contract, or may be allowed as the means of inducing him to perform it. The state may withhold this mean and leave the contract in full force. Imprisonment is no part of the contract, and simply to release the prisoner does not impair its obligation.

14

JOSEPH STORY, COMMENTARIES ON THE
CONSTITUTION 3:§§ 1100–10
1833

§ 1100. The power to pass laws on the subject of bankruptcies was not in the original draft of the constitution.

The original article was committed to a committee together with the following proposition: "to establish uniform laws upon the subject of bankruptcies, and respecting the damages arising on the protest of foreign bills of exchange." The committee subsequently made a report in favour of incorporating the clause on the subject of bankruptcies into the constitution; and it was adopted by a vote of nine states against one. The brevity, with which this subject is treated by the Federalist, is quite remarkable. The only passage in that elaborate commentary, in which the subject is treated, is as follows: "The power of establishing uniform laws of bankruptcy is so intimately connected with the regulation of commerce, and will prevent so many frauds, where the parties or their property may lie, or be removed into different states, that the expediency of it seems not likely to be drawn in question."

§ 1101. The subject, however, deserves a more exact consideration. Before the adoption of the constitution the states severally possessed the exclusive right, as matter belonging to their general sovereignty, to pass laws upon the subject of bankruptcy and insolvency. Without stopping at present to consider, what is the precise meaning of each of these terms, as contradistinguished from the other; it may be stated, that the general object of all bankrupt and insolvent laws is, on the one hand, to secure to creditors an appropriation of the property of their debtors *pro tanto* to the discharge of their debts, whenever the latter are unable to discharge the whole amount; and, on the other hand, to relieve unfortunate and honest debtors from perpetual bondage to their creditors, either in the shape of unlimited imprisonment to coerce payment of their debts, or of an absolute right to appropriate and monopolize all their future earnings. The latter course obviously destroys all encouragement to industry and enterprize on the part of the unfortunate debtor, by taking from him all the just rewards of his labour, and leaving him a miserable pittance, dependent upon the bounty or forbearance of his creditors. The former is, if possible, more harsh, severe, and indefensible. It makes poverty and misfortune, in themselves sufficiently heavy burthens, the subject or the occasion of penalties and punishments. Imprisonment, as a civil remedy, admits of no defence, except as it is used to coerce fraudulent debtors to yield up their present property to their creditors, in discharge of their engagements. But when the debtors have no property, or have yielded up the whole to their creditors, to allow the latter at their mere pleasure to imprison them, is a refinement in cruelty, and an indulgence of private passions, which could hardly find apology in an enlightened despotism; and are utterly at war with all the rights and duties of free governments. Such a system of legislation is as unjust, as it is unfeeling. It is incompatible with the first precepts of Christianity; and is a living reproach to the nations of christendom, carrying them back to the worst ages of paganism. One of the first duties of legislation, while it provides amply for the sacred obligation of contracts, and the remedies to enforce them, certainly is, *pari passu*, to relieve the unfortunate and meritorious debtor from a slavery of mind and body, which cuts him off from a fair enjoyment of the common benefits of society, and robs his family of the fruits of his labour, and the benefits of his paternal superintendence. A national government, which did not possess this power of legislation, would be little worthy of the exalted functions of guarding the happiness, and supporting the rights of a free people. It might guard against political oppressions, only to render private oppressions more intolerable, and more glaring.

§ 1102. But there are peculiar reasons, independent of these general considerations, why the government of the United States should be entrusted with this power. They result from the importance of preserving harmony, promoting justice, and securing equality of rights and remedies among the citizens of all the states. It is obvious, that if the power is exclusively vested in the states, each one will be at liberty to frame such a system of legislation upon the subject of bankruptcy and insolvency, as best suits its own local interests, and pursuits. Under such circumstances no uniformity of system or operations can be expected. One state may adopt a system of general insolvency; another, a limited or temporary system; one may relieve from the obligation of contracts; another only from imprisonment; another may adopt a still more restrictive course of occasional relief; and another may refuse to act in any manner upon the subject. The laws of one state may give undue preferences to one class of creditors, as for instance, to creditors by bond, or judgment; another may provide for an equality of debts, and a distribution *pro ratâ* without distinction among all. One may prefer creditors living within the state to all living without; securing to the former an entire priority of payment out of the assets. Another may, with a more liberal justice, provide for the equal payment of all, at home and abroad, without favour or preference. In short, diversities of almost infinite variety and object may be introduced into the local system, which may work gross injustice and inequality, and nourish feuds and discontents in neighbouring states. What is here stated, is not purely speculative. It has occurred among the American states in the most offensive forms, without any apparent reluctance or compunction on the part of the offending state. There will always be found in every state a large mass of politicians, who will deem it more safe to consult their own temporary interests and popularity, by a narrow system of preferences, than to enlarge the boundaries, so as to give to distant creditors a fair share of the fortune of a ruined debtor. There can be no other adequate remedy, than giving a power to the general government, to introduce and perpetuate a uniform system.

§ 1103. In the next place it is clear, that no state can introduce any system, which shall extend beyond its own territorial limits, and the persons, who are subject to its jurisdiction. Creditors residing in other states cannot be bound by its laws; and debts contracted in other states are beyond the reach of its legislation. It can neither discharge the obligation of such contracts, nor touch the remedies, which relate to them in any other jurisdiction. So that the most meritorious insolvent debtor will be harassed by new suits, and new litigations, as often as he moves out of the state boundaries. His whole property may be absorbed by his creditors residing in a single state, and he may be left to the severe retributions of judicial process in every other state in the Union. Among a people, whose general and commercial intercourse must be so great, and so constantly increasing, as in the United States, this alone would be a most enormous evil, and bear with peculiar severity upon all the commercial states. Very few persons engaged in active business will be without debtors or creditors in many states in the Union. The evil is incapable of being redressed by the states. It can be adequately redressed only by the power of the Union. One of the most pressing grievances, bearing upon commercial, manufacturing, and agricultural interests at the present moment, is the total want of a general system of bankruptcy. It is well known, that the power has lain dormant, except for a short period, ever since the constitution was adopted; and the excellent system, then put into operation, was repealed, before it had any fair trial, upon grounds generally believed to be wholly beside its merits, and from causes more easily understood, than deliberately vindicated.

§ 1104. In the next place, the power is important in regard to foreign countries, and to our commercial credits and intercourse with them. Unless the general government were invested with authority to pass suitable laws, which should give reciprocity and equality in cases of bankruptcies here, there would be danger, that the state legislation might, by undue domestic preferences and favours, compel foreign countries to retaliate; and instead of allowing creditors in the United States to partake an equality of benefits in cases of bankruptcies, to postpone them to all others. The existence of the power is, therefore, eminently useful; first, as a check upon undue state legislation; and secondly, as a means of redressing any grievances sustained by foreigners in commercial transactions.

§ 1105. It cannot but be matter of regret, that a power so salutary should have hitherto remained (as has been already intimated) a mere dead letter. It is extraordinary, that a commercial nation, spreading its enterprise through the whole world, and possessing such an infinitely varied, internal trade, reaching almost to every cottage in the most distant states, should voluntarily surrender up a system, which has elsewhere enjoyed such general favour, as the best security of creditors against fraud, and the best protection of debtors against oppression.

§ 1106. What laws are to be deemed bankrupt laws within the meaning of the constitution has been a matter of much forensic discussion and argument. Attempts have been made to distinguish between bankrupt laws and insolvent laws. For example, it has been said, that laws, which merely liberate the person of the debtor, are insolvent laws, and those, which discharge the contract, are bankrupt laws. But it would be very difficult to sustain this distinction by any uniformity of laws at home or abroad. In some of the states, laws, known as insolvent laws, discharge the person only; in others, they discharge the contract. And if congress were to pass a bankrupt act, which should discharge the person only of the bankrupt, and leave his future acquisitions liable to his creditors, there would be great difficulty in saying, that such an act was not in the sense of the constitution a bankrupt act, and so within the power of congress. Again; it has been said, that

insolvent laws act on imprisoned debtors only at their own instance; and bankrupt laws only at the instance of creditors. But, however true this may have been in past times, as the actual course of English legislation, it is not true, and never was true, as a distinction in colonial legislation. In England it was an accident in the system, and not a material ground to discriminate, who were to be deemed in a legal sense insolvents, or bankrupts. And if an act of congress should be passed, which should authorize a commission of bankruptcy to issue at the instance of the debtor, no court would on this account be warranted in saying, that the act was unconstitutional, and the commission a nullity. It is believed, that no laws ever were passed in America by the colonies or states, which had the technical denomination of "bankrupt laws." But insolvent laws, quite co-extensive with the English bankrupt system in their operations and objects, have not been unfrequent in colonial and state legislation. No distinction was ever practically, or even theoretically attempted to be made between bankruptcies and insolvencies. And an historical review of the colonial and state legislation will abundantly show, that a bankrupt law may contain those regulations, which are generally found in insolvent laws; and that an insolvent law may contain those, which are common to bankrupt laws.

§ 1107. The truth is, that the English system of bankruptcy, as well as the name, was borrowed from the continental jurisprudence, and derivatively from the Roman law. "We have fetched," says Lord Coke, "as well the name, as the wickedness of bankrupts, from foreign nations; for *banque* in the French is *mensa,* and a banquer or eschanger is *mensarius;* and *route* is a sign or mark, as we say a cart route is the sign or mark, where the cart hath gone. Metaphorically it is taken for him, that hath wasted his estate, and removed his bank, so as there is left but a mention thereof. Some say it should be derived from *banque* and *rumpue,* as he that hath broken his bank or state. Mr. Justice Blackstone inclines strongly to this latter intimation, saying, that the word is derived from the word *bancus,* or *banque,* which signifies the table or counter of a tradesman, and *ruptus,* broken; denoting thereby one, whose shop or place of trade is broken and gone. It is observable, that the first statute against bankrupt, is 'against such persons, as do make bankrupt,' (34 Hen. 8, ch. 4,) which is a literal translation of the French idiom, *qui font banque route.*"

§ 1108. The system of discharging persons, who were unable to pay their debts, was transferred from the Roman law into continental jurisprudence at an early period. To the glory of Christianity let it be said, that the law of cession (*cessio bonorum*) was introduced by the Christian emperors of Rome, whereby, if a debtor ceded, or yielded up all his property to his creditors, he was secured from being dragged to gaol, *omni quoque corporali cruciau semoto;* for as the emperor (Justinian) justly observed, *inhumanum erat spoliatum fortunis suis in solidum damnari;* a noble declaration, which the American republics would do well to follow, and not merely to praise. Neither by the Roman, nor the continental law, was the *cessio bonorum* confined to traders, but it extended to all persons. It may be added, that the *cessio bonorum* of the Roman law, and that, which at present prevails in most parts of the continent of Europe, only exempted the debtor from imprisonment. It did not release or discharge the debt, or exempt the future acquisitions of the debtor from execution for the debt. The English statute, commonly called the "Lords' Act," went no farther, than to discharge the debtor's person. And it may be laid down, as the law of Germany, France, Holland, Scotland, and England, that their insolvent laws are not more extensive in their operation, than the *cessio bonorum* of the civil law. In some parts of Germany, we are informed by Huberus and Heineccius, a *cessio bonorum* does not even work a discharge of the debtor's person, and much less of his future effects. But with a view to the advancement of commerce, and the benefit of creditors, the systems, now commonly known by the name of "bankrupt laws," were introduced; and allowed a proceeding to be had at the instance of the creditors against an unwilling debtor, when he did not choose to yield up his property; or, as it is phrased in our law, bankrupt laws were originally proceedings *in invitum*. In the English system the bankrupt laws are limited to persons, who are traders, or connected with matters of trade and commerce, as such persons are peculiarly liable to accidental losses, and to an inability of paying their debts without any fault of their own. But this is a mere matter of policy, and by no means enters into the nature of such laws. There is nothing in the nature, or reason of such laws to prevent their being applied to any other class of unfortunate and meritorious debtors.

§ 1109. How far the power of congress to pass uniform laws on the subject of bankruptcies supersedes the authority of state legislation on the same subject, has been a matter of much elaborate forensic discussion. It has been strenuously maintained by some learned minds, that the power in congress is exclusive of that of the states; and, whether exerted or not, it supersedes state legislation. On the other hand, it has been maintained, that the power in congress is not exclusive; that when congress has acted upon the subject, to the extent of the national legislation the power of the states is controlled and limited; but when unexerted, the states are at liberty to exercise the power in its full extent, unless so far as they are controlled by other constitutional provisions. And this latter opinion is now firmly established by judicial decisions. As this doctrine seems now to have obtained a general acquiescence, it does not seem necessary to review the reasoning, on which the different opinions are founded; although, as a new question, it is probably as much open to controversy, as any one, which has ever given rise to judicial argumentation. But upon all such subjects it seems desirable to adopt the sound practical maxim, *Interest reipublicae, ut finis sit litium*.

§ 1110. It is, however, to be understood, that although the states still retain the power to pass insolvent and bankrupt laws, that power is not unlimited, as it was before the constitution. It does not, as will be presently seen, extend to the passing of insolvent or bankrupt acts, which shall discharge the obligation of antecedent contracts. It can discharge such contracts only, as are made subsequently to the passing of such acts, and such, as are made within the state between citizens of the same state. It does not extend to contracts made with a citizen of another state within the state, nor to any contracts made in other states.

SEE ALSO:

Generally 1.10.1

An Act to Establish a Uniform System of Bankruptcy throughout the United States, 2 Stat. 19 (1800)

House of Representatives, Uniform Bankruptcy Law, 16–19 Feb. 1818, Annals 31:905, 907–35, 936–53, 954–61, 963–67, 970–72

Senate, Bankrupt Bill, 16, 17 Mar. 1820, Annals 35:502–21

United States v. *Wilson*, 8 Wheat. 253 (1823)

Glenn v. *Humphreys*, 10 Fed. Cas. 471, no. 5,480 (C.C.E.D.Pa. 1823)

James Kent, Commentaries 1:356–58 (1826)

Mason v. *Haile*, 12 Wheat. 370 (1827)

Boyle v. *Zacharie & Turner*, 6 Pet. 348 (1832)

Betts v. *Bagley*, 29 Mass. 571 (1832)

Field v. *United States*, 9 Pet. 182 (1835)

Constitution of the United States and the First Twelve Amendments

We the People of the United States, in Order to form a more perfect Union, establish Justice, insure domestic Tranquility, provide for the common defence, promote the general Welfare, and secure the Blessings of Liberty to ourselves and our Posterity, do ordain and establish this Constitution for the United States of America.

Article. I.

SECTION 1. All legislative Powers herein granted shall be vested in a Congress of the United States, which shall consist of a Senate and House of Representatives.

SECTION 2. The House of Representatives shall be composed of Members chosen every second Year by the People of the several States, and the Electors in each State shall have the Qualifications requisite for Electors of the most numerous Branch of the State Legislature.

No person shall be a Representative who shall not have attained to the Age of twenty five Years, and been seven Years a Citizen of the United States, and who shall not, when elected, be an Inhabitant of that State in which he shall be chosen.

Representatives and direct Taxes shall be apportioned among the several States which may be included within this Union, according to their respective Numbers, which shall be determined by adding to the whole Number of free Persons, including those bound to Service for a Term of Years, and excluding Indians not taxed, three fifths of all other Persons. The actual Enumeration shall be made within three Years after the first Meeting of the Congress of the United States, and within every subsequent Term of ten Years, in such Manner as they shall by Law direct. The Number of Representatives shall not exceed one for every thirty Thousand, but each State shall have at Least one Representative; and until such enumeration shall be made, the State of New Hampshire shall be entitled to chuse three, Massachusetts eight, Rhode-Island and Providence Plantations one, Connecticut five, New-York six, New Jersey four, Pennsylvania eight, Delaware one, Maryland six, Virginia ten, North Carolina five, South Carolina five, and Georgia three.

When vacancies happen in the Representation from any State, the Executive Authority thereof shall issue Writs of Election to fill such Vacancies.

The House of Representatives shall chuse their Speaker and other Officers; and shall have the sole Power of Impeachment.

SECTION 3. The Senate of the United States shall be composed of two Senators from each State, chosen by the Legislature thereof, for six Years; and each Senator shall have one Vote.

Immediately after they shall be assembled in Consequence of the first Election, they shall be divided as equally as may be into three Classes. The Seats of the Senators of the first Class shall be vacated at the Expiration of the second Year, of the second Class at the Expiration of the fourth Year, and of the third Class at the Expiration of the sixth Year, so that one third may be chosen every second Year; and if Vacancies happen by Resignation, or otherwise, during the Recess of the Legislature of any State, the Executive thereof may make temporary Appointments until the next Meeting of the Legislature, which shall then fill such Vacancies.

No Person shall be a Senator who shall not have attained to the Age of thirty Years, and been nine Years a Citizen of the United States, and who shall not, when elected, be an Inhabitant of that State for which he shall be chosen.

The Vice President of the United States shall be President of the Senate, but shall have no Vote, unless they be equally divided.

The Senate shall chuse their other Officers, and also a President pro tempore, in the Absence of the Vice President, or when he shall exercise the Office of President of the United States.

The Senate shall have the sole Power to try all Impeachments. When sitting for that Purpose, they shall be on Oath or Affirmation. When the President of the United States is tried, the Chief Justice shall preside: And no Person shall be convicted without the Concurrence of two thirds of the Members present.

Judgment in Cases of Impeachment shall not extend further than to removal from Office, and disqualification to hold and enjoy any Office of honor, Trust or Profit under the United States: but the Party convicted shall nevertheless be liable and subject to Indictment, Trial, Judgment and Punishment, according to Law.

SECTION 4. The Times, Places and Manner of holding Elections for Senators and Representatives, shall be prescribed in each State by the Legislature thereof; but the Congress may at any time by Law make or alter such Regulations, except as to the Places of chusing Senators.

The Congress shall assemble at least once in every Year, and such Meeting shall be on the first Monday in December, unless they shall by Law appoint a different Day.

SECTION 5. Each House shall be the Judge of the Elections, Returns and Qualifications of its own Members, and a Majority of each shall constitute a Quorum to do Business; but a smaller Number may adjourn from day to day, and may be authorized to compel the Attendance of absent Members, in such Manner, and under such Penalties as each House may provide.

Each House may determine the Rules of its Proceedings, punish its Members for disorderly Behaviour, and, with the Concurrence of two thirds, expel a Member.

Each House shall keep a Journal of its Proceedings, and from time to time publish the same, excepting such Parts as may in their Judgment require Secrecy; and the Yeas and Nays of the Members of either House on any question shall, at the Desire of one fifth of those Present, be entered on the Journal.

Neither House, during the Session of Congress, shall, without the Consent of the other, adjourn for more than three days, nor to any other Place than that in which the two Houses shall be sitting.

SECTION 6. The Senators and Representatives shall receive a Compensation for their Services, to be ascertained by Law, and paid out of the Treasury of the United States. They shall in all Cases, except Treason, Felony and Breach of the Peace, be privileged from Arrest during their Attendance at the Session of their respective Houses, and in going to and returning from the same; and for any Speech or Debate in either House, they shall not be questioned in any other Place.

No Senator or Representative shall, during the Time for which he was elected, be appointed to any civil Office under the Authority of the United States, which shall have been created, or the Emoluments whereof shall have been encreased during such time; and no Person holding any Office under the United States, shall be a Member of either House during his Continuance in Office.

SECTION 7. All Bills for raising Revenue shall originate in the House of Representatives; but the Senate may propose or concur with Amendments as on other Bills.

Every Bill which shall have passed the House of Representatives and the Senate, shall, before it become a Law, be presented to the President of the United States; If he approve he shall sign it, but if not he shall return it, with his Objections to that House in which it shall have originated, who shall enter the Objections at large on their Journal, and proceed to reconsider it. If after such Reconsideration two thirds of that House shall agree to pass the Bill, it shall be sent, together with the Objections, to the other House, by which it shall likewise be reconsidered, and if approved by two thirds of that House, it shall become a Law. But in all such Cases the Votes of both Houses shall be determined by yeas and Nays, and the Names of the Persons voting for and against the Bill shall be entered on the Journal of each House respectively. If any Bill shall not be returned by the President within ten days (Sundays excepted) after it shall have been presented to him, the Same shall be a Law, in like Manner as if he had signed it, unless the Congress by their Adjournment prevent its Return in which Case it shall not be a Law.

Every Order, Resolution, or Vote to which the Concurrence of the Senate and House of Representatives may be necessary (except on a question of Adjournment) shall be presented to the President of the United States; and before the Same shall take Effect, shall be approved by him, or being disapproved by him, shall be repassed by two thirds of the Senate and House of Representatives, according to the Rules and Limitations prescribed in the Case of a Bill.

SECTION 8. The Congress shall have Power To lay and collect Taxes, Duties, Imposts and Excises, to pay the Debts and provide for the common Defence and general Welfare of the United States; but all Duties, Imposts and Excises shall be uniform throughout the United States;

To borrow Money on the credit of the United States;

To regulate Commerce with foreign Nations, and among the several States, and with the Indian Tribes;

To establish an uniform Rule of Naturalization, and uniform Laws on the subject of Bankruptcies throughout the United States;

To coin Money, regulate the Value thereof, and of foreign Coin, and fix the Standard of Weights and Measures;

To provide for the Punishment of counterfeiting the Securities and current Coin of the United States;

To establish Post Offices and post Roads;

To promote the progress of Science and useful Arts, by securing for limited Times to Authors and Inventors the exclusive Right to their respective Writings and Discoveries;

To constitute Tribunals inferior to the supreme Court;

To define and punish Piracies and Felonies committed on the high Seas, and Offences against the Law of Nations;

To declare War, grant Letters of Marque and Reprisal, and make Rules concerning Captures on Land and Water;

To raise and support Armies, but no Appropriation of Money to that Use shall be for a longer Term than two Years;

To provide and maintain a Navy;

To make Rules for the Government and Regulation of the land and naval Forces;

To provide for calling forth the Militia to execute the Laws of the Union, suppress Insurrections and repel Invasions;

To provide for organizing, arming, and disciplining, the Militia, and for governing such Part of them as may be employed in the Service of the United States, reserving to the States respectively, the Appointment of the Officers, and the Authority of training the Militia according to the discipline prescribed by Congress;

To exercise exclusive Legislation in all Cases whatsoever, over such District (not exceeding ten Miles square) as may, by Cession of particular States, and the Acceptance of Congress, become the Seat of the Government of the United States, and to exercise like Authority over all Places purchased by the Consent of the Legislature of the State in which the Same shall be, for the Erection of Forts, Magazines, Arsenals, dock-Yards, and other needful Buildings;—And

To make all Laws which shall be necessary and proper for carrying into Execution the foregoing Powers, and all other Powers vested by this Constitution in the Government of the United States, or in any Department or Officer thereof.

SECTION 9. The Migration or Importation of such Persons as any of the States now existing shall think proper to admit, shall not be prohibited by the Congress prior to the Year one thousand eight hundred and eight, but a Tax or duty may be imposed on such Importation, not exceeding ten dollars for each Person.

The Privilege of the Writ of Habeas Corpus shall not be suspended, unless when in Cases of Rebellion or Invasion the public Safety may require it.

No Bill of Attainder or ex post facto Law shall be passed.

No Capitation, or other direct, Tax shall be laid, unless in Proportion to the Census or Enumeration herein before directed to be taken.

No Tax or Duty shall be laid on Articles exported from any State.

No Preference shall be given by any Regulation of Commerce or Revenue to the Ports of one State over those of another: nor shall Vessels bound to, or from, one State, be obliged to enter, clear, or pay Duties in another.

No Money shall be drawn from the Treasury, but in Consequence of Appropriations made by Law; and a regular Statement and Account of the Receipts and Expenditures of all public Money shall be published from time to time.

No Title of Nobility shall be granted by the United States: And no Person holding any Office of Profit or Trust under them, shall, without the Consent of the Congress, accept of any present, Emolument, Office, or Title, of any kind whatever, from any King, Prince, or foreign State.

SECTION 10. No State shall enter into any Treaty, Alliance, or Confederation; grant Letters of Marque and Reprisal; coin Money; emit Bills of Credit; make any Thing but gold and silver Coin a Tender in Payment of Debts; pass any Bill of Attainder, ex post facto Law, or Law impairing the Obligation of Contracts, or grant any Title of Nobility.

No State shall, without the Consent of the Congress, lay any Imposts or Duties on Imports or Exports, except what may be absolutely necessary for executing it's inspection Laws: and the net Produce of all Duties and Imposts, laid by any State on Imports or Exports, shall be for the Use of the Treasury of the United States; and all such Laws shall be subject to the Revision and Controul of the Congress.

No State shall, without the Consent of Congress, lay any Duty of Tonnage, keep Troops, or Ships of War in time of Peace, enter into any Agreement or Compact with another State, or with a foreign Power, or engage in War, unless actually invaded, or in such imminent Danger as will not admit of delay.

Article. II.

SECTION 1. The executive Power shall be vested in a President of the United States of America. He shall hold his Office during the Term of four Years, and, together with the Vice President, chosen for the same Term, be elected as follows

Each State shall appoint, in such Manner as the Legislature thereof may direct, a Number of Electors, equal to the whole Number of Senators and Representatives to which the State may be entitled in the Congress: but no Senator or Representative, or Person holding an Office of Trust or Profit under the United States, shall be appointed an Elector.

The Electors shall meet in their respective States, and vote by Ballot for two Persons, of whom one at least shall not be an Inhabitant of the same State with themselves. And they shall make a List of all the Persons voted for, and of the Number of Votes for each; which List they shall sign and certify, and transmit sealed to the Seat of the Government of the United States, directed to the President of the Senate. The President of the Senate shall, in the Presence of the Senate and House of Representatives, open all the Certificates, and the Votes shall then be counted. The Person having the greatest Number of Votes shall be the President, if such Number be a Majority of the whole Number of Electors appointed; and if there be more than one who have such Majority, and have an equal Number of Votes, then the House of Representatives shall immediately chuse by Ballot one of them for President; and if no Person have a Majority, then from the five highest on the List the said House shall in like Manner chuse the President. But in chusing the President, the Votes shall be taken by States, the Representation from each State having one Vote; A quorum for this Purpose shall consist of a Member or Members from two thirds of the States, and a Majority of all the States shall be necessary to a Choice. In every Case, after the Choice of the President, the Person having the greatest Number of Votes of the Electors shall be the Vice President. But if there should remain two or more who have equal Votes, the Senate shall chuse from them by Ballot the Vice President.

The Congress may determine the Time of chusing the Electors, and the Day on which they shall give their Votes; which Day shall be the same throughout the United States.

No Person except a natural born Citizen, or a Citizen of the United States, at the time of the Adoption of this Constitution, shall be eligible to the Office of President; neither shall any Person be eligible to that Office who shall not have attained to the Age of thirty five Years, and been fourteen Years a Resident within the United States.

In Case of the Removal of the President from Office, or of his Death, Resignation, or Inability to discharge the Powers and Duties of the said Office, the Same shall devolve on the Vice President, and the Congress may by Law provide for the Case of Removal, Death, Resignation or Inability, both of the President and Vice President, declaring what Officer shall then act as President, and such Officer shall act accordingly, until the Disability be removed, or a President shall be elected.

The President shall, at stated Times, receive for his Services, a Compensation, which shall neither be encreased nor diminished during the Period for which he shall have been elected, and he shall not receive within that Period any other Emolument from the United States, or any of them.

Before he enter on the Execution of his Office, he shall take the following Oath or Affirmation:—"I do solemnly swear (or affirm) that I will faithfully execute the Office of President of the United States, and will to the best of my Ability, preserve, protect and defend the Constitution of the United States."

SECTION 2. The President shall be Commander in Chief of the Army and Navy of the United States, and of the Militia of the several States, when called into the actual Service of the United States; he may require the Opinion, in writing, of the principal Officer in each of the executive Departments, upon any Subject relating to the Duties of their respective Offices, and he shall have Power to grant Reprieves and Pardons for Offences against the United States, except in Cases of Impeachment.

He shall have Power, by and with the Advice and Consent of the Senate, to make Treaties, provided two thirds of the Senators present concur; and he shall nominate, and by and with the Advice and Consent of the Senate, shall appoint Ambassadors, other public Ministers and Consuls, Judges of the supreme Court, and all other Officers of the United States, whose Appointments are not herein otherwise provided for, and which shall be established by Law: but the Congress may by Law vest the Appointment of such inferior Officers, as they think proper, in the President alone, in the Courts of Law, or in the Heads of Departments.

The President shall have Power to fill up all Vacancies that may happen during the Recess of the Senate, by granting Commissions which shall expire at the End of their next Session.

SECTION 3. He shall from time to time give to the Congress Information of the State of the Union, and recommend to their Consideration such Measures as he shall judge necessary and expedient; he may, on extraordinary Occasions, convene both Houses, or either of them, and in Case of Disagreement between them, with Respect to the Time of Adjournment, he may adjourn them to such Time as he shall think proper; he shall receive Ambassadors and other public Ministers; he shall take Care that the Laws be faithfully executed, and shall Commission all the Officers of the United States.

SECTION 4. The President, Vice President and all civil Officers of the United States, shall be removed from Office on Impeachment for, and Conviction of, Treason, Bribery, or other high Crimes and Misdemeanors.

Article. III.

SECTION 1. The judicial Power of the United States, shall be vested in one supreme Court, and in such inferior Courts as the Congress may from time to time ordain and establish. The Judges, both of the supreme and inferior Courts, shall hold their Offices during good Behaviour, and shall, at stated Times, receive for their Services, a Compensation, which shall not be diminished during their Continuance in Office.

SECTION 2. The judicial Power shall extend to all Cases, in Law and Equity, arising under this Constitution, the Laws of the United States, and Treaties made, or which shall be made, under their Authority;—to all Cases affecting Ambassadors, other public Ministers and Consuls;—to all Cases of admiralty and maritime Jurisdiction;—to Controversies to which the United States shall be a Party;—to Controversies between two or more States;—between a State and Citizens of another State;—between Citizens of different States,—between Citizens of the same State claiming Lands under Grants of different States, and between a State, or the Citizens thereof, and foreign States, Citizens or Subjects.

In all Cases affecting Ambassadors, other public Ministers and Consuls, and those in which a State shall be Party, the supreme Court shall have original Jurisdiction. In all the other Cases before mentioned, the supreme Court shall have appellate Jurisdiction, both as to Law and Fact, with such Exceptions, and under such Regulations as the Congress shall make.

The Trial of all Crimes, except in Cases of Impeachment, shall be by Jury; and such Trial shall be held in the State where the said Crimes shall have been committed; but when not committed within any State, the Trial shall be at such Place or Places as the Congress may by Law have directed.

SECTION 3. Treason against the United States, shall consist only in levying War against them, or in adhering to their Enemies, giving them Aid and Comfort. No Person shall be convicted of Treason unless on the Testimony of two Witnesses to the same overt Act, or on Confession in open Court.

The Congress shall have Power to declare the Punishment of Treason, but no Attainder of Treason shall work Corruption of Blood, or Forfeiture except during the Life of the Person attainted.

Article. IV.

SECTION 1. Full Faith and Credit shall be given in each State to the public Acts, Records, and judicial Proceedings of every other State. And the Congress may by general Laws prescribe the Manner in which such Acts, Records and Proceedings shall be proved, and the Effect thereof.

SECTION 2. The Citizens of each State shall be entitled to all Privileges and Immunities of Citizens in the several States.

A Person charged in any State with Treason, Felony, or other Crime, who shall flee from Justice, and be found in another State, shall on Demand of the executive Authority of the State from which he fled, be delivered up, to be removed to the State having Jurisdiction of the Crime.

No Person held to Service or Labour in one State, under the Laws thereof, escaping into another, shall, in Consequence of any Law or Regulation therein, be discharged from such Service or Labour, but shall be delivered up on

Claim of the Party to whom such Service or Labour may be due.

SECTION 3. New States may be admitted by the Congress into this Union; but no new State shall be formed or erected within the Jurisdiction of any other State; nor any State be formed by the Junction of two or more States, or Parts of States, without the Consent of the Legislatures of the States concerned as well as of the Congress.

The Congress shall have Power to dispose of and make all needful Rules and Regulations respecting the Territory or other Property belonging to the United States; and nothing in this Constitution shall be so construed as to Prejudice any Claims of the United States, or of any particular State.

SECTION 4. The United States shall guarantee to every State in this Union a Republican Form of Government, and shall protect each of them against Invasion; and on Application of the Legislature, or of the Executive (when the Legislature cannot be convened) against domestic Violence.

Article. V.

The Congress, whenever two thirds of both Houses shall deem it necessary, shall propose Amendments to this Constitution, or, on the Application of the Legislatures of two thirds of the several States, shall call a Convention for proposing Amendments, which, in either Case, shall be valid to all Intents and Purposes, as Part of this Constitution, when ratified by the Legislatures of three fourths of the several States, or by Conventions in three fourths thereof, as the one or the other Mode of Ratification may be proposed by the Congress; Provided that no Amendment which may be made prior to the Year One thousand eight hundred and eight shall in any Manner affect the first and fourth Clauses in the Ninth Section of the first Article; and that no State, without its Consent, shall be deprived of it's equal Suffrage in the Senate.

Article. VI.

All Debts contracted and Engagements entered into, before the Adoption of this Constitution, shall be as valid against the United States under this Constitution, as under the Confederation.

This Constitution, and the Laws of the United States which shall be made in Pursuance thereof; and all Treaties made, or which shall be made, under the Authority of the United States, shall be the supreme Law of the Land; and the Judges in every State shall be bound thereby, any Thing in the Constitution or Laws of any State to the Contrary notwithstanding.

The Senators and Representatives before mentioned, and the Members of the several State Legislatures, and all executive and judicial Officers, both of the United States and of the several States, shall be bound by Oath or Affirmation, to support this Constitution; but no religious Test shall ever be required as a Qualification to any Office or public Trust under the United States.

Article. VII.

The Ratification of the Conventions of nine States, shall be sufficient for the Establishment of this Constitution between the States so ratifying the Same.

The Word, "the," being interlined between the seventh and eighth Lines of the first Page, The Word "Thirty" being partly written on an Erazure in the fifteenth Line of the first Page, The Words "is tried" being interlined between the thirty second and thirty third Lines of the first Page and the Word "the" being interlined between the forty third and forty fourth Lines of the second Page. Attest WILLIAM JACKSON Secretary

done in Convention by the Unanimous Consent of the States present the Seventeenth Day of September in the Year of our Lord one thousand seven hundred and Eighty seven and of the Independance of the United States of America the Twelfth In witness whereof We have hereunto subscribed our Names,

Go: WASHINGTON—Presidt. and deputy from Virginia

New Hampshire	John Langdon Nicholas Gilman
Massachusetts	Nathaniel Gorham Rufus King
Connecticut	Wm. Saml. Johnson Roger Sherman
New York	Alexander Hamilton
New Jersey	Wil: Livingston David Brearley. Wm. Paterson. Jona: Dayton
Pensylvania	B Franklin Thomas Mifflin Robt Morris Geo. Clymer Thos. FitzSimons Jared Ingersoll James Wilson Gouv Morris
Delaware	Geo: Read Gunning Bedford jun John Dickinson Richard Bassett Jaco: Broom
Maryland	James McHenry Dan of St Thos. Jenifer Danl Carroll
Virginia	John Blair— James Madison Jr.
North Carolina	Wm. Blount Richd. Dobbs Spaight. Hu Williamson
South Carolina	J. Rutledge Charles Cotesworth Pinckney Charles Pinckney Pierce Butler.
Georgia	William Few Abr Baldwin

Amendments to the Constitution

Article I

Congress shall make no law respecting an establishment of religion, or prohibiting the free exercise thereof; or abridging the freedom of speech, or of the press; or the right of the people peaceably to assemble, and to petition the Government for a redress of grievances.

Article II

A well regulated Militia, being necessary to the security of a free State, the right of the people to keep and bear Arms, shall not be infringed.

Article III

No Soldier shall, in time of peace be quartered in any house, without the consent of the Owner, nor in time of war, but in a manner to be prescribed by law.

Article IV

The right of the people to be secure in their persons, houses, papers, and effects, against unreasonable searches and seizures, shall not be violated, and no Warrants shall issue, but upon probable cause, supported by Oath or affirmation, and particularly describing the place to be searched, and the persons or things to be seized.

Article V

No person shall be held to answer for a capital, or otherwise infamous crime, unless on a presentment or indictment of a Grand Jury, except in cases arising in the land or naval forces, or in the Militia, when in actual service in time of War or public danger; nor shall any person be subject for the same offence to be twice put in jeopardy of life or limb; nor shall be compelled in any criminal case to be a witness against himself, nor be deprived of life, liberty, or property, without due process of law; nor shall private property be taken for public use, without just compensation.

Article VI

In all criminal prosecutions, the accused shall enjoy the right to a speedy and public trial, by an impartial jury of the State and district wherein the crime shall have been committed, which district shall have been previously ascertained by law, and to be informed of the nature and cause of the accusation; to be confronted with the witnesses against him; to have compulsory process for obtaining witnesses in his favor, and to have the Assistance of Counsel for his defence.

Article VII

In Suits at common law, where the value in controversy shall exceed twenty dollars, the right of trial by jury shall be preserved, and no fact tried by a jury, shall be otherwise re-examined in any Court of the United States, than according to the rules of the common law.

Article VIII

Excessive bail shall not be required, nor excessive fines imposed, nor cruel and unusual punishments inflicted.

Article IX

The enumeration in the Constitution, of certain rights, shall not be construed to deny or disparage others retained by the people.

Article X

The powers not delegated to the United States by the Constitution, nor prohibited by it to the States, are reserved to the States respectively, or to the people.

Article XI

The Judicial power of the United States shall not be construed to extend to any suit in law or equity, commenced or prosecuted against one of the United States by Citizens of another State, or by Citizens or Subjects of any Foreign State.

Article XII

The Electors shall meet in their respective states, and vote by ballot for President and Vice-President, one of whom, at least, shall not be an inhabitant of the same state with themselves; they shall name in their ballots the person voted for as President, and in distinct ballots the person voted for as Vice-President, and they shall make distinct lists of all persons voted for as President, and of all persons voted for as Vice-President, and of the number of votes for each, which lists they shall sign and certify, and transmit sealed to the seat of the government of the United States, directed to the President of the Senate;—The President of the Senate shall, in the presence of the Senate and House of Representatives, open all the certificates and the votes shall then be counted;—The person having the greatest number of votes for President, shall be the President, if such number be a majority of the whole number of Electors appointed; and if no person have such majority, then from the persons having the highest numbers not exceeding three on the list of those voted for as President, the House of Representatives shall choose immediately, by ballot, the President. But in choosing the President, the votes shall be taken by states, the representation from each state having one vote; a quorum for this purpose shall consist of a member or members from two-thirds of the states, and a majority of all the states shall be necessary to a choice. And if the House of Representatives shall not choose a President whenever the right of choice shall devolve upon them, before the fourth day of March next following, then the Vice-President shall act as President, as in the case of the death or other constitutional disability of the President. The person having the greatest number of votes as Vice-President, shall be the Vice-President, if such number be a majority of the whole number of Electors appointed, and if no person have a majority, then from the two highest numbers on the list, the Senate shall choose the Vice-President; a quorum for the purpose shall consist of two-thirds of the whole number of Senators, and a majority of the whole number shall be necessary to a choice. But no person constitutionally ineligible to the office of President shall be eligible to that of Vice-President of the United States.

.   .   .

Short Titles Used

Documentary citations given in short-title forms as "Life," "Papers," "Works," etc., are to be understood as referring to editions of the author of that particular document. Exceptions are clearly noted.

John Adams, Diary *Diary and Autobiography of John Adams.* Edited by L. H. Butterfield et al. 4 vols. Cambridge: Belknap Press of Harvard University Press, 1961.

John Adams, Papers *Papers of John Adams.* Edited by Robert J. Taylor et al. Cambridge: Belknap Press of Harvard University Press, 1977–.

John Adams, Works *The Works of John Adams.* Edited by Charles Francis Adams. 10 vols. Boston: Little, Brown & Co., 1850–56.
See also: Butterfield; Cappon; Warren-Adams Letters

J. Q. Adams, Writings *Writings of John Quincy Adams.* Edited by Worthington Chauncey Ford. 7 vols. New York: Macmillan Co., 1913–17.

Samuel Adams, Writings *The Writings of Samuel Adams.* Edited by Harry Alonzo Cushing. 4 vols. New York: G. P. Putnam's Sons, 1904–8.

American Archives *American Archives.* Edited by M. St. Clair Clarke and Peter Force. 4th ser., 6 vols. Washington, D.C., 1837–46. 5th ser., 3 vols. Washington, D.C., 1848–53.

American Colonial Documents Jensen, Merrill, ed. *American Colonial Documents to 1776.* English Historical Documents, edited by David C. Douglas, vol. 9. New York: Oxford University Press, 1969.

Annals *Annals of Congress. The Debates and Proceedings in the Congress of the United States.* "History of Congress." 42 vols. Washington, D.C.: Gales & Seaton, 1834–56.

Bailyn Bailyn, Bernard, ed. *Pamphlets of the American Revolution, 1750–1776.* Vol. 1, *1750–1765.* Cambridge: Belknap Press of Harvard University Press, 1965.

Blackstone, Commentaries Blackstone, William. *Commentaries on the Laws of England: A Facsimile of the First Edition of 1765–1769.* Chicago: University of Chicago Press, 1979.

Boyd Boyd, Julian P., ed. *Fundamental Laws and Constitutions of New Jersey, 1664–1964.* New Jersey Historical Series, vol. 17. Princeton: D. Van Nostrand Co., Inc., 1964.

Bradford, Of Plymouth Plantation Bradford, William. *Of Plymouth Plantation, 1620–1647.* Edited by Samuel Eliot Morison. New York: Modern Library, 1967.

Burgh [Burgh, James.] *Political Disquisitions: or, An Enquiry into Public Errors, Defects, and Abuses. . . .* 3 vols. London, 1774–75.

Burke, Works *The Works of the Right Honourable Edmund Burke.* 6 vols. London: Henry G. Bohn, 1854–56.

Burnett Burnett, Edmund C., ed. *Letters of Members of the Continental Congress.* 8 vols. Washington: Carnegie Institution of Washington, 1921–36.

Butterfield Adams, Abigail Smith. *The Book of Abigail and John: Selected Letters of the Adams Family, 1762–1784.* Edited by L. H. Butterfield et al. Cambridge: Harvard University Press, 1975.

Cannon *The Letters of Junius.* Edited by John Cannon. Oxford: At the Clarendon Press, 1978.

Cappon *The Adams-Jefferson Letters: The Complete Correspondence between Thomas Jefferson and Abigail and John Adams.* Edited by Lester J. Cappon. 2 vols. Chapel Hill: University of North Carolina Press for the Institute of Early American History and Culture, Williamsburg, Virginia, 1959.

Chase Chase, Frederick. *A History of Dartmouth College and the Town of Hanover New Hampshire.* Edited by John K. Lord. 2 vols. Cambridge: John Wilson & Son, 1891.

Colonial Records *The Colonial Records of North Carolina.* Edited by William L. Saunders. 10 vols. Raleigh: Josephus Daniels, 1886–90.

Crèvecoeur Crèvecoeur, J. Hector St. John. *Letters from an American Farmer.* New York: Albert & Charles Boni, 1925.

Documentary History *Documentary History of the Constitution of the United States of America, 1786–1870.* 5 vols. Washington, D.C.: Department of State, 1901–5.

Dumbauld Dumbauld, Edward. *The Bill of Rights and What It Means Today.* Norman: University of Oklahoma Press, 1957.

Early History *Early History of the University of Virginia, as Contained in the Letters of Thomas Jefferson and Joseph C. Cabell, Hitherto Unpublished. . . .* Richmond: J. W. Randolph, 1856.

Elliot Elliot, Jonathan, ed. *The Debates in the Several State Conventions on the Adoption of the Federal Constitution as Recommended by the General Convention at Philadelphia in 1787. . . .* 5 vols. 2d ed. 1888. Reprint. New York: Burt Franklin, n.d.

Emlyn Hale, Sir Matthew. *Historia Placitorum Coronae. The History of the Pleas of the Crown.* Edited by Sollom Emlyn. 2 vols. London, 1736. Reprint. Classical English Law Texts. London: Professional Books, Ltd., 1971.

Essays Ford, Paul Leicester, ed. *Essays on the Constitution of the United States, Published during Its Discussion by the People, 1787–1788.* Brooklyn: Historical Printing Club, 1892.

Farrand Farrand, Max, ed. *The Records of the Federal Convention of 1787.* Rev. ed. 4 vols. New Haven and London: Yale University Press, 1937.

Federalist Hamilton, Alexander; Madison, James; and Jay, John. *The Federalist.* Edited by Jacob E. Cooke. Middletown, Conn.: Wesleyan University Press, 1961.

Foster Foster, Sir Michael. *A Report of Some Proceedings on the Commission . . . for the Trial of the Rebels in the Year 1746 . . . , and of Other Crown Cases*. London, 1762. Reprint. Classical English Law Texts. Abingdon, England: Professional Books, Ltd., 1982.

Four Letters on Interesting Subjects *Four Letters on Interesting Subjects*. Philadelphia: 1776. Evans 14759.

Franklin, Papers *The Papers of Benjamin Franklin*. Edited by Leonard W. Labaree et al. New Haven: Yale University Press, 1959–.

Franklin, Writings *The Writings of Benjamin Franklin*. Edited by Albert Henry Smyth. 10 vols. New York: Macmillan Co., 1905–7.

Gerry, Life Austin, James T. *The Life of Elbridge Gerry. With Contemporary Letters*. 2 vols. Boston, 1828–29.

Gray Hale, Sir Matthew. *The History of the Common Law of England*. Edited by Charles M. Gray. Classics of British Historical Literature. Chicago: University of Chicago Press, 1971.

Gwyn Gwyn, W. B. *The Meaning of the Separation of Powers: An Analysis of the Doctrine from Its Origin to the Adoption of the United States Constitution*. Tulane Studies in Political Science, vol. 9. New Orleans: Tulane University, 1965.

Hamilton, Papers *The Papers of Alexander Hamilton*. Edited by Harold C. Syrett et al. 26 vols. New York and London: Columbia University Press, 1961–79.

See also: Federalist

Handlin Handlin, Oscar, and Handlin, Mary, eds. *The Popular Sources of Political Authority: Documents on the Massachusetts Constitution of 1780*. Cambridge: Belknap Press of Harvard University Press, 1966.

Harrington *The Political Writings of James Harrington: Representative Selections*. Edited by Charles Blitzer. New York: Liberal Arts Press, 1955.

History of Congress *History of Congress; Exhibiting a Classification of the Proceedings of the Senate, and the House of Representatives, from March 4, 1789, to March 3, 1793. . . .* Philadelphia: Lea & Blanchard, 1843.

Hume Hume, David. *Essays Moral, Political and Literary*. 1742, 1752.

Hurst Hurst, James Willard. *The Law of Treason in the United States: Collected Essays*. Westport, Conn.: Greenwood Publishing Corp., 1971.

Iredell, Life *Life and Correspondence of James Iredell*. Edited by Griffith J. McRee. 2 vols. New York: D. Appleton & Co., 1857.

Iredell, Papers *The Papers of James Iredell*. Edited by Don Higginbotham. Raleigh: North Carolina Division of Archives and History, 1976–.

Jacobson Trenchard, John, and Gordon, Thomas. *Cato's Letters*. In *The English Libertarian Heritage*, edited by David L. Jacobson. American Heritage Series. Indianapolis: Bobbs-Merrill, 1965.

Jamestown, The Three Charters of the Virginia Company of London *The Three Charters of the Virginia Company of London*. Jamestown 350th Anniversary Historical Booklet, no. 4. 1957

Jay, Correspondence *The Correspondence and Public Papers of John Jay*. Edited by Henry P. Johnston. 4 vols. New York and London: G. P. Putnam's Sons, 1890–93.

Jay, Unpublished Papers *John Jay: Unpublished Papers*. Edited by Richard B. Morris et al. New York: Harper & Row, 1975–.

See also: Federalist

Jefferson, Notes on the State of Virginia Jefferson, Thomas. *Notes on the State of Virginia*. Edited by William Peden. Chapel Hill: University of North Carolina Press for the Institute of Early American History and Culture, Williamsburg, Virginia, 1954.

Jefferson, Papers *The Papers of Thomas Jefferson*. Edited by Julian P. Boyd et al. Princeton: Princeton University Press, 1950–.

Jefferson, Works *The Works of Thomas Jefferson*. Collected and edited by Paul Leicester Ford. Federal Edition. 12 vols. New York and London: G. P. Putnam's Sons, 1904–5.

Jefferson, Writings *The Writings of Thomas Jefferson*. Edited by Andrew A. Lipscomb and Albert Ellery Bergh. 20 vols. Washington: Thomas Jefferson Memorial Association, 1905.

Jensen *The Documentary History of the Ratification of the Constitution*. Edited by Merrill Jensen et al. Madison: State Historical Society of Wisconsin, 1976–.

Journals *Journals of the Continental Congress, 1774–1789*. Edited by Worthington C. Ford et al. 34 vols. Washington, D.C.: Government Printing Office, 1904–37.

Kent Kent, James. *Commentaries on American Law*. 4 vols. New York, 1826–30.

King, Life *The Life and Correspondence of Rufus King*. Edited by Charles R. King. 6 vols. New York: G. P. Putnam's Sons, 1894–1900.

Land Eddis, William. *Letters from America*. Edited by Aubrey C. Land. Cambridge: Belknap Press of Harvard University Press, 1969.

Leake Leake, Isaac Q. *Memoir of the Life and Times of General John Lamb*. Albany, N.Y., 1857.

Lee, Letters *The Letters of Richard Henry Lee*. Edited by James Curtis Ballagh. 2 vols. New York: Macmillan Co., 1911–14.

Lincoln, Collected Works *The Collected Works of Abraham Lincoln*. Edited by Roy P. Basler et al. 8 vols. New Brunswick, N.J.: Rutgers University Press, 1953.

Locke, Second Treatise Locke, John. *Two Treatises of Government*. Edited by Peter Laslett. New York: Mentor Books, New American Library, 1965.

See also: Montuori

Machiavelli Machiavelli, Niccolò. *Discourses on the First Ten Books of Titus Livius*. Translated by Christian E. Detmold. New York: Modern Library, 1940.

McMaster McMaster, John Bach, and Stone, Frederick D., eds. *Pennsylvania and the Federal Constitution, 1787–1788*. Lancaster: Published for the Subscribers by the Historical Society of Pennsylvania, 1888.

Madison, Letters *Letters and Other Writings of James Madison*. Published by order of Congress. 4 vols. Philadelphia: J. B. Lippincott & Co., 1865.

Madison, Papers *The Papers of James Madison.* Edited by William T. Hutchinson et al. Chicago and London: University of Chicago Press, 1962–77 (vols. 1–10); Charlottesville: University Press of Virginia, 1977– (vols. 11–).

Madison, W. & M. Q. Fleet, Elizabeth. "Madison's 'Detached Memoranda.'" *William and Mary Quarterly*, 3d ser., 3 (1946): 534–68.

Madison, Writings *The Writings of James Madison.* Edited by Gaillard Hunt. 9 vols. New York: G. P. Putnam's Sons, 1900–1910.

See also: Federalist

Marshall, Life Beveridge, Albert J. *The Life of John Marshall.* 4 vols. Boston: Houghton Mifflin Co., 1916–19.

Marshall, Papers *The Papers of John Marshall.* Edited by Herbert A. Johnson et al. Chapel Hill: University of North Carolina Press, in association with the Institute of Early American History and Culture, Williamsburg, Virginia, 1974–.

Maryland Archives *Archives of Maryland: Proceedings and Acts of the General Assembly of Maryland.* Edited by William Hand Browne. Vol. 1. Baltimore: Maryland Historical Society, 1883.

Mason, Papers *The Papers of George Mason, 1725–1792.* Edited by Robert A. Rutland. 3 vols. Chapel Hill: University of North Carolina Press, 1970.

Meade Meade, Robert Douthat. *Patrick Henry: Patriot in the Making.* Philadelphia: J. B. Lippincott Co., 1957.

MHS Collections *Collections of the Massachusetts Historical Society.*

Monroe, Writings *The Writings of James Monroe.* Edited by Stanislaus Murray Hamilton. 7 vols. New York and London: G. P. Putnam's Sons, 1898–1903.

Montesquieu *The Spirit of Laws.* 1748. Translated by Thomas Nugent, 1750.

Montuori Locke, John. *A Letter concerning Toleration.* Latin and English texts revised and edited by Mario Montuori. The Hague: Martinus Nijhoff, 1963.

Gouverneur Morris, Amerikastudien Adams, Willi Paul. "'The Spirit of Commerce Requires that Property be Sacred': Gouverneur Morris and the American Revolution." *Amerikastudien* 21 (1976): 309–31.

Gouverneur Morris, Life *The Life of Gouverneur Morris, with Selections from His Correspondence and Miscellaneous Papers.* Edited by Jared Sparks. 3 vols. Boston, 1832.

Robert Morris, Papers *The Papers of Robert Morris, 1781–1784.* Edited by E. James Ferguson et al. Pittsburgh: University of Pittsburgh Press, 1973–.

New England Federalism Adams, Henry, ed. *Documents Relating to New-England Federalism.* Boston: Little, Brown & Co., 1877.

Niles Niles, Hezekiah, *Principles and Acts of the Revolution in America.* Centennial Offering. New York: A. S. Barnes & Co., 1876.

Old Family Letters Biddle, Alexander. *Old Family Letters.* Ser. A. Philadelphia: J. B. Lippincott Co., 1892.

Otis, Political Writings "Some Political Writings of James Otis." Collected by Charles F. Mullett. *University of Missouri Studies* 4 (1929): 257–432.

Paine, Life *The Life and Works of Thomas Paine.* Edited by William M. Van der Weyde. Patriots' Edition. 10 vols. New Rochelle, N.Y.: Thomas Paine National Historical Association, 1925.

Pamphlets Ford, Paul Leicester, ed. *Pamphlets on the Constitution of the United States, Published during Its Discussion by the People, 1787–1788.* Brooklyn, 1888. Reprint. New York: De Capo Press, 1968.

Penn, Select Works *The Select Works of William Penn.* 5 vols. 3d ed. London, 1782.

Pickering, Life Upham, Charles W. *The Life of Timothy Pickering.* 2 vols. Boston: Little, Brown & Co., 1873.

Pinkney Wheaton, Henry. *Some Account of the Life, Writings, and Speeches of William Pinkney.* Baltimore: E. J. Coale, 1826.

Randolph, History of Virginia Randolph, Edmund. *History of Virginia.* Edited by Arthur H. Shaffer. Charlottesville: University Press of Virginia for the Virginia Historical Society, 1970.

Rawle Rawle, William. *A View of the Constitution of the United States of America.* 2d ed. Philadelphia, 1829. Reprint. New York: Da Capo Press, 1970.

Read, Life Read, William Thompson. *Life and Correspondence of George Read.* Philadelphia: J. B. Lippincott & Co., 1870.

Records of the Federal Convention. *See* Farrand

Remonstrance and Petition, W. & M. Q. Schmidt, F. T., and Wilhelm, B. R. "Early Proslavery Petitions in Virginia." *William and Mary Quarterly*, 3d ser., 30 (1973): 133–46.

Richardson Richardson, James D., comp. *A Compilation of the Messages and Papers of the Presidents, 1789–1897.* 10 vols. Washington, D.C.: Government Printing Office, 1896–99.

Robertson Robertson, C. Grant, ed. *Select Statutes, Cases and Documents to Illustrate English Constitutional History, 1660–1832.* 4th ed., rev. London: Methuen & Co., Ltd., 1923.

Rush, Letters *Letters of Benjamin Rush.* Edited by L. H. Butterfield. 2 vols. Memoirs of the American Philosophical Society, vol. 30, parts 1 and 2. Princeton: Princeton University Press, for the American Philosophical Society, 1951.

Rush, Selected Writings *The Selected Writings of Benjamin Rush.* Edited by Dagobert D. Runes. New York: Philosophical Library, 1947.

Scribner *Revolutionary Virginia: The Road to Independence.* Vol 6, *The Time for Decision, 1776: A Documentary Record*, edited by Robert L. Scribner and Brent Tarter. Charlottesville: University Press of Virginia for the Virginia Independence Bicentennial Commission, 1981.

Sidney, Works *The Works of Algernon Sydney. A New Edition.* London, 1772.

Sources *Sources of Our Liberties.* Edited by Richard L. Perry under the general supervision of John C. Cooper. [Chicago:] American Bar Foundation, 1952.

State Trials *State Trials of the United States during the Administrations of Washington and Adams.* Edited by Francis Wharton. Philadelphia: Carey & Hart, 1849.

Stokes Stokes, Anton Phelps, ed. *Church and State in the United States.* 3 vols. New York: Harper & Bros., 1950.

Storing Storing, Herbert J., ed. *The Complete Anti-Federalist.* 7 vols. Chicago: University of Chicago Press, 1981.

Story Story, Joseph. *Commentaries on the Constitution of the United States.* 3 vols. Boston, 1833.

Tansill *Documents Illustrative of the Formation of the Union of the American States.* Edited by Charles C. Tansill. 69th Cong., 1st sess. House Doc. No. 398. Washington, D.C.: Government Printing Office, 1927.

Taylor Taylor, Robert J., ed. *Massachusetts, Colony to Commonwealth: Documents on the Formation of Its Constitution, 1775–1780.* Chapel Hill: University of North Carolina Press for the Institute of Early American History and Culture, Williamsburg, Virginia, 1961.

Thorpe Thorpe, Francis Newton, ed. *The Federal and State Constitutions, Colonial Charters, and Other Organic Laws of the States, Territories, and Colonies Now or Heretofore Forming the United States of America.* 7 vols. Washington, D.C.: Government Printing Office, 1909.

Tucker, Blackstone's Commentaries Tucker, St. George. *Blackstone's Commentaries: With Notes of Reference to the Constitution and Laws of the Federal Government of the United States and of the Commonwealth of Virginia.* 5 vols. Philadelphia, 1803. Reprint. South Hackensack, N.J.: Rothman Reprints, 1969.

Walker, U. Pa. L. Rev. Radin, Max. "The Doctrine of the Separation of Powers in Seventeenth Century Controversies." *University of Pennsylvania Law Review* 86 (1938): 842–66.

Warren, Life Frothingham, Richard. *Life and Times of Joseph Warren.* Boston: Little, Brown & Co., 1865.

Warren-Adams Letters *Warren-Adams Letters, Being Chiefly a Correspondence among John Adams, Samuel Adams, and James Warren.* Vol. 2, 1778–1814. Collections of the Massachusetts Historical Society, vol. 73. [Boston:] Massachusetts Historical Society, 1925.

Washington, Writings *The Writings of George Washington from the Original Manuscript Sources, 1745–1799.* Edited by John C. Fitzpatrick. 39 vols. Washington, D.C.: Government Printing Office, 1931–44.

Webster, Collection Webster, Noah. *A Collection of Essays and Fugitiv Writings on Moral, Historical, Political and Literary Subjects.* Boston, 1790. Reprint. Delmar, N.Y.: Scholars' Facsimiles & Reprints, 1977.

Webster, Political Papers Webster, Noah. *A Collection of Papers on Political, Literary and Moral Subjects.* New York, 1843. Reprint. New York: Burt Franklin, 1968.

Wharton Wharton, Francis, ed. *The Revolutionary Diplomatic Correspondence of the United States.* 6 vols. Washington, D.C.: Government Printing Office, 1889.

Wilson, Works *The Works of James Wilson.* Edited by Robert Green McCloskey. 2 vols. Cambridge: Belknap Press of Harvard University Press, 1967.

Winthrop Winthrop, John. *The History of New England from 1630 to 1649.* Edited by James Savage. 2 vols. Boston: Little, Brown & Co., 1853.

Woodhouse Woodhouse, A. S. P., ed. *Puritanism and Liberty, Being the Army Debates (1647–9) from the Clarke Manuscripts with Supplementary Documents.* 2d ed. London: J. M. Dent & Sons Ltd., 1951.

Index of Constitutional Provisions

Table of Cases

Index of Authors and Documents

References are to chapter or to constitutional section, and to document number. References to volume 1 are by chapter and document number (e.g., ch. 15, no. 23); references to constitutional provisions in volumes 2–4 are by article, section, clause, and document number (e.g., 1.8.8, no. 12); and references to volume 5 are by Amendment and document number (e.g., Amend. I [religion], no. 66). In the case of documents whose several clauses are ranged under a large number of headings (e.g., the Bill of Rights of 1689, the Massachusetts Constitution of 1780, and the like), reference is made only to appearances of the complete text.